ADVANCED TORTS

CASES AND MATERIALS

Second Edition

■ ■ ■

By

George C. Christie

James B. Duke Professor of Law
Duke University

Joseph Sanders

A. A. White Professor of Law
University of Houston

AMERICAN CASEBOOK SERIES®

WEST®

A Thomson Reuters business

Mat #41290518

610 Opperman Drive
St. Paul, MN 55123
1–800–313–9378

Printed in the United States of America

ISBN: 978–0–314–28182–1

To Our Students

Preface

This Advanced Torts Casebook is designed for a two or three hour tort course for students who have had a basic torts course and wish to pursue in depth some of the important topics of tort law that are either not covered or not covered in much depth in their basic tort course. Unlike some advanced torts texts that devote most of their attention to economic and business torts, products liability, or toxic torts, this book offers materials on a number of areas: trespass and nuisance, economic torts, products liability, insurance, tort reform and non-tort compensation systems, intentional infliction of emotional distress, defamation, privacy, misuse of legal process, and constitutional torts.

Although this casebook builds on the materials in the authors' **Cases and Materials on the Law of Torts, Fifth Edition,** they have added some problems and some chapters have been rewritten or expanded to reflect their purpose of making this an advanced torts casebook suitable for upper level students. For example, Chapter One includes materials allowing the professor to devote attention to the use of public nuisance law to pursue environmental and toxic tort issues. Chapters Two and Three expand the coverage of economic torts to include longer discussions of the economic loss rule in the context of toxic spills, fiduciary duties, fraud and negligent misrepresentation, tortious interference with contract and prospective contract, and damages for economic torts. Chapter Six discusses the empirical evidence relevant to the long-standing tort reform debate as well as an overview of a number of non-tort systems such as worker's compensation and no-fault automobile insurance. There have also been modifications and some reference to more recent developments in the products liability, defamation, and privacy materials.

George C. Christie
Durham, North Carolina

Joseph Sanders
Houston, Texas

Summary of Contents

TABLE OF CONTENTS

Table of Cases

The principal cases are in bold type. Cases cited or discussed in the text are in roman type. References are to pages. Cases cited in principal cases and within other quoted materials are not included.

ADVANCED TORTS

CASES AND MATERIALS

Second Edition

CHAPTER 1

INTERESTS IN LAND (NUISANCE AND TRESPASS)

■ ■ ■

A. OVERVIEW

BROWN v. COUNTY COMMISSIONERS OF SCIOTO COUNTY

Court of Appeals of Ohio, 1993.
87 Ohio App.3d 704, 622 N.E.2d 1153.

HARSHA, PRESIDING JUDGE.

Jack D. Brown and Barbara Brown filed a complaint which alleged that the Scioto County Commissioners had failed to properly maintain and operate a sewage treatment plant and thereby created a nuisance and trespass to the Browns' neighboring property. After the trial court granted the commissioners' motion for summary judgment, Barbara Brown took this appeal.

* * *

For the sum of $50,000, the Browns purchased a house located approximately one-quarter of a mile from the sewage treatment plant. They moved into the house on March 12, 1978. Prior to moving into the house, they did not perceive any odor from the plant. However, within the first week after they moved in, they noticed some odor coming from the plant. The odor was not very noticeable the first few years, but became worse and more frequent during the early 1980s. The odor was particularly bad when the weather was hot and humid or when the wind was blowing in a particular direction. The worst period for the noxious odors emanating from the sewage treatment plant was the summer of 1983, when there was an odor comparable to having their septic tank cleaned. The extreme odor during that period lasted twenty-four hours every day and prompted the Browns to file their initial complaint. Additionally, the odors from the plant increased the number of insects of all kinds on the Browns' property, requiring them to call an exterminating company two or three times a month during one period of time. The Browns became nauseated due to the odors, and in 1984, a physician indicated that it was a "probability" that appellant's stomach problems, including loss of appetite, were related to the treatment plant odors. The odors made it uncomfortable and, at times, impossible to be outside their house.

According to Jack D. Brown, the sewage treatment plant emitted germs and bacteria that rotted the ears off two rabbits that the Browns owned. Although unsure of the exact date, the Browns had their home listed for sale at $65,000 and a woman interested in purchasing it was driven away by the plant odors. Although the Browns and several neighbors complained to appellees, as well as state and federal officials, no action was taken by appellees to remedy the problems associated with their operation and maintenance of the sewage treatment plant.

Appellees operated the sewage treatment plant from its inception under a lease with the state. The lease was extended for a few brief periods until it was determined that the state could more efficiently operate the plant. Accordingly, appellees relinquished operation and maintenance of the plant to the state on June 1, 1985. During appellees' period of operation of the plant, the condition of the plant was deplorable. The Ohio Environmental Protection Agency cited the plant for violations concerning the level of bacteria and suspended solids contained in the effluent discharged into an adjacent stream. Most of the equipment was old and worn out. A comminutor, which was utilized to break down the raw sewage, had not been operable for several months, and the screen used to filter the sewage through the treatment process had a large hole in it. One of the two oxidation ditches was idle and the other ditch was only operating at twenty-five to fifty percent of its capacity. The idle oxidation ditch had become septic, breeding anaerobic bacteria that emitted the gaseous substance causing the noxious odors.

When appellees operated the sewage treatment facility, they rarely stocked an inventory of spare parts for the plant machinery. Consequently, there were occasions when an old part malfunctioned and the plant would be shut down until a new part was back-ordered. The plant shutdowns caused untreated sewage to remain idle and contributed to the noxious odors.

* * *

Appellees * * * contended that the Browns had failed to introduce evidence which would preclude summary judgment on their nuisance and trespass claims. We will initially consider appellant's claim for relief based upon nuisance. Appellees asserted that there was no genuine issue of material fact as to the existence of either an absolute nuisance, a qualified nuisance, a public nuisance, or a private nuisance.

As stated by Professor Keeton in Prosser & Keeton, The Law of Torts (5th Ed.1984) 616, Section 86: "There is perhaps no more impenetrable jungle in the entire law than that which surrounds the word 'nuisance.' " Nuisance describes two separate fields of tort liability that through the accident of historical development are called by the same name. See

Restatement of the Law 2d, Torts (1979) 84, Introductory Note. One of these two fields of liability bears the name of public nuisance and covers the invasion of public rights, i.e., rights common to all members of the public. Historically, public nuisance was criminal in nature and recovery in damages is limited to those who can show particular harm of a kind different from that suffered by the general public. Id.

The other field of liability is called private nuisance. This tort covers the invasion of the private interest in the use and enjoyment of land. As such, plaintiff's action must always be founded upon her interest in the land. Id. * * *

Restatement of the Law 2d, Torts (1979) 87, Section 821B, defines public nuisance as an unreasonable interference with a right common to the general public. Conduct does not become a public nuisance merely because it interferes with a large number of people. At common law, there must be some interference with a public right which is common to all members of the general public. In addition to common-law public nuisance, Ohio has adopted statutes and administrative regulations which define certain conduct as being a public nuisance. These statutes amount to a legislative declaration that the proscribed conduct is an unreasonable interference with a public right.

Restatement of the Law 2d, Torts (1979) 100, Section 821D, defines private nuisance as a nontrespassory invasion of another's interest in the private use and enjoyment of land. Section 822 of Restatement of the Law 2d, Torts provides that in order to be actionable, the invasion must be either (a) intentional and unreasonable, or (b) unintentional and caused by negligent, reckless or abnormally dangerous conduct (negligent and reckless conduct carry with them a degree of unreasonableness; abnormally dangerous activity is not treated in the same sense, but the balancing effort necessary to determine liability has the same effect). Id. at 113–115.

While the law in Ohio is far from clear in this area, absolute nuisance and nuisance per se seem to be the same. The essence of these two characterizations of nuisance is that no matter how careful one is, such activities are inherently injurious and cannot be conducted without damaging someone else's property or rights. They are based upon either intentional conduct or abnormally dangerous conditions, and as such the rule of absolute liability applies. A modern example would be a neighborhood "crack house."

Conversely, qualified nuisance is premised upon negligence. It consists of a lawful act that is so negligently or carelessly done as to have created an unreasonable risk of harm which in due course results in injury to another. Obviously, both public and private nuisances may be either absolute or qualified.

* * *

Having reviewed the appropriate law, we look first to see if appellant has presented sufficient evidence to allow her complaint to proceed in the area of either common law or statutory public nuisance. * * *

Since a pollution control facility operates under the sanction of law, it cannot be a common-law public nuisance.

* * *

In any event, Ohio Adm. Code 3745–15–07(A) states:

"Except as provided in paragraph (B) of this rule, the emission or escape into the open air from any source or sources whatsoever, of smoke, ashes, dust, dirt, grime, acids, fumes, gases, vapors, odors, or any other substances or combinations of substances, in such manner or in such amounts as to endanger the health, safety or welfare of the public, or cause unreasonable injury or damage to property, is hereby found and declared to be a public nuisance. It shall be unlawful for any person to cause, permit or maintain any such public nuisance."

* * *

Appellees did not argue below nor do they argue on appeal that subsection (A) is not applicable * * *. Accordingly, there remains a genuine issue of material fact as to whether their conduct constitutes a public nuisance pursuant to Ohio Adm. Code 3745–15–07(A). In this regard, the evidence indicated that appellees maintained the plant in "deplorable" condition, with numerous Ohio EPA violations.

* * *

A public nuisance as such does not afford a basis for recovery of damages in tort unless there is particular harm to the plaintiff that is of a different kind than that suffered by the public in general. See Restatement of the Law 2d, Torts (1979) 94, Section 821C(1). When the particular harm involved consists of interference with the use and enjoyment of land, the landowner may recover either on the basis of the particular harm to her resulting from the public nuisance or on the basis of private nuisance. See Restatement of the Law 2d, Torts (1979) 93, Section 821B, Comment h. Here appellant contends that she lost an opportunity to sell her property and was unable to use and enjoy it. This is a sufficiently distinct or particular harm from the public right so as to allow recovery under a statutory public nuisance theory.

However, just as the appellees' sewage disposal plant cannot be a common-law public nuisance because of the governmental authorization to operate, it likewise cannot be an absolute statutory nuisance. * * * In order for a duly licensed and regulated sanitary landfill to be found liable for maintaining a nuisance, negligence must be established, i.e., a qualified nuisance. * * *

As stated above, appellant introduced no evidence that appellees were not licensed to operate the sewage disposal plant. * * * [S]he failed to raise a genuine issue of material fact as to the presence of absolute public nuisance, but may proceed on the theory of qualified statutory nuisance.

We turn now to the cause of action for private nuisance. * * * [A]ppellant did not present sufficient evidence to withstand a motion for summary judgment on the issue of absolute private nuisance.

A civil action based upon the maintenance of a qualified private nuisance is essentially an action in tort for the negligent maintenance of a condition, which, of itself, creates an unreasonable risk of harm, ultimately resulting in injury. In such a case, negligence must be alleged and proven to warrant a recovery.

Appellees contend that there was no evidence of a qualified nuisance since there was no indication that appellant suffered any injury during the period when appellees operated the plant. * * * However, there was evidence that a prospective purchaser was lost due to the offensive odors from the plant. There was also evidence that appellant suffered nausea and was unable to fully use her property. To entitle adjoining property owners to recover damages for the maintenance of a nuisance, it is not necessary that they should be driven from their dwellings, or that the defendants' acts create a positive unhealthy condition; it is enough that their enjoyment of life and property is rendered uncomfortable, for in some circumstances discomfort and annoyance may constitute a nuisance. See, generally, 61 American Jurisprudence 2d (1981) 950, Pollution Control, Section 531. Accordingly, there remains a genuine issue of material fact as to whether appellees' conduct constituted a qualified private nuisance.

* * *

Additionally, construing the evidence most strongly in appellant's favor, we are persuaded that her evidence of loss of at least one prospective purchaser, increase in insects necessitating extermination expenses, nausea, and inability to use her property fully constituted sufficient evidence to raise a genuine issue of material fact as to whether appellees' interference with her property was substantial and unreasonable. Accordingly, a genuine issue of material fact remains on the question of qualified private nuisance.

Appellees further claim that there was no showing of trespass. The essential elements necessary to state a cause of action in trespass are: (1) an unauthorized intentional act, and (2) entry upon land in the possession of another. Traditionally, an invasion of the exclusive possession of land by intangible substances, such as an airborne pollutant, was usually held by the courts not to constitute a trespass since a trespass involved a physical invasion by tangible matters. See Annotation, Recovery in Trespass for Injury to Land Caused by Airborne Pollutants (1980), 2 A.L.R. 4th 1054. However, there has been a growing trend among jurisdictions to hold that the test for whether an invasion of a property interest is a trespass does not depend upon whether the intruding agent is an intangible or tangible substance, but whether the intrusion interferes with the right to the exclusive possession of property. Id. at 1055. However, odors emanating from a facility, see Born v. Exxon Corp. (Ala.1980), 388 So.2d 933, or mere diminution of value, see Maddy v. Vulcan Materials Co. (D.Kan.1990), 737 F.Supp. 1528, are insufficient to state a trespass claim even under the modern view.

The Supreme Court of Alabama in *Born* cited its previous decision in Borland v. Sanders Lead Co., Inc. (Ala.1979), 369 So.2d 523, 530, to note the following distinction between trespass under the modern trend and nuisance at 388 So.2d at 934:

"For an indirect invasion to amount to an actionable trespass, there must be an interference with plaintiff's exclusive possessory interest; that is, through the defendant's intentional conduct, and with reasonable foreseeability, some substance has entered upon the land itself, affecting its nature and character, and causing substantial actual damage to the res. For example, if the smoke or polluting substance emitting from a defendant's operation causes discomfort and annoyance to the plaintiff in his use and enjoyment of the property, then the plaintiff's remedy is for nuisance; but if, as a result of the defendant's operation, the polluting substance is deposited upon the plaintiff's property, thus interfering with his exclusive possessory interest by causing substantial damage to the res, then the plaintiff may seek his remedy in trespass, though his alternative remedy in nuisance may co-exist."

There is no summary judgment evidence of the polluting substance, i.e., noxious odors, depositing particulate matter on appellant's real property or causing physical damage to it. We are persuaded that under either the traditional or modern views, since appellant has failed to adduce summary judgment evidence of physical damage to her real property, appellees were entitled to summary judgment on appellant's trespass claim.

* * *

Appellant's assignment of error is sustained in part and overruled in part. Accordingly, the summary judgment entered by the common pleas court is affirmed as to appellant's claims of absolute nuisance, common-law public nuisance, trespass to real property, and injunctive relief, and is reversed and remanded for further proceedings consistent with this opinion * * *.

Judgment affirmed in part, reversed in part, and cause remanded.

PETER B. ABELE and STEPHENSON, JJ., concur.

NOTE

1. The Browns claimed that acts of the Scioto County Commissioners constituted a trespass, a private nuisance, and a public nuisance. In the next three sections we discuss each of these causes of action. All three causes of

action typically involve conflicts in land use and, therefore, while historically are torts, they have very close ties to property and land use law. The topic is often taught in property courses related to land use and environment. It also relates today to zoning law, the law of covenants regarding land use, and statutory law related to water and air pollution and hazardous waste. We provide a mere introduction to this fascinating area of the law.

B. TRESPASS

Trespass to land may be conceived of as an intentional tort. However, the intent necessary to commit a trespass is quite minimal. Culpability is unnecessary and even mistaken, non-culpable entries may count as a trespass. See Restatement (Second) of Torts § 163, comment *b*. Moreover, because of its roots in the writ of trespass, modern trespass actions do not require proof of damages. As a result, a trespass action may appear to be an attractive alternative to nuisance actions which often require culpable action on the part of the defendant and always require proof of damages. Inevitably, courts have been called upon repeatedly to determine whether a particular invasion is a trespass, a nuisance, neither, or perhaps both.

JOHN LARKIN, INC. v. MARCEAU

Supreme Court of Vermont, 2008.
184 Vt. 207, 959 A.2d 551.

JOHNSON, J.

Real estate developers, who sued a neighboring landowner for trespass based on the neighbor's spraying of pesticides in his apple orchard, appeal the superior court's decision rejecting their trespass theory. Because the developers failed to make a showing sufficient to survive the neighbor's motion for summary judgment, we affirm the court's judgment in favor of the neighbor.

Plaintiffs John Larkin, Inc. and Larkin Family Partnership (Larkin) own undeveloped land adjoining that of defendant J. Edward Marceau, Jr., who operates an apple orchard on his property. Larkin purchased the property from Marceau's former spouse in 2001 for the purpose of building a residential development. To increase the density of the proposed development, Larkin later obtained a transfer of the development rights from Marceau's property and another adjoining parcel of land.

* * *

In March 2005, * * * Larkin filed suit against Marceau, seeking injunctive and compensatory relief based on Marceau's spraying of pesticides in his orchard. The lawsuit sounded in trespass, with Larkin alleging that winds carried detectable levels of pesticides onto its property, thereby damaging the property. In his answer to the complaint, Marceau asserted, among other things, that Larkin had failed to state a claim upon which relief could be granted, that the claims were not ripe, and that the claims were barred by Vermont's right-to-farm law, 12 V.S.A. §§ 5751–5754, which establishes a rebuttable presumption that agricultural activities are not a nuisance. *Id.* § 5753(a)(1). The superior court initially dismissed the trespass claim, but later allowed it to proceed beyond the pleadings stage.

In January 2007, after discovery was closed, Marceau moved for summary judgment, arguing that Larkin was in fact making a nuisance claim but couching the complaint in terms of trespass to circumvent the right-to-farm law. Larkin opposed the motion and filed a cross-motion for summary judgment * * *. Concluding that Larkin's suit actually sounded in nuisance rather than trespass, the superior court stated that it would not endorse the fiction that Marceau's pesticides occupied Larkin's land, which would allow Larkin to evade the Legislature's plain intent to offer heightened protection to agricultural activities with respect to claims of this nature. The court declined to grant either party summary judgment, however, stating that the right-to-farm law did not necessarily preclude Larkin's complaint from surviving a motion for summary judgment insofar as the law established only a rebuttable presumption that no nuisance existed. The parties later stipulated to dismissal of Larkin's claims to the extent that they sounded in nuisance, and the superior court entered a final judgment against Larkin.

On appeal, Larkin argues that: (1) the superior court erred by recharacterizing its trespass action as a nuisance action subject to the right-to-farm law and thus effectively dismissing its trespass claim; (2) the right-to-farm law does not insulate farmers from liability for trespass, regardless of the nature of the trespass * * *. In response, Marceau argues that Larkin's claims are actually nuisance claims subject to the right-to-farm law, and that Larkin cannot avoid that law by alleging trespass. * * * We conclude that Larkin failed to make a showing sufficient to survive summary judgment on its trespass claim, and thus affirm the superior court's judgment in favor of Marceau.

The parties frame the primary issue as whether the deposit of airborne particulates on land may sound in trespass rather than nuisance. They both acknowledge the accepted distinction "that trespass is an invasion of the plaintiff's interest in the exclusive possession of his land, while nuisance is an interference with his use and enjoyment of it." W. Keeton et al., Prosser and Keeton on the Law of Torts § 87, at 622 (5th ed.1984). Compare Restatement (Second) of Torts § 158 cmt. c, at 277 (1965) (describing trespass as an "intrusion" invading "the possessor's interest in the exclusive possession of his land" (internal quotations omitted)) with Restatement (Second) of Torts § 821D cmt. d, at 101 (1979) (defining nuisance as "an interference with the interest in the private use and enjoyment of the land [that] does not require interference with the possession," and distinguishing trespass as "an invasion of the interest in the exclusive possession of land"). Larkin claims that Marceau's application of pesticides that settle onto its property effectively ousted it from the property. Marceau counters that Larkin is actually asserting a loss in the use and enjoyment of its property, which is a claim sounding in nuisance.

Traditionally, courts held that although a personal entry is unnecessary for trespass to take place, a defendant's act "must cause an invasion of the plaintiff's property by some tangible matter." See *Maddy v. Vulcan Materials Co.,* 737 F.Supp. 1528, 1539 (D.Kan.1990) (citing cases); see also *Adams v. Cleveland–Cliffs Iron Co.,* 237 Mich.App. 51, 602 N.W.2d 215, 219 (Ct.App.1999) (citing cases); D. Dobbs, The Law of Torts § 50, at 96 (2001) ("The law of nuisance deals with indirect or intangible interference with an owner's use and enjoyment of land, while trespass deals with direct and tangible interferences with the right to exclusive possession of land.") * * *. Plaintiffs showing a direct and tangible invasion of their property may obtain injunctive relief and at least nominal damages without proof of any other injury. *Adams,* 602 N.W.2d at 219.

On the other hand, plaintiffs claiming a nuisance have to demonstrate actual and substantial injury. *Id.* Under this traditional view, the intrusion of smoke, gas, noise, or other invisible particles onto another's property is not actionable as a trespass, but only as a private nuisance. Keeton, *supra,* § 13, at 71; see Dobbs, *supra,* § 53, at 105 (explaining that courts have been reluctant to allow trespass actions based on the invasion of microscopic or intangible particles because trespass "provided no mechanism for limiting liability to serious or substantial invasions").

Some courts eventually adopted a so-called "modern" theory of trespass that permits actions based on the invasion of intangible airborne particulates. Compare *Maddy,* 737 F.Supp. at 1539–40 (explaining and adopting "modern trend" of trespass) with *Adams,* 602 N.W.2d at 220–21 (explaining and rejecting "modern view" of trespass). Under this modern theory, invasions of intangible matter are actionable in trespass only if they cause substantial damage to the plaintiff's property, sufficient to be considered an infringement on the plaintiff's right to exclusive possession of the property. Hence, the modern view "departs from traditional trespass rules by refusing to infer damages as a matter of law" with respect to intangible invasions of property, as would be the case with direct, tangible invasions of property. *Maddy,* 737 F.Supp. at 1539; see *Borland v. Sanders Lead Co.,* 369 So.2d 523, 530 (Ala.1979) (explaining that invasion of polluting particulates is actionable as trespass only if invasion interferes with exclusive possessory interest of plaintiff's property by causing substantial damage to property); *Bradley v. Am. Smelting & Ref. Co.,* 104 Wash.2d 677, 709 P.2d 782, 791 (1985) (en banc) (explaining that trespass from airborne particles cannot occur unless plaintiff has suffered actual and substantial damages).

At least one court has rejected this modern view and held that recovery for trespass is available "only upon proof of an unauthorized direct or immediate intrusion of a physical, tangible object onto land over which the plaintiff has a right of exclusive possession." *Adams,* 602 N.W.2d at 222. In so holding, the Michigan court reasoned that requiring a showing of substantial damage for a trespass of intangible matter would "conflate [ ] nuisance with trespass to the point of rendering it difficult to delineate the difference between the two theories of recovery" and would weaken property owners' automatic right of exclusion in traditional trespass cases involving invasions of tangible objects. *Id.* at 221; see Keeton, *supra,* § 13, at 72 ("The historical requirement of an intrusion by a person or some tangible thing seems the sounder way to go about protecting the exclusive right to the use of property.").

In considering these alternatives, we note that Vermont law is silent on this issue, although we have recently looked to the Restatement of Torts for guidance on the law of trespass and nuisance. See, e.g., *Harris v. Carbonneau,* 165 Vt. 433, 437, 685 A.2d 296, 299 (1996) (citing Restatement § 158 in defining liability for trespass); *Canton,* 171 Vt. at 552, 762 A.2d at 810 (citing Restatement §§ 158. 821D, and 833 in defining liability for trespass and comparing nuisance). But neither the Restatement provisions nor their accompanying commentaries address the thorny question of whether the dispersion of particulate matter on property may be actionable as a trespass in addition to a nuisance. The Restatement does note, however, that the two actions are not necessarily exclusive and may overlap. Restatement (Second) of Torts § 821D cmt. e, at 102; see *Bradley,* 709 P.2d at 790 (noting that "remedies of trespass and nuisance are not necessarily mutually exclusive") (quotations omitted).

We recognize that the dispersion of airborne particles, whatever their nature, may technically be considered an entry onto land creating liability for trespass irrespective of whether any damage was caused. Because the ambient environment always contains particulate matter from many sources, such a technical reading of trespass would subject countless persons and entities to automatic liability for trespass absent any demonstrated injury. Plainly, that cannot be the law-and, as far as we can tell, no jurisdiction has so held. The question, then, is whether the physical entry onto land of intangible airborne particulates can ever be a trespass, or whether such an invasion may be actionable only as a nuisance. Because Larkin has failed to demonstrate any impact on its property from Marceau's pesticides, we find it unnecessary in this case to adopt a hard-line position that the dispersion of airborne particulates on property may never be actionable as a trespass, irrespective of the nature of the invasion or the right invaded. We leave for another day the question of whether the intrusion of airborne particulates may ever be a trespass, and, if so, what impact is required to sustain such an action.

Here, absent a demonstrated physical impact on Larkin's property resulting from the airborne particulates, the superior court did not err in granting summary judgment to Marceau. When particles enter the ambient environment without any demonstrated impact on the land, we fail to see how a trespass has occurred. In such a case, there is no ouster from the land, as Larkin claims here, and no interference with the landowner's right to exclusive possession of the land. Hence, under such circumstances, the landowner has no action in trespass. In a traditional trespass action, the right to exclusive possession of property may not depend on an analysis of the impact on the use of the land, but we cannot presume an intrusion on that right in situations where the plaintiff fails to show that an intangible invasion of airborne particulates had a demonstrated physical impact.

Despite having an opportunity during discovery to make out a case of trespass under the modern view examining the nature of the right invaded, Larkin failed to make any showing whatsoever that the presumed dispersion of detectable levels of pesticides onto its property from Marceau's orchard deprived it of exclusive possession of its property or had any other impact on the property. * * * Nor did Larkin proffer evidence indicating the extent of the dispersion of pesticides on its property or any potential safety or health concerns related to the pesticide use. * * *

Without question, there are situations in which both trespass and nuisance—two distinct actions that are not mutually exclusive—will be cognizable in the same lawsuit. This is not such a case, however.

* * *

Affirmed.

NOTES

1. *Nuisance and Trespass*

a. *Borland v. Sanders Lead Co.* is mentioned in both *Brown* and *Larkin*. The case offered the following analysis of why the boundary between the two torts is sometimes confused.

> The [court in Martin v. Reynolds Metals Co., 221 Or. 86, 342 P.2d 790 (1959), *cert. denied* 362 U.S. 918, 80 S.Ct. 672, 4 L.Ed.2d 739 (1960)] pointed out that trespass and nuisance are separate torts for the protection of different interests invaded—trespass protecting the possessor's interest in exclusive possession of property and nuisance protecting the interest in use and enjoyment. The Court noted, and we agree, that the same conduct on the part of a defendant may, and often does, result in the actionable invasion of both interests.
>
> The confusion surrounding trespass and nuisance is due in a large part to the influence of common law forms of action. The modern action for trespass to land stemmed inexorably from the common law action for trespass which lay when the injury was both direct and substantial. Nuisance, on the other hand, would lie when injuries were indirect and less substantial. *See* Winfield, *Nuisance as a Tort,* 4 Camb.L.J., 189, 201–06 (1931). A fictitious "dimensional" test arose, which obviated the necessity of determining whether the intrusion was "direct" and "substantial." If the intruding agent could be seen by the naked eye, the intrusion was considered a trespass. If the agent could not be seen, it was considered indirect and less substantial, hence, a nuisance. * * *
>
> * * * Whether an invasion of a property interest is a trespass or a nuisance does not depend upon whether the intruding agent is "tangible"

> or "intangible." Instead, an analysis must be made to determine the interest interfered with. If the intrusion interferes with the right to exclusive possession of property, the law of trespass applies. If the intrusion is to the interest in use and enjoyment of property, the law of nuisance applies. As previously observed, however, the remedies of trespass and nuisance are not necessarily mutually exclusive.

Borland v. Sanders Lead Co., 369 So.2d 523, 527, 529 (Ala.1979). Bradley v. American Smelting & Refining Co., 104 Wash.2d 677, 691, 709 P.2d 782, 791 (1985) adopts a similar position.

> When airborne particles are transitory and quickly dissipate, they do not interfere with a property owner's possessory rights and, therefore, are properly denominated as nuisances. * * * When, however, the particles or substance accumulate on the land and do not pass away, then a trespass has occurred.

b. The *Larkin* opinion notes that the "modern trend" of determining whether an invasion constitutes a trespass or a nuisance depending on the nature of interest interfered with was rejected in Adams v. Cleveland–Cliffs Iron Co., 237 Mich.App. 51, 602 N.W.2d 215 (1999). In *Adams*, the plaintiffs complained that the operation of a nearby iron mine invaded their property with noise, vibrations due to blasting, and a fine, gritty, oily, difficult to clean dust. A jury found for the plaintiffs on a trespass claim, but were hung on the plaintiffs' nuisance claim. As to the "modern trend," the *Adams* court had this to say:

> [T]he traditional view of trespass required a direct entry onto the land by a tangible object. However, recent trends have led to an erosion of these requirements. Some courts have eliminated the requirement of a direct entry onto the land.* * *. Some courts have likewise eliminated the requirement of a tangible object.
>
> * * *
>
> The courts that have deviated from the traditional requirements of trespass, however, have consequently found troublesome the traditional principle that at least nominal damages are presumed in cases of trespass. Thus, under the so-called modern view of trespass, in order to avoid subjecting manufacturing plants to potential liability to every landowner on whose parcel some incidental residue of industrial activity might come to rest, these courts have grafted onto the law of trespass a requirement of actual and substantial damages.
>
> * * *
>
> We do not welcome this redirection of trespass law toward nuisance law. The requirement that real and substantial damages be proved, and balanced against the usefulness of the offending activity, is appropriate where the issue is interference with one's use or enjoyment of one's land; applying it where a landowner has had to endure an unauthorized physical occupation of the landowner's land, however, offends traditional principles of ownership. The law should not require a property owner to justify exercising the right to exclude. To countenance the erosion of

presumed damages in cases of trespass is to endanger the right of exclusion itself.

As the *Larkin* opinion indicates, *Adams* to the contrary notwithstanding, the trend toward the "modern view" goes on apace. *See* Stevenson v. E.I DuPont De Nemours & Co., 327 F.3d 400 (5th Cir. 2003).

2. Trespass is an intentional tort in this sense. The defendant must intend to enter the property or cause an entry into the property. Surely it was not defendant Marceau's purpose to put his valuable pesticide onto adjacent property. In what sense then, did the defendants intend to trespass on the plaintiff's property?

3. What of "stray electricity" and electromagnetic waves escaping onto plaintiff's land? Trespass? *See,* Fletcher v. Conoco Pipe Line Co., 129 F.Supp.2d 1255 (W.D. Mo. 2001); Public Service Co. of Colorado v. Van Wyk, 27 P.3d 377 (Colo. 2001); Beal v. Western Farmers Elec. Co-op., 228 P.3d 538 (Okla.Civ.App. 2009). If the answer is no, does this mean that a "fictitious 'dimensional' test" still plays some role in distinguishing trespasses and nuisances?

C. PRIVATE NUISANCE

Unlike trespass, which protects a property right that may be thought of as inviolate, nuisance almost always involves competing uses of property. Unsurprisingly, the tort involves the difficult task of balancing rights and interests of neighboring land owners.

PESTEY v. CUSHMAN

Supreme Court of Connecticut, 2002.
259 Conn. 345, 788 A.2d 496.

[The defendant operated a dairy farm one-third of a mile from plaintiffs' home. The farm generated a substantial amount of manure which was stored in a pit near a 42,000 square foot barn built to house the cows. Over time, the odor from the pit became more pungent. A few years after the construction of the barn, the defendant installed an anaerobic digestion system to process the manure. However, due to the overloading of the system, this made the odors even worse, becoming more acrid and evincing the smells of sulphur and sewage. At times, the odor was sufficiently strong to awaken the plaintiffs in the middle of the night and force them to close the windows in their home. They brought a private nuisance lawsuit. After a lengthy trial, a jury found for the plaintiffs and awarded them $100,000.]

VERTEFEUILLE, J.

The principal issues in this appeal are whether: (1) the trial court properly instructed the jury with respect to the unreasonableness element of the common-law private nuisance claim * * *.

[W]e adopt the basic principles of § 822 of the Restatement (Second) of Torts and conclude that in order to recover damages in a common-law private nuisance cause of action, a plaintiff must show that the defendant's conduct was the proximate cause of an unreasonable interference with the plaintiff's use and enjoyment of his or her property. The interference may be either intentional or the result of the defendant's negligence. Whether the interference is unreasonable depends upon a balancing of the interests involved under the circumstances of each individual case. In balancing the interests, the fact finder must take into consideration all relevant factors, including the nature of both the interfering use and the use and enjoyment invaded, the nature, extent and duration of the interference, the suitability for the locality of both the interfering conduct and the particular use and enjoyment invaded, whether the defendant is taking all feasible precautions to avoid any unnecessary interference with the plaintiff's use and enjoyment of his or her property, and any other factors that the fact finder deems relevant to the question of whether the interference is unreasonable. No one factor should dominate this balancing of interests; all relevant factors must be considered in determining whether the interference is unreasonable.

The determination of whether the interference is unreasonable should be made in light of the fact that some level of interference is inherent in modern society. There are few, if any, places remaining where an individual may rest assured that he will be able to use and enjoy his property free from all interference. Accordingly, the interference must be substantial to be unreasonable.

Ultimately, the question of reasonableness is whether the interference is beyond that which the plaintiff should bear, under all of the circumstances of the particular case, without being compensated. See Restatement (Second), supra, § 822, comment (g), and § 826, comment (e). With these standards in mind, we turn to the present case.

In reaching its verdict, the jury completed a set of interrogatories provided by the trial court. Each interrogatory asked the jury whether the plaintiffs had proven a specific element of the private nuisance claim, and the jury answered each interrogatory affirmatively. The first interrogatory asked: "Did the plaintiffs prove [that] the defendants' dairy farm produced odors which unreasonably interfered with [the] plaintiffs' enjoyment of their property?" This interrogatory correctly captured the crux of a common-law private nuisance cause of action for damages, i.e., whether the defendants' conduct unreasonably interfered with the plaintiffs' use and enjoyment of their property. It correctly stated that the focus in such a cause of action is on the reasonableness of the interference and not on the use that is causing the interference. * * * As our previous discussion herein demonstrates, a plaintiff seeking damages in a common-law private nuisance cause of action is not required to prove that the defendant's conduct was unreasonable. Rather, the plaintiff must show that the interference with his or her property was unreasonable. * * * We conclude that the jury interrogatories and the jury charge, considered together, properly informed the jury of the necessary elements of a common-law private nuisance cause of action for damages and provided the jury with adequate guidance with which to reach its verdict. Accordingly, the trial court's jury charge was proper under the law as clarified herein.

* * *

The judgment is affirmed.

NOTES

1. The black letter of Section 822 of the Second Restatement adopted by *Pestey* provides as follows:

§ 822. General Rule

One is subject to liability for a private nuisance if, but only if, his conduct is a legal cause of an invasion of another's interest in the private use and enjoyment of land, and the invasion is either

(a) intentional and unreasonable, or

(b) unintentional and otherwise actionable under the rules controlling liability for negligent or reckless conduct, or for abnormally dangerous conditions or activities.

Nuisance, like trespass, is about a type of harm, not a type of conduct. The essence of the private nuisance tort is the disruption of another's quiet use and enjoyment of their property. "If the condition constituting the nuisance exists, the person responsible for it is liable for resulting damages to others even though the person acted reasonably to prevent or minimize the deleterious effects of the nuisance." Bormann v. Board of Sup'rs In and For Kossuth County, 584 N.W.2d 309, 315 (Iowa 1998).

2. Nuisances resulting solely from the defendant's negligence may be relatively easy to resolve because, by definition, had the defendant exercised due care the nuisance would be abated. This, apparently was the situation in *Brown*. Do you think it is the case in *Pestey*?

3. Most nuisance cases involve intentional conduct in the sense that the defendant intends the course of conduct giving rise to the nuisance. Indeed, is it not the case that any defendant who continues his activity after being sued is intending to create the alleged nuisance? *Restatement (Second) of Torts* § 825, comment *d* contains the following relevant observation.

> *Continuing or recurrent invasions*. Most of the litigation over private nuisances involves situations in which there are continuing or recurrent invasions resulting from continuing or recurrent conduct; and the same is true of many public nuisances. In these cases the first invasion resulting from the actor's conduct may be either intentional or unintentional; but when the conduct is continued after the actor knows that the invasion is resulting from it, further invasions are intentional.

4. Unlike trespass, even intentional nuisances must be unreasonable to be actionable. As the *Pestey* court points out, what must be unreasonable is not the defendant's conduct but the disruption of the plaintiff's quiet use and enjoyment and whether this disruption is unreasonable involves the balancing of a number of factors.

5. Sections 826–831 of the Second Restatement, flesh out these reasonableness factors in the context of an intentional nuisance.

§ 826. Unreasonableness of Intentional Invasion

An intentional invasion of another's interest in the use and enjoyment of land is unreasonable if

(a) the gravity of the harm outweighs the utility of the actor's conduct, or

(b) the harm caused by the conduct is serious and the financial burden of compensating for this and similar harm to others would not make the continuation of the conduct not feasible.

§ 827. Gravity of Harm—Factors Involved

In determining the gravity of the harm from an intentional invasion of another's interest in the use and enjoyment of land, the following factors are important:

(a) The extent of the harm involved;

(b) the character of the harm involved;

(c) the social value that the law attaches to the type of use or enjoyment invaded;

(d) the suitability of the particular use or enjoyment invaded to the character of the locality; and

(e) the burden on the person harmed of avoiding the harm.

§ 828. Utility of Conduct—Factors Involved

In determining the utility of conduct that causes an intentional invasion of another's interest in the use and enjoyment of land, the following factors are important:

(a) the social value that the law attaches to the primary purpose of the conduct;

(b) the suitability of the conduct to the character of the locality; and

(c) the impracticability of preventing or avoiding the invasion.

§ 829. Gravity vs. Utility—Conduct Malicious or Indecent

An intentional invasion of another's interest in the use and enjoyment of land is unreasonable if the harm is significant and the actor's conduct is

(a) for the sole purpose of causing harm to the other; or

(b) contrary to common standards of decency.

§ 829A. Gravity vs. Utility—Severe Harm

An intentional invasion of another's interest in the use and enjoyment of land is unreasonable if the harm resulting from the invasion is severe and greater than the other should be required to bear without compensation.

§ 830. Gravity vs. Utility—invasion Avoidable

An intentional invasion of another's interest in the use and enjoyment of land is unreasonable if the harm is significant and it would be practicable for the actor to avoid the harm in whole or in part without undue hardship.

§ 831. Gravity vs. Utility—conduct Unsuited to Locality

An intentional invasion of another's interest in the use and enjoyment of land is unreasonable if the harm is significant, and

(a) the particular use or enjoyment interfered with is well suited to the character of the locality; and

(b) the actor's conduct is unsuited to the character of that locality.

Do these sections remind you of the factors courts are asked to use when determining whether some activity is abnormally dangerous? Are they dealing with a similar problem?

6. The defendant's dairy operation in *Pestey* was protected by a right-to-farm statute. The Connecticut statute contains the following provisions:

> (a) Notwithstanding any general statute or municipal ordinance or regulation pertaining to nuisances to the contrary, no agricultural or farming operation, place, establishment or facility, or any of its appurtenances, or the operation thereof, shall be deemed to constitute a nuisance, either public or private, due to alleged objectionable (1) odor from livestock, manure, fertilizer or feed ... provided such agricultural or farming operation, place, establishment or facility has been in operation for one year or more and has not been substantially changed, and such operation follows generally accepted agricultural practices ...
>
> * * *
>
> "(c) The provisions of this section shall not apply whenever a nuisance results from negligence or willful or reckless misconduct in the operation of any such agricultural or farming operation, place, establishment or facility, or any of its appurtenances."

Conn. General Statutes § 19a–341

Thus, in order to prevail on their nuisance claim the plaintiffs had to prove negligence on the part of the defendants. That is, they must show the defendants operated their dairy farm in an unreasonable fashion. In response to a special interrogatory, the *Pestey* jury explicitly found that § 19a–341 did not apply because the plaintiffs had proven that the offensive odors produced by the defendants' farm were the result of the defendants' negligence in the operation of their farm. Presumably, this was because of the use of an undersized anaerobic digestion system. What result in *Pestey* if the defendants had never installed this device and in all other regards followed generally accepted agricultural practices?

Recall the *Larkin* case also involved a right-to-farm law. Apparently every states has passed some form of a right-to-farm statute. In Bormann v. Board of Supervisors, 584 N.W.2d 309 (Iowa 1998), the county board of supervisors approved a landowners' application for establishment of an "agricultural area." The consequence, under Iowa's agricultural land preservation statute, was to provide the landowner with immunity against nuisance suits brought by adjoining landowners. The Iowa Supreme Court held that this resulted in condemnation by nuisance of neighbors' property without just compensation, and, therefore, the nuisance immunity provision in agricultural land preservation statute violated both the state and federal constitutions. *Id.* at 321. In Buchanan v. Simplot Feeders, Ltd. Partnership, 134 Wash.2d 673, 952 P.2d 610 (1998) the Washington Supreme Court affirmed that state's right to farm statute, albeit only in the situation where a nuisance suit arises because of urban encroachment into an established agricultural area. *See* Alexander A. Reinert, *The Right to Farm: Hog-tied and Nuisance Bound,* 73 N.Y.U. L. Rev. 1694 (1998); Jesse Richardson, Jr. and Theodore A. Feitshans, *Nuisance Revisited after Buchanan and Bormann*, 5 Drake J. Agric. L. 121 (2000); Terence J. Centner, *Governments and Unconstitutional Takings: When Do Right–To–Farm Laws Go Too Far?*, 33 B.C. Envtl. Aff. L. Rev. 87 (2006).

7. In Carpenter v. Double R Cattle Co., 108 Idaho 602, 701 P.2d 222, 224 (1985), the court refused to adopt *Restatement (Second) of Torts* § 826(b) and concluded the defendant's feed lot was not a nuisance because its utility outweighed the costs. In a dissenting opinion, Justice Bistline accused the majority of adhering to "ideas on the law of nuisance that should have gone out with the use of buffalo chips as fuel."

> The majority's rule today suggests that part of the cost of industry, agriculture or development must be borne by those unfortunate few who have the fortuitous luck to live in the immediate vicinity of a nuisance producing facility. Frankly, I think this naive economic view is ridiculous in both its simplicity and its outdated view of modern economic society. The "cost" of a product includes not only the amount it takes to produce such a product but also includes the external costs: the damage done to the environment through pollution of air or water is an example of an external cost. In the instant case, the nuisance suffered by the homeowners should be considered an external cost of operating a feedlot and producing beef for public consumption. I do not believe that a few should be required to pay this extra cost of doing business by going uncompensated for a nuisance of this sort. If a feedlot wants to continue, I say fine, providing compensation is paid for the serious invasion (the odors, flies, dust, etc.) of the homeowner's interest. My only qualification is that the financial burden of compensating for this harm should not be such as to force the feedlot (or any other industry) out of business. The true cost can then be shifted to the consumer who rightfully should pay for the entire cost of producing the product he desires to obtain.

Carpenter, 701 P.2d at 229. How, if at all, is the *Carpenter* rule any different than that created by right-to-farm laws? *Compare* Jost v. Dairyland Power Cooperative, 45 Wis.2d 164, 172 N.W.2d 647, 653 (1969) ("We therefore conclude that the court properly excluded all evidence that tended to show the utility of the Dairyland Cooperative's enterprise. * * * We know of no acceptable rule of jurisprudence that permits those who are engaged in important and desirable enterprises to injure with impunity those who are engaged in enterprises of lesser economic significance.") Does the *Jost* court mean to reject *Restatement (Second) of* Torts § 826(a)?

8. The growth of renewable energy in the form of wind farms presents a new, fertile area for nuisance suits. Neighbors near wind farms may complain of noise, a "flicker effect" from the turning blades, and diminution of property values. See Rankin v. FPL Energy, LLC, 266 S.W.3d 506 (Tex. App. 2008); Burch v. Nedpower Mount Storm, LLC, 220 W.Va. 443, 647 S.E.2d 879 (2007). Nor do the potential causes of action run in only one direction. Owners of wind farms or solar collection systems may claim that any structure that blocks their access to wind or sunlight constitutes a nuisance. For useful discussions of this emerging area, *see* Susan Lorde Martin, *Wind Farms and NIMBYs: Generating Conflict, Reducing Litigation*, 20 Fordham Environmental L. Rev. 427 (2010); Megan Hiorth, *Are Traditional Property Rights Receding With Renewable Energy on the Horizon?* 62 Rutgers L. Rev. 527 (2010).

9. In an analysis which contributed to his winning the Nobel Prize in Economics, Ronald Coase argued that under certain circumstances the law's choice of liability rules will not alter the efficient allocation of resources. Ronald H. Coase, *The Problem of Social Cost*, 3 J. Law and Econ. 1 (1960). These circumstances include, a) zero transaction costs, i.e. perfectly costless bargaining between parties, b) the alienability of entitlements, i.e. individuals are free to buy and sell the rights and obligations imposed by the liability rule, c) the absence of wealth effects, and d) profit-maximizing bargainers. *See* Herbert Hovenkamp, *Marginal Utility and the Coase Theorem*, 75 Cornell L. Rev. 783, 785 (1990). Under these circumstances, once a liability rule is assigned the parties will bargain to the same efficient result, regardless of to whom liability was initially assigned.

A simple hypothetical taken from the case *Foster v. Preston Mill Co.*, 44 Wash.2d 440, 443, 268 P.2d 645 (1954) may be used to illustrate this point. Imagine that the vibrations caused by the defendant's blasting to build a logging road so frightens mother minks that they devour their young. Coase begins with the central observation that it is incorrect to say simply that the blasting causes injury to the mink. The causation is "reciprocal" in the sense that it is the joint presence of both the logging and the mink ranch that is a prerequisite to any damage. If liability is placed on the mink rancher, the damage to his animals is a cost added to the cost of production of pelts. The blasting caused his costs to rise. If, on the other hand, the liability is placed on the logger, the damage to the minks is a cost added to the cost of logging. The existence of nearby minks caused the price of logging to increase.

In order to see how the Theorem applies to this and similar competing land use circumstances, it is useful to imagine two different situations: one in which blasting is worth more to the logger than the damage it causes the mink rancher, and another in which blasting is worth less to the logger than the mink damage it causes. The first situation would exist if blasting is worth $100 to the logger (*i.e.* is $100 cheaper than any alternative way of building logging roads), but costs $90 worth of injuries to the mink rancher. The efficient allocation of resources is to continue to blast, for this creates $100 in value at a $90 cost. If the legal system were to force the logger to cease this method of construction, the collective wealth of the rancher and the logger would be $10 less. However, if the logger only has to pay damages to the rancher for the injuries he causes, he will continue to blast, for blasting is still

$10 cheaper ($100 savings less the $90 he must pay the rancher) than his next best alternative. The logger may wish to avoid the cost of litigation and simply pay the rancher directly. He might, for example, pay the rancher $91 for the right to blast and still realize a benefit of $9. If, on the other hand, the law refuses to assign liability to the logger, i.e., he is not legally responsible for injuries to the mink, then the mink rancher will simply have to live with the blasting. It is only worth $90 to him to have the blasting cease, and if he were to offer this sum to the logger, the logger would decline for it is worth $100 to continue blasting.

Now imagine the second situation, where the injuries caused to the minks is greater than the benefits derived from blasting as a method of constructing logging roads. This situation would exist if blasting is $90 cheaper than its alternatives, but costs $100 worth of injuries to the mink rancher. If the logger is liable for the damages he causes the minks, presumably he will turn to another way of building the road, for the cost of blasting ($100 in damages) is not worth the benefit. If, on the other hand, the logger may blast with impunity, the mink rancher will bargain with the logger to cease blasting. For example, the rancher might offer the logger $91 dollars to cease blasting, and still realize a benefit of $9. The central idea of the Coase Theorem is that in both situations, regardless of the initial assignment of liability, the parties achieve the same, efficient allocation resources.

The parties in the *Pestey* case were unable to reach an agreement. Why do you think they failed to come to an accommodation? Consider the assumptions underlying the Coase Theorem.

The Theorem generated a large number of articles, criticizing, explaining, and expanding on Coase's analysis. *See* Ian Ayres and Eric Talley, *Solomonic Bargaining: Dividing A Legal Entitlement to Facilitate Coasean Trade*, 104 Yale L.J. 1027 (1995); Robert Cooter, *The Cost of Coase*, 11 J. Legal Stud. 1 (1982); Harold Demsetz, *When Does The Rule Of Liability Matter?* 1 J. Legal Stud. 13 (1972); Donald H. Gjerdingen, *The Coase Theorem and the Psychology of Common–Law Thought,* 56 S. Cal. L. Rev. 711 (1983); Elizabeth Hoffman and Matthew L. Spitzer, *The Coase Theorem: Some Experimental Tests*, 25 J.L. & Econ. 73 (1982); Christine Jolls, Cass R. Sunstein, and Richard Thaler, *A Behavioral Approach to Law and Economics*, 50 Stan. L. Rev. 1471 (1998); Mark Kelman, *Consumption Theory, Production Theory, and Ideology in the Coase Theorem,* 52 S. Cal. L. Rev. 669 (1979).

IMPELLIZERRI v. JAMESVILLE FEDERATED CHURCH

Supreme Court of New York, Onondaga County, 1979.
104 Misc.2d 620, 428 N.Y.S.2d 550.

JOHN R. TENNEY, JUSTICE.

Anthony and Luana Impellizerri are seeking an injunction to restrain the Jamesville Federated Church from playing its carillon. They contend that the playing of the carillon is an invasion of privacy and a nuisance. The carillon is a series of bells which are played in various musical arrangements. It is played three times a day and four times on Sundays at regular hours for a period of approximately four minutes each time. Many attempts have been made to compromise. The speakers have been moved, playing time curtailed and the sound intensity reduced to no avail. Plaintiffs want it stopped. There is no dispute as to the facts and neither party has requested a hearing.

Life is full of sounds. The same sound can be pleasant in one moment and unpleasant in another. Children at play can be a refreshing sound to some and an annoyance to others. Unwanted sound is called noise, and it can produce unwanted effects. It may even reach the point where it becomes a restrainable pollutant. * * * However, there are many noises which are part of life and which all of us have to learn to accept. Plaintiffs admit that on occasion the normal village and traffic sounds drown out the bells.

In an industrial society, there are many noises which the courts have considered and have found not subject to restraint; trains and whistles, low flying planes, manufacturing noises, loud music * * *.

The plaintiffs contend that the volume of the bells affects their son who has a neurological disease and is kept awake. Luana Impellizerri claims she has migraine headaches and muscle spasms as the result of an accident which are aggravated by the bells. Generally, the claim is that conversation is disrupted, and the sounds cause severe anxiety and emotional stress to plaintiffs.

Bells in one form or another are a tradition throughout the world. In the Koran, they are considered the music of God. In the Christian world, every church is proud of its bells. The bells are rung for joy, for sadness, for warnings and for worship.

There are people who find total beauty in the sounds of bells in the Tower of Parliament in London or the daily ritual ringing at the Cathedral of Notre Dame in Paris. There is little question that the sound is often deafening when these bells start to ring, but for the general enjoyment of the public, it is considered acceptable.

It is often said that what is beauty to one may be ugly to another. A person with a special problem or an extra sensitive ear will be upset by any but the purest sound. That is not enough to justify the interference of the law.

The right to make a reasonable use of one's property has been long protected. Such a right is limited only if it unreasonably interferes with the rights of others.

There must be a material interference with the physical comfort and financial injury before there can be a nuisance. Stated another way, an early Massachusetts case held that the test should be the "common care of persons of ordinary prudence" and not as to those with "peculiar condition[s]". Rogers v. Elliott, 146 Mass. 349, 15 N.E. 768, 772 (1888). The alleged nuisance must be such as would cause an unwanted effect on the health and comfort of an ordinary person in the same or a similar situation. * * *

It seems that the plaintiffs have a special problem because of their own special condition. There are no other complainants, although there are several neighbors who live closer to the church than plaintiffs. It cannot be said that the ringing of the bell is such that would produce an unwanted effect on the ordinary person in the same circumstances.

Plaintiffs also argue that the playing of the music is an infringement on their right to religious freedom. This argument has no merit. The music is played without words although it is the music of well-known Christian hymns. There is no attempt to preach or impose any unwanted views.

Therefore, the plaintiffs' motion for an injunction is denied, and the defendant's cross-motion to dismiss the complaint is granted.

NOTES

1. In Rogers v. Elliott, 146 Mass. 349, 15 N.E. 768 (1888), discussed by the court, the plaintiff alleged that he had been suffering from sun stroke. His physician asked the pastor of the adjoining church to keep the church bells from being rung as the noise was interfering with the patient's recovery. The action was dismissed.

2. In Langan v. Bellinger, 203 A.D.2d 857, 611 N.Y.S.2d 59 (1994) the plaintiff objected to the chiming of the hour by the Presbyterian Church clarion. Defendant presented affidavits from 15 residents, some living closer to the church than the plaintiffs, saying they enjoyed the bells. Suppose there were fifty householders within two blocks of the church and fifteen found the bells as offensive as did the plaintiff but the other thirty-five were indifferent. Private nuisance? Public nuisance?

3. *The extra-sensitive plaintiff.* In negligence law it is often said the plaintiff must take his victim as he finds him, a concept reflected in the egg-shell skull metaphor. In other areas of the law, however, there is an often unstated premise that in order for the defendant to recover he or his property must be of a reasonable constitution. Can you explain the difference in approach in these two areas?

4. An extreme case of an idiosyncratic plaintiff (and defendant) is Amphitheaters, Inc. v. Portland Meadows, 184 Or. 336, 198 P.2d 847 (1948). The plaintiff owned a drive-in theater which was adjacent to the defendant's stock car race track at which night racing was held. During night races, the floodlights from the race track cast sufficient light upon the plaintiff's movie screen so as to interfere with the quality of the picture. On one occasion, the admission price to the drive-in theater had to be returned. The amount of light reaching the screen was equivalent to the light of a full moon on a cloudless night. The court held that, *vis-à-vis* the drive-in theater, the race track was not a nuisance. It also held that the casting of light upon the plaintiff's property did not constitute a trespass. Belmar Drive–In Theatre Co. v. Illinois State Toll Highway Commission, 34 Ill.2d 544, 216 N.E.2d 788 (1966) reached a similar result.

5. What about recovery for diminution in property value because substantial portions of the public incorrectly believe that something built next door, e.g., a high voltage power line, emits dangerous radiation?

Remedies

BOOMER v. ATLANTIC CEMENT COMPANY, INC.

Court of Appeals of New York, 1970.
26 N.Y.2d 219, 309 N.Y.S.2d 312, 257 N.E.2d 870.

BERGAN, JUDGE.

Defendant operates a large cement plant near Albany. These are actions for injunction and damages by neighboring land owners alleging injury to property from dirt, smoke and vibration emanating from the plant. A nuisance has been found after trial, temporary damages have been allowed; but an injunction has been denied.

The public concern with air pollution arising from many sources in industry and in transportation is currently accorded ever wider recognition accompanied by a growing sense of responsibility in State and Federal Governments to control it. Cement plants are obvious sources of air pollution in the neighborhoods where they operate.

But there is now before the court private litigation in which individual property owners have sought specific relief from a single plant operation. The threshold question raised by the division of view on this appeal is whether the court should resolve the litigation between the parties now before it as equitably as seems possible; or whether, seeking promotion of the general public welfare, it should channel private litigation into broad public objectives.

A court performs its essential function when it decides the rights of parties before it. Its decision of private controversies may sometimes greatly affect public issues. Large questions of law are often resolved by the manner in which private litigation is decided. But this is normally an incident to the court's main function to settle controversy. It is a rare exercise of judicial power to use a decision in private litigation as a purposeful mechanism to achieve direct public objectives greatly beyond the rights and interests before the court.

Effective control of air pollution is a problem presently far from solution even with the full public and financial powers of government. In large measure adequate technical procedures are yet to be developed and some that appear possible may be economically impracticable.

It seems apparent that the amelioration of air pollution will depend on technical research in great depth; on a carefully balanced consideration of the economic impact of close regulation; and of the actual effect on public health. It is likely to require massive public expenditure and to demand more than any local community can accomplish and to depend on regional and interstate controls.

A court should not try to do this on its own as a by-product of private litigation and it seems manifest that the judicial establishment is neither equipped in the limited nature of any judgment it can pronounce nor prepared to lay down and implement an effective policy for the elimination of air pollution. This is an area beyond the circumference of one private lawsuit. It is a direct responsibility for government and should not thus be undertaken as an incident to solving a dispute between property owners and a single cement plant—one of many—in the Hudson River valley.

The cement making operations of defendant have been found by the court at Special Term to have damaged the nearby properties of plaintiffs in these two actions. That court, as it has been noted, accordingly found defendant maintained a nuisance and this has been affirmed at the Appellate Division. The total damage to plaintiffs' properties is, however, relatively small in comparison with the value of defendant's operation and with the consequences of the injunction which plaintiffs seek.

The ground for the denial of injunction, notwithstanding the finding both that there is a nuisance and that plaintiffs have been damaged substantially, is the large disparity in economic consequences of the nuisance and of the injunction. This theory cannot, however, be sustained without overruling a doctrine which has been consistently reaffirmed in several leading cases in this court and which has never been disavowed here, namely that where a nuisance has been found and where there has been any substantial damage shown by the party complaining an injunction will be granted.

The rule in New York has been that such a nuisance will be enjoined although marked disparity be shown in economic consequence between the effect of the injunction and the effect of the nuisance.

The problem of disparity in economic consequence was sharply in focus in Whalen v. Union Bag & Paper Co., 208 N.Y. 1, 101 N.E. 805. A pulp mill entailing an investment of more than a million dollars polluted a stream in which plaintiff, who owned a farm, was "a lower riparian owner". The economic loss to plaintiff from this pollution was small. This court, reversing the Appellate Division, reinstated the injunction granted by the Special Term against the argument of the mill owner that in view of "the slight advantage to plaintiff and the great loss that will be inflicted on defendant" an injunction should not be granted (p. 2, 101 N.E. p. 805). "Such a balancing of injuries cannot be justified by the circumstances of this case", Judge Werner noted (p. 4, 101 N.E. p. 805). He continued: "Although the damage to the plaintiff may be slight as compared with the defendant's expense of abating the condition, that is not a good reason for refusing an injunction" (p. 5, 101 N.E. p. 806).

Thus the unconditional injunction granted at Special Term was reinstated. The rule laid down in that case, then, is that whenever the damage resulting from a nuisance is found not "unsubstantial", viz., $100 a year, injunction would follow. This states a rule that had been followed in this court with marked consistency * * *.

* * * Thus if, within Whalen v. Union Bag & Paper Co., *supra* which authoritatively states the rule in New York, the damage to plaintiffs in these present cases from defendant's cement plant is "not unsubstantial," an injunction should follow.

Although the court at Special Term and the Appellate Division held that injunction should be denied, it was found that plaintiffs had been damaged in various specific amounts up to the time of the trial and damages to the respective plaintiffs were awarded for those amounts. The effect of this was, injunction having been denied, plaintiffs could maintain successive actions at law for damages thereafter as further damage was incurred.

The court at Special Term also found the amount of permanent damage attributable to each plaintiff, for the guidance of the parties in the event both sides stipulated to the payment and acceptance of such permanent damage as a settlement of all the controversies among the parties. The total of permanent damages to all plaintiffs thus found was $185,000. This basis of adjustment has not resulted in any stipulation by the parties.

This result at Special Term and at the Appellate Division is a departure from a rule that has become settled; but to follow the rule literally in these cases would be to close down the plant at once. This court is fully agreed to avoid that immediately drastic remedy; the difference in view is how best to avoid it.*

One alternative is to grant the injunction but postpone its effect to a specified future date to give opportunity for technical advances to permit defendant to eliminate the nuisance; another is to grant the injunction conditioned on the payment of permanent damages to plaintiffs which would compensate them for the total economic loss to their property present and future caused by defendant's operations. For reasons which will be developed the court chooses the latter alternative.

If the injunction were to be granted unless within a short period—e.g., 18 months—the nuisance be abated by improved methods, there would be no assurance that any significant technical improvement would occur.

The parties could settle this private litigation at any time if defendant paid enough money and the imminent threat of closing the plant would build up the pressure on defendant. If there were no improved techniques found, there would inevitably be applications to the court at Special Term for extensions of time to perform on showing of good faith efforts to find such techniques.

Moreover, techniques to eliminate dust and other annoying by-products of cement making are unlikely to be developed by any research the

* Respondent's investment in the plant is in excess of $45,000,000. There are over 300 people employed there.

defendant can undertake within any short period, but will depend on the total resources of the cement industry nationwide and throughout the world. The problem is universal wherever cement is made.

For obvious reasons the rate of the research is beyond control of defendant. If at the end of 18 months the whole industry has not found a technical solution a court would be hard put to close down this one cement plant if due regard be given to equitable principles.

On the other hand, to grant the injunction unless defendant pays plaintiffs such permanent damages as may be fixed by the court seems to do justice between the contending parties. All of the attributions of economic loss to the properties on which plaintiffs' complaints are based will have been redressed.

The nuisance complained of by these plaintiffs may have other public or private consequences, but these particular parties are the only ones who have sought remedies and the judgment proposed will fully redress them. The limitation of relief granted is a limitation only within the four corners of these actions and does not foreclose public health or other public agencies from seeking proper relief in a proper court.

It seems reasonable to think that the risk of being required to pay permanent damages to injured property owners by cement plant owners would itself be a reasonable effective spur to research for improved techniques to minimize nuisance.

The power of the court to condition on equitable grounds the continuance of an injunction on the payment of permanent damages seems undoubted. * * *

Thus it seems fair to both sides to grant permanent damages to plaintiffs which will terminate this private litigation. * * *

The judgment, by allowance of permanent damages imposing a servitude on land, which is the basis of the actions, would preclude future recovery by plaintiffs or their grantees * * *.

This should be placed beyond debate by a provision of the judgment that the payment by defendant and the acceptance by plaintiffs of permanent damages found by the court shall be in compensation for a servitude on the land.

Although the Trial Term has found permanent damages as a possible basis of settlement of the litigation, on remission the court should be entirely free to re-examine this subject. It may again find the permanent damage already found; or make new findings.

The orders should be reversed, without costs, and the cases remitted to Supreme Court, Albany County to grant an injunction which shall be vacated upon payment by defendant of such amounts of permanent damage to the respective plaintiffs as shall for this purpose be determined by the court.

JASEN, JUDGE (dissenting).

I agree with the majority that a reversal is required here, but I do not subscribe to the newly enunciated doctrine of assessment of permanent damages, in lieu of an injunction, where substantial property rights have been impaired by the creation of a nuisance.

It has long been the rule in this State, as the majority acknowledges, that a nuisance which results in substantial continuing damage to neighbors must be enjoined. (Whalen v. Union Bag & Paper Co., 208 N.Y. 1, 101 N.E. 805; Campbell v. Seaman, 63 N.Y. 568; see, also, Kennedy v. Moog Servocontrols, 21 N.Y.2d 966, 290 N.Y.S.2d 193, 237 N.E.2d 356.) To now change the rule to permit the cement company to continue polluting the air indefinitely upon the payment of permanent damages is, in my opinion, compounding the magnitude of a very serious problem in our State and Nation today.

In recognition of this problem, the Legislature of this State has enacted the Air Pollution Control Act (Public Health Law, Consol. Laws, c. 45, §§ 1264 to 1299–m) declaring that it is the State policy to require the use of all available and reasonable methods to prevent and control air pollution (Public Health Law § 1265).

The harmful nature and widespread occurrence of air pollution have been extensively documented. Congressional hearings have revealed that air pollution causes substantial property damage, as well as being a contributing factor to a rising incidence of lung cancer, emphysema, bronchitis and asthma.

The specific problem faced here is known as particulate contamination because of the fine dust particles emanating from defendant's cement plant. The particular type of nuisance is not new, having appeared in many cases for at least the past 60 years. * * * It is interesting to note that cement production has recently been identified as a significant source of particulate contamination in the Hudson Valley. This type of pollution, wherein very small particles escape and stay in the atmosphere, has been denominated as the type of air pollution which produces the greatest hazard to human health. We have thus a nuisance which not only is damaging to the plaintiffs, but also is decidedly harmful to the general public.

I see grave dangers in overruling our long-established rule of granting an injunction where a nuisance results in substantial continuing damage. In permitting the injunction to become inoperative upon the payment of permanent damages, the majority is, in effect, licensing a continuing wrong. It is the same as saying to the cement company, you may continue to do harm to your neighbors so long as you pay a fee for it. Furthermore, once such permanent damages are assessed and paid, the incentive to alleviate the wrong would be eliminated, thereby continuing air pollution of an area without abatement.

It is true that some courts have sanctioned the remedy here proposed by the majority in a number of cases, but none of the authorities relied upon by the majority are analogous to the situation before us. In those cases, the courts, in denying an injunction and awarding money damages, grounded their decision on a showing that the use to which the property was intended to be put was primarily for the public benefit. Here, on the other hand, it is clearly established that the cement company is creating a continuing air pollution nuisance primarily for its own private interest with no public benefit.

This kind of inverse condemnation * * * may not be invoked by a private person or corporation for private gain or advantage. Inverse condemnation should only be permitted when the public is primarily served in the taking or impairment of property. * * * The promotion of the interests of the polluting cement company has, in my opinion, no public use or benefit.

Nor is it constitutionally permissible to impose servitude on land, without consent of the owner, by payment of permanent damages where the continuing impairment of the land is for a private use. * * * This is made clear by the State Constitution (art. I, § 7, subd. [a]) which provides that "[p]rivate property shall not be taken for *public use* without just compensation" (emphasis added). It is, of course, significant that the section makes no mention of taking for a *private* use.

In sum, then, by constitutional mandate as well as by judicial pronouncement, the permanent impairment of private property for private purposes is not authorized in the absence of clearly demonstrated public benefit and use.

I would enjoin the defendant cement company from continuing the discharge of dust particles upon its neighbors' properties unless, within 18 months, the cement company abated this nuisance.

It is not my intention to cause the removal of the cement plant from the Albany area, but to recognize the urgency of the problem stemming from this stationary source of air pollution, and to allow the company a specified period of time to develop a means to alleviate this nuisance.

I am aware that the trial court found that the most modern dust control devices available have been installed in defendant's plant, but, I submit, this does not mean that *better* and more effective dust control devices could not be developed within the time allowed to abate the pollution.

Moreover, I believe it is incumbent upon the defendant to develop such devices, since the cement company, at the time the plant commenced production (1962), was well aware of the plaintiffs' presence in the area, as well as the probable consequences of its contemplated operation. Yet, it still chose to build and operate the plant at this site.

In a day when there is a growing concern for clean air, highly developed industry should not expect acquiescence by the courts, but should, instead, plan its operations to eliminate contamination of our air and damage to its neighbors.

FULD, C.J., and BURKE and SCILEPPI, JJ., concur with BERGAN, J.

JASEN, J., dissents in part and votes to reverse in a separate opinion.

BREITEL and GIBSON, JJ., taking no part.

NOTES

1. As *Boomer* makes clear, whether the defendant's behavior constitutes a nuisance and whether the plaintiff is entitled to injunctive relief are two separate questions.

2. In Penland v. Redwood Sanitary Sewer Service District, 156 Or.App. 311, 965 P.2d 433 (1998), the court granted an injunction to a group of residents who lived near the defendant's substantial composting operation. Many lived there long before the sanitary district began composting in 1991. Beginning in 1992 the plaintiffs and others complained. The district's remedial actions proved ineffective and the plaintiffs brought an action seeking an injunction 1994. After affirming that the operation was nuisance, the court of appeals discussed possible remedies.

> Thus, we must compare the benefit to plaintiffs with the hardship to the District resulting from a permanent injunction. The benefit to plaintiffs is the ability to enjoy their property in a manner consistent with its rural character—to garden, and eat outside, and keep their windows open on summer evenings. For plaintiffs, an injunction would mean being able to use and enjoy their property as they did before the nuisance came to them—to live, and breathe, free from a pervasive, nauseating odor.
>
> * * *
>
> In contrast, the District's objections to relocating the composting operation to an alternative, non-residential site appear to be purely financial. That is, in contrast to land application, there is no evidence that practical or legal impediments, including land use or environmental restrictions, would somehow preclude such relocation. The capital cost of relocating the existing composting operation (as distinct from any expansion of that operation to accommodate projected population growth and demands) would be approximately $1,000,000. The District currently serves approximately 1,800 households. The additional capital costs associated with relocating, amortized over a 20–year period, would result in a $5.00 per month rate increase per household over that period. In addition the District's annual operating costs would increase by approximately $100,000, representing the expense of trucking the present volume of biosolids/sludge from the existing treatment plant to the newly-relocated composting operation.
>
> Assessing those alternatives, we conclude, as did the trial court, that the hardship to the District from the issuance of an injunction does not "greatly outweigh" the benefit to plaintiffs. There is no question that relocating the composting operation will, in fact, be expensive. Nevertheless, two factors especially bear on our assessment of the equities.
>
> First, although a precise apportionment is impossible, the District's relocation expenses have been exacerbated by actions and additional expenditures that the District undertook after becoming aware of the

Penlands' initial complaints in 1991 and of other plaintiffs' complaints by late 1992. This was not merely a case of the nuisance coming to the homeowners, but of the District expanding its operations after plaintiffs protested.

* * *

Second, although the additional cost to the District will be substantial, the impact will be ameliorated because it can be spread among the District's rate-payers-over 1,800 households.

* * *

If the District and those whom it serves are committed to the environmental values and benefits of composting, that may well be laudable. But the cost of that commitment should be commonly borne and not visited solely upon a handful of "involuntary contributors who happen to lie in the path of progress." We emphasize that this is not a case of simple-minded "NIMBY" parochialism—of narrow-minded refusal to assume burdens that are, reasonably and necessarily, part of living as a community. It is, rather, a clear and compelling case of living next to a * * * nuisance. The equities favor the issuance of an injunction.

3. In *Penland,* damages were not a possible remedy because of governmental immunity barring damages for injuries caused by the exercise of a discretionary function. In the absence of governmental immunity, do you think that *Penland* would have reached the same result as *Boomer*? If not, can the cases be reconciled? Do you agree with the *Penland* court that the costs of an injunction are somehow ameliorated because they can be spread among all the ratepayers? Can a similar argument be made in the *Boomer* case?

4. *Permanent Damages.* The *Boomer* court's justification of the permanent damages solution assumes that it is possible to calculate the present value of both past and future harm. Do you think this possible? For what types of damages? *Restatement (Second) of Torts* § 929 discusses the types of damages one is entitled to for past invasions.

§ 929. Harm To Land From Past Invasions

(1) If one is entitled to a judgment for harm to land resulting from a past invasion and not amounting to a total destruction of value, the damages include compensation for

(a) the difference between the value of the land before the harm and the value after the harm, or at his election in an appropriate case, the cost of restoration that has been or may be reasonably incurred,

(b) the loss of use of the land, and

(c) discomfort and annoyance to him as an occupant.

Comment *e.* Has the following to say about discomfort and annoyance damages:

Discomfort and other bodily and mental harms. Discomfort and annoyance to an occupant of the land and to the members of the household are distinct grounds of compensation for which in ordinary cases the person in possession is allowed to recover in addition to the harm to his proprietary interests. He is also allowed to recover for his own serious sickness or other substantial bodily harm but is not allowed to recover for serious harm to other members of the household, except so far as he maintains an action as a spouse or parent, under the rules stated in §§ 693 and 703. The owner of land who is not an occupant is not entitled to recover for these harms except as they may have affected the rental value of his land.

Do you think the *Boomer* court was thinking about "discomfort and annoyance" damages when it crafted its remedy? The *Penland* court clearly considered these damages when it compared the plaintiffs' interest in breathing odorless air and the defendant's cost of moving its operation. Once one introduces these "discomfort" damages into the balancing equation how is one ever to arrive at an objective determination of whether the gravity of the plaintiff's harm outweighs the utility of the defendant's conduct?

5. If, at a later point in time, a *Borland* plaintiff were able to prove that exposure to cement dust caused a respiratory disease, would he be able to bring a personal injury claim? What if he could only prove that he developed a cement dust allergy? On the use of nuisance law to recover for personal injury, *see* Burns v. Jaquays Mining Corp., 156 Ariz. 375, 752 P.2d 28 (1987).

6. In *Penland* the defendant had increased the capacity of the composting operation during the time of the suit. Absent an injunction, there is the possibility that in the future it would have chosen to once again increase capacity to meet growing needs. Can permanent damages deal with this problem? What if the defendant in *Boomer* decided to increase the size of its facility in the future? Would the plaintiffs have any remedy? If so, do permanent damages really achieve anything that temporary damages do not? If not, is the solution of permanent damages seriously flawed?

7. In *Pestey*, the plaintiffs were only awarded money damages? Why?

8. *Coming to the nuisance.* In Spur Industries, Inc. v. Del E. Webb Development Co, 108 Ariz. 178, 494 P.2d 700 (1972) plaintiff's burgeoning Sun City development on the outskirts of Phoenix moved closer and closer to defendant's feed lot which, by the time the development approached to within 500 feet, was producing over 1,000,000 pounds of wet manure per day. The court declared the feedlot to be both a private and a public nuisance. Should the plaintiff be entitled to damages? To an injunction? *Restatement (Second) of Torts* § 840D provides: "The fact that the plaintiff has acquired or improved his land after a nuisance interfering with it has come into existence is not in itself sufficient to bar his action, but is a factor to be considered in determining whether the nuisance is actionable." What are the arguments against allowing the defendant to prevail on a "coming to the nuisance" defense every time the plaintiff moves near the defendant's activity? The issue is discussed in Donald Wittman, *First Come, First Served: An Economic Analysis of "Coming to the Nuisance,"* 9 J. Legal Studies 557 (1980).

9. In *Spur Industries* the court dealt with the competing equities in the following manner:

> There was no indication in the instant case at the time Spur and its predecessors located in western Maricopa County that a new city would spring up, full-blown, alongside the feeding operation and that the developer of that city would ask the court to order Spur to move because of the new city. Spur is required to move not because of any wrongdoing on the part of Spur, but because of a proper and legitimate regard of the courts for the rights and interests of the public.
>
> Del Webb, on the other hand, is entitled to the relief prayed for (a permanent injunction), not because Webb is blameless, but because of the damage to the people who have been encouraged to purchase homes in Sun City. It does not equitably or legally follow, however, that Webb, being entitled to the injunction, is then free of any liability to Spur if Webb has in fact been the cause of the damage Spur has sustained. It does not seem harsh to require a developer, who has taken advantage of the lesser land values in a rural area as well as the availability of large tracts of land on which to build and develop a new town or city in the area, to indemnify those who are forced to leave as a result.
>
> Having brought people to the nuisance to the foreseeable detriment of Spur, Webb must indemnify Spur for a reasonable amount of the cost of moving or shutting down. It should be noted that this relief to Spur is limited to a case wherein a developer has, with foreseeability, brought into a previously agricultural or industrial area the population which makes necessary the granting of an injunction against a lawful business and for which the business has no adequate relief.

Spur Industries, Inc. v. Del E. Webb Development Co., 108 Ariz. 178, 185–86, 494 P.2d 700, 707–08 (1972).

10. Guido Calabresi and A. Douglas Melamed, *Property Rules, Liability Rules, and Inalienability: One View of the Cathedral*, 85 Harv.L.Rev. 1089 (1972), point out that nuisance situations can be resolved in one of four ways:

> a. The complaining "victim" can stop the nuisance by securing an injunction.
>
> b. The complaining "victim" can receive damages for the loss incurred as a result of the invasion.
>
> c. The court can hold that there is no nuisance thus placing the cost of the loss upon the complaining "victim".
>
> d. The court can find that there is an invasion but that the complaining "victim" must bear the cost of removing the offensive activity.

Go back over the cases you have read in this chapter and identify which fit into which category.

How should the courts decide which rule to apply? If one applies an economic analysis, does it make any difference? To the contesting parties? To society as a whole? Robert Rabin, *Nuisance Law: Rethinking Fundamental Assumptions*, 63 Va. L.Rev. 1299 (1977), does a particularly good job of tracing through this analysis as applied to the facts in Amphitheaters, Inc. v. Portland Meadows, 184 Or. 336, 198 P.2d 847 (1948), discussed p. 22, *supra*.

11. The law of nuisance has given rise to a very large body of published scholarship in both law and economics. Much of it starts with the Coase Theorem, discussed in the notes after *Pestey*. *See, e.g.*, Leslie Rosenthal, *Economic Efficiency, Nuisance, and Sewage: New Lessons from Attorney–General v. Council of the Borough of Birmingham*, 1858–95, 36 J. Legal Stud 27 (2007); Henry E. Smith, *Exclusion and Property Rules in the Law of Nuisance*, 90 Va. L. Rev. 965 (2004); Ward Farnsworth, *Do Parties to Nuisance Cases Bargain After Judgment? A Glimpse Inside the Cathedral*, 66 U. Chi. L. Rev. 473 (1999); Louis Kaplow and Steven Shavell, *Property Rules Versus Liability Rules: An Economic Analysis*, 109 Harv. L. Rev. 713 (1996); James E. Krier and Stewart J. Schwab, *Property Rules and Liability Rules: The Cathedral In Another Light*, 70 N.Y.U. L. Rev. 440 (1995); Herbert Hovenkamp, *Marginal Utility and the Coase Theorem,* 75 Cornell L. Rev. 783 (1990); Mitchell Polinsky, *Resolving Nuisance Disputes: The Simple Economics of Injunctive and Damage Remedies*, 32 Stan.L.Rev. 1075 (1980).

D. PUBLIC NUISANCE

In its earliest forms in the twelfth century, public nuisance was a criminal writ used to prosecute individuals or abatement of activities considered to be invasions on the rights of the public. In the fourteenth century courts began to apply public nuisance principles to protect rights common to the public, such as air and water pollution, and public health. In the sixteenth century the crime of public nuisance was transformed into the tort with which we are familiar today, "an act or omission which obstructs or causes inconvenience or damage to the public in the exercise of rights common to all." *Iafrate v. Ramsden,* 96 R.I. 216, 222, 190 A.2d 473, 476 (1963).

In recent years, plaintiffs have attempted to expand the modern scope of this ancient tort to achieve remedies that for whatever reason are unattainable using other tort causes of action such as negligence or products liability and which, in the plaintiffs' opinion, have been inadequately dealt with by the legislature. In the following case, the Rhode Island Supreme Court addresses one such effort.

STATE v. LEAD INDUSTRIES ASS'N

Supreme Court of Rhode Island, 2008.
951 A.2d 428.

CHIEF JUSTICE WILLIAMS, for the Court.

It is undisputed that lead poisoning constitutes a public health crisis that has plagued and continues to plague this country, particularly its children. * * * There seems to be little public debate that exposure to lead can have a wide range of effects on a child's development and behavior. Contact with low levels of lead may lead to "permanent learning disabilities, reduced concentration and attentiveness and behavior problems, problems which may persist and adversely affect the child's chances for success in school and life." * * * Children exposed to elevated levels of lead can suffer from comas, convulsions, and even death.

Lead was widely used in residential paints in the United States until the mid–1970s. There is no doubt that lead-based paint is the primary source of childhood lead exposure. In the United States, children most often are lead-poisoned by ingesting lead paint chips from deteriorating walls or inhaling lead-contaminated surface dust.

Children under six years of age are the most susceptible to lead poisoning * * *.

On October 12, 1999, the Attorney General, on behalf of the state filed a ten-count complaint against eight former lead pigment manufacturers * * *.

The state alleged that the manufacturers or their predecessors-in-interest had manufactured, promoted, distributed, and sold lead pigment for use in residential paint, despite that they knew or should have known, since the early 1900s, that lead is hazardous to human health. * * * The state further alleged that defendants' actions caused it to incur substantial damages. As such, the state asserted, defendants were liable for public nuisance, violations of Rhode Island's Unfair Trade Practices and Consumer Protection Act, strict liability, negligence, negligent misrepresentation, fraudulent misrepresentation, civil conspiracy, unjust enrichment, and indemnity. The state also requested equitable relief to protect children in Rhode Island. The state sought compensatory and punitive damages, in addition to an order requiring defendants to (1) abate lead pigment in all Rhode Island buildings accessible to children and (2) fund educational and lead-poisoning prevention programs.

In January 2000, defendants moved to dismiss all counts of the state's complaint pursuant to Rule 12(b)(6) of the Superior Court Rules of Civil Procedure. * * * Eventually, only the state's public nuisance claim proceeded to trial. After a seven-week trial, however, the jury was deadlocked and the trial justice declared a mistrial.

Before a second trial commenced, the state moved to strike defendants' demand for a jury trial, contending that its public nuisance claim was equitable in nature and that defendants had no right to a jury trial on that issue. At that time, the state voluntarily dismissed with prejudice all other non-equitable claims remaining in the case, including the following counts: strict liability, negligence, negligent misrepresentation, and fraudulent misrepresentation. The trial justice, however, denied the state's motion to strike the jury demand, concluding that the existence of a nuisance was a factual issue to be resolved by a jury and, further, that the state's demand for compensatory and punitive damages entitled defendants to a jury trial.

* * *

[T]he second trial proceeded * * *. The jury * * * found that the "cumulative presence of lead pigment in paints and coatings on buildings throughout the State of Rhode Island" constituted a public nuisance. The jury further found that defendants * * * were liable for causing or substantially contributing to the creation of the public nuisance. Lastly, the jury concluded that those three defendants "should be ordered to abate the public nuisance."

* * *

After the verdict, defendants renewed their motions for judgment as a matter of law pursuant to Rule 50 and moved alternatively for a new trial pursuant to Rule 59 of the Superior Court Rules of Civil Procedure. The trial justice denied both these motions. * * * On March 16, 2007, the court entered a judgment of abatement in favor of the state against defendants, Millennium, NL, and Sherwin–Williams, from which they appeal.

* * *

The defendants first argue that the trial justice erred in refusing to dismiss the public nuisance count set forth in the state's complaint. * * * We agree with defendants that the public nuisance claim should have been dismissed at the outset because the state has not and cannot allege that defendants' conduct interfered with a public right or that defendants were in control of lead pigment at the time it caused harm to children in Rhode Island. We reach this conclusion with a keen realization of how limited the judicial system often is. We believe that the following recent observation by this Court in another case is equally applicable to this case:

> "The American judicial system as it exists today is admirable: it is the product of many decades of fine-tuning of an already excellent substantive and procedural construct which this country took with it when it parted ways with England. Nevertheless, our judicial system is not a panacea that can satisfy everyone who has recourse to it. Some wrongs and injuries do not lend themselves to *full* redressment by the judicial system." *Ryan v. Roman Catholic Bishop of Providence,* 941 A.2d 174, 188 (R.I.2008).

* * *

Today, public nuisance and private nuisance are separate and distinct causes of action, but both torts are inextricably linked by their joint origin as a common writ, dating to twelfth-century English common law. *See* * * * Donald G. Gifford, Public Nuisance as a Mass Products Liability Tort, 71 U. Cin. L. Rev. 741, 790–91, 794 (2003).

* * *

In time, public nuisance became better known as a tort, and its criminal counterpart began to fade away in American jurisprudence. As state legislatures started enacting statutes prohibiting particular conduct and setting forth criminal penalties there was little need for the broad, vague, and anachronistic crime of nuisance. Restatement (Second) Torts § 821B, cmt. c.

The criminal origins of public nuisance in Rhode Island still can be found in statutes designating certain criminal activities and the places in which they are conducted as "common nuisances." * * *

This Court has defined public nuisance as "an unreasonable interference with a right common to the general public." *Citizens for Preservation of Waterman Lake v. Davis,* 420 A.2d 53, 59 (R.I.1980). "[I]t is behavior that unreasonably interferes with the health, safety, peace, comfort or convenience of the general community." Put another way, "public nuisance is an act or omission which obstructs or causes inconvenience or damage to the public in the exercise of rights common to all." *Iafrate v. Ramsden,* 96 R.I. 216, 222, 190 A.2d 473, 476 (1963) (citing Prosser, *Torts,* ch. 14, § 71 at 401 (2d ed. 1955)).

* * *

Whether the Presence of Lead Paint Constitutes a Public Nuisance

After thoroughly reviewing the complaint filed by the state in this case, we are of the opinion that the trial justice erred in denying defendants' motion to dismiss under Rule 12(b)(6) of the Superior Court Rules of Civil Procedure.

As the foregoing analysis demonstrates, under Rhode Island law, a complaint for public nuisance minimally must allege: (1) an unreasonable interference; (2) with a right common to the general public; (3) by a person or people with control over the instrumentality alleged to have created the nuisance when the damage occurred; and (4) causation. Even considering the allegations of fact as set forth in the complaint, we cannot ascertain allegations in the complaint that support each of these elements. * * * Absent from the state's complaint is any allegation that defendants have interfered with a public right as that term long has been understood in the law of public nuisance. Equally problematic is the absence of any allegation that defendants had control over the lead pigment at the time it caused harm to children.

* * *

A necessary element of public nuisance is an interference with a public right—those indivisible resources shared by the public at large, such as air, water, or public rights of way. The interference must deprive all members of the community of a right to some resource to which they otherwise are entitled. *See* Restatement (Second) Torts § 821B, cmt. *g.* The Restatement (Second) provides much guidance in ascertaining the fine distinction between a public right and an aggregation of private rights. "Conduct does not become a public nuisance merely because it interferes with the use and enjoyment of land by a large number of persons." *Id.*

Although the state asserts that the public's right to be free from the hazards of unabated lead had been infringed, this contention falls far short of alleging an interference with a public right as that term traditionally has been understood in the law of public nuisance. The state's allegation that defendants have interfered with the "health, safety, peace, comfort or convenience of the residents of the [s]tate" standing alone does not constitute an allegation of interference with a public right. The term public right is reserved more appropriately for those indivisible resources shared by the public at large, such as air, water, or public rights of way. Expanding the definition of public right based on the allegations in the complaint would be antithetical to the common law and would lead to a widespread expansion of public nuisance law that never was intended * * *.

The right of an individual child not to be poisoned by lead paint is strikingly similar to other examples of nonpublic rights cited by courts, the Restatement (Second), and several leading commentators. *See Beretta U.S.A. Corp.*, 290 Ill.Dec. 525, 821 N.E.2d at 1114 (concluding that there is no public right to be "free from unreasonable jeopardy to health, welfare, and safety, and from unreasonable threats of danger to person and property, caused by the presence of illegal weapons in the city of Chicago"); Restatement (Second) Torts § 821B, cmt. g (the individual right that everyone has not to be assaulted or defamed or defrauded or negligently injured is not a public right); Gifford, 71 U. Cin. L. Rev. at 815 (there is no common law public right to a certain standard of living, to a certain standard of medical care, or to a certain standard of housing). * * *

The enormous leap that the state urges us to take is wholly inconsistent with the widely recognized principle that the evolution of the common law should occur gradually, predictably, and incrementally. Were we to hold otherwise, we would change the meaning of public right to encompass all behavior that causes a widespread interference with the private rights of numerous individuals.

* * *

Even had the state adequately alleged an interference with a right common to the general public, which we conclude it did not, the state's complaint also fails to allege any facts that would support a conclusion that defendants were in control of the lead pigment at the time it harmed Rhode Island's children.

The state filed suit against defendants in their capacity "either as the manufacturer of * * * lead pigment * * * or as the successors in interest to such manufacturers" for "the cumulative presence of lead pigment in paints and coatings in or on buildings throughout the [s]tate of Rhode Island." For the alleged public nuisance to be actionable, the state would have had to assert that defendants not only manufactured the lead pigment but also controlled that pigment at the time it caused injury to children in Rhode Island—and there is no allegation of such control.

The New Jersey Supreme Court applied these same elements to the lead paint litigation in that jurisdiction and likewise held that public nuisance was an improper cause of action. The court emphasized that were it "to permit these complaints to proceed, [it] would stretch the concept of public nuisance far beyond recognition and would create a new and entirely unbounded tort antithetical to the meaning and inherent theoretical limitations of the tort of public nuisance." [*In re Lead Paint Litigation,* 924 A.2d 484, 494.] We agree.

We conclude, therefore, that there was no set of facts alleged in the state's complaint that, even if proven, could have demonstrated that defendants' conduct, however unreasonable, interfered with a public right or that defendants had control over the product causing the alleged nuisance at the time children were injured. Accordingly, we need not decide whether defendants' conduct was unreasonable or whether defendants caused an injury to children in Rhode Island.

* * *

Finally, our decision that defendants' conduct does not constitute a public nuisance as that term has for centuries been understood in Anglo–American law does not leave Rhode Islanders without a remedy. For example, an injunction requiring abatement may be sought against landlords who allow lead paint on their property to decay. In addition, the [Lead Poisoning Prevention Act] (LPPA), provides for penalties and fines against those property owners who violate its rules or procedures. Sections 23–24.6–23 and 23–24.6–27. The [Lead Hazard Mitigation Act] (LHMA) further authorizes a private cause of action to be brought on behalf of households with at-risk occupants to seek injunctive relief to compel property owners to comply with the act. G.L. 1956 § 42–128.1–10.

Apart from these actions, the proper means of commencing a lawsuit against a manufacturer of lead pigments for the sale of an unsafe product is a products liability action.

* * *

[E]ven if a lawsuit is characterized as a public nuisance cause of action, the suit nonetheless sounds in products liability if it is against a manufacturer based on harm caused by its products. Regardless of the label placed on the cause of action, the elements of products liability still must be met to properly maintain such a product-based proceeding. It is essential that these two causes of action remain just that—two separate and distinct causes of action.

* * *

For the foregoing reasons, we conclude that the trial justice erred in denying defendants' motion to dismiss.

NOTES

1. For a study of the history and development of public nuisance, *see* J. Spencer, *Public Nuisance—A Critical Examination*, [1989] Camb.L.J. 55.

2. Why, according to the court, did the plaintiff fail to state a cause of action? Are there other parties against whom the state might be more likely to prevail in a public nuisance claim? Why do you believe the state has not pursued such defendants?

3. The Rhode Island court suggests that if the state wants to pursue lead pigment manufacturers it should do so in products liability. Given what you learned when you studied products, what barriers confront the state in pursuing this cause of action?

4. Efforts to use public nuisance law to control other products have met with limited success.

a. The most noteworthy cases attempted to use public nuisance law a means of gun control. Most courts that have considered public nuisance claims against the gun industry dismissed the claims, but a substantial minority have not done so. *Compare* City of Cincinnati v. Beretta U.S.A. Corp., 95 Ohio St.3d 416, 768 N.E.2d 1136, 1143–44 (2002) (upholding the viability of a public action for public nuisance), *with* Camden County Bd. of Chosen Freeholders v. Beretta, U.S.A. Corp., 273 F.3d 536, 540 (3d Cir. 2001). In 2005, Congress barred such suits with the passage of the Protection of Lawful Commerce in Arms Act, 15 U.S.C. §§ 7901–03. The purpose of the act is "to prohibit causes of action against manufacturers, distributors, dealers, and importers of firearms or ammunition products, and their trade associations, for the harm solely caused by the criminal or unlawful misuses of firearm products or ammunition products by others when the product functioned as designed and intended." 15 U.S.C. § 7901.

b. In City of Cleveland v. Ameriquest Mortg. Securities, Inc., 621 F.Supp.2d 513 (N.D.Ohio 2009), *aff'd* City of Cleveland v. Ameriquest Mortg. Securities, Inc., 615 F.3d 496 (6th Cir. 2010), the plaintiff claimed that defendant's sub-prime lending practices were a public nuisance. The City sought damages for costs associated with the foreclosed and abandoned properties that increasingly plagued its neighborhoods and which, according to the plaintiff, were the result of these lending practices. How might the Rhode Island Supreme Court resolve this case?

c. In a number of cases, plaintiffs pressed public nuisance claims against emitters of greenhouse gases. Most noteworthy among these cases was Connecticut v. American Electric Power, Co., 582 F.3d 309 (2d Cir. 2009). There, the Court of Appeals held that several states and some private entities stated a federal common law public nuisance cause of action against the owners of a number of fossil-fuel-fired power plants for contribution to global warming and thereby impacting the welfare of their citizens. However, the United States Supreme Court reversed and remanded. American Elec. Power Co., Inc. v. Connecticut, ___ U.S. ___, 131 S.Ct. 2527, 180 L.Ed.2d 435 (2011). It held that the Clean Air Act and EPA actions it authorizes displace any federal common law right to seek abatement of carbon dioxide emissions from fossil-fuel fired power plants. It did, however, remanded the case on the question of whether the plaintiffs could state a claim under state nuisance law. If the suit were brought in Rhode Island, how would the Supreme Court resolve it? See also, Native Village of Kivalina v. Exxon Mobil Corp., 663 F. Supp. 2d 863 (N.D. Cal. 2009). For a useful discussion of this use of public nuisance law, *see*

Donald G. Gifford, *Climate Change and the Public Law Model of Torts: Reinvigorating Judicial Restraint Doctrines,* 62 S.C. L. Rev. 201 (2010).

5. Were the plaintiffs in *American Electric Power* ultimately to prevail, what problems do you foresee in crafting a remedy, either in terms of damages or abatement of the nuisance.

Private Enforcement of Public Nuisance

Ordinarily, public nuisances do not give rise to a private cause of action. However, as noted in *Brown*, private individuals may bring a claim if they have suffered a harm different in kind from that suffered by the public. The following case addresses this somewhat slippery concept.

GRACELAND CORP. v. CONSOLIDATED LAUNDRIES CORP.

Supreme Court of New York, Appellate Division, 1958.
7 A.D.2d 89, 180 N.Y.S.2d 644, aff'd 6 N.Y.2d 900,
190 N.Y.S.2d 708, 160 N.E.2d 926 (1959).

BREITEL, J. Defendant laundry appeals from a judgment granting to plaintiff apartment house owner a permanent injunction and nominal damages following a trial at Special Term. Involved is the obstruction by the laundry of the north sidewalk of East 94th Street, between First and Second Avenues in the City of New York. The laundry parks and stores its trucks on the pedestrian sidewalk in front of its own building. Plaintiff owns three partially renovated "new law" tenement houses on the same side of the street adjacent to the laundry. The issue in the case is whether the owner is entitled to enjoin the illegal use of the sidewalk by the laundry.

The laundry contends that, although it be assumed that its use is illegal (which it denies), and that such use constitutes a public nuisance, nevertheless, the adjacent owner is debarred from any private remedy because it cannot satisfy the legal requirement of showing special damage.

In substance the judgment should be affirmed, although it should be modified to make clear that the laundry is permitted to use the sidewalk for loading and unloading its commercial vehicles for reasonable periods of time under the provisions of the Administrative Code of the City * * *. Under the rules which obtain in regard to bringing private actions to enjoin a public nuisance, the owner has made a sufficient showing.

The laundry has operated at the site in question for some 25 years. It claims to have used the sidewalk in the same manner for 10 years. The owner purchased its property in late 1955 and remodeled the lower stories in early 1956. The property is used and rented as a multiple dwelling, and the owner claims that its rental value has been adversely affected by the obstruction of the adjacent sidewalk. To prove this the owner offered the testimony of a real estate expert and the rentals obtained from the entire property.

The laundry is, even by city standards, a large one. It uses large trucks, and the photographs submitted in evidence show that these trucks and some passenger automobiles are parked and stored on the public sidewalk. It is clear that this occurs while the trucks are not being loaded or unloaded. The effect is to block the sidewalk substantially with respect to access to the owner's premises, but not to preclude entirely pedestrian traffic. The court found, and it is not seriously disputed, that the practice is a continual one.

While it is variously argued that the laundry does no more than have its trucks "stand" while being loaded and unloaded, that is not the issue in the case. Such standing or parking is a permitted use. The issue turns on the finding supported by the evidence that the laundry "parks" and "stores" its vehicles on the pedestrian sidewalk.

The obstruction of a public street or sidewalk beyond the reasonable uses permitted to abutting owners is a public nuisance. (Administrative Code, §§ 82d7–15.0, 755(2)–4.0; Penal Law, §§ 1530, 1532.) In the absence of special damage to another, such public nuisance is subject only to correction at the hands of public authority. It is equally clear, however, that one who suffers damage or injury, beyond that of the general inconvenience to the public at large, may recover for such nuisance in damages or obtain injunction to prevent its continuance. This is old law. (Callanan v. Gilman, 107 N.Y. 360 * * *.)

While there has been suggestion that the obstruction of a street must be total before there is a remedy, the cases do not support such a total requirement. There must, of course, be a substantial impairment of the use of the street. This is exemplified by the very illustrations and the earlier precedents cited in the *Callanan* case (*supra*). Moreover, when the question has come up sharply, the courts have granted an injunction to a plaintiff although the obstruction was not total. * * *

As a matter of logic and common sense, the preceding analysis could hardly be otherwise. The key to the private remedy is special damage, and substantial obstruction may accomplish that result just as effectively, in some cases, as total obstruction. Of course, in other cases, it may well be that only total obstruction will be sufficient to incur special damage.

On the matter of special damage, moreover, there is no requirement that there be directness of such damage, or that there be any particular quantum, before there is a right to a private remedy, such as injunction * * * provided it is established that the plaintiff must have sustained some material injury peculiar to himself. * * *

In the cases, almost always involved was a conflict between merchants or a conflict between a merchant and an owner of a private dwelling. In this case the apartment house owner partakes of both merchant and owner of a private dwelling. Thus, in this case the owner provides dwellings for a price to members of the public. There was expert evidence, although it was hardly necessary, that a multiple dwelling the adjacent sidewalk to which is illegally obstructed by trucks and passenger automobiles will suffer depreciated rentals, and thereby reduce its value. This, of course, provides the commercial damage which has been stressed in some of the cases. But it is important to note that insofar as the owners of private dwellings are concerned there has not been such a necessity. In other words, a man may suffer special damage in his dwelling apart from commercial or even visible pecuniary damage, and that is just as actionable as the commercial damage suffered by a merchant from a diversion of potential customers.

The laundry has stressed, in a phrase not unfamiliar to the law, that the present owner has "come to the nuisance", that is, it purchased the building knowing of the obstruction of the adjacent sidewalk by the laundry of at least 10 years standing. Considering the illegality of the use by the laundry this is hardly a persuasive position. Nor is it one addressed to any equity that the court is obliged to recognize. (Campbell v. Seaman, 63 N.Y. 568, 584 * * *). Interestingly enough, in the *Campbell* case, there was some evidence that the defendant's brickyard had been such, albeit not continuously, for some 25 years, the precise period of the laundry's ownership. Of greater significance is that the factor of "coming to the nuisance", and factor is all that it is, is most often applied to private rather than to public nuisance * * *.

The laundry has also stressed that the owner's proper remedies lie with the Police Department of the City. One may not conjecture as to why that remedy has not sufficed during the period of the owner's interest in the adjacent property or the decade preceding. But it does not follow that because equity will decline to exercise its power where there is an adequate remedy at law, meaning an action at law, that, therefore, its doors are closed to petitioners because of the existence of an administrative remedy, an appropriate criminal proceeding—or even the availability of self-help. * * * It suffices, in any event, that equity, traditionally, in this country and in England, has granted injunctions in cases of public nuisance, although even from the days of the common law, indictment lay, and still lies, for a public nuisance * * *. Indeed, if the situation were otherwise, there never could be an injunction to restrain a public nuisance, because, by its very nature and nomenclature, a public nuisance is one for which there is a public remedy * * *.

[Order affirmed as modified.]

Settle order.

VALENTE, J. (dissenting). * * *

I dissent and would reverse the judgment and dismiss the complaint because plaintiff did not prove any special injury resulting from the alleged unreasonable use of the public streets which was peculiar to plaintiff as distinct from that suffered by the general public. * * *

The conduct of which plaintiff complains is singularly a matter for correction by the appropriate law enforcement agencies. It is not without significance that no reported cases involving grants of injunctions in similar matters have appeared in the books for many years. Quite clearly, the authorities have dealt with such complaints in adequate fashion. We should not open the door to pleas to a court of equity for injunctive relief unless there is sufficient evidence of special damage over and above the inconvenience to the general public. The showing in the instant case falls far short of the well-settled legal requirements.

It must also be pointed out that plaintiff became the owner of the three adjoining apartment houses in 1955. Defendant operates a large commercial laundry on East 94th Street between First and Second Avenues in the Borough of Manhattan, City of New York. It had continuously operated that laundry for 25 years before plaintiff purchased its properties. Plaintiff's agent admitted that he knew, during the last 10 years, that defendant had been backing up its trucks perpendicularly for loading and unloading. With knowledge of this practice, plaintiff nevertheless purchased the property. The requirement of a clear demonstration of special damage becomes even more warranted under such circumstances.

NOTES

1. A somewhat similar case, decided the other way, is Hay v. Oregon Dep't of Transp., 301 Or. 129, 719 P.2d 860 (1986). The court found neither a public nor a private nuisance. The case involved the defendant allowing parking on a beach in front of plaintiff's motel.

2. As noted in the *Brown* case that opened this chapter, most states statutorily declare activities such as gambling, public nudity, prostitution, and selling controlled substances to be public nuisances. *See* Texas Civ. Prac. & Rem. Code § 125.021 (1997). The use of nuisance law to control immoral activities now confronts a number of legal and constitutional challenges. *See* John Copeland Nagle, *Moral Nuisances*, 50 Emory L.J. 265 (2001); City of Erie v. Pap's A.M., 529 U.S. 277, 120 S.Ct. 1382, 146 L.Ed.2d 265 (2000).

3. The difficulty in applying the special injury rule is highlighted in a group of public nuisance claims arising out of the crash of the Exxon Valdez. Following *Oppen* the district court allowed plaintiffs to proceed with their commercial fishing claims. In re Exxon Valdez, 1994 WL 182856, at *6. However, it rejected a similar claim by sports fishers. In re Exxon Valdez, 1993 WL 735037, at *1, aff'd on other grounds, Alaska Sport Fishing Ass'n v. Exxon Corp., 34 F.3d 769 (9th Cir. 1994). And in In re The Exxon Valdez: Alaska Native Class v. Exxon Corp., 104 F.3d 1196 (9th Cir. 1997), the appellate court affirmed the district court's summary judgment in favor of the defendant on all noneconomic claims for injury to culture or a subsistence way of life asserted by a class of Alaskan natives. The trial court noted that all Alaskans have the right to lead subsistence lifestyles. "Admittedly, the oil spill affected the communal life of Alaska Natives, but whatever injury they suffered (other than the harvest loss), though potentially different in degree than that suffered by other Alaskans, was not different in kind." *Id.* at 1198.

Would the native Americans have a claim if others were not permitted to engage in a subsistence way-of-life? How is the native American claim any weaker than that of commercial fishermen? Is there any principle that can justify the distinction? Should we care? *See* George Christie, *The Uneasy Place of Principle in Tort Law*, 49 SMU L. Rev. 525 (1996). For a useful discussion of the special injury rule in public nuisance law, *see* Denise E. Antolini, *Modernizing Public Nuisance: Solving the Paradox of the Special Injury Rule*, 28 Ecology L.Q. 755 (2001).

CHAPTER 2

TORTS FOR ECONOMIC INJURY: THE ECONOMIC LOSS RULE, BREACH OF FIDUCIARY DUTY, FRAUDULENT AND NEGLIGENT MISREPRESENTATION

■ ■ ■

A. INTRODUCTION TO TORTS FOR ECONOMIC INJURY

This chapter addresses tort theories of liability relating to economic injury. Several introductory points should be noted.

First, in contrast to the world of personal injury (in which the accident is often between strangers), economic tort cases frequently involve parties who are not complete strangers. Often the parties to an economic tort cause of action will have been in a contractual relationship. Examples include: accountant-client; attorney-client; partners in a limited partnership; etc. Even when they are not in a contractual relationship, often the parties to an economic tort have some previous contact or nexus with each other. Examples are: business competitors, persons who will predictably make use of the information or expertise that the one might have (for instance, the investors who rely on accountant report of company solidity; the beneficiaries of a will drafted by a lawyer for a client).

Unsurprisingly, then, the scope and content of tort liability for economic injury differ somewhat from liability for personal injury. One important reason for this difference is that the world of contract law—including warranty law—provides a way of ordering the relationships that we discuss in this chapter. Unlike a car accident between strangers, people and entities involved in economic transactions can use contracts for "private ordering" of the risks posed by these transactions. Thus, for every theory of noncontractual liability for economic harm, one could fairly start by asking two basic questions, one practical and one theoretical: (1) what, if anything, does this theory provide to the plaintiff that is different from a contract remedy?; and (2) what in theory explains the existence of this other remedy, given the availability of contract law? At least implicitly and often explicitly, the answers to these questions affect the shape of existing and still-evolving doctrines. For example, consider the tort that many jurisdictions recognize for the breach of the duty of good faith and fair dealing. This cause of action does not usually exist, as a tort, in all contract relationships, but only in relationships that courts have determined justify the special protections of a tort remedy for at least one party to the transaction. A good example is the insurer-insured relationship, which in most states can give rise to this tort.

A second general observation about litigation relating to economic injury is that it usually involves multiple theories of liability, some that overlap substantially and some that do not. (Of course, multiple theories of liability often are advanced in personal injury torts, so this point applies to personal injury contexts as well.) The points of overlap or non-overlap can relate to the elements of liability, to the available damages, or both.

Third, litigation relating to economic injury covers a vast variety of commercial actors and transactions, from a lawyer writing a simple will to the hundreds of transactions by multinational corporations. Cases may involve many types of relationships, including: partners (general or limited); a corporation and its directors and officers; a corporation and its shareholders; brokers or agents and their clients; lawyers and their clients; banks and investors or clients; trustees and the beneficiary or estate; the list could go on.

Fourth, litigation relating to economic injury involves many common law theories and concepts, but also frequently relies on statutory theories, such as the Lanham Act, antitrust laws, or state and federal laws relating to unfair trade practices. This Chapter primarily addresses common law theories, with text notes referencing some of the major statutory causes of action that address the underlying conduct.

Fifth, claims for economic injury involve a much wider range of remedial and damages theories than do claims for personal injury. Actual damages are available, of course, but the doctrines relating to actual damages are different in important ways. In addition, equitable remedies such as recision, disgorgement, and unjust enrichment frequently appear.

B. THE ECONOMIC LOSS RULE

Before looking at economic torts, we address a basic doctrine in tort law, usually known as the "economic loss rule." The doctrine, often framed as a "no duty" rule, states that, as a general default matter with some exceptions, tort law does not allow recovery for pure economic loss. *See Restatement (Third) of Torts: Liability for Economic* Harm § 1 (Preliminary Draft No. 1, 2011). To understand the rule, we must first realize what it does not mean. First, the rule does not mean that all losses that are economic are not recoverable. Lost wages and medical expenses are purely economic losses; damage to property usually is only economic. Yet all these are recoverable when the plaintiff can otherwise establish breach, causation, etc. This is because all these cases involve either an initial personal injury or some type of physical damage to property.

Second, the rule does not mean that tort law altogether exempts wrongful conduct that causes only economic loss. Most jurisdictions, for instance, recognize the tort of professional negligence for attorney and accountant misconduct, as well as claims for tortious interference with contract, misrepresentation, etc. These are usually claims for purely economic losses, yet tort avenues exist for them in most jurisdictions. We address many such claims later in this chapter and in the chapter following.

Still, the economic loss rule has extensive application. Most jurisdictions follow some version of the rule, and thus bar many claims for pure economic loss. On inspection, one can see that claims for purely economic loss arise in two general types of scenarios: "non-stranger" contexts and "stranger" contexts. For a general discussion of the economic loss rule and the stranger-nonstranger distinction, *see* William Powers, Jr. & Margaret Niver, *Negligence, Breach of Contract, and the "Economic Loss" Rule*, 23 Tex. Tech L. Rev. 477, 488–89 (1992); Mark P. Gergen, *The Ambit of Negligence Liability for Pure Economic Loss*, 48 Ariz. L. Rev. 749 (2006).

Nonstranger contexts are those in which the plaintiff and defendant are in a contractual relationship (such as when a purchaser sues a product manufacturer that sold the product directly to the consumer) or at least are indirectly connected through a market transaction (such as when a consumer sues a product manufacturer that sold the product through a wholesaler or retailer). Stranger contexts are those in which the plaintiff and defendant are not in contractual privity and are not even indirectly connected to the same market transaction (such as when a tanker negligently spills oil into the ocean and thus harms the commercial interests of those affected by the spill). The next two cases deal with each of these situations in turn.

RARDIN v. T & D MACHINE HANDLING, INC.

United States Court of Appeals, Seventh Circuit, 1989.
890 F.2d 24.

POSNER, CIRCUIT JUDGE.

Jack Rardin, the plaintiff, bought for use in his printing business a used printing press from Whitacre–Sunbelt, Inc. for $47,700. The price included an allowance of $1,200 to cover the cost of dismantling the press for shipment and loading it on a truck at Whitacre's premises in Georgia for transportation to Rardin in Illinois. The contract of sale provided that the press was to be "Sold As Is, Where Is," that payment was to be made before the removal of the press from Whitacre's premises, and that Whitacre was to be responsible only for such damage to the press as might be "incurred by reason of the fault or negligence of [Whitacre's] employees, agents, contractors or representatives." To dismantle and load the press, Whitacre hired T & D Machine Handling, Inc., which performed these tasks carelessly; as a result the press was damaged. Not only did

Rardin incur costs to repair the press; he also lost profits in his printing business during the time it took to put the press into operating order. He brought this suit against Whitacre, T & D, and others; settled with Whitacre; dismissed all the other defendants except T & D; and now appeals from the dismissal of his case against T & D for failure to state a claim. (The facts we recited are all taken from the complaint.) The only issue is whether Rardin stated a claim against T & D under Illinois law, which the parties agree controls this diversity suit.

The contract indemnified Rardin against physical damage to the press caused by the negligence of Whitacre's contractor, T & D, and the settlement with Whitacre extinguished Rardin's claim for the cost of repairing the damage. The damages that Rardin seeks from T & D are the profits that he lost as a result of the delay in putting the press into operation in his business, a delay caused by T & D's negligence in damaging the press. Rardin could not have sought these damages from Whitacre under the warranty, because consequential damages (of which a loss of profits that is due to delay is the classic example) are not recoverable in a breach of contract suit, with exceptions not applicable here. Rardin had no contract with T & D, and his claim against T & D is a tort claim; consequential damages are the norm in tort law.

We agree with the district judge that Illinois law does not provide a tort remedy in a case such as this. We may put a simpler version of the case, as follows: A takes his watch to a retail store, B, for repair. B sends it out to a watchmaker, C. Through negligence, C damages the watch, and when it is returned to A via B it does not tell time accurately. As a result, A misses an important meeting with his creditors. They petition him into bankruptcy. He loses everything. Can he obtain damages from C, the watchmaker, for the consequences of C's negligence? There is no issue of causation in our hypothetical case; there is none in Rardin's. We may assume that but for C's negligence A would have made the meeting and averted the bankruptcy, just as but for T & D's negligence the press would have arrived in working condition. The issue is not causation; it is duty.

The basic reason why no court (we believe) would impose liability on C in a suit by A is that C could not estimate the consequences of his carelessness, ignorant as he was of the circumstances of A, who is B's customer. In principle, it is true, merely to conclude that C was negligent is to affirm that the costs of care to him were less than the costs of his carelessness to all who might be hurt by it; that, essentially, is what negligence means, in Illinois as elsewhere. So in a perfect world of rational actors and complete information, and with damages set equal to the plaintiff's injury, there would be no negligence: the costs of negligence would be greater to the defendant than the costs of care and therefore it would never pay to be negligent. And if there were no negligence, the scope of liability for negligence would have no practical significance. But all this is a matter of abstract principle, and it is not realistic to assume that *every* responsible citizen can and will avoid *ever* being negligent. In fact, all that taking care does is make it less likely that one will commit a careless act. In deciding how much effort to expend on being careful-and therefore how far to reduce the probability of a careless accident-the potential injurer must have at least a rough idea of the extent of liability. C in our example could not form such an idea. He does not know the circumstances of the myriad owners of watches sent him to repair. He cannot know what costs he will impose if through momentary inattention he negligently damages one of the watches in his charge.

Two further points argue against liability. The first is that A could by his contract with B have protected himself against the consequences of C's negligence. He could have insisted that B guarantee him against all untoward consequences, however remote or difficult to foresee, of a failure to redeliver the watch in working order. The fact that B would in all likelihood refuse to give such a guaranty for a consideration acceptable to A is evidence that liability for all the consequences of every negligent act is not in fact optimal. Second, A could have protected himself not through guarantees but simply by reducing his dependence on his watch. Knowing how important the meeting was he could have left himself a margin for error or consulted another timepiece. Why impose liability for a harm that the victim could easily have prevented himself?

The present case is essentially the same as our hypothetical example. T & D is in the business of dismantling and loading printing presses. It is not privy to the circumstances of the owners of those presses. It did not deal directly with the owner, that is, with Rardin. It knew nothing about his business and could not without an inquiry that Rardin would have considered intrusive (indeed bizarre) have determined the financial consequences to Rardin if the press arrived in damaged condition.

The spirit of *Hadley v. Baxendale,* 9 Ex. 341, 156 Eng.Rep. 145 (1854), still the leading case on the nonrecoverability of consequential damages in breach of contract suits, broods over this case although not cited by either party or by the district court and although the present case is a tort case rather than a contract case. The plaintiffs in *Hadley v. Baxendale* owned a mill, and the defendants were in business as a common carrier. The defendants agreed to carry the plaintiffs' broken mill shaft to its original manufacturer, who was to make a new shaft using the broken one as a model. The defendants failed to deliver the broken shaft within the time required by the contract. Meanwhile, the plaintiffs, having no spare shaft, had been forced to shut down the mill. The plaintiffs sued the defendants for the profits lost during the additional period the mill remained closed as a result of the defendants' delay in delivering the shaft to the manufacturer. The plaintiffs lost the case. The defendants were not privy to the mill's finances and hence could not form an accurate estimate of how costly delay would be and therefore how much care to take to prevent it. The plaintiffs, however, as the court noted, could have protected themselves from the consequences of a delay by keeping a spare shaft on hand. See 9 Ex. at 355–56, 156 Eng.Rep. at 151. Indeed, simple prudence dictated such a precaution, both because a replacement shaft could not be obtained immediately in any event (it had to be manufactured), and because conditions beyond the defendants' control could easily cause delay in the delivery of a broken shaft to the manufacturer should the shaft ever break. See also *EVRA Corp. v. Swiss Bank Corp.*, 673 F.2d 951, 957 (7th Cir.1982); Rardin, too, could have taken measures to protect himself against the financial consequences of unexpected delay. He could have arranged in advance to contract out some of his printing work, he could have bought business insurance, or he could have negotiated for a liquidated-damages clause in his contract with Whitacre that would have compensated him for delay in putting the press into working condition after it arrived.

* * * Illinois follows *Hadley v. Baxendale.* So if this were a contract case, Rardin would lose-and this regardless of whether the breach of contract were involuntary or, as he alleges, due to the promisor's negligence. It is a tort case, but so was *EVRA,* where, applying Illinois law, we concluded that the plaintiff could not recover consequential damages. The plaintiff had instructed its bank to deposit a payment in the bank account of a firm with which the plaintiff had a contract. The bank telexed its correspondent bank in Geneva-which happened to be Swiss Bank Corporation-to make the transaction. As a result of negligence by Swiss Bank, the transaction was not completed, whereupon the plaintiff lost its contract because the other party to it declared a default. The plaintiff sued Swiss Bank for the lost contract profits, and lost. We held that the principle of *Hadley v. Baxendale* is not limited to cases in which there is privity of contract between the plaintiff and the defendant. Swiss Bank could not have estimated the consequences of its negligence and the plaintiff, like the plaintiffs in *Hadley,* could have averted disaster by simple precautions. See 673 F.2d at 955–59. This case differs from both *Hadley* and *EVRA* in that there is no suggestion that Rardin was imprudent in failing to take precautions against damage or delay. But as in those cases the defendant was not in a position to assess the consequences of its negligence. In this respect the present case and *EVRA* are actually stronger for defendants even though these are tort rather than contract cases since neither case involves a defendant who is dealing face-to-face with the plaintiff. While it is generally true that consequential damages are recoverable in tort law although not in contract law, *EVRA* shows that the classification of a case as a tort case or a contract case is not decisive on this question.

We are reinforced in our conclusion that T & D is not liable to Rardin by a series of cases-beginning with *Moorman Mfg. Co. v. National Tank Co.,* 91 Ill.2d 69, 61 Ill.Dec. 746, 435 N.E.2d 443 (1982) * * * in which the Supreme Court of Illinois has held that damages for "purely economic loss" cannot be recovered in tort cases. The doctrine is not unique to Illinois. Originating in Chief Justice Traynor's opinion in Seely v. White Motor Co., 63 Cal.2d 9, 45 Cal.Rptr. 17, 403 P.2d 145 (1965), it has become the majority rule * * * and was adopted as the rule for admiralty as well in East River S.S. Corp. v. Transamerica Delaval Inc., 476 U.S. 858, 106 S.Ct. 2295, 90 L.Ed.2d 865 (1986). We need not consider the outer boundaries of the doctrine; it is enough that it bars liability in a suit for lost profits resulting from negligence in carrying out a commercial undertaking.

The doctrine (called in Illinois the *Moorman* doctrine) rests on the insight, which is consistent with the analysis in *EVRA,* that contractual-type limitations on liability may make sense in many tort cases that are not contract cases only because there is no privity of contract between the parties. The contractual linkage between Rardin and T & D was indirect but unmistakable, and Rardin could as we have said have protected himself through his contractual arrangements with Whitacre, while there was little that T & D could do to shield itself from liability to Whitacre's customer except be more careful-and we have explained why a finding of negligence alone should not expose a defendant to unlimited liability.

The *Moorman* doctrine goes further than is necessary to resolve this case. Once a case is held to fall within it, the plaintiff has no tort remedy. In our hypothetical case about the watch, the plaintiff could not sue the repairer even for property damage. *Moorman* itself was a case in which there was a contract between the parties, so there was no reason to allow a tort remedy. The present case * * * is one where, although there is no contract, the policies that animate the principle which denies recovery of consequential damages in contract cases apply fully and forbid a tort end-run around that principle.

The "economic loss" doctrine of *Moorman* and of its counterpart cases in other jurisdictions is not the only tort doctrine that limits for-want-of-a-nail-the-kingdom-was-lost liability. It is closely related to the doctrine, thoroughly discussed in *Barber Lines A/S v. M/V Donau Maru,* 764 F.2d 50 (1st Cir.1985), that bars recovery for economic loss even if the loss does not arise from a commercial relationship between the parties-even if for example a negligent accident in the Holland Tunnel backs up traffic for hours, imposing cumulatively enormous and readily monetizable costs of delay. See *Petition of Kinsman Transit Co.,* 388 F.2d 821, 825 n. 8 (2d Cir.1968). Admittedly these doctrines are in tension with other doctrines of tort law that appear to expose the tortfeasor to unlimited liability. One is the principle that allows recovery of full tort damages in a personal-injury suit for injury resulting from a defective or unreasonably dangerous product-a form of legal action that arises in a contractual setting and indeed originated in suits for breach of warranty. Another is the principle, also of personal-injury law, that the injurer takes his victim as he finds him and is therefore liable for the full extent of the injury even if unforeseeable-even if the person he runs down is Henry Ford and sustains a huge earnings loss, or because of a preexisting injury sustains a much greater loss than the average victim would have done. Both are doctrines of personal-injury law, however, and there are at least three differences between the personal-injury case and the economic-loss case, whether in a stranger or in a contractual setting. The first difference is that the potential variance in liability is larger when the victim of a tort is a business, because businesses vary in their financial magnitude more than individuals do; more precisely, physical capital is more variable than human capital. The second is that many business losses are offset elsewhere in the system: Rardin's competitors undoubtedly picked up much or all of the business he lost as a result of the delay in putting the press into operation, so that his loss overstates the social loss caused by T & D's negligence. Third, tort law is a field largely shaped by the special considerations involved in personal-injury cases, as contract law is not. Tort doctrines are, therefore, prima facie more suitable for the governance of such cases than contract doctrines are.

* * *

Although cases barring the recovery, whether under tort or contract law, of consequential damages in contractual settings ordinarily involve smaller potential losses than pure stranger cases do (such as the Lincoln Tunnel hypothetical discussed in *Kinsman*), this is not always so. In our watch hypothetical, in *EVRA,* and for all we know in *Hadley* and in the present case, the financial consequences of a seemingly trivial slip might be enormous. And it is in contractual settings that the potential victim ordinarily is best able to work out alternative protective arrangements and need not rely on tort law. Our conclusion that there is no tort liability in this case does not, therefore, leave buyers in the plaintiff's position remediless. Rardin could have sought guarantees from Whitacre (at a price, of course), but what he could not do was require the tort system to compensate him for business losses occasioned by negligent damage to his property.

* * *

The protracted analysis that we have thought necessary to address the parties' contentions underscores the desirability-perhaps urgency-of harmonizing the entire complex and confusing pattern of liability and nonliability for tortious conduct in contractual settings. But that is a task for the Supreme Court of Illinois rather than for us in this diversity case governed by Illinois law. It is enough for us that Illinois law does not permit a tort suit for profits lost as the result of the failure to complete a commercial undertaking.

NOTE

1. In Chapter 5 (p. 180 *infra*) we discuss one particular application of the economic loss rule in non-stranger cases: the rule that when a defective product damages only itself the plaintiff's remedy is in contract and not tort. One can see that the justifications for the rule in that context are similar to the justification for the rule in other non-stranger situations; non-strangers are able to use the law of contract and warranty to allocate the risk of disappointed economic expectations.

2. In nonstranger cases outside the products context—for instance, in the area of services or professional services—courts still apply the economic loss rule. Probably the most dominant approach is the following: a plaintiff

can bring a claim for a tort, even if the recovery sought is purely economic and even if the claim has a contractual nexus—if the plaintiff can establish the elements of an "independent" tort. That is, plaintiff cannot simply present a theory that the defendant breached a contract negligently. Rather, the plaintiff must show some other, independent tort. This might be fraud, negligent misrepresentation, breach of fiduciary duty, etc. *See* Southwestern Bell Telephone Co. v. DeLanney, 809 S.W.2d 493, 494 (Tex. 1991) (stating that a tort claim will be available if the plaintiff could establish the elements of some independent tort, other than negligence); Freeman & Mills, Inc. v. Belcher Oil Co., 11 Cal.4th 85, 44 Cal.Rptr.2d 420, 900 P.2d 669 (1995) (concluding that the economic loss case law in California "strongly suggests courts should limit tort recovery in contract breach situations to the insurance area, at least in the absence of violation of an independent duty arising from principles of tort law"). A minority of courts maintain even a stricter boundary on possible tort claims for economic loss. *See* Hoseline, Inc. v. U.S.A. Diversified Products, Inc., 40 F.3d 1198 (11th Cir. 1994) (holding that, if the plaintiff does not sustain personal injury or property damage, then the plaintiff has no tort cause of action, even if he could establish an independent tort such as fraud). Werwinski v. Ford Motor Co., 286 F.3d 661 (3d Cir. 2002).

STATE OF LOUISIANA, EX REL. GUSTE v. M/V TESTBANK

United States Court of Appeals, Fifth Circuit, 1985.
752 F.2d 1019.

PATRICK E. HIGGINBOTHAM, CIRCUIT JUDGE:

We are asked to abandon physical damage to a proprietary interest as a prerequisite to recovery for economic loss in cases of unintentional maritime tort. We decline the invitation

I

In the early evening of July 22, 1980, the M/V SEA DANIEL, an inbound bulk carrier, and the M/V TESTBANK, an outbound container ship, collided at approximately mile forty-one of the Mississippi River Gulf outlet. At impact, a white haze enveloped the ships until carried away by prevailing winds, and containers aboard TESTBANK were damaged and lost overboard. The white haze proved to be hydrobromic acid and the contents of the containers which went overboard proved to be approximately twelve tons of pentachlorophenol, PCP, assertedly the largest such spill in United States history. The United States Coast Guard closed the outlet to navigation until August 10, 1980 and all fishing, shrimping, and related activity was temporarily suspended in the outlet and four hundred square miles of surrounding marsh and waterways.

Forty-one lawsuits were filed and consolidated before the same judge in the Eastern District of Louisiana. These suits presented claims of shipping interests, marina and boat rental operators, wholesale and retail seafood enterprises not actually engaged in fishing, seafood restaurants, tackle and bait shops, and recreational fishermen. They proffered an assortment of liability theories, including maritime tort, private actions pursuant to various sections of the Rivers & Harbors Appropriation Act of 1899 and rights of action under Louisiana law. Jurisdiction rested on the proposition that the collision and contamination were maritime torts and within the court's maritime jurisdiction. *See* 28 U.S.C. § 1333.

Defendants moved for summary judgment as to all claims for economic loss unaccompanied by physical damage to property. The district court granted the requested summary judgment as to all such claims except those asserted by commercial oystermen, shrimpers, crabbers and fishermen who had been making a commercial use of the embargoed waters. The district court found these commercial fishing interests deserving of a special protection akin to that enjoyed by seamen. *See State of Louisiana ex rel. Guste v. M/V Testbank,* 524 F.Supp. 1170, 1173–74 (E.D.La.1981).[2]

On appeal a panel of this court affirmed, concluding that claims for economic loss unaccompanied by physical damage to a proprietary interest were not recoverable in maritime tort. 728 F.2d 748 (5th Cir.1984). The panel, as did the district court, pointed to the doctrine of *Robins Dry Dock & Repair Co. v. Flint,* 275 U.S. 303, 48 S.Ct. 134, 72 L.Ed. 290 (1927), and its development in this circuit. Judge Wisdom specially concurred, agreeing that the denial of these claims was required by precedent, but urging reexamination en banc. We then took the case en banc for that purpose. * * * [W]e are unpersuaded that we ought to drop physical damage to a proprietary interest as a prerequisite to recovery for economic loss. To the contrary, our reexamination of the history and central purpose of this pragmatic restriction on the doctrine of foreseeability heightens our commitment to it. Ultimately we conclude that without this limitation foreseeability loses much of its ability to function as a rule of law.

II

Plaintiffs first argue that the "rule" of *Robins Dry Dock* is that "a tort to the property of one which results in the negligent interference with contractual relationships of another does not state a claim," and that so defined, *Robins Dry Dock* is here inapplicable. Next and relatedly, plaintiffs urge that physical damage is not a prerequisite to recovery of economic loss where the damages suffered were foreseeable. Third, plaintiffs argue that their claims are cognizable in maritime tort because the pollution from the collision constituted a public nuisance and violated the Rivers and Harbors Appropriation Act of 1899, as well as Louisiana law.

* * *

2. Stated more generally, the summary judgment denied the claims asserted by shipping interests suffering losses from delays or rerouting, marina and boat operators, wholesale and retail seafood enterprises not actually engaged in fishing, shrimping, crabbing or oystering in the area, seafood restaurants, tackle and bait shops, and recreational fishermen, oystermen, shrimpers and crabbers. The rights of commercial fishermen who survived summary judgment are not before us.

III

The meaning of *Robins Dry Dock v. Flint,* (Holmes, J.) is the flag all litigants here seek to capture. We turn first to that case and to its historical setting.

Robins broke no new ground but instead applied a principle, then settled both in the United States and England, which refused recovery for negligent interference with "contractual rights." Stated more broadly, the prevailing rule denied a plaintiff recovery for economic loss if that loss resulted from physical damage to property in which he had no proprietary interest. *See, e.g., Byrd v. English,* 117 Ga. 191, 43 S.E. 419 (1903); *Cattle v. Stockton Waterworks Co.,* 10 Q.B. 453, 457 (C.A.1875). *See also* James, *Limitations on Liability for Economic Loss Caused by Negligence: A Pragmatic Appraisal,* 25 Vand.L.Rev. 43, 44–46 (1972) (discussing history of the rule); Carpenter, *Interference with Contract Relations,* 41 Harv. L.Rev. 728 (1928). Professor James explains this limitation on recovery of pure economic loss: "The explanation . . . is a pragmatic one: the physical consequences of negligence usually have been limited, but the indirect economic repercussions of negligence may be far wider, indeed virtually open-ended." James, *supra,* at 45.

Decisions such as *Stockton* illustrate the application of this pragmatic limitation on the doctrine of foreseeability. The defendant negligently caused its pipes to leak, thereby increasing the plaintiff's cost in performing its contract to dig a tunnel. The British court, writing fifty-two years before *Robins,* denied the plaintiff's claim. The court explained that if recovery were not contained, then in cases such as *Rylands v. Fletcher,* 1 L.R.–Ex. 265 (1866), the defendant would be liable not only to the owner of the mine and its workers "but also to . . . every workman and person employed in the mine, who in consequence of its stoppage made less wages than he would otherwise have done." *Id.* at 457.

–1–

In *Robins,* the time charterer of a steamship sued for profits lost when the defendant dry dock negligently damaged the vessel's propeller. The propeller had to be replaced, thus extending by two weeks the time the vessel was laid up in dry dock, and it was for the loss of use of the vessel for that period that the charterer sued. The Supreme Court denied recovery to the charterer, noting:

> . . . no authority need be cited to show that, as a general rule, at least, a tort to the person or property of one man does not make the tort-feasor liable to another merely because the injured person was under a contract with that other unknown to the doer of the wrong. (citation omitted). The law does not spread its protection so far.

275 U.S. at 309, 48 S.Ct. at 135.

* * *

–2–

The principle that there could be no recovery for economic loss absent physical injury to a proprietary interest was not only well established when *Robins Dry Dock* was decided, but was remarkably resilient as well. Its strength is demonstrated by the circumstance that *Robins Dry Dock* came ten years after Judge Cardozo's shattering of privity in *MacPherson v. Buick Motor Co.,* 217 N.Y. 382, 111 N.E. 1050 (1916). Indeed this limit on liability stood against a sea of change in the tort law. Retention of this conspicuous bright-line rule in the face of the reforms brought by the increased influence of the school of legal realism is strong testament both to the rule's utility and to the absence of a more "conceptually pure" substitute[3]. The push to delete the restrictions on recovery for economic loss lost its support and by the early 1940's had failed. *See* W. Prosser, *Law of Torts* § 129, at 938–940 (4th ed. 1971). In sum, it is an old sword that plaintiffs have here picked up.

–3–

Plaintiffs would confine *Robins* to losses suffered for inability to perform contracts between a plaintiff and others, categorizing the tort as a species of interference with contract. When seen in the historical context described above, however, it is apparent that *Robins Dry Dock* represents more than a limit on recovery for interference with contractual rights. Apart from what it represented and certainly apart from what it became, its literal holding was not so restricted. If a time charterer's relationship to its negligently injured vessel is too remote, other claimants without even the connection of a contract are even more remote.

It is true that in *Robins* the lower courts had sustained recovery on contract principles, but the Supreme Court pushed the steamship company's contract arguments aside and directly addressed its effort to recover in tort. The *Robins* court, however, pushed the steamship company's contract arguments aside and directly addressed its effort to recover in tort. The language and the cases the *Robins* Court pointed to as "good statement[s]" of the principle make plain that the charterer failed to recover its delay claims from the dry dock because the Court believed them to be too remote. Notably, although the dry dock company did not know of the charter party when it damaged the propeller, delay losses by

3. Professor Carpenter's article, *supra*, came within months of *Robins Dry Dock,* and sounded the drumbeat for change with arguments similar to those now urged. What is relevant here is that the courts did not follow Professor Carpenter's call to abandon the physical injury requirement. As Professor James pointed out:

> The failure of the movement to gain momentum takes on added significance when it is put into context. It coincided with a veritable ground swell in the law of negligence that pushed liability for physical injuries toward the full extent of what was foreseeable and shattered ancient barriers to recovery based on limitations associated with privity of contract and similar restrictive concepts.

James, supra, at 47 (citing 2 Harper & James §§ 18.3, 18.5, chs. 27–29 (1956 & Supp.1968); Prosser, *The Fall of the Citadel,* 50 Minn.L.Rev. 791 (1966); Wade, *Strict Tort Liability of Manufacturers,* 19 Sw.L.J. 5 (1965)).

users of the vessel were certainly foreseeable. Thus *Robins* was a pragmatic limitation imposed by the Court upon the tort doctrine of foreseeability.

* * *

If a plaintiff connected to the damaged chattels by contract cannot recover, others more remotely situated are foreclosed *a fortiori*. Indisputably, the *Robins Dry Dock* principle is not as easily contained as plaintiff would have it. We turn to our application of the principle, its application in other circuits, and the tort law of our Gulf states before returning to the doctrine itself.

–4–

This circuit has consistently refused to allow recovery for economic loss absent physical damage to a proprietary interest. * * *

We denied recovery to the Louisville & Nashville Railroad for its loss suffered when the M/V BAYOU LACOMBE damaged a bridge that the railroad had a contract right to use. *Louisville & Nashville R.R. Co. v. M/V BAYOU LACOMBE,* 597 F.2d 469 (5th Cir.1979). We rejected the railroad's argument that its right to use the damaged bridge was a property right sufficient to support recovery, concluding that whatever its label, recovery was sought for loss of an economic expectancy. *Id.* at 474. * * *

–5–

Nor has this circuit been the sole guardian of the *Robins Dry Dock* principle. *Rederi A/B Soya v. Evergreen Marine Corp.,* 1972 A.M.C. 1555, (E.D.Va.1971), *aff'd,* 1972 A.M.C. 538 (4th Cir.1972), was a case factually similar to *Robins.* There the Fourth Circuit adopted the opinion of the district court that had denied on the basis of *Robins* a time charterer's claim for profits lost when his leased vessel was negligently damaged. * * *

In *Henderson v. Arundel Corp.,* 262 F.Supp. 152 (D.Md.1966), *aff'd,* 384 F.2d 998 (4th Cir.1967), the court applied *Robins* to deny claims by seamen for wages lost when the vessel on which they worked was negligently damaged in a collision * * *.[4]

The court in *General Foods Corp. v. United States,* 448 F.Supp. 111 (D.Md.1978), faced a situation similar to that presented to us in *M/V BAYOU LACOMBE.* A ship collided with a railroad bridge over the Chesapeake and Delaware Canal, forcing General Foods to ship by truck goods moving to and from one of its plants. Relying on *Robins Dry Dock,* the court denied General Foods recovery for these additional costs. The

4. We note that both the Ninth and Eleventh Circuits have permitted crewmembers of a fishing boat to recover for their share of the lost catch when the vessel was negligently damaged. *See Carbone v. Ursich,* 209 F.2d 178, 181–82 (9th Cir.1953); *Miller Industries v. Caterpillar Tractor Co.,* 733 F.2d 813, 818–20 (11th Cir.1984). Both courts recognized, however, that such recovery was an exception to the general rule.

court discussed *Robins,* the decisions applying its rule, as well as decisions which assertedly undermined the doctrine and concluded:

> Imposition of liability in the present case involves precisely the limitless type of liability which courts have consistently considered excessive for negligence. Neither the case law nor the sound policy considerations on which the decisions are bottomed support plaintiff's claims for its economic losses. Even assuming General Foods is a foreseeable plaintiff, "the law does not spread its protection so far."

Id. at 116.

Plaintiffs urge that the decisions in *Petition of Kinsman Transit Co.,* 388 F.2d 821 (2d Cir.1968) (*Kinsman II*), and *Union Oil Co. v. Oppen,* 501 F.2d 558 (9th Cir.1974), support their arguments that the *Robins Dry Dock* principle should be abandoned. We disagree. The policy considerations on which both those decisions are bottomed confirm our opinion that pragmatic limitations on the doctrine of foreseeability are both desirable and necessary.

In *Kinsman* "an unusual concatenation of events on the Buffalo River" resulted in a disaster which disrupted river traffic for several months. Because of the disruption, the plaintiffs incurred extra expenses in fulfilling their contracts to supply and transport wheat and corn. In a previous panel decision arising out of the same facts, the court had rejected the defendants' arguments that recovery by such plaintiffs should be disallowed because their injuries were not foreseeable. Judge Friendly stated that while "[f]oreseeability of danger [was] necessary to render conduct negligent," it was not required that the defendants envision the precise harm resulting from their conduct before liability could be imposed. *Petition of Kinsman Transit Co.,* 338 F.2d 708, 724 (2d Cir.1964) (*Kinsman I*).

In *Kinsman II* the defendants argued that the plaintiffs' claims should be denied because there was no cause of action for negligent interference with a contractual right. The court dismissed the claims, but did so on the basis that the damages were too remote.* * * While rejecting any bright line rule, the court recognized that foreseeability was not a panacea and that limits on that concept should be maintained.

As we explain in Part IV of this opinion, we disagree with a case-by-case approach because we think the value of a rule is significant in these maritime decisions. *Kinsman II's* general analysis of the problem, however, recognizing as it does the need for the imposition of limitations on recovery for the foreseeable consequences of an act of negligence, is compatible with our own.

In *Union Oil,* vast quantities of raw crude were released when the defendant oil company negligently caused an oil spill. The oil was carried by wind, wave, and tidal currents over large stretches of the California coast disrupting, among other things, commercial fishing operations. While conceding that ordinarily there is no recovery for economic losses unaccompanied by physical damage, the court concluded that commercial fishermen were foreseeable plaintiffs whose interests the oil company had a duty to protect when conducting drilling operations. The opinion pointed out that the fishermen's losses were foreseeable and direct consequences of the spill, that fishermen have historically enjoyed a protected position under maritime law, and suggested that economic considerations also supported permitting recovery.

Yet *Union Oil's* holding was carefully limited to commercial fishermen, plaintiffs whose economic losses were characterized as "of a particular and special nature." *Union Oil,* 501 F.2d at 570. The *Union Oil* panel expressly declined to "open the door to claims that may be asserted by ... other[s] ... whose economic or personal affairs were discommoded by the oil spill" and noted that the general rule denying recovery for pure economic loss had "a legitimate sphere within which to operate." *Id.*[5]

A substantial argument can be made that commercial fishermen possess a proprietary interest in fish in waters they normally harvest sufficient to allow recovery for their loss. Whether the claims of commercial fishermen ought to be analyzed in this manner or simply carved from the rule today announced, in the fashion of *Union Oil,* or allowed at all, we leave for later. That is, today's decision does not foreclose free consideration by a court panel of the claims of commercial fishermen.

In sum, the decisions of courts in other circuits convince us that *Robins Dry Dock* is both a widely used and necessary limitation on recovery for economic losses. The holdings in *Kinsman* and *Union Oil* are not to the contrary. The courts in both those cases made plain that restrictions on the concept of foreseeability ought to be imposed where recovery is sought for pure economic losses.

–6–

Jurisprudence developed in the Gulf states informs our maritime decisions. It supports the *Robins* rule. Courts applying the tort law of Texas, Georgia, Florida, Alabama, Mississippi and Louisiana have consistently denied recovery for economic losses negligently inflicted where there was no physical damage to a proprietary interest.

* * *

5. Judge Sneed wrote:

Nothing said in this opinion is intended to suggest, for example, that every decline in the general commercial activity of every business in the Santa Barbara area following the occurrences of 1969 constitutes a legally cognizable injury for which the defendants may be responsible. The plaintiffs in the present action lawfully and directly make use of a resource of the sea, *viz,* its fish, in the ordinary course of their business. This type of use is entitled to protection from negligent conduct by the defendants in their drilling operations. Both the plaintiffs and defendants conduct their business operations away from land and in, on and under the sea. Both must carry on their commercial enterprises in a reasonably prudent manner. Neither should be permitted negligently to inflict commercial injury on the other. We decide no more than this.

501 F.2d at 570–71.

IV

Plaintiffs urge that the requirement of physical injury to a proprietary interest is arbitrary, unfair, and illogical, as it denies recovery for foreseeable injury caused by negligent acts. At its bottom the argument is that questions of remoteness ought to be left to the trier of fact. Ultimately the question becomes who ought to decide-judge or jury-and whether there will be a rule beyond the jacket of a given case. The plaintiffs contend that the "problem" need not be separately addressed, but instead should be handled by "traditional" principles of tort law. Putting the problem of which doctrine is the traditional one aside, their rhetorical questions are flawed in several respects.

Those who would delete the requirement of physical damage have no rule or principle to substitute. Their approach fails to recognize limits upon the adjudicating ability of courts. * * *

Review of the foreseeable consequences of the collision of the SEA DANIEL and TESTBANK demonstrates the wave upon wave of successive economic consequences and the managerial role plaintiffs would have us assume. The vessel delayed in St. Louis may be unable to fulfill its obligation to haul from Memphis, to the injury of the shipper, to the injury of the buyers, to the injury of their customers. Plaintiffs concede, as do all who attack the requirement of physical damage, that a line would need to be drawn-somewhere on the other side, each plaintiff would say in turn, of its recovery. Plaintiffs advocate not only that the lines be drawn elsewhere but also that they be drawn on an ad hoc and discrete basis. The result would be that no determinable measure of the limit of foreseeability would precede the decision on liability. We are told that when the claim is too remote, or too tenuous, recovery will be denied. Presumably then, as among all plaintiffs suffering foreseeable economic loss, recovery will turn on a judge or jury's decision. There will be no rationale for the differing results save the "judgment" of the trier of fact. Concededly, it can "decide" all the claims presented, and with comparative if not absolute ease. The point is not that such a process cannot be administered but rather that its judgments would be much less the products of a determinable rule of law. In this important sense, the resulting decisions would be judicial products only in their draw upon judicial resources.

The bright line rule of damage to a proprietary interest, as most, has the virtue of predictability with the vice of creating results in cases at its edge that are said to be "unjust" or "unfair." Plaintiffs point to seemingly perverse results, where claims the rule allows and those it disallows are juxtaposed-such as vessels striking a dock, causing minor but recoverable damage, then lurching athwart a channel causing great but unrecoverable economic loss. The answer is that when lines are drawn sufficiently sharp in their definitional edges to be reasonable and predictable, such differing results are the inevitable result-indeed, decisions are the desired product. But there is more. The line drawing sought by plaintiffs is no less arbitrary because the line drawing appears only in the outcome-as one claimant is found too remote and another is allowed to recover. The true difference is that plaintiffs' approach would mask the results. The present rule would be more candid, and in addition, by making results more predictable, serves a normative function. It operates as a rule of law and allows a court to adjudicate rather than manage.[6]

V

That the rule is identifiable and will predict outcomes in advance of the ultimate decision about recovery enables it to play additional roles. Here we agree with plaintiffs that economic analysis, even at the rudimentary level of jurists, is helpful both in the identification of such roles and the essaying of how the roles play. Thus it is suggested that placing all the consequence of its error on the maritime industry will enhance its incentive for safety. While correct, as far as such analysis goes, such *in terrorem* benefits have an optimal level. Presumably, when the cost of an unsafe condition exceeds its utility there is an incentive to change. As the costs of an accident become increasing multiples of its utility, however, there is a point at which greater accident costs lose meaning, and the incentive curve flattens. When the accident costs are added in large but unknowable amounts the value of the exercise is diminished.

With a disaster inflicting large and reverberating injuries through the economy, as here, we believe the more important economic inquiry is that of relative cost of administration, and in maritime matters administration quickly involves insurance. Those economic losses not recoverable under the present rule for lack of physical damage to a proprietary interest are the subject of first party or loss insurance. The rule change would work a shift to the more costly liability system of third party insurance. For the same reasons that courts have imposed limits on the concept of foreseeability, liability insurance might not be readily obtainable for the types of losses asserted here. As Professor James has noted, "[s]erious practical problems face insurers in handling insurance against potentially wide, open-ended liability. From an insurer's point of view it is not practical to cover, without limit, a liability that may reach catastrophic proportions, or to fix a reasonable premium on a risk that does not lend itself to actuarial measurement." James, *supra,* at 53. By contrast, first party insurance is feasible for many of the economic losses claimed here. Each businessman who might be affected by a disruption of river traffic or by a halt in fishing activities can protect against that eventuality at a relatively low cost since his own potential losses are finite and readily discernible. Thus, to the extent that economic analysis informs our decision here, we think that it favors retention of the present rule.

6. Fuller, *The Forms and Limits of Adjudication,* 92 Harv.L.Rev. 353, 396 (1978). This case illustrates how our technocratic tradition masks a deep difference in attitudes toward the roles of a judiciary. The difference between the majority and dissenting opinions is far more than a choice between competing maritime rules. The majority is driven by the principle of self ordering and modesty for the judicial role; the dissent accepts a role of management which can strain the limits of adjudication

VI

Plaintiffs argue alternatively that their claims of economic losses are cognizable in maritime tort because the pollution from the collision constituted a public nuisance, and violated the Rivers and Harbors Appropriation Act of 1899 and Louisiana law. We look to each in turn.

–1–

Plaintiffs seek to avoid the *Robins* rule by characterizing their claims as damages caused by a public nuisance. They suggest that when a defendant unreasonably interferes with public rights by obstructing navigation or negligently polluting a waterway he creates a public nuisance for which recovery is available to all who have sustained "particular damages." As defined at common law such damages are those which are substantially greater than the presumed-at-law damages suffered by the general public as a result of the nuisance. *See generally Restatement (Second) of Torts* §§ 821B, 821C (1977); Prosser, *Private Action For Public Nuisance,* 52 Va.L.Rev. 997 (1966). Characterizing the problem as one of public nuisance, however, does not immediately solve the problems with plaintiffs' damage claims for pure economic losses. As Dean Prosser has explained, "courts have not always found it at all easy to determine what is sufficient 'particular damage' to support [a] private action [for a public nuisance], and some rather fine lines have been drawn in the decisions." W. Prosser, *Law of Torts* § 88 (4th ed. 1971). In drawing such lines today we are unconvinced that we should abandon the physical damage limitation as a prerequisite to recovery for economic loss.

The problem in public nuisance theory of determining when private damages are sufficiently distinct from those suffered by the general public so as to justify recovery is as difficult, if not more so, as determining which foreseeable damages are too remote to justify recovery in negligence. In each case it is a matter of degree, and in each case lines must be drawn. With economic losses such as the ones claimed here the problem is to determine who among an entire community that has been commercially affected by an accident has sustained a pecuniary loss so great as to justify distinguishing his losses from similar losses suffered by others. Given the difficulty of this task, we see no jurisprudential advantage in permitting the use of nuisance theory to skirt the *Robins* rule.

* * *

–2–

Plaintiffs' arguments that the Rivers and Harbors Appropriation Act affords them an avenue of relief are foreclosed by Supreme Court decision. Plaintiffs suggest that both Section 10 of the Act, which prohibits the obstruction of navigable waters, and Section 13 of the Act, which prohibits the deposit of refuse into navigable waters, have been violated, and that such violations provide a basis for civil liability. In *California v. Sierra Club,* 451 U.S. 287, 101 S.Ct. 1775, 68 L.Ed.2d 101 (1981), the Court held that the Rivers and Harbors Appropriation Act did not authorize private actions to be brought for violation of its provisions. Accordingly, plaintiffs' claims under the Rivers and Harbors Act may not be maintained.

–3–

Plaintiffs also urge that their economic losses are recoverable as state law claims in negligence, nuisance or under the Louisiana Environmental Affairs Act of 1980. Because established principles of general maritime law govern the issue of recovery in this case, we reject these state law theories.

* * *

It is well-settled that the invocation of federal admiralty jurisdiction results in the application of federal admiralty law rather than state law.

* * *

VII

In conclusion, having reexamined the history and central purpose of the doctrine of *Robins Dry Dock* as developed in this circuit, we remain committed to its teaching. Denying recovery for pure economic losses is a pragmatic limitation on the doctrine of foreseeability, a limitation we find to be both workable and useful. Nor do we find persuasive plaintiffs' arguments that their economic losses are recoverable under a public nuisance theory, as damages for violation of federal statutes, or under state law.Accordingly, the decision of the district court granting summary judgment to defendants on all claims for economic losses unaccompanied by physical damage to property is AFFIRMED

GEE, CIRCUIT JUDGE, with whom CLARK, CHIEF JUDGE, joins, concurring:

Both the majority opinion and the dissent do our Court proud, joining a few others on that relatively short list of truly distinguished and thoughtful legal writings of which it or any court can boast.

* * *

If the rule which Judge Wisdom espouses were one written in stone, I would be the first to enforce it by whatever means and procedures, inadequate or no, were available. That is not the question. The question is whether we should *ourselves adopt* such a rule and then proceed to apply it. My answer is that since I do not believe we are capable of administering such a procedure justly, we should not set ourselves the task. Nor am I so clear as my dissenting brethren seem to be about where the high ground lies in these premises. Extending theories of liability may not always be the more moral course, especially in such a case as this, where the extension, in the course of awarding damages to unnumbered claimants for injuries that are unavoidably speculative, may well visit destruction on enterprise after enterprise, with the consequent loss of employment and productive capacity which that entails.

JERRE S. WILLIAMS, CIRCUIT JUDGE, concurring specially:

My brother Higginbotham in his opinion for the Court correctly points out in footnote [2] that the issue of liability to the commercial fishermen who were financially injured because of this ship collision and resultant spillage is not before us and is an undecided issue in this Circuit.

I am not in serious disagreement with the Court's approach on this issue as set out in the footnote. I write for purposes of emphasis more than to differ. My concern is that I have considerable doubt that commercial fishermen can establish a proprietary interest in the right to fish in their fishing waters. Certainly the common legal synonym for "proprietary interest" is "ownership", as legal lexicons attest. Yet the bright line rule of the Court's opinion places emphasis upon a requisite proprietary interest.

It would be preferable, in my view, to have the rule include a clear recognition that the rights of commercial fishermen were more accurately defined by the Court in *Union Oil Co. v. Oppen,* 501 F.2d 558 (9th Cir.1974), one of the cases discussed by Judge Higginbotham. The Court agreed that ordinarily there is no recovery for economic losses unaccompanied by physical damage. It found, however, that commercial fishermen were foreseeable plaintiffs whose interests the oil company had a duty to protect when conducting its operations which resulted in the spillage. The rule that should prevail was effectively stated by Judge Sneed in that case in the quotation set out in Judge Higginbotham's opinion. I repeat it here for emphasis:

> Nothing said in this opinion is intended to suggest, for example, that every decline in the general commercial activity of every business in the Santa Barbara area following the occurrences of 1969 constitutes a legally cognizable injury for which the defendants may be responsible. *The plaintiffs in the present action lawfully and directly make use of a resource of the sea, viz,* its fish, in the ordinary course of their business. This type of use is entitled to protection from negligent conduct by the defendants in their drilling operations. Both the plaintiffs and defendants conduct their business operations away from land and in, on and under the sea. Both must carry on their commercial enterprises in a reasonably prudent manner. Neither should be permitted negligently to inflict commercial injury on the other. We decide no more than this. (Emphasis added.) 501 F.2d at 570.

The commercial fishermen properly recover because their livelihood comes from a "resource" of the water which was polluted. Yet, physical property owned by them was not damaged and it is doubtful that a proprietary interest could have been shown.

I recognize that the Court's opinion in footnote 10 accepted *Union Oil* as a possible alternative analysis as to the rights of the commercial fishermen. I write to give it greater emphasis than is to be found in the footnote reference and to stress it as the more realistic alternative than a proprietary interest analysis. I would prefer that the rule be stated with enough additional breadth to allow recovery for those who are damaged because they make their living out of a "resource" of the water.

I concur fully in the result in this case because I am in full agreement with the decision of the Court as to all the claimants who are before us. But I have the reservation expressed above as to the rule of law which is stated in the Court's opinion.

* * *

WISDOM, CIRCUIT JUDGE, with whom ALVIN B. RUBIN, POLITZ, TATE, and JOHNSON, CIRCUIT JUDGES, join, dissenting.

Robins is the Tar Baby of tort law in this circuit. And the brier-patch is far away. This Court's application of *Robins* is out of step with contemporary tort doctrine, works substantial injustice on innocent victims, and is unsupported by the considerations that justified the Supreme Court's 1927 decision.

Robins was a tort case grounded on a contract. Whatever the justification for the original holding, this Court's requirement of physical injury as a condition to recovery is an unwarranted step backwards in torts jurisprudence. The resulting bar for claims of economic loss unaccompanied by any physical damage conflicts with conventional tort principles of foreseeability and proximate cause. I would analyze the plaintiffs' claims under these principles, using the "particular damage" requirement of public nuisance law as an additional means of limiting claims. Although this approach requires a case-by-case analysis, it comports with the fundamental idea of fairness that innocent plaintiffs should receive compensation and negligent defendants should bear the cost of their tortious acts. Such a result is worth the additional costs of adjudicating these claims, and this rule of liability appears to be more economically efficient. Finally, this result would relieve courts of the necessity of manufacturing exceptions totally inconsistent with the expanded *Robins* rule of requiring physical injury as a prerequisite to recovery.

* * *

The enduring appeal of *Robins,* despite its inapplicability to cases such as this one, seems to spring from the administrative convenience of a "conspicuous bright-line rule" and from "the virtue of predictability". In a frequently cited extension of *Robins,* an Ohio Court of Appeals was remarkably candid in its justification for relying on *Robins. Stevenson v. East Oil & Gas Co.,* Ohio Ct.App. 1946, 73 N.E.2d 200. In *Stevenson* a defendant negligently obstructed a factory building, necessitating a large-scale lay-off. The court felt that it would be impossible to draw a workable line of liability between workers out of their jobs and restaurant owners supplying the workers' lunches:

> "While the reason usually given for the refusal to permit recovery in this class of cases is that the damages are 'indirect' or are 'too remote' it is our opinion that the principal reason that has motivated the

courts in denying recovery in this class of cases is that to permit recovery of damages in such cases would open the door to a mass of litigation which might very well overwhelm the courts so that in the long run while injustice might result in special cases, the ends of justice are conserved by laying down and enforcing the general rule so well stated by Mr. Justice Holmes. . . ."

73 N.E.2d at 202

Our notions of proximate cause and foreseeability are admittedly less adequate in truncating a chain of claims where the conduit through which the harm passes is contract. If a contract between *A* and *B* provides sufficient nexus for *B* to recover after *A*'s physical injury, then it is difficult to distinguish *C*'s contract with *B,* or *D*'s contract with *C.* In short, one contract seems as good as the next for establishing proximate cause and foreseeability once the first claim is allowed. *Robins* resolves this dilemma by disallowing all third party claims based solely upon a contractual relationship with the injured party.

There are sound reasons for such a rule. Courts recognize that once they permit recovery for economic loss to parties linked in a serial chain of contracts, defining a stopping point becomes nearly impossible. In *Robins,* for example, the shipowner had settled his claim against the drydocker, apparently for the rents the shipowner would have received from the charterer had there not been an additional delay. *Robins,* 2 Cir.1926, 13 F.2d 3, 4. Had Justice Holmes imposed liability again in the *Robins* appeal for the charterer's lost profits, the tortfeasor would have been required to make good the still better bargain of the charterer. Similarly, if the charterer had a contract with parties on shore to clean the charterer's catch, the drydock would have been required to make good on this bargain as well. This iteration of compensation could conceivably run without limit. Liability would accrue "in an indeterminate amount for an indeterminate time to an indeterminate class". *Ultramares Corp. v. Touche,* N.Y. 1931, 255 N.Y. 170, 179, 174 N.E. 441, 444 (Cardozo, C.J.). In limiting recovery in a chain of contractual relations, the Supreme Court drew the line after the first claim for damages. Justice Holmes had thus fashioned a rule in claims arising from a chain of contracts that would avoid a multiplicity of actions and prevent a vast extension of liability. * * *

II. THE INAPPLICABILITY OF *Robins Dry Dock* TO THIS CASE

Whatever the pragmatic justification for the original holding in *Robins,* the majority has extended the case beyond the warrant of clear necessity in requiring *a physical injury* for a recovery of economic loss in cases such as the one before the court. *Robins* prevented plaintiffs who were neither proximately nor foreseeably injured by a tortious act or product from recovering solely by claiming a contract with the injured party. The wisdom of this rule is apparent. This rule, however, has been expanded now to bar recovery by plaintiffs who would be allowed to recover if judged under conventional principles of foreseeability and proximate cause.

A. The Precise Holding of Robins Applies Only to Claims for Negligent Interference with Contract.

Because the centerpiece of this litigation has been *Robins,* the holding of this oft-cited case merits scrutiny. A ship's time charterer was required under contract to turn the vessel over to a dry dock for maintenance. The charterer owed no rent during the time the ship was under repair. The drydocker, who had contracted with the owner of the ship for the work, negligently damaged the ship's propeller. During the additional delay caused by repairs to the propeller, the charterer lost expected profits from the use of the ship. The charterer sued the shipyard for these economic losses. The Supreme Court denied relief, holding that the shipyard's damage to the propeller wronged only the owner of the ship. The Court further held that the charterer had lost merely the benefit of his contract for hire and had suffered no legally cognizable claim:

> "[The plaintiff's] loss arose only through [its] contract with the owners-and while intentionally to bring about a breach of contract may give rise to a cause of action, no authority need be cited to show that, as a general rule, at least, a tort to the person or property of one man does not make the tort-feasor liable to another merely because the injured person was under a contract with that other, unknown to the doer of the wrong. The law does not spread its protection so far."

275 U.S. at 308–09, 48 S.Ct. at 135, 72 L.Ed. at 292 (citations omitted).

Robins held only that if a defendant's negligence injures party *A,* and the plaintiff suffers loss of expected income or profits because it had a contract with *A,* then the plaintiff has no cause of action based on the defendant's negligence.

* * *

Although the majority says that this Court has not "been the sole guardian of the *Robins Dry Dock* principle", the majority's support is reminiscent of the Potemkin Village set up for Catherine the Great to visit. In both the Second and the Fourth Circuits courts have recently limited the applicability of the *Robins* rule in maritime torts.

The Second Circuit's opening volley on *Robins* was *Petition of Kinsman Transit Co.,* 2 Cir.1968, 388 F.2d 821 (*Kinsman II*), which has effectively limited the applicability of *Robins* to a small number of maritime torts. * * *

In the Fourth Circuit, District Judge Merhige refused to dismiss claims for economic losses suffered by commercial fishermen, local boat, and tackle and bait shop owners, but did dismiss claims by the plaintiffs who purchased and marketed seafood from commercial fishermen. Those losses, although foreseeable, were too indirect. *Pruitt v. Allied Chemical Corp.,* E.D.Va.1981, 523 F.Supp. 975.

Finally, the ramparts have been breached in the Ninth Circuit. Although the majority says that *Union Oil Co. v. Oppen,* 9 Cir.1974, 501

F.2d 558, is "not contrary" to our Court's affirmation of the *Robins* rule, a close reading of *Oppen* indicates that this is incorrect. In *Oppen,* a mishap in 1969 at an offshore oil drilling platform introduced hundreds of thousands of gallons of oil into the ocean off the coast of Santa Barbara, California. Although a strict application of the extensions of *Robins* would have barred all recovery, the Ninth Circuit allowed fishermen to recover for the loss of their livelihood. After acknowledging the "widely recognized principle" that a plaintiff could not recover for the negligently induced loss of "a prospective pecuniary advantage", *id.* at 563, the Court noted the many exceptions to this rule, "in which defendants engaged in certain professions, businesses, or trades have been held liable for economic losses resulting from the negligent performance of tasks within the course of their callings", *id.* 566. The Court regarded the real question to be whether Union owed a duty to the fishermen. This in turn depended on whether Union could foresee a risk of harm to fishermen:

> [W]e can not escape the conclusion that under California law the presence of a duty on the part of the defendants in this case would turn *substantially on foreseeability. That being the crucial determinant,* the question must be asked whether the defendants could reasonably have foreseen that negligently conducted drilling operations might diminish aquatic life and thus injure the business of commercial fishermen. We believe the answer is yes.

Id. at 569 (emphasis added).[7]

* * *

---

7. Judge Sneed also based his holding on the traditional deference accorded to fishermen under maritime law: * * *

I would go further than *Oppen* in repudiating the applicability of *Robins. Oppen* allowed the fishermen to recover-a result that all on our Court seem to agree with-but the opinion fails to draw a very convincing line between the rights of fishermen and the rights of others who draw their living from the water. Certainly the injury from the oil spill to others who make their living upon the water, such as boat charterers who are unable to put to sea, is as foreseeable and as direct as the injury to the fishermen. It is therefore unclear why these parties should not also be entitled to recovery. The court did attempt to distinguish fishermen in that they "lawfully and directly make use of a resource of the sea, *viz.* its fish, in the ordinary course of their business". *Id.* at 570. Yet, if those who make use of a "resource of the sea" are entitled to recovery, then it seems *a fortiori* that those who make use of the sea itself in their business-a boat charterer, for example-would be entitled to recovery. Nor can *Oppen*'s restricted recovery be explained in terms of special property rights in the fish. No one owns a wild animal, or fish, until achieving capture, and under this rule, the fishermen had no rights to the fish superior to those of Union Oil. *See* Epstein, *Nuisance Law: Corrective Justice and Its Utilitarian Constraints,* 8 J.Legal Stud. 49 (1979). After reminding us that no one owns a wild animal until after achieving capture, he argues:

> "[S]o it is with unowned fish in *Oppen.* The plaintiffs who do not own the fish cannot complain if the Union Oil Company captures them. As they cannot complain of capture, they cannot complain of destruction after capture. As they cannot complain of destruction after capture, they cannot complain of it before capture. No theory of tortious liability can make up the plaintiffs' deficit attributable to their want of ownership."

Id. at 52. *See also* Posner, *Some Uses and Abuses of Economics in Law,* 46 U.Chi.L.Rev. 281, 305 (1979).

The *Oppen* court's stopping point is no more logical than that of courts that have followed *Robins*'s extensions. Today, the majority has difficulty in justifying recovery for fishermen while at the same time denying recovery to all other parties. This difficulty highlights *Oppen*'s failure to

With deference to the majority, I suggest, notwithstanding their well reasoned opinion, that the utility derived from having a "bright line" boundary does not outweigh the disutility caused by the limitation on recovery imposed by the physical-damage requirement. *Robins* and its progeny represent a wide departure from the usual tort doctrines of foreseeability and proximate cause. Those doctrines, as refined in the law of public nuisance, provide a rule of recovery that compensates innocent plaintiffs and holds the defendants liable for much of the harm proximately caused by their negligence.

* * *

V. CONCLUSION

The *Robins* approach restricts liability more severely than the policies behind limitations on liability require and imposes the cost of the accident on the victim, who is usually not in a superior position to obtain insurance to cover this loss. I would apply a rule of recovery based on conventional tort principles of proximate cause and foreseeability and limit eligibility only by the requirement that a claimant prove "particular" damages.

* * *

Robins should not be extended beyond its actual holding and should not be applied in cases like this, for the result is a denial of recompense to innocent persons who have suffered a real injury as a result of someone else's fault. We should not flinch from redressing injury because Congress has been indifferent to the problem.

[The concurring opinion of JUDGE GARWOOD is omitted]

NOTES

1. In omitted portions of Judge Wisdom's lengthy dissent, he basically adopts the public nuisance approach to the problem and then offers a detailed analysis of who has suffered a sufficiently "particular injury" to recover for pure economic loss. He would provide recovery to commercial fishermen and to owners of vessels trapped in the river during the cleanup process. He then offers the following analysis of who, beyond this set of defendants can recover.

> The land-based businesses that have claimed damages include drydocks, marinas, bait and tackle shops, seafood processors, seafood wholesalers, and restaurants. It is here that drawing the line becomes difficult, for these businesses have been affected by the PCP spill, but all would agree that a seafood restaurant in New Orleans should not recover for a loss of business from consumers' concern over contaminated products.
>
> The general test of recovery for these claimants is whether their business of supplying a vital commodity or service to those engaged in the

---

have a conceptually tenable stopping point for the imposition of liability and the denial of recovery. If *Oppen* is consistent with *Robins*'s extensions, it is only because *Oppen* attempts to limit liability on as arbitrary a basis as *Robins*'s progeny.

> maritime industry has been interrupted by the collision, the closure, or the embargo. Marinas, for example, in the afflicted area should be allowed to recover. If all shipping and boating is suspended, then a marina or drydock in the area affected is unable to supply docking or repair services to users of the waterway.[8] No mitigation of damages is possible. The same would be true for similarly situated boat charterers who supply marine "common carrier" services. Bait and tackle shops present a similar situation: The condemnation of a large fishing area damages or destroys the livelihood of those shops whose business is exclusively predicated upon supplying direct inputs (bait, fuel) to those whose commercial undertakings have been foreclosed by the quarantine and embargo.[9] Finally, seafood processors and seafood wholesalers that provide services for the condemned area should recover.
>
> There is a point beyond which we cannot allow recovery. Seafood restaurants, for example, are not providers of a vital service to the afflicted area. Their damage is not sufficiently distinguishable from general economic dislocation to allow for recovery. They are too removed from the tortious act. A plaintiff may also be barred because it is not sufficiently involved with the afflicted area as a supplier of vital inputs peculiar to maritime activities. The bar would arise, for example, if a bait and tackle shop were only partially connected with a foreclosed area. Basically, a claim for damages that is indistinguishable from a general grievance furnishes no basis for recovery.

Testbank at. 1050–51. Is this careful parsing of who can and who cannot recover the very type of thing that concerns the majority? Should it?

2. The economic loss rule in stranger cases is more difficult to justify because the main argument in favor of the rule in non-stranger situations—the parties are in a better position to allocate risks through contract provisions—is missing or at least greatly weakened. For instance, if a professional basketball star is negligently run over by a motorist, the injured player can recover for his physical injuries and his loss of earning capacity, but the owner of an arena who suffers diminution in attendance because the star is unable to perform will not have any remedy against the negligent motorist. In these stranger cases, the parties had no opportunity to allocate, via their bargain, the risks of poor performance or negligence. Thus, the stranger cases do not so clearly rest on the availability and superiority of the contract regime for allocating loss. However, as the majority notes, the risks of economic loss may be allocated through insurance. Indeed, many enterprises carry business interruption policies. Is this a superior way to deal with the problem of pure economic loss? Why or why not?

3. In the absence of the superiority-of-contract justification the economic loss rule in stranger cases is most frequently justified on the basis of a fear of unlimited and unpredictable liability and, therefore, a disproportionality

---

8. A marina could not recover for losses from the poor business or closure of its restaurant or a gift shop because these businesses do not provide a vital service to a primary maritime industry.

9. Bait shops that had long-term contracts would be unable to recover under *Robins*. I would limit *Robins* to express contracts.

between liability and fault. There are, however, a number of additional arguments in favor of the rule.

Several instrumental arguments in favor of the economic loss rule have been advanced. One argument is a concern that full compensation for all economic losses will over-deter and potentially drive valuable enterprises into bankruptcy. This argument is picked up in Judge Gee's concurring opinion in *Testbank,* when he notes that extending liability to a substantial number of entities suffering economic harm "may well visit destruction on enterprise after enterprise, with the consequent loss of employment and productive capacity which that entails." *Testbank* at 1034.

A second instrumental argument relates to the availability of third party insurance. Insofar as liability is open ended, insurance companies will be reluctant to write policies that cover any more than a small percentage of potential losses. Indeed, it is not clear that all but the largest firms would even chose to insure against such catastrophic liability. Recall that the majority in *Testbank* pit this relative unavailability against the supposed availability of first party insurance individuals and businesses may purchase to cover economic losses.

A third argument focuses on the threat that over-deterrence will cause firms to adopt an overly-cautious approach. But, one might argue, if this is so, so be it. If in fact the costs of a line of conduct include these pure economic losses, should they not be internalized? Perhaps surprisingly, a number of scholars have said no. As Judge Posner suggested in *Rardin* they argue that many economic losses are not true social costs. The economic losses that befall some result in economic gain for others. See generally, Eric Kades, Windfalls, 108 Yale L. J. 1489, 1531 (1999). If, due to an oil spill, a family does not go to the gulf coast for a vacation, undoubtedly this harms commercial interests along that coast. If, however, the family chooses instead to vacation on Florida's east coast, well away from the effects of the oil spill, this produces an offsetting gain for commercial interests along that coastline. If the tortfeasor is compelled to pay for the economic loss it caused gulf coast interests, by what argument should it not be permitted to recapture the economic gains enjoyed by the east coast interests? For a useful elaboration on this issue, *see* Ronen Perry, The Deepwater Horizon Oil Spill and the Limits of Civil Liability, 86 Wash. L. Rev. 1, 16–17 (2011).

4. The extended discussion of the *Oppen* case in both the majority and dissent highlights the difficulty of justifying the commercial fisherman exception to the economic loss rule. The pre-*Oppen* opinion in Burgess v. M/V Tamano, 370 F.Supp. 247 (D. Maine 1973) justified the exception using a public nuisance theory as did the court in Leo v. General Electric Co., 145 A.D.2d 291, 538 N.Y.S.2d 844 (1989). In Chapter 1, p. 43, *supra*, we noted the difficulty of applying the special injury rule in this context. Here is the *Burgess* court's attempt to explain why fishermen, but not others, suffer a particular injury necessary to bring a private cause of action for a public nuisance:

> The commercial fishermen and clam diggers in the present cases clearly have a special interest, quite apart from that of the public generally, to take fish and harvest clams from the coastal waters of the State of Maine.

> The injury of which they complain has resulted from defendants' alleged interference with *their* direct exercise of the public right to fish and to dig clams.
>
> * * *
>
> Unlike the commercial fishermen and clam diggers, the Old Orchard Beach businessmen do not assert any interference with *their* direct exercise of a public right. They complain only of loss of customers indirectly resulting from alleged pollution of the coastal waters and beaches in which they do not have a property interest. Although in some instances their damage may be greater in degree, the injury of which they complain, which is derivative from that of the public at large, is common to all businesses and residents of the Old Orchard Beach area. In such circumstances, the line is drawn and the courts have consistently denied recovery.

Burgess at 250–51. One might wonder if simply italicizing the word "their" twice actually clarifies why gathering the fish in the sea is a special right of commercial fishermen and not common to all who fish while the use of the public beach by economic interests with businesses along the shore is not. It is not surprising, therefore, that the court concedes that "the line between damages different in kind and those different only in degree from those suffered by the public at large has been difficult to draw."

Other courts have focused on the license justification, suggested by the majority in *Testbank*, This approach is adopted in Curd v. Mosaic Fertilizer, LLC, 39 So.3d 1216, 1228 (Fla. 2010). This approach, too, is open to critique. In his dissent in *Curd*, Justice Polston noted:

> Although the majority rules that the commercial fishermen's state licenses set them apart from the general population, if every state-licensed Floridian has a "special" or "unique" interest, then it seems there is endless "foreseeable" liability. Commercial fishermen are a small group, among thousands of licensed Floridians, who can claim economic damages from pollution of coastal waters. For example, hotels and restaurants near the beach, seafood truck drivers, beach community realtors, and yacht salesmen are all licensed by the State to conduct commercial activities that may be negatively affected by pollution of coastal waters. *Curd* at 1233.

Some courts are prepared to allow others to fit within exceptions to the economic loss rule, but ultimately they, too, draw a line excluding other claims. *See Pruitt v. Allied Chemical Corp.*, 523 F.Supp. 975 (E.D.Va.1981).

Regardless of its theoretical underpinnings, the commercial fisherman exception is now well established. Given the problems facing these justifications, is Judge Wisdom correct in saying that drawing the line so as to include commercial fishermen but no others is just as arbitrary as an economic loss rule that denies recovery to everyone? Perhaps the commercial fisherman exception may be best thought of as simply that: the fisherman exception. *See* George Christie, *The Uneasy Place of Principle in Tort Law*, 49 SMU L. Rev. 525 (1996).

5. *The Deepwater Horizon spill.* The economic loss rule once again emerged in the aftermath of the Deepwaer Horizon drilling rig explosion and the blow out of the Macando well in the summer of 2010. Before the well was finally capped, approximately 200 million gallons of oil escaped into the Gulf of Mexico off the coast of Louisiana—18 times more oil than was spilled in the Exxon Valdez disaster. The majority owner of the well was BP. Liability for the spill is set forth in the Oil Pollution Liability and Compensation Act of 1990, 33 U.S.C.§§ 2701—2720, passed in the aftermath of the Exxon Valdez spill. Liability under the act is capped at $75 million unless the incident was proximately caused by the gross negligence or willful misconduct of the responsible party, or its violation of an applicable Federal safety, construction, or operating regulations. § 2704.

Section 2702 of the Act provides in relevant part:

Elements of liability

(a) In general

Notwithstanding any other provision or rule of law, and subject to the provisions of this Act, each responsible party for a vessel or a facility from which oil is discharged, or which poses the substantial threat of a discharge of oil, into or upon the navigable waters or adjoining shorelines or the exclusive economic zone is liable for the removal costs and damages specified in subsection (b) of this section that result from such incident.

(b) Covered removal costs and damages

* * *

2) Damages: The damages referred to in subsection (a) of this section are the following: . . .

B) Real or personal property

Damages for injury to, or economic losses resulting from destruction of, real or personal property, which shall be recoverable by a claimant who owns or leases that property.

* * *

(E) Profits and earning capacity

Damages equal to the loss of profits or impairment of earning capacity due to the injury, destruction, or loss of real property, personal property, or natural resources, which shall be recoverable by any claimant.

Thus § 2702(b)(2)(E) provides for the recovery of some pure economic loss. The provision undoubtedly permits recovery by commercial fisherman, but who else can recover under this provision? Does this cover the lost profits of a beachfront hotel that lost customers because of oil on its beach? Does it cover lost profits of the laundry that had a contract to clean the towels and sheets used by hotel guests? Does it cover lost sales of new linens to the hotel by a company in Wisconsin that has an exclusive contract with the hotel to provide such linens when it proves its total sales to the hotel declined 10% during the summer and fall of 2010? Does it cover a catering company in New York City that people a BP headquarters often used to cater events, and who has suffered a substantial downturn in this business because BP has decided to tighten its belt and have fewer catered events in an attempt to save money? Does the statute offer any help in answering these questions?

BP chose to set up a $20 billion fund operated by the Gulf Coast Claims Facility to compensate those affected by the spill. The fund sought legal advice as to which economic loss claims it should honor. Professor John Goldberg offered his assessment in a memo to the GCCF. John C.P. Goldberg, *Liability for Economic Loss in Connection With the Deepwater Horizon Spill*. The memorandum my be found at http://www.gulfcoastclaimsfacility.com/Goldberg.Memorandum.of.Law.2010.pdf. Professor Robertson offers a rebuttal to this analysis in David W. Robertson, *The Oil Pollution Act's Provisions on Damages for Economic Loss*, 30 Miss. C. L. Rev. 157 (2011). *See also*, Andrew B. Davis, *Pure Economic Loss Claims Under the Oil Pollution Act: Combining Police and Congressional Intent*, 45 Colum. J.L. & Soc. Probs. 1 (2011); Robert Force, *Deepwater Horizon: Removal Costs, Civil Damages, Crimes, Civil Penalties, and State Remedies in Oil Spill Cases,* 85 Tul. L. Rev. 889, 936 (2011).

C. FIDUCIARY DUTY

Claims for breach of fiduciary duty exist under the common law of torts, and also under a number of state and federal statutes. As a common law doctrine, an important early pronouncement was Justice Cardozo's opinion in Meinhard v. Salmon, 249 N.Y. 458, 164 N.E. 545, 546 (N.Y. 1928). Discussing the duties of partners and co-adventurers in real estate contexts, he commented: "Many forms of conduct permissible in a workaday world for those acting at arm's length are forbidden to those bound by fiduciary ties. A trustee is held to something stricter than the morals of the market place. Not honesty alone, but the punctilio of an honor the most sensitive, is then the standard of behavior. As to this there has developed a tradition that is unbending and inveterate."

Breach of fiduciary duty is a tort cause of action in most states, and has become an increasingly significant part of modern business tort litigation. Although the emphasis in this book is on the common law of fiduciary duty, many of the principles discussed here apply in various statutory settings, because many statutory fiduciary principles borrow from common law concepts.

1. DEFINITIONS AND ELEMENTS OF PROOF

A fiduciary relationship can exist in a broad range of contexts. Definitions vary; a basic formulation is that a fiduciary is one in whom another has justifiably placed trust and confidence to act in the best interest of the other. A fiduciary relationship is not created just because X requests or pays Y to do something for X. Rather, the fiduciary "obtains power . . . for the sole purpose of enabling the fiduciary to act effectively" in the interests of the one on whose behalf the power has been given. Tamar Franklin, *Fiduciary Law*, 71 Cal. L. Rev. 795, 809 (1983). Tamar Franklin, FIDUCIARY LAW (2011). A fiduciary might obtain any of a wide variety of delegated powers depending on the needs of the entrustor.

An understanding of fiduciary obligations requires attention to the closely related, but not identical, notion of agency. According to the *Restatement (Third) of Agency* § 1.01, an agency relationship exists when (1) a person (the principal) manifests assent to another person (the agent) that the agent will act on the principal's behalf and subject to the principal's control, and (2) the agent manifests assent or otherwise consents to act. If an agency relationship exists, the relationship is fiduciary in nature. Thus, an agent is always a fiduciary of the principal with respect to activities within the scope of the agency relationship. It is important to realize, however, that fiduciary relationships can arise even when the relationship is not one of agency.

Establishing that a breach of fiduciary relationship has occurred requires analysis of several points: (1) At the time of the alleged misconduct, did a fiduciary relationship exist? (2) If the answer to the first question is yes, then what was the scope of the fiduciary relationship? and (3) Did the fiduciary breach the duties that existed within the scope of that relationship? Robert Kutcher & Benjamin W. Bronston, Breach of Fiduciary Duties, in ABA Section of Litigation, Business Torts Litigation, Chapter 1, at 1 (1992). Remedies for breach of fiduciary duty can include compensatory damages or equitable relief.

2. EXISTENCE OF A FIDUCIARY RELATIONSHIP

Courts have found that some relationships are fiduciary as a matter of law. Examples include: attorney-client (attorney is fiduciary); principal-agent (agent is a fiduciary); partner-partner (partners stand in fiduciary relationships to each other); trustee of a trust; estate executor. When the relationship is in one of these or other "as a matter of law" categories, the factfinder does not have to make a finding on the existence of a fiduciary relationship. Outside of these "as a matter of law" categories, a fiduciary relationship can exist on the facts of a given case. The facts must give rise to a finding that the parties had a special relationship under which one party places confidence in the other, giving the other a position of superiority and influence. As one court put it, "A fiduciary relationship may arise as a matter of law by virtue of the parties' relationship, e.g., attorney-client, or it may arise as a result of the special circumstances of the parties' relationship where one places trust in another so that the latter gains superiority and influence over the other." Shervin v. Huntleigh Securities Corp., 85 S.W.3d 737, 740 (Mo. Ct. App. 2002). This does not mean, however, that a fiduciary relationship exists whenever one party places trust in another. The unilateral investment of confidence by one party in the other is usually not enough, by itself, to create a fiduciary relationship. Unless the fiduciary relationship can be established as a matter of law, it is a question for the factfinder.

Two examples can illustrate relationships that might be fiduciary on the facts, but that are not fiduciary as a matter of law. One is the relationship between a franchisor and franchisee. Courts have held that this relationship is not fiduciary as a matter of law, but that a particular franchisor/franchisee relationship might rise to the level of a fiduciary relationship on certain facts. *See* Crim Truck & Tractor Co. v. Navistar Int'l Transportation Corp., 823 S.W.2d 591 (Tex. 1992). Likewise, the relationship between a borrower and lender (bank) is not usually deemed fiduciary as a matter of law. Yet a bank might "owe a fiduciary duty to a customer if special circumstances exist where the bank acts as an advisor or asserts influence in the customer's business." Kondelik v. First Fidelity Bank, 259 Mont. 446, 857 P.2d 687, 691 (Mont. 1993).

Courts vary in their approach to the question of when fiduciary duties should attach to relationships that are not held to be of a fiduciary nature as a matter of law. Some courts are reluctant to recognize fiduciary relationships when they are not similar to traditional fiduciary relationships. *See* Wolf v. Superior Court of Los Angeles County, 130 Cal.Rptr.2d 860 (Cal.App. 2003). Other courts are more open to imposing fiduciary duties whenever the principles on which fiduciary relationships rest are met. In Roberts v. Sears, Roebuck & Co, 573 F.2d 976 (7th Cir. 1978) the plaintiff, a sales clerk for the defendant, invented a new type of socket wrench in his off hours. He showed the invention to his manager. The defendant persuaded the inventor that the idea had limited patentability, and appeal and induced him into agreeing to assign all his rights in return for royalty payments to a maximum of $10,000. Sears then proceeded to mass produce the item, eventually selling millions of units. In affirming a jury verdict for the plaintiff, the court noted there are no hard and fast rules for determining whether a relationship exists. However, the focus should be on whether "one person reposes trust and confidence in another who thereby gains a resulting influence and superiority over the first." In the case at hand factors relevant to that inquiry included the disparity of age, education and business experience between the parties as well as the existence of an employment relationship and the exchange of confidential information from one party to the other.

> All five of those factors are present in this case. In addition, one of Sears' witnesses admitted that the company expected plaintiff to "believe" and to "rely" on various representations that Sears made to him. Obviously, this question is best left to the trier of fact, and this court under any circumstances would hesitate to disturb the jury's findings. That hesitation is especially strong here where so many factors suggest that a confidential relationship in fact existed.

Id. at 983. *See generally*, Leonard Rotman, *Fiduciary Law's "Holy Grail": Reconciling Theory and Practice in Fiduciary Jurisprudence*, 91 B.U. L. Rev. 921 (2011)

3. SCOPE OF THE FIDUCIARY RELATIONSHIP

When a fiduciary relationship exists, this does not mean that the person is a fiduciary with respect to the entire sphere of possible activities that the fiduciary might take. Obviously, the fiduciary relationship must have some boundaries; it must have a scope. For instance, if a client retains an attorney to represent her in connection with a personal injury suit, the client cannot later complain that the attorney breached a fiduciary duty by failing to update the client's will. The scope of the retention, in this situation, determines the scope of the fiduciary relationship. Or suppose that X retains a financial advisor to review X's portfolio for the purpose of advising X about the most financial sensible mechanism for financing the college education of X's four grandchildren, and then maintaining that investment mechanism. X could not later complain that the financial advisor failed to inform X that X was woefully underinsured with respect to disability insurance. The scope of the fiduciary relationship will not always be easy to determine. The scope might be determined by statute, or it might be clear from a written or oral agreement between the parties.

4. BREACH OF FIDUCIARY OBLIGATIONS

Jurisdictions vary in the exact phrasing of the duties of a fiduciary, but the core duties that attach to the fiduciary's role include: duty of loyalty; confidence (both in terms of use of confidences and disclosure of confidences); communication, and competence. Note that, when one focuses only on the duty of competence, a claim for breach of fiduciary duty seems hard to distinguish, factually or in principle, from a claim for negligence or professional negligence. Most claims for breach of fiduciary duty implicate, in some way, the duties of loyalty, confidence, and communication. Breaches of fiduciary duty can take hundreds of forms. The most common include: self-dealing; acting with conflict of interest; usurping a business or corporate opportunity; misappropriating funds; neglect; failure to act in the other's best interest; misrepresenting or omitting a material fact; misuse of confidential information or breach of confidentiality. When a fact issue exists as to whether a breach occurred, a jury typically receives instructions that specify the duties of loyalty, confidence, communication, etc. For instance, consider the following jury instruction from State Bar of Texas, Pattern Jury Charge 104.2 (2000), which is substantively similar to the obligations imposed on fiduciaries under the common law of most states:

- The transaction[s] in question was/were fair and equitable to P;
- D made reasonable use of the confidence that P placed in him;
- D acted in the utmost good faith and exercised the most scrupulous honesty toward P;
- D placed the interests of P before D's own, did not use the advantage of his position to gain any benefit for himself at the expense of P, and did

not place himself in any position where his self-interest might conflict with his obligations as a fiduciary; and

- D fully and fairly disclosed all important information to P concerning the transactions

D. MISREPRESENTATION: INTENTIONAL AND NEGLIGENT

1. INTRODUCTION

Consider the following two scenarios:

Example 1. A farmer applies for a loan from a bank, pledging as collateral most of his farm machinery. The bank agrees to lend the farmer $1,000,000, but on one condition: the farmer must obtain a letter from a lawyer certifying that there are no prior liens on the machinery. The farmer asks a friend of his, who is a lawyer, to prepare a letter. The lawyer does so, and gives the letter to the farmer. The letter states that the lawyer "conducted a thorough search" and that "the machinery is free and clear of all liens." But the lawyer never conducted such a search, and the machinery indeed did have prior liens. The farmer defaults on the loan, and the bank is unable to obtain the collateral because it is pledged to other creditors.

Example 2. A weight control clinic enrolls clients and recommends that they take a dietary supplement manufactured by the clinic. The clinic's literature claims that the supplement provides "full nutritional needs" and is "safe, with no side effects." A client of the clinic suffers an adverse reaction to a dose of the supplement that has been tainted with a toxic substance.

These two simple scenarios pose a number of themes that the materials in this section explore.

Personal Injury Versus Purely Economic Loss. Misrepresentations can lead either to personal injury or to purely economic loss. Liability for misrepresentation exists for both contexts. With respect to personal injury contexts, if a defendant intentionally or negligently gives false information, and if a person suffers physical harm as a result of reasonably relying on this information, then the defendant is liable for full tort damages. *See Restatement (Second) of Torts* § 311 (1965). In a somewhat later doctrinal development, courts also developed a theory of liability for personal injury based on "innocent" misrepresentations; that is, false statements of fact that were not made either fraudulently or as a result of lack of due care. Section 402B of the *Restatement (Second) of Torts* and § 9 of the *Restatement (Third) of Torts: Products Liability* provide for a cause of action in such cases if (1) the defendant is engaged in the business of selling chattels, (2) the defendant misrepresents to the public a material fact relating to the quality or character of the chattel, and (3) physical harm is caused by justifiable reliance on the misrepresentation. *See* page 175, *infra*.

On the facts of Example 2, the plaintiff might not be able to show either that the clinic made the false statement with knowledge of its falsity, or that the clinic made the statement without having taken reasonable care. But in any event the clinic would be subject to liability if the jurisdiction had adopted the theory of liability based on section 402B.

This section primarily addresses the use of misrepresentation theories to recover for purely economic losses. From one perspective, misrepresentation law stands as an exception to the general "economic loss rule," in tort law. As you consider this area of law in more detail, consider whether and to what extent the reasons for tort's traditional economic loss rule do or do not apply to misrepresentation contexts.

The Defendant's State of Mind. The examples illustrate that a misrepresentation might be the product of different states of mind and different motives. A defendant might have made the statement knowing it to be false, with or without a purpose to harm. Or a defendant might have been reckless about the truth of the statement, or negligent. Finally, a defendant might have made a statement that is false even though the speaker neither knew this nor could have known it was false, even by exercising reasonable care. These differences are reflected in the law of misrepresentation, which has developed three theories of liability: fraud, negligent misrepresentation, and innocent misrepresentation.

Reliance, Justified Reliance, Materiality, and Contributory Negligence. The examples raise the issues of reliance, materiality, justified reliance, and contributory negligence. Should it matter whether the bank in Example 1 could have easily obtained a second opinion? Should it matter whether the client of the weight loss clinic was reasonable in believing that the vitamin supplement was safe, or should it be enough to show that she did in fact believe it to be safe? Even if she can state a prima facie case, should the defendant be able to raise a contributory negligence defense against the client?

Who May Sue. The examples also raise the issue of *who* may sue for misrepresentation. The bank was not in contractual privity with the lawyer; rather, the lawyer was in a contractual, lawyer-client relationship with the farmer. Should the law of misrepresentation extend to "third parties" such as the bank? If so, should it matter whether the defendant knew about third party's likely reliance on the letter?

One additional point should be noted at the outset. Misrepresentations by one contracting party have often formed the basis of a claim by the other party for rescission of the contract. If a person is merely seeking rescission of a transaction, he may be entitled to relief on the basis of negligent or even innocent misrepresentations. Indeed rescission, under these circumstances, is merely part of the general question of when a reasonable mistake can justify equitable relief. *See* H. McClintock, Equity

253–55 (1948). The following materials, however, focus on the use of misrepresentation theories as a basis for affirmative relief in tort.

2. FRAUDULENT MISREPRESENTATION

The oldest form of misrepresentation-based tort liability is that for fraudulent misrepresentation, sometimes known as "deceit" or "intentional misrepresentation." The following gives some history about this theory.

1 T. Street, The Foundations of Legal Liability, 374–377 (1906).

> Deceit consists of the fraudulent imposition of damage, and this damage commonly takes the form of pecuniary loss or risk of pecuniary loss. The idea which is at the root of liability in deceit is that of a detriment imposed by fraud. It corresponds with the conception of *dolus* in the Roman law. Let us proceed to discover the process by which the common law was led to grasp this notion of liability arising from dishonesty.
>
> One of the very oldest of common-law writs is the writ of deceit *(breve de deceptione).*[10] Consideration of the scope of this early writ shows where legal evolution in the field of fraud began. The first form of deceit which was recognized by the common law as a ground of legal liability was that which embodied a deception of the court and a consequent perversion of the ordinary course of legal proceeding. Of such a wrong the common law could take notice because it was an interference with the administration of royal justice. The wrong was viewed as an offense against the king as well as a wrong against the individual who happened to be damaged. Hence the wrongdoer had to pay a fine to the king as well as damages to the individual. False personation in court proceedings, whereby actions were brought without authority or judgments recovered against persons ignorant of the pendency of a suit, was the most common grievance for which the writ of deceit was used.
>
> Deceit was one of the first of common-law actions to feel the stimulus of the statute specially authorizing the issuance of writs *in consimili casu* with writs already formed; and under the influence of that statute, the action of deceit or case in the nature of deceit began to be used for many other purposes than that of recovering damages for deceitful practices in court proceedings. Illustrations of the extended use of the action on the case in the nature of deceit are found in situations like these: If one who had been retained as legal counsel fraudulently colluded with his client's adversary; or if one who had been retained of counsel to be at court on a certain day, failed to come, whereby the cause was lost; or if a man who professed skill in a common calling like that of a smith, lamed the horse that he had

10. The writ of deceit was already known in the time of John. 2 Poll. & Mait. Hist.Eng.Law, 2d ed., 535, citing Select Civil Pleas, pl. III (A.D.1201).

undertaken to shoe; or if a farrier undertook to cure a graveled horse, but on the contrary killed him; in all these cases, it was held, an action on the case in the nature of deceit lay at common law.

Reference to the authorities * * * will show that the old writ of deceit was entirely merged in or superseded by the action on the case in the nature of deceit and that in the latter form it became the general common-law remedy for fraudulent acts of any kind which result in actual damage. The remedy was broad enough to cover such wrongs as malicious prosecution and abuse of legal process, and, indeed, much of the old law on these topics is tucked away under the heading 'Deceit' in the old books.

FOLLO v. FLORINDO

Supreme Court of Vermont, 2009.
185 Vt. 390, 970 A.2d 1230.

BURGESS, J.

Defendants Paul Florindo and Susan Morency appeal from a jury verdict and judgment against them for common-law fraud * * * in connection with their sale of a bed and breakfast business. Both defendants claim that the evidence did not support the verdict, that the jury instructions regarding common law and consumer fraud were plainly erroneous * * *. We affirm on all counts.

Plaintiff, Carl Follo, the purchaser and current operator of the bed and breakfast, cross-appeals on two issues. First, he claims error in the trial court's exclusion of punitive damages as a matter of law. Second, plaintiff argues that it was improper for the trial court to order remittitur of a portion of the jury award. We reverse the trial court's punitive-damages decision and affirm the remittitur order.

I. Background

A. History of the Real Estate Transactions

In 2000, defendants formed a Vermont limited liability company, Cranberry Farm, LLC. Defendant Morency owned 51% of the LLC and was president and treasurer while defendant Florindo owned 49% and was vice-president, secretary, and assistant treasurer of the company. Defendants created Cranberry Farm, LLC to acquire an inn in Vermont, and soon after it was formed, the company purchased an inn on twenty-seven acres of land in Rockingham, Vermont (the Inn) for $825,000. Defendants' lenders required an appraisal of the parcel, and the appraised value was the same as the purchase price. * * * In the same year, 2000, but acting as individuals instead of through either of their companies, defendants purchased a single-family house (the Cottage) on twenty acres of land adjacent to the Inn for $175,000.

Over the next two years, defendants redecorated and operated the Inn while also separately renting out the Cottage.* * * [I]n the summer of

2002, defendants decided to sell the Inn and the Cottage. Defendants listed the properties with a real estate company, Hospitality Consultants. Hospitality Consultants marketed the Inn and the Cottage together in one brochure, listing the Inn for $1,195,000 and the Cottage for $225,000.

Around the time that defendants decided to get out of the innkeeping business, plaintiff decided to enter it. When plaintiff decided he wanted to buy a bed and breakfast, he began researching methods for evaluating inns listed for sale. During his research, plaintiff learned about a "gross revenue multiplier" approach to calculating sales prices for inns. Under this approach, a prospective buyer multiplies the inn's gross earnings by a number between three and seven to determine an appropriate sales price. Plaintiff decided he would buy only an inn that showed it was profitable, that he could acquire for a maximum of five times the inn's gross sales, and that would cost less than $1 million.

Plaintiff entered into negotiations to purchase defendants' Inn late in 2002. He specifically pursued the Inn, even though the listed sales price was above his $1 million limit, because the profit-and-loss statement included in the marketing brochure for the Inn showed that it was a solid business. During negotiations, plaintiff asked for and received reports, including tax returns, from defendants (via the real estate agent) on the revenues, sales, expenses, and net income of the Inn during 2001 and 2002. Relying on these reports, plaintiff used the "gross revenue multiplier" approach to calculate that the property was worth $1,130,000 by multiplying the Inn's reported 2001 sales of $226,000 by five. Plaintiff then offered $1,080,000 for the Inn. However, in order to succeed with his bid for the Inn, plaintiff felt it was necessary to bid simultaneously on the Cottage because another bidder was prepared to make a bid on both properties at the same time. Plaintiff discussed with the real estate agent and defendant Florindo whether they thought he could raise sufficient revenue from the Cottage to cover its purchase price if he remodeled the Cottage to contain three suites, then rented those as part of the Inn business. According to plaintiff, both the real estate agent and Florindo expressed the opinion that he would "absolutely" get his money back using that plan, at least in part due to the occupancy rates and demand during certain times of the year as represented by defendants when they operated the Inn. Plaintiff purchased both the Inn and the Cottage for $1,245,000 in March 2003.

As he began to operate the Inn during the spring of 2003, plaintiff realized that the Inn's sales for the first few months of his ownership were less than one-quarter of the sales figures he expected based on the information defendants provided prior to sale. To boost sales, plaintiff decided to try a mailing directed at the Inn's former customers and requested guest registration information from defendant Florindo. Subsequent communications between the parties led plaintiff to suspect that defendants had not truthfully represented the Inn's actual revenues and occupancy rates in the realtor's marketing brochure and the various reports and tax returns defendants provided plaintiff during sale negotiations. His exchanges with defendants eventually led plaintiff to file this lawsuit in early 2004.

* * *

After deliberating, the jury returned a verdict against defendants Florindo and Morency for common-law fraud * * *, but found in favor of the realtor and its agents. The jury awarded damages for plaintiff in the amount of $645,000.

* * *

However, the trial court held that the jury's damages award was higher than it could be under the law of the case and the evidence presented by plaintiff. The court concluded that the evidence presented was sufficient to support a damages award of only $295,000. Based on this determination, the court conditionally denied defendant's motion for a new trial on damages subject to plaintiff's agreement to remit any claim of damages above $295,000. Plaintiff agreed to the remittitur, and the court entered final judgment against defendants for damages of $295,000 plus prejudgment interest, costs, and attorney's fees. Defendants appealed here and plaintiff filed his cross-appeal.

* * *

D. The Common–Law Fraud Claims

We turn now to defendants' contests of their common-law fraud liability.

* * *

The trial court's instructions on common-law fraud stated, in relevant part:

> In order to prove fraud, plaintiffs must demonstrate by clear and convincing evidence each of the following essential elements. One, that defendants misrepresented an existing fact which affected the essence of the transaction with plaintiffs or knowingly allowed another to make such a representation on defendants' behalf; two, that defendants did so intentionally; three, that the misrepresentation was false when made and known at the time to be false by a defendant, or that the representation was recklessly made as being within the defendants' own knowledge without defendant in fact knowing whether it was true or not.

Both defendants argue that they were entitled to judgment as a matter of law on common-law fraud mainly because they claim there was insufficient evidence to show that they knew their misrepresentations were false when made. The jury instructions allow a fraud verdict both for defendants' actual knowledge of the falsity of their representations and for recklessly making misrepresentations without actual knowledge. To evaluate whether the evidence fairly and reasonably supports the jury's fraud verdict, it is helpful to flesh out the meaning of "recklessly" in the context of common-law fraud.

Fraud exists not only when speakers knows their statements are false, but also when the statements are "made in such a reckless manner that the law will presume them to be made with knowledge." *Town of Townshend v. Howard's Estate,* 94 Vt. 215, 217, 109 A. 903, 904 (1920); see also *Bennington Housing Auth. v. Bush,* 182 Vt. 133, 933 A.2d 207 (fraud can consist in making a false statement "with reckless indifference as to its truth") (quotation omitted).

The Restatement (Second) of Torts provides guidance on this issue. According to the Restatement, an actual fraudulent representation occurs when a person misrepresents a fact in a way that "assert[s] that the maker knows it" to be so, but in fact "has merely a belief in its existence and recognizes that there is a chance . . . that the fact may not be as it is represented." Restatement (Second) of Torts § 526 cmt. e (1977). Fraud perpetrated in this manner is characterized as a "false representation . . . made . . . *recklessly*" because the person making the misrepresentation asserts something as fact regardless of "whether it is true or false." *Id.* (emphasis added). Additionally, when someone makes a false representation of fact and expressly states that it is based upon the

> maker's personal knowledge of the fact in question or even upon his personal investigation of the matter. . . . [or] though not expressly so stated, the representation [is] made in a form or under such circumstances as to imply that this is the case. . . . [then the] misrepresentation so made is fraudulent even though the maker is honestly convinced of its truth from hearsay or other sources that he believes to be reliable.

Id. cmt. f. These two comments explain situations where actual fraud lies even when there is no proof that the reporter of a material fact has actual knowledge of the falsity of the representation. See also *Powell v. D.C. Hous. Auth.,* 818 A.2d 188, 197–98 (D.C.2003) ("To find that a misstatement was made with knowledge of its falsity, the person accused . . . must be found to have known that the statement was false, or to have made that statement with reckless indifference as to its truth.") * * * These explanations are consistent with the trial court's jury instruction, and we hold that there was sufficient evidence for a reasonable jury to find that defendants committed fraud under the actual knowledge and the reckless standard.

Taking the evidence in the light most favorable to the jury's verdict and to plaintiff, the following facts were established at trial. Plaintiff's decision to buy the Inn and Cottage for $1,245,000 was founded in large part on his belief that the Inn generated certain levels of revenue and maintained certain occupancy rates during the years of defendants' operation. Plaintiff's beliefs on these subjects came from several documents that were either created by defendants or by third parties based on information that defendants provided. One of the documents was the brochure produced by the real estate agency, misrepresenting the Inn's profits and losses, occupancy information, and room rates for 2001. Another document was a separate profit-and-loss statement for the Inn for 2002, which the real estate agent provided plaintiff. The real estate agent also provided plaintiff with Cranberry Farm, LLC's 2001 income tax return. These documents indicated that the Inn had over $226,000 in gross revenue in 2001 and over $250,000 in gross revenue in 2002. In discussions with the real estate agency, plaintiff was told that those numbers represented the Inn's revenues without including the additional nine percent rooms-and-meals tax. At trial, the real estate agents testified that all of the financial information about the Inn that they presented to plaintiff came from defendants, although their direct dealings were with defendant Florindo.

Data gathered by plaintiff after he purchased the Inn, and in discovery after commencing this lawsuit, contradicted the representations contained in the brochure, the profit-and-loss statements, and the 2001 tax return. Before filing this suit, plaintiff obtained from defendants the original guest-information forms defendants kept for the Inn's 2002 reservations, which revealed the actual room sales for 2002 amounted to only about one-fifth of the sales defendants claimed in the 2002 profit-and-loss statement provided to plaintiff via the real estate agency. During discovery, plaintiff received defendants' room-assignment book for August 2002 through January 2003. According to defendants' bookkeeping system, the guest-information forms and room-assignment book should have contained duplicative information regarding room sales and occupancy. However, trial testimony by both plaintiff and defendant Morency revealed that the guest-information forms, which defendants had provided plaintiff before this lawsuit was commenced, listed many customers not corroborated by the room assignment book. As noted above, even the occupancy rates culled by plaintiff from the guest-information forms fell far short of the occupancy rate represented in the documents provided by defendants before plaintiff purchased the Inn.

Other documents contradicted defendants' representations to plaintiff prior to purchase. An audit of defendants' tax and bank records, obtained in discovery, documented far less income than the approximately $226,000 and $250,000 represented in defendants' disclosures to plaintiff prior to the sale of the Inn. The Inn's tax returns indicated room sales of just over $54,000 in 2001 and a little more than $49,000 in 2002. All of the Inn's bank deposits for the relevant years showed the Inn's 2001 total sales at about $88,000 and their 2002 sales at just under $110,000. Plaintiff's evidence of misrepresentation was ample.

Moreover, Mr. Florindo's testimony supplied evidence that his misrepresentations were knowingly or recklessly made. The trial court found that Mr. Florindo's testimony could be construed as unresponsive or evasive by a reasonable jury. The court concluded that a reasonable jury could imply from this evasiveness that defendant Florindo intentionally falsified the figures shared with plaintiff. Additionally, the court concluded that even if the jury would not find that Mr. Florindo was being evasive or that he had provided false numbers intentionally, the jury could believe that it was reckless for him to provide the revenue numbers for potential buyers of the property given how little understanding he claimed to have about the revenues and sales, and how little data and supporting evidence he could provide for those numbers.

Our review of the record supports the trial court's characterization of Mr. Florindo's testimony. * * *

Ms. Morency argues that all of the trial testimony, including that of plaintiff's and her co-defendants', revealed that she, personally, never made any representations to plaintiff regarding the Inn's finances. She notes that there was no evidence that she communicated any financial information about the Inn to the real estate agents who marketed the Inn and Cottage to plaintiff. Further, Ms. Morency claims that she never knew that the companies' tax returns contained any inaccuracies or that defendant Florindo provided the tax returns to the real estate agents for use in marketing the Inn. Ms. Morency argues that all of this evidence shows that she did not take any actions that could be considered fraudulent and that she did not have the requisite knowledge of the misrepresentations of the Inn's finances made to plaintiff to be liable for fraud.

We agree that the record does not reveal any evidence that Ms. Morency made misrepresentations directly to plaintiff or directly to the real estate agents, as Mr. Florindo did. Instead, the evidence of fraud by defendant Morency subsists in her documented involvement in the companies and the business of operating the Inn and in her trial testimony.

* * *

[T]he guest-information forms and room-assignment book that plaintiff introduced at trial were filled out, for the most part, in Ms. Morency's handwriting. Even though she had filled out those forms, she could not explain why the 2002 guest-information forms contained many customer names and reservations that never appeared in the corresponding room-assignment book. This provides sufficient information for a reasonable jury to conclude that defendant Morency made misrepresentations by aiding in supplying false statements of occupancy rates to plaintiff while he was deciding to purchase the Inn. * * *

Although she testified that she had no idea that Mr. Florindo supplied the false documentation to plaintiff, a reasonable jury simply could have discredited her testimony, under the circumstances, as a false, and inculpatory, protestation of innocence. * * *

In sum, given the jury instructions and the totality of the evidence presented at trial, there is no basis for reversing the jury's verdict or ordering a new trial as a matter of law. Coupling her trial testimony with her background and experience with the Inn and Mr. Florindo, there is sufficient evidence to support the jury's verdict that defendant Morency participated in the fraud. The evidence fairly and reasonably supports the charges of common-law fraud against both defendants.

III. Plaintiff's Issues on Cross–Appeal

A. Punitive Damages

* * *

Because the jury in the present case found defendants liable for actual common-law fraud, an intentional act with a specific intent to defraud the buyer, the trial court erred in not sending the issue of punitive damages to the jury.

B. Remittitur

The final issue before us is plaintiff's cross-appeal on the issue of whether it was appropriate for the trial court to have ordered either remittitur of part of the jury's damages award or a new trial. * * * [T]he court gave plaintiff the option of accepting a remittitur of any damages above $295,000 or a new trial. While a party who accepts a remittitur, as plaintiff did here, may not then appeal it directly, it may cross-appeal on that issue if the opposing party appeals on other issues. As thus allowed in response to defendants' appeal, plaintiff now argues that the court's order of remittitur was error because the jury's award was consistent with the jury instructions on damages and with the evidence presented at trial.

In this case, the jury was instructed that it could measure damages either by "the difference between the purchase price paid by Plaintiffs and the actual fair market value of the business as it existed at the time of any fraudulent . . . misrepresentations or deceptive statements" or by the benefit-of-the-bargain measure. The benefit-of-the-bargain measure of damages was defined as the "amounts [plaintiff] believe[s] the business would have generated in profit had the income and expenses been as represented by Defendants." The trial court explicitly stated that the jury could award damages under only one of these measures, not both. * * *

There was arguably evidence to support either approach. The jury had before it plaintiff's purchase price of $1,245,000, and plaintiff's expert witness's market price appraisal of the property of $950,000. Also for the jury's consideration was evidence of the revenues and profit-and-loss statements that defendants presented to plaintiff before plaintiff purchased the property, and the evidence of the profits actually produced by the property under defendants' ownership.

At closing, however, not relying on this evidence, plaintiff argued instead that he would have paid only $600,000 for the Inn had he known the Inn's actual revenue figures. This argument arose from plaintiff's own purchasing guidelines employed when shopping for a bed and breakfast, specifically the "gross revenue multiplier" approach to valuing businesses. Plaintiff stated he would have paid, at most, $600,000 for the Inn because that amount was just over five times the Inn's actual gross revenues, as calculated by plaintiff's accountant, for the last full year of defendants' ownership. Plaintiff argued to the jury for a recovery of the difference between the $1,245,000 purchase price and the "gross revenue multiplier" figure of $600,000.

The jury returned damages for plaintiff in the amount of $645,000, which is the exact difference between plaintiff's actual purchase price and his hypothetical purchase price using the "gross revenue multiplier." The trial court granted defendants' motion for remittitur because it concluded that this award had no basis in the court's jury instructions on damages, and that the "gross revenue multiplier" approach was not an accepted method for calculating damages. It also noted that the benefit-of-the-bargain instruction focused on profits plaintiff would have received, not revenues, and that the "gross revenue multiplier" approach was focused wholly on revenues. Determination of loss, or damages, cannot be achieved by measuring revenue alone. The trial court explained that plaintiff did not make any "effort to demonstrate from the evidence how they had realized smaller profits than they reasonably ought to have expected given the deceptive representations." Further, plaintiff had not even offered evidence regarding his actual revenues. Thus, there was no basis for the jury to measure benefit-of-the-bargain damages based on plaintiff's case. It was equally evident that the $600,000 figure was not a reasonable fair market value of the property in light of plaintiff's own expert's appraisal value of $950,000. The trial court noted, reasonably, that it was "inconceivable" that defendants would have accepted an offer of $600,000 given plaintiff's own expert appraisal of the property at the time of trial. For these reasons, the trial court determined that the jury's award was excessive and that "the only fair measure of damages which the jury could have assessed" was the difference between the purchase price and the properties' fair market value as presented by plaintiff's expert appraiser, which difference was $295,000.

"Remittitur is within the sound discretion of the trial court, and its ruling will not be set aside on appeal absent abuse of discretion." *Lent v. Huntoon,* 143 Vt. 539, 553, 470 A.2d 1162, 1172 (1983). Considering the trial court's close examination and analysis of the jury instructions, the jury's damages award, and the evidence presented at trial, we cannot say that it abused its discretion here. The jury's award far exceeds the amount it could have calculated based on market value and purchase price, and, as the trial court stated, plaintiff gave the jury no basis to find that the Inn would have generated profits of $645,000 more than it did had the business' income and expenses been as defendants represented them.

We also hold that the remittitur amount ordered by the trial court was appropriate.

* * *

Affirmed in part and reversed in part. Remanded for jury determination of punitive damages, if any, to be awarded.

NOTES

1. *Elements of Fraud*. There are several formulations of the elements of fraud depending on the particularity with which each aspect of the tort is defined. Here are two statements of the elements:

> Under Missouri law, the elements of an action for fraudulent misrepresentation are: 1) a false, material representation; 2) the speaker's knowledge of its falsity or his ignorance of its truth; 3) the speaker's intent that it should be acted upon by the hearer in the manner reasonably contemplated; 4) the hearer's ignorance of the falsity of the statement; 5) the hearer's reliance on its truth; 6) the hearer's right to rely thereon; and 7) the hearer's consequent and proximately caused injury.

Reding v. Goldman Sachs & Co., 382 F. Supp. 2d 1112, 1117 (E.D. Mo. 2005).

In Delaware, common law fraud consists of:

> (1) a false representation, usually one of fact, made by the defendant; (2) the defendant's knowledge or belief that the representation was false, or was made with reckless indifference to the truth; (3) an intent to induce the plaintiff to act or to refrain from acting; (4) the plaintiff's action or inaction taken in justifiable reliance upon the representation; and (5) damage to the plaintiff as a result of such reliance.

Snowstorm Acquisition Corp. v. Tecumseh Products Co., 739 F.Supp.2d 686, 708 (D. Del. 2010). As one can see, both definitions basically say the same thing.

2. *Falsity, Fraud, Purpose, and Intent*. The second element in both of these definitions, paralleling *Restatement (Second) of Torts* § 526, requires proof of a particular state of mind with regard to the statement's truth or falsity. This is often known as the scienter requirement. The third element requires proof that the defendant had the purpose to induce reliance; some courts require either "purpose or intent" to induce reliance. Notice that the plaintiff does not need to prove that the defendant intended or had a purpose *to cause harm* to the plaintiff. The scienter requirement can be established by proof that the defendant knew the statement was false. But, as the Restatement and *Follo* reflect, something less than knowledge of falsity can suffice. For example, a deceit occurs when the defendant states that something is true but knows that he has no present basis for making that statement, although he hopes that the statement might be true or that subsequent events will make it true.

Given the evidence as recounted in the court's opinion, and using the Restatement formulation, what arguments could Follo make to establish each element of the cause of action for fraudulent misrepresentation? Could the defendants make any plausible arguments that one or more of the elements were not established?

3. *Remedies*. Because fraudulent misrepresentation is a tort, tort's general damage principle is usually thought to apply: restoring the plaintiff, to the degree money can do so, to the position plaintiff occupied before the

wrongful act. Applying this general principle to misrepresentation scenarios has raised a number of interesting damages issues.

a. Benefit of the bargain vs. out-of-pocket damages. The first issue is whether the "benefit of the bargain" or the "out-of-pocket" measure should be used to compensate for the plaintiff's pecuniary harm. Most courts agree with *Follo* and allow a plaintiff who succeeds on a fraudulent misrepresentation claim to recover under either measure. A good number of courts, however, only allow the out-of-pocket measure if the claim is for negligent, rather than fraudulent, misrepresentation. *See* D. Dobbs, Law of Remedies (553–54 2d ed.). Some courts generally use only the out-of-pocket measure, but will allow the benefit of the bargain measure if the out-of-pocket measure seems particularly inappropriate. *See* B.F. Goodrich v. Mesabi Tire Co., 430 N.W.2d 180 (Minn.1988).

The *Follo* court gave the plaintiff his out-of-pocket damages because he failed to present evidence on what he would have been entitled to under the benefit of the bargain test. As the court notes, benefit-of-the-bargain damages are not simply lost revenue but lost revenue minus expenses, i.e. lost profits. Exactly what evidence would Mr. Follo have needed to present to recover under this test? How hard would it have been for him to produce such evidence?

If the question is one of lost profits, how long into the future will the courts look to assess this loss? For example, could Mr. Follo collect damages for (discounted) lost profits twenty years hence? Most courts limit what can be recovered by requiring that benefit of the bargain damages must be proven with some degree of specificity and they must be the natural, probable, and foreseeable consequence of the defendant's fraud. See Formosa Plastics Corp. USA v. Presidio Engineers and Contractors, Inc., 960 S.W.2d 41 (Tex. 1998). In this regard, does it matter that Mr. Follo has never been in the bed and breakfast business before? Why or why not?

The potential difference between these two measures of damages are easier to see with respect to the sale of a piece of personal property. To take a simple example, suppose a piece of furniture is represented to be an antique and the buyer pays $3000 for it. If the furniture were really an antique, it would be worth $6000. In fact, however, the piece is not an antique and is worth only $2000. The out-of-pocket measure of damages is $1000; the benefit of the bargain measure is $4000. Another example that arises not infrequently is life insurance. Suppose a person has paid premiums totaling $20,000 on a life insurance policy that is represented to cover a spouse and that pays $1 million on death. The spouse dies, but the policy contains an exclusion whose terms were misrepresented when the policy was purchased. The out-of-pocket measure is $20,000, but the benefit of the bargain would yield the $1 million. *See* Jill Wieber Lens, *Honest Confusion: The Purpose of Compensatory Damages in Tort and Fraudulent Misrepresentation*, 59 U. Kan. L. Rev. 231 (2011) for an argument that benefit of the bargain damages in fraud cases are punitive in nature.

If Mr. Follo truly wanted to pay no more than $600,000 for this property, presumably he could have chosen to rescind the sales contract. However, in this context it is generally held that rescission and money damages are inconsistent remedies and he cannot have both. *See* Timmons v. Bender, 601 S.W.2d 688 (Mo. Ct. App. 1980) (holding that plaintiffs in real estate transaction could not sue for fraud where they had elected inconsistent remedy of rescission of the contract of sale); Barnco Int'l, Inc. v. Arkla, Inc., 628 So.2d 162 (La. Ct. App. 1993) (holding that plaintiff could be denied damages based on lost profits where he had elected dissolution of contract).

b. Consequential damages. A second damages issue relates to "consequential" pecuniary damages; that is, damages in addition to those measured by the out-of-pocket or benefit of bargain measure and sustained, allegedly, as a consequence of the defendant's misrepresentation. For instance, suppose that the spouse in the life insurance example is unable to pay her mortgage and loses her home as a result of the insurer's nonpayment (and original misrepresentation). In this regard, lost profits often straddle the boundary between benefit of the bargain damages and consequential damages. The lost profits under discussion in *Follo* are generally thought to be direct damages. Sometime, however, parties seek damages for the loss of profits they would have realized from other business opportunities lost as a result of the fraudulent misrepresentation. These are generally categorized as consequential damages. See Springs Window Fashions Div., Inc. v. Blind Maker, Inc., 184 S.W.3d 840, 882–83 (Tex. App. 2006).

In general, tort law places fewer restrictions on the recovery of consequential damages than does contract law. Thus, courts in misrepresentation cases are more likely to allow consequential damages, in addition to those damages measured by the out-of-pocket or benefit of bargain standards. We say more about consequential damages in Chapter 3, *infra*.

c. Mental anguish. A third damages issue is whether mental anguish should be allowed. The majority of courts and the Restatement take the position that mental anguish is not recoverable for misrepresentation, even for fraudulent misrepresentation. The following case explains the divergent views on the issue.

> Some courts take the approach that the purpose of fraud or deceit cases is to put the plaintiff in the position that he would have been in had he not been defrauded. For example, in Cornell v. Wunschel, 408 N.W.2d 369, 382 (Iowa 1987), in considering damages on a claim for fraudulent misrepresentation, the court noted that emotional distress damages "are not ordinarily contemplated in a business transaction." Since deceit is an economic tort and resembles more a contract claim than a tort claim, the court held that emotional distress damages were not recoverable in fraud actions. Other courts, by contrast, have stressed that fraud is a tort cause of action and that even though it may arise out of a contractual dispute, intentional or reckless conduct justifies a broadened scope of damages. * * *
>
> We hold that, upon proof of intentional misrepresentation, a plaintiff may recover "emotional damages that are the natural and proximate result" of the defendant's conduct. * * * While the underlying dispute here is contractual in nature, defendants are alleged to have committed an intentional tort when they misrepresented the payoff amount of the note. Whether or not the tort was committed in a contractual context is

> not dispositive; mental suffering is a "natural and proximate" consequence of intentional fraud and should be a compensable injury. * * *

Osbourne v. Capital City Mortgage Corp., 667 A.2d 1321, 1328 (D.C.App. 1995).

Consider the arguments for and against recovery of mental anguish damages in personal injury torts. Which of these arguments applies to the question of mental anguish recoveries when the plaintiff has suffered pecuniary loss from an intentional misrepresentation? Can business entities collect mental anguish damages?

4. *Justifiable Reliance.* Most courts require that the plaintiff have relied in fact on the representation, and that the reliance be justifiable. According to the Restatement, justifiable reliance requires that the matter misrepresented be a "material" one; materiality is defined as follows:

> (2) The matter is material if
>
> (a) a reasonable man would attach importance to its existence or nonexistence in determining his choice of action in the transaction in question; or
>
> (b) the maker of the representation knows or has reason to know that its recipient regards or is likely to regard the matter as important in determining his choice of action, although a reasonable man would not so regard it.

Restatement (Second) Torts § 538 (1965). The option set out in (a) employs the objective "reasonable man" standard, but option (b) offers a way to bypass the objective standard. For example, if A wishes to induce B to buy stock in a corporation, knows that B believes heavily in astrology, and tells B that the horoscope favors the purchase, then B can establish justifiable reliance even if B's behavior does not comport with that of the reasonable person. For this and other examples and explanations, *see Restatement (Second) Torts* § 538, comment *f* and illustrations.

Why retain an objective standard for all occasions when the maker of the representation does not know or have reason to know of the recipient's unusual beliefs or qualities? We return to a discussion of remedies in the next chapter when we discuss damages for economic torts. See p. 142 *infra.*

5. *Opinion.* The area of opinion has posed special challenges for the law of misrepresentation. An early and much-cited discussion of the subject appeared in Judge Learned Hand's opinion in Vulcan Metals Co. v. Simmons Manufacturing Co., 248 Fed. 853 (2nd Cir. 1918). Simmons Manufacturing had allegedly made a number of representations about the qualities of certain tools, dies, and equipment sold by Simmons for the manufacture of vacuum cleaners. The representations included statements that the machines were perfect in even small details, that water power was the most economical and efficient way of operating a vacuum cleaner, and that it was simple, long-lived, easily operated, and effective, etc.

> [The case raises], therefore, the question of law how far general 'puffing' or 'dealers' talk' can be the basis of an action for deceit.

> The conceded exception in such cases has generally rested upon the distinction between 'opinion' and 'fact'; but that distinction has not escaped the criticism it deserves. An opinion is a fact, and it may be a very relevant fact; the expression of an opinion is the assertion of a belief, and any rule which condones the expression of a consciously false opinion condones a consciously false statement of fact. When the parties are so situated that the buyer may reasonably rely upon the expression of the seller's opinion, it is no excuse to give a false one. Bigler v. Flickinger, 55 Pa. 279. And so it makes much difference whether the parties stand 'on an equality.' For example, we should treat very differently the expressed opinion of a chemist to a layman about the properties of a composition from the same opinion between chemist and chemist, when the buyer had full opportunity to examine. The reason of the rule lies, we think, in this: There are some kinds of talk which no sensible man takes seriously, and if he does he suffers from his credulity. If we were all scrupulously honest, it would not be so; but, as it is, neither party usually believes what the seller says about his own opinions, and each knows it. Such statements, like the claims of campaign managers before election, are rather designed to allay the suspicion which would attend their absence than to be understood as having any relation to objective truth. It is quite true that they induce a compliant temper in the buyer, but it is by a much more subtle process than through the acceptance of his claims for his wares.
>
> * * *
>
> In the case at bar, since the buyer was allowed full opportunity to examine the cleaner and to test it out, we put the parties upon an equality. It seems to us that general statements as to what the cleaner would do, even though consciously false, were not of a kind to be taken literally by the buyer. As between manufacturer and customer, it may not be so; but this was the case of taking over a business, after ample chance to investigate. Such a buyer, who the seller rightly expects will undertake an independent and adequate inquiry into the actual merits of what he gets, has no right to treat as material in his determination statements like these. The standard of honesty permitted by the rule may not be the best; but, as Holmes, J., says in Deming v. Darling, 148 Mass. 504, 20 N.E. 107, 2 L.R.A. 743, the chance that the higgling preparatory to a bargain may be afterwards translated into assurances of quality may perhaps be a set-off to the actual wrong allowed by the rule as it stands.

Id. at 856–58. Was Judge Hand suggesting that an average individual consumer would not be "in equality" with the commercial seller and thus would have a cause of action for representations of the sort that Simmons made? What does the following rationale, set out in the Restatement, suggest should be the outcome if Simmons made such representations to an average individual consumer?

> The law assumes that the ordinary man has a reasonable competence to form his own opinion as to the advisability of entering into those transactions that form part of the ordinary routine of life. The fact that one of the two parties to a bargain is less astute than the other does not

> justify him in relying upon the judgment of the other. This is true even though the transaction in question is one in which the one party knows that the other is somewhat more conversant with the value and quality of the things about which they are bargaining. Thus the purchaser of an ordinary commodity is not justified in relying upon the vendor's opinion of its quality or worth. For example, one who is purchasing a horse from a dealer is not justified in relying upon the dealer's opinion, although the latter has a greater experience in judging the effect of the factors which determine its value.

Restatement (Second) of Torts § 542, comment *d* (1965).

Doctrinally, therefore, courts treat opinions differently than representations of fact, although the precise doctrinal contours diverge somewhat among the jurisdictions. Some courts announce that "pure opinion" cannot as a matter of law serve as a representation for purposes of the law of misrepresentation, unless certain circumstances exist. *See* Transport Ins. Co. v. Faircloth, 898 S.W.2d 269 (Tex.1995). Others courts, and the Restatement, focus not on whether an opinion can constitute a misrepresentation, but on the circumstances when "justifiable reliance" on an opinion can be established. Although these two approaches appear to concentrate on different "elements" of the cause of action, the approaches are fundamentally the same because each allows the recipient to recover if certain circumstances are present. These circumstances include: (1) the maker purports to have special knowledge that the recipient does not have; (2) the maker is in a fiduciary relation with the recipient; or (3) the maker has some special reason to expect that the recipient will rely on the opinion. *See Restatement (Second) of Torts* § 542 (1965).

6. *Statements of Law*. Statements about law also have posed challenges for the law of misrepresentation. Obviously, the litigants in such a context might be a lawyer and the client. If so, the client may have, in addition to the misrepresentation cause of action, a claim for breach of contract, breach of fiduciary duty, or professional negligence. The client might be able to recover under all theories, or perhaps only one or two.

The older view was that misrepresentations of law could not form the basis of a misrepresentation action. Consider two common types of representations of law: a prediction or assertion about a legal outcome ("We will win the case"), and a conclusion about an issue of law ("The procedures that the city followed comply with all applicable state law"; "Exclusion A of the insurance policy excludes coverage in this case"). Under the older view, such representations could not form the basis of a tort cause of action because the recipient should know that no lawyer or layperson can be certain of a legal outcome or issue, and thus the recipient cannot justifiably rely on such statements. Does this rationale convince you that none of the statements just noted should form the basis of a misrepresentation cause of action?

Most jurisdictions now recognize that misrepresentations of law in some circumstances can form the basis of a tort cause of action. Common circumstances include when the opinion contains a material misstatement of fact, when the maker of the opinion purports to have special knowledge of the matter, or when the maker stands in a fiduciary relationship with the recipient. Even when these circumstances are present, however, the question of justifiable reliance will usually be for the factfinder. *See generally Restatement (Second) of Torts* § 545; *see* Nagashima v. Busck, 541 So.2d 783, 783–84 (Fla.App.1989) (discussing traditional approach in this area, exceptions to it, and the "modern" approach).

Consider again the two types of statements mentioned at the beginning of this note: predictions of a legal outcome and conclusions about a legal issue. Would a recipient be justified in relying on any or all of the statements given as examples?

7. *Nondisclosure and Concealment.* Suppose the defendant has not made a representation, but instead has remained silent about or has concealed some material fact. Many such cases arise from real estate transactions. A number of jurisdictions have passed legislation relating to what must be disclosed in real estate transactions. Outside the real estate context, there is no general duty to disclose, unless special circumstances are present. These can include the presence of a fiduciary relationship or some other legal duty. *See Restatement (Second) of* Torts § 551. Ollerman v. O'Rourke Co., Inc., 94 Wis.2d 17, 288 N.W.2d 95(1980).

Here it is often important to distinguish nondisclosure from concealment.

> [E]ven in the absence of a fiduciary, statutory, or other independent legal duty to disclose material information, common-law fraud includes acts taken to conceal, create a false impression, mislead, or otherwise deceive in order to "prevent[ ] the other [party] from acquiring material information." *(Second) of* Torts § 550 (1977); see also W. Page Keeton et al., Prosser and Keeton on Torts § 106 (5th ed. 1984) ("Any words or acts which create a false impression covering up the truth, or which remove an opportunity that might otherwise have led to the discovery of a material fact . . . are classed as misrepresentation, no less than a verbal assurance that the fact is not true.").
>
> Thus, fraudulent concealment-without any misrepresentation or duty to disclose-can constitute common-law fraud. This does not mean, however, that simple nondisclosure similarly constitutes a basis for fraud. Rather, the common law clearly distinguishes between concealment and nondisclosure. The former is characterized by deceptive acts or contrivances intended to hide information, mislead, avoid suspicion, or prevent further inquiry into a material matter. The latter is characterized by mere silence. Although silence as to a material fact (nondisclosure), without an independent disclosure duty, usually does not give rise to an action for fraud, suppression of the truth with the intent to deceive (concealment) does. See, e.g., Stewart v. Wyoming Cattle Ranche Co., 128 U.S. 383, 388, 9 S.Ct. 101, 32 L.Ed. 439 (1888).

United States v. Colton, 231 F.3d 890, 898–99 (4th Cir. 2000).

What of partial disclosures? *See* In re Enron Corp. Securities, Derivative & ERISA Litigation, 761 F.Supp.2d 504 (S.D. Tex. 2011).

8. *Third–Party Recipients.* The defendant might make the misrepresentation directly to the recipient, who then acts in reliance on it. This is the typical pattern in fraudulent misrepresentation cases. But a third party also

might act in reliance on the misrepresentation, even though the defendant did not make the representation directly to him. Most courts allow such a third party to establish fraudulent misrepresentation, so long as the maker "intends or has reason to expect" that the substance of the misrepresentation will be communicated to the third party and will influence the conduct of the third party. *Restatement (Second) of* Torts § 533. The question of misrepresentation-based liability to third parties has arisen most often, and has posed the most difficult questions, in the context of negligent rather than intentional misrepresentation. Thus, we take up the third-party question in more detail in the next subsection.

9. *Breach of Contract Versus Fraudulent Misrepresentation.* In some cases, fraudulent misrepresentation claims often are joined with claims for breach of contract. It is important to appreciate several features of the relationship between the causes of action.

First, and most obviously, the contract claim might exist without a misrepresentation claim, and vice versa. The misrepresentation cause of action does not require a contractual relationship, and breaches of contract can occur without misrepresentation. Second, different remedies are available for the two causes of action. Third, despite the analytical distinctions, in particular cases there may be factual overlap between the two causes of action, and courts have devoted considerable attention to deciding whether, in a given case, the plaintiff has proven only breach of contract or also a misrepresentation case. An illustrative case is Smehlik v. Athletes and Artists, Inc., 861 F.Supp. 1162 (W.D.N.Y.1994), in which a professional hockey player sued the agency that had represented him in connection with efforts to obtain a contract. According to the plaintiff, the agency had represented (1) that the agency could obtain a contract for him with the Buffalo Sabres for the 1991/92 season; (2) that it could "make a deal right away;" (3) that it would arrange for him to participate in the Sabres' 1991 training camp; and (4) that it would make all necessary arrangements to enable him to attend the Sabres' 1991 training camp, which required obtaining a release from his Czech hockey club.

> A mere "promissory statement [ ] as to what will be done in the future" may give rise only to a breach of contract claim. [citation omitted] However, a false representation of a present fact may give rise to a separable claim for fraudulent inducement, and generally speaking, if a promise is "made with a preconceived and undisclosed intention of not performing it, it constitutes a misrepresentation of material existing fact" upon which an action for fraudulent inducement may be predicated. * * * Thus, it is clear that a cause of action for fraudulent inducement may be sustained on the basis of an allegation that the defendant made a promise to undertake some action separate and apart from his obligations under the express terms of the contract, if it is also alleged that he made the promise with no intention of making good on that commitment.
>
> What is much less clear is whether a cause of action for fraud may properly be sustained on the basis of an allegation that the defendant made a promise to perform under the express terms of the contract while intending not to abide by its terms. The New York courts are split on this issue. * * * The Second Department has recently stated, for example,

> that where a fraud claim "is premised upon an alleged breach of contractual duties and the supporting allegations do not concern representations which are collateral or extraneous to the terms of the parties' agreement, a cause of action sounding in fraud does not lie." McKernin v. Fanny Farmer Candy Shops, Inc., 176 A.D.2d 233, 574 N.Y.S.2d 58, 59 (2d Dept.1991) (citing Mastropieri v. Solmar Construction Co., Inc., 159 A.D.2d 698, 553 N.Y.S.2d 187 (2d Dept.1990)) * * * On the other hand, the Third Department has recently held that "a party who is fraudulently induced to enter a contract may join a cause of action for fraud with one for breach of the same contract" where the misrepresentations alleged are "misstatements of material fact or promises [to perform under the contract] made with a present, albeit undisclosed, intent not to perform them." Shlang v. Bear's Estates Development of Smallwood, N.Y., Inc., 194 A.D.2d 914, 599 N.Y.S.2d 141, 142–143 (3d Dept.1993). * * *

Id. at 1171–72.

One reason for the requirement that the fraudulent promise relate to action separate from the actions promised in the contract is the concern that otherwise ordinary breach of contract claims will be converted into claims for fraudulent misrepresentation. The resulting litigation, it is feared, would be more lengthy, expensive, and uncertain in outcome (because it requires the factfinder to look into the defendant's state of mind and not just to the more objective circumstances of whether a breach has occurred). Note, however, that even in the jurisdictions which do not impose the "separate from the contract" requirement the plaintiff must prove that the defendant made the promise with a present intent not to perform. In practice, would this requirement allay concerns about excessive use of the misrepresentation theory in breach of contract contexts?

3. NEGLIGENT MISREPRESENTATION

a. Elements and Development

Section 552 of the *Restatement (Second) of Torts* outlines the cause of action for negligent misrepresentation:

> One who, in the course of his business, profession or employment, or in any other transaction in which he has a pecuniary interest, supplies false information for the guidance of others in their business transactions, is subject to liability for pecuniary loss caused to them by their justifiable reliance upon the information, if he fails to exercise reasonable care or competence in obtaining or communicating the information.

The cause of action for negligent misrepresentation includes many of the same elements as the cause of action for fraudulent misrepresentation: there must be a misrepresentation, there must be justifiable reliance, and the plaintiff must have suffered harm as a result of the reliance. The primary difference between the two causes of action relates to the defendant's state of mind. Negligent misrepresentation, unlike fraudulent misrepresentation, requires only that the plaintiff show the defendant failed to exercise reasonable care with regard to whether or not the representation was true.

As the common law of misrepresentation developed, it was initially doubtful whether a cause of action for negligent misrepresentation would be recognized at all. In Derry v. Peek, 14 App. Cas. 337 (House of Lords 1889), Lord Herschell's opinion explained:

> First, in order to sustain an action of deceit, there must be proof of fraud, and nothing short of that will suffice. Secondly, fraud is proved when it is shewn that a false representation has been made (1) knowingly, or (2) without belief in its truth, or (3) recklessly, careless whether it be true or false.
>
> * * *
>
> In my opinion making a false statement through want of care falls far short of, and is a very different thing from, fraud, and the same may be said of a false representation honestly believed though on insufficient grounds.

Derry v. Peek was immediately interpreted by the English legal profession to stand for the proposition that, absent privity of contract or some special relationship such as attorney/client or trustee/beneficiary, no action would lie for negligent misrepresentation, 34 Solicitors J. 140 (1889); and the Court of Appeal so held, shortly thereafter, in Le Lievre v. Gould, [1893] 1 Q.B. 491 (C.A.).

Derry v. Peek received a more guarded reaction in the United States. A number of United States cases allowed a cause of action for negligent misrepresentation in certain circumstances, such as cases involving certificates of title abstractors. *See, e.g.,* Anderson v. Spriestersbach, 69 Wash. 393, 125 P. 166 (1912).

In 1890, Parliament responded to *Derry v. Peek* by enacting the Directors Liability Act of 1890 (53 & 54 Vict., c. 64), later incorporated in the Companies Act of 1948 (11 & 12 Geo. 6, c. 38, § 43). Under this statute persons who have suffered damages as a result of acting upon incorrect statements negligently inserted in a prospectus issued by the promoters or directors of a company are given an action for damages.

In Hedley Byrne & Co. v. Heller & Partners Ltd., [1964] A.C. 465, (1963) [1963] 3 W.L.R. 101, 2 All E.R. 575, the House of Lords declared that all *Derry v. Peek* had held was that the allegation of outright fraud made in that case had not been proved rather than that an action for negligent misrepresentation would not lie on the facts of that case. That's one way, one supposes, of dispensing with an unwanted precedent.

b. Extent of Liability to Third–Parties

ELLIS v. GRANT THORNTON LLP

United States Court of Appeals, Fourth Circuit, 2008.
530 F.3d 280.

HAMILTON, SENIOR CIRCUIT JUDGE:

The principal issue presented in this appeal is whether Grant Thornton LLP (Grant Thornton), an accounting firm retained by First National Bank of Keystone (Keystone), in response to an investigation by the Office of the Comptroller of the Currency (OCC) into Keystone's banking activities, owed a duty of care under the West Virginia law of negligent misrepresentation to Gary Ellis, who allegedly relied on oral statements made by Stan Quay (Quay), a Grant Thornton partner, and a Grant Thornton audit report of Keystone's 1998 financial statements in deciding to accept the job as president of Keystone. We hold that Grant Thornton owed Ellis no such duty under West Virginia law. Accordingly, we reverse the judgment of the district court, which found in favor of Ellis on his negligent misrepresentation claim against Grant Thornton.

I

In late June 1999, the OCC began to intensify its ongoing investigation into Keystone's banking activities. The OCC's investigation revealed that Keystone's books overstated the value of the loans Keystone owned by over $515 million. Based on these overstatements, Keystone was declared insolvent and was closed on September 1, 1999. This case is yet another case that comes before this court in the wake of Keystone's collapse. This case concerns Ellis, who took the job as president of Keystone in April 1999. According to Ellis, he took the position only because he relied on negligent misrepresentations made by Quay and made by Grant Thornton in the audit report.

A

Prior to 1992, Keystone was a small community bank providing banking services to clients located primarily in McDowell County, West Virginia. Before its collapse, Keystone was a national banking association within the Federal Reserve System, the deposits of which were insured by the FDIC.

In 1992, Keystone began to engage in an investment strategy that involved the securitization of high risk mortgage loans. Between 1992 and 1998, Keystone originated nineteen securitizations. In general, Keystone would acquire Federal Housing Authority or high loan to value real estate mortgage loans from around the United States, pool a group of these loans, and sell interests in the pool through underwriters to investors. The pooled loans were serviced by third-party loan servicers, including companies like Advanta and Compu–Link. Keystone retained residual interests (residuals) in each loan securitization. The residuals were subordinated securities that would receive payments only after all expenses were paid and all investors in each securitization pool were paid. Thus, Keystone stood to profit from a securitization only after everyone else was paid in full. The residuals were assigned a value that was carried on the books of Keystone as an asset. Over time, the residual valuations came to represent a significant portion of Keystone's book value.

From 1993 until 1998, when the last loan securitization was completed, the size and frequency of these transactions expanded from about $33 million to approximately $565 million for the last one in September 1998. All told, Keystone acquired and securitized over 120,000 loans with a total value in excess of $2.6 billion.

The loan securitization business appeared to be quite profitable. On paper, Keystone's assets grew from $107 million in 1992 to over $1.1 billion in 1999. In reality, however, the securitization program proved highly unprofitable. Due to the risky nature of many of the underlying mortgage loans, the failure rate was excessive. As a result, the residual interests retained by Keystone proved highly speculative and, in actuality, they did not perform well.

Keystone's valuation of the residuals was greater than their market value. J. Knox McConnell, Keystone's largest shareholder until his death, Terry Church (Church), another Keystone director, and others concealed the failure of the securitizations by falsifying Keystone's books. Bogus entries and documents hid the true financial condition of Keystone from the bank's directors, shareholders, depositors, and federal regulators.

Keystone's irregular bank records drew the attention of the OCC, which began an investigation into Keystone's banking activities. This investigation revealed major errors in Keystone's accounting records that financially jeopardized Keystone. In May 1998, the OCC required Keystone to enter into an agreement obligating Keystone to take specific steps to improve its regulatory posture and financial condition. This agreement required Keystone to, among other things, retain a nationally recognized independent accounting firm "to perform an audit of the Bank's mortgage banking operations and determine the appropriateness of the Bank's accounting for purchased loans and all securitizations." (J.A. 3043). In August 1998, Keystone retained Grant Thornton as its outside auditor.

Under the agreement between Grant Thornton and Keystone, Grant Thornton was to, among other things, perform for Keystone, in accordance with Generally Accepted Auditing Standards (GAAS), an audit of Keystone's consolidated financial statements as of December 31, 1998. Quay was the lead Grant Thornton partner on the Keystone audit. Susan Buenger (Buenger), a junior manager, performed substantial work on the audit as well.

Grant Thornton performed the audit on Keystone's 1998 financial statements. Keystone's 1998 financial statements reflected ownership of more than $515 million in loans that it did not own. Due to negligence on the part of both Quay and Buenger, Grant Thornton's audit did not uncover the $515 million discrepancy.[11] In fact, on March 24, 1999, Quay presented several members and prospective members of Keystone's board and Keystone's shareholders with draft copies of Keystone's 1998 financial statements and told them that Keystone was going to get an unqualified or "clean" audit opinion on its 1998 financial statements. (J.A. 2701). At the shareholders meeting the next day, Quay also distributed copies of Keystone's financial statements. At that time, Quay reiterated that Keystone was going to get a clean audit opinion on its 1998 financial statements.

On April 19, 1999, even though Keystone was, in fact, insolvent as of the end of 1998, Grant Thornton issued and delivered to Keystone's board its audit opinion stating that Keystone's financial statements were fairly stated in accordance with the GAAP and reflecting a shareholder's equity of $184 million. The intent of the report was plainly stated on the first page of the report: "This report is intended for the information and use of the Board of Directors and Management of The First National Bank of Keystone and its regulatory agencies and should not be used by third parties for any other purpose." (J.A. 2903).

The audited financial statements provided by Quay to the board on April 19, 1999 were substantially the same as the financial statements Quay had provided board members and shareholders in March 1999. Based on Grant Thornton's audit report, Keystone's board continued to declare dividends and operate the bank.

B

In 1984, Gary Ellis was President of the Bank of Dunbar. The Bank of Dunbar was later merged into United National Bank (United) at which time Ellis joined the management team at United, eventually becoming its president. From the time of the merger with the Bank of Dunbar until the time Ellis left United, United more than doubled in size. In 1998, United merged with George Mason Bankshares of Virginia. In the spring of 1999, following the merger, Ellis voluntarily began looking for employment outside United. Ellis had dealt with Keystone in the past, and, on March 19, 1999, Billie Cherry (Cherry), chairman of Keystone's board, called Ellis and invited Ellis to attend Keystone's annual shareholders meeting on March 25, 1999. During the call, Cherry suggested that Ellis should consider becoming president of Keystone.

Ellis was not fired or told to leave United, had no deadline for leaving United, and could have remained at United rather than leaving for the Keystone position. Ellis attended Keystone's board meeting on March 24, 1999, at which the board granted Ellis' request to review, upon the signing of a confidentiality agreement, the financial condition of the bank. * * * [T]he Keystone board permitted Ellis to discuss the financial condition of the bank with Quay * * *. Consequently, following the Keystone

11. Grant Thornton does not challenge the district court's finding of negligence in this appeal * * *. [W]e, too, will assume, without deciding, that Quay and Buenger were negligent in preparing the audit * * *.

board meeting on March 24, 1999, Ellis met Quay and two other outside directors * * *. Quay told Ellis and the two outside directors that Keystone was going to receive a "clean [audit] opinion." (J.A. 401). Ellis also attended the March 25, 1999 shareholders' meeting at which Quay informed the group that Grant Thornton was going to give Keystone a clean audit opinion for 1998. On March 30, 1999, Ellis visited Keystone. During this visit, Quay told Ellis once again that Keystone would receive a clean audit opinion for 1998.

On April 2, 1999, Ellis met with his attorneys to draft a proposed employment agreement with Keystone. * * * It was decided that Ellis would be responsible for the "banking" business at Keystone as opposed to the mortgage loan securitizations. On April 19, 1999, at a Keystone board meeting, Ellis reviewed Grant Thornton's final audit report on Keystone for 1998. The board voted to approve Ellis' hiring as president of Keystone. Ellis officially resigned from United by letter dated April 20, 1999. Ellis' employment contract was signed on April 26, 1999. According to Ellis, he relied on Grant Thornton's audit, which was consistent with Quay's earlier March 1999 statements that Grant Thornton was going to issue a clean audit opinion for 1998, in deciding to accept the job as president of Keystone.

C

After being named as a defendant in the Gariety v. Grant Thornton, LLP securities class action, Ellis filed a cross-claim against Grant Thornton for negligent misrepresentation under West Virginia law in which he sought to recover damages in the form of lost earnings. The district court * * * ruled in favor of Ellis on his negligent misrepresentation claim and found that he was entitled to $2,419,233 in damages. The district court found that, in accepting the job as president of Keystone, "Ellis relied on the financial statements Quay gave him," "Quay's oral representations," and the Grant Thornton audit report. (J.A. 2706). The district court also found that "Quay intended and knew that Ellis would rely on his statements." (J.A. 2707). In view of these findings of fact, the district court concluded that Grant Thornton, as the auditor of Keystone, was liable to Ellis under the West Virginia law of negligent misrepresentation, citing *First National Bank of Bluefield v. Crawford,* 182 W.Va. 107, 386 S.E.2d 310 (1989), because Grant Thornton (through Quay's oral statements and the audit report) made negligent misrepresentations concerning the financial condition of Keystone knowing that Ellis would receive and rely upon those representations in making his decision to accept or reject employment with Keystone. * * *

II

* * *

As a federal court sitting in diversity, we have an obligation to apply the jurisprudence of West Virginia's highest court, the Supreme Court of

Appeals of West Virginia.* * * In this case, we are called upon to predict whether, under the facts of this case, Grant Thornton owed Ellis a duty of care under the West Virginia law of misrepresentation.

In *Bank of Bluefield,* the Supreme Court of Appeals of West Virginia addressed the question of whether the lack of privity of contract between an accountant and a bank was a complete defense to the bank's suit against the accountant for professional negligence in preparing a financial statement. The court answered that question in the negative.

In resolving the issue before it, the court in *Bank of Bluefield* discussed the four approaches to resolving the question of under what circumstances an accountant can be liable to third parties for a negligent misrepresentation. The first of these approaches was announced in *Ultramares Corp. v. Touche,* 255 N.Y. 170, 174 N.E. 441 (1931), which held that negligence actions were only permitted by parties in privity of contract or in a situation so close as to approach that of privity. The second approach was also developed by the New York Court of Appeals, which slightly modified the *Ultramares Corp.* approach in 1985. *See Credit Alliance Corp. v. Arthur Andersen & Co.,* 65 N.Y.2d 536, 493 N.Y.S.2d 435, 483 N.E.2d 110 (1985) (relaxing the strict *Ultramares Corp.* privity doctrine by requiring a relationship "sufficiently approaching privity").[12] The third approach is set forth in § 552 of the *Restatement (Second) of Torts.* Under this approach, a person or a limited class of persons who the auditor can foresee as parties who will (and do) rely upon financial statements are allowed to recover. *Restatement (Second) of Torts* § 552(1)–(2). The fourth approach is the reasonably foreseeable approach, which permits all parties who are reasonably foreseeable recipients of financial statements for business purposes to recover as long as they rely on the statements for those business purposes. *See, e.g., H. Rosenblum, Inc. v. Adler,* 93 N.J. 324, 461 A.2d 138, 142–46 (1983).[13]

---

12. *Credit Alliance Corp.* announced the following three-prong test for determining whether an accountant can be held liable for negligence to a third party who has detrimentally relied on inaccurate financial statements: (1) the accountant must have been aware that the financial reports were to be used for a particular purpose or purposes; (2) in the furtherance of which a known party or parties was intended to rely; and (3) there must have been some conduct on the part of the accountant linking him to that party or parties, which evinces the accountant's understanding of that party or parties' reliance. 493 N.Y.S.2d 435, 483 N.E.2d at 118. The *Credit Alliance Corp.* approach is often referred to as the "near-privity" approach. *First Nat'l Bank of Commerce v. Monco Agency, Inc.,* 911 F.2d 1053, 1058 (5th Cir. 1990).

13. Although it is sometimes difficult to discern the differences between the four approaches, appropriate lines can be drawn between the restrictive *Ultramares Corp., Credit Alliance Corp.,* and Restatement approaches and the nonrestrictive foreseeability approach. For example, although the Restatement's approach expands liability to a larger potential class of third parties than do the *Ultramares Corp.* and *Credit Alliance Corp.* approaches, it does not extend liability beyond an identified third party, a known third party, or third parties who enter into the same type of transaction as originally contemplated. In other words, under the *Ultramares Corp.* and *Credit Alliance Corp.* approaches, "the precise identity of the informational consumer [must] be foreseen by the auditor," *Monco Agency, Inc.,* 911 F.2d at 1059, but, under the Restatement approach, the precise "informational consumer" need not be known, rather the Restatement approach "contemplates identification of a narrow group, not necessarily the specific membership within that group." *Id.* Moreover, unlike the foreseeability approach, the Restatement approach does not extend to "every reasonably foreseeable consumer of financial information." *Id.* at 1060.

After summarizing these four approaches, the court in *Bank of Bluefield* adopted the Restatement § 552 approach for West Virginia, finding that the rule stated therein was "more appropriate because it imposes a standard of care only to known users who will actually be relying on the information provided by the accountant." 386 S.E.2d at 313 * * *.[14] In view of the court's adoption of the Restatement approach in *Bank of Bluefield,* the court answered the certified question-was privity a defense-in the negative. Consequently, other than the adoption of the Restatement approach, the *Bank of Bluefield* court gave no further meaningful guidance concerning under what circumstances an accountant can be liable to third parties for negligent misrepresentations under § 552

Restatement (Second) of Torts § 552 provides in relevant part:

> (1) One who, in the course of his business, profession or employment, or in any other transaction in which he has a pecuniary interest, supplies false information for the guidance of others in their business transactions, is subject to liability for pecuniary loss caused to them by their justifiable reliance upon the information, if he fails to exercise reasonable care or competence in obtaining or communicating the information.

[T]he liability stated in Subsection (1) is limited to loss suffered

> (a) by the person or one of a limited group of persons for whose benefit and guidance he intends to supply the information or knows that the recipient intends to supply it; and
>
> (b) through reliance upon it in a transaction that he intends the information to influence or knows that the recipient so intends or in a substantially similar transaction.

Restatement (Second) of Torts § 552(1)–(2).

The Restatement approach is deliberately restrictive to encourage the free flow of commercial information. *See id.* § 552, cmt. *a* ("By limiting the liability for negligence of a supplier of information to be used in commercial transactions to cases in which he manifests an intent to supply the information for the sort of use in which the plaintiff's loss occurs, the law promotes the important social policy of encouraging the flow of commercial information upon which the operation of the economy rests."). It also seeks to protect suppliers of commercial information from liability in instances in which they oblige themselves to provide information but the terms of the obligation are unknown to them. *See id.* ("A user of commercial information cannot reasonably expect its maker to have undertaken to satisfy this obligation unless the terms of the obligation were known to him.").

---

14. We note that the *Bank of Bluefield* court did not identify what constitutes a "known" user, the definition of which is important to separate the third parties entitled to recover under the Restatement approach and not entitled to recover under the *Ultramares Corp.* and *Credit Alliance Corp.* approaches. Such a demarcation, however, was not essential to the *Bank of Bluefield* court's rejection of these approaches, so its failure to employ precise cabining language is understandable.

Although the West Virginia Supreme Court of Appeals in *Bank of Bluefield* did not set forth what must be proven by an injured third party proceeding under § 552 against an accountant for the accountant's negligent misrepresentations, other courts have set forth six elements that essentially track the language of the Restatement. *See, e.g., N. Am. Specialty Ins. Co. v. Lapalme,* 258 F.3d 35, 41–42 (1st Cir.2001) (setting forth six elements). Under this authority, a finding of liability requires the injured party to prove (1) inaccurate information, (2) negligently supplied, (3) in the course of an accountant's professional endeavors, (4) to a third person or limited group of third persons for whose benefit and guidance the accountant actually intends or knows will receive the information, (5) for a transaction (or for a substantially similar transaction) that the accountant actually intends to influence or knows that the recipient so intends, (6) with the result that the third party justifiably relies on such misinformation to his detriment. The third party has the burden of proving each of these elements. Moreover, the accountant's "actual knowledge . . . should be ascertained at the time the audit report or financial statement is issued." *Id.* at 39, 42.

In this case, the record simply is devoid of evidence suggesting that Ellis proved the fourth, fifth, and sixth elements. With regard to the fourth element, it is clear that Ellis failed to show that Grant Thornton knew (or intended) that potential employees, like Ellis, were intended to receive the audit report for their benefit and guidance. The audit report was delivered to the board of directors of Keystone. The audit report plainly states that the audit report was *not* intended for use by third parties. Rather, the audit report was prepared for the benefit of Keystone and the OCC, which is entirely consistent with the agreements between Keystone and the OCC and between Keystone and Grant Thornton. Thus, Ellis, or any other potential employee, was not a member of any limited group of persons for whose benefit the audit report was prepared.

* * * Indeed, throughout most of the course of the audit report's preparation, Ellis was an unknown, unidentified potential employee of Keystone. Grant Thornton was not aware of the existence of the potential employment transaction between Ellis and Keystone until *after* Grant Thornton reached its decision to give Keystone a clean audit opinion. * * *

Thus, the clean audit opinion information was disclosed for the benefit of Keystone's board and not potential employees such as Ellis. * * * [A]ny release of information to Ellis was done at the behest of Keystone, not Grant Thornton. There is no evidence in the record to support the conclusion that Ellis was a member of any limited group of persons for whose benefit Quay's statements were made.

Our conclusion concerning the fourth element is buttressed by Illustration 10 in § 552. That illustration provides:

> A, an independent public accountant, is retained by B Company to conduct an annual audit of the customary scope for the corporation

and to furnish his opinion on the corporation's financial statements. A is not informed of any intended use of the financial statements; but A knows that the financial statements, accompanied by an auditor's opinion, are customarily used in a wide variety of financial transactions by the corporation and that they may be relied upon by lenders, investors, shareholders, creditors, purchasers and the like, in numerous possible kinds of transactions. In fact B Company uses the financial statements and accompanying auditor's opinion to obtain a loan from X Bank. Because of A's negligence, he issues an unqualifiedly favorable opinion upon a balance sheet that materially misstates the financial position of B Company, and through reliance upon it X Bank suffers pecuniary loss. A is not liable to X bank.

Id. § 552, cmt. h, illus. 10.

Illustration 10, we believe, is materially indistinguishable from our case. Like the accountant in the illustration, Grant Thornton was not aware of an intended use of its audit opinion beyond the customary business planning use of an audit opinion by a corporation such as Keystone and the use by the OCC for oversight * * *. Indeed, Grant Thornton was not aware that any potential employee of Keystone was going to base their decision to seek employment with Keystone on the outcome of the audit. Rather, in performing its audit function, Grant Thornton was aware that its audit opinion and any statements made leading up to the issuance of the audit opinion *may* be relied upon by shareholders, investors, and perhaps potential employees such as Ellis. However, more than a tenuous awareness of this sort is required to impose liability on Grant Thornton. To hold otherwise would transform the Restatement approach into the foreseeability approach, which the court in *Bank of Bluefield* clearly rejected. Ellis was required to show that Grant Thornton knew that its audit opinion would be used by Keystone to assist potential employees in making their decision concerning whether to come to work for Keystone. The record simply does not demonstrate that Ellis made such a showing.

With regard to the fifth element's substantiality requirement, we examine two questions. First, we examine, from the accountant's standpoint, what risks he reasonably perceived he was undertaking when he delivered the challenged report or financial statement. If the accountant is unaware of a potential risk, then liability cannot attach. Next, we make an objective comparison between the transaction to which the accountant had actual knowledge and the transaction that in fact occurred. This comparison cannot be hypertechnical, but, rather, must be conducted in light of customary business world practices and attitudes. Restatement (Second) of Torts § 552, cmt. j. * * *

When Grant Thornton issued its audit report, it was not assuming the risk that third parties would rely on the report. As noted above, the report itself states that it is not to be used by third parties. To the extent that Ellis relied on Quay's statements, it cannot be said that Grant Thornton was assuming the risk of being liable for Ellis' future lost earnings. The audit opinion was formed by the time Quay met with Ellis, and Quay was simply repeating information that was earlier disclosed to the Keystone board in his presence.

With regard to the objective comparison, the liability of the maker of a negligent misrepresentation extends "to all transactions of the type or kind that the maker intends or has reason to expect." Restatement (Second) of Torts § 552, cmt. j. For example, "independent public accountants who negligently make an audit of books of a corporation, which they are told is to be used only for the purpose of obtaining a particular line of banking credit, are not subject to liability to a wholesale merchant whom the corporation induces to supply it with goods on credit by showing him the financial statements and the accountant's opinion." *Id.* Moreover, an accountant who negligently conducts an audit for A corporation knowing that A corporation is going to show the audit to B corporation as a basis for the extension of credit from B corporation is not liable to B corporation if B corporation buys a controlling interest in A corporation in reliance upon the audit. *Id.* § 552, cmt. j, illus. 14.

* * *

In short, to find the fifth element satisfied, we would have to materially change the transaction from an audit undertaken to benefit Keystone and the OCC to one intended to benefit potential employees of Keystone. Such a material change to the nature of the transaction is prohibited under the Restatement approach.

Ellis fares no better on the sixth element. Unquestionably, given that the audit report stated that it was not intended for use by third parties, Ellis could not justifiably rely on the audit report in signing his employment contract with Keystone. With regard to Quay's oral assurances, likewise, Ellis could not justifiably rely on those statements. First, Ellis was aware at the time he signed his employment contract that the audit report was not to be used by third parties. A person as sophisticated and experienced in the banking business as Ellis is, he knew he could not justifiably rely on Quay's statements when the report itself stated otherwise. Moreover, as previously noted, Quay's statements concerning the clean audit opinion were offered by Quay to the board and the shareholders to apprise the board and the OCC of Keystone's financial condition. They were not offered to induce individuals to accept employment with Keystone. As such, it is difficult to discern how an individual as sophisticated and experienced as Ellis would justifiably rely on this information in accepting a job at Keystone.

III

For the reasons stated herein, the judgment of the district court is reversed.

REVERSED

NOTES

1. *The scope and results of audits.* In an omitted footnote, the court offers the following description of the accounting process.

> Although accountants provide a variety of services to clients, their primary function is auditing. Samuel S. Paschall, *Liability to Non–Clients: The Accountant's Role and Responsibility,* 53 Mo. L.Rev. 693, 698 (1988). In a typical audit, the financial statements of an entity, usually a corporation, are verified by examining the corporation's accounting records and supporting evidence. After examining such records and evidence, the accountant expresses an opinion as to whether such statements fairly represent the corporation's actual financial position in accordance with the Generally Accepted Accounting Principles (GAAP). For practical reasons of cost and time, an accountant is rarely able to examine every accounting transaction of a corporation. Denise M. Orlinsky, Note, *An Accountant's Liability to Third Parties: Bily v. Arthur Young & Co.,* 43 DePaul L.Rev. 859, 862 (1994). Therefore, the performance of an audit requires a high degree of professional skill and judgment, as the accountant can only test the output of the corporation's accounting systems. In performing an audit, an accountant follows procedures outlined in the GAAS. The end result of an audit is the audit report or opinion, which evaluates the information obtained to determine whether the corporation's financial statements fairly represent the financial position of the corporation in accordance with the GAAP. The audit opinion is usually expressed in a letter addressed to the client and can be one of four types: an unqualified audit opinion, a qualified audit opinion, an adverse audit opinion, or a disclaimer audit opinion. An unqualified audit opinion is an expression of opinion by the accountant without any exceptions, reservations, or qualifications that the financial statements of the corporation represent its financial position and the results of its operations. A qualified audit opinion, on the other hand, states that improper accounting treatment has been applied to one or more items and that, consequently, the financial statements are not in compliance with the GAAP. An adverse audit opinion is issued if any items have a material and pervasive effect on the financial statement, thus destroying their fairness of presentation. *Id.* A disclaimer audit opinion is issued if the accountant is unable to form an opinion because of serious limitations on the scope of the examination of the audit. Typically, the corporation then uses this audit opinion for its own business planning, and the audit opinion is used to inform outside parties as to the financial health of the audited company.

The *Bily* case is the leading case adopting the Restatement position. Robert R. Bily v. Arthur Young & Co., 3 Cal.4th 370, 11 Cal.Rptr.2d 51, 834 P.2d 745 (1992). The *Bily* court echoes this view of the scope of audits:

> An auditor is a watchdog, not a bloodhound. As a matter of commercial reality, audits are performed in a client-controlled environment. The client typically prepares its own financial statements; it has direct control over and assumes primary responsibility for their contents. The client

> engages the auditor, pays for the audit, and communicates with audit personnel throughout the engagement. Because the auditor cannot in the time available become an expert in the client's business and record-keeping systems, the client necessarily furnishes the information base for the audit.

834 P.2d 745, 762

All of this is well and good in the ordinary audit, but recall that Grant Thornton knew in this case that it was conducting an audit precisely because the OCC was concerned about the financial health of Keystone. Should this change the auditor's approach? Should the auditor act as a bloodhound? Does this mean it should have charged much more than it would for an ordinary audit? Clearly, one would have to dig deeper to discover all the shenanigans involved in the Keystone Bank collapse. *See* Grant Thornton, LLP v. F.D.I.C., 694 F.Supp.2d 506 (S.D.W.Va. 2010). There is some research indicating that accounting firms do adjust their fees according to the perceived risks posed by different audits. *See* C. Bryan Cloyd et al., *Independent Auditor Litigation: Recent Events and Related Research*, 17 J. Acct. & Pub. Pol'y 121 (1998); Jay Feinman, *Liability of Accountants for Negligent Auditing: Doctrine, Policy and Ideology*, 31 Fla. St. U L.Rev. 17 (2003).

2. As we noted earlier in this chapter, the American Law Institute has begun work on the *Restatement (Third) of Torts: Liability for Economic Harm, Preliminary* Draft No. 1 (2011). The proposed Section 4 of the new restatement retains the "limited group" rule of the Second Restatement with minor wording changes. Comment *a* provides the following gloss on the rule:

> A plaintiff's reliance alone, even if foreseeable, is not a sufficient basis for a suit. * * *[A] defendant must act with the apparent purpose of providing a basis for the reliance. It may be useful to say that a defendant held liable * * * must "invite reliance" by the plaintiff, so long as the expression is understood to refer to the defendant's apparent purpose and not to a temptation incidently created by the defendant's words or acts.

By this test, should Mr. Ellis have a cause of action?

3. In the *Rosenblum* opinion, cited by *Ellis*, the New Jersey Supreme Court justified the foreseeability test because it would serve "the dual functions of compensation for injury and deterrence of negligent conduct. Moreover, it is a just and rational judicial policy that the same criteria govern the imposition of negligence liability, regardless of the context in which it arises. The accountant, the investor, and the general public will in the long run benefit when the liability of the certified public accountant for negligent misrepresentation is measured by the foreseeability standard." Rosenblum, Inc. v. Adler, 93 N.J. 324, 461 A.2d 138, 260 (1983). How would the *Ellis* court respond to this argument?

4. *Insurance and the pricing of audits.* In the *Bily* case the majority and dissent sparred over the consequence of a foreseeability test on the availability of insurance. This debate was carried on in the absence of any empirical evidence on point. Apparently, the ensuing years have not changed the situation. *See* Daniel Tinkelman, *Reconsidering the "Lack of Duty" Defense to State Auditor Negligence Claims*, 25 J. Corp. L. 489, 509 (2000). In fact, this

may be a relatively difficult area to study. One obvious approach would be to examine insurance rates in states with a foresight test and states with the Restatement or New York tests. This approach assumes, however, that the volume and success of negligent audit litigation is higher in foresight states. There is little evidence that this is the case. Although New Jersey was the first state to adopt a foresight test, in 1995 the New Jersey legislature effectively overruled the *Rosenblum* opinion by adopting N.J.S.A. 2A:53A–25, which adopted a rule similar to the New York rule.

Today, only two states, Mississippi and Wisconsin retain the foresight rule. It is unclear, however, whether this has had much impact on subsequent cases. The Mississippi court adopted the foresight test in Touche Ross & Co. v. Commercial Union Ins. Co., 514 So.2d 315 (Miss. 1987) and apparently there is no subsequent Mississippi case affirming an auditors liability in negligence to third parties. Only slightly more litigation has occurred in Wisconsin. *See* Citizens State Bank v. Timm, Schmidt & Co., S.C., 113 Wis.2d 376, 335 N.W.2d 361 (1983); Chevron Chemical Co. v. Deloitte & Touche, 168 Wis.2d 323, 483 N.W.2d 314 (Ct.App.1992); Krier v. Vilione, 317 Wis.2d 288, 766 N.W.2d 517 (2009). Because the trend is clearly away from broad liability for negligent audits, it may be that the insurance question will remain unanswered. *See* Carl Pacini, *At the Interface of Law and Accounting: An Examination of a Trend Toward A Reduction in the Scope of Auditor Liability to Third Parties in the Common Law Countries*, 37 Am. Bus. L.J. 171(2000). For a general discussion of the hardening and softening of accountant liability insurance markets, *see* Lawrence A. Cunningham, *Securitizing Audit Failure Risk: An Alternative to Caps on Damages*, 49 Wm. & Mary L. Rev. 711 (2007).

5. *Contributory Negligence*. Contributory negligence is not a defense—either as an absolute bar or in a comparative way—as to intentional misrepresentation claims. Some jurisdictions, however, have allowed a contributory negligence defense (now a comparative defense in most jurisdictions) to claims of negligent misrepresentation. Courts and commentators continue to disagree about whether and when such a defense should be recognized when the claim concerns the tort liability of an accountant or attorney. *See, e.g.*, Greenstein, Logan & Co. v. Burgess Marketing, Inc., 744 S.W.2d 170 (Tex. App. 1987) (stating that the defense should be available only if the client's negligence caused the accountant's failure to perform the contract).

In considering the question, it is useful to appreciate that the comparative negligence argument might arise from several different categories of fact patterns. First, a plaintiff's negligence might have contributed to the alleged error in the audit in the first instance. For instance, suppose the client keeps sloppy records and that the accountant alleges that this sloppiness contributed to the error in the audit. Should this form of "pre-error" negligence by the client be allowed to form the basis of a comparative negligence defense?

Second, the plaintiff's alleged negligence might be in relying on the results of the audit or the professional advice. For instance, in a case brought by investors such as in *Bily*, the accounting firm might argue that the plaintiffs had or could reasonably have obtained independent information that would have indicated problems with the finances of the audited company. These same allegations, of course, would be relevant to a different aspect of the case: whether or not the plaintiff can prove "justifiable reliance." Still, a defendant who loses on the "no justifiable reliance" point still might try the comparative negligence argument and seek a comparative reduction in the damages. Does it seem likely that a defendant could ever persuade a factfinder that the plaintiff "justifiably relied" and yet was "unreasonable" in relying? In any event, courts have not been sympathetic to comparative negligence arguments that fit this fact pattern.

Third, the plaintiff's negligence might increase the size of the losses caused by the audit. This would be akin to the failure to mitigate (although some jurisdictions now treat the failure to mitigate as a species of contributory negligence). Courts have been willing to allow such conduct to form the basis of a comparative defense.

6. *Statutory Remedies for Financial Misrepresentations.* In the United States, a number of statutes have, either expressly or by judicial construction, provided remedies for misrepresentations made in the course of certain kinds of transactions. Among the principal such statutory schemes is the one that, as a result of judicial construction, arises under § 10(b) of the Securities Exchange Act of 1934 (15 U.S.C. § 77j(b)), and SEC Rule 10b–5 issued under the authority of that statutory provision. Disagreeing with a number of lower courts, the Supreme Court ruled that an action for damages based upon Rule 10b–5 cannot be maintained on a showing merely of negligence. Some kind of scienter is necessary, perhaps even as culpable as "an intent to deceive, manipulate, or defraud." Ernst & Ernst v. Hochfelder, 425 U.S. 185, 96 S.Ct. 1375, 47 L.Ed.2d 668 (1976). Exactly who has to know what to meet the scienter requirement? *See* Patricia S. Abril, *The Locus of Corporate Scienter*, 2006 Colum. Bus. L. Rev. 81 (1996); Bradley J. Bondi, *Dangerous Liaisons: Collective Scienter in SEC Enforcement Actions*, 6 N.Y.U. J. L. & Bus. 1 (2009).

In a subsequent case, Basic, Inc. v. Levinson, 485 U.S. 224, 108 S.Ct. 978, 99 L.Ed.2d 194 (1988), the Court reaffirmed that the standard of materiality in actions brought under Rule 10b–5, was whether there was a substantial likelihood that a reasonable investor would consider the matter important in deciding what course of conduct to pursue. *See* TSC Industries, Inc. v. Northway, Inc., 426 U.S. 438, 96 S.Ct. 2126, 48 L.Ed.2d 757 (1976). The *Basic, Inc.* case involved the possible liability of a corporation for falsely denying that any preliminary discussions concerning a merger were taking place. The major problem facing the plaintiffs, who sold their shares for a lower price than they would have received if they had continued to hold the shares until a merger was eventually agreed upon, was to show that they had relied on the company's misrepresentations. The Court, by a 5–2 majority, adopted the so-called "fraud on the market theory"—namely, that an investor who buys or sells stock at the market price does so in reliance upon the "integrity of that price. Because most publicly available information is reflected in market price, an investor's reliance on any public material misrepresentations, therefore, may be presumed for purposes of a Rule 10b–5 action." 485 U.S. at 247, 108 S.Ct. at 992, 99 L.Ed.2d at 218. The defendant could rebut the presumption by showing that the plaintiff would have sold his stock for other reasons regardless of the misrepresented facts or that the market-makers were aware of the falsity of the statement, so that the stock was, in point of fact, not artificially underpriced. Under some other statutory schemes, however, liability will lie for negligent misrepresentation and even, occasionally, for innocent misrepresentation.

In the English case, Caparo Industries PLC v. Dickman, [1989] Q.B. 653, 2 W.L.R. 316, 1 All E.R. 798 (C.A.1988), the Court of Appeal held that the auditors of a public company who had negligently conducted their audit owed a duty of care to the plaintiffs who were already shareholders in the company and who, on the basis of the defendants' audit, made a successful takeover bid for the company, but declared that no such duty would be owed to other investors who may have purchased shares on the strength of the auditors' report. The House of Lords, however, reversed; no such duty was owed to existing shareholders who purchased additional shares. [1990] 2 A. C. 605, 1 All E.R. 568, 2 W.L.R. 358. New Zealand has limited auditor liability along similar lines. *See* Boyd Knight v. Purdue [1999] 2 N.Z.L.R. 276.

7. *Legal malpractice*

a. *Client Claims*. As in the accounting context, negligence claims against lawyers in theory could take one or both of two forms: professional negligence, and negligent misrepresentation. A client who receives bad advice from a lawyer may be able to pursue both theories. In fact, however, most clients rely primarily on the professional negligence theory. Lawyers may commit malpractice against their clients in many ways. Most frequently, they fail to exercise due diligence with respect to the client's case. For example, they miss filing deadlines. Less frequently, clients may prevail by arguing that the attorney made negligent recommendations. *See* Grayson v. Wofsey, Rosen, Kweskin and Kuriansky, 231 Conn. 168, 646 A.2d 195 (1994). As a separate matter, lawyers may breach their fiduciary duty by failing to provide undivided loyalty to the client. *See* Sande Buhai, *Lawyers as Fiduciaries*, 53 St. Louis U. L.J. 553 (2009). In all of these cases, clients sometimes have a difficult time proving the causal connection between the lawyer's malfeasance and an injury. For example, when arguing a lawyer committed malpractice by missing a filing deadline, the client usually must show that the action, if filed, would have been successful.

b. *Third–Party Claims*. The question of attorney liability to nonclients has proved no less vexing than that of accountant liability. "If attorney third-party liability law is, as one commentator has lamented, 'hopelessly confused,' the law addressing third-party negligence claims against counsel deserves much of the blame." Kevin H. Michels, *Third–Party Negligence Claims Against Counsel: A Proposed Unified Liability Standard*, 22 Geo. J. Legal Ethics 143, 146 (2009). In considering the question, several examples should be useful.

Example A. Attorney prepares a will for a client who wants to bequeath half the estate to his spouse and half to his best friend. The will is not executed properly, and so when the client dies the estate is distributed according to the laws of intestacy. The friend thus receives nothing, and sues the lawyer on a theory of professional negligence.

Example B. Attorney for a defendant in a personal injury claim offers the plaintiff (who is not yet represented by counsel) $20,000 to settle the case, telling the plaintiff that "most cases of this sort don't settle for as much as this." The plaintiff accepts the offer, and then learns that the settlement value of the case was considerably more, given clear liability and high damages. She sues the attorney for negligent and intentional misrepresentation.

Example C. An attorney prepares an opinion letter for client, declaring that certain real property has no easements and is not burdened by any lien. The client shows the letter to prospective purchasers, one of whom relies on it and buys the land, only to discover that it does have several easements that diminish its value to him. He sues the attorney for negligent misrepresentation and for professional negligence.

Example D. A woman hires a lawyer to represent her in a personal injury claim arising from an injury she sustained in an accident. Only the woman, and not her husband, signs the contract with the lawyer. The lawyer never advises the client or her husband that the husband might have a claim for loss of consortium. The statute of limitations expires on the husband's potential claim for loss of consortium.

How do the policy concerns discussed in *Ellis* apply to the context of attorney liability to nonclients? Does the attorney liability context raise concerns different from those discussed in *Ellis*? For instance, lawyers owe an undivided duty of loyalty and duties of confidentiality to their clients. Do these duties affect the analysis?

Which of the approaches outlined in *Ellis* would you consider most desirable as a general rule for attorney liability to third parties? Does any one approach seem workable or defensible with respect to all four examples given above? If you believe that there are occasions when no attorney liability to third-parties should be recognized as a matter of law, can you articulate a "bright line" definition of those occasions?

Courts have adopted a number of approaches to this problem. Some adopt a privity or near-privity rule. Others have adopted a third party beneficiary rule, at least in some contexts. The *Restatement (Third) of Law Governing Lawyers* § 51, eschews a general rule and instead seeks to define the specific instances in which attorneys owe a duty of care to nonclients. *See* R. Mallen & J. Smith, LEGAL MALPRACTICE, CHAPTER 7: LIABILITY TO THE NONCLIENT (2011). The outcome is now fairly predictable in a few fact patterns. For example, in almost all jurisdictions, beneficiaries of wills are allowed to sue the attorney who did not prepare the will properly. Moreover, the ambit of attorney liability to third parties does not generally extend to adversaries. *See* Onita Pacific Corp. v. Trustees of Bronson, 315 Or. 149, 843 P.2d 890 (1992); United Bank of Kuwait v. Enventure Energy Enhanced Oil, 755 F.Supp. 1195 (S.D.N.Y.1989).

8. *Products and audits.* Recall that in *McPherson v. Buick Motors,* while striking down the privity barrier in products liability cases, Judge Cardozo noted that by limiting liability to those with whom Buick Motors was in privity of contract the courts provided a vacuous remedy. The automobile dealer who purchased the automobile from Buick Motors "was indeed the one person of whom it might be said with some approach to certainty that by him the car would not be used. Yet the defendant would have us say that he was the one person who it was under a legal duty to protect." Could not the same

thing be said in some audit cases, especially those where the audited firm is fraudulently misrepresenting its financial situation to the auditor, as occurred in H. Rosenblum, Inc. v. Adler, 93 N.J. 324, 461 A.2d 138 (1983), the New Jersey case that adopted a foreseeability test? Why, then, do you think Judge Cardozo was unwilling to "assault the citadel of privity" in *Ultramares*? Why have so few courts been willing to do so?

Part of the answer may be that unlike relatively powerless consumers, third parties in audit negligence cases have other options. As noted by the court in the *Bily* case:

> For example, a third party might expend its own resources to verify the client's financial statements or selected portions of them that were particularly material to its transaction with the client. Or it might commission its own audit or investigation, thus establishing privity between itself and an auditor or investigator to whom it could look for protection. In addition, it might bargain with the client for special security or improved terms in a credit or investment transaction. Finally, the third party could seek to bring itself within the Glanzer exception to Ultramares by insisting that an audit be conducted on its behalf or establishing direct communications with the auditor with respect to its transaction with the client.

Bily v. Arthur Young & Co., 834 P.2d at 765 (1992), citing John A. Siliciano, *Negligent Accounting and the Limits of Instrumental Tort Reform*, 86 Mich. L.Rev.1929, 1956–57 (1988). In this regard, what steps might Mr. Ellis have taken to protect himself?

CHAPTER 3

TORTIOUS INTERFERENCE WITH CONTRACT AND PROSPECTIVE CONTRACT; DAMAGES FOR ECONOMIC TORTS

■ ■ ■

A. TORTIOUS INTERFERENCE WITH CONTRACT AND PROSPECTIVE CONTRACTUAL RELATIONS

The tort causes of action for intentional interference with contract and intentional interference with prospective contractual relations are only several strands in a much larger and quite complex fabric regulating the protection of economic interests. Some of the other strands in the fabric are also common law in origin, such as the cause of action for breach of contract itself, as well as tort claims for misrepresentation. Many other crucial strands of the fabric are statutory, including the antitrust laws and the many statutes regulating intellectual property, such as the laws relating to trademark, copyright, and patents.

Protection for trademarks derives from the Lanham Act, 15 U.S.C. §§ 1051–1128 (1994). The Act makes actionable the deceptive or misleading use of trademarks and unfair competition with respect to trademarks. The statute protects many forms of marks, symbols, designs, and other product-identifying features. Federal law also includes an elaborate system for protecting patents, a system that includes a procedure for obtaining a new patent and substantive rights and remedies for the possessor of a patent. *See* 35 U.S.C. §§ 100–293 (1994). Federal law also protects copyrights, and expressly preempts state law with respect to some copyright issues. *See* 17 U.S.C. § 301 (1994). As we shall see in the following case, litigation arising out of economic injury often includes a mixture of common law and statutory claims.

The cause of action for tortious interference with contract is outlined in Section 766 of the *Restatement (Second) Torts*:

> One who intentionally and improperly interferes with the performance of a contract (except a contract to marry) between another and a third person by inducing or otherwise causing the third person not to

> perform the contract, is subject to liability to the other for the pecuniary loss resulting to the other from the failure of the third person to perform the contract.

Section 766B outlines the cause of action for tortious interference with prospective contractual relations:

> One who intentionally and improperly interferes with another's prospective contractual relation (except a contract to marry) is subject to liability to the other for the pecuniary harm resulting from loss of the benefits of the relation, whether the interference consists of (a) inducing or otherwise causing a third person not to enter into or continue the prospective relation or (b) preventing the other from acquiring or continuing the prospective relation.

Most authorities agree that intent for purposes of this tort, as with other intentional tort claims, can be established either by proof of subjective purpose or knowledge with substantial certainty. The additional element—an "improper" interference—was not included as an element under the first Restatement's formulation of the tort. Rather, the first Restatement placed the burden on the defendant to prove that the interference was in some way proper or privileged. The Restatement (Second) declines to take a position as to who bears the burden of proof on the issue of whether the interference was proper or improper.

WAL–MART STORES, INC. v. STURGES

Supreme Court of Texas, 2001.
52 S.W.3d 711.

JUSTICE HECHT delivered the opinion of the Court, in which CHIEF JUSTICE PHILLIPS, JUSTICE ENOCH, JUSTICE OWEN, and JUSTICE ABBOTT joined, and in Parts I, IV and V of which JUSTICE HANKINSON and JUSTICE O'NEILL joined.

Texas, like most states, has long recognized a tort cause of action for interference with a prospective contractual or business relation even though the core concept of liability—what conduct is prohibited—has never been clearly defined. Texas courts have variously stated that a defendant may be liable for conduct that is "wrongful", "malicious", "improper", of "no useful purpose", "below the behavior of fair men similarly situated", or done "with the purpose of harming the plaintiff", but not for conduct that is "competitive", "privileged", or "justified", even if intended to harm the plaintiff. Repetition of these abstractions in the case law has not imbued them with content or made them more useful, and tensions among them, which exist not only in Texas law but American law generally, have for decades been the subject of considerable critical commentary.

This case affords us the opportunity to bring a measure of clarity to this body of law. From the history of the tort in Texas and elsewhere, and from the scholarly efforts to analyze its boundaries, we conclude that to establish liability for interference with a prospective contractual or business relation the plaintiff must prove that it was harmed by the defendant's conduct that was either independently tortious or unlawful. By "independently tortious" we mean conduct that would violate some other recognized tort duty. We must explain this at greater length, but by way of example, a defendant who threatened a customer with bodily harm if he did business with the plaintiff would be liable for interference because his conduct toward the customer—assault—was independently tortious, while a defendant who competed legally for the customer's business would not be liable for interference. Thus defined, an action for interference with a prospective contractual or business relation provides a remedy for injurious conduct that other tort actions might not reach (in the example above, the plaintiff could not sue for assault), but only for conduct that is already recognized to be wrongful under the common law or by statute.

Because the defendant's conduct in this case was not independently tortious or unlawful, and because the defendant did not breach its contract, we reverse the court of appeals' judgment and render judgment for the defendant.

I

Plaintiff Harry W. Sturges, III contracted for himself and plaintiffs Dick Ford, Bruce Whitehead, and J.D. Martin, III to purchase from Bank One, Texas a vacant parcel of commercial property in Nederland, Texas, referred to as Tract 2. The contract, dated December 29, 1989, gave purchasers the right to terminate if within sixty days they were unable to lease the property and "to secure the written approval of Wal–Mart Corporation to the intended use of the Property, in accordance with the right so given to Wal–Mart pursuant to certain restrictions on the Property." The right referred to was the right to approve modifications in a site plan for the property that Wal–Mart Stores, Inc. and Wal–Mart Properties, Inc. (collectively, "Wal–Mart") held under two recorded instruments, each entitled "Easements with Covenants and Restrictions Affecting Land" ("ECRs"), one filed in 1982 and the other in 1988. The purpose of the ECRs was to assure the commercial development of Tract 2 and an adjacent tract, Tract 1, according to a prescribed plan.

The 1982 ECR was between Wal–Mart, which owned Tract 2 at the time, and the State Teachers Retirement System of Ohio ("OTR"), which owned Tract 1, having acquired it from Wal–Mart under a sale and leaseback agreement. OTR leased Tract 1 to Wal–Mart to use for a store. In 1984, Wal–Mart sold Tract 2 to a joint venture that included a partnership, Gulf Coast Investment Group. Gulf Coast later acquired Tract 2 from the joint venture. The 1988 ECR, made by Gulf Coast, OTR, and Wal–Mart, modified the site plan for the tracts and otherwise incorporated the terms of the 1982 ECR.

Gulf Coast's efforts to develop Tract 2 failed, and in 1989 Bank One acquired the property by foreclosure. Two of Gulf Coast's partners, plaintiffs Whitehead and Martin, along with two other investors, plaintiffs

Sturges and Ford, continued to look for a way to develop the property. When Sturges learned that Fleming Foods of Texas, Inc. was interested in building a food store in the area, he contracted with Bank One to purchase Tract 2 for the plaintiffs in hopes of leasing the property to Fleming Foods.

As soon as the agreement with Bank One was executed, Sturges contacted Wal–Mart to request a modification of the 1982/1988 ECRs to permit construction on Tract 2 of a food store to Fleming's specifications. A modification was necessary in part because Fleming wanted to construct a 51,000 square foot store, and the site plan permitted only a 36,000 square foot structure. A manager in Wal–Mart's property management department, DeLee Wood, told Sturges to submit a revised site plan, and though she did not have authority to approve the modification herself, she indicated to Sturges that Wal–Mart would approve it. About the same time, Sturges obtained from Fleming a non-binding memorandum of understanding that it would lease Tract 2.

Unbeknownst to Wood, a manager in another Wal–Mart department, Sandra Watson, had been evaluating the possibilities for expanding stores at various locations, including the Nederland store. If a store could not be expanded, Watson's assignment was to consider relocating the store. In July 1989 Watson hired a realtor, Tom Hudson, to help Wal–Mart acquire Tract 2 for purposes of expansion. When Hudson learned of Sturges's contract with Bank One, he suggested to Watson that Wal–Mart could thwart Sturges's efforts to purchase the property by refusing to approve the requested modification of the 1982/1988 ECRs. At the time, neither Watson nor Hudson knew of Wood's conversations with Sturges.

When Wood's and Watson's conflicting activities came to the attention of the head of Wal–Mart's property management department, Tony Fuller, he agreed with Watson that Wal–Mart should try to acquire Tract 2 and told Wood to deny Sturges's request to modify the ECR, which she did in a letter to Sturges without explanation. Fuller then instructed Hudson to contact Fleming and communicate Wal–Mart's desire to expand onto Tract 2. Hudson complied, telling L.G. Callaway, Fleming's manager of store development who had been working on the deal with Sturges, that if Wal–Mart could not acquire Tract 2, it would close its store on Tract 1 and relocate. Since Fleming was not interested in Tract 2 without a Wal–Mart store next door, Callaway took Hudson's call to be an ultimatum not to move forward on the proposed lease with Sturges. Consequently, Fleming canceled its letter of intent with Sturges, and the plaintiffs opted out of their contract with Bank One. Several months later, Wal–Mart purchased Tract 2 and expanded its store.

The plaintiffs sued Wal–Mart for tortiously interfering with their prospective lease with Fleming and for breaching the 1982/1988 ECRs by unreasonably refusing to approve the requested site plan modification. The plaintiffs' actual damages claim under both theories was the same-the profits the plaintiffs would have made on the Fleming lease. The jury found Wal–Mart liable on both theories. Concerning the plaintiffs' interference claim, the district court submitted to the jury two questions with accompanying instructions as follows:

> Did Wal–Mart wrongfully interfere with Plaintiffs' prospective contractual agreement to lease the property to Fleming?
>
> Wrongful interference occurred if (a) there was a reasonable probability that Plaintiffs would have entered into the contractual relation, and (b) Wal–Mart intentionally prevented the contractual relation from occurring with the purpose of harming Plaintiffs.
>
> Was Wal–Mart's intentional interference with Plaintiffs' prospective lease agreement with Fleming justified?
>
> An interference is "justified" if a party possesses an interest in the subject matter equal or superior to that of the other party, or if it results from the good faith exercise of a party's rights, or the good faith exercise of a party's mistaken belief of its rights.

The jury answered "yes" to the first question and "no" to the second. Wal–Mart offered no objection to this part of the jury charge that is relevant to our consideration of the case. The jury assessed $1 million actual damages on the contract claim and on the interference claim, assessed $500,000 punitive damages on the interference claim, and found that reasonable attorney fees for each side were $145,000. At the plaintiffs' election, the trial court rendered judgment on the interference claim, awarding actual and punitive damages but not attorney fees.

All parties appealed. The court of appeals affirmed the award of actual damages but remanded for a retrial of punitive damages, holding that the trial court had improperly excluded evidence offered by the plaintiffs during the punitive damages phase of the trial.

We granted Wal–Mart's petition for review.

II

Wal–Mart argues that there is no evidence to support the jury's verdict that it wrongfully interfered with the plaintiffs' prospective lease with Fleming or that it was not justified in acting as it did. * * * Whenever two competitors vie for the same business advantage, as Wal–Mart and Sturges did over the acquisition of Tract 2, one's success over the other can almost always be said to harm the other. Wal–Mart's evidentiary challenge here raises the question of what harm must be proved to constitute tortious interference. To answer this question, we look to the historical development of the interference torts in other jurisdictions and in Texas * * *. We then analyze the evidence in this case.

A

The origins of civil liability for interference have been traced to Roman law that permitted a man to sue for violence done to members of his household. Francis Bowes Sayre, *Inducing Breach of Contract,* 36 Harv. L. Rev. 663, 663–664 (1923). The common law also recognized such liability as early as the fourteenth century and extended it to include driving away a business's customers or a church's donors. But a common-law cause of action was strictly limited to cases in which actual violence or other such improper means were used. For centuries the common law continued to allow civil actions for interference with one's customers or other prospective business relationships, but as the *Restatement (Second) of Torts* summarizes, "in all of them the actor's conduct was characterized by violence, fraud or defamation, and was tortious in character."

The common law departed from this requirement in 1853 in the English case of *Lumley v. Gye,* 2 El. & Bl. 216, 118 Eng. Rep. 749 (Q.B.1853). which held that liability could be imposed for interference with a contract if the defendant acted "wrongfully and maliciously", even if the defendant's conduct was not tortious or illegal. In that case, Gye induced an opera singer to sing for him instead of Lumley, for whom she had contracted to perform, not with threats of violence but by offering her a higher fee. Forty years later in *Temperton v. Russell,* 1 Q.B. 715 (1893). the English court reaffirmed its decision in *Lumley,* holding that trade union officials could be liable to a building materials supplier for threatening his customers with labor disturbances if they continued to purchase supplies from him The court announced that the rule in *Lumley* would apply not only to interference with all contracts, regardless of the subject matter, but to interference with prospective or potential relations as well.

Temperton's treatment of interference with prospective relations as simply another aspect of interference with contract was a mistake. It is one thing for *A* and *B* to compete for *C*'s business, and quite another for *A* to persuade or force *C* to break his contract with *B.* Tortious interference with contract contemplates that competition may be lawful and yet limited by promises already made. Absent any such promises, competitors should be free to use any lawful means to obtain advantage. As one commentator has observed:

> [A]lthough one who interferes with the stability of a contractual relationship may be seen as an interloper and possibly a tortfeasor, one who interferes merely with a "prospective business advantage" may be essentially a competitor. In an economic system founded upon the principle of free competition, competitors should not be liable in tort for seeking a legitimate business advantage.

Gary Myers, *The Differing Treatment of Efficiency and Competition in Antitrust and Tortious Interference Law,* 77 Minn. L. Rev. 1097, 1121–1122 (1993).

Lumley's holding that unlawful conduct was not a prerequisite for liability for tortious interference with contract was understandable; *Temperton*'s extension of the same rule to situations involving only prospective relations was not.

The use of "malice" to denote the touchstone of liability for tortious interference with contract was not well explained in *Lumley* and the cases that followed. "Malice" appeared at first to signify malevolence, although it soon became apparent that that definition would not work. As we have explained in a similar context, lawful conduct is not made tortious by the actor's ill will towards another, nor does an actor's lack of ill will make his tortious conduct any less so. "Malice" obviously meant that character of conduct that would not justify inducing a breach of contract, but that was an obviously circular definition (a person is not justified in inducing a breach of contract if he acts with malice, that is, if he acts in such a way that does not justify inducing a breach of contract). Exactly what conduct was culpable, and therefore "malicious", went undefined.

As clumsy as the idea of "malice" was in describing liability for tortious interference with contract, it made no sense at all in trying to describe liability for tortious interference with prospective advantage. Competitors could quite naturally be expected, well within the bounds of law, to try to achieve the best for themselves and, consequently, harm to each other. In a society built around business competition, interference with prospective business relations has never been thought to be wrongful in and of itself. That some liability factor was essential has never been in doubt. If that factor was not unlawful conduct, discarded by *Lumley* for tortious interference with contract, then it was not clear what it should be.

These two problems—the misassociation of the two torts and the confusion regarding their standards of liability—may have been due to, and were certainly exacerbated by, the concept of a prima facie tort that was being advanced about the same time. As explained by Justice Holmes: "It has been considered that, prima facie, the intentional infliction of temporal damages is a cause of action, which, as a matter of substantive law, whatever may be the form of pleading, requires a justification if the defendant is to escape." *Aikens v. Wisconsin*, 195 U.S. 194, 204, 25 S.Ct. 3, 49 L.Ed. 154 (1904) (citations omitted). In other words, intentionally inflicting harm is tortious unless justified. Consistent with this idea, and with the association of the two interference torts, the 1939 *Restatement of Torts* defined tortious interference as simply this:

> [O]ne who, without a privilege to do so, induces or otherwise purposely causes a third person not to (a) perform a contract with another, or (b) enter into or continue a business relation with another is liable to the other for the harm caused thereby. Restatement of Torts § 766 (1939).

In determining the existence of a privilege, the *Restatement* called for consideration of

> (a) the nature of the actor's conduct, (b) the nature of the expectancy with which his conduct interferes, (c) the relations between the parties, (d) the interest sought to be advanced by the actor and (e) the

> social interests in protecting the expectancy on the one hand and the actor's freedom of action on the other hand. Id. § 767.

The *Restatement* also stated a privilege for competition when, among other things, "the actor does not employ improper means". *Id.* § 768.

The *Restatement*'s broad statements did almost nothing to define the parameters of tortious conduct. What was it about the nature of an actor's conduct, or of the expectancy at issue, or of any of the other considerations that should or should not result in liability in specific circumstances? Were the considerations the same for interference with a contract and interference with a prospective business relation? When were means of competition "improper"? The *Restatement*'s provisions gave no more guidance than the concept of prima facie tort. Not surprisingly, when the second *Restatement* was published forty years later, it commented:

> [T]here is no clearcut distinction between the requirements for a prima facie case and the requirements for a recognized privilege. Initial liability depends upon the interplay of several factors and is not reducible to a single rule; and privileges, too, are not clearly established but depend upon a consideration of much the same factors. Moreover, there is considerable disagreement on who has the burden of pleading and proving certain matters, such for example, as the existence and effect of competition for prospective business.
>
> This has occurred for two reasons. First, the law in this area has not fully congealed but is still in a formative stage. The several forms of the [interference] tort . . . are often not distinguished by the courts, and cases have been cited among them somewhat indiscriminately. This has produced a blurring of the significance of the factors involved in determining liability. . . .
>
> The second reason grows out of use of the term "malicious" in [*Lumley v. Gye*] and other early cases. It soon came to be realized that the term was not being used in a literal sense, requiring ill will toward the plaintiff as a requirement for imposing liability. Many courts came to call this "legal malice," and to hold that in this sense the requirement means that the infliction of the harm must be intentional and "without justification." "Justification" is a broader and looser term than "privilege," and the consequence has been that its meaning has not been very clear. Restatement (Second) of Torts, intro to ch. 37, at 5 (1979).

Having recognized these problems, the *Restatement* did little to solve them. Concluding that "it has seemed desirable to make use of a single word that will indicate for this tort the balancing process expressed by the two terms, 'culpable and not justified,' " the *Restatement* chose "improper" as a word "neutral enough to acquire a specialized meaning of its own" for purposes of defining the interference torts. The *Restatement* separated interference with contract and interference with prospective business relations, previously combined as one, but it used the same new standard—"improper"—to define liability for each. Hence, section 766B states with respect to intentional interference with prospective contractual relations:

> One who intentionally and improperly interferes with another's prospective contractual relation (except a contract to marry) is subject to liability to the other for the pecuniary harm resulting from loss of the benefits of the relation, whether the interference consists of (a) inducing or otherwise causing a third person not to enter into or continue the prospective relation or (b) preventing the other from acquiring or continuing the prospective relation.

The *Restatement* then states that whether conduct was "improper" for both interference torts should be determined from consideration of the same broad factors:

> In determining whether an actor's conduct in intentionally interfering with a contract or a prospective contractual relation of another is improper or not, consideration is given to the following factors: (a) the nature of the actor's conduct, (b) the actor's motive, (c) the interests of the other with which the actor's conduct interferes, (d) the interests sought to be advanced by the actor, (e) the social interests in protecting the freedom of action of the actor and the contractual interests of the other, (f) the proximity or remoteness of the actor's conduct to the interference, and (g) the relations between the parties. *Id.* § 767.

The second *Restatement,* like the first, provided that lawful competition was not tortious interference with a prospective business relation although it might be tortious interference with any contract not terminable at will. *Id.* § 768.

Thus, the second *Restatement* abandoned the confusing and overlapping notions of "malice", "privilege", and "justification", but it made little more than a formal distinction between the two interference torts, setting the liability standard for both at "improper" conduct, and it continued the idea that the considerations for determining what was improper were, except for lawful competition, similar for both torts. Commentators since have criticized the *Restatement* as overstating case law. * * *

Two recent cases of note have echoed the same idea after surveying existing case law. In *Della Penna v. Toyota Motor Sales, Inc.,* a car manufacturer required dealers not to sell its vehicles for resale outside the United States in order to protect its dealership network. An exporter sued the manufacturer for tortious interference with his business prospects. The Supreme Court of California rejected the claim as a matter of law, concluding that the manufacturer's conduct was not actionable. Abandoning notions of "malice" and "justification", the court held

> that a plaintiff seeking to recover for an alleged interference with prospective contractual or economic relations must plead and prove as part of its case-in-chief that the defendant not only knowingly inter-

fered with the plaintiff's expectancy, but engaged in conduct that was wrongful by some legal measure other than the fact of interference itself. 11 Cal.4th 376, 45 Cal.Rptr.2d 436, 902 P.2d 740, 751 (1995).

The "legal measures" identified by the court were existing tort law and statutes.

Similarly, in Speakers of Sport, Inc. v. ProServ, Inc., 178 F.3d 862 (7th Cir.1999). the Seventh Circuit concluded that under Illinois law, actionable interference requires conduct that is independently tortious by nature. In that case, one sports agency sued another for interference in obtaining Texas Rangers' catcher Ivan Rodriguez as a client by promising him more than it could deliver. The plaintiff agency sought damages alleging that the defendant agency's conduct was unfair, unethical, and deceitful. The court rejected the argument that actionable interference could be based on conduct that was not independently tortious or otherwise unlawful. * * *

Della Penna and *Speakers of Sport* demonstrate the importance of decoupling interference with contract from interference with prospective relations, and of grounding liability for the latter in conduct that is independently tortious by nature or otherwise unlawful.

B

* * *

It appears that in most Texas cases in which plaintiffs have actually recovered damages for tortious interference with prospective business relations, the defendants' conduct was either independently tortious—in the four cases noted, defamatory or fraudulent—or in violation of state law. For the same reasons accepted by the Supreme Court of California in *Della Penna,* and by the Seventh Circuit in *Speakers of Sport,* and advanced by Professor Perlman and other legal commentators, we see no need for a definition of tortious interference with prospective business relations that would encompass other conduct. The historical limitation of the tort to unlawful conduct * * * provides a viable definition and preserves the tort's utility of filling a gap in affording compensation in situations where a wrong has been done. The concepts of malice, justification, and privilege have not only proved to be overlapping and confusing, they provide no meaningful description of culpable conduct, as the *Restatement (Second) of Torts* concluded more than twenty years ago.

We therefore hold that to recover for tortious interference with a prospective business relation a plaintiff must prove that the defendant's conduct was independently tortious or wrongful. By independently tortious we do not mean that the plaintiff must be able to prove an independent tort. Rather, we mean only that the plaintiff must prove that the defendant's conduct would be actionable under a recognized tort. Thus, for example, a plaintiff may recover for tortious interference from a defendant who makes fraudulent statements about the plaintiff to a third person without proving that the third person was actually defrauded. If, on the other hand, the defendant's statements are not intended to deceive, as in *Speakers of Sport,* then they are not actionable. Likewise, a plaintiff may recover for tortious interference from a defendant who threatens a person with physical harm if he does business with the plaintiff. The plaintiff need prove only that the defendant's conduct toward the prospective customer would constitute assault. Also, a plaintiff could recover for tortious interference by showing an illegal boycott, although a plaintiff could not recover against a defendant whose persuasion of others not to deal with the plaintiff was lawful. Conduct that is merely "sharp" or unfair is not actionable and cannot be the basis for an action for tortious interference with prospective relations, and we disapprove of cases that suggest the contrary. These examples are not exhaustive, but they illustrate what conduct can constitute tortious interference with prospective relations.

The concepts of justification and privilege are subsumed in the plaintiff's proof, except insofar as they may be defenses to the wrongfulness of the alleged conduct. For example, a statement made against the plaintiff, though defamatory, may be protected by a complete or qualified privilege. Justification and privilege are defenses in a claim for tortious interference with prospective relations only to the extent that they are defenses to the independent tortiousness of the defendant's conduct. Otherwise, the plaintiff need not prove that the defendant's conduct was not justified or privileged, nor can a defendant assert such defenses.

In reaching this conclusion we treat tortious interference with prospective business relations differently than tortious interference with contract. It makes sense to require a defendant who induces a breach of contract to show some justification or privilege for depriving another of benefits to which the agreement entitled him. But when two parties are competing for interests to which neither is entitled, then neither can be said to be more justified or privileged in his pursuit. If the conduct of each is lawful, neither should be heard to complain that mere unfairness is actionable. Justification and privilege are not useful concepts in assessing interference with prospective relations, as they are in assessing interference with an existing contract.

III

With this understanding of what conduct is prohibited by the tort of interference with prospective contractual or business relations and what conduct is not prohibited, we return to the evidence of this case. * * * We must look to see whether there is evidence of harm from some independently tortious or unlawful activity by Wal–Mart.

The plaintiffs tell us that their interference claim is based on the telephone conversation between Hudson, Wal–Mart's relator, and Callaway, Fleming's manager of store development. Specifically, the plaintiffs complain of Hudson's "ultimatum" to Callaway that if Wal–Mart were not able to acquire Tract 2 for expansion, it would relocate its store. The plaintiffs contend that Hudson's statement was false and therefore fraudulent. To be fraudulent a statement must be material and false, the speaker must have known it was false or acted recklessly without regard to its falsity, the speaker must have intended that the statement be acted on, and hearer must have relied on it. The plaintiffs do not dispute that Wal–Mart had undertaken to identify stores which could not be expanded and to relocate them, that it attempted to acquire Tract 2 as an alternative to relocating the Nederland store, and that as Hudson told Callaway, if Wal–Mart could not acquire Tract 2 it would relocate. * * * The fact that Wal–Mart had not begun to relocate its store when Hudson talked with Callaway is no evidence that his statement was false. The plaintiffs point to no evidence that Wal–Mart's general preference for expansion over relocation, or the possibilities for some expansion on Tract 1, would have made it decide not to relocate. Indeed, if Tract 1 had been adequate for Wal–Mart's intended expansion, it would not have needed to acquire Tract 2.

Thus, no evidence supports the plaintiffs' contention that Hudson's statement to Callaway was fraudulent or that Hudson intended to deceive Callaway, and the plaintiffs do not contend that Wal–Mart's conduct was otherwise illegal or tortious. The record contains no evidence to indicate that Wal–Mart intended the plaintiffs any harm other than what they would necessarily suffer by Wal–Mart's successful acquisition of Tract 2, which they were both pursuing, by entirely lawful means. We therefore conclude that there is no evidence to support a judgment for the plaintiffs on their interference claim.

* * *

For the reasons we have explained, we reverse the judgment of the court of appeals and render judgment that the plaintiffs take nothing.

[The concurring opinion of JUSTICE O'NEILL is omitted.]

NOTES

1. *Privileges and Burden of Proof.* The case illustrates the complexity of the interrelated topics of "improper interference," privilege, and burden of proof. With respect to other intentional torts, justification or privilege is an affirmative defense for the defendant. In seeming contrast to other intentional torts, the Second Restatement's formulation of both interference torts includes the requirement that the interference be not just intentional but improper. Yet, as we have seen, the comments to the *Restatement (Second)* acknowledge that the caselaw is unsettled as to whether the plaintiff or defendant bears the burden of proof with respect to showing that the interference was improper or unprivileged. *See Restatement (Second) Torts* § 767, comment b (1965).

Courts in theory could adopt one of three approaches to the privilege-burden of proof question: (1) require only that the plaintiff show an intentional interference, placing on defendant the burden of proving that the interference was privileged and proper; (2) require that the plaintiff also show the interference was "improper," meaning that the plaintiff must both show some level of impropriety and negate any possible justification or excuse; or (3) require that the plaintiff show that the interference was "improper" in some sense, but leave the burden of proof on the defendant with respect to at least some privileges. To illustrate (3), courts might allow the plaintiff to satisfy the requirement of "improper" by showing that the interference was motivated partly by malice, and yet allow the defendant to escape liability by proving that the interference fell within the privilege of fair competition because it was motivated at least in part by a competitive goal and involved no illegal means. The current trend is to move away from (1), but much of the case law is murky about whether the second or third approach applies.

Which of the three approaches does the *Wal–Mart v. Sturges* court identify as applying to tortious interference with prospective business relations? Assuming that a court is persuaded to reject the first approach, what rationales might explain choosing (3) over (2); that is, does it make sense to parse the general topic of whether the interference was proper into a burden that is partly the plaintiff's (a showing of improper) and partly the defendant's (a showing that the conduct was privileged)?

2. *Questioning an Inquiry into Subjective Wrongful Purpose.* In Leigh Furniture & Carpet Co. v. Isom, 657 P.2d 293, 304 (Utah 1982), the court stated that the plaintiff could satisfy the requirement of proving an improper interference by proving that the defendant interfered either "for an improper purpose or by improper means." An improper means would be shown if the plaintiff proved that the defendant's means of interference violated statutory or regulatory standards, common law standards, or an "established standard of a trade or profession." *Id.* at 308 (quoting Top Serv. Body Shop, Inc. v. Allstate Ins. Co., 283 Or. 201, 582 P.2d 1365, 1371 & n. 11 (1978)). Plaintiff could prove an improper purpose by showing that the defendant's ill will predominated over all legitimate economic motivations. A plaintiff, therefore, could prevail on the tort claim by showing an improper purpose even if the means were proper. Subsequently, the Utah Supreme Court expressed reservations about the wisdom of the two-part test:

> The author of this opinion has grave doubts about the future vitality of Leigh's improper-purpose prong, especially in the context of commercial dealings. * * * [T]he operative test set out in Leigh—a test under which all relevant considerations are issues of fact, which insulates improper-purpose findings from meaningful appellate review—gives no guidance as to which activities qualify as "commercial conduct" and provides no standards by which a court or jury can determine when to apply the improper-purpose test to "commercial conduct." Absent such standards, Leigh's improper-purpose test creates a trap for the wary and unwary alike: business practices that are found to be "proper means" by a finder of fact and may otherwise be regarded as wholly legitimate under our capitalistic economic system may be recast through a jury's unguided exercise of its moral judgment into examples of spite or malice. For example, the enforcement of a binding, valid contractual noncompete provision can result in liability under Leigh merely upon a jury finding of some ill-defined "improper purpose." For these reasons, the author of this opinion thinks Leigh's improper-purpose test should be revisited and

> recast to minimize its potential for misuse. However, neither [party] has asked this court to modify Leigh's improper-purpose prong. Therefore, the issue of whether lawful means can result in liability for an improper purpose is not before the court today.

Pratt v. Prodata, Inc., 885 P.2d 786, 789 n. 3 (Utah 1994) (Zimmerman, C.J.).

Iowa also makes use of an "improper purpose" standard, but under the Iowa formulation the plaintiff must show that "the sole or predominant purpose of the actor's conduct was to financially injure or destroy the plaintiff." *See* Willey v. Riley, 541 N.W.2d 521, 527 (Iowa 1995). Would this formulation satisfy the concerns expressed about the "purpose" inquiry by the Utah Supreme Court?

3. *The Interference Torts in the Employment Context.* The traditional rule is that a party cannot be liable for interfering with its own contract. This requirement that the interference be by a "third-party" and not a party to the contract has arisen in a number of employment cases. For example, in McGanty v. Staudenraus, 321 Or. 532, 901 P.2d 841 (1995), plaintiff sued her former employer, a collection agency, as well as the individual who was the president and owner of the agency; the president and owner had been her immediate supervisor. He allegedly had made unwelcome sexual advances and comments, and plaintiff sued on a variety of theories, including tortious interference with contract. Applying the law of respondeat superior, the court reasoned that the supervisor had been acting as the employer if he had made the advances during the course and scope of his employment. Thus, the supervisor could not be a third-party to the contract for the purposes of the tort of intentional interference.

Another issue that often arises when intentional interference is alleged in connection with an employment relationship is whether a contract for employment at will can serve as the basis for the tort cause of action. A number of courts have answered affirmatively. New York courts have cautioned that a plaintiff should not "be allowed to evade the employment at-will rule and relationship by recasting his cause of action in the garb of a tortious interference with his employment." Ingle v. Glamore Motor Sales, Inc., 73 N.Y.2d 183, 189, 535 N.E.2d 1311, 1313–14, 538 N.Y.S.2d 771, 774 (1989). New York courts, nonetheless, allow an at-will employee to maintain a claim for tortious interference in limited circumstances; if, for instance, the defendant used wrongful means (such as fraud or misrepresentation) to effect the termination, the defendant acted with malice, or the means used violated a duty to the plaintiff. *See generally* Finley v. Giacobbe, 79 F.3d 1285 (2d Cir.1996).

4. *Litigation as the Basis for the Interference Torts?* Suppose that the means of the alleged interference is a lawsuit. In applying the interference torts in such contexts, courts have tended to look to the law of malicious prosecution and vexatious litigation for guidance. As one court explained, "these kindred torts have also had to address the competing policies of deterrence of groundless litigation and protection of good faith access to the courts." Blake v. Levy, 191 Conn. 257, 464 A.2d 52 (1983). Thus, some courts have imported the standards governing vexatious litigation into the interference torts when plaintiff bases the latter on litigation. These standards often

require that plaintiff show that the lawsuit was initiated maliciously, was initiated without probable cause, and terminated in the plaintiff's favor.

5. *False statements about a competitor's product.* Claims for "trade libel," "disparagement" or "injurious falsehood" are different names for the same tort. The action has evolved to cover untrue statements about the quality of goods. To state a claim for commercial disparagement or trade libel, the claimant must allege (1) publication; (2) with malice; (3) of false allegations concerning another party's property or product; (4) causing special damages (pecuniary harm). Several states have enacted disparagement statutes that apply to anyone maliciously disparaging a product. *See* Texas Beef Group v. Winfrey, 201 F.3d 680 (5th Cir. 2000). Because the malice requirement sets a high bar for recovery and because the tort sometimes comes up against First Amendment concerns (see the discussion of defamation in Chapter 8, *infra*), neither common law nor statutory claims meet with frequent success. *But see* Vascular Solutions, Inc. v. Marine Polymer Technologies, Inc., 590 F.3d 56 (1st Cir. 2009).

6. *The Pennzoil–Texaco Verdict.* In a now-famous chapter in the history of American civil litigation, Pennzoil sued Texaco in Texas state court for interfering with Pennzoil's contractual relations with Getty Oil Co. The underlying events behind the suit began with Pennzoil's and Getty's negotiations over an acquisition by Pennzoil of Getty Oil. The two companies drafted a memorandum of agreement, which stated that it was subject to approval by the Getty board. Yet the memorandum was signed by parties who controlled a majority of the outstanding shares of Getty, and eventually the Getty board voted to accept Pennzoil's proposal of $110 per share on the condition that the Pennzoil also pay a "stub" of $5 per share. There was evidence that Pennzoil then accepted the counteroffer. Yet Getty eventually accepted an offer from Texaco of $125 per share and signed a merger agreement with Texaco that gave Texaco control over Getty.

The jury returned a verdict for Pennzoil of $7.53 billion compensatory damages and $3 billion in punitive damages. The Texas Court of Appeals affirmed the liability aspects of the case and the award of compensatory damages, but reduced the punitive damage award to $1 billion. Texaco, Inc. v. Pennzoil Co., 729 S.W.2d 768 (Tex.App.1987) *cert. denied* 485 U.S. 994, 108 S.Ct. 1305, 99 L.Ed.2d 686 (1988). After the Texas Supreme Court declined review, Texaco filed for bankruptcy and appealed to the United States Supreme Court. While this appeal was pending, the parties settled the case for $3 billion, at the time the largest settlement or judgment in history. The case is discussed in Michael Ansaldi, *Texaco, Pennzoil and the Revolt of the Masses*, 27 Hous. L. Rev. 733 (1990).

PROBLEM: TRUCK LEASING

Geltman counsels companies that lease trucks. He educates his customers about the truck leasing business so that they may obtain more favorable leases. He helps in soliciting and critiquing bids from lessors and sometimes negotiates leases. Geltman also attempts to obtain changes in existing leases that will be beneficial to his clients. The plaintiff (United) operates a large truck leasing company in the Commonwealth.

United sues Geltman on claims of (1) intentional interference with contract, and (2) intentional interference with prospective contractual relations. The first claim is based on United's contention that Geltman caused one of his customers (Universal Fixtures) to break its contract with United and to enter into a lease with Flexi–Van, the lessor with whom Universal Fixtures had had a lease prior to its lease with United. It is clear, on the plaintiff's evidence, that Geltman knew of the existing lease between United and Universal Fixtures and recognized the possibility that, if Universal Fixtures signed on with Flexi–Van, United might sue Universal Fixtures for breach of contract. There was evidence that United lost $60,000 because of Universal Fixtures's repudiation of the contract.

United's claim for intentional interference with prospective contractual relations concerns United's inability to obtain a lease with Matthew's Salad House (Matthew's). United had been trying to arrange a lease with Matthew's for about six years. Matthew's retained Geltman to advise it concerning the lease of refrigerated trucks. Geltman did not invite United to bid on the Matthew's account, although there were good reasons why United might have been invited to do so. When asked by a United representative why he had not invited United to bid, Geltman replied that other leasing companies gave him leads for new accounts but that United did not. After learning the amount of its competitor's bid, United did bid on the Matthew's account but was not awarded the account.

Evaluate the strength and weakness of United's two claims. If either claim were allowed to go to the jury, what would the jury issues on liability look like?

(Adapted from United Truck Leasing Corp. v. Geltman, 406 Mass. 811, 551 N.E.2d 20 (1990).)

PROBLEM: HIGH-RISK FISHERMEN

Molltopia is a small fishing town. Owners of fishing vessels in Molltopia employ the local fishermen as crewmen. As a matter of state law, the owners-employers are required to provide insurance for all of their employee fishermen to protect the employees from potential injuries sustained while working aboard the vessels. Thus, the owners-employers purchase individual insurance policies from Security Insurance Company ("Security") for each of their employees and pay the necessary premiums as they became due.

Security keeps a record of fishermen who allegedly create a "special risk of loss." These fishermen are designated "high-risk" not for legitimate risk-related reasons, but because they have previously submitted personal injury claims to Security and have spurned Security's settlement offers, choosing instead to hire attorneys and to sue Security. Because of the litigation expenses from these "high-risk" fishermen, Security's insurance costs have risen steadily over the past few years. This has resulted in increased premiums for all Security policyholders. When such "high-risk" fishermen are identified, Security informs the owners-employers that they will have to pay significantly higher premiums to cover these employees. As a result, the owners-employers usually terminate the employment of the designated "high-risk'' fishermen (the fishermen are ''at-will'' employees and can be terminated, in most instances, at the whim of the employer).

Recently, the ''high-risk'' fishermen sued Security in a state court for tortious interference with their employment relationships.

What are the Plaintiffs' best arguments in support of their claims? What are Security's best responses? As a matter of policy, who should bear the burden of proof on the element of ''impropriety?'' What considerations support placing the burden on plaintiffs, and what considerations support placing the burden on defendants?

B. DAMAGES FOR ECONOMIC TORTS

1. INTRODUCTION

The world of damages for economic torts has important differences from, and important similarities to, the world of damages for noneconomic torts. Before turning specifically to the main doctrines relating to damages for noneconomic torts, it might be helpful to gain an overview of these general differences and similarities.

Categories of damages. The first and most obvious difference is that the categories of available damages are different. In the world of personal injury torts, damage take three forms: nominal (available for intentional torts), compensatory, and punitive/exemplary. The compensatory damage categories include: past and future lost earnings or earning capacity; past and future medical and rehabilitative expenses; past and future mental anguish; past and future pain and suffering; past and future impairment and disfigurement. Exemplary damages are available only for intentional torts, or gross negligence. These general categories apply across the world of personal injury torts.

In the economic tort arena, as noted in the preceding chapter, the categories of available relief are more wide-ranging, yet not all categories are available for every economic tort. For instance, damages for negligent misrepresentation usually are limited to economic injury. By contrast, damages for fraud can include mental anguish in some jurisdictions.

The theoretical principles of damages. In the personal injury world, the damages principle (aside from cases of punitive damages) is compensatory: returning the plaintiff, to the extent money can do so, to the position he or she occupied before the injury. In the economic tort context, principles of equitable relief play an important role in addition to compensatory relief. Thus, for instance, damages include fee forfeiture, constructive trusts, etc.

Comparative Fault and Apportionment. Comparative fault and apportionment are not rules of damages, but obviously they affect the calculation of the final judgment for claimants. Thus, this section's discussion of damages also will include some attention to defenses and apportionment in economic injury cases.

Equitable Relief. In the personal injury context, one rarely if ever sees reference to "equitable" final relief. Rather, the overriding principle is the payment of compensatory damages, and the purported goal of compensation is to restore the plaintiff, to the extent money can do so, to the plaintiff's pre-injury position. In the economic tort context, compensatory damages are available, but plaintiffs can sometimes seek what are often termed "equitable" forms of relief. Some of the most common examples include: constructive trust, fee forfeiture, and profit disgorgement. This is not to say that all these remedies are available for every economic tort. Rather, the menu of possible relief tends to include offerings that were traditionally viewed as equitable relief. Whether a particular remedy (such as profit disgorgement) is available in a given case depends on the general doctrine surrounding the tort at issue, and the particular facts of the case.

An explanatory note about the term "equitable relief" may also be useful. A complete treatment of equitable versus legal relief is beyond the scope of this book. Briefly, however, under English common law, some courts were equity courts and empowered to issue equity-based remedies. Law courts, by contrast, had the power to issue legal remedies. In American common law, judicial powers have merged. But the distinction between equitable and legal relief remains important, if sometimes opaque. A plaintiff in an economic tort case might seek a remedy that is not considered equitable, such as compensatory damages. Or a plaintiff might also seek an equitable remedy such as fee forfeiture. The distinction can matter because a plaintiff often has to make a different showing, or complete a different procedural step, before obtaining equitable relief. Likewise, depending on the particular tort, equitable remedies might be more readily available.

2. BASIC PRINCIPLES FOR DAMAGES AND CAUSATION IN ECONOMIC TORTS

A treatment of damages in economic torts requires an understanding of terms that often appear in both contract cases and in economic tort cases: "general damages" and "consequential" damages. Although these specific terms do not always appear in tort cases, they come up frequently enough to be confusing for someone who does not understand them or how they fit into tort damages. An excellent source for this purpose (as well as personal injury and other causes of action) is the three-volume treatise, Dan B. Dobbs, Law of Remedies (2d ed. 1993).

The phrases themselves—"general damages" and "consequential damages"—tend to refer to the same things in either contract or tort, but tort law is normally viewed as allowing "consequential damages" more often than does contract law. "General damages" refers to the damages that a defendant's contract breach or tort has caused in net worth or loss of value, akin to a before-and-after balance sheet. *See* 1 Dobbs, *supra*, at 288. For instance, suppose that the defendant negligently drives a car into the plaintiff's garage, smashing many of the items (tools, bicycles, etc.) in the garage. The general damages turn on the value of the items in the garage before the defendant's negligence and after the defendant's negligence. So, for instance, if the items in the garage were worth $5000 before the crash and only $800 after the crash, the general damages are $4200. *See id.* A similar approach could be used in a contract case. For instance, suppose that the defendant promises to sell to plaintiff all the bicycles and tools in his garage, for the sum of $2000. The defendant breaches this promise. The actual market value of the bicycles and tools was $2,800. Therefore, the plaintiff has suffered $800 in general damages. *See id.*

Consequential damages refer to damages other than general damages that are, in a "but for" cause sense, arguably linked to the defendant's conduct. Often, consequential damages take the form of a claim for lost profits, although this is not the only type of consequential damage. Rather, consequential damages are very case-specific. For instance, in the example just given, suppose that the crash into the garage damages the structure of the house in a way that requires repairs that render the house uninhabitable during repairs. The costs of repairs, and the costs of living away from the home, are consequential losses.

Under the famous contract rule of *Hadley v. Baxendale*, 9 Ex. 341, 156 Eng. Rep. 145 (1854), consequential damages are available in contract only if they were within the contemplation of the parties at the time of contracting. *See id.* at 321. A tort theory does not throw open the door to recovery of all consequential damages. Rather, as with any tort damages, an economic tort plaintiff must show that the consequential damages satisfy the tests of factual causation and proximate causation.

As a very general matter, then, tort law allows, for economic tort cases, what courts sometimes (but not always) term "general" and "consequential" damages. Yet the plaintiff bears the burden of proving factual cause and proximate cause. In addition, plaintiff must prove the amount of the resulting damages with reasonable certainty. This requirement is an obvious one in theory, and it parallels the requirement in personal injury contexts. But, in economic torts, the need to prove the amount of damages with reasonable certainty often presents complex and fascinating issues of proof. The challenges of proving the amount (and the causation) of economic loss have intensified since the United States Supreme Court, in Kumho Tire Co. v. Carmichael, 526 U.S. 137, 119 S.Ct. 1167, 143 L.Ed.2d 238 (1999) (reprinted on p. 306, *infra*) extended the ruling of *Daubert* to all expert testimony.

3. LOST PROFITS VERSUS LOSS OF VALUE OF THE BUSINESS

It is important to understand two possible measures of tort damages to a business: lost profits, and loss of the value of the business. The two phrases are closely connected, because in economic theory the value of a business can be characterized as the "net present value of all future benefits (i.e., cash flows) that the owner may expect to derive from it." Kenneth M. Kolaski & Mark Kuga, *Measuring Commercial Damages Via Lost Profits or Loss of Business Value: Are These Measures Redundant or Distinguishable?*, 18 J.L. & Com. 1 (1998). Thus, to cause lost profits is also to cause a diminution of business value. Used this way, however, the notion of diminished business value is the same as lost profits.

A somewhat different situation occurs when the tortious conduct essentially destroys the business—for instance, by physically destroying the business or causing financial ruination. When this is the case, plaintiffs sometimes seek as damages the "value of the business." Different methods of measuring this are available. The methods include the following: (1) Discounted Net Cash Flow, which is based on the premise that the value of the business is the present value of all the future income to be derived by the owners of the business; (2) Capital Market Approach, which is based on "the premise that the value of a business enterprise should be determined based on what astute and rational capital market investors would pay to own the stock in the subject company," and (3) Comparative Market Transaction Approach, which "determines the value of the business by comparing the subject firm to comparable firms that have been bought or sold during a reasonably recent period of time." Kolaski & Kuga, *supra*.

4. OUT OF POCKET MEASURE VERSUS BENEFIT OF THE BARGAIN MEASURE

We discussed the distinction between the out of pocket measure and the benefit of bargain measure in the context of misrepresentation cases in the last chapter (see p. 90 *supra*). Recall that former assesses damages by what it would cost to replace the money that the plaintiff has paid out; the latter assesses damages by the value that the bargain or contract would have produced. These are alternative ways of measuring the "general damages" that a plaintiff might have suffered as a result of a contract breach or a tort. Under many tort theories, a plaintiff is entitled to use either measure. In such cases, a plaintiff will use the measure that yields the highest number if the plaintiff is able to satisfy the requirement that the plaintiff prove the amount of damages to a reasonable degree of certainty. Of course, sometimes the plaintiff will not be able to prove, with a reasonable degree of certainty, the benefit of the bargain. Thus, even if in theory this measure of damages is allowed under a certain tort cause of action, a plaintiff might not be able to prove the damages to a reasonable degree of certainty.

5. FREQUENT CATEGORIES OF DAMAGES SOUGHT UNDER VARIOUS ECONOMIC TORT THEORIES

Having seen the basic principles that applies to all compensatory damages in economic torts—requirements of proving actual cause, proximate cause, and the amount of loss with reasonable certainty—it should be useful to summarize the types of damage that plaintiffs often allege, and that courts have allowed, in various economic tort cases.

Intentional Interference with Contract and Prospective Contract. Suppose that D intentionally interferes with a contract between P and X. P can recover: the market value of the contract (measured either by benefit of the bargain or out of pocket measure); consequential damages including lost profits; punitive damages; and, in some limited cases, emotional distress. *See* 2 Dobbs, *supra*, at 134. Of course, as to any of these categories, the plaintiff must satisfy the requirements of factual causation and proximate causation, and must prove the amount of damages to a reasonable degree of certainty.

Negligent Misrepresentation. Most cases, along with the Restatement (Second) of Torts, take the position that plaintiffs are limited to the out-of-pocket measure for negligent misrepresentation. Most courts do not allow emotional distress.

Fraudulent Misrepresentation. Plaintiff can recover damages under either the out of pocket or benefit of bargain measure. Consequential damages are available. In only rare instances is emotional distress available. Again, the plaintiff must satisfy the requirements of factual cause, proximate cause, and proof of the damages amount to a reasonable degree of certainty.

Breach of fiduciary duty. The plaintiff may recover: (1) damages under either a benefit of the bargain or out of pocket measure; (2) consequential damages; (3) in certain cases, emotional distress.

6. OTHER REMEDIES

As noted earlier, equitable remedies are also available in many economic tort contexts. In breach of fiduciary duty, the full scope of equitable remedies is available, including disgorgement of profits, fee forfeiture, constructive trust. For breach of fiduciary duty by lawyers, some courts have allowed fee forfeiture as a remedy, even when the client has not suffered actual compensatory damages. *See* Burrow v. Arce, 997 S.W.2d 229 (Tex. 1999). For the interference torts and fraudulent misrepresentation, equitable remedies are often available.

7. CAUSATION OF DAMAGES

In general, the economic tort world operates under the same causation principles as personal injury cases. In most economic tort cases, the plaintiff must prove both factual causation ("but for" causation) and proximate cause. As a practical matter, of course, the methods of proving these points are very different than evidence in personal injury contexts. The proof of causation is often particularly difficult in the economic tort context. The next three cases demonstrate the nature of this problem, first in the context of lawyer malpractice and second with respect to tortious interference damages.

a. But–For Causation in the Legal Malpractice Setting

VINER v. SWEET

Supreme Court of California, 2003.
30 Cal.4th 1232, 135 Cal.Rptr.2d 629, 70 P.3d 1046.

KENNARD, J.

In a client's action against an attorney for legal malpractice, the client must prove, among other things, that the attorney's negligent acts or omissions caused the client to suffer some financial harm or loss. When the alleged malpractice occurred in the performance of transactional work (giving advice or preparing documents for a business transaction), must the client prove this causation element according to the "but for" test, meaning that the harm or loss would not have occurred without the attorney's malpractice? The answer is yes.[1]

I

In 1984, plaintiffs Michael Viner and his wife, Deborah Raffin Viner, founded Dove Audio, Inc. (Dove). The company produced audio versions of books read by the authors or by celebrities, and it did television and movie projects.

In 1994, Dove went public by issuing stock at $10 a share. In 1995, the Viners and Dove entered into long-term employment contracts guaranteeing the Viners, among other things, a certain level of salaries, and containing indemnification provisions favorable to the Viners. The Viners received a large share of Dove's common stock and all of its preferred cumulative dividend series "A" stock.

Thereafter, Michael Viner discussed with longtime friend David Povich, a partner in defendant law firm Williams & Connolly in Washington, D.C., the possibility of selling the Viners' interest in Dove. In the fall of 1996, Norton Herrick proposed buying the Viners' entire interest in Dove.

1. Causation analysis in tort law generally proceeds in two stages: determining cause in fact and considering various policy factors that may preclude imposition of liability. * * * This case concerns only the element of cause in fact.

Attorney Povich assigned the matter to his partner, defendant Charles A. Sweet, a corporate transactional attorney. Sweet was not a member of the California Bar and was not familiar with California law. During the negotiations with Herrick, Sweet learned that under the Viners' employment agreements with Dove, the latter owed the Viners a substantial amount of unpaid dividends on their preferred stock. Sweet also learned that the Viners wanted to preserve their right to engage in the television and movie businesses.

When the negotiations with Herrick were unsuccessful, Ronald Lightstone of Media Equities International (MEI) approached the Viners. Thereafter, in March 1997, the Viners and MEI entered into an agreement under which MEI was to invest $4 million, and the Viners $2 million, to buy Dove stock. By May 1997, disputes arose, and the parties to the agreement each threatened litigation. That same month, Ronald Lightstone of MEI and Michael Viner, without defendant attorney Sweet's involvement, agreed that MEI would buy the Viners' stock in Dove and the Viners would terminate their employment with Dove.

Defendant attorney Sweet and Lightstone of MEI negotiated the final agreement, which the parties signed on June 10, 1997. The deal consisted of a securities purchase agreement and an employment termination agreement. Under the former, MEI agreed to buy a significant portion of the Viners' stock for more than $3 million. Under the latter agreement, the Viners' employment with Dove was terminated, mutual general releases were given, and Dove was to pay the Viners a total of $1.5 million over five years in monthly payments, with Dove's series "E" preferred stock to be held in escrow for distribution to the Viners if Dove defaulted on the monthly payments to them.

The employment termination agreement contained a noncompetition provision stating that the Viners would not " 'compete' in any way, directly or indirectly, in the audio book business for a period of four years" in any state in which Dove was doing business. The agreement also had a nonsolicitation provision that the Viners would not "directly or indirectly contract with, hire, solicit, encourage the departure of or in any manner engage or seek to employ any author or, for purposes of audio books, reader, currently under contract or included in the Company's book or audio catalogues for a period of four years."

In addition, the employment termination agreement provided that Deborah Raffin Viner would receive "Producer Credit" on audiobook work initiated during her employment with Dove; that Dove would not amend documents to terminate or reduce its obligation to indemnify the Viners; and that disputes would be submitted to arbitration, whose costs were to be split equally between the parties, with attorney fees to the party seeking to enforce the arbitration in court.

Defendant attorney Sweet led the Viners to believe that the employment termination agreement gave them three years of monthly payments by Dove, retained the indemnity protection they had with Dove, and provided credit for work done before their departure from Dove. The Viners also thought that they could use their celebrity contacts for any work that did not compete with Dove's audiobook business and involvement in film and television productions, and that if Dove defaulted on the agreed-upon monthly payments to them, the noncompetition clauses would be voided. The contracts did not so provide.

Later, several arbitration proceedings took place to resolve disputes between the Viners and MEI, including a claim by the Viners that the noncompetition provision of the employment termination agreement violated Business and Professions Code section 16600's restrictions on noncompetition agreements. The arbitrator rejected the claim, and the superior court confirmed the arbitrator's decision.

On June 3, 1998, the Viners brought a malpractice action against Attorney Sweet and the law firm of Williams & Connolly. Presented at trial were these seven claims: (1) Sweet told the Viners that the nonsolicitation clause of the employment termination agreement prohibiting plaintiffs from using their contacts to obtain work in television and movie projects applied only to the book and audio book parts of Dove's business, but Dove, because the clause was ambiguous, asserted that the clause also encompassed Dove's television and movie projects; (2) Sweet negligently agreed to the noncompetition provision, which violated Business and Professions Code section 16600's restrictions on such provisions; (3) the Viners had asked for an attorney fees provision, but the employment termination agreement disallowed attorney fees in any disputes, permitting them only in enforcing an arbitration award; (4) ambiguous language in the Producer Credit provision caused Dove not to give Deborah Raffin Viner credit as a producer; (5) the Viners lost rights to dividends on Dove's series "A" preferred stock; (6) the employment termination agreement did not contain an indemnity provision providing the same level of protection as the Viners' agreement with Dove; and (7) the series "E" stock afforded inadequate security to the Viners if Dove defaulted on the monthly payments due them under the employment termination agreement.

After deliberating five days, the jury found defendants liable on all seven claims of malpractice, awarding the Viners $13,291,532 in damages. Defendants moved for judgment notwithstanding the verdict or in the alternative for a new trial, arguing that the trial court erred in not instructing the jury that the Viners needed to prove they would have received a better deal "but for" defendant attorney Sweet's negligence. The trial court denied both motions.

The Court of Appeal reduced the damage award to $8,085,732, but otherwise affirmed the judgment. * * * It held that the "but for" test of causation did not apply to transactional malpractice.

The Court of Appeal distinguished transactional malpractice from litigation malpractice, in which the plaintiff is required to prove the harm would not have occurred without the alleged negligence, and it offered three reasons for treating the two forms of malpractice differently. First, the court asserted that in litigation a gain for one side is always a loss for the other, whereas in transactional work a gain for one side could also be a gain for the other side. Second, the court observed that litigation malpractice involves past historical facts while transactional malpractice involves what parties would have been willing to accept for the future. Third, the court stated that "business transactions generally involve a much larger universe of variables than litigation matters." According to the Court of Appeal, in "contract negotiations the number of possible terms and outcomes is virtually unlimited," and therefore the "jury would have to evaluate a nearly infinite array of 'what-ifs,' to say nothing of 'if that, then whats,' in order to determine whether the plaintiff would have ended up with a better outcome 'but for' the malpractice."

We granted defendants' petition for review, and thereafter limited the issues to whether the plaintiff in a transactional legal malpractice action must prove that a more favorable result would have been obtained *but for* the alleged negligence.* * *

II

Defendants contend that in a transactional malpractice action, the plaintiff must show that *but for* the alleged malpractice, a more favorable result would have been obtained. Thus, defendants argue, the Viners had to show that without defendants' negligence (1) they would have had a more advantageous agreement (the "better deal" scenario), or (2) they would not have entered into the transaction with MEI and therefore would have been better off (the "no deal" scenario).

* * * The Court of Appeal here held that a plaintiff suing an attorney for transactional malpractice need not show that the harm would not have occurred in the absence of the attorney's negligence. We disagree. We see nothing distinctive about transactional malpractice that would justify a relaxation of, or departure from, the well-established requirement in negligence cases that the plaintiff establish causation* * *.

"When a business transaction goes awry, a natural target of the disappointed principals is the attorneys who arranged or advised the deal. Clients predictably attempt to shift some part of the loss and disappointment of a deal that goes sour onto the shoulders of persons who were responsible for the underlying legal work. Before the loss can be shifted, however, the client has an initial hurdle to clear. *It must be shown that the loss suffered was in fact caused by the alleged attorney malpractice*. It is far too easy to make the legal advisor a scapegoat for a variety of business misjudgments unless the courts pay close attention to the cause in fact element, and deny recovery where the unfavorable outcome was likely to occur anyway, the client already knew the problems with the deal, or where the client's own misconduct or misjudgment caused the problems. It is the failure of the client to establish the causal link that explains decisions where the loss is termed remote or speculative. Courts are properly cautious about making attorneys guarantors of their clients' faulty business judgment." (Bauman, *Damages for Legal Malpractice: An Appraisal of the Crumbling Dike and Threatening Flood* (1988) 61 Temp. L.Rev. 1127, 1154–1155, fns. omitted, italics added (hereafter Bauman, *Damages for Legal Malpractice*).)

In a litigation malpractice action, the plaintiff must establish that *but for* the alleged negligence of the defendant attorney, the plaintiff would have obtained a more favorable judgment or settlement in the action in which the malpractice allegedly occurred. The purpose of this requirement, which has been in use for more than 120 years, is to safeguard against speculative and conjectural claims. * * * It serves the essential purpose of ensuring that damages awarded for the attorney's malpractice actually have been caused by the malpractice. * * *

The Court of Appeal here attempted to distinguish litigation malpractice from transactional malpractice in order to justify a relaxation of the "but for" test of causation in transactional malpractice cases. One of the distinguishing features, according to the court, was that in litigation a gain for one side necessarily entails a corresponding loss for the other, whereas in transactional representation a gain for one side does not necessarily result in a loss for the other. We question both the accuracy and the relevance of this generalization. In litigation, as in transactional work, a gain for one side does not necessarily result in a loss for the other side. Litigation may involve multiple claims and issues arising from complaints and cross-complaints, and parties in such litigation may prevail on some issues and not others, so that in the end there is no clear winner or loser and no exact correlation between one side's gains and the other side's losses. In addition, an attorney's representation of a client often combines litigation and transactional work, as when the attorney effects a settlement of pending litigation. The "but for" test of causation applies to a claim of legal malpractice in the settlement of litigation* * *, even though the settlement is itself a form of business transaction.

Nor do we agree with the Court of Appeal that litigation is inherently or necessarily less complex than transactional work. Some litigation, such as many lawsuits involving car accidents, is relatively uncomplicated, but so too is much transactional work, such as the negotiation of a simple lease or a purchase and sale agreement. But some litigation, such as a beneficiary's action against a trustee challenging the trustee's management of trust property over a period of decades, is as complex as most transactional work.

It is true, as the Court of Appeal pointed out, that litigation generally involves an examination of past events whereas transactional work involves anticipating and guiding the course of future events. But this distinction makes little difference for purposes of selecting an appropriate test of causation. Determining causation always requires evaluation of hypothetical situations concerning what might have happened, but did not. In both litigation and transactional malpractice cases, the crucial causation inquiry is *what would have happened* if the defendant attorney had not been negligent. This is so because the very idea of causation necessarily involves comparing historical events to a hypothetical alternative.* * *

The Viners also contend that the "but for" test of causation should not apply to transactional malpractice cases because it is too difficult to obtain the evidence needed to satisfy this standard of proof. In particular, they argue that proving causation under the "but for" test would require them to obtain the testimony of the other parties to the transaction, who have since become their adversaries, to the effect that they would have given the Viners more favorable terms had the Viners' attorneys not performed negligently. Not so. In transactional malpractice cases, as in other cases, the plaintiff may use circumstantial evidence to satisfy his or her burden. An express concession by the other parties to the negotiation that they would have accepted other or additional terms is not necessary. And the plaintiff need not prove causation with absolute certainty. Rather, the plaintiff need only " 'introduce evidence which affords a reasonable basis for the conclusion that it is more likely than not that the conduct of the defendant was a cause in fact of the result.' " (*Ortega v. Kmart Corp.* (2001) 26 Cal.4th 1200, 1205, 114 Cal.Rptr.2d 470, 36 P.3d 11, quoting Prosser & Keeton on Torts, (5th ed.1984) § 41, p. 269, fns. omitted.) In any event, difficulties of proof cannot justify imposing liability for injuries that the attorney could not have prevented by performing according to the required standard of care.* * *

For the reasons given above, we conclude that, just as in litigation malpractice actions, a plaintiff in a transactional malpractice action must show that *but for* the alleged malpractice, it is more likely than not that the plaintiff would have obtained a more favorable result.

DISPOSITION

The judgment of the Court of Appeal is reversed, and the matter is remanded to the Court of Appeal for proceedings consistent with the views expressed here

NOTES

1. *Proving but-for.* The bulk of the earliest case law on causation in legal malpractice arose from malpractice in a litigation setting. This gave rise to the phrase "case within a case." The plaintiff in the malpractice action, to prove but-for causation, had to prove in some detail how the underlying litigation would have played out had the lawyer not malpracticed. "Proving the case within a case is often a time-consuming and expensive exercise. It requires, among other things, attempting to replicate the underlying case by calling the witnesses that should have been called, offering the exhibits that should have been offered, litigating all the motions that should have been filed, and instructing the jury as it should have been instructed. Occasionally, attempts have been made to short-cut the process by calling lawyer-experts to opine about what the outcome should have been." Michael T. McConnell, *Proximate*

Causation in Colorado Legal Malpractice Litigation, 31 Colo. Lawyer 9 (Jan. 2002). Even before the *Daubert* line of cases, *see* Daubert v. Merrell Dow Pharmaceuticals, Inc., 516 U.S. 869, 116 S.Ct. 189, 133 L.Ed.2d 126 (1995), courts differed over the admissibility of exert testimony to establish the likely outcome of the case within a case. See Wilburn Brewer, Jr., *Expert Witness Testimony in Legal Malpractice Cases,* 45 S.C. L. Rev. 727 (1994).

2. *Causation in criminal representation*. Suppose that a criminal defense lawyer fails to tell the criminal defendant about a possible deal under which the criminal defendant will be given immunity in exchange for agreeing to testify against others involved in the alleged criminal activity. The criminal defendant then pleads guilty to several counts and is sentenced to prison. Suppose the criminal defendant can prove (1) that the lawyer failed to advise her of the immunity deal and that this was malpractice; and (2) that the criminal defendant would have taken the immunity deal if she had known of it. Has the criminal defendant proven "but for" causation for purposes of legal malpractice? Most courts, on public policy grounds, have ruled that, in such circumstances, the legal malpractice plaintiff cannot succeed on cause unless he or she has been exonerated on direct appeal, through post-conviction relief, or otherwise. As the court explained in Peeler v. Hughes & Luce, 909 S.W.2d 494 (Tex. 1995), "[An] opportunity to shift much, if not all, of the punishment assessed against convicts for their criminal acts to their former attorneys, drastically diminishes the consequences of the convicts' criminal conduct and seriously undermines our system of criminal justice.* * * We therefore hold that, as a matter of law, it is the illegal conduct rather than the negligence of a convict's counsel that is the cause in fact of any injuries flowing from the conviction, unless the conviction has been overturned." See Kevin Bennardo, *A Defense Bar: The "Proof of Innocence" Requirement in Criminal Malpractice Claims*, 5 Ohio St. J. Crim. L. 341 (2007) for an argument that the proof of innocence requirement sets the bar too high.

3. *Comparative responsibility*. Most jurisdictions allow the defense of comparative negligence as to lawyer malpractice claims. *See* Note, *Comparative Fault in Legal Malpractice and Insurance Bad Faith: An Argument for Symmetry*, 21 Rev. Litig. 663 (2002). This does not mean, however, that every instance of client negligence or inattention will permit the lawyer to raise a defense of comparative negligence. Assertions about client negligence can take many forms, including the client's failure or neglect in supervising, reviewing, or inquiring about matters relevant to the representation; failure to follow the lawyer's advice or instructions; actively interfering with the attorney's representation or failing to finish tasks relating to the representation; and failing to mitigate the effects of the lawyer's malpractice.

b. Damages in Tortious Interference Cases

VANDERBEEK v. VERNON CORPORATION

Supreme Court of Colorado, En Banc., 2002.
50 P.3d 866.

[The Petitioners were three individuals, including Robert R. Vanderbeek, who served as co-trustees of a trust. This action began when they filed an action for attachment of $1 million that was to be paid into the account of Vernon Corporation, the Respondent in this case. The attachment was successful, and approximately $1 million in the Vernon Corporation's account was frozen. After another hearing, the garnishment was dissolved, given the trial court's conclusion that it had no jurisdiction over the action. Vernon Bank then filed a motion seeking damages caused by the allegedly wrongful attachment of the funds. Vernon Corp. claimed that it had intended to use $450,000 to purchase shares of Osicom. (Vanderbeek and the others had no knowledge of this intent.) Had the money not been frozen, Vernon Corp. alleged, it would have been able to buy 200,000 shares of Osicom for approximately $436,000 plus commission. Instead, Vernon Corp. was unable to purchase Osicom until the release of the funds. At that time, given the rise in the value of Osicom stock, Vernon Corp. was able to purchase only 95,000 shares for a cost of $449,828.15.

Vernon Corp. sought damages, under a tort theory of wrongful attachment, for $331,015.65. This figure represented the sum of: the additional $242,728.15 that Vernon Corp. had to pay for the 95,000 shares it did purchase, and the $88,287.50 in lost profits on the 105,000 shares that it was unable to purchase. The trial court denied recovery for both parts of this sum. In the trial court's view, Osicom's rise in value between the time of attachment and the time the funds were released (from December 23, 1997 to January 13, 1998) was unforeseeable. Thus, damages relating to that increase were speculative, in the view of the trial court. The court held that the correct measure of damages was the interest on the amount of the funds during the time they were frozen.

After the trial court reversed in part, the co-trustees appealed to the Colorado Supreme Court. Given that the theory of the action was a tort cause of action, the Supreme Court addressed the general damage principles applicable to economic torts.]

* * *

B. The Appropriate Measure of Damage for Economic Torts

Central to our determination of the appropriate measure of damage is a determination of the nature of the duty breached in economic torts. Where the duty breached stems from a contract, redress must be under the contract, and the rule derived from *Hadley [Hadley v. Baxendale*, 9 Ex. 341, 156 Eng. Rep. 145 (1854)] is the appropriate standard by which to assess the consequential damages of the breach. However, [when a tort action will lie,] consequential damages should be assessed under traditional tort standards.

We have recently had occasion to fully examine the boundary between contract and tort law in upholding the validity of the economic loss rule. *See Town of Alma v. Azco Constr., Inc.*, 10 P.3d 1256 (Colo.2000). In *Town of Alma,* we explained that "[t]he essential difference between a tort obligation and a contract obligation is the source of the duties of the parties." 10 P.3d at 1262. Tort law is designed to protect all citizens from the risk of harm to their persons or their property. *Id.* Accordingly, tort duties are generally imposed by law "without regard to any agreement or contract." *Id.* Contract obligations, in contrast, arise from promises between the parties. *Id.*

The rationale behind *Hadley v. Baxendale's* contract measure of damages demonstrates why it is an inappropriate standard for assessing consequential damages when the duty breached arises independently of any agreement between the parties. The *Hadley* rule is designed to further a fundamental principle of contract law: parties must be able to confidently allocate risks and costs during their bargaining without fear that unanticipated liability may arise in the future, effectively negating the parties' efforts to build these cost considerations into the contract. Under *Hadley,* a party to a contract is only responsible for those damages that he should reasonably have contemplated as the probable result of a breach at the time the contract was entered into. Because the party is aware, or should be aware, that these damages are a potential consequence of breach, he presumably will take into account the risk that these contingencies will occur while negotiating the contract. Thus, by limiting contractual liability to those damages foreseen by the parties at the time the contract was formed, *Hadley* ensures that the bargain struck reflects a mutually agreeable allocation of the risks and costs of breach. In other words, *Hadley* guarantees the fairness of a bilateral agreement by protecting the parties from unanticipated liability arising in the future.

But a tortious act is a unilateral invasion of a right taken "without regard to any agreement or contract." *Town of Alma,* 10 P.3d at 1262. The victim of a tort has no opportunity to negotiate with the tortfeasor—no opportunity to allocate the risk that a particular consequence will occur or evaluate the cost if it should. Therefore, whether he reasonably contemplated a particular consequence as the probable result of the tort at the time it occurred is irrelevant. * * *

Accordingly, * * * we hold that the appropriate measure of the damages * * * is such damage as is "the natural and probable result of the injury sustained by virtue of the tortious act." [ ] As is the case in other tort actions, the recovery of these damages is limited by the requirements that such damages be proximately caused by the tortious act, and that they be reasonably ascertainable.

C. The Tortious Act Must Proximately Cause The Consequential Damages

In torts involving interference with contract and economic opportunity "[m]ost courts award damages under tort principles . . . with damages limits based upon proximate cause rather than contemplation of the parties." Dan B. Dobbs, *The Law of Torts,* § 455, at 1297 (2000) [hereinafter *Law of Torts*]; *see also Dean v. James McHugh Constr. Co.,* 56 A.D.2d 716, 392 N.Y.S.2d 946, 948 (N.Y.App.Div.1977) (holding that there is "no reason why a party who is wrongfully deprived of the use of his funds may not recover damages representing more than the legal interest rate, provided that he can prove that such damages were actually sustained as a proximate result of the deprivation"). "Under this view, the plaintiff can recover all proximately caused damages, including consequential damages, even if those damages were greater than the damages the plaintiff could recover against [a] contract breacher." *Law of Torts, supra,* § 455, at 1297. The proximate cause standard requires only that the damages be "reasonably foreseeable." *Ekberg v. Greene,* 196 Colo. 494, 496–97, 588 P.2d 375, 376–77 (1978); *see also Walcott v. Total Petroleum, Inc.,* 964 P.2d 609, 611 (Colo.App.1998) ("[F]oreseeability is the touchstone of proximate cause."); *cf.* C.J.I.–Civ.3d 9:30 ("The negligence, if any, of the defendant . . . is not a cause of any . . . damage . . . to the plaintiff . . . unless injury to a person in the plaintiff's situation was a reasonably foreseeable consequence of that negligence."). "The exact or precise injury need not have been foreseeable, but it is sufficient if a reasonably careful person, under the same or similar circumstances, would have anticipated that injury to a person in the plaintiff's situation might result from the defendant's conduct." C.J.I.–Civ.3d 9:30. Thus, although broader than *Hadley,* proximate cause serves as a very real limit on liability. Melvin Aron Eisenberg, *The Principle of Hadley v. Baxendale,* 80 Calif. L.Rev. 563, 567 (1992) ("[T]he choice between a regime based on *Hadley v. Baxendale* and a regime based on proximate cause is not a choice between liability for foreseeable losses and liability for all losses caused in fact. Rather it is a choice between competing standards of foreseeability. . . ."). In sum, because damages resulting from wrongful attachment are governed by tort principles, proximate cause is the appropriate standard by which to assess their extent.

D. Damages Must Be Reasonably Ascertainable

Whether *Hadley* or proximate cause serves to limit liability for consequential damages, a plaintiff must prove the damages he has suffered with reasonable certainty. Dobbs, *supra,* § 6.6(2), at 137. "When the issue of causation is resolved, the question is whether the evidence of loss . . . contains sufficient certainty and proximity upon which to base an award of special or consequential damages." *Cope v. Vermeer Sales & Serv. of Colo.,* 650 P.2d 1307, 1309 (Colo.App.1982). "The purpose of the reasonable certainty rule is to avoid making compensatory damages awards for lost profits which are fabricated or based on mere conjecture or speculation." *Nora v. Safeco Ins. Co.,* 99 Idaho 60, 577 P.2d 347, 350 (1978) (internal quotations omitted). The rule only applies to situations where the fact of damages is uncertain, not where the amount is uncertain. *Peterson v. Colo. Potato Flake & Mfg. Co.,* 164 Colo. 304, 310, 435 P.2d 237, 239 (1967).

Hornblower v. Lazere, 301 Minn. 462, 222 N.W.2d 799 (1974), provides a relevant application of this rule. In that case, the defendant alleged in his counterclaim that by mispaying him $8,000, the plaintiff had caused him to forbear selling stock that he otherwise would have sold. *Hornblower,* 222 N.W.2d at 803. This stock declined in value between the time that the mispayment was made and the time the plaintiff demanded that defendant return the $8,000. *Id.*

Citing the rule that speculative, remote or conjectural damages are not recoverable, the Minnesota Supreme Court held that an award of damages could not be sustained on this basis. *Id.* It noted that "[a]lthough defendant alleged that the negligent payment caused him to forbear selling stock which later declined in value, he was unable at trial to state specifically what stock he would have sold, and on what date he would have sold it, had he been informed of the correct state of his account." *Id.* Accordingly, the court reasoned that "since it would have been impossible for the jury to have determined with any accuracy what stocks defendant would have sold and on what date, . . . we hold that the evidence, viewed in the light most favorable to the verdict, is too speculative to afford a reasonable basis for that portion of the verdict granting damages to defendant for plaintiff's negligent mispayment of the $8,000." *Id.*

With these principles in mind, we turn to the merits of the case at hand.

III. *APPLICATION*

The parties are former partners who had an established business relationship. Not only did Petitioners [the co-trustees] know the approximate amount of money Respondent [Vernon Corp.] was transferring into the state, they knew precisely when this transfer would take place, and at what bank. Furthermore, the parties stipulated that Respondent intended to use the funds frozen by the writ of garnishment to purchase 200,000 shares of Osicom. Given these undisputed facts, we hold that the damages sought by Petitioner are the natural and probable result of the injuries they sustained by virtue of the tortious act. In addition, although Petitioners had no actual knowledge that Respondent intended to purchase Osicom, it was reasonably foreseeable that the money attached was to be used for investment purposes of some kind. Likewise, it was reasonably foreseeable that attachment of the funds would prevent, or at least delay, such an investment and cause damage thereby. Accordingly, we hold as a matter of law that Petitioners' wrongful attachment of Respondent's funds proximately caused: (1) an increase in the price Respondent paid to acquire 95,000 shares of Osicom stock; and (2) Respondent's inability to purchase an additional 105,000 shares of Osicom stock. *See Pioneer Constr. Co. v. Richardson,* 176 Colo. 254, 259, 490 P.2d 71, 74 (1971) (holding that the question of proximate cause is for the court in the absence of conflicting testimony); *see also Lyons v. Nasby,* 770 P.2d 1250, 1256 (Colo.1989) (holding that "where reasonable minds can draw but one inference from the evidence," the question of proximate cause becomes one of law); *Samuelson v. Chutich,* 187 Colo. 155, 160, 529 P.2d 631, 634 (1974) (holding that the question of "proximate cause [is] for the court where the evidence, and the inferences to be drawn therefrom, are such that reasonable men, giving fair consideration thereto, must reach the same conclusion").

We now turn our attention to whether the damages claimed by the Respondent are reasonably ascertainable. First, we consider Respondent's claim that it had to pay a higher price to acquire 95,000 shares of Osicom stock as a result of Petitioner's wrongful attachment. It is undisputed that, at the time of attachment, Respondent intended to buy 200,000 shares of Osicom stock and had earmarked a certain sum of money for this purpose. Because these funds were frozen, however, it was unable to purchase Osicom stock until approximately one month later when the writ of garnishment was released. Since the price of Osicom stock increased dramatically while the funds were frozen, Respondent was able to purchase only 95,000 shares of Osicom with the money it had set aside to purchase 200,000 shares. These facts are reasonably ascertainable from the parties' stipulation. [According to that stipulation, on December 24, 1997—the day after the writ was issued—Respondent could have acquired 95,000 shares of Osicom stock for $207,100. Instead, after the writ was released in January 1998, Respondent paid $449,828.15 for 95,000 shares of Osicom. Thus, the wrongful attachment caused Vernon Corporation to pay an additional $242,728.15 to obtain 95,000 shares of Osicom stock.] Therefore, not only is the additional amount paid for the 95,000 shares reasonably ascertainable, it is "a concrete figure that [can] be calculated given the time frame and the differences in the price of the stock." *Vanderbeek,* 25 P.3d at 1246.

We approve of the court of appeals' assessment of this element of the consequential damages claimed by Respondent:

[D]espite the trial court's conclusion that "money [can] be put to innumerable uses," an identifiable portion of the wrongfully attached money here had been set aside for a particular purpose. Accordingly, defendant is entitled to . . . the additional amount paid for the 95,000 shares . . . of the wrongfully attached $450,000 that he had intended to spend, and indeed, did spend on Osicom stock. *Vanderbeek,* 25 P.3d at 1246. Because the increase in the price Respondent paid to acquire 95,000 shares of Osicom stock is a reasonably ascertainable consequential damage of Petitioners' wrongful attachment, it is recoverable. Accordingly, we affirm the court of appeals' judgment awarding Respondent the increase in the price it paid to acquire 95,000 shares of Osicom stock.

In contrast, whether, and to what extent, Respondent lost profits on the 105,000 shares he never purchased is speculative and conjectural. Generally, damages based on lost profits are disfavored when the venture from which the projected profit is derived is speculative or conjectural. *Lee v. Durango Music,* 144 Colo. 270, 278, 355 P.2d 1083, 1087 (1960) (holding that a claim for future profits may not be sustained by evidence which is speculative, remote, imaginary, or impossible of ascertainment); *Milheim v. Baxter,* 46 Colo. 155, 103 P. 376 (1909); *see also* Restatement (Second) of Torts § 912 cmt. f (1979) (requiring that an injured party have a "substantial and measurable chance of a profit without chance of loss" to satisfy the requirement of "certainty"). As the trial court pointed out, "stock trading is a gambler's business, the very nature of which is speculative and conjectural."

Profits from a stock investment are not realized until the stock is sold at a higher price than that at which it was bought. These 105,000 shares of Osicom stock were neither bought nor sold. Thus, unlike the increased cost Respondent actually paid to acquire the 95,000 shares of Osicom, determining the profits Respondent could have realized had he purchased the 105,000 shares of Osicom the day after the earmarked funds were frozen is entirely dependent on an arbitrarily chosen "sell" date.

On December 24, 1997—the day after Respondent's earmarked funds were frozen—Osicom stock was trading at $2 3/16 per share. Subsequent to this date, the value of Osicom's stock has varied tremendously. Adjusted to reflect a reverse split of the stock on a one for three basis that Osicom completed on July 24, 1998, it has ranged from $1 7/8 to $19 1/2 according to the parties' stipulation. Respondent chose to calculate profits lost on the 105,000 shares they were unable to purchase as a result of Petitioners' wrongful attachment based on the value of Osicom stock on November 30, 1998—the day before the trial court hearing on this issue. On this date, Osicom stock closed at $9 1/16 per share. Accordingly, Respondent claimed the difference in value between Osicom's stock on this date and its value the day after the earmarked funds were frozen, or $88,287.50, as the profits it had lost.[2] If Respondent had instead chosen the date on which Osicom stock was trading at $19 1/2 per share, its "lost profits" would have been much more. In contrast, if lost profits had been measured from the date that Osicom was trading at 1 7/8, Respondent would not have been damaged at all. This uncertainty precludes an award of damage for lost profits. *Cf. Hornblower,* 222 N.W.2d at 803 (holding that although plaintiff caused defendant to forbear selling stock which later declined in value, damages therefor were too speculative to be recovered because defendant was unable at trial to state specifically what stock he would have sold, and on what date he would have sold it). We therefore affirm the court of appeals' judgment denying Respondent lost profits on the 105,000 shares of Osicom stock it was unable to purchase because of Petitioners wrongful attachment.

IV. CONCLUSION

We hold that consequential damages are recoverable in torts of economic interference, such as the wrongful attachment here. As in any other tort action, the appropriate measure of the damage a victim of an economic tort may recover is that amount which is the natural and probable result of the injury sustained by virtue of the tortious act. In order to be recoverable, such damages must be proximately caused by the tortious act and must be reasonably ascertainable.

2. Respondent's calculation of the profits it claims to have lost takes into account the 3 to 1 reverse stock split that occurred on July 24, 1998

Given the undisputed facts in this case, we hold that the damages sought by Petitioner are the natural and probable result of the injury they sustained by virtue of the tortious act. In addition, we hold that Petitioners' wrongful attachment of Respondent's funds was the proximate cause of: (1) an increase in the price Respondent paid to acquire 95,000 shares of Osicom stock; and (2) Respondent's inability to purchase an additional 105,000 shares of Osicom stock. The increased cost of acquiring 95,000 shares of Osicom stock due to the wrongful attachment is reasonably ascertainable and therefore recoverable. However, the lost profits on 105,000 shares of Osicom stock not purchased because of the wrongful attachment is not reasonably ascertainable and therefore not recoverable. We therefore affirm the court of appeals judgment. We remand the case to the court of appeals to return it to the trial court to recalculate the Respondent's damages consistent with this opinion.

NOTES

1. The court emphasizes that it is applying the tort principles of proximate cause and damages, rather than the contract approach of *Hadley v. Baxendale*. What is the difference between tort law's general principles for economic damages—and specifically proximate cause—and the *Hadley v. Baxendale* approach? In the end, does the use of the tort standard rather than the contract approach make any difference? Put another way, would Vernon Corp. have recovered the same damages even if the court had used the *Hadley v. Baxendale* requirement?

2. Why does the court uphold the recovery of the increased price that VernonCorp. had to pay for the stock it obtained, but disallow recovery for the lost profits on the stock it was unable to buy? Does the court's disallowance of the lost profits turn on "proximate cause" or on the requirement of proving damages, and specifically the requirement of proving damages with reasonable certainty. Could Vernon Corp. have presented any other evidence—expert or otherwise—that would have strengthened the chances of recovering for lost profits?

c. New or Emerging Businesses

BEVERLY HILLS CONCEPTS, INC. v. SCHATZ AND SCHATZ, RIBICOFF AND KOTKIN

Supreme Court of Connecticut, 1998.
247 Conn. 48, 717 A.2d 724.

KATZ, ASSOCIATE JUSTICE.

The principal issue in this appeal is the proper method for calculating damages for the destruction of a nascent business. We conclude that: (1) unestablished enterprises must be permitted to recover damages for legal malpractice and that a flexible approach in determining those damages generally is appropriate; (2) lost profits for a reasonable period of time may serve as an appropriate measure of damages under certain circumstances; and (3) the plaintiff bears the burden of proving lost profits to a reasonable certainty. As applied to the facts of this case, however, we conclude that the plaintiff has not sustained its burden of proof regarding damages.

This appeal arises from a malpractice action brought by Beverly Hills Concepts, Inc. (plaintiff) * * * against the named defendant, the law firm, Schatz and Schatz, Ribicoff and Kotkin (Schatz & Schatz), and the individual defendants, attorneys Stanford Goldman, Ira Dansky and Jane Seidl. In its complaint, dated November 2, 1989, the plaintiff alleged legal malpractice (first count), breach of contract (second count), intentional misrepresentation (third and fifth counts), negligent misrepresentation (fourth count), breach of fiduciary duty (sixth count), breach of the covenant of good faith and fair dealing (seventh count), and violation of the Connecticut Unfair Trade Practices Act (CUTPA)* * *.

On January 27, 1997, following a trial to the court, Hon. Robert J. Hale, judge trial referee, rendered judgment for the plaintiff on the first, second, fourth, sixth and seventh counts, and for the defendants on the third, fifth and eighth counts. The trial court awarded the plaintiff damages in the amount of $15,931,289.

On February 6, 1997, the defendants filed a motion to reargue and/or open or set aside the judgment, for a new trial, and/or for judgment, which the trial court denied.* * *

The defendants appealed the judgment to the Appellate Court.* * * We transferred the appeal and the cross appeal to this court pursuant to [Connecticut statute allowing the Supreme Court to transfer to itself a case in the appellate court].

[The trier of fact, in the Supreme Court's view, could have found the following facts. Three individuals incorporated the plaintiff corporation with the aim of selling fitness equipment with a distinctive color scheme, as well as a plan to operate a fitness club for women. The plaintiff began to license purchasers to use its concept, and it sold distributorships to investors who would gain the exclusive right to sell the plaintiff's product and to sublicense the name within a region. One of the three individuals behind the company contact the firm of Schatz & Schatz to clear up a legal problem regarding the trademark in California. The firm mistakenly thought that the plaintiff had a "federally registered trademark," and thus the firm assumed incorrectly that the company did not have to register as a "business opportunity" under a Connecticut statute. The partner who first handled the file told the plaintiff that the firm possessed expertise in the field of franchising and was well-qualified to handle the matter; he also said he would be personally involved in the firm's representation. Despite several incidents that should have alerted the firm to the fact that the plaintiff was operating in violation of the Connecticut law, the firm did not advise the plaintiff to this effect, at most saying that this was a "gray area." Eventually, the firm terminated its representation because a contract lawyer with the firm stated that he was concerned that the plaintiff's operating documents overstated the company's financial position. The plaintiff company retained other counsel. Soon after, an official with the state banking commissioner notified plaintiff that it was in violation of the state law. Although the plaintiff ceased its advertising and franchising activities and sought to file a post-sale registration, the banking commissioner issued a cease-and-desist order and a notice of intent to fine. Eventually, after hearing, the cease and desist order became final.]

For purposes of this appeal, the defendants do not challenge the trial court's determination that they breached the applicable professional standard of care. Rather, they raise claims regarding the issues of causation and damages. Specifically, the defendants argue that the trial court improperly: (1) rendered judgment against Seidl on the negligent misrepresentation and breach of fiduciary duty claims based on the same conduct underlying the judgment of malpractice; (2) concluded that the defendants' failure to advise the plaintiff of its violation of the act caused its demise; (3) awarded damages based on lost profits rather than the going concern value of the business at the date of destruction; (4) awarded the plaintiff approximately $15.9 million in lost profits calculated over a period of twelve years* * *.

We agree with the defendants' first and fourth claims. Accordingly, we reverse the judgment of the trial court and render judgment for the defendants.

[Discussion of fiduciary duty claim against Seidl omitted]

II

We turn next to the defendants' claim that the trial court improperly determined that their malpractice caused the demise of the plaintiff. We review a trial court's determination of causation under the clearly erroneous standard.* * *

In its memorandum of decision, the trial court concluded that the defendants' malpractice had constituted a proximate cause of the plaintiff's failure. Applying the "substantial factor" test of causation, the trial court concluded: "The [defendants'] inept legal representation, inordinate delays in completing their work, and . . . fundamental failure to recognize [the plaintiff] as a seller of business opportunities were, as claimed by the plaintiff, substantial factors in causing damage to the plaintiff and this damage, the forced closing of the business, was a natural and foreseeable consequence of the defendants' neglect and incompetence." In support of its determination, the trial court cited, inter alia, portions of the testimony of Harold Brown, the plaintiff's expert on franchising and business opportunities.

* * * Even if we were to assume that the trial court properly determined that the defendants' malpractice had constituted a proximate cause of the plaintiff's failure, we conclude, for the reasons that follow,

that the trial court improperly concluded that the plaintiff had established its damages to a reasonable certainty.

III

The defendants' third claim on appeal challenges the trial court's award of damages. * * * We conclude that: (1) the plaintiff's expert was qualified; (2) unestablished enterprises must be permitted to recover damages for legal malpractice and that a flexible approach in determining those damages generally is appropriate; (3) lost profits for a reasonable period of time may serve as an appropriate measure of damages under certain circumstances; and (4) the plaintiff bears the burden of proving lost profits to a reasonable certainty. As applied to the facts of this case, however, we conclude that the plaintiff has not sustained its burden of proof regarding damages.

We begin with a brief overview of additional facts that are relevant to the correct determination of damages in this case. The plaintiff had been operating for approximately one year at the time it retained the defendants. It therefore had a business track record by which to measure the likely success of its planned franchising operation. As the defendants correctly point out, despite its initial sales of exercise equipment, the plaintiff was in poor financial condition. The plaintiff owed approximately $80,000 in unpaid federal and state payroll taxes and had never paid unemployment taxes, a decision that its own expert witness, Thomas Ferreira, a certified public accountant, characterized as not a good business practice. Significantly, the plaintiff had not filed federal or state income tax returns for 1987, 1988 or 1989. The plaintiff's financial statement, prepared by Coopers, revealed that it was insolvent as of November 30, 1987, and its situation had deteriorated even further by January, 1988. It is particularly telling that the plaintiff had attempted to obtain financing from a number of banks as well as from the Small Business Administration and that it had been rejected by all of these institutions. According to Charles Remington, one of the plaintiff's officers, this financing was necessary to the proposed franchising operation. Additionally, the model franchise opened by the plaintiff in East Hartford quickly failed. Finally, despite several months of trying, the plaintiff never sold a single franchise. Moreover, its own damages expert, Ferreira, characterized the plaintiff as a poor credit risk. These facts serve to indicate that the plaintiff was not financially stable and that its prospects for earning profits in the future were, at best, questionable.

A

We first address the defendants' claim that Ferreira was not qualified to render an expert opinion regarding the value of the plaintiff. We conclude that the trial court did not abuse its discretion in determining that Ferreira was sufficiently qualified.

"The determination of the qualification of an expert is largely a matter for the discretion of the trial court." (Internal quotation marks omitted.) * * *

In its memorandum of decision, the trial court noted that Ferreira had fifteen years of experience as a certified public accountant, and that he had prepared business projections on numerous prior occasions. The court also noted that Ferreira had prepared the projections in this case in compliance with the standards of the American Institute of Certified Public Accountants and with generally accepted accounting procedures.

The defendants challenge the trial court's determination on several grounds. They argue that Ferreira was not properly qualified because he: (1) is an accountant rather than an economist; and (2) lacked prior experience in the personal fitness industry. We disagree.

"Generally, expert testimony is admissible if (1) the witness has a special skill or knowledge directly applicable to a matter in issue, (2) that skill or knowledge is not common to the average person, and (3) the testimony would be helpful to the court or jury in considering the issues." *Id.* "[I]t is not essential that an expert witness possess any particular credential, such as a license, in order to be qualified to testify, so long as his education or experience indicate that he has knowledge on a relevant subject significantly greater than that of persons lacking such education or experience." *Conway v. American Excavating, Inc.,* 41 Conn.App. 437, 448–49, 676 A.2d 881 (1996).

The defendants argue that Ferreira was not qualified to make business projections because the plaintiff had introduced no evidence that he was well versed in economic skills such as regression analysis. It is true that "[a]n accounting degree alone should not qualify a witness to testify that a given volume of sales, for example, will continue in the future." 2 R. Dunn, Recovery of Damages for Lost Profits (4th Ed.1992) § 7.3, p. 443. Nevertheless, we have affirmed the admission of testimony regarding lost profit damages by an accountant who had based his projections on the "standard valuation procedures recognized in the accounting profession." *West Haven Sound Development Corp. v. West Haven,* 201 Conn. 305, 321, 514 A.2d 734 (1986). As noted above, Ferreira had prior experience in making business projections. We conclude that, in this regard, the trial court did not abuse its discretion in allowing him to testify.

The defendants further argue that the trial court abused its discretion in allowing Ferreira to testify because he lacked prior experience in the personal fitness industry. * * * Generally, if a proponent of testimony establishes reasonable expert qualifications for a witness, further objections to that expert's testimony go to its weight, not its admissibility. C. Tait & J. LaPlante, supra, § 7.16.7, p. 179. We are not persuaded to abandon this principle in favor of a bright line rule that expert witnesses must possess prior industry-specific experience. Industries may be segmented infinitesimally. Some economists' and accounting professionals' skills may be transferred between industries. Under these circumstances, we conclude that the trial court did not abuse its discretion in concluding that Ferreira was qualified to testify regarding the valuation of the plaintiff's business.

B

We next address the question of whether lost profits are an appropriate measure of damages for the destruction of a nascent enterprise. The defendants argue that the appropriate measure of damages for the destruction of a business is its going concern value at the time of its destruction rather than lost profits. The plaintiff argues that the present value of a stream of expected future profits is an appropriate way to value a business and that it is therefore an appropriate measure of damages. We conclude that it is proper to award damages for the destruction of an unestablished enterprise and that lost profits may constitute an appropriate measure of damages for the destruction of such an enterprise.

We begin with a brief history of the evolution of the law on the determination of damages with respect to a business that has been destroyed by the conduct of a third party. A principle component of damages in such a situation is the present value of the profits lost as a result of the defendant's wrongdoing. * * * Although the guiding principle of tort law is to compensate parties for harm to their protected interests; W. Prosser & W. Keeton, Torts (5th Ed.1984) § 1, pp. 5–6; recovery for lost profits has not always been available. The "new business rule" in particular forbade the recovery of lost profits for an unestablished enterprise. * * * "Originally the speculative and contingent nature of profits was regarded as a complete bar to their recovery in any case. Gradually, however, came recognition that difficulties of proof and the speculative nature of profits were not uniform for all situations; and the rigid prohibition has given way to a more flexible requirement of 'reasonable certainty.' " 4 F. Harper, F. James & O. Gray, Torts (2d Ed.1986) § 25.3, pp. 502–503. "A common thread running through opinions expressing the liberal standard of proof in lost profit damages cases is that there is really no alternative: [A] [d]efendant will get away with its wrongdoing if the court requires [the] plaintiff to prove damages to the dollar.... The wrongdoer has created the problem; its conduct has interfered with [the] plaintiff and caused damages. The wrongdoer cannot now complain that the damages cannot be measured exactly." 1 R. Dunn, supra, § 5.2, p. 314. The former rule forbidding lost profit damages for new enterprises has thus given way to the general view that such damages ought to be recoverable where the likelihood of future profits can be established with reasonable certainty.

* * *

In accordance with these principles, we have approved the recovery of lost profits where the defendant has destroyed the plaintiff's opportunity to earn profits in the future. * * * Furthermore, we note that, "[i]n economic theory ... the current market value of a company is the discounted present value of the estimated flow of future earnings." Note, "Private Treble Damage Antitrust Suits: Measure of Damages For Destruction of All or Part of a Business," 80 Harv. L.Rev. 1566, 1580 (1967). Thus, determining a business' future lost profits is one generally accepted way of calculating its market value at the time of its destruction.

* * *

For the foregoing reasons, we conclude that lost profits may provide an appropriate measure of damages for the destruction of an unestablished enterprise, and further, that a flexible approach is best suited to ensuring that new businesses are compensated fully if they suffer damages as a result of a breach of contract, professional malpractice, or similar injuries.

C

We next consider whether the trial court improperly awarded the plaintiff approximately $15.9 million in lost profits calculated over a period of twelve years. In challenging the award, the defendants contest the assumptions upon which Ferreira based his projections and the court's acceptance of his choice of a twelve year time span. We conclude that the trial court abused its discretion because the plaintiff did not prove the lost profit damages to a reasonable certainty.

We recognize that "[t]he trial court has broad discretion in determining damages. * * * The determination of damages involves a question of fact that will not be overturned unless it is clearly erroneous. * * *

We are, therefore, constrained to accord substantial deference to the fact finder on the issue of damages. In deciding whether damages properly have been awarded, however, we are guided by the well established principle that such damages must be proved with reasonable certainty. *Gargano v. Heyman,* 203 Conn. 616, 621, 525 A.2d 1343 (1987). "Although we recognize that damages for lost profits may be difficult to prove with exactitude; * * * such damages are recoverable only to the extent that the evidence affords a sufficient basis for estimating their amount with *reasonable certainty.* * * * Consequently, we have permitted lost profits to be calculated by extrapolating from past profits. * * * We have stated, however, that the plaintiff cannot recover for "the mere possibility" of making a profit. * * *

In order to recover lost profits, therefore, the plaintiff must present sufficiently accurate and complete evidence for the trier of fact to be able to estimate those profits with reasonable certainty. The trial court in this case, although cognizant of this standard, nevertheless assessed damages based upon assumptions that were not supported by the record. The trial court's determination that the plaintiff would have earned approximately $15.9 million in profits over the course of twelve years had it not been for the defendants' conduct, therefore, constituted an abuse of discretion.

We will first address the defendants' claims regarding the assumptions upon which the plaintiff's expert, Ferreira, based his projections. Ferreira assumed that a substantial number of the people who had purchased toning tables would also have purchased franchises. He also assumed that the plaintiff would sell twenty franchises per year for the first five years and would progressively increase sales until it was selling forty franchises per year by year twelve. The defendants have claimed that these assumptions were speculative and therefore could not have formed a reasonable basis from which to estimate damages with any degree of certainty. We agree with the defendants and therefore conclude that the trial court abused its discretion in determining that the plaintiff had established lost profits to a reasonable certainty.

The weakness underlying the assumptions challenged by the defendants is that the plaintiff's sales of toning tables, which had been declining, could be extrapolated to predict future success in selling franchises. The testimony indicates that there is no reasonable basis to compare the two products other than the possibility that they might be marketed to the same customer base. The toning table transactions cost from $45,000 to $50,000 per location, whereas each franchise cost $116,500 to $172,500. That figure included a $20,000 franchise fee and $90,000 in equipment, or approximately twice the initial expenditure required for toning table packages. Additionally, a franchise involves a much greater commitment in terms of expenditures, opportunity costs and effort than does the purchase of equipment. Purchasers of toning tables were not required to make any further expenditures. Franchisees, on the other hand, would have been required to pay the plaintiff a monthly service fee of 5 percent of gross revenue, but not less than $349 per month and would have had to contribute 3 percent of monthly gross revenues, but not less than $200, to an advertising fund. It is also significant that the plaintiff, by its own estimate, needed $300,000 in new capital to launch its proposed franchising business and, in its investment proposal, stated that it was seeking to raise between $250,000 and $500,000 for that purpose. Ferreira's projections, however, were based on the assumption that the plaintiff needed only $100,000 to enter the franchise business.

Ferreira's assumption that the plaintiff would, in fact, have sold franchises is also directly contradicted by the record. The model franchise opened by the plaintiff failed shortly after it began operation. Additionally, the plaintiff attempted for months to sell franchises but was unable to sell even one. Ferreira's reliance on the performance of World Gym Licensing Limited (World Gym) as a model for predicting the plaintiff's future success was also unreasonable. Ferreira himself conceded that World Gym and the plaintiff were not similar. Additionally, he appears to have based his information about World Gym on a magazine article. Although he assumed that the plaintiff would grow at a slower rate than World Gym, Ferreira did not explain how he arrived at the projected rate of sale for the plaintiff's franchises other than to state that he had discounted the rates reported by World Gym. Therefore, even reducing the plaintiff's sales of sixty-five toning tables in a one and one-half year period to a projection that twenty franchises per year would be sold is contradicted by the available evidence of the plaintiff's failed attempts to sell the actual franchises. Moreover, no evidence was presented to support the contention that even the sales of toning tables would continue at their prior rate.

This court and courts of other jurisdictions have looked to a number of factors in evaluating whether the plaintiff has proved lost profits to a reasonable certainty. A plaintiff's prior experience in the same business has been held to be probative; * * * as has a plaintiff's experience in the same enterprise subsequent to the interference. * * * In jurisdictions that have been faced with assessing damages for the destruction of a new business, the experience of the plaintiff and that of third parties in a similar business have been admitted to prove lost profits. * * * In addition, the average experience of participants in the same line of business as the injured party has been approved as a method of proving lost profits. * * * The underlying requirement for each of these types of evidence is a substantial similarity between the facts forming the basis of the profit projections and the business opportunity that was destroyed.

* * *

We note that lack of prior profitability does not *necessarily* prohibit a trial court from awarding future lost profits, although it serves as a strong indicator that future profits are uncertain. The plaintiff must carry the burden of proving that prior losses will be turned around to provide future gains. In the present case, the plaintiff has failed to come forward with evidence showing, to a reasonable degree of certainty, that it would become profitable.

Finally, we disagree with the trial court's decision to award lost profits over a twelve year period. We agree with the plaintiff that there is nothing inherently improper about allowing damages for lost profits over a twelve year period. What is improper, however, is to award damages over such a long time span when there is no evidence that the plaintiff would have survived for twelve years, let alone that it would have remained profitable for that length of time. In order to remove the assessment of damages from the realm of speculation, it is necessary to tie the award of damages to objective verifiable facts that bear a logical relationship to projected future profitability.

Where the lost business opportunity is grounded in a contract or a lease, it is sometimes appropriate to award damages for a period commensurate with the term of that contract or lease. We have stated that, where the claimed damages are not the result of a breach of contract or lease of express duration, damages for future losses are permitted "as long as they are limited to a *reasonable time* and are supported by the evidence." * * * In *Westport Taxi Service, Inc. v. Westport Transit District,* supra, 235 Conn. at 33–36, 664 A.2d 719, this court approved the trial court's damage award consisting of one year of lost profits and the value of the business based on its actual earnings in the year before it ceased operating. * * *

A survey of cases permitting the recovery of lost profits over long periods of time reveals that, in these cases, the recovery period frequently is based on contracts or lease terms of fixed duration. * * * In the present case, by contrast, the choice of a twelve year time span appears quite arbitrary. The example case study prepared by the American Institute of Certified Public Accountants that was introduced by the plaintiff, and noted by the trial court in its memorandum of decision, was based on a proposed twelve year contractual agreement, and was therefore not comparable to the present case. The time span applied in the present case was not tied to any objective facts that reasonably could be construed as supporting the plaintiff's claim that the sale of fitness center franchises would have become profitable and would have remained so for twelve years. We conclude, therefore, that the trial court abused its discretion in failing to limit the recovery of lost profits to a reasonable time period.

We recognize that our decision that the plaintiff failed to prove damages means that the defendants, whose malpractice caused the plaintiff's harm, escape virtually unscathed. * * * This is a case in which we reverse the judgment not for lack of "mathematical exactitude"; * * * but because the plaintiff failed to provide sufficient evidence. This outcome is a direct result of the plaintiff's choice of evidence.

[Discussion of state statutory cause of action omitted]

The judgment with respect to the appeal is reversed and the case is remanded with direction to render judgment for the defendants; the judgment is affirmed with respect to the cross appeal.

In this opinion NORCOTT, PALMER and EDWARD Y. O'CONNELL, JJ., concurred.

PETERS, ASSOCIATE JUSTICE, dissenting.

I respectfully dissent. * * * I disagree with parts II and III concerning the liability of the defendant law firm and the other individual defendants.

As a matter of principle, the majority opinion subscribes to the position advanced by the defendants that, no matter how egregious and protracted their professional misconduct, it is more appropriate for this court to take an unnecessarily rigorous view of proof of damages than to provide relief for the plaintiff, * * * a client whom the defendants have put out of business. I disagree with so constricted a view of professional and fiduciary responsibility. Clients aggrieved by the misconduct of their attorneys are entitled to rely on courts to recognize that such misconduct may impair not only the clients' business but also the clients' ability to prove, with complete precision, the extent to which their business has been impaired. Having substantially created the problem, the defendants now should not be allowed to walk away from all responsibility for its solution.

Secondarily, as a matter of appellate practice, the majority opinion departs from the deference ordinarily accorded to a trial court's discretionary role as the finder of facts. The trial court found the plaintiff's evidence of causation and damages to have been proved sufficiently to justify a large amount of damages. Even if the court reasonably might have found to the contrary, its view of the evidence should not be set aside lightly. This is not a case in which the plaintiff produced no evidence in support of causation and damages. The weight to be assigned to disputed evidence ordinarily is determined by the trial court and not an appellate tribunal.

* * *

B

I turn next to the issue of damages.* * *

In addressing this issue, the majority opinion starts out with an accurate description of the rocky state of the plaintiff's finances when it came to the defendants for legal representation. To my mind, it is not surprising that start-up companies, in the first years of their operation, would have a difficult time making ends meet. It is not far-fetched to assume that Steve Jobs, when he started Apple Computers, might have had difficulty in obtaining financing for so untested an idea as a personal computer. At that time, how could he have projected future profits with analytic precision? In negligence actions, defendants take their plaintiffs as they find them and cannot excuse their own misconduct because of a plaintiff's preexisting infirmities. * * * The time for the defendants to have considered the financial circumstances of the plaintiff was when they agreed to represent the plaintiff, not after they assured its demise. Accordingly, the trial court reasonably might have assigned little or no probative weight to the evidence of the plaintiff's straitened financial circumstances.

I also disagree with the majority opinion's reasoning with respect to the remaining issues concerning damages. These issues are whether the trial court improperly: (1) awarded the plaintiff approximately $16 million in lost profits calculated over a period of twelve years; and (2) included prejudgment interest in the damages award. I would reject both of the defendants' claims.

* * *

1

I turn first to whether twelve years was a reasonable time frame for projecting future lost profits. I am persuaded that the trial court did not abuse its discretion in accepting a valuation of the business that projected lost profits over a twelve year period.

* * *

The defendants urge us to adopt a rule that damages based on a twelve year projection of future lost profits inherently are so speculative as to be contrary to law. * * *

The majority opinion rejects the defendants' bright line approach, but decides that damages over a twelve year period are inappropriate without "objective verifiable facts" to prove that the plaintiff would have survived and would have remained profitable for that period. In the circumstances of a plaintiff in the early days of an uncertain new venture, this harsh requirement inevitably will preclude any award of damages. If it is the misconduct of the defendants that is a substantial cause of a plaintiff's early demise, and the reason for its inability to make a more precise showing of damages, I disagree with requiring the level of proof of damages demanded by the majority.

* * *

"It has been suggested that profits cannot reliably be forecast for any business beyond a ten year period, and that consequently this is the maximum for which they should be awarded. But the span of time for which profits can be predicted varies from business to business according to a great many factors; this makes any standard less flexible than a 'reasonable' time seem unwise." Note, "Private Treble Damage Antitrust Suits: Measure of Damages for Destruction of All or Part of a Business," 80 Harv. L.Rev. 1566, 1577 (1967). Such a flexible approach might take into account factors including: (1) a business' past profit record, if any; (2) "the experience and ability of its management"; (3) "the quality and goodwill of its product"; (4) "the firm's comparative standing among its competitors"; (5) "the future of the particular industry as a whole"; (6) the behavior of comparable or competitor "yardstick" firms; and (7) "the average lifespan of the type of business destroyed. . . ." *Id.*

I note, moreover, that other jurisdictions have awarded future lost profits projected over a period of ten or more years, even to unestablished businesses. * * *

A flexible approach is best suited to ensuring that new businesses are compensated fully if they suffer damages as the result of professional malpractice, breach of contract and failure to comply with fiduciary duty.* * *

2

The majority opinion's principal reason for overturning the trial court's award of damages is that, in its view, certain of Ferreira's underlying assumptions were so speculative as to make the trial court's acceptance of his projection an abuse of its discretion. The majority opinion agrees with the defendants' argument that Ferreira's expert opinion was flawed because he assumed that: (1) the plaintiff would have sold franchises; (2) the thirty-five people who had purchased fitness equipment from the plaintiff would have converted their operations into franchises; and (3) the plaintiff would have sold at least twenty new franchises each year for twelve years, and would have derived additional revenues from the sale of "super centers." I am not persuaded that the trial court abused its discretion in accepting Ferreira's opinion.

In this situation, as in the antitrust context, "[t]he vagaries of the marketplace usually deny us sure knowledge of what [the] plaintiff's situation would have been in the absence of the defendant's ... violation." (Internal quotation marks omitted.) *Westport Taxi Service, Inc. v. Westport Transit District,* supra, 235 Conn. at 28, 664 A.2d 719. Accordingly, "[a] damage theory may be based on assumptions so long as the assumptions are reasonable in light of the record evidence." (Internal quotation marks omitted.) *Id.* * * *

In this case, Ferreira testified that the plaintiff already had sold about sixty-five locations, nationwide, through licensing arrangements, in a period of about one and one-half years. Ferreira projected a slower growth rate of twenty locations per year for the plaintiff's franchise sales. He explained that purchasing a franchise required "more of a commitment" for buyers than purchasing a business opportunity, including paying the franchise, royalties and advertising fees. Accordingly, in order to ensure a conservative projection, he estimated sales of twenty franchises per year, the actual growth rate of World Gym Licensing Limited. He checked this assumption with at least two people who had been associated with the sales of the plaintiff's business locations, and he concluded that it was reasonable, if not conservative.

As for the role of the "super centers" in Ferreira's projection, Ferreira estimated the plaintiff's revenues based, in part, on the probable equipment sales to future clubs under the plaintiff's name. The plaintiff's clubs initially were about 2000 square feet and were designed to serve women exclusively. The plaintiff planned, however, to expand its clubs to a larger floor plan of 4000 or 5000 square feet, the super center format, serving both men and women.

In projecting equipment sales to the plaintiff's clubs, Ferreira based his estimates on figures contained in the plaintiff's Uniform Franchise Offering Circular (circular). Ferreira projected equipment sales on the basis of the expected average sales to clubs with the super center floor plan, as outlined in the circular. According to Ferreira's interviews and research, the super center was the style of club that the plaintiff had planned for the future, and, in fact, the format that had become more popular in the industry. Again, to be conservative, Ferreira estimated $90,000 in initial equipment sales, the lower end of the range of average expected equipment sales to super centers listed in the plaintiff's circular.

On the basis of this record, I would conclude that the trial court, in the exercise of its discretion, reasonably might have found that the plaintiff had adduced sufficient evidence to support Ferreira's assumptions. The fact that the record is thin would have supported the trial court's decision to the contrary, but it does not make it clearly erroneous for the court to find as it did.* * *

* * *

In conclusion, the majority opinion, in my view, reaches out to reverse a trial court judgment on grounds that are far from compelling. We condone professional misconduct if we discharge these defendants of all liability to a plaintiff that has tried, as best it could, to quantify the loss that the defendants' misconduct has caused it to suffer. Such a result, it seems to me, turns the law of professional responsibility on its head. Those members of the legal profession who engage in egregious and protracted misconduct bear the responsibility, fiscally as well as morally, for the harm that they have caused. It is our responsibility to search for ways to reinforce that professional commitment.

Accordingly, I respectfully dissent.

NOTES

1. The majority agrees with the principle that lost profits—reduced of course to present value—can be an appropriate measure of tort damages for destruction of a nascent business. Why did courts once reject this principle, and why have the majority of courts now accepted it?

2. The majority concluded that the trial court's lost profits assessment was based on several assumptions that were not supported by the record. What were these assumptions? Would the plaintiff have been able to recover if the plaintiff had reduced the length of the time period for which plaintiff sought lost profits?

3. Does the dissent disagree with the trial court about the strength of the assumptions underlying the lost profit projections? If the dissent also views these assumptions as "thin," what is the basis for the dissent's view that the judgment should be affirmed?

4. For a valuable discussion of causation in fiduciary cases, *see* Deborah A. DeMott, *Causation in the Fiduciary Realm*, 91 B.U. L. Rev. 851 (2011).

CHAPTER 4

PRODUCTS LIABILITY

■ ■ ■

Perhaps all law is better understood if we are aware of its historical development. This is especially true with respect to products liability, which may usefully be thought of in terms of four separate eras, the first three of which are marked by landmark cases—*Winterbottom v. Wright*, *MacPherson v. Buick Motors, Co.*, and *Greenman v. Yuba Power Products Inc.*—and the last of which is marked by the adoption of the *Restatement (Third) of Torts: Products Liability*. During different eras, products liability moved into and out of the mainstream of negligence law and has been influenced to a greater or lesser extent by the law of contracts. For a useful discussion of the history of this fascinating area of law see David G. Owen, *The Evolution of Products Liability Law*, 26 Rev. Litig. 955 (2007).

A. NEGLIGENCE ACTIONS–OVERCOMING THE PRIVITY BARRIER

THOMAS v. WINCHESTER

Court of Appeals of New York, 1852.
6 N.Y. 397.

RUGGLES, CH. J. delivered the opinion of the court. This is an action brought to recover damages from the defendant for negligently putting up, labeling and selling as and for the extract of *dandelion*, which is a simple and harmless medicine, a jar of the extract of *belladonna*, which is a deadly poison; by means of which the plaintiff Mary Ann Thomas, to whom, being sick, a dose of dandelion was prescribed by a physician, and a portion of the contents of the jar, was administered as and for the extract of dandelion, was greatly injured, & c.

The facts proved were briefly these: Mrs. Thomas being in ill health, her physician prescribed for her a dose of dandelion. Her husband purchased what was believed to be the medicine prescribed, at the store of Dr. Foord, a physician and druggist in Cazenovia, Madison county, where the plaintiffs reside.

A small quantity of the medicine thus purchased was administered to Mrs. Thomas, on whom it produced very alarming effects; such as coldness of the surface and extremities, feebleness of circulation, spasms of the muscles, giddiness of the head, dilation of the pupils of the eyes, and derangement of mind. She recovered however, after some time, from its effects, although for a short time her life was thought to be in great danger. The medicine administered was *belladonna, and not dandelion.* The jar from which it was taken was labeled "*½ lb. dandelion, prepared by A. Gilbert, No. 108, John-street, N.Y. Jar 8 oz.*" It was sold for and believed by Dr. Foord to be the extract of dandelion as labeled. Dr. Foord purchased the article as the extract of dandelion from Jas. S. Aspinwall, a druggist at New–York. Aspinwall bought it of the defendant as extract of dandelion, believing it to be such. The defendant was engaged at No. 108 John-street, New–York, in the manufacture and sale of certain vegetable extracts for medicinal purposes, and in the purchase and sale of others. The extracts manufactured by him were put up in jars for sale, and those which he purchased were put up by him in like manner. The jars containing extracts manufactured by himself and those containing extracts purchased by him from others, were labeled alike. Both were labeled like the jar in question, as "prepared by A. Gilbert." Gilbert was a person employed by the defendant at a salary, as an assistant in his business. The jars were labeled in Gilbert's name because he had been previously engaged in the same business on his own account at No. 108 John-street, and probably because Gilbert's labels rendered the articles more salable. The extract contained in the jar sold to Aspinwall, and by him to Foord, was not manufactured by the defendant, but was purchased by him from another manufacturer or dealer. The extract of dandelion and the extract of belladonna resemble each other in color, consistence, smell and taste; but may on careful examination be distinguished the one from the other by those who are well acquainted with these articles. Gilbert's labels were paid for by Winchester and used in his business with his knowledge and assent.

The case depends on the first point taken by the defendant on his motion for a nonsuit; and the question is, whether the defendant, being a remote vendor of the medicine, and there being no privity or connection between him and the plaintiffs, the action can be maintained.[a]

If, in labeling a poisonous drug with the name of a harmless medicine, for public market, no duty was violated by the defendant, excepting that which he owed to Aspinwall, his immediate vendee, in virtue of his contract of sale, this action cannot be maintained. If A. build a wagon and sell it to B., who sells its to C., and C. hires it to D., who in consequence of the gross negligence of A. in building the wagon is overturned and injured, D. cannot recover damages against A., the builder. A.'s obligation to build the wagon faithfully, arises solely out of his contract with B. The public have nothing to do with it. Misfortune to third persons, not parties to the contract, would not be a natural and necessary consequence of the builder's negligence; and such negligence is not an act imminently dangerous to human life.

---

a. [Ed. note] The jury had returned a verdict of $800 against Winchester.

So, for the same reason, if a horse be defectively shod by a smith, and a person hiring the horse from the owner is thrown and injured in consequence of the smith's negligence in shoeing; the smith is not liable for the injury. The smith's duty in such case grows exclusively out of his contract with the owner of the horse; it was a duty which the smith owed to him alone, and to no one else. And although the injury to the rider may have happened in consequence of the negligence of the smith, the latter was not bound, either by his contract or by any considerations of public policy or safety, to respond for his breach of duty to any one except the person he contracted with.

This was the ground on which the case of *Winterbottom v. Wright*, (10 *Mees. & Welsb.* 109,) was decided. A. contracted with the postmaster general to provide a coach to convey the mail bags along a certain line of road, and B. and others, also contracted to horse the coach along the same line. B. and his co-contractors hired C., who was the plaintiff, to drive the coach. The coach, in consequence of some latent defect, broke down; the plaintiff was thrown from his seat and lamed. It was held that C. could not maintain an action against A. for the injury thus sustained. The reason of the decision is best stated by Baron Rolfe. A.'s duty to keep the coach in good condition, was a duty to the postmaster general, with whom he made his contract, and not a duty to the driver employed by the owners of the horses.

But the case in hand stands on a different ground. The defendant was a dealer in poisonous drugs. Gilbert was his agent in preparing them for market. The death or great bodily harm of some person was the natural and almost inevitable consequence of the sale of belladonna by means of the false label.

Gilbert, the defendant's agent, would have been punishable for manslaughter if Mrs. Thomas had died in consequence of taking the falsely labeled medicine. Every man who, by his culpable negligence, causes the death of another, although without intent to kill, is guilty of manslaughter. (2 *R.S.* 662, § 19.) * * * Although the defendant Winchester may not be answerable criminally for the negligence of his agent, there can be no doubt of his liability in a civil action, in which the act of the agent is to be regarded as the act of the principal.

In respect to the wrongful and criminal character of the negligence complained of, this case differs widely from those put by the defendant's counsel. No such imminent danger existed in those cases. In the present case the sale of the poisonous article was made to a dealer in drugs, and not to a consumer. The injury therefore was not likely to fall on him, or on his vendee who was also a dealer; but much more likely to be visited on a remote purchaser, as actually happened. The defendant's negligence put human life in imminent danger. Can it be said that there was no duty on the part of the defendant, to avoid the creation of that danger by the exercise of greater caution? or that the exercise of that caution was a duty only to his immediate vendee, whose life was not endangered? * * * The duty of exercising caution in this respect did not arise out of the defendant's contract of sale to Aspinwall. The wrong done by the defendant was in putting the poison, mislabeled, into the hands of Aspinwall as an article of merchandise to be sold and afterwards used as the extract of dandelion, by some person then unknown. The owner of a horse and cart who leaves them unattended in the street is liable for any damage which may result from his negligence. * * * The owner of a loaded gun who puts it into the hands of a child by whose indiscretion it is discharged, is liable for the damage occasioned by the discharge. * * * The defendant's contract of sale to Aspinwall does not excuse the wrong done to the plaintiffs. It was a part of the means by which the wrong was effected. The plaintiffs' injury and their remedy would have stood on the same principle, if the defendant had given the belladonna to Dr. Foord without price, or if he had put it in his shop without his knowledge, under circumstances which would probably have led to its sale on the faith of the label.

In *Longmeid v. Holliday*, (6 *Law and Eq.Rep.* 562) the distinction is recognized between an act of negligence imminently dangerous to the lives of others, and one that is not so. In the former case, the party guilty of the negligence is liable to the party injured, whether there be a contract between them or not; in the latter, the negligent party is liable only to the party with whom he contracted, and on the ground that negligence is a breach of the contract.

The defendant, on the trial, insisted that Aspinwall and Foord were guilty of negligence in selling the article in question for what it was represented to be in the label; and that the suit, if it could be sustained at all, should have been brought against Foord. * * * If the case really depended on the point thus raised, the question was properly left to the jury. But I think it did not. The defendant, by affixing the label to the jar, represented its contents to be dandelion; and to have been "prepared" by his agent Gilbert. The word 'prepared' on the label, must be understood to mean that the article was manufactured by him, or that it had passed through some process under his hands, which would give him personal knowledge of its true name and quality. Whether Foord was justified in selling the article upon the faith of the defendant's label, would have been an open question in an action by the plaintiffs against him, and I wish to be understood as giving no opinion on that point. But it seems to me to be clear that the defendant cannot, in this case, set up as a defense, that Foord sold the contents of the jar as and for what the defendant represented it to be. The label conveyed the idea distinctly to Foord that the contents of the jar was the extract of dandelion; and that the defendant knew it to be such. So far as the defendant is concerned, Foord was under no obligation to test the truth of the representation. * * *

GARDINER, J. concurred in affirming the judgment, on the ground that selling the belladonna without a label indicating that it was a *poison*, was declared a misdemeanor by statute; * * * but expressed no opinion upon the question whether, independent of the statute, the defendant would have been liable to these plaintiffs.

Judgment affirmed.

NOTES

1. Winterbottom v. Wright, 10 M. & W. 109, 152 Eng.Rep. 402 (Exch. 1842), which was discussed at some length in Chief Judge Ruggles' opinion in *Thomas v. Winchester*, is the most famous expression of the old common-law privity requirement. The following statement from the judgment of Lord Abinger, C.B., is often cited:

> * * * It is however contended, that this contract being made on behalf of the public by the Postmaster–General, no action could be maintained against him, and therefore the plaintiff must have a remedy against the defendant. But that is by no means a necessary consequence—he may be remediless altogether. There is no privity of contract between these parties; and if the plaintiff can sue, every passenger, or even any person passing along the road, who was injured by the upsetting of the coach, might bring a similar action. Unless we confine the operation of such contracts as this to the parties who entered into them, the most absurd and outrageous consequences, to which I can see no limit, would ensue. * * *

10 M. & W. at 114, 152 Eng.Rep. at 404–05.

2. In Loop v. Litchfield, 42 N.Y. 351 (1870), a circular saw was constructed with a balance (or fly) wheel which had been improperly cast. The defect apparently had been pointed out to the original purchaser but was not readily detectable because lead had been used to give the wheel a uniform appearance. Some three years after the saw had been acquired by the original purchaser, it was leased to the plaintiffs' decedent, who was unaware of the problem with the balance wheel. About two years later the wheel burst and killed the decedent. The trial court let the case go to the jury on the theory that the plaintiffs were entitled to recover if the balance wheel was negligently constructed. The General Term reversed a judgment for the plaintiff and the New York Court of Appeals affirmed this reversal. In distinguishing *Thomas v. Winchester*, it declared:

> The appellants recognize the principle of this decision, and seek to bring their case within it, by asserting that the fly wheel in question was a dangerous instrument. Poison is a dangerous subject. Gunpowder is the same. A torpedo is a dangerous instrument as is a spring gun, a loaded rifle or the like. They are instruments and articles in their nature calculated to do injury to mankind, and generally intended to accomplish that purpose. They are essentially, and in their elements, instruments of danger. Not so, however, an iron wheel a few feet in diameter and a few inches in thickness, although one part may be weaker than another.

42 N.Y. at 358–59 (per Hunt, J.). The court also stressed that the wheel had lasted for five years.

Losee v. Clute, 51 N.Y. 494 (1873), involved litigation that arose out of the same accident as that which generated *Losee v. Buchanan*, 51 N.Y. 476 (1873). In the *Buchanan* case, the plaintiff sought recovery for damage to his property against the owners of a bursting boiler on a *Rylands v. Fletcher* theory of strict liability. In *Losee v. Clute*, the plaintiff brought a negligence action against the manufacturer of the boiler. The court reaffirmed the privity rule, noting that "the opinion of Hunt, J. in Loop v. Litchfield * * * clearly shows that the principle decided in [Thomas v. Winchester] case has no application to this [case]." 51 N.Y. at 497.

3. The next important New York case was Devlin v. Smith, 89 N.Y. 470 (1882). The defendants were Smith, who had contracted to paint the dome of a county court-house, and Stevenson, whom Smith had employed to construct a scaffold upon which the painters would work. Hugh Devlin, the plaintiff's intestate, was one of the painters employed by Smith. The scaffold collapsed hurtling Devlin to his death. The court first held that there was sufficient evidence to go to the jury on the questions of whether the scaffold had been negligently built by Stevenson and of whether that negligence had caused the collapse. The court continued:

> Stevenson undertook to build a scaffold ninety feet in height, for the express purpose of enabling the workmen of Smith to stand upon it to paint the interior of the dome. Any defect or negligence in its construction, which should cause it to give way, would naturally result in these men being precipitated from that great height. A stronger case where misfortune to third persons not parties to the contract would be a natural and necessary consequence of the builder's negligence, can hardly be supposed, nor is it easy to imagine a more apt illustration of a case where such negligence would be an act imminently dangerous to human life. These circumstances seem to us to bring the case fairly within the principle of *Thomas v. Winchester*.
>
> * * *
>
> Loop v. Litchfield (42 N.Y. 351, 1 Am.Rep. 543) was decided upon the ground that the wheel which caused the injury was not in itself a dangerous instrument, and that the injury was not a natural consequence of the defect, or one reasonably to be anticipated. Losee v. Clute (51 N.Y. 494, 10 Am.Rep. 638) was distinguished from *Thomas v. Winchester*, upon the authority of *Loop v. Litchfield*.

89 N.Y. at 477–79.

MacPHERSON v. BUICK MOTOR CO.

Court of Appeals of New York, 1916.
217 N.Y. 382, 111 N.E. 1050.

CARDOZO, J. The defendant is a manufacturer of automobiles. It sold an automobile to a retail dealer. The retail dealer resold to the plaintiff. While the plaintiff was in the car, it suddenly collapsed. He was thrown out and injured. One of the wheels was made of defective wood, and its spokes crumbled into fragments. The wheel was not made by the defendant; it was bought from another manufacturer. There is evidence, however, that its defects could have been discovered by reasonable inspection, and that inspection was omitted. There is no claim that the defendant knew of the defect and willfully concealed it. * * * The question to be determined is whether the defendant owed a duty of care and vigilance to any one but the immediate purchaser.

The foundations of this branch of the law, at least in this state, were laid in Thomas v. Winchester (6 N.Y. 397). A poison was falsely labeled. The sale was made to a druggist, who in turn sold to a customer. The customer recovered damages from the seller who affixed the label. "The defendant's negligence," it was said, "put human life in imminent danger." A poison falsely labeled is likely to injure any one who gets it. Because the danger is to be foreseen, there is a duty to avoid the injury. Cases were cited by way of illustration in which manufacturers were not subject to any duty irrespective of contract. The distinction was said to be that their conduct, though negligent, was not likely to result in injury to any one except the purchaser. We are not required to say whether the chance of injury was always as remote as the distinction assumes. Some of the illustrations might be rejected to-day. The *principle* of the distinction is for present purposes the important thing.

Thomas v. Winchester became quickly a landmark of the law. In the application of its principle there may at times have been uncertainty or even error. There has never in this state been doubt or disavowal of the principle itself. The chief cases are well known, yet to recall some of them will be helpful. Loop v. Litchfield (42 N.Y. 351) is the earliest. It was the case of a defect in a small balance wheel used on a circular saw. The manufacturer pointed out the defect to the buyer, who wished a cheap article and was ready to assume the risk. The risk can hardly have been an imminent one, for the wheel lasted five years before it broke. In the meanwhile the buyer had made a lease of the machinery. It was held that the manufacturer was not answerable to the lessee. *Loop v. Litchfield* was followed in Losee v. Clute (51 N.Y. 494), the case of the explosion of a steam boiler. That decision has been criticised * * *; but it must be confined to its special facts. It was put upon the ground that the risk of injury was too remote. The buyer in that case had not only accepted the boiler, but had tested it. The manufacturer knew that his own test was not the final one. The finality of the test has a bearing on the measure of diligence owing to persons other than the purchaser * * *.

These early cases suggest a narrow construction of the rule. Later cases, however, evince a more liberal spirit. First in importance is Devlin v. Smith (89 N.Y. 470). The defendant, a contractor, built a scaffold for a painter. The painter's servants were injured. The contractor was held liable. He knew that the scaffold, if improperly constructed, was a most dangerous trap. He knew that it was to be used by the workmen. He was building it for that very purpose. Building it for their use, he owed them a duty, irrespective of his contract with their master, to build it with care.

From *Devlin v. Smith* we pass over intermediate cases and turn to the latest case in this court in which *Thomas v. Winchester* was followed. That case is Statler v. Ray Mfg. Co. (195 N.Y. 478, 480). The defendant manufactured a large coffee urn. It was installed in a restaurant. When heated, the urn exploded and injured the plaintiff. We held that the manufacturer was liable. We said that the urn "was of such a character inherently that, when applied to the purposes for which it was designed, it was liable to become a source of great danger to many people if not carefully and properly constructed."

It may be that *Devlin v. Smith* and *Statler v. Ray Mfg. Co.* have extended the rule of *Thomas v. Winchester*. If so, this court is committed to the extension. The defendant argues that things imminently dangerous to life are poisons, explosives, deadly weapons—things whose normal function it is to injure or destroy. But whatever the rule in *Thomas v. Winchester* may once have been, it has no longer that restricted meaning. A scaffold * * * is not inherently a destructive instrument. It becomes destructive only if imperfectly constructed. A large coffee urn * * * may have within itself, if negligently made, the potency of danger, yet no one thinks of it as an implement whose normal function is destruction. What is true of the coffee urn is equally true of bottles of aerated water (Torgesen v. Schultz, 192 N.Y. 156). We have mentioned only cases in this court. But the rule has received a like extension in our courts of intermediate appeal. * * * We are not required at this time either to approve or to disapprove the application of the rule that was made in these cases. It is enough that they help to characterize the trend of judicial thought.

Devlin v. Smith was decided in 1882. A year later a very similar case came before the Court of Appeal in England (Heaven v. Pender, L.R. [11 Q.B.D.] 503). We find in the opinion of BRETT, M. R., afterwards Lord ESHER (p. 510), the same conception of a duty, irrespective of contract, imposed upon the manufacturer by the law itself: "Whenever one person supplies goods, or machinery, or the like, for the purpose of their being used by another person under such circumstances that every one of ordinary sense would, if he thought, recognize at once that unless he used ordinary care and skill with regard to the condition of the thing supplied or the mode of supplying it, there will be danger of injury to the person or property of him for whose use the thing is supplied, and who is to use it, a duty arises to use ordinary care and skill as to the condition or manner of supplying such thing." He then points out that for a neglect of such ordinary care or skill whereby injury happens, the appropriate remedy is an action for negligence. The right to enforce this liability is not to be confined to the immediate buyer. The right, he says, extends to the persons or class of persons for whose use the thing is supplied. It is enough that the goods "would in all probability be used at once * * * before a reasonable opportunity for discovering any defect which might exist," and that the thing supplied is of such a nature "that a neglect of ordinary care or skill as to its condition or the manner of supplying it would probably cause danger to the person or property of the person for whose use it was supplied, and who was about to use it." On the other hand, he would exclude a case "in which the goods are supplied under circumstances in which it would be a chance by whom they would be used or whether they would be used or not, or whether they would be used before there would probably be means of observing any defect," or where the goods are of such a nature that "a want of care or skill as to their condition or the manner of supplying them would not probably produce danger of injury to person or property." What was said by Lord ESHER in that case did not command the full assent of his associates. His opinion has been criticised "as requiring every man to take affirmative precautions to protect his neighbors as well as to refrain from injuring them" (Bohlen, Affirmative Obligations in the Law of Torts, 44 Am.Law Reg. [N.S.] 341). It may not be an accurate exposition of the law of England. Perhaps it may need some qualification even in our own state. Like most attempts at comprehensive definition, it may involve errors of inclusion and of exclusion. But its tests and standards, at least in their underlying principles, with whatever qualification may be called for as they are applied to varying conditions, are the tests and standards of our law.

We hold, then, that the principle of *Thomas v. Winchester* is not limited to poisons, explosives, and things of like nature, to things which in their normal operation are implements of destruction. If the nature of a thing is such that it is reasonably certain to place life and limb in peril when negligently made, it is then a thing of danger. Its nature gives warning of the consequences to be expected. If to the element of danger there is added knowledge that the thing will be used by persons other than the purchaser, and used without new tests, then, irrespective of contract, the manufacturer of this thing of danger is under a duty to make it carefully. That is as far as we are required to go for the decision of this case. There must be knowledge of a danger, not merely possible, but probable. It is *possible* to use almost anything in a way that will make it dangerous if defective. That is not enough to charge the manufacturer with a duty independent of his contract. Whether a given thing is dangerous may be sometimes a question for the court and sometimes a question for the jury. There must also be knowledge that in the usual course of events the danger will be shared by others than the buyer. Such knowledge may often be inferred from the nature of the transaction. But it is possible that even knowledge of the danger and of the use will not always be enough. The proximity or remoteness of the relation is a factor to be considered. We are dealing now with the liability of the manufacturer of the finished product, who puts it on the market to be used without inspection by his customers. If he is negligent, where danger is to be foreseen, a liability will follow. We are not required at this time to say that it is legitimate to go back of the manufacturer of the finished product and hold the manufacturers of the component parts. To make their negligence a cause of imminent danger, an independent cause must often intervene; the manufacturer of the finished product must also fail in *his* duty of inspection. It may be that in those circumstances the negligence of the earlier members of the series is too remote to constitute, as to the ultimate user, an actionable wrong * * *. We leave that question open. * * * There is here no break in the chain of cause and effect. In such circumstances, the presence of a known danger, attendant upon a known use, makes vigilance a duty. We have put aside the notion that the duty to safeguard life and limb, when the consequences of negligence may be foreseen, grows out of contract and nothing else. We have put the source of the obligation where it ought to be. We have put its source in the law.

* * * Beyond all question, the nature of an automobile gives warning of probable danger if its construction is defective. This automobile was designed to go fifty miles an hour. Unless its wheels were sound and strong, injury was almost certain. It was as much a thing of danger as a defective engine for a railroad. The defendant knew the danger. It knew also that the car would be used by persons other than the buyer. This was apparent from its size; there were seats for three persons. It was apparent also from the fact that the buyer was a dealer in cars, who bought to resell. The maker of this car supplied it for the use of purchasers from the dealer just as plainly as the contractor in *Devlin v. Smith* supplied the scaffold for use by the servants of the owner. The dealer was indeed the one person of whom it might be said with some approach to certainty that by him the car would not be used. Yet the defendant would have us say that he was the one person whom it was under a legal duty to protect. The law does not lead us to so inconsequent a conclusion. Precedents drawn from the days of travel by stage coach do not fit the conditions of travel today. The principle that the danger must be imminent does not change, but the things subject to the principle do change. They are whatever the needs of life in a developing civilization require them to be.

In reaching this conclusion, we do not ignore the decisions to the contrary in other jurisdictions. It was held in Cadillac M. C. Co. v. Johnson (221 Fed.Rep. 801) that an automobile is not within the rule of *Thomas v. Winchester*. There was, however, a vigorous dissent. Opposed to that decision is one of the Court of Appeals of Kentucky (Olds Motor Works v. Shaffer, 145 Ky. 616). The earlier cases are summarized by Judge Sanborn in Huset v. J. I. Case Threshing Machine Co. (120 Fed.Rep. 865). Some of them, at first sight inconsistent with our conclusion may be reconciled upon the ground that the negligence was too remote, and that another cause had intervened. But even when they cannot be reconciled, the difference is rather in the application of the principle than in the principle itself. Judge Sanborn says, for example, that the contractor who builds a bridge, or the manufacturer who builds a car, cannot ordinarily foresee injury to other persons than the owner as the probable result * * *. We take a different view. We think that injury to others is to be foreseen not merely as a possible, but as an almost inevitable result. Indeed, Judge Sanborn concedes that his view is not to be reconciled with our decision in *Devlin v. Smith (supra)*. The doctrine of that decision has now become the settled law of this state, and we have no desire to depart from it.

There is nothing anomalous in a rule which imposes upon A, who has contracted with B, a duty to C and D and others according as he knows or does not know that the subject-matter of the contract is intended for their use. We may find an analogy in the law which measures the liability of landlords. If A leases to B a tumbledown house he is not liable, in the absence of fraud, to B's guests who enter it and are injured. This is because B is then under the duty to repair it, the lessor has the right to suppose that he will fulfill that duty, and, if he omits to do so, his guests must look to him * * *. But if A leases a building to be used by the lessee at once as a place of public entertainment, the rule is different. There injury to persons other than the lessee is to be foreseen, and foresight of the consequences involves the creation of a duty * * *.

We think the defendant was not absolved from a duty of inspection because it bought the wheels from a reputable manufacturer. It was not merely a dealer in automobiles. It was a manufacturer of automobiles. It was responsible for the finished product. It was not at liberty to put the finished product on the market without subjecting the component parts to ordinary and simple tests * * *. Under the charge of the trial judge nothing more was required of it. * * *

Other rulings complained of have been considered, but no error has been found in them.

The judgment should be affirmed with costs.

WILLARD BARTLETT, CH. J. (dissenting). * * *

I do not see how we can uphold the judgment in the present case without overruling what has been so often said by this court and other courts of like authority in reference to the absence of any liability for negligence on the part of the original vendor of an ordinary carriage to any one except his immediate vendee. The absence of such liability was the very point actually decided in the English case of *Winterbottom v. Wright (supra)*, and the illustration quoted from the opinion of Chief Judge Ruggles in *Thomas v. Winchester (supra)* assumes that the law on the subject was so plain that the statement would be accepted almost as a matter of course. In the case at bar the defective wheel on an automobile moving only eight miles an hour was not any more dangerous to the occupants of the car than a similarly defective wheel would be to the occupants of a carriage drawn by a horse at the same speed; and yet unless the courts have been all wrong on this question up to the present time there would be no liability to strangers to the original sale in the case of the horse-drawn carriage.

NOTES

1. Cardozo, J., stresses very heavily that New York law on the subject of a manufacturer's liability to third parties was laid down in *Devlin v. Smith* and that the *MacPherson* case is merely an application of the doctrine of *Devlin v. Smith*. Willard Bartlett, Ch. J., in his dissent declares that the court that decided *Devlin v. Smith* would not have found the automobile in *MacPherson* analogous to the scaffold in *Devlin v. Smith* which was some 90 feet high. Which judge do you think has the better of this argument? Does it matter how fast Mr. MacPherson's car was going at the time of the accident?

The *MacPherson* case is a textbook illustration of the technique of legal argument in which a court, when confronted with a potentially controversial decision, asserts that the point at issue was really decided previously. By making this move, the present court rather than being obliged to accept responsibility for its decision can assert that it is merely following the law established by prior courts.

2. Judge Cardozo's opinion in *MacPherson* marked the beginning of the end of the privity rule in products liability cases. Any lingering notion that liability to persons not in privity of contract for negligently manufactured products depends on some finding that the product is in some way imminently dangerous was soon abandoned in most jurisdictions. All that is necessary is that the product presents a foreseeable risk of physical injury to persons or property if it should be negligently manufactured. The extensive development of this type of liability is summed up in Dix W. Noel, *Manufacturers' Liability for Negligence*, 33 Tenn.L.Rev. 444 (1966). As we have seen in the economic tort area, versions of the privity rule have survived in other contexts. *See* William L. Prosser, *The Assault Upon the Citadel (Strict Liability to the Consumer)*, 69 Yale L.J. 1099 (1960).

3. Once it was generally accepted that an action for negligence would lie against the manufacturer of a defective product, the doctrine of res ipsa loquitur became available to the plaintiff. That is, it was often possible to argue that, since the product was defective, the defect was the result of the defendant's negligence. In Escola v. Coca Cola Bottling Co., 24 Cal.2d 453, 150 P.2d 436 (1944), Traynor, J., in a concurring opinion, argued that the use of res ipsa loquitur in products liability cases was often tantamount to permitting the jury to impose liability without proof of fault. We shall return to Justice Traynor's opinion in *Escola* shortly.

B. MISREPRESENTATION AND BREACH OF WARRANTY

Negligence law is not the only possible approach to product disappointments. Because product sales are often accompanied by representations concerning the goods and because they typically involve a contract between the buyer and seller, both misrepresentation and warranty law offer potential remedies to plaintiffs

1. MISREPRESENTATION

We dealt with misrepresentation at much greater depth in Chapter Two. Here, we briefly mention the use of this remedy in the products context. In Baxter v. Ford Motor Co., 168 Wash. 456, 12 P.2d 409 (1932); 179 Wash. 123, 35 P.2d 1090 (1934), the defendant advertised that its wind shield was made of "shatter-proof glass." Plaintiff was injured when a rock from a passing car broke his windshield, causing him to lose the sight of one eye. The Washington Supreme Court rejected the defendant's privity defense and ruled that he could rely on Ford's representation to the public that the windshield was shatter-proof. This position was extended in *Restatement (Second) of Torts* § 402B, which deals with liability for misrepresenting a material fact in advertising or other promotional material.

§ 402B. Misrepresentation by Seller of Chattels to Consumer

One engaged in the business of selling chattels who, by advertising, labels, or otherwise, makes to the public a misrepresentation of a material fact concerning the character or quality of a chattel sold by him is subject to liability for physical harm to a consumer of the chattel caused by justifiable reliance upon the misrepresentation, even though

(a) it is not made fraudulently or negligently, and

(b) the consumer has not bought the chattel from or entered into any contractual relation with the seller.

Note that the plaintiff may recover on a § 402B misrepresentation claim even in the absence of manufacturer negligence. An interesting case applying § 402B is Crocker v. Winthrop Laboratories, 514 S.W.2d 429 (Tex. 1974). There defendant had represented its painkiller product as "free and safe from all dangers of addiction." Plaintiff had an unforeseeable, idiosyncratic reaction to the drug and became addicted. As we shall see later, the fact that a manufacturer could not know of a danger will often relieve the manufacturer of liability under products liability doctrines. The *Crocker* court held, however, that a cause of action based upon misrepresentation would lie even when the manufacturer had no basis in currently available knowledge to believe that the statement was untrue.

The *Restatement (Third) of Torts: Products Liability* includes the following provision on misrepresentation.

§ 9. Liability Of Commercial Product Seller Or Distributor For Harm Caused By Misrepresentation

One engaged in the business of selling or otherwise distributing products who, in connection with the sale of a product, makes a fraudulent, negligent, or innocent misrepresentation of material fact concerning the product is subject to liability for harm to persons or property caused by the misrepresentation.

Comment *b. Liability for innocent misrepresentation.* The rules governing liability for innocent product misrepresentation are stated in the Restatement, Second, of Torts § 402B. Case law has followed that Section. Section 402B contains two caveats. The first caveat leaves open the question whether a seller should be liable under § 402B for an innocent misrepresentation that is made to an individual and not to the public at large. This question remains open. Case law on the subject of liability for innocent misrepresentation has dealt exclusively with public misrepresentations. The second caveat to § 402B leaves open the question whether a seller should be liable for an innocent misrepresentation that causes harm to the person or property of one who is not a consumer of the product. Case law has not resolved the issue of whether an innocent misrepresentation may, in the absence of a product defect, be a basis of liability to a non-consumer who suffers harm as a result of reliance by an intermediary.

2. BREACH OF WARRANTY

a. Introduction

When there is a direct contractual relationship between the injured plaintiff and the seller of a product, a breach of contract action is possible if the injury has occurred as the result of the breach of an warranty expressly made by the seller or implied by law regarding the nature or condition of the product. Today, warranty law is important to our study of products liability in torts because it played an important role historically in the evolution of tort theory. Moreover, although a majority of the states have now recognized the tort approach, some states have continued to rely upon the contract-warranty approach to the exclusion of the tort remedy. Even in those states in which products liability law is the primary means of resolving cases involving injuries caused by defective products, lawyers often plead alternatively for breach of warranty and, in most cases, also in negligence.

b. General Background

The traditional legal remedy by which a buyer of goods sought to recover from the seller, if the goods proved to be defective, was an action for breach of warranty. Prior to the late eighteenth century any such actions were brought as instances of trespass on the case for deceit or on what we would now call a tort theory. Towards the end of the eighteenth century, the action started to become merged with the action for express assumpsit which itself had also evolved out of trespass on the case.

An action for breach of warranty, whether considered as a tort or contract remedy, originally required some kind of express representation, what we would now call an *express* warranty. Gradually, over the course of the nineteenth century a number of *implied* warranties evolved. These were warranties that, in the absence of an effective disclaimer, were read into sales transaction by the courts as a matter of law and which operated as legally enforceable guarantees that the goods sold met certain standards. The two most important of such warranties for our purposes were the implied warranty of fitness for a particular purpose and the implied warranty of merchantability. These types of implied warranties were recognized under the Uniform Sales Act of 1906—eventually adopted in 34 states, the then territories of Alaska and Hawaii, and the District of Columbia—and now under the Uniform Commercial Code which, since 1967, has been in effect in 49 states and the District of Columbia. Portions of the UCC, but not the provisions on sales with which we shall be concerned, have also been adopted by Louisiana.

The implied warranty of fitness for a particular purpose arises when, at the *time of contracting*, the seller has reason to know both the particular purpose for which the goods are required and that the buyer is relying on the seller's skill or judgment [UCC § 2–315 set out below]. The implied warranty of merchantability applies only if the seller is a merchant with regard to goods of that kind [UCC § 2–314 set out below]. For our purposes, it suffices to state that, in order to be merchantable, goods must pass without objection in the trade under the contract description and the goods must be fit for the ordinary purposes for which such goods are used. It is obvious that some defective goods may be both not of merchantable quality and not fit for a particular purpose. But there will be instances where the two implied warranties will not both be applicable. Gasoline, for example, can be of merchantable quality even if it is unfit for the particular purpose of starting a fire in your barbecue pit.

Traditionally before an action for breach of an express or implied warranty could be brought there had to be a sale and there had to be privity of contract between the parties. That is, the plaintiff had to have bought the goods from the seller. As people turned to these essentially commercial remedies in order to avoid the need for showing fault as a precondition to recovering damages for physical injuries caused by defective products, pressure developed to relax the privity requirement.

Originally, in § 2–318, the UCC abolished the privity requirement only with respect to a very narrow group of individuals. It extended seller warranties to "any natural person who is in the family or household of his buyer or who is a guest in his home if it is reasonable to expect that such person may use, consume or be affected by the goods and who is injured in person by the breach of warranty." In 1966, the sponsors of the UCC provided two alternatives to this provision, which was renamed "Alternative A." "Alternative B" extends a seller's warranties to "any natural person who may reasonably be expected to use, consume or be affected by the goods" and who suffers personal injuries as a result of any breach of warranty. "Alternative C" extends a seller's warranties to "any person * * * who is injured" as a result of any breach of warranty. By 1966, however, judicial solutions to the privity problem were already beginning to be found. As a result, neither Alternative B nor Alternative C was widely adopted.

c. Current State of the Law

UNIFORM COMMERCIAL CODE (1966)

§ 2–313. Express Warranties by Affirmation, Promise, Description, Sample

(1) Express warranties by the seller are created as follows:

(a) Any affirmation of fact or promise made by the seller to the buyer which relates to the goods and becomes part of the basis of the bargain creates an express warranty that the goods shall conform to the affirmation or promise.

(b) Any description of the goods which is made part of the basis of the bargain creates an express warranty that the goods shall conform to the description.

(c) Any sample or model which is made part of the basis of the bargain creates an express warranty that the whole of the goods shall conform to the sample or model.

(2) It is not necessary to the creation of an express warranty that the seller use formal words such as "warrant" or "guarantee" or that he have a specific intention to make a warranty, but an affirmation merely of the value of the goods or a statement purporting to be merely the seller's opinion or commendation of the goods does not create a warranty.

§ 2–314. Implied Warranty: Merchantability; Usage of Trade

(1) Unless excluded or modified (Section 2–316), a warranty that the goods shall be merchantable is implied in a contract for their sale if the seller is a merchant with respect to goods of that kind. Under this section the serving for value of food or drink to be consumed either on the premises or elsewhere is a sale.

(2) Goods to be merchantable must be at least such as

(a) pass without objection in the trade under the contract description; and

(b) in the case of fungible goods, are of fair average quality within the description; and

(c) are fit for the ordinary purposes for which such goods are used; and

(d) run, within the variations permitted by the agreement, of even kind, quality and quantity within each unit and among all units involved; and

(e) are adequately contained, packaged, and labeled as the agreement may require; and

(f) conform to the promises or affirmations of fact made on the container or label if any.

(3) Unless excluded or modified (Section 2–316) other implied warranties may arise from course of dealing or usage of trade.

§ 2–315. Implied Warranty: Fitness for Particular Purpose

Where the seller at the time of contracting has reason to know any particular purpose for which the goods are required and that the buyer is relying on the seller's skill or judgment to select or furnish suitable goods, there is unless excluded or modified under the next section an implied warranty that the goods shall be fit for such purpose.

§ 2–316. Exclusion or Modification of Warranties

(1) Words or conduct relevant to the creation of an express warranty and words or conduct tending to negate or limit warranty shall be construed wherever reasonable as consistent with each other; but subject to the provisions of this Article on parol or extrinsic evidence (Section 2–202) negation or limitation is inoperative to the extent that such construction is unreasonable.

(2) Subject to subsection (3), to exclude or modify the implied warranty of merchantability or any part of it the language must mention merchantability and in case of a writing must be conspicuous, and to exclude or modify any implied warranty of fitness the exclusion must be by a writing and conspicuous. Language to exclude all implied warranties of fitness is sufficient if it states, for example, that "There are no warranties which extend beyond the description on the face hereof."

(3) Notwithstanding subsection (2)

(a) unless the circumstances indicate otherwise, all implied warranties are excluded by expressions like "as is", "with all faults" or other language which in common understanding calls the buyer's attention to the exclusion of warranties and makes plain that there is no implied warranty; and

(b) when the buyer before entering into the contract has examined the goods or the sample or model as fully as he desired or has refused to examine the goods there is no implied warranty with regard to defects which an examination ought in the circumstances to have revealed to him; and

(c) an implied warranty can also be excluded or modified by course of dealing or course of performance or usage of trade.

(4) Remedies for breach of warranty can be limited in accordance with the provisions of this Article on liquidation or limitation of damages and on contractual modification of remedy (Sections 2–718 and 2–719).

NOTES

1. The leading case marking the modern development of liability under the warranty approach is Henningsen v. Bloomfield Motors, Inc., 32 N.J. 358, 161 A.2d 69 (1960). Mr. Henningsen bought a new automobile for his wife. Ten days later, while Mrs. Henningsen was driving the car, she was involved in a one car accident in which the automobile was completely destroyed and she was seriously injured. The accident allegedly occurred as a result of a mechanical failure or defect in the steering mechanism. The Henningsens brought an action based on, among other grounds, breach of warranty. The court examined the modern merchandising approach in some detail and "adapted" warranty law to the consumer interests presented. The court held, in a manner similar to *MacPherson* in the negligence area, that a warranty runs to a foreseeable third party and thus Mrs. Henningsen was covered. Not only was the retail dealer who had sold the car responsible, but also the manufacturer of the automobile.

The court accordingly held that an implied warranty of merchantability and fitness for its intended purpose ran both from the dealer and the manufacturer. Moreover, the efforts of the dealer and manufacturer to disclaim implied warranties were found to be inadequate. They were in small print buried in an unlabeled paragraph on the back of the sales contract. The terms of the warranty were quite harsh. The manufacturer limited the warranty to "making good at its factory any part or parts thereof which shall, within ninety (90) days after delivery of such vehicle to the original purchaser or before such vehicle has been driven 4,000 mile, whichever event shall first occur, be returned to it with transportation charges prepaid and which its examination shall disclose to its satisfaction to have been thus defective." Although the disclaimer never said so, the provision effectively disclaimed all liability for personal injuries incurred as a result of a vehicle defect. The court further noted that, as a practical matter, the buyer had no choice in the marketing context presented by this case and therefore the disclaimer was not a freely bargained for provision of the contract. One could not buy an extended warranty of any kind and no other automobile manufacturer offered a superior warranty. In sum: a) the disclaimer was not conspicuous; b) the buyer was likely to be surprised by the scope of the warranty; c) the parties enjoyed unequal bargaining strength; d) the terms were harsh; e) no alternative products offered better warranties; and f) the seller offered no alternative (extended) warranty. One might ask which of these shortcomings was fatal to the defendant's case? In dicta, the court, consistent with UCC § 316, suggested that disclaimers could be valid if clearly stated and prominently displayed in the contract.

2. Several states adopted *Henningsen*, at least to some extent and the UCC provisions, set out above, were greatly influenced by the decision. In most contexts, the decision was soon rendered moot by the development of products liability under tort theory, to which we will shortly turn. Nevertheless, the case is still important in at least two categories of cases.

First, a few states (e.g. Delaware, Massachusetts, North Carolina) have not adopted the tort products liability approach. *See* Smith v. Fiber Controls Corp., 300 N.C. 669, 268 S.E.2d 504 (1980); Cline v. Prowler Industries of Maryland, Inc., 418 A.2d 968 (Del. 1980). In tort law in those states, one must still make out a case of negligence, although the courts will generally follow *MacPherson* on the question of privity. Alternatively, one may plead breach of warranty along the lines of the *Henningsen* case.

3. The second class of cases in which the contract-warranty approach to strict liability is still critical are those cases in which the claim is for damage to the product itself or for consequential economic loss. The lines are not always easy to draw, but most courts have held that a tort remedy is only available for personal injuries and property damage caused by the defective product. For property damage solely to the product itself and consequential economic loss most courts require the plaintiff to rely upon the UCC warranty provisions instead. Neibarger v. Universal Cooperatives, Inc., 439 Mich. 512, 486 N.W.2d 612 (1992); Florida Power & Light Co. v. Westinghouse Electric Corp., 510 So.2d 899 (Fla. 1987); 2000 Watermark Ass'n Inc. v. Celotex Corp., 784 F.2d 1183 (4th Cir. 1986) (applying South Carolina law); East River Steamship Corp. v. Transamerica Delaval, Inc., 476 U.S. 858, 106 S.Ct. 2295,

90 L.Ed.2d 865 (1986) (applying admiralty law); Seely v. White Motor Co., 63 Cal.2d 9, 45 Cal.Rptr. 17, 403 P.2d 145 (1965). Indiana has given the same interpretation to its products liability statute. Reed v. Central Soya Company, Inc., 621 N.E.2d 1069 (Ind. 1993). This, of course, is a specific application of the economic loss rule discussed in Chapter Two.

The *Seely* case has been very influential because the opinion was authored by Justice Traynor, one of the principal architects in the development of products liability law. There the court allowed recovery under the warranty theory but held that the tort remedy was not available. In the *2000 Watermark* case, *supra*, the court said:

> Contract law permits the parties to negotiate the allocation of risk. Even where the law acts to assign risk through implied warranties, it can easily be shifted by the use of disclaimers. No such freedom is available under tort law, which assigns risk as a matter of law. Once assigned, the risk cannot be easily disclaimed. This lack of freedom seems harsh in the context of a commercial transaction, and thus the majority of courts have required that there be injury to person or property before imposing tort liability.
>
> * * *
>
> If intangible economic loss were actionable under a tort theory, the UCC provisions permitting assignment of risk by means of warranties and disclaimers would be rendered meaningless. It would be virtually impossible for a seller to sell a product "as is" because if the product did not meet the economic expectations of the buyer, the buyer would have an action under tort law. The UCC represents a comprehensive statutory scheme which satisfies the needs of the world of commerce * * *.

The leading case to the contrary was Santor v. A & M Karagheusian, Inc., 44 N.J. 52, 207 A.2d 305 (1965). However, in Alloway v. General Marine Industries, L.P., 149 N.J. 620, 695 A.2d 264 (1997), New Jersey retreated from the position that one could sue in tort when damage is restricted to the product itself. At least where the parties are of similar bargaining strength, the product is not a necessity, and the nature of the defect does not pose a serious risk to other property, the buyer's remedy for damage to the product lies only in contract.

Some jurisdictions have created a "sudden and calamitous" exception to the economic loss rule. Under this exception, if property damage results from a sudden or dangerous occurrence, then tort theory may provide recovery. Vulcan Materials Co. Inc. v. Driltech Inc., 251 Ga. 383, 306 S.E.2d 253 (1983); Capitol Fuels Inc. v. Clark Equipment Co., 181 W.Va. 258, 382 S.E.2d 311 (1989). Some states may apply the exception only in the case of consumer transactions. See Ford Motor Co. Speed Control Deactivation Switch Products Liability Litigation, 664 F.Supp.2d 752 (E.D. Mich. 2009) (discussing the economic loss rule in several states, including Illinois, Georgia, Michigan, North Carolina, and Texas). Courts that do adopt this exception face the sometimes difficult question of what constitutes such an occurrence. *See* ExxonMobil Oil Corp. v. Amex Construction Co. Inc., 702 F.Supp.2d 942 (N.D. Ill. 2010).

The United States Supreme Court rejected this intermediate position in *East River, supra*. It noted that, "[e]ven when the harm to the product itself occurs through an abrupt, accident-like event, the resulting loss due to repair costs, decreased value, and lost profits is essentially the failure of the purchaser to receive the benefit of its bargain—traditionally the core concern of contract law." 476 U.S. at 871. The *Restatement (Third) of Torts: Products Liability* § 21 adopts the majority position. Comment *d.* affirms the position taken in *East River*.

Seely distinguishes situations where only the product in question is harmed—where one's remedy lies in contract—and situations where the product and other property is harmed—where there is a tort remedy. The line, however is not easy to draw. What if the other property is trivial in nature, i.e. a car burns up due to a defect and a $10 present in the trunk is also destroyed? What if the allegedly defective product is a component of a larger product and the entire product is destroyed due to the defect? *See* Albers v. Deere & Co., 599 F.Supp.2d 1142 (D.N.D 2008) for a discussion of various approaches to this problem.

4. When the claim is between two business entities that have a continuing commercial relationship, it is relatively rare to see a products liability claim filed in court when the only injury is the failure of the product to perform as expected. Commonly such claims are handled by some form of mediation or arbitration in order to protect the on-going relationship. *See* Stuart Macaulay, *Non-Contractual Relations in Business: A Preliminary Study,* 28 Am. Soc. Rev. 55 (1963); Thomas Palay, *Comparative Institutional Economics: The Governance of Rail Freight Contracting*, 13 J. Legal Stu. 265 (1984); Cary Coglianese, *Litigating Within Relationships: Disputes and Disturbances in the Regulatory Process,* 30 Law & Soc'y Rev. 735 (1996). Several states have also passed "lemon laws" of one sort or another, typically dealing with automobiles. These are designed to give the ordinary consumer a relatively easy remedy for products that do not live up to expectations, but which have not caused any physical injury. Frequently, some alternative dispute resolution, such as mediation, is provided in lieu of the traditional tort or contract law suit. *See* Ohio Rev. Code §§ 1345.71–1345.77.

5. If the *Henningsen* court had been unwilling to strike down the privity barrier in breach of warranty cases, what would the plaintiff have had to show to prove a case based upon negligence? THEY WERE IN PRIVITY

6. Because plaintiffs frequently plead misrepresentation and warranty theories as part of their products liability cases, the student may find it helpful to consider how one would frame various fact patterns in terms of these different causes of action. Consider the "Golfing Gizmo." As described by the court in Hauter v. Zogarts, 14 Cal.3d 104, 120 Cal.Rptr. 681, 534 P.2d 377 (1975), the Gizmo,

> [I]s a simple device consisting of two metal pegs, two cords—one elastic, one cotton—and a regulation golf ball. After the pegs are driven into the ground approximately 25 inches apart, the elastic cord is looped over them. The cotton cord, measuring 21 feet in length, ties to the middle of the elastic cord. The ball is attached to the end of the cotton cord. When

the cords are extended, the Gizmo resembles the shape of a large letter "T," with the ball resting at the base.

The user stands by the ball in order to hit his practice shots. The instructions state that when hit correctly, the ball will fly out and spring back near the point of impact; if the ball returns to the left, it indicates a right hander's "slice"; a shot returning to the right indicates a right-hander's "hook." * * * The label on the shipping carton and the cover of the instruction booklet urge players to " 'drive the ball with full power' and further state: 'COMPLETELY SAFE BALL WILL NOT HIT PLAYER.' "

534 P.2d at 379. The plaintiff, a thirteen year old boy, was seriously injured when he apparently swung under the teed-up ball and his club became entangled in the cotton cord. The ball looped over the club producing a "bolo" effect, and struck the plaintiff in the temple. The plaintiff's mother had purchased the Gizmo as a Christmas present. What result under misrepresentation and warranty theories?

7. In a well-known article, *The Model of Rules*, 35 U.Chi.L.Rev. 14 (1967) (reprinted in Taking Rights Seriously 14 (1977)), Ronald Dworkin referred to *Henningsen* as an illustration of a situation in which the settled rules of law dictated a particular solution but in which the court relied upon legal "principles" to reach a result more in accord with its notions of what the law should be, the settled law being that in the absence of fraud contractual disclaimers were valid even against one who had not read the clause. In point of fact, however, prior cases in New Jersey and other jurisdictions, cited in the *Henningsen* opinion, had held disclaimers and limitations in contracts of adhesion invalid. For a critique of Dworkin's thesis, *see* George Christie, *The Model of Principles,* 1968 Duke L.J. 649.

8. One criticism of the contract approach to product disappointments is that the language of the UCC is primarily designed with dealings between businesses in mind and is not always well suited to the business-consumer relationship. What are some examples of this problem?

C. STRICT (DEFECT) LIABILITY IN TORTS

1. HISTORICAL DEVELOPMENT

Many cases refer to present day products liability as "strict products liability." As we discuss in the following sections, if this terminology is mean to imply that products liability is liability without fault, then it is often misleading. The expression came into widespread use following the adoption of *Restatement (Second) of Torts* § 402A in 1965. This section discusses developments leading up to the adoption of 402A. Today, however, products law is much less "strict" than it was in the first decade following the promulgation of this section of the Restatement. We begin the discussion of modern products liability law in Section D. What does remain true in both periods is that modern product liability focuses on the alleged defect in the product rather than the alleged negligence of its manufacturer.

The first important judicial discussion of strict liability for defective products based upon tort law was in a concurring opinion by Justice Roger Traynor, of the California Supreme Court, in Escola v. Coca Cola Bottling Co., 24 Cal.2d 453, 150 P.2d 436 (1944). The case involved an exploding pop bottle. The majority had approved a jury verdict based upon a finding of negligence, which in turn had been based upon the use of res ipsa loquitur. Justice Traynor argued that "[i]f public policy demands that a manufacturer of goods be responsible for their quality regardless of negligence there is no reason not to fix that responsibility openly." Justice Traynor went on to argue:

> Even if there is no negligence, * * * public policy demands that responsibility be fixed wherever it will most effectively reduce the hazards to life and health inherent in defective products that reach the market. It is evident that the manufacturer can anticipate some hazards and guard against the recurrence of others, as the public cannot. Those who suffer injury from defective products are unprepared to meet its consequences. The cost of an injury and the loss of time or health may be an overwhelming misfortune to the person injured, and a needless one, for the risk of injury can be insured by the manufacturer and distributed among the public as a cost of doing business. It is to the public interest to discourage the marketing of products having defects that are a menace to the public. If such products nevertheless find their way into the market it is to the public interest to place the responsibility for whatever injury they may cause upon the manufacturer, who, even if he is not negligent in the manufacture of the product, is responsible for its reaching the market. However intermittently such injuries may occur and however haphazardly they may strike, the risk of their occurrence is a constant risk and a general one. Against such a risk there should be general and constant protection and the manufacturer is best situated to afford such protection.
>
> * * *
>
> As handicrafts have been replaced by mass production with its great markets and transportation facilities, the close relationship between the producer and consumer of a product has been altered. Manufacturing processes, frequently valuable secrets, are ordinarily either inaccessible to or beyond the ken of the general public. The consumer no longer has means or skill enough to investigate for himself the soundness of a product, even when it is not contained in a sealed package, and his erstwhile vigilance has been lulled by the steady efforts of manufacturers to build up confidence by advertising and marketing devices such as trade-marks. Consumers no longer approach products warily but accept them on faith, relying on the reputation of the manufacturer or the trade mark. Manufacturers have sought to justify that faith by increasingly high standards of inspection and a readiness to make good on defective products by way

> of replacements and refunds. The manufacturer's obligation to the consumer must keep pace with the changing relationship between them; it cannot be escaped because the marketing of a product has become so complicated as to require one or more intermediaries. Certainly there is greater reason to impose liability on the manufacturer than on the retailer who is but a conduit of a product that he is not himself able to test.
>
> The manufacturer's liability should, of course, be defined in terms of the safety of the product in normal and proper use, and should not extend to injuries that cannot be traced to the product as it reached the market.

Nearly 20 years later Traynor wrote the opinion in *Greenman* that fulfilled his invitation to move to a regime of strict liability.

GREENMAN v. YUBA POWER PRODUCTS, INC.

Supreme Court of California, 1963.
59 Cal.2d 57, 27 Cal.Rptr. 697, 377 P.2d 897.

TRAYNOR, JUSTICE.

Plaintiff brought this action for damages against the retailer and the manufacturer of a Shopsmith, a combination power tool that could be used as a saw, drill, and wood lathe. He saw a Shopsmith demonstrated by the retailer and studied a brochure prepared by the manufacturer. He decided he wanted a Shopsmith for his home workshop, and his wife bought and gave him one for Christmas in 1955. In 1957 he bought the necessary attachments to use the Shopsmith as a lathe for turning a large piece of wood he wished to make into a chalice. After he had worked on the piece of wood several times without difficulty, it suddenly flew out of the machine and struck him on the forehead, inflicting serious injuries. About ten and a half months later, he gave the retailer and the manufacturer written notice of claimed breaches of warranties and filed a complaint against them alleging such breaches and negligence.

After a trial before a jury, the court ruled that there was no evidence that the retailer was negligent or had breached any express warranty and that the manufacturer was not liable for the breach of any implied warranty. Accordingly, it submitted to the jury only the cause of action alleging breach of implied warranties against the retailer and the causes of action alleging negligence and breach of express warranties against the manufacturer. The jury returned a verdict for the retailer against plaintiff and for plaintiff against the manufacturer in the amount of $65,000. The trial court denied the manufacturer's motion for a new trial and entered judgment on the verdict. The manufacturer and plaintiff appeal. Plaintiff seeks a reversal of the part of the judgment in favor of the retailer, however, only in the event that the part of the judgment against the manufacturer is reversed.

Plaintiff introduced substantial evidence that his injuries were caused by defective design and construction of the Shopsmith. His expert witnesses testified that inadequate set screws were used to hold parts of the machine together so that normal vibration caused the tailstock of the lathe to move away from the piece of wood being turned permitting it to fly out of the lathe. They also testified that there were other more positive ways of fastening the parts of the machine together, the use of which would have prevented the accident. The jury could therefore reasonably have concluded that the manufacturer negligently constructed the Shopsmith. The jury could also reasonably have concluded that statements in the manufacturer's brochure were untrue, that they constituted express warranties,[1] and that plaintiff's injuries were caused by their breach.

The manufacturer contends, however, that plaintiff did not give it notice of breach of warranty within a reasonable time and that therefore his cause of action for breach of warranty is barred by section 1769 of the Civil Code. Since it cannot be determined whether the verdict against it was based on the negligence or warranty cause of action or both, the manufacturer concludes that the error in presenting the warranty cause of action to the jury was prejudicial.

Section 1769 of the Civil Code provides: "In the absence of express or implied agreement of the parties, acceptance of the goods by the buyer shall not discharge the seller from liability in damages or other legal remedy for breach of any promise or warranty in the contract to sell or the sale. But, if, after acceptance of the goods, the buyer fails to give notice to the seller of the breach of any promise or warranty within a reasonable time after the buyer knows, or ought to know of such breach, the seller shall not be liable therefor."

Like other provisions of the uniform sales act * * *, section 1769 deals with the rights of the parties to a contract of sale or a sale. It does not provide that notice must be given of the breach of a warranty that arises independently of a contract of sale between the parties. Such warranties are not imposed by the sales act, but are the product of common-law decisions that have recognized them in a variety of situations. * * *

The notice requirement of section 1769, however, is not an appropriate one for the court to adopt in actions by injured consumers against manufacturers with whom they have not dealt. "As between the immediate parties to the sale [the notice requirement] is a sound commercial rule, designed to protect the seller against unduly delayed claims for damages. As applied to personal injuries, and notice to a remote seller, it becomes a booby-trap for the unwary. The injured consumer is seldom 'steeped in the

1. In this respect the trial court limited the jury to a consideration of two statements in the manufacturer's brochure. (1) "WHEN SHOPSMITH IS IN HORIZONTAL POSITION—Rugged construction of frame provides rigid support from end to end. Heavy centerless-ground steel tubing insures perfect alignment of components." (2) "SHOPSMITH maintains its accuracy because every component has positive locks that hold adjustments through rough or precision work."

business practice which justifies the rule,' [James, Product Liability, 34 Texas L.Rev. 44, 192, 197] and at least until he has had legal advice it will not occur to him to give notice to one with whom he has had no dealings." (Prosser, Strict Liability to the Consumer, 69 Yale L.J. 1099, 1150, footnotes omitted). * * * We conclude, therefore, that even if plaintiff did not give timely notice of breach of warranty to the manufacturer, his cause of action based on the representations contained in the brochure was not barred.

Moreover, to impose strict liability on the manufacturer under the circumstances of this case, it was not necessary for plaintiff to establish an express warranty as defined in section 1732 of the Civil Code. A manufacturer is strictly liable in tort when an article he places on the market, knowing that it is to be used without inspection for defects, proves to have a defect that causes injury to a human being. Recognized first in the case of unwholesome food products, such liability has now been extended to a variety of other products that create as great or greater hazards if defective. * * *

Although in these cases strict liability has usually been based on the theory of an express or implied warranty running from the manufacturer to the plaintiff, the abandonment of the requirement of a contract between them, the recognition that the liability is not assumed by agreement but imposed by law * * * and the refusal to permit the manufacturer to define the scope of its own responsibility for defective products * * * make clear that the liability is not one governed by the law of contract warranties but by the law of strict liability in tort. Accordingly, rules defining and governing warranties that were developed to meet the needs of commercial transactions cannot properly be invoked to govern the manufacturer's liability to those injured by their defective products unless those rules also serve the purposes for which such liability is imposed.

We need not recanvass the reasons for imposing strict liability on the manufacturer. They have been fully articulated in the cases cited above. * * * The purpose of such liability is to insure that the costs of injuries resulting from defective products are borne by the manufacturers that put such products on the market rather than by the injured persons who are powerless to protect themselves. Sales warranties serve this purpose fitfully at best. * * * In the present case, for example, plaintiff was able to plead and prove an express warranty only because he read and relied on the representations of the Shopsmith's ruggedness contained in the manufacturer's brochure. Implicit in the machine's presence on the market, however, was a representation that it would safely do the jobs for which it was built. Under these circumstances, it should not be controlling whether plaintiff selected the machine because of the statements in the brochure, or because of the machine's own appearance of excellence that belied the defect lurking beneath the surface, or because he merely assumed that it would safely do the jobs it was built to do. It should not be controlling whether the details of the sales from manufacturer to retailer and from retailer to plaintiff's wife were such that one or more of the implied warranties of the sales act arose. * * * To establish the manufacturer's liability it was sufficient that plaintiff proved that he was injured while using the Shopsmith in a way it was intended to be used as a result of a defect in design and manufacture of which plaintiff was not aware that made the Shopsmith unsafe for its intended use.

The judgment is affirmed.

Shortly after *Greenman* was decided the American Law Institute promulgated Section 402A.

RESTATEMENT (SECOND) OF TORTS (1965)

§ 402A. Special Liability of Seller of Product for Physical Harm to User or Consumer

(1) One who sells any product in a defective condition unreasonably dangerous to the user or consumer or to his property is subject to liability for physical harm thereby caused to the ultimate user or consumer, or to his property, if

(a) the seller is engaged in the business of selling such a product, and

(b) it is expected to and does reach the user or consumer without substantial change in the condition in which it is sold.

(2) The rule stated in Subsection (1) applies although

(a) the seller has exercised all possible care in the preparation and sale of his product, and

(b) the user or consumer has not bought the product from or entered into any contractual relation with the seller.

Caveat:

The Institute expresses no opinion as to whether the rules stated in this Section may not apply

(1) to harm to persons other than users or consumers;

(2) to the seller of a product expected to be processed or otherwise substantially changed before it reaches the user or consumer; or

(3) to the seller of a component part of a product to be assembled.

James R. Hackney, Jr., *The Intellectual Origins of American Strict Products Liability: A Case Study in American Pragmatic Instrumentalism*, 39 Am. J. Legal Hist. 443 (1995) offers a fascinating discussion of the intellectual roots of the products liability revolution. For a critique of many of the assumptions underlying *Greenman* and Section 402A *see* Alan Schwartz, *The Case Against Strict Liability*, 60 Fordham L. Rev. 819 (1992).

Section 402A became the cornerstone of a rapid movement toward "strict" products liability. *See, e.g.*, Suvada v. White Motor Co., 32 Ill.2d 612, 210 N.E.2d 182 (1965); McKisson v. Sales Affiliates, Inc., 416 S.W.2d 787 (Tex. 1967). The importance of this provision can hardly be overstated. As Professor Vandall put it:

> Only rarely do provisions of the American Law Institute's Restatements of the Law rise to the dignity of holy writ. Even more rarely do individual comments to Restatement sections come to symbolize important, decisive developments that dominate judicial thinking. Nevertheless, section 402A of the Restatement (Second) of Torts is such a provision. Literally thousands upon thousands of products liability decisions in the past thirty years have explicitly referred to, and come to grips with, that section.

Frank J. Vandall, *The Restatement (Third) of Torts, Products Liability, Section 2(B): Design Defect*, 68 Temp. L. Rev. 167 (1995).

2. PLAINTIFFS AND DEFENDANTS

A. *Beyond users or consumers—liability to bystanders.* Shortly after Section 402 of the Restatement (Second) was published in final form, with its *caveat* as to whether liability extended to persons other than those who might be classified as "users or consumers," the cases started to extend strict liability for defective products to "mere bystanders," at least if they were foreseeable victims. *See, e.g.,* Elmore v. American Motors, 70 Cal.2d 578, 75 Cal.Rptr. 652, 451 P.2d 84 (1969); Piercefield v. Remington Arms Co., 375 Mich. 85, 133 N.W.2d 129 (1965). To hold that foreseeable third parties are not within the scope of a strict liability action for defective products is to be caught up in the contractual concerns that gave rise to the original privity problem. A typical case is illustrated by Haumersen v. Ford Motor Co., 257 N.W.2d 7 (Iowa 1977) in which a seven year old boy was killed while playing on a school playground when an automobile using an adjoining street went out of control due to an alleged product defect. The automobile manufacturer was held liable.

B. *Business of Selling.* The comments to Section 402A were nearly as important as the black letter in shaping the development of this new approach to products liability. One important comment defined the defendants against whom a Section 402A claim might be brought.

> *Comment f. Business of selling.* The rule stated in this Section applies to any person engaged in the business of selling products for use or consumption. It therefore applies to any manufacturer of such a product, to any wholesale or retail dealer or distributor, and to the operator of a restaurant. It is not necessary that the seller be engaged solely in the business of selling such products. Thus the rule applies to the owner of a motion picture theatre who sells popcorn or ice cream, either for consumption on the premises or in packages to be taken home.

> The rule does not, however, apply to the occasional seller of food or other such products who is not engaged in that activity as a part of his business. Thus it does not apply to the housewife who, on one occasion, sells to her neighbor a jar of jam or a pound of sugar. Nor does it apply to the owner of an automobile who, on one occasion, sells it to his neighbor, or even sells it to a dealer in used cars, and this even though he is fully aware that the dealer plans to resell it. * * *

One important consequence of the movement to strict liability was that everyone in the chain of distribution who sells a defective product became a proper defendant. Plaintiffs no longer needed to search out the negligent defendant in the chain of distribution. As Judge Traynor noted in Vandermark v. Ford Motor Co. 61 Cal.2d 256, 391 P.2d 168, 37 Cal.Rptr. 896 (1964): "In some cases the retailer may be the only member of the enterprise reasonably available to the injured plaintiff." When "middlemen" such as a retailers or wholesalers are held liable for a defect caused by the manufacturer they usually have an indemnity claim against the manufacturer. Sometimes, this claim is defined by statute. *See* Tex. Civ. Prac. & Rem. Code § 82.002. The practical effect of this legislation is that the wholesalers and retailers are liable only when they have been negligent or when the manufacturer has gone out of business or is unreachable through judicial process.

3. DEFINING A DEFECT

Greenman and the *Restatement (Second) of Torts* Section 402A did not alter the elements the plaintiff must prove in order to prevail. The plaintiff must still show that the defendant owed a duty to the plaintiff and breached that duty. The plaintiff must also prove damages and a causal connection between the breach of duty and the damages. What is the nature of that duty? As the court in the influential early case of Phillips v. Kimwood Machine Co., 269 Or. 485, 525 P.2d 1033 (1974) said:

> No one wants absolute liability where all the article has to do is to cause injury. To impose liability there has to be something about the article which makes it dangerously defective without regard to whether the manufacturer was or was not at fault for such condition.

As this quote suggests, what *Greenman* and Section 402A did accomplish was to change the language of duty. They replaced the concept of *negligence* with the concept of *defect.* Over the course of the following 20 years, with many false starts, including occasional flirtations with the possibility of abolishing the requirement of proving a defect, the courts worked out the definition(s) of this new concept within the context of a wide variety of product disappointments. *See* James A. Henderson and Aaron D. Twerski, *Closing the American Products Liability Frontier: The Rejection of Liability Without Defect,* 66 N.Y.U. L. Rev. 1263 (1991).

B. *Section 402A's definition of defectiveness*. Two of the most important, comments to § 402A, *g* and *i,* define the key concepts of "defective condition" and "unreasonably dangerous."

g. Defective condition. The rule stated in this Section applies only where the product is, at the time it leaves the seller's hands, in a condition not contemplated by the ultimate consumer, which will be unreasonably dangerous to him. The seller is not liable when he delivers the product in a safe condition, and subsequent mishandling or other causes make it harmful by the time it is consumed. The burden of proof that the product was in a defective condition at the time that it left the hands of the particular seller is upon the injured plaintiff; and unless evidence can be produced which will support the conclusion that it was then defective, the burden is not sustained.

Safe condition at the time of delivery by the seller will, however, include proper packaging, necessary sterilization, and other precautions required to permit the product to remain safe for a normal length of time when handled in a normal manner.

i. Unreasonably dangerous. The rule stated in this Section applies only where the defective condition of the product makes it unreasonably dangerous to the user or consumer. Many products cannot possibly be made entirely safe for all consumption, and any food or drug necessarily involves some risk of harm, if only from overconsumption. Ordinary sugar is a deadly poison to diabetics, and castor oil found use under Mussolini as an instrument of torture. That is not what is meant by "unreasonably dangerous" in this Section. The article sold must be dangerous to an extent beyond that which would be contemplated by the ordinary consumer who purchases it, with the ordinary knowledge common to the community as to its characteristics. Good whiskey is not unreasonably dangerous merely because it will make some people drunk, and is especially dangerous to alcoholics; but bad whiskey, containing a dangerous amount of fusel oil, is unreasonably dangerous. Good tobacco is not unreasonably dangerous merely because the effects of smoking may be harmful; but tobacco containing something like marijuana may be unreasonably dangerous. Good butter is not unreasonably dangerous merely because, if such be the case, it deposits cholesterol in the arteries and leads to heart attacks; but bad butter, contaminated with poisonous fish oil, is unreasonably dangerous.

When Section 402A was first drafted it was applicable only to food and drink. These roots are visible in the examples accompanying Comment *i*. Both Comments *g* and *i* adopt a "consumer expectations" test. A product is defective and unreasonably dangerous when the risks it poses are "beyond the contemplation" of the of the ordinary consumer. The consumer expectations test works well when the products under consideration are whiskey and butter. As we shall see, it proved less successful when the courts were confronted with cases involving complex machinery such as automobiles and airplanes.

Why do you think the Restatement required a product to be in a defective condition and also to be unreasonably dangerous to the user? In

Cronin v. J.B.E. Olson Corp., 8 Cal.3d 121, 104 Cal.Rptr. 433, 501 P.2d 1153 (1972) the California Supreme Court rejected the Restatement language. It believed that the "unreasonably dangerous" requirement "has burdened the injured plaintiff with proof of an element which rings of negligence." Moreover, the court felt Section 402A was susceptible "to a literal reading which would require the finder of fact to conclude that the product is, first, defective and, second, unreasonably dangerous. A bifurcated standard is of necessity more difficult to prove than a unitary one. But merely proclaiming that the phrase 'defective condition unreasonably dangerous' requires only a single finding would not purge that phrase of its negligence complexion. We think that a requirement that a plaintiff also prove that the defect made the product 'unreasonably dangerous' places upon him a significantly increased burden and represents a step backward in the area pioneered by this court." *Cronin*, 8 Cal.3d at 133, 501 P.2d at 1162, 104 Cal.Rptr. at 442.

Given that both "defective condition" and "unreasonably dangerous" are defined in terms of consumer expectations, do you think there is a substantial danger that plaintiffs will lose their lawsuit because they were able to prove only one prong of the "bifurcated standard?" Can you think of a situation where this might occur? What do you think the court meant when it said that the term unreasonably dangerous "rings of negligence?" Do you agree?

C. *The variety of defects.* In *MacPherson* and *Escola* the defect was unique to the particular item in question. Mr. MacPherson's Buick had a bad wheel, but not all Buick wheels were alleged to be bad. These came to be known as manufacturing or construction defects. On the other hand, the defect in Mr. Greenman's Shopsmith, the inadequate set-screw, may have been present in all Shopsmiths. Such defects came to be known as design defects. Neither Justice Traynor's *Greenman* opinion nor the *Restatement (Second)* § 402A envisions different legal rules for these different types of defect. In time, however, the case law came to recognize three distinct types of defect: manufacture, design, and warning, all with somewhat different legal definitions.

D. THE CONCEPT OF DEFECT IN PRODUCTS LIABILITY LAW TODAY

In 1991, the American Law Institute began work on a new restatement. The initial focus was on products liability, in large part because § 402A no longer reflected the state of products liability law as it had developed in most jurisdictions. The *Restatement (Third) of Torts: Products Liability* was approved by the Institute in 1997 and published in early 1998. As an indication of the enormous growth and change in this area of torts, the new Restatement replaces Section 402A with 21 separate sections. For an initial assessment of the adoption of the Third Restatement by it reporters, *see* James A. Henderson, Jr. and Aaron D. Twerski, *The*

Products Liability Restatement in the Courts: An Initial Assessment, 27 Wm. Mitchell L. Rev. 7 (2000). *See also* a symposium issue of the Seton Hall Law Review (1999) and a symposium ten years later in the Spring 2009 Brooklyn Law Review (74 Brook. L. Rev. 633) asking whether the new Restatement has been a success.

RESTATEMENT (THIRD) OF TORTS: PRODUCTS LIABILITY (1997)

§ 1. Liability of Commercial Seller or Distributor for Harm Caused by Defective Products

One engaged in the business of selling or otherwise distributing products who sells or distributes a defective product is subject to liability for harm to persons or property caused by the defect.

§ 2. Categories of Product Defect

A product is defective when, at the time of sale or distribution, it contains a manufacturing defect, is defective in design, or is defective because of inadequate instructions or warnings. A product:

(a) contains a manufacturing defect when the product departs from its intended design even though all possible care was exercised in the preparation and marketing of the product;

(b) is defective in design when the foreseeable risks of harm posed by the product could have been reduced or avoided by the adoption of a reasonable alternative design by the seller or other distributor, or a predecessor in the commercial chain of distribution, and the omission of the alternative design renders the product not reasonably safe;

(c) is defective because of inadequate instructions or warnings when the foreseeable risks of harm posed by the product could have been reduced or avoided by the provision of reasonable instructions or warnings by the seller or other distributor, or a predecessor in the commercial chain of distribution, and the omission of the instructions or warnings renders the product not reasonably safe.

As one can see by reading these provisions, under the Restatement approach strict liability in the sense of liability without fault exists only for manufacturing defects. The existence of both design and warning defects turns on the "reasonableness" of the design or warning.

Unlike § 402A, which literally pioneered the strict products liability movement, with very little precedent to support it, the Third Restatement provisions were much more reactive. They were an attempt to restate the law of products liability as it had developed in the case law in the years following the promulgation of § 402A. We explore these developments by looking at current approaches to manufacturing defects, design defects, and warning defects in each of the next three sub-sections.

1. MANUFACTURING DEFECTS

SMOOT v. MAZDA MOTORS OF AMERICA, INC.

United States Court of Appeals, Seventh Circuit, 2006.
469 F.3d 675.

POSNER, CIRCUIT JUDGE.

The district judge, after barring the plaintiffs' expert from testifying, dismissed this diversity personal-injury suit (the substantive issues in which are governed by Wisconsin law) on the ground that without expert testimony the plaintiffs could not prove their case.

* * *

Mrs. Smoot was driving her one-year-old Mazda at 35 to 40 m.p.h. when she struck either a chunk of asphalt that had been dislodged from the pavement (her current version) or, more likely, a large pothole (the defendants' version—but also what Mrs. Smoot told the police officer who investigated the accident). Deployment of the airbags was triggered by the collision, causing the injuries of which she complains. The day before the accident she had received a notice from Mazda that there was "an increased risk of airbag deployment in a low speed crash or minor impact to the undercarriage" in the model that Mrs. Smoot was driving, and that the owner should contact a Mazda dealer to have the airbag control unit reprogrammed. Her husband had made an appointment with the dealer for a few days later—too late.

The windshield and front left wheel and tire of the car were damaged in the accident, apparently from the impact with whatever it collided with—asphalt or pothole. Photographs were taken, which of course did not show the airbag mechanism. The car was repaired and sold before the lawsuit and cannot be traced.

The Smoots' lawyer wanted to base their case on the venerable common law doctrine of res ipsa loquitur (the thing speaks for itself). A plaintiff who establishes that the accident in which he was injured was of a kind that could not reasonably have been expected to occur unless the injurer had been negligent has made out a prima facie case of tort liability, which is to say has presented enough evidence to withstand a directed verdict or equivalent—enough in other words to get his case to a jury. E.g., *Lambrecht v. Estate of Kaczmarczyk,* 241 Wis.2d 804, 623 N.W.2d 751, 761 (2001); *Peplinski v. Fobe's Roofing, Inc.,* 193 Wis.2d 6, 531 N.W.2d 597, 600 (1995).

Canonical statements of the doctrine, in Wisconsin as elsewhere, require that the defendant have had exclusive control of whatever it was that caused the accident. If taken literally, this would bar applying the doctrine to a products liability case, as this case is, since "unlike an ordinary accident case the defendant in a products case has parted with possession and control of the harmful object before the accident occurs."

Welge v. Planters Lifesavers Co., 17 F.3d 209, 211 (7th Cir.1994). But as we went on to explain, "the doctrine [of res ipsa loquitur] instantiates the broader principle, which is as applicable to a products case as to any other tort case, that an accident can itself be evidence of liability." *Id. Welge* was a case governed by Illinois law, not as here by Wisconsin law. But Wisconsin too allows the doctrine to be applied in a products case as long as the product defect that is claimed to have caused the accident existed before the defendant shipped the product rather than being created by tampering or use after he parted with it.

The defendant can contest the prima facie case with evidence that this particular accident could and did occur without negligence on his part, but unless the defendant's evidence is conclusive the jury will have to weigh it against the general probability that established the prima facie case. *Turk v. H.C. Prange Co.,* 18 Wis.2d 547, 119 N.W.2d 365, 370 (1963). An older view was that if the defendant presented evidence, the presumption of liability created by evidence of res ipsa loquitur evaporated. *Bollenbach v. Bloomenthal,* 341 Ill. 539, 173 N.E. 670, 672–73 (1930), overruled by *Metz v. Central Illinois Electric & Gas Co.,* 32 Ill.2d 446, 207 N.E.2d 305 (1965). That view was unsound, and has long been rejected by the Wisconsin courts. The presumption created by res ipsa loquitur is not a device for forcing the defendant to present evidence, if he has any; it is, rather, the acknowledgment of a probability (what statistical theorists call a "prior probability") that the accident was due to the defendant's negligence. That probability is weakened, but not necessarily to the point of extinction, by contrary evidence presented by the defendant, though the probability is not so great that it entitles the plaintiff to a directed verdict if the defendant presents no evidence. So really the term "presumption" is a misnomer as applied to res ipsa loquitur and should be replaced by "permissible inference of negligence"—as the Wisconsin cases have done.

Turning to the specific issue presented by the appeal, we agree with the plaintiffs that in a proper case of res ipsa loquitur the plaintiff does not, at least initially, have to present expert testimony; it may be obvious to judges and jurors that the accident that befell him is the kind that rarely occurs without negligence on the part of the injurer. A typical example is where the plaintiff is discovered after his appendectomy to have a surgeon's sponge where his appendix was. This would be a similar case had the airbags deployed when Mrs. Smoot parked her car and turned off the ignition, or when while driving steadily she had blown the car's horn.

Expert testimony on behalf of the plaintiff in a case based on res ipsa loquitur might seem mandatory (and this regardless of the character or strength of the defendant's evidence) if the inference of negligence from the accident itself was obvious only to an expert. Suppose there is no sponge but when the patient wakes up he discovers that his right leg is paralyzed. A medical expert might testify that it was obvious to him (the expert) that the surgeon had sliced a nerve in the patient's abdomen rather than that the nerve had snapped spontaneously. But at this point the doctrine of res ipsa loquitur would drop out of the case because the expert's evidence would have provided a complete explanation of the accident, superseding any inference that might have been drawn from the accident itself. To instruct the jury on res ipsa loquitur in such a case would merely confuse.

It would be different if all the expert had done had been to rebut evidence given by the defendant that indeed the accident might well have occurred without negligence on the defendant's part. Refuting that evidence would just repel a challenge to the inference created by the accident itself. Despite this point, the courts are divided over whether it is ever appropriate to permit expert testimony to be given to bolster the plaintiff's invocation of res ipsa loquitur. *Connors v. University Associates in Obstetrics & Gynecology, Inc.*, 4 F.3d 123, 127 (2d Cir. 1993). But Wisconsin, consistent with its view that the function of res ipsa loquitur is just to identify a ground for an inference of negligence, allows the plaintiff to present expert testimony to show that such an injury would indeed, despite what the defendant may have tried to show, not ordinarily occur in the absence of negligence.

Although we have been speaking so far of "negligence" because it is primarily in negligence cases that res ipsa loquitur is invoked, this is a products liability case and the issue is not whether the defendant was negligent but whether its product, namely the car in which Mrs. Smoot was injured, was defective. However, there need be no practical difference between a claim that a product was negligently manufactured and a claim that it has a defect rendering it unreasonably dangerous, and so it is no surprise that, as we have seen, res ipsa loquitur is applied in products cases. It would make no difference, so far as application of the doctrine was concerned, if a car accelerated when the brake was depressed because the brake had been manufactured negligently or designed improperly.

The district judge was correct, however, to reject the plaintiffs' attempt to invoke the doctrine in this case, or, to state the point more practically, was correct to rule that the plaintiff could not prove a product defect without expert testimony. What triggers an airbag is not the speed at which the car is traveling, but the rate of deceleration. Adnan Shaout & Charles A. Mallon, "Automotive Airbag Technology Past, Present and Future," 13 *Int'l J. Computer Applications in Technology* 159, 160 (2000). By our rough calculation, if you hit a wall head on while driving at 35 miles per hour and decelerate to zero miles per hour in a tenth of a second, you'll want your airbag to deploy because you'll have hit the wall with the same force as if you had fallen from a window 40 feet above the ground. We don't know the rate of deceleration of Mrs. Smoot's car when it hit the obstacle that triggered the airbag. Even if it was a chunk of asphalt rather than a pothole, the fact that the front of the car was damaged suggests rapid deceleration, and one could not allow a jury to speculate that it was not rapid enough to trigger a properly controlled airbag. The plaintiffs concede that a "sudden slowing" in the speed of the car by only 8 m.p.h. would have triggered a properly controlled airbag, and we cannot say as a matter of common sense or common experience that hitting a pothole or a chunk of asphalt could not cause a "sudden slowing" of the car from 35 to 27 m.p.h. The investigator's report depicts a pothole approximately two feet in diameter, though its depth is not indicated.

By the time the judge ruled against the plaintiffs on res ipsa loquitur, discovery was closed and the plaintiffs had not retained an expert. But the judge gave them time to find one, and they did. His qualifications to testify about airbags were poor, but passing that, his study of the accident was so perfunctory that he quite rightly was barred from testifying. He flunked all three requirements of Fed.R.Evid. 702—that the expert's testimony be "based upon sufficient facts or data," that it be "the product of reliable principles and methods," and that the expert have "applied the principles and methods reliably to the facts of the case."

The plaintiffs' expert cannot be faulted for not having inspected the car's airbag control unit, though his clients can be. The car should not have been sold or repaired (it was repaired before it was sold, and the repairs included replacing the airbag control unit) before the unit was inspected. And whether or not a "spoliation of evidence" instruction would have been proper had this case gotten to a jury, the plaintiffs cannot escape the responsibility for having placed their expert in a difficult position. Even so, he could have inquired into the circumstances behind the recall notice, into the results of the recalls (were the airbag control units found to be defective in all of the recalled vehicles? Some? None?), and into the experience of premature deployment of the airbags in Mrs. Smoot's Mazda model. He could have tried to infer deceleration from the car's weight and the damage to it. He did none of these things. He also did not examine another car of the same model; interview Mrs. Smoot, the investigating police officer, or any of the mechanics who repaired the vehicle; review crash testing data for the model involved; or review technical specifications or other literature regarding the manufacture, design, or functioning of airbag systems in Mazdas. He offered the naked unsubstantiated opinion that an airbag should not deploy when the car is traveling at a speed of only 35 to 40 m.p.h. and hits something unlikely to have brought the car to a complete and sudden stop-yet Mrs. Smoot had told the police investigator that the car had been "severely jolted" by the collision.

Without expert testimony, the plaintiffs were left essentially with the recall notice plus a certain implausibility in the notion that a properly controlled airbag would deploy when a car traveling at a relatively low speed hit a chunk of asphalt (though probably it really hit a pothole). The plaintiffs have not shared with us the details of the recall. But according to the documents available at the National Highway Traffic Safety Administration's website, http:// www-odi. nhtsa. dot. gov, the percentage of the recalled Mazdas that turned out to have a defect that would trigger airbag deployments prematurely is unknown. The recall covered approximately 214,270 vehicles. NHTSA's investigation preceding the recall discovered 88 incidents, causing a total of 56 injuries. In 2002, Mazda stated that the complaint rate for improper airbag deployment for the recalled vehicles had been 14.6 per 100,000 vehicles per year. These numbers would preclude inferring liability from the recall alone, which anyway the plaintiffs do not ask us to do.

A case based on so little evidence gives rise to an inference that the plaintiffs searched no further because they were pessimistic that their case had any real merit. The judge was right to keep the case from reaching a jury.

AFFIRMED.

NOTES

1. The problems that confront plaintiffs in manufacturing defect cases almost uniformly involve proving the existence of a defect at the time the product left the possession of the defendant. The difficulty arises in several forms. In some cases the product is literally destroyed in the accident, leaving little evidence of what went wrong. This frequently occurs in house fires. *See* Speller ex rel. Miller v. Sears, Roebuck and Co., 100 N.Y.2d 38, 760 N.Y.S.2d 79, 790 N.E.2d 252 (2003).

In Welge v. Planters Lifesavers Co., 17 F.3d 209, 211 (7th Cir.1994), a glass jar of peanuts smashed as the plaintiff tried to re-fasten the lid. The fragments were preserved and the parties agreed that it must have contained a defect but they could not find the fracture that caused the jar to shatter. More importantly, they did not agree when the defect had come into existence. Not surprisingly, the defendant argued that the defect was introduced due to rough handling and the plaintiff's evidence suggested nothing unusual had happened to the jar. Summary judgment against the plaintiff was held to be inappropriate.

In another group of cases there is a controversy as to whether the defect caused the accident or the accident caused the "defect." For example, in Johnson v. Michelin Tire Corp., 812 F.2d 200 (5th Cir.1987) plaintiff was injured when his car, equipped with four-year-old tires, crossed two lanes and ran into a guard rail. The question in the case was whether a defect in the tire caused a blow-out which led to the wreck, or, on the other hand, whether the tire damage was caused by the accident. In many of these situations, if the plaintiff is to prevail at all she must make out a case using circumstantial evidence.

The problem in *Johnson* is nothing new. In *MacPherson v. Buick*, the appellate opinion adopts facts most favorable to the plaintiff, who had won at trial before a jury. In this version we are led to believe the automobile was being driven eight miles an hour when, inexplicitly, a wheel simply collapsed. In a wonderful essay on the case, Professor Henderson notes that the facts introduced at trial paint a much different picture. Far from going eight miles an hour, Mr. MacPherson, in a rush to get a friend to the hospital, was going over thirty (at that time most motor cars traveled between fifteen and twenty miles per hour). The Buick hit a patch of loose gravel, slid off the road, struck a telephone pole, and spun around 180 degrees before falling into a three foot ditch. The fall apparently caused the wheel to break. No spokes or spoke parts were found anywhere except near the damaged car. As a result of the broken wheel, the automobile rolled over and landed on top of Mr. MacPherson, breaking his wrist and cracking several ribs. James A. Henderson, Jr., *MacPherson v. Buick Motor Co.: Simplifying the Facts While Reshaping the Law,* p. 43, in ROBERT RABIN AND STEPHEN SUGARMAN (EDS.) TORTS STORIES (2003).

2. The *Restatement (Third) of Torts: Products Liability* (1997) clarifies any ambiguity concerning the application of a circumstantial evidence rule in products liability cases with the following provision:

§ 3. Circumstantial Evidence Supporting Inference of Product Defect.

It may be inferred that the harm sustained by the plaintiff was caused by a product defect existing at the time of sale or distribution, without proof of a specific defect, when the incident that harmed the plaintiff:

(a) was of a kind that ordinarily occurs as a result of product defect; and

(b) was not, in the particular case, solely the result of causes other than product defect existing at the time of sale or distribution.

3. In the *Welge* opinion, Judge Posner noted that there are significant differences between res ipsa loquitor and the circumstantial evidence rule in products cases. Res ipsa loquitur is a negligence doctrine, directed to the question of whether the defendant exercised due care, whereas products liability focuses on the product only. Moreover, the second element of res ipsa loquitur, which is critical to the theory, requires that the defendant have control of the instrumentality, whereas, as Judge Posner points out above, the second element of strict products liability requires the product to have left the defendant's control in a defective condition. In the *Smoot* opinion, however, he says in passing that there need be no practical difference between a claim that a product was negligently manufactured and a claim that it has a defect rendering it unreasonably dangerous. Are these consistent positions?

4. The New Jersey Supreme Court adopted the Restatement approach in Myrlak v. Port Authority of New York and New Jersey. 157 N.J. 84, 723 A.2d 45 (1999). There, a 6′6″, 325 pound man was injured when the back of an office swivel chair gave way while he was at work. The plaintiff used the chair during one shift, but it was also used by several other employees twenty-four hours each day. What legal difficulties do you anticipate the plaintiff will face at the new trial ordered by the Supreme Court?

In Cooper Tire & Rubber Co. v. Mendez, 204 S.W.3d 797 (Tex. 2006), the court refused to decide whether or not to adopt Section 3, but it did note that even if an inference of a product defect can be made from the fact of the product failure, this inference would generally apply only to new or almost new products. *Cooper* involved a tire failure on a tire that had been driven 30,000 miles. Why isn't the circumstantial evidence rule available here?

5. Harrison v. Bill Cairns Pontiac, Inc., 77 Md.App. 41, 549 A.2d 385 (1988) noted five factors to be considered in determining whether a product defect may be inferred from circumstantial evidence: (1) expert testimony on possible causes; (2) the length of time between the sale and the accident; (3) the occurrence of similar accidents in similar products; (4) the elimination of

other causes of the accident; (5) whether the accident is a type that does not happen without a defect. What evidence might have the plaintiff's expert in *Smoot* have presented to get to the jury?

6. The frequent focus on circumstantial evidence in manufacturing defect cases should not cause us to lose sight of the fact that under the Third Restatement this remains a matter of strict liability. The plaintiff must prove that when the product left the hands of the manufacturer it deviated from its design specifications in a manner that rendered it unreasonably dangerous. The plaintiff does not have to demonstrate that this deviation was the result of negligence. *See* Ford Motor Co. v. Ledesma, 242 S.W.3d 32 (Tex. 2007).

7. The trial judge excluded the plaintiff's expert testimony under Federal Rule of Evidence 702. We discuss the admissibility of expert testimony in greater depth in the *Kumho Tire* case, p. 306 *infra*.

8. Judge Posner suggests that spoliation of evidence might be a reason to deny a party the use of res ipsa loquitor or its products liability analog. On this point, see Lawson v. Mitsubishi Motor Sales of America, Inc., 938 So.2d 35 (La. 2006), where the court held in a manufacturing defect case that application of res ipsa loquitur was inappropriate when direct evidence had been tampered with.

9. In the first few years after the adoption of *Restatement (Second) of Torts* § 402A a substantial number of appellate opinions involved manufacturing defects. As the field matured, plaintiffs more frequently advanced design and marketing defects. Most products with obvious manufacturing flaws do not pass inspection and, therefore, never enter the stream of commerce. Products with latent defects, such as the alleged defect in *Smoot,* are another matter. As Justice Mosk said in his dissent to Daly v. General Motors Corp., 20 Cal.3d 725, 760, 144 Cal.Rptr. 380, 401, 575 P.2d 1162, 1183 (1978), often such defects are time bombs, waiting to explode at an inappropriate time.

10. What about food? How should products liability law deal with food that is tainted or in some other way causes harm to an individual, e.g. a broken tooth as the result of biting down on a shell in a container of "shelled" nuts? The *Restatement (Third) of Torts: Products Liability* contains a separate section to deal with these cases.

§ 7. Liability Of Commercial Seller Or Distributor For Harm Caused By Defective Food Products

> One engaged in the business of selling or otherwise distributing food products who sells or distributes a food product that is defective * * * is subject to liability for harm to persons or property caused by the defect. Under § 2(a), a harm-causing ingredient of the food product constitutes a defect if a reasonable consumer would not expect the food product to contain that ingredient.

Note, that § 7 employs a consumer expectation test to assess whether a food is defective. What result if a person is injured at a restaurant by a fishbone in fish chowder? *See* Webster v. Blue Ship Tea Room, 347 Mass. 421, 198 N.E.2d 309 (1964).

PROBLEM: MANUFACTURING DEFECT

Jack Ridgway sustained serious injuries when his two-year-old Ford F–150 pick-up truck caught fire while he was driving. Ridgway was the truck's second owner. The first owner drove the truck approximately 21,000 miles and had the truck repaired four times at the Red McCombs Ford dealership in San Antonio, Texas ("Red McCombs"). Each repair attempted to fix a clunking noise that occurred during hard turns. One repair also involved the fuel system in an attempt to improve the truck's poor gas mileage. Ridgway drove the truck for only one month before the fire, making no repairs or modifications.

The fire occurred when Ridgway was driving home from work on a paved county road in Bandera County. Driving at or below the speed limit, he looked into the rear-view mirror and noticed flames curling up around the cab of the truck. Before he could jump out, Ridgway sustained second-degree burns to 20 percent of his body.

Ridgway and his wife Linda sued Red McCombs and Ford, alleging, negligence and a products liability manufacturing defect claim. Texas adopts the Restatement (Third) of Torts: Products Liability § 2(a) rule that a manufacturing defect exists when a product deviates, in its construction or quality, from the specifications or planned output in a manner that renders it unreasonably dangerous. A plaintiff must prove that the product was defective when it left the hands of the manufacturer and that the defect was a cause of the plaintiff's injuries.

Ford moved for summary judgment. In an attempt to defeat Ford's motion, the Ridgways presented affidavits from the truck's owner and from Bill Greenlees, an expert who inspected the truck after the accident. The previous owner explained when and where he purchased the truck, how many miles he drove it, and any modifications or repairs he made. In addition, Ridgway described when he first noticed the fire, how he reacted, and the injuries he sustained. Greenlees explained that his expert opinion was based on his visual inspection of the truck after the accident, a visual comparison of a similar but undamaged truck, a review of Ford service manuals, and a review of the National Highway Traffic Safety Administration's database.

Based on the areas of greatest damage to the truck and an indication of a "hot spot in the left center area of the engine compartment," Greenlees concluded that the fire originated within the engine compartment and opined that "a malfunction of the electrical system in the engine compartment is suspected of having caused this accident." Greenlees, however, declined to eliminate all portions of the fuel system as a possible cause of the accident and conceded that "the actual cause of the fire has not been determined yet." Although Greenlees suggested that further investigation might yield a more definitive conclusion, particularly if the vehicle were disassembled, the Ridgways made no motion for further testing and did not complain that the trial court failed to allow adequate time for or sufficient scope of discovery.

Write a memo assessing whether an appellate court should affirm the trial court's grant of a summary judgment in favor of the defendant on the plaintiff's negligence and products liability claims.

2. DESIGN DEFECTS

BRANHAM v. FORD MOTOR CO.

Supreme Court of South Carolina, 2010.
390 S.C. 203, 701 S.E.2d 5.

JUSTICE KITTREDGE.

This is a direct appeal in a product liability case tried to a jury in Hampton County. * * * We affirm in part, reverse in part and remand for a new trial.

I.

This product liability action involves a 1987 Ford Bronco II 4x2, manufactured in 1986. Cheryl Hale (or her husband) purchased the 1987 Ford Bronco in June of 1999 for a nominal sum. At the time of sale, the Bronco had 137,500 miles on it.

On June 17, 2001, Hale was driving her Bronco along Cromwell Road in Colleton County. Hale was driving several children to her house. Hale's daughter was seated in the front passenger seat. Plaintiff Jesse Branham, III, was riding in the backseat. Hale recalled that the children were "all excited." No one was wearing a seatbelt.

The weather was clear and, according to Hale, she was not speeding. Hale admittedly took her eyes off the road and turned to the backseat to ask the children to quiet down. When she took her eyes off the road, the Bronco veered towards the shoulder of the road, and the rear right wheel left the roadway. When Hale realized that her inattention resulted in the vehicle leaving the roadway, she responded by overcorrecting to the left. Hale's overcorrection led to the vehicle "shaking." The vehicle rolled over. Branham was thrown from the vehicle and was injured.

Branham filed this lawsuit against Ford Motor Company and Hale in Hampton County. At trial, Branham did not seriously pursue the claim against Hale. The case against Ford was based on two product liability claims, one a defective seatbelt sleeve claim and the other, a "handling and stability" design defect claim related to the vehicle's tendency to rollover. Both of these claims were pursued in negligence and strict liability. Ford denied liability and, among other things, asserted Hale's negligence caused the accident. The jury, in a general verdict, found both Ford and Hale responsible and awarded Branham $16,000,000 in actual damages and $15,000,000 in punitive damages. Only Ford appeals. The direct appeal is before us pursuant to Rule 204(b), SCACR, certification.[a]

[a] [Ed. Note: Rule 204(b) permits the South Carolina Supreme Court to certify a case for review by the Supreme Court before it has been considered by the Court of Appeals. Such certification is normally reserved for cases that involve "an issue of significant public interest or a legal principle of major importance."]

II.

A.

The Seatbelt Sleeve Negligence Claim

Branham alleged Ford was negligent "[i]n selling the Bronco II with a defective rear occupant restraint system." The amended complaint contains no specifications of Ford's purported negligence. At trial, Branham claimed Ford was negligent in failing to adequately test the seatbelt sleeve, but he did not challenge the seatbelt sleeve design. Branham filed a companion strict liability claim concerning the seatbelt sleeve. Ford successfully moved for a directed verdict on the strict liability seatbelt sleeve claim.

The trial court dismissed the strict liability claim on the ground that the seatbelt sleeve was not as a matter of law in a defective condition unreasonably dangerous to the user at the time of manufacture. Based on this premise, Ford contends the companion negligence claim must fail, for all products liability actions, regardless of the stated theory, have common elements. *Madden v. Cox,* 284 S.C. 574, 579, 328 S.E.2d 108, 112 (Ct.App. 1985) [("In a products liability action the plaintiff must establish three things, regardless of the theory on which he seeks recovery: (1) that he was injured by the product; (2) that the product, at the time of the accident, was in essentially the same condition as when it left the hands of the defendant; and (3) that the injury occurred because the product was in a defective condition unreasonably dangerous to the user.")]. Ford, therefore, concludes that the negligence claim (which required Branham to prove that the seatbelt sleeve was in a defective condition unreasonably dangerous to the user) should have been dismissed. We agree. When an element common to multiple claims is not established, all related claims must fail.

A negligence theory imposes the additional burden on a plaintiff "of demonstrating the defendant (seller or manufacturer) failed to exercise due care in some respect, and, unlike strict liability, the focus is on the conduct of the seller or manufacturer, and liability is determined according to fault." *Bragg v. Hi–Ranger, Inc.,* 319 S.C. 531, 539, 462 S.E.2d 321, 326 (Ct.App.1995). The fault-based element is of no moment where, as here, there is no showing in the first instance of a product in a defective condition unreasonably dangerous to the user.

In addition, Ford asserts there is no separate "failure to test claim" apart from the duty to design and manufacture a product that is not defective and unreasonably dangerous. We agree, for if a product is not in a defective condition unreasonably dangerous to the user, an alleged failure to test cannot be the proximate cause of an injury. The failure to establish that the seatbelt sleeve was in a defective condition unreasonably dangerous to the user for purposes of the strict liability claim requires the dismissal of the companion negligence claim. * * *

B.

The "Handling and Stability" Design Defect Claim

The "handling and stability" design defect claim (strict liability and negligence) is the gravamen of Branham's case. Branham alleged a design defect related to the rollover propensity of the Bronco. Ford appeals from the denial of its motions to dismiss the strict liability and negligence design defect claims. Viewing the evidence in a light most favorable to Branham, we find no error in the submission of these design defect claims to the jury. * * *

We begin with an overview of the technical information involved in the design defect claims. Ford uses the term "stability index" to describe the overall stability of a vehicle. The stability index is a comparison of the height and width of the vehicle, expressed in a numerical term. A closely connected term is the center of gravity. A vehicle's center of gravity relates to what one usually thinks of as "top heavy" or "stable." The lower the center of gravity in a vehicle, the more stable it is. Conversely, the higher the center of gravity (top heavy), the less stable the vehicle is.

The stability of a vehicle is related in part to its suspension. According to Branham's expert, Dr. Melvin Richardson, a vehicle with a stable suspension is able to make a turn in the road, and "as the vehicle goes around the curve, it leans over some and . . . the tires stay the same distance apart where they touch the ground." A vehicle with an unstable suspension will cause the tires to "scrub" the ground during a turn, which "cuts down friction, [and] increases tire wear," causing the vehicle to handle poorly. When a vehicle is turning and the tires begin to scrub, "you lose some of [the tire's] capabilities to keep the vehicle going in the right direction and lose some of the ability to control the vehicle."

Ford primarily employed two engineering tests as a means of determining whether the Bronco II was ready for manufacturing. The first test is called a "J" turn. In this test, as described by Dr. Richardson, the vehicle is driven down a roadway, and "as quickly as possible the driver turns [the wheel to a] predetermined angle and just holds it there" for the remainder of the turn.

The second test is called an accident avoidance maneuver test. This is where the vehicle is turned in an abrupt fashion one way, like in the "J" turn, but with the added maneuver of an immediate turn back in the opposite direction. With these engineering concepts in mind, we turn to the design defect evidence presented.

Thomas Feaheny, a former vice president at Ford, testified for Branham. Feaheny described the marketing forces and engineering insights that led to the development of the Bronco II. The genesis of the Bronco II spawned from the YUMA Program, which came into being in the late 1970s. YUMA was Ford's code name for the study of small trucks, which eventually resulted in the Ford Ranger, and later the Bronco II. The YUMA prototypes initially had a MacPherson front suspension, which, according to Feaheny, is a "type of independent front suspension that is used on a lot of small cars and trucks." Ford's engineers requested the MacPherson front suspension for the Bronco II when communicating with management on how best to address the Bronco II's handling and stability concerns raised during the prototype stage.

Feaheny opined that the MacPherson strut was the "best, most feasible suspension from a functional standpoint and also from a cost and weight standpoint." However, there was a divergence in viewpoints between corporate executives and engineers, as Ford's engineers advocated the use of the MacPherson strut for the small truck program. Since the mid–1960s Ford had employed a Twin I–Beam suspension on its bigger trucks. Feaheny testified that "there was a belief that [Ford] should adapt [the] Twin I–Beam suspension to the new small trucks."

The engineers at Ford believed the MacPherson suspension the better choice and "opposed [the Twin I–Beam suspension] because it was directionally wrong from the standpoint of steering, handling and rollover propensity and other characteristics." Because the Twin I–Beam suspension was physically larger than the MacPherson suspension, using it required the entire vehicle to be lifted higher. This had a cascading effect on the composite makeup of the vehicle, which detrimentally moved the center of gravity higher off the ground. To make room for the Twin I–Beam suspension, the engine had to be raised "two to three" inches. With the engine raised a few inches, the transmission had to be raised, which caused the hood to be raised, which then caused the seating to be raised. The net effect of this was a higher center of gravity, "which add[ed] a rollover propensity."

Feaheny also noted that the Twin I–Beam had a tendency for "jacking." Feaheny stated that jacking is a term used to describe an occurrence when the "vehicle will slide out in a severe handling maneuver. The outboard wheel would tend to dig into . . . the suspension arm, which was strong and stiff, [and it] would have to move with that wheel and the inner pivot would go up in the air." When a vehicle jacks, there is an instantaneous raising of the center of gravity, which further "increase[s] the propensity for rollover."

Use of the Twin I–Beam and its attendant safety concerns came to a head in the late 1970s. A group of engineers approached Feaheny and recommended that Ford use either the MacPherson suspension or the SLA (short long arm) suspension for the YUMA prototypes. The engineers made it clear that they were "very concerned" with the Twin I–Beam. Feaheny directed the engineers to one of his colleagues, Jim Capalongo, and Feaheny later met with Capalongo to discuss the engineers' concerns. After this meeting, alternative suspension designs were discussed and tested for "about a year" but the Twin I–Beam was still selected.

The reason the Twin I–Beam was selected in the face of engineering concerns was that it served a "major marketing advantage," as Ford had promoted this form of suspension on its full size trucks since the mid–

1960s. In the minds of the marketing executives, the Twin I–Beam was part and parcel of a tough truck, and it made business sense to carry that suspension into the smaller trucks.

The testimony of Dr. Richardson buttressed the evidence supplied by Feaheny and Ford's internal documents. Dr. Richardson opined that the use of the Twin I–Beam suspension led to the Bronco II being unreasonably dangerous. Dr. Richardson described three common suspension systems referenced above: (1) the SLA; (2) the MacPherson; and (3) the Twin I–Beam. It was through Dr. Richardson that Branham introduced many of Ford's internal documents showing the competing concerns and interests of the engineers and management over the proper suspension.

The Bronco II was designed from the existing "bones" of the Ford Ranger. Dr. Richardson opined that using the Ranger as the design platform was an appropriate engineering decision, and that it gave Ford the advantage of using components that had already been made.

Dr. Richardson testified to a Ford document dated February 5, 1981, and titled "Revised Stability Index for Utility." The stated objective of the document was to "review alternatives to increase stability index." Reading from the document, he stated that, "a study of methods to improve the stability index for the Bronco II has resulted in several design alternatives to achieve an improvement . . . from 1.85 to maximum achievable of 2.25 without a totally new concept vehicle."

The document made a general assessment about improving the stability index. "In order to improve stability index substantially, the following are required: widen track width, and lower center of gravity achieved by raising the wheel center lines with respect to body with trade-offs in ground clearance and vehicle package." The document also made five proposals to achieve a higher stability index. The first two proposals did not jeopardize the target release date for the Bronco II, but the latter three did. Only one of the proposals would have achieved a stability index of 2.25 for the Bronco II, but it was not selected.

Ford selected what is referred to as "proposal two," and it had a target stability index of 2.02. Dr. Richardson pointed out that proposal two saved Ford money. None of the proposals on this document argued for a change in the suspension system. But Dr. Richardson opined that had Ford opted to use an SLA or a MacPherson suspension system, then it could have achieved a stability index of 2.25. At that point, however, Ford had already decided to employ the Twin I–Beam suspension notwithstanding its engineers' criticisms.

* * *

Dr. Richardson testified to a Ford document dated May 4, 1982. The document identified the current stability index of the Bronco II at 2.03. Dr. Richardson noted that any change to the Bronco II after the date of this document "had to be very small if [Ford] w[as] going to still put [the Bronco II] on the market in the beginning of [1983]." He went on to testify that in the state the Bronco II was then in, with a stability index of 2.03 the vehicle would be "dangerously unstable."

Branham introduced a Ford document from September 14, 1982, with the following stated purpose: "To identify advanced engineering projects that will be undertaken to provide for continued improvement, Bronco II handling, during its cycle life." Dr. Richardson responded to the document as follows:

> The vehicle should have been made reasonably safe when it was first designed and built. There was time to do that, the discussions in the engineering documents, to me as an engineer, show me that the engineers knew how to do that, could have done it, and that should have been done. To release it without it being reasonably safe then subjects those people who buy it to risk. Now, if it is released in that configuration, it certainly should be improved as time goes along because it shouldn't be left that way.

Following up on his expert's opinion, Branham asked whether improvements were ever made to correct the problems in the Bronco II when it was released. Dr. Richardson responded, "there were no improvements made that would correct this defect."

The rollover propensity in the Bronco II 4x4, as reflected in the stability index and elevated center of gravity, was increased in the Bronco II 4x2. The two-wheel drive Bronco was lighter than its four-wheel version, resulting in reduced stability and an even higher center of gravity. The Bronco II involved in this litigation is a 4x2.

The foregoing is not an exhaustive review of the evidence presented by Branham, but it serves to support the able trial judge's determination that Branham presented sufficient evidence of a design defect known to Ford at or prior to the date of manufacture to withstand a directed verdict motion. We make this determination without having to rely on the further body of evidence of the Bronco II's rollover tendencies found in the substantial post-distribution evidence which the trial court allowed.

C.

We next address Ford's two-fold argument that: (1) Branham failed to prove a reasonable alternative design pursuant to the risk-utility test; and (2) South Carolina law requires a risk-utility test in design defect cases to the exclusion of the consumer expectations test.

For a plaintiff to successfully advance a design defect claim, he must show that the design of the product caused it to be "unreasonably dangerous." *Madden v. Cox,* 284 S.C. 574, 579–80, 328 S.E.2d 108, 112 (Ct.App.1985). In South Carolina, we have traditionally employed two tests to determine whether a product was unreasonably dangerous as a result of a design defect: (1) the consumer expectations test and (2) the risk-utility test.

In *Claytor v. General Motors Corp.*, this Court phrased the consumer expectations test as follows: "The test of whether a product is or is not defective is whether the product is unreasonably dangerous to the consumer or user given the conditions and circumstances that foreseeably attend use of the product." 277 S.C. 259, 262, 286 S.E.2d 129, 131 (1982).

The *Claytor* Court articulated the risk-utility test in the following manner: "[N]umerous factors must be considered [when determining whether a product is unreasonably dangerous], including the usefulness and desirability of the product, the cost involved for added safety, the likelihood and potential seriousness of injury, and the obviousness of danger." *Id.* at 265, 286 S.E.2d at 132.

* * *

Ford contends Branham failed to present evidence of a feasible alternative design. Implicit in Ford's argument is the contention that a product may only be shown to be defective and unreasonably dangerous by way of a risk-utility test, for by its very nature, the risk-utility test requires a showing of a reasonable alternative design.[9] Branham counters, arguing that under *Claytor* he may prove a design defect by resort to the consumer expectations test or the risk-utility test. Branham also argues that regardless of which test is required, he has met both, including evidence of a feasible alternative design. We agree with Branham's contention that he produced evidence of a feasible alternative design. Branham additionally points out that the jury was charged on the consumer expectations test *and* the risk-utility test.

As discussed above, Branham challenged the design of the Ford Bronco II by pointing to the MacPherson suspension as a reasonable alternative design. A former Ford vice president, Thomas Feaheny, testified that the MacPherson suspension system would have significantly increased the handling and stability of the Bronco II, making it less prone to rollovers. Branham's expert, Dr. Richardson, also noted that the MacPherson suspension system would have enhanced vehicle stability by lowering the vehicle center of gravity. There was further evidence that the desired sport utility features of the Bronco II would not have been compromised by using the MacPherson suspension. Moreover, there is evidence that use of the MacPherson suspension would not have increased costs. Whether this evidence satisfies the risk-utility test is ultimately a jury question. But it is evidence of a feasible alternative design, sufficient to survive a directed verdict motion.

While the consumer expectations test fits well in manufacturing defect cases, we do agree with Ford that the test is ill-suited in design defect cases. We hold today that the exclusive test in a products liability design case is the risk-utility test with its requirement of showing a

---

9. One commentator has noted that, "one simply cannot talk meaningfully about a risk-[utility] defect in a product design until and unless one has identified some design alternative (including any design omission) that can serve as the basis for a risk-[utility] analysis." Gary T. Schwartz, *Foreword: Understanding Products Liability,* 67 CAL.L.REV. 435, 468 (1979).

feasible alternative design. In doing so, we recognize our Legislature's presence in the area of strict liability for products liability.

In 1974, our Legislature adopted the *Restatement (Second) of Torts* § 402A (1965), and identified its comments as legislative intent. S.C.Code Ann. §§ 15–73–10–30 (2005). The comments in section 402A are pointed to as the basis for the consumer expectations test. Since the adoption of section 402A, the American Law Institute published the *Restatement (Third) of Torts: Products Liability* (1998). The third edition effectively moved away from the consumer expectations test for design defects, and towards a risk-utility test. We believe the Legislature's foresight in looking to the American Law Institute for guidance in this area is instructive.

The Legislature has expressed no intention to foreclose court consideration of developments in products liability law. For example, this Court's approval of the risk-utility test in *Claytor* yielded no legislative response. We thus believe the adoption of the risk-utility test in design defect cases in no manner infringes on the Legislature's presence in this area.

Some form of a risk-utility test is employed by an overwhelming majority of the jurisdictions in this country.[11] Some of these jurisdictions exclusively employ a risk-utility test[12], while others do so with a hybrid of the risk-utility and the consumer expectations test, or an explicit either-or option.[13] States that exclusively employ the consumer expectations test are a decided minority.[14]

We believe that in design defect cases the risk-utility test provides the best means for analyzing whether a product is designed defectively. Unlike the consumer expectations test, the focus of a risk-utility test centers upon the alleged defectively designed product. The risk-utility test provides objective factors for a trier of fact to analyze when presented with a challenge to a manufacturer's design. Conversely, we find the consumer expectations test and its focus on the consumer ill-suited to determine whether a product's design is unreasonably dangerous.

---

11. By our count 35 of the 46 states that recognize strict products liability utilize some form of risk-utility analysis in their approach to determine whether a product is defectively designed. Four states do not recognize strict liability claims at all. Those four states are Delaware, Massachusetts, North Carolina, and Virginia. [citations omitted] Another state, Missouri, rejects altogether any test in the form of a jury charge to determine whether a product is unreasonably dangerous, leaving that determination instead to the "collective intelligence and experience" of the jury. *Rodriguez v. Suzuki Motor Corp.*, 996 S.W.2d 47, 64–65 (Mo.1999).

12. [In this footnote, the court lists cases from the following states: Alabama, Colorado, Iowa. Kentucky, Louisiana, Maine, Michigan, Minnesota, Mississippi, Montana, New Jersey, New Mexico, New York, Pennsylvania, Texas, and West Virginia—Eds.]

13. [In this footnote, the court lists cases from the following states: Alaska, Arizona, Arkansas, California, Connecticut, Florida, Hawai'i, Illinois, Maryland, New Hampshire, North Dakota, Ohio, Oregon, South Dakota, Tennessee, Utah, and Washington—Eds.]

14. [In this footnote, the court lists cases from the following states: Idaho, Indiana, Kansas, Nebraska, Nevada, Oklahoma, Rhode Island, Vermont, Wisconsin, and Wyoming. It notes, however, that in several of these states courts have from time to time recognized the relevance of a reasonable alternative design in design defect cases.—Eds.]

We believe the rule we announce today in design defect cases adheres to the approach the trial and appellate courts in this state have been following.

* * *

This approach is in accord with the current edition of the Restatement of Torts:

> A product ... is defective in design when the foreseeable risks of harm posed by the product could have been reduced or avoided by the adoption of a reasonable alternative design by the seller or other distributor, or a predecessor in the commercial chain of distribution, and the omission of the alternative design renders the product not reasonably safe.

RESTATEMENT (THIRD) OF TORTS: PRODUCTS LIABILITY § 2(b) (1998). Concerning the framework for the risk-utility test, we agree with Professor David G. Owen, who observed:

> [T]he basic liability test should be congruent with the basic issue that in most cases must be proved. In design defect litigation, that basic issue involves the following fundamental ... question: whether the manufacturer's failure to adopt a particular design feature proposed by the plaintiff was, on balance, right or wrong. A congruence between this central issue and the liability test requires that the test focus squarely on the issue of what, in particular, allegedly was wrong with the manufacturer's design decision. More specifically, this inquiry asks whether the increased costs (lost dollars, lost utility, and lost safety) of altering the design—in the particular manner the plaintiff claims was reasonably necessary to the product's safety—would have been worth the resulting safety benefits.

David G. Owen, *Toward a Proper Test for Design Defectiveness: "Micro–Balancing" Costs and Benefits,* 75 TEX.L.REV. 1661, 1687 (1997).

In every design defect case the central recurring fact will be a product that failed causing damage to a person or his property. Consequently, the focus will be whether the product was made safe enough. This inquiry is the core of the risk-utility balancing test in design defect cases, yet we do not suggest a jury question is created merely because a product can be made safer. We adhere to our longstanding approval of the principle that a product is not in a defective condition unreasonably dangerous merely because it "can be made more safe." As we observed in *Marchant v. Mitchell Distributing Co.:*

> Most any product can be made more safe. Automobiles would be more safe with disc brakes and steel-belted radial tires than with ordinary brakes and ordinary tires, but this does not mean that an automobile dealer would be held to have sold a defective product merely because the most safe equipment is not installed. By a like token, a bicycle is more safe if equipped with lights and a bell, but the fact that one is

not so equipped does not create the inference that the bicycle is defective and unreasonably dangerous.

. . . .

There is, of course, some danger incident to the use of any product.

270 S.C. 29, 35–36, 36, 240 S.E.2d 511, 513, 514 (1977).

In sum, in a product liability design defect action, the plaintiff must present evidence of a reasonable alternative design. The plaintiff will be required to point to a design flaw in the product and show how his alternative design would have prevented the product from being unreasonably dangerous. This presentation of an alternative design must include consideration of the costs, safety and functionality associated with the alternative design. On retrial, Branham's design defect claim will proceed pursuant to the risk-utility test and not the consumer expectations test.

III.

Notwithstanding the existence of ample evidence to withstand a directed verdict motion on the handling and stability design defect claim, we reverse and remand for a new trial. There are three reasons we reverse and remand the finding of liability and award of actual damages. First, this case implicates two evidentiary rules related to products liability cases. The first rule provides that whether a product is defective must be measured against information known at the time the product was placed into the stream of commerce. When a claim is asserted against a manufacturer, post-manufacture evidence is generally not admissible. The second rule provides that evidence of similar incidents is admissible where there is a substantial similarity between the other incidents and the accident in dispute tending to prove or disprove some fact in controversy. Evidence was introduced that violated both of these rules. Third, Branham's closing argument was a direct appeal to the passion and prejudice of the jury. And although not a standalone ground for reversal, we find that because Ford and Hale were joint tortfeasors, it was error to require the jury to apportion responsibility between the defendants.

A.

Post-distribution evidence

In order for a plaintiff to prove his case in a product liability action, he must show that the "product was in a defective condition at the time that it left the hands of the particular seller . . . and unless evidence can be produced which will support the conclusion that it was *then* defective, the burden is not sustained." *Claytor v. Gen. Motors Corp.*, 277 S.C. 259, 264, 286 S.E.2d 129, 131–32 (1982) (emphasis added) (quoting RESTATEMENT (SECOND) OF TORTS § 402A, cmt. g. (1965) adopted as legislative intent via S.C.Code Ann. § 15–73–30 (2005)) * * *.

[W]e find Branham presented sufficient evidence to create a jury question on his design defect claim, we further find Ford was prejudiced by Branham's unrelenting pursuit of post-distribution evidence on the issue of liability. Given the extent of the improper post-distribution evidence introduced, the error cannot be considered harmless.

We first clarify what is post-distribution evidence. Simply defined, post-distribution evidence is evidence of facts neither known nor available at the time of distribution. When assessing liability in a design defect claim against a manufacturer, the judgment and ultimate decision of the manufacturer must be evaluated based on what was known or "reasonably attainable" at the time of manufacture. RESTATEMENT (THIRD) OF TORTS: PRODUCTS LIABILITY § 2, cmt. a. (1998). The use of post-distribution evidence to evaluate a product's design through the lens of hindsight is improper.

* * *

Dr. Richardson * * * testified to a document * * * referencing post-manufacture evidence that compared a 1989 Bronco II (referred to in the document as BII) to the UN46 prototype, now known as the Ford Explorer. This exhibit shows the additional evidence of the rollover tendency of the Bronco II that came to light after 1986:

> Current "strategies" for development of utility vehicle stability have changed over the past few years due (sic) the increased availability of rollover accident data and analyses. Previous strategies were partially driven by the Insurance Institute tests of the Jeep CJ7 in the early 80's which emphasized risk from rollovers caused by extreme (rate and magnitude) steering inputs in emergency maneuvers. Independent DOT, GM and Ford studies have confirmed that rollovers directly induced by extreme steering inputs are rare for any Utility vehicle (including the CJ7). The following quote from GM's recent SAE Paper (Reconstruction of Rollover Collisions, SAE 890857) summarizes current wisdom. "A common pre-rollover maneuver is an off-road path by the car, followed by heavy steer correction back towards the road leading to a side slide, and, ultimately, a trip followed by the rollover." Based on this new information, the UN46 was developed using a handling philosophy notably different from the BII.

* * *

There are other examples of post-manufacture evidence, but the few examples cited illustrate the inherent prejudice that flows from post-distribution evidence. It is good when a manufacturer continues to test and evaluate its product after initial manufacture. As additional information is learned, changes may be made that improve product safety and function. As a matter of policy, the law should encourage the design and manufacture of safe, functional products. In holding manufacturers accountable for unreasonably dangerous products pursuant to a fair system, products liability law serves that goal. Moreover, the law should encourage manufacturers to continue to improve their products in terms of utility and safety free from prior design decisions judged through the lens of hindsight.

Whether the 1987 Ford Bronco II was defectively designed and in a defective condition unreasonably dangerous must be determined as of the 1986 manufacture date of the vehicle. Ford's 1986 design and manufacture decision should be assessed on the evidence available at that time, not the increased evidence of additional rollover data that came to light after 1986.

B.

Other Similar Incidents

In *Whaley v. CSX Transportation Inc.,* this Court recognized that similar accidents are admissible if they "tend [ ] to prove or disprove some fact in dispute." 362 S.C. 456, 483, 609 S.E.2d 286, 300 (2005). The Court also recognized that this type of evidence has the potential to be "highly prejudicial." *Id.* at 483, 609 S.E.2d at 300. Accordingly, it set forth a stringent standard for admissibility: " '[A] plaintiff must present a factual foundation for the court to determine that the other accidents were substantially similar to the accident at issue.' " *Id.* at 483, 609 S.E.2d at 300.

* * *

Branham introduced evidence of rollover accidents involving the Bronco II and other vehicles in the same class that was known at or prior to the 1986 manufacture of Hale's Bronco II. Ford claims the pre-manufacture comparative evidence of rollover accidents violates the Whaley * * * "substantially similar" test because there was no showing that the cause of the other accidents was similar to the cause of the rollover accident at issue.

* * *

[W]e disagree with Ford. Admittedly, a showing of comparative rollover accident rates does not establish the manner in which any particular accident occurred. But Ford misconstrues the essence of Branham's design defect claim. To the extent Branham is able to establish (at or prior to the manufacture date of the subject vehicle) the rate or number of rollover accidents of the Bronco II was greater as compared to other vehicles in its class, such evidence may well be relevant on whether the Bronco II was unreasonably dangerous.

We do agree with Ford that if the cause of an accident is known and the cause is not substantially similar to the accident at issue, evidence of the other accident should be excluded. Yet, where the precise cause of an accident is not known, Bronco II rollover accident data has relevance when compared to rollover accident data of other vehicles in class. This relevance is linked directly to Branham's claim that the design of the

Bronco II caused it to have an unreasonably dangerous tendency to rollover.

* * *

Assuming a number of rollover accidents are caused by inexperienced or impaired drivers, there is no suggestion in this record that inexperienced or impaired drivers disproportionately favored the Bronco II, thus skewing the comparative rollover accident data. It is inferable that rollover accidents caused by inexperienced or impaired drivers are shared by all vehicles in the class, not just the Bronco II. * * *

Second, there may be little or no doubt as to Hale's negligence, but that misses the point in terms of the admissibility of comparative rollover accident data. A car manufacturer must design and produce vehicles that are not in a defective condition unreasonably dangerous to the user. Cars are designed with utility and safety in mind, and careless driving is a foreseeable reality. The general nature of the alleged negligent driving on the part of Hale was (or should have been) part of the evaluative process that culminated in the ultimate decision of Ford to design, manufacture and market the Bronco II to the driving public. Ford had a duty to design and manufacture the Bronco II as a reasonably safe vehicle.

We believe our consideration of the admissibility of the pre-manufacture rollover accident data necessarily flows from the risk-utility test for products liability design defect cases.

C.

Closing Argument

It is improper for counsel to make a "closing argument to the jury . . . calculated to arouse passion or prejudice." The closing argument of Branham's counsel was designed to inflame and prejudice the jury.

* * *

It is unmistakable that the closing argument relied heavily on inadmissible evidence. * * * The closing argument invited the jury to base its verdict on passion rather than reason. The closing argument denied Ford a fair trial.

* * *

VI.

The judgment of the trial court is affirmed in part, reversed in part and the case is remanded for a new trial.

NOTES

1. *Consumer expectations versus risk utility.* As the *Branham* court notes, the Second Restatement's consumer expectation test has largely been replaced by a risk-utility analysis. Only a handful of states have retained

consumer expectations as the sole test in design defect cases. The movement away from only a consumer expectations test in design defect cases came relatively shortly after the adoption of Section 402A. By the mid 1970s, commentators were proposing alternatives. The most influential alternative came from Professor John Wade. He proposed the following seven factor test:

> (1) The usefulness and desirability of the product—its utility to the user and to the public as a whole.
>
> (2) The safety aspects of the product—the likelihood that it will cause injury and the probable seriousness of the injury.
>
> (3) The availability of a substitute product which would meet the same need and not be as unsafe.
>
> (4) The manufacturer's ability to eliminate the unsafe character of the product without impairing its usefulness or making it too expensive to maintain its utility.
>
> (5) The user's ability to avoid danger by the exercise of care in the use of the product.
>
> (6) The user's anticipated awareness of the dangers inherent in the product and their avoidability because of general public knowledge of the obvious condition of the product, or of the existence of suitable warnings or instructions.
>
> (7) The feasibility, on the part of the manufacturer, of spreading the loss by setting the price of the product or carrying liability insurance.

John Wade, *On the Nature of Strict Tort Liability for Products*, 44 Miss.L.J. 825, 837–38 (1973).

Note that factors five and six of the Wade test in fact incorporate consumer expectations as part of his risk-utility equation. The Third Restatement retains this perspective. Comment *f* of Section 2 notes that among the factors relevant to assessing the existence of a design defect under its risk-utility test are:

> the magnitude and probability of the foreseeable risks of harm, the instructions and warnings accompanying the product, and the nature and strength of consumer expectations regarding the product, including expectations arising from product portrayal and marketing . . .

And in comment *g* the Third Restatement notes:

> Consumer expectations, standing alone, do not take into account whether the proposed alternative design could be implemented at reasonable cost, or whether an alternative design would provide greater overall safety. Nevertheless, consumer expectations about product performance and the dangers attendant to product use affect how risks are perceived and relate to foreseeability and frequency of the risks of harm, both of which are relevant under Subsection (b). See Comment f. Such expectations are often influenced by how products are portrayed and marketed and can have a significant impact on consumer behavior. Thus, although consumer expectations do not constitute an independent standard for judging the defectiveness of product designs, they may substantially influence or even be ultimately determinative on risk-utility balancing in judging whether

the omission of a proposed alternative design renders the product not reasonably safe.

What position does the South Carolina take on this question?

2. The leading case in retaining both a consumer expectations and risk-utility test is Barker v. Lull Eng'g Co., 20 Cal.3d 413, 143 Cal.Rptr. 225, 573 P.2d 443 (1978). Under *Barker* a plaintiff could prevail by showing that the product failed to meet the consumer expectation test or that the risk of the design outweighed its utility. The California Supreme Court shifted the burden of persuasion on risk-utility issue to the defendant. As noted in *Branham,* many states adopted the *Barker* two pronged test. However, only a few courts followed the case in shifting the burden of persuasion to the defendant. *See* Caterpillar Tractor Co. v. Beck, 593 P.2d 871 (Alaska 1979).

The scope of *Barker's* consumer-expectation prong was narrowed in Soule v. General Motors Corp., 8 Cal.4th 548, 34 Cal.Rptr.2d 607, 882 P.2d 298 (1994). The *Soule* court held that "the jury may not be left free to find a violation of ordinary consumer expectations whenever it chooses. * * * Instructions based on the ordinary consumer expectations prong of *Barker* are not appropriate where, as a matter of law, the evidence would not support a jury verdict on that theory. * * * The crucial question in each individual case is whether the circumstances of the product's failure permit an inference that the product's design performed below the legitimate, commonly accepted minimum safety assumptions of its ordinary consumers." *Soule,* 8 Cal.4th at 567–68, 34 Cal.Rptr.2d at 617–18. The court found the consumer expectations was inappropriate on the facts of *Soule*, which involved a complex claim involving the design of the wheel assembly on the plaintiff's automobile.

In *Soule*, General Motors gave the following reasons for completely abandoning the consumer expectations test in design cases:

> First, it defies definition. Second, it focuses not on the objective condition of products, but on the subjective, unstable, and often unreasonable opinions of consumers. Third, it ignores the reality that ordinary consumers know little about how safe the complex products they use can or should be made. Fourth, it invites the jury to isolate the particular consumer, component, accident, and injury before it instead of considering whether the whole product fairly accommodates the competing expectations of all consumers in all situations. Fifth, it eliminates the careful balancing of risks and benefits which is essential to any design issue.

Soule, 8 Cal.4th at 569. Assess the merits of each of these arguments. Which do you think is the strongest?

3. *Risk-utility versus negligence.* In the early years following the adoption of 402A, some courts were reluctant to move toward a risk-utility standard to judge design defects because they felt that this would reintroduce negligence ideas into an area designed to be free of such concepts. On the other hand, some courts forthrightly stated that a risk-utility analysis in design defect cases is very similar to the negligence test as it was formulated by Learned Hand in *Carroll Towing*. The Michigan Supreme Court took this position in Prentis v. Yale Manufacturing Co., 421 Mich. 670, 365 N.W.2d 176

(1984). The opinion included the following comments about the appropriate test in design defect cases.

> Like the courts in every other state, whether a suit is based upon negligence or implied warranty, we require the plaintiff to prove that the product itself is actionable—that something is wrong with it that makes it dangerous. This idea of "something wrong" is usually expressed by the adjective "defective" and the plaintiff must, *in every case, in every jurisdiction,* show that the product was defective. * * *
>
> * * *
>
> At present, questions related to "design defects" and the determination of when a product is defective, because of the nature of its design, appear to be the most agitated and controversial issues before the courts in the field of products liability. * * *
>
> The approaches for determination of the meaning of "defect" in design cases fall into four general categories. The first, usually associated with Dean Wade, employs a negligence risk-utility analysis, but focuses upon whether the manufacturer would be judged negligent if it had known of the product's dangerous condition at the time it was marketed. The second, associated with Dean Keeton, compares the risk and utility of the product at the time of trial. The third focuses on consumer expectations about the product. The fourth combines the risk-utility and consumer-expectation tests. While courts have included many other individual variations in their formulations, the overwhelming consensus among courts deciding defective design cases is in the use of some form of risk-utility analysis, either as an exclusive or alternative ground of liability. Risk-utility analysis in this context always involves assessment of the decisions made by manufacturers with respect to the design of their products.
>
> * * *
>
> The risk-utility balancing test is merely a detailed version of Judge Learned Hand's negligence calculus. See *United States v. Carroll Towing Co.*, 159 F.2d 169, 173 (2d Cir. 1947). * * *
>
> Although many courts have insisted that the risk-utility tests they are applying are not negligence tests because their focus is on the *product* rather than the manufacturer's *conduct,* see, *e.g., Barker v. Lull Engineering Co., Inc.,* 20 Cal.3d 413, 418, 143 Cal.Rptr. 225, 573 P.2d 443 (1978), the distinction on closer examination appears to be nothing more than semantic. As a common-sense matter, the jury weighs competing factors presented in evidence and reaches a conclusion about the judgment or decision (*i.e., conduct*) of the manufacturer. The underlying negligence calculus is inescapable.

Do you agree that the negligence and risk-utility tests are fundamentally the same? At least with respect to design defects, has products liability returned to fault principles? *See* David G. Owen, *The Fault Pit*, 26 Ga. L. Rev. 703 (1992). As a result, has it somehow betrayed the strict liability promise of 402A? *See* Michael D. Green, *The Unappreciated Congruity of the Second and*

Third Torts Restatements on Design Defects, 74 Brook. L. Rev. 807 (2009); David G. Owen, *Design Defect Ghosts*, 74 Brook. L. Rev. 927 (2009); Aaron D. Twerski, *Manufacturers' Liability for Defective Product Designs: The Triumph of Risk–Utility*, 74 Brook. L. Rev. 1061 (2009). Not everyone is happy with the move toward a risk utility model. *See* Richard A. Epstein, *The Risks of Risk/Utility*, 48 Ohio St. L.J. 469 (1987).

4. *Products liability and Negligence.* Why did the South Carolina Supreme Court refuse to allow the plaintiff to pursue his negligent testing of the seatbelt claim? This claim raises the interesting question of the congruence of these causes of action. What did the Court say with respect to whether a jury could find negligence but no manufacturing defect? What about a verdict that finds a manufacturing defect but no negligence? The *Restatement (Third) of Torts: Products Liability* § 2, comment *n* echoes the South Carolina Supreme Court's analysis of Branham's seat belt claim.

> [C]learly it would be inconsistent for a trier of fact to find no manufacturing defect on a § 2(a) claim and yet return a verdict of liability because the defendant was negligent in having poor quality control. What must be shown under either theory is that the product in question did, in fact, have a manufacturing defect at time of sale that contributed to causing the plaintiff's harm.

Problems also arise when the jury is asked to resolve both a products liability and negligence claim with respect to an alleged design defect. If a court has adopted a risk utility test, and a jury is asked to decide both a products liability and a negligence claim with respect to the same defect, is there any way to resolve inconsistent verdicts, e.g. the defendant was negligent but the product was not defectively designed? How should courts respond when this does occur? See Ford Motor Co. v. Miles, 141 S.W.3d 309 (Tex. App. 2004). What steps might a court take to avoid this outcome?

The *Restatement (Third) of Torts: Products Liability* § 2, comment *n* argues against instructing juries on multiple theories of recovery when the underlying products liability issue is to be resolved by a risk utility test.

> To allow two or more factually identical risk-utility claims to go to a jury under different labels, whether "strict liability," "negligence," or "implied warranty of merchantability," would generate confusion and may well result in inconsistent verdicts.

5. *Alternative Design*. Under the South Carolina Supreme Court's risk utility test the plaintiff must introduce evidence of a feasible alternative in order to reach a jury. The case is typical of jurisdictions that apply the risk utility rigorously, carefully weighing costs and benefits in deciding whether plaintiff's evidence of a safer alternative design is sufficient to create a jury question. *See* Smith v. Louisville Ladder Co., 237 F.3d 515 (5th Cir. 2001) (applying Texas law). Other states adopt a much softer approach and make the availability of a safer design a factor the jury may consider. See Kallio v. Ford Motor Co. 407 N.W.2d 92 (Minn. 1987). The *Restatement (Third) of Torts: Products Liability* § 2, comment *f* takes the position that the plaintiff normally must prove the existence of a safer alternative design as an element of her prima facie case. On these various approaches see Michael Green, *The*

Schizophrenia of Risk-benefit Analysis in Design Defect Litigation, 48 Vand. L. Rev. 609 (1995).

Regardless of the approach taken, courts generally agree with the South Carolina court that there can be more than one safe design and a product is not defective simply because the plaintiff can point to some other competing product that is safer still. Is this the position adopted by the *Restatement (Third) of Torts: Products Liability* § 2(b)? We revisit and expand on the central topic topic of alternative design in Note 4, p. 232, *infra,* following the next case.

6. *The time dimension*. As noted in the *Prentis* opinion, Dean Keeton's design defect test weighs the risks and benefits of a product as they are understood at the time of trial, not the time of manufacture. *See* W. Page Keeton, *Product Liability and the Meaning of Defect*, 5 St. Mary's L.J. 30, 34–35 (1973). This test was adopted in Phillips v. Kimwood Machine Co., 269 Or. 485, 525 P.2d 1033 (1974).

> A dangerously defective article would be one which a reasonable person would not put into the stream of commerce if he had knowledge of its harmful character. The test, therefore, is whether the seller would be negligent if he sold the article knowing of the risk involved. Strict liability imposed what amounts to constructive knowledge of the condition of the product.

Phillips, 269 Or. at 492, 525 P.2d at 1036.

The time dimension is most important in cases where risks associated with a product are discovered only after manufacture. The *Phillips* court was not confronted with this situation and, therefore, its comment about "constructive knowledge" might be viewed as dicta. Recall that § 2 of the *Restatement (Third) of Torts: Products Liability* assesses defectiveness at the time the manufacturer puts the product into the stream of commerce. Some jurisdictions continue to reject this position. *See* Green v. Smith & Nephew AHP, Inc., 245 Wis.2d 772, 629 N.W.2d 727 (2001). What position does the South Carolina Supreme Court take on this position?

In most jurisdictions, when a risk becomes known only subsequent to manufacture, the defendant may present a state-of-the-art defense. We return to state-of-the-art in the section on warning defects. *See* James Henderson, *Coping with the Time Dimension in Products Liability,* 69 Calif.L.Rev. 919 (1981).

7. *Obvious defects.* The details of the front suspension in Ford Broncos are largely unknown to the consumer. Such defects are often called latent defects. What if the alleged defect is in plain view? In Camacho v. Honda Motor Co. Ltd., 741 P.2d 1240 (Colo. 1987), the court had to assess whether a motorcycle without crash bars was defective. Crash bars are tubular steel bars attached to the motorcycle to protect the rider's legs in the event of a collision. The absence of crash bars is an obvious feature of a motorcycle, including the Honda Hawk involved in this litigation. Is a product with an obvious danger defective? Does this turn on whether a court uses a consumer expectation or a risk utility test?

Following Campo v. Scofield, 301 N.Y. 468, 95 N.E.2d 802 (1950), it was held by a number of courts that, if the dangerousness of a product was obvious (or "patent"), there could be no recovery under either a negligence theory or later a strict products liability theory. This insistence that the defect be "latent" could be rationalized under Section 402A's requirement that a product be "in a condition not contemplated by the ultimate consumer which will be unreasonably dangerous to him." *Campo* was overruled in Micallef v. Miehle Co., 39 N.Y.2d 376, 384 N.Y.S.2d 115, 348 N.E.2d 571 (1976), and there is little validity now left to the proposition that there is no liability, as a matter of law, for patent defects in manufacturing defect or design defect cases. As the *Camacho* court concluded, obvious dangers have become a matter to be balanced in the cost-benefit analysis as to whether the product is defective. Should a defendant be able to avoid liability for a design defect by warning the consumer of the defect and instructing her how to avoid it?

In warning defect cases the obvious danger issue is still alive. The basic idea is that obvious danger conveys its own warning and moots any need for the manufacturer to give a warning.

8. *Crashworthiness.* Both *Branham* and *Camacho* are crashworthiness cases. They involve claims that the product was not designed to minimize injuries even though the user failed to use it as the manufacturer intended. As explained in Reed v. Chrysler Corp., 494 N.W.2d 224 (Iowa 1992), "The [crashworthiness] doctrine imposes liability on manufacturers for design defects which only enhance injuries rather than cause them. The doctrine is applicable when a design defect, not causally connected to the accident, results in injuries greater than those which would have resulted from the accident had there been no design defect. In other words, enhancement of injuries is the gist of crashworthiness cases, not the precipitating cause of the accident." *Reed,* 494 N.W.2d at 226.

The focus of a crashworthiness case is on the enhanced injuries suffered by the plaintiff, not injuries suffered due to the underlying accident. Where it is possible to divide plaintiff's injuries in this way, courts will instruct the jury to do so. *See Restatement (Third) of Torts: Products Liability* § 16. Problems arise when the injuries are indivisible, that is when the fact finder cannot apportion injuries to causes. Today, most courts only require the plaintiff to show that the product defect was a substantial factor in producing her injuries and places the burden of proving injuries are divisible on the product manufacturer. They also follow the approach adopted in Restatement (Third) of Torts: Products Liability § 16 and hold that when injuries are indivisible the product seller is liable for all the plaintiff's harm attributable to the defect *and* other causes. *See* Trull v. Volkswagen of America, Inc., 145 N.H. 259, 761 A.2d 477 (2000). In this situation, however, the jury would still be asked to divide liability under the state's comparative responsibility rules. *See* Egbert v. Nissan Motor Co., Ltd., 228 P.3d 737 (Utah 2010). Are Jesse Branham's injuries causally divisible between Mrs. Hale and Ford? How would you divide them based on comparative responsibility?

At the time of the Branham accident, South Carolina still held all defendants jointly and severally liable for a plaintiff's injuries. As between themselves, the defendants were liable pro rata for the injuries, e.g. if there are two defendants each is responsible for half the damages. Do you believe that in this legal environment Mrs. Hale and Ford are allies? Do you believe Mrs. Hale and the Branham's are adversaries? How should courts respond to this reality?

9. *Consumer tastes and product desirability*. The *Claytor* court, cited in *Branham* states that a product's desirability should play a role in the risk benefit analysis. Desirability is closely related to consumer tastes. Indeed, some "obvious defects" that may reduce crashworthiness are the very reason the consumer chooses the product. Consider the convertible. Should a plaintiff be able to purchase a convertible and then claim it is defective when he is injured in a rollover accident? Why not?

RILEY v. BECTON DICKSON VASCULAR ACCESS, INC.

U.S. District Court, E.D. Pennsylvania, 1995.
913 F.Supp. 879.

Memorandum

TROUTMAN, SENIOR DISTRICT JUDGE.

[T]he plaintiff, a twenty-three year old nurse, contracted the HIV virus as a result of being stuck with an I.V. catheter needle after initiating an I.V. in a patient in the Intensive Care Unit of Community Hospital of Lancaster where she was employed.[1]

Plaintiff asserts that defendant, Becton Dickinson Vascular Access, Inc., is strictly liable for her injury in that the I.V. catheter, an Angiocath manufactured by defendant and used by plaintiff to initiate the I.V., is unsafe for its intended use because the needle, contaminated by the patient's blood, remains exposed after it is withdrawn from the catheter, thus permitting a needle-stick accident to occur. Plaintiff contends that such design is defective and that an available and feasible alternative design of the catheter, in which the needle is retracted into a plastic sheath as it is withdrawn, would have prevented her accident and consequent injury if she had been using such alternative device at the time the incident in which she was injured occurred.

Presently before the Court is defendant's motion for summary judgment. * * *

* * *

II. Strict Liability Claims

* * *

[W]hen presented with claims arising under s 402A of the RESTATEMENT (SECOND) OF TORTS, it is necessary for courts applying Penn-

1. The device here involved is a peripheral I.V. catheter, which consists of a needle and a slender flexible, hollow tube designed to be inserted into a vein in the patient's arm, hand, leg or foot. The needle is used to gain access to the patient's vein and is then withdrawn through the catheter tubing, which remains attached to the patient's vein for infusion of fluids and/or medications as needed.

sylvania law to determine, initially and as a matter of law, whether the product in question is "unreasonably dangerous." Such determination is to be made by weighing the utility of the product against the likelihood and seriousness of the injury claimed and the availability of precautions which might have prevented the injury in order to reach the ultimate conclusion whether, as a matter of social policy, the risk of loss is appropriately placed upon the supplier of the product.

We will first consider the danger inherent in the Angiocath under the unquestionably applicable risk/utility analysis to determine whether the product is unreasonably dangerous in light of its utility and the availability of similarly useful devices which might reduce or eliminate the risk to healthcare workers from exposed I.V. catheter needles. * * *

III. Risk/Utility Analysis Under Pennsylvania Law

The parties agree that the Pennsylvania courts have adopted a risk/utility test which requires consideration of the following factors in aid of the determination whether a product is unreasonably dangerous: 1. The usefulness and desirability of the product—its utility to the user and to the public as a whole. 2. The safety aspects of a product—the likelihood that it will cause injury, and the probable seriousness of the injury. 3. The availability of a substitute product which would meet the same need and not be as unsafe. 4. The manufacturer's ability to eliminate the unsafe character of the product without impairing its usefulness or making it too expensive to maintain its utility. 5. The user's ability to avoid danger by the exercise of care in the use of the product. 6. The user's anticipated awareness of the dangers inherent in the product and their avoidability, because of general public knowledge of the obvious condition of the product, or of the existence of suitable warnings or instructions. 7. The feasibility, on the part of the manufacturer, of spreading the loss of setting the price of the product or carrying liability insurance.[a]

* * *

Although the parties agree on the applicable legal standards, they obviously disagree as to the outcome when such standards are properly applied in this action. Upon review of the parties' respective arguments, it appears that their differing conclusions are based upon the different emphasis placed by each party on the various factors.

Plaintiff focuses almost exclusively upon the devastating potential effects of a needle stick accident which, as here, can lead to the transmission of a serious, even deadly, blood-borne disease, as well as upon the ready availability of an alternative design, already on the market, which plaintiff contends is feasible and eliminates the danger inherent in the design of the Angiocath.

a. [Ed. Note: These, of course, are the seven factor proposed by John Wade. *See* note 1, *supra* following *Branham*.]

Defendant, on the other hand, argues that although each needle stick accident involving HIV exposure is potentially very serious, there are very few accidents given the widespread use of the product. Defendant also contends that the alternative product touted by plaintiff does not meet the same equipment needs as the Angiocath and does not eliminate the potentially serious risk of needle sticks or other blood exposure. * * *

It is difficult, but absolutely essential, for the Court to be completely dispassionate in weighing the risks and benefits of the Angiocath in order to make the required social policy determination concerning the allocation of the risk of loss resulting from an accident such as that here involved. The social policy issue before the Court is not whether plaintiff deserves compensation for a terrible accident, but whether the manufacturer of the device through which she was injured is appropriately subject to liability for the accident, and, therefore, can be required to provide such compensation.

We also note that defendant bears the burden of proof on the threshold determination of allocation of risk and that all of the evidence on the threshold issue must be viewed in the light most favorable to the plaintiff.

It is with these principles firmly in mind that we consider each specific factor of the risk/utility analysis.

A. Utility of the Angiocath to the User and to the Public

It is obvious that many medical procedures depend upon the use of sharp needles to deliver vaccines and medication, to take blood samples, and, as here, to provide a means for intravenous delivery of fluids, nutrients and medicine. Thus, the availability of products such as the Angiocath is absolutely essential to modern medicine. Products which incorporate a sharp needle, therefore, are highly useful to the public as well as to medical professionals, who require devices which function well for their intended purpose, piercing skin and subcutaneous tissue.

* * *

B. Safety Aspects

In analyzing this factor, we consider both the likelihood of injury from use of the product and the probable seriousness of the injury. To make that assessment in this case is somewhat less straightforward than usual in that the term "injury" has several meanings in the present circumstances. The needle stick itself is an injury of which there is a determinable likelihood, while exposure to HIV or another blood-borne disease is likewise an injury that is more serious but less likely, since most patients are neither HIV positive nor infected with any blood-borne disease. Finally, contracting such a disease is still less likely than exposure thereto, albeit far more serious. Thus, although it is indisputable that all exposures to HIV which result in infection are terribly serious, and, because of the deadly consequences of infection, all needle stick exposures to HIV contaminated blood are serious, it does not follow that all needle stick incidents present a risk of serious injury.[3]

To properly assess this factor in terms of social policy concerns, therefore, the Court must avoid undue consideration of the indisputable fact that whatever the theoretical risk to plaintiff of serious consequent injury from the initial needle stick injury, plaintiff did sustain that most serious of injuries. Nevertheless, that fact alters neither her theoretical risk of serious injury at the time of the initial needle stick injury, nor the theoretical risk of serious injury to all other users of the product in question. To make the requisite social policy determination, which obviously affects every potential user of the Angiocath, the Court must focus on the general, theoretical risks inherent in the use of the product in terms of the likelihood that any needle stick injury involving an Angiocath will result in a serious injury, as that term is used herein, i.e., exposure to HIV/HIV infection.

Calculations from the evidence submitted by both parties to this action indicate that the risks of HIV exposure/HIV infection from an I.V. catheter are quite small. We note, first, that estimates of the rate of HIV infection from HIV exposure range from 0.3–0.47%. * * *

[T]he Court, in order to fulfill our obligation to view the evidence in the light most favorable to the plaintiff, has attempted to calculate the likelihood of HIV exposure/HIV infection from additional data included in evidence submitted by both parties. We begin with the estimate of the number of needle sticks to healthcare workers each year, which ranges from 800,000 to 1,000,000. Next we consider the percentage of all needle sticks attributable to I.V. catheter stylets, which has been documented in a relatively small sample at approximately 2.0%, and was then projected to be approximately 18.4/100,000 uses. Finally, based upon plaintiff's evidence, our estimate of the likely rate of HIV contamination is 2% of all needle sticks. Thus, using the figures most favorable to the plaintiff, 20,000 out of 1,000,000 needle sticks per year are likely to be attributable to an I.V. catheter stylet and 400 such needle sticks are likely to be HIV contaminated. At the previously estimated infection rate of .3–.47%, it appears that there are likely to be 1–2 HIV infections to healthcare workers per year from use of all I.V. catheter sets, both conventional and protected.

Stated in other terms, if we assume that there are 18.4 I.V. catheter needle sticks per 100,000 uses of such devices, assume an HIV contamination rate of 2%, and assume the highest likely infection rate, .47%, there could be 17 HIV infections per 1 billion I.V. catheters used, both protected

3. Our discussion of the risk of injury from a needle stick will be limited to the risk of exposure to and risk of contracting HIV for several reasons: (1) That is the injury involved in this action; (2) actual data available in the record is limited primarily to assessing the risk of exposure to HIV and HBV, (Hepatitis B Virus); (3) although the risk of contracting HBV after exposure via a needle stick is significantly greater than that of contracting HIV, the evidence discloses that healthcare workers can readily protect themselves by receiving the HBV vaccine, which provides over 90% protection from infection for seven years, and which OSHA regulations require hospitals to make available to healthcare workers free of charge.

and conventional, or between 8 and 9 infections per 500,000,000 uses of an I.V. catheter set.

* * *

Moreover, we note that the Court's calculations overstate the true risk, since the actual rate of HIV infection from exposure lies somewhere between .3% and .47%. With that consideration in mind, we further note that even using the lower infection rate as an estimate of the incidence of HIV infection from exposure, our projected risk calculation still overstates the actual incidence of HIV infection from defendant's products. Defendant has had only three reports of HIV infection from conventional I.V. catheters since 1981, a period during which defendant estimates that it sold 1.5 billion such devices.

From the available evidence and projections based thereon, the Court concludes that the risk of serious injury from use of an I.V. catheter such as the Angiocath is quite low.

C. Availability of a Safer, Substitute Product

Plaintiff does not argue that there is an acceptable substitute for an I.V. catheter. Plaintiff points out, however, that there is an available substitute for a conventional I.V. catheter which leaves the introducing needle exposed after it is withdrawn from the flexible tube. The ProtectIV, an I.V. catheter manufactured by Critikon, a competitor of defendant, permits the needle to be retracted into a plastic sheath as it is withdrawn from the tube attached to the patient's vein. Indeed, at the time of plaintiff's injury, defendant itself was marketing a similar device known as the Insyte Saf–T–Cath.[7]

A study of 1024 healthcare workers at nine hospitals in 6 states over a period of six months revealed that the incidence of needle sticks was lower with the ProtectIV, i.e., 2.25 injuries per 100,000 compared to 7.48 injuries per 100,000 conventional devices. * * *

Although a reduction in the total number of needle sticks would obviously lessen the likelihood of serious injury, the projected risks of HIV exposure and infection from any one such needle stick are identical to the risks associated with a needle stick from a conventional catheter, since the rate of HIV exposure and infection depend upon the patient population, not the type of I.V. catheter used. Based upon a projected incidence of 2.25 needle sticks per 100,000 uses of a protected catheter, the projected risk of HIV infection from an I.V. catheter needle stick would be reduced from 3.5/500,000,000 uses with a conventional catheter to 2/1,000,000,000 uses or 1/500,000,000 uses with a protected catheter. Consequently, it appears that an already small risk might be somewhat reduced, but would not be eliminated, by use of a protected rather than a conventional I.V. catheter.

* * *

7. Defendant's alternative catheter was later withdrawn from the market when an injunction was entered in a patent infringement suit brought by Critikon against Becton–Dickinson.

[T]he actual experience of one hospital in the use of conventional and protected catheters confirms that the * * * the projected decrease in that risk with the use of a protected catheter is not likely to be achieved in practice until and unless the healthcare workers using the new device become proficient with it. Indeed, such experience indicates that the risk of injury could initially increase.

Such conclusion is supported by anecdotal evidence relating to certain difficulties and drawbacks inherent in the design of the protected catheter which became evident during the early clinical experiences at Community Hospital of Lancaster. We note, e.g., that contrary to plaintiff's argument that the ProtectIV provides "automatic" protection from an exposed needle, the record shows that the introducer needle is retracted into the protective sheath only if the person initiating the I.V. activates that mechanism by sliding the sheath front, over the needle, as the needle is withdrawn through the catheter. Failure to properly engage the mechanism by fully extending the sheath until it "clicks" allows the sharp tip of the needle to remain exposed, which can, and at Community Hospital of Lancaster did, result in a needle stick.[10]

Moreover, the available evidence also discloses that even if the incidence of needle sticks is ultimately somewhat reduced by using the ProtectIV, a healthcare worker's exposure to a patient's blood may not be significantly reduced since more blood escapes from the catheter as the needle is withdrawn than occurs with a conventional I.V. catheter. * * *

Other problems with the ProtectIV were also reported at Community Hospital of Lancaster, such as: faster deterioration of IV sites; failure of the catheters to lock in place because the catheter, not the needle, penetrated the patient's vein; malfunction, such as the needle penetrating the catheter shaft as it was withdrawn; catheter kinking and bending; difficulty using the catheters on infants, small children, elderly patients and others with difficult veins. Many such problems would likely result in the need for additional I.V. initiations, thereby actually increasing the potential for a needle stick by increasing the number of times an I.V. introducer needle is used.

* * *

Finally, the evidence discloses that the experience of Community Hospital of Lancaster appears to be neither unusual nor unique. In a September, 1992, article in a publication for healthcare workers, a San Francisco hospital employee stated that the design of the protected cathe-

10. As defendant points out, given the undisputed circumstances of plaintiff's accident and the operation of the ProtectIV, it is not at all certain that she could have avoided the needle stick if she had been using it, since she reacted to a patient's sudden movement by an apparently reflexive movement of her own. It is not possible, therefore, to infer that plaintiff would have been able to completely engage the protective mechanism of the ProtectIV before the incident occurred. Had the needle been suddenly withdrawn from the catheter in response to the patient's movement and the tip remained exposed, a needle stick could have occurred, just as it did when a nurse in the hospital's birthing center failed to fully engage the sheath of the ProtectIV in August, 1993.

ter requires improvement and described similar complaints and concerns about the protected catheters as those noted by the staff of the Lancaster hospital. * * *

We conclude, therefore, that although the small projected risk of a needle stick might be further reduced by substituting a protected I.V. catheter for a conventional device, assuming that the user is proficient with the new device, the danger of a needle stick cannot be eliminated. Moreover, a reduction in the incidence of needle sticks is by no means assured, and, even if achieved, blood exposure may not be significantly reduced, if at all, due to a generally recognized "backflow" problem which occurs when the needle is withdrawn from the catheter and the I.V. connection is not completed quickly. We further conclude that other design features of the available substitute product render it less effective, in general, than the Angiocath for its intended purpose, since use of the protected catheter may not be appropriate in some situations due to difficulties that cannot be easily overcome, if at all, with certain patients.

Thus, although a substitute for a conventional I.V. catheter is available which may reduce the incidence of needle sticks, it is not entirely certain that such substitute is safer overall when other aspects of the alternative design are considered and it does not appear to be an alternative which can feasibly replace conventional I.V. catheters completely.

D. Elimination of the Unsafe Character of the Product without Impairing Usefulness or Making It Too Expensive

As already discussed in detail in connection with the availability of a safer, comparable product, there is only one substitute for a conventional I.V. catheter on the market at present. With proper use, the alternative product does not leave the introducer needle exposed after it is withdrawn from the catheter. The protective design, however, does not completely eliminate the danger of a needle stick since failure to properly activate the shielding device still leaves the needle exposed, and, in gaining a small safety improvement with respect to the risk of a needle stick, the alternative product creates other problems which do not occur with the use of a conventional I.V. catheter and which render the redesigned product less suitable for some uses.

In addition, the cost of the protected catheter far exceeds that of the conventional device. At the time the Community Hospital of Lancaster first evaluated the ProtectIV in 1992, the cost was $1.40 per unit compared to $.78 for the Angiocath. Moreover, the unit cost of the catheters is not the only cost consideration. As noted, the evidence establishes the need for extensive training with the ProtectIV in order to gain the benefit of somewhat fewer needle sticks and to overcome the problems inherent in other aspects of the product to the greatest possible extent. The additional costs associated with training hundreds of hospital workers prior to introducing the protected device for general use, combined with the potential need for follow-up in-servicing, as occurred at Community Hospital of Lancaster, are also costs associated with use of the alternative product.

Although plaintiff argues that such increased costs of a substitute product are defensible in light of the devastating effects of the injury that she sustained, we note again that we are here concerned with the magnitude of the increased costs in light of the magnitude of the theoretical risks of a needle stick and the consequent costs associated with that risk of injury. In that regard, a discussion of the feasibility and desirability of using products designed to prevent needle sticks noted that "Hospitals should not pay an excessive amount to achieve only a minimal reduction in risk." The authors of the study also suggested an appropriate cost differential based upon the average costs of any needle stick injury: "On average, needlesticks cost an overall 36% above the purchase price of the devices. Thus, a hospital could pay an additional 36% for preventive devices (assuming that they would totally eliminate the costs associated with needle sticks) without increasing total costs."

It is clear, however, that needle sticks, and their associated increased costs, cannot be completely eliminated. Moreover, the authors of the discussion quoted above based their recommendation on the average costs associated with injuries from all types of needles likely to be encountered in a hospital. For present purposes, however, it is more accurate to use the increased needle stick costs associated only with I.V. stylets, which the authors estimate at 10% of the cost of such devices.

Based upon evidence submitted by plaintiff, therefore, it appears that the higher unit cost of a protected catheter would be reasonable in light of its expected benefits if it were 10%–36% above the cost of an unprotected device.

By that measure, it is clear that the unit cost of the ProtectIV, approximately 80% above the cost of the Angiocath, is very high in light of the small benefit likely to be derived from the possible reduction, but not elimination, of the risk of a needle stick. Moreover, the increased unit cost does not include the costs of inservice training or the potential for higher usage due to faster deterioration of I.V. sites.

Thus, we conclude that it is not possible to eliminate the unsafe feature of the Angiocath without impairing its utility since the costs of the only available alternative product are much higher; the risk associated with the allegedly unsafe design cannot be completely eliminated; and there are problems other than the risk of a needle stick associated with the use of the alternative design which require extensive training to diminish and which cannot be entirely eliminated.

E. The User's Ability to Avoid Danger by Exercising Care in the Use of the Product

* * *

We conclude that just as the design of the protected catheter cannot completely prevent needle sticks from the use of I.V. catheters, it is unlikely that even extreme caution and punctilious adherence to recommended procedures can enable a healthcare worker to completely avoid that danger. Nevertheless, it does appear that healthcare facilities and healthcare workers themselves have some ability to reduce the risk inherent in the use of any I.V. catheter by taking appropriate precautions.

F. The User's Anticipated Awareness of the Dangers and Their Avoidability

The sheer size of the record produced in support of and in opposition to the instant motion, including many articles written for healthcare providers concerning the risks of exposure to blood-borne diseases from needle sticks, indicates that there is widespread knowledge of the potential danger of a needle stick accident among healthcare workers. Indeed, plaintiff does not contend that the danger inherent in an exposed needle is hidden, generally unknown to healthcare workers, or that she was personally unaware of such danger.

G. Feasibility on the Part of the Manufacturer of Spreading the Loss

* * *

As plaintiff suggests, a conclusion by the Court that the manufacturer of the Angiocath may be required to assume responsibility for compensating those injured while using it could lead to its withdrawal from the market, or, at least, to such a substantial increase in its cost as to minimize or eliminate the cost differential between the Angiocath and the alternative product, the ProtectIV, potentially leading to increased acceptance of the needle-sheathing design. The Court must, therefore, determine whether, as the plaintiff vigorously contends, that result is desirable and should be encouraged.

Based upon a consideration of all the evidence, we conclude that such a potential manipulation of the market for peripheral I.V. catheters should not be undertaken as a consequence of one of three tragic accidents which occurred during 16 years of experience with defendant's I.V. catheter products by a multitude of healthcare workers, especially where the alternative product is certainly not without its own dangers and other drawbacks and where the product in question appears to be functionally superior to the alternative in all respects other than leaving the needle exposed after it is withdrawn from the catheter.

Moreover, we conclude that in this case, there would be no adverse effect to plaintiff or to the public in general as a result of not shifting the costs of plaintiff's injury to the manufacturer of the product, thereby allowing the costs to remain where they are currently allocated: on the plaintiff's employer via the Workmen's Compensation system. At the time of plaintiff's accident, Community Hospital of Lancaster required the use of the Angiocath by refusing to purchase the alternative product. * * *

[I]f the Angiocath was not the best or safest product for plaintiff to use under the circumstances which existed at the time of her accident, the fact that she had no choice but to proceed with the use of a less desirable alternative was due entirely her employer's decision. Hence, it would be unfair to expect the manufacturer of the Angiocath to spread the costs of plaintiff's injury to all users thereof, including those healthcare facilities which might take more care to assure that a variety of products are available to their staffs in order to permit their employees to select the most appropriate device for various circumstances.

* * *

H. Summary

Having examined each factor in the risk/utility analysis which both parties agree is applicable to this case in the light of the available evidence, we conclude that the Angiocath, although dangerous because it is capable of causing serious injury, is not unreasonably dangerous as that term is defined in Pennsylvania law.

* * *

VI. Conclusion

Having carefully considered the extensive evidence, arguments of counsel and other submissions of the parties in connection with a risk/utility analysis undertaken pursuant to Pennsylvania law governing strict liability claims, we conclude that the product in question, the Angiocath peripheral I.V. catheter manufactured and sold by defendant, is not unreasonably dangerous, and, therefore, is not defective as a matter of law. Accordingly, defendant's motion for summary judgment will be granted and judgment will be entered in favor of the defendant.

Order

And now, this 27th day of December, 1995, upon consideration of defendant's Motion for Summary Judgment, and plaintiff's response thereto, IT IS HEREBY ORDERED that the motion is GRANTED.

IT IS FURTHER ORDERED that judgment is entered in favor of the defendant and against the plaintiff.

NOTES

1. Why aren't all of the issues discussed by the court properly questions for the jury? Do you think the plaintiff failed to present a prima facie case? Do you believe that the trial court's grant of a summary judgment would be overturned on appeal?

2. At several points in his opinion, Judge Troutman noted that the focus of the risk-utility analysis should be on the theoretical risk of injury to all users of the product, not the particular injury suffered by the plaintiff. Do you

agree? Do you believe the average jury would adopt this point of view? Consider the comments of Judge Easterbrook in Carroll v. Otis Elevator Co., 896 F.2d 210 (7th Cir. 1990). In *Carroll,* an unidentified child pushed the emergency stop button on an escalator, causing the plaintiff to fall and injure her knee. The plaintiff argued that the escalator was defectively designed because the "emergency stop button was unguarded and unreasonably attractive and operable by children." The jury awarded the plaintiff $43,000.

> The *ex post* perspective of litigation exerts a hydraulic force that distorts judgment. Engineers design escalators to minimize the sum of construction, operation, and injury costs. Department stores, which have nothing to gain from maiming their customers and employees, willingly pay for cost-effective precautions. Some persons will be injured when caught in the escalator; these costs go down as emergency stop buttons are easy to find and press. Others will be injured as escalators suddenly stop; these costs will go down as stop buttons are hard to find and press. Escalators move slowly, so stops rarely cause falls (and falls rarely cause serious injuries); passengers with poor balance or frail constitution may protect themselves by holding the handrails. Because the expected costs of stops are small, designers make buttons easy to find and press, to reduce the costs of the rarer, but much more serious, entanglements. The machines they have designed are safer than stairs.
>
> Come the lawsuit, however, the passenger injured by a stop presents himself as a person, not a probability. Jurors see today's injury; persons who would be injured if buttons were harder to find and use are invisible. Although witnesses may talk about them, they are spectral figures, insubstantial compared to the injured plaintiff, who appears in the flesh. * * * [N]o matter how conscientious jurors may be, there is a bias in the system. *Ex post* claims are overvalued and technical arguments discounted in the process of litigation.

Carroll, 896 F.2d at 215–16. If Judge Easterbrook is correct, how should products defendants respond? Should they, for example report in detail on their risk assessment studies so as to demonstrate to jurors that they have made the correct risk-utility tradeoff? *See* W. Kip Viscusi, *Corporate Risk Analysis: A Reckless Act?*, 52 Stan. L. Rev. 547 (2000); Robert J. MacCoun, *The Costs and Benefits of Letting Juries Punish Corporations: Comment on Viscusi*, 52 Stan. L. Rev. 1821 (2000).

3. The court clearly places much of the responsibility for the plaintiff's injury in *Riley* on her employer. Many products liability cases arise in the employment context, frequently involving machinery by the use of which the plaintiff has been injured. As indicated in the *Riley* opinion, most states have adopted workers' compensation statutes, discussed in more detail in Chapter Six, *infra,* which replace tort law in this situation with a no-fault, statutory remedy. However, these statutes limit the damages that may be recovered. Thus, there is a strong incentive to sue the manufacturer under products liability. Occasionally, these cases have involved situations in which the employer has been given an equipment option and has chosen the less safe design. The manufacturer is nevertheless held liable. Hammond v. International Harvester Co., 691 F.2d 646 (3d Cir. 1982) (applying Pennsylvania

law). *But see* Caterpillar, Inc. v. Shears, 911 S.W.2d 379 (Tex. 1995). The same result has sometimes occurred where the employer or even the employee has altered the machine to eliminate safety provisions, at least if the machine could have been designed to make such alteration difficult. The theory is that the employer's motive to speed up production by eliminating safety provisions, or pressuring workers to do so, is foreseeable and, failure to anticipate this potential alteration in the design of the machine, makes the product defective. *See* Knitz v. Minster Machine Co., 69 Ohio St.2d 460, 432 N.E.2d 814 (1982). What role should employer negligence play in products cases?

4. *More on Reasonable Alternative Design.* The existence of an alternative design is central to both *Branham* and *Riley*. The most controversial provision in *Restatement (Third) of Torts: Products Liability* was § 2(b)'s requirement that the plaintiff demonstrate a reasonable alternative design in order to prevail in a design defect case.

Comment *d.* elaborates:

> Subsection (b) adopts a reasonableness ("risk-utility balancing") test as the standard for judging the defectiveness of product designs. More specifically, the test is whether a reasonable alternative design would, at reasonable cost, have reduced the foreseeable risks of harm posed by the product and, if so, whether the omission of the alternative design by the seller or a predecessor in the distributive chain rendered the product not reasonably safe. (This is the primary, but not the exclusive, test for defective design. See Comment *b*). Under prevailing rules concerning allocation of burden of proof, the plaintiff must prove that such a reasonable alternative was, or reasonably could have been, available at time of sale or distribution.

Comment *b*, referred to in the above passage, acknowledges that sometimes a plaintiff may be able to prove a design defect through circumstantial evidence arising from the way a product malfunctions. *See Restatement (Third) of Torts: Products Liability* § 3, *supra*, p. 199. The plaintiff also may be able to prove a product is defectively designed by showing that it failed to comply with government product safety statutes or regulations. *See Restatement (Third) of Torts: Products Liability* § 4. Finally, Comment *e* to Section 2 recognizes the possibility that when a design is manifestly unreasonable a seller may be subject to liability even absent a reasonable alternative design.

Even with these caveats, some courts have rejected the Restatement's position. Potter v. Chicago Pneumatic Tool Co., 241 Conn. 199, 694 A.2d 1319 (1997); Delaney v. Deere and Co. 268 Kan. 769, 999 P.2d 930 (2000). *But see* Wright v. Brooke Group Ltd., 652 N.W.2d 159 (Iowa 2002) (adopting §§ 1 and 2 of the Third Restatement).

The plaintiffs in *Potter* were injured as a result of using pneumatic hand tools that were allegedly defectively designed because they exposed the plaintiffs to excessive vibration. The court refused to adopt the Third Restatement's risk utility approach because of its alternative design requirement. Instead, it reaffirmed the State's reliance on the consumer expectations test for design defects.

And what of the fact that consumers have no reasonable expectations with respect to many complex products? The *Potter* court addressed the problem in the following passage:

> Although today we continue to adhere to our long-standing rule that a product's defectiveness is to be determined by the expectations of an ordinary consumer, we nevertheless recognize that there may be instances involving complex product designs in which an ordinary consumer may not be able to form expectations of safety. * * * In such cases, a consumer's expectations may be viewed in light of various factors that balance the utility of the product's design with the magnitude of its risks. We find persuasive the reasoning of those jurisdictions that have modified their formulation of the consumer expectation test by incorporating risk-utility factors into the ordinary consumer expectation analysis. * * * Thus, the modified consumer expectation test provides the jury with the product's risks and utility and then inquires whether a reasonable consumer would consider the product unreasonably dangerous.
>
> * * *
>
> In our view, the relevant factors that a jury *may* consider include, but are not limited to, the usefulness of the product, the likelihood and severity of the danger posed by the design, the feasibility of an alternative design, the financial cost of an improved design, the ability to reduce the product's danger without impairing its usefulness or making it too expensive, and the feasibility of spreading the loss by increasing the product's price.

Potter, 694 A.2d at 1333–334.

Which approach is preferable, *Potter* or the Restatement?

O'Brien v. Muskin, 94 N.J. 169, 463 A.2d 298 (1983) is an earlier opinion adopting the position that the plaintiff does not need to show an alternative design. O'Brien suffered a serious injury when he dove head first into an above-ground swimming pool. His outstretched hands hit the pool bottom and slid apart, allowing his head to strike the bottom of the pool. The plaintiff claimed that the pool was defectively designed because it was lined with vinyl, which became slippery when wet. One of the plaintiff's expert witnesses contended that vinyl should not be used in above-ground pools, even though no alternative was available. The trial court refused to allow the plaintiff's design defect claim go to the jury, but the New Jersey Supreme Court affirmed an appellate court reversal. With respect to design alternatives, the court said:

> The evaluation of the utility of a product also involves the relative need for that product; some products are essentials, while others are luxuries. A product that fills a critical need and can be designed in only one way should be viewed differently from a luxury item. Still other products, including some for which no alternative exists, are so dangerous and of such little use that under the risk-utility analysis, a manufacturer would bear the cost of liability of harm to others. That cost might dissuade a manufacturer from placing the product on the market, even if the product has been made as safely as possible. Indeed, plaintiff contends that above-

> ground pools with vinyl liners are such products and that manufacturers who market those pools should bear the cost of injuries they cause to foreseeable users.
>
> A critical issue at trial was whether the design of the pool, calling for a vinyl bottom in a pool four feet deep, was defective. The trial court should have permitted the jury to consider whether, because of the dimensions of the pool and slipperiness of the bottom, the risks of injury so outweighed the utility of the product as to constitute a defect. In removing that issue from consideration by the jury, the trial court erred. To establish sufficient proof to compel submission of the issue to the jury for appropriate fact-finding under risk-utility analysis, it was not necessary for plaintiff to prove the existence of alternative, safer designs. Viewing the evidence in the light most favorable to plaintiff, even if there are no alternative methods of making bottoms for above-ground pools, the jury might have found that the risk posed by the pool outweighed its utility.

O'Brien, 463 A.2d at 306.

New Jersey subsequently passed a products liability statute, which provided in part:

> In any product liability action against a manufacturer or seller for harm allegedly caused by a product that was designed in a defective manner, the manufacturer or seller shall not be liable if: (1) At the time the product left the control of the manufacturer, there was not a practical and technically feasible alternative design that would have prevented the harm without substantially impairing the reasonably anticipated or intended function of the product;

NJ ST 2A: 58C–3(a)(1).

In light of the statute, it is not surprising that the expansive language of *O'Brien* has been reined in by subsequent opinions. In Smith v. Keller Ladder Co., 275 N.J.Super. 280, 645 A.2d 1269 (1994), a jury returned a verdict of $115,000 for the plaintiff who fell off of the defendant's ladder. The appellate court affirmed a trial court j.n.o.v. because the plaintiff "failed to present any evidence suggesting either that there was a reasonably feasible alternative design which would have made defendant's ladder safer, or that the ladder was so dangerous and of so little use that defendant should bear the liability." *Smith*, 645 A.2d at 1271.

The New Jersey statute is one of many that have been passed in recent years, a number of which, like New Jersey, require the plaintiff to present evidence of an alternative design in order to prevail. Following, is the relevant Texas provision.

> **Design Defects**
>
> (a) In a products liability action in which a claimant alleges a design defect, the burden is on the claimant to prove by a preponderance of the evidence that:
>
> (1) there was a safer alternative design; and
>
> (2) the defect was a producing cause of the personal injury, property damage, or death for which the claimant seeks recovery.

(b) In this section, "safer alternative design" means a product design other than the one actually used that in reasonable probability:

(1) would have prevented or significantly reduced the risk of the claimant's personal injury, property damage, or death without substantially impairing the product's utility; and

(2) was economically and technologically feasible at the time the product left the control of the manufacturer or seller by the application of existing or reasonably achievable scientific knowledge.

Tex. Civ. Prac. & Rem. Code § 82.005.

As a practical matter, in most cases isn't it unlikely that the plaintiff will be able to persuade the trier of fact that the defendant's design is defective without introducing some evidence of a safer alternative?

5. Cigarettes could be thought of as a good example of a product whose risks outweigh its utility even in the absence of an alternative design. In fact, in Horton v. American Tobacco Company, 667 So.2d 1289 (Miss. 1995), a jury returned a verdict for the plaintiff on an undifferentiated risk-utility products liability theory. (However, the jury awarded zero damages because of plaintiff's contributory negligence. Plaintiff admitted that since 1966 he had read and disregarded the warnings on packs of cigarettes. *Id.* at 1290).

In 1993 the Mississippi legislature passed a products liability statute that on its face would prevent such findings in the future by requiring proof of an alternative feasible design. Similarly, earlier New Jersey cases that suggested a plaintiff might proceed with a design defect claim in a tobacco case without showing an alternative feasible design (Dewey v. R.J. Reynolds Tobacco Co., 216 N.J.Super. 347, 523 A.2d 712 (Law Div.1986), *rev'd in part, aff'd in part,* Dewey v. R.J. Reynolds Tobacco Co., 121 N.J. 69, 577 A.2d 1239 (1990)) were rendered moot by the New Jersey products liability statute cited above. Courts in other jurisdictions have rejected a general risk/utility test under which a tobacco product could be found to be "unreasonable per se," thereby making it a tort to market the product at all. Hite v. R.J. Reynolds Tobacco Co., 396 Pa.Super. 82, 578 A.2d 417 (1990); Kotler v. American Tobacco Co., 926 F.2d 1217, 1225–26 (1st Cir.1990), *vacated*, 505 U.S. 1215, 112 S.Ct. 3019, 120 L.Ed.2d 891 (1992), *reaff'd*, 981 F.2d 7 (1st Cir.1992) (interpreting Massachusetts law); Brown v. R.J. Reynolds Tobacco Co., 852 F.Supp. 8 (E.D.La.1994) (applying Louisiana products liability statute). For general assessments of the litigation surrounding tobacco, *see* Gary Schwartz, *Tobacco Liability in the Courts in* SMOKING POLICY: LAW, POLITICS AND CULTURE pp. 131–160 (Robert Rabin & Stephen Sugarman eds., 1993); Carl T. Bogus, *War on the Common Law: The Struggle at the Center of Products Liability,* 60 Mo. L. Rev. 1 (1995); Robert L. Rabin, *The Tobacco Litigation: A Tentative Assessment*, 51 DePaul L. Rev. 331 (2001); Robert L. Rabin, *Tobacco Control Strategies: Past Efficacy and Future Promise*, 41 Loy. L.A. L. Rev. 1721 (2008); James A. Henderson and Aaron Twerski, *Reaching Equilibrium in Tobacco Litigation*, 62 S.C. L. Rev. 67 (2010).

6. In footnote 7 of the *Riley* opinion, the court noted that the defendant's introduction of a retractable catheter was met with an injunction in a patent infringement claim brought by its competitor. Is it possible for one

company to patent the best feasible design and effectively force all other manufacturers to use an inferior design that might be considered defective in subsequent products liability litigation? If a design is patented, does this mean that the design is not "feasible" for other manufacturers? One way to think about this issue is to ask whether products liability law requires the manufacturer to use the "best" design. What position did the *Branham* court take on this question?

PROBLEM: DESIGN DEFECT

Samuel Bailey was killed in a boating accident. Mr. Bailey was alone in the boat when the accident occurred. According to witnesses in other boats, Bailey's bass boat struck an underwater tree stump, throwing him into the water. With its motor still running, the boat turned sharply and circled back toward the stump. Bailey was killed by the propeller, but it is unclear whether he was struck when first thrown out or after the boat circled back toward him. Bailey's widow has filed a wrongful death claim against the boat manufacturer. The plaintiff claims the product was defectively designed because of the failure of the motor to turn off automatically when Bailey was thrown from the boat.

Bailey's expert is prepared to argue that the boat should have been equipped with a safety device known as a "kill switch." At the time of Bailey's death several types of kill switches were available on new boats. However, at the time the Bailey boat was manufactured in 1973 such switches were not installed on new boats.

George Horton, Bailey's expert, was the inventor of a kill switch designed for bass boats such as Bailey's. Horton began developing his "Quick Kill" in November of 1972 and applied for a patent in January of 1973. According to Horton, his invention required no breakthroughs in the state of the art of manufacturing or production. He stated that his invention was simple: a lanyard connects the operator's body to a device that fits over the ignition key. If the operator moves, the lanyard is pulled, the device rotates, and the ignition switch turns off. When he began to market his "Quick Kill," the response by boat dealers was very positive, which Horton perceived to be due to the filling of a recognized need. He considered the kill switch to be a necessary safety device for a bass boat with stick steering. If the kill switch were hooked up and the operator thrown out, the killing of the motor would prevent the boat from circling back where it came from. Horton also testified that for 30 years racing boats had been using various types of kill switches. Thus, the concept of kill switches was not new.

Defense experts challenge the feasibility of equipping bass boats with kill switches or similar devices in March of 1973, when the boat was assembled and sold. The defense got plaintiff's expert, Horton to admit at deposition that until he obtained the patent for his "Quick Kill" in 1974 he kept the idea to himself. Before he began to manufacture them, he investigated the market for competitive devices and found none. Horton, first became aware of competitive devices in August of 1974. Other individuals in the bass boat business are prepared to testify that kill switches were not available in 1973. The first time they sold bass boats with such devices was in 1974 although homemade foot buttons had long been in use on high speed racing boats.

The Bailey accident occurred on a lake that constitutes the border between two states. It is not as yet clear in which state the accident occurred and because both states strongly adhere to a choice of law rule that applies the law of the state in which an accident occurs, it is not clear which law will apply. Unfortunately, the law in the two states could not be much more different. State A law on design defects is similar to that in *Branham* and the *Restatement (Third) of Torts: Products Liability*. However, State B law on this issue is similar to that in *Potter* (*supra* note 4, p. 232)

A partner in the firm representing the defendant asks you to write a memo assessing the merits of the plaintiff's design defect claim in each state.

GRUNDBERG v. UPJOHN CO.

Supreme Court of Utah, 1991.
813 P.2d 89.

DURHAM, JUSTICE:

* * * The issue before us is whether Utah adopts the "unavoidably unsafe products" exception to strict products liability as set forth in Comment k to section 402A of the Restatement (Second) of Torts (1965) ("comment k"). This question presents an unanswered issue of law for original disposition by this court.

We hold that a drug approved by the United States Food and Drug Administration ("FDA"), properly prepared, compounded, packaged, and distributed, cannot as a matter of law be "defective" in the absence of proof of inaccurate, incomplete, misleading, or fraudulent information furnished by the manufacturer in connection with FDA approval. We acknowledge that by characterizing all FDA-approved prescription medications as "unavoidably unsafe," we are expanding the literal interpretation of comment k.

The following facts are taken from the federal district court's certification order. Mildred Lucille Coats died at age 83 from gunshot wounds inflicted by her daughter, Ilo Grundberg, on June 19, 1988. Grundberg and Janice Gray, the personal representative of Coat's estate, brought this action, alleging that Grundberg shot her mother as a result of ingesting the drug Halcion, a prescription drug manufactured by defendant Upjohn to treat insomnia.[11]

Plaintiffs allege that Grundberg took a .5 milligram dose of Halcion the day she shot her mother. They allege that this dose was recommended by her physician and was consistent with Upjohn's recommended dosage. Plaintiffs assert that Grundberg shot her mother while in a state of Halcion-induced intoxication, which allegedly included side effects such as depression, psychosis, depersonalization, aggressive assaultive behavior, and homicidal compulsion.

11. Halcion is the trade name of the drug triazolam.

* * * Plaintiffs claim that Upjohn failed to adequately warn about certain adverse side effects of Halcion and that Halcion was defectively designed. The failure-to-warn claim is scheduled for trial. The strict liability claim based on design defect is the subject of Upjohn's pending summary judgment motion, the outcome of which depends on this court's resolution of the certified question.

The parties agree that the Restatement (Second) of Torts section 402A, comment k (1965) and the principles it embodies provide an exemption from strict liability for a claimed design defect in the case of products that are "unavoidably unsafe." * * *

Specifically, the issues we address at the request of the federal court are:

1. Does Utah adopt the "unavoidably unsafe products" exception to strict products liability as set forth in comment k to section 402A of the *Restatement (Second) of Torts* (1965)?

(a) If Utah does adopt comment k, should FDA-approved prescription drugs be deemed as a matter of law to have satisfied the "unavoidably unsafe" prerequisite to the comment k exception, or should that determination be made on a case-by-case basis?

(b) If Utah does adopt comment k, and if it is further determined that its application to FDA-approved prescription drugs ought to be made on a case-by-case basis, is such determination a threshold question for the trial court or a question properly to be presented to the jury?

* * *

In its entirety, comment k reads:

k. Unavoidably unsafe products. There are some products which, in the present state of human knowledge, are quite incapable of being made safe for their intended and ordinary use. These are especially common in the field of drugs. An outstanding example is the vaccine for the Pasteur treatment of rabies, which not uncommonly leads to very serious and damaging consequences when it is injected. Since the disease itself invariably leads to a dreadful death, both the marketing and the use of the vaccine are fully justified, notwithstanding the unavoidable high degree of risk which they involve. Such a product, properly prepared, and accompanied by proper directions and warning, is not defective, nor is it unreasonably dangerous. The same is true of many other drugs, vaccines, and the like, many of which for this very reason cannot legally be sold except to physicians, or under the prescription of a physician. It is also true in particular of many new or experimental drugs as to which, because of lack of time and opportunity for sufficient medical experience, there can be no assurance of safety, or perhaps even of purity of ingredients, but such experience as there is justifies the marketing and use of the drug notwithstanding a medically recognizable risk. The seller of such products, again with the qualification that they are properly prepared and marketed, and proper warning is given, where the situation calls for it, is not to be held to strict liability for unfortunate consequences attending their use, merely because he has undertaken to supply the public with an apparently useful and desirable product, attended with a known but apparently reasonable risk.

* * *

We agree with comment k's basic proposition—that there are some products that have dangers associated with their use even though they are used as intended. We also agree that the seller of such products, when the products are properly prepared and marketed and distributed with appropriate warnings, should not be held strictly liable for the "unfortunate consequences" attending their use. Thus, we adopt comment k's basic policy as the law to be applied in this state and must now turn to the issue of how to apply that policy.

* * *

By its terms, comment k excepts unavoidably unsafe products from strict liability only to the extent that the plaintiff alleges a design defect; comment k's immunity from strict liability does not extend to strict liability claims based on a manufacturing flaw or an inadequate warning. The purpose of comment k is to protect from strict liability products that cannot be designed more safely. If, however, such products are mismanufactured or unaccompanied by adequate warnings, the seller may be liable even if the plaintiff cannot establish the seller's negligence.

* * *

Even in the case of a clearly alleged design defect, however, comment k is unclear on the scope of its protection.

* * *

Some courts have applied comment k on a case-by-case basis, conditioning application of the exemption on a finding that the drug is in fact "unavoidably unsafe." see Feldman v. Lederle Laboratories, 97 N.J. 429, 479 A.2d 374, 382–83 (1984) (involving allegations of failure to warn, but stating, "Whether a drug is unavoidably unsafe should be decided on a case-by-case basis....")

California was the first state to fashion a risk/benefit test to determine which drugs are entitled to comment k protection. In Kearl v. Lederle Laboratories, 172 Cal.App.3d 812, 218 Cal.Rptr. 453 (1985), the California Court of Appeal specifically discussed the problems society would face by subjecting drugs to the same accountability as other products, allowing unlimited redress for plaintiffs injured by pharmaceutical products. Such problems, the court noted, include delayed availability of needed drugs and imposition of the costs of research, development, and marketing of new products beyond that which manufacturers, especially small manufacturers, might be willing to risk. (quoting Feldman, 460 A.2d at 209).

The Kearl court expressed discomfort, however, with the "mechanical" method by which many appellate courts had concluded that drugs are entitled to special treatment. Thus, Kearl set forth a risk/benefit analysis to be carried out by the trial court on a case-by-case basis. Under this approach, a product may be deemed unavoidably unsafe and thus exempt from a strict liability design defect cause of action only if the court concludes that (1) the product was intended to provide an exceptionally important benefit, and (2) the risk posed was substantial and unavoidable when distributed.

Idaho adopted and to some extent refined the Kearl approach in Toner v. Lederle Laboratories, 112 Idaho 328, 732 P.2d 297 (1987), a case addressing a suit against the manufacturer of a vaccine to immunize against diphtheria, pertussis, and tetanus ("DPT").

* * *

In direct contrast to those courts applying comment k's immunity on a case-by-case basis are courts holding that all prescription drugs are entitled as a matter of law to the exemption from strict liability claims based on design defect. In Brown v. Superior Court, 44 Cal.3d 1049, 245 Cal.Rptr. 412, 751 P.2d 470 (1988), the court addressed claims brought by plaintiffs who sued drug companies for injuries allegedly arising from their mothers' in utero exposure to diethylstilbestrol, a synthetic hormone marketed for use during pregnancy. The court weighed the problem of whether imposing strict liability on drug manufacturers comports with the traditional goals of tort law, namely, deterrence and cost distribution. The court acknowledged that a drug might be safer if pharmaceutical companies withheld it from the market until scientific skill and knowledge advanced to the point where all dangerous side effects could be discovered. There was concern, however, that this delay, when added to the delay normally required for the FDA to approve a new drug, would not serve the public welfare. The court cited examples of several potentially useful drugs being withdrawn from the market or their availability seriously curtailed because of the liability crisis.

The Brown court acknowledged the appeal of the Kearl cost/benefit approach, yet found the "mini-trial" procedure unworkable because of its negative impact on the development and marketing of new drugs. Another of the Brown court's objections to Kearl was that it left the trial court to hear and resolve mixed questions of law and fact, placing the trial court in the role of fact finder. The court found the cost/benefit test too open-ended and predicted that it would lead to disparate treatment of the same drug by different judges.

The Brown court stressed three public policies mitigating against imposing strict liability for prescription drugs. First, drug manufacturers might stop producing valuable drugs because of lost profits resulting from lawsuits or the inability to secure adequate insurance. Second, consumers have a vested interest in prompt availability of new pharmaceutical products. Imposing strict liability for design defects might cause manufacturers to delay placing new products on the market, even after those products receive FDA approval. Finally, the added expense of insuring against strict liability and additional research programs might cause the cost of medication to increase to the extent that it would no longer be affordable to consumers.

* * *

In reviewing the approaches of other jurisdictions toward strict products liability for design defects in drug products, we are troubled by the lack of uniformity and certainty inherent in the case-by-case approach and fear the resulting disincentive for pharmaceutical manufacturers to develop new products.

* * *

We agree with Brown that the case-by-case method first articulated in Kearl is unworkable.* * * We find the Brown result more in line with the public policy considerations in the important area of pharmaceutical product design. We do not agree, however, with the Brown court's apparent attempt to use the plain language of comment k as the vehicle for exempting all prescription drugs from strict liability rather than relying on the policies underlying that comment.

The American Law Institute's restatements are drafted by legal scholars who attempt to summarize the state of the law in a given area, predict how the law is changing, and suggest the direction the law should take. The restatement serves an appropriate advisory role to courts in approaching unsettled areas of law. We emphasize, however, that section 402A of the Restatement (Second) of Torts, as drafted in 1965, is not binding on our decision in this case except insofar as we explicitly adopt its various doctrinal principles. We agree with the principle comment k embodies, that manufacturers of unavoidably dangerous products should not be liable for a claim of design defect. We are persuaded that all prescription drugs should be classified as unavoidably dangerous in design because of their unique nature and value, the elaborate regulatory system overseen by the FDA, the difficulties of relying on individual lawsuits as a forum in which to review a prescription drug's design, and the significant public policy considerations noted in Brown. We therefore reach the same conclusion as did the California Supreme Court in Brown, albeit pursuant to a slightly different rationale.

III. Unique Characteristics of Drugs

* * *

Despite inherent risks, and in contrast to any other product, society has determined that prescription medications provide a unique benefit and so should be available to physicians with appropriate warnings and guidance as to use. The federal government has established an elaborate regulatory system, overseen by the FDA, to control the approval and distribution of these drugs. See 21 U.S.C. §§ 301–393. No other class of products is subject to such special restrictions or protections in our society.

IV. FDA Regulation

Congress created the FDA to "protect consumers from dangerous products." United States v. Sullivan, 332 U.S. 689, 696, 68 S.Ct. 331, 335, 92 L.Ed. 297 (1948). In its role as "both a health promoter . . . and . . . a public protector," the FDA employs a comprehensive scheme of premarket screening and post-market surveillance to ensure the safety and efficacy of all licensed medications. 50 Fed.Reg. 7452 (1985).

Before licensing a new medication, the FDA employs an extensive screening mechanism to ensure that the potential benefits of the product outweigh any associated risks. The manufacturer initiates the review by submitting an Investigational New Drug Application ("IND"), containing information about the drug's chemistry, manufacturing, pharmacology, and toxicology. See 21 U.S.C. s 355(b)(1)(Supp.1991); 21 C.F.R. s 312.21 (1990). If the FDA approves the IND, the drug's sponsor may gather data on clinical safety and efficacy needed for a New Drug Application ("NDA"), the formal license application. The NDA must include very detailed reports of all animal studies and clinical testing performed with the drug, reports of any adverse reactions, and any other pertinent information from world-wide scientific literature. 21 U.S.C. § 355(b) (Supp.1991); 21 C.F.R. § 314.50 (1990).

The new drug approval process can require years of testing and review. By the time an NDA is submitted, it often consists of thousands of pages of material describing studies of the drug in several hundred to several thousand patients. See 47 Fed.Reg. 46626 (Oct. 19, 1982). The FDA carefully scrutinizes the data supporting the NDA, requiring "substantial evidence" consisting of adequate and well-controlled investigations. 21 U.S.C. § 355(d) (Supp.1991). The application is reviewed by physicians, pharmacologists, chemists, microbiologists, statisticians, and other professionals within the FDA's National Center for Drugs and Biologics who are experienced in evaluating new drugs. 47 Fed.Reg. 46626 (Oct. 19, 1982). Recommendations by those professionals are then reviewed by management personnel within the National Center for Drugs and Biologics before the FDA makes a final determination to approve or reject the new drug application. Id.

Elaborate premarket screening, however, does not ensure review of approved prescription medications where adverse reactions may appear after extensive preapproval testing. For this reason, the FDA also conducts extensive post-market surveillance. All reports of adverse drug reactions ("ADRs") must be reported to the FDA, regardless of whether the physician, the manufacturer, or others believe the reaction to be drug-related. 21 C.F.R. § 314.80(b). The manufacturer must also periodically submit reports as to what actions it took in response to ADRs and must submit data from any post-marketing studies, reports in the scientific literature, and foreign marketing experience. 21 C.F.R. §§ 314.80(b),

.80(c). The FDA has authority to enforce these reporting requirements; any failure to comply may subject a manufacturer to civil and criminal penalties. 21 U.S.C. §§ 332–34 (1972 & Supp.1991). In response to its surveillance findings, the FDA may require labeling changes or if necessary withdraw NDA approval and thereby revoke the license to market the medication. Id. at § 355(e).

We find this extensive regulatory scheme capable of and appropriate for making the preliminary determination regarding whether a prescription drug's benefits outweigh its risks. The structured follow-up program imposed by law ensures that drugs are not placed on the market without continued monitoring for adverse consequences that would render the FDA's initial risk/benefit analysis invalid. Allowing individual courts and/or juries to continually reevaluate a drug's risks and benefits ignores the processes of this expert regulatory body and the other avenues of recovery available to plaintiffs.

* * *

V. Proper Forum for Risk/Benefit Analysis

Finally, we do not believe that a trial court in the context of a products liability action is the proper forum to determine whether, as a whole, a particular prescription drug's benefits outweighed its risks at the time of distribution. In a case-by-case analysis, one court or jury's determination that a particular drug is or is not "defectively designed" has no bearing on any future case. As a result, differences of opinion among courts in differing jurisdictions leaves unsettled a drug manufacturer's liability for any given drug. Although the FDA may have internal differences of opinion regarding whether a particular new drug application should be approved, the individuals making the ultimate judgment will have the benefit of years of experience in reviewing such products, scientific expertise in the area, and access to the volumes of data they can compel manufacturers to produce. Nor is the FDA subject to the inherent limitations of the trial process, such as the rules of evidence, restrictions on expert testimony, and scheduling demands.[9]

One commentator has argued that courts as a whole are unsuited to render responsible judgments in the design defect area generally. See Henderson, Judicial Review of Manufacturers' Conscious Design Choices: The Limits of Adjudication, 73 Colum.L.Rev. 1531 (1973). He argues that decisions in this area are arbitrary due to their "polycentric" nature in

9. There is also a certain moral question to be addressed when determining whether a product's benefit outweighs its risk when faced with the reality of an injured plaintiff. For example, in the case of a vaccine, certain benefits of the drug's availability will accrue to group A, the individuals who are prevented from contracting the disease. A smaller number of individuals, however, may contract the disease and react violently to a component of the drug or, as some other result of the drug's properties, suffer terribly. Under a case-by-case approach, courts or juries must ask which is a more significant interest: efficacy with respect to group A versus harm to group B? The FDA must ask the same question: Does the benefit of this product outweigh its risk? The distinction is that the FDA is in a more objective and informed posture to make that determination.

which "each point for decision is related to all the others as are the strands of a spider web." Id. at 1536. These issues are difficult to litigate because

> [i]f one strand is pulled, a complex pattern of readjustments will occur throughout the entire web. If another strand is pulled, the relationships among all the strands will again be readjusted. A lawyer seeking to base [an] argument upon established principle and required to address himself in discourse to each of a dozen strands, or issues, would find [the] task frustratingly impossible. Id.

Although we do not accept the notion that courts are unsuited to address design defect claims in any products liability action, we do agree that prescription drug design presents precisely this type of "polycentric" problem. A drug is designed to be effectively administered to specific individuals for one or a number of indications. To determine whether a drug's benefit outweighs its risk is inherently complex because of the manufacturer's conscious design choices regarding the numerous chemical properties of the product and their relationship to the vast physiologic idiosyncracies of each consumer for whom the drug is designed. Society has recognized this complexity and in response has reposed regulatory authority in the FDA. Relying on the FDA's screening and surveillance standards enables courts to find liability under circumstances of inadequate warning, mismanufacture, improper marketing, or misinforming the FDA—avenues for which courts are better suited. Although this approach denies plaintiffs one potential theory on which to rely in a drug products liability action, the benefits to society in promoting the development, availability, and reasonable price of drugs justifies this conclusion.

In light of the strong public interest in the availability and affordability of prescription medications, the extensive regulatory system of the FDA, and the avenues of recovery still available to plaintiffs by claiming inadequate warning, mismanufacture, improper marketing, or misrepresenting information to the FDA, we conclude that a broad grant of immunity from strict liability claims based on design defects should be extended to FDA-approved prescription drugs in Utah.

HALL, C.J., and ZIMMERMAN, J., concur.

STEWART, JUSTICE (dissenting):

I dissent. The majority holds that a drug that is avoidably unsafe to human life or health is exempt from strict liability for design defects if approved by the FDA, even though alternative drugs can provide the same, or even better, therapy, with less risk to life or health. Thus, such FDA-approved drugs as various decongestants, expectorants, deodorants, hair growth stimulants, skin moisturizers, and cough and cold remedies,[1] for example, have the same immunity as rabies or polio vaccines or medications essential in the treatment of cancer, heart disease, or AIDS. I see no basis for according drugs used to treat comparatively minor

1. The Physicians' Desk Reference (1990 ed.) includes prescription drugs in each of the categories stated in the text.

ailments a blanket immunity from strict liability for design defects if they are unreasonably dangerous to those who use them.

* * *

I agree with Justice Huntley of the Idaho Supreme Court, who stated:

> [N]o state supreme court has yet become convinced that the FDA has either adequate staffing, expertise, or data base to warrant its being substituted for the judicial system.... I fear the day when any supreme court can be convinced that an agency such as the FDA, no matter how well-intentioned, can supplant the American judicial system.

Toner v. Lederle Laboratories, 112 Idaho 328, 344, 732 P.2d 297, 313 (1987) (Huntley, J., concurring specially).

* * *

Numerous congressional investigations have demonstrated that the FDA has often approved drugs in complete ignorance of critical information relating to the hazards of such drugs which was contained either in its own files or in the published medical literature, or both.

* * *

In relying on the efficacy of FDA approval procedures as the basis for dispensing with the judicial remedy of product liability, the majority simply ignores FDA failures to protect the public against unnecessary and unacceptable risks.

* * *

Proposals before Congress and rules promulgated by the FDA to make it easier for pharmaceutical companies to obtain FDA approval for new drugs would dilute even further the safety and efficacy standards for FDA approval of drugs. See Note, Regulation of Investigational New Drugs: "Giant Step for the Sick and Dying?", 77 Georgetown L.J. 463 (1988). Perhaps truly unavoidably unsafe drugs intended to treat life-threatening ailments should be more easily available to the public, but a lessening of safety standards is an argument for strict liability, not against. Profit motivation is likely to lead to many more unnecessarily dangerous drugs.

* * *

Certain drugs clearly qualify for comment k exemption, even though the drugs' risk may be comparatively great. A drug's social utility may be so great, for example, a chemotherapeutic agent used for treatment of cancer, that it would obviously qualify for comment k exemption. Other drugs, such as sleeping compounds or dandruff cures, whose social utility may not be of such a high order, would not automatically qualify.

* * *

The majority opinion states that a case-by-case analysis would leave drug companies uncertain regarding questions of immunity and would result in patchwork verdicts when a drug may be found to be subject to comment k exemption in one case but not subject to the exemption in another case. That consideration has little merit, in my view. We tolerate nonuniformity of result in negligence cases all the time. Nothing this Court does can bring about uniformity of result with respect to drugs. The states are already divided on the issue of whether FDA approval of a drug should confer immunity from design defects, although it appears that no state has gone as far as Utah now does. Suffice to say, a number of courts apply comment k on a case-by-case basis—a task that cannot be avoided even under the majority's position if a strict liability claim is coupled with a negligence claim, as is usually the case.

* * *

In this case, plaintiff Ilo Marie Grundberg was taking a variety of medications for chronic depression and anxiety. Halcion, the medication at issue here, had first been prescribed for Mrs. Grundberg on May 21, 1987. In December 1987, Mrs. Grundberg lost her job and, shortly thereafter, moved with her mother, Mildred Coats, to Hurricane, Utah, where they lived together in a mobile home. On June 19, 1988, Mrs. Grundberg took three medications: Valium, codeine, and Halcion. Later that night, she shot and killed her mother. Mrs. Grundberg was charged with criminal homicide. Because of alienists' reports, the Washington County prosecutor dropped all criminal charges on February 7, 1989. Mrs. Grundberg and Janice Gray, the personal representative of Mrs. Coats' estate, filed this civil action later in 1989. At issue in this case is whether Halcion was the cause of Mrs. Grundberg's bizarre behavior on the night of the homicide.

* * *

[The dissenting opinion of ASSOCIATE CHIEF JUSTICE HOWE is omitted.]

NOTES

1. Why do you think Justice Stewart is willing to grant Comment *k* immunity to chemotherapy drugs used to fight cancer and not to drugs used for more mundane purposes such as fighting dandruff or insomnia? Is it clear that the utility of first type of drug always outweighs its risk? Which type of drug is most likely to skate closer to the risk-benefit tipping point? What about drugs designed to treat chronic conditions such as arthritis, high blood pressure, high cholesterol, and depression?

2. For a review of cases discussing whether products, including drugs, are unavoidably unsafe, *see* Annotation, Products Liability: What is an "Unavoidably Unsafe" Product, 70 A.L.R.4th 16.

3. Most jurisdictions agree with Justice Stewart and have refused to conclude that all prescription drugs are unavoidably unsafe. Rather, Comment *k* is an affirmative defense to be assessed on a case-by-case basis. *See* Savina

v. Sterling Drug, Inc., 247 Kan. 105, 115, 795 P.2d 915, 924 (1990); White v. Wyeth Lab., 40 Ohio St.3d 390, 394, 533 N.E.2d 748, 752 (1988); Freeman v. Hoffman–La Roche, Inc., 260 Neb. 552, 618 N.W.2d 827 (2000); Vondra v. Chevron U.S.A., Inc., 652 F.Supp.2d 999 (D.Neb. 2009) (applying Nebraska law). *But see* Young v. Key Pharmaceuticals, Inc., 130 Wn.2d 160, 922 P.2d 59 (1996). If a jurisdiction does follow the case-by-case approach, should the initial determination as to whether the drug is unavoidably unsafe be made by the judge or left to the jury?

A few cases have completely rejected Comment *k* for all drugs. *See* Shanks v. Upjohn Co., 835 P.2d 1189 (Alaska 1992); Allison v. Merck and Co., Inc., 110 Nev. 762, 878 P.2d 948 (1994). One of the reasons the Alaska court gave for rejecting Comment *k* was that a risk-benefit test "offers the manufacturers of those products intended to be protected by Comment *k* an opportunity to avoid liability for strict liability claims based on a design defect theory. * * * We recognize that by holding that the liability of drug manufacturers should be measured by the second prong of the Barker test, we are taking a position similar to those jurisdictions which apply Comment k to prescription drugs on a case-by-case basis. However, we arrive at this result without specifically relying on Comment k." *Shanks*, 835 P.2d at 1198. Is Comment *k* an unnecessary redundancy in jurisdictions that have adopted a risk-utility test in design defect cases?

4. Most courts that have considered the question have found that Comment *k* applies to medical devices, especially those which are implanted in the human body. See Harwell v. American Med. Systems, Inc., 803 F.Supp. 1287 (M.D.Tenn. 1992) and Tansy v. Dacomed Corp., 890 P.2d 881 (Okl. 1994) (penile prosthesis protected under Comment *k*); McKee v. Moore, 648 P.2d 21 (Okla. 1982) and Terhune v. A.H. Robins, 90 Wn.2d 9, 577 P.2d 975 (1978) (Comment *k* applied to an IUD); Phelps v. Sherwood Medical Industries, 836 F.2d 296 (7th Cir. 1987) and Brooks v. Medtronic, Inc., 750 F.2d 1227 (4th Cir. 1984) (pacemaker and heart catheter covered under Comment *k*); Soufflas v. Zimmer, Inc., 474 F.Supp.2d 737 (E.D.Pa. 2007) (polyethylene tibial components); Breen v. Synthes–Stratec, Inc., 108 Conn.App. 105, 947 A.2d 383 (2008) (dynamic condylar screw plate). *But see* Hawkinson v. A.H. Robins Co., 595 F.Supp. 1290 (D.Colo.1984) (Dalkon Shield); Coursen v. A.H. Robins Co., 764 F.2d 1329 (9th Cir. 1985) (Dalkon Shield). Courts have been reluctant to extend unavoidably unsafe status to products other than prescription medical devices. *See* 70 A.L.R.4th 16 for a review of these cases.

5. The *Restatement (Third) of Torts: Products Liability* (1997) takes a different approach to prescription drugs and medical devices.

§ 6 Liability of Commercial Seller or Distributor for Harm Caused by Prescription Drugs and Medical Devices

(a) A manufacturer of a prescription drug or medical device who sells or otherwise distributes a defective drug or medical device is subject to liability for harm to persons caused by the defect. A prescription drug or medical device is one that may be legally sold or otherwise distributed only pursuant to a health-care provider's prescription.

(b) For purposes of liability under Subsection (a), a prescription drug or medical device is defective if at the time of sale or other distribution the drug or medical device:

(1) contains a manufacturing defect as defined in § 2(a); or

(2) is not reasonably safe due to defective design as defined in Subsection (c); or

(3) is not reasonably safe due to inadequate instructions or warnings as defined in Subsection (d).

(c) A prescription drug or medical device is not reasonably safe due to defective design if the foreseeable risks of harm posed by the drug or medical device are sufficiently great in relation to its foreseeable therapeutic benefits that reasonable health-care providers, knowing of such foreseeable risks and therapeutic benefits, would not prescribe the drug or medical device for any class of patients.

(d) A prescription drug or medical device is not reasonably safe due to inadequate instructions or warnings if reasonable instructions or warnings regarding foreseeable risks of harm are not provided to:

(1) prescribing and other health-care providers who are in a position to reduce the risks of harm in accordance with the instructions or warnings; or

(2) the patient when the manufacturer knows or has reason to know that health-care providers will not be in a position to reduce the risks of harm in accordance with the instructions or warnings.

(e) A retail seller or other distributor of a prescription drug or medical device is subject to liability for harm caused by the drug or device if:

(1) at the time of sale or other distribution the drug or medical device contains a manufacturing defect as defined in § 2(a); or

(2) at or before the time of sale or other distribution of the drug or medical device the retail seller or other distributor fails to exercise reasonable care and such failure causes harm to persons.

As noted in Comment *f* accompanying § 6,

> Subsection (c) reflects the judgment that, as long as a given drug or device provides net benefits for a class of patients, it should be available to them, accompanied by appropriate warnings and instructions. * * * A defendant prescription drug or device manufacturer defeats plaintiff's design claim by establishing one or more contexts in which its product would be prescribed by a reasonable, informed health care provider. * * * Given this very demanding standard, liability is likely to be imposed only under unusual circumstances. The court has the responsibility to determine when the plaintiff has introduced sufficient evidence so that reasonable persons could conclude that plaintiff has met this demanding standard.

This provision has made almost no headway as a replacement for comment *k*. At least one jurisdiction has rejected the Third Restatement approach in favor of the earlier Second Restatement approach. Freeman v. Hoffman–La Roche,

Inc., 260 Neb. 552, 618 N.W.2d 827 (2000). Other courts seem to be satisfied with the Second Restatement approach. *See*, Bryant v. Hoffmann–La Roche, Inc., 262 Ga.App. 401, 585 S.E.2d 723 (2003); Doe v. Solvay Pharmaceuticals, Inc., 350 F.Supp.2d 257 (D.Me. 2004). Why do you think the Third Restatement approach has made so little headway? *See* Teresa Moran Schwartz, *Prescription Products and the Proposed Restatement (Third)*, 61 Tenn. L. Rev. 1357(1994).

6. *Why are drugs special?* Comment *b* of § 6 offers three rationales for giving special treatment to prescription drugs and medical devices: (1) these products present a unique set of risks and benefits because what may be harmful to one person may provide net benefits to another, (2) governmental regulatory agencies adequately review new prescription drugs and devices, effectively keeping dangerous designs from consumers, (3) there is a "learned intermediary" (a treating physician) between the consumer and the manufacturer who is able to direct the right drugs and devices to the right patients. (We discuss the "learned intermediary rule" in the warning defect section, *infra*).

With respect to the first two rationales, could not the same arguments be made about many other products, including automobiles and motorcycles? How about aircraft?

3. WARNING DEFECTS

JOHNSON v. AMERICAN CYANAMID CO.

Supreme Court of Kansas, 1986.
239 Kan. 279, 718 P.2d 1318.

MCFARLAND, JUSTICE:

Emil E. Johnson brought this personal injury action alleging he had contracted poliomyelitis as a result of his infant daughter having been vaccinated by defendant physician, Vernon Branson, utilizing Orimune, an oral polio vaccine manufactured by Lederle Laboratories (a division of defendant American Cyanamid Company). Henceforth in the opinion, the manufacturer of the vaccine will be referred to as American Cyanamid. The jury was instructed on comparison of fault as between the two defendants (no issue of fault was submitted as to the plaintiff). The jury assessed 100% of fault against defendant American Cyanamid and awarded $2,000,000.00 actual damages and $8,000,000.00 punitive damages. American Cyanamid appeals from the judgment against it but specifically does not appeal from the jury's finding of zero fault on the part of defendant Branson.

Facts Relative to Plaintiff's Illness

On September 26, 1975, plaintiff took his infant daughter Laurie to the child's pediatrician, Dr. Vernon Branson, where Orimune, an oral polio vaccine manufactured by American Cyanamid, was administered to her. The sequence of polio vaccination was completed by additional administration of the same vaccine by the same physician on November 24,

1975, and January 14, 1976. In December of 1975 plaintiff became ill and was admitted to the University of Kansas Medical Center on December 9 where his illness was diagnosed as bulbar paralytic poliomyelitis. Plaintiff contends he is totally disabled as a result of the disease. At trial, it was contested whether or not Laurie's vaccination program was the cause of plaintiff's illness, but this is not an issue on appeal.

History of Polio Vaccines

By virtue of the nature of claims of liability asserted against American Cyanamid, much of the evidence at trial concerned the history of the disease poliomyelitis and efforts to control the disease, namely, the development of vaccines and the federal government's efforts to vaccinate the public. Polio was first identified as a disease in the 19th century. Its occurrence became more frequent and in 1952 it claimed 57,897 victims in the United States alone. The federal government and private medical research facilities commenced an all-out effort to conquer the dreaded killer and crippler of so many children and adults. A major breakthrough occurred when Dr. Jonas Salk developed a killed or "inactivated" polio vaccine. This vaccine must be administered by injection. By 1955 the Salk vaccine was being distributed extensively in the United States and new cases of polio were reduced to less than 5,000 per year by 1959. In the late 1950's a new polio vaccine was developed by Dr. Albert Sabin and was widely tested in Europe. The Sabin vaccine is a live polio vaccine which contains greatly weakened or attenuated polio virus. The Sabin vaccine must be given orally.

Although the Salk vaccine had greatly reduced the incidence of polio, the disease remained a significant health threat and pressure was mounting for a federally funded immunization program to bring the disease under control and, it was hoped, eliminate it. By 1961, the bitter controversy was in full bloom as to which of the two types of vaccines—Sabin or Salk—should be the weapon used in the battle against the disease. At that time only the Salk vaccine was being produced in this country although the Sabin vaccine had been used very successfully in Europe. The American Medical Association urged, in 1961, the use of the Sabin vaccine. The federal government solicited American drug firms to produce the Sabin vaccine. United States manufacturers of the Salk vaccine opposed the introduction of the Sabin vaccine. Three manufacturers agreed to manufacture the Sabin vaccine (including American Cyanamid). The Sabin vaccine rapidly replaced the Salk vaccine in the United States and no Salk vaccine has been manufactured in this country since 1968. American Cyanamid is the only United States firm manufacturing polio vaccine at the present time and it manufactures the Sabin type.

* * *

There are advantages to the Sabin vaccine. It is administered orally—usually on a sugar cube to individuals old enough to eat sugar cubes. The Salk vaccine can only be injected through a needle. The injections are time-consuming and require individual administration by trained medical personnel. Further, injections are less well received by poorly educated persons and resistance thereto is stronger. Additionally, there is substantial medical evidence that the immunity induced by the Sabin vaccine is longer lasting and does not require boosters as may be necessary with the Salk vaccine.

Ironically, the very cause of the longer-lasting immunity of the Sabin vaccine gives rise to the major drawback of this vaccine. The Sabin vaccine must be given orally, as the weakened virus gives immunity by proliferating in the intestines, thereby triggering the body's immune system. For reasons unknown, occasionally, but on a rather predictable ratio of incidence, the virus reproduced in the intestinal tract is a virulent virus, not the weakened Sabin virus. When this occurs, the individual receiving the virus, and persons in close contact with such individual, may acquire polio as a result of the vaccination. This unfortunate event occurs some five to ten times each year in the United States. This risk from the Sabin vaccine has been there from the beginning of its usage. It is a known risk and has been argued at every phase in the long-standing Salk–Sabin controversy.

The very ability of the Sabin vaccine to infest others is, in the broad public health view, a plus factor. Unlike the Salk vaccine, the Sabin vaccine can vaccinate persons in contact with vaccinated persons because the intestines secrete the virus. Usually, the virus so secreted is the same weakened type as was used in the vaccine. Hence, such individuals are vaccinated without actual medical vaccinations. From a public health standpoint, more people can be so vaccinated than could otherwise be reached. Kansas requires polio vaccination before children are admitted to elementary school or state licensed child care centers or preschools.

Being fully informed of this known risk, the federal government approved the Sabin vaccine and purchased large quantities of it for its mass public immunization program. The decision was made that the Sabin vaccine would be the weapon utilized to fight the serious public health problem of polio. The program has been so successful in reducing the incidence of "wild" polio that an individual in the United States now has about the same risk of contracting "wild" polio as he or she does of contracting polio through vaccination or contact with a vaccinee. Virtually all of the Western world utilizes the Sabin vaccine over the Salk vaccine in its public health programs. Finland, by virtue of a recent polio outbreak which included some individuals previously immunized by the Salk vaccine, is now using the Sabin vaccine in its public health program.

* * *

The Sabin-type vaccine was the vaccine of choice recommended by all major health organizations in the United States in 1975. Its production by American Cyanamid was the result of the federal government's solicitation of the firm to manufacture the Sabin vaccine which public health authorities believed, based on a vast array of scientific literature, was necessary to combat a major health problem. The seed strains of virus utilized in the manufacture of the vaccine by American Cyanamid are supplied by the federal government and the vaccine's manufacture is closely monitored by the federal government.

Plaintiff acquired contact polio from his child, the vaccinee. The fact that this type of occurrence would happen on an extremely infrequent, but rather predictable, ratio was known from the time Sabin-type vaccines were introduced. The remote risk of contact polio is inherent in the Sabin-type vaccine and cannot be eliminated. The risk could not be altered by a change in the manufacturing process. The phenomenon of contact polio was not newly discovered information acquired by American Cyanamid and hidden from public view. * * * Plaintiff seeks to impose liability, in the first instance, on what is, in essence, a design defect theory. That is, that the Salk-type vaccine (a killed virus vaccine) is a better product and American Cyanamid should be held liable for producing a Sabin-type vaccine (live virus vaccine) rather than the Salk-type vaccine. Plaintiff is seeking to impose strict liability in tort based upon design defect (the inadequate warning claim of liability will be discussed later). Section 402A of the Restatement (Second) of Torts (1963) states: [The court here quotes § 402A and Comment *k*.]

* * *

Orimune, the Sabin-type vaccine, is an "unavoidably unsafe product" that is an "apparently useful and desirable product, attended with a known but apparently reasonable risk" as a matter of law. Public policy requires that the mere manufacture of the vaccine not be actionable on the ground of design defect. The trial judge should have heard the evidence on this issue outside the presence of the jury and made the determination thereon. There is no claim that the vaccine administered to plaintiff's child was improperly manufactured or that a defective product was delivered. The vaccine was properly prepared and marketed and was exactly what it was intended to be. As a matter of law there is no manufacturing or design defect in the product at issue herein.

This leaves the only possible liability in the adequacy of the warning provided by the manufacturer.

In Wooderson v. Ortho Pharmaceutical Corp., 235 Kan. 387, 681 P.2d 1038, previously cited, this court discusses the duty to warn relative to drugs. As in the case before us, the drug in Wooderson was sold to a physician who, in turn, prescribed/administered the drug to the patient. As recognized in Wooderson, under such circumstances the "learned intermediary" concept comes into play. The manufacturer's duty is to adequately warn the physician of a known risk.

In determining warning issues, the test is reasonableness. To impose liability on a manufacturer, the plaintiff must show negligence on the part of the manufacturer.

* * *

Was the warning adequate as a matter of law? That is, was it a reasonable warning by a manufacturer to a learned intermediary? Was the manufacturer negligent in the warning supplied?

The warning provided herein states:

"ADVERSE REACTIONS

"Individual patients have at times attributed symptoms or conditions to the vaccine by reason of time relationship, but these in general have been minor and apparently unrelated. * * *

"Expert opinion is in agreement that the administration of live oral poliovirus vaccines is generally an effective and safe method of protecting populations against the natural disease. *Paralytic disease following the ingestion of live poliovirus vaccines has been reported in individuals receiving the vaccine, and* in some instances, in persons who were in close *contact with subjects who had been given live oral poliovirus vaccine.* Fortunately, *such occurrences are rare,* but considering the epidemiological evidence developed with respect to the total group of 'vaccine related cases' it is believed by some that at least some of the cases were caused by the vaccine.

"*The estimated risk of vaccine-induced paralytic disease occurring in vaccinees or those in close contact with vaccinees is extremely low. A total of approximately 30 of such cases were reported for the 8 year period covering 1963 to 1970, during which time about 147,000,000 doses of the vaccine were distributed nationally. Even though this risk is low, it should always be a source of consideration.*" (Emphasis supplied.)

The warning obviously warns that in rare instances a person in close contact with a vaccinee may develop polio. This is exactly what happened to the plaintiff herein. This, then, is not a failure to warn question, but rather a question of the adequacy of the warning. Wooderson v. Ortho Pharmaceutical Corp., 235 Kan. 387, 681 P.2d 1038, previously cited, although couched in terms of an "adequacy of warning" issue, actually involves a failure to warn, as the injury received by plaintiff was not included in the warning.

Plaintiff contends the first paragraph of the warning waters down the total warning. We do not believe so. It deals with what patients have reported rather than scientific fact. If a lay person takes a drug or receives a vaccine and two days later is suffering from an abscessed tooth, an attack of appendicitis, or whatever, he or she tends to link the two occurrences as cause and effect regardless of any medical connection. The paragraph leaves in the possibility some minor side effects reported by patients might be medically possible.

The balance of the warning clearly states the scientific fact that some persons in close contact with vaccinees may develop a paralytic disease from such contact. It is unnecessary to describe to a physician what paralytic disease is and the seriousness of it. The warning then states the chances of this happening are "extremely low." The figures of 30 cases in a particular eight-year period during which time 147,000,000 doses were distributed are included. These figures are consistent with those provided in 1972 by the Public Health Service, and the Advisory Committee on Immunization Practices and were current in 1975 when the vaccine herein was administered.

* * *

Plaintiff contends that the warning was also inadequate because it failed to state that individuals who were not immune to the disease were at greater risk than those who were immune. It hardly takes a medical degree to know that a person immune to a virus cannot acquire the disease. Later warnings spelled this out, but this is not evidence of negligence.

Plaintiff also argues that the warning was inadequate because it did not provide information on alternate vaccines. No Salk-type vaccine was being manufactured in the United States in 1975. Although unclear, there was evidence that a Salk vaccine might have been available at that time through a Canadian source. Sabin-type vaccines were the vaccines of choice and recommended at the time (1975) by all major health organizations involved therein. The general consensus was that the Sabin-type vaccine was superior to the Salk-type vaccine. American Cyanamid had no special knowledge or new information tending to refute this. Further, this is not a case where the drug manufacturer attempted to water down the warning by direct contact with physicians intending to lull the physicians into believing the stated risk was less than the required warning indicated * * *. The warning given herein had been approved by the Federal Drug Administration and was consistent with an overwhelming bulk of the current medical opinion.

We conclude that the trial court erred in denying American Cyanamid's motion for a directed verdict herein. As a matter of law, there was no submissible theory of liability on the part of American Cyanamid.

* * *

As a note of explanation, American Cyanamid originally appealed from the entire verdict, but later specifically dismissed its appeal relative to the jury's finding that Dr. Branson had zero percentage of fault. There was no cross-appeal filed by the plaintiff herein. Does this court have any jurisdiction under these circumstances to remand the case for retrial of the issues between plaintiff and defendant Branson? We believe not. All issues between these two parties were fully litigated in the trial herein, and no party to the appeal claims any error in the trial of said issues.

The judgment against American Cyanamid is reversed.

PRAGER, JUSTICE, dissenting:

I respectfully dissent. By this decision, the majority has denied to the plaintiff his right to trial by jury and has substituted its judgment for that of the jury and the trial judge who heard the testimony of the witnesses and determined the case.

* * *

The law requires that the warning be communicated to the user of the product who may be injured by the use of the product. In situations where a product is sold and delivered to a treating physician, who then administers the product to the patient, the law requires that the manufacturer of the drug provide information and a sufficient warning to the physician who in turn is required to advise the patient or user of the drug of its dangers so that the ultimate user may make an informed decision whether to expose himself or herself to it. In the present case, the evidence is undisputed that the defendant, Dr. Vernon L. Branson, the treating physician, never at any time conveyed to the plaintiff, Emil E. Johnson, any warning whatsoever that the use of Orimune by Mr. Johnson's daughter could transmit paralytic polio either to the child or to Mr. Johnson as the parent and custodian of the child. Both Dr. Branson and Mr. Johnson testified without equivocation that no warning was ever given by the doctor to Johnson.

The evidence was likewise undisputed that some information about the drug and a warning were given by the defendants, American Cyanamid Company and Lederle Laboratories, to Dr. Branson. The primary issue presented to the jury was whether or not the warning was adequate to inform Dr. Branson of the nature of the drug, its dangers, and the possibility of using less dangerous alternatives.

In determining this case, this court must first consider the nature and scope of the warning requirement in mass inoculation cases. In this regard, the cases generally agree that an adequate warning in mass inoculation cases requires that vaccinees be directly informed in clear and simple terms by the drug manufacturer of (1) the reasonably foreseeable risk inherent in the product; (2) reasonable available alternative products and the reasonably foreseeable risks posed by such alternatives; and perhaps—in appropriate cases—(3) the reasonably foreseeable results of remaining untreated.

* * *

This rule is recognized and applied in Kearl v. Lederle Laboratories, 172 Cal.App.3d 812, 218 Cal.Rptr. 453 (1985) * * *. In Kearl, the package of OPV polio vaccine which was sold and delivered by Lederle to the doctor in 1978 contained a one-page warning insert which was described by the Kearl court as follows:

> " 'IMPORTANT INFORMATION ABOUT POLIO AND POLIO VACCINE. *Please read this carefully.*' The information sheet briefly described polio, stated that the risk of contracting it is very low '[e]ven for someone who is not vaccinated,' and explained inter alia that oral live polio vaccine is '*one* of the best ways to prevent polio' in young children. (Italics added.) It provided: 'POSSIBLE SIDE EFFECTS

FROM THE VACCINE: Oral live polio vaccine rarely produces side effects. *However, once in about every 4 million vaccinations, persons who have been vaccinated or who come in close contact with those who have recently been vaccinated are permanently crippled and may die.* Even though these risks are very low, they should be recognized. The risk of side effects from the vaccine must be balanced against the risk of the disease, both now and in the future.' (Italics added.) The information sheet suggested that pregnant women should consult a physician before taking the vaccine, and listed other persons who should not take the vaccine without consulting a doctor. It then informed the prospective vaccinee of the alternative vaccine: 'NOTE ON INJECTABLE (KILLED) POLIO VACCINE: Besides the oral polio vaccine, there is also a killed polio vaccine given by injection which protects against polio after several shots. *It has no known risk of causing paralysis.* Most polio experts do not feel it is as effective as the oral vaccine for controlling polio in the United States. It is recommended for persons needing polio vaccination who have low resistance to infections (or those who live with them) and for unprotected adults traveling to a place where polio is common. It is not widely used in this country at the present time, but it is available. If you would like to know more about this type of polio vaccine, please ask us.' (Italics added.)" pp. 818–19, 218 Cal.Rptr. 453.

* * *

In considering the adequacy or inadequacy of the warning in this case, the language should be carefully analyzed.

* * *

It seems to me that, from a reading of the warning given in this case, a reasonable person might conclude that the danger of total paralysis is not emphasized with the same intensity which is present in the warning which was found adequate in *Kearl v. Lederle Laboratories*, mentioned heretofore. *It must also be emphasized that the warning in the present case did not in any way convey to Dr. Branson the fact that there was a reasonably available alternative product and the reasonable risks posed by such alternative product.* This element of an adequate warning was considered as essential by the court in Kearl.

* * *

Dr. Branson was called as a witness. He testified without equivocation that the 1975 insert involved in this case did not tell him enough. He testified that he would have liked to have known as a practicing physician that Lederle was expecting a certain number of contacts to get polio from the vaccine he was giving to his babies. If he had known about it, he would have passed the information on to Emil Johnson. He did not consider the warning adequate, because it was not made clear that the vaccine would cause paralytic disease. Dr. Branson testified that, since he has learned about the use of IPV vaccine, he has used it in his practice, and, if Lederle had told him about IPV vaccine in 1975, he would have done so then. Dr. Branson, a competent Kansas physician, clearly testified that the warning provided by the defendants was inadequate. Why has the majority rejected his testimony as a matter of law?

* * *

I respectfully question how the four-person majority can hold, from the evidence in this case, that no reasonable person could conclude that the warning failed to meet the standard required by law for the protection of the American people. In my judgment, a legitimate fact issue was presented in the case which was for the jury to determine.

* * *

HERD and LOCKETT, JJ., join the foregoing dissenting opinion.

NOTES

1. What do you think of the plaintiff's lawyer's failure to appeal the jury verdict in favor of Dr. Branson? Did his behavior constitute malpractice? Remember that Dr. Branson testified very persuasively for the plaintiff and was the plaintiff's personal family doctor.

2. *Design defect revisited.* It is reported that as of 1996 wild polio virus has been entirely eradicated from the Western Hemisphere. There are no known human cases and wild polio virus cannot be found. J.L. Melnick, *Poliomyelitis Vaccination: What Are The Options*, 6 Clinical Immunotherapeutics, 1172 (1996). As of 2000, the Centers for Disease Control has recommend that children receive the Salk Vaccine. Given this state of affairs, is it now the case that the use of the Sabin vaccine in the United States is malpractice? Is the Sabin vaccine defectively designed under the Comment *k* approach? How about under the Third Restatement approach?

Is your answer affected by the fact that the Sabin vaccine is much cheaper? Is your answer different in those parts of the world where wild polio can still be detected and where public health funds may be in short supply? *See* George W. Conk, *The True Test: Alternative Safer Designs for Drugs and Medical Devices in a Patent–Constrained Market*, 49 UCLA L. Rev. 737 (2002).

3. Most courts agree with *Johnson* that in the case of prescription drugs the manufacturer's obligation to warn extends only to doctors who prescribe the drug. This is referred to as the "learned intermediary" doctrine. *See* Niemiera v. Schneider, 114 N.J. 550, 555 A.2d 1112 (1989); Felix v. Hoffmann–LaRoche, Inc., 540 So.2d 102 (Fla.1989). Some cases hold that there is a duty to warn the consumer directly if the doctor plays a nominal rule in the decision to use the drug. *See* MacDonald v. Ortho Pharm. Corp., 394 Mass. 131, 475 N.E.2d 65 (1985), cert. denied 474 U.S. 920, 106 S.Ct. 250, 88 L.Ed.2d 258; Hill v. Searle Labs., 884 F.2d 1064 (8th Cir. 1989) (IUD). *But see*, Martin v. Ortho Pharmaceutical Corp., 169 Ill.2d 234, 214 Ill.Dec. 498, 661 N.E.2d 352 (1996) (the existence of a Federal regulation requiring manufacturers to inform patients directly of the risks and benefits involved in

the use of oral contraceptives does not create a common law duty to do so. Defendant only had a duty to adequately inform the learned intermediary.)

Many pharmaceutical companies now advertise prescription drugs directly to potential patients. One court has held that the learned intermediary doctrine does not apply when drug manufacturer engages in direct-to-consumer advertising. Perez v. Wyeth Laboratories Inc., 161 N.J. 1, 734 A.2d 1245 (1999). Pharmaceutical companies also must warn consumers directly. The court notes that there is a rebuttable presumption that a warning is adequate when the manufacturer complies with FDA advertising, labeling and warning requirements. It is not clear, however, exactly what a manufacturer needs to do to meet the duty to warn individuals directly. The *Perez* court refers to FDA guidelines set forth in Guidance for Industry: Consumer-directed Broadcast Advertisements <http://www.fda.gov/Drugs/GuidanceCompliance RegulatoryInformation/Guidances/> (last visited July 12, 2012). Among other things, the guidelines note that the ad should have a thorough major statement conveying all of the product's most important risk information in consumer-friendly language and that it should present a fair balance between information about effectiveness and information about risk. In addition, the advertisement should provide a toll-free number and an Internet web page that consumers could use to receive the approved package labeling, and it should note that health care providers may provide additional information to consumers. For discussions of the *Perez* opinion, *see* Jeffrey J. Wiseman, *Another Factor in the "Decisional Calculus": The Learned Intermediary Doctrine, The Physician–Patient Relationship, and Direct–To–Consumer Marketing*, 52 S.C. L. Rev. 993 (2001); Richard C. Ausness, *Will More Aggressive Marketing Practices Lead to Greater Tort Liability For Prescription Drug Manufacturers?*, 37 Wake Forest L. Rev. 97 (2002).

In New Jersey, if the pharmaceutical company fails to warn consumers, but the patient's physician in fact apprises the plaintiff of the drug's risks, what result? *See Perez*, 734 A.2d at 1260.

4. Problems with the learned intermediary rule also arise in mass immunization situations where the person being immunized is not under the care of some physician. In litigation arising out of the polio immunization campaigns of the 1960's, some courts held drug manufacturers to be under an obligation to warn the people participating in the program of the dangers. *See, e.g.,* Davis v. Wyeth Labs., Inc., 399 F.2d 121 (9th Cir. 1968); Reyes v. Wyeth Labs., 498 F.2d 1264 (5th Cir. 1974), cert. denied, 419 U.S. 1096, 95 S.Ct. 687, 42 L.Ed.2d 688 (1974).

5. In another direct-to-consumer advertising case, the West Virginia Supreme Court took the much more radical step of completely abolishing the learned intermediary rule. State ex rel. Johnson & Johnson Corp. v. Karl, 220 W.Va. 463, 647 S.E.2d 899 (2007).

It is said that no other state has refused to apply the rule in all circumstances, although two states, Rhode Island and Vermont, have yet to consider the issue. See Drug and Device Law, Headcount II: The Learned Intermediary Rule and Medical Devices, available at http://druganddevicelaw.blogspot.com/2008/07/headcount-ii-learned-intermediary-rule.html (last visited October 5, 2011). What are the arguments for and against the West Virginia position? With the adoption of this rule, in the absence of advertising, how should drug manufacturers convey warning information to consumers? Would an insert accompanying the drug suffice? Should this rule also apply to medical devices such as joint implants that usually are chosen by the physician?

6. *Read and heed presumption.* A problem for the plaintiff is establishing that, if a warning had been given, the plaintiff might have avoided the injury. In the *Reyes* case, the court held that there was a rebuttable presumption that the consumer would have read a warning provided by the manufacturer and would have acted "so as to minimize the risks." 498 F.2d at 1281. *Accord* Cunningham v. Charles Pfizer & Co., 532 P.2d 1377 (Okla.1974). In *Cunningham* the court nevertheless held that, given the presence of rebutting evidence—12 cases of polio in Tulsa in October and November 1962 and Oklahoma's history as an "epidemic state"—"the issue of whether the plaintiff as a reasonably prudent person would have refused to take the vaccine if adequate warning had been given should have been submitted to the jury." *Cunningham,* 532 P.2d at 1382.

Most jurisdictions follow *Reyes* and entitle a plaintiff to a rebuttable presumption that he would have read and heeded an adequate warning. *See*, e.g. Coffman v. Keene Corp., 133 N.J. 581, 628 A.2d 710 (1993) (listing the states that have applied the presumption). *But see*, Riley v. American Honda Motor Co., 259 Mont. 128, 856 P.2d 196 (1993); Thomas v. Hoffman–LaRoche, Inc. 949 F.2d 806 (5th Cir.1992) (applying Mississippi law); and Rivera v. Philip Morris, Inc., 125 Nev. 185, 209 P.3d 271 (2009) ("Shifting the burden of proving causation to the manufacturer in a strict product liability case, even if it is a temporary shift, is contrary to this state's law, as well as public policy.")

A separate question is whether the presumption also works in favor of the seller. Comment *j* of § 402A of the Second Restatement supported a presumption that when an adequate warning is given the consumer will read and heed it. However, this provision was omitted in the *Restatement (Third) of Torts: Products Liability* and a number of courts have rejected the Second Restatement Position. *See* Uniroyal Goodrich Tire Co. v. Martinez, 977 S.W.2d 328 (Tex. 1998) (reproduced on p. 286 *infra.*) Why might these courts have adopted this position?

7. In response to the unavoidable risk of injury associated with the Sabin vaccine and other vaccines for childhood diseases, Congress passed the National Childhood Vaccine Injury Act of 1986, 42 U.S.C.A. §§ 30aa–1 to –34. (*See* p. 333, *infra.*) The statute provides for a system of no-fault compensation for individuals injured by vaccines, but limits recovery for pain and suffering. The Act is funded by a tax on drug manufacturers. Is this a reasonable response to the vaccine problem? Should it be expanded to cover other drugs and other products? *See* Victor E. Schwartz and Liberty Mahshigian, *National Childhood Vaccine Injury Act of 1986: An Ad Hoc Remedy or a Window For The Future?* 48 Ohio St. L. J. 387 (1987); Lars Noah, *Triage in the Nation's Medicine Cabinet: the Puzzling Scarcity of Vaccines and Other Drugs*, 54 S.C. L. Rev. 371 (2002).

8. In Bruesewitz v. Wyeth LLC, ___ U.S. ___, 131 S.Ct. 1068, 179 L.Ed.2d 1 (2011) the Court was asked to determine whether the Vaccine Act preempts all design-defect claims against vaccine manufacturers brought by plaintiffs who seek compensation for injury or death caused by vaccine side effects. We return to a discussion of preemption on page 321, *infra*.

9. The word "warnings" is often used as a generic term to describe two somewhat different types of information the manufacturer (and others in the chain of distribution) may provide the user. Warnings in the form of safety instructions inform consumers how to minimize any risks associated with the use of the product. Other warnings may simply notify the consumer of an irreducible risk associated with a product, which the consumer can avoid only by choosing not to use the product at all. Which type of "warning" was at issue in the *Johnson* case?

By and large, the duty to provide warnings apprising the user of irreducible risks has been imposed with respect to toxic agents and drugs. It has not expanded to products such as automobiles. Why do you think this is the case? *See Restatement (Third) of Torts: Products Liability* § 2, Comment *i*.

10. *Adequacy*. The adequacy of warnings and instructions has been a troublesome area of law. As the principal case suggests, after the fact it is often possible to imagine that a somewhat different warning might have caused the plaintiff to take precautions that would have prevented disaster. Questions of adequacy are particularly thorny in cases that do not involve the learned intermediary rule. For example, in Burch v. Amsterdam Corp., 366 A.2d 1079 (D.C.App.1976) the plaintiff was badly burned in an explosion that occurred while he was putting down floor tile using the defendant's mastic adhesive. The warning on the adhesive read as follows:

DANGER! EXTREMELY FLAMMABLE: See Cautions elsewhere on label.
CAUTION: FLAMMABLE MIXTURE. DO NOT USE NEAR FIRE OR FLAME USE WITH ADEQUATE VENTILATION

The plaintiff read the label and checked to see if all flames were out but did not think of the pilot light in the kitchen stove where he was working. The appellate court reversed a trial court summary judgment for the defendant. "Given the potential for serious injury we cannot say as a matter of law that this warning adequately alerted users of the dangers inherent in the product. Among other things, an ordinary user might not have realized that 'near fire or flame' included nearby pilot lights or that fumes and vapors, as well as the adhesive itself, were extremely flammable." *Burch*, 366 A.2d at 1087–88.

Murray v. Wilson Oak Flooring Co., 475 F.2d 129 (7th Cir.1973) also involved a fire that erupted when the vapors of a mastic adhesive were ignited by a pilot light. This time the warning read (in part) as follows:

CAUTION: INFLAMMABLE MIXTURE DO NOT USE NEAR FIRE OR FLAME

Contains Heptane—use in Well Ventilated Area

Do not smoke—Extinguish flame—including pilot lights.

Reversing a judgment n.o.v. and reinstating a plaintiff verdict, the appellate court said: "We cannot say as a matter of law that the term 'near' was sufficient to inform Murray that his spreading adhesive within four feet of a pilot light located behind a closed door and within eight feet of stove pilot lights three feet off the floor exposed him to the risk of an explosion." *Murray,* 475 F.2d at 132. Do you think you could craft a warning for this product that would result in a directed verdict in similar accidents?

In *Burch*, Chief Judge Reilly dissented. He asked: "if there was a duty to advert expressly to pilot lights in addition to 'fire and flame', it would seem equally incumbent upon the vendors to devise a label warning against lighted pipes, cigars and cigarettes, vigil lights, candles, sparks from an electric lamp switch, a running fan or motor, and the other myriad of things which could possibly ignite vapors." Do you agree, or are pilot lights in a special category?

Is there any warning that the majorities in these two cases are likely to find to be adequate as a matter of law? Perhaps the problem is not one of warnings, but of design.

Judicial attitudes toward the costs and benefits of warnings have varied substantially. *Compare* Moran v. Faberge, Inc., 273 Md. 538, 332 A.2d 11 (1975) *with* Cotton v. Buckeye Gas Products Co., 840 F.2d 935 (D.C.Cir.1988). In *Moran,* two teenage girls attempted to scent a candle by pouring perfume slightly below the burning flame. The perfume was 82% alcohol and the ensuing fire seriously burned one of the girls. The perfume contained no warnings that it was highly flammable. In reversing a trial court judgment n.o.v. for the defendant, the court made the following comment: "[W]e observe that in cases such as this the cost of giving an adequate warning is usually so minimal, amounting only to the expense of adding some more printing to a label, that this balancing process will almost always weigh in favor of an obligation to warn of latent dangers. . . ." *Moran,* 273 Md. at 543–44, 332 A.2d at 15.

In *Cotton*, plaintiff's job was to monitor portable propane heaters used to cure concrete in cold weather and to change propane cylinders supplied by the defendant when they ran low. He failed to close the valves on the used cylinders and stored them near the active heaters. Gas escaped from the used cylinders and badly burned the plaintiff. The cylinders did have a conspicuous label warning that they contained flammable gas and should be stored in a well ventilated area. The label did not warn that gas might escape from used cylinders believed to be empty or instruct the user to shut the valves on used cylinders. However, the cylinders were accompanied by a pamphlet, posted on a bulletin board at the construction site. The pamphlet did instruct the user to close the valve on used cylinders and store them in a well ventilated area. The plaintiff argued that these warnings should have been placed on the cylinders themselves. This time the appellate court affirmed a trial court judgment n.o.v. for the defendant. With respect to the plaintiff's requested warnings, it made the following comment:

> Failure-to-warn cases have the curious property that, when the episode is examined in hindsight, it appears as though addition of warnings keyed to a particular accident would be virtually cost free. What could be simpler than for the manufacturer to add the few simple items noted above? The primary cost is, in fact, the increase in time and effort required for the user to grasp the message. The inclusion of each extra item dilutes the

punch of every other item. Given short attention spans, items crowd each other out; they get lost in fine print. Here, in fact, Buckeye responded to the information-cost problem with a dual approach: a brief message on the canisters themselves and a more detailed one in the NLPGA pamphlet * * *.

Plaintiff's analysis completely disregards the problem of information costs. He asserts that "it would have been neither difficult nor costly for Buckeye to have purchased or created for attachment to its propane cylinders a clearer, more explicit label, such as the alternatives introduced at trial, warning of propane's dangers and instructing how to avoid them." Brief for Appellant at 25. But he offers no reason to suppose that any alternative package of warnings was preferable. He discounts altogether the warnings in the pamphlet, without even considering what the canister warning would have looked like if Buckeye had supplemented it not only with the special items he is personally interested in—in hindsight—but also with all other equally valuable items (i.e., "equally" in terms of the scope and probability of the danger likely to be averted and the incremental impact of the information on user conduct). If every foreseeable possibility must be covered, "[T]he list of foolish practices warned against would be so long, it would fill a volume." Kerr v. Koemm, 557 F.Supp. 283, 288 n. 2 (S.D.N.Y.1983).

How do these two approaches differ in their assumptions about how humans respond to danger and warnings of danger? *See* Howard Latin, *"Good" Warnings, Bad Products, and Cognitive Limitations*, 41 UCLA L. Rev. 1193 (1994); W. Kip Viscusi, *Individual Rationality, Hazard Warnings, and the Foundations of Tort Law*, 48 Rutgers L. Rev. 625 (1996). Both of these articles report on research assessing how individuals perceive risks and respond to warnings. For a very useful pair of articles discussing the empirical research on human rationality and its limits, *see* Gregory Mitchell, *Why Law and Economics' Perfect Rationality Should Not be Traded For Behavioral Law and Economics' Equal Incompetence*, 91 Geo. L.J. 67 (2002); Gregory Mitchell, *Taking Behavioralism Too Seriously? The Unwarranted Pessimism of the New Behavioral Analysis of Law*, 43 Wm. & Mary L. Rev. 1907 (2002). Experts in areas such as cognitive psychology, communications psychology and human factors engineering frequently offer testimony on such issues. *See, e.g.*, Long v. Deere & Co., 238 Kan. 766, 715 P.2d 1023 (1986).

11. *Assessing adequacy*. Warnings may suffer from both substantive and procedural inadequacy. A warning is substantively inadequate when it fails provide the consumer with the information necessary to properly assess the risk. A warning may also be "procedurally inadequate." Procedural adequacy involves such things as conspicuousness, i.e. the size and location of warnings, the need for pictorial and other non-verbal warnings such as buzzers or bells, and the adequacy warnings only in English. A number of courts have developed criteria for assessing adequacy. *See*, Pittman v. Upjohn Co., 890 S.W.2d 425 (Tenn.1994); Pavlides v. Galveston Yacht Basin, Inc., 727 F.2d 330, 338 (5th Cir.1984).

[I]n order for a warning to be adequate, it must provide 'a complete disclosure of the existence and extent of the risk involved.' A warning must (1) be designed so it can reasonable be expected to catch the attention of the consumer; (2) be comprehensible and give a fair indication of the specific risks involved with the product; and (3) be of an intensity justified by the magnitude of the risk.

12. *Bulk suppliers*. The learned intermediary rule is an exception to the general rule that the manufacturer must warn the user of risks associated with a product. A second exception has been created for bulk suppliers. Higgins v. E.I. DuPont de Nemours & Co., Inc., 671 F.Supp. 1055 (1987), *aff'd* 863 F.2d 1162 (4th Cir.1988) is a representative case. Plaintiffs sued DuPont, the manufacturer of a paint called Imron, claiming it failed to warn them of the paint's possible teratogenic effects. They also sued Eastman Chemical Co. and Union Carbide, two firms that supplied DuPont with the chemical ingredients with which it made Imron. The court granted summary judgment to Eastman and Union Carbide:

> DuPont manufactured (from various chemicals including the glycol ether acetates supplied by Eastman and Union Carbide), packaged, labeled, and distributed the finished product denominated Imron paint. The facility with which DuPont could communicate an effective labeling warning to its customers is apparent. By comparison, Eastman and Union Carbide supplied in bulk *via* railroad tank cars and tank trucks, vast amounts of liquid chemicals which were subsequently reprocessed and repackaged by DuPont as Imron paint, rendering these bulk suppliers unable, as a practical matter, to communicate any warning to the ultimate purchasers. * * * The suppliers' apparent reliance upon DuPont to communicate an effective warning to its customers was also clearly reasonable.

Higgins, 671 F.Supp. at 1062.

The *Higgins* court considered DuPont to be a sophisticated user who could be relied upon to warn the ultimate consumer. Almost all bulk supplier cases involve a sophisticated user, that is a buyer who appreciates the risks associated with the product. What duty does the bulk supplier have if the buyer is not sophisticated? What if the bulk supplier knows from past experience that the buyer has failed to pass a warning along to the consumer? *See* Hunnings v. Texaco, Inc., 29 F.3d 1480 (11th Cir.1994); *Restatement (Second) of Torts* § 388, Comment *n*.

A large number of lawsuits were brought against DuPont, the bulk supplier of Teflon to Vitek, a company which used the product to make implants for individuals with problems in their temporomandibular joint, the joint connecting the upper and lower jaw. Over 25,000 TMJ implants were done before trouble arose. The cases are interesting because they involve both bulk supplier and learned intermediary issues. The plaintiffs claim that the bulk supplier should have warned physicians that Teflon was not suitable for this purpose. In almost all cases DuPont was granted a summary judgment. *See* Edward M. Mansfield, *Reflections on Current Limits on Component and Raw Material Supplier Liability and the Proposed Third Restatement*, 84 Ky. L.J 221 (1995–96); David A. Fischer, *Products Liability: A Commentary on the Liability of Suppliers of Component Parts and Raw Materials*, 53 S.C. L. Rev. 1137 (2002). For a further discussion of component part manufacturer liability, see page 306 *infra*.

PROBLEM: WARNING DEFECT

Mildredge Broussard brought a personal injury suit against Black & Decker (U.S.), Inc. after he was badly burned in an explosion of natural gas sparked by a Black & Decker hand drill. Broussard was using the drill while working at a Continental Oil Company (Conoco) plant at Grand Chenier, Louisiana. Other parties to the suit settled with the plaintiff before trial.

On the day of the accident, plaintiff and four other men, including Sanders Miller, were in the process of building a sump box enclosure at the end of a natural gas vent line (pipe) at the Grand Chenier plant. Plaintiff was a carpenter's helper and Miller was a carpenter. Upon arriving at the site, both men noticed that natural gas could be heard and smelled coming from the vent line. Miller immediately notified Conoco's relief plant foreman about the escaping gas and asked if it could be shut off. The foreman refused to do so because the whole plant would have had to be shut down to prevent the gas from being vented at the location of the sump box. After Miller requested a shut down a second time, the foreman talked to Mr. Leeman, another Conoco employee and the plant supervisor. Miller was again told nothing could be done.

Miller testified that he recognized the danger of working around the flammable natural gas. The workers took what precautions they could to minimize the risk of igniting the natural gas fumes. Cigarettes, cigarette lighters and matches were left in the work vehicles. The vehicles were parked some distance away from the site. A gasoline powered electricity generator was placed at the end of two 50–foot extension cords. Miller warned the plaintiff to be careful not to cause a spark, especially when the fumes were heavy.

The explosion occurred as plaintiff was standing inside a plywood box loosely held together and being constructed as a concrete form. He was positioned inside the form to drill holes in its sides through which rods were to be inserted. It is not seriously contested that sparks from the drill plaintiff was using ignited the natural gas fumes coming from the vent line. Such sparks are normally emitted from this and similar type drills when the "brushes" inside the armature of the drill contact and slide along the inside surface of the rapidly spinning cylinder in which the brushes sit. There is no evidence that the design which allows the creation and emission of these sparks constitutes a design defect. Rather, the issues relate to the failure to warn on the part of the defendant manufacturer of the hazard of explosion.

Both the plaintiff Broussard and Sanders Miller testified that they were unaware at the time of the accident that sparks from electrical power drills could ignite gaseous atmospheres. Allen Nunez, the relief foreman, likewise testified that neither he nor anyone at the Conoco plant knew of the potential of explosion in a like situation before the accident occurred. However, the owner's manual that Black & Decker claims is placed in every box containing one of their drills as it leaves the manufacturer's control, warns of 18 separate dangers involved in using their product and instructs the user as to proper use in the face of these dangers.

The owner's manual is not attached to the drill but is loosely placed in the box. Thus, unless the box with the owner's manual inside (or the owner's manual itself, with the safety warnings inside its folded pamphlet form) is kept with the drill, the warning is not available to users other than the buyer. In addition to the owner's manual warning, there is a small notice on the side of the drill which simply reads, "CAUTION: For Safe Operation See Owner's Manual." This notice is approximately one-eighth inch high and one inch long.

Sanders Miller originally received the drill at the plant office from the secretary who worked in the office. The secretary asked Miller if he wanted the box the drill came in. Miller replied he had no use for it, and the box was thrown away. Neither Miller nor the plaintiff saw the owner's manual. Item eighteen in the owner's manual reads as follows:

> "18. DO NOT OPERATE portable electric tools in gaseous or explosive atmospheres. Motors in these tools normally spark, and the sparks might ignite fumes."
>
> Broussard contends that Black & Decker should have placed the warning on the drill itself. Plaintiff introduced into evidence a proposed label measuring approximately 2 5/8 inches by 1 3/4 inches on which the following words were typed:
>
> Safety Rules
>
> Don't abuse cord
>
> Wear proper apparel
>
> Don't use in damp areas
>
> Use proper extension cords outdoors
>
> Don't touch metal parts when drilling near any electrical wiring
>
> Remove tightening key
>
> Unplug to change bits
>
> Use safety glasses
>
> Avoid gaseous areas
>
> Secure work
>
> SEE MANUAL FOR COMPLETE TEXTS

The warning advises of 10 of the 18 dangers discussed in the manual. The material is typed in small letters written in a slant-wise or diagonal fashion on the label in order to fit on the handle of the drill.

Alternatively, plaintiff's expert argued that warnings should be placed on the drill through the use of symbols rather than words. The expert devised a series of symbols of his own creation designed to represent ten of the eighteen warnings that Black & Decker sets forth in the owner's manual. The expert admitted, however, that some of the symbols are not generally recognizable by the general public

Write a memo assessing the merits of plaintiff's warning defect claim.

BURKE v. SPARTANICS LTD.

United States Court of Appeals, Second Circuit, 2001.
252 F.3d 131.

CALABRESI, CIRCUIT JUDGE:

A metal shearing machine severed the fingers of plaintiff-appellant Alphonso Burke's right hand while he was at work. Burke brought suit in the United States District Court for the Eastern District of New York (Joanna Seybert, *Judge*), invoking the court's diversity jurisdiction. In his suit Burke asserted various New York State tort claims against the machine's manufacturer, defendant-appellee Spartanics Ltd. ("Spartanics"), which in turn impleaded Burke's employer, Metal Etching Company ("Metal Etching"), as a third-party defendant. The case proceeded to trial on Burke's claims, principally that the machine was defectively designed, and that Spartanics failed to provide adequate warnings of the dangers of using the machine. The jury returned a verdict against plaintiff on all counts. Burke now appeals from the judgment entered pursuant to that verdict and also from the district court's denial of his post-trial motion for judgment as a matter of law or for a new trial. We affirm.

Background

The Accident

The accident occurred while Burke was receiving instruction from a supervisor, Mr. O'Neill, on how to perform a particular job with the machine in question, which cuts sheets of metal with a shear. Believing that O'Neill had finished setting up the job, Burke went to the rear of the machine to clear out some cut pieces of metal. After being cut, the pieces of metal had fallen and accumulated in a ramp mounted behind the machine. As was the usual practice in Metal Etching's shop, in order to gain leverage while removing the metal with his left hand, Burke placed his right hand on the machine's cutting surface. Apparently unaware of what Burke was doing, O'Neill attempted to make a cut and, in doing so, severed Burke's fingers, which were in the cutting plane.

The ramp from which Burke was removing the metal when the accident occurred had been installed by Metal Etching. This ramp altered a feature of the machine as initially delivered by Spartanics. The original machine had another ramp with a conveyor belt that ran across the rear of the machine leading to a stacking bin at the machine's side. Metal Etching installed its own ramp above the conveyor system in order to catch the metal cuttings before they hit the conveyor. It did so allegedly to avoid a totally different hazard that the original ramp would supposedly have created. With the original conveyor system in place, however, there was no need for workers to clear cut material from the rear of the machine. But with the new ramp installed, employees not only had to remove the cut material but found that doing so required bracing themselves with one hand on the cutting surface.

By the time of the accident, Burke had been using the machine for about seven months. He fully understood how it worked, where the cutting plane was, and how dangerous it was to place one's hand in the plane while the machine was in operation. He was also aware of the warning label on the front of the machine that specifically warned against getting near the cutting mechanism. There was no warning label on the rear of the machine.

* * *

The Instruction on Duty to Warn

At the charging conference, plaintiff's counsel requested that the court's instructions on the manufacturer's duty to warn include the statement that "even if Mr. Burke was aware of a danger, that did not obviate the need of Spartanics to warn." Judge Seybert rejected this proposal, and, instead, instructed the jury that "[i]f you find that Alphonso Burke already knew of the danger or dangers associated with the Spartanics WL–2 metal shearing machine, you will find that the defendant had no duty to warn him of the dangers associated with the machine."

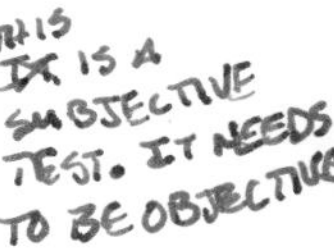

The Post–Trial Motions

After the jury returned its verdict finding for defendants on August 3, 1999, Burke moved for judgment as a matter of law. The district court reserved decision, received written motion papers several weeks later, and subsequently denied the motion on January 20, 2000. Burke now appeals from the judgment, entered immediately after trial, pursuant to the jury verdict and from the district court's disposition of his post-trial motion, which had raised issues similar to those now presented on appeal. * * *

Discussion

Burke argues * * * that the court incorrectly instructed the jury on the standard governing Spartanics' duty to warn. * * *

The Instruction on Spartanics' Duty to Warn

At trial, Burke objected to the district court's instruction to the jury that, if it found that "[1] Burke already knew of the danger or dangers associated with the Spartanics metal shearing machine, or [2] that the dangers associated with the machine were obvious, and generally known and recognized, you will find that the defendant Spartanics had no duty to warn Mr. Burke of the dangers associated with the metal shearing machine." Based on Burke's own requested instruction, his statements to the trial judge, and his briefing on appeal, we discern two discrete arguments put forward by appellant: first, that the court below erred in instructing the jury that Spartanics had no duty to warn of risks that were "obvious"; second, that the court erred in instructing the jury that Spartanics had no duty to warn of risks about which Burke himself was aware. For both propositions appellant relies on our recent decision in *Liriano v. Hobart Corp.*, 170 F.3d 264, 269 (2d Cir.1999) ("*Liriano III*"), in which we applied New York's failure-to-warn law as set forth by the New York Court of Appeals' in *Liriano v. Hobart Corp.*, 700 N.E.2d 303, 308 (N.Y.1998) (*"Liriano II"*), *answering questions certified by Liriano v. Hobart Corp.*, 132 F.3d 124 (2d Cir.1998) (*"Liriano I"*).

The first of these arguments is plainly wrong. It is a well-established principle of New York law that "a limited class of hazards need not be warned of as a matter of law because they are patently dangerous or pose open and obvious risks." *Liriano II,* 700 N.E.2d 303, 308; *accord, e.g., Bazerman v. Gardall Safe Corp.,* 609 N.Y.S.2d 610, 611 (App. Div., 1st Dep't 1994). This is just another way of saying that a reasonable person would not warn of obvious dangers, *i.e.* those harms that most all people know about. As a result, as to these risks, it cannot be negligent to fail to warn.

Not only did the New York Court of Appeals in *Liriano II* reaffirm the "obviousness" exception to a manufacturer's duty to warn, *see Lauber v. Sears, Roebuck and Co.,* 709 N.Y.S.2d 325, 326 (App. Div., 4th Dep't 2000); *Brady v. Dunlop Tire Corp.,* 711 N.Y.S.2d 633, 634–35 (App. Div., 3d Dep't 2000), but nothing in our opinion in *Liriano III* suggests the contrary. The question in *Liriano III* was simply "obviousness of what?" The *Liriano* cases involved an employee who injured his hand in the course of using a meat grinder that was manufactured with a safety guard but from which the guard had been removed. In *Liriano III* we upheld the verdict for the plaintiff because the jury could have found that, absent an appropriate warning, it was not obvious "(a) that it is feasible to reduce the risk with safety guards, (b) that such guards are made available with the grinders, and (c) that the grinders should be used only with the guards." *Liriano III,* 170 F.3d at 271. Because the *existence of a safer method* of using the grinder was not obvious, a jury could have found that a duty to warn, *i.e.* to inform the plaintiff that the machine should not be used in the absence of that safer method, was violated. Accordingly, it was unnecessary in *Liriano III* to decide whether it was obvious that the method plaintiff actually used was dangerous. * * *

At oral argument, Burke made clear that his contention is that Spartanics should have placed a warning, at the rear approach to the machine, about the dangers of placing one's hand in the cutting plane. His argument was *expressly not* that Spartanics should have warned that the (perhaps obvious) dangers associated with access to the machine from the back could be obviated by use of the original conveyor system, and that the machine should not be used without that conveyor system. Nor was this latter argument, an analogue to that upheld in *Liriano III,* put forward below. Accordingly, *Liriano III* is of no benefit to plaintiff, and the trial court was correct in charging the jury that there was no duty to warn if "the dangers associated with the machine were obvious, and generally known and recognized."

Burke's second argument—that *his own* knowledge of the machine's dangerousness did not negate Spartanics' duty to warn—is essentially correct, but for reasons that do not ultimately undermine our confidence in the jury verdict. The problem with the court's instruction lies in its conflation of two separate issues: (1) whether the manufacturer, considering the reasonably foreseeable uses to which its product might be put, had a duty to warn potential users in general about the machine's dangers; and (2) whether, in retrospect, giving a warning would have made any difference *to this particular plaintiff.* The first question concerns the "open and obvious risks" exception, which goes to the manufacturer's *duty.* The second question, in contrast, goes to the analytically distinct issue of whether a putative breach of that duty was a *cause* of this plaintiff's injury.

Whether a given risk is "obvious" depends in large part on what the mass of users knows and understands. Thus, "[a] manufacturer has a duty to warn against latent dangers resulting from *foreseeable uses* of its product of which it knew or should have known." *Liriano II,* 700 N.E.2d at 305 (emphasis added). Accordingly, "courts treat obvious danger as 'a condition that would ordinarily be seen and the danger of which would ordinarily be appreciated by *those who would be expected to use the product.*' " *Id.* at 308 (quoting Prosser and Keeton, *Torts* § 96, at 686–87 (5th ed.1984)) (emphasis added).

The class of reasonably foreseeable users will, of course, encompass a spectrum of persons with widely varying abilities and experience bearing on their perception of the hazards at hand. Some may be practiced and skilled operators, while others may be novices, or may use the machine in adverse conditions that, though atypical, are still foreseeable. *See id.* at 305 ("A manufacturer also has a duty to warn of the danger of unintended uses of a product provided these uses are reasonably foreseeable."); *id.* at 307 (duty to warn of dangers arising from foreseeable alterations to a product).

So long as the relevant risks are not obvious to *some* members of the class of foreseeable users, a reasonable manufacturer might well be expected to warn. And, as a result, a duty to warn will generally be said to exist. * * * *See id.* at 308 (the purpose of the "open and obvious" exception is to identify "dangers of which a user might not otherwise be aware," thereby enabling "consumers to adjust their behavior"). This is so, moreover, notwithstanding the fact that there may also be foreseeable users for whom the warning is superfluous. It is always possible that a particular plaintiff has a greater awareness of the risks in question than do other users who are or ought to be foreseeable to the manufacturer, and it is, therefore, error to instruct the jury, as was done here, that there is no duty to warn simply because *the particular plaintiff* was cognizant of the relevant hazards.[4]

4. In assessing the manufacturer's duty, we ask, essentially, what it ought to have done when distributing its product * * *, a question that necessarily arises *before* the particular accident forming the basis for litigation. The content of this duty, therefore, cannot vary depending on who, among foreseeable users, ultimately happens to be injured by the product. * * *

But of course a defendant's *liability* will not arise from a breach of duty alone. Instead, the plaintiff must show, in addition, that "the failure to warn [was] a substantial cause of the events which produced the injury." *Billsborrow v. Dow Chem.*, 579 N.Y.S.2d 728, 733 (App. Div., 2d Dep't 1992). And "where the injured party was fully aware of the hazard through general knowledge, observation or common sense, or participated in the removal of the safety device whose purpose is obvious, lack of a warning about that danger may well obviate the failure to warn as a legal cause of an injury resulting from that danger." *Liriano II,* 700 N.E.2d at 308 * * *. Thus, it may well be the case that a given risk is not "obvious," in the sense of precluding any duty to warn, but that nevertheless, because the risk was well understood by the plaintiff, a warning would have made no difference. *See Brady,* 711 N.Y.S.2d at 634–36 (distinguishing issue of whether risk was "open and obvious" from issue of whether plaintiff had "actual knowledge of the hazard"). And the failure to warn was therefore not a cause of the harm.

There are sufficient similarities between the issues of (a) whether a hazard was sufficiently obvious to all *foreseeable users* to preclude any *duty to warn,* and (b) whether the danger was sufficiently well known to *the plaintiff* to preclude a showing of *causation,* that confusion between them is not surprising. This is especially so because the concrete experiences of individual plaintiffs understandably, and properly, provide an important reference point in assessing the range of knowledge among reasonably foreseeable users. *See Liriano III,* 170 F.3d at 268–69. Nonetheless, recognizing the difference between these questions is important.

If the distinction is not observed, manufacturers' duties may be diluted by cases in which the particular plaintiff happens to have had a greater appreciation of the risks than would the mass of other foreseeable users. Where such greater individual awareness of the risk means that a warning would not have prevented the injury, failure to distinguish *duty* from *cause* may lead to an (erroneous) finding of no duty to warn notwithstanding the fact that foreseeable users would in fact be significantly aided by a warning. And, as a result of such a holding, subsequent plaintiffs injured by the same instrumentality would be faced with a prior ruling establishing the absence of any duty to warn, even though their appreciation of the risk might well be low enough to establish causation. Conversely, the distinction protects manufacturers against suits by plaintiffs who, though sufficiently ignorant that a warning would have enabled them to avoid an accident, were so unforeseeable that the manufacturer had no duty to provide them with notice of what to foreseeable users would be obvious. *Cf. Liriano II,* 700 N.E.2d at 308 (noting that requiring warnings against obvious dangers would tend to "trivialize[ ] and undermine[ ] the entire purpose of the rule [by] drowning out cautions against latent dangers").

Harmless Error

The same fact—Burke's awareness of the risk of placing his hand in the cutting plane while removing metal from the ramp—that appellant urges (correctly) should not have been permitted to negate Spartanics' duty to warn *does,* however, fully negate any causal connection between the absence of a rear warning and his injuries. *See, e.g., Smith,* 490 N.E.2d at 842 (finding no causation because plaintiff must have known based on his "general knowledge of pools, his observations prior to the accident, and plain common sense . . . that, if he dove into the pool, the area into which he dove contained shallow water"); *McMurry v. Inmont Corp.,* 694 N.Y.S.2d 157, 158–59 (App. Div., 2d Dep't 1999) (holding that, given plaintiff's experience and training, "a warning would not have added anything to the appreciation of this hazard"). The erroneous instruction was therefore harmless. * * *

In reaching this conclusion, we are cognizant that the essence of Burke's claim is that a warning on the rear of the machine would have *reminded* him of the danger of placing his hand near the cutting mechanism, not simply that a warning would have *informed* him of that danger. Warnings, of course, can serve to bring dangerous conditions to a user's attention, not merely to explain that they are dangerous. Thus, the mere fact that Burke already knew that it was dangerous to put his hand in the cutting plane (in the sense that, had he been asked whether it was dangerous, he would have answered that it was and would have understood why), is compatible with the notion that, had he seen a warning at the time he was choosing to put his hand there, such a warning might have prompted him to exercise greater care (whether by finding another source of leverage or by making sure that O'Neill knew not to engage the blade). *Cf. Liriano II,* 700 N.E.2d at 308 (noting that ultimate measure of need for warnings is whether they aid or hinder customers in adjusting their behavior to avoid accidents).

Nonetheless, on the facts presented here, we have no doubt that the lack of a warning on the rear of the machine was not a cause-in-fact of the accident. This is not a case in which a usually careful employee uncharacteristically forgot to take a safety precaution, nor one in which a plaintiff, though fully apprised of a machine's dangers, simply forgot to take care in the course of using the machine for the first time, or after a long hiatus. In such circumstances, it might be the case that a reminder could avert an accident. * * *

Here, instead, the method by which plaintiff removed cut metal from the ramp (*i.e.,* by bracing himself with one hand on the machine's cutting surface) was the routine manner in which this task was carried out at Metal Etching. Indeed, plaintiff testified that he had been trained to act in this way, that his supervisor acted in this way, and that he had never been instructed by his employer to clear out the machine in any other manner. Burke also testified that putting his hand near the blade "caused [him] concern" but that he never complained because he did not want to cause trouble, because it was the only way to accomplish the task, and because it was understood that, precisely to mitigate the maneuver's well-known dangers, one did not operate the machine while someone else was behind it retrieving materials.

If we assume—as we must—that the jury, based on the incorrect instruction, found that these facts concerning Burke's awareness of the machine's dangers precluded any duty on defendant to provide a rear warning, then we must also say, as a matter of law, that the same jury, properly instructed, would have found that Burke was sufficiently aware of the danger to preclude the required causal connection between the absence of a warning and the accident in question. In circumstances such as these, an erroneous instruction is harmless. * * *

Conclusion

We hold * * * that the jury charge on defendant's duty to warn, though in part erroneous, was harmless. Accordingly, and having considered and rejected all of appellant's other arguments, we AFFIRM.

NOTES

1. The *Burke* case states the majority rule that the defendant is not required to warn about obvious defects. *See, e.g.,* Motley v. Bell Helicopter Textron, Inc., 892 F.Supp. 249 (M.D.Ala.1995) (rotating helicopter swash plate); Smith v. American Motors Sales Corp., 215 Ill.App.3d 951, 159 Ill.Dec. 477, 576 N.E.2d 146 (1991) (driving Jeep CJ–7 with barefoot hanging outside passenger compartment). Comment *j.* of § 2, *Restatement (Third) of Torts: Products Liability* reflects this position:

> j. *Warnings: obvious and generally known risks.* In general, a product seller is not subject to liability for failing to warn or instruct regarding risks and risk-avoidance measures that should be obvious to, or generally known by, foreseeable product users. When a risk is obvious or generally known, the prospective addressee of a warning will or should already know of its existence. Warning of an obvious or generally known risk in most instances will not provide an effective additional measure of safety. Furthermore, warnings that deal with obvious or generally known risks may be ignored by users and consumers and may diminish the significance of warnings about non-obvious, not-generally-known risks. Thus, requiring warnings of obvious or generally known risks could reduce the efficacy of warnings generally. When reasonable minds may differ as to whether the risk was obvious or generally known, the issue is to be decided by the trier of fact. The obviousness of risk may bear on the issue of design defect rather than failure to warn.

Also relevant is Comment *k* of *Restatement (Second) of Torts* § 388, a section dealing with the duty of suppliers of chattel to warn users of dangers associated with the chattel under negligence principles.

> Comment *k.* One who supplies a chattel to others to use for any purpose is under a duty to exercise reasonable care to inform them of its dangerous character in so far as it is known to him, or of facts which to his knowledge make it likely to be dangerous, if, but only if, he has no reason to expect that those for whose use the chattel is supplied will discover its condition and realize the danger involved. It is not necessary for the supplier to inform those for whose use the chattel is supplied of a

condition which a mere casual looking over will disclose, unless the circumstances under which the chattel is supplied are such as to make it likely that even so casual an inspection will not be made. However, the condition, although readily observable, may be one which only persons of special experience would realize to be dangerous. In such case, if the supplier, having such special experience, knows that the condition involves danger and has no reason to believe that those who use it will have such special experience as will enable them to perceive the danger, he is required to inform them of the risk of which he himself knows and which he has no reason to suppose that they will realize.

2. In *Liriano III*, referred to frequently in *Burke*, Judge Calabresi affirmed a jury verdict for a plaintiff against his employer and the manufacturer of a meat grinder in whose product he badly injured his hand. The meat grinder was manufactured with a safety guard, but the guard had been removed by the employer. The manufacturer claimed it had no duty to warn Liriano of the obvious danger posed by the product. However, the Second Circuit argued that warnings may do more than exhort people to be careful. In addition, they may assist people in making choices by advising them of the existence of alternatives. *Liriano III,* 170 F.3d at 270.

> Consequently, the instant case does not require us to decide the difficult question of whether New York would consider the risk posed by meat grinders to be obvious as a matter of law. A jury could reasonably find that there exist people who are employed as meat grinders and who do not know (a) that it is feasible to reduce the risk with safety guards, (b) that such guards are made available with the grinders, and (c) that the grinders should be used only with the guards. Moreover, a jury can also reasonably find that there are enough such people, and that warning them is sufficiently inexpensive, that a reasonable manufacturer would inform them that safety guards exist and that the grinder is meant to be used only with such guards.

Id. at 271.

The causal question that proved decisive in *Burke* did not arise in *Liriano* because in the latter case the plaintiff was an inexperienced 17 year old recent immigrant who had been on the job for only one week. Thus, it could less easily be said of him than of Mr. Burke that he actually knew of the danger posed by the machine.

3. Nevertheless, the final result of *Liriano* was that the plaintiff was assigned one-third of the responsibility for the accident, the employer 63.3% of the responsibility and the manufacturer 3.3% of the responsibility. Does this seem so out of line? Note, however, that New York is perhaps the only state that permits a defendant to implead the plaintiff's employer and obtain full contribution based on the employer's proportionate fault regardless of the level of worker's compensation benefits paid by the employer. *See* Dole v. Dow Chem. Co., 30 N.Y.2d 143, 331 N.Y.S.2d 382, 282 N.E.2d 288 (1972). Most jurisdictions either permit no contribution or limit contributions up to an amount equal to the plaintiff's worker's compensation benefits.

4. *Liriano III* is roundly criticized in Hildy Bowbeer and David S. Killoran, *Liriano v. Hobart Corp.: Obvious Dangers, the Duty to Warn of Safer*

Alternatives, and the Heeding Presumption, 65 Brook. L. Rev. 717 (1999). As to the duty to warn of ways to reduce risk, the authors argue:

> The fallacies of the Second Circuit's analysis become evident when one considers its ramifications for meat grinder manufacturers alone. First, any grinder manufacturer would have to conclude from this opinion that it should provide an on-product warning capable of informing even uneducated, inexperienced, non-English speaking users about the existence of every machine part that is capable of being removed (however forcibly) and the safety consequences (however obvious) of its absence. * * * Indeed, by the same rationale, the Liriano duty to warn should be extended to cover not only the removal but the potential modification of machine parts that could have safety consequences.
>
> * * *
>
> Consider, for example, the protective guard on the meat grinder in Liriano. It seems easy enough for the court to suggest a warning indicating that a guard is available and that the machine should only be used with the guard in place. Even if the user knows what is meant by a guard and could tell whether it was missing, what if the guard was not removed, but instead modified by enlarging the holes to accommodate a larger "stomper"? The warning that focuses solely on the presence of the guard rather than its performance characteristics might well lead to a false sense of security. Thus, the warning would have to caution against using the product with the guard removed or modified. But, the question arises: How will the user recognize whether the guard is in its original condition? Will the warning need to include a picture? A set of dimensions and specifications?

Id. at 737–38.

Do you agree? Does the *Liriano* analysis destroy the obvious danger rule? Is *Burke* a retreat from *Liriano*? For an influential law review article on duty to warn, see James A. Henderson Jr. and Aaron Twerski, *Doctrinal Collapse in Products Liability: The Empty Shell of Failure to Warn* 65 N.Y.U. L.Rev. 265 (1990).

5. The "obviousness" of a risk may turn in part on how the risk is defined. In Caterpillar, Inc. v. Shears, 911 S.W.2d 379 (Tex.1995), the plaintiff was injured in a collision of two front-end loaders. The loader operated by the plaintiff had a removable rollover protective structure (ROPS), that had been removed by his employer so that the loader could be used to load and unload the cargo of ships with limited clearance between decks. While operating the vehicle in a warehouse where blowing sulphate dust limited visibility to a few feet. Shears was struck from behind and seriously injured. Had the ROPS been in place, he would not have been harmed. Shears proceeded on both a design defect and warning defect theory. With respect to the latter theory, the court said:

> The inquiry is not whether the average person would know that a ROPS makes a loader safer. Rather, the proper inquiry is whether an average person would recognize that operating an industrial vehicle with open sides and top presents a degree of risk of serious harm to the operator.

> We believe it beyond dispute that the average person, looking at the open cab of a Caterpillar 920 front-end loader, would understand that nothing stands in the way of an intrusion from the rear or above. As a matter of law, Caterpillar and B.D. Holt did not have the duty to warn of the dangers of operating the loader as an open cab without a ROPS.

Id. at 383.

Do you agree with the *Shears* court that it is "beyond dispute that the average person, looking at the open cab of a Caterpillar 920 front-end loader, would understand that nothing stands in the way of an intrusion from the rear or above?" Is this the right way to phrase the question?

6. Is it "beyond dispute" that Mr. Shears understood the risk he was running? Do you think there would be a different outcome if he had no previous experience operating the loader? Compare *Shears* with Rowson v. Kawasaki Heavy Industries, Ltd., 866 F.Supp. 1221 (N.D.Iowa 1994). In that case the judge concluded that the jury should determine whether a lack of a ROPS on an all-terrain vehicle presented an open and obvious danger. At the time of his accident the plaintiff had never ridden an ATV before. *Rowson*, 866 F.Supp. at 1227. How would Judge Calabresi analyze these two cases?

7. *Duty or Causation?* Glittenberg v. Doughboy Recreational Industries, 441 Mich. 379, 491 N.W.2d 208 (1992) discusses the choice between a duty analysis and a causation analysis in a case involving an individual who dove head first into an above ground swimming pool.

> Most jurisdictions that have addressed similar cases have been unwilling to impose liability on the pool manufacturer or seller. Summary judgment in favor of the defendant has been based on lack of a causal connection between the alleged negligent failure to warn and the plaintiff's injury. Courts typically focus on the plaintiff's deposition testimony, establishing familiarity with the pool and awareness of the depth of the water in relation to the body, and hence recognition of the need to execute a shallow, flat dive in order to avoid contact with the bottom of the pool and injury. From this, it is concluded that, because the plaintiff was aware of the shallow condition of the pool's water and the dangers inherent in a headfirst dive into observably shallow water, the absence of a warning conveying those very facts could not be a proximate cause of the plaintiff's injuries.
>
> Although these cases could be decided on the fact specific basis of causation, the temptation to do so or to rely on the observation that a jury should be permitted to determine whether the asserted danger is latent, simply postpones to another day the need to grapple with the more difficult duty analysis. On the record here presented, we find that the plaintiffs' evidence fails to demonstrate the existence of a necessary antecedent to resolution of the causation issue, i.e., that the defendants owe the plaintiffs a duty to warn.

491 N.W.2d at 211. Other cases involving the open and obvious danger rule include Timpte Industries, Inc. v. Gish, 286 S.W.3d 306 (Tex. 2009); Walker v. George Koch Sons, Inc., 610 F.Supp.2d 551 (S.D.Miss. 2009).

8. *The ongoing battle between judge and jury.* As the *Glittenberg* court indicates, if a court determines that the question of open and obvious defect is a duty issue then it is more nearly a question of law, and the court may have more latitude in taking the case from the jury. If, on the other hand, open and obvious danger is a question of causation, it is more nearly a factual question for the trier of fact. Throughout this chapter we have seen that some courts have become more aggressive in their willingness to take cases from juries, either through summary judgment, directed verdict, or judgment n.o.v. There is some evidence that this is a general trend. *See* James A. Henderson, Jr. and Theodore Eisenberg, *The Quiet Revolution in Products Liability: An Empirical Study of Legal Change,* 37 UCLA L. Rev. 479 (1990); Theodore Eisenberg and James A. Henderson, Jr., *Inside The Quiet Revolution in Products Liability,* 39 UCLA L. Rev. 731(1992); Philip H. Corboy, *The Not–So–Quiet Revolution: Rebuilding Barriers to Jury Trial in the Proposed Restatement (Third) of Torts: Products Liability*, 61 Tenn. L. Rev. 1043 (1994). Why do you think this is the case?

FELDMAN v. LEDERLE LABORATORIES

Supreme Court of New Jersey, 1984.
97 N.J. 429, 479 A.2d 374.

SCHREIBER, J.

* * *

Plaintiff, Carol Ann Feldman, has gray teeth as a result of taking a tetracyline drug, Declomycin. Plaintiff's father, a pharmacist and a medical doctor, prescribed and administered the drug to her when she was an infant to control upper respiratory and other secondary types of infections. Since Dr. Feldman claimed that he had administered Declomycin, suit was instituted against defendant, Lederle Laboratories, which manufactured and marketed Declomycin. The action was presented to the jury on the theory that the defendant was strictly liable, not because the drug was ineffective as an antibiotic, but because defendant had failed to warn physicians of the drug's side effect, tooth discoloration.

* * *

[D]efendant argued that it had complied with the state of the art in its warning literature. It had not warned of possible tooth discoloration because, the defendant claimed, the possibility of that side effect was not known at the time its literature was disseminated.

The jury found for the defendant. * * *

Defendant first marketed Declomycin in 1959. The Physicians' Desk Reference (PDR), a book used by doctors to determine effects of drugs, contains data furnished by drug manufacturers about drugs, their compositions, usages, and reactions. The 1959 PDR entry for Declomycin stated that it had a greater antibiotic potency that made it possible to achieve therapeutic activity with less weight of antibiotic; it had a reduced renal clearance rate that produced a prolongation of the antibacterial levels in the body; and it was therapeutically equally effective as other tetracyclines in infections caused by organisms sensitive to the tetracyclines. The PDR is produced annually. Until the 1965 or 1966 edition, the PDR did not mention that tooth discoloration was a possible side effect of Declomycin. Since 1965 or 1966 the PDR has stated that the drug, when administered to infants and children, could cause tooth discoloration that would be permanent if the drug were given during the developmental stage of the permanent teeth.

Plaintiff, Carol Ann Feldman, was born on February 8, 1960. Her father, Dr. Harold Feldman, asserted that he prescribed Declomycin for her approximately seven or more times from September or October, 1960, when she was eight or nine months old, until the end of 1963.

* * *

Plaintiff's baby teeth were discolored gray-brown. Her permanent teeth were more deeply discolored, being primarily gray. The parties agreed that this discoloration had resulted from use of a tetracycline * * *.

The respective experts, Dr. Bonda for the plaintiff and Dr. Guggenheimer for the defendant, agreed that scientific literature existed by 1960 that referred to tooth staining being caused by tetracycline. Dr. Bonda specifically mentioned a 1956 article by Dr. Andre reciting that tetracycline accumulated in mineralized portions of growing bones and teeth of mice; an article by Dr. Milch in the July, 1957 Journal of the National Cancer Institute reporting that laboratory animals had yellow fluorescents in bones, including teeth, following dosages of tetracycline; a second article by Dr. Milch in the July, 1958 issue of the Journal of Bone and Joint Surgery again describing fluorescents in the bones and incisor teeth of rodents that had been fed tetracycline; a 1959 article by Dr. Swackman noting that of 50 children with cystic fibrosis who had received massive doses of tetracycline, 40 had dark tooth staining; a 1960 letter from Dr. Sigrelli, a Columbia University professor, to the Pediatric Journal observing that patients with cystic fibrosis of the pancreas who had received tetracyclines as an antibiotic suffered severe discoloration of their teeth, possibly as a result of their tetracycline use; a May, 1961 article by Dr. Sigrelli in the New Jersey/New York State Dental Journal containing the same information; and an essay by Dr. Bevlander on "The Effect of the Administration of Tetracycline on the Development of Teeth" in the October, 1961 issue of the Journal of Dental Research reflecting the adverse effect of tetracycline on developing teeth in young laboratory animals. Dr. Bonda concluded the defendant should have begun to investigate the possible effects of all forms of tetracycline on teeth no later than 1956, when the Andre article appeared.

Defendant's expert, Dr. Guggenheimer, on the other hand, noted that before 1962 the literature on tooth discoloration concerned only patients with cystic fibrosis who had been receiving massive doses of tetracyclines. He pointed out that Dr. Milch's papers described only fluorescents, not tooth staining. He testified that Declomycin did not become available until 1959 and that it would take 2½ years for permanent teeth developing in 1959 to erupt. The completion of accurate controlled studies of multiple well-documented cases would have been the only way one could really know whether Declomycin caused tooth discoloration in permanent teeth. Dr. Guggenheimer's testimony is unclear as to whether a correlation between tetracycline and tooth discoloration had been established in 1962. One reading of his testimony indicates that such a correlation was not known to exist and that only by hindsight could that conclusion be drawn. It is also possible to interpret his opinion to be that such correlation had been established in 1962. In any event it is significant that Dr. Guggenheimer gave no opinion as to 1963.

On November 16, 1962, Dr. Swanzey, defendant's Director of Regulatory Agencies Relations, wrote to the Federal Food and Drug Administration (FDA) that the defendant proposed to add to the labels on all its tetracycline products the following warning: "During therapy tetracyclines may form a stable calcium complex in bone-forming tissue with no known harmful effects. Use of any tetracycline during teeth development in the neonatal period or early childhood may cause discoloration of the teeth." Dr. Swanzey explained that it was not necessary to obtain FDA approval before placing a warning on a label, but it was the practice to do so. On cross-examination, however, he indicated that although no FDA approval was needed to write letters to doctors informing them of this correlation, labeling the product without FDA approval could be considered a misbranding.

The FDA acknowledged receipt of Dr. Swanzey's letter on December 3, 1962, and advised him that the FDA "has been acutely interested by the increasing number of new and/or undesirable effects accompanying or following the use of these products," and would notify the defendant "as soon as any conclusion is reached." Dr. Swanzey telephoned Dr. Barzilai of the FDA, who advised against putting any statement in a circular proposed to be distributed by the defendant and that the FDA had the matter under study. On January 15, 1963, Dr. Swanzey sent to the FDA two articles on bone effects, including a copy of the Bevlander article. Dr. Swanzey also spoke with Dr. Sigrelli, who advised that staining would occur with some tetracyclines, but he had not observed that it occurred with Declomycin.

The FDA, in a letter dated February 4, 1963, proposed that the defendant insert the following warning statement in "all" its tetracycline products: Tetracyclines may form a stable calcium complex in any bone forming tissue with no serious harmful effects reported thus far in humans. However, use of any tetracycline drug during tooth development (= last trimester of pregnancy, neonatal period and early childhood) may cause discoloration of the teeth (= yellow-grey-brownish). This effect occurs mostly during long-term use of the drug but it has also been observed in usual short treatment courses.

Dr. Swanzey responded that the suggested statement was satisfactory and would be incorporated in its literature. He added that he assumed that the directive was applicable to Declomycin as well as other tetracycline drugs. The FDA replied that "[t]here is practically no specific clinical evidence to substantiate such a labeling requirement" for Declomycin and the warning would have to appear only on labeling of other tetracycline drugs. On April 12, 1963, the FDA made it clear that the warning statement was to refer not to tetracyclines generally but only to the specific brand names of the implicated products.

In 1963, the defendant received complaints from eight doctors that Declomycin was causing tooth staining. In May, 1963 the defendant referred the FDA again to the side effect of Declomycin. Commencing in mid-December, 1963, after receipt of FDA approval, it included the same warning in the Declomycin literature as in other tetracyclines.

* * *

The trial court's charge to the jury was directed to * * * whether the defendant knew or should have known of the need to place a warning on its literature accompanying the sale of Declomycin and in the literature distributed to the medical profession. The trial court also stated that if the defendant did not know of the danger of tooth discoloration, and if the application of reasonably developed human skill and foresight consistent with the state of the art and the knowledge of the scientific community existing during the periods in question would not have alerted defendant to the danger, then there would have to be a finding for the defendant. The trial court also charged that the defendant's reliance on the FDA would not serve to relieve defendant of its duty to insert a warning if it knew or should have known of the need for such a warning. No exceptions were taken to the charge.

* * *

[In an omitted portion of the opinion the court addresses the question of whether strict liability applies to prescription drugs. The court determined that Comment *k.* of § 402A should be applied on a case-by-case basis]

III

We commence our strict liability analysis with the now familiar refrain that to establish strict liability a plaintiff must prove that the product was defective, that the defect existed when the product left the defendant's control, and that the defect caused injury to a reasonably foreseeable user. * * *

This is a strict-liability-warning case. The product has been made as the manufacturer intended. The plaintiff does not contend that it contained a manufacturing defect. Declomycin's purpose was to act as did other tetracyclines—as an antibiotic. However, it had several advantages over other antimicrobial therapeutics. The plaintiff does not dispute this. Indeed, there is no evidence that plaintiff's usage of Declomycin was not adequate in this respect. Nor was there any proof that it was improperly designed. The crux of the plaintiff's complaint is that her doctor should have been warned of a possible side effect of the drug in infants, discoloration of teeth.

The failure-to-warn strict liability classification is similar to the improper design category. The manufacturer is under a duty to produce and distribute a product that is reasonably fit, suitable, and safe. It has not met that obligation if it puts a defective article into the stream of commerce that causes injury or damage. * * *

The emphasis of the strict liability doctrine is upon the safety of the product, rather than the reasonableness of the manufacturer's conduct. * * *

* * * Th[e] difference between strict liability and negligence is commonly expressed by stating that in a strict liability analysis, the defendant is assumed to know of the dangerous propensity of the product, whereas in a negligence case, the plaintiff must prove that the defendant knew or should have known of the danger. This distinction is particularly pertinent in a manufacturing defect context.

When the strict liability defect consists of an improper design or warning, reasonableness of the defendant's conduct is a factor in determining liability. The question in strict liability design defect and warning cases is whether, assuming that the manufacturer knew of the defect in the product, he acted in a reasonably prudent manner in marketing the product or in providing the warnings given. Thus, once the defendant's knowledge of the defect is imputed, strict liability analysis becomes almost identical to negligence analysis in its focus on the reasonableness of the defendant's conduct. * * *

Generally, the state of the art in design defect cases and available knowledge in defect warning situations are relevant factors in measuring reasonableness of conduct. Thus * * * we [have] explained that other than assuming that the manufacturer knew of the harmful propensity of the product, the jury could consider "the technological feasibility of manufacturing a product whose design would have prevented or avoided the accident, given the known state of the art." We observed that "the state of the art refers not only to the common practice and standards in the industry but also to the other design alternatives within practical and technological limits at the time of distribution." [W]e again referred to the state of the art as an appropriate factor to be considered by the jury to determine whether feasible alternatives existed when the product was marketed.

Similarly, as to warnings, generally conduct should be measured by knowledge at the time the manufacturer distributed the product. Did the defendant know, or should he have known, of the danger, given the scientific, technological, and other information available when the product was distributed; or, in other words, did he have actual or constructive knowledge of the danger? The Restatement, supra, has adopted this test in Comment j to section 402A, which reads in pertinent part as follows:

> *Directions or warning.* In order to prevent the product from being unreasonably dangerous, the seller may be required to give directions or warning, on the container, as to its use. * * * Where the product contains an ingredient * * * whose danger is not generally known, or if known is one which the consumer would reasonably not expect to find in the product, the seller is required to give warning against it, *if he has knowledge, or by the application of reasonable, developed human skill and foresight should have knowledge,* of the presence of the ingredient and the danger. [Emphasis added.]

Under this standard negligence and strict liability in warning cases may be deemed to be functional equivalents. * * * Constructive knowledge embraces knowledge that should have been known based on information that was reasonably available or obtainable and should have alerted a reasonably prudent person to act. Put another way, would a person of reasonable intelligence or of the superior expertise of the defendant charged with such knowledge conclude that defendant should have alerted the consuming public?

Further, a manufacturer is held to the standard of an expert in the field. A manufacturer should keep abreast of scientific advances. * * *

Furthermore, a reasonably prudent manufacturer will be deemed to know of reliable information generally available or reasonably obtainable in the industry or in the particular field involved. Such information need not be limited to that furnished by experts in the field, but may also include material provided by others. Thus, for example, if a substantial number of doctors or consumers had complained to a drug manufacturer of an untoward effect of a drug, that would have constituted sufficient information requiring an appropriate warning. * * *

This test does not conflict with the assumption made in strict liability design defect and warning cases that the defendant knew of the dangerous propensity of the product, if the knowledge that is assumed is reasonably knowable in the sense of actual or constructive knowledge. A warning that a product may have an unknowable danger warns one of nothing. * * * [T]he manufacturer would [not] be deemed to know of the dangerous propensity of the chattel when the danger was unknowable. In our opinion [Beshada v. Johns–Manville Products Corp., 90 N.J. 191, 447 A.2d 539 (1982)] * * * would not demand a contrary conclusion in the typical design defect or warning case. If *Beshada* were deemed to hold generally or in all cases, particularly with respect to a situation like the present one involving drugs vital to health, that in a warning context knowledge of the unknowable is irrelevant in determining the applicability of strict liability, we would not agree. Many commentators have criticized this aspect of the *Beshada* reasoning and the public policies on which it is based. * * * The rationale of *Beshada* is not applicable to this case. We do not overrule

Beshada, but restrict Beshada to the circumstances giving rise to its holding. * * *

In strict liability warning cases, unlike negligence cases, however, the defendant should properly bear the burden of proving that the information was not reasonably available or obtainable and that it therefore lacked actual or constructive knowledge of the defect. * * * The defendant is in a superior position to know the technological material or data in the particular field or specialty. The defendant is the expert, often performing self-testing. It is the defendant that injected the product in the stream of commerce for its economic gain. As a matter of policy the burden of proving the status of knowledge in the field at the time of distribution is properly placed on the defendant. * * *

One other aspect with respect to warnings based on subsequently obtained knowledge should be considered. Communication of the new warning should unquestionably be given to prescribing physicians as soon as reasonably feasible. Although a manufacturer may not have actual or constructive knowledge of a danger so as to impose upon it a duty to warn, subsequently acquired knowledge, both actual and constructive, also may obligate the manufacturer to take reasonable steps to notify purchasers and consumers of the newly-discovered danger. * * *

The timeliness of the warning issue is obliquely present in this case. It is possible that Dr. Feldman already had Declomycin on hand when defendant became aware of Declomycin's side effect. If that state of affairs existed, defendant would have had an obligation to warn doctors and others promptly. This most assuredly would include those to whom defendant had already furnished the product. * * * The extent and nature of post-distribution warnings may vary depending on the circumstances, but in the context of this case, the defendant at a minimum would have had a duty of advising physicians, including plaintiff's father, whom it had directly solicited to use Declomycin.

* * *

We reverse and remand for a new trial.

NOTES

1. How long after the first hints that there may be a problem with a product should the manufacturer issue a warning? What factors should be considered in making this determination?

2. As you will recall from the discussion in the notes following the *Branham* case, the position taken by the *Feldman* court is often called a foresight test. The adequacy of a warning is to be judged by what the manufacturer reasonably should have known at the time the product entered the stream of commerce. This may be distinguished from a hindsight test. The adequacy of the warning is to be judged by looking backward from the time of the accident to ask what, given what we know at that time, the manufacturer

should have told the plaintiff. With the adoption of a foresight test in warning cases, what, if anything, distinguishes this area of products law from negligence?

3. As noted earlier, state-of-the-art issues arise in design defect cases as well. A discussion of the state-of-the-art defense in the design defect context can be found in Hughes v. Massey–Ferguson, Inc., 522 N.W.2d 294 (Iowa 1994). *See also* Boatland of Houston v. Bailey, 609 S.W.2d 743 (Tex.1980). Some older opinions refused to consider state-of-the-art evidence in design defect cases. *See* Elmore v. Owens–Illinois, Inc., 673 S.W.2d 434 (Mo.1984).

4. The *Beshada* case referred to in *Feldman* rejected a state-of-the-art defense in warning cases. *Beshada* involved a group of plaintiffs suffering from asbestosis, mesothelioma, and other asbestos related diseases. They claimed the defendants failed to warn them of the dangers of exposure to airborne asbestos and the defendants responded that they did not know of the risks at the time the plaintiffs were exposed. The court justified its rejection of the state-of-the-art defense on three grounds: a) denying this defense will maximize the strict liability goal of risk spreading, b) by imposing liability on manufacturers for unknown risks the courts will create additional incentives to invest in safety research, and c) denying the defense will reduce the costs of litigation. With respect to this last point, the court said:

> Proof of what could have been known will inevitably be complicated, costly, confusing, and time consuming. * * * We doubt that juries will be capable of even understanding the concept of scientific knowability, much less be able to resolve such a complex issue. Moreover, we should resist legal rules that will so greatly add to the costs both sides incur in trying a case.

Beshada, 90 N.J. at 207–08, 447 A.2d at 548.

Assess each of these grounds for rejecting a state-of-the-art defense. Most commentators agree with the majority rule set forth in *Feldman. See* David Owen, *The Moral Foundation of Products Liability Law: Toward First Principles*, 68 Notre Dame L. Rev. 427 (1993); John Wade, *On the Effect in Product Liability of Knowledge Unavailable Prior to Marketing*, 58 N.Y.U. L. Rev. 734 (1983); Gary Schwartz, *The Vitality of Negligence and the Ethics of Strict Liability*, 15 Ga. L. Rev. 963 (1981). *But see* Ellen Wertheimer, *Unknowable Dangers and the Death of Strict Products Liability: The Empire Strikes Back*, 60 U. Cin. L. Rev. 1183 (1992) for a criticism of judicial unwillingness to impute knowledge to manufacturers in state-of-the-art cases.

5. Today, there is very little support for the *Beshada* position. Recall that Massachusetts has never adopted *Restatement (Second) of Torts* § 402A; but it has developed a parallel body of warranty law. In Vassallo v. Baxter Healthcare Corp., 428 Mass. 1, 696 N.E.2d 909 (1998), it adopted the majority position:

> Our current law, regarding the duty to warn under the implied warranty of merchantability, presumes that a manufacturer was fully informed of all risks associated with the product at issue, regardless of the state of the

art at the time of the sale, and amounts to strict liability for failure to warn of these risks.

* * *

[W]e recognize that we are among a distinct minority of States that applies a hindsight analysis to the duty to warn. * * * At least three jurisdictions that previously applied strict liability to the duty to warn in a products liability claim have reversed themselves, either by statute or by decision, and now require knowledge, or reasonable knowability as a component of such a claim. See * * * *Feldman v. Lederle Labs.*, 97 N.J. 429, 455, 479 A.2d 374 (1984) * * *. The change in the law of New Jersey is particularly relevant, because we relied in part on New Jersey law in formulating the strict liability standard expressed in the *Hayes* decision. See Hayes, supra at 413, 462 N.E.2d 273, citing *Beshada v. Johns–Manville Prods. Corp.*, 90 N.J. 191, 202–207, 447 A.2d 539 (1982). The thin judicial support for a hindsight approach to the duty to warn is easily explained. The goal of the law is to induce conduct that is capable of being performed. This goal is not advanced by imposing liability for failure to warn of risks that were not capable of being known. * * * Restatement (Third) of Torts: Products Liability § 2(c) (1997), recently approved by the American Law Institute, reaffirms the principle expressed in Restatement (Second) of Torts, *supra* at § 402A comment j, by stating that a product "is defective because of inadequate instructions or warnings when the foreseeable risks of harm posed by the product could have been reduced or avoided by the provision of reasonable instructions or warnings ... and the omission of the instructions or warnings renders the product not reasonably safe." The rationale behind the principle is explained by stating that "[u]nforeseeable risks arising from foreseeable product use ... by definition cannot specifically be warned against." Restatement (Third) of Torts: Products Liability, *supra* at § 2 comment m, at 34. However, comment m also clarifies the manufacturer's duty "to perform reasonable testing prior to marketing a product and to discover risks and risk-avoidance measures that such testing would reveal. A seller is charged with knowledge of what reasonable testing would reveal." *Id.*

* * *

In recognition of the clear judicial trend regarding the duty to warn in products liability cases, and the principles stated in Restatement (Third) of Torts: Products Liability, *supra* at § 2(c) and comment m, we hereby revise our law to state that a defendant will not be held liable under an implied warranty of merchantability for failure to warn or provide instructions about risks that were not reasonably foreseeable at the time of sale or could not have been discovered by way of reasonable testing prior to marketing the product. A manufacturer will be held to the standard of knowledge of an expert in the appropriate field, and will remain subject to a continuing duty to warn (at least purchasers) of risks discovered following the sale of the product at issue.

Opinions admitting state-of-the-art evidence in warning cases include Anderson v. Owens–Corning Fiberglas Corp., 53 Cal.3d 987, 281 Cal.Rptr.

528, 810 P.2d 549 (1991); Fibreboard Corp. v. Fenton, 845 P.2d 1168 (Colo. 1993); Powers v. Taser Int'l, Inc., 217 Ariz. 398, 174 P.3d 777, 779–84 (Ct. App. 2007). *But see* Sternhagen v. Dow Co., 282 Mont. 168, 935 P.2d 1139 (1997).

6. *Custom and industry practice.* Courts generally distinguish a state-of-the-art defense from industry custom. In design defect cases, the issue is usually put as one of feasibility. As the *Hughes* court (*supra* note 3) noted: "custom refers to what was being done in the industry; state-of-the-art refers to what feasibly could have been done." *Hughes*, 522 N.W.2d at 295. The *Boatland* court (*supra* note 3) used similar language: "In our view, 'custom' is distinguishable from 'state of the art.' The state of the art with respect to a particular product refers to the technological environment at the time of its manufacture. This technological environment includes the scientific knowledge, economic feasibility, and the practicalities of implementation when the product was manufactured." *Boatland*, 609 S.W.2d at 748. Likewise, in warning cases the issue is not what warnings firms in the industry actually gave, but what knowledge reasonably should have been possessed concerning the risks associated with the product.

7. *Feldman* viewed state-of-the-art as an affirmative defense. The *Restatement (Third) of Torts: Products Liability* § 2, Comment *m*, cited above in *Vassallo*, places the burden of showing that a risk was known or should have been known to the relevant manufacturing community on the plaintiff.

8. *Post Sale duties.* What duty did Lederle have to warn earlier purchasers of its product once it discovered Declomycin may cause tooth discoloration? This is part of a larger question of a seller's post sale conduct. The *Restatement (Third) of Torts: Products* Liability § 10 contains the following provision:

§ 10. Liability of Commercial Seller or Distributor for Harm Caused by Post–Sale Failure to Warn

(a) One engaged in the business of selling or otherwise distributing products is subject to liability for harm to persons or property caused by the seller's failure to provide a warning after the time of sale or distribution of a product if a reasonable person in the seller's position would provide such a warning.

(b) A reasonable person in the seller's position would provide a warning after the time of sale if:

(1) the seller knows or reasonably should know that the product poses a substantial risk of harm to persons or property; and

(2) those to whom a warning might be provided can be identified and can reasonably be assumed to be unaware of the risk of harm; and

(3) a warning can be effectively communicated to and acted on by those to whom a warning might be provided; and

(4) the risk of harm is sufficiently great to justify the burden of providing a warning.

For cases supporting this position, *see* Patton v. Hutchinson Wil–Rich Manufacturing Co., 253 Kan. 741, 861 P.2d 1299 (1993); Crowston v. Goodyear Tire & Rubber Co., 521 N.W.2d 401 (N.D. 1994); Rash v. Stryker Corp., 589 F.Supp.2d 733 (W.D.Va. 2008). In Robinson v. Brandtjen & Kluge, Inc., 500 F.3d 691 (8th Cir. 2007), plaintiff was injured in 2001 when her hand became caught between two large surfaces of a printing press manufactured in 1939 and originally sold to a newspaper in Deadwood, South Dakota in 1940. Plaintiff argued that the manufacturer was negligent in failing to provide the current owner with post-sale warnings against manually feeding sheets into the press. What result under Restatement Section 10?

Section 10 is intended specifically to cover those situations where the courts would not say a product was defective at the time of sale, perhaps because the newly discovered risks were unknowable at that time. If the product was defective at the time of sale, liability exists even in the absence of a post-sale duty to warn and such a warning does not necessarily relieve the seller of liability for any injuries caused by the defect. *See* Flax v. DaimlerChrysler Corp., 272 S.W.3d 521 (Tenn. 2008).

Courts have not been willing to impose a post-sale duty to recall or repair absent some ongoing relationship, e.g. a maintenance contract, between the seller and buyer. *See Restatement (Third) of Torts: Products Liability* § 11.

4. THE CONTINUING TENSION BETWEEN WARNING AND DESIGN

Under a consumer expectation test of defect, warnings often trump design. For example, a warning might make a design defect obvious and, therefore, not dangerous beyond the expectations of the ordinary consumer. The movement to a risk-utility test of defect reverses this relationship. An adequate warning that draws the consumer's attention to a design flaw will not necessarily absolve the manufacturer of liability. However, as we saw in the *Riley* case, *supra* p. 221, the user's awareness of danger is one of the factors courts may consider in assessing whether a design is defective. In the following case, the Texas Supreme Court is sharply divided on the continuing question of the proper relationship between warning and design.

UNIROYAL GOODRICH TIRE CO. v. MARTINEZ

Supreme Court of Texas, 1998.
977 S.W.2d 328.

PHILLIPS, CHIEF JUSTICE, delivered the opinion of the Court, in which GONZALEZ, SPECTOR, ABBOTT and HANKINSON, JUSTICES, join.

* * *

We must decide whether a manufacturer who knew of a safer alternative product design is liable in strict products liability for injuries caused by the use of its product that the user could have avoided by following the product's warnings. The court of appeals held that the mere fact that a product bears an adequate warning does not conclusively establish that the product is not defective. * * * Because we agree, we affirm the judgment of the court of appeals.

I

Roberto Martinez, together with his wife and children, sued Uniroyal Goodrich Tire Company ("Goodrich"), The Budd Company, and Ford Motor Company for personal injuries Martinez suffered when he was struck by an exploding 16″ Goodrich tire that he was mounting on a 16.5″ rim. Attached to the tire was a prominent warning label containing yellow and red highlights and a pictograph of a worker being thrown into the air by an exploding tire. The label stated conspicuously:

DANGER

> NEVER MOUNT A 16″ SIZE DIAMETER TIRE ON A 16.5″ RIM. Mounting a 16″ tire on a 16.5″ rim can cause severe injury or death. While it is possible to pass a 16″ diameter tire over the lip or flange of a 16.5″ size diameter rim, it cannot position itself against the rim flange. If an attempt is made to seat the bead by inflating the tire, the tire bead will break with explosive force.
>
> . . .
>
> NEVER inflate a tire which is lying on the floor or other flat surface. Always use a tire mounting machine with a hold-down device or safety cage or bolt to vehicle axle.
>
> NEVER inflate to seat beads without using an extension hose with gauge and clip-on chuck.
>
> NEVER stand, lean or reach over the assembly during inflation.
>
> . . .
>
> Failure to comply with these safety precautions can cause the bead to break and the assembly to burst with sufficient force to cause serious injury or death.

Unfortunately, Martinez ignored every one of these warnings. While leaning over the assembly, he attempted to mount a 16″ tire on a 16.5″ rim without a tire mounting machine, a safety cage, or an extension hose. Martinez explained, however, that because he had removed a 16″ tire from the 16.5″ rim, he believed that he was mounting the new 16″ tire on a 16″ rim. Moreover, the evidence revealed that Martinez's employer failed to make an operable tire-mounting machine available to him at the time he was injured, and there was no evidence that the other safety devices mentioned in the warning were available.

In their suit, the Martinezes did not claim that the warnings were inadequate, but instead alleged that Goodrich, the manufacturer of the tire, Budd, the manufacturer of the rim, and Ford, the designer of the rim, were each negligent and strictly liable for designing and manufacturing a defective tire and rim. Budd and Ford settled with the Martinezes before trial, and the case proceeded solely against Goodrich.

At trial, the Martinezes claimed that the tire manufactured by Goodrich was defective because it failed to incorporate a safer alternative bead design that would have kept the tire from exploding. This defect, they asserted, was the producing cause of Martinez's injuries. * * *

The bead is the portion of the tire that holds the tire to the rim when inflated. A bead consists of rubber-encased steel wiring that encircles the tire a number of times. When the tire is placed inside the wheel rim and inflated, the bead is forced onto the bead-seating ledge of the rim and pressed against the lip of the rim, or the wheel flange. When the last portion of the bead is forced onto this ledge, the tire has "seated," and the air is properly sealed inside the tire. The bead holds the tire to the rim because the steel wire, unlike rubber, does not expand when the tire is inflating. The tire in this case was a 16″ bias-ply light truck tire with a 0.037″ gauge multi-strand weftless bead, or tape bead, manufactured in 1990. A tape bead consists of several strands of parallel unwoven steel wires circling the tire with each layer resting on top of the last, similar to tape wound on a roll. After a number of layers have been wound, the end of the bead is joined, or spliced, to the beginning of the same bead to form a continuous loop.

The Martinezes' expert, Alan Milner, a metallurgical engineer, testified that a tape bead is prone to break when the spliced portion of the bead is the last portion of the bead to seat. This is commonly called a hang-up. Milner testified that an alternative bead design, a 0.050″ gauge single strand programmed bead, would have prevented Martinez's injuries because its strength and uniformity make it more resistant to breaking during a hang-up. Milner explained that the 0.050″ single strand programmed bead is stronger because it is 0.013″ thicker and that it is uniform because it is wound, or programmed, by a computer, eliminating the spliced portion of the bead that can cause the tire to explode during a hang-up.

* * *

In 1966, 16.5″ wheel rims were first introduced into the American market.[1] Milner testified that Uniroyal, Inc. and B.F. Goodrich Company, who in 1986 merged to form Goodrich, soon became aware that mismatching their 16″ tires with the new wheel rims often caused hang-ups that resulted in broken beads. * * *

Finally, Milner testified that B.F. Goodrich's own testing department was aware by at least 1976 that a 16″ tire mounted on a 16.5″ rim would explode during a hang-up. * * * A B.F. Goodrich "test request" of that year was entered into evidence indicating that a 16″ tire would explode when mounted on a 16.5″ rim at 73 psi (pounds of pressure per square inch). The test request further indicated that "inspection revealed break

1. The rim involved in this case was manufactured in 1979. The Budd Company ceased manufacturing 16.5″ rims in 1983.

was at [illegible] ends of bottom layer of [bead] wires as anticipated." The stated "Object of Test" was: "To develop demonstrative evidence & data for use in lawsuits involving broken beads."

Milner explained that the computer technology required to manufacture the programmed bead was developed in 1972 and widely available by 1975. Milner testified that Goodyear began using a 0.051″ gauge single strand programmed bead in its radial light truck tires in 1977, and that Yokohama began using a single strand programmed bead in its radial light truck tires in 1981. Milner also testified that General Tire began using a single strand programmed bead in its bias-ply light truck tires in 1982. Finally, Milner testified that Goodrich itself began using the single strand programmed bead in its 16″ radial light truck tires in 1991. * * *

Milner also testified that the rim designed by Ford and manufactured by Budd was defective because its size was not clearly marked on it and because it could have been redesigned to prevent a 16″ tire from passing over its flange.

The jury found that Goodrich's conduct was the sole proximate cause of Martinez's injuries and that Goodrich was grossly negligent. Furthermore, the jury found that the tire manufactured by Goodrich was defective, while the wheel rim designed by Ford and manufactured by Budd was not defective. The jury allocated 100% of the producing cause of Martinez's injuries to the acts and omissions of Goodrich.

The jury awarded the Martinezes $5.5 million in actual damages and $11.5 million in punitive damages. After reducing the award of actual damages by $1.4 million pursuant to a settlement agreement between the Martinezes, Ford, and Budd, reducing the punitive damages to the amount of actual damages pursuant to a pretrial agreement between Goodrich and the Martinezes, and awarding prejudgment interest, the trial court rendered judgment for the Martinezes for $10,308,792.45.

The court of appeals affirmed the award of actual damages * * *. However, the court of appeals reversed and rendered the award of punitive damages, holding that there was no evidence to support the jury's finding of gross negligence.

Only Goodrich applied to this Court for writ of error. As in the court of appeals, Goodrich's principal argument here is that no evidence supports the jury finding that the tire was defective because "the tire bore a warning which was unambiguous and conspicuously visible (and not claimed to be inadequate); the tire was safe for use if the warning was followed; and the cause of the accident was mounting and inflating a tire in direct contravention of those warnings."

* * *

II

A

This Court has adopted the products liability standard set forth in section 402A of the Restatement (Second) of Torts. * * * A product may be unreasonably dangerous because of a defect in manufacturing, design, or marketing. *See Caterpillar, Inc. v. Shears,* 911 S.W.2d 379, 382 (Tex. 1995) * * *. To prove a design defect, a claimant must establish, among other things, that the defendant could have provided a safer alternative design. *See Caterpillar,* 911 S.W.2d at 384 ("[I]f there are no safer alternatives, a product is not unreasonably dangerous as a matter of law."). * * * Implicit in this holding is that the safer alternative design must be reasonable, *i.e.,* that it can be implemented without destroying the utility of the product. * * *

The newly released Restatement (Third) of Torts: Products Liability carries forward this focus on reasonable alternative design. *See* RESTATEMENT (THIRD) OF TORTS: PRODUCTS LIABILITY § 2(b). Section 2(b) provides:

> A product ... is defective in design when the foreseeable risks of harm posed by the product could have been reduced or avoided by the adoption of a reasonable alternative design by the seller or other distributor, or a predecessor in the commercial chain of distribution, and the omission of the alternative design renders the product not reasonably safe.

To determine whether a reasonable alternative design exists, and if so whether its omission renders the product unreasonably dangerous (or in the words of the new Restatement, not reasonably safe), the finder of fact may weigh various factors bearing on the risk and utility of the product. *See Caterpillar,* 911 S.W.2d at 383–84; *Turner v. General Motors Corp.,* 584 S.W.2d 844, 848 (Tex.1979). One of these factors is whether the product contains suitable warnings and instructions. *See Turner,* 584 S.W.2d at 847. The new Restatement likewise carries forward this approach:

> A broad range of factors may be considered in determining whether an alternative design is reasonable and whether its omission renders a product not reasonably safe. The factors include, among others, the magnitude and probability of the foreseeable risks of harm, *the instructions and warnings accompanying the product,* and the nature and strength of consumer expectations regarding the product, including expectations arising from product portrayal and marketing.... The relative advantages and disadvantages of the product as designed and as it alternatively could have been designed may also be considered. Thus, the likely effects of the alternative design on production costs; the effects of the alternative design on product longevity, maintenance, repair, and esthetics; and the range of consumer choice among products are factors that may be taken into account....

Restatement (Third) of Torts: Products Liability § 2 cmt. f (emphasis added).

Goodrich urges this Court to depart from this standard by following certain language from Comment j of the Restatement (Second) of Torts. Comment j provides in part:

> Where warning is given, the seller may reasonably assume that it will be read and heeded; and a product bearing such a warning, which is safe for use if it is followed, is not in defective condition, nor is it unreasonably dangerous.

Restatement (Second) of Torts § 402A cmt. j (1965). The new Restatement, however, expressly rejects the Comment j approach:

> Reasonable designs and instructions or warnings both play important roles in the production and distribution of reasonably safe products. In general, when a safer design can reasonably be implemented and risks can reasonably be designed out of a product, adoption of the safer design is required over a warning that leaves a significant residuum of such risks. For example, instructions and warnings may be ineffective because users of the product may not be adequately reached, may be likely to be inattentive, or may be insufficiently motivated to follow the instructions or heed the warnings. However, when an alternative design to avoid risks cannot reasonably be implemented, adequate instructions and warnings will normally be sufficient to render the product reasonably safe. *Compare* Comment *e*. *Warnings are not, however, a substitute for the provision of a reasonably safe design.*

Restatement (Third) of Torts: Products Liability § 2 cmt. *l* (emphasis added). The Reporters' Notes in the new Restatement refer to Comment j as "unfortunate language" that "has elicited heavy criticism from a host of commentators." Restatement (Third) of Torts: Products Liability § 2, Reporters' Note, cmt. *l* * * * Similarly, this Court has indicated that the fact that a danger is open and obvious (and thus need not be warned against) does not preclude a finding of product defect when a safer, reasonable alternative design exists.

* * *

B

We do not hold, as the dissenting justices claim, that "a product is defective whenever it could be more safely designed without substantially impairing its utility," *post* at 344, or that "warnings are irrelevant in determining whether a product is reasonably safe." *Post* at 345. Rather, as we have explained, we agree with the new Restatement that warnings and safer alternative designs are factors, among others, for the jury to consider in determining whether the product as designed is reasonably safe. *See* Restatement (Third) of Torts: Products Liability § 2 cmt. f. While the dissenting justices say that they also agree with the Restatement's approach, they would, at least in this case, remove the balancing process from the jury. Instead, they would hold that Goodrich's warning rendered the tape bead design reasonably safe as a matter of law.

* * *

V

Goodrich also argues that the evidence conclusively establishes that Martinez was negligent and that he contributed to his own injuries. Specifically, Goodrich argues that unless some defect in the warning hinders a plaintiff's ability to see and heed it, the failure to see and heed a warning is conclusive proof of contributory negligence.

In reviewing a conclusive evidence point, we must determine whether the proffered evidence as a whole rises to a level that reasonable people could not differ in their conclusions. *Transportation Ins. Co. v. Moriel,* 879 S.W.2d 10, 25 (Tex.1994); Powers & Ratliff, *Another Look at "No Evidence" and "Insufficient Evidence,"* 69 TEX. L.REV. 515, 523 (1991) ("Ultimately, the test for 'conclusive evidence' . . . is similar to the test for 'no evidence' . . .; the court asks whether reasonable minds could differ about the fact determination to be made by the jury."). The jury was asked to decide whether Martinez was negligent, that is, whether he failed to exercise ordinary prudence. Both Martinez and his co-worker Ramundo Regalado testified that, because they had removed 16″ tires from the rims on which they were working, they assumed that the rims were also 16″. Also, although there was a tire-changing machine on the premises, the evidence was conflicting as to whether Martinez could have used it to secure the tire. Rene Vera, Martinez and Regalado's employer, testified that the tire-changing machine, although inoperable for dismounting tires, could have nonetheless been used to secure the tire during inflation. Regalado testified, however, that the tire-changing machine did not work, despite his repeated requests to the safety foreman to have it repaired, and that had it worked he and Martinez would have been using it on the day of the accident to secure the tire. Thus, Goodrich failed to conclusively prove that Martinez was negligent in failing to use the machine. There is no evidence that the other safety devices referenced in the tire warning—a safety cage or an extension hose—were available to Martinez. Further, Goodrich offered no evidence as to whether it was practical or feasible under the circumstances for Martinez to bolt the rim to a vehicle axle in order to inflate the tire and seat the bead. Both Martinez and Regalado testified that the manner in which Martinez was inflating the tire was customary in their shop. Based upon this evidence, we cannot conclude that reasonable people could not differ about whether Martinez failed to exercise ordinary prudence under the circumstances.

Because we conclude that Goodrich did not conclusively establish that Martinez was negligent, we do not address Goodrich's argument that there is no evidence to support the jury's allocation of causation.

* * *

VI

Goodrich next argues that even if it is not entitled to a rendition of judgment, it is entitled to a new trial because of * * * the admission of evidence that Goodrich had subsequently redesigned its radial light truck tires to incorporate the single strand programmed bead * * *.

Goodrich * * * complains that the trial court erred by admitting evidence that Goodrich subsequently redesigned its radial light truck tires to incorporate the single strand programmed bead, because radial tires are fundamentally different from the bias-ply tire that injured Martinez, and the bead change was not made in the radial tires for safety reasons. Goodrich first argues that, under these circumstances, the evidence regarding radial tires violates Texas Rule of Civil Evidence 407(a).

Rule 407(a) states:

> Subsequent Remedial Measures. When, after an event, measures are taken which, if taken previously, would have made the event less likely to occur, evidence of the subsequent remedial measures is not admissible to prove negligence or culpable conduct in connection with the event. This rule does not require the exclusion of evidence of subsequent remedial measures when offered for another purpose, such as proving ownership, control or feasibility of precautionary measures, if controverted, or impeachment. *Nothing in this rule shall preclude admissibility in products liability cases based on strict liability.*

Tex.R. Civ. Evid. 407(a) (emphasis added). Goodrich argues that this rule only permits the admission of subsequent remedial measures involving the product at issue, and that such measures must have been made for safety reasons. However, the rule does not contain these limitations. Rather, under the express language emphasized above, Rule 407(a) simply does not apply in products liability cases based on strict liability. Thus, the trial court did not violate Rule 407(a).

* * *

Because we conclude that there is some evidence to support the judgment of the court below on the theory of products liability, we need not consider Goodrich's claim that there is no evidence as to negligence. For the foregoing reasons, we affirm the judgment of the court of appeals.

HECHT, JUSTICE, joined by ENOCH and BAKER, JUSTICES, and by OWEN, JUSTICE, in all but Part II, dissenting.

* * *

Having changed about a thousand tires in his life, Roberto Martinez admits he knew better than to lean over a tire while inflating it. Besides, he had seen the pictographic warning on the very tire he was changing which showed a worker being hurt by an exploding tire and warned: "NEVER stand, lean or reach over the assembly during inflation." Ignoring this warning and his own good sense, Martinez was leaning over the tire, inflating it, when it exploded in his face.

The 16″ tire exploded because it would not fit the 16.5″ wheel on which Martinez was trying to mount it. Martinez knew it was very dangerous to try to mount a 16″ tire on a 16.5″ wheel, and he would never knowingly have tried to do it, but the size of the wheel was not marked where he could find it. He understood that his co-worker had taken a 16″ tire off the wheel, and he was simply trying to put the same size tire back on. The Budd Company, which manufactured the wheel to Ford Motor Company's specifications, knew, as did Ford, that people sometimes try to mount 16″ tires on 16.5″ wheels, not realizing that tire and wheel are mismatched. To minimize the risk of such mistakes, Budd and Ford could have changed the design of the wheel to prevent mounting mismatched tires, but they did not do so. Budd could also have simply stamped the size in plain view on the outboard side of the wheel near the valve stem where it was almost sure to be seen, but it did not do that, either. Instead it encoded the size in small letters on the inboard side, where it was hard to find if the wheel was clean, and indecipherable if the wheel was dirty, as it was in this case.

Although a 16.5″ wheel can be designed so that a 16″ tire cannot be mounted on it, a 16″ tire cannot be designed so that it cannot be mounted on a 16.5″ wheel. A tire manufacturer's only options to reduce the risk of injury from attempting to mount a 16″ tire on a 16.5″ wheel are to place a warning on the tire or to design the bead wire so that it will withstand higher inflation pressure before exploding. The Uniroyal Goodrich Tire Company, which made the tire Martinez was using, chose to put a prominent, pictographic label on it, which, as I have said, Martinez actually saw but did not heed. Had he done so, he would not have been injured. In fact, according to the record, only one other person has ever claimed to have been injured attempting to mount a 16″ tire with a warning label like Goodrich's on a 16.5″ wheel, although thousands of labeled tires and more than thirty million 16.5″ wheels have been manufactured in the past two decades.

Now as among Martinez, the wheel manufacturers, and Goodrich, how should responsibility for Martinez's accident be apportioned? The reader may be surprised at the answer in this case. Martinez, though negligent by his own admission, is held to bear no responsibility for the accident. The wheel manufacturers, too, are held to be free of responsibility (they settled with Martinez before trial) although the undisputed testimony by both Martinez's and Goodrich's experts is that Budd and Ford defectively designed the wheel. Only Goodrich is held liable—and for providing a warning on the tire that would have prevented Martinez's accident altogether instead of redesigning the bead wire so that the accident would only have been less likely. This aberrant result flows from * * * serious flaws in the Court's opinion which, even more importantly, misstate the law that will be applied in other cases.

First, the Court holds that a product can be found to be defective whenever it could be more safely designed without substantially impairing its utility. This is not, and should not be, the law. As the *Restatement (Third) of Torts: Products Liability* advises, a "broad range of factors" besides the utility of a reasonable alternate design should be considered in determining whether its use is necessary to keep the product reasonably safe, including "the magnitude and probability of the foreseeable risks of harm [and] the instructions and warnings accompanying the product". When the undisputed evidence is that the magnitude and probability of a risk are low, an alternative design could reduce but not eliminate that risk, and the instructions and warnings given do eliminate the risk, the product should be determined not to be defective as a matter of law.

* * *

I

Comment j to Section 402A of the *Restatement (Second) of Torts* states: Where warning is given, the seller may reasonably assume that it will be read and heeded; and a product bearing such a warning, which is safe for use if it is followed, is not in defective condition, nor is it unreasonably dangerous.

We have followed the first clause of comment j, but only to the extent of holding that a plaintiff is entitled to a rebuttable presumption that had he been adequately warned of the dangers of a product, he would have avoided injury, despite the fact that experience teaches that "it is not at all unusual for a person to fail to follow basic warnings and instructions."[7] The presumption is merely a procedural device to obviate the necessity of plaintiff's self-serving testimony that he would have heeded adequate warnings. In making the presumption rebuttable we recognized that the first clause is not always true. Further, we have never followed the second clause of comment j, and now the *Restatement (Third) of Torts: Products Liability* has withdrawn comment j altogether as "unfortunate language" that "has elicited heavy criticism from a host of commentators." The Court's firm rejection of comment j, which the Court has never adopted and the *Restatement* has now itself rejected, is perhaps beating a dead horse, but I agree that comment j does not correctly state what the law is or should be.

Since it is human nature to disregard instructions, a rule that any product is reasonably safe as long as it bears an adequate warning of the risks of its use is not feasible. Such behavior, however, does not warrant the opposite rule that warnings are irrelevant in determining whether a product is reasonably safe. I agree with the Court that comment *l* to Section 2 of the *Restatement (Third) of Torts: Products Liability* now has it about right:

* * *

I do not agree, however, that the Court correctly reads or follows comment *l*. Comment *l* limits but does not foreclose the role of warnings in making products reasonably safe, even when there is a safer alternative design. * * *

7. *General Motors Corp. v. Saenz,* 873 S.W.2d 353, 358 (Tex.1993) * * *.

Section 2(b) of the *Restatement (Third) of Torts: Products Liability* states the applicable rule: A product ... is defective in design when the foreseeable risks of harm posed by the product could have been reduced or avoided by the adoption of a reasonable alternative design by the seller or other distributor, or a predecessor in the commercial chain of distribution, *and* the omission of the alternative design renders the product not reasonably safe.

There are two components to this rule: the possibility of a safer, reasonable alternative design, *and* a product that is not reasonably safe without that design. Both are required. Even if a reasonable alternative design would make a product safer, the product is not defective unless the omission of the design makes the product not reasonably safe. The comparison is not between the two designs, but between the product alternatively designed and the product including any warning.

* * *

[An] example * * * is aerosol cans. Such cans are not defective merely because they could be redesigned so as not to explode if punctured or incinerated. A warning against such misuse ought to be sufficient.

The Court protests that it has not disregarded the effect of warnings in determining whether the possibility of a safer alternative design makes a product defective but has merely left the matter to the jury. But the question remains: can any product be shown not to be defective as a matter of law if a reasonable alternative design could have avoided plaintiff's injury? The Court suggests no such possibility. The *Restatement* appears to contemplate that a product is not defective as a matter of law if the safer design does not eliminate the risks, or if the warning on the product does not leave a significant residuum of risk, as when "users of the product may not be adequately reached, may be likely to be inattentive, or may be insufficiently motivated to follow the instructions or heed the warnings."[16] The present case illustrates this rule. Concededly, the evidence favorable to Martinez shows that * * * an alternative design is * * * reasonable and safer. But it only reduces—it does not eliminate—the risk that a tire being mounted on a mismatched wheel will explode. The undisputed evidence in this case is that a 16″ tire cannot be mounted on a 16.5″ wheel, and that if the tire continues to be inflated in an effort to force it to seat on the wheel rim, it will explode. Redesigning the bead wire only means that the tire will withstand higher inflation pressure before exploding. * * * Because the risk of explosion cannot be eliminated, omission of the alternative design may not make the tire not reasonably safe under comment l of the *Restatement*.

* * *

Martinez does not question the adequacy of the warning. It cautions not only against mismatching tires and wheels but against inflating tires in certain ways under *any* circumstances. The record in this case does not

16. Restatement (Third) of Torts: Products Liability § 2, cmt. *l* (1998).

show that a warning against mismatching tires and wheels will not reach users. On the contrary, Martinez testified that he saw the warning on the tire, and anyway, he knew that it would be very dangerous to try to mount a 16″ tire on a 16.5″ wheel. As Martinez put it, "common sense also tells you that where you have a mismatch you can get injured." Martinez was not inattentive, as the garbage truck worker who lost his balance. He knew better than to lean over a tire—any tire—while inflating it. None of the reasons in comment l that warnings may be ineffective apply in this case.

Nor were the warnings impractical. Despite the fact that Martinez was not provided with any of the safety devices prescribed in the warning—a workable tire mounting machine, a cage, or an extension hose with gauge and clip-on chuck—and may not have been able to bolt the wheel back on the trailer from which it had been removed before mounting the tire, he could have avoided injury by simply not leaning over the tire while inflating it. Martinez testified as follows:

> Q. Now, I believe you have also testified, Roberto, that while you are inflating a tire you would not want to be leaning over the tire as you inflate it.
>
> A. No.
>
> Q. And by that I mean when you are airing it up during the mounting process you would want to lean away from it; would you not?
>
> A. Well, just don't get over it, you know, just be right beside it.
>
> Q. Why would you not want to be leaning over it?
>
> A. Because that's the way I was caught.
>
> Q. Okay. Do you feel it would be a safety consideration, to be safer to not be over the tire—
>
> A. Yes.
>
> Q.—while you're inflating it?
>
> A. Yes.

The inboard side of the tire, next to the ground, exploded. Martinez was injured when the wheel struck his head. The wheel also struck the roof of the shop overhead and dented it. Clearly, had Martinez not been leaning over the wheel, as he knew not to do and as the tire label warned against, the tire would not have struck his head.

* * * [T]here is no evidence that redesigning the bead wire will eliminate a "significant residuum of risk" in the tire as designed with the warning label. In fact, Martinez's own evidence is to the contrary. The record establishes that there has been only one other claimed injury caused by attempting to mount a 16″ tire with a warning label on a 16.5″ wheel. The record does not reflect whether that claim was ever proved. * * * The tire industry should not be compelled to redesign bead wires to make tires harder to explode—or pay damages for failing to do so—simply

because one or perhaps two mechanics over the years failed to follow directions or their own good sense.

> From a fairness perspective, requiring individual users and consumers to bear appropriate responsibility for proper product use prevents careless users and consumers from being subsidized by more careful users and consumers, when the former are paid damages out of funds to which the latter are forced to contribute through higher product prices.

Restatement (Third) of Torts: Products Liability § 2, cmt. *a* (1998).

Thus, under comment *l*, there is no evidence that omission of the safer bead wire design made Goodrich's tire not reasonably safe. The risk of explosion could not be eliminated, the warning was clear, effective, and easy to follow, and thus no significant residuum of risk remained in the tire as designed with the warning label attached. In the Court's view, a product manufacturer may be liable for failing to make any feasible design change that does not significantly impair a product's utility, if only to prevent rare mishaps from conscious disregard of adequate warnings. That is all the evidence in this case shows. The Court appropriately rejects one extreme position—comment j to Section 402A of the *Restatement (Second) of Torts*—but then adopts the opposite and equally extreme position.

* * *

The record in this case shows that Goodrich's tire including the warning label was not defectively designed as a matter of law. * * * Because the Court denies Goodrich any relief, I respectfully dissent.

NOTES

1. On exactly what issues do the majority and the dissent disagree? On what issues do they agree?

2. How would a court that continues to use a consumer expectation test deal with this problem? *See* Delaney v. Deere and Company, 268 Kan. 769, 999 P.2d 930 (Kan. 2000).

3. The Texas Rule of Evidence 407 in force at the time *Uniroyal* was decided is rare in that specifically states that the subsequent remedial measure rule does not apply in products liability cases. A number of states have reached the same position even in the absence of a specific clause. *See* Ault v. International Harvester Co., 13 Cal.3d 113, 117 Cal.Rptr. 812, 528 P.2d 1148 (1974).

Some courts have distinguished between types of products claims. For example, Colorado apparently would bar subsequent remedial measure evidence in cases based on a warning defect theory but permits it in design defect cases. Forma Scientific, Inc. v. BioSera, Inc., 960 P.2d 108 (Colo. 1998). The court justifies this distinction because "strict liability cases based on design defect theories do not entail considerations of "fault" in the traditional tort sense as do strict liability cases grounded in failure to warn claims." *Id.*

at 118. The dissent in *Forma Scientific* disagreed with the majority as to whether design defect and negligence cases are so analytically similar that they should be treated alike. Who has the best of this argument under RESTATEMENT (SECOND) OF TORTS § 402A? Who has the best of the argument under RESTATEMENT (THIRD) OF TORTS: PRODUCTS LIABILITY § 2?

A number of states and the federal courts have concluded that the Rule does apply to all products cases. Recently, the federal rule has been changed to cover products liability claims specifically. The Federal Rule now provides:

> When measures are taken that would have made an earlier injury or harm less likely to occur, evidence of the subsequent measures is not admissible to prove:
>
> - negligence;
> - culpable conduct;
> - a defect in a product or its design; or
> - a need for a warning or instruction.
>
> But the court may admit this evidence for another purpose, such as impeachment or—if disputed—proving ownership, control, or the feasibility or precautionary measures.

FEDERAL RULE OF EVIDENCE 407

4. The majority implies that the primary reason the plaintiff was not negligent as a matter of law is because of the substantial negligence on the part of his employer who failed to provide an operating changing machine despite repeated employee requests and who permitted employees to customarily inflate tires in a dangerous fashion. In Texas, as in most states employers are immune from common law liability and the jury is not permitted to include the employer when assigning percentages of responsibility to responsible parties. Indeed, in most states the employer or the employer's worker's compensation insurance carrier can recoup its entire worker's compensation payment from the joint tortfeasor or, by way of subrogation, out of the plaintiff's recovery from the joint tortfeasor. The result of this rule is to cast the risk of a negligent employer largely on other defendants. As part of tort reform in Texas, it is now possible for other defendants to add the employer as a designated third party potentially responsible for part of the plaintiff's damages. Texas Civ. Pract. & Remedy Code §§ 33.002–33.004, 33.011. The employer is still immune from common law liability even though the jury assigns a percentage of responsibility to the employer. The employee is restricted to her worker's compensation remedy. Other defendants cannot obtain contributions from the employer. However, if they are not jointly and severally liable, their total percentage of responsibility will be reduced by the percentage of responsibility assigned to the employer. Moreover, the employer's insurance company's subrogation rights are reduced by the percentage of responsibility the trier of fact assigns to the employer.This solution casts more of the risk of a negligent employer on the plaintiff-employee.

In Lambertson v. Cincinnati Welding Corp., 312 Minn. 114, 257 N.W.2d 679 (1977), the court held that a joint tortfeasor can recover contribution from the plaintiff's negligent employer, even though the plaintiff himself would be barred from recovering common law damages from his employer. The employer's contribution obligation is limited, however, to the total amount of worker's compensation paid by the employer. *See* Kotecki v. Cyclops Welding Corp., 146 Ill.2d 155, 166 Ill.Dec. 1, 585 N.E.2d 1023 (Ill. 1991) for another opinion permitting contribution in an amount not greater than worker's compensation liability.

Which of these solutions is preferable? Are any preferable to the New York rule that the employer is fully liable for contribution damages in products liability cases? Why?

E. THE PARTIES AND INTERESTS COVERED BY PRODUCTS LIABILITY

What are the boundaries of products liability law? This question has two parts: who can be a proper defendant, and what types of transactions are included?

1. *Manufacturers of component parts.* Section 402A's caveat as to whether strict liability extended to the maker of defective component parts was soon resolved in favor of liability. *See, e.g.,* Deveny v. Rheem Manufacturing Co., 319 F.2d 124 (2d Cir.1963); Suvada v. White Motor Co., 32 Ill.2d 612, 210 N.E.2d 182 (1965); Rosenau v. City of New Brunswick, 51 N.J. 130, 238 A.2d 169 (1968). One must be careful in applying the majority rule, however, because it only applies if the defect in the product causing the injury was in the component part. If the defect was the result of the installation of the component part or the incompatibility of the component with some other aspect of the product, the component part manufacturer will not be liable. *See* Mitchell v. Sky Climber, Inc., 396 Mass. 629, 487 N.E.2d 1374 (1986); Zaza v. Marquess and Nell, Inc., 144 N.J. 34, 675 A.2d 620 (1996) (interpreting the New Jersey Products Liability Statute); Kohler Co. v. Marcotte, 907 So.2d 596 (Fla. App. 2005); Ranger Conveying & Supply Co. v. Davis, 254 S.W.3d 471 (Tex. App. 2007). However, if the component part maker knows that the assembler is using the part in a dangerous or inappropriate way and does not warn, the component part maker may be liable. *See* Maake v. Ross Operating Valve Co., 149 Ariz. 244, 717 P.2d 923 (App. 1985); J. Meade Williamson and F.D.I.B., Inc. v. Piper Aircraft Corp., 968 F.2d 380 (3d Cir. 1992) (manufacturer of vacuum pump for aircraft engine had duty to instruct manufacturer on proper method of attachment to engine); Apperson v. E.I. du Pont de Nemours & Co., 41 F.3d 1103 (7th Cir. 1994) (du Pont, manufacturer of Teflon, did provide manufacturer of artificial temporomandibular joint (TMJ) with data indicating that Teflon had failed when used in hip implants. Held: Teflon itself is not defective and du Pont's warnings were sufficient as a matter of law.) The *Restatement (Third) of Torts: Products Liability* § 5 agrees (no liability unless the component part itself is defective *or* the component part manufacturer substantially participates in the integration of the component into the

design of the completed product and the integration of the component part causes the product to be defective).

2. *Successor liability.* A more difficult problem has been whether the liability extends to successor corporations after the manufacturer has ceased to exist in the corporate form that it had at the time of the sale of the product. When the manufacturer sells its assets and then ceases business, the liability does not pass to the successor firm unless:

(1) the buyer expressly or impliedly agrees to assume such liability;

(2) the transaction amounts to a *de facto* consolidation or merger;

(3) the buyer corporation is merely a continuation of the seller corporation; or

(4) the transaction is entered into fraudulently for the purpose of escaping liability.

Flaugher v. Cone Automatic Machine Co., 30 Ohio St.3d 60, 62, 507 N.E.2d 331, 334 (1987). *See also* George v. Parke–Davis, 684 F.Supp. 249 (E.D.Wash.1988); Bernard v. Kee Mfg. Co., 409 So.2d 1047 (Fla.1982). California introduced a fifth circumstance under which the successor will be held liable when it continues to market the same product line. Ray v. Alad Corp., 19 Cal.3d 22, 136 Cal.Rptr. 574, 560 P.2d 3 (1977). The court reasoned that the successor corporation enjoys the benefits of the good will associated with the product and therefore should bear the burden of the defects as well. This approach was endorsed in Ramirez v. Amsted Indus., Inc., 86 N.J. 332, 431 A.2d 811 (1981) but it was specifically rejected in the *Flaugher* case, *supra,* on the grounds that "[t]he adoption of the product line theory would cast a potentially devastating burden on business transfers and would convert sales of corporate assets into traps for the unwary." *Id.* at 66, 507 N.E.2d at 337. Most states that have considered the issue have refused to adopt the product line exception. *See* Fish v. Amsted Indus., Inc., 126 Wis.2d 293, 376 N.W.2d 820 (1985); DeLapp v. Xtraman, Inc., 417 N.W.2d 219 (Iowa 1987); Simoneau v. South Bend Lathe, Inc., 130 N.H. 466, 543 A.2d 407 (1988); Nissen Corp. v. Miller, 323 Md. 613, 594 A.2d 564 (1991).

A second line of cases has used a broad reading of the "mere continuation" exception to expand liability. Under the "continuity of enterprise" exception, courts may look at a number of factors in assessing whether to impose liability. These include: whether the purchaser (1) retains the same employees; (2) retains the same supervisory personnel; (3) retains the same production facilities in the same location; (4) produces the same product; (5) retains the same name; (6) maintains the same assets; (7) continues the same general business operations; and (8) holds itself out as a continuation of the previous enterprise. United States v. Carolina Transformer Co., 978 F.2d 832, 838 (4th Cir.1992). *See, for example*, Savage Arms, Inc. v. Western Auto Supply Co., 18 P.3d 49 (Alaska 2001). For a discussion of this trend, *see* Richard L. Cupp Jr., *Redesigning Successor Liability*, 1999 U. Ill. L. Rev. 845 (1999). To date, only a few states have adopted this approach, and The *Restatement (Third) of Torts: Products Liability* § 12 does not extend liability beyond the original four exceptions to non-liability. See Kenneth R. Meyer, et al., *Buyer Beware: You May Be Liable For the Defective Products of Your Predecessor*, 75 Def. Couns. J. 161 (2008).

In the *Nissen* case noted above, the acquired company maintained its corporate existence for five years after the sale of assets to Nissen. Plaintiff was injured six years after the sale. Do you think rules requiring enterprises to maintain some existence and to post a bond against future tort claims would be a wise policy?

3. *The Sale of Real Estate.* The sale of real estate is not a sale of goods. Nevertheless, some courts have come to recognize an "implied warranty of habitability" in the sale of new housing. Several of the cases have explicitly allowed recovery by persons not in privity with the builder. Schipper v. Levitt & Sons, 44 N.J. 70, 207 A.2d 314 (1965), is a leading case. *See also* Kirk v. Ridgway, 373 N.W.2d 491 (Iowa 1985); Richards v. Powercraft Homes, Inc., 139 Ariz. 242, 678 P.2d 427 (1984); Lempke v. Dagenais, 130 N.H. 782, 547 A.2d 290 (1988) (overruling an earlier New Hampshire case holding that strict liability only applies to the first buyer).

In Becker v. IRM Corp., 38 Cal.3d 454, 213 Cal.Rptr. 213, 698 P.2d 116 (1985), California applied products liability law to a landlord of a dwelling unit that contained a latent defect at the time of lease. However, in Peterson v. Superior Court, 10 Cal.4th 1185, 43 Cal.Rptr.2d 836, 899 P.2d 905 (1995), the Supreme Court overruled *Becker*, and refused to hold a hotel owner liable to a guest who slipped in a defective bathtub. The *Becker* case had been virtually alone in imposing liability in such cases.

What posture should courts adopt with respect to manufactured housing that is built in a factory and later moved to a homesite? *See Restatement (Third) of Torts: Products Liability* § 19, comment *e*.

4. *Used goods.* Although there is case authority to the contrary, it is generally thought that one selling used goods is not liable under products liability law. The policy objective here seems to be to facilitate a market for inexpensive, used products and is built upon the assumption that the buyer is taking the goods "as is"—a variety of assumption of the risk. Moreover, because sellers of used goods are not in the original chain of distribution they have no direct relationship with the manufacturer and, therefore, are not in a position to influence product safety. Tillman v. Vance Equipment Co., 286 Or. 747, 596 P.2d 1299 (1979); Peterson v. Idaho First National Bank, 117 Idaho 724, 791 P.2d 1303 (1990). However, where the seller of used goods extensively modifies the goods before resale, there is an obvious analogy to the status of a manufacturer, especially if the defect is related to the modification. *See* Green v. City of Los Angeles, 40 Cal.App.3d 819, 115 Cal.Rptr. 685 (1974). A difficult case arises when the seller of used goods is "regularly" engaged in that business, as opposed to engaging in an occasional transaction, but makes no modification in the goods. This frequently happens in the purchase and

resale of used commercial machinery. Indeed the used machinery dealer may never take physical possession of the goods. Here one arguably faces a different policy balance since the seller is in a position to spread the costs over the second hand market, analogous to the manufacturer, but one still has the concern about inhibiting a viable second hand market. Moreover, such a seller is unlikely to be in a position to obtain indemnification from the manufacturer who will claim that the product was not defective when it left the manufacturer's hands. An older case holding that in this situation there is no products liability action and discussing the few cases and secondary authority on the subject is LaRosa v. Superior Court, 122 Cal.App.3d 741, 176 Cal.Rptr. 224 (1981). *See also* Cataldo v. Lazy Days R.V. Center, Inc., 920 So.2d 174 (Fla. App. 2006). The New York Court of Appeals, in response to a certified question, was prepared to recognize regular seller liability but conclude the defendant was not a regular seller of goods. Jaramillo v. Weyerhaeuser Co., 12 N.Y.3d 181, 878 N.Y.S.2d 659, 906 N.E.2d 387 (2009).

Should it make any difference if the seller of a used product refurbished or reconditioned it? *See Restatement (Third) of Torts: Products* Liability § 8(c).

Restatement (Third) of Torts: Products Liability § 18 declares that seller disclaimers do not bar otherwise valid products liability claims. Should a seller of used products be permitted to disclaim liability? Even if your answer is no, what affect might a disclaimer have on the legal question of whether a product is defective?

5. *Franchisors.* Extending products liability to franchisors for sales to customers by a franchisee poses a number of problems. If the franchisor is the manufacturer of the defective product there is no problem. Frequently, however, the franchisor simply furnishes a trade-name, training, recipes or directions and the like. Actual "manufacturing" of the product is done by the franchisee. *See* S. Sandrock, *Tort Liability for a Non–Manufacturing Franchisor for Acts of Its Franchisee,* 48 U.Cin.L.Rev. 699 (1979). A few cases have found liability, the theory being either that sufficient control was exerted or that consumers relied upon the name of the product as a statement of responsibility. Kosters v. Seven–Up Co., 595 F.2d 347 (6th Cir.1979); City of Hartford v. Associated Construction Co., 34 Conn.Sup. 204, 384 A.2d 390 (1978); Torres v. Goodyear Tire and Rubber Co., 163 Ariz. 88, 786 P.2d 939 (1990); Nadel v. Burger King Corp., 119 Ohio App.3d 578, 695 N.E.2d 1185 (1997); Automobile Ins. Co. Of Hartford Conn. v. Murray, Inc., 571 F.Supp.2d 408 (W.D. N.Y. 2008) (New York law recognizes that imposition of products liability is proper where the party can exercise leverage or control over its manufacturer to improve product safety through approval of the product's design applications and manufacturing quality controls).

Restatement (Third) of Torts: Products Liability § 14 contains the following provision:

§ 14. Selling Or Distributing As One's Own A Product Manufactured By Another

One engaged in the business of selling or otherwise distributing products who sells or distributes as its own a product manufactured by another is subject to the same liability as though the seller or distributor were the product's manufacturer.

Comment *d. Liability of trademark licensors.* The rule stated in this Section does not, by its terms, apply to the owner of a trademark who licenses a manufacturer to place the licensor's trademark or logo on the manufacturer's product and distribute it as though manufactured by the licensor. In such a case, even if purchasers of the product might assume that the trademark owner was the manufacturer, the licensor does not "sell or distribute as its own a product manufactured by another." Thus, the manufacturer may be liable under §§ 1–4, but the licensor, who does not sell or otherwise distribute products, is not liable under this Section of this Restatement.

Trademark licensors are liable for harm caused by defective products distributed under the licensor's trademark or logo when they participate substantially in the design, manufacture, or distribution of the licensee's products. In these circumstances they are treated as sellers of the products bearing their trademarks.

6. *Non-sales situations—services.* Products liability has been extended to a number of non-sales situations. Thus commercial lessors of automobiles have been held liable for supplying defective vehicles. *See, e.g.,* Cintrone v. Hertz Truck Leasing & Rental Service, 45 N.J. 434, 212 A.2d 769 (1965); Price v. Shell Oil Co., 2 Cal.3d 245, 85 Cal.Rptr. 178, 466 P.2d 722 (1970). *See also,* Samuel Friedland Family Enterprises v. Amoroso, 630 So.2d 1067 (Fla.1994) (liability applies to hotel and sailboat concession that leased defective sailboat to guest). However, most courts that have passed on the question have rejected liability on the part of one who only finances the sale or lease, even in a lease-for-purchase arrangement. *See* AgriStor Leasing v. Meuli, 634 F.Supp. 1208 (D.Kan. 1986); Ames v. Ford Motor Co., 299 F.Supp.2d 678, 679 (S.D. Tex. 2003). Nor do most courts apply products liability law to repairers, refurbishers, and installers, usually holding those pursuits to be services and not sales. Barry v. Stevens Equip. Co., 176 Ga.App. 27, 335 S.E.2d 129 (1985). *But see* O'Laughlin v. Minnesota Natural Gas Co., 253 N.W.2d 826 (Minn. 1977) (installer).

A large number of activities such as the provision of legal advice have been excluded from the scope of products liability law because the defendant's activity was categorized as a "service" rather than a "sale." *See* William Powers, *Distinguishing Between Products and Services in Strict Liability,* 62 N.C.L.Rev. 415 (1984). Difficult cases arise when a product is sold to an individual as part of providing a service. Compare Newmark v. Gimbel's Inc., 54 N.J. 585, 258 A.2d 697 (1969) (defective permanent wave solution used on the plaintiff when she visited a beauty parlor) with

Magrine v. Spector, 53 N.J. 259, 250 A.2d 129 (1969) (hypodermic needle used by defendant dentist broke off in plaintiff's gum).

Doctors, hospitals and pharmacies are rarely held responsible for defects in the products they use or dispense when providing their services. For useful discussions of why this is so see Cafazzo v. Central Medical Health Services, Inc. 542 Pa. 526, 668 A.2d 521 (1995); Madison v. American Home Products Corp., 358 S.C. 449, 595 S.E.2d 493 (2004). The Third Restatement: Products Liability wrestles with the sales/service issue in Sections 19 and 20.

Blood transfusions have been the subject of much controversy in this regard, primarily due to litigation with respect to blood transmitted diseases such as hepatitis and A.I.D.S. Because some tainted blood may go undetected even when blood banks exercise the utmost care, the question of whether to impose liability for a defective product is presented in a most dramatic situation. Several states have passed statutes that define blood transfusions as a service and not a sale. For example, the Ohio statute provides:

> [T]he procuring, furnishing, donating, processing, distributing, or using human whole blood, plasma, blood products, blood derivatives, and products, corneas, bones, organs, or other human tissue except hair, for the purpose of injecting, transfusing, or transplanting the fluid or body part in another human body, is considered for all purposes as the rendition of a service by every person participating in the act and not a sale of any such fluid or body part. No warranties of any kind or description are applicable to the act.

Ohio Rev. Code § 2108.11. Moreover, the Ohio Products Liability Statute provides that blood and blood products are not a "product" and therefore are not covered by products liability law. Ohio Rev. Code § 2307.71(L)(2). The *Restatement (Third) of Torts: Products Liability* § 19(c) bluntly declares that "Human blood and human tissue, even when provided commercially, are not subject to the rules of this Restatement." Blood banks may still be responsible, of course, for negligent conduct. *See* J.K. and Susie L. Wadley Research Institute v. Beeson, 835 S.W.2d 689 (Tex.App. 1992); Patin v. Administrators of Tulane Educational Fund, 2004–2040, 907 So.2d 164 (La. App. 2005).

7. *Intangible property*. Products liability law is usually restricted to tangible personal property. See *Restatement (Third) of Torts: Products Liability* § 19. There are two types of intangible property against which products liability claims are occasionally made. The first consists of information in books, maps and other media. When the information contained therein proves to be erroneous, causing harm to individuals who relied on it, they may seek to recover against the publisher, claiming that the product, e.g. the book, is defective. With a few exceptions involving navigational charts, courts have rejected such claims. See Winter v. G.P. Putnam's Sons, 938 F.2d 1033, 1034 (9th Cir.1991); Gorran v. Atkins

Nutritionals, Inc., 464 F.Supp.2d 315, 324 (S.D. N.Y. 2006), affirmed 279 Fed.Appx. 40 (2d Cir.2008).

The second type of intangible property occasionally subject to products liability suits includes such things as electricity. Most courts have held that electricity is not a product until it enters the customer's premises. Until that point, it is not a product, but a service and it is sometimes also said that until it has passed the customer's meter it has not "entered the stream of commerce." *See* Smith v. Home Light and Power Co., 734 P.2d 1051, 1055 (Colo. 1987); Monroe v. Savannah Elec. & Power Co., 267 Ga. 26, 471 S.E.2d 854 (1996).

F. ADMISSIBILITY OF EXPERT TESTIMONY TO PROVE DEFECT AND CAUSATION

KUMHO TIRE CO., LTD. v. CARMICHAEL

Supreme Court of the United States, 1999.
526 U.S. 137, 119 S.Ct. 1167, 143 L.Ed.2d 238.

JUSTICE BREYER delivered the opinion of the Court.

In *Daubert v. Merrell Dow Pharmaceuticals, Inc.,* 509 U.S. 579, 113 S.Ct. 2786, 125 L.Ed.2d 469 (1993), this Court focused upon the admissibility of scientific expert testimony. It pointed out that such testimony is admissible only if it is both relevant and reliable. And it held that the Federal Rules of Evidence "assign to the trial judge the task of ensuring that an expert's testimony both rests on a reliable foundation and is relevant to the task at hand." * * * The Court also discussed certain more specific factors, such as testing, peer review, error rates, and "acceptability" in the relevant scientific community, some or all of which might prove helpful in determining the reliability of a particular scientific "theory or technique." * * *

This case requires us to decide how *Daubert* applies to the testimony of engineers and other experts who are not scientists. We conclude that *Daubert's* general holding—setting forth the trial judge's general "gatekeeping" obligation—applies not only to testimony based on "scientific" knowledge, but also to testimony based on "technical" and "other specialized" knowledge. See Fed. Rule Evid. 702. We also conclude that a trial court *may* consider one or more of the more specific factors that *Daubert* mentioned when doing so will help determine that testimony's reliability. But, as the Court stated in *Daubert,* the test of reliability is "flexible," and *Daubert's* list of specific factors neither necessarily nor exclusively applies to all experts or in every case. Rather, the law grants a district court the same broad latitude when it decides *how* to determine reliability as it enjoys in respect to its ultimate reliability determination. See *General Electric Co. v. Joiner,* 522 U.S. 136, 143, 118 S.Ct. 512, 139 L.Ed.2d 508 (1997) (courts of appeals are to apply "abuse of discretion" standard when reviewing district court's reliability determination). Applying these standards, we determine that the District Court's decision in this case—not to admit certain expert testimony—was within its discretion and therefore lawful.

I

On July 6, 1993, the right rear tire of a minivan driven by Patrick Carmichael blew out. In the accident that followed, one of the passengers died, and others were severely injured. In October 1993, the Carmichaels brought this diversity suit against the tire's maker and its distributor, whom we refer to collectively as Kumho Tire, claiming that the tire was defective. The plaintiffs rested their case in significant part upon deposition testimony provided by an expert in tire failure analysis, Dennis Carlson, Jr., who intended to testify in support of their conclusion.

Carlson's depositions relied upon certain features of tire technology that are not in dispute. A steel-belted radial tire like the Carmichaels' is made up of a "carcass" containing many layers of flexible cords, called "plies," along which (between the cords and the outer tread) are laid steel strips called "belts." Steel wire loops, called "beads," hold the cords together at the plies' bottom edges. An outer layer, called the "tread," encases the carcass, and the entire tire is bound together in rubber, through the application of heat and various chemicals. * * * The bead of the tire sits upon a "bead seat," which is part of the wheel assembly. That assembly contains a "rim flange," which extends over the bead and rests against the side of the tire. * * *

Carlson's testimony also accepted certain background facts about the tire in question. He assumed that before the blowout the tire had traveled far. (The tire was made in 1988 and had been installed some time before the Carmichaels bought the used minivan in March 1993; the Carmichaels had driven the van approximately 7,000 additional miles in the two months they had owned it.) Carlson noted that the tire's tread depth, which was 11/32 of an inch when new, * * * had been worn down to depths that ranged from 3/32 of an inch along some parts of the tire, to nothing at all along others. * * * He conceded that the tire tread had at least two punctures which had been inadequately repaired. * * *

Despite the tire's age and history, Carlson concluded that a defect in its manufacture or design caused the blow-out. He rested this conclusion in part upon three premises which, for present purposes, we must assume are not in dispute: First, a tire's carcass should stay bound to the inner side of the tread for a significant period of time after its tread depth has worn away. * * * Second, the tread of the tire at issue had separated from its inner steel-belted carcass prior to the accident. * * Third, this "separation" caused the blowout. * * *

Carlson's conclusion that a defect caused the separation, however, rested upon certain other propositions, several of which the defendants strongly dispute. First, Carlson said that if a separation is *not* caused by a certain kind of tire misuse called "overdeflection" (which consists of underinflating the tire or causing it to carry too much weight, thereby generating heat that can undo the chemical tread/carcass bond), then, ordinarily, its cause is a tire defect. * * * Second, he said that if a tire has been subject to sufficient overdeflection to cause a separation, it should reveal certain physical symptoms. These symptoms include (a) tread wear on the tire's shoulder that is greater than the tread wear along the tire's center; * * * (b) signs of a "bead groove," where the beads have been pushed too hard against the bead seat on the inside of the tire's rim; * * * (c) sidewalls of the tire with physical signs of deterioration, such as discoloration: * * * and/or (d) marks on the tire's rim flange. * * * Third, Carlson said that where he does not find *at least two* of the four physical signs just mentioned (and presumably where there is no reason to suspect a less common cause of separation), he concludes that a manufacturing or design defect caused the separation. * * *

Carlson added that he had inspected the tire in question. He conceded that the tire to a limited degree showed greater wear on the shoulder than in the center, some signs of "bead groove," some discoloration, a few marks on the rim flange, and inadequately filled puncture holes (which can also cause heat that might lead to separation). * * * But, in each instance, he testified that the symptoms were not significant, and he explained why he believed that they did not reveal overdeflection. For example, the extra shoulder wear, he said, appeared primarily on one shoulder, whereas an overdeflected tire would reveal equally abnormal wear on both shoulders. * * * Carlson concluded that the tire did not bear at least two of the four overdeflection symptoms, nor was there any less obvious cause of separation; and since neither overdeflection nor the punctures caused the blowout, a defect must have done so.

Kumho Tire moved the District Court to exclude Carlson's testimony on the ground that his methodology failed Rule 702's reliability requirement. The court agreed with Kumho that it should act as a *Daubert*-type reliability "gatekeeper," even though one might consider Carlson's testimony as "technical," rather than "scientific."

* * *

It conceded that there may be widespread acceptance of a "visual-inspection method" for some relevant purposes. But the court found insufficient indications of the reliability of

> "the component of Carlson's tire failure analysis which most concerned the Court, namely, the methodology employed by the expert in analyzing the data obtained in the visual inspection, and the scientific basis, if any, for such an analysis." * * *

It consequently affirmed its * * * order declaring Carlson's testimony inadmissable and granting the defendants' motion for summary judgment.

The Eleventh Circuit reversed. See *Carmichael v. Samyang Tire, Inc.*, 131 F.3d 1433 (1997). It "review[ed] ... *de novo*" the "district court's legal decision to apply *Daubert*." * * * It noted that "the Supreme Court in *Daubert* explicitly limited its holding to cover only the 'scientific context,' " adding that "a *Daubert* analysis" applies only where an expert relies "on the application of scientific principles," rather than "on skill-or experience-based observation." * * * It concluded that Carlson's testimony, which it viewed as relying on experience, "falls outside the scope of *Daubert*," that "the district court erred as a matter of law by applying *Daubert* in this case," and that the case must be remanded for further (non-*Daubert*-type) consideration under Rule 702. * * *

We granted certiorari in light of uncertainty among the lower courts about whether, or how, *Daubert* applies to expert testimony that might be characterized as based not upon "scientific" knowledge, but rather upon "technical" or "other specialized" knowledge. Fed. Rule Evid. 702 * * *.

II

A

In *Daubert,* this Court held that Federal Rule of Evidence 702 imposes a special obligation upon a trial judge to "ensure that any and all scientific testimony ... is not only relevant, but reliable." 509 U.S., at 589. The initial question before us is whether this basic gatekeeping obligation applies only to "scientific" testimony or to all expert testimony. We, like the parties, believe that it applies to all expert testimony. * * *

For one thing, Rule 702 itself says:

> "If scientific, technical, or other specialized knowledge will assist the trier of fact to understand the evidence or to determine a fact in issue, a witness qualified as an expert by knowledge, skill, experience, training, or education, may testify thereto in the form of an opinion or otherwise."

This language makes no relevant distinction between "scientific" knowledge and "technical" or "other specialized" knowledge. It makes clear that any such knowledge might become the subject of expert testimony. In *Daubert,* the Court specified that it is the Rule's word "knowledge," not the words (like "scientific") that modify that word, that "establishes a standard of evidentiary reliability." * * * Hence, as a matter of language, the Rule applies its reliability standard to all "scientific," "technical," or "other specialized" matters within its scope. We concede that the Court in *Daubert* referred only to "scientific" knowledge. But as the Court there said, it referred to "scientific" testimony "because that [wa]s the nature of the expertise" at issue. * * *

Neither is the evidentiary rationale that underlay the Court's basic *Daubert* "gatekeeping" determination limited to "scientific" knowledge. *Daubert* pointed out that Federal Rules 702 and 703 grant expert witnesses testimonial latitude unavailable to other witnesses on the "assumption that the expert's opinion will have a reliable basis in the knowledge and experience of his discipline." * * * (pointing out that experts may testify to opinions, including those that are not based on firsthand knowledge or observation). The Rules grant that latitude to all experts, not just to "scientific" ones.

Finally, it would prove difficult, if not impossible, for judges to administer evidentiary rules under which a gatekeeping obligation depended upon a distinction between "scientific" knowledge and "technical" or "other specialized" knowledge. There is no clear line that divides the one from the others. Disciplines such as engineering rest upon scientific knowledge. Pure scientific theory itself may depend for its development upon observation and properly engineered machinery. And conceptual efforts to distinguish the two are unlikely to produce clear legal lines capable of application in particular cases. * * *

Neither is there a convincing need to make such distinctions. Experts of all kinds tie observations to conclusions through the use of what Judge Learned Hand called "general truths derived from ... specialized experience." Hand, Historical and Practical Considerations Regarding Expert Testimony, 15 Harv. L.Rev. 40, 54 (1901). And whether the specific expert testimony focuses upon specialized observations, the specialized translation of those observations into theory, a specialized theory itself, or the application of such a theory in a particular case, the expert's testimony often will rest "upon an experience confessedly foreign in kind to [the jury's] own." * * * The trial judge's effort to assure that the specialized testimony is reliable and relevant can help the jury evaluate that foreign experience, whether the testimony reflects scientific, technical, or other specialized knowledge.

We conclude that *Daubert's* general principles apply to the expert matters described in Rule 702. The Rule * * * "requires a valid ... connection to the pertinent inquiry as a precondition to admissibility." *Id.*, at 592. And where such testimony's factual basis, data, principles, methods, or their application are called sufficiently into question, see Part III, *infra,* the trial judge must determine whether the testimony has "a reliable basis in the knowledge and experience of [the relevant] discipline." 509 U.S., at 592.

B

The petitioners ask more specifically whether a trial judge determining the "admissibility of an engineering expert's testimony" *may* consider several more specific factors that *Daubert* said might "bear on" a judge's gate-keeping determination. These factors include:

—Whether a "theory or technique ... can be (and has been) tested";

—Whether it "has been subjected to peer review and publication";

—Whether, in respect to a particular technique, there is a high "known or potential rate of error" and whether there are "standards controlling the technique's operation"; and

—Whether the theory or technique enjoys "general acceptance" within a "relevant scientific community." * * *

Emphasizing the word "may" in the question, we answer that question yes.

Engineering testimony rests upon scientific foundations, the reliability of which will be at issue in some cases. * * * In other cases, the relevant reliability concerns may focus upon personal knowledge or experience. As the Solicitor General points out, there are many different kinds of experts, and many different kinds of expertise. * * * (citing cases involving experts in drug terms, handwriting analysis, criminal *modus operandi,* land valuation, agricultural practices, railroad procedures, attorney's fee valuation, and others). Our emphasis on the word "may" thus reflects *Daubert's* description of the Rule 702 inquiry as "a flexible one." 509 U.S., at 594. *Daubert* makes clear that the factors it mentions do *not* constitute a "definitive checklist or test." *Id.* at 593, 113 S.Ct. 2786. And *Daubert* adds that the gatekeeping inquiry must be " 'tied to the facts' " of a particular "case." *Id.,* at 591 (quoting *United States v. Downing,* 753 F.2d 1224, 1242 (C.A.3 1985)). * * * The conclusion, in our view, is that we can neither rule out, nor rule in, for all cases and for all time the applicability of the factors mentioned in *Daubert,* nor can we now do so for subsets of cases categorized by category of expert or by kind of evidence. Too much depends upon the particular circumstances of the particular case at issue.

Daubert itself is not to the contrary. It made clear that its list of factors was meant to be helpful, not definitive. Indeed, those factors do not all necessarily apply even in every instance in which the reliability of scientific testimony is challenged. It might not be surprising in a particular case, for example, that a claim made by a scientific witness has never been the subject of peer review, for the particular application at issue may never previously have interested any scientist. Nor, on the other hand, does the presence of *Daubert's* general acceptance factor help show that an expert's testimony is reliable where the discipline itself lacks reliability, as, for example, do theories grounded in any so-called generally accepted principles of astrology or necromancy.

At the same time, and contrary to the Court of Appeals' view, some of *Daubert's* questions can help to evaluate the reliability even of experience-based testimony. In certain cases, it will be appropriate for the trial judge to ask, for example, how often an engineering expert's experience-based methodology has produced erroneous results, or whether such a method is generally accepted in the relevant engineering community. Likewise, it will at times be useful to ask even of a witness whose expertise is based purely on experience, say, a perfume tester able to distinguish among 140 odors at a sniff, whether his preparation is of a kind that others in the field would recognize as acceptable.

* * * We do not believe that Rule 702 creates a schematism that segregates expertise by type while mapping certain kinds of questions to certain kinds of experts. Life and the legal cases that it generates are too complex to warrant so definitive a match.

To say this is not to deny the importance of *Daubert's* gatekeeping requirement. The objective of that requirement is to ensure the reliability and relevancy of expert testimony. It is to make certain that an expert, whether basing testimony upon professional studies or personal experience, employs in the courtroom the same level of intellectual rigor that characterizes the practice of an expert in the relevant field. Nor do we deny that, as stated in *Daubert,* the particular questions that it mentioned will often be appropriate for use in determining the reliability of challenged expert testimony. Rather, we conclude that the trial judge must have considerable leeway in deciding in a particular case how to go about determining whether particular expert testimony is reliable. That is to say, a trial court should consider the specific factors identified in *Daubert* where they are reasonable measures of the reliability of expert testimony.

C

The trial court must have the same kind of latitude in deciding *how* to test an expert's reliability, and to decide whether or when special briefing or other proceedings are needed to investigate reliability, as it enjoys when it decides *whether or not* that expert's relevant testimony is reliable. Our opinion in *Joiner* makes clear that a court of appeals is to apply an abuse-of-discretion standard when it "review[s] a trial court's decision to admit or exclude expert testimony." 522 U.S., at 138–139. That standard applies as much to the trial court's decisions about how to determine reliability as to its ultimate conclusion. Otherwise, the trial judge would lack the discretionary authority needed both to avoid unnecessary "reliability" proceedings in ordinary cases where the reliability of an expert's methods is properly taken for granted, and to require appropriate proceedings in the less usual or more complex cases where cause for questioning the expert's reliability arises. Indeed, the Rules seek to avoid "unjustifiable expense and delay" as part of their search for "truth" and the "jus[t] determin[ation]" of proceedings. Fed. Rule Evid. 102. Thus, whether *Daubert's* specific factors are, or are not, reasonable measures of reliability in a particular case is a matter that the law grants the trial judge broad latitude to determine. * * *

III

We further explain the way in which a trial judge "may" consider *Daubert's* factors by applying these considerations to the case at hand, a matter that has been briefed exhaustively by the parties and their 19 *amici*. The District Court did not doubt Carlson's qualifications, which included a masters degree in mechanical engineering, 10 years' work at Michelin America, Inc., and testimony as a tire failure consultant in other tort cases. Rather, it excluded the testimony because, despite those qualifications, it initially doubted, and then found unreliable, "the methodology employed by the expert in analyzing the data obtained in the visual inspection, and the scientific basis, if any, for such an analysis." * * * It fell outside the range where experts might reasonably differ, and where the jury must decide among the conflicting views of different experts, even though the evidence is "shaky." *Daubert,* 509 U.S., at 596. In our view, the doubts that triggered the District Court's initial inquiry here were reasonable, as was the court's ultimate conclusion.

For one thing, and contrary to respondents' suggestion, the specific issue before the court was not the reasonableness *in general* of a tire expert's use of a visual and tactile inspection to determine whether overdeflection had caused the tire's tread to separate from its steel-belted carcass. Rather, it was the reasonableness of using such an approach, along with Carlson's particular method of analyzing the data thereby obtained, to draw a conclusion regarding *the particular matter to which the expert testimony was directly relevant.* That matter concerned the likelihood that a defect in the tire at issue caused its tread to separate from its carcass. The tire in question, the expert conceded, had traveled far enough so that some of the tread had been worn bald; it should have been taken out of service; it had been repaired (inadequately) for punctures; and it bore some of the very marks that the expert said indicated, not a defect, but abuse through overdeflection. * * * The relevant issue was whether the expert could reliably determine the cause of *this* tire's separation.

Nor was the basis for Carlson's conclusion simply the general theory that, in the absence of evidence of abuse, a defect will normally have caused a tire's separation. Rather, the expert employed a more specific theory to establish the existence (or absence) of such abuse. Carlson testified precisely that in the absence of *at least two* of four signs of abuse (proportionately greater tread wear on the shoulder; signs of grooves caused by the beads; discolored sidewalls; marks on the rim flange) he concludes that a defect caused the separation. And his analysis depended upon acceptance of a further implicit proposition, namely, that his visual and tactile inspection could determine that the tire before him had not been abused despite some evidence of the presence of the very signs for which he looked (and two punctures).

For another thing, the transcripts of Carlson's depositions support both the trial court's initial uncertainty and its final conclusion. Those transcripts cast considerable doubt upon the reliability of both the explicit theory (about the need for two signs of abuse) and the implicit proposition (about the significance of visual inspection in this case). Among other things, the expert could not say whether the tire had traveled more than 10, or 20, or 30, or 40, or 50 thousand miles, adding that 6,000 miles was "about how far" he could "say with any certainty." * * * The court could reasonably have wondered about the reliability of a method of visual and tactile inspection sufficiently precise to ascertain with some certainty the abuse-related significance of minute shoulder/center relative tread wear differences, but insufficiently precise to tell "with any certainty" from the tread wear whether a tire had traveled less than 10,000 or more than 50,000 miles. And these concerns might have been augmented by Carlson's repeated reliance on the "subjective[ness]" of his mode of analysis in response to questions seeking specific information regarding how he could differentiate between a tire that actually had been overdeflected and a tire that merely looked as though it had been. * * * They would have been further augmented by the fact that Carlson said he had inspected the tire itself for the first time the morning of his first deposition, and then only for a few hours. (His initial conclusions were based on photographs.) * * *

[T]he court, after looking for a defense of Carlson's methodology as applied in these circumstances, found no convincing defense. Rather, it found (1) that "none" of the *Daubert* factors, including that of "general acceptance" in the relevant expert community, indicated that Carlson's testimony was reliable; * * * (2) that its own analysis "revealed no countervailing factors operating in favor of admissibility which could outweigh those identified in Daubert" * * *; and (3) that the "parties identified no such factors in their briefs." * * * For these three reasons *taken together,* it concluded that Carlson's testimony was unreliable.

Respondents now argue to us, as they did to the District Court, that a method of tire failure analysis that employs a visual/tactile inspection is a reliable method, and they point both to its use by other experts and to Carlson's long experience working for Michelin as sufficient indication that that is so. But no one denies that an expert might draw a conclusion from a set of observations based on extensive and specialized experience. Nor does anyone deny that, as a general matter, tire abuse may often be identified by qualified experts through visual or tactile inspection of the tire. * * * As we said before, * * * the question before the trial court was specific, not general. The trial court had to decide whether this particular expert had sufficient specialized knowledge to assist the jurors "in deciding the particular issues in the case." * * *

The particular issue in this case concerned the use of Carlson's two-factor test and his related use of visual/tactile inspection to draw conclusions on the basis of what seemed small observational differences. We have found no indication in the record that other experts in the industry use Carlson's two-factor test or that tire experts such as Carlson normally make the very fine distinctions about, say, the symmetry of comparatively greater shoulder tread wear that were necessary, on Carlson's own theory, to support his conclusions. Nor, despite the prevalence of tire testing, does anyone refer to any articles or papers that validate Carlson's approach. * * * Indeed, no one has argued that Carlson himself, were he still working for Michelin, would have concluded in a report to his employer that a similar tire was similarly defective on grounds identical to those upon which he rested his conclusion here. Of course, Carlson himself claimed that his method was accurate, but, as we pointed out in *Joiner,* "nothing in either *Daubert* or the Federal Rules of Evidence requires a district court to admit opinion evidence that is connected to existing data only by the *ipse dixit* of the expert." 522 U.S. at 146.

Respondents additionally argue that the District Court too rigidly applied *Daubert's* criteria. They read its opinion to hold that a failure to satisfy any one of those criteria automatically renders expert testimony inadmissible. The District Court's initial opinion might have been vulnerable to a form of this argument. There, the court, after rejecting respondents' claim that Carlson's testimony was "exempted from *Daubert*-style scrutiny" because it was "technical analysis" rather than "scientific evidence," simply added that "none of the four admissibility criteria outlined by the *Daubert* court are satisfied." * * * Subsequently, however, the court granted respondents' motion for reconsideration. It then explicitly recognized that the relevant reliability inquiry "should be 'flexible,' " that its " 'overarching subject [should be] . . . validity' and reliability," and that "*Daubert* was intended neither to be exhaustive nor to apply in every case." * * * And the court ultimately based its decision upon Carlson's failure to satisfy either *Daubert's* factors *or any other* set of reasonable reliability criteria. In light of the record as developed by the parties, that conclusion was within the District Court's lawful discretion.

In sum, Rule 702 grants the district judge the discretionary authority, reviewable for its abuse, to determine reliability in light of the particular facts and circumstances of the particular case. The District Court did not abuse its discretionary authority in this case. Hence, the judgment of the Court of Appeals is

Reversed.

JUSTICE SCALIA, with whom JUSTICE O'CONNOR and JUSTICE THOMAS join, concurring.

I join the opinion of the Court, which makes clear that the discretion it endorses—trial-court discretion in choosing the manner of testing expert reliability—is not discretion to abandon the gatekeeping function. I think it worth adding that it is not discretion to perform the function inadequately. Rather, it is discretion to choose among *reasonable* means of excluding expertise that is *fausse* and science that is junky. Though, as the Court makes clear today, the *Daubert* factors are not holy writ, in a particular case the failure to apply one or another of them may be unreasonable, and hence an abuse of discretion.

NOTES

1. Subsequent to *Kumho Tire*, Federal Rule of Evidence 702 was modified to reflect the holdings in *Daubert, Joiner,* and *Kumho Tire.* Rule 702 now provides:

> A witness who is qualified as an expert by knowledge, skill, experience, training, or education may testify in the form of an opinion or otherwise if:
>
> (a) the expert's scientific, technical, or other specialized knowledge will help the trier of fact to understand the evidence or to determine a fact in issue;
>
> (b) the testimony is based on sufficient facts or data;
>
> (c) the testimony is the product of reliable principles and methods; and
>
> (d) the expert has reliably applied the principles and methods to the facts of the case

Courts increasingly refer to this language in making admissibility rulings. *See e,g,* In re Prempro Products Liability Litigation, 765 F.Supp.2d 1113 (W.D.Ark. 2011).

2. Justice Stevens dissented from Part III of the court's opinion, believing that the case should have been sent back to the appellate court for its assessment of whether the trial judge abused his discretion. In Weisgram v. Marley Co., 528 U.S. 440, 120 S.Ct. 1011, 145 L.Ed.2d 958 (2000) the district court entered a judgment on a jury verdict for plaintiff and denied defendants motion for a judgment as a matter of law or a new trial. The Eighth Circuit vacated and directed entry of judgment as a matter of law for manufacturer after concluding the trial court had erred in admitting expert testimony. The plaintiff appealed, arguing the appellate court abused its discretion when it failed to remand the case to the trial court. The Supreme Court affirmed and held that appellate courts may direct entry of judgment as a matter of law for a verdict loser, upon determining that after the exclusion there is no longer sufficient evidence to sustain the verdict.

3. Admissibility issues now arise in a wide variety of products contexts. In *Daubert* and *Joiner* the issue was whether a drug (Bendectin) or a toxic substance (PCB's) caused the plaintiff's injury. Experts are increasingly challenged in design defect cases. *See* Jaurequi v. Carter Manufacturing Co., Inc., 173 F.3d 1076 (8th Cir. 1999) (expert testimony excluded because he had not studied the feasibility of "awareness barriers" intended to protect workers from the gathering hooks on a combine); Bourelle v. Crown Equipment Corp., 220 F.3d 532 (7th Cir. 2000) (expert's testimony regarding alternative design of forklift unreliable and inadmissible); Smith v. Ingersoll–Rand Co., 214 F.3d 1235 (10th Cir. 2000) (human factors engineer testimony that lack of visibility around machine used to remove pavement prior to resurfacing a road made it defective held to be admissible); Graves v. Mazda Motor Corp., 675 F.Supp.2d 1082 (W.D.Okla. 2009) (automobile gear shift); Kilpatrick v. Breg, Inc., 613 F.3d 1329 (11th Cir. 2010) (pain pump).

4. Most states have evidence codes patterned after the Federal Rules of Evidence and, therefore, it is not surprising that a majority of jurisdictions have adopted a Daubert-like admissibility standard. *See* E.I. du Pont de Nemours & Co. v. Robinson, 923 S.W.2d 549, 554 (Tex. 1995); Schafersman v. Agland Coop, 262 Neb. 215, 631 N.W.2d 862, 876–877 (2001); Christian v. Gray, 65 P.3d 591 (Okla. 2003). Some states have refused to follow the Federal courts' lead and retain the earlier Frye Rule (Frye v. United States, 293 Fed. 1013 (D.C.Cir. 1923)), under which an expert opinion based on a scientific technique is inadmissible unless the technique is "generally accepted" in the relevant scientific community. *See* People v. Leahy, 8 Cal.4th 587, 591, 34 Cal.Rptr.2d 663, 882 P.2d 321 (1994). However, in some of these states, Daubert-like issues have come to influence admissibility decisions. *See* Goeb v. Tharaldson, 615 N.W.2d 800 (Minn. 2000). *See generally* DAVID FAIGMAN, ET AL., MODERN SCIENTIFIC EVIDENCE. CH. 1 (2011).

5. *Restatement (Third) of Torts: Liability for Physical and Emotional Harm* § 28, Comment *c* notes that although the admissibility of expert testimony is covered by the law of evidence, admissibility cannot be determined without reference to the substantive law of torts. This law generally

requires the plaintiff to show both that a product is capable of causing injury (general causation) and that it caused the plaintiff's injury in this particular case (specific causation). On which causal question did the Carmichael's claim fail?

G. DEFENSES

1. PLAINTIFF'S BEHAVIOR

A. *The movement from contributory to comparative negligence.* The *Restatement (Second) of Torts* § 402A was adopted when the overwhelming majority of American jurisdictions held that plaintiff's contributory negligence was a total bar to recovery. In this context, should plaintiff negligence bar recovery against a manufacturer of a defective product? § 402A, Comment *n* provided the following answer:

> n. Contributory negligence. Since the liability with which this Section deals is not based upon negligence of the seller, but is strict liability, the rule applied to strict liability cases (see § 524) applies. Contributory negligence of the plaintiff is not a defense when such negligence consists merely in a failure to discover the defect in the product, or to guard against the possibility of its existence. On the other hand the form of contributory negligence which consists in voluntarily and unreasonably proceeding to encounter a known danger, and commonly passes under the name of assumption of risk, is a defense under this Section as in other cases of strict liability. If the user or consumer discovers the defect and is aware of the danger, and nevertheless proceeds unreasonably to make use of the product and is injured by it, he is barred from recovery.

Comment *n* seemingly divides plaintiff misconduct into three categories: failure to discover or guard against a product defect (which should not affect the plaintiff's recovery), assumption of the risk (which should affect plaintiff's recovery), and negligent use of a product (about which the Restatement takes no position). However, in short order most courts concluded that this third type of plaintiff misconduct should not affect the plaintiff's recovery. *See* McCown v. International Harvester Co., 463 Pa. 13, 342 A.2d 381 (1975); Mauch v. Manufacturers Sales & Service, Inc., 345 N.W.2d 338 (N.D.1984).

The wholesale movement from contributory negligence to comparative fault caused courts to reconsider the effect of plaintiff's negligence in products liability actions. Over time, most jurisdictions concluded, either by legislative enactment or by judicial opinion, that comparative responsibility principles applies in products liability cases. For example, in the leading case of Daly v. General Motors Corp., 20 Cal.3d 725, 144 Cal.Rptr. 380, 575 P.2d 1162 (1978), the California Supreme Court concluded that "a system of comparative fault should be and it is hereby extended to actions founded on strict products liability. In such cases the separate defense of 'assumption of risk,' to the extent that it is a form of contributory negligence, is abolished." 575 P.2d at 1172.

One objection to adopting comparative principles in products cases is that it would be difficult or impossible to compare the plaintiff's negligence with the defendant's defective product. For example, in his concurring and dissenting opinion in *Daly*, Justice Jefferson, argued:

> The majority rejects what I consider to be a sound criticism of its holding that it is illogical and illusory to compare elements or factors that are not reasonably subject to comparison. The majority states that it is convinced that jurors will be able to compare the noncomparables plaintiff's negligence with defendant's strict liability for a defective product and still reach a fair apportionment of liability.
>
> I consider the majority conclusion a case of wishful thinking and an application of an impractical, ivory-tower approach. The majority's assumption that a jury is capable of making a fair apportionment between a plaintiff's negligent conduct and a defendant's defective product is no more logical or convincing than if a jury were to be instructed that it should add a quart of milk (representing plaintiff's negligence) and a metal bar three feet in length (representing defendant's strict liability for a defective product), and that the two added together equal 100 percent the total fault for plaintiff's injuries; that plaintiff's quart of milk is then to be assigned its percentage of the 100 percent total and defendant's metal bar is to be assigned the remaining percentage of the total. * * * Because the legal concept of negligence is so utterly different from the legal concept of a product defective by reason of manufacture or design, a plaintiff's negligence is no more capable of being rationally compared with a defendant's defective product to determine what percentage each contributes to plaintiff's total damages than is the quart of milk with the metal bar posed in the above illustration.

575 P.2d at 1178.

The problem that seemed so perplexing in theory, comparing the plaintiff's fault to the defendant's defect, has turned out to be a relatively straightforward task in practice. Why do you think this is the case?

Most jurisdictions have adopted comparative fault principles in products liability cases through legislation. *See* Smith v. Ingersoll–Rand Co., 14 P.3d 990 (Alaska 2000) (interpreting the 1986 Alaska tort reform act). When first enacted, many "comparative negligence" statutes by their own terms were limited to negligence cases. As time has passed, however, many of these statutes were modified to include products claims. *See* Ga. Code Ann., § 51–12–33; Ohio Revised Code R.C. § 2315.32.

There is a declaration in Murray v. Fairbanks Morse, 610 F.2d 149 (3d Cir. 1979) that, in products liability actions, the comparison should be on the basis of causal contribution to the injuries, and not on the basis of fault. Texas adopted a comparative causation approach for products liability claims in Duncan v. Cessna Aircraft Co., 665 S.W.2d 414 (Tex. 1984). Subsequently, this special rule was merged into a general comparative responsibility statute, which reads as follows:

> (a) The trier of fact, as to each cause of action asserted, shall determine the percentage of responsibility, stated in whole numbers, for the following persons with respect to each person's causing or contributing to cause in any way the harm for which recovery of damages is sought, whether by negligent act or omission, by any defective or unreasonably dangerous product, by other conduct or activity that violates an applicable legal standard, or by any combination of these:

Tex. Civ. Pract. & Rem. Code § 33.003. Does this statute call for comparative fault, comparative causation, or a combination of both?

Consider also the language in the Uniform Comparative Fault Act § 2(b)

> In determining the percentages of fault, the trier of fact shall consider both the nature of the conduct of each party at fault and the extent of the causal relation between the conduct and the damages claimed.

What type of a comparison does it call for? When, if ever, do you think comparing causation versus comparing fault matters in the outcome of cases?

B. *Apportionment in crashworthiness cases. Daly* is another crashworthiness case. The plaintiff's decedent was killed when he was ejected from his car while driving down the freeway. He claimed that when his Opel struck the divider fence the door was thrown open because of an improperly designed door latch. Mr. Daly was not wearing his seat belt and he was intoxicated at the time of the crash. The plaintiffs only claimed enhancement injuries from General Motors. On retrial, should the court permit the jury to consider Mr. Daly's intoxication in apportioning fault? Should they be allowed to consider the fact that he was not wearing his seat belt? *See* D'Amario v. Ford Motor Co., 806 So.2d 424, 441 (Fla. 2001); Ellen M. Bublick, *The Tort–Proof Plaintiff: The Drunk in the Automobile Crashworthiness Claims, and the Restatement (Third) of Torts*, 74 Brook. L. Rev. 707 (2009). Does your answer depend on whether the plaintiff's injuries are indivisible, i.e., if it is possible to determine which injuries were caused by the initial crash and which were caused by the automobile's lack of crashworthiness? *See* Note 8, page 220, *supra* following the *Branham* case.

C. *Failure to discover a defect.* Still following Comment *n.* to *Restatement (Second) of Torts* § 402A, some courts refuse to apply comparative responsibility when plaintiff's only fault is in failing to discover or guard against a defect in the product. *See* West v. Caterpillar Tractor Co., 336 So.2d 80 (Fla.1976); General Motors Corp. v. Sanchez, 997 S.W.2d 584 (Tex. 1999).

D. *Assumption of the risk and misuse.* On the other hand, some jurisdictions have retained assumption of risk as a complete defense that, if proven, bars the plaintiff from all recovery. *See* Ind. Code § 34–20–6–3 (1999); Sheehan v. The North American Marketing Corp., 610 F.3d 144 (1st Cir. 2010) (applying Rhode Island law). In addition, some jurisdictions continue to hold that a misuse of a product is a separate defense that acts as a complete bar to recovery, although it is frequently said that misuse is not a defense at all but rather a failure by the plaintiff to show either causation or defect. *See* Lightolier, A Div. of Genlyte Thomas Group, LLC v. Hoon, 387 Md. 539, 876 A.2d 100 (2005).

E. *Third Restatement.* The *Restatement (Third) of Torts: Products Liability* reflects the majority view on comparative fault while at the same time rejecting any special status for failure to discover or assumption of the risk. All types of plaintiff behavior should be considered when apportioning responsibility.

§ 17. Apportionment Of Responsibility Between Or Among Plaintiff, Sellers And Distributors Of Defective Products, And Others

(a) A plaintiff's recovery of damages for harm caused by a product defect may be reduced if the conduct of the plaintiff combines with the product defect to cause the harm and the plaintiff's conduct fails to conform to generally applicable rules establishing appropriate standards of care.

(b) The manner and extent of the reduction under Subsection (a) and the apportionment of plaintiff's recovery among multiple defendants are governed by generally applicable rules apportioning responsibility.

However, comment *d* notes, "[W]hen the defendant claims that the plaintiff failed to discover a defect, there must be evidence that the plaintiff's conduct in failing to discover a defect did, in fact, fail to meet a standard of reasonable care. In general, a plaintiff has no reason to expect that a new product contains a defect and would have little reason to be on guard to discover it." Does this language resurrect the Second Restatement's distinction between "failure to discover" and other types of plaintiff misconduct? The *Sanchez* opinion cited above provides one answer. *See* William J. McNichols, *The Relevance of the Plaintiff's Misconduct in Strict Tort Products Liability, The Advent of Comparative Responsibility, and the Proposed Restatement (Third) of Torts*, 47 Okla. L. Rev. 201 (1994).

F. *Bankruptcy.* Although not a defense, Chapter 11 of the U.S. Bankruptcy Code, 11 U.S.C. § 101 *et seq.*, has been used by corporations facing massive products liability claims. For a look at the effect bankruptcy laws may have on pending product liability claims, *see* Susan S. Ford, *Who Will Compensate the Victims of Asbestos–Related Diseases? Manville's Chapter 11 Fuels the Fire,* 14 Enviro.Law 465 (1983–84); Note, *Strategic Bankruptcies: Class Actions, Classification & the Dalkon Shield Cases,* 7 Cardozo L.Rev. 817 (1985–86); Kesner, *Future Asbestos Related Litigants as Holders of Statutory Claims Under Chapter 11 of the Bankruptcy Code and Their Place in the Johns–Manville Reorganization,* 62 Am.Bankruptcy

L.J. 69 (1988). The asbestos litigation, in particular, has driven a substantial number of firms into bankruptcy. *See* DEBORAH HENSLER ET AL., RAND INSTITUTE FOR CIVIL JUSTICE, ASBESTOS LITIGATION IN THE U.S.: A NEW LOOK AT AN OLD ISSUE, 4–5, 12–13 (Aug. 2001); Paul Carrington, *Asbestos Lessons: the Consequences of Asbestos Litigation*, 26 Rev. Litig. 583 (2007).

The effectiveness and fairness of bankruptcy proceedings as a way to resolve mass torts is a matter of debate. *See* Alan N. Resnick, *Bankruptcy as a Vehicle for Resolving Enterprise–Threatening Mass Tort Liability*, 148 U. Pa. L. Rev. 2045 (2000); Douglas G. Smith, *Resolution of Mass Tort Claims in the Bankruptcy System*, 41 U.C. Davis L. Rev. 1613 (2008).

2. PRE–EMPTION

BATES v. DOW AGROSCIENCES LLC

Supreme Court of the United States, 2005.
544 U.S. 431, 125 S.Ct. 1788, 161 L.Ed.2d 687.

JUSTICE STEVENS delivered the opinion of the Court.

Petitioners are 29 Texas peanut farmers who allege that in the 2000 growing season their crops were severely damaged by the application of respondent's newly marketed pesticide named "Strongarm." The question presented is whether the Federal Insecticide, Fungicide, and Rodenticide Act (FIFRA), 7 U.S.C. § 136 *et seq.* (2000 ed. and Supp. II), pre-empts their state-law claims for damages.

I

Pursuant to its authority under FIFRA, the Environmental Protection Agency (EPA) conditionally registered Strongarm on March 8, 2000, thereby granting respondent (Dow) permission to sell this pesticide—a weed killer—in the United States. Dow obtained this registration in time to market Strongarm to Texas farmers, who normally plant their peanut crops around May 1. According to petitioners-whose version of the facts we assume to be true at this stage-Dow knew, or should have known, that Strongarm would stunt the growth of peanuts in soils with pH levels of 7.0 or greater. Nevertheless, Strongarm's label stated, "Use of Strongarm is recommended in all areas where peanuts are grown," App. 108, and Dow's agents made equivalent representations in their sales pitches to petitioners. When petitioners applied Strongarm on their farms-whose soils have pH levels of 7.2 or higher, as is typical in western Texas-the pesticide severely damaged their peanut crops while failing to control the growth of weeds. The farmers reported these problems to Dow, which sent its experts to inspect the crops.

* * *

After unsuccessful negotiations with Dow, petitioners gave Dow notice of their intent to bring suit as required by the Texas Deceptive Trade

Practices–Consumer Protection Act[3] (hereinafter Texas DTPA). In response, Dow filed a declaratory judgment action in Federal District Court, asserting that petitioners' claims were expressly or impliedly pre-empted by FIFRA. Petitioners, in turn, brought counterclaims, including tort claims sounding in strict liability and negligence. They also alleged fraud, breach of warranty, and violation of the Texas DTPA. The District Court granted Dow's motion for summary judgment, rejecting one claim on state-law grounds and dismissing the remainder as expressly pre-empted by 7 U.S.C. § 136v(b), which provides that States "shall not impose or continue in effect any requirements for labeling or packaging in addition to or different from those required under this subchapter."

The Court of Appeals affirmed. It read § 136v(b) to pre-empt any state-law claim in which "a judgment against Dow would induce it to alter its product label." The court held that because petitioners' fraud, warranty, and deceptive trade practices claims focused on oral statements by Dow's agents that did not differ from statements made on the product's label, success on those claims would give Dow a "strong incentive" to change its label. Those claims were thus pre-empted. The court also found that petitioners' strict liability claim alleging defective design was essentially a "disguised" failure-to-warn claim and therefore pre-empted. It reasoned: "One cannot escape the heart of the farmers' grievance: Strongarm is dangerous to peanut crops in soil with a pH level over 7.0, and that was not disclosed to them.... It is inescapable that success on this claim would again necessarily induce Dow to alter the Strongarm label." The court employed similar reasoning to find the negligent testing and negligent manufacture claims pre-empted as well.

This decision was consistent with those of a majority of the Courts of Appeals, as well of several state high courts but conflicted with the decisions of other courts and with the views of EPA set forth in an *amicus curiae* brief filed with the California Supreme Court in 2000. We granted certiorari to resolve this conflict.

II

Prior to 1910 the States provided the primary and possibly the exclusive source of regulatory control over the distribution of poisonous substances. Both the Federal Government's first effort at regulation in this area, the Insecticide Act of 1910, 36 Stat. 331, and FIFRA as originally enacted in 1947, ch. 125, 61 Stat. 163, primarily dealt with licensing and labeling. Under the original version of FIFRA, all pesticides sold in interstate commerce had to be registered with the Secretary of Agriculture. The Secretary would register a pesticide if it complied with the statute's labeling standards and was determined to be efficacious and safe. In 1970, EPA assumed responsibility for this registration process.

In 1972, spurred by growing environmental and safety concerns, Congress adopted the extensive amendments that "transformed FIFRA

3. Tex. Bus. & Com.Code Ann. § 17.01 *et seq.* (West 2002).

from a labeling law into a comprehensive regulatory statute." *Ruckelshaus v. Monsanto Co.,* 467 U.S. 986, 991, 104 S.Ct. 2862, 81 L.Ed.2d 815 (1984). "As amended, FIFRA regulated the use, as well as the sale and labeling, of pesticides; regulated pesticides produced and sold in both intrastate and interstate commerce; provided for review, cancellation, and suspension of registration; and gave EPA greater enforcement authority." *Id.,* at 991–992. The 1972 amendments also imposed a new criterion for registration-environmental safety. *Id.,* at 992.

Under FIFRA as it currently stands, a manufacturer seeking to register a pesticide must submit a proposed label to EPA as well as certain supporting data. 7 U.S.C. §§ 136a(c)(1)(C), (F). The agency will register the pesticide if it determines that the pesticide is efficacious (with the caveat discussed below), § 136a(c)(5)(A); that it will not cause unreasonable adverse effects on humans and the environment, §§ 136a(c)(5)(C), (D); § 136(bb); and that its label complies with the statute's prohibition on misbranding, § 136a(c)(5)(B); 40 CFR § 152.112(f) (2004). A pesticide is "misbranded" if its label contains a statement that is "false or misleading in any particular," including a false or misleading statement concerning the efficacy of the pesticide. 7 U.S.C. § 136(q)(1)(A); 40 CFR § 156.10(a)(5)(ii). A pesticide is also misbranded if its label does not contain adequate instructions for use, or if its label omits necessary warnings or cautionary statements. 7 U.S.C. §§ 136(q)(1)(F), (G).

Because it is unlawful under the statute to sell a pesticide that is registered but nevertheless misbranded, manufacturers have a continuing obligation to adhere to FIFRA's labeling requirements. § 136j(a)(1)(E); see also § 136a(f)(2) (registration is prima facie evidence that the pesticide and its labeling comply with the statute's requirements, but registration does not provide a defense to the violation of the statute); § 136a(f)(1) (a manufacturer may seek approval to amend its label). Additionally, manufacturers have a duty to report incidents involving a pesticide's toxic effects that may not be adequately reflected in its label's warnings, 40 CFR §§ 159.184(a), (b) (2004), and EPA may institute cancellation proceedings, 7 U.S.C. § 136d(b), and take other enforcement action if it determines that a registered pesticide is misbranded.

Section 136v, which was added in the 1972 amendments, addresses the States' continuing role in pesticide regulation. As currently codified, § 136v provides:

> "(a) In general
>
> "A State may regulate the sale or use of any federally registered pesticide or device in the State, but only if and to the extent the regulation does not permit any sale or use prohibited by this subchapter.
>
> "(b) Uniformity
>
> "Such State shall not impose or continue in effect any requirements for labeling or packaging in addition to or different from those required under this subchapter.

"(c) Additional uses

"(1) A State may provide registration for additional uses of federally registered pesticides formulated for distribution and use within that State to meet special local needs in accord with the purposes of this subchapter and if registration for such use has not previously been denied, disapproved, or canceled by the Administrator. Such registration shall be deemed registration under section 136a of this title for all purposes of this subchapter, but shall authorize distribution and use only within such State. . . ."

In 1978, Congress once again amended FIFRA, this time in response to EPA's concern that its evaluation of pesticide efficacy during the registration process diverted too many resources from its task of assessing the environmental and health dangers posed by pesticides. Congress addressed this problem by authorizing EPA to waive data requirements pertaining to efficacy, thus permitting the agency to register a pesticide without confirming the efficacy claims made on its label. § 136a(c)(5). In 1979, EPA invoked this grant of permission and issued a general waiver of efficacy review, with only limited qualifications not applicable here. In a notice published years later in 1996, EPA confirmed that it had "stopped evaluating pesticide efficacy for routine label approvals almost two decades ago," and clarified that "EPA's approval of a pesticide label does not reflect any determination on the part of EPA that the pesticide will be efficacious or will not damage crops or cause other property damage," The notice also referred to an earlier statement in which EPA observed that " 'pesticide producers are aware that they are potentially subject to damage suits by the user community if their products prove ineffective in actual use.' " This general waiver was in place at the time of Strongarm's registration; thus, EPA never passed on the accuracy of the statement in Strongarm's original label recommending the product's use "in all areas where peanuts are grown."

Although the modern version of FIFRA was enacted over three decades ago, this Court has never addressed whether that statute pre-empts tort and other common-law claims arising under state law. Courts entertained tort litigation against pesticide manufacturers since well before the passage of FIFRA in 1947, and such litigation was a common feature of the legal landscape at the time of the 1972 amendments. Indeed, for at least a decade after those amendments, arguments that such tort suits were pre-empted by § 136v(b) either were not advanced or were unsuccessful. See, *e.g., Ferebee v. Chevron Chemical Co.,* 736 F.2d 1529 (C.A.D.C.1984). It was only after 1992 when we held in *Cipollone v. Liggett Group, Inc.,* 505 U.S. 504, 112 S.Ct. 2608, 120 L.Ed.2d 407, that the term "requirement * * * or prohibition" in the Public Health Cigarette Smoking Act of 1969 included common-law duties, and therefore pre-empted certain tort claims against cigarette companies, that a groundswell of federal and state decisions emerged holding that § 136v(b) pre-empted claims like those advanced in this litigation.

This Court has addressed FIFRA pre-emption in a different context. In *Wisconsin Public Intervenor v. Mortier,* 501 U.S. 597, 111 S.Ct. 2476, 115 L.Ed.2d 532 (1991), we considered a claim that § 136v(b) pre-empted a small town's ordinance requiring a special permit for the aerial application of pesticides. Although the ordinance imposed restrictions not required by FIFRA or any EPA regulation, we unanimously rejected the pre-emption claim. In our opinion we noted that FIFRA was not "a sufficiently comprehensive statute to justify an inference that Congress had occupied the field to the exclusion of the States." *Id.,* at 607. "To the contrary, the statute leaves ample room for States and localities to supplement federal efforts even absent the express regulatory authorization of § 136v(a)." *Id.,* at 613.

As a part of their supplementary role, States have ample authority to review pesticide labels to ensure that they comply with both federal and state labeling requirements. Nothing in the text of FIFRA would prevent a State from making the violation of a federal labeling or packaging requirement a state offense, thereby imposing its own sanctions on pesticide manufacturers who violate federal law. The imposition of state sanctions for violating state rules that merely duplicate federal requirements is equally consistent with the text of § 136v.

III

Against this background, we consider whether petitioners' claims[15] are pre-empted by § 136v(b), which, again, reads as follows: "Such State shall not impose or continue in effect any requirements for labeling or packaging in addition to or different from those required under this subchapter."

* * *

The prohibitions in § 136v(b) apply only to "requirements." An occurrence that merely motivates an optional decision does not qualify as a requirement. The Court of Appeals was therefore quite wrong when it assumed that any event, such as a jury verdict, that might "induce" a pesticide manufacturer to change its label should be viewed as a requirement. The Court of Appeals did, however, correctly hold that the term "requirements" in § 136v(b) reaches beyond positive enactments, such as statutes and regulations, to embrace common-law duties. Our decision in *Cipollone* supports this conclusion. While the use of "requirements" in a pre-emption clause may not invariably carry this meaning, we think this is the best reading of § 136v(b).

That § 136v(b) may pre-empt judge-made rules, as well as statutes and regulations, says nothing about the *scope* of that pre-emption. For a particular state rule to be pre-empted, it must satisfy two conditions.

15. * * * Of course, we express no view as to whether any of these claims are viable as a matter of Texas law. Nor do we, given the early stage of this litigation, opine on whether petitioners can adduce sufficient evidence in support of their claims to survive summary judgment.

First, it must be a requirement *"for labeling or packaging"*; rules governing the design of a product, for example, are not pre-empted. Second, it must impose a labeling or packaging requirement that is *"in addition to or different from* those required under this subchapter." A state regulation requiring the word "poison" to appear in red letters, for instance, would not be pre-empted if an EPA regulation imposed the same requirement.

It is perfectly clear that many of the common-law rules upon which petitioners rely do not satisfy the first condition. Rules that require manufacturers to design reasonably safe products, to use due care in conducting appropriate testing of their products, to market products free of manufacturing defects, and to honor their express warranties or other contractual commitments plainly do not qualify as requirements for "labeling or packaging." None of these common-law rules requires that manufacturers label or package their products in any particular way. Thus, petitioners' claims for defective design, defective manufacture, negligent testing, and breach of express warranty are not pre-empted.

To be sure, Dow's express warranty was located on Strongarm's label.[16] But a cause of action on an express warranty asks only that a manufacturer make good on the contractual commitment that it voluntarily undertook by placing that warranty on its product. Because this common-law rule does not require the manufacturer to make an express warranty, or in the event that the manufacturer elects to do so, to say anything in particular in that warranty, the rule does not impose a requirement "for labeling or packaging."

In arriving at a different conclusion, the court below reasoned that a finding of liability on these claims would "induce Dow to alter [its] label." 332 F.3d, at 332. This effects-based test finds no support in the text of § 136v(b), which speaks only of "requirements." A requirement is a rule of law that must be obeyed; an event, such as a jury verdict, that merely motivates an optional decision is not a requirement. The proper inquiry calls for an examination of the elements of the common-law duty at issue; it does not call for speculation as to whether a jury verdict will prompt the manufacturer to take any particular action (a question, in any event, that will depend on a variety of cost/benefit calculations best left to the manufacturer's accountants).

The inducement test is unquestionably overbroad because it would impeach many "genuine" design defect claims that Dow concedes are not pre-empted. A design defect claim, if successful, would surely induce a manufacturer to alter its label to reflect a change in the list of ingredients or a change in the instructions for use necessitated by the improvement in the product's design. Moreover, the inducement test is not entirely consistent with § 136v(a), which confirms the State's broad authority to regulate the sale and use of pesticides. Under § 136v(a), a state agency may

16. The label stated: "Dow AgroSciences warrants that this product conforms to the chemical description on the label and is reasonably fit for the purposes stated on the label when used in strict accordance with the directions, subject to the inherent risks set forth below."

ban the sale of a pesticide if it finds, for instance, that one of the pesticide's label-approved uses is unsafe. This ban might well induce the manufacturer to change its label to warn against this questioned use. Under the inducement test, however, such a restriction would anomalously qualify as a "labeling" requirement. It is highly unlikely that Congress endeavored to draw a line between the type of indirect pressure caused by a State's power to impose sales and use restrictions and the even more attenuated pressure exerted by common-law suits. The inducement test is not supported by either the text or the structure of the statute.

Unlike their other claims, petitioners' fraud and negligent-failure-to-warn claims are premised on common-law rules that qualify as "requirements for labeling or packaging." These rules set a standard for a product's labeling that the Strongarm label is alleged to have violated by containing false statements and inadequate warnings. While the courts of appeals have rightly found guidance in *Cipollone's* interpretation of "requirements," some of those courts too quickly concluded that failure-to-warn claims were pre-empted under FIFRA, as they were in *Cipollone,* without paying attention to the rather obvious textual differences between the two pre-emption clauses.

Unlike the pre-emption clause at issue in *Cipollone,*[22] § 136v(b) prohibits only state-law labeling and packaging requirements that are "*in addition to or different from*" the labeling and packaging requirements under FIFRA. Thus, a state-law labeling requirement is not pre-empted by § 136v(b) if it is equivalent to, and fully consistent with, FIFRA's misbranding provisions. * * *

The "parallel requirements" reading of § 136v(b) that we adopt today finds strong support in *Medtronic, Inc. v. Lohr,* 518 U.S. 470, 116 S.Ct. 2240, 135 L.Ed.2d 700 (1996). In addressing a similarly worded pre-emption provision in a statute regulating medical devices, we found that "[n]othing in [21 U.S.C.] § 360k denies Florida the right to provide a traditional damages remedy for violations of common-law duties when those duties parallel federal requirements." *Id.,* at 495, As Justice O'CONNOR explained in her separate opinion, a state cause of action that seeks to enforce a federal requirement "does not impose a requirement that is 'different from, or in addition to,' requirements under federal law. To be sure, the threat of a damages remedy will give manufacturers an additional cause to comply, but the requirements imposed on them under state and federal law do not differ. Section 360k does not preclude States from imposing different or additional *remedies,* but only different or additional *requirements.*" *Id.,* at 513. Accordingly, although FIFRA does not provide a federal remedy to farmers and others who are injured as a result of a manufacturer's violation of FIFRA's labeling requirements, nothing in § 136v(b) precludes States from providing such a remedy.

22. "No requirement or prohibition based on smoking and health shall be imposed under State law with respect to the advertising or promotion of any cigarettes the packages of which are labeled in conformity with the provisions of this [Act]." 15 U.S.C. § 1334(b).

Dow, joined by the United States as *amicus curiae,* argues that the "parallel requirements" reading of § 136v(b) would "give juries in 50 States the authority to give content to FIFRA's misbranding prohibition, establishing a crazy-quilt of anti-misbranding requirements different from the one defined by FIFRA itself and intended by Congress to be interpreted authoritatively by EPA." In our view, however, the clear text of § 136v(b) and the authority of *Medtronic* cannot be so easily avoided. Conspicuously absent from the submissions by Dow and the United States is any plausible alternative interpretation of "in addition to or different from" that would give that phrase meaning. Instead, they appear to favor reading those words out of the statute, which would leave the following: "Such State shall not impose or continue in effect any requirements for labeling or packaging." This amputated version of § 136v(b) would no doubt have clearly and succinctly commanded the pre-emption of *all* state requirements concerning labeling. That Congress added the remainder of the provision is evidence of its intent to draw a distinction between state labeling requirements that are pre-empted and those that are not.

* * *

Finally, we find the policy objections raised against our reading of § 136v(b) to be unpersuasive. Dow and the United States greatly overstate the degree of uniformity and centralization that characterizes FIFRA. In fact, the statute authorizes a relatively decentralized scheme that preserves a broad role for state regulation. Most significantly, States may ban or restrict the uses of pesticides that EPA has approved, § 136v(a); they may also register, subject to certain restrictions, pesticides for uses beyond those approved by EPA, § 136v(c). A literal reading of § 136v(b) is fully consistent with the concurrent authority of the Federal and State Governments in this sphere.

Private remedies that enforce federal misbranding requirements would seem to aid, rather than hinder, the functioning of FIFRA. Unlike the cigarette labeling law at issue in *Cipollone,* which prescribed certain immutable warning statements, FIFRA contemplates that pesticide labels will evolve over time, as manufacturers gain more information about their products' performance in diverse settings. As one court explained, tort suits can serve as a catalyst in this process:

> "By encouraging plaintiffs to bring suit for injuries not previously recognized as traceable to pesticides such as [the pesticide there at issue], a state tort action of the kind under review may aid in the exposure of new dangers associated with pesticides. Successful actions of this sort may lead manufacturers to petition EPA to allow more detailed labelling of their products; alternatively, EPA itself may decide that revised labels are required in light of the new information that has been brought to its attention through common law suits. In addition, the specter of damage actions may provide manufacturers with added dynamic incentives to continue to keep abreast of all possible injuries stemming from use of their product so as to forestall

such actions through product improvement." *Ferebee,* 736 F.2d, at 1541–1542.

Dow and the United States exaggerate the disruptive effects of using common-law suits to enforce the prohibition on misbranding. FIFRA has prohibited inaccurate representations and inadequate warnings since its enactment in 1947, while tort suits alleging failure-to-warn claims were common well before that date and continued beyond the 1972 amendments. We have been pointed to no evidence that such tort suits led to a "crazy-quilt" of FIFRA standards or otherwise created any real hardship for manufacturers or for EPA. Indeed, for much of this period EPA appears to have welcomed these tort suits. While it is true that properly instructed juries might on occasion reach contrary conclusions on a similar issue of misbranding, there is no reason to think such occurrences would be frequent or that they would result in difficulties beyond those regularly experienced by manufacturers of other products that every day bear the risk of conflicting jury verdicts. * * *

In sum, under our interpretation, § 136v(b) retains a narrow, but still important, role. In the main, it pre-empts competing state labeling standards-imagine 50 different labeling regimes prescribing the color, font size, and wording of warnings-that would create significant inefficiencies for manufacturers. The provision also pre-empts any statutory or common-law rule that would impose a labeling requirement that diverges from those set out in FIFRA and its implementing regulations. It does not, however, pre-empt any state rules that are fully consistent with federal requirements.

Having settled on our interpretation of § 136v(b), it still remains to be decided whether that provision pre-empts petitioners' fraud and failure-to-warn claims. Because we have not received sufficient briefing on this issue, which involves questions of Texas law, we remand it to the Court of Appeals. We emphasize that a state-law labeling requirement must in fact be equivalent to a requirement under FIFRA in order to survive pre-emption. For example, were the Court of Appeals to determine that the element of falsity in Texas' common-law definition of fraud imposed a broader obligation than FIFRA's requirement that labels not contain "false or misleading statements," that state-law cause of action would be pre-empted by § 136v(b) to the extent of that difference. State-law requirements must also be measured against any relevant EPA regulations that give content to FIFRA's misbranding standards. For example, a failure-to-warn claim alleging that a given pesticide's label should have stated "DANGER" instead of the more subdued "CAUTION" would be pre-empted because it is inconsistent with 40 CFR § 156.64 (2004), which specifically assigns these warnings to particular classes of pesticides based on their toxicity.

* * *

The judgment of the Court of Appeals is vacated, and the case is remanded for further proceedings consistent with this opinion.

It is so ordered.

JUSTICE THOMAS, with whom JUSTICE SCALIA joins, concurring in the judgment in part and dissenting in part.

I agree with the Court that the term "requirements" in § 24(b) of the Federal Insecticide, Fungicide, and Rodenticide Act (FIFRA), 7 U.S.C. § 136v(b), includes common-law duties for labeling or packaging. I also agree that state-law damages claims may not impose requirements "in addition to or different from" FIFRA's. *Ante,* at 1803–1804. While States are free to impose liability predicated on a violation of the federal standards set forth in FIFRA and in any accompanying regulations promulgated by the Environmental Protection Agency, they may not impose liability for labeling requirements predicated on distinct state standards of care. Section 136v(b) permits States to add remedies-not to alter or augment the substantive rules governing liability for labeling. Because the parties have not argued that Dow violated FIFRA's labeling standards, the majority properly remands for the District Court to consider whether Texas law mirrors the federal standards.

However, the majority omits a step in its reasoning that should be made explicit: A state-law cause of action, even if not specific to labeling, nevertheless imposes a labeling requirement "in addition to or different from" FIFRA's when it attaches liability to statements on the label that do not produce liability under FIFRA. The state-law cause of action then adds some supplemental requirement of truthfulness to FIFRA's requirement that labeling statements not be "false or misleading." 7 U.S.C. § 136(q)(1)(A). That is why the fraud claims here are properly remanded to determine whether the state and federal standards for liability-incurring statements are, in their application to this case, the same.

Under that reasoning, the majority mistreats two sets of petitioners' claims. First, petitioners' breach-of-warranty claims should be remanded for pre-emption analysis, contrary to the majority's disposition, see *ante,* at 1798–1799. To the extent that Texas' law of warranty imposes liability for statements on the label where FIFRA would not, Texas' law is pre-empted. Second, the majority holds that petitioners' claim under the Texas Deceptive Trade Practices–Consumer Protection Act (DTPA) is not pre-empted to the extent it is a breach-of-warranty claim. However, the DTPA claim is also (and, in fact, perhaps exclusively) a claim for false or misleading representations on the label. Therefore, all aspects of the DTPA claim should be remanded. The DTPA claim, like petitioners' fraud claims, should be pre-empted insofar as it imposes liability for label content where FIFRA would not. * * *

NOTES

1. *Types of Preemption.* In Louisiana Public Service Commission v. FCC, 476 U.S. 355, 106 S.Ct. 1890, 90 L.Ed.2d 369 (1986), the Supreme Court stated:

> Preemption occurs when Congress, in enacting a federal statute, expresses a clear intent to preempt state law, when there is outright or actual conflict between federal and state law, where compliance with both federal and state law is in effect physically impossible, where there is implicit in federal law a barrier to state regulation, where Congress has legislated comprehensively, thus occupying an entire field of regulation and leaving no room for the states to supplement federal law, or where the state law stands as an obstacle to the accomplishment and execution of the full objectives of Congress.

476 U.S. at 368–69.

2. *Field preemption.* The most extensive preemption occurs when the courts determine that Congress has "occupied the field" in a given area. An example of a statute that occupies the field, leaving no room for the states to supplement federal law is the Atomic Energy Act on matters of nuclear safety. See Pacific Gas & Elec. Co. v. State Energy Res. Conservation & Dev. Comm'n, 461 U.S. 190, 212, 103 S.Ct. 1713, 75 L.Ed.2d 752 (1983). Likewise, the Supreme Court has held that because the Natural Gas Act, 15 U.S.C. §§ 717–717w, gives the Federal Energy Regulatory Commission "exclusive" jurisdiction over the transportation and sale of natural gas in interstate commerce, Congress intended to occupy the field of natural gas regulation, including regulation of natural gas pipelines. Schneidewind v. ANR Pipeline Co., 485 U.S. 293, 108 S.Ct. 1145, 99 L.Ed.2d 316 (1988). Could the defendant in *Bates* have argued that FIFRA occupies the field? Why or why not?

3. *Express Preemption.* Second, there is express preemption. In *Bates* the court addressed the preemptive effect of express language contained in the federal statute. Why did the Court conclude that the plaintiff's suit was not preempted?

Riegel v. Medtronic, Inc., 552 U.S. 312, 128 S.Ct. 999, 169 L.Ed.2d 892 (2008) involved the Medical Device Amendments of 1976. The Statute's preemption clause provides that a state shall not "establish or continue in effect with respect to a device intended for human use any requirement-. . . (1) which is different from, or in addition to, any requirement applicable under [federal law] to the device, and . . . (2) which relates to the safety or effectiveness of the device . . ." The court concluded the purpose of the statute was to create a general scheme of federal safety oversight for medical devices while sweeping back state oversight. It held that this language expressly preempted common-law claims challenging the safety or effectiveness of a medical device marketed in a form that received premarket approval from the FDA.

4. *Implied conflict preemption.* Recall that the third type of preemption, implied preemption, is often divided into two sub-categories, conflict (obstacle) and impossibility. Conflict preemption occurs when a state statute or favorable plaintiff lawsuit creates a rule that conflicts with the purpose of a federal statute.

Some case involve more than one type of preemption. For example, in Geier v. American Honda Motor Co., 529 U.S. 861, 120 S.Ct. 1913, 146 L.Ed.2d 914 (2000), the court held that an express preemption clause in the National Traffic and Motor Vehicle Safety Act of 1966 did not bar plaintiff's suit. Unlike the "requirement" language in the statutes in *Bates* and *Cipollone* the statute preempted "any safety *standard*" that was not identical to any federal safety standard promulgated under the NTMVSA. The court declined to interpret "standard" to include state tort actions, in large part because the statute included a "saving clause" that stated compliance with a safety standard "does not exempt any person from any liability under common law." However, it then proceeded to hold that plaintiffs' tort claim was impliedly preempted. Plaintiff claimed the defendant's car, a 1987 Honda Accord, was defectively designed because it was not equipped with airbags. The court held that a ruling in favor of the plaintiff would conflict with the statutory goal of achieving greater passenger safety either through the use of airbags or seatbelts. In reaching this conclusion, the court engaged in an historical analysis of the statute and Congress' overall purpose.

Two years later in Sprietsma v. Mercury Marine, 537 U.S. 51, 123 S.Ct. 518, 154 L.Ed.2d 466 (2002), the plaintiff's decedent was killed in a boating accident when she was struck by the propeller of a boat. The plaintiff argued there should have been a guard over the propeller. The plaintiff's claim was met with a preemption argument, based on the fact that the Coast Guard, to which the Secretary of Transportation delegated the task of adopting boating safety regulations, had considered, but not adopted any regulation concerning propeller guards. The relevant statute, like the statute in *Geier*, contained both a preemption clause and a savings clause. The Supreme Court engaged in a historical analysis similar to that in *Geier*, and concluded that the failure to adopt a regulation concerning propeller guards did not preempt civil design defect suits against manufacturers.

With respect to the defendant's conflict preemption argument, the court said that is quite wrong to equate the Coast Guard's decision not to adopt a regulation requiring propeller guards on motorboats with a regulation prohibiting states from adopting such a regulation. Moreover, unlike the position taken by the Government and the DOT in *Geier*, neither the Coast Guard nor the Solicitor General viewed the Coast Guard's refusal to regulate in the area of propeller guards as having any pre-emptive effect. Insofar as the *Geier* decision rested on the interpretation of the executive branch, the reasoning in *Geier* supported the conclusion that there should be no preemption in the current situation.

Still more recently, in Wyeth v. Levine, 555 U.S. 555, 129 S.Ct. 1187, 173 L.Ed.2d 51 (2009), the court concluded defendant's warning defect claim with respect to a prescription drug was not preempted by language in the Food Drug and Cosmetic Act because the act contained a so-called "changes being effected" provision permitting a defendant to alter the warnings accompanying a drug prior to receiving FDA approval of the change. Thus, short term changes would not conflict with the overall statutory purpose of FDA approval of drug labels.

5. *Implied impossibility preemption*. Impossibility preemption occurs when it is impossible for a defendant to comply with both federal and state requirements. For example, if in *Geier* the federal rule had mandated seat belts only and the state suit were to define as defective any 1987 automobile without airbags, Honda could not comply with both rules.

PLIVA, Inc. v. Mensing, ___ U.S. ___, 131 S.Ct. 2567, 180 L.Ed.2d 580 (2011) concerned only a slight variation on the *Wyeth* case cited in the previous note. The Food Drug and Cosmetic Act distinguishes between drugs manufactured by the original brand-name developer of a prescription drug and manufacturers of generic versions of the drug. Generic versions routinely appear on the market immediately after the drug patent expires. In order to encourage competition, the Hatch–Waxman Amendments to the Act does not require generic manufacturers to replicate the research done by the original developer in order to have their identical drug approved by the FDA. The Amendments also adopts separate rules concerning the warnings obligations of generic drug manufacturers. Under the Hatch–Waxman Amendments, generic manufacturers seeking approval of their version of the drug, must initially ensure that their warning is the same as the brand name's. The issue in the litigation was whether the Act permits the generic manufacturers to make unilateral changes to their labels after initial FDA approval. The FDA took the position that they may not. The brand name and generic labels must always be the same. The "changes-being-effected" process does not apply to generic versions of the drug.

The *Pliva* plaintiffs argued that even though the generic warnings were identical to the brand-name warnings, they were defective because they failed to warn against known dangers involved in the long term use of Metoclopramide, a drug designed to speed the movement of food through the digestive system. In a 5–4 opinion, the court sided with the FDA's interpretation of the Act and said that the plaintiffs' claims, if successful, would make it impossible for the manufacturer to comply with federal law and do what state law required of them.

If nothing else, the case demonstrates the perverse outcomes that may occur in the preemption arena. As Justice Thomas noted,

> We recognize that from the perspective of [the plaintiffs] finding preemption here but not in *Wyeth* makes little sense. Had [they] taken Reglan, the brand-name drug prescribed by their doctors, *Wyeth* would control and their lawsuits would not be pre-empted. But because pharmacists, acting in full accord with state law, substituted generic Metoclopramide instead, federal law preempts these suits. We acknowledge the unfortunate hand that federal drug regulation has dealt [the plaintiffs] and others similarly situated.
>
> But "it is not this Court's task to decide whether the statutory scheme established by Congress is unusual or even bizarre." * * * As always, Congress and the FDA retain the authority to change the law and regulations if they so desire.

131 S.Ct. at 2581–82.

On this last note, what would you propose the Congress or the FDA do? Why?

6. Bruesewitz v. Wyeth L.L.C., ___ U.S. ___, 131 S.Ct. 1068, 179 L.Ed.2d 1 (2011) involved the question of whether the National Childhood Vaccine Injury Act of 1986 (NCVIA) expressly bars state law design-defect claims

against vaccine manufacturers. The relevant statutory provision reads as follows:

> "No vaccine manufacturer shall be liable in a civil action for damages arising from a vaccine-related injury or death associated with the administration of a vaccine after October 1, 1988, if the injury or death resulted from side effects that were unavoidable even though the vaccine was properly prepared and was accompanied by proper directions and warnings."

42 U.S.C. § 300aa–22(b)(1).

How would you interpret this provision so that it preempts vaccine design defect claims? How would you interpret the provision so that it does not preempt such claims? What weight should be given to the fact that amicus briefs filed by the United States (per the Department of Health and Human Services) and leading public health organizations, including the American Academy of Pediatrics, the American Academy of Family Physicians, the American College of Preventive Medicine, the American Public Health Association, the American Medical Association, and the March of Dimes Foundation support the preemption position?

7. In addition to the cases discussed above, preemption litigation sweeps across numerous additional areas of products liability law, involving both design defect and warning defect claims. *See*, e.g. West v. Mattel, Inc., 246 F.Supp.2d 640 (S.D.Tex. 2003) (Child swallowed toy. Warning defect claim, but not design defect claim, preempted by Child Safety Protection Act.); Choate v. Champion Home Builders Co., 222 F.3d 788 (10th Cir. 2000) (National Manufactured Housing Construction and Safety Standards Act does not preempt claim that manufactured home is unreasonably dangerous because it did not have a battery-powered backup smoke detection device or a warning about the absence of such a device); Scheiding v. General Motors Corp., 22 Cal.4th 471, 993 P.2d 996, 93 Cal.Rptr.2d 342 (2000) (claims for asbestos related injuries against manufacturer of railroad locomotives preempted by the Locomotive Boiler Inspection Act); Comeaux v. National Tea Co., 81 F.3d 42 (5th Cir. 1996) (alleged inadequate warning accompanying lighter fluid preempted by Federal Hazardous Substances Act); Cipollone v. Liggett Group, 505 U.S. 504, 112 S.Ct. 2608, 120 L.Ed.2d 407 (1992) and Altria Group, Inc. v. Good, 555 U.S. 70, 129 S.Ct. 538, 172 L.Ed.2d 398 (2008) (preemption under the Cigarette Labeling and Advertising Act).

For useful discussions of preemption law, *see* Stuart Madden, *Federal Preemption of Inconsistent State Safety Obligations*, 21 Pace. L. Rev. 103 (2000); Jamelle C. Sharpe, *Toward (A) Faithful Agency in the Supreme Courts' Preemption Jurisprudence*, 18 Geo. Mason L. Rev. 367 (2011); Mary J. Davis, *The "New" Presumption Against Preemption,* 61 Hastings L.J. 1217 (2010); Symposium issue, *Federal Preemption of State Tort Law*. 84 Tul. L. Rev. No. 5 (2010).

3. COMPLIANCE WITH REGULATIONS

Failure to comply with state or government regulations is, of course, often held to be negligence *per se*. The *Restatement (Third) of Torts:*

Products Liability § 4 takes the position that noncompliance with an applicable product safety statute or regulation "renders the product defective with respect to the risks sought to be reduced by the statute or regulation."

As we saw in *Grundberg* (*supra*, p. 237), a number of courts have used comment *k* of the *Restatement of Torts (Second)* § 402A to declare that some or all prescription drugs approved by the Food and Drug Administration are not defectively designed as a matter of law. In these jurisdictions, compliance with FDA regulations provides the pharmaceutical manufacturer with broad immunity. Most courts permit the defendant to introduce compliance evidence as a fact tending to support the defendant's position that its product is non-defective, but the overwhelming majority of courts have said that such evidence is not conclusive. For example, most courts have now held that approval by the Federal Food and Drug Administration, pursuant to the Federal Food, Drug, and Cosmetic Act, 21 U.S.C. § 301 *et seq.* and the Public Health Service Act, 42 U.S.C. § 201 *et seq.*, may be evidence of lack of defect but is not determinative. *See, e.g.*, Feldman v. Lederle Laboratories, 97 N.J. 429, 479 A.2d 374 (1984). This is the position taken by the *Restatement (Third) of Torts: Products Liability* § 4. A few state product liability statutes contain provisions that state compliance with appropriate government standards creates a rebuttable presumption that the product is not defective. For example, the Colorado statute contains the following provision:

Colo. Rev. Stat. § 13–21–403. Presumptions

(1) In any product liability action, it shall be rebuttably presumed that the product which caused the injury, death, or property damage was not defective and that the manufacturer or seller thereof was not negligent if the product:

(a) Prior to sale by the manufacturer, conformed to the state of the art, as distinguished from industry standards, applicable to such product in existence at the time of sale; or

(b) Complied with, at the time of sale by the manufacturer, any applicable code, standard, or regulation adopted or promulgated by the United States or by this state, or by any agency of the United States or of this state.

(2) In like manner, noncompliance with a government code, standard, or regulation existing and in effect at the time of sale of the product by the manufacturer which contributed to the claim or injury shall create a rebuttable presumption that the product was defective or negligently manufactured.

(3) Ten years after a product is first sold for use or consumption, it shall be rebuttably presumed that the product was not defective and that the manufacturer or seller thereof was not negligent and that all warnings and instructions were proper and adequate.

In Lorenz v. Celotex, 896 F.2d 148 (5th Cir. 1990), the court affirmed a jury instruction that "Compliance with government safety standards constitutes strong and substantial evidence that a product is not defective."

4. GOVERNMENT CONTRACTORS

In Boyle v. United Technologies Corp., 487 U.S. 500, 108 S.Ct. 2510, 101 L.Ed.2d 442 (1988), a soldier drowned when his United States Marine helicopter crashed into the water. The plaintiff claimed the craft was defectively designed because the copilot escape hatch opened out instead of in, and, therefore, because of water pressure it was very difficult to open. The design was in accordance with specifications set forth by the government. The jury returned a verdict for $725,000 for the plaintiff. The court of appeals reversed the trial court's judgment for the plaintiff. The Supreme Court affirmed. It held that civil liabilities arising out of the performance of federal procurement contracts is an area of "uniquely federal interest." When this is the case and when the application of state law would create a "significant conflict" with an identifiable federal policy or interest or would "frustrate specific objectives" of federal legislation, "state law is preempted and replaced, where necessary, by federal law of a content prescribed (absent explicit statutory directive) by the courts—so-called 'federal common law.' " 487 U.S. at 504. On this latter issue, the court concluded that:

> Here the state-imposed duty of care that is the asserted basis of the contractor's liability (specifically, the duty to equip helicopters with the sort of escape-hatch mechanism petitioner claims was necessary) is precisely contrary to the duty imposed by the Government contract (the duty to manufacture and deliver helicopters with the sort of escape-hatch mechanism shown by the specifications).

487 U.S. at 509.

In such situations, the Supreme Court held that:

> Liability for design defects in military equipment cannot be imposed, pursuant to state law, when (1) the United States approved reasonably precise specifications; (2) the equipment conformed to those specifications; and (3) the supplier warned the United States about the dangers in the use of the equipment that were known to the supplier but not to the United States.

Id. at 512.

Boyle has been applied to a wide variety of design defect claims. *See* In re "Agent Orange" Product Liability Litigation, 517 F.3d 76 (2d Cir. 2008). Does the government contractor defense apply to manufacturing defects? *See* McGonigal v. Gearhart Industries, Inc., 851 F.2d 774 (5th Cir.1988); Rodriguez v. Lockheed Martin Corp., 627 F.3d 1259 (9th Cir. 2010). Does the defense apply to warning defects? *See* Tate v. Boeing Helicopters, 140 F.3d 654 (6th Cir. 1998); Jowers v. Lincoln Electric Co.,

617 F.3d 346 (5th Cir. 2010). What about civilian products manufactured for the government? *See* Carley v. Wheeled Coach, 991 F.2d 1117 (3d Cir. 1993).

H. RELEVANT STATUTES

An attorney consulted in a potential products liability action would be obliged to examine the growing state and federal regulation of consumer products. Potentially the most pervasive and important legislation of this kind thus far enacted is the Consumer Products Safety Act (now, as amended, 15 U.S.C. §§ 2051–81).

For purposes of a torts lawyer the most important provisions of the Consumer Products Safety Act are those that provide for actions for damages by those persons injured by any violations of the Commission's rules. The Act (15 U.S.C. § 2072) authorizes "[a]ny person who shall sustain injury by reason of any knowing (including willful) violation of a consumer product safety rule * * * or order issued by the Commission" to "sue any person who knowingly (including willfully) violated any such rule." If the plaintiff can meet the jurisdictional amount required for the exercise of federal jurisdiction, the action may be brought in the appropriate federal district court, which is authorized, if "the court determines it to be in the interests of justice" to award the plaintiff in addition to his damages, "the costs of suit, including reasonable attorneys' fees * * * and reasonable expert witness fees." It should be pointed out that, in an action based upon a violation of the Act, the plaintiff is not obliged to litigate the question of the dangerousness or the degree of dangerousness of the product. All the plaintiff must show is the knowing violation of a rule promulgated by the Commission and a sufficient causal connection between that violation and the plaintiff's injuries.

The Act specifically provides that the damage remedy provided "shall be in addition to and not in lieu of any other remedies provided by common law or under Federal or State law" (15 U.S.C. § 2072), and that compliance with a consumer product safety rule "shall not relieve any person from liability at common law or under State statutory law." (15 U.S.C. § 2074). Undoubtedly, however, in an action in the state courts the existence of a federal safety rule will be a highly relevant factor. Many if not most state courts can be expected to treat a violation of the federal rule as negligence *per se* or as an instance in which absolute liability should be imposed.

Another important federal statute for products liability lawyers is the Magnuson–Moss Act of 1975, 15 U.S.C. §§ 2301–2312. The Act was designed to make warranties on consumer products more understandable to consumers and authorizes the Federal Trade Commission to issue regulations implementing the Act's provisions. Written warranties are not required but, if offered, must meet disclosure requirements specified in the regulations. The Act encourages warrantors to establish informal dispute settlement procedures and provides that, where acceptable procedures are established and incorporated in the warranty, a consumer may initiate a civil action only after first resorting to the settlement procedures. 15 U.S.C. § 2310(a).

Many states have now passed tort reform statutes. These measures vary but in general they have been aimed at (1) limiting non-economic damages; (2) limiting the occasions upon which punitive damages could be awarded; (3) limiting lawyer's fees; (4) limiting the time within which suits can be brought (a statute of repose); (5) defining a product defect to include the state-of-the-art concept and applying it at the point of first sale to a consumer (or a similar point in time); (6) eliminating joint and several liability, at least in comparative negligence states; (7) applying comparative negligence principles in states that have not already done so; (8) making compliance with statutory or administratively set standards a defense; and (9) eliminating suits against retailers or others in the distribution network. *See, e.g.,* Ohio Rev.Code §§ 2307.71–80, 2315.20 (Page); N.J.Stat.Ann. 2A:58C–1 *et seq.* (West); Tex. Civil Prac. & Rem. Code §§ 33.001 et seq. Some state Supreme Courts have found all or parts of particular statutes unconstitutional under state constitutions. *See* Best v. Taylor Mach. Works, 179 Ill.2d 367, 689 N.E.2d 1057, 228 Ill.Dec. 636 (1997). The number of states that have enacted some type of tort reform continues to grow. *See* 2011 Wis. Act 2, 2011 S.B.1. To date, no legislation has been enacted at the federal level.

Earlier reform efforts are discussed in Joseph Sanders and Craig Joyce, *"Off to the Races": The 1980s Tort Crisis and the Law Reform Process,* 27 Hous. L. Rev. 207(1990) (summarizing tort reform provisions adopted in 48 jurisdictions between 1985 and 1988) and Warren Eginton, *Products Liability Legislation Update*, 4 Prod. Liab. L.J. 181 (1993). For a more recent set of articles on tort reform see Winter 2008 volume the Roger Williams University Law Review. *See generally*, Alan Schwartz, *Proposals for Products Liability Reform: A Theoretical Synthesis,* 97 Yale L.J. 353 (1988). Tort Reform is discussed at greater length in Chapter Six.

Section § 13–21–403(3) of the Colorado presumption statute quoted above creates a rebuttable presumption that products more than ten years old are not defective. Several states have repose statutes that absolutely bar suits after a product has reached a certain age. For example, Ind. Stat. § 34–20–3–1(1998) provides as follows:

Negligence and strict liability in tort actions

Sec. 1.

(a) This section applies to all persons regardless of minority or legal disability. Notwithstanding IC 34–11–6–1 [on legal disabilities], this section applies in any product liability action in which the theory of liability is negligence or strict liability in tort.

(b) Except as provided in section 2 of this chapter, a product liability action must be commenced:

(1) within two (2) years after the cause of action accrues; or

(2) within ten (10) years after the delivery of the product to the initial user or consumer.

However, if the cause of action accrues at least eight (8) years but less than ten (10) years after that initial delivery, the action may be commenced at any time within two (2) years after the cause of action accrues.

Statutes of repose are a response to the fact that products liability actions have long "tails." That is, many years may pass between the time a product is first put into the stream of commerce and the last lawsuit concerning the product is brought. *See*, George Priest, *The Current Insurance Crisis and Modern Tort Law*, 96 Yale L. J. 1521 (1987); Michael Faure and Paul Fenn, *Retroactive Liability and the Insurability of Long–Tail Risks*, 19 Int'l Rev. L. & Econ. 487 (1999) for discussions of the special problems this creates for insurance markets.

Statutes of repose have met mixed reactions. *See* Jones v. Five Star Engineering, Inc., 717 S.W.2d 882 (Tenn.1986) (suit must be filed within 10 years of the product's first sale for use, constitutional); Dague v. Piper Aircraft Corp., 275 Ind. 520, 418 N.E.2d 207 (1981) (within 10 years after delivery to initial user, constitutional); Radke v. H.C. Davis Sons' Manufacturing Co., Inc., 241 Neb. 21, 486 N.W.2d 204 (1992) (within 10 years after product was first sold or leased for use or consumption, constitutional); Hanson v. Williams County, 389 N.W.2d 319 (N.D.1986) (within 10 years from date of purchase or 11 years from date of manufacture, violates equal protection); Kennedy v. Cumberland Engineering Co., 471 A.2d 195 (R.I. 1984) (within 10 years, violates access to courts guarantee); McIntosh v. Melroe Co., 729 N.E.2d 972 (Ind. 2000). (ten year statute of repose ruled constitutional).

I. PRODUCTS LIABILITY IN OTHER COUNTRIES

1. THE EUROPEAN ECONOMIC UNION DIRECTIVE

The European Economic Union has adopted a Directive providing a uniform code of products liability. O.J.Eur.Comm. (No. L 210) 29–33 (1985). The Directive is a good example of a simple attempt to codify products liability law. A "producer" is liable for damages caused by a defect in his product without proof of negligence. Article 2 of the Directive defines a "product" to "mean all movables." Article 6 defines a "defect."

Article 6.

1. A product is defective when it does not provide the safety which a person is entitled to expect, taking all circumstances into account, including:

(a) the presentation of the product;

(b) the use to which it could reasonably be expected that the product would be put;

(c) the time when the product was put into circulation.

2. A product shall not be considered defective for the sole reason that a better product is subsequently put into circulation.

How would you describe the European Directive test for defectiveness in American terms? Do you see any problems with this test?

Article 7 provides the producer with a set of defenses to a products liability claim.

Article 7.

The producer shall not be liable as a result of this Directive if he proves:

(a) that he did not put the product into circulation; or

(b) that, having regard to the circumstances, it is probable that the defects which caused the damage did not exist at the time when the product was put into circulation by him or that this defect came into being afterwards; or

(c) that the product was neither manufactured by him for sale or any form of distribution for economic purpose nor manufactured or distributed by him in the course of his business; or

(d) that the defect is due to compliance of the product with mandatory regulations issued by the public authorities; or

(e) that the state of scientific and technical knowledge at the time when he put the product into circulation was not such as to enable the existence of the defect to be discovered; or

(f) in the case of a manufacturer of a component, that the defect is attributable to the design of the product in which the component has been fitted or the instructions given by the manufacturer of the product.

Article 7(e) establishes what American courts would call a state-of-the-art defense. In Europe this is called "development risk." The development risk defense set forth in Article 7(e) was quite controversial and in response Article 15(1)(b) permits member states to exclude this provision. Member states may "provide * * * that the producer shall be liable even if he proves that the state of scientific and technical knowledge at the time when he put the product into circulation was not such as to enable the existence of a defect to be discovered." *See*, Lori M. Linger, *The Products Liability Directive: A Mandatory Development Risk Defense*, 14 Fordham Int'l L. J. 487 (1991), for a discussion of which alternative member states had adopted as of 1990.

The Directive has the following provision with respect to plaintiff behavior.

Article 8.

* * *

2. The liability of the producer may be reduced or disallowed, when having regard to all the circumstances, the damages is caused both by a defect in the product and by the fault of the injured person or any person for whom the injured person is responsible.

The Directive has a three year statute of limitations, governed by a discovery rule. It also contains a 10 year statute of repose. For useful discussions of the E.U. directive *see*, Mary J. Davis, *Individual and Institutional Responsibility: A Vision for Comparative Fault in Products Liability*, 39 Vill. L. Rev. 281 (1994); John G. Culhane, *The Limits of Products Liability Reform Within A Consumer Expectation Model: A Comparison of Approaches Taken by the United States and the European Union*, 19 Hastings Int'l & Comp. L. Rev. 1 (1995).

2. SOUTH AMERICA

In South America, products liability laws are usually part of a consumer protection code. These codes frequently impose an a quality requirement similar to that expressed in the idea of merchantability. They also typically impose liability for injuries caused by dangerous products. As is the case in Europe, a dangerous product is usually defined as one that poses risks of harm beyond those risks considered normal and foreseeable given the nature of the product. For example, Article 13, Paragraph 1 of the Brazilian Code states:

> A product is defective when it does not offer the safety rightly expected of it, taking relevant circumstances into consideration, including:
>
> I. The presentation of the product
>
> II. The uses and risks reasonably expected of it; and
>
> III. The time when it was distributed.

The statutes do not distinguish among types of defects. *See* David B. Jaffe and Robert G. Vaughn, SOUTH AMERICAN CONSUMER PROTECTION LAWS (1996).

3. JAPAN

Japan passed a products liability statute in 1994. The statute is modeled on the European Economic Union Directive. As in Europe, a producer is strictly liable for injuries caused by his defective product. Article 2 of the statute defines a defect as a lack of safety which the product should ordinarily provide considering its ordinary use, its specific characteristics, the time it was put on the market, and other considerations. The level of safety that a product is generally expected to meet is judged by the expectations of the ordinary person under normal circumstances. Article 4 provides for a "development risk" defense. As in Europe, there is a three year statute of limitations and a ten year statute of repose. *See* Catherine Dauvergne, *The Enactment of Japan's Product Liability*

Law, 28 U.B.C. L. Rev. 403, 413–14 (1994); Anita Bernstein and Paul Fanning, *"Weightier Than A Mountain": Duty, Hierarchy, and the Consumer in Japan*, 29 Vand. J. Transnat'l L. 45 (1996); Hideyuki Kobayashi and Yoshimasa Futura, *Products Liability Act and Transnational Litigation in Japan*, 34 Tex. Int'l L. J. 93 (1999).

Statutes alone do not make a legal system or a legal culture. Japan is a less litigious and less individualistic society than the United States. Even with the passage of the products liability statute, litigation remains quite rare by American standards. *See* Susan H. Easton, *The Path for Japan?: An Examination of Product Liability Laws in the United States, The United Kingdom, and Japan*, 23 B.C. Int'l & Comp. L. Rev. 311 (2000); Phil Rothenberg, *Japan's New Product Liability Law: Achieving Modest Success*, 31 Law and Policy in International Business 453 (2000); ROBERT A. KAGAN, ADVERSARIAL LEGALISM: THE AMERICAN WAY OF LAW (2001).

Prior to the passage of the products liability statute, Japan had enacted the Consumer Products Safety Act. This 1973 statute created the Products Safety Council which began coordinating a privately ordered, voluntary products liability system. The Council established safety standards for over 100 products. Manufacturers whose products meet the standards attach a S ("safety") label to the goods. In addition, manufactures could opt to attach a SG ("safety goods") label. By doing so, they agreed that their product would be judged by a strict liability standard (i.e. a defectiveness standard) rather than the prevailing negligence standard. *See* J. Mark Ramseyer, *Products Liability Through Private Ordering: Notes on a Japanese Experiment*, 144 U. Pa. L. Rev. 1823 (1996). As Ramseyer notes, this system allows individuals who want to purchase "strict liability" to do so while allowing others who do not choose to pay a higher price for similar goods to rely on a negligence regime. What are the arguments for and against this method of achieving consumer protection against product caused injuries?

4. COMPARISON OF EUROPEAN, SOUTH AMERICAN, AND JAPANESE APPROACHES TO THE UNITED STATES

In an instructive article, the Reporters of the *Restatement (Third) of Torts: Products Liability*, James Henderson and Aaron Twerski, compare the approaches of the United States, Europe, and Japan and other countries. James Henderson and Aaron Twerski, *What Europe, Japan, and Other Countries Can Learn From the New American Restatement of Products Liability*, 34 Tex. Int'l L.J. 1 (1999). The authors review the history of products liability law in the United States from the time of the Second Restatement to the adoption of the Third Restatement, focusing most of their attention on the decision to move from a consumer expectations test to a risk-utility test for "classic design defects," i.e. design defect cases that do not involve product malfunctions, violations of safety regulations, or egregiously dangerous products. They conclude their article with the following observation:

> [D]rafters of the EC Directive and the Product Liability Act in Japan have made a rather substantial mistake. Apparently believing that they were taking a page from the United States' book by following Comment i to Section 402A of the Restatement (Second), they have unfortunately adopted a page from American legal history that the new Restatement has properly relegated to the waste basket. As this article explains, the consumer expectations test for defect adopted recently in Europe and Japan has been thoroughly discredited in the United States as a way to decide classic product design cases.

Id. at 20.

After reading this chapter, do you agree? In the European case, has the Directive really adopted a consumer expectations test? Recall that the Directive states that "a product is defective when it does not provide the safety which a person is entitled to expect . . ." How should one understand this phrase? Should consumers be entitled to expect greater safety than is technologically or economically feasible? See David G. Owen, *Design Defects*, 73 Mo. L. Rev. 291, 307 (2008); See Geraint G. Howells & Mark Mildred, *Is European Products Liability More Protective Than the Restatement (Third) of Torts: Products Liability?*, 65 Tenn. L. Rev. 985, 994 (1998). For a view that the Europeans had their eye on a different set of product problems, *see* Jane Stapleton, *Bugs in Anglo–American Products Liability*, 53 S.C.L. Rev. 1225 (2002).

CHAPTER 5

LIABILITY INSURANCE

■ ■ ■

Tort litigation and liability insurance are, in Kent Syverud's words, "symbiotic institutions." Without tort litigation, the institution of liability insurance would wither away, and without liability insurance many potential tort suits would never be brought. "The insurance industry and the [plaintiffs'] trial lawyers may take potshots at each other in attempts to reform aspects of the relationship, but they cannot afford to shoot to kill." Kent D. Syverud, *The Duty to Settle*, 76 Va. L. Rev. 1113, 1114 (1990). Tort doctrine and liability insurance have evolved together; changes in tort doctrine have affected the shape and scope of insurance, and vice versa. *See* David A. Fischer & Robert H. Jerry, II, *Teaching Torts Without Insurance: A Second–Best Solution*, 45 St. Louis U. L. J. 857 (2001); Kenneth S. Abraham, THE LIABILITY CENTURY: INSURANCE AND TORT LAW FROM THE PROGRESSIVE ERA TO 9/11 (2008).

Liability insurance premiums in the United States reached a peak of approximated $250 billion dollars in the mid 2000s and have declined somewhat since then to approximately $220 billion. Automobile insurance accounts for over $100 billion of this total. This represents between 1.5 and 1.7% of the Gross Domestic Product. See Tom Baker, *The Shifting Terrain of Risk and Uncertainty On the Liability Insurance Field*, 60 DePaul L. Rev. 521 (2011).

This chapter offers an introduction to the fascinating and critical issues posed by the interaction of tort doctrine and liability insurance. (Chapter Six, on existing and proposed alternatives to tort, discusses other forms of insurance, such as workers' compensation insurance and automobile no-fault insurance.) The first two sections of this chapter examine the most basic functions that the liability insurance carrier performs in standard tort litigation: the duty to defend the suit and to pay judgments on behalf of the insured (Part A) and the duty to respond reasonably to settlement offers made by the plaintiff (Part B). Part C briefly discusses the issue of subrogation.

A. THE DUTY TO DEFEND AND THE DUTY TO INDEMNIFY

FLOMERFELT v. CARDIELLO

Supreme Court of New Jersey, 2010.
202 N.J. 423, 997 A.2D 991.

JUSTICE HOENS delivered the opinion of the Court.

Plaintiff Wendy Flomerfelt sustained temporary and permanent injuries after she overdosed on alcohol and drugs during a party hosted by defendant Matthew Cardiello at his parents' home while they were out of town. Plaintiff has little recollection of what she drank or ingested either before she arrived or during the party itself. Her complaint, however, asserted that her injuries were caused by defendant, who provided her with drugs and alcohol, served her alcohol when she was visibly intoxicated, and failed to promptly summon the rescue squad when she was found, unconscious, on the porch the next day.

Defendant turned to Pennsylvania General Insurance Company, his parents' homeowners' insurer, tendering to it the defense of Flomerfelt's complaint and seeking indemnification under the terms of the policy. Pennsylvania General, in response, declined either to provide a defense against the claim or to indemnify him, pointing to the language of its policy that excluded claims "[a]rising out of the use, ... transfer or possession" of controlled dangerous substances.

The parties dispute the meaning of that language and the scope of the exclusion as it bears on both the insurer's duty to defend and its obligation to indemnify. Accordingly, this appeal requires us to consider the insurer's duties to defend and indemnify when the precise manner in which the injury was caused is in dispute and when the parties disagree about the role that controlled dangerous substances, for which the policy excludes coverage, played in bringing about plaintiff's injury.

I.

Plaintiff was a guest at a Saturday evening party hosted by defendant Matthew Cardiello while his parents, the owners of the home, were out of town. At the time, Flomerfelt was twenty-one years old. Cardiello, who was only twenty years old, admitted that he provided his guests with beer, that he was aware that a variety of drugs were being used at the event, and that during the party he saw Flomerfelt ingest cocaine. * * *

Flomerfelt * * * concedes that prior to arriving at defendant's home she may have smoked marijuana, but cannot recall what else she might have ingested either before or during the party. In her complaint, however, plaintiff alleged that defendant provided her with alcohol and drugs * * *. Each of those allegations is connected to a toxicology report that identified traces of numerous substances in her urine.

Late Saturday evening or early Sunday morning, Flomerfelt became ill and unresponsive, although precisely when that occurred is unclear from the record. Defendant denies that he was aware of Flomerfelt's plight prior to Sunday afternoon when he finally awoke for the day. According to several of the partygoers, it was not until then that defendant and others found plaintiff on the porch and were unable to rouse her. Defendant admits that he first tried to have plaintiff's sister come to the house and transport her to the hospital. Only after that effort failed did he summon rescue personnel, who took her to the emergency room. Plaintiff contends that defendant delayed calling for help because he was afraid that the police would discover the illegal drugs in the house and because he did not want his parents to learn about the party he had hosted in their absence.

Plaintiff was treated in the Emergency Room and in the Intensive Care Unit for kidney and liver failure. A toxicology report identified alcohol, marijuana, opiates and cocaine in plaintiff's system and her hospital discharge summary included an initial diagnosis of numerous conditions "probably secondary to drug overdose." When plaintiff was released from the hospital, she had recovered from the effects of the acute liver and kidney conditions but she contends that she suffers from permanent partial hearing loss.

During discovery, two experts provided opinions concerning the cause of plaintiff's injuries, both temporary and permanent. Plaintiff's expert, Dr. Michael Buccigrossi, concluded that her injuries were caused by the ingestion of multiple drugs and alcohol, and that the injuries were exacerbated by a delay in receiving medical attention. He did not attempt to quantify the amounts of each of the substances found in her system or to determine when each substance may have been ingested. Rather, he based his conclusions on reports identifying each of the substances, that is drugs or alcohol ingestion alone, as the potential causative agent for each of plaintiff's injuries.

Defendant offered the expert opinion of Dr. James Cinberg, who concluded that "[t]he toxins found in Wendy Flomerfelt's urine have been associated with rapid and irreversible high frequency loss of hearing and with tinnitus." Dr. Cinberg suggested that plaintiff's injuries might have resulted from prior drug abuse, pointing to a reported case history in which hearing loss was linked to regular marijuana use and other drug ingestion that preceded an overdose. He also noted the possibility that Flomerfelt had a genetic predisposition to hearing loss that contributed to her injury. Finally, Dr. Cinberg rejected plaintiff's assertion that defendant's delay in summoning aid had caused or contributed to her injuries. He opined that "[t]reatment that might have been instituted hours earlier would not be expected to have improved her current status."

II.

Following the service of plaintiff's complaint, defendant tendered the defense and sought indemnification for plaintiff's claims to Pennsylvania

General, his parents' homeowners' insurer. Pennsylvania General declined to defend or indemnify, pointing to the exclusion in the policy for claims "[a]rising out of the use, . . . transfer or possession" of controlled dangerous substances. In April 2007, defendant filed a declaratory judgment action, seeking a declaration that Pennsylvania General was obligated both to defend and to indemnify him. That complaint was consolidated with plaintiff's pending personal injury action for discovery and trial.

Early in 2008, Pennsylvania General and defendant cross-moved for summary judgment on the issues raised in the declaratory judgment aspect of the litigation. The insurer argued that the "arising out of" language is unrelated to causation, but instead equates with concepts such as "incident to" or "in connection with." Asserting that all of the evidence ties plaintiff's injuries at least in part to her ingestion of illegal drugs at the party, the insurer argued that it had neither a duty to defend nor a duty to indemnify.

Defendant opposed that motion, arguing that the "arising out of" language is ambiguous. He asserted that because the complaint also alleged that the injuries were caused by alcohol or by the failure to promptly summon assistance, judgment could not be entered in favor of the insurer. Based upon the ambiguity in the phrase, defendant argued that the insurer was obligated to provide him with a defense unless and until it could be proven that alcohol was neither the sole nor a contributing cause and, depending on the outcome of the trial of plaintiff's complaint, that it was obligated to indemnify him as well.

The trial court denied the insurer's motion and granted defendant's, directing Pennsylvania General to provide both a defense and indemnity pursuant to the policy. In a brief statement of reasons, the court explained that the insurer has the burden of proving that the exclusion applies and that in the context of a summary judgment motion, defendant was entitled to the benefit of factual inferences in his favor. The court then commented that the insurer could not rely on the exclusion because the experts were not able to specifically attribute plaintiff's injuries to either the drugs or the alcohol. The court reasoned that although plaintiff's complaint referred to both drugs and alcohol, defendant was entitled to the benefit of an inference that the injuries were caused by a covered, as opposed to an excluded, risk. The court therefore concluded that the insurer was required to defend and indemnify defendant.

The Appellate Division, in an interlocutory appeal, reversed the trial court's denial of Pennsylvania General's motion and its grant of relief in favor of defendant. In doing so, the panel employed a broad interpretation of the phrase "arising out of" as it was used in the policy's exclusion and utilized a substantial nexus test for purposes of evaluating the indemnification question. Following that logic, the panel concluded that because the expert proofs linked plaintiff's injuries to both drugs and alcohol, those injuries "arose out of" the excluded acts of "use, . . . transfer or possession" of illegal drugs. The panel did not engage in a separate analysis of the duty to defend, because it concluded that the exclusion barred coverage under any circumstances. The panel therefore directed that judgment be entered in favor of Pennsylvania General.

We granted defendant's motion for leave to appeal, and we reverse.

III.

We begin by reciting briefly some familiar principles that bear upon the question before this Court. An insurance policy is a contract that will be enforced as written when its terms are clear in order that the expectations of the parties will be fulfilled. In considering the meaning of an insurance policy, we interpret the language "according to its plain and ordinary meaning."

If the terms are not clear, but instead are ambiguous, they are construed against the insurer and in favor of the insured, in order to give effect to the insured's reasonable expectations. * * *

Exclusionary clauses are presumptively valid and are enforced if they are "specific, plain, clear, prominent, and not contrary to public policy." *Princeton Ins. Co. v. Chunmuang,* 151 N.J. 80, 95, 698 A.2d 9 (1997). * * *

We have observed that "[i]n general, insurance policy exclusions must be narrowly construed; the burden is on the insurer to bring the case within the exclusion." *Am. Motorists Ins. Co. v. L–C–A Sales Co.,* 155 N.J. 29, 41, 713 A.2d 1007 (1998). * * * As a result, exclusions are ordinarily strictly construed against the insurer, and if there is more than one possible interpretation of the language, courts apply the meaning that supports coverage rather than the one that limits it.

* * *

If the language of an exclusion requires a causal link, courts must consider its nature and extent because evaluating that link will determine the meaning and application of the exclusion.

On the other hand, if the exclusion uses terms that make it plain that coverage is unrelated to any causal link, it will be applied as written. Thus, an exclusion for damage to an aircraft while it was being "operated in flight by a pilot who is not approved" barred coverage for damage sustained while an unapproved pilot was in control, even though the damage itself was caused by a mechanical failure and through no fault of the pilot. The exclusion applied because, by definition, it included no causal element.

* * *

A.

In addition to those basic tenets of construction, this matter requires an evaluation of the principles governing the insurer's duties to defend and to indemnify. Those duties are neither identical nor coextensive, and therefore must be analyzed separately. Although a definitive conclusion that a policy by its terms affords no coverage, and therefore that there is no duty of indemnification, also means that there is no duty to defend, coverage questions may not have clear answers in advance of discovery or trial. As a result, courts are often required to evaluate whether the insurer owes its insured a duty to defend in advance of a conclusive decision about coverage. In those circumstances, the separate principles that govern the duty to defend must be considered and applied.

An insurer's duty to defend an action brought against its insured depends upon a comparison between the allegations set forth in the complainant's pleading and the language of the insurance policy. In making that comparison, it is the nature of the claim asserted, rather than the specific details of the incident or the litigation's possible outcome, that governs the insurer's obligation.

In evaluating the complaint for this purpose, doubts are resolved in favor of the insured and, therefore, in favor of reading claims that are ambiguously pleaded, but potentially covered, in a manner that obligates the insurer to provide a defense. Similarly, if a complaint includes multiple or alternative causes of action, the duty to defend will attach as long as any of them would be a covered claim and it continues until all of the covered claims have been resolved.

* * *

The analysis of the duty to defend is more complex if there are multiple theories of recovery or claims, some of which would be or arguably would be covered and others of which certainly would not. * * *

[A]lthough the duty to defend arises because of an underlying obligation to pay the claim, the insurer may not refuse to provide a defense merely because it believes the claim is weak or not likely to succeed. However, * * * if there are multiple theories of liability, only some of which would be covered, the interests of the insured and insurer may not coincide. * * *

[I]f a factual dispute central to deciding whether a policy provides coverage cannot be decided absent a trial, "an insured must initially assume the costs of defense . . . subject to reimbursement by the insurer if [the insured] prevails on the coverage question." *Hartford Accident & Indem. Co. v. Aetna Life & Cas. Ins. Co.*, 98 N.J. 18, 24 n. 3, 483 A.2d 402 (1984). That does not mean, however, that factual disputes will always require the insured to assume the defense initially; on the contrary, * * * it might be appropriate to decide the coverage question, and thus the insurer's duty to defend, before trial of the underlying claim. * * *

In short, in circumstances in which the underlying coverage question cannot be decided from the face of the complaint, the insurer is obligated to provide a defense until all potentially covered claims are resolved, but the resolution may be through adjudication of the complaint or in a separate proceeding between insured and insurer either before or after that decision is reached.

B.

Complaints resting on multiple claimed causes present additional challenges for courts considering an insurer's duty to defend or indemnify.

* * *

This Court has only once addressed a concurrent cause question in the third-party insurance context, and only as it concerned the insurer's duty to defend. *See Salem Group v. Oliver,* 128 N.J. 1, 607 A.2d 138 (1992). In *Salem Group,* the Court affirmed, per curiam, the Appellate Division's decision that an insurer had a duty to defend its insured * * *. In that matter, the Court concluded that the insurer was obligated to defend the homeowner who had served alcohol to his underage nephew who then drove an all-terrain vehicle (ATV) and had an off-premises accident. Even though the policy excluded a loss "arising out of" the use of the insured's motor vehicle, this Court noted that "insurers are generally obligated to defend their insureds on social host claims" and held that the insurer "may not avoid that obligation simply because the operation of the ATV constitutes an additional cause of the injury."

For purposes of the duty to defend, this Court highlighted evidence that the nephew's consumption of alcohol, a covered event, was a causal factor in the accident because the nephew had driven "harder, faster and recklessly" as a result of it. The Court commented that the policy's silence about concurrent causation made the exclusion ambiguous, and concluded that allowing the insurer to refuse to defend "could defeat the reasonable expectations of the insured, which should be respected to the extent the policy's language allows." *Id.* at 4, 607 A.2d 138.

In reaching its conclusion, * * * the Court reasoned that the duty to defend turned on whether the insured could be found liable based on a theory completely independent of the excluded cause, such as social host liability, rather than one that was intertwined with the excluded cause, such as negligent supervision. That is, if the claim could be based on social host liability, a covered event, rather than solely based on the insured's failure to exercise sufficient control and supervision over a child in the operation of a motor vehicle, an excluded event, the insurer would be obligated to defend it.

* * *

C.

As with all disputes about an insurer's duty to defend or indemnify, this appeal turns on the particular language of the policy that defines the coverage and the exclusion. Those provisions are:

Coverage E–Personal Liability

If a claim or suit is brought against an insured for damages because of **bodily injury** or **property damage** caused by an occurrence to which this coverage applies, we will:

1. pay up to our limit of liability for the damages for which the insured is legally liable. . . .

2. provide a defense at our expense by counsel of our choice, even if the suit is groundless, false or fraudulent. . . .

. . . .

Coverage E–Personal Liability . . . **[does] not apply to bodily injury or property damage:**

. . . .

m. Arising out of the use, sale, manufacture, delivery, transfer or possession by any person of a controlled substance(s). . . . Controlled Substances include, but are not limited to, cocaine, LSD, marijuana and all narcotic drugs.

The critical language in the exclusion as it relates to both the duty of defense and indemnity is the phrase "arising out of," a phrase this Court has considered in the context of a Comprehensive General Liability policy that excluded claims "arising out of and in the course of employment." *Am. Motorists, supra,* 155 N.J. at 34, 713 A.2d 1007. In concluding that the insured's claim for defense and indemnity against its employee's wrongful termination claim was within the exclusion, this Court commented on the different tests that could be applied to interpret the "arising out of" language. After canvassing appellate court decisions that had analyzed the phrase, this Court noted that it has been read expansively to define the link between the conduct and the covered activity as " 'originating from,' 'growing out of' or having a 'substantial nexus.' " *Id.* at 35, 713 A.2d 1007.

* * *

Only one published decision has addressed the phrase "arising out of the use, . . . transfer or possession" of illegal drugs as used in an exclusion in a homeowners' policy. *See Prudential Prop. & Cas. Ins. Co. v. Brenner,* 350 N.J. Super. 316, 795 A.2d 286 (App. Div. 2002). In that matter, the trial court had used a substantial nexus analysis to conclude that a complaint against the insured's son for the shooting death of plaintiff's decedent sustained in a drug deal was excluded from coverage.

The factual setting in which the injury occurred was central to the appellate court's decision to affirm. In short, the insured's son, along with others, went to the decedent's residence to get marijuana. He hoped that he and his friends could persuade the decedent to "loan" it to them based on prior transactions, but he was aware that the others were prepared to steal it if need be and that they were armed. As Judge Cuff, writing for the Appellate Division, concluded, the nexus between the claim and the excluded act was plain, because the focus of the events that led to the shooting was the use and possession of illegal drugs. As Judge Cuff explained, "[i]t is this activity which the exclusion clearly and expressly addresses. In the face of clear and unambiguous language and undisputed conduct encompassed by the policy language, we decline to engage in a strained construction to impose coverage." *Id.* at 322, 795 A.2d 286. Quoting this Court's analysis of the "arising out of" phrase in *American Motorists,* Judge Cuff concluded that there was a "clear nexus between the fatal shooting . . . and [the insured's] attempt to obtain illegal drugs" that fit this Court's interpretation of the exclusionary clause.

IV.

Although in *American Motorists* we referred to the "arising out of" language of the exclusion as clear and unambiguous, the circumstances presented in this appeal reveal an inherent and heretofore unseen ambiguity that requires us to consider the phrase in a new and different context. At a minimum, the facts before us demonstrate the complexity of interpreting the exclusion when a claim for a personal injury asserts multiple possible causes and theories for recovery against the insured. Plaintiff's complaint asserted that she was entitled to recover from defendant because her injuries were caused by drugs, by alcohol, by a combination of drugs and alcohol, by serving alcohol to her when she was visibly intoxicated, or by the negligent failure to summon aid promptly. On the face of the complaint, only some of those theories would support defendant's demand that his homeowners' insurer defend and indemnify him. That is, some claims made against defendant potentially would be covered but others would not.

We begin with the principles we announced in *American Motorists,* where we interpreted the "arising out of" language to mean " 'originating from,' 'growing out of' or having a 'substantial nexus,' " * * *

[T]he three definitions are not identical, because two of them could be read to apply where multiple potential causes are sequential and severable, with the third having a broader preclusive scope. That is, the definitions that exclude injuries that "originate from" or "grow out of" drug use at the party suggest both a close causal connection and a temporal relationship in which the injury is part of a chain of events that began with the use of a drug at the party. That reading would mean that neither an injury that occurred as a result of multiple or concurrent causes, nor an injury that resulted because drugs were used before the party, nor an injury that began with alcohol ingestion would be excluded.

However, "having a 'substantial nexus,' " the other definition of the phrase we used in *American Motorists,* is broader. It could operate to exclude coverage if drug use was part of interrelated or concurrent causes. That is, if the evidence demonstrates, or if there is a finding of fact, that the excluded act, here the use of drugs, has a substantial nexus to the temporary or permanent injury, then there will be no coverage for that injury, even if there are other contributing causes. On the other hand, if the finder of fact were to conclude that plaintiff's use of drugs before she arrived at the party or a prior history of drug use caused her injury, and that her use of drugs at the party did not also have a substantial nexus to the injury, then the exclusion would not apply. Similarly, if the finder of fact were to conclude that the use of alcohol was the cause of the injury and that there was no substantial nexus between her use of drugs at the party and her injury, the exclusion would not bar coverage of the claim.

Regardless of which definition for the phrase we utilize, the exclusion, for example, would not bar a claim by another guest at the same party who had neither participated in nor been aware of the drug use and who fell off the deck and was injured. Likewise, if a partygoer suffered injuries that were solely alcohol-induced, the exclusion would not bar that person's claim even if others at the party were using drugs. In neither situation would there be a substantial nexus between drugs and the injury, with the result that the exclusion would not apply.

Our well-established principles require that the insurer bear the burden of demonstrating that the exclusion applies, and that the duty to defend continues as long as there is a potentially covered claim. More to the point, in light of the principles we announced in *American Motorists,* the insurer's decision to use the phrase "arising out of" with no further qualification imposes upon it the meaning we ascribed when explaining our understanding of that phrase. At a minimum, as we observed in *Salem Group,* the insurer's use of the phrase with no clarification of its intended meaning in circumstances arising from potentially concurrent causes makes the phrase ambiguous, calling for an interpretation consistent with the reasonable expectations of the insured.

Applying those meanings and those precedents, the insurer's proposed construction that we read the phrase in the exclusion to mean "incident to" or "in connection with" cannot be correct. That reading would expand the phrase "arising out of" to mean that the injury is connected in any fashion, however remote or tangential, to the excluded act, rather than one that "originates in," "grows out of" or has a "substantial nexus" to the excluded act. It is a suggested reading so at odds with our case law that we decline to embrace it.

We turn then to our consideration of the insurer's duties to defend and indemnify in light of plaintiff's claims and the policy's language. Confounding our analysis in this case is the state of the record relating to the experts and their opinions. The toxicology report merely identified substances, both drugs and alcohol, that were found in plaintiff's system. Plaintiff's expert Buccigrossi conceded that there is insufficient evidence on which to base an opinion about which substance was ingested when and with what effect on plaintiff's temporary and permanent injuries. His opinion referred to literature that would permit a finder of fact to attribute each of the injuries to drugs, or to alcohol, or to a combination of substances plaintiff ingested. Defendant's expert Cinberg did not dispute that any of the substances individually could have caused the injuries, but suggested other potential causes including genetic predispositions and a prior history of drug abuse.

The procedural posture in which this matter has reached us therefore does not permit a definitive answer to the question, as a matter of fact, about the cause or causes that led to plaintiff's injuries, either temporary or permanent. Nor can we determine the sequence of events that led to the injuries or whether drugs provided or used at the party, that is the excluded acts, had a substantial nexus to those injuries. The question, therefore, is what the language of the exclusion means in this context and, more to the point, how the duties to defend and indemnify should be evaluated. Although the record is not sufficiently developed to decide the question of the insurer's liability for indemnity, the duty to defend can be resolved utilizing our traditional analysis.

In evaluating the duty to defend, we can lay the complaint and the policy side by side and see that in this dispute some theories of liability would be covered and others would not. If, for example, the finder of fact were to conclude that alcohol ingestion, either in the context of the social host serving plaintiff when she was visibly intoxicated, or in combination with a delay in summoning aid, was the cause for the injuries, or set the chain of events in motion, and that there was not a substantial nexus between drugs at the party and the injuries, the claim would fall within the coverage of the policy and would not be barred by the exclusion. If the finder of fact were to conclude that plaintiff's injuries were caused by use of drugs before she arrived at the party, by genetic predisposition, or by long-term drug use such that the injuries did not "originate in," "grow out of" or have a "substantial nexus" to her use of drugs at the party, the claim would also be covered. Whether any of those possibilities is the likeliest outcome is of no consequence, because our traditional analysis of the duty to defend requires that Pennsylvania General provide a defense.

The record before us does not permit us to resolve the question of the insurer's duty to indemnify. * * * [I]n those thorny situations in which there are some covered theories coupled with alternatives in which the claim would not be covered, the insurer has several options available to it. They include opting to defend under a reservation of rights, declining to do so, preferring to await the outcome and to reimburse its insured if the finder of fact decides the injury did not "arise out of" drug use, as we have defined it, or electing to litigate the coverage issue in advance of a trial on plaintiff's claim, disputing the proof of causation against its insured first. The duty to defend, however, is not dependent upon whether there is a finding that the claim is covered; instead it attaches because our analysis of the exclusion demonstrates that there are potentially covered claims.

V.

The judgment of the Appellate Division is reversed and the matter is remanded to the trial court for further proceedings consistent with this opinion.

JUSTICE LAVECCHIA, concurring in judgment.

I concur in the judgment of the Court for the simple reason that I find the Court's decision in *The Salem Group v. Oliver,* 128 N.J. 1, 607 A.2d 138 (1992), to be controlling. * * * [T]he majority in that case * * * established a dual or concurring causation test for determining whether there exists a duty to defend under a homeowner's policy notwithstanding a specific policy exclusion, a test that Pennsylvania General Insurance Company (Penn General) did not ask us to reconsider. * * * That holding * * * set the stage for subsequent case law, which has required that, to eliminate a duty to defend, an insurance policy must unambiguously state that an exclusion will operate notwithstanding any concurrent or sequential causation issues even when the policy's exclusion is otherwise clear and specific. * * *

No doubt, in drafting the policy that is in dispute in the present matter the insurer attempted to distance itself as far as possible from behavior inconsistent with public policy-namely, the use of illegal drugs-to avoid any obligation to provide coverage for injuries that arise from the use of such contraband. The policy reflects a clear desire not to be liable for any injuries having a substantial nexus to the illegal behavior associated with drugs and their use, hence the policy exclusion's use of the words "arising out of," which convey a broader reach than a direct causative effect. * * *

This case presents an even more compelling basis to find that the insurer has no more duty to the insured than existed in *Salem Group,* because the exclusion in issue here is in accord with the public policy of our state, which clearly opposes the use of illegal drugs. *See, e.g., N.J.S.A.* 2C:35–1.1(b) ("[T]he unlawful use . . . of [illegal drugs] continues to pose a serious and pervasive threat to the health, safety and welfare of the citizens of this State."). New Jersey courts have not hesitated to look to public policy when interpreting insurance contracts. And, not only does the exclusion support public policy by disapproving of the use of illegal drugs, it is also sensible from the point-of-view of an insurer who cannot accurately formulate underwriting guidelines because the use of illegal drugs is by its very nature an illicit activity.

Here, however, the complaint did not allege that plaintiff was injured due to the use of illegal drugs alone, but rather that plaintiff was injured due to a mixed cause: a drug she claimed was provided by the insured's son and alcohol provided and served to her at the party when she already was inebriated. Plainly, the latter addresses a social host theory of liability that is independent of the policy exclusion for illegal drugs and would be covered under the policy. But, wrapped together-as the claims are in the complaint and in the experts' reports opining as to the cause of Wendy Flomerfelt's injuries-the two are intertwined. How those claims sort out at trial remains to be seen.

In this setting, and for purposes of resolving whether there exists a duty to defend plaintiff's third-party complaint, the issue has been settled by *Salem Group*. Because the instant policy did not unambiguously declare that coverage would be excluded for injuries arising out of the use of illegal drugs "*regardless of any other cause or event contributing concurrently or in any sequence to the loss*," or words to that effect,[3] the holding in *Salem Group* is controlling. If Penn General had included a clause excluding coverage in cases where the use of illegal drugs was a concurrent or contributing cause of personal injury, it would not have a duty to defend Matthew Cardiello. But, because Penn General did not include such a clause in the insurance policy, a defense must be provided until more is known about the cause or causes of Wendy Flomerfelt's injuries.[4]

For that reason, and that reason alone, I concur in the judgment reached today. As stated, a different outcome is preferable because the better-reasoned view in *Salem Group* was expressed by Justices Clifford and Garibaldi in dissent; however, that perspective did not prevail. Accordingly, although I do not embrace the reasoning espoused by the majority in *Salem Group,* it nevertheless remains precedent deserving of respect. That respect for stare decisis is the simple, and sole, reason for my concurrence in the judgment reached today.

JUSTICE RIVERA-SOTO joins in this opinion.

NOTES

1. *Liability Insurance ("Third Party" Insurance) Versus First Party Insurance*. An understanding of insurance begins with the distinction between liability insurance ("third party" insurance) and "first party" insurance. The heart of liability insurance consists of the insurer's promise to pay *a third party*—the injured plaintiff—if the insured causes an injury of the sort covered under the policy. In contrast, first party insurance is the term that applies to the promise by the insurer to pay *the insured* when the insured himself sustains a loss. Examples include health insurance, property insurance, and disability insurance—all these pay money to the insured when he has sustained a particular loss (medical bills, damaged property, or disability rendering him unable to work). A typical homeowner's insurance policy consists of both first and third party insurance: liability insurance that will indemnify someone injured by the homeowner's actions, and first party insurance for damage to the home.

---

3. Penn General obviously knew how to incorporate that language because it included such a clause in the same policy's provisions concerning exclusions applicable to property damage. The policy provides, in the context of property damage only, that coverage for direct or indirect loss "is excluded regardless of any other cause or event contributing concurrently or in any sequence to the loss."

4. The majority in *Salem Group, supra,* was careful to limit its holding to an insurer's duty to defend, and did not suggest that the insurer had a duty to indemnify the insured under a concurrent causation theory. The majority opinion in the present matter is similarly limited. If it is established that Wendy Flomerfelt suffered injuries "arising out of" the use of illegal drugs she ingested at the party and that Matthew Cardiello had knowledge of such use, Penn General will have no duty to indemnify Matthew Cardiello. Again, I understand the majority to be in accord with that conclusion. *See ante* at 454–56, 997 *A.*2d at 1004–05.

When significant numbers of people first started purchasing insurance to protect themselves against tort liability to third persons, in the latter part of the nineteenth century, the insurance was typically written as indemnity insurance. That is, the insurance company promised the insured to reimburse him, up to the policy limits, for any loss he might suffer as a result of a tort judgment, arising out of a covered risk, entered against him. Such contracts were open to abuse in that, if the insured were adjudicated a bankrupt after entry of a judgment against him, the insurance company would have no liability under the policy. The abuses are described in Roth v. National Automobile Mutual Casualty Co., 202 App. Div. 667, 195 N.Y.S. 865 (1922). Massachusetts in 1914, and New York in 1918, enacted statutes to prevent these abuses. In Merchants' Mutual Automobile Liability Insurance Co. v. Smart, 267 U.S. 126, 45 S.Ct. 320, 69 L.Ed. 538 (1925), the Court upheld the constitutionality of these statutes. By 1933, about half of the states had enacted such statutes. For these and other reasons the standard policies were changed by the insurance companies from contracts of indemnity into true liability policies. That is, the insurance contract provided that the company would pay on behalf of the insured all sums up to the policy limits "which the insured shall become legally *obligated* to pay" as a result of a covered risk.

The standard policy has traditionally stipulated that no action may be brought against the insurance company until the amount of the insured's obligation to pay has been finally determined by a judgment entered against the insured or a written settlement agreement signed by the insured, the claimant, and the company. Most courts uphold such clauses. Nevertheless in some states, *e.g.*, Louisiana and Wisconsin, by statute the claimant is permitted to join the insurance company as a defendant or even bring a direct action against the insurance carrier without joining the insured as a defendant.

2. *Insurance, Deterrence, and Fairness.* Does liability insurance blunt the potential deterrent impact of tort doctrine? This depends on how closely linked the insured's premiums are to the actual risks that the insured's behavior causes. Consider an example from Gary T. Schwartz, *The Ethics and the Economics of Tort Liability Insurance*, 75 Cornell L. Rev. 313 (1990). A manufacturer could alter a product design for a cost of $700 per unit and thereby avoid expected injuries per unit of $1000 (probability times magnitude of potential loss). If liability insurance is priced in a way that is perfectly tailored to the risk, then the manufacturer will know that it can either (1) pay $700 to alter the design, thereby lessening its insurance premium by $1000; or (2) refuse to alter the design and pay an increased premium of $1000. Plainly, the manufacturer would choose the first. Of course, insurance premiums are not perfectly tailored, for many reasons. Still, "[m]ost liability insurance is written so as to render its premium somewhat responsive to the level of tortious risktaking engaged in by the insured." Schwartz, *supra,* at 363.

How does liability insurance relate to the aim of corrective justice? Does this depend on how well-tailored the insurance is to the risks posed by the insured? Why? Do you suppose that the parents of the plaintiff in *Flomerfelt* paid homeowner's insurance premiums that were linked at all to the types of activities that occurred in that case?

3. *The decision to buy insurance*. Why do people purchase insurance against tort liability? The reason is applicable to all forms of insurance: individuals are generally risk-averse with respect to losses that are significant in relation to the individual's wealth. To take a simplified example, suppose an individual faces a 2% chance that her $100,000 home will burn down. Her "expected loss"—the magnitude of the loss times the probability of its occurrence—is $2,000. So the following two items are an even bet: (1) paying $2000 now, or (2) facing a 2% chance that her home will burn down. A risk-neutral person would have no reason to prefer option 1 over option 2. Yet many individuals prefer option 1, and they implement that preference by paying insurance premiums. Insurers are willing to accept these premiums and to bear the risk not because they are risk-preferring, but because they can use the law of large numbers to their advantage. Insurers can pool together many similar risks to reduce random variation, and then can calculate the premiums that will be necessary to pay claims and still leave room for profit. More detail, as well as a rich discussion of insurance generally, appears in KENNETH S. ABRAHAM, DISTRIBUTING RISK (1986).

4. *Standard Liability Policies: The Duty to Defend and the Duty to Indemnify*. Most standard liability policies, such as the liability insurance involved in *Flomerfelt*, contain two promises by the insurer: (1) to provide a defense to the insured when the insured is sued on a claim potentially within policy coverage, even if the claim is frivolous (the "duty to defend"); and (2) to pay—up to policy limits—the injured party (or indemnify the insured for his payments to the injured party) for any tort judgment obtained against the insured so long as the judgment is within the scope of the policy's coverage (the "duty to indemnify"). The duty to defend is not capped by the policy limits; only the duty to indemnify is. Suppose, for instance, that an insured with a $50,000 liability policy is sued on a tort claim, that the insurer spends $15,000 for attorney's fees in defending the case; and that the tort plaintiff obtains a judgment for $75,000. The insurer will be obligated to pay the full $50,000 of the policy amount, notwithstanding the insurer's expense for attorneys' fees. Of course, to the extent that an insurer will have to satisfy some or all of the insured's legal obligations, it also has an incentive to try to control and limit the extent of those obligations and thus to manage the insured's legal defense. For analysis of the theory and practice of the duty to defend and its effect on the tort system, see Ellen S. Pryor, *The Tort Liability Regime and the Duty to Defend*, 58 Md. L. Rev. 1 (1999).

The duty to defend is commonly said to be broader than the duty to indemnify. There is no duty to defend only if it is clear that under no set of facts will the insurer be obligated to indemnify under the policy. As the court in City of Willoughby Hills v. Cincinnati Insurance Co., 9 Ohio St.3d 177, 459 N.E.2d 555, 558 (1984) noted, "where the insurer's duty to defend is apparent from the pleadings in the case against the insured, but the allegations do state a claim which is potentially or arguably within the policy coverage, or there is some doubt as to whether a theory of recovery within the policy coverage has been pleaded, the insurer must accept the defense of the claim."

What reasons might explain and support the rules that have evolved about the duty to defend? One way to get at this question is to envision the alternative: the carrier is allowed to deny a defense whenever it believes that the "true" facts will show the case really is not covered; the carrier would be liable for breach of the duty to defend only if ultimately (after adjudication in an insurance coverage dispute) the carrier's view of the true facts were rejected by the factfinder. Presumably, we would all pay lower premiums for this type of defense insurance, but the certainty of protection would be diminished. Which version of defense insurance would you prefer?

As was the case in *Flomerfelt*, conflicts over the duty to defend frequently arise when there are multiple theories of recovery or multiple claims, some of which would be or arguably would be covered and others which would not.

5. *Exclusions*. The *Flomerfelt* litigation was occasioned by the drug use exclusion in the policy. Why do insurers choose to insert exclusions in their policies? In the *Flomerfelt* situation, one reason presumably is set forth in the concurring opinion. The insurer does not wish to be seen to be insuring against the adverse effects of drug use. That is, the exclusion is normative. A second reason is that the insured simply does not want some coverage and would prefer not to pay a premium needed to include it in the policy. For instance, a homeowner would prefer a policy with an exclusion for products liability coverage: the homeowner knows she has virtually no chance of being found liable as a products manufacturer or supplier, and she would not want to be lumped together in the same risk pool as product suppliers and be charged the resulting higher premium. If there were no exclusions for products liability, then the costs of losses resulting from products injuries would be spread through a risk pool that included not just products manufacturers and suppliers but also homeowners and business owners that have little to do with products.

Many exclusions are included in policies because the insurer does not believe it can properly assess a risk, and therefore will be unable to charge an appropriate premium. The clearest example is an exclusion for intentional acts. The underlying concern of the insurer is that injuries occasioned by intentional conduct are more completely in the control of the insured and thus less predictable in an actuarial sense. Insurers frequently employ the term "moral hazard" to describe this problem.

Moral hazard exists when an insured enters into an insurance contract in bad faith. This purposeful misrepresentation is a greater risk in first party insurance policies. For example, insurers routinely include a suicide exclusion clause in life insurance policies to guard against the possibility that an individual would buy a policy in contemplation of suicide. Today these clauses typically exclude coverage if the insured takes his own life during the first two years the policy is in place.

The moral hazard terminology is also used to refer to the danger that a party insulated from a risk may behave differently than if that party were fully exposed to the risk. *See* Tom Baker, *On the Genealogy of Moral Hazard*, 75 Tex. L. Rev. 237, 239 (1996). All insurance has the potential to create this type of a moral hazard. For example, people may exercise less care if they know their negligent acts are insured. Often insurers seek to control this type of moral hazard by using less extreme measures than a complete exclusion of coverage. For example, insurance companies routinely include a deductible in policies so that part of the loss associated with accidents falls on the insured.

For valuable discussions of ways insurers control moral hazard *see* CAROL HEIMER, REACTIVE RISK AND RATIONAL ACTION: MANAGING MORAL HAZARD IN INSURANCE CONTRACTS (1985); PAT O'MALLEY, RISK, UNCERTAINTY AND GOVERNMENT (2004).

It is commonly believed, however, that with respect to intentional acts, these alternatives are not sufficient and the better course is to exclude coverage. An intentional tort exclusion is also understandable from the standpoint of some insureds, for at least some conduct. Suppose that you were choosing between two homeowners' insurance policies: Policy A would cover you only for negligently-caused injuries; Policy B would cover you for negligently and intentionally caused injuries, but this policy would cost you a substantially higher premium. Which would you choose, and why?

Moral hazard is not the only reason insurance companies cannot estimate risks. Almost all Commercial General Liability (CGL) policies contain a pollution exclusion.The more recent version of these policies has what is called an "absolute pollution exclusion" designed to exclude liability for anything except acute, accidental spills. The insurers wish to exclude coverage for pollution because the cleanup costs may be very large and are quite unpredictable. Moreover, since the passage of the Comprehensive Environmental Response, Compensation, and Liability Act (CERCLA) in 1980, 42 U.S.C. §§ 9601–9675 entities that made relatively minor contributions to a contaminated "Super Fund" site may become a "potentially responsible party" and as a result may be jointly and severally liable for cleanup costs. *See* Quadrant Corp. v. American States Insurance Co., 154 Wash.2d 165, 110 P.3d 733 (2005) for a discussion of the exclusion.

6. *Litigating Exclusions*. Exclusions are one of the most frequently litigated issues in insurance. There are two central reasons why these provisions are litigated: alleged ambiguity in the exclusion language and uncertainty as to whether the cause of the alleged harm fell within the scope of the exclusion. The exclusion issue in *Flomerfelt* is a particularly thorny one because it involves both of these issues. The phrase "arising out of" is ambiguous and the cause of Ms Flomerfelt's injury is uncertain.

a. *Ambiguity*. The concurring opinion in *Flomerfelt* suggests that the insurer could have clarified the uncertainty surrounding the term "arising out of" by including an additional sentence such as the following: "*regardless of any other cause or event contributing concurrently or in any sequence to the loss*" and notes the insurer had included similar language in other policies. Would this have permitted the insurer to avoid its obligation to defend the insured?

Ambiguity has been at the heart of litigation surrounding the CGL pollution exclusion. Initially, insurers attempted to exclude coverage by inserting a clause that they thought would exclude harms caused by long term release of hazardous waste. The policies precluded coverage unless the release of pollutants was "sudden and accidental." This so-called "qualified pollution exclusion" lead to litigation that is still going on. The fight was often over the meaning of the word "sudden." A rather obvious issue is how sudden is sudden. What of a leak over several days? *See* Sauer v. Home Indem. Co., 841 P.2d 176 (Alaska 1992). Another question is whether suddenness should apply to the initial release or to the entire pollution process. What of a relatively sudden release which leads to the slow contamination of groundwater over the course of several years?

Many cases, however, involved much more fundamental interpretive conflicts. Insurers argued that the term "sudden" in the phrase "sudden and accidental" was designed to permit recovery only when a release was abrupt, e.g., the bursting of a tank containing toxic chemicals, and this abrupt release was not intended, i.e., it was accidental. Even accidental pollution would not be covered if it were not sudden. Insureds argued that the term "sudden" did not have a temporal dimension. Rather, it was synonymous with accidental and thus the qualified pollution policies covered all pollution that was not intended. *See* Sharon M. Murphy, *The "Sudden and Accidental" Exception to the Pollution Exclusion Clause in Comprehensive General Liability Insurance Policies: The Gordian Knot of Environmental Liability*, 45 Vand. L. Rev. 161 (1992).

Although insurance companies moved away from the qualified exclusion language in the mid 1980s, the very long tail of environmental harms insured that litigation over the meaning of these policies would continue for at least a quarter of a century. *See* Coffeyville Resources Refining & Marketing, LLC v. Liberty, 714 F.Supp.2d 1119 (D. Kan. 2010). Even the new, "absolute pollution exclusion" language that replaced the earlier qualified pollution language has led to litigation over the allegedly ambiguous meaning of the exclusion language. *See, e.g.* Nautilus Ins. Co. v. Jabar, 188 F.3d 27 (1st Cir. 1999).

In sum, many insurance cases begin with the preliminary question of whether the language in insurance contract is "ambiguous." In this context, ambiguous is itself an ambiguous term. Perhaps courts can do no better than assessing whether language is ambiguous within the facts of each case. If this is so, does it mean that it is impossible to draft unambiguous contracts? Is it possible to draft any unambiguous document? Literary deconstructionists would answer with a resounding no. Deconstruction ideas have slowly seeped into legal discourse. *See* Jack M. Balkin, *Deconstruction's Legal Career*, 27 Cardozo L. Rev. 719 (2005). Is the task of an insured's lawyer to play the role of a deconstructionist and attempt to render all text unclear? *See* Peter Nash Swisher *Judicial Interpretations of Insurance Contract Disputes: Toward a Realistic Middle Ground Approach*, 57 Ohio St. L. J. 543 (1996).

b. *Uncertainty*. In *Flomerfelt*, the court refused to resolve the issue of a duty to defend because of uncertainty concerning what caused Ms Flomerfelt's injuries. With respect to the intentional acts exclusion, uncertainty often arises when the insured's behavior could be characterized either as intentional or negligent. In North Star Mutual Insurance Co. v. R.W., 431 N.W.2d 138 (Minn. App. 1988), the insurance company sought a declaratory judgment in a case where the defendant was sued by a young woman who claimed that he negligently infected her with herpes during consensual sex. The insurance policy contained an exclusion for intentional acts. The trial court grated the insurer a summary judgment. The court of appeals reversed. It held that until the factual question of the insured's knowledge of his illness was resolved the insurer must defend T.F. in the underlying case.

7. *Resolving conflicts by changing the policy.* Once an insurer recognizes its homeowner's policy will cover some judgments for injuries related to the use of drugs or, as in the *North Star* case, will not exclude judgments for negligently transmitted sexual diseases, in theory several options are available: (1) predict the overall risks of such judgments posed by the complete pool of homeowners, and spread that aggregate risk to all homeowners by eliminating the exclusion and increasing the premium charged to every homeowner; (2) insert a provision in all homeowners' policies similar to the concurring opinion in *Flomerfelt* that attempts to broaden the exclusion. In the *North Star* context this might mean an exclusion for harms arising out of intentional or negligent consensual sexual conduct; (3) charge a higher premium to those homeowners who might predictably be at higher risk for such judgments, just as a higher premium is charged to certain business owners who don't have fire sprinkler systems; or (4) write an exclusion into most policies, but offer such coverage to insureds willing to pay an extra premium for this coverage.

What are the possible concerns raised by the first and second options? The third option might sound fine in theory, but in practice would it be possible for insurers to identify—except according to crude and perhaps objectionable criteria—which types of people are more at risk for these sorts of tort judgments? The fourth option also might sound promising, but insurers would be wary of it because of moral hazard concerns.

8. *Public policy considerations.* The concurring opinion in *Flomerfelt* was sympathetic to the insurer's exclusion on public policy grounds. Some jurisdictions go further and mandate certain exclusions, either through court opinions or legislation. For example, some jurisdictions prohibit coverage for intentional torts. In California, for instance, an "insurer is not liable for a loss caused by the willful act of the insured; but he is not exonerated by the negligence of the insured * * *." Cal. Ins. Code § 553 (2010). Some have argued, however, that public policy supports coverage for intentional acts. See James M. Fischer, *The Exclusion From Insurance Coverage of Losses Caused by the Intentional Acts of the Insured: A Policy in Search of a Justification*, 30 Santa Clara L. Rev. 95 (1990). What are the issues?

Punitive damages are another area where courts or legislatures frequently prohibit coverage, even when the policy is written only to cover the insureds for punitive damages arising out of reckless conduct. *See* Alan, I. Widiss, *Liability Insurance Coverage for Punitive Damages? Discerning Answers to the Conundrum Created by Disputes Involving Conflicting Public Policies, Pragmatic Considerations and Political Actions,* 39 Vill. L. Rev. 455 (1994).

9. *Pleading With the Aim of Accessing Insurance.* Given the systemic objectives of tort law—efficiency, corrective justice, recognition of the victim's loss, distributive justice—should we care that, in gray cases, the existence of insurance might cause the tort plaintiff to "underlitigate," that is to characterize intentional conduct as merely negligent? For more detail on the topic, *see* Ellen S. Pryor, *The Stories We Tell: Intentional Harm and the Quest for Insurance Funding,* 75 Tex. L. Rev. (1997).

Pleadings, of course, do not insure success on the merits. The insurer only has a duty to indemnify if the fact finder concludes that the plaintiff's harm was the result of covered actions by the insured. That is, while allegations alone may be sufficient to trigger a duty to defend, they do not trigger the duty to indemnify or pay. What, then, is the incentive for the plaintiff to plead a case in a way that triggers the duty to defend if it does not also trigger a duty to indemnify? For one thing, the very fact that a carrier has to pay defense costs might create some incentive for the carrier to settle the case. Moreover, in some jurisdictions, a carrier that breaches its duty to defend is considered "estopped" from arguing that it has no duty to pay. This means that pleading the case in a way which triggers a duty to defend might create a back door to insurance coverage, even though the front door—the policy language itself—is closed. These and other reasons are explored more fully in Pryor, *supra*. This leads to the question of what alternatives are available to the insurer when it does contest coverage.

10. *Challenging coverage*. Insurers may pursue several alternatives when they contest coverage. They can refuse to defend, they can defend under a reservation of rights, or they can defend without a reservation of rights. As occurred in *Flomerfelt*, the insurer may also attempt to litigate the question of coverage in advance in a declaratory judgment action. The availability and consequences of each of these alternatives varies from state to state. For a discussion of the risks and benefits of these various alternatives in two jurisdictions, *see* Ellen S. Pryor, *Mapping the Changing Boundaries of the Duty to Defend in Texas*, 31 Tex. Tech L. Rev. 869 (2000); Gregor J. Schwinghammer, Jr., *Insurance Litigation in Florida—Declaratory Judgments and the Duty to Defend*, 50 U. Miami L. Rev. 945 (1996).

11. *Conflict of Interest*. Once a coverage question has arisen, there is a potential conflict of interest between the insurer and the insured. The *Flomerfelt* court noted the potential for conflict in that case. Exactly what is the nature of that conflict? A close reading of the *Flomerfelt* opinion suggests that the following are potential causes of the plaintiff's hearing impairment: 1) genetic predisposition, 2) prior drug use, 3) drug consumption at the party, 4) alcohol consumption at the party, 5) alcohol consumed at the party that was served to her by the defendant after she was obviously intoxicated, 6) delay in receiving treatment, and 7) delay in receiving treatment due to the defendant's negligent failure to render aid. With respect to each of these, which, if proven to be a cause, would lead to liability? Which would lead to liability that the insurer would be required to indemnify?

What outcome if a fact finder concludes that the plaintiff's hearing loss injury is an indivisible result of all of the above? Would a finding of indivisibility benefit or harm the insured? Would it benefit or harm the insurance company's duty to indemnify? Why?

All of this highlights the fact that in this situation the interests of the insurer and insured are not identical. The *Flomerfelt* opinion suggests that when this situation arises it would be best for the insurer to seek a declaratory judgment, but offers no suggestions about what to do when this is impossible. The prevailing rule now is that, when a conflict of interest relating to coverage exists and the conflict may affect how the tort claim is litigated, the carrier must provide "independent counsel." That is, the insurance carrier must pay the lawyer's bills but does not have the right to control or direct the defense or the defense strategy. This is in contrast to the pattern in garden-variety claims where no conflict of interest exists—for instance, when the insured is sued for negligence in causing a car crash and the insurer does not dispute coverage. Then the insurance company will select the defense lawyer and has the right to control the defense.

Suppose the insurance company in *Flomerfelt* does provide the insured with independent counsel and he and the plaintiff emphasize the failure to render prompt aid as the cause of the plaintiff's injury. Suppose then that the jury returns a verdict for the plaintiff solely based on this negligence. Would this trigger the duty to indemnify, since the theory on which the judgment rested—failure to aid—was indeed covered? Although some doctrinal differences exist on the question, the general rule now seems to be that the carrier will not be bound to the finding of negligence and will be able to contest—in a separate action on the coverage question—whether or not the injury fell within the exclusion. Put another way, the finding of negligence in the tort action will not have collateral estoppel effect in the coverage action between the insurance carrier and the insured. *See* Commercial Insurance Company of Newark, New Jersey v. Popadich, 68 A.D.3d 401, 890 N.Y.S.2d 36 (2009). For more detail, see ALLAN D. WINDT, 2 INSURANCE CLAIMS AND DISPUTES, § 6:22 (5TH ED. 2010).

B. THE DUTY TO SETTLE

CRISCI v. SECURITY INSURANCE COMPANY OF NEW HAVEN, CONNECTICUT

Supreme Court of California, 1967.
66 Cal.2d 425, 58 Cal.Rptr. 13, 426 P.2d 173.

PETERS, JUSTICE.

In an action against The Security Insurance Company of New Haven, Connecticut, the trial court awarded Rosina Crisci $91,000 (plus interest) because she suffered a judgment in a personal injury action after Security, her insurer, refused to settle the claim. Mrs. Crisci was also awarded $25,000 for mental suffering. Security has appealed.

June DiMare and her husband were tenants in an apartment building owned by Rosina Crisci. Mrs. DiMare was descending the apartment's outside wooden staircase when a tread gave way. She fell through the resulting opening up to her waist and was left hanging 15 feet above the ground. Mrs. DiMare suffered physical injuries and developed a very severe psychosis. In a suit brought against Mrs. Crisci the DiMares alleged that the step broke because Mrs. Crisci was negligent in inspecting and maintaining the stairs. They contended that Mrs. DiMare's mental condition was caused by the accident, and they asked for $400,000 as compensation for physical and mental injuries and medical expenses.

Mrs. Crisci had $10,000 of insurance coverage under a general liability policy issued by Security. The policy obligated Security to defend the suit against Mrs. Crisci and authorized the company to make any settlement it deemed expedient. * * * Security hired an experienced lawyer, Mr. Healy, to handle the case. Both he and defendant's claims manager believed that unless evidence was discovered showing that Mrs. DiMare had a prior mental illness, a jury would probably find that the accident precipitated Mrs. DiMare's psychosis. And both men believed that if the jury felt that the fall triggered the psychosis, a verdict of not less than $100,000 would be returned.

An extensive search turned up no evidence that Mrs. DiMare had any prior mental abnormality. As a teenager Mrs. DiMare had been in a Washington mental hospital, but only to have an abortion. Both Mrs. DiMare and Mrs. Crisci found psychiatrists who would testify that the accident caused Mrs. DiMare's illness, and the insurance company knew of this testimony. Among those who felt the psychosis was not related to the accident were the doctors at the state mental hospital where Mrs. DiMare had been committed following the accident. All the psychiatrists agreed, however, that a psychosis could be triggered by a sudden fear of falling to one's death.

The exact chronology of settlement offers is not established by the record. However, by the time the DiMares' attorney reduced his settlement demands to $10,000, Security had doctors prepared to support its position and was only willing to pay $3,000 for Mrs. DiMare's physical injuries. Security was unwilling to pay one cent for the possibility of a plaintiff's verdict on the mental illness issue. This conclusion was based on the assumption that the jury would believe all of the defendant's psychiatric evidence and none of the plaintiff's. Security also rejected a $9,000 settlement demand at a time when Mrs. Crisci offered to pay $2,500 of the settlement.

A jury awarded Mrs. DiMare $100,000 and her husband $1,000. After an appeal * * * the insurance company paid $10,000 of this amount, the amount of its policy. The DiMares then sought to collect the balance from Mrs. Crisci. A settlement was arranged by which the DiMares received $22,000, a 40 percent interest in Mrs. Crisci's claim to a particular piece of property, and an assignment of Mrs. Crisci's cause of action against Security. Mrs. Crisci, an immigrant widow of 70, became indigent. She worked as a babysitter, and her grandchildren paid her rent. The change in her financial condition was accompanied by a decline in physical health, hysteria, and suicide attempts. Mrs. Crisci then brought this action.

The liability of an insurer in excess of its policy limits for failure to accept a settlement offer within those limits was considered by this court in Comunale v. Traders & General Ins. Co., 50 Cal.2d 654, 328 P.2d 198, 68 A.L.R.2d 883. It was there reasoned that in every contract, including policies of insurance, there is an implied covenant of good faith and fair dealing that neither party will do anything which will injure the right of the other to receive the benefits of the agreement; that it is common knowledge that one of the usual methods by which an insured receives protection under a liability insurance policy is by settlement of claims without litigation; that the implied obligation of good faith and fair dealing requires the insurer to settle in an appropriate case although the express terms of the policy do not impose the duty; that in determining whether to settle the insurer must give the interests of the insured at least as much consideration as it gives to its own interests; and that when "there is great risk of a recovery beyond the policy limits so that the most reasonable manner of disposing of the claim is a settlement which can be made within those limits, a consideration in good faith of the insured's interest requires the insurer to settle the claim." * * *

In determining whether an insurer has given consideration to the interests of the insured, the test is whether a prudent insurer without policy limits would have accepted the settlement offer. * * *

Several cases, in considering the liability of the insurer, contain language to the effect that bad faith is the equivalent of dishonesty, fraud, and concealment. * * * Obviously a showing that the insurer has been guilty of actual dishonesty, fraud, or concealment is relevant to the determination whether it has given consideration to the insured's interest in considering a settlement offer within the policy limits. The language used in the cases, however, should not be understood as meaning that in the absence of evidence establishing actual dishonesty, fraud, or concealment no recovery may be had for a judgment in excess of the policy limits. Comunale v. Traders & General Ins. Co., supra, 50 Cal.2d 654, 658–659, 328 P.2d 198, makes it clear that liability based or an implied covenant exists whenever the insurer refuses to settle in an appropriate case and that liability may exist when the insurer unwarrantedly refuses an offered settlement where the most reasonable manner of disposing of the claim is by accepting the settlement. Liability is imposed not for a bad faith breach of the contract but for failure to meet the duty to accept reasonable settlements, a duty included within the implied covenant of good faith and fair dealing. Moreover, * * * recovery may be based on unwarranted rejection of a reasonable settlement offer and * * * the absence of evidence, circumstantial or direct, showing actual dishonesty, fraud, or concealment is not fatal to the cause of action.

Amicus curiae argues that, whenever an insurer receives an offer to settle within the policy limits and rejects it, the insurer should be liable in every case for the amount of any final judgment whether or not within the policy limits. As we have seen, the duty of the insurer to consider the insured's interest in settlement offers within the policy limits arises from an implied covenant in the contract, and ordinarily contract duties are strictly enforced and not subject to a standard of reasonableness. Obviously, it will always be in the insured's interest to settle within the policy limits when there is any danger, however slight, of a judgment in excess of those limits. Accordingly the rejection of a settlement within the limits where there is any danger of a judgment in excess of the limits can be justified, if at all, only on the basis of interests of the insurer, and, in light of the common knowledge that settlement is one of the usual methods by which an insured receives protection under a liability policy, it may not be unreasonable for an insured who purchases a policy with limits to believe that a sum of money equal to the limits is available and will be used so as to avoid liability on his part with regard to any covered accident. In view of such expectation an insurer should not be permitted to further its own interests by rejecting opportunities to settle within the policy limits unless it is also willing to absorb losses which may result from its failure to settle.

The proposed rule is a simple one to apply and avoids the burdens of a determination whether a settlement offer within the policy limits was reasonable. The proposed rule would also eliminate the danger that an insurer, faced with a settlement offer at or near the policy limits, will reject it and gamble with the insured's money to further its own interests. Moreover, it is not entirely clear that the proposed rule would place a burden on insurers substantially greater than that which is present under existing law. The size of the judgment recovered in the personal injury action when it exceeds the policy limits, although not conclusive, furnishes an inference that the value of the claim is the equivalent of the amount of the judgment and that acceptance of an offer within those limits was the most reasonable method of dealing with the claim.

Finally, and most importantly, there is more than a small amount of elementary justice in a rule that would require that, in this situation where the insurer's and insured's interests necessarily conflict, the insurer, which may reap the benefits of its determination not to settle, should also suffer the detriments of its decision. On the basis of these and other considerations, a number of commentators have urged that the insurer should be liable for any resulting judgment where it refuses to settle within the policy limits. * * *

We need not, however, here determine whether there might be some countervailing considerations precluding adoption of the proposed rule because, under Comunale v. Traders & General Ins. Co., supra, 50 Cal.2d 654, 328 P.2d 198, and the cases following it, the evidence is clearly sufficient to support the determination that Security breached its duty to consider the interests of Mrs. Crisci in proposed settlements. Both Security's attorney and its claims manager agreed that if Mrs. DiMare won an award for her psychosis, that award would be at least $100,000. Security attempts to justify its rejection of a settlement by contending that it believed Mrs. DiMare had no chance of winning on the mental suffering issue. That belief in the circumstances present could be found to be unreasonable. Security was putting blind faith in the power of its psychiatrists to convince the jury when it knew that the accident could have caused the psychosis, that its agents had told it that without evidence of prior mental defects a jury was likely to believe the fall precipitated the psychosis, and that Mrs. DiMare had reputable psychiatrists on her side. Further, the company had been told by a psychiatrist that in a group of 24 psychiatrists, 12 could be found to support each side.

The trial court found that defendant "knew that there was a considerable risk of substantial recovery beyond said policy limits" and that "the defendant did not give as much consideration to the financial interests of its said insured as it gave to its own interests." That is all that was required. The award of $91,000 must therefore be affirmed.

We must next determine the propriety of the award of Mrs. Crisci of $25,000 for her mental suffering. In Comunale v. Traders & General Ins. Co., supra, 50 Cal.2d 654, 663, 328 P.2d 198, 203, it was held that an action of the type involved here sounds in both contract and tort and that "where a case sounds both in contract and tort the plaintiff will ordinarily have freedom of election between an action of tort and one of contract. An exception to this rule is made in suits for personal injury caused by negligence, where the tort character of the action is considered to prevail (citations), but no such exception is applied in cases, like the present one, which relate to financial damage (citations)." * * *

Fundamental in our jurisprudence is the principle that for every wrong there is a remedy and that an injured party should be compensated for all damage proximately caused by the wrongdoer. Although we recognize exceptions from these fundamental principles, no departure should be sanctioned unless there is a strong necessity therefor.

The general rule of damages in tort is that the injured party may recover for all detriment caused whether it could have been anticipated or not. * * * In accordance with the general rule, it is settled in this state that mental suffering constitutes an aggravation of damages when it naturally ensues from the act complained of, and in this connection mental suffering includes nervousness, grief, anxiety, worry, shock, humiliation and indignity as well as physical pain. * * * Such awards are not confined to cases where the mental suffering award was in addition to an award for personal injuries; damages for mental distress have also been awarded in cases where the tortious conduct was an interference with property rights without any personal injuries apart from the mental distress.

We are satisfied that a plaintiff who as a result of a defendant's tortious conduct loses his property and suffers mental distress may recover not only for the pecuniary loss but also for his mental distress. No substantial reason exists to distinguish the cases which have permitted recovery for mental distress in actions for invasion of property rights. The principal reason for limiting recovery of damages for mental distress is that to permit recovery of such damages would open the door to fictitious claims, to recovery for mere bad manners, and to litigation in the field of trivialities. * * * Obviously, where, as here, the claim is actionable and has resulted in substantial damages apart from those due to mental distress, the danger of fictitious claims is reduced, and we are not here concerned with mere bad manners or trivialities but tortious conduct resulting in substantial invasions of clearly protected interests. * * *

Recovery of damages for mental suffering in the instant case does not mean that in every case of breach of contract the injured party may recover such damages. Here the breach also constitutes a tort. Moreover, plaintiff did not seek by the contract involved here to obtain a commercial advantage but to protect herself against the risks of accidental losses, including the mental distress which might follow from the losses. Among the considerations in purchasing liability insurance, as insurers are well aware, is the peace of mind and security it will provide in the event of an accidental loss, and recovery of damages for mental suffering has been permitted for breach of contracts which directly concern the comfort, happiness or personal esteem of one of the parties. * * *

It is not claimed that plaintiff's mental distress was not caused by defendant's refusal to settle or that the damages awarded were excessive in the light of plaintiff's substantial suffering.

The judgment is affirmed.

TRAYNOR, C.J., and MCCOMB, TOBRINER, MOSK and BURKE, JJ., concur.

NOTES

1. *The Insurer's Contractual Right to Control Defense and Settlement.* Most standard liability policies give the insurance company the "right and duty to defend the suit," and many policies provide that the company may "investigate and settle any claim or 'suit' at [the company's] discretion." As Professor Charles Silver has explained:

> These contract provisions are generally interpreted as granting the company plenary and exclusive control of the defense. Ordinarily, the company can select counsel to defend the insured, discharge appointed counsel and name a replacement without the insured's consent, bargain with appointed counsel over fees, monitor counsel and direct litigation strategy, require counsel to inform the company of settlement demands and procedural developments, direct counsel to initiate settlement discussions, settle claims without an insured's consent and decline to settle claims over an insured's objection, and file appeals.

Charles Silver, *Does Insurance Defense Counsel Represent the Company or the Insured?*, 72 Tex. L. Rev. 1583, 1594–95 (1994).

Why would insurers, under standard liability policies, be unwilling to yield to insureds the ability to choose defense counsel, select defense strategy, and make settlement decisions? Why might it be in insureds' interests (in at least some situations) to agree to give insurers control over the defense and settlement of the case?

The relationship between the insured, the insurance defense counsel, and the insurance carrier is often known as the "tripartite" relationship. It has generated complex and still unsettled questions relating to when an attorney-client relationship exists, what the scope of that relationship is, and what the duties of the attorney are in various insurance defense situations. To illustrate some of these questions, suppose that the tort plaintiff brings an action against the insured for injuries arising from a boating accident. The insured defendant forwards the complaint to the insurance company, which then hires insurance defense counsel to represent the insured. Who is or are the client or clients of the insurance defense counsel—the insured only, or also the insurance company? See Charles Silver, *Does Insurance Defense Counsel Represent the Company or the Insured?*, 72 Tex. L. Rev. 1583 (1994); Ellen S. Pryor & Charles Silver, *Defense Lawyers' Professional Responsibilities: Part I—Excess Exposure Cases*, 78 Tex. L. Rev. 599 (2000); Ellen S. Pryor & Charles Silver, *Defense Lawyers' Professional Responsibilities: Part II—Contested Coverage Cases*, 15 Geo. J. Leg. Ethics 29 (2001).

2. *Evaluating Settlement Demands in the Absence of Insurance.* To understand why courts have imposed certain standards on insurers when evaluating settlement offers, one must first appreciate some basics about settlement evaluation when no insurance is involved. In the absence of insurance, whether and when a defendant will accept a plaintiff's "demand" to settle will turn in large part on the expected costs of going to trial. These costs consist of the expected judgment if defendant loses, multiplied by the expected probability of loss at trial, plus the additional attorneys' fees and court costs that defendant will incur by going to trial. Consider the following example. Plaintiff demands $45,000 to settle her tort suit. Defendant evaluates the chances of a plaintiff verdict at 80%, the chances of a no-liability verdict at 20%, and the amount of the verdict if plaintiff wins as $50,000. Thus, the "expected value" of the case is .8 * $50,000 = $40,000. Defendant also realizes that he will spend another $10,000 in fees and costs if the case goes to trial. Thus, defendant's full expected costs of turning down the settlement demand and proceeding to trial are: $40,000 + $10,000 = $50,000. The defendant would rationally accept the plaintiff's demand.

Of course, if the plaintiff faces similar litigation costs and evaluates the case similarly, the above logic would cause a plaintiff to rationally accept any offer greater than $40,000 − $10,000 = $30,000. The point is that the litigation costs involved in going to trial create a bargaining space in which both parties would be better off by settling than by going to trial. Given this logic, why do cases ever go to trial? *See* RICHARD LEMPERT AND JOSEPH SANDERS, AN INVITATION TO LAW AND SOCIAL SCIENCE. pp. 137–168 (1986); Kent Syverud, *The Duty to Settle*, 76 Va. L. Rev. 1113, 1128–29 (1990).

3. *How Liability Insurance Affects the Evaluation of Settlement Offers.* Suppose that the defendant in the above example has liability insurance of $100,000. Both the insurer and the defendant have a common interest in defeating the tort claim entirely. But their interests diverge with respect to settlement demands. Suppose again that the expected costs of going to trial are $50,000, ($40,000 + $10,000 litigation costs) and that the plaintiff submits a settlement demand of $99,000. What will the insurer prefer—accepting or rejecting the offer? What will the insured defendant prefer?

Now suppose that the plaintiff has a 90% chance of obtaining a liability verdict, and that the expected judgment amount should the plaintiff win is $200,000. Given these assumptions, the expected value of the plaintiff's claim is $180,000. Suppose the plaintiff offers to settle the case for $99,000. If the insurer rejects the demand and goes on to trial, it will risk only an additional $1,000 (plus costs of defense) and will still have a small chance (10%) that it will win altogether. What will the insurer prefer? What will the insured defendant prefer?

The presence of a policy limit—$100,000 in our example—creates a conflict of interest with respect to settlement demands within policy limits. In the *Crisci* case, was there a conflict of interest between Mrs. Crisci and the insurer?

4. *The Judicially Imposed Duty to Settle*. Most jurisdictions, many of them following *Crisci* explicitly, have recognized an extra-contractual duty to settle on the part of liability insurers. Like the *Crisci* court, most jurisdictions hold that a claim for breach of the duty to settle sounds in tort; the factfinder in this tort action will be asked to evaluate whether the insurer's conduct comported with the required standard. Jurisdictions use one or more of the following standards: (1) The insurer must act with reasonable care in evaluating settlement demands; (2) The insurer must act with good faith in evaluating settlement demands; (3) The insurer must give equal consideration to the interests of the insured and the insurer when evaluating settlement demands; and (4) The insurance company, when evaluating a settlement demand, must view the situation as it would if there were no policy limit applicable to the claim. Some courts have added a requirement that the insurer have acted "recklessly" or with some gross absence of care. For instance, in Pavia v. State Farm Mutual Automobile Ins. Co., 82 N.Y.2d 445, 626 N.E.2d 24, 605 N.Y.S.2d 208 (1993), the court held that the insured must show a "gross disregard' of the insured's interests—that is, a deliberate or reckless failure to place on equal footing the interests of its insured with its own interests when considering a settlement offer."

What are the benefits of a judicially imposed duty to settle? What are the costs? One obvious cost is that insurers, when defending tort suits against insureds, spend money and extend effort "to document the reasonableness of the insurer's behavior as much as to assist the insurer in resolving the underlying litigation." Syverud, *supra*, at 1165–1166. Another potential cost is that insurers will essentially overpay some tort claims—a cost passed on to all insureds—when there is considerable ambiguity about how a jury in the later duty-to-settle suit will assess the insurer's conduct. These concerns are parallel to "overdeterrence" concerns raised in other tort contexts. Is the zone of uncertainty greater as to duty-to-settle contexts than as to, say, predictions about whether particular product design decisions will be found to be negligent by a jury?

The *amicus curiae* in *Crisci* argued for a version of strict liability: the insurer will be liable any time it rejects a within-limits demand and the trial results in a verdict in excess of policy limits. No state has adopted this position. Why not?

For additional discussions of the rationale for duty to settle, see Robert Heidt, *The Unappreciated Importance, For Small Business Defendants, of the Duty to Settle,* 62 Me. L. Rev. 75 (2010); Kyle D. Logue, *Solving the Judgment–Proof Problem*, 72 Tex. L. Rev. 1375 (1994); Seth J. Chandler, *Reconsidering the Duty to Settle*, 42 Drake L. Rev. 741 (1993); Charles Silver, *A Missed Misalignment of Interests: A Comment on Syverud*, 77 Va. L. Rev. 1585 (1991); KENNETH S. ABRAHAM, DISTRIBUTING RISK 188–95 (1986). One commentator finds unpersuasive the theoretical and practical arguments for a judicially imposed duty to settle. *See* Alan O. Sykes, *Judicial Limitations on the Discretion of Liability Insurers to Settle or Litigate: An Economic Critique*, 72 Tex. L. Rev. 1345 (1994).

5. *No Direct Claim Against Insurer by the Tort Claimant.* If an insurer unreasonably fails to respond to a settlement initiative made by the tort plaintiff, may the tort plaintiff directly sue the insurer? What are the issues? *See* Moradi–Shalal v. Fireman's Fund Ins. Cos., 46 Cal.3d 287, 250 Cal.Rptr. 116, 758 P.2d 58 (1988).

6. *Exclusions and Settlements.* The problems of exclusions and settlements sometimes intersect to create truly thorny problems. For instance, suppose that the plaintiff was shot by a neighbor with a gun following an argument. The plaintiff's lawyer files the case and pleads negligence; the insurance company provides a defense (because the complaint states a potentially covered claim) but reserves its right to contest coverage of the incident. The policy limits are $20,000. The plaintiff's lawyer makes a demand for $20,000. If the injury was only negligently inflicted, then the insurer would pay the demand because this is reasonable in light of the potential tort judgment against the insured. But if the injury was intentionally inflicted, then the policy does not cover it and in theory the insurer owes nothing. But whether the injury was or was not intentionally inflicted has not yet been adjudicated, and the insurer is now faced with the settlement demand.

If the insurer turns out to be incorrect about the coverage issue, some courts hold that the insurer has breached the duty to settle even if its coverage decision was based on a good faith appraisal of the facts at the time. For further discussion, *see* Stephen S. Ashley, *Coverage Doubts and the Insurer's Duty to Settle*, 4 Bad Faith L. Rep. 27 (1988); ALLAN D. WINDT, 1 INSURANCE CLAIMS AND DISPUTES § 5:10 (5TH ED. 2010). If you were in-house counsel to the insurer in the above example, what would you advise the insurer to do with respect to the $20,000 demand from the plaintiff if the potential excess verdict against the insured defendant is extremely high?

C. INTERACTION OF LIABILITY INSURANCE AND FIRST–PARTY INSURANCE SOURCES: SUBROGATION

First-party insurers often assert rights of subrogation in tort litigation. Consider an example. A fire breaks out in the insured's home and is not quenched until it has caused $50,000 to the dwelling and to insured contents. The insured has a property loss limit of $100,000, and recovers $48,000 from the insurer (the amount of damage, less the deductible). The fire began because a neighbor negligently allowed a trash fire to get out of control and spread to the insured's house. The property insurer will assert a right of subrogation against the negligent neighbor. Such a right is derivative: it allows the insurer to step into the shoes of the insured and make a claim for the insured's loss, to the extent the insurer has paid that loss. Most property insurance policies contain express subrogation clauses;

but when the policies do not include such clauses, most courts nevertheless will allow subrogation on equitable grounds.

Subrogation interacts with the collateral source rule to achieve two aims: visiting upon negligent actors the full cost of the injuries they cause, and avoiding duplicative recoveries by the injured person. In the fire example, for instance, the collateral source rule would allow the insured to recover the full $50,000 from the negligent neighbor, notwithstanding that the insured already had recovered $48,000 from the property insurer. The insurer's subrogation interest will allow it to recoup that payment, leaving the insured $2,000, the amount of the deductible. Thus, the negligent neighbor still bears the full cost of his conduct, and the insured is not overcompensated for his loss.

The theory and workings of subrogation are relatively simple in this fire example. However, subrogation can present complex theoretical and practical issues in tort litigation. Consider another example. The insured is a 16–year old girl who is an insured under her mother's health insurance policy. The girl sustains serious head injuries in a car accident, and will require expensive therapy and personal assistance for many years, perhaps even throughout her life. By the end of the first year following the accident, the health insurer has paid hospital and medical bills totaling $250,000; the health insurance has a total cap of $1 million as to any single insured. The girl's parents, as guardians, file a lawsuit on the girl's behalf against the driver whose negligence caused the accident. The driver has liability limits of $300,000. The liability insurer, after a short investigation, determines that this is a policy-limits case, and is willing to tender the full $300,000 to settle the claim. The health insurer, however, has notified the parents that it will seek subrogation to the extent of the $250,000 it has already paid.

What options does the plaintiff's lawyer have? She could try to settle the lawsuit for the full $300,000 liability limits and not notify the health insurer of the settlement. This option is unattractive for many reasons: the settlement might require judicial approval and the health insurer could intervene in the proceeding, thus rendering impossible a back-door deal that cuts out the health insurer. The liability insurer might be unwilling to settle without assurance that all subrogation interests are adequately dealt with and a back-door deal would likely be deemed a breach by the insured of the insured's duties under the health insurance policy, thus forfeiting rights to further coverage under the health policy.

So the plaintiff's lawyer's options do not look promising unless there is some chink in the health insurer's assertion of a subrogation right. In fact, several types of chinks exist in different jurisdictions. First, some jurisdictions hold that the health insurer has no subrogation right unless the health insurance policy contains an explicit clause entitling it to subrogation; such jurisdictions do not recognize an equitable right of subrogation for health insurers. *See* Wolters v. American Republic Insurance Co., 149 N.H. 599, 827 A.2d 197 (2003).

Second, even if the jurisdiction recognizes an equitable right of subrogation for health insurers, or even if the health insurance policy contains a subrogation clause, a number of jurisdictions hold that the right does not exist unless the injured person has first been "fully compensated" for the loss by the tort recovery. *See, e.g.*, Powell v. Blue Cross and Blue Shield, 581 So.2d 772 (Ala.1990). The full compensation rule has been enshrined in a statute in several states. *See* Colo. Rev. Stat. § 10–1–135. If we apply this full compensation requirement to the fire example, it is easy to see that the insured, after payment of the tort recovery ($50,000) and the insurance funds ($48,000), has been fully compensated for his loss of $50,000; thus the insurer is entitled to subrogation above that amount. But, in the personal injury example, even the girl's receipt of the full $300,000 liability limit does not come close to "full compensation." Thus the health insurer will not receive any subrogation. Given that one aim of subrogation is to prevent duplicative recoveries, does the "full compensation" requirement seem justifiable?

Not every state has adopted the above approach. When there is a statutory or contractual right to subrogation, these jurisdictions compel some allocation. *See* Texas Health Insurance Risk Pool v. Sigmundik, 315 S.W.3d 12 (Tex. 2010). For discussion of the theory and history of subrogation, as well as an argument for pro tanto subrogation as a default rule, *see* Jeffrey A. Greenblatt, *Insurance and Subrogation: When the Pie Isn't Big Enough, Who Eats Last?*, 64 U. Chi. L. Rev. 1337 (1997); Brandan S. Mahler and Radha A. Pathak, *Understanding and Problematizing Contractual Tort Subrogation*, 40 Loy. U. Chi. L. J. 49 (2008).

CHAPTER 6

TORT REFORM AND NONTORT COMPENSATION PROGRAMS

■ ■ ■

A. INTRODUCTION

This chapter discusses two related topics. It begins with discussion of the substantial body of "tort reform" legislation that has been enacted over the last thirty plus years. Tort reforms are generally modest changes that keep in place the basic structure of torts while modifying many of its collateral rules, most frequently rules about damages. The following part of the chapter discusses more radical alternatives: various existing and proposed nontort compensation programs, such as workers' compensation, automobile no-fault, and social security disability that have the goal of entirely replacing tort with a no-fault compensation system. The chapter also examines New Zealand's decision, in 1972, to abolish tort for most personal injuries and to replace it with a comprehensive no-fault compensation program.

Before we begin this discussion, it may be worthwhile to review the goals of tort law: deterrence, compensation, and corrective justice.

Deterrence

The Hand Formula and similar statements of what it is to be negligent emphasize the deterrent function of tort. The ability of tort law to achieve this goal has been critiqued from many perspectives. Tort law fails to produce optimal reductions in unsafe conduct due to: a lack of knowledge about tort liability; the unpredictability of potential tort liability; psychological factors that lead people to discount the threat of potential liability; and widespread liability insurance that, even if priced partly according to the risks that the insured poses, still blunts the deterrent impact of potential tort liability. As a result of all these factors, the law underdeters. According to some, not only does tort fail to add meaningfully to the reduction of unreasonably unsafe conduct, it overdeters some desirable although risky social conduct because it holds out the prospect of occasional, unpredictable, and possibly "incorrect" enormous verdicts. *See generally* Gary T. Schwartz, *Reality in the Economic Analysis of Tort Law:*

Does Tort Law Really Matter?, 42 U.C.L.A. L.Rev. 377 (1994); Joseph Sanders, *Firm Risk Management in the Face of Product Liability Rules*. 11 Law and Policy 253 (1989); Richard J. Pierce, Jr., *Encouraging Safety: The Limits of Tort Law and Government Regulation,* 33 Vand. L. Rev. 1281 (1980); Daniel W. Shuman, *The Psychology of Deterrence in Tort Law,* 42 U. Kan. L. Rev. 115 (1993).

Compensation

A second goal, compensation of victims once was thought by some to be the paramount goal of torts. *See* Glanville Williams, *The Aims of the Law of Tort*, 4 Current Legal Problems 137 (1951). Williams thought that deterrence and retribution should be left to the criminal law. Because of the perceived shortcomings of tort as a compensation scheme, few would take this view today.

As we note below, empirical research indicates that tort law overcompensates smaller injuries, undercompensates larger injuries, and fails to produce "horizontal consistency"—that is, juries award significantly different damages to basically similar injuries. Added to these criticisms is the "lottery" nature of tort compensation: whether and how much a deserving victim recovers in tort depends on the fortuity of whether the defendant has liability insurance or funds to satisfy a judgment. (This element of fortuity is only slightly reduced by minimum insurance laws in some areas.) And tort is an extremely expensive form of compensation insurance when compared to first-party insurance or social insurance. Much more of our "tort premium" goes to the payment of administrative overhead, court costs, and attorneys' fees than is the case with any other form of insurance.

In addition, tort's compensation regime has a regressive impact on the poor. Both the rich and poor must pay when the prospect of tort liability increases the prices for goods and services. Yet, high income individuals receive more from a successful tort claim than individuals with a low income, despite the fact that both usually have paid a similar tort "premium" in the form of an increased price for or reduced availability of the good or service. A final criticism of tort compensation is that it forces us to buy a type of insurance—for pain and suffering—that most of us do not desire and would not purchase if given a choice. For details on these criticisms, *see* Marc A. Franklin, *Replacing the Negligence Lottery: Compensation and Selective Reimbursement*, 53 Vir. L. Rev. 774 (1967); George L. Priest, *The Current Insurance Crisis and Modern Tort Law*, 96 Yale L.J. 1521 (1986); Alan Schwartz, *Proposals for Products Liability Reform: A Theoretical Synthesis,* 97 Yale L.J. 353 (1988); F. Patrick Hubbard, *The Nature and Impact of the "Tort Reform" Movement*, 35 Hofstra L. Rev. 437 (2006); Ellen S. Pryor, *Parts of the Whole: Tort Law's Compensatory Failures Through a Wider Lens*, 27 Rev. Litig. 307 (2008). These shortcomings have caused some to argue for the abolition of the tort system as we know it, to be replaced with other methods to compensate victims.

Stephen D. Sugarman, DOING AWAY WITH PERSONAL INJURY LAW: NEW COMPENSATION MECHANISMS FOR VICTIMS, CONSUMERS, AND BUSINESS (1989).

Corrective Justice

These critiques of law's ability to achieve deterrence and compensation have caused some to view tort primarily as an instrument of corrective justice.

> If achieving important compensatory and regulatory goals is really what a government wants to do, it would do best to give up the presumption that tort law stands ready to deliver on these goals. While tort law does permit injured victims to gain compensation and does provide financial incentives for actors to address the potential harmfulness of their conduct, it is a remarkably inconsistent, blunt, and expensive tool for these tasks. Other forms of public and private legal arrangements are demonstrably superior in a wide range of cases.

John C.P. Goldberg & Benjamin C. Zipursky, *Torts as Wrongs*, 88 Tex. L. Rev. 917, 978–79 (2010)

Corrective justice is a somewhat slippery concept that in recent decades has become littered with different definitions. However, as Keating notes, at bottom it "holds that negligence law is (and should be) an articulation of our ordinary moral conceptions of agency and responsibility, carelessness and wrongdoing, harm and reparation." Gregory C. Keating, *Distributive and Corrective Justice in the Tort Law of Accidents*, 74 S. Cal. L. Rev. 193 (2000). More formally, the theories argue that tort law embodies a set of first order duties not to injure. The scope of these duties is defined by social norms. When these first order duties are breached, there arise second order duties of repair—one has a duty to repair the losses created by wrongful conduct. *See* Jules L. Coleman, *The Practice of Corrective Justice*, in PHILOSOPHICAL FOUNDATIONS OF TORT LAW 53 (DAVID G. OWEN ED., 1995).

Supporters of this perspective argue that tort law functions to resolve disputes arising from perceived violations of social norms, *see* Stephen D. Smith, *The Critics and the Crisis: A Reassessment of Current Conceptions of Tort Law,* 72 Cornell L.Rev. 765 (1987), and that tort law's reliance on jury adjudication comports with a view of tort law as enforcing community standards of financial responsibility and just compensation, *see* Catherine Pierce Wells, *Tort Law As Corrective Justice: A Pragmatic Justification for Jury Adjudication*, 88 Mich.L.Rev. 2348 (1990). They view the corrective justice perspective as an alternative to an instrumentalist-deterrence based approaches that view tort as a system of encouraging efficient safety precautions. *See* Benjamin C. Zipursky, *Civil Recourse, Not Corrective Justice*, 91 Geo. L.J. 695 (2003); John C.P. Goldberg & Benjamin C. Zipursky, *Torts as Wrongs*, 88 Texas L. Rev. 917 (2010); Jane Stapleton, *Evaluating Goldberg and Zipursky's Civil Recourse Theory*, 75 Fordham L. Rev. 1529 (2006).

Note, that while this approach de-emphasizes tort law's deterrence goal, it generally offers no systematic discussion of remedies for the perceived shortcomings of the current compensation scheme. Consequently, some would argue that even in terms of corrective justice, the system falls short. As Professor Sugarman has argued, the "current system functions whimsically and doesn't accord with anyone's sense of justice. The much-vaunted individualized attention to victims in practice sanctions flagrant horizontal inequity because of settlement practices, trial theatrics, and other reasons already discussed." Stephen Sugarman, DOING AWAY WITH PERSONAL INJURY LAW: NEW COMPENSATION MECHANISMS FOR VICTIMS, CONSUMERS, AND BUSINESS 604 (1989).

While reading the following materials, the student would be well served by stopping from time to time to ask how, if at all, tort reform and alternatives to tort address perceived problems in achieving these three goals.

B. TORT REFORM

"Tort reform" could mean many things ranging from minor alterations of the duty owed to people who come on your land to the wholesale abandonment of the traditional tort regime such as has occurred with respect to workers compensation. At a middle level, the term could describe a debate about the traditional goals of tort law: retribution, deterrence, and compensation and how we might alter the tort regime to better achieve one or more of these goals. Most frequently, however, the term is used to describe a specific set of legislative initiatives reaching back to the 1970s that, in the eyes of their supporters, redress problems created by a long term drift toward greater litigiousness and uncertainty in the tort system. All, or nearly all of these reforms are supported by defense interests and opposed by the plaintiff's personal injury bar. As a subject of interest, tort reform has moved from the academy to every state legislature and to a lively societal debate. Well over 40 states have passed major tort reform legislation packages at least once (and often several times) since the medical malpractice insurance-tort problems of the mid–1970s. The general public is well aware of complaints about excessive verdicts, overlitigiousness, "frivolous lawsuits," "junk science," and many high-profile cases, such as the McDonald's coffee spill case and litigation over diet drugs, tire failures, and other products. As two respected researchers have explained, those who seek tort reform "are, of course, seeking sympathetic rule-makers and favorable rule changes; they also want to affect the way in which the media, intellectuals, key elites, and ultimately the public at large think about the civil justice system. Consequently, this political conflict has always been waged on multiple fronts, in legislatures, in the courts, in elections, in the worlds of various elites, including academe, and in the world of public perception. More than just the formal legal changes it seeks, tort reform has also been about altering the cultural environment surrounding civil litigation—e.g., what is perceived as an injury; whom to blame for an injury; what to do about it; and even how to respond to what others (especially plaintiffs and their lawyers) do with regard to naming and blaming." *See* Stephen Daniels & Joanne Martin, *"The Impact It Has Had Is Between People's Ears": Tort Reform, Mass Culture, and Plaintiff's Lawyers*, 50 DePaul L. Rev. 453, 453 (2000). The reform-seeking vision of tort is concerned with reducing the number of personal injury suits, limiting the size of awards and the unpredictability of jury outcomes, and controlling costs. Much of this is surrounded with a fair amount of rhetoric, i.e. "frivolous lawsuits," "outrageous awards," "the lawsuit lottery."

A full look at all aspects of tort reform would require a book in itself—indeed, many books have been devoted to one or more of these topics, such as tort reform, "junk science," particular lawsuits, etc. In this chapter, we distill the main features of the tort reform debate in a way that fairly represents the arguments on both sides, the empirical evidence supporting various claims, and the statutory reforms.

Before dealing with the specifics of tort reform as it is commonly understood, we offer a brief review of some of the empirical research about the workings of the tort system. Academic consensus is clearer on some issues than others but political agreement is elusive and popular opinions about the tort system are often formed without benefit of the more careful empirical research.

Next we turn to a discussion of the major tort reforms passed since the mid–1970s and the empirical evidence on their effects. This is followed by a short discussion of state constitutional law challenges to these reforms. We conclude with a discussion of legislation aimed at allowing or encouraging plaintiffs to "opt out" of the tort system and choose a no-fault package of benefits. This last topic includes discussion of the legislation creating the September 11 victims' compensation fund.

1. EMPIRICAL EVIDENCE

The onset of the modern tort reform debates has prompted a considerable body of empirical research about the workings of the tort system. The research contradicts many of the popular contentions about the problems with the jury system or tort law, and it raises some concerns that rarely make their way into the popular debate. The following discussion focuses on a number of empirical issues that have been especially important in the debate over whether tort meaningfully advances any of its major goals. Consider how each point relates to the various systemic goals of tort, and what type of tort reform might be responsive to the issue.

a. Overcompensating Small Injuries, Undercompensating Large Injuries

One of the most consistent findings of many studies is that the tort system, via both settlement and trial, yields overcompensation as to smaller injuries and undercompensation of larger injuries. Many of these studies have compared actual settlement amounts with independent assessments of the value of the claim. Many small injury victims, of course, never file a claim and receive no compensation. But some who do are overcompensated, given the nuisance value to the defendant or its insurer of paying off the claim.

Factors that might explain undercompensation relative to the true value of a case involving more serious injuries include inadequate insurance or defendant solvency; the plaintiff's need for money and the inability to bear the delay of going to trial; uncertainties about the value of the claim; and cognitive or psychological factors that result in a discounting of higher damages.

For discussion of the issues, *see* Patricia Munch, Costs and Benefits of the Torts System If Viewed As a Compensation System 14, 38–39, 76–81 (1977); Marc Galanter, *Real World Torts: An Antidote to Anecdote,* 55 Md.L.Rev. 1093, 1116–20 (1996); Michael J. Saks, *Do We Really Know Anything About the Behavior of the Tort Litigation System—And Why Not?,* 140 U.Pa.L.Rev. 1147, 1216–20 (1992); Deborah L. Rhode, *Frivolous Litigation and Civil Justice Reform: Miscasting the Problem, Recasting the Solution*, 54 Duke L.J. 447 (2004).

b. Vertical Consistency and Horizontal Inconsistency

Another persistent finding from a number of studies relates to how well jury verdicts correspond to the severity of injuries. Most studies find that jury awards over time reflect a high degree of "vertical consistency"—that is, juries tend to award higher damage amounts for more serious injuries, and lower damage amounts for less serious injuries. But jury awards over time do a poorer job of achieving "horizontal consistency"—that is, giving roughly similar damage awards for roughly similar injuries (after accounting for other reasons that might explain the variation). See Neil Vidmar, *et al., Jury Awards for Medical Malpractice and Post–Verdict Adjustments of Those Awards*, 48 DePaul L. Rev. 265 (1999).

To illustrate by an example, consider an injury severity scale from 1 to 9, with 1 and 2 corresponding to insignificant and temporary injury, and 8 and 9 corresponding, respectively, to permanent grave injury and to death. Juries over time are consistent in awarding higher amounts for each successive level of severity. But the variation of awards within any given category is very high, even after accounting for legitimate reasons for variation (such as the reducing effect of a finding of contributory negligence). So, for instance, the amount of money given for all Category 7 injuries will vary considerably. Of course, much of this variation can be explained by factors that are appropriate to the decision. An injury to A could have very different effects than that same injury to B, depending on A's and B's health before injury, occupation, family circumstances, age, level and quality of post-injury medical care. *See* Roselle L. Wissler, et al., *Instructing Jurors on General Damages in Personal Injury Cases*, 6 Psych. Pub. Pol'y & Law 712, 713 (2000).

Nonetheless, a number of empirical studies have shown that some of the variation—anywhere between one-third and one-fourth—cannot be explained by factors that legitimately bear on the damages calculation. For instance, one study found that awards for level 8 injuries ranged from a low of $147,000 to a high of $18,100,000, and that all awards in the top quartile for this severity level were at least six times as high as awards in the bottom quartile. Some of the variation could be explained by legitimate factors, such as variation in the plaintiff's age or pre-injury earnings. "No amount of adjusting, however, is likely to fully account for the extreme values." Randall R. Bovbjerg, Frank A. Sloan & James F. Blumstein, *Valuing Life and Limb in Tort: Scheduling "Pain and Suffering,"* 83 Nw. U. L. Rev. 908, 919–24 (1989). *See also* Michael J. Saks, *Do We Really Know Anything About the Behavior of the Tort Litigation System—And Why Not?,* 140 U.Pa.L.Rev. 1147, 1274–77 (1992) (discussing variation in awards); David Schkade et al., *Deliberating About Dollars: The Severity Shift,* 100 Colum. L. Rev. 1139, 1142–43 (2000); Joseph Sanders, *Why Do Proposals Designed to Control Variability in General Damages (Generally) Fall on Deaf Ears? (And Why This is too Bad)*, 55 DePaul L. Rev. 489 (2006) (discussing why proposed reforms in this area have gone nowhere).

c. Number of Claims

The tort reform debate has frequently included contentions that too many frivolous tort claims are filed and that too many excessive verdicts are returned in favor of plaintiffs. Anecdotal evidence—descriptions of seemingly ridiculous claims or recoveries—has played a large role in this portion of the debate. But "if we want to know how the system is really performing, and we are not merely trying to provoke people to despise it or fear losing it, then we must do more than fling anecdotes back and forth." Michael J. Saks, *Do We Really Know Anything About the Behavior of the Tort Litigation System—And Why Not?,* 140 U.Pa.L.Rev. 1147, 1160 (1992).

An important limitation of any discussion of whether or not there are too many lawsuits is that filing rates, standing alone, do not tell us very much.

> Any assessment of whether the propensity to sue is increasing, decreasing, or remaining the same can be made only in relation to the waxing or waning of the pool of injuries from which suits properly arise. Any inference about whether the average size of awards or settlements has gone up, down, or remained level, in real terms, depends upon knowing what the pool of injuries looks like. If the pool of injuries has increased and the inherent seriousness of the injuries or the cost of repairing them has increased, one should not be surprised to find a commensurate increase in cases or awards. If the pool has shrunk either in size or cost of injuries, even a seemingly level number of filings or payments should in real terms be regarded as an increase.

Saks, *supra*, at 1174–75.

The most rigorous studies of *filing rates relative to the injury pool* have taken place in the medical malpractice arena. A group of investigators led by the former Dean of the Harvard School of Public Health undertook a major study in the mid–1980s. The aim was to answer several questions: (1) How frequent are medical injuries, and negligence-caused injuries, in hospitals? (2) What portion of those injuries results in litigation, and how frequent is litigation in the absence of such injuries? (3) What are the economic consequences of these injuries? Among other tasks, the research team selected a representative sample of 52 hospitals in the state of New York, randomly sampled medical records from those hospitals, reviewed each record looking for evidence of "adverse events," and assessed whether the adverse event had been caused by negligence (deviation from the standard of care in the practice area). Paul C. Weiler et al., A MEASURE OF MALPRACTICE: MEDICAL INJURY, MALPRACTICE LITIGATION, AND PATIENT COMPENSATION (1993). The study is described in detail in David M. Studdert, *et al., Beyond Dead Reckoning: Measures of Medical Injury Burden, Malpractice Litigation, and Alternative Compensation Models from Utah and California*, 33 Ind. L. Rev. 1643, 1648–51 (2000). Studdert also reports on a second large-scale medical injury study in Utah and Colorado between 1995 and 1998. The researchers essentially replicated the careful methods used ten years previously in the Harvard Medical Practice Study. The results of the Utah–Colorado study are similar in many ways to the New York study: adverse medical events occurred in about the same percentage of hospitalizations; negligently caused adverse events were 5 or 6 times more common than the number of filed claims; and a significant percentage of the claims that were actually filed had not been identified by the researchers as involving negligence.

In sum, both studies suggest a stability about certain features of the current system: negligent injury occurs at a rate, and in medical contexts (*e.g.*, emergency rooms), that remain consistent across states and across time (from mid–1980s to mid–1990s); the number of negligently caused injuries is from 5 to 7 times greater than the number of claims; a significant percentage of the claims actually filed involve adverse events that were not negligently caused. "[C]laims lag well behind the incidence of negligent injury, and the two are seldom connected in the current system." David M. Studdert, *et al., Beyond Dead Reckoning: Measures of Medical Injury Burden, Malpractice Litigation, and Alternative Compensation Models from Utah and Colorado*, 33 Ind. L. Rev. 1643, 1667 (2000). *See also* A. Russell Localio, *et al., Relation Between Malpractice Claims and Adverse Events to Negligence: Results of the Harvard Medical Practice Study III*, 325 New Eng. J. Med. 245 (1991); David M. Studdert, et al., *Claims, Errors, and Compensation Payments in Medical Malpractice Litigation*, 354 New Eng. J. Med. 2024 (2006).

d. Size of Verdicts

What about the contention that the tort system produces too many excessive settlements and verdicts? As noted, most studies continue to show a pattern of overcompensation of smaller injuries and undercompensation of larger injuries. Adequate study into the issue requires controlling for variables such as changes in severity of injury and inflation. Once this is done, the data show that there was only a slight, if any, general increase in damages awards during the period leading up to the tort crisis. But there was a significant increase in the number of very large jury awards, even if the average amount paid per claim across the board has not increased much. American Law Institute, Reporters' Study on Enterprise Responsibility for Personal Injury, Vol. II, 64–66 (1991). Between 1992 and 2001 it appears that the size of median jury awards actually declined. However, this effect masks large large increases in median awards in those areas of tort law that have been most central to the tort reform movement: medical malpractice and products liability. Median malpractice awards trebled and median products awards doubled. Bureau of Justice Statistics, TORT TRIALS AND VERDICTS IN LARGE COUNTIES, 2001 (2004). More information is necessary, of course, to judge whether this increase reflects inappropriately high verdicts or instead results from other factors, such as changes in "case mix" (the number of serious injury cases filed), or higher survival rates (and thus higher long-term care and rehabilitation expenses) for injuries that in the past would have proved fatal.

e. Juries as Decisionmakers on Damages

A vast literature—from popular fiction to scholarly articles working analytically or empirically—explores the ability of the jury to "get it right." We have already addressed parts of this literature that touch on horizontal variability, excessiveness and frequency of verdicts.

Juries, judges, and lawyers are similar in their thinking about injury severity and injury awards. "[S]imilarity exists in the injury attributes that drive their decisions, the weight given to those attributes, and the shared sense of vertical equity held by jurors, judges, plaintiffs' lawyers, and defense lawyers alike." Roselle L. Wissler, *et al., Decisionmaking About General Damages: A Comparison of Jurors, Judges, and Lawyers*, 98 Mich. L. Rev. 751, 812 (1999). The greater concern is not with jurors' assessments about injury and severity, but in the translation of that assessment into dollar values. This is the point when predictability diminishes and variability increases. Variability also increases, in this area, when the decisionmaker is a judge or lawyer, but not by as large an amount. Jennifer K. Robbennolt, *Evaluating Juries by Comparison to Judges: a Benchmark for Judging*?, 32 Fla. St. U. L. Rev. 469 (2005).The central problem here appears to be the absence of any clear guideline to assist the fact finder in assessing damages, especially non-economic damages. See Michael J. Saks et al., *Reducing Variability in Civil Jury Awards*, 21 Law & Hum. Behav. 243, 252 (1997); Joseph Sanders, *Reforming General Damages: A Good Tort Reform,* 13 Roger Williams U. L. Rev. 115 (2008).

Professor Neil Vidmar, analyzing the empirical evidence about jury awards in the medical malpractice area, concludes that the data do "not support the widely made claims that jury damage awards are based on the depths of defendants' pockets, sympathies for plaintiffs, caprice, or excessive generosity." Neil Vidmar, MEDICAL MALPRACTICE AND THE AMERICAN JURY 259 (1995); Neil Vidmar, *The Performance of the American Civil Jury: An Empirical Perspective*, 40 Ariz. L. Rev. 849, 868 (1998).

f. Juries as Decisionmakers About Expert Scientific and Technical Information

A common concern is that juries are confused and misled by expert testimony on complex issues, such as scientific causation, statistics, and economics. One fear is that juries are unable to distinguish between their impressions of the expert and the substantive meaning of the testimony. Sanja Kutnjak Ivkovi & Valerie P. Hans, *Jurors' Evaluations of Expert Testimony: Judging the Messenger and the Message*, 28 Law & Soc. Inquiry (2003) present research showing that jurors "consider both the messenger and the message in the course of evaluating the expert's credibility." Various studies have focused on how well juries make decisions about liability, causation, and damages in these complex cases. For instance, Professor Sanders conducted interviews with members of the jury in a Bendectin case, which involved difficult issues of causation. His study revealed a "substantial spread" among the jurors with respect to their ability to understand the scientific evidence; unsurprisingly, jurors with more education or more skilled occupations had a better understanding. *See* Joseph Sanders, BENDECTIN ON TRIAL: A STUDY OF MASS TORT LITIGATION (1998).

Other studies show that jurors have trouble with statistical evidence, especially with understanding the process of reasoning from "base rates" of disease (such as epidemiological studies that look at rates of disease in exposed versus unexposed populations). Neil Vidmar, *The Performance of the American Civil Jury: An Empirical Perspective*, 40 Ariz. L. Rev. 849, 859 (1998). However, judges also are prone to having difficulties in this area. Reid Hastie & W. Kip Viscusi, *What Juries Can't Do Well: The Jury's Performance as a Risk Manager*, 40 Ariz. L. Rev. 901, 917 (1998); Chris Guthrie et al., *Inside the Judicial Mind*, 86 Cornell L. Rev. 777, 808 (2001).

When jurors, or indeed anyone, is confronted with a problem, they may chose to decide based on the evidence for and against a proposition. This is commonly called central processing. On the other hand, they may decide based on other factors such as the credentials or status of the individual arguing for a position. This is commonly called peripheral processing. Peripheral processing per se is not necessarily a bad thing. When judges decide about the admissibility of certain testimony based on the opinions of the experts in the field about its reliability, this is a form of peripheral processing that seems quite legitimate. On the other hand, were a jury to decide to believe an expert based solely on the expert's presentational style, many would find this to be a less legitimate type of peripheral processing. There is some evidence that as decisions become more difficult people, including jurors retreat to peripheral processing, not always in a particularly legitimate way. See Joel Cooper & Isaak M. Neuhaus, *The "Hired Gun" Effect: Assessing the Effect of Pay, Frequency of Testifying, and Credentials on the Perception of Expert Testimony*, 24 Law & Hum. Behav. 149 (2000); Daniel A. Krauss & Bruce D. Sales, *The Effects of Clinical and Scientific Expert Testimony on Juror Decision Making in Capital Sentencing*, 7 Psychol. Pub. Pol'y & L. 267 (2002); Eugene Morgulis, *Juror Reactions to Scientific Testimony: Unique Challenges in Complex Mass Torts*, 15 B.U. J. Sci. & Tech. L. 252 (2009). But see Neil Vidmar & Shari S. Diamond, *Juries and Expert Evidence*, 66 Brook. L. Rev. 1121 (2001).

Proposals to assist juries in this task often involve changing the way expert testimony is presented to the jury. See Samuel R. Gross, *Expert Evidence*, 1991 Wis. L. Rev. 1113; Christopher Tarver Robertson, *Blind Expertise*, 85 N.Y.U. L. Rev. 174 (2010).

g. Uncertainty and Overdeterrence

A critical though sometimes overlooked issue is the level of uncertainty that the tort system creates for individuals and corporations as they make decisions about which activities to engage in, which safety-related precautions to adopt, and how much liability insurance to purchase (or how to self-insure). If actors are highly uncertain about whether and for how much they will be liable for a given action, then this uncertainty obviously interferes both with optimal deterrence and with optimal insurance. Even liability insurers, whose very livelihood depends on risk, dislike unpredictable or uncertain liability:

> Insurers do not support abolition of liability, for liability is their business. Many do not even object in principle to growth in liability. In this respect, they (partly) resemble attorneys. However, they vehemently object to unpredictable change, for they have to pay for the changed risk from unchanged, previously collected premiums. The two types of uncertainty that they appear to dislike the most are (1) tort law's unlimited damages and (2) its propensity to change legal rules over time with what appears to them to be essentially retroactive effect.

Randall R. Bovbjerg, *Liability and Liability Insurance: Chicken and Egg, Destructive Spiral, or Risk and Reaction?*, 72 Tex. L. Rev. 1655, 1668 (1994).

If actors resolve uncertainty by assuming error in favor of the victim (incorrect liability findings or excessive damage awards), then actors might be "overdeterred"; that is, fail to engage in risky though socially desirable conduct or engage in risk-reduction whose costs outweigh its benefits. And the price of liability insurance will increase as well. Disagreement persists about whether tort law has overdeterred in various areas, such as medical practice, aviation, pharmaceuticals, and products in general. Some argue that the withdrawal or limited availability of certain goods and services, e.g. vaccines, reflects overdeterrence. *See* THE LIABILITY MAZE; THE IMPACT OF LIABILITY LAW ON SAFETY AND INNOVATION (PETER W. HUBER & ROBERT E. LITAN EDS. 1991); George L. Priest, *The Current Insurance Crisis and Modern Tort Law*, 96 Yale L.J. 1521 (1986). Others offer a different view. They argue that the reduction of certain goods and services instead reflects that consumers were no longer willing to pay the full cost of the product or service once tort law forced consumers to internalize the full cost of the product. *See* Steven P. Croley & Jon D. Hanson, *What Liability Crisis? An Alternative Explanation for Recent Events in Products Liability*, 8 Yale J. Reg. 1, 84–90 (1991).

The overdeterrence debate is often conducted around the issue of defensive medicine, i.e. the alleged tendency of physicians to order more tests and other procedures than are medically justified as a way to insure against adverse malpractice verdicts. for fear of litigation. Early research indicated that differences in malpractice risk may have a substantial effect on the practice of defensive medicine but later research shows a more modest effect. *See* Daniel Kessler & Mark McClellan, *Do Doctors Practice Defensive Medicine?* 111 Quarterly Journal of Economics 931 (1996); David Dranove & Yasutora Watanabe, *Influence and Deterrence: How Obstetricians Respond to Litigation Against Themselves and Their Colleagues*, 12 Am. L. & Econ. Rev. 69 (2010); Tom Baker, THE MEDICAL MALPRACTICE MYTH (2005). And as Baker points out, "[N]one of the researchers who have studied defensive medicine have claimed that they are able to separate the wasteful effects of malpractice lawsuits from the good, injury-prevention effects." Baker, p. 119.

A related debate is whether litigation deters physicians from entering high-risk specialities. Studies exploring this question have produced ambiguous results. *See* Jonathan Klick & Thomas Stratmann, *Medical Malpractice Reform and Physicians in High–Risk Specialties*, 36 J. Legal Stud. S121 (2007); David A. Matsa, *Does Malpractice Liability Keep the Doctor Away? Evidence from Tort Reform Damage Caps*, 36 J. Legal Stud. S143 (2007).

h. High Transaction Costs

There is general agreement that the tort system is expensive to administer. According to one respected study, each dollar expended on auto tort litigation was divided as follows: 52 cents in net compensation to the claimant; 24 cents to plaintiff's legal fees and expenses; 13 cents to defendants' fees and expenses; and 13 cents to various other costs. Non-auto tort liability cases delivered even less to victims: 43 cents was paid to the plaintiff in compensation; 20 cents went to plaintiff's legal fees and expenses; 18 cents went to defendants' fees and expenses; and 20 cents was absorbed by other costs. Deborah R. Hensler, *et al.*, TRENDS IN TORT LITIGATION: THE STORY BEHIND THE STATISTICS 26–29 (1987). In asbestos cases, even less went to plaintiffs and more to transaction costs. The large percentage of funds going to transaction costs is reflected in mass torts as well. Howard M. Erichson & Benjamin C. Zipersky, *Consent Versus*

Closure, 96 Cornell L. Rev. 265 (2011) report that, "Of the roughly $7 billion Merck will have spent on the Vioxx litigation, approximately $3.5 billion will have been on attorneys' fees (including roughly $2 billion for defense litigation fees)."

By contrast, first-party insurance (such as medical and private disability), and social insurance such as social security disability, deliver to the insured a far greater percentage of each dollar expended by the system. Thus, if the tort system is justified solely on an insurance rationale, it is too expensive. The high administrative overhead of the tort system must be justified on the basis of deterrence or corrective justice rationales.

i. Insurance Availability and Affordability

Policymakers have given much attention to several "crises" of insurance availability and affordability. The first occurred in the mid–1970s in the context of medical malpractice liability insurance. Numerous medical malpractice insurers withdrew from some state markets or raised prices significantly; some physicians could not find insurance at any price; and some doctors as a result slowed down certain medical services and lobbied for emergency legislation. Most states passed tort reform legislation aimed at alleviating the crisis.

The immediate crisis abated within two years as a result of several factors: new physician-run insurance associations entered the market; many states mandated that other private insurers participate in "joint underwriting associations" that provide coverage to physicians unable to procure it otherwise; there was a decline in the degree to which claims filing increased; and insurance increasingly was written on a "claims-made" rather than "occurrence" basis. Claims-made policies cover only claims that are made during the year of coverage; occurrence policies provide coverage for any malpractice incident that occurred during the year of coverage. Suppose, for instance, that an insurer provides occurrence-based coverage for the year of 1970. The patient does not discover her impairment until 1973, sues in 1974 (given a "discovery" exception to the normal two-year statute of limitations), and receives a settlement in 1976. The insurer must cover the settlement. The "long tail" nature of much medical malpractice liability (the long time between occurrence, discovery, and claim recovery) means that occurrence-based exposures are harder to predict.

For more detail on the medical malpractice crisis, *see* Patricia Danzon, MEDICAL MALPRACTICE: THEORY, EVIDENCE, AND PUBLIC POLICY (1985); Frank A. Sloan, Randall R. Bovbjerg & Penny B. Githens, INSURING MEDICAL MALPRACTICE (1991); Paul Weiler, MEDICAL MALPRACTICE ON TRIAL (1991).

A second insurance crisis occurred in the mid–1980s and involved not just medical malpractice in particular but also the general commercial general liability insurance market for products and services across the economy. Premiums rose sharply in this period; coverage reportedly became unavailable at any price as to certain products and services (such as IUDs and day care), forcing the withdrawal of some goods and services altogether. Forty-six states passed tort reform legislation aimed at responding to the crisis. *See* Joseph Sanders & Craig Joyce, *"Off to the Races": The 1980s Tort Crisis and the Law Reform Process* 27 Hou. L. Rev. 207 (1990).

Within several years, there was a slowdown in the rapid rise of insurer losses and premium increases. But many contend that high premiums and reduced availability of insurance are still basic features of the landscape, resulting in higher prices for, and reduced availability of, products and services.

Less disagreement exists now than in the past over the origins of the insurance crises. Some have persuasively argued that the problems largely resulted from insurance "cycles" (aggressively underwriting new risks at times of high interest on premium investment). See Tom Baker, *Medical Malpractice and the Insurance Underwriting Cycle*, 54 DePaul L. Rev. 393 (2005). There now seems to be less support for the explanation offered by a 1986 Department of Justice Report: that the crisis resulted from sharp increases in the number of tort claims filed and in the number of plaintiff recoveries. *See* REPORT OF THE TORT POLICY WORKING GROUP ON THE CAUSES, EXTENT AND POLICY IMPLICATIONS OF THE CURRENT CRISIS IN INSURANCE AVAILABILITY AND AFFORDABILITY (1986). Nevertheless, it undoubtedly is the case that hard insurance medical malpractice markets have played an important role in driving tort reform. Tom Baker, *The Shifting Terrain of Risk and Uncertainty on the Liability Insurance Field*, 60 DePaul L. Rev. 521 (2011).

Regardless of tort law's role in insurances crises, some have argued that it is a mistake to view tort law as an appropriate insurance mechanism, rather than a means of achieving deterrence. *See* George L. Priest, *The Current Insurance Crisis and Modern Tort Law*, 96 Yale L.J. 1521 (1986). Professor Priest argues that, since tort law is inferior to first-party insurance sources as an insurance mechanism, tort doctrines cannot and should not be justified in light of an insurance goal. Rather, tort liability doctrines can and should be justified only in light of the deterrence aim. For a contrary view, see Steven P. Croley & Jon D. Hanson, *What Liability Crisis? An Alternative Explanation for Recent Events in Products Liability*, 8 Yale J. Reg. 1, 9 (1991). Interestingly, Baker argues that the medical malpractice insurance underwriting cycle may promote patient safety by drawing attention to the problem of medical malpractice in a manner that makes medical liability more salient and induces greater efforts to prevent medical injuries.

2. LEGISLATIVE TORT REFORM

a. The Reforms

In the states. The first wave of legislative tort reform, which occurred in the mid–1970s, was primarily in response to the perceived liability-insurance crisis stemming from medical malpractice, and the reforms usually related specifically to that area. The second wave of tort reform, consisting of legislation passed by over forty states in the mid–1980s, applied more generally.

Although over forty states passed reform legislation in 1986, that year does not mark the end of the reform movement. Rather, many states have passed additional measures in the past few years, and calls for further tort reform continue at the state level.

The most commonly enacted tort reforms are the following: caps on nonpecuniary damages (generally in the range of $250,000 to $500,000); modification of the collateral source rule under which an individual's recovery is not reduced based on funds the individual receives from collateral sources such as health insurance; elimination of, or modifications to joint and several liability; restrictions on punitive damages; and changes in the substantive standards governing product liability claims. Other reforms enacted by some states include: sanctions for filing frivolous suits; limits on attorneys' contingency fees; class action reforms; and provisions encouraging or requiring the periodic payment of judgments. The American Tort Reform Association, a pro-tort reform organization, keeps a running tab on the reforms enacted in each state. *See* http://www.atra.org/.

Still on the tort reformers' national and state agendas are the following desired changes: complete abolition of joint and several liability; national product liability reform, including a "governmental compliance defense"; restrictions on contingency fees; national caps on non-pecuniary damages in medical malpractice.

At the Federal level. At the federal level, a number of tort reform bills have been introduced over the years, including many efforts to provide for an administrative solution to the asbestos crisis. However, there has been little action at the federal level and it seems unlikely that anything of major significance will occur on this front in the near future.

One exception is the passage of the Class Action Fairness Act, which expands federal diversity jurisdiction for class action cases. The federal diversity statute has been amended so that district courts have original jurisdiction over civil class action cases, before or after the entry of a class certification order, involving (1) an aggregate amount in controversy in excess of $5,000,000, exclusive of interest and costs, and (2) diversity of citizenship between one plaintiff class member and one defendant, instead of complete diversity between all plaintiffs and all defendants. 28 U.S.C.A. § 1332. Because federal class certification requirements are higher than those in a number of states, the act tends to favor defendants in large class actions.

Another set of developments at the federal level merits attention. This is the passage, over the past 15 years, of a number of statutes that carve out a specific area of potential tort liability and create federal standards for liability and compensation. These statutes generally preempt state tort law. For discussion and analysis, *see* Perry H. Apelbaum & Samara T. Ryder, *The Third Wave of Federal Tort Reform: Protecting the Public or Pushing the Constitutional Envelope?*, 8 Cornell J. Law & Pub. Pol'y 591 (1999). Examples are:

— General Aviation Revitalization Act of 1994, 49 U.S.C. § 40101 (2003). This includes an 18–year federal statute of repose for those who manufacture "general aviation aircraft"; the statute includes several exceptions, including cases when the manufacturer has misrepresented safety information to the Federal Aviation Administration.

— The Volunteer Protection Act of 1997, 42 U.S.C. §§ 14501 et seq. (2003). This exempts from negligence liability individuals who volunteer for nonprofit organizations or government agencies; the exemption does not apply to volunteers acting outside the scope of their responsibility; volunteers who act without a required license, certification, or authorization; or harm caused by a motor vehicle. The Act also: allows punitive damages only if plaintiff establishes by clear and convincing evidence that the harm was caused by willful misconduct, criminal misconduct, or conscious and flagrant indifference to safety; eliminates joint and several liability for non-economic damages.

— The Bill Emerson Good Samaritan Food Donation Act of 1996, 42 U.S.C. § 1791 (2003). This exempts from tort liability persons who donate food and grocery products to nonprofits to give to the needy; the nonprofits also are exempted. The exemption applies if the food is "apparently wholesome" and if grocery products "apparently fit" (that is, the products meet quality and labeling standards). In addition, the Act exempts from liability a person who donates food and grocery products that do not meet applicable quality and labeling standards as long as the nonprofit organization is informed of this, agrees to remedy the defect, and has the knowledge to do so.

— The Biomaterials Access Assurance Act of 1998, 21 U.S.C. § 1601 (2003). This Act applies to suppliers of raw materials and medical implant component parts. If these parties meet certain contractual and product requirements, they can be dismissed from product liability actions.

b. The Effects of the Reforms

There now exists a substantial body of empirical research on the effects of tort reforms. Some results are fairly well established but the research produces contradictory results with respect to a number of issues. More empirical information is available about medical tort reforms than general tort reform. The research has focused on two basic, interrelated questions: a) what impact have reforms had on various outcomes, and b) which reforms have had the greatest impact?

An early important study by Patricia Danzon, examined the effects of the medical malpractice tort reforms of the mid–1970s. She found that several reforms had an appreciable effect on the number of claims filed: alterations of the collateral source rule and tighter controls on the statute of limitations (that is, eliminating or greatly restricting the "discovery rule" exception to the usual two-year statute of limitations). Several reforms appreciably reduced the amounts paid out on claims: caps on non-economic damages, alterations of the collateral source rule, and arbitration procedures. Patricia M. Danzon, NEW EVIDENCE ON THE FREQUENCY AND SEVERITY OF MEDICAL MALPRACTICE CLAIMS (1986). Subsequent research, much of which is described below, confirm that caps on non-economic damages and changes in joint and several liability rules have had the greatest impact on recoveries.

The number of tort filings appears to have declined in the 2000s. Patricia W. Hatamyar, *The Effects of "Tort Reform" on Tort Case Filings*, 43 Val. U. L. Rev. 559 (2009); Nat'l Ctr. for State Courts, Examining the Work of State Courts, 2002: A National Perspective from the Court Statistics Project 23–29 (Brian J. Ostrom et al. eds., 2003). As we noted above, however, interpreting such findings is very difficult in the absence of data on injury rates. In this regard, the tort system may usefully be thought of as a disputing pyramid as diagramed in the following figure.

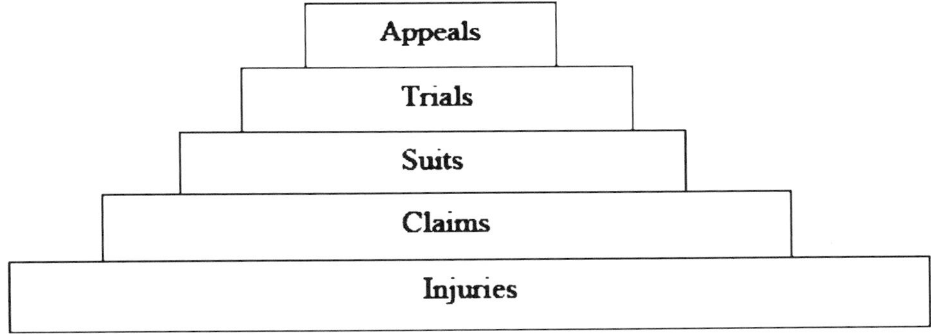

The bottom tier of the pyramid is the number of injuries occurring in the jurisdiction in a relevant time period. Note, this tier is designed to reflect injuries, i.e., those events that might give rise to a claim against someone. Above injuries are claims, but of course all claims to not lead to the filing of a lawsuit. Thus, in order to properly interpret changing filing rates we need to know something about the underlying injury rate and how it might have changed over the relevant time span. We also need to know something about the transition rate between injuries and claims and then again the transition rate between claims and suits, i.e. the percentage of claims that ripen into a suit. Thus, while it is tempting to attribute a decline in filings to tort reform, we rarely have sufficient information about the entire pyramid to do so with any confidence. The one exception is in the malpractice area where, as we noted above, several large studies do indicate that the transition rate from injury to claim is low, on the order of 10 to 20 percent. However, there is good reason to believe this transition rate is much higher in other areas such as automobile accidents. For more complete discussions of the disputing pyramid, *see* Michael J.

Saks, *Do We Really Know Anything About the Behavior of the Tort Litigation System—And Why Not?*, 140 U.Pa.L.Rev. 1147, 1216–20 (1992); Joseph Sanders & Craig Joyce, *"Off to the Races": The 1980s Tort Crisis and the Law Reform Process* 27 Hou. L. Rev. 207 (1990). Because of this lack of information, Professor Eisenberg has called for a national survey of injury rates and claiming behavior. Theodore Eisenberg, *The Need For a National Civil Justice Survey of Incidence and Claiming Behavior*, 37 Fordham Urb. L.J. 17 (2010).

As we also noted above, one important question is whether tort law causes physicians to practice defensive medicine and, if so whether tort reform reduces the extent of this behavior. Unfortunately, as we also noted above, the extent of defensive medicine is difficult to measure and, therefore, it is not surprising that persuasive evidence on the effect of tort reform on this practice is even more elusive. See Randall R. Bovbjerg, *et al., Defensive Medicine and Tort Reform: New Evidence in an Old Bottle*, 21 J. Health Pol. Pol'y & L. 267, 282–83 (1996); Michelle M. Mello & Troyen A. Brennan, *Deterrence of Medical Errors: Theory and Evidence for Malpractice Reform*, 80 Tex. L. Rev. 1595, 1610 (2002) (arguing that studies of defensive medicine have been inconclusive). More recent research has focused on the question of whether caps on non-economic damages reduces the level of defensive medicine. The results are mixed. *Compare* Frank A. Sloan & John H. Shadle, *Is There Empirical Evidence for "Defensive Medicine"? A Reassessment*, 28 J. Health Econ. 481, 481 (2009) (no) *with* Daniel P. Kessler & Mark B. McClellan, *How Liability Law Affects Medical Productivity*, 21 J. Health Econ. 931, 932 (2002) (yes). *See generally* Vasanthakumar N. Bhat, MEDICAL MALPRACTICE (2001)

Are doctors more likely to gravitate toward states with tort reform and away from states without tort reform? Again, there are no clear answers. The Bovbjerg study found that damage caps in Indiana did not seem to increase physician supply. David A. Matsa, *Does Malpractice Liability Keep the Doctor Away? Evidence From Tort Reform Damage Caps*, 36 J. Legal Stud. S143 (2007) confirmed this general conclusion but did find that caps did have an effect on the speciality physician supply in rural areas. On the other hand studies by Michelle Mello & Carly Kelly, *Effects of a Professional Liability Crisis on Residents' Practice Decisions*, 106 Obstetrics and Gynecology 1287 (2005) and Daniel Kessler, et al., *Impact of Malpractice Reforms on the Supply of Physician Services*. 293 J. Amer. Med. Assn. 2618 (2005) find an effect. The latter study finds that "direct reforms led to increased growth in the supply of emergency medicine physicians of approximately 11.5%" *Id.* at 2622. *See also* Joanna Shepherd, *Tort Reforms' Winners and Losers: The Competing Effects of Care and Activity Levels,* 55 UCLA L. Rev. 905 (2008).

Still another question is the effect of reforms on the frequency and size of malpractice awards. Here, as in much of the literature discussed above, the largest effect is produced by caps on non-economic damages and, to a lesser extent limitations on joint and several liability. Vidmar reports a reduction in mean and median tort awards in at least some areas. Neil Vidmar, *The Performance of the American Civil Jury: An Empirical Perspective*, 40 Ariz. L. Rev. 849, 878 (1998). Other research confirms that certain tort reforms, especially caps on non-economic loss and restrictions on joint and several liability have reduced average malpractice settlements. Ronen Avraham, *An Empirical Study of the Impact of Tort Reforms on Medical Malpractice Settlement Payments,* 36 J. Legal Stud. 183 (2007). *See also*, Charles R. Ellington, et al., *State Tort Reforms and Hospital Malpractice Costs*, 38 J. L. Med. & Ethics 127 (2010) (finding that caps on non-economic damages are associated with significantly lower average hospital malpractice costs per bed.) Insofar as this has occurred, in large part it is probably due to mandated reductions in jury awards. David Hyman, et al., *Estimating the Effect of Damage Caps in Medical Malpractice Cases: Evidence From Texas*, 1 J. of Legal Analysis S9 (2009) estimate that in Texas caps resulted in a 73% reduction in non-economic damage awards. Other studies reporting reforms lowered malpractice costs include Glenn Blackmon & Richard Zeckhauser, *State Tort Reform Legislation: Assessing Our Control of Risks*, in Tort Law and the Public Interest 272, 273 (Peter H. Schuck, ed. 1991); Albert Yoon, *Damage Caps and Civil Litigation: An Empirical Study of Medical Malpractice Litigation in the South,* 3 Amer, L. & Econ. Rev. 199 (2001) (damage caps reduced total awards 28% in Alabama); David M. Studdert et al., *Are Damages Caps Regressive? A Study of Malpractice Jury Verdicts in California*, 23 Health Aff. 54, 57 (2007) (caps reduced total awards 34% in California); Patricia W. Hatamyar, *The Effect of "Tort Reform" on Tort Case Filings*, 43 Val. L. Rev. 559 (2009). With respect to a slightly different question, Christine Durrance, *Noneconomic Damage Caps and Medical Malpractice Claim Frequencey: A Policy Endogeneity Approach*, 26 J. of Law, Econ. & Org. 569 (2010) found that caps did not alter claim frequency.

Some studies report that certain tort reforms will have a disparate impact on women. The authors contend that limiting recoveries for punitive damages and noneconomic damages in medical malpractice and medical device litigation adversely affect women because women more often than men receive such damage awards. Thomas Koenig & Michael Rustad, *His and Her Tort Reform: Gender Injustice in Disguise*, 70 Wash. L. Rev. 1 (1995); Lucinda M. Finley, *The Hidden Victims of Tort Reform: Women, Children, and the Elderly*, 53 Emory L.J. 1263 (2004). The data reported in these studies are open to various interpretations, however. *See* Joseph Sanders, *Reforming General Damages: A Good Tort Reform,* 13 Roger Williams U. L. Rev. 115, 138–139 (2008).

The careful reader may have surmised by now that the reforms enacted in the states do not always speak directly to the problems uncovered in earlier research and often do not seem to be the best way to address specific issues. Take, for example, the most "effective" reform, caps on non-economic damages. Statutory caps have been enacted in a majority of the states. Lee Harris, *Tort Reform as Carrot and Stick*, 46 Harv. J. on Legis. 163 (2009). Insofar as they are a response to the variability in jury awards, they are a very blunt instrument, the effects of which fall disproportionately on the most seriously injured individuals, the very individuals that research indicates are the most under compensated by the tort system. It is not surprising, therefore, that many observers have argued the reforms are not well tailored to the larger problems confronting tort law. *See* Robert Rabin, *Some Reflections on the Process of Tort Reform*, 25 San Diego L. Rev.13 (1988); Joseph Sanders & Craig Joyce, *"Off To The Races": The 1980s Tort Crisis and the Law Reform Process*, 27 Hous. L. Rev. 207 (1990); Paul C. Weiler, MEDICAL MALPRACTICE ON TRIAL 50 (1991).

3. CONSTITUTIONAL CHALLENGES TO TORT REFORM LEGISLATION

A number of lawsuits have challenged the constitutionality of tort reform legislation under the respective state constitutions. Several state supreme courts have struck down various tort reforms on this ground; others have upheld the reforms in question. For cases striking down tort reforms, *see* Best v. Taylor Machine Works, 179 Ill.2d 367, 228 Ill.Dec. 636, 689 N.E.2d 1057 (1997); Smothers v. Gresham Transfer, Inc., 332 Or. 83, 23 P.3d 333 (2001). For cases upholding specific tort reforms, *see* Phillips v. Mirac, Inc., 251 Mich.App. 586, 651 N.W.2d 437 (2002); Guzman v. St. Francis Hospital, Inc., 240 Wis.2d 559, 623 N.W.2d 776 (App.2000); Scholz v. Metropolitan Pathologists, P.C., 851 P.2d 901 (Colo. 1993) (en banc); Murphy v. Edmonds, 325 Md. 342, 601 A.2d 102 (1992). Generalizations about this area are difficult because state constitutions differ in content and historical background. Most constitutional challenges, however, center on various states' equal protection clauses, due process clauses, and clauses often termed an "open courts" provision which state that the courts of the state shall remain open to all citizens of the state.

Ohio offers a particularly interesting interaction between the legislature and the courts that extended over two decades. The Ohio Constitution contains the following provisions:

> Art. I, sec. 2—Equal Protection:
>
> All political power is inherent in the people. Government is instituted for their equal protection and benefit, and they have the right to alter, reform, or abolish the same, whenever they may deem it necessary.
>
> Art. I, sec. 5—Trial by Jury:
>
> The right of trial by jury shall be inviolate, except that, in civil cases laws may be passed to authorize the rendering of a verdict by the concurrence of no less than three-fourths of the jury.
>
> Art. I, sec. 16—Open Courts/Right to Remedy/Due Process:
>
> All courts shall be open, and every person for an injury done him in his land, goods, person or reputation, shall have remedy by due course of law....

How should one apply these particular provisions to tort reform efforts? In a series of cases in the mid to late 1990s the Ohio Supreme Court struck down a number of tort reform provisions because they were held to infringe on the jury's fact finding role and because they violated the plaintiff's right to trial by jury. Moreover, it held that the statutes denied due process because there was insufficient evidence of a relationship between tort reform and affordable medical malpractice insurance. See Galayda v. Lake Hosp. Sys. Inc., 71 Ohio St.3d 421, 644 N.E.2d 298 (1994); Zoppo v. Homestead Ins. Co., 71 Ohio St.3d 552, 644 N.E.2d 397 (1994); State ex rel. Ohio Acad. of Trial Lawyers v. Sheward, 86 Ohio St.3d 451, 715 N.E.2d 1062 (1999). However, in Arbino v. Johnson & Johnson, 116 Ohio St.3d 468, 880 N.E.2d 420 (2007), in the face of still another legislative effort to enact tort reform, the court relented. It held that 2004 enactments limiting non-economic and punitive damages in tort actions are facially constitutional. Ohio Revised Code §§ 2315.18, 2315.21. For interesting discussions of this long-drawn-out contest between the legislative and judicial branches *see* Symposium, *Ohio: A Microcosm of Tort Reform versus State Constitutional Mandates*, 32 Rutgers L.J. 1045 (2001); Symposium, *Tort Liability, the Structural Constitution, and the States*, 31 Seton Hall L. Rev. 563 (2001); Kara Lee Monahan. *State Constitutional Law—Tort Reform—Supreme Court of Ohio Reverses Course and Upholds Limits on Noneconomic and Punitive Damages as Constitutional*, 40 Rutgers L.J. 953 (2009). For a discussion of how possible future federal tort reforms might fare under federal constitutional analysis, *see* Betsy J. Grey, *The New Federalism Jurisprudence and National Tort Reform*, 59 Wash. & Lee L. Rev. 475 (2002).

4. LEGISLATION ALLOWING OR ENCOURAGING OPTING OUT OF TORT IN EXCHANGE FOR AN ALTERNATIVE PACKAGE OF BENEFITS (INCLUDING THE SEPTEMBER 11TH VICTIM COMPENSATION FUND)

a. Opt–Out Plans

An additional feature of the changing tort landscape is legislation that allows or encourages plaintiffs to "opt out" of tort law at some point, in exchange for a package of benefits. Within this general category are a number of approaches:

— An early offer system under which a defendant may make a plaintiff an offer to pay for the full economic costs (medical, rehabilitative, lost earning capacity) of the plaintiff's injury; if plaintiff does not accept the offer, plaintiff can still go forward with the case, but now will face additional obstacles, such as a higher standard of proof, a fee-shifting provision, etc. *See generally* Jeffrey O'Connell & Geoffrey Paul Eaton, *Binding Early Offers as a Simple, if Second Best, Alternative to Tort Law*, 78 Neb. L. Rev. 858 (1999). A number of bills to this effect have been introduced in state legislatures and in Congress.

For instance, Florida statutes provide that either a plaintiff or defendant may make an offer to enter into binding arbitration. If the defendant refuses the plaintiff's offer to arbitrate and if the plaintiff prevails at trial the plaintiff will be entitled to reasonable attorney's fees up to 25 percent of the award reduced to present value.If the plaintiff rejects a defendant's offer to settle, then the plaintiff's damages will be limited to no more than $350,000. *See* Fla. Stat. Ch. 766.209(3)(4). New Jersey rules for compulsory auto liability insurance now provide that an individual may select either of two tort options: (1) opting out of coverage for nonpecuniary damages, so that the insured will not be able to recover for noneconomic damages and will not be liable for such damages to any individual also selecting this coverage; or (2) opting for the right to recover noneconomic damages, but also being liable for such damages to other drivers. *See* N.J. Rev. Stat. § 39:6A–8 (2003).

— Legislation that creates a no-fault compensation program for claimants who fit certain criteria; such claimants can opt for the no-fault package of benefits, or can instead choose to bring a tort claim. The compensation system that Congress passed soon after the September 11 attacks, designed to compensate individuals who were present at the World Trade Center, Pentagon, or Shanksville, Pennsylvania, falls into this category and will be discussed shortly. Earlier examples of such a system include the National Childhood Vaccine Injury Act of 1986 (the Vaccine Act), and no-fault medical schemes enacted by Virginia and Florida for babies who are born with severe brain or neurological damage.

The National Childhood Vaccine Injury Act, 42 U.S.C. §§ 300aa–1 et seq. provides no-fault compensation benefits to a narrow category of victims: children injured by exposure to particular government-mandated vaccines. The Act is financed by an excise tax on each dose of vaccine given. If the injured claimant pursues the statutory remedy, a special master gathers the evidence and renders a decision. The claimant must prove that he or she suffers an injury from a vaccine. Once the claimant makes this proof, he or she is entitled to no-fault benefits that consist of medical, rehabilitative, custodial, and counseling services, as well as lost income and lost earning capacity. U.S.C. § 300aa–15 (2003). Once the master renders a benefit decision, the claimant is entitled to reject it and pursue tort remedies instead. But, if the claimant chooses the tort route, he will face several obstacles, including the "learned intermediary doctrine" (which requires the manufacturer only to give adequate warning to the learned intermediary, such as the doctor) and immunity of the manufacturer from punitive damages if it complied with federal legislation. Few vaccine victims who are awarded compensation under the Act reject the statutory benefits and opt for a tort remedy. One early analysis concluded that the Act has "achieved its goal of protecting the nation's vaccine supplies while providing compensation for the unavoidable injuries resulting from the administration of vaccines. * * * " Theodore H. Davis, Jr. & Catherine B. Bowman, *No–Fault Compensation for Unavoidable Injuries: Evaluating the National Childhood Vaccine Injury Compensation*

Program, 16 U. Dayton L. Rev. 277, 279 (1991). More recently the program has come under substantial pressure by parents claiming their child's autism is a result of vaccines or mercury based additives to vaccines. However, these claims have met with no success before the Court of Federal Claims, which hears appeals from the special masters who act as judges with respect to claims under the Act. *See e.g.*, Snyder ex rel. Snyder v. Secretary of Health and Human Services, 88 Fed.Cl. 706 (2009). The controversy highlights the fact that although claimants need not prove fault they must still present evidence establishing a causal link between a vaccine and an injury. *See* Brandon L. Boxler, *What to do With Daubert: How to Bring Standards of Reliable Scientific Evidence to the National Vaccine Injury Compensation Program*, 52 Wm. & Mary L. Rev. 1319 (2011). Note that in Bruesewitz v. Wyeth LLC, ___ U.S. ___, 131 S.Ct. 1068, 179 L.Ed.2d 1 (2011) the Supreme Court concluded that the Act preempts state law design defect claims, thereby reducing the viability of any opt-out solution on the part of those injured by vaccines.

b. The September 11 Victim Compensation Fund

The most well-known of the opt-out approaches is the September 11 Victim Compensation Fund. The statute creating this fund was passed on September 22, 2001, only 11 days after the terrorist attacks; the fund was one part of the statute titled the "Air Transportation Safety and System Stabilization Act." 49 U.S.C. § 40101 (2003). The fund was designed as a no-fault alternative to tort litigation for all eligible claimants. Those who chose to file a claim for compensation under the fund waived any right to file a civil action (or be a party to any civil action) in any federal or state court for any damages resulting from the attacks (aside from suits against the terrorists or conspirators or suits seeking to recover from collateral sources—for instance, a suit against an insurer for failing to pay disability insurance).

The Act itself was scanty on the details, and provided that a Special Master appointed by the Attorney General would "administer the compensation program," "promulgate all procedural and substantive rules for administration" of the program, and employ the hearing officers and other persons necessary for implementation. The Attorney General Appointed Kenneth R. Feinberg as the special master and in March 2002 issued the final rule for the terms of recovery, 28 C.F.R. Pt. 104.

The final rule varied in important ways from the ordinary operation of the tort system. Awards were reduced by the amount of "all collateral source compensation." This includes pension plans, life insurance, death benefits, disability insurance. For deceased victim, lost earnings calculations were tied to actual income, but only up to the ninety-eighth percentile of individual income in the United States. Non-economic damage recoveries were governed by a "presumptive award methodology" under which presumed *non-economic* loss, for deceased victims, is $250,000 plus an additional $100,000 for the spouse and each dependent. For physical injury claimants, the presumed non-economic loss is an amount determined by the special master, who relies on the presumptive non-economic losses for death and then may adjust these amounts depending on the extent of the victim's physical harm. The result of the non-economic loss rules was to substantially shrink variability in non-economic damage awards.

In all of these ways, the compensation fund was at variance with the "individualized justice" ideal of the tort system where each case is to be judged on its own merits and not in comparison with other awards. As we discuss below, this tradeoff between certainty and no need to show fault on the one hand and fixed limited payments on the other hand is typical of all non-tort plans. What are the pros and cons of each of these variations from common law recoveries—collateral source, economic damage limitation, and lack of variability in non-economic damage—in the September 11 context?

Ultimately, nearly all the 9/11 victims opted to take money from the fund rather than litigate and the fund awarded over $7 billion to 5560 victims and their families in the course of two years. Robert M. Ackerman, *The September 11th Victim Compensation Fund: An Effective Administrative Response to National Tragedy*, 10 Harv. Negot. L. Rev. 135, 227 (2005). Professor Mullenix infers from this that "it seems that rational people would select a modified regime—i.e., some aspects of tort reform—if they believed that such a regime would fairly and expeditiously compensate them for their injuries, even at the cost of forgoing potentially greater compensatory damages, windfall exemplary damages, and a jury trial." Linda S. Mullenix, *The Future of Tort Reform: Possible Lessons From the World Trade Center Victim Compensation Fund*, 53 Emory L.J. 1315, 1347 (2004). For a useful discussion of the process from the perspective of the Fund Special Master see Kenneth R. Feinberg, WHAT IS LIFE WORTH? THE UNPRECEDENTED EFFORT TO COMPENSATE THE VICTIMS OF 9/11 (2005).

One should note, however, that a handful of victims—approximately 100—refused money from the fund, primarily it seems because they felt that only through litigation could they achieve other goals, including: 1) getting information about what happened and what various entities such as the airlines or government agencies did and did not do prior to the attacks and 2) achieving accountability based on these factual findings. As two individuals who did not join the fund noted

> [Litigation] is one way of saying no, it wasn't just the terrorists. There was a lot of ordinary negligence that led to people's deaths.... It's not just about the facts; there is a need to bring those facts to accountability.... It's not about winning;.... It's about shining a very bright light on the facts.... I just want that to be a historical conclusion: more people could have been saved, there was truth.
>
> What I'm looking for is justice—someone held accountable for the murder. There are people who did not do their job. No one has been fired, demoted.

Gillian K. Hadfield, *Framing the Choice Between Cash and the Courthouse Experiences With the 9/11 Victim Compensation Fund,* 42 Law & Soc'y Rev. 645, 662 (2008). Given what you now know about the tort system in the United States, do you think these individuals had realistic views about what could be accomplished through litigation? Should Congress create a permanent fund for such disasters? See Betsy J. Grey, *Homeland Security and Federal Relief: A Proposal for a Permanent Compensation System for Domestic Terrorist Victims*, 9 N.Y.U. J. Legis. & Pub. Pol'y 663 (2005–2006). If so, how should it be structured? For a general criticism of the structure of the 9/11 Fund, *see* John G. Culhane, *Tort, Compensation, and Two Kinds of Justice*, 55 Rutgers L. Rev. 1027 (2003).

C. AN INTRODUCTION TO NONTORT COMPENSATION PROGRAMS

1. WHY STUDY NONTORT PROGRAMS?

The tort liability structure forms just one, albeit crucial, strand in the complex fabric that American society has developed for addressing the problems of injury and disease. Other strands include no-fault schemes such as workers' compensation and automobile no-fault; private first-party insurance sources such as health insurance, long-term care insurance, and disability insurance; social insurance such as social security disability insurance and the federal-state rehabilitation system; and federal and state "disability-rights" statutes mandating reasonable accommodation in employment settings, schools, etc.

Even if one were altogether satisfied with current American tort doctrine, these nontort programs would deserve attention because they represent a large proportion of the total dollars paid for illness and injury, and because they present intriguing and critical policy issues in their own right. According to one study, tort payments constitute only about 10% of all benefits paid for illness and injury; nontort sources (including private and social insurance and workers' compensation) account for the rest. *See* J. O'Connell & J. Guinivan, *An Irrational Combination: The Relative Expansion of Liability Insurance and Contraction of Loss Insurance*, 49 Ohio St. L.J. 757, 766 (1988).

Of course, there is much dissatisfaction with the traditional tort system, as the tort reform debates of the past twenty years attest. Therefore these nontort programs also have attracted attention because they represent potential models for more substantial tort reform. For instance, policymakers and legislatures, when considering the desirability of additional no-fault compensation schemes in the medical injury context, have looked to workers' compensation as at least a partial sketch of the potential benefits and drawbacks of such a scheme.

2. INJURY, DISEASE, AND DISABILITY

Because all the existing and proposed alternatives to traditional tort are aimed at addressing disabilities caused by injury or illness, we should consider at the outset some basic data about (1) injury, disease, and disability in the United States, and (2) what the sources and amounts of payments are for injury, disease, and disability.

An injury or disease might be so minor that it results in nothing but the most temporary of consequences, such as a scrape that heals within a day or a mild throat irritation that resolves within a week. Or injury and disease could lead to more substantial temporary or permanent consequences. Usually the terms "impairment" and "disability" are used to describe these consequences. Consider a serious knee injury that, for the first six weeks, prevents the individual from using the knee or leg at all. After surgery and rehabilitation, the knee eventually returns to a level of functioning, but will never have the strength or mobility it once had. Often the term "impairment" is used to refer to the person's organ-level or person-level reduced ability to function as measured by standard medical norms. For instance, the organ-level impairment would be the knee's reduced range of motion and strength; the person-level impairment would be the person's reduced mobility and capacity to bend or stoop.

The term "disability" often is used to refer to the consequences of the impairment on a particular person's life. For instance, the knee injury just described would produce a different level of disability for an accountant than for a professional tennis player. Both would have the same impairment, as measured by standard medical norms, but the consequences on work or social roles would be very different.

Reliable measures of impairment in the United States are difficult to obtain. If we focus just on impairments, then by some estimates half the United States population has some type of medical impairment. A more useful approach is to focus on disability and to define disability as the reduced ability or inability to function in some major life activity (such as going to school, working, or performing basic daily activities such as dressing and eating), due to impairment. The 2000 census indicated that approximately 9.7% of the population reported such disability. The 2009 Current Population Survey indicated that approximately 12% of the population report a disability and 8% report a disability leading to a work limitation. *See* Cornell Employment and Disability Institute, Disability Statistics at http://www.disabilitystatistics.org/.

3. PROGRAM CATEGORIES AND PURPOSES

When examining the disability fabric, it is helpful to realize that each of these compensation programs can be placed into one of three general categories, corresponding to the basis upon which the program awards compensation: fault, cause, or loss. Kenneth S. Abraham & Lance Liebman, *Private Insurance, Social Insurance, and Tort Reform: Toward a*

New Vision of Compensation for Illness and Injury, 93 Colum. L. Rev. 75 (1993).

Except for pockets of strict liability, tort represents a fault-based compensation approach. By contrast, cause-based compensation programs do not depend on a finding of fault, but they do limit benefits to losses resulting from particular causes. Examples include workers' compensation (which requires an injury or disease causally linked to employment); automobile no-fault (which requires losses caused by automobile accidents); the National Vaccine Injury Compensation Fund (which requires an injury caused by the administration of a vaccine); and service-connected veteran's benefits.

The third category consists of programs that do not require either fault or a particular causal origin, and instead are based solely on whether a covered individual has sustained a loss of a certain sort. These include primarily (1) private health, life, and disability insurance; and (2) social insurance such as Medicare, Medicaid, and Social Security disability insurance (SSDI). Under all these programs, if a person is covered and if the loss is covered, then benefits are payable without regard to the causal source or fault. For instance, an individual disabled by a car accident may receive SSDI, but so too may an individual disabled by multiple sclerosis.

It is also useful to appreciate the amount of benefits delivered by each of the three categories. In 1990, the tort system paid about $50 billion annually to its beneficiaries. Cause-based systems in combination paid approximately $55 billion. Loss-based programs paid far more: private insurance pays about $220 billion annually, and social insurance in excess of $235 billion. Abraham & Liebman, *supra*.

Just as the basis of compensation differs among various programs, so does the primary systemic purpose or purposes of the programs. As we discussed above, any program will aim at one or more of four primary goals. The first is corrective justice: identifying wrongful injurious conduct and requiring correction of that wrong by compensation of the victim. The second is deterring unreasonably unsafe conduct, usually defined as conduct whose social costs outweigh its social benefits. Third is the aim of insurance. That is, even if all wrongful injurious conduct were corrected, and even if all unreasonably unsafe conduct were deterred, some injuries and illnesses still would occur. There will be victims of multiple sclerosis and cerebral palsy; there will be victims of car accidents even when people drive as safely as possible in well-designed cars. The mechanism of insurance helps cushion these losses both by spreading them over time (the individual pays a series of smaller insurance premiums over time and thus can more easily absorb the large loss) and by spreading them among many people.

Finally, a compensation program might aim at income redistribution. For instance, federal "supplemental security income" makes payments to those (1) who are considered disabled and (2) whose income falls below a certain level. The aim is to provide some basic subsistence-level income for those who are both disabled and poor. On the whole, the American disability fabric is not primarily occupied with income redistribution, and instead is more understandable in terms of the other three goals.

In most programs, only one or two of these goals will dominate. For instance, social insurance (such as social security disability insurance) cannot be viewed as aimed at deterrence because the costs of such insurance are not linked at all to the origin of or responsibility for the loss. By contrast, workers' compensation, though not fault-based, includes deterrence as an aim because insurance premiums or self-insurance costs are linked to the employer's actual injury costs, thus creating incentives to reduce injuries when it is cost-justified to do so. For more detail on these goals and how they relate to the various programs, *see* Abraham & Liebman, *supra*.

When considering any existing or proposed compensation program in light of these goals, keep in mind that two other mechanisms in theory can be used in service of the goal of optimal deterrence: direct government safety regulation, and the marketplace (consumers' own preferences for safety, translated into willingness to pay for safety). Thus, when considering whether an existing or proposed nontort compensation program would produce too little deterrence, one needs to consider whether the marketplace or direct government regulation could take up the deterrence slack.

4. THE "ACCIDENT PREFERENCE"

Analysts have long noted that both tort and cause-based nontort programs (such as workers' compensation and auto no-fault) traditionally have been more likely to allow compensation for traumatic injuries than for injuries resulting from disease, even "man-made" disease. As Professor Jane Stapleton has explained, tort law does not officially prefer accident over disease victims, but tort law's conceptual structure—particularly the requirement of actual cause—makes it less likely that victims of disease will recover in tort than will accident victims. *See* Jane Stapleton, DISEASE AND THE COMPENSATION DEBATE 3, 10–11, 116 (1986).

As you read the following materials, consider a number of questions about this "accident preference." How do the various existing and proposed nontort compensation programs address the issue of disease? For instance, do they allow compensation for some diseases but not others, and if so why? Are there theoretical reasons for distinguishing diseases with their origins in human activity such as such as asbestos-related disease, cancers and immunological disorders arising from chemical exposure, from diseases that (at least given current knowledge) are so-called "natural" diseases? If so, how should a particular nontort program address the practical problems of distinguishing between these two categories? Does the overall fabric of American compensation programs (including tort and nontort) provide adequate compensation for disabilities due to disease?

D. CAUSE-BASED COMPENSATION PROGRAMS

The most prominent existing cause-based compensation schemes are workers' compensation and automobile no-fault. These are cause-based because they do not require a showing of fault, but instead turn on whether the injury or disease had a particular causal origin (arising out of and in the course and scope of employment; arising out of use of an automobile).

The design of any cause-based compensation program must come to grips with several questions. First, what will be the causal trigger? If the causal trigger is vague and often contestable, then the system will be plagued by the high administrative costs of making that determination from case to case. And, if the causal trigger is too broad, then the system will allocate to a particular activity or industry costs that have nothing to do with that activity or industry.

A second question that a cause-based system must confront is whether the system will entirely supplant tort within a particular sphere, or instead will simply be added on to tort. As we will see, workers' compensation generally supplants tort entirely with regard to most work-related injuries. With respect to auto no-fault, sometimes it is simply added to existing tort remedies, but in some states it supplants tort at least for less severe injuries. Whether the causal scheme supplants or simply supplements tort obviously affects many issues, including the cost of the system and its deterrent consequences.

A third question is how the cause-based system will be funded, including the degree to which system costs will be tied to the riskiness of a particular actor's conduct. For instance, in workers' compensation, employers pay insurance premiums that are tied in part to the number and severity of work-related injuries. As you read the following materials about workers' compensation, auto no-fault, and other existing and proposed no-fault programs, consider how each system addresses these basic design questions.

1. WORKERS' COMPENSATION

FENWICK v. OKLAHOMA STATE PENITENTIARY

Supreme Court of Oklahoma, 1990.
792 P.2d 60.

HODGES, JUSTICE.

This case arose after James R. Fenwick (Claimant) sought workers' compensation for permanent partial disability. The Workers' Compensation Court found that Claimant had not suffered an accidental injury. The Oklahoma Court of Appeals reversed the Workers' Compensation Court, and this Court granted the Petition for Writ of Certiorari. The issue on appeal is whether the claimant's mental stress, which arose out of an isolated incident, without any accompanying physical injury is compensable under the Workers' Compensation Act. We find that it is not.

On August 8, 1979, Claimant, while working as a psychological assistant at the Oklahoma State Penitentiary, encountered a situation where four women were being held hostage by an inmate. Claimant negotiated the release of three of the hostages in exchange for himself. Subsequently, the fourth woman was released. After being held hostage for approximately four and one-half hours, Claimant was released without physical injury.

Although Claimant took two days off work immediately following the hostage incident, he continued to work in the same position until October 1, 1982. At that time he resigned to take a similar job with the Carl Albert Community Mental Health Center.

On July 9, 1982, Claimant filed his Form 3 seeking disability compensation. The State Insurance Fund paid for Claimant's medical and psychiatric treatment until April, 1986. Then on January 6, 1987, Claimant filed a Form 9 seeking permanent partial disability.

Claimant was diagnosed by Dr. Nolan L. Armstrong as suffering from major depression, generalized anxiety disorder, and post-traumatic stress disorder. He was diagnosed by Dr. Larry M. Prater as suffering from post-traumatic stress disorder and personality disorder. Although Claimant complains of periodic shakiness, headaches, tingling in the hands, discomfort in the pit of his stomach, and several other physical disorders, none of the diagnosis included physical injury.

An employee is entitled to compensation, regardless of fault, when the employee suffers disability or death "resulting from an accidental personal injury ... arising out of and in the course of his employment."[1] The causation of the claimant's mental disorders are not disputed leaving the question of accidental personal injury as the only issue.

A definition of injury is provided in the Workers' Compensation Act (the Act) itself[2] This definition is more repetitive of the requirements set out under section 11 than it is definitive. Since the definition in the Act is not comprehensive, it has been the duty of the courts to further define "accidental personal injury."

This Court has long recognized that "[a] disease of the mind or body which arises in the course of employment, with nothing more" is not an accidental injury and, thus, not compensable. * * * Claimant argues that the additional element requirement of "nothing more" is satisfied by the

1. Okla.Stat. tit. 85, § 11 (1981).

2. Okla.Stat. tit. 85, § 3(7) (1981) provides: "Injury or personal injury" means only accidental injuries arising out of and in the course of employment and such disease or infection as may naturally result therefrom and occupational disease arising out of and in the course of employment as herein defined. Provided, only injuries having as their source a risk not purely personal but one that is reasonably connected with the conditions of employment shall be deemed to arise out of the employment.

fact that the event which caused his stress is a definite and identifiable occurrence. This is not the case. This Court has consistently held that physical injury must be present for a disability to be compensable. * * * Just as physical symptoms such as pain, tingling of the limbs, and nausea do not constitute accidental injury, * * * neither does mental stress. Because there is no evidence in the present case that Claimant suffered any physical injury, * * * he has not shown that he suffered an accidental injury. Therefore, his disability is not compensable under the Act.

* * *

[Previous cases have] involved mental stress or physical pain unaccompanied by a physical injury and caused by an identifiable event which occurred at a definite time. Yet, in all previous cases, the claimant's disability was not compensable. The present case presents the same situation. Here we have a disability without any evidence of a physical injury, caused by an identifiable event which occurred at a definite time.

For the first time in 1977, the American Medical Association (AMA) included a chapter on the evaluation of mental disorders in its guidelines[9] Then in 1985, the Legislature mandated that the AMA's guidelines were to be used by physicians when evaluating impairment[10] The legislative intent behind this mandate was to provide some consistency in the evaluations of mental disorders accompanied by physical injury. Had the Legislature intended to make disabilities from mental disorders without accompanying physical injury compensable, they would have changed the statutory definition of injury * * * rather than only including a method for consistently evaluating mental disorders.

It has long been the rule that disability, either mental or physical, which is not accompanied by a physical injury is not compensable under the Act. * * * This rule is based on the statutory definition of injury. * * * This definition has remained substantially unchanged since 1915 * * * even though the Act has frequently been amended. In fact, the Act has been amended annually since the establishment of this rule.

* * *

Since the Legislature has not substantially changed the statutory definition of injury, nor has it enacted any statute which would conflict with our prior decision, we must presume that the Legislature is in agreement with our judicial interpretation. Therefore, without a legislative mandate, we decline to alter the rule that disability unaccompanied by physical injury is not compensable under the Act. The Workers'

9. American Medical Association, Guides to Evaluation of Permanent Impairment, p. 149 (AMA 1977).

10. Okla.Stat. tit. 85, § 3(11) (Supp.1985) provides in part: [A]ny examining physician shall evaluate impairment in substantial accordance with such guides to the evaluation of permanent impairment as have been officially approved by a majority of the Workers' Compensation Court. These guides may include, but shall not be limited to, the "Guides to the Evaluation of Permanent Impairment" published in 1971 by the American Medical Association. . . .

Compensation Court was correct in ruling that Claimant was not entitled to compensation.

* * * COURT OF APPEALS' OPINION VACATED; ORDER OF THE WORKERS' COMPENSATION COURT SUSTAINED.

* * *

Dissenting Opinion by KAUGER, J., joined by OPALA, V.C.J., and DOOLIN, J.

* * *

The claimant, who offered himself as a hostage to secure the release of three female hostages while attempting to mediate a crisis at the Oklahoma State Penitentiary on August 8, 1979, first suffered serious psychological problems in December of that year when he experienced marital dysfunction and extreme anxiety. Because of Fenwick's mental condition, he left the stress of the prison job, and accepted a position with a community mental health center. It is undisputed that in order to continue even at this occupation, he needs the benefit of counseling.

The State Insurance Fund recognized that Fenwick had been harmed—it paid for his medical and psychiatric treatment for almost four years. It was only after he filed a claim for permanent partial disability that the Fund denied that he had been injured in the course of his employment. * * * Recovery would surely have been granted to the hostage's survivors had he been killed while being held hostage; however, he is denied recovery for a life-altering trauma.

* * *

There are three types of psychic injury: 1) a mental stimulus which causes a physical injury; 2) a physical trauma which causes a nervous injury; and 3) a mental stimulus which causes a nervous injury. * * * Here, recovery is denied not because of lack of evidence of injury, but on the basis that there was no evidence of bleeding, bruising, or tearing, or of lasting physical injury, i.e., accidental personal injury. * * * It is undisputed that the Act has never specifically excluded recovery for mental stress in the absence of physical injury. Nor has it specifically provided that physical trauma is a prerequisite to recovery for mental stress. The Court has engrafted this requirement to its definition of personal injury just as the Court had engrafted sovereign immunity into the common law—* * * by judicial fiat, not by legislative enactment.

* * *

An increasing number of courts are recognizing that recovery is proper for mental injuries not associated with physical impact. There is already visible a distinct majority position supporting compensability for nervous injuries. * * * The courts which find that mental injuries may be compensable absent physical impact reason that there is no valid justification for distinguishing between mental disorders—whether caused by physical impact or injury caused or aggravated by emotional stimuli—in view of the policy of workmens' compensation statutes to provide for work-related disabilities. * * * Courts which do not allow compensation for disabling mental disorders resulting from a work-related emotional stimulus reason that an emotional stimulus is not an "accident" or "injury" within the meaning of the compensation statutes. * * * Some states prohibit recovery for mental or nervous injury by statutorily excluding such events from the definition of an injury arising out of the employment. * * * Although we have relied on this premise to deny recovery in the past, the Oklahoma Act does not specifically exempt mental or neurological illness from its application. * * * Denial of recovery for purely psychological injuries has been a judicial limitation rather than a statutory one. * * * Twenty-six jurisdictions, with similar statutes, allow recovery for properly documented cases of mental disability caused by on-the-job stress and strain. * * *

Adoption of the majority rule will not disrupt the ordinary evidentiary burden. Rule 20 * * * of the Act sets forth the requirements for expert medical testimony. The difficulty of requiring physicians to appear at trials is recognized. The Rule provides the standards necessary for verified reports. Reports prepared for trial must contain a statement that "the evaluation is in substantial accordance with the latest 'Guides to the Evaluation of Permanent Impairment'." * * * Chapter 14 of the Guide is devoted to the consideration of mental and behavioral disorders. The Guide provides a method of evaluation of diseases causing psychiatric impairment, and it is attached hereto as Appendix I.

The use of the Guide as an evaluative tool is also required by 85 O.S.Supp.1988 § 3(11). * * * This section defines "permanent impairment" as "any anatomical or functional abnormality or loss after reasonable medical treatment has been achieved, which abnormality or loss the physician considers to be capable of being evaluated at the time the rating is made." This definition, like those of "injury or personal injury" and "occupational disease" does not specifically exclude mental injuries. Instead, its reference to "any abnormality" encompasses the physical as well as mental condition of the claimant.

* * *

The nature of compensable injuries has changed since workers' compensation laws were originally enacted. What was once a severed limb or debilitating lung disease has become a stress-induced heart attack or a permanent psychic injury. Out of a total of 29,030 workers surveyed in 1900, only 5,115 were white-collar workers. The other 23,915 were manual and farm laborers. By 1970 the figures had changed. Of 79,802 laborers surveyed, 37,857 of those counted were in white-collar jobs. The rest, 41,868 were manual and farm workers. By 1987 in Oklahoma, there were only 40,400 agricultural workers compared to 1,104,783 wage and salary earners. * * * Blue-collar workers have gone from 40 percent of the national workforce in 1950 to 30 percent in 1982. The service sector has grown from 55 percent of the workforce to over 70 percent. Over two-thirds of today's laborers are found in the fields of accounting, banking, engineering, consumer services, education, health care, legal work, transportation, wholesale, and retail trade. * * * Instead of recognizing this shift, the majority mechanically transfers the non-physical injury concept designed to deter false claims by blue collar workers in routine industrial jobs to an environment where psychic trauma is a routine component of working conditions.

In the past, before the recognition of the relationship of mental and nervous injuries to physical symptoms and behavior, there was an understandable basis, i.e., apparently insoluble evidentiary difficulties, for denying recoveries based on such injuries, both in tort and in workers' compensation law. That justification is no longer valid. The present Act predicates indemnification based, not on the label assigned to the injury—whether mental or physical, but upon the employee's inability to work because of impairments flowing from his/her employment conditions.

* * *

A human being is not constituted of mere blood, bones, muscles, ligaments, and tissues. He/she also has a nervous system, a brain and a psyche. * * * The majority opinion ignores one of the major portions of the body—the nervous system. Mental stimuli may cause either physical or mental disease, and there is no creditable distinction, nor can a valid line be drawn under contemporary medical standards, between what is totally psychological and what is purely physical. * * * No reason is suggested, and none appears, why injury in the form of debilitating depression, insomnia, and headaches, as well as injury to the cardiovascular system * * * and other internal organs caused by work induced mental or emotional stress and strain, should not be covered if the cause and effect are established by competent evidence.

* * *

NOTES

1. *History*. Workers' compensation programs exist in all fifty states and also for federal workers. Their origins trace back to nineteenth century Europe. The first European legislation dealing with industrial accidents was enacted in Prussia in 1838 and made railroads strictly liable to passengers and employees for all accidents occurring in the course of their operations except those arising from an act of God or the negligence of the claimant. In subsequent years legislation was passed requiring employers in certain industries to contribute to local "sickness-association funds." Finally in 1884, Germany (the modern German state having been formed in 1871) adopted the first modern comprehensive compensation scheme. The German plan included also provision for disability arising from old age and causes not specifically covered under the heading of industrial accidents. *See* 1 A. Larson, WORKMEN'S COMPENSATION LAW § 5.10 (1989).

In 1897 the Workmen's Compensation Act introduced the idea of accident compensation independent of tort into Great Britain. This legislation, as gradually extended, was consolidated in the Workmen's Compensation Act of 1925, 15 & 16 Geo. 5, c. 84. In 1946 Great Britain adopted (effective in 1948) a comprehensive scheme of National Insurance which replaced the Workmen's Compensation Act. Under this legislation, benefits are paid by the state. Of interest to the tort lawyer is the fact that an award under the social insurance scheme does not bar a common-law action by a worker against the employer.

The first workers' compensation act passed in this country was that of New York in the first decade of the Twentieth Century. After some initial uncertainty about whether the acts would pass constitutional muster, *see* Ives v. South Buffalo Ry. Co., 201 N.Y. 271, 94 N.E. 431 (1911) (invalidating the 1910 New York act on due process grounds); New York Central R.R. Co. v. White, 243 U.S. 188, 37 S.Ct. 247, 61 L.Ed. 667 (1917) (upholding the 1914 New York act), within short order most states had passed a workers' compensation statute, and constitutional challenges proved unavailing. The main impetus behind the acts was the widespread belief that tort law was a deficient vehicle for compensating and deterring the injury toll of an increasingly industrialized society. Several common-law tort doctrines combined to make especially unlikely a worker's recovery in tort: contributory negligence, the "fellow-servant rule" (under which the employer generally was not liable for injuries caused by the fault of another employee), and assumption of the risk.

2. *Basic Features.* Although workers' compensation statutes vary in a number of particulars, all statutes share basic similarities.

Quid Pro Quo. All workers' compensation acts reflect a basic quid-pro-quo. The employer agrees to provide (by insurance or self-insurance) certain no-fault benefits (medical benefits, cash disability benefits, and sometimes vocational rehabilitation benefits) for virtually all work-related injuries and for many occupational diseases. The benefits are payable without a showing of the employer's fault, and the employee's own fault (save certain limited exceptions, such as willful injury or intoxication) does not bar or limit recovery. The employer (or its insurer) is supposed to pay the benefits immediately as they are due, and penalties accrue for delay or unjustified opposition to the claim.

In exchange for these benefits, the employee gives up his or her common law right to sue in tort for the full spectrum of tort damages. Instead, for virtually all work-related injuries, the workers' compensation benefit structure is the employee's exclusive remedy (the "exclusivity" doctrine). There are some exceptions to the exclusivity doctrine; for instance, some states allow the employee's family to sue in tort if the employee dies as a result of gross negligence.

Compulsory Coverage. In most states, workers' compensation is compulsory for the great majority of wage and salary workers. (The most common coverage exclusions are for domestic workers and farm workers.) Workers' compensation has covered approximately 87% of all wage and salary workers. *See* 56 Social Security Bulletin, Fall 1993, at 68. A few states allow the employer to "opt out" of the system. If the employer does opt out, it is fully exposed to tort suits by employees. Indeed, Texas, one of the few opt-out states, removes the defense of comparative negligence from any employer who opts out. Tex.Lab.Code Ann. § 406.033(a).

Benefits But Not "Full" Compensation. Workers' compensation benefits are of three types: medical, cash for disability, and (in some states) vocational rehabilitation. Originally, the medical benefits under all state workers' compensation programs had few of the restrictions now common to private health insurance—deductibles, coinsurance provisions, and various managed care features, such as restrictions on choice of physician. Now, many states are allowing utilization review and restrictions on choice of physician.

Cash disability benefits are available both for partial and for total disability, and both for temporary and for permanent disabilities. The benefits are not aimed at complete compensation for lost earnings, but instead at replacing some substantial portion of the employee's lost earning capacity.

Administrative Adjudication. All workers' compensation programs replace tort's adjudicative approach with an administrative decision making scheme. If a dispute over benefits arises, the dispute first is heard by an administrative hearing officer, whose decision may be appealed at one or more administrative levels. The final administrative decision—such as the decision of the state workers' compensation commission—usually is subject to judicial review.

3. *The Work–Relation Requirement.* All workers' compensation programs contain some type of work-relation test—a requirement that the injury be one "arising out of and in the course of" the employment. To understand the theoretical reasons for the work-relation requirement, consider the basic systemic aims of workers' compensation. First, worker's compensation has been viewed as serving a social justice aim: industry—and those who consume its products and services—should bear the cost of industry-related injury just as it does any other cost of business. Second, worker's compensation aims at deterrence. Workers' compensation internalizes to the employer many of the costs of untaken yet cost-justified safety precautions, thus inducing the employer to take cost-justified preventative steps. An extensive literature supports the conclusion that workers' compensation results in significant safety advantages not produced by the private market or regulatory structures. *See* Michael J. Moore & W. Kip Viscusi, COMPENSATION MECHANISMS FOR JOB RISKS 121–35 (1990). Third, workers' compensation in essence forces the purchase of insurance for income-replacement and medical costs arising from work-related injuries.

From either a justice-based or deterrence-based perspective, why would a work-relation test of some sort be necessary? Given the systemic aims that underlie workers' compensation in general and the work-relation requirement in particular, should Fenwick's injury have been covered?

The work-relation boundary is often tested with respect to the "going-and-coming" rule. This rule bars workers' compensation recovery to those employees who are injured while off the employer's premises. However, the rule is subject to many qualifications. There may be a "parking lot" exception if an employee is attacked while going to her car after work. See Fred Meyer, Inc. v. Hayes, 325 Or. 592, 943 P.2d 197 (1997). Even greater difficulties arise when the employee has no fixed place of employment. *See* Andover Volunteer

Fire Dept. v. Grinnell Mut. Reinsurance Co., 787 N.W.2d 75 (Iowa 2010); McGloin v. Trammellcrow Services, Inc., 987 A.2d 881 (R.I. 2010).

What about acts of God, as when an employee is injured by a tornado or a bolt of lightning? See Lane v. G & M Statuary, Inc., 156 S.W.3d 498 (Mo.App. 2005); Ex parte Byrom, 895 So.2d 942 (Ala. 2004); Decatur–Macon County Fair Ass'n v. Industrial Commission, 69 Ill.2d 262, 13 Ill.Dec. 662, 371 N.E.2d 597 (1977). What are the issues?

4. *Mental Disabilities*. A minority of jurisdictions have interpreted references to injury in their workers compensation statutes to include emotional harm. See DePaoli v. Great A & P Tea Co., 94 N.Y.2d 377, 704 N.Y.S.2d 527, 725 N.E.2d 1089 (2000). Even when workers compensation statutes are revised to permit recovery for emotional harm, they may include some restrictions. For example, the Missouri statute contains the following provision:

> Mental injury resulting from work-related stress does not arise out of and in the course of the employment, unless it is demonstrated that the stress is work related and was extraordinary and unusual. The amount of work stress shall be measured by objective standards and actual events.

Mo. Stat. § 287.120.8 *See* Schaffer v. Litton Interconnect Technology, 274 S.W.3d 597 (Mo. App. 2009) for an application of this statute denying recovery to an individual suffering from Generalized Anxiety Disorder because he could not show that his work-related stress was extraordinary or unusual when compared to other similar positions. For a similar statutory provision, *see* 39–A Me. Rev, Stat., § 201(3)(a)

As the *Schaffer* and *Fenwick* cases indicate, mental disabilities in general have received less coverage under workers' compensation than have physical injuries. Indeed, after the opinion in Fenwick, the Oklahoma legislature modified the statute to make clear that an "injury or personal injury" would not include "mental injury that is unaccompanied by physical injury." 85 Okla. Stat. § 3(7)(c) (2003). If a physical injury results in a mental disability (such as depression following a back injury), then usually the mental disability is covered. But coverage is much less likely when the precipitating event is not a physical injury. Several rationales might be advanced for such restrictions: a concern about the quality of proof available with respect to the existence and causal source of mental disabilities; the view that mental disabilities in general are not work-related or cannot reliably be proven to be; and concerns about the predictability and insurability of mental disabilities as distinct from physical disabilities.

Do these rationales convincingly support *some* form of restriction on coverage for mental disabilities? If so, do they convincingly support the approach embodied in the Oklahoma statute—the requirement of a physical injury? Some jurisdictions have tried other approaches to mental disabilities: (1) allow coverage if the source of the mental impairment is a sudden or shocking event; (2) allow coverage if the mental disability stems from employment-related stress which exceeds that of ordinary life or that of other workers; (3) allow coverage but only if the claimant can satisfy a high causal threshold, such as showing that the employment contributed to the impairment by at least 50%; or (4) allow coverage for most work-related mental disabilities but exclude particular types of claims, such as mental disabilities arising from bona fide personnel actions. For more detail, *see* Ellen S. Pryor, *Mental Disabilities and the Disability Fabric,* in MENTAL DISORDER, WORK DISABILITY, AND THE LAW 153 (R.J. BONNIE & J. MONAHAN, EDS., 1997). *Right to Workers' Compensation for Emotional Distress or Like Injury Suffered by Claimant as Result of Nonsudden Stimuli—Right to Compensation Under Particular Statutory Provisions*, 97 A.L.R.5th 1 collects the cases.

Which of these coverage approaches seems most defensible in theory and workable in practice?

5. *Occupational Disease*. Earlier versions of workers' compensation statutes restricted recoveries to "accidental injury." Thus, the statutes contained large gaps for the victims of occupational diseases, such as victims of asbestos-related illnesses arising from longer-term exposure to asbestos. All workers' compensation programs now cover at least some occupational diseases. Drawing the appropriate boundaries, however, has posed both theoretical and practical difficulties. From a theoretical perspective, coverage for disease should be restricted to work-related diseases, for the same theoretical reasons that explain the work-relation requirement in general. The challenge is devising a theoretically sound and practically workable causal test.

> The real source of the problem is the inherent mismatch between the characteristics of such disease conditions and the nature of the liability systems through which sufferers of these diseases might seek compensation, whether the basis of liability is fault or simply cause. * * * [E]ven if a disease such as lung cancer is clearly attributable to a variety of exposures in the workplace, it is even more likely to be caused by a variety of other toxic substances to which the worker is exposed in his daily life. Given the practical difficulties posed by a lengthy latency period between initial exposure and ultimate manifestation of the disease, together with the logical difficulties of using epidemiological statistics to establish causal connections in individual cases, any program offering benefits that rest on proof of cause (rather than simply loss) will likely reject more claims than it accepts and will actually attract an even smaller proportion of such claims in the first instance.

American Law Institute, Reporters' Study on Enterprise Responsibility for Personal Injury, Vol. I, at 112 (1991).

Common formulations of the work-relation test are (1) the disease must be "peculiar to the occupation," Conn. Gen. Stat. § 31–275(15) (2003); (2) the disease must be characteristic of and peculiar to the employment, but excluding ordinary diseases of life to which the public is equally exposed, N.C Stat. 97–53 (2002). Even if the worker can show that the disease has an occupational link, what if some portion of the disease is linked to nonoccupational factors? Again, jurisdictions differ. One approach is to reduce the compensation award by a percentage reflecting nonoccupational factors. *See* Price v. Lithonia Lighting Co., 256 Ga. 49, 343 S.E.2d 688 (1986). Other jurisdictions adopt an either-or approach: the worker must prove that the work "significantly contributed to" the disease; if so the claim is covered, and if not no partial benefits are due. Lindquist v. City of Jersey City Fire Department, 175 N.J. 244, 814 A.2d 1069 (2003) provides a discussion of New Jersey's slow acceptance of recovery for occupational diseases under its workers compensation act. In *Lindquist*, the plaintiff claimed his years as a firefighter contributed to his chronic obstructive pulmonary disease. However, his employer claimed this injury and plaintiff's emphysema were caused by his cigarette smoking. The court permitted recovery because his exposure to smoke as a firefighter substantially contributed to the development or aggravation of emphysema. How, if at all, should worker compensation systems take plaintiff's non-job related behavior into account?

Given the problems with the causal test for occupational disease, would it be preferable to eliminate workers' compensation coverage for occupational disease claims and create a single "loss-based" compensation program for the most seriously disabling and fatal diseases, regardless of whether the disease was causally linked to the workplace? What would be the drawbacks of such an approach? For an article supporting this general approach, *see* Leslie I. Boden, *Problems in Occupational Disease Compensation,* in Current Issues in WORKERS' COMPENSATION 313 (J. CHELIUS ED., 1986).

6. *Exclusivity, and Tort Options*. Workers' compensation carves out a no-fault system that generally displaces tort, by means of the exclusivity doctrine. Most courts, legislatures, and analysts consider the exclusivity principle to be central to the viability of workers' compensation. The exclusivity principle also applies to tort claims brought by family members of the injured worker. For instance, a spouse's tort claim for loss of consortium is generally disallowed, *see, e.g.*, Mardian Construction Co. v. Superior Court, 157 Ariz. 103, 754 P.2d 1378 (App.1988), as are wrongful death actions by family members, *see, e.g.*, Morrill v. J & M Construction Co., 635 P.2d 88 (Utah 1981).

Despite general agreement over the importance of exclusivity, challenging issues continue to arise about the boundary between tort and workers' compensation. One such "boundary" issue is raised by Fenwick's situation: may a worker sue in tort if the worker is or would be unsuccessful in recovering workers' compensation benefits? Several guidelines have emerged. If an injury is "covered"—that is, arises out of and in the course and scope of employment—but is simply not compensable, then the exclusivity doctrine bars a tort suit. Depending on the jurisdiction, examples of such covered but noncompensable injuries include: a back injury that causes pain but does not impair earning capacity; an injury to the worker's reproductive system that does not produce any rated impairment under the state's impairment schedule.

If the injury is not "covered"—that is, it does not arise out of and in the course and scope of employment—then the worker is not barred. Suppose, for instance, that the employer provides a remote parking facility and negligently fails to notify workers that there has been a series of assaults and robberies in the parking lot. A worker is physically assaulted when he arrives at the parking lot one evening. Many jurisdictions consider an injury sustained while driving to and from work, or in parking lots, to be outside the course and scope of employment. Thus, the worker in theory could sue the employer in tort.

Does this distinction between "covered but noncompensable" and "non-covered" flow from any of the purposes of workers' compensation and the need for an exclusivity rule? How does the distinction apply to Fenwick's injury; that is, would the exclusivity doctrine bar a tort claim by Fenwick? (Of course, even if the exclusivity doctrine would not bar a tort claim by Fenwick, the tort claim might run into other obstacles, such as governmental immunity or rules restricting recoveries for emotional distress.)

How does the exclusivity doctrine apply to claims of injury arising from sexual harassment? A leading case is Byrd v. Richardson–Greenshields Securities, Inc., 552 So.2d 1099 (Fla.1989).

> Our analysis must begin with the premise, now well established in our law, that workers' compensation generally is the sole tort remedy available to a worker injured in a manner that falls within the broad scope and policies of the workers' compensation statute. * * * This statute expresses a plain legislative intent that any potential liability arising from "injury or death" is abolished in favor of the exclusive remedy available under workers' compensation. However, if the liability arises from something other than "injury or death," the other potential bases of liability remain viable.
>
> * * *
>
> * * * [W]e cannot find that acts constituting sexual harassment were ever meant to fall under workers' compensation. Moreover, we have an equal obligation to honor the intent and policy of other enactments and, accordingly, may not apply the exclusivity rule in a manner that effectively abrogates the policies of other law. * * *
>
> There can be no doubt at this point in time that both the state of Florida and the federal government have committed themselves strongly to outlawing and eliminating sexual discrimination in the workplace, including the related evil of sexual harassment. The statutes, case law, and administrative regulations uniformly and without exception condemn sexual harassment in the strongest possible terms. We find that the present case strongly implicates these sexual harassment policies and, accordingly, may not be decided by a blind adherence to the exclusivity rule of the workers' compensation statute alone. Our clear obligation is to construe both the workers' compensation statute and the enactments dealing with sexual harassment so that the policies of both are preserved to the greatest extent possible. [The court reviews the federal and state statutes outlawing workplace sexual harassment.]
>
> * * *
>
> In light of this overwhelming public policy, we cannot say that the exclusivity rule of the workers' compensation statute should exist to shield an employer from all tort liability based on incidents of sexual harassment. The clear public policy emanating from federal and Florida law holds that an employer is charged with maintaining a workplace free from sexual harassment. Applying the exclusivity rule of workers' compensation to preclude any and all tort liability effectively would abrogate

> this policy, undermine the Florida Human Rights Act, and flout Title VII of the Civil Rights Act of 1964.
>
> This, we cannot condone. Public policy now requires that employers be held accountable in tort for the sexually harassing environments they permit to exist, whether the tort claim is premised on a remedial statute or on the common law.
>
> We find this conclusion harmonizes with the policies and scope of workers' compensation. As often has been noted, workers' compensation is directed essentially at compensating a worker for lost resources and earnings. This is a vastly different concern than is addressed by the sexual harassment laws. While workplace injuries rob a person of resources, sexual harassment robs the person of dignity and self esteem. Workers' compensation addresses purely economic injury; sexual harassment laws are concerned with a much more intangible injury to personal rights. * * * To the extent these injuries are separable, we believe that they both should be, and can be, enforced separately.

522 So.2d at 1100–04.

Most courts, like *Byrd,* have allowed workers to pursue tort and civil rights claims for sexual harassment. *E.g.*, O'Connell v. Chasdi, 400 Mass. 686, 511 N.E.2d 349 (1987). A few, however, hold that workers' compensation is the exclusive avenue for mental anguish claims resulting from sexual harassment. *See* Knox v. Combined Insurance Co., 542 A.2d 363 (Me.1988). Does allowing tort and civil rights claims for sexual harassment undermine the purposes behind the exclusivity doctrine?

Suppose that sexual harassment caused a worker to experience anxiety or depression debilitating enough to cause at least a temporary disability and the need for medical and psychological treatment. According to the *Byrd* court's analysis, would the worker's injury be covered by workers' compensation? In Ramada Inn Surfside v. Swanson, 560 So.2d 300 (Fla.Ct.App.1990), the court was faced with such a claim. Citing *Byrd* and its reasoning, the court held that workers' compensation covered the claim. Do you agree with this reading of *Byrd*? If the result is correct as an interpretation of *Byrd,* do you see any problems with this way of addressing the relation of workers' compensation and sexual harassment claims?

7. *Other exceptions to exclusivity: Intentional acts and the "dual capacity" doctrine.*

a. *Intentional Harms*. In *Beauchamp v. Dow Chemical Co.*, 427 Mich. 1, 398 N.W.2d 882 (1986) the court discussed circumstances where the employer's intentional acts would not be covered by the exclusivity provision of the worker's compensation statute, permitting the employee to bring a common law tort suit. In deciding the nature of the intention necessary to sidestep worker's compensation, the court adopted the "substantial certainty" test from the Second Restatement. Other decisions have adopted a more stringent position, requiring an actual subjective intent to injure. See Rainer v. Union Carbide Corp. 402 F.3d 608 (6th Cir. 2005), interpreting the Kentucky workers' compensation statute that reserves a common law cause of action for a worker who is injured "through the deliberate intention of his employer to produce such injury or death." Ky. Rev. Stat. § 342.610(4) (2004). The West Virginia statute contains similar language, providing an exception only if the employer "consciously, subjectively and deliberately formed [the intent] to produce the specific result of injury or death." W.Va.Code § 23–4–2(2)(i) (2003). *See also* Bardere v. Zafir, 102 App. Div.2d 422, 477 N.Y.S.2d 131, *aff'd on other grounds*, 63 N.Y.2d 850, 472 N.E.2d 37, 482 N.Y.S.2d 261 (1984). Why have courts and legislatures been reluctant to use the "knowledge with substantial certainty" formulation when drawing the boundary of the exclusivity doctrine?

b. *Dual Capacity*. Another exception is the "dual capacity" doctrine that courts fashioned in limited instances. If the employer acted in dual capacities—for instance, as both product manufacturer of the product that injured the worker, and as the worker's employer—then some courts allowed the worker to sue the employer in tort in the manufacturer's capacity. *See* Bell v. Industrial Vangas, Inc., 30 Cal.3d 268, 179 Cal.Rptr. 30, 637 P.2d 266 (1981). After some initial judicial acceptance of the doctrine, however, most courts now reject the dual capacity doctrine when the injury results from a product manufactured or sold by the employer. *See* Schump v. Firestone Tire and Rubber Co., 44 Ohio St.3d 148, 541 N.E.2d 1040 (1989). Following the *Bell* decision, California eliminated the dual capacity doctrine by statute. *See* Cal. Labor Code § 3602(a).

8. *Tort Suits Against Third Parties*. Consider the following scenario. A worker sustains a serious arm injury when using an industrial tool that is not equipped with a handguard. When the employer first purchased the tool from the manufacturer, the tool came with a handguard that could be attached and removed, depending on the uses to which the tool was put. The employer fails to attach the handguard when appropriate or to instruct workers about this, and eventually the handguard is simply lost. The worker sues the manufacturer, alleging negligent design and failure to warn, as well as products liability claims. Suppose that the jury finds liability on the manufacturer's part and awards tort damages of $500,000. The total medical and disability benefits paid by the workers' compensation insurer amount to $150,000.

Until recently, most jurisdictions handled this scenario in the following way: (1) the manufacturer was not allowed to bring a claim against the employer for contribution; and (2) the employer (or employer's insurer) could bring a claim for subrogation, requiring the repayment of the $150,000 in worker's compensation benefits. Thus, even if the employer's own negligence was a contributing factor in bringing about the injury, the manufacturer paid the full bill for the injury, and the employer could be relieved of even its workers' compensation bill. *See* Arthur Larson, *Third–Party Action Over Against Workers' Compensation Employer*, 1982 Duke L.J. 483.

It is not difficult to understand the reluctance to allow the manufacturer's claim for contribution. "If contribution or indemnity is allowed, the employer may be forced to pay his employee—through the conduit of the third-party tortfeasor—an amount in excess of his statutory workers' compensation liability. This arguably thwarts the central concept of workers' compensation. * * *." Lambertson v. Cincinnati Welding Corp., 312 Minn. 114, 119,

257 N.W.2d 679, 684 (1977). What are the drawbacks of the traditional approach?

Some jurisdictions and commentators have endorsed other approaches. Under one approach, the manufacturer could indeed bring a contribution claim against the employer and try to establish a percentage of fault or responsibility; the employer's contribution, however, would be capped by the amount of workers' compensation benefits. So, in our example, if the employer was found 80% responsible for the injury, the employer would owe contribution to the manufacturer not in the amount of $400,000 (80% of the tort damages) but only for the sum of $150,000. Note, though, that this approach would expose the employer to litigation costs, which might be considerable since the suit would need to determine percentages of fault for the accident. For one discussion of the approach, *see* Paul Weiler, *Workers' Compensation and Product Liability: The Interaction of a Tort and Non–Tort Regime*, 50 Ohio St. L.J. 825 (1989).

A second approach allows the manufacturer to add the employer as a potentially responsible party under the state's comparative responsibility statute, but solely for the purpose of permitting the fact finder to assign a percentage of responsibility to the employer. The plaintiff-employee could not collect any sums from the employer beyond sums available under workers' compensation nor would the manufacturer be entitled to any contribution from the employer. However, insofar as the manufacturer is not jointly and severally liable for the plaintiff's damages, this alternative does reduce the total amount the plaintiff may recover from the manufacturer. Employer's subrogation rights are unaffected by the fact finder determination of employer responsibility.

A third approach would simply reduce the plaintiff's total tort judgment against any third party, dollar for dollar, by the amount of the benefits paid in workers' compensation. So, in our example, the manufacturer would not be allowed to bring a contribution claim, but would be liable to the claimant only for $350,000. The employer (or workers' compensation insurer) would not be allowed to recoup, via subrogation, the amount of benefits paid out.

This approach avoids litigation costs for the employer, and it also allocates some of the loss to the employer, rather than shifting it to the manufacturer. This is an attractive result when the employer has been partially at fault. But what if the accident involves no employer fault? Then the employer, under this approach, still would be unable to obtain subrogation from the product manufacturer, and the product manufacturer will bear less than the full costs of the accident. This may seem unappealing, yet the only way out is to have some type of factfinding about the employer's fault in each case, and this of course will raise again the problem of litigation costs. Which of the approaches seems most likely to achieve appropriate allocation of accident costs at an acceptable level of transaction costs?

9. *Disability Benefits*. Throughout the 1980s and early 1990s, many employers, insurers, and analysts contended that the workers' compensation system was in need of serious reform. One item high on the reform agenda has been the escalating costs of medical benefits, which during the 1980s and early 1990s exceeded the rate of growth in non-workers' compensation health

care costs. As noted earlier, many states now have implemented some type of managed care approach.

Another key target of reformers has been the approach for calculating and awarding cash disability benefits. Both employers and employees have had complaints: the cost of providing disability benefits continued to increase rapidly, yet the actual amount of benefits delivered to workers is often below the recommendation, made by the 1972 National Commission on State Workmen's Compensation Laws, that workers' compensation replace two-thirds of a worker's lost wages. Analysts have contended that these dual deficiencies are in large part the product of an excessively costly and inefficient system for measuring and awarding one category of disability benefits: "permanent partial" disability benefits ("PPD"). (The other categories are temporary total, temporary partial, and permanent total.)

To understand PPD benefits and the problems they have generated, consider a worker whose left hand is amputated after an industrial accident. He is unable to work at all for six months; during that time he will receive weekly or bi-weekly workers' compensation checks for temporary total disability. The amount of such benefits is based on the worker's "average weekly wage" before injury; depending on how generous the state's benefits are, the worker will receive from 66⅔% to 80% of his average weekly wage (subject to maximum caps or minimum benefit levels). During months 7 through 11 post-injury, the worker is able to return to a modified-duty position, earning less than he did before injury; he still undergoes another prosthetic surgery and some rehabilitation. During these 4 months, he will receive temporary partial disability payments, which also are based on the degree to which the injury has diminished his average weekly wages.

By month 12, the worker has reached medical stabilization. He still is working in the "light duty" position. The question now is what amount he should receive for the permanent though partial disability the injury has caused him. Until legislative reforms, two approaches dominated.

First, some jurisdictions based awards of PPD, for all types of injuries, on an assessment of how the disability affects the worker's lost-earning capacity. For instance, the administrative judge might determine, based on medical and vocational reports and given the worker's particular education, age, and background, that the worker has suffered a 30% loss of his wage-earning capacity. Suppose, too, that the jurisdiction specifies that the maximum duration of PPD payments is 450 weeks. The worker then would receive either (1) a lump sum award equal to the present value of 30% times his average pre-injury weekly wage, multiplied by 450; or (2) weekly or biweekly checks equal to 30% of that average weekly wage.

Second, some jurisdictions used an anatomical "schedule" for determining PPD for at least some injuries—for instance, loss of a thumb might receive 75 weeks of compensation. The schedules usually applied only to anatomical members such as arm, hand, finger, leg, foot, toe, eye, ear; the schedules did not apply to "general" injuries such as back injuries, respiratory disabilities, etc. If the worker had only a partial loss of a thumb or a leg, then the worker received some portion of the scheduled amount. If the injury is a "general" one not governed by the schedule, then the PPD benefits depend on an assessment of how the injury has reduced the worker's wage-earning capacity. Thus, most schedule jurisdictions actually use two approaches: schedules for specific injuries, and lost-earning assessment for general injuries. Disputes often arose over whether an injury was really specific (thus governed only by the schedule) or whether it had "extended to and affected" some nonscheduled body part and thus had become a general injury.

In a schedule jurisdiction, then, our worker would receive the specified amount of compensation—such as an amount equal to 311 (number of weeks for loss of hand) times two-thirds of the average pre-injury weekly wage. Under the schedule approach, it would not matter whether the worker's occupation and training heavily required use of the hand (the worker is an artist or mechanic) or whether the worker will suffer little permanent wage loss as a result of the injury (the worker is an accountant).

What are the benefits and drawbacks of, respectively, the schedule approach and the lost wage-earning approach?

In both schedule and nonschedule jurisdictions, lengthy disputes over PPD have been common. Lawyers are often hired; administrative appeals and judicial review are common; and expert assessments of disability frequently diverge significantly.

In response, many jurisdictions have significantly altered the traditional approaches. Although the particulars vary somewhat among jurisdictions, the Texas reforms are representative of the newer approach. Consider again the worker with the amputated hand. In the Texas scheme, once the worker reaches maximum medical improvement—that is, once no further substantial medical recovery from the injury can be expected—the worker will be evaluated according to a comprehensive "impairment rating schedule." Texas has adopted the American Medical Association's schedule, known as the *Guides to the Evaluation of Permanent Impairment*, which undergoes revision every several years. The schedule consists of several hundred pages, and provides evaluative protocols for rating—in terms of a single "whole person" percentage—the anatomical impairment that an injury has produced. The schedule does not try to measure lost earning capacity, but only the "impairment." According to the *Guides,* a hand amputation translates into a 100% impairment of the hand, which in turn translates into a 90% impairment of the "upper extremity," which in turn translates into the final, whole-person impairment of 54%. In Texas, each percentage of whole-person impairment entitles the worker to 3 weeks of compensation at the rate of 70% of the worker's average weekly wage. Thus, our worker will be entitled to 162 weeks of compensation in the amount just noted. This amount is payable even if the worker has gone back to work at the full wages he once was earning. The percentage of impairment is the sole consideration. And Texas, like many states, resolves differences in ratings by giving presumptive weight to the rating provided by a "designated" physician—one agreed to by the parties or chosen by the administrative agency.

The aim here is to substitute a predictable, "objective" measurement method—the impairment rating schedule—for the unpredictable and disputed ratings generated by previous schedules and lost earnings assessments. But there is an obvious danger. What if the worker's injury, given his education, occupation, age, and background, prevents him from returning to the workforce, even after the allotted 162 weeks? Texas provides a "supplemental" form of benefits to address this scenario. If, after 162 weeks following the date of medical stabilization, our worker has not returned to work or is earning less than 80% of his previous average weekly wages, then the worker is entitled to additional benefits based on his lost earnings. The worker must show good faith efforts to obtain a job.

What are the possible benefits and disadvantages of reforms such as that of Texas, compared to the two more traditional approaches just described?

Legislative reforms directed at disability and medical payments apparently have resulted in lower costs and more compensation dollars are being delivered to workers for each dollar expended for administrative overhead. *See* Jack Schmulowitz, *Workers' Compensation: Coverage, Benefits, and Costs,* 1992–93, in 1996 WORKERS' COMPENSATION YEARBOOK, AT I–33 (J. BURTON ED. 1996). Still, important questions remain unanswered, including the distributional equity of payments and the measurement accuracy, in practice, of the *AMA Guides* or other comprehensive impairment schedules. Although almost 40 states now mandate or recommend use of the *Guides* for use in workers' compensation claims, little research has been conducted as to whether measurements produced by the *Guides* correlate to lost-earning capacity in the short or long run. For more detail on the *Guides, see* Ellen S. Pryor, *Flawed Promises: A Critical Evaluation of the American Medical Association's Guides to the Evaluation of Permanent Impairment (Book Review),* 103 Harv. L. Rev. 964 (1990).

2. AUTOMOBILE NO–FAULT

Before beginning a look at auto no-fault, it is important to address several other strands in the current fabric for compensating auto injuries: financial responsibility and compulsory insurance laws; unsatisfied judgment funds; and uninsured and underinsured motorist coverage. As you read these materials, consider whether any one of these strands, or some combination of them, can effectively address the persistent concern about victims of insolvent or uninsured drivers.

a. Financial Responsibility and Compulsory Insurance Laws, Unsatisfied Judgment Funds, and Uninsured Motorists Coverage

Compulsory Insurance and Financial Responsibility Laws

Beginning in the 1920s, every state eventually enacted some form of "financial responsibility" or "compulsory insurance" legislation. These statutes usually require that every motorist have a certain minimum level of liability insurance, or be able to demonstrate—in lieu of having such insurance—the financial ability to satisfy a tort judgment, up to some point. Although over the years many states have improved enforcement of such laws, the minimum amounts are not high enough to ensure basic coverage for many severe injuries. The minimum levels are commonly

$20,000/$40,000/$10,000 (the first figure is the coverage amount for a single bodily injury; the second figure is the total amount required for the aggregate bodily injury if more than one person is injured in a single accident; and the third figure is the amount for property damage covered).

The enactment of compulsory insurance laws has raised thorny problems relating to the availability and affordability of insurance. Consider, for instance, a driver who has had two previous accidents, lives in an urban area, is under the age of 25, and drives a sports car. On the basis of these factors this driver and others who share these characteristics form a "risk pool" with a far greater chance than some other drivers of being involved in a serious accident. Without any regulatory constraints, private insurers either will not write coverage for this driver or will charge a rate considerably higher than those for many other drivers. This problem of differential risks creates competing political interests: drivers who fall in the riskier categories demand available and affordable insurance, especially because insurers' risk classifications (based on age, geography, and sometimes even credit history) may seem subjective or contestable; insurers warn that heavy regulation of rates will force insurers out of the market and thus reduce coverage for less risky drivers; and less risky drivers wish to avoid paying increased premiums for the risks posed by the risky drivers.

States have varied in their approaches to these competing demands, and all approaches have posed some problems. One approach, taken by just a handful of states, is to allow private insurers to operate with little regulation of rates. Three basic categories then emerge: many drivers will be charged basically standard rates; other drivers will pay high-risk rates; and a few drivers will be unable to obtain coverage at all in the "voluntary" market (that is, insurance voluntarily provided by private insurers). The state thus also creates a mechanism, often known as an "assigned risk plan," that will provide insurance for this "involuntary" market. Usually an assigned risk pool works as follows. The state requires that each insurer be assigned some proportion of the uninsurable drivers; the proportion depends on the total volume of auto insurance that the insurer writes in the state. A driver who is unable to obtain insurance in the standard voluntary market is then able to obtain insurance as an assigned risk, and must pay higher premiums. (The person will be altogether ineligible under certain circumstances, such as drug use, felony conviction, or habitual violation of law.) Insurers may sustain net losses on these assigned risks, even given higher premiums, and so the hope is that the size of the "involuntary market" or assigned risk pool is small.

Some have argued that this approach—minimal rate regulation—works best. Most drivers find coverage at standard rates, a smaller percentage must pay higher-risk rates, and a still-smaller percentage is unable to obtain insurance except through the involuntary system. Insurers are able to engage in risk differentiation among lower and higher risk insureds. In addition, although insurers are required to write insurance for a proportion of the assigned risks, insurers still can achieve an overall adequate return on auto insurance because, by slightly increasing the rates charged to all insureds, insurers can offset the losses that will be posed by the small percentage of assigned risks. Others criticize the approach because they maintain that regulation of rates is necessary to prevent excessive profits, or because they dispute the insurers' risk classifications, such as those based on geography, age, or sex. Many other states, therefore, have taken an approach that more heavily regulates rates charged for auto insurance.

Although the debate over these various mechanisms will continue, consider a few points that emerge from this brief description. First, absent restrictions, insurers will engage in considerable risk differentiation among drivers, differentiation that may depend on geography, age, sex, marital status, use of the auto, driver education, and driving record. Higher-risk insureds will pay higher rates (or will simply opt not to carry insurance and risk the consequences). Second, regulation of rates in the voluntary market has seemed to increase the number of drivers to whom insurers are unwilling to sell coverage at the regulated rate. Put another way, the number of drivers in the "voluntary market" decreases and the number in the "involuntary" market increases. Why? Third, under any system, the state needs some mechanism for providing insurance to the involuntary market. These mechanisms end up transferring, to the voluntary market or to state coffers, the costs of higher risk insureds.

Uninsured/Underinsured Motorist Coverage

Uninsured and underinsured motorist coverage is a feature of the liability insurance offered in most states. Basically, it works as follows. If the insured under a liability policy is injured by another party, and if that other party is underinsured or uninsured (or was a hit and run driver), then the injured person can recover against his own insurance company, up to the limits of the coverage, if he can show that the other party would have been liable for the injuries.

This coverage originated from the voluntary efforts of insurers seeking to avoid the imposition of compulsory insurance laws. Eventually all states required that uninsured coverage either be provided or offered. Many states have enacted similar provisions relating to underinsured motorist coverage.

b. History of Auto No–Fault

Early consideration of no-fault concepts was not limited to the employment arena. A study published in 1932, by the Committee to Study Compensation for Automobile Accidents of the Columbia University Council for Research in the Social Sciences, examined thousands of auto liability cases and criticized several features of the tort liability system. The study proposed making automobile insurance compulsory and imposing upon the owners of motor vehicles a limited absolute liability for personal injuries or death arising out of the operation of their vehicles. The plan adopted the compensation schedules used in the workers' compensation schemes of New York and Massachusetts. As under workers' compensation, the remedy under the proposed automobile compensation scheme was to be exclusive. The Columbia Plan, as might be expected, generated a great amount of often bitter controversy. Although never enacted into law, the Columbia Plan was the influential forerunner of a plan adopted in 1946 in the Canadian province of Saskatchewan (10 Geo. 6, c. 11), a plan that has been frequently amended since its initial adoption.

In 1965, Professors Robert E. Keeton and Jeffrey O'Connell published their BASIC PROTECTION FOR THE TRAFFIC VICTIM (hereafter *Basic Protection*), which proposed an auto no-fault system. Their proposed scheme applied to all injuries except severe injuries; a person with a severe injury retained the right to sue in tort. For anyone with a nonsevere injury, the no-fault scheme would be the only recourse. Under the no-fault scheme, benefits were to be paid by the injured person's own insurer, not the insurer of other individuals. Payment of benefits did not require a showing of anyone's fault. But benefits did not include payment for pain and suffering; rather, benefits were limited to net economic loss. An insured could buy a policy with greater protection (such as coverage for pain and suffering), but the premiums for this would be higher.

Almost contemporaneous with the publication of *Basic Protection*, another publication appeared that strongly argued against auto no-fault. W. Blum & H. Kalven, Jr., PUBLIC LAW PERSPECTIVES ON A PRIVATE LAW PROBLEM (1965). Blum and Kalven argued that a no-fault auto system would place on motorists both the costs of accidents caused by motorist fault and those not caused by motorist fault. In their view, there was no defensible reason for placing on motorists the costs of non-fault accidents. Rather, such costs in principle should be borne by the population as a whole, through the general tax and welfare system. And this result deserved rejection, in their view, because it simply created a form of social insurance for the victims of auto accidents, leaving victims of other injuries or illnesses uncovered or at least uncovered to such a degree. Do you find this criticism convincing?

In 1970, Massachusetts became the first state to adopt a no-fault plan. Since then several dozen states have adopted some version of auto no-fault. It is fair to say, however, that in recent years no-fault plans have lost much of their appeal as some insurers and consumer groups have ceased supporting this reform largely because no-fault auto-insurance claim costs proved to be higher than other auto-insurance systems.

c. Current Types of Auto No-Fault

Auto no-fault schemes vary in important ways. No state has entirely replaced the tort system with no-fault for all auto-related injuries although Michigan, New York, and Florida have adopted programs that eliminate a large proportion of tort suits relating to auto injuries. The no-fault schemes that do exist fall into several categories. One category is "add on" or "personal injury protection" no-fault, which exists in at least

20 states. These provisions pay the insured directly in the event of injury. They are either mandatory or optional. The tort system, however, remains fully in operation, and the injured driver still can pursue the other driver in tort.

Another type is partial no-fault. Under this category, which approximately twelve states allow, no-fault compensation is the only remedy for injuries that do not exceed a particular level of seriousness, defined either in terms of monetary damages caused or medical severity. That is, if the case falls below the threshold, then the person may not sue in tort and is limited to the no-fault benefits. Most of these states use a monetary threshold. When the threshold is higher, more cases will fall within the no-fault scheme; when the threshold is lower, more cases will remain within the traditional tort realm.

A third category of no-fault is a choice system. Under such a system, the insured driver would choose whether to be covered under the traditional tort system or under no-fault. Currently, only a few states have a limited form of choice. *See* James M. Anderson, et al., THE U.S. EXPERIENCE WITH NO-FAULT AUTOMOBILE INSURANCE: A RETROSPECTIVE 11–16 (RAND 2010).

The following is an excerpt of New York's auto no-fault statute.

McKINNEY'S CONSOLIDATED LAWS OF NEW YORK ARTICLE 51—COMPREHENSIVE MOTOR VEHICLE INSURANCE REPARATIONS

§ 5102. Definitions

In this chapter: (a) "Basic economic loss" means, up to fifty thousand dollars per person of the following combined items * * *: [All necessary medical care, including psychiatric and rehabilitative services; lost earnings; expenditures made to obtain services in lieu of those that the injured person would have performed for income; and other reasonable and necessary expenses up to $25 a day.]

* * *

(c) "Non-economic loss" means pain and suffering and similar non-monetary detriment.

(d) "Serious injury" means a personal injury which results in death; dismemberment; significant disfigurement; a fracture; loss of a fetus; permanent loss of use of a body organ, member, function or system; permanent consequential limitation of use of a body organ or member; significant limitation of use of a body function or system; or a medically determined injury or impairment of a non-permanent nature which prevents the injured person from performing substantially all of the material acts which constitute such person's usual and customary daily activities for not less than ninety days during the one hundred eighty days immediately following the occurrence of the injury or impairment.

* * *

(j) "Covered person" means any pedestrian injured through the use or operation of, or any owner, operator or occupant of, a motor vehicle which has in effect the financial security required by article six or eight of the vehicle and traffic law or which is referred to in subdivision two of section three hundred twenty-one of such law; or any other person entitled to first party benefits.

§ 5103. Entitlement to first party benefits; additional financial security required

(a) Every owner's policy of liability insurance issued [in compliance with the state compulsory insurance law] shall also provide for * * * the payment of first party benefits to:

(1) Persons, other than occupants of another motor vehicle or a motorcycle, for loss arising out of the use or operation in this state of such motor vehicle. * * *

(2) The named insured and members of his household, other than occupants of a motorcycle, for loss arising out of the use or operation of (i) an uninsured motor vehicle or motorcycle, within the United States, its territories or possessions, or Canada; and (ii) an insured motor vehicle or motorcycle outside of this state and within the United States, its territories or possessions, or Canada.

* * *

(b) An insurer may exclude from coverage required by subsection (a) hereof a person who:

(1) Intentionally causes his own injury.

(2) Is injured as a result of operating a motor vehicle while in an intoxicated condition or while his ability to operate such vehicle is impaired by the use of a drug. * * *

* * *

§ 5104. Causes of action for personal injury

(a) Notwithstanding any other law, in any action by or on behalf of a covered person against another covered person for personal injuries arising out of negligence in the use or operation of a motor vehicle in this state, there shall be no right of recovery for non-economic loss, except in the case of a serious injury, or for basic economic loss.

§ 5106. Fair claims settlement

(a) Payments of first party benefits and additional first party benefits shall be made as the loss is incurred. Such benefits are overdue if not paid within thirty days after the claimant supplies proof of the fact and amount of loss sustained. If proof is not supplied as to the entire claim, the amount which is supported by proof is overdue if not paid within thirty days after such proof is supplied. All overdue payments shall bear interest at the rate of two percent per month. If a valid claim or portion was overdue, the claimant shall also be entitled to recover his attorney's reasonable fee, for services necessarily performed in connection with securing payment of the overdue claim, subject to limitations promulgated by the superintendent in regulations.

NOTES

1. *Evaluating No–Fault.* From the standpoint of timely, certain, and complete compensation, what are the advantages and disadvantages of New York's no-fault scheme as compared to traditional tort? From the standpoint of deterrence, does the no-fault scheme achieve less of the desirable level of deterrence than the tort system? In addressing this question, consider how auto insurance rates will be set under, respectively, the traditional tort system and under a no-fault scheme such as that of New York, under which more severe injuries can remain in the tort system.

Early summaries of the empirical and analytic literature on auto no-fault systems (including true no-fault and the more common partial no-fault) concluded that, as compared to tort, no-fault approaches: (1) deliver a higher portion of premium payments to claimants than does tort; (2) deliver compensation to more accident victims; (3) reduce under-compensation and over-compensation; (4) deliver compensation more quickly; (5) reduce the number of lawsuits. No-fault has not, however, reduced premiums; indeed, premiums seem to be higher in no-fault states. In part, this is because the thresholds for filing a tort suit have not been high enough to prevent frequent filing of tort suits. In addition, the no-fault component compensates more people. Mark M. Hager, *No–Fault Drives Again: A Contemporary Primer*, 52 U. Miami L. Rev. 793 (1998). A 2010 Rand study confirms the cost conclusions and finds that the primary source of this difference is increased medical costs. It reports that whereas injury costs under no-fault were only 12 percent higher in 1987 than those under tort, this difference had ballooned to 73 percent by 2004. James M. Anderson, et al., THE U.S. EXPERIENCE WITH NO–FAULT AUTOMOBILE INSURANCE: A RETROSPECTIVE xv (RAND 2010). States that have repealed no-fault acts have experienced a substantial decline in premiums. *Id.* at 74–75

Moreover, originally no-fault states had lower levels of litigation activity and devoted a smaller share of payments to noneconomic damages in the 1980s than did tort states, but "by 2007, the two systems had largely converged on these characteristics. No-fault has shifted over time from a system with better medical benefits but reduced access to the courts to a system that simply offers more-generous medical benefits." *Id.* at xv–xvi.

The empirical and analytical studies addressing the deterrent impact of no-fault have reached mixed results. The Rand report summarizes eight studies of the effect of no-fault on fatal accidents, generally by comparing fatal-accident rates across states covered by no-fault and other systems while controlling for such things as aggregate driver and vehicle characteristics. Four of the studies find that no-fault coverage increases fatal accidents, while the other half find no evidence of such an effect. *Id.* at 81, Table 5.1 One study that examines the effect of no-fault laws on both fatal and non-fatal accidents finds no evidence of an effect of no-fault on accident rates.

2. *Retaining Tort for Severe Injuries.* As already noted, some states provide for some no-fault benefits in addition to full rights under the tort system. The New York statute does not simply add on no-fault benefits, but instead supplants the tort system in certain cases with the no-fault system. However, the New York statute has lead to a substantial amount of litigation over whether a particular injury is above or below the threshold. *See* 33 A.L.R.4th 767.

Assuming the desirability of no-fault for some injuries, what is the rationale for retaining tort as to more severe injuries? Is the rationale linked to the aim of compensation? The aim of deterrence? The aim of corrective justice? Or is the retention of tort for more severe injuries difficult to justify theoretically and thus reflective of a political compromise? Professors Keeton and O'Connell, in their initial landmark proposal, suggested retaining tort for more severe injuries. They explained that this would "retain most of whatever deterrent value tort liability engenders under the present system," and that it would also have a chance of political survival, in contrast to complete abolition of tort for auto-related injuries. *See* Robert E. Keeton & Jeffrey O'Connell, BASIC PROTECTION FOR THE TRAFFIC VICTIM 270–71 (1965). On the other hand Professor Schwartz concludes, "Those who support no-fault should support pure no-fault." Gary T. Schwartz, *Auto No-Fault and First-Party Insurance: Advantages and Problems*, 73 S. Cal. L. Rev. 611, 629 (2000).

If one is theoretically attracted to a two-tier approach, the remaining question is whether the two tiers can be effectively administered in practice. If the threshold is vague, then the threshold itself will generate litigation; if the doorway to tort is too wide or malleable, then injuries that in theory should be handled via no-fault will instead become tort claims. In light of these considerations, what is your evaluation of the threshold that the New York statute establishes? Can you suggest improvements?

3. *Choosing No-Fault and Pain and Suffering.* Under the New York scheme, pain and suffering damages are available only if a tort suit is available; pain and suffering are not included in no-fault benefits. New Jersey is an example of a state that has enacted a form of "choice" legislation. In New Jersey, auto owners are required to purchase no-fault insurance along with liability coverage, but they have two choices with respect to the no-fault coverage. If an owner chooses option 1, he retains the right to sue in tort for full tort damages (including pain and suffering) as to any injury, including less severe injuries. If an owner chooses option 2, he may sue in tort only if he meets a threshold that is quite similar to the one contained in the New York statute. The choice must be made in writing, on a form approved by the Insurance Commissioner. An owner who chooses option 2 will pay a smaller premium. N.J. Stat. 39:6A–8 (2003).

What factors might go into an individual's choice under New Jersey's choice approach? Would the wealth of the individual affect the choice? Would the individual's level of insurance coverage under other insurance, such as private medical and disability insurance? How about the individual's level of risk aversion?

3. NO–FAULT PROPOSALS FOR MEDICAL INJURIES AND FOR MASS TORT

Scholars and policymakers have also considered nontort alternatives for compensating medical injuries and mass tort injuries, especially mass tort claims resulting from toxic substances. Aside from specific categories of injuries (such as Vaccine Act discussed above), designing and implementing a general medical no-fault system would face substantial theoretical and practical (not to mention political) problems. One of the main challenges for such a program would be the difficulty of distinguishing between losses caused by a medical incident ("iatrogenic losses") versus losses due to other causes, such as preexisting illness. "Indeed, [opponents to medical no-fault] argue, in the medical context determining the actual *cause* of the patient's injury is typically as difficult as determining the doctor's fault. If that is the case, there would be higher administrative costs under no-fault because much larger numbers of patients would be making claims. * * * In practice it would likely be too costly and burdensome to have a patient compensation program try in each case to isolate precisely which of the immediate economic consequences were attributable to the original unhealthy condition and which to the iatrogenic injury, even after determining that such an injury had in fact occurred. Instead, the program would have to feature an across-the-board rule that no-fault insurance would be available only after a certain period of disability had elapsed, perhaps six months." American Law Institute, Reporters' Study on Enterprise Responsibility for Personal Injury, Vol. II, at 492–50. But medical researchers and policymakers point to strong advantages of a no-fault system as both a compensatory vehicle and as a more likely tool for implementing systemic risk management systems that could reduce the incidence of medical error. *See generally* David M. Studdert, *et al.*, *Beyond Dead Reckoning: Measures of Medical Injury Burden, Malpractice Litigation, and Alternative Compensation Models from Utah and California*, 33 Ind. L. Rev. 1643 (2000); Paul Barringer, et al., *Administrative Compensation of Medical Injuries: A Hardy Perennial Blooms Again*, 33 J. Health Pol. Pol'y & L. 725, 752 (2008) (noting that such reforms face fundamental political barriers, including: "the energetic opposition of the trial bar and the cautious response of health care providers to proposals that might lead to an increase in insurance costs.").

Addressing the broader topic of all types of tort reform that eliminate fault concepts, Professor Rabin has this to say:

> Is the renaissance of nonfault activity * * * now a historical artifact? That would be too strong a conclusion to draw from my survey of the ensuing years. But surely it has failed to ripen into a new era of transformed responsibility for accidental harm. I have suggested that political cross-currents have played the dominant role in stunting the growth of nonfault systems in the legislative arena. Absent the sense of urgency that is triggered by a perceived crisis in the delivery of

public health services, for example, or the human devastation of an unprecedented terrorist attack, legislative embrace of a tort replacement system has been hard to come by. Instead of a bold move to nonfault approaches, the legislative proclivity has been to whittle away at the borders of the traditional fault system through incremental reform, predominantly limitations on recoverable damages.

Robert L. Rabin, *The Renaissance of Accident Law Plans Revisited*, 64 Md. L. Rev. 699, 733 (2005).

E. LOSS-BASED PROGRAMS AND PROPOSALS

1. COMPREHENSIVE LOSS-BASED COMPENSATION: DOING AWAY WITH TORT LAW; THE NEW ZEALAND SYSTEM

In 1967, a Royal Commission, headed by Justice Woodhouse, proposed abolishing the common law of accidental injuries and replacing it with a unified compensation system not contingent on fault or the cause of an injury. The Accident Compensation Act was enacted in 1972. It abolished tort remedies for "personal injury by accident," a phrase interpreted to exclude ordinary sickness but to include occupational disease. As originally enacted, the Act covered only "earners," that is, people who worked for a wage or salary or self-employed persons. Before the Act became effective in 1974, however, it was amended to include homemakers and other non-earners. The Act also included periodic payments for permanent partial incapacity, and lump sums for loss or impairment of bodily functions and for loss of amenities or capacity to enjoy life, including disfigurement, pain and suffering, and nervous shock. Non-earners receive all the benefits of the Act with the important exception that they are not awarded anything for loss of earnings. Loss of earnings are computed at 80% of earnings over a base period with an upper limit that has been periodically increased. In the case of certain low-wage workers, compensation is provided at 90% of earnings over the base period.

To finance the scheme, which is administered by the New Zealand Accident Compensation Commission, an Earners Fund and a Motor Vehicle Fund were established. The Earners Fund is financed by levies on employers as a certain percentage of their payroll costs. Rates vary according to industry and occupation. Self-employed persons are taxed at a flat 1% of earnings. The Motor Vehicle Fund is financed by a levy on automobile owners. Unless an "earner" injured in an automobile accident was injured while acting in the course of employment, he is compensated from the Motor Vehicle Fund. When the Act was amended to include non-earners—that is, people not covered by the Earners Fund—a supplementary fund, dependent upon sums appropriated from general revenues, was established to provide compensation for non-earners for all accidents not covered by the Motor Vehicle Fund.

Criticisms of the scheme over the years have included its increasing costs, and its exclusion for non-occupational illnesses. On all these matters, see G. Palmer, COMPENSATION FOR INCAPACITY (1979). The increased costliness of the New Zealand scheme has presented some problems. These problems and the proposed solutions are discussed extensively in Richard S. Miller, *The Future of New Zealand's Accident Compensation Scheme*, 11 U.Haw.L.Rev. 1 (1989). For a critical assessment of the possible adoption of a New Zealand type plan in the United States, *see* James Henderson, *The New Zealand Accident Compensation Reform*, 48 U.Chi.L.Rev. 781 (1981). Another comparative law discussion of tort reform is Jeffrey O'Connell and Donald Partlett, *An America's Cup for Tort Reform? Australia and America Compared*, 21 J.L. Reform 443 (1988).

In 1992, New Zealand significantly modified the accident compensation scheme with the passage of the Accident Rehabilitation and Compensation Act. First, the scope of the scheme's application was cut back. Coverage now required injury by "by an accident" rather than just "by accident." The latter formulation was interpreted to extend coverage when the disability or problem was accidental even if the injury could not be linked to a particular external event or cause, or when the person suffered injury from witnessing a physical injury to another person. These instances no longer were covered. Second, the 1992 amendments cut back on benefits. Lump-sum payments for nonpecuniary losses now were not available, and instead were replaced by a more modest "independence allowance." Third, mental injury now was not compensable unless it resulted from an independent physical injury. Fourth, the pre–1992 scheme allowed compensation for injuries resulting from medical, surgical, or dental "misadventure," without further definition or restriction. The 1992 amendments include a two-page definition of a compensable "medical misadventure" that essentially required a showing of negligence. The 1992 amendments created an additional source of funding from premiums charged to health professionals. This change, along with the move to essentially a negligence requirement for victims of medical accidents, reflected a move toward deterrence objectives in the medical arena. For analysis of the 1992 changes, *see* Richard S. Miller, *An Analysis and Critique of the 1992 Changes to New Zealand's Accident Compensation Scheme*, 52 Md. L. Rev. 1070 (1993).

The statute was revised once again in 2005. It relaxed the qualifying criteria for claims relating to the adverse outcomes of medical care and abandoned the fault-based test of medical error in the 1992 reforms. Nevertheless, it retained a distinction between injury caused by medical treatment and injury attributable to the individual's underlying medical condition. Ken Oliphant summarizes:

> In the Woodhouse Commission's analysis of its foundational principle of community responsibility, it was possible to discern two distinct theories, one based on social solidarity, the other on causality * * * Social solidarity, it is generally agreed, points irresistibly towards a comprehensive compensation scheme encompassing incapacity in gen-

> eral, and cannot provide convincing criteria by which to determine the boundaries of a scheme limited by and large to injury. The principle of causal community responsibility, in contrast, suggests that [the Accident Compensation Act] boundaries might be set by reference to a distinction between natural conditions and incapacities resulting from the interplay of social forces. And, this is very substantially the approach adopted in the 2005 reform in respect of the adverse outcomes of medical treatment. Under the treatment injury provisions, the fundamental question (as it has been described here) is posed directly and without adornment, namely whether the injury is attributable to the patient's underlying health (natural) or the treatment (social).

Ken Oliphant, *Beyond Misadventure: Compensation for Medical Injuries in New Zealand*, 15 Med. L. Rev. 357, 390–91 (2007).

Thus even the New Zealand plan must deal with the boundaries between a fully loss based system and one that retains some causation components. In his timely review of the New Zealand approach, Professor Schuck notes that:

> By focusing on accident outcomes rather than on the process by which they occurred, a no-fault scheme can reduce some of the difficulties in establishing tort-relevant causation, but it cannot eliminate them. This truth is particularly relevant in the area of medical treatment, where adverse outcomes often are caused more by a patient's preexisting physical condition or bad luck than the treatment itself. So long as society is unwilling to compensate for the former, the causation issue will remain....

Peter H. Schuck, *Tort Reform, Kiwi–Style*, 27 Yale L. & Pol'y Rev. 187, 199 (2008).

Scholars have proposed a more dramatic reform than the New Zealand plan: a general loss-based compensation scheme that would replace tort and that would apply to both partial and total disabilities. One proposal, made by Professor Richard Pierce, would create a new federal agency that would compensate victims of accidents and disease and regulate safety in all areas of the economy. Compensation would not depend on fault, and the amount of compensation due for particular injuries or diseases would be determined according to formulas and schedules similar to those used in workers' compensation programs. Funding for the agency and its compensation would depend in part on general tax revenues, but the agency also would assess costs against various types of industries, based on the number and severity of accidents caused. For more detail, *see* Richard J. Pierce, Jr., *Encouraging Safety: The Limits of Tort Law and Government Regulation*, 33 Vand. L. Rev. 1281 (1980).

Professor Stephen Sugarman set out one of the most detailed critiques of tort and proposals for comprehensive tort replacement. The basics of his proposal include the following. All Americans would be assured income for periods of temporary and permanent disability, and would also receive medical expense protection that would include traditional medical needs, rehabilitation, and assistant care. Safety regulation should remain the province of regulatory agencies, but individuals might be afforded private rights of action against injurers, not for compensatory but for injunctive relief against plainly and unreasonably dangerous conduct. *See* Stephen Sugarman, DOING AWAY WITH PERSONAL INJURY LAW (1989).

2. SOCIAL SECURITY DISABILITY

As noted at the outset of this chapter, the major loss-based programs in the United States are the social security disability system and private health care insurance. These systems are not fault-based (coverage does not require a showing of fault) or cause-based (coverage does not depend on a causal link such as work relation or arising out of the use of an auto). Rather, coverage depends on whether the person is enrolled in the program and whether the person has sustained the type of loss covered.

Social Security disability insurance (SSDI) was added to the Social Security program in 1956. It pays cash benefits to workers (and to their eligible spouses, children, and survivors) who have been employed for the requisite number of quarters and who are found to be disabled. "Disability" is defined as "inability to engage in any substantial gainful activity by reason of any medically determinable physical or mental impairment which can be expected to result in death or has lasted or can be expected to last for a continuous period of not less than 12 months", 42 U.S.C. § 423 (1990). The program is not means-tested; that is, it does not depend on the claimant's financial need. Monthly benefits are based on the worker's annual taxable earnings, averaged over most of the worker's adult years; the payment is subject to a maximum family benefit amount. Supplemental security income (SSI), added to the Social Security program in 1972, pays additional benefits to individuals who fall below a certain income level and are disabled.

Statutes and regulations set out extremely detailed substantive and procedural requirements governing the determination of disability. A multi-layered administrative decisional process, including a hearing by an administrative law judge, is responsible for the determination of disability. The results of the administrative decisional process are reviewable in federal district court.

One might suppose that, since the program does not require proof of fault or causation, the program has been relatively free of decisional controversies and difficulties. Yet the social security disability program has been the subject of intense political, scholarly, and judicial controversy. Points of controversy have included the following: the increase in numbers and size of disability payments and whether funding is adequate; the fairness of the decisional criteria and processes, including when a disability recipient may be cut off on the grounds that he or she is no longer disabled; the extreme inefficiencies and delay in making decisions; the standards governing disability for children with disabilities; and the standards governing mental disabilities. For more detail on these issues, *see* Jerry L. Mashaw, BUREAUCRATIC JUSTICE (1983); Ellen S. Pryor, *Compensation and the Ineradicable Problems of Pain,* 59 Geo.Wash.L.Rev. 239 (1991); Kenneth Abraham and Lance Liebman, *Private Insurance, Social Insurance and Tort Reform: Toward a New Vision of Compensation for Illness and Injury*, 93 Colum. L. Rev. 75 (1993). For a detailed analysis of the role the SSD program plays, see Matthew Diller, *Entitlement and Exclusion: the Role of Disability in the Social Welfare System,* 44 U.C.L.A. L.Rev. 361 (1996); Frank S. Bloch, *Medical Proof, Social Policy, and Social Security's Medically Centered Definition of Disability*, 92 Cornell L. Rev. 189 (2007); Jon C. Dubin, *Overcoming Gridlock: Campbell After a Quarter–Century and Bureaucratically Rational Gap–Filling in Mass Justice Adjudication in the Social Security Administration's Disability Programs,* 62 Admin. L. Rev. 937 (2010).

Professor Deborah Stone, in her study of disability policy, offers insights into why the design and administration of disability programs may remain difficult even when they do not require adjudication of fault or causal origin. Clinical tests cannot answer the question of whether one is "impaired" or "disabled" or still able to work. Someone must decide this issue and decide what to do when there are contradictory tests or conflicting expert opinions. The opinions themselves are somewhat subjective. The building blocks of clinical practice: medical history, blood pressure, pulse, and temperature measurements, X-rays, and laboratory tests do not "speak for themselves." Numerous studies have demonstrated significant variations among physicians and laboratory technicians in interpreting them. Moreover, patients themselves may influence test results, by, for example, failing to make a serious effort when asked to take a cardiac stress test or a pulmonary function test. She concludes

> Thus, one can trace in one particular type of disability—respiratory disease—a hierarchy of criteria from highly subjective to more objective. But ultimately, even the most objective criteria are subject to manipulation, and in the end the decision about what constitutes a legitimate medical impairment is still a matter of judgment. Given, this analysis of factors that influence clinical judgment, it is not surprising to find substantial inconsistencies in disability determination in a program whose definition rests on clinical judgment.

Deborah Stone, THE DISABLED STATE 127–33 (1984).

CHAPTER 7

INTENTIONAL INFLICTION OF EMOTIONAL DISTRESS

■ ■ ■

TEXAS & PACIFIC RAILWAY v. JONES

Court of Civil Appeals of Texas, 1897.
39 S.W. 124.

HUNTER, J. On the 5th day of April, 1892, appellee Jessie Jones, about 45 minutes before train time, walked into the waiting room of appellant's station at Millsap, Tex., carrying some bundles in her arms, which she laid down on the seat, and sat down by them, intending to purchase a ticket to a small station on appellant's road, and to become a passenger on appellant's train, which was soon to arrive. She was called across the street by a friend, and, leaving her bundles in her seat, she left the waiting room, went across, the street, and returned in about 15 minutes, when she found her bundles had been thrown out of the waiting room on the platform. She inquired of the station agent's wife, who was at the ticket window, where her bundles were, when the agent's wife told her she knew nothing about them, and cared nothing about them, nor about her either, and then and there used insulting and abusive language about appellee, accusing her of being indecent, in having undressed before men, and of stealing her scissors, and continued the abuse for some 10 minutes, so that persons on the platform heard the abusive and insulting language, and saw the agent's wife throw the bundles out the window. The appellant's agent was in the ticket office, within a few feet of his wife, and heard, or could have heard, his wife's language and made no effort to protect appellee, or restrain his wife in her rude and abusive conduct towards her. Appellee was behaving herself properly at the time, and did nothing to call forth the abuse. Appellee was much humiliated and mortified in feelings from the abusive and insulting language used, had a severe headache consequent upon the nervous excitement produced thereby, and was made sick, and cried, and suffered pain and mental anguish by reason thereof, and was damaged in the amount of the verdict found by the jury, to wit, $450.

* * *

On her right to recover damages for mental suffering, we think that it was the duty of the appellant's station agent to protect appellee from insult and abuse from all persons while she was at its station, waiting to become a passenger on its train, whether she received physical injuries or did not. *Leach v. Leach* (Tex.Civ.App.) 33 S.W. 703. In the Leach Case there was no bodily injury, but only the mental suffering of a virtuous woman consequent upon an unwarranted proposal for sexual intercourse; and the supreme court refused a writ of error in that case. The right of a lady passenger to be secure from personal insult and abuse in the waiting room of a railroad station, and the correlative obligation of the railroad company, who has invited her there, to protect her in such right while there, is as clear in the one case as in the other. * * * We find no error in the judgment, and it is affirmed.

NOTES

1. A later Texas case held that, in determining whether the behavior of the carrier's employees was tortious, the age as well as the sex of the plaintiff must be taken into account. Fort Worth & Rio Grande Railway v. Bryant, 210 S.W. 556 (Tex.Civ.App.1919) ("obscene, vulgar, and profane language" actionable by ten year old girl but not by her father). Nevertheless there are cases allowing recovery by grown men. *See* Lipman v. Atlantic Coast Line Railroad, 108 S.C. 151, 93 S.E. 714 (1917). The first of the carrier cases seems to have been Chamberlain v. Chandler, 5 Fed.Cas. 413 (C.C.D.Mass.1823) (ship's captain insulted and mistreated passengers). The *Restatement of Torts* § 48 (1934) summarized these early cases by providing for the liability of a common carrier "for the offense reasonably suffered" by its passengers "through the insulting conduct of its servants while otherwise acting within the scope of their employment." The Restatement added a *caveat* as to whether this liability extends to "public utilities other than common carriers and to the possessors of land who for their business purposes hold it open as a place of public resort." In 1965, the American Law Institute extended the liability to public utilities (Restatement (Second) of Torts § 48), but retained a *caveat* as to whether "this Section may also be applicable to possessors of land whose premises are held open to the public for a business or other purpose." The extension of liability to public utilities whose employees, such as telephone repairmen or meter readers, often enter their customers' residences seems particularly warranted. Liability for insulting behavior has also been imposed upon innkeepers who were required, at least by English common law, to serve anyone who was prepared to pay the innkeeper's charges and deport himself properly.

2. In 1934, the American Law Institute confined recovery for conduct "intended or * * * likely to cause only mental or emotional disturbance" to cases of assault and the common carrier situations just discussed. *Restatement of Torts* § 46. As we shall soon see, this situation has now changed.

3. Even when recovery for intentional infliction of emotional distress was not generally recognized, recovery was occasionally had in some other limited types of circumstances. Thus, in Wilkinson v. Downton, [1897] 2 Q.B.

57, a practical joker told the plaintiff that her husband had been badly injured in an accident. She rushed off in a cab to get her husband. "The effect of this statement upon the plaintiff was a violent shock to her nervous system, producing vomiting and other more serious and permanent physical consequences at one time threatening her reason, and entailing weeks of suffering and incapacity as well as expense to her husband for medical attendance." The court would only allow the plaintiff to recover her cab fare on a fraud count. It nevertheless upheld a jury award of £100 for injuries caused by nervous shock because the defendant had "wilfully done an act calculated to cause physical harm to the plaintiff * * * and has in fact thereby caused physical harm to her." *Wilkinson* is often classed as a case of "intangible battery." *Cf.* Price v. Yellow Pine Paper Mill Co., 240 S.W. 588 (Tex.Civ.App. 1922), where an injured employee was carried to his home over his objections, and his wife, on seeing him bloody and battered, became ill and miscarried. On developments in English law, *see* R. Townshend–Smith, *Harassment as a Tort in English and American Law: The Boundaries of* Wilkinson v. Downton, 24 Anglo–Am.L.Rev. 299 (1995).

Another cruel practical joke case is Nickerson v. Hodges, 146 La. 735, 84 So. 37 (1920). The plaintiff, who died while the case was pending, was a spinster who had an obsession about finding a pot of gold coins supposedly buried by her ancestors on or near some land which had passed into the ownership of one of the defendants. Some twenty years earlier the plaintiff had actually been institutionalized "in an insane asylum, to the knowledge" of the defendants. What the defendants did was to bury an old pot containing rocks at a place where Miss Nickerson and those who were helping her in the search would find it. When the pot was found, arrangements were made to have it opened at a local bank in which Miss Nickerson had left the pot for safekeeping. A sizeable crowd attended the opening. When the pot proved to contain rocks and dirt, Miss Nickerson flew into a rage and had to be physically restrained from assaulting some of the defendants. The defendants claimed, *inter alia,* that they were trying to show Miss Nickerson that her obsession was a folly.

Section 306 of the *Restatement of Torts* tried to accommodate, at least the result, in cases like *Wilkinson,* by providing that "[a]n act may be negligent, as creating an unreasonable risk of bodily harm * * * if the actor intends to subject, * * * or should realize that his act involves an unreasonable risk of subjecting, the other to an emotional disturbance of such a character as to be likely to result in illness or other bodily harm." *See also id.* § 312 which is a companion provision. The provisions were retained *verbatim* in the *Restatement (Second).* A case going beyond § 306 was Blakeley v. Shortal's Estate, 236 Iowa 787, 20 N.W.2d 28 (1945). In that case, Shortal, a farmer, had recently been divorced. A day or so following "a sale" and division of the property with his ex-wife, Shortal went to the neighboring Blakeley farm and asked to spend the night. The next morning, after breakfast, Shortal asked for paper and pencil because he felt that "in the division of his property he had been beaten out of some money." At noon the plaintiff and her husband went to town to do some shopping. When they returned at four, the plaintiff opened the kitchen door to find Shortal lying in pools of blood. He had killed himself with a skinning knife belonging to the plaintiff's son. In bringing an action for mental and physical shock, the only allegations of physical injury were difficulty in sleeping, nervousness, and restlessness. The trial court granted a directed verdict for the defendant. The Supreme Court of Iowa reversed and directed that the case be submitted to the jury to decide whether Shortal could be said to have willfully inflicted shock and fright in subjecting the plaintiff to "the gory and ghastly sight."

STATE RUBBISH COLLECTORS ASSOCIATION v. SILIZNOFF

Supreme Court of California, 1952.
38 Cal.2d 330, 240 P.2d 282.

TRAYNOR, JUSTICE.

On February 1, 1948, Peter Kobzeff signed a contract with the Acme Brewing Company to collect rubbish from the latter's brewery. Kobzeff had been in the rubbish business for several years and was able to secure the contract because Acme was dissatisfied with the service then being provided by another collector, one Abramoff. Although Kobzeff signed the contract, it was understood that the work should be done by John Siliznoff, Kobzeff's son-in-law, whom Kobzeff wished to assist in establishing a rubbish collection business.

Both Kobzeff and Abramoff were members of the plaintiff State Rubbish Collectors Association, but Siliznoff was not. The by-laws of the association provided that one member should not take an account from another member without paying for it. Usual prices ranged from five to ten times the monthly rate paid by the customer, and disputes were referred to the board of directors for settlement. After Abramoff lost the Acme account he complained to the association, and Kobzeff was called upon to settle the matter. Kobzeff and Siliznoff took the position that the Acme account belonged to Siliznoff, and that he was under no obligation to pay for it. After attending several meetings of plaintiff's board of directors Siliznoff finally agreed, however, to pay Abramoff $1,850 for the Acme account and join the association. The agreement provided that he should pay $500 in thirty days and $75 per month thereafter until the whole sum agreed upon was paid. Payments were to be made through the association, and Siliznoff executed a series of promissory notes totaling $1,850. None of these notes was paid, and in 1949 plaintiff association brought this action to collect the notes then payable. Defendant cross-complained and asked that the notes be cancelled because of duress and want of consideration. In addition he sought general and exemplary damages because of assaults made by plaintiff and its agents to compel him to join the association and pay Abramoff for the Acme account. The jury returned a verdict against plaintiff and for defendant on the complaint and for defendant on his cross-complaint. It awarded him $1,250 general and special damages and $7,500 exemplary damages. The trial court denied a motion for a new trial on the condition that defendant consent to a reduction of the exemplary damages to $4,000. Defendant filed the required consent, and plaintiff has appealed from the judgment.

Plaintiff's primary contention is that the evidence is insufficient to support the judgment. Defendant testified that shortly after he secured the Acme account, the president of the association and its inspector, John Andikian, called on him and Kobzeff. They suggested that either a settlement be made with Abramoff or that the job be dropped, and requested Kobzeff and defendant to attend a meeting of the association. At this meeting defendant was told that the association "ran all the rubbish from that office, all the rubbish hauling," and that if he did not pay for the job they would take it away from him. " 'We would take it away, even if we had to haul for nothing.' * * * [O]ne of them mentioned that I had better pay up, or else." Thereafter, on the day when defendant finally agreed to pay for the account, Andikian visited defendant at the Rainier Brewing Company, where he was collecting rubbish. Andikian told defendant that " 'We will give you up till tonight to get down to the board meeting and make some kind of arrangements or agreements about the Acme Brewery, or otherwise we are going to beat you up.' * * * He says he either would hire somebody or do it himself. And I says, 'Well, what would they do to me?' He says, well, they would physically beat me up first, cut up the truck tires or burn the truck, or otherwise put me out of business completely. He said if I didn't appear at that meeting and make some kind of an agreement that they would do that, but he says up to then they would let me alone, but if I walked out of that meeting that night they would beat me up for sure." Defendant attended the meeting and protested that he owed nothing for the Acme account and in any event could not pay the amount demanded. He was again told by the president of the association that "that table right there [the board of directors] ran all the rubbish collecting in Los Angeles and if there was any routes to be gotten that they would get them and distribute them among their members * * *." After two hours of further discussion defendant agreed to join the association and pay for the Acme account. He promised to return the next day and sign the necessary papers. He testified that the only reason "they let me go home, is that I promised that I would sign the notes the very next morning." The president "made me promise on my honor and everything else, and I was scared, and I knew I had to come back, so I believed he knew I was scared and that I would come back. That's the only reason they let me go home." Defendant also testified that because of the fright he suffered during his dispute with the association he became ill and vomited several times and had to remain away from work for a period of several days.

Plaintiff contends that the evidence does not establish an assault against defendant because the threats made all related to action that might take place in the future; that neither Andikian nor members of the board of directors threatened immediate physical harm to defendant. * * * We have concluded, however, that a cause of action is established when it is shown that one, in the absence of any privilege, intentionally subjects another to the mental suffering incident to serious threats to his physical well-being, whether or not the threats are made under such circumstances as to constitute a technical assault.

In the past it has frequently been stated that the interest in emotional and mental tranquillity is not one that the law will protect from invasion in its own right. * * * As late as 1934 the Restatement of Torts took the position that "The interest in mental and emotional tranquillity and, therefore, in freedom from mental and emotional disturbance is not, as a thing in itself, regarded as of sufficient importance to require others to refrain from conduct intended or recognizably likely to cause such a disturbance." Restatement, Torts, § 46, comment c. The Restatement explained the rule allowing recovery for the mere apprehension of bodily harm in traditional assault cases as an historical anomaly, § 24, comment c, and the rule allowing recovery for insulting conduct by an employee of a common carrier as justified by the necessity of securing for the public comfortable as well as safe service. § 48, comment c.

The Restatement recognized, however, that in many cases mental distress could be so intense that it could reasonably be foreseen that illness or other bodily harm might result. If the defendant intentionally subjected the plaintiff to such distress and bodily harm resulted, the defendant would be liable for negligently causing the plaintiff bodily harm. Restatement, Torts, §§ 306, 312. Under this theory the cause of action was not founded on a right to be free from intentional interference with mental tranquillity, but on the right to be free from negligent interference with physical well-being. A defendant who intentionally subjected another to mental distress without intending to cause bodily harm would nevertheless be liable for resulting bodily harm if he should have foreseen that the mental distress might cause such harm.

The California cases have been in accord with the Restatement in allowing recovery where physical injury resulted from intentionally subjecting the plaintiff to serious mental distress. * * *

The view has been forcefully advocated that the law should protect emotional and mental tranquillity as such against serious and intentional invasions * * * and there is a growing body of case law supporting this position. * * * In recognition of this development the American Law Institute amended section 46 of the Restatement of Torts in 1947 to provide: "One who, without a privilege to do so, intentionally causes severe emotional distress to another is liable (a) for such emotional distress, and (b) for bodily harm resulting from it."

In explanation it stated that "The interest in freedom from severe emotional distress is regarded as of sufficient importance to require others to refrain from conduct intended to invade it. Such conduct is tortious. The injury suffered by the one whose interest is invaded is frequently far more serious to him than certain tortious invasions of the interest in bodily integrity and other legally protected interests. * * *."

There are persuasive arguments and analogies that support the recognition of a right to be free from serious, intentional, and unprivileged invasions of mental and emotional tranquillity. If a cause of action is otherwise established, it is settled that damages may be given for mental suffering naturally ensuing from the acts complained of, * * * and in the case of many torts, such as assault, battery, false imprisonment, and defamation, mental suffering will frequently constitute the principal element of damages. * * * In cases where mental suffering constitutes a major element of damages it is anomalous to deny recovery because the defendant's intentional misconduct fell short of producing some physical injury.

It may be contended that to allow recovery in the absence of physical injury will open the door to unfounded claims and a flood of litigation, and that the requirement that there be physical injury is necessary to insure that serious mental suffering actually occurred. The jury is ordinarily in a better position, however, to determine whether outrageous conduct results in mental distress than whether that distress in turn results in physical injury. From their own experience jurors are aware of the extent and character of the disagreeable emotions that may result from the defendant's conduct, but a difficult medical question is presented when it must be determined if emotional distress resulted in physical injury. See, Smith, Relation of Emotions to Injury and Disease, 30 Va.L.Rev. 193, 303–306. Greater proof that mental suffering occurred is found in the defendant's conduct designed to bring it about than in physical injury that may or may not have resulted therefrom.

That administrative difficulties do not justify the denial of relief for serious invasions of mental and emotional tranquillity is demonstrated by the cases recognizing the right of privacy. Recognition of that right protects mental tranquillity from invasion by unwarranted and undesired publicity. Melvin v. Reid, 112 Cal.App. 285, 289, 297 P. 91 * * *. As in the case of the protection of mental tranquillity from other forms of invasion, difficult problems in determining the kind and extent of invasions that are sufficiently serious to be actionable are presented. Also the public interest in the free dissemination of news must be considered. Nevertheless courts have concluded that the problems presented are not so insuperable that they warrant the denial of relief altogether.

In the present case plaintiff caused defendant to suffer extreme fright. By intentionally producing such fright it endeavored to compel him either to give up the Acme account or pay for it, and it had no right or privilege to adopt such coercive methods, in competing for business. In these circumstances liability is clear.

* * *

The judgment is affirmed.

NOTES

1. The subject of invasion of privacy is discussed in Chapter Nine, *infra.*

2. Although Traynor, J.'s, discussion is wide-ranging, is it not the case that *Siliznoff* involved conduct that, while not an assault (either criminally or

civilly) because the threat of physical harm was not immediate enough, was nevertheless arguably criminal, namely attempted extortion? Under this view of the matter *Siliznoff* could be viewed as another limited exception to the no-liability rule. The bill collector cases, to be considered at pp. 451–54, *infra,* would, under this approach, constitute another limited exception to the no-liability rule. After finishing the chapter one might consider whether this piecemeal approach might have been better. As noted by Traynor, J., however, the *Restatement* took a more expansive approach, the ramifications of which will be considered in the next few cases.

KORBIN v. BERLIN

District Court of Appeal of Florida, 1965.
177 So.2d 551.

CARROLL, JUDGE.

This appeal is from an order dismissing an amended complaint in an action brought by a six year old girl through her guardian and next friend. It was alleged in the amended complaint that at a certain time and place the defendant "Willfully and maliciously approached the said plaintiff * * * and made the following statement to her: 'Do you know that your mother took a man away from his wife? Do you know God is going to punish them? Do you know that a man is sleeping in your mother's room?' She then again repeated, 'God will punish them.'" It was alleged the statements were knowingly false, "made maliciously, willfully and with utter disregard to the feelings of the six-year-old Plaintiff," and it was further alleged that the statements were made "for the purpose of causing the plaintiff-child undue emotional stress, mental pain and anguish." Resultant injuries were alleged, and damages were sought.

In our opinion the trial judge was in error in holding that a cause of action was not stated, and we reverse * * *.

The law in this state with reference to the cause of action declared on is dealt with in the cited cases. Thus, in Kirksey v. Jernigan, supra (45 So.2d at 189), the Supreme Court said:

> "This court is committed to the rule, and we re-affirm it herein, that there can be no recovery for mental pain and anguish unconnected with physical injury in an action arising out of the negligent breach of a contract whereby simple negligence is involved. * * *
>
> "But we do not feel constrained to extend this rule to cases founded purely in tort, where the wrongful act is such as to reasonably imply malice, or where, from the entire want of care of attention to duty, or great indifference to the persons, property, or rights of others, such malice will be imputed as would justify the assessment of exemplary or punitive damages. * * * "

Later, in Slocum v. Food Fair Stores of Florida, supra (100 So.2d at 397–398) it was said:

"A most cogent statement of the doctrine covering tort liability for insult has been incorporated in the Restatement of the Law of Torts, 1948 supplement, sec. 46, entitled 'Conduct intended to cause emotional distress only.' It makes a blanket provision for liability on the part of 'one, who, without a privilege to do so, intentionally causes severe emotional distress to another,' indicating that the requisite intention exists 'when the act is done for the purpose of causing the distress or with knowledge * * * that severe emotional distress is substantially certain to be produced by [such] conduct.' Comment (a), sec. 46, supra. Abusive language is, of course, only one of the many means by which the tort could be committed.

"However, even if we assume, without deciding, the legal propriety of that doctrine, a study of its factual applications shows that a line of demarcation should be drawn between conduct likely to cause mere 'emotional distress' and that causing 'severe emotional distress,' so as to exclude the situation at bar. Illus. 5, sec. 46, supra. * * *

"This tendency to hinge the cause of action upon the degree of the insult has led some courts to reject the doctrine in toto. Wallace v. Shoreham Hotel Corp., D.C.Mun.App., 49 A.2d 81. Whether or not this is desirable, it is uniformly agreed that the determination of whether words or conduct are actionable in character is to be made on an objective rather than subjective standard, from common acceptation. The unwarranted intrusion must be calculated to cause 'severe emotional distress' to a person of ordinary sensibilities, in the absence of special knowledge or notice. * * * "

The complaint in the instant case met the requirements for validity as outlined in Kirksey v. Jernigan, supra, as quoted above. This is so because the claim presented here for damages "for mental pain and anguish unconnected with physical injury" did not arise "out of the negligent breach of a contract whereby simple negligence is involved" but from action "founded purely in tort, where the wrongful act is such as to reasonably imply malice," or "great indifference" to the rights of others. The alleged tortious injury did not occur incident to violation of a contract obligation, but in the course of a tortious act, which, if the facts so established, was a slander of the plaintiff's mother.

In the later Slocum case, the Supreme Court showed readiness to apply the rule discussed and quoted * * *. However, in the Slocum case it was held the words used were not of such consequence.

Therefore, the determinative question here is whether what was said to the child was intended or reasonably calculated to cause the child "severe emotional distress." The alleged statements and the manner and circumstances under which they were communicated to the child leave little room to doubt they were made with a purpose and intent to shame her, and to shock the sensibilities of this child of tender years. Relating, as they did, to the child's mother, the content and import of the statements were such that it can not be said as a matter of law that this alleged deliberately harmful act was not one "calculated to cause 'severe emotional distress' to a person [child] of ordinary sensibilities." See Slocum v. Food Fair Stores of Florida, supra.

Accordingly, the order dismissing the amended complaint is reversed and the cause is remanded for further proceedings.

SWANN, JUDGE (dissenting).

I dissent on the authority of Slocum v. Food Fair Stores of Florida, Inc., Fla.1958, 100 So.2d 396, and Mann v. Roosevelt Shop, Inc., Fla.1949, 41 So.2d 894.

NOTES

1. Suppose it proved to be true that the girl's mother, in some manner of speaking, "took a man away from his wife?" Should recovery be permitted then? Would allowing recovery interfere not only with the defendant's "freedom of speech" but also the "free exercise" of her religion? If the truth of the charge is a defense, is the court then merely expanding the class of potential plaintiffs in defamation actions to include the young children of persons who have been defamed?

2. In Slocum v. Food Fair Stores of Florida, Inc., 100 So.2d 396 (Fla. 1958), relied on in *Korbin,* one of the defendant's employees was asked the price of an item he was in the process of marking. He was alleged to have responded: "If you want to know the price, you'll have to find out the best way you can * * * you stink to me." The Supreme Court of Florida upheld the dismissal of the complaint.

3. Undoubtedly in reaction to the potential constitutional issues and the reluctant attitude adopted by courts in cases like *Slocum,* § 46 was again revised in 1965 with the publication of the *Restatement (Second) of Torts* § 46(1). Those changes, with minor alterations in wording, have been incorporated in *Restatement (Third) of Torts, Liability for Physical and Emotional Harm* § 46 which is about to be published and provides as follows:

> An actor who by extreme and outrageous conduct intentionally or recklessly causes severe emotional harm to another is subject to liability for that emotional harm and, if the emotional harm causes bodily harm, also for the bodily harm.

Thus, unlike the original 1948 revision referred to in the *Korbin* case, the intentional infliction of severe emotional distress is, by itself, not enough to result in liability. The severe emotional distress must be caused by "extreme and outrageous conduct." At the same time the *Restatement (Second)* and *Restatement (Third)* extended liability beyond that encompassed in the 1948 revision to recklessly caused severe emotional distress. The 1948 revision only applied to *intentionally* caused severe emotional distress. As the subsequent cases to be presented indicate, it is not at all clear that these changes avoid the constitutional problems that will be discussed later in this chapter. It has been questioned whether, if the defendant's conduct is "extreme and outrageous" enough, the plaintiff should be under any obligation to show that he suffered "severe emotional distress." *See* W. Pedrick, *Should Section 46 Be*

Revised?, 13 Pepp.L.Rev. 1 (1985). Do you agree? There is normally no such requirement in most intentional torts. *See, e.g.*, Niblo v. Parr Mfg., Inc., 445 N.W.2d 351 (Iowa 1989) a wrongful discharge case where the plaintiff showed that the defendant's conduct was "willful" and which has numerous citations to cases involving other types of intentional torts.

4. Several states still have so-called insult statutes. *See* Miss.Code 1972 Ann., § 95–1–1; Va.Code § 18.2–416 (1996); W.Va.Code, 55–7–2 (1994). Statutes of this type had their origin in the anti-dueling codes of the nineteenth century. Generally they provide for liability for words which from their "usual construction and common acceptance" are considered as "insults" and lead to violence and breach of the peace. For a variety of reasons, including very definitely the possible conflict with a speaker's First Amendment rights, in modern times these statutes have tended to be construed as imposing no more than a statutory remedy for defamation, the subject which will be discussed in the next chapter.

WOMACK v. ELDRIDGE

Supreme Court of Virginia, 1974.
215 Va. 338, 210 S.E.2d 145.

I'ANSON, CHIEF JUSTICE.

Plaintiff, Danny Lee Womack, instituted this action against the defendant, Rosalie Eldridge, to recover compensatory and punitive damages for mental shock and distress allegedly caused by the defendant's willful, wanton, malicious, fraudulent and deceitful acts and conduct toward him. The question of punitive damages was stricken by the trial court and the jury returned a verdict for the plaintiff in the amount of $45,000. The trial court set aside the verdict *non obstante veredicto* on the ground that there could be no recovery for emotional distress in the absence of "physical damage or other bodily harm." We granted plaintiff a writ of error. Defendant did not assign cross-error, although the record shows she excepted to many rulings in the court below and several of them are relied upon in her brief and argument before us.

Plaintiff assigned numerous errors, but the controlling question is whether one who by extreme and outrageous conduct intentionally or recklessly causes severe emotional distress to another is subject to liability for such emotional distress absent any bodily injury.

The evidence shows that defendant had been engaged in the business of investigating cases for attorneys for many years. She was employed by Richard E. Seifert and his attorney to obtain a photograph of the plaintiff to be used as evidence in the trial of Seifert, who was charged with sexually molesting two young boys. On May 27, 1970, about 8 a.m., defendant went to plaintiff's home and upon gaining admittance told him that she was a Mrs. Jackson from the newspaper and that she was writing an article on Skateland. Defendant asked plaintiff, who was a coach at Skateland, if she could take a picture of him for publication with the article, and he readily consented.

Shortly thereafter defendant delivered the photograph to Seifert's counsel while he was representing Seifert at his preliminary hearing. Seifert's counsel showed plaintiff's photograph to the two young boys and asked if he was the one who molested them. When they replied that he was not, counsel withdrew the photograph and put it in his briefcase. However, the Commonwealth's Attorney then asked to see the photograph and requested additional information about the person shown in it. Defendant was then called to the stand and she supplied the plaintiff's name and address. Plaintiff's photograph in no way resembled Seifert, and the only excuse given by defendant for taking plaintiff's picture was that he was at Skateland when Seifert was arrested. However, the offenses alleged against Seifert did not occur at Skateland.

The Commonwealth's Attorney then directed a detective to go to plaintiff's home and bring him to court. The detective told plaintiff that his photograph had been presented in court; that the Commonwealth's Attorney wanted him to appear at the proceedings; and that he could either appear voluntarily then or he would be summoned. Plaintiff agreed to go voluntarily. When called as a witness, plaintiff testified as to the circumstances under which defendant had obtained his photograph. He also said that he had not molested any children and that he knew nothing about the charges against Seifert.

A police officer questioned plaintiff several times thereafter. Plaintiff was also summoned to appear as a witness before the grand jury but he was not called. However, he was summoned to appear several times at Seifert's trial in the circuit court because of continuances of the cases.

Plaintiff testified that he suffered great shock, distress and nervousness because of defendant's fraud and deceit and her wanton, willful and malicious conduct in obtaining his photograph and turning it over to Seifert's attorney to be used in court. He suffered great anxiety as to what people would think of him and feared that he would be accused of molesting the boys. He had been unable to sleep while the matter was being investigated. While testifying in the instant case he became emotional and incoherent. Plaintiff's wife also testified that her husband experienced great shock and mental depression from the involvement.

* * *

In the case at bar, reasonable men may disagree as to whether defendant's conduct was extreme and outrageous and whether plaintiff's emotional distress was severe. Thus, the questions presented were for a jury to determine. A jury could conclude from the evidence presented that defendant willfully, recklessly, intentionally and deceitfully obtained plaintiff's photograph for the purpose of permitting her employers to use it as a defense in a criminal case without considering the effect it would have on the plaintiff. There is nothing in the evidence that even suggests that plaintiff may have been involved in the child molesting cases. The record shows that the only possible excuse for involving the plaintiff was that Seifert was arrested at the place where plaintiff was employed. A reasonable person would or should have recognized the likelihood of the serious mental distress that would be caused in involving an innocent person in child molesting cases. If the two boys had hesitated in answering that the man in the photograph was not the one who had molested them, it is evident that the finger of suspicion would have been pointed at the plaintiff.

* * *

Judgment reversed, jury verdict reinstated, and final judgment.

MEITER v. CAVANAUGH

Court of Appeals of Colorado, 1978.
40 Colo.App. 454, 580 P.2d 399.

PIERCE, JUDGE.

Defendant appeals from an adverse judgment entered upon a jury verdict, alleging that plaintiff failed to establish a prima facie case of intentional infliction of emotional distress by outrageous conduct. Defendant also argues that the evidence is insufficient to justify the award of $5,500 in actual and $10,000 in exemplary damages. We affirm the judgment in its entirety.

* * *

In March of 1973, plaintiff and defendant entered into a specific performance contract, under which plaintiff was to purchase defendant's home. Plaintiff wanted to buy the house for her grandchildren and recently widowed daughter-in-law. The contract provided that defendant would have a right to retain possession of the property on a rental basis for a period not to exceed six weeks after the delivery of the deed. Since the deed was delivered at the closing on April 12, 1973, defendant's rental period ended on May 25, and plaintiff was entitled to exclusive possession on May 26.

Sometime in late May or early June, plaintiff went to the house to inquire about the surrender of possession. Defendant informed her, for the first time, that he would be unable to move until the end of his children's school term, sometime in early June. Plaintiff explained that her daughter-in-law desperately needed a place to stay. Defendant became quite belligerent, and responded, "Well, as far as that's concerned, you can move [her furniture] up in that shanty. When I get out, you can roll it down the hill."

During another early June encounter, defendant told plaintiff, "I'm an attorney. I know my rights. I'll move when I'm damn well ready." He also called plaintiff, who was visibly bandaged after recent cancer surgery, a "sick old woman."

On June 7, 1973, defendant mailed a letter to plaintiff notifying her that he was considering legal action. The letter implied that defendant had some special influence with the court:

"I am sure the local court known personally to me over the years, will appreciate my problem * * *. In fact, he may just break our contract, which would satisfy me and I will repay every cent of your money."

Meanwhile, plaintiff had to find another home for her daughter-in-law, and she purchased one on June 13, 1973. When defendant finally vacated in early July, plaintiff found that the premises had been damaged. Some windows were broken, a few sliding doors were untracked, and the lock on the back door was broken. Several outdoor light fixtures had been removed, and a built-in barbeque had been dismantled. After repairing some of this damage, plaintiff sold the house in December.

I.

The first question we must address is whether this conduct was sufficiently "outrageous" to withstand defendant's motions for a directed verdict and judgment notwithstanding the verdict. We hold that it was.

* * *

II.

Defendant argues that the award of damages was excessive and unsupported by the evidence. Again, we disagree.

The amount of damages is within the sole province of the jury, and an award will not be disturbed unless it is completely unsupported by the record. * * *

Here, there was evidence that plaintiff spent over $900 in repairing the damage to the house. There was also evidence that she suffered a loss exceeding $1,700 in re-selling the house, as well as incurring a substantial sum in brokerage fees. These out-of-pocket expenses, in addition to the damages attributable to the mental distress alone, were sufficient to support the award. The individual acts, or failures to act, which resulted in these expenditures, could be considered by reasonable jurors to be part of the total scheme of outrageous conduct directed at this plaintiff by this defendant. The isolated fact that plaintiff may not have incurred medical expenses immediately after the incidents does not require reversal. * * *

Nor does the fact that these out-of-pocket expenses may have been recoverable in an action for breach of the lease preclude their recovery in tort. * * *

Since the award of actual damages was supported by the record, and since the exemplary damages are not manifestly exorbitant, we affirm the judgment as to exemplary damages as well. * * *

* * *

The judgment is affirmed.

COYTE, JUDGE, concurring in part and dissenting in part:

I agree that the conduct of defendant toward the plaintiff constituted outrageous conduct. However, I feel that the award of damages is excessive and not supported by the evidence, where to justify the award, the majority has to point to the consequential damages suffered by plaintiff because of defendant's breach of contract. The cause should be remanded for a new trial on the damage issue but limited to mental suffering and the consequential damages flowing from the mental suffering and not the breach of contract.

HOOD v. NAETER BROTHERS PUBLISHING CO.

Court of Appeals of Missouri, 1978.
562 S.W.2d 770.

CLEMENS, PRESIDING JUDGE.

Action for damages for allegedly outrageous conduct by a newspaper in publishing plaintiff's name as witness to a murder. The trial court sustained defendants' motion for summary judgment and plaintiff has appealed.

Plaintiff pleaded he was an employee of a liquor store and was working on the evening of August 7, 1976 when the store was robbed by two masked black men. Plaintiff witnessed the fatal shooting of a fellow employee. The next day the Cape Girardeau police department released its report to the press, giving details of the robbery, including plaintiff's name and address. At this time, plaintiff, a recent resident of Cape Girardeau, was not listed in the telephone directory. The following day defendant Naeter Brothers published a front-page article, written by defendant Don Smith, reporting the robbery and murder in the "Southeast Missourian." The article identified plaintiff as a witness and printed his address. The two suspects were still at large.

Plaintiff further pleaded that as a result of the publication he has been in constant fear, has been forced to change his residence repeatedly, has become suspicious of all black persons and has been under the care of a psychiatrist.

Plaintiff contends defendants' publication of his name and address constituted outrageous conduct because defendants knew or should have known the killers were still at large. He argues that the issue of culpability is for a jury to determine and, accordingly, the trial court erred in granting summary judgment for defendant.

The issue is whether the alleged acts constitute outrageous conduct as a matter of law. We say no. In Pretsky v. Southwestern Bell Telephone Co., 396 S.W.2d 566, 568 (Mo.1965), our supreme court adopted § 46 of the Restatement of the Law of Torts and its comment (d):

* * *

Comment (d) gives guidance on the meaning of "extreme" and "outrageous."

"(d) Extreme and outrageous conduct. The cases thus far decided have found liability only where the defendant's conduct has been extreme and outrageous * * *. Liability has been found only where the conduct has been so outrageous in character, and so extreme in degree, as to go beyond all possible bounds of decency, and to be regarded as atrocious, and utterly intolerable in a civilized community. Generally, the case is one in which the recitation of the facts to an average member of the community would arouse his resentment against the actor, and lead him to exclaim, 'Outrageous!'

The liability clearly does not extend to mere insults, indignities, threats, arrogancies, petty oppression, or other trivialities. The rough edges of our society are still in need of a good deal of filing down, and in the meantime plaintiffs must necessarily be expected and required to be hardened to a certain amount of rough language, and to occasional acts that are definitely inconsiderate and unkind * * *."

Cases from other jurisdictions illustrate the type of conduct held to be outrageous. In Blakeley v. Shortal's Estate, 236 Iowa 787, 20 N.W.2d 28 (1945), the court upheld recovery against decedent's estate where the deceased slit his throat in plaintiff's kitchen and plaintiff suffered shock upon finding the body. And in Great Atlantic and Pacific Tea Co. v. Roch, 160 Md. 189, 153 A. 22 (1931), the court affirmed a jury verdict for plaintiff where defendant delivered a dead rat in a package instead of the bread plaintiff had ordered.[a]

Missouri cases involving outrageous conduct have dealt with creditors harassing debtors. In Liberty Loan Corp. of Antioch v. Brown, 493 S.W.2d 664[4] (Mo.App.1973), the court upheld a verdict for plaintiff where defendant made harassing, abusive and threatening phone calls to plaintiff in order to collect a debt. In Warrem v. Parrish, 436 S.W.2d 670[6] (Mo.1969), the court upheld a count of plaintiff's petition alleging outrageous conduct where plaintiff pleaded that defendant, in order to collect a debt, put plaintiff's car on a lift for three hours, threatened plaintiff and refused to return the car until payment was made.

In contrast, in *Pretsky, supra,* at 396 S.W.2d 566 the court ruled plaintiff failed to state a cause of action for outrageous conduct where she alleged defendant's employee gained entrance to her house by falsely stating there was trouble on her telephone line and that he must enter to correct the problem. The court followed § 46 of the Restatement and held defendant's conduct was not actionable, ruling:

"The facts pleaded do not constitute what could be considered to be extreme and outrageous conduct * * * "and the petition "does not contain averments which invoke substantive principles of law which entitle plaintiff to relief."[b]

---

a. [Ed. note] In *Roch,* the plaintiff alleged, and the evidence introduced supported the allegation, that she had suffered physical injuries as a result of her fright. The physical injuries included those suffered when she fainted and fell to the floor on seeing the dead rat.

b. [Ed. note] In *Pretsky,* the plaintiff also unsuccessfully sought relief under § 48 of the *Restatement (Second) of Torts* dealing with gross insults by servants of common carriers or public utilities. There were no allegations of any insults. The plaintiff relied exclusively on the entry under false pretenses.

Similarly, in Nelson v. Grice, 411 S.W.2d 117[4] (Mo.1967), the court held no outrageous conduct was shown. There, defendants had leased property to plaintiff on which he ran a grocery store. Subsequently, defendants built a second building on the property and told plaintiff he could rent it at the same rate. Instead, defendants raised the rent, harassed plaintiff and operated their own store in competition. As a result, plaintiff suffered a heart attack and attempted suicide. The supreme court, based on that part of Restatement quoted in *Presky, supra,* reversed a jury verdict for plaintiff, holding no outrageous conduct was shown.

We hold the conduct alleged here is not of the extreme and outrageous nature contemplated by § 46 of the Restatement. The publication of the name and address of the sole witness to a violent crime at a time when the criminals are at large may be unwise but it does not go beyond the bounds of human decency. Furthermore, the published information was a matter of public record and readily available to all interested persons.[1]

We hold the trial court did not err in rendering summary judgment against plaintiff.

Judgment affirmed.

NOTES

1. In Hyde v. City of Columbia, 637 S.W.2d 251 (Mo.Ct.App.1982), the court upheld a cause of action based on a negligent publication theory brought by a woman whose name, as the victim of a kidnaping, and address were revealed by the defendant city to the defendant newspaper which then published the information. The plaintiff alleged that her unknown assailant thereafter "terrorized her on seven different occasions." With regard to the action against the newspaper, the court held that the police report upon which the newspaper's story was based was not a "public record," and that the "dictum" of the *Hood* case that such reports were matters of public record was ill-advised. Whether the *Hyde* court's conclusion, that police reports about private persons are not matters of public record or interest, can support an action against a newspaper now seems questionable in the light of The Florida Star v. B.J.F., 491 U.S. 524, 109 S.Ct. 2603, 105 L.Ed.2d 443 (1989), which will be discussed at p. 681, *infra*, when we consider the tort of invasion of privacy.

2. In Harris v. Jones, 281 Md. 560, 380 A.2d 611 (1977), the defendant, the plaintiff's supervisor at a factory, had ridiculed and mimicked the plaintiff who had a severe stuttering problem. The defendant's conduct was held not to be actionable. The court did not feel compelled to decide whether the supervisor's conduct was "extreme or outrageous" because it concluded that the plaintiff had made an insufficient showing that the humiliation he had suffered had led to "severe emotional distress." For the emotional distress to be sufficiently severe, the court opined that it must be a "*severely* disabling

1. Plaintiff complains of the dissemination of his name and address to the public. Although neither party has raised the first amendment issue, the case of Cox Broadcasting Corp. v. Cohn, 420 U.S. 469, 95 S.Ct. 1029, 43 L.Ed.2d 328 (1975), is relevant. [p. 695, *infra.*] * * *

emotional response." In Pankratz v. Willis, 155 Ariz. 8, 744 P.2d 1182 (App.1987), the court concluded that all that was required was that the distress be severe; not that it be in any way disabling. The *Pankratz* case involved a father's action against his former wife's parents for their complicity in their daughter's absconding from the United States with the child born during the plaintiff's marriage to the defendants' daughter.

3. Solicitations to sexual intercourse are generally held not to be actionable. *See* C. Magruder, *Mental and Emotional Disturbance in the Law of Torts,* 49 Harv.L.Rev. 1033, 1055 (1936) (" * * * the view being, apparently, that there is no harm in asking.") Nevertheless, repeated solicitations, under some instances, have been held to be actionable. *See, e.g.,* Samms v. Eccles, 11 Utah 2d 289, 358 P.2d 344 (1961); Mitran v. Williamson, 21 Misc.2d 106, 197 N.Y.S.2d 689 (1960). The fact that the solicitation or other sexual advance was made in a context in which the person making the solicitation or advances is in a position of actual or apparent power over the person who is the object of the solicitation or advances is a relevant factor. *See e.g.* Howard University v. Best, 484 A.2d 958 (D.C.1984) (Dean with supervisory power over plaintiff faculty member); McDaniel v. Gile, 230 Cal.App.3d 363, 281 Cal.Rptr. 242 (1991) (Attorney threatened to withhold legal services from client). It has been held, however, that a single solicitation by a professor for oral sex in return for a higher grade, where there was no evidence of any retaliation against the student who rebuffed the solicitation, was not enough to support a claim for intentional infliction of emotional distress, even if it might support an action based on some other theory against either the individual defendant or the defendant community college. Slaughter v. Waubonsee Community College, 1994 WL 663596 (N.D.Ill.1994). These cases are but a small subset of a much larger set of cases, namely those alleging sexual harassment, particularly in the workplace. Harassment on a religious, sexual, or racial basis in the workplace, when condoned by the employer, is a form of discrimination prohibited by Title VII of the Civil Rights Act of 1964, as amended, 42 U.S.C. §§ 2000e *et seq.* (1988). The more difficult cases concern harassment based upon verbal conduct. Robinson v. Jacksonville Shipyards, Inc., 760 F.Supp. 1486 (M.D.Fla.1991), which involved a claim largely based on the presence of nude pin-ups in the workplace, has received a fair amount of notoriety. The question of verbal harassment in the workplace is a vast subject raising questions that are far beyond the purview of a general torts course. For conflicting perspectives, *compare* E. Volokh, *Freedom of Speech and Appellate Review in Workplace Harassment Cases,* 90 Nw.U.L.Rev. 1009 (1996), *with* B. Wolman, *Verbal Sexual Harassment on the Job as Intentional Infliction of Emotional Distress*, 17 Cap.U.L.Rev. 245 (1988). *See also* K. Browne, *Title VII as Censorship: Hostile–Environment Harassment and the First Amendment*, 52 Ohio St.L.J. 481 (1991). For a more recent discussion, *see* M. Chaplin, *Workplace Bullying: The Problem and the Cure,* 12 U. Pa. J. Bus. L. 437 (2010).

4. As the discussion in the *Hood* case makes clear, many of the cases in which a cause of action for the intentional infliction of severe emotional distress has been sustained have involved bill collectors. A good illustration is Ford Motor Credit Co. v. Sheehan, 373 So.2d 956 (Fla.App.1979). The relevant facts of that case were as follows:

> On October 28, 1974, Sheehan purchased a Ford automobile which was financed by Ford Credit pursuant to the terms of a retail installment contract. Later, Sheehan moved to various locations and became delinquent on his account. Ford Credit was unable to locate Sheehan and assigned the account to a central recovery office maintained by it in Michigan. On May 1, 1975, Sheehan's mother, who lived in Coventry, Rhode Island, received a telephone call from a woman who identified herself as being employed by Mercy Hospital in San Francisco, California. She was advised that one or both of Sheehan's children had been involved in a serious automobile accident and that the caller was attempting to locate Sheehan. The mother supplied information to the caller concerning his home and business addresses and phone numbers located in Jacksonville, Florida.
>
> Sheehan testified that on May 1, 1975, he returned a call to his mother's home in Rhode Island, spoke to his sister, and as a result of information received in that telephone conversation, placed calls during a seven-hour period to hospitals and police departments in San Francisco, California until he finally discovered the information was false. The following day, Sheehan's automobile was repossessed by Search International, an independent contractor with Ford Credit.

There was no indication that any physical harm was sustained by the plaintiff. The court affirmed a judgment, entered on a jury verdict, awarding $4,000 in compensatory damages and $11,000 in punitive damages. The Supreme Court of Florida refused to review the case. 379 So.2d 204 (Fla. 1979). The plaintiff in *Sheehan* also relied on a Florida statute prohibiting, *inter alia,* anyone while collecting a debt to "willfully communicate with the debtor or any other member of his family with such frequency as can reasonably be expected to harass the debtor or his family, or willfully engage in other conduct which can reasonably be expected to abuse or harass the debtor or any member of his family." West's Fla.Stat.Ann. § 559.72(7). The district court of appeal held the statute inapplicable to the case before it because the phone call had been made from Michigan. On the other hand, in Public Finance Corp. v. Davis, 66 Ill.2d 85, 4 Ill.Dec. 652, 360 N.E.2d 765 (1976), it was held that the following conduct which accompanied the finance company's judicial foreclosure of its security interest was not actionable:

> Count I of the amended counterclaim alleges the conduct of Public Finance which Davis claims entitles her to recover. Stripped of the conclusions, it is charged that on or about September 1, 1974, Davis informed Public Finance she was no longer employed, was on public aid and did not have enough money to make regular payments on her obligations; that in order to collect the account Public Finance from September 1, 1974, to April 4, 1975, called Davis several times weekly, frequently more than once a day; that in order to collect the account agents of Public Finance went to Davis' home one or more times a week; that on October 15, 1974, when Davis' daughter was in the hospital, an agent of Public Finance, in order to collect the account, called the defendant at the hospital; that on that day Davis informed the agent of the severity of her daughter's condition, that she, herself, was sick and nervous and asked that Public Finance refrain from calling her at the

hospital; that on the same day an agent of Public Finance again called Davis at the hospital; that after an employee of Public Finance induced Davis to write a check and promised that the check would not be processed, Public Finance phoned an acquaintance of Davis and informed her that Davis was writing bad checks; that in November 1974 an employee of Public Finance called at Davis' home and after being told that Davis had no money with which to make a payment, with Davis' permission, used her phone to call Public Finance and to describe and report the items of Davis' household goods; that on that day the employee "failed or refused" to leave Davis' home until her son entered the room.

The Illinois Supreme Court felt that "a creditor must be given some latitude to pursue reasonable methods of collecting debts even though such methods may result in some inconvenience, embarrassment or annoyance to the debtor." The court felt that the finance company's conduct was neither abrasive enough nor prolonged enough to subject it to liability. Two justices dissented to the denial of a rehearing of the case. For other debt collector cases, *see* 87 A.L.R.3d 201 (1978). An illustrative case is Etchart v. Bank One, 773 F.Supp. 239 (D.Nev.1991) in which the court refused to grant summary judgment for the defendant in an action for intentional infliction of emotional distress based on a bank's refusal to provide written notice that the plaintiff no longer owed the bank anything and the bank's failure to stop reporting the outstanding debt to a credit reporting agency after settlement of earlier litigation between the parties. The outrageousness of the defendants' conduct and the severity of the plaintiff's emotional distress were issues for the jury.

5. Not only are there state statutes regulating the conduct of bill collectors, such as the one involved in the *Sheehan* case which also regulates approaches to a debtor's employer and the public dissemination of the fact of a debtor's indebtedness, but there is also federal legislation on the subject. Under the Fair Debt Collection Practices Act of 1977, 15 U.S.C. § 1692 *et seq.*, certain types of debt collectors are forbidden to communicate with a consumer at "any unusual time or place." Such a debt collector is required to assume, in the absence of knowledge of circumstances to the contrary, that times before 8:00 a.m. and after 9:00 p.m. are not convenient. Among other prohibitions, the debt collector may not communicate with third parties about the consumer more than once, unless requested to do so by that third person, nor may the debt collector use any symbol or words on the envelope of a mail communication that indicate that the debt collector is in the debt collection business. The debt collector is also forbidden to communicate with a consumer by post card. The Act provides for the civil liability of a debt collector who fails to comply with the provisions of the Act. The debt collector may only escape liability if it can show that any violations of the Act were both unintentional *and* the result of what the Act calls a "bona fide error." The Act was amended in 1986 to cover the activities of lawyers who regularly engage in debt collection. The Court has held that the Act applies even to lawyers regularly engaging in debt collection litigation. Heintz v. Jenkins, 514 U.S. 291, 115 S.Ct. 1489, 131 L.Ed.2d 395 (1995). For more recent successful actions for the intentional infliction of emotional distress *see, e.g.*, Young v. Allstate Ins. Co., 119 Hawai'i 403, 198 P.3d 666 (2008) (action against an insurance company for mistreating a policy holder who refused to settle a

claim without consulting a lawyer); DeGolyer v. Green Tree Servicing, LLC, 291 Ga.App. 444, 662 S.E.2d 141 (2008) (action against a mortgage servicing company that continued to pursue a foreclosure proceeding after it had been informed by the defendant in the foreclosure action and by a third party that it was foreclosing on the wrong property).

STAR v. RABELLO

Supreme Court of Nevada, 1981.
97 Nev. 124, 625 P.2d 90.

SPRINGER, JUSTICE.

Respondent Rabello sued appellant Star for special, general and punitive damages for assault and battery. Rabello also sued as Guardian ad Litem for her daughter, Lisa Rabello, who was a witness to the attack, for intentional infliction of emotional distress. Star counterclaimed for assault and battery, alleging that Rabello initiated the fight. * * *

At trial, both sides presented conflicting evidence as to who started the fight and who was the more aggressive during its course. After hearing testimony from fifteen witnesses, the trial judge dismissed Star's counterclaim, stating that Rabello's version of the fight was corroborated by two disinterested witnesses. He then found that Star precipitated the fight, and awarded Rabello special, general and punitive damages. He also awarded Lisa Rabello, Rabello's daughter, $300.00 in general damages for intentional infliction of emotional distress.

Star appeals from the damages awarded to Lisa Rabello, arguing that Lisa should not be entitled to recovery under an intentional infliction of emotional distress cause of action. We agree.

The fight occurred at Lisa's school after the opening of a school play. Star testified that she knew Lisa was present at the time. As a result of witnessing the altercation and her "embarrassment" at being the daughter of one of the participants, Lisa has suffered from intermittent headaches, sleeplessness and an upset stomach.

There are no reported cases in this jurisdiction concerning the intentional infliction of emotional distress—the tort of "outrage." * * *

Recovery on the part of a third party witness to an outrageous act is permitted if that third party is a close relative of the person against whom the outrage was directed. Restatement of Torts 2d § 46(2). Most plaintiffs who have been permitted recovery *as bystanders,* however, have witnessed acts which were not only outrageous but unquestionably violent and shocking.

Prosser's analysis of witness recovery indicates that the outrage requirement is more difficult to meet when the act has been directed against a third party in cases in which the plaintiff has been a mere witness to the occurrence. * * *

Thus, recovery has been allowed when a husband watched his wife die because the doctor refused to treat her, Grimsby v. Samson, 85 Wash.2d

52, 530 P.2d 291 (1975), and when an illegitimate five year old sued her father's estate after she had witnessed her father kill her mother, was kept in a room with the body for seven days, and was forced to watch her father commit suicide, Mahnke v. Moore, 197 Md. 61, 77 A.2d 923 (1951). Recovery was denied when, after a boundary line dispute, plaintiff's husband was verbally abused and assaulted with a pitchfork by an irate neighbor. Wiehe v. Kukal, 225 Kan. 478, 592 P.2d 860 (1979).

In urging that Star's conduct was sufficiently outrageous to sustain her cause of action, Rabello relies on three cases.[1] In each case, the defendant had knowledge that the witness was either pregnant or had recently given birth and was in a weakened state. Knowledge of a witness's condition tends to increase the outrageous nature of the act.

There is very little case law relating to recovery based on the mere observation of outrageous acts aimed at third parties. In instances where recovery has been allowed, the observed conduct has been outrageous in the extreme. Although the trial judge found that Star's conduct was outrageous, we rule, as a matter of law, that an assault of the kind presented in this appeal is insufficient to warrant recovery by a witness to such an assault; accordingly, the judgment in favor of Lisa must be reversed.

* * *

The judgment in favor of Sandra Rabello is affirmed; the judgment in favor of Lisa Rabello is reversed.

NOTE

The *Restatement (Second)* had a separate subsection, § 46 (2), that, where the conduct in question was "directed at a third person, the actor is subject to liability if he intentionally or recklessly causes severe emotional distress (a) to a member of such person's immediate family who is present at the time . . . or (b) to any other person who is present at the time" but only if such persons who are not immediate relatives suffer "bodily harm". It seems like an odd provision because, as intent is defined in the law of torts, one can say that if one is aware of the presence of third persons he can be said to know with substantial certainty that emotional harm will be suffered by those persons by any sufficiently outrageous conduct on his part. The *Restatement (Third) of Torts, Liability for Physical and Emotional Harm* § 46 has no specific reference to liability to third persons in the black letter. It covers the matter in Comment *m.* If there is any such liability to third parties who are present, surely it must be limited to threats of physical violence. It is hard to believe that, if one insults a relative let alone a third party, one would be liable to an observer for the discomfort that such persons might experience. Whatever the nature of the conduct directed against the primary victim may be there is

1. Jeppsen v. Jensen, 47 Utah 536, 155 P. 429 (1916) (defendant, while in plaintiff's home and in front of her children, threatened her husband with a gun); Lambert v. Brewster, 97 W.Va. 124, 125 S.E. 244 (W.Va.1924) (plaintiff witnessed forcible assault on her father); Rogers v. Williard, 144 Ark. 587, 223 S.W. 15 (1920) (defendant threatened to shoot plaintiff's husband).

always the question of what it means for third parties to be present at the time of the original tort. In Garland v. Herrin, 724 F.2d 16 (2d Cir.1983), an action brought by the parents of a girl who, while the parents were asleep in their bedroom, had been bludgeoned to death by her boyfriend in one of the other bedrooms of the house. The trial court had held that the parents were sufficiently "present" within the meaning of *Restatement (Second) of Torts* § 46(2) to be entitled to recover, 554 F.Supp. 308 (S.D.N.Y.1983), but the Second Circuit reversed.

PAUL v. WATCHTOWER BIBLE AND TRACT SOCIETY OF NEW YORK, INC.

United States Court of Appeals, Ninth Circuit, 1987.
819 F.2d 875, cert. denied 484 U.S. 926, 108 S.Ct. 289, 98 L.Ed.2d 249.

REINHARDT, CIRCUIT JUDGE:

Janice Paul, a former member of the Jehovah's Witness Church, appeals from the grant of summary judgment in favor of defendants, the corporate arms of the Governing Body of Jehovah's Witnesses. Paul contends that she is being "shunned" by adherents of the Jehovah's Witness faith. She initially filed suit in state court, setting forth various tort claims. Defendants removed the action on the ground of diversity. Because the practice of shunning is a part of the faith of the Jehovah's Witness, we find that the "free exercise" provision of the United States Constitution and thus of the Washington State Constitution precludes the plaintiff from prevailing. The defendants have a constitutionally protected privilege to engage in the practice of shunning. Accordingly, we affirm the grant of summary judgment, although for reasons different from those of the district court. * * *

I. Facts

Janice Paul was raised as a Jehovah's Witness. Her mother was very active in the Church and, from the age of four, Paul attended church meetings. In 1962, when Paul was 11 years old, her mother married the overseer of the Ephrata, Washington congregation of Jehovah's Witnesses. In 1967, Paul officially joined the Witnesses and was baptized.

According to Paul, she was an active member of the congregation, devoting an average of 40 hours per month in door-to-door distribution of the Witnesses' publications. In addition to engaging in evening home bible study, she attended church with her family approximately 20 hours per month. She eventually married another member of the Jehovah's Witnesses.

In 1975, Paul's parents were "disfellowshiped" from the Church. According to Paul, her parents' expulsion resulted from internal discord within their congregation. The Elders of the Lower Valley Congregation told Paul that she and her husband should not discuss with other members their feeling that her parents had been unjustly disfellowshiped.

That advice was underscored by the potential sanction of her own disfellowship were she to challenge the decision.

Sometime after the Elders' warning, Paul decided that she no longer wished to belong to the congregation, or to remain affiliated with the Jehovah's Witnesses. In November 1975, Paul wrote a letter to the congregation withdrawing from the Church.

The Witnesses are a very close community and have developed an elaborate set of rules governing membership. The Church has four basic categories of membership, non-membership or former membership status; they are: members, non-members, disfellowshiped persons, and disassociated persons. "Disfellowshiped persons" are former members who have been excommunicated from the Church. One consequence of disfellowship is "shunning," a form of ostracism. Members of the Jehovah's Witness community are prohibited—under threat of their own disfellowship—from having any contact with disfellowshiped persons and may not even greet them. Family members who do not live in the same house may conduct necessary family business with disfellowshiped relatives but may not communicate with them on any other subject. Shunning purportedly has its roots in early Christianity and various religious groups in our country engage in the practice including the Amish, the Mennonites, and, of course, the Jehovah's Witnesses.

"Disassociated persons" are former members who have voluntarily left the Jehovah's Witness faith. At the time Paul disassociated, there was no express sanction for withdrawing from membership. In fact, because of the close nature of many Jehovah's Witness communities, disassociated persons were still consulted in secular matters, e.g. legal or business advice, although they were no longer members of the Church. In Paul's case, for example, after having moved from the area, she returned for a visit in 1980, saw Church members and was warmly greeted.

In September 1981, the Governing Body of Jehovah's Witnesses, acting through the defendants—Watchtower Bible and Tract Society of Pennsylvania, Inc., and the Watchtower Bible and Tract Society of New York, Inc.—issued a new interpretation of the rules governing disassociated persons. The distinction between disfellowshiped and disassociated persons was, for all practical purposes, abolished and disassociated persons were to be treated in the same manner as the disfellowshiped. The September 15, 1981 issue of *The Watchtower,* an official publication of the Church, contained an article entitled "Disfellowshiping—how to view it." The article included the following discussion:

> *THOSE WHO DISASSOCIATE THEMSELVES*
>
> * * * Persons who make themselves 'not of our sort' by deliberately rejecting the faith and beliefs of Jehovah's Witnesses should appropriately be viewed and treated as are those who have been disfellowshiped for wrongdoing.

The Watchtower article based its announcement on a reading of various passages of the Bible, including 1 John 2:19 and Revelations 19:17–21. The article noted further that "[a]s distinct from some personal 'enemy' or worldly man in authority who opposed Christians, a * * * disassociated person who is trying to promote or justify his apostate thinking or is continuing in his ungodly conduct is certainly not one to whom to wish 'Peace' [understood as a greeting]. (1 Tim. 2:1, 2)." Finally, the article stated that if "a Christian were to throw in his lot with a wrongdoer who * * * has disassociated himself, * * * the Elders * * * would admonish him and, if necessary, 'reprove him with severity.'" (citing, *inter alia,* Matt. 18:18, Gal. 6:1, Titus 1:13).

Three years after this announcement in *The Watchtower,* Paul visited her parents, who at that time lived in Soap Lake, Washington. There, she approached a Witness who had been a close childhood friend and was told by this person: "I can't speak to you. You are disfellowshiped." Similarly, in August 1984, Paul returned to the area of her former congregation. She tried to call on some of her friends. These people told Paul that she was to be treated as if she had been disfellowshiped and that they could not speak with her. At one point, she attempted to attend a Tupperware party at the home of a Witness. Paul was informed by the Church members present that the Elders had instructed them not to speak with her.

Upset by her shunning by her former friends and co-religionists, Paul, a resident of Alaska, brought suit in Washington State Superior Court alleging common law torts of defamation, invasion of privacy, fraud, and outrageous conduct. Defendants, Watchtower Bible and Tract Associations, removed the action to federal court pursuant to 28 U.S.C. § 1441 (1982). Watchtower moved to dismiss for lack of subject matter jurisdiction and for failure to state a claim under Washington law. Fed.R.Civ.P. 12(b)(1) & (6). In the alternative, Watchtower sought summary judgment. Fed.R.Civ.P. 56(b).

The district court denied the 12(b)(1) motion to dismiss for lack of subject matter jurisdiction and the 12(b)(6) motion to dismiss for failure to state a claim, but granted the motion for summary judgment. The court ruled that it had jurisdiction over the case because the state court properly had jurisdiction originally. * * * The court also held that Paul's affidavits did not set forth facts that would establish a prima facie case for relief. Moreover, the court ruled that even if the practice of shunning was actionable, the court was prohibited from ruling on the issue on the ground of ecclesiastical abstention. That doctrine prohibits courts from determining issues of canon law. *See generally Serbian Eastern Orthodox Diocese v. Milivojevich,* 426 U.S. 696, 96 S.Ct. 2372, 49 L.Ed.2d 151 (1976).[1]

1. The doctrine of ecclesiastical abstention is not pertinent here. * * * Ecclesiastical abstention thus provides that civil courts may not redetermine the correctness of an interpretation of canonical text or some decision relating to government of the religious polity. Rather, we must accept as a given whatever the entity decides. * * *

II. The Plaintiff's Cause of Action

Janice Paul seeks relief against the Church and several Church officials under Washington state law and pleads various causes of action in tort. She claims in essence that the practice of shunning invades interests that the state does or should protect through its tort law.

* * *

We note at the outset that in this case the actions of Church officials and members were clearly taken pursuant to Church policy. * * * Although shunning is intentional, the activity is not malum in se. The state is legitimately concerned with its regulation only to the extent that individuals are directly harmed.

One state has recently recognized a cause of action in tort arising from the practice of shunning. Although it did not purport to create a new tort, the Supreme Court of Pennsylvania, in *Bear v. Reformed Mennonite Church,* 462 Pa. 330, 341 A.2d 105 (1975), noted that certain interests protected by the state may be invaded when shunning occurs. As the Court stated:

> the "shunning" practice of appellee church and the conduct of the individuals may be an excessive interference within areas of "paramount state concern," i.e. the maintenance of marriage and family relationship, alienation of affection, and the tortious interference with a business relationship. * * *

Id. at 107.

Under Washington tort law there are at least three basic categories of intentional conduct that are relevant here: conduct causing emotional distress, conduct causing alienation of affections, and conduct causing harm to reputation. Paul claims to have suffered injuries in all three categories as a result of the intentional actions of the Jehovah's Witnesses. Under Washington law, "intangible-emotional" harm is, at least in some circumstances, sufficient to support a claim in tort. * * *

Federal courts are not precluded from affording relief simply because neither the state Supreme Court nor the state legislature has enunciated a clear rule governing a particular type of controversy. Were we able to invoke only clearly established state law, litigants seeking to protect their rights in federal courts by availing themselves of our diversity jurisdiction would face an inhospitable forum for claims not identical to those resolved in prior cases. Equally important, a policy by the federal courts never to advance beyond existing state court precedent would vest in defendants the power to bar the successful adjudication of plaintiffs' claims in cases with novel issues; defendants could ensure a decision in their favor simply

---

This limited abstention doctrine is not relevant here because Paul is not alleging that the new rules governing disassociation are improper under Church law. * * * Nor does she seek relief for having been "wrongfully" disfellowshiped. Rather, she seeks relief for the harms she has suffered as a result of conduct engaged in by the Jehovah's Witnesses that is presumably consistent with the governing law of the Church. Accordingly, the doctrine of *Serbian Orthodox Diocese* does not apply.

by removing the case to federal court. Congress, in providing for removal, certainly did not intend to provide such a weapon to defendants.

Nonetheless, we need not decide here whether Washington courts would ultimately rule that Paul has set forth a prima facie claim for relief in tort because the defendants, in any event, possess an affirmative defense of privilege—a defense that permits them to engage in the practice of shunning pursuant to their religious beliefs without incurring tort liability. Were shunning considered to be tortious conduct, the guarantee of the free exercise of religion would provide that it is, nonetheless, privileged conduct. In theory, we could examine the question whether the shunning of a former member of a church is, in itself, tortious; however, we will follow the practice of Washington courts which safeguard the free exercise of religion through the recognition of substantive defenses to torts, rather than by negating the plaintiff's cause of action itself (i.e. ruling that the conduct in question is not tortious). *See Carrieri v. Bush,* 69 Wash.2d 536, 419 P.2d 132, 137 (1966). The Washington practice, in addition to being the governing rule here is, in our view, the most sensible juridical approach. * * *

III. The Defendants' Privilege

Shunning is a practice engaged in by Jehovah's Witnesses pursuant to their interpretation of canonical text, and we are not free to reinterpret that text.[2] Under both the United States and Washington Constitutions, the defendants are entitled to the free exercise of their religious beliefs.

State laws whether statutory or common law, including tort rules, constitute state action. Clearly, the application of tort law to activities of a church or its adherents in their furtherance of their religious belief is an exercise of state power. When the imposition of liability would result in the abridgement of the right to free exercise of religious beliefs, recovery in tort is barred.

The Jehovah's Witnesses argue that their right to exercise their religion freely entitles them to engage in the practice of shunning. The Church further claims that assessing damages against them for engaging in that practice would directly burden that right.

We agree that the imposition of tort damages on the Jehovah's Witnesses for engaging in the religious practice of shunning would constitute a direct burden on religion. The free exercise claim here is unlike the one in *Braunfeld v. Brown;* 366 U.S. 599, 81 S.Ct. 1144, 6 L.Ed.2d 563 (1961). In *Braunfeld,* the United States Supreme Court upheld Sunday closing laws even though it acknowledged that Sunday closings made the practice of their religious beliefs more expensive for Saturday Sabbatarians, by forcing them to close their businesses two days a week—Saturday (per religious compulsion) and Sunday (per state compulsion). In upholding the Pennsylvania statute, the Court stated that "to strike down ... legislation which imposes only an indirect burden on the exercise of

2. *See supra* note 1.

religion, i.e. legislation which does not make unlawful the religious practice itself, would radically restrict the operating latitude of the legislature." *Id.* at 606, 81 S.Ct. at 1147.

* * * In the Court's view, the law did not regulate or prohibit Saturday closings, (in which case it would have constituted a direct burden on Saturday Sabbatarians) but only Sunday operations. From this, the Court concluded that the statute did not directly regulate or prohibit a religious practice (Saturday closings) but merely regulated a non-religious one (Sunday business operations); accordingly, any effect on the religious practice was, in the Court's view, "indirect."[4]

Here, by contrast, shunning is an actual practice of the Church itself, and the burden of tort damages is direct. Permitting prosecution of a cause of action in tort, while not criminalizing the conduct at issue, would make shunning an "unlawful act." * * * The Church and its members would risk substantial damages every time a former Church member was shunned. In sum, a state tort law prohibition against shunning would directly restrict the free exercise of the Jehovah's Witnesses' religious faith.[5]

* * *

We find the practice of shunning not to constitute a sufficient threat to the peace, safety, or morality of the community as to warrant state intervention. The test for upholding a direct burden on religious practices is as stringent as any imposed under our Constitution. Only in extreme and unusual cases has the imposition of a direct burden on religion been upheld. *See, e.g., Reynolds v. United States,* 98 U.S. (8 Otto) 145, 25 L.Ed. 244 (1878) (polygamy); *Hill v. State,* 38 Ala.App. 404, 88 So.2d 880 (1956) (snake handling). The harms suffered by Paul as a result of her shunning by the Jehovah's Witnesses are clearly not of the type that would justify the imposition of tort liability for religious conduct. No physical assault or battery occurred. Intangible or emotional harms cannot ordinarily serve as a basis for maintaining a tort cause of action against a church for its practices—or against its members. * * *

A religious organization has a defense of constitutional privilege to claims that it has caused intangible harms—in most, if not all, circumstances. * * *

Providing the Church with a defense to tort is particularly appropriate here because Paul is a former Church member. Courts generally do not scrutinize closely the relationship among members (or former mem-

4. The reasoning of *Braunfeld* has been substantially undermined by subsequent cases. * * * In any event, for reasons set forth in the text immediately following, *Braunfeld* is not controlling.

5. At oral argument, both counsel seem to agree on the principle that if the behavior of the religious organization in question were criminal, the state would have a sufficient interest to overcome first amendment protections. This position is clearly incorrect. Whether a state labels a particular type of behavior criminal or whether it enables private citizens to enforce substantive rules of behavior through tort laws is not dispositive of the constitutional question. * * *

bers) of a church. Churches are afforded great latitude when they impose discipline on members or former members. * * *

The members of the Church Paul decided to abandon have concluded that they no longer want to associate with her. We hold that they are free to make that choice. The Jehovah's Witnesses' practice of shunning is protected under the first amendment of the United States Constitution and therefore under the provisions of the Washington state constitution.

IV. Conclusion

We affirm the district court's grant of summary judgment in favor of the defendants, Watchtower Bible Societies of New York and Philadelphia. Although we recognize that the harms suffered by Janice Paul are real and not insubstantial, permitting her to recover for intangible or emotional injuries would unconstitutionally restrict the Jehovah's Witnesses free exercise of religion. The First Amendment of the United States Constitution and therefore the protections of the Washington Constitution provide the Jehovah's Witnesses' with a defense to the plaintiff's cause of action—the defense of privilege. The constitutional guarantee of the free exercise of religion requires that society tolerate the type of harms suffered by Paul as a price well worth paying to safeguard the right of religious difference that all citizens enjoy. Affirmed.

NOTES

1. Bear v. Reformed Mennonite Church, 462 Pa. 330, 341 A.2d 105 (1975), which was briefly discussed in the court's opinion in *Paul,* was a case brought by a man who alleged that he had been excommunicated from the church and that as part of the excommunication process all members of the church had been ordered to "shun" him. As a result, he complained that his business was collapsing, since he was unable to hire workers, obtain loans, or market his products. Furthermore, he alleged that neither his wife nor his children would speak to him. The Supreme Court of Pennsylvania, in a very brief opinion, reversed the trial court's granting of a demurrer to the complaint. The Pennsylvania Supreme Court only held that the plaintiff had pleaded sufficient facts to entitle him to proceed with his action. It expressly stated that it did not rule out the possibility that "the First Amendment may present a complete and valid defense to the allegations of the complaint." On the general subject, *see* Comment, *Damned If You Do, Damned If You Don't: Religious Shunning and the Free Exercise Clause,* 137 U.Pa.L.Rev. 27 (1988). For a more recent case denying a cause of action for the shunning of members of one church congregation by a rival congregation, *see* Sands v. Living Word Fellowship, 34 P.3d 955 (Alaska, 2001), although it permitted an action against some of the members of the defendant based on conduct not prompted by religious belief and that was alleged to be in fact fraudulent. The courts are also reluctant to enter into disputes between family members involving allegations that one member of the family has engaged in efforts to estrange one member of the family from another member of the family. *See* Lopacich v. Falk, 5 F.3d 210 (7th Cir. 1993).

2. In Guinn v. Church of Christ of Collinsville, Oklahoma, 775 P.2d 766 (Okl.1989), the Supreme Court of Oklahoma partially upheld an award of damages against the defendant church. The plaintiff had been confronted by the elders of the church with an allegation that she had been engaging in fornication. The initial confrontation was in a laundromat in front of her children. She admitted having an affair. The elders then requested that she appear before the church and repent of her sin and that she refrain from seeing her companion. After several other meetings, the elders told the plaintiff that if she did not repent they would initiate a withdrawal of fellowship process against her. This process involved the elders informing the congregation of her sexual involvement. After seeking legal advice, she wrote the elders imploring them not to publicize her sexual involvement and resigning from the church. Apparently the Church of Christ does not permit a member to disassociate from it. She was therefore publicly branded a fornicator. A letter was sent to four other Church of Christ congregations in the area advising them that the Collinsville church had withdrawn its fellowship from the plaintiff and the reasons for its having done so. The membership of the Church of Christ comprised about five percent of the population in the Collinsville area. The majority of the Oklahoma Supreme Court ruled that both compensatory and punitive damages could be awarded for invasion of privacy and intentional infliction of emotional distress for the actions of the elders subsequent to the plaintiff's attempt to resign from the church. It held that, regardless of church doctrine, the plaintiff had a right to resign from the church. A judgment for substantial damages was vacated, and the case was returned to the trial court, because it was not clear from the jury's award to what extent it had taken into account the actions of the elders prior to the plaintiff's attempt to resign from the church. One judge dissented on the issue of whether punitive damages could be awarded, and two judges would not have allowed any award of damages at all. Having joined the church voluntarily, they argued, the plaintiff was obliged to accept the consequences, including the church doctrine refusing to recognize any attempt at disassociation. The case is somewhat unclear because there is some basis in the record to support the conclusion that the plaintiff had admitted her sexual dalliance under some promise of confidentiality. The major thrust of the case would thus appear to be one involving an invasion of privacy, a subject that will be discussed in Chapter Nine, *infra,* in which emotional distress is merely one component of the damage award. In Hadnot v. Shaw, 826 P.2d 978 (Okla.1992), the court reaffirmed its holding that, after excommunication or expulsion or the voluntary withdrawal of an individual from membership in the church, a church no longer enjoys any general immunity from tort liability in an action brought by former members who alleged that the church had publicly explained their expulsion from the local Mormon church as being based on grounds of "fornication." A more recent case denying recovery for emotional distress caused by "disfellowship" is Anderson v. Watchtower Bible and Tract Society of New York, Inc., 2007 WL 161035 (Tenn. App.), *cert. denied*, 552 U.S. 891, 128 S.Ct. 323, 169 L.Ed.2d 153 (2007).

3. The reluctance of courts to get involved in ecclesiastical doctrinal disputes is well illustrated by O'Connor v. Diocese of Honolulu, 77 Haw. 383, 885 P.2d 361 (1994), in which the plaintiff, the publisher of a lay religious

newspaper who had been excommunicated by the local Catholic Bishop for supporting the late Archbishop Marcel Lefebre, unsuccessfully sought to bring an action seeking *inter alia*, damages for mental distress, on a variety of theories. *See also* Williams v. Episcopal Diocese of Mass., 436 Mass. 574, 766 N.E.2d 820 (2002) where the court refused to recognize a claim by a female Episcopal priest that she had been discriminated on the basis of her sex in the conditions, largely pay and allowances, of her employment.

The courts are reluctant to intervene in the activities of religious bodies even when the content of the religious belief in question is not in dispute. For example, in Murphy v. I.S.K. Con. of New England, Inc., 409 Mass. 842, 571 N.E.2d 340 (1991), the court vacated a substantial judgment and dismissed that portion of the complaint based on a theory of intentional infliction of emotional distress when the supporting evidence was that the plaintiff's daughter had, when a minor, as a member of the Hare Krishna religion been exposed to the church's teaching on the inferior status of women and its claims that the "earthly family was a perversion of the Krishna family." It was not for the courts "to consider the propriety of constitutionally protected religious beliefs." Nevertheless, in Wollersheim v. Church of Scientology, 15 Cal.App.4th 1426, 6 Cal.Rptr.2d 532 (1992), it was held that, even accepting that the church's practices of "auditing," "disconnect" and "fair game" were religious practices, they nevertheless could be the basis of an action for intentional infliction of emotional distress when it was found that they were conducted in a coercive environment and were thus not truly "voluntary." The jury awarded a total of $30,000,000 in compensatory and punitive damages. This award was reduced on appeal to $500,000 in compensatory damages and $2,000,000 in punitive damages. Before its final disposition in the California Court of Appeals, the case reached the United States Supreme Court which, 499 U.S. 914, 111 S.Ct. 1298, 113 L.Ed.2d 234 (1991), vacated the initial California appellate judgment for reconsideration on the punitive damage issue in the light of Pacific Mutual Life Insurance Company v. Haslip, 499 U.S. 1, 111 S.Ct. 1032, 113 L.Ed.2d 1 (1991). As already indicated, on reconsideration, the California Court of Appeal held that the punitive damage award met the *Haslip* criteria. For the difficulties the plaintiff encountered in trying to enforce the judgment, *see* 69 Cal.App.4th 1012, 81 Cal.Rptr.2d 896 (1999). *But cf.* Lewis v. Holy Spirit Ass'n for Unification, 589 F.Supp. 10 (D. Mass. 1983). In Peterson v. Sorlien, 299 N.W.2d 123 (Minn. 1980), *cert.* denied, 450 U.S. 1031, 101 S.Ct. 1742, 68 L.Ed.2d 227 (1981), a young woman was unsuccessful in her attempt to recover against her parents for forcing her to undergo "re-programming," but was awarded damages for intentional infliction of emotional distress against the deprogrammers. On the general subject of religion and the tort of intentional infliction of emotional distress, *see* P. Hayden, *Religiously Motivated "Outrageous" Conduct: Intentional Infliction of Emotional Distress as a Weapon Against "Other People's Faiths,"* 34 Wm. & Mary L.Rev. 580 (1993).

HUSTLER MAGAZINE v. FALWELL

Supreme Court of the United States, 1988.
485 U.S. 46, 108 S.Ct. 876, 99 L.Ed.2d 41.

CHIEF JUSTICE REHNQUIST delivered the opinion of the Court.

Petitioner Hustler Magazine, Inc., is a magazine of nationwide circulation. Respondent Jerry Falwell, a nationally known minister who has been active as a commentator on politics and public affairs, sued petitioner and its publisher, petitioner Larry Flynt, to recover damages for invasion of privacy, libel, and intentional infliction of emotional distress. The District Court directed a verdict against respondent on the privacy claim, and submitted the other two claims to a jury. The jury found for petitioners on the defamation claim, but found for respondent on the claim for intentional infliction of emotional distress and awarded damages. We now consider whether this award is consistent with the First and Fourteenth Amendments of the United States Constitution.

The inside front cover of the November 1983 issue of Hustler Magazine featured a "parody" of an advertisement for Campari Liqueur that contained the name and picture of respondent and was entitled "Jerry Falwell talks about his first time." This parody was modeled after actual Campari ads that included interviews with various celebrities about their "first times." Although it was apparent by the end of each interview that this meant the first time they sampled Campari, the ads clearly played on the sexual double entendre of the general subject of "first times." Copying the form and layout of these Campari ads, Hustler's editors chose respondent as the featured celebrity and drafted an alleged "interview" with him in which he states that his "first time" was during a drunken incestuous rendezvous with his mother in an outhouse. The Hustler parody portrays respondent and his mother as drunk and immoral, and suggests that respondent is a hypocrite who preaches only when he is drunk. In small print at the bottom of the page, the ad contains the disclaimer, "ad parody—not to be taken seriously." The magazine's table of contents also lists the ad as "Fiction; Ad and Personality Parody."

Soon after the November issue of Hustler became available to the public, respondent brought this diversity action in the United States District Court for the Western District of Virginia against Hustler Magazine, Inc., Larry C. Flynt, and Flynt Distributing Co. Respondent stated in his complaint that publication of the ad parody in Hustler entitled him to recover damages for libel, invasion of privacy, and intentional infliction of emotional distress. The case proceeded to trial.[1] At the close of the evidence, the District Court granted a directed verdict for petitioners on the invasion of privacy claim. The jury then found against respondent on the libel claim, specifically finding that the ad parody could not "reasonably be understood as describing actual facts about [respondent] or actual

1. While the case was pending, the ad parody was published in Hustler magazine a second time.

events in which [he] participated." App. to Pet. for Cert. C1. The jury ruled for respondent on the intentional infliction of emotional distress claim, however, and stated that he should be awarded $100,000 in compensatory damages, as well as $50,000 each in punitive damages from petitioners.[2] Petitioners' motion for judgment notwithstanding the verdict was denied.

On appeal, the United States Court of Appeals for the Fourth Circuit affirmed the judgment against petitioners. *Falwell v. Flynt,* 797 F.2d 1270 (C.A.4 1986). The court rejected petitioners' argument that the "actual malice" standard of *New York Times Co. v. Sullivan,* 376 U.S. 254, 84 S.Ct. 710, 11 L.Ed.2d 686 (1964), must be met before respondent can recover for emotional distress. The court agreed that because respondent is concededly a public figure, petitioners are "entitled to the same level of first amendment protection in the claim for intentional infliction of emotional distress that they received in [respondent's] claim for libel." 797 F.2d, at 1274. But this does not mean that a literal application of the actual malice rule is appropriate in the context of an emotional distress claim. In the court's view, the *New York Times* decision emphasized the constitutional importance not of the falsity of the statement or the defendant's disregard for the truth, but of the heightened level of culpability embodied in the requirement of "knowing * * * or reckless" conduct. Here, the *New York Times* standard is satisfied by the state-law requirement, and the jury's finding, that the defendants have acted intentionally or recklessly.[3] The Court of Appeals then went on to reject the contention that because the jury found that the ad parody did not describe actual facts about respondent, the ad was an opinion that is protected by the First Amendment. As the court put it, this was "irrelevant," as the issue is "whether [the ad's] publication was sufficiently outrageous to constitute intentional infliction of emotional distress." *Id.,* at 1276. Petitioners then filed a petition for rehearing en banc, but this was denied by a divided court. Given the importance of the constitutional issues involved, we granted certiorari.

This case presents us with a novel question involving First Amendment limitations upon a State's authority to protect its citizens from the intentional infliction of emotional distress. We must decide whether a public figure may recover damages for emotional harm caused by the publication of an ad parody offensive to him, and doubtless gross and repugnant in the eyes of most. Respondent would have us find that a State's interest in protecting public figures from emotional distress is sufficient to deny First Amendment protection to speech that is patently

2. The jury found no liability on the part of Flynt Distributing Co., Inc. It is consequently not a party to this appeal.

3. Under Virginia law, in an action for intentional infliction of emotional distress a plaintiff must show that the defendant's conduct (1) is intentional or reckless; (2) offends generally accepted standards of decency or morality; (3) is causally connected with the plaintiff's emotional distress; and (4) caused emotional distress that was severe. 797 F.2d, at 1275, n. 4 (citing *Womack v. Eldridge,* 215 Va. 338, 210 S.E.2d 145 (1974)). [Ed. note] This case was presented at p. 444, *supra*.

offensive and is intended to inflict emotional injury, even when that speech could not reasonably have been interpreted as stating actual facts about the public figure involved. This we decline to do.

At the heart of the First Amendment is the recognition of the fundamental importance of the free flow of ideas and opinions on matters of public interest and concern. * * * We have therefore been particularly vigilant to ensure that individual expressions of ideas remain free from governmentally imposed sanctions. The First Amendment recognizes no such thing as a "false" idea. *Gertz v. Robert Welch, Inc.,* 418 U.S. 323, 339, 94 S.Ct. 2997, 3007, 41 L.Ed.2d 789 (1974). * * *

The sort of robust political debate encouraged by the First Amendment is bound to produce speech that is critical of those who hold public office or those public figures who are "intimately involved in the resolution of important public questions or, by reason of their fame, shape events in areas of concern to society at large." *Associated Press v. Walker,* decided with *Curtis Publishing Co. v. Butts,* 388 U.S. 130, 164, 87 S.Ct. 1975, 1996, 18 L.Ed.2d 1094 (1967) (Warren, C.J., concurring in result). * * *

Of course, this does not mean that *any* speech about a public figure is immune from sanction in the form of damages. Since *New York Times Co. v. Sullivan, supra,* we have consistently ruled that a public figure may hold a speaker liable for the damage to reputation caused by publication of a defamatory falsehood, but only if the statement was made "with knowledge that it was false or with reckless disregard of whether it was false or not." *Id.,* 376 U.S., at 279–280, 84 S.Ct., at 726. False statements of fact are particularly valueless; they interfere with the truth-seeking function of the marketplace of ideas, and they cause damage to an individual's reputation that cannot easily be repaired by counterspeech, however persuasive or effective. * * * But even though falsehoods have little value in and of themselves, * * * a rule that would impose strict liability on a publisher for false factual assertions would have an undoubted "chilling" effect on speech relating to public figures that does have constitutional value. "Freedoms of expression require 'breathing space.'" *Philadelphia Newspapers, Inc. v. Hepps,* 475 U.S. 767, 772, 106 S.Ct. 1558, 1561, 89 L.Ed.2d 783 (1986) (quoting *New York Times,* 376 U.S., at 272, 84 S.Ct., at 721). This breathing space is provided by a constitutional rule that allows public figures to recover for libel or defamation only when they can prove *both* that the statement was false and that the statement was made with the requisite level of culpability.

Respondent argues, however, that a different standard should apply in this case because here the State seeks to prevent not reputational damage, but the severe emotional distress suffered by the person who is the subject of an offensive publication. * * * In respondent's view, and in the view of the Court of Appeals, so long as the utterance was intended to inflict emotional distress, was outrageous, and did in fact inflict serious emotional distress, it is of no constitutional import whether the statement was a fact or an opinion, or whether it was true or false. It is the intent to cause injury that is the gravamen of the tort, and the State's interest in preventing emotional harm simply outweighs whatever interest a speaker may have in speech of this type.

Generally speaking the law does not regard the intent to inflict emotional distress as one which should receive much solicitude, and it is quite understandable that most if not all jurisdictions have chosen to make it civilly culpable where the conduct in question is sufficiently "outrageous." But in the world of debate about public affairs, many things done with motives that are less than admirable are protected by the First Amendment. In *Garrison v. Louisiana,* 379 U.S. 64, 85 S.Ct. 209, 13 L.Ed.2d 125 (1964), we held that even when a speaker or writer is motivated by hatred or ill-will his expression was protected by the First Amendment:

> "Debate on public issues will not be uninhibited if the speaker must run the risk that it will be proved in court that he spoke out of hatred; even if he did speak out of hatred, utterances honestly believed contribute to the free interchange of ideas and the ascertainment of truth." *Id.,* at 73, 85 S.Ct., at 215.

Thus while such a bad motive may be deemed controlling for purposes of tort liability in other areas of the law, we think the First Amendment prohibits such a result in the area of public debate about public figures.

Were we to hold otherwise, there can be little doubt that political cartoonists and satirists would be subjected to damages awards without any showing that their work falsely defamed its subject. Webster's defines a caricature as "the deliberately distorted picturing or imitating of a person, literary style, etc. by exaggerating features or mannerisms for satirical effect." Webster's New Unabridged Twentieth Century Dictionary of the English Language 275 (2d ed. 1979). The appeal of the political cartoon or caricature is often based on exploration of unfortunate physical traits or politically embarrassing events—an exploration often calculated to injure the feelings of the subject of the portrayal. The art of the cartoonist is often not reasoned or evenhanded, but slashing and one-sided. One cartoonist expressed the nature of the art in these words:

> "The political cartoon is a weapon of attack, of scorn and ridicule and satire; it is least effective when it tries to pat some politician on the back. It is usually as welcome as a bee sting and is always controversial in some quarters." Long, The Political Cartoon: Journalism's Strongest Weapon, The Quill, 56, 57 (Nov.1962).

Several famous examples of this type of intentionally injurious speech were drawn by Thomas Nast, probably the greatest American cartoonist to date, who was associated for many years during the post-Civil War era with Harper's Weekly. In the pages of that publication Nast conducted a graphic vendetta against William M. "Boss" Tweed and his corrupt associates in New York City's "Tweed Ring." It has been described by one historian of the subject as "a sustained attack which in its passion and effectiveness stands alone in the history of American graphic art." M. Keller, The Art and Politics of Thomas Nast 177 (1968). Another writer explains that the success of the Nast cartoon was achieved "because of the emotional impact of its presentation. It continuously goes beyond the bounds of good taste and conventional manners." C. Press, The Political Cartoon 251 (1981).

Despite their sometimes caustic nature, from the early cartoon portraying George Washington as an ass down to the present day, graphic depictions and satirical cartoons have played a prominent role in public and political debate. Nast's castigation of the Tweed Ring, Walt McDougall's characterization of presidential candidate James G. Blaine's banquet with the millionaires at Delmonico's as "The Royal Feast of Belshazzar," and numerous other efforts have undoubtedly had an effect on the course and outcome of contemporaneous debate. Lincoln's tall, gangling posture, Teddy Roosevelt's glasses and teeth, and Franklin D. Roosevelt's jutting jaw and cigarette holder have been memorialized by political cartoons with an effect that could not have been obtained by the photographer or the portrait artist. From the viewpoint of history it is clear that our political discourse would have been considerably poorer without them.

Respondent contends, however, that the caricature in question here was so "outrageous" as to distinguish it from more traditional political cartoons. There is no doubt that the caricature of respondent and his mother published in Hustler is at best a distant cousin of the political cartoons described above, and a rather poor relation at that. If it were possible by laying down a principled standard to separate the one from the other, public discourse would probably suffer little or no harm. But we doubt that there is any such standard, and we are quite sure that the pejorative description "outrageous" does not supply one. "Outrageousness" in the area of political and social discourse has an inherent subjectiveness about it which would allow a jury to impose liability on the basis of the jurors' tastes or views, or perhaps on the basis of their dislike of a particular expression. An "outrageousness" standard thus runs afoul of our longstanding refusal to allow damages to be awarded because the speech in question may have an adverse emotional impact on the audience. * * *

Admittedly, these oft-repeated First Amendment principles, like other principles, are subject to limitations. We recognized in *Pacifica Foundation,* that speech that is " 'vulgar,' 'offensive,' and 'shocking' " is "not entitled to absolute constitutional protection under all circumstances." 438 U.S., at 747, 98 S.Ct., at 3039. * * * But the sort of expression involved in this case does not seem to us to be governed by any exception to the general First Amendment principles stated above.

We conclude that public figures and public officials may not recover for the tort of intentional infliction of emotional distress by reason of publications such as the one here at issue without showing in addition that the publication contains a false statement of fact which was made with "actual malice," *i.e.,* with knowledge that the statement was false or with reckless disregard as to whether or not it was true. This is not merely a "blind application" of the *New York Times* standard, see *Time, Inc. v. Hill,* 385 U.S. 374, 390, 87 S.Ct. 534, 543, 17 L.Ed.2d 456 (1967), it reflects our considered judgment that such a standard is necessary to give adequate "breathing space" to the freedoms protected by the First Amendment.

Here it is clear that respondent Falwell is a "public figure" for purposes of First Amendment law.[5] The jury found against respondent on his libel claim when it decided that the Hustler ad parody could not "reasonably be understood as describing actual facts about [respondent] or actual events in which [he] participated." App. to Pet. for Cert. Cl. The Court of Appeals interpreted the jury's finding to be that the ad parody "was not reasonably believable," 797 F.2d, at 1278, and in accordance with our custom we accept this finding. Respondent is thus relegated to his claim for damages awarded by the jury for the intentional infliction of emotional distress by "outrageous" conduct. But for reasons heretofore stated this claim cannot, consistently with the First Amendment, form a basis for the award of damages when the conduct in question is the publication of a caricature such as the ad parody involved here. The judgment of the Court of Appeals is accordingly reversed.

JUSTICE WHITE, concurring in the judgment.

As I see it, the decision in *New York Times v. Sullivan,* 376 U.S. 254, 84 S.Ct. 710, 11 L.Ed.2d 686 (1964), has little to do with this case, for here the jury found that the ad contained no assertion of fact. But I agree with the Court that the judgment below, which penalized the publication of the parody, cannot be squared with the First Amendment.

NOTE

For a similar case, *see* Dworkin v. Hustler Magazine Inc., 867 F.2d 1188 (9th Cir.1989), *cert. denied* 493 U.S. 812, 110 S.Ct. 59, 107 L.Ed.2d 26 (1989). On the general subject of the constitutional problems raised by the tort of intentional infliction of emotional distress, *see* Note, *First Amendment Limits on Tort Liability for Words Intended to Inflict Severe Emotional Distress,* 85 Colum.L.Rev. 1749 (1985). The next case presents an important illustration of the situations in which the courts will have to tangle with the question of when the intentional infliction of emotional distress is actionable. Do you think the previous cases adequately took into account the constitutional considerations which were the focus of *Paul* and *Falwell?* What do you think of a doctrine that permits so-called "ordinary people," but not public figures, to recover for the intentional infliction of emotional distress by virtue of speech-related activities? What result would you expect if Falwell's mother had brought suit?

5. Neither party disputes this conclusion. Respondent is the host of a nationally syndicated television show and was the founder and president of a political organization formerly known as the Moral Majority. He is also the founder of Liberty University in Lynchburg, Virginia, and is the author of several books and publications. Who's Who in America 849 (44th ed. 1986–1987).

SNYDER v. PHELPS

Supreme Court of the United States, 2011.
562 U.S. ___, 131 S.Ct. 1207, 179 L.Ed.2d 172.

CHIEF JUSTICE ROBERTS delivered the opinion of the Court.

A jury held members of the Westboro Baptist Church liable for millions of dollars in damages for picketing near a soldier's funeral service. The picket signs reflected the church's view that the United States is overly tolerant of sin and that God kills American soldiers as punishment. The question presented is whether the First Amendment shields the church members from tort liability for their speech in this case.

I

A

Fred Phelps founded the Westboro Baptist Church in Topeka, Kansas, in 1955. The church's congregation believes that God hates and punishes the United States for its tolerance of homosexuality, particularly in America's military. The church frequently communicates its views by picketing, often at military funerals. In the more than 20 years that the members of Westboro Baptist have publicized their message, they have picketed nearly 600 funerals. * * *

Marine Lance Corporal Matthew Snyder was killed in Iraq in the line of duty. Lance Corporal Snyder's father selected the Catholic church in the Snyders' hometown of Westminster, Maryland, as the site for his son's funeral. Local newspapers provided notice of the time and location of the service.

Phelps became aware of Matthew Snyder's funeral and decided to travel to Maryland with six other Westboro Baptist parishioners (two of his daughters and four of his grandchildren) to picket. On the day of the memorial service, the Westboro congregation members picketed on public land adjacent to public streets near the Maryland State House, the United States Naval Academy, and Matthew Snyder's funeral. The Westboro picketers carried signs that were largely the same at all three locations. They stated, for instance: "God Hates the USA/Thank God for 9/11," "America is Doomed," "Don't Pray for the USA," "Thank God for IEDs," "Thank God for Dead Soldiers," "Pope in Hell," "Priests Rape Boys," "God Hates Fags," "You're Going to Hell," and "God Hates You."

The church had notified the authorities in advance of its intent to picket at the time of the funeral, and the picketers complied with police instructions in staging their demonstration. The picketing took place within a 10–by–25–foot plot of public land adjacent to a public street, behind a temporary fence. * * * That plot was approximately 1,000 feet from the church where the funeral was held. Several buildings separated the picket site from the church. * * *The Westboro picketers displayed their signs for about 30 minutes before the funeral began and sang hymns and recited Bible verses. None of the picketers entered church property or went to the cemetery. They did not yell or use profanity, and there was no violence associated with the picketing.* * *

The funeral procession passed within 200 to 300 feet of the picket site. Although Snyder testified that he could see the tops of the picket signs as he drove to the funeral, he did not see what was written on the signs until later that night, while watching a news broadcast covering the event.

B

Snyder filed suit against Phelps, Phelps's daughters, and the Westboro Baptist Church (collectively Westboro or the church) in the United States District Court for the District of Maryland under that court's diversity jurisdiction. Snyder alleged five state tort law claims: defamation, publicity given to private life, intentional infliction of emotional distress, intrusion upon seclusion, and civil conspiracy. Westboro moved for summary judgment contending, in part, that the church's speech was insulated from liability by the First Amendment. * * *

The District Court awarded Westboro summary judgment on Snyder's claims for defamation and publicity given to private life, concluding that Snyder could not prove the necessary elements of those torts. * * * A trial was held on the remaining claims. At trial, Snyder described the severity of his emotional injuries. He testified that he is unable to separate the thought of his dead son from his thoughts of Westboro's picketing, and that he often becomes tearful, angry, and physically ill when he thinks about it. * * * Expert witnesses testified that Snyder's emotional anguish had resulted in severe depression and had exacerbated pre-existing health conditions.

A jury found for Snyder on the intentional infliction of emotional distress, intrusion upon seclusion, and civil conspiracy claims, and held Westboro liable for $2.9 million in compensatory damages and $8 million in punitive damages. Westboro filed several post-trial motions, including a motion contending that the jury verdict was grossly excessive and a motion seeking judgment as a matter of law on all claims on First Amendment grounds. The District Court remitted the punitive damages award to $2.1 million, but left the jury verdict otherwise intact. * * *

In the Court of Appeals, Westboro's primary argument was that the church was entitled to judgment as a matter of law because the First Amendment fully protected Westboro's speech. The Court of Appeals agreed. The court reviewed the picket signs and concluded that Westboro's statements were entitled to First Amendment protection because those statements were on matters of public concern, were not provably false, and were expressed solely through hyperbolic rhetoric.

We granted certiorari.

II

To succeed on a claim for intentional infliction of emotional distress in Maryland, a plaintiff must demonstrate that the defendant intentionally or recklessly engaged in extreme and outrageous conduct that caused the plaintiff to suffer severe emotional distress. See Harris v. Jones, 281 Md. 560, 565–566, 380 A.2d 611, 614 (1977). The Free Speech Clause of the First Amendment—"Congress shall make no law ... abridging the freedom of speech"—can serve as a defense in state tort suits, including suits for intentional infliction of emotional distress. See, e.g., Hustler Magazine, Inc. v. Falwell * * *.

Whether the First Amendment prohibits holding Westboro liable for its speech in this case turns largely on whether that speech is of public or private concern, as determined by all the circumstances of the case. "[S]peech on 'matters of public concern' ... is 'at the heart of the First Amendment's protection.' ". * * * The First Amendment reflects "a profound national commitment to the principle that debate on public issues should be uninhibited, robust, and wide-open." * * * That is because "speech concerning public affairs is more than self-expression; it is the essence of self-government." * * * Accordingly, "speech on public issues occupies the highest rung of the hierarchy of First Amendment values, and is entitled to special protection. * * *

" '[N]ot all speech is of equal First Amendment importance,' " however, and where matters of purely private significance are at issue, First Amendment protections are often less rigorous. * * *. That is because restricting speech on purely private matters does not implicate the same constitutional concerns as limiting speech on matters of public interest: "[T]here is no threat to the free and robust debate of public issues; there is no potential interference with a meaningful dialogue of ideas"; and the "threat of liability" does not pose the risk of "a reaction of self-censorship" on matters of public interest. * * *

We noted a short time ago, in considering whether public employee speech addressed a matter of public concern, that "the boundaries of the public concern test are not well defined." * * * Although that remains true today, we have articulated some guiding principles, principles that accord broad protection to speech to ensure that courts themselves do not become inadvertent censors.

Speech deals with matters of public concern when it can "be fairly considered as relating to any matter of political, social, or other concern to the community* * *, or when it "is a subject of legitimate news interest; that is, a subject of general interest and of value and concern to the public"; * * *. The arguably "inappropriate or controversial character of a statement is irrelevant to the question whether it deals with a matter of public concern." * * *

Our opinion in Dun & Bradstreet, on the other hand, provides an example of speech of only private concern. In that case we held, as a general matter, that information about a particular individual's credit report "concerns no public issue." 472 U.S., at 762, 105 S. Ct. 2939, 86 L. Ed. 2d 593. The content of the report, we explained, "was speech solely in the individual interest of the speaker and its specific business audience." Ibid. That was confirmed by the fact that the particular report was sent to only five subscribers to the reporting service, who were bound not to disseminate it further. Ibid. To cite another example, we concluded in San Diego v. Roe that, in the context of a government employer regulating the speech of its employees, videos of an employee engaging in sexually explicit acts did not address a public concern; the videos "did nothing to inform the public about any aspect of the [employing agency's] functioning or operation." 543 U.S., at 84, 125 S. Ct. 521, 160 L. Ed. 2d 410.

Deciding whether speech is of public or private concern requires us to examine the " 'content, form, and context' " of that speech, " 'as revealed by the whole record.' " * * *. As in other First Amendment cases, the court is obligated "to 'make an independent examination of the whole record' in order to make sure that 'the judgment does not constitute a forbidden intrusion on the field of free expression.' " * * *In considering content, form, and context, no factor is dispositive, and it is necessary to evaluate all the circumstances of the speech, including what was said, where it was said, and how it was said.

The "content" of Westboro's signs plainly relates to broad issues of interest to society at large, rather than matters of "purely private concern." * * *. While these messages may fall short of refined social or political commentary, the issues they highlight—the political and moral conduct of the United States and its citizens, the fate of our Nation, homosexuality in the military, and scandals involving the Catholic clergy—are matters of public import. The signs certainly convey Westboro's position on those issues, in a manner designed, unlike 'the private speech' in Dun & Bradstreet, to reach as broad a public audience as possible. And even if a few of the signs—such as "You're Going to Hell" and "God Hates You"—were viewed as containing messages related to Matthew Snyder or the Snyders specifically, that would not change the fact that the overall thrust and dominant theme of Westboro's demonstration spoke to broader public issues.

Apart from the content of Westboro's signs, Snyder contends that the "context" of the speech—its connection with his son's funeral—makes the speech a matter of private rather than public concern. The fact that Westboro spoke in connection with a funeral, however, cannot by itself transform the nature of Westboro's speech. Westboro's signs, displayed on public land next to a public street, reflect the fact that the church finds much to condemn in modern society. Its speech is "fairly characterized as constituting speech on a matter of public concern," * * *, and the funeral setting does not alter that conclusion.

Snyder argues that the church members in fact mounted a personal attack on Snyder and his family, and then attempted to "immunize their conduct by claiming that they were actually protesting the United States' tolerance of homosexuality or the supposed evils of the Catholic Church* * *. We are not concerned in this case that Westboro's speech on public matters was in any way contrived to insulate speech on a private matter from liability. Westboro had been actively engaged in speaking on the subjects addressed in its picketing long before it became aware of Matthew Snyder, and there can be no serious claim that Westboro's picketing did not represent its "honestly believed" views on public issues. There was no pre-existing relationship or conflict between Westboro and Snyder that might suggest Westboro's speech on public matters was intended to mask an attack on Snyder over a private matter. Contrast Connick, * * * (finding public employee speech a matter of private concern when it was "no coincidence that [the speech] followed upon the heels of [a] transfer notice" affecting the employee).

Snyder goes on to argue that Westboro's speech should be afforded less than full First Amendment protection "not only because of the words" but also because the church members exploited the funeral "as a platform to bring their message to a broader audience." * * * There is no doubt that Westboro chose to stage its picketing at the Naval Academy, the Maryland State House, and Matthew Snyder's funeral to increase publicity for its views and because of the relation between those sites and its views—in the case of the military funeral, because Westboro believes that God is killing American soldiers as punishment for the Nation's sinful policies.

Westboro's choice to convey its views in conjunction with Matthew Snyder's funeral made the expression of those views particularly hurtful to many, especially to Matthew's father. The record makes clear that the applicable legal term—"emotional distress"—fails to capture fully the anguish Westboro's choice added to Mr. Snyder's already incalculable grief. But Westboro conducted its picketing peacefully on matters of public concern at a public place adjacent to a public street. Such space occupies a "special position in terms of First Amendment protection." * * *. "[W]e have repeatedly referred to public streets as the archetype of a traditional public forum," noting that " '[t]ime out of mind' public streets and sidewalks have been used for public assembly and debate. * * *.[1]

That said, "[e]ven protected speech is not equally permissible in all places and at all times." * * *. Westboro's choice of where and when to conduct its picketing is not beyond the Government's regulatory reach—it is "subject to reasonable time, place, or manner restrictions" that are consistent with the standards announced in this Court's precedents. * * *. Maryland now has a law imposing restrictions on funeral picketing, Md. Crim. Law Code Ann. § 10–205 (Lexis Supp. 2010), as do 43 other States and the Federal Government. * * *. To the extent these laws are

---

1. The dissent is wrong to suggest that the Court considers a public street "a free-fire zone in which otherwise actionable verbal attacks are shielded from liability." * * * The fact that Westboro conducted its picketing adjacent to a public street does not insulate the speech from liability, but instead heightens concerns that what is at issue is an effort to communicate to the public the church's views on matters of public concern. That is why our precedents so clearly recognize the special significance of this traditional public forum.

content neutral, they raise very different questions from the tort verdict at issue in this case. Maryland's law, however, was not in effect at the time of the events at issue here, so we have no occasion to consider how it might apply to facts such as those before us, or whether it or other similar regulations are constitutional.

We have identified a few limited situations where the location of targeted picketing can be regulated under provisions that the Court has determined to be content neutral. In Frisby, for example, we upheld a ban on such picketing "before or about" a particular residence* * *. In Madsen v. Women's Health Center, Inc., we approved an injunction requiring a buffer zone between protesters and an abortion clinic entrance* * *. The facts here are obviously quite different, both with respect to the activity being regulated and the means of restricting those activities.

Simply put, the church members had the right to be where they were. Westboro alerted local authorities to its funeral protest and fully complied with police guidance on where the picketing could be staged. The picketing was conducted under police supervision some 1,000 feet from the church, out of the sight of those at the church. The protest was not unruly; there was no shouting, profanity, or violence.

The record confirms that any distress occasioned by Westboro's picketing turned on the content and viewpoint of the message conveyed, rather than any interference with the funeral itself. A group of parishioners standing at the very spot where Westboro stood, holding signs that said "God Bless America" and "God Loves You," would not have been subjected to liability. It was what Westboro said that exposed it to tort damages.

Given that Westboro's speech was at a public place on a matter of public concern, that speech is entitled to "special protection" under the First Amendment. Such speech cannot be restricted simply because it is upsetting or arouses contempt. "If there is a bedrock principle underlying the First Amendment, it is that the government may not prohibit the expression of an idea simply because society finds the idea itself offensive or disagreeable." * * *. Indeed, "the point of all speech protection . . . is to shield just those choices of content that in someone's eyes are misguided, or even hurtful."

The jury here was instructed that it could hold Westboro liable for intentional infliction of emotional distress based on a finding that Westboro's picketing was "outrageous." "Outrageousness," however, is a highly malleable standard with "an inherent subjectiveness about it which would allow a jury to impose liability on the basis of the jurors' tastes or views, or perhaps on the basis of their dislike of a particular expression." Hustler, 485 U.S., at 55, 108 S. Ct. 876, 99 L. Ed. 2d 41 (internal quotation marks omitted). In a case such as this, a jury is "unlikely to be neutral with respect to the content of [the] speech," posing "a real danger of becoming an instrument for the suppression of . . . 'vehement, caustic, and sometimes unpleasan[t]' "expression. Bose Corp., 466 U.S., at 510, 104 S. Ct. 1949, 80 L. Ed. 2d 502 (quoting New York Times, * * *. Such a risk is unacceptable; "in public debate [we] must tolerate insulting, and even outrageous, speech in order to provide adequate 'breathing space' to the freedoms protected by the First Amendment." Boos v. Barry, 485 U.S. 312, 322, 108 S. Ct. 1157, 99 L. Ed. 2d 333 (1988) (some internal quotation marks omitted). What Westboro said, in the whole context of how and where it chose to say it, is entitled to "special protection" under the First Amendment, and that protection cannot be overcome by a jury finding that the picketing was outrageous.

For all these reasons, the jury verdict imposing tort liability on Westboro for intentional infliction of emotional distress must be set aside.

III

The jury also found Westboro liable for the state law torts of intrusion upon seclusion and civil conspiracy. The Court of Appeals did not examine these torts independently of the intentional infliction of emotional distress tort. Instead, the Court of Appeals reversed the District Court wholesale, holding that the judgment wrongly "attache[d] tort liability to constitutionally protected speech." * * *.

Snyder argues that even assuming Westboro's speech is entitled to First Amendment protection generally, the church is not immunized from liability for intrusion upon seclusion because Snyder was a member of a captive audience at his son's funeral. * * * We do not agree. In most circumstances, "the Constitution does not permit the government to decide which types of otherwise protected speech are sufficiently offensive to require protection for the unwilling listener or viewer. Rather, . . . the burden normally falls upon the viewer to avoid further bombardment of [his] sensibilities simply by averting [his] eyes." * * *.

As a general matter, we have applied the captive audience doctrine only sparingly to protect unwilling listeners from protected speech. For example, we have upheld a statute allowing a homeowner to restrict the delivery of offensive mail to his home, * * * and an ordinance prohibiting picketing "before or about" any individual's residence, * * *.

Here, Westboro stayed well away from the memorial service. Snyder could see no more than the tops of the signs when driving to the funeral. And there is no indication that the picketing in any way interfered with the funeral service itself. We decline to expand the captive audience doctrine to the circumstances presented here.

Because we find that the First Amendment bars Snyder from recovery for intentional infliction of emotional distress or intrusion upon seclusion—the alleged unlawful activity Westboro conspired to accomplish—we must likewise hold that Snyder cannot recover for civil conspiracy based on those torts.

* * *

The judgment of the United States Court of Appeals for the Fourth Circuit is affirmed.

* * *

It is so ordered.

JUSTICE ALITO, dissenting.

Our profound national commitment to free and open debate is not a license for the vicious verbal assault that occurred in this case.

Petitioner Albert Snyder is not a public figure. He is simply a parent whose son, Marine Lance Corporal Matthew Snyder, was killed in Iraq. Mr. Snyder wanted what is surely the right of any parent who experiences such an incalculable loss: to bury his son in peace. But respondents, members of the Westboro Baptist Church, deprived him of that elementary right. They first issued a press release and thus turned Matthew's funeral into a tumultuous media event. They then appeared at the church, approached as closely as they could without trespassing, and launched a malevolent verbal attack on Matthew and his family at a time of acute emotional vulnerability. As a result, Albert Snyder suffered severe and lasting emotional injury. The Court now holds that the First Amendment protected respondents' right to brutalize Mr. Snyder. I cannot agree.

I

Respondents and other members of their church have strong opinions on certain moral, religious, and political issues, and the First Amendment ensures that they have almost limitless opportunities to express their views. They may write and distribute books, articles, and other texts; they may create and disseminate video and audio recordings; they may circulate petitions; they may speak to individuals and groups in public forums and in any private venue that wishes to accommodate them; they may picket peacefully in countless locations; they may appear on television and speak on the radio; they may post messages on the Internet and send out e-mails. And they may express their views in terms that are "uninhibited," "vehement," and "caustic." * * *

It does not follow, however, that they may intentionally inflict severe emotional injury on private persons at a time of intense emotional sensitivity by launching vicious verbal attacks that make no contribution to public debate. To protect against such injury, "most if not all jurisdictions" permit recovery in tort for the intentional infliction of emotional distress (or IIED). * * *

This is a very narrow tort with requirements that "are rigorous, and difficult to satisfy." * * *. To recover, a plaintiff must show that the conduct at issue caused harm that was truly severe. * * *

A plaintiff must also establish that the defendant's conduct was " 'so outrageous in character, and so extreme in degree, as to go beyond all possible bounds of decency, and to be regarded as atrocious, and utterly intolerable in a civilized community.' " * * *

Although the elements of the IIED tort are difficult to meet, respondents long ago abandoned any effort to show that those tough standards were not satisfied here. On appeal, they chose not to contest the sufficiency of the evidence. * * *. They did not dispute that Mr. Snyder suffered " 'wounds that are truly severe and incapable of healing themselves.' " * * *. Nor did they dispute that their speech was " 'so outrageous in character, and so extreme in degree, as to go beyond all possible bounds of decency, and to be regarded as atrocious, and utterly intolerable in a civilized community.' " * * *. Instead, they maintained that the First Amendment gave them a license to engage in such conduct. They are wrong.

II

It is well established that a claim for the intentional infliction of emotional distress can be satisfied by speech. Indeed, what has been described as "[t]he leading case" recognizing this tort involved speech. Prosser and Keeton, *supra,* § 12, at 60 (citing *Wilkinson* v. *Downton,* [1897] 2 Q. B. 57); see also Restatement (Second) of Torts § 46, illustration 1. And although this Court has not decided the question, I think it is clear that the First Amendment does not entirely preclude liability for the intentional infliction of emotional distress by means of speech. * * *

* * *

NOTES

Justice Breyer concurred in the Court's opinion but wrote a brief concurrence in which he posed some hypothetical cases in which even speech on a matter of public concern could be suppressed or regulated. These included someone staging a violent demonstration with the idea that it would be recorded and then shown on television. He also found some merit in Justice Alito's assertion that the English case, Wilkinson v. Downton, [1897] 2 QB. 57, discussed earlier in this chapter at p. 435, and *Restatement (Second) of Torts* § 46 showed that intentional infliction of emotional distress could be committed by verbal means. Justice Breyer likewise found some merit in Justice Alito's contention, in a part of his dissent that has not been reprinted here, that the fighting words exception of Chaplinsky v. New Hampshire, 315 U.S. 568, 62 S.Ct. 766, 86 L.Ed. 1031 (1942) demonstrated the Court's acceptance of some constitutionally recognized power to regulate even public speech. *Chaplinsky,* and other similar cases are discussed in the next chapter, at p. 525, when we consider the question of group defamation. To the extent that there is such a thing as a "fighting words" exception to the First Amendment's protection of speech, it seems to be extremely doubtful that the speech involved in the *Chaplinsky* case, calling a law enforcement officer a " 'God damned racketeer' and a 'damned fascist,' " would now be considered to be fighting words. As we shall see subsequent cases have confined the "fighting words" exception to speech advocating immediate violence.

A more serious issue from the perspective of the present discussion is the use of cases from the area of defamation law, where the speech in question is by definition false, to establish the governing law in areas in which the speech in question is either true or opinion or invective that is neither true nor false. For example in the *Dun & Bradstreet* case which Chief Justice Roberts discussed and upon which he relied, the speech in question was both false and confidential. Putting the burden on the defendant to show that such speech must involve a matter of public concern in order to escape liability is one thing. To put that burden on a defendant who speaks in a public space and makes no false statements is another matter. In the guise of deciding what is a matter of public concern or interest, are courts to impose a core of civility on society? For a general discussion of the philosophical and policy issues involved in the judicial regulation of speech, *see* G. Christie, Philosopher Kings? The Adjudication of Conflicting Human Rights and Values (2011).

As we shall again see in Chapter 9, p. 675 *infra*, Congress, in 2006, amended the interstate stalking statute (18 U.S.C. § 2261A), to cover causing "substantial emotional distress" not only by stalking but by the use of the mail or interactive internet services. An attempt to apply the statute to postings on Twitter and internet websites was held to be unconstitutional in United States v. Cassidy, 814 F.Supp.2d 574 (D.Md.2011).

CHAPTER 8

DEFAMATION

■ ■ ■

A. COMMON-LAW DEVELOPMENT

STANDIFER v. VAL GENE MANAGEMENT SERVICES, INC.

Court of Appeals of Oklahoma, 1974.
527 P.2d 28.

BRIGHTMIRE, PRESIDING JUDGE.

This is a slander action. The trial court disposed of it by granting defendant a summary judgment. Whether he was correct in doing so is the only issue presented for review. We think he was and affirm.

In her petition, plaintiff stated that through the mouth of its agent, 24–year–old redheaded Sharon Gayle Wright, defendant corporation maliciously spoke and published to several people certain slanderous, false and defamatory words about plaintiff, "to-wit: That the plaintiff was a constant troublemaker; that the plaintiff was not a fit tenant; that the plaintiff was harassing her; that the plaintiff had 'cussed her out'; that the plaintiff was disruptive in nature and was bothering the other tenants; and various and numerous statements tending to degrade the plaintiff * * * and * * * spoken * * * to blacken and injure the honesty, virtue, integrity, morality and reputation of * * * plaintiff and to thereby expose her to public contempt and ridicule." As a "direct * * * result" of all this she "was compelled to move from her residence of many years and incurred [these] actual damages * * * Moving expense—$375.00; Telephone—$15.00; Automobile expense—$20.00; and additional rent—$80.00." She asked for these amounts plus $5,000 general damages and $25,000 punitive damages.

A demurrer challenging the sufficiency of the petition was overruled. Defendant's short answer did nothing more than deny the allegations regarding slander.

Following the taking of agent Wright's deposition and plaintiff's, defendant filed an amended answer adding that if the alleged statements were made, they "are true."

A pretrial conference was held a short time later. And then defendant filed a motion for summary judgment stating in substance that plaintiff's deposition testimony generally supported the factual allegations in her petition and "assuming that all the statements said to have been made by defendant were in fact made, they are insufficient as a matter of law to be the foundation for recovery."

A short time later the court agreed and in sustaining the motion said:

"The remarks under consideration, although undeniably vulgar and offensive, do not fall within any of the various categories of publications recognized by the Oklahoma statute to be slanderous *per se* * * *."

The first question to be resolved is whether under District Court Rule 13, 12 O.S.1971, Ch. 2, App., the pleadings and depositions on file in this case require a finding that no substantial controversy as to any material fact exists and if not whether under the admitted facts defendant is entitled to judgment as a matter of law.

This question involves consideration of one or two more basic issues: (1) is the alleged publication slanderous per se; or if not, (2) has special resulting damage been adequately alleged?

To start our probe of these points we quote the statute defining slander—12 O.S.1971 § 1442:

"Slander is a false and unprivileged publication, other than libel, which:

"1. Charges any person with crime, or with having been indicted, convicted or punished for crime.

"2. Imputes in him the present existence of an infectious, contagious or loathsome disease.

"3. Tends directly to injure him in respect to his office, profession, trade or business, either by imputing to him general disqualification in those respects which the office or other occupation peculiarly requires, or by imputing something with reference to his office, profession, trade or business that has a natural tendency to lessen its profit.

"4. Imputes to him impotence or want of chastity; or,

"5. Which, by natural consequences, causes actual damage."

We can dismiss from consideration those paragraphs numbered one through four as being irrelevant because not alleged by plaintiff.

Slander is one of the two torts comprising the law of defamation. In general it is an oral publication while its mate, libel, is generally a written one. The distinction between the two developed haphazardly in old English courts from as far back as Runnymede. Their decisional expediencies were influenced considerably by the rise and fall in popularity of the actions at various points in time and—during the 14th and 15th centuries—by the ecclesiastical courts' punishment of defamation as a "sin." A jurisdictional dispute between church and common law courts was temporarily resolved by allowing the latter tribunals to act if "temporal" damage could be proved and if not then the defamation was deemed a "spiritual" matter for the church to handle. In its early development slander was thought to be within the province of ecclesiastical law prompting secular courts to hold the action would not lie without proof of "temporal" damages. Eventually proof of actual damage became an essential element of slander. Then in deference to reality courts began to recognize various exceptions such as imputations of a crime, of a loathsome disease, and those adversely affecting plaintiff's trade, business, or profession—exceptions which required no proof of damages.[1] This historical distinction between libel and slander eventually found its way into the statutory law of this area while Oklahoma was still Indian Territory, along with—as can be seen above—the addition of a fourth category regarding imputation of unchastity or impotency to one.

To compare our libel statute with the one defining slander is to dramatize the distinction and underscore the former's much larger "temporal" base. It is 12 O.S.1971 § 1441 and reads:

> "Libel is a false or malicious unprivileged publication by writing, printing, picture, or effigy or other fixed representation to the eye, *which exposes any person to public hatred,* contempt, ridicule or obloquy, *or which tends to deprive him of public confidence, or to injure him in his occupation,* or any malicious publication as aforesaid, designed to blacken or vilify the memory of one who is dead, and tending to scandalize his surviving relatives or friends." (emphasis ours)

At once it can be seen libel has quite a bit broader statutory definition than slander. That the historical basis for the difference is irrational is beside the point. The statute being what it is must determine human rights until otherwise legally changed.

Turning now to the case at bar, it is conceded that plaintiff has not attempted to plead or complain of any statement which would be actionable slander without proof of damages under the first four numbered paragraphs of § 1442. These are the only "per se" slanders actionable in this state. All others are "per quod." Thus if an action she has it must be in terms of paragraph five requiring pleading and proof of "actual damage."

The words said to have been spoken by defendant's agent were, we think, defamatory on their face in that they have a clear tendency to injure plaintiff's reputation. By natural import they diminish the esteem, respect, and confidence in which she is held by others. They would, had the publication been written, be actionable without proof of damages.

1. Holdsworth, Defamation in the Sixteenth and Seventeenth Centuries, 40 L.Q.Rev. 302, 397 (1924), 41 L.Q.Rev. 13 (1925); Carr, The English Law of Defamation, 18 L.Q.Rev. 255, 388 (1902); Veeder, History and Theory of the Law of Defamation, 3 Col.L.Rev. 546 (1903), 4 Col.L.Rev. 33 (1904).

But it was not written and so—because they neither charge a crime, impute disease or sexual irregularity, nor tend to injure plaintiff in respect to any known office or calling—it matters not how grossly defamatory or insulting the words may be they are actionable only upon proof of "special damage." * * *

The next question then is does plaintiff claim actual damages which the slander "by natural consequences" caused?

The phrase "by natural consequences" is another way of saying there must be a causal connection between the slanderous statement and the damage sought—one that is reasonably direct.

As mentioned earlier the special damages plaintiff says she sustained as a "direct result" of the defamation were various items relating to moving from defendant's apartment to another.

The only conceivable basis upon which the moving expenses could be the natural consequences of the alleged slander would be that the defamation published to plaintiff's fellow tenants caused them to react toward and treat her in such a manner as to significantly interfere with the enjoyment of her habitation and effectuate a constructive ouster therefrom.

Such causal connection is not perceptible on the face of plaintiff's petition. And since this would not necessarily foreclose proof of the consequence at trial we will examine the record to see if it discloses any admission by plaintiff fatally inconsistent with a cause and effect relationship between the slander and the move.

* * *

Interpreting the foregoing in a light most favorable to plaintiff we can see no way the alleged defamation could have caused the move for the simple reason plaintiff was unaware of it until after she vacated defendant's apartment where she presumably would still be had she not been asked to move. The cause of the move was a request by the manager to do so—a request involving neither a tortious nor anti-contractual act—not the defamation. Injured reputation there may have been but unless it in some way precipitated the change of apartments the latter could not be a natural consequence of the former.

We therefore hold the facts admitted by plaintiff disclose she is without an actionable cause for lack of special damages hence the trial court did not err in awarding defendant a summary judgment.

Affirmed.

NOTES

1. As will be seen when we reach Section C of this chapter, the Supreme Court of the United States has held some parts of the common law of defamation to be unconstitutional. It is nevertheless important to begin this chapter with a somewhat detailed examination of the common law on this

subject for a number of significant reasons. First, the Court acted with the common law in mind and left much of the common law unchanged. Second, the law of defamation is much more technical than most other parts of the law of tort and most of these technical aspects have been left unchanged. Third, not only is the law of defamation evolving, but, as we shall see in Section C, many Justices continue to press for a rejection of some of the constitutional restrictions imposed by the Court and a return to the common law as to those aspects of the current American law of defamation.

2. The Oklahoma statute defining slander, quoted in the court's opinion, in large part tracks the common law. *See Restatement (Second) of Torts* §§ 570–74.

3. The provision making it slander per se to say of someone that he is impotent is somewhat unusual. As will be seen in the next principal case, at common law, slander imputing lack of chastity was not actionable without proof of special damages. In 1891 Parliament enacted the Slander of Women Act, 54 & 55 Vict. c. 51, making it slander per se to impute lack of chastity to a woman. By statute or common law a similar change was accepted in the United States. *See, e.g.,* Hollman v. Brady, 16 Alaska 308, 233 F.2d 877 (9th Cir.1956); Biggerstaff v. Zimmerman, 108 Colo. 194, 114 P.2d 1098 (1941). *See also* A. King, *Constructing Gender: Sexual Slander in Nineteenth Century America,* 13 Law & Hist. Rev. 63 (1995). In 1937 *Restatement of Torts* § 574 limited the lack of chastity category to women. The *Restatement (Second)* provision, published in 1977, extends this category of slander per se to all "serious sexual misconduct" including the lack of chastity of men and homosexuality. It remains to be seen whether the majority of courts will follow this extension. *Cf.* P. Arend, *Defamation in an Age of Political Correctness: Should a False Public Statement that a Person is Gay be Defamatory?*, 18 No.Ill.Rev. 99 (1997). In considering whether false allegations of engaging in sexual activities should be actionable without proof of special damages one must be aware that the sexual mores of American society are changing. This is particularly true concerning charges of homosexuality. A number of courts have now held that an imputation of homosexuality is not defamatory per se. *See, e.g.,* Stern v. Cosby, 645 F.Supp.2d 258 (S.D.N.Y. 2009) (interpreting New York law at the time the action was brought). *But see* Robinson v. Radio One, Inc., 695 F.Supp.2d 425 (N.D.Tex. 2010) which was decided on the basis that, although Lawrence v. Texas, 539 U.S. 558, 123 S.Ct. 2472, 156 L.Ed.2d 508 (2003), struck down the Texas statute criminalizing sodomy, a false charge of homosexuality was nevertheless still considered defamatory in Texas. As more states permit same sex marriage or civil unions, one can expect more and more states to hold that false charges of homosexuality are not defamatory of and by themselves. Would one expect the same of false charges of pre-marital sex?

4. The Oklahoma statutory codification of libel, quoted in *Standifer,* includes defamation of the dead. This is an extension of the common law. In most jurisdictions an action will *not* lie for defamation of the dead. *See, e.g.,* Lee v. Weston, 402 N.E.2d 23 (Ind.App.1980).[1] For the contention that such a

1. One should also note that, in perhaps as many as one half of the states, a defamation action still will not survive the death of either the plaintiff or the defendant. For an examination of

cause of action should be generally recognized, *see* Note, *Dead But Not Forgotten: Proposals for Imposing Liability for Defamation of the Dead*, 67 Tex.L.Rev. 1525 (1989). Defamation by the dead is another matter. It has, for example, been held that the estate of the testatrix was liable for defamatory statements made in her will. Brown v. Du Frey, 1 N.Y.2d 190, 151 N.Y.S.2d 649, 134 N.E.2d 469 (1956).

5. As noted in *Standifer,* if the slander does not fall within one of the per se categories, an action will not lie without allegation and proof of special damages. In many jurisdictions such allegations and proof must be quite specific and detailed. Special damages are pecuniary losses flowing from the defamatory statement, but not all such pecuniary losses will qualify as special damages. The pecuniary loss must be more than a consequence of the defamatory statement; it must be *the direct result of the plaintiff's lowered reputation in the community* that has been brought about by the defendant's statement. A classic case is Terwilliger v. Wands, 17 N.Y. 54, 72 Am.Dec. 420 (1858). The defendant had told third persons that the plaintiff was having intercourse with the wife of a man serving time in the state penitentiary. The plaintiff's proof showed that he had become distraught, was unable to work, and that he had incurred medical expenses. All this was held not to be a sufficient showing of special damages.

> Where there is no proof that the character has suffered from the words, if sickness results it must be attributed to apprehension of loss of character, and such fear of harm to character, with resulting sickness and bodily prostration, cannot be such special damages as the law requires for the action. The loss of character must be a substantive loss, one which has actually taken place.

17 N.Y. at 63. Citing a leading treatise of the period, examples of special damages were "loss of a marriage, loss of hospitable gratuitous entertainment, preventing a servant or bailiff from getting a place, the loss of customers by a tradesman." *Id.* at 60.

6. With regard to the category of slander per se involving imputation of criminal conduct, many of the older cases declared that the crime must be one involving moral turpitude or, in the alternative, an indictable offense. More recent authority has held that imputation of *any* criminal conduct is enough, whether punishable by imprisonment or fine. Starobin v. Northridge Lakes Development, 94 Wis.2d 1, 287 N.W.2d 747 (1980). This shift is partially reflected in the Restatements. *Restatement of Torts* § 571 required the crime to be indictable at common law and punishable by death or imprisonment rather than a fine. *Restatement (Second) of Torts* § 571 requires either that the conduct charged be punishable by imprisonment or involve moral turpitude.

7. The category of slander per se involving the imputation of loathsome or infectious diseases is generally restricted to venereal diseases and leprosy. *Cf. Restatement (Second) of Torts* § 572 and comments.

---

developments in this area, *see* Note, *Defamation, Survivability, and the Demise of the Antiquated "Actio Personalis" Doctrine*, 85 Colum.L.Rev. 1833 (1985).

JONES v. JONES

House of Lords, 1916.
[1916] 2 A.C. 481.

* * *

VISCOUNT HALDANE. My Lords, the question in this appeal is whether the appellant, who was plaintiff in the action, can recover general damages for an untrue verbal imputation of immoral conduct with a married woman. He is a certificated teacher and is the senior master of a council school in Wales. It is not in dispute that the imputation of such conduct, if believed, would be seriously prejudicial to a person in his position, and might lead to the loss of an appointment which, concerned as it is with the teaching of the young, implies in the person who holds it freedom from reproach of this kind. At the same time it must be remembered that the position of a certificated teacher is not unique in this respect, for there are many other appointments that are held on a similar condition, express or implied.

The school in which the appellant was employed was looked after by his aunt, as caretaker, and she was in the habit of employing the husband of a Mrs. Ellen Roberts to do some of the cleaning. The respondent, Mrs. Jones, is found by the jury before which the action was tried to have spoken words imputing moral misconduct between the appellant and Mrs. Roberts. Mrs. Jones was the defendant in the action, and her husband was joined as being liable for his wife's tort.[a] The jury found further, in response to questions from Lush J., who tried the case, that the words "were spoken of him in the way of his calling, that is, in such a way as to imperil the retention of his office," and further that "the words imputed that he was unfit to hold his office." It is, however, clear that there was no evidence that any words were used which referred to his office or his conduct in it, and the first part of the finding cannot be relied on as anything more than an inference. Nor was there any evidence of the use of words which could, by the terms used, bear out the second part of the finding. It was, moreover, not alleged that the appellant had been dismissed or otherwise pecuniarily injured in his calling, and indeed there was no evidence whatever of special damage. The jury, however, assessed general damages, at 10*l*. Upon these findings Lush J. reserved the question of law, whether the appellant was entitled to judgment, and afterwards, having heard arguments, delivered a considered opinion, as the result of which, after examining the authorities, he decided for the appellant. In the course of the argument before him, counsel for the present respondents admitted that the local educational authority would naturally not allow a teacher to remain in the school and teach children if he were carrying on an immoral intercourse. But he said that his admission was meant to have nothing in it distinctive of the office of a teacher,

a. [Ed. note] At common law a husband was responsible for his wife's torts. This is no longer the case.

and that he admitted only what would apply equally in the case of other offices.

The Court of Appeal reversed the judgment of Lush J. and entered judgment for the respondents.

After examining the authorities, I have come to the conclusion that the Court of Appeal were right, and that the judgment of Lush J., notwithstanding the care which he had obviously bestowed on it, cannot be supported. He seems to have regarded the decided cases as having laid down a broad principle, which could be legitimately extended to a case like the present. My Lords, I think that is not so. The action for slander has been evolved by the Courts of common law in a fashion different from that which obtains elsewhere. As one of the consequences the scope of the remedy is in an unusual degree confined by exactness of precedent. It is not for reasons of mere timidity that the Courts have shown themselves indisposed to widen that scope, nor do I think your Lordships are free to regard the question in this case as one in which a clear principle may be freely extended. * * * There is a difference between slander and libel which has been established by the authorities, and which is not the less real and far-reaching because of the fact that it is explicable almost exclusively by the different histories of the remedies for two wrongs that are in other respects analogous in their characters. The greater importance and scope of the action for libel was mainly attributable to the appearance of the printing press. The Court of Star Chamber quickly took special cognizance of libel, regarding it not merely as a crime punishable as such, but as a wrong carrying the penalty of general damages. After the Star Chamber was abolished by the Long Parliament much of the jurisdiction which its decisions had established and developed in cases of libel survived, and was carried on by the Courts of common law to whom it passed.

The history of the action for slander is radically different. Slander never became punishable in the civil Courts as a crime. In early days the old local Courts took cognizance of it as giving rise to claims for compensation. When these Courts decayed, the entire jurisdiction in cases of defamation appears to have passed, not to the Courts of the King, but, at first at all events, to the Courts of the Church. However, after the Statute of Westminster the Second had enabled novel writs in consimili casu to be issued, the action on the case for spoken words began to appear as one which the Courts of the King might entertain. Subsequently to the Reformation, when the authority of the Courts of the Church received a heavy blow and began to wane, the Courts of the King commenced the full assertion of a jurisdiction in claims arising out of spoken defamation concurrent with that of the spiritual tribunals. As might have been expected of civil Courts, whose concern had been primarily with material rights and not with discipline as such, the new jurisdiction in claims based on slander appears to have been directed to the ascertainment of actual damage suffered and to a remedy limited to such damage. This explains the restricted character of the development of the remedy and the tendency to confine its scope by the assertion that actual damage was the gist of the action. * * * The rule thus established was to some extent relaxed in its form by decisions which in certain nominate cases treated particular types of slander as so injurious by their very nature that the suffering of actual damage might be presumed and need not be proved. These exceptional types of slander comprised imputations of the commission of serious criminal offenses, imputations of suffering from certain noxious diseases, and imputations of special forms of misconduct which would manifestly prejudice a man in his calling. But, as a general principle, as to the actionable character of words spoken of a man to his disparagement in his calling the Courts, with an exception to which I will refer later, appear on the balance of authority to have laid down the limitation that the words must have been actually spoken of him "touching" or "in the way" of that calling. In *Lumby v. Allday*[1] Bayley B. said: "Every authority which I have been able to find, either shows the want of some general requisite, as honesty, capacity, fidelity & c., or connects the imputation with the plaintiff's office, trade, or business." In speaking of the imputation of such a want of "general requisite" as actionable in itself I think that Bayley B. was referring to certain decisions which show that, in the case of a trader, the Courts construed language which might affect his credit to be presumed to be directed against his credit as a trader, although no express "colloquium" touching his trade had been proved. The Courts, who leaned specially to the protection of traders, appear to have made this presumption almost, if not quite, as matter of law for the security of commerce. But Bayley B. observed that the words must be such as to have "a natural" as distinguished from a merely probable tendency to damage the plaintiff's reputation in his calling. In *Jones v. Littler*[2] Parke B. laid down this exception to much the same effect. A brewer was alleged to have been locked up for debt. It was found that in the "colloquium" he had been referred to as a brewer. But Parke B. said that "even if" the words "were spoken of him in his private character, I think the case of *Stanton v. Smith*[3] is an authority to shew that the words would have been actionable, because they must necessarily affect him in his trade." * * * This readiness to make a presumption as regards language which might affect the credit of a trader of damage arising from words alleging insolvency, notwithstanding that the imputation is not in terms made about him in his capacity of trader, has not been extended to other callings. There is indeed at least one other illustration of such readiness disclosed by the books in the case of a clergyman who holds a benefice or an ecclesiastical position of temporal profit which may, by the very terms on which it is held, be put in peril of forfeiture by the slander. But this is an exception which has no application, notwithstanding peril of injury to his reputation in his calling, if the clergyman does not hold his benefice or position actually on these terms. Subject to the carefully-guarded exceptions to

1. 1 Cr. & J. 301, 305.

2. 7 M. & W. 423, 426.

3. 2 Ld.Raym. 1480.

which I have referred, the rule is that laid down in Comyns' Digest, "Action upon the Case for Defamation" (D. 27): "But words not actionable in themselves, are not actionable, when spoken of one in an office, profession or trade, unless they touch him in his office, & c." In *Doyley v. Roberts*[1] Tindal C.J. applied the law as laid down in this passage by refusing relief to an attorney of whom it was falsely said that he had defrauded his creditors and been horsewhipped off the course at Doncaster. That this is the basic principle which limits the cases in which the common law permits general damages to be awarded was laid down in striking language in the judgment of the Court of King's Bench in *Ayre v. Craven*[2], delivered by Lord Denman C.J. "Some of the cases," he said, "have proceeded to a length which can hardly fail to excite surprise; a clergyman having failed to obtain redress for the imputation of adultery; and a schoolmistress having been declared incompetent to maintain an action for a charge of prostitution. Such words were undeniably calculated to injure the success of the plaintiffs in their several professions; but not being applicable to their conduct therein, no action lay." There a physician had been accused of adultery, but the words did not in terms connect the imputation with anything done by him when acting in a professional capacity. * * *

My Lords, I think that these authorities and others which were referred to in the arguments at the Bar have settled the law too firmly to admit of our extending the exceptions which have been made further than the decided cases go. * * * If we were to admit that an action for slander can lie in the case of a schoolmaster who has not proved either that the words were spoken of him "touching or in the way of his calling," or that he has suffered the actual damage which is the historical foundation of the action, and is even now its normal requisite, I think we should be overruling *Ayre v. Craven* and other decisions of great authority, and should be doing what only the Legislature can do to-day. It required an Act of Parliament, the Slander of Women Act, 1891, to enable a woman to recover general damages for an imputation of unchastity. In my opinion it would require an analogous Act to enable the present appellant to recover such damages for an imputation of adultery which was not obviously directed to his reputation as a schoolmaster. I am therefore of opinion that we have no option to do anything but dismiss this appeal with costs.

LORD SUMNER. My Lords, the facts of this case are of a familiar kind. The appellant, Mr. David Jones, is headmaster of the Llidiardau Council school, Rhoshirwaen, Pwllheli. He is an unmarried man and lives with his aunt. In May, 1914, Ellen Jones, who is a farmer's wife, told Elizabeth Jones, and, as was alleged, Eliza Griffiths too, that Mr. David Jones had committed adultery with Ellen Roberts. What is more, she added that Ellen Roberts herself had told her so. This came to the appellant's ears, and no doubt not to his alone, and he sued Ellen Jones and her husband for slander. A Carnarvon common jury awarded him 10*l.*, which seems to

1. 3 Bing.N.C. 835.

2. 2 Ad. & E. 2, 7.

show that they thought it an ordinary matter, but it is only fair to him to say that the defendants did not venture to support the charge, and for their part had no merits whatever. It is accordingly just the sort of case in which a contention fundamentally challenging long-settled law would be brought before your Lordships.

Lush J. at the trial put to the jury, with other questions, these two: "Were they (the words charged) spoken of him (the plaintiff) in the way of his calling, i.e., in such a way as to imperil the retention of his office?" and "Did they impute that he was unfit to hold his office?" The jury said "Yes" to both. Evidence of the suggested tendency to affect the plaintiff in his office was not called, an admission having been made by counsel for the defendants. Of this admission two versions exist. The difference in form is slight, and no difference in substance was intended, but I think that the one actually made before verdict, in the hearing of the jury, is the one that should prevail. The substance of it, according to the shorthand note, is:—

> "Lush J.: 'Can you suggest, Mr. Artemus Jones, that if a schoolmaster, in a place like this, is found misconducting himself with a married woman he is not likely to suffer in his employment?'
>
> "Mr. Artemus Jones (for the defendants): 'I submit that he would suffer no more than a man following any other occupation, and I submit again that in order to get this evidence in, the foundation-stone must be laid—that the words were spoken of him in the way of his profession.'
>
> "Lush J.: 'But you don't want evidence to show that he would not be kept in his employment if he misconducted himself in this way, but it does not follow that the words were spoken of him in the way of his profession.'
>
> "Mr. Montgomery (for the plaintiff): 'This is a fact upon which evidence ought to be given.'
>
> "Lush J.: 'Then you may take it that it would be injurious.' "

The words of the slander itself made no allusion to the appellant's calling at all, and Elizabeth Jones, to whom they were spoken, when asked in cross-examination "The words were spoken to you not in reference to his position as a schoolmaster at all?" said "Not at all." * * * The question, therefore, comes to be this: "In the absence of proof of special damage, of which none was given, is an imputation of adultery made against a man, who is in fact a schoolmaster but is not spoken of as such, a matter which is actionable per se?"

* * *

Thirdly, except in the case of slanders imputing incontinence to beneficed clergymen of the Church of England and slanders imputing insolvency to persons who in fact are tradesmen (which last is probably not a real exception), no plaintiff, at least since the time of Comyns'

Digest, has ever recovered damages for a spoken imputation of incontinence, unless he either showed that the words were spoken of him in his calling or proved actual damage. Earlier cases, so far as they seem to be to the contrary, can, I think, be accounted for. They are often badly or too briefly reported; they are often cases in which after verdict the necessary allegation and proof that the words were spoken of and touched the plaintiff in his calling were presumed as a matter of course. How is this blank in the authorities to be explained, if the appellant's proposition be sound? For three centuries the Courts have been dealing with such imputations. They are, and long have been,—such is the weakness of our nature—a favourite weapon in the armoury of controversialists, male and female, in private life, and mankind has so often acted on the proverb that "hard words break no bones," that special damage has rarely been proved to have occurred. My Lords, before these considerations can be answered, it must be shown that the law has long been grievously misunderstood, and that requires cogent proof indeed.

* * *

Order of the Court of Appeal affirmed and appeal dismissed with costs.

NOTES

1. The Artemus Jones referred to in Lord Sumner's speech may well be the plaintiff in the famous case of Hulton & Co. v. Jones, [1910] A.C. 20, a case that will be referred to and discussed in some of the subsequent cases and their accompanying notes. Artemus Jones, the plaintiff in that case, was a barrister, apparently of Welsh origin.

2. For a more recent discussion of the history of libel and slander, see J. M. Kaye, *Libel and Slander—Two Torts or One?,* 91 L.Q.Rev. 524 (1975). With the coming of the Protestant Reformation and the decline of the ecclesiastical courts, the petty complaints, most of which were about oral statements that would now be classified as slander, increasingly were brought to the common-law courts. Since much of this litigation was regarded as a nuisance not only was the special damage requirement imposed but the courts developed a doctrine known as *mitiore sensu,* under which, if a statement were capable of an innocent as well as a defamatory meaning, the more innocent meaning would be ascribed to it even if that meaning were the least plausible. The most extreme of these early cases is the ludicrous Holt v. Astgrigg, Cro.Jac. 184, 79 Eng.Rep. 161 (K.B.1608). The complaint alleged that the defendant had said: "Sir Thomas Holt struck his cook on the head with a cleaver, and cleaved his head; the one part lay on one shoulder, and another part on the other." It was held that this was not slander per se for imputing the crime of murder to the plaintiff because "it is not averred that the cook was killed." See also the perhaps more subtle Miles v. Jacob, Hob. 6, 80 Eng.Rep. 156 (Ex.Ch.1610), in which the words were "Thou hast poisoned Smith." It was held that the words were not actionable for "it doth not

appear by the words that he poisoned him willingly, neither that Smith was dead at the time the words spoken."

The Star Chamber's concern with defamation was undoubtedly stimulated by the development of the printing press and the circulation of religious and political tracts. It was concerned on the whole with socially more important contexts and most, though not all, of the matters brought before it concerned written statements. Star Chamber was most interested in prosecuting criminal libel, in which the defendant was prosecuted for undermining public confidence in authority, but it also provided remedies for aggrieved private persons. Star Chamber was abolished in 1641 and, on the restoration of the monarchy in 1660, Charles II promised not to reestablish it. The common law courts thus came to take on this jurisdiction as well. In the process the *mitiore sensu* rule fell into disuse.

Kaye contends that in the latter part of the seventeenth century the options for the courts were to make all defamation actionable without proof of special damages where aggravating circumstances were present or to treat libel cases differently by in effect making written defamation a new category of slander per se. Eventually the latter alternative prevailed. The early history of the law of defamation is also discussed in R. Post, *The Social Foundations of Defamation Law: Reputation and the Constitution*, 74 Calif.L.Rev. 691 (1986). For even more recent scholarship on the subject, *see* P. Mitchell, The Making of the Modern Law of Defamation (2005).

It has been more or less taken for granted by most observers that the slander per se categories are fixed even if there is room for movement within the commonly recognized categories. In Ward v. Zelikovsky, 263 N.J.Super. 497, 623 A.2d 285 (App.Div.1993), however, the court created a new category of slander per se to cover charges of social and ethnic bigotry. At a board meeting of a condominium association the defendant shouted "Don't listen to these people * * * She's a bitch * * * These people hate jews." Do you think that expansion of the categories of slander per se to include charges of racial or ethnic bigotry is a wise development? The Supreme Court of New Jersey did not and reversed. 136 N.J. 516, 643 A.2d 972 (1994). It also held that, in the context in which they were made, the statements were mere invective. A factual charge of bigotry could be defamatory but, if the action is brought as one of slander, special damages must be shown.

3. *Who can be a plaintiff?* As will be illustrated in many of the cases that we shall subsequently consider, it is uncontroversial that corporations and other juridical entities, so long as they have standing to sue, may bring an action for statements that injure their reputation. It has been held, however, both in Great Britain and the United States, that public bodies cannot bring a civil action for defamation. *See* Derbyshire County Council v. Times Newspapers, Ltd., [1993] A.C. 534, 2 W.L.R. 449, 1 All E.R. 1011; City of Chicago v. Tribune Co., 307 Ill. 595, 139 N.E. 86 (1923). Allowing a civil action by a public body would be too great an inhibition on the freedom of speech of the citizens. A prosecution for criminal libel is more politically difficult to bring and provides the defendant with greater procedural protection, as well as a much lower exposure to monetary damages. What about an action by a

political party? *See* Goldsmith v. Bhoyrul, [1998] Q.B. 459, [1997] 4 All E.R. 268 (1997).

4. *Criminal libel.* Criminal libel was an indictable offense at common law. As already indicated, it was aimed at suppressing sedition and later extended to reach written materials likely to lead to breaches of the peace. There never was any such thing as criminal slander. Unlike the situation with regards to civil actions for libel, for a considerable period of time, truth was *not* a defense to criminal libel. The old saw was, "the greater the truth, the greater the libel." That state of the law was largely altered in England by the Libel Act of 1843, 6 & 7 Vict. c. 96, § 6, and eventually in most American jurisdictions, to make truth a defense if the matter was published for a proper motive. Previously in Fox's Libel Act, 32 Geo. 3, c. 60 (1792), in order to prevent judges from taking from the jury the issue of the defamatory nature of a publication, juries were empowered to bring in a general verdict in prosecutions for criminal libel. Finally, in Garrison v. Louisiana, 379 U.S. 64, 85 S.Ct. 209, 13 L.Ed.2d 125 (1964), as part of the "revolution" precipitated by the Supreme Court's insistence that constitutional considerations be taken into consideration in defamation litigation, it was held that truth is an absolute defense in a prosecution for criminal libel. In contrast to criminal libel, with some qualifications that will be touched on in some of the succeeding principal cases, and their accompanying notes, truth seems to have always been accepted as a defense to a tort action for defamation whether for libel or slander. A good discussion of the law of criminal libel in England is contained in The Law Commission, Working Paper No. 84, Criminal Libel (1982), which proposed the abolition of criminal libel and its replacement with a few narrowly focused statutory crimes.

5. An attempt to abolish the distinction between libel and slander was made in Thorley v. Lord Kerry, 4 Taunt. 355, 128 Eng.Rep. 367 (Ex.Ch. 1812), but Lord Chief Justice Mansfield felt the distinction was too firmly established although "[i]f the matter were for the first time to be decided at this day, I should have no hesitation in saying, that no action could be maintained for written scandal which could not be maintained for the words if they had been spoken."

6. *Mitiore sensu* may be dead but it is not quite completely buried. In Hewitt v. Wasek, 35 Misc.2d 946, 231 N.Y.S.2d 884 (1962), the defendant had said that the plaintiff, a married woman, was having an affair with a married man. The court held that special damages had to be alleged. The statement did not necessarily impute lack of chastity because it could be taken to mean the woman and the man were having an affair that was "both romantic and platonic." Likewise it has been held that an assertion that the plaintiff was a "slum landlord" was not defamatory because it was susceptible of the innocent interpretation that he was "a landlord in a slum," i.e., someone who "owned buildings in a poor and dirty neighborhood." Rasky v. Columbia Broadcasting System, Inc., 103 Ill.App.3d 577, 59 Ill.Dec. 298, 431 N.E.2d 1055 (1981).

7. The most open-ended of the slander per se categories is that involving imputations affecting the business, trade, profession, or office of the plaintiff. Nevertheless, as the *Jones* case indicates, making the connection between the

statement and the trade or profession is not always easy. In Gunsberg v. Roseland Corp., 34 Misc.2d 220, 225 N.Y.S.2d 1020 (1962), an employee of the defendant had said to the plaintiff, who was a patron at the defendant's dance hall: "Get out of here you silly, stupid senile bum; you are a troublemaker and should be confined to an asylum." The plaintiff was a stockbroker. It was held that the statement did not injure him in his trade or profession and was thus not actionable without allegation and proof of special damages.

8. *Pleading an action for defamation.* In an action for defamation the customary practice is for the plaintiff (a) to insert a verbatim description of the actual defamatory statements in his complaint, (b) to allege the publication of the defamatory statement to third parties, (c) to explain how the statements in question relate to him and why they are defamatory, and (d) to make a claim for damages. If the defamation is of the type for which special damages must be alleged and proved, (e) these special damages must be described in the complaint with some specificity. Insofar as the plaintiff's complaint includes a request for punitive damages, he must in most cases, also (f) allege actual malice in the sense of knowledge of falsity or reckless disregard of truth or falsity. At common law, actual malice could also be established by showing ill-will toward the plaintiff or a desire to injure him on the part of the defendant. As we shall see below, when we discuss the impact of the United States Constitution on defamation law, common-law malice may now no longer be by itself a sufficient basis upon which to premise an award of punitive damages. Pleading an action for defamation has continued to have a certain technical character and the following special technical vocabulary has developed to describe various components of the complaint:

> *The Inducement.* Sometimes neither the defamatory character of a publication nor its connection with the plaintiff is evident from the actual words used in the allegedly defamatory statement. The plaintiff will therefore have to allege in his complaint the facts that are necessary to support his claim that the statements are defamatory and that they refer to him. The portion of the complaint in which these extrinsic facts are alleged is called the *inducement.* An alternate terminology sometimes used is to state that these extrinsic facts are "alleged by way of inducement."
>
> *The Colloquium.* The *colloquium* is that portion of the complaint in which the plaintiff, making use if necessary of the facts alleged in the inducement, states that the allegedly defamatory statements were *about* him. That is, at the very least, that some reasonable people would take these statements as referring to the plaintiff.
>
> *The Innuendo.* The *innuendo* is that portion of the complaint in which the plaintiff explains *what is defamatory about the statements made about him.* Some courts speak of the plaintiff making this showing "by way of innuendo." In this usage the courts are referring to the method by which the plaintiff makes out the defamatory meaning rather than to some discreet portion of the complaint. The meaning which the plaintiff attempts to engraft upon the allegedly defamatory statement must be a reasonable one. In this regard, it is a question for the court, in the first instance, whether reasonable people could so construe the challenged

statement. It is then for the jury to decide whether, in point of fact, those to whom the communication was addressed did understand it in a defamatory sense.

9. It is possible to say things without words. For example, stopping someone on the suspicion that he is a shop-lifter can be said to convey to reasonable observers that the person is being accused of the crime of shop-lifting. *See. e.g.,* Aker v. New York & Co., 364 F.Supp.2d 661 (N.D.Ohio 2005); Street v. Shoe Carnival, Inc., 660 N.E.2d 1054 (Ind. App. 1996). More difficult are cases in which an employee is seen being disciplined. *Compare* Phelan v. May Dept. Stores Co., 443 Mass. 52, 819 N.E.2d 550 (Mass. 2004) *with* Tyler v. Macks Stores of So. Carolina, Inc., 275 S.C. 456, 272 S.E.2d 633 (1980).

HINSDALE v. ORANGE COUNTY PUBLICATIONS, INC.

Court of Appeals of New York, 1966.
17 N.Y.2d 284, 270 N.Y.S.2d 592, 217 N.E.2d 650.

DESMOND, CHIEF JUDGE.

The plaintiffs in these two libel actions demand damages because of an article published in defendant's newspaper. Their complaints have been dismissed for insufficiency on the ground that the newspaper story was not libelous per se and that no special damages are pleaded as is required when the words are libelous *per quod* but not per se.

On July 7, 1964 defendant's daily newspaper *The Times Herald Record* (of Middletown, N.Y.) contained this:

"Mr. and Mrs. Paul M. Hinsdale of Balmville Gardens, Newburgh, have announced the engagement of their son, Robert W., to Concetta Kay Rieber of 43 Knox Drive, New Windsor.

"Miss Rieber, a native of Brooklyn, was educated in Brooklyn and Newburgh schools. She is employed by Jack Wilkins Associates, Inc., at Newburgh.

"Her fiance attended Newburgh and Connecticut schools. He is the president of the Jack Wilkins Associates insurance agency.

"The wedding is set for August."

Plaintiff Hinsdale's complaint asserts that at the time of the publication defendant knew or by reasonable diligence could have learned that Mr. Hinsdale was and is married and the father of two children, and that Concetta Kay Rieber was and is married and the mother of three sons, and that there was and is no engagement to marry between Robert Hinsdale and Mrs. Rieber. The Hinsdale pleading alleges that defendant's newspaper was of general circulation not only in Middletown, New York, but also in the City of Newburgh and its environs, that plaintiff lives and is in business in Newburgh and that he has been defamed by the newspaper announcement and held up to public disgrace, scorn and ridicule.

The Rieber complaint, besides repeating some of Hinsdale's allegations, says that Mr. and Mrs. Rieber live in New Windsor, that the wife was and is employed in the City of Newburgh, that because of the newspaper item Mrs. Rieber's reputation has been damaged and an evil opinion of her induced in the minds of the people of the community and that because of her pain, shock, fright and physical and mental suffering the husband has been deprived of his wife's services and society and put to expense, etc.

Special Term, although it dismissed the complaints, conceded that the facts in Sydney v. Macfadden Newspaper Pub. Corp. (242 N.Y. 208, 151 N.E. 209, 44 A.L.R. 1419) were "practically identical" to those in the present cases, holding that the controlling decision was the earlier one of O'Connell v. Press Pub. Co. (214 N.Y. 352, 108 N.E. 556). *O'Connell,* so the court reasoned, was not overruled by *Sydney* which expresses the rule that for a libel per se to be actionable without special damages the damage must arise from the publication itself "without any reference to extrinsic facts, except those generally known to a substantial number of the community of the general reading public." The court thought, apparently, that these complaints did not meet the *O'Connell* test. The Appellate Division unanimously affirmed and gave plaintiffs leave to replead, a permission of which they did not make use. We granted plaintiffs leave to appeal to this court.

It is not defamatory to say of a man or woman that he or she is engaged to be married but an announcement that an already married male or female is about to be married to a new partner imputes a violation of commonly accepted rules of marital morality, a deviation from community norms. It does not necessarily charge sexual immorality but to many minds it suggests a disregard of existing commitments and obligations * * *. Surely such an announcement about a seemingly happily married person comes as a surprise and shock to relatives and acquaintances. To publicize an imminent marriage between two already married persons who work in the same office and live in the same lightly populated area would normally cause a local scandal of considerable size. This announcement amounted, therefore, to a written accusation which tended to hold plaintiffs up to "ridicule, contempt, shame, disgrace or obloquy, to degrade [them] in the estimation of the community, * * * to diminish [their] respectability." * * *

* * * Other courts in this State and elsewhere have agreed that a false statement as to a married person that he or she is about to be or has been divorced is defamatory * * *.

Printed material is, because of the relative permanency of its impact, more readily held to be defamatory per se than are oral utterances of similar import * * * We conclude, therefore, that printed statements like those in this newspaper announcement about married people are libelous per se, that is, that, without a showing of "special" damage, they raise a presumption of inevitable actual damage to reputation * * *.

But the newspaper article here complained of does not itself refer to the fact (alleged in the complaint and now conceded) that the "engaged" couple were in truth already married to others and living with their respective spouses. Defendant says—and the courts below agreed—that since the published material needs the allegation of existing facts the libel, if any, is not per se but *per quod* and, lacking any allegation of special damages, is not actionable. The authority cited for this "rule" is O'Connell v. Press Pub. Co. * * *.

The Sydney v. Macfadden Newspaper Pub. Corp. * * * decision would seem to control here. The plaintiff was a well-known actress of the day, known professionally under her maiden name of Doris Keane but married to one Basil Sydney. That latter fact was alleged in the complaint but nowhere alluded to in the newspaper column which was held to be libelous per se. The offending newspaper article said that Doris Keane was the "latest lady love" of Fatty Arbuckle, a movie comedian of the day whose claims to fame did not include a reputation for virtuous life. The columnist intimated that Doris Keane and Arbuckle were to marry. Defendant argued that the extrinsic fact of plaintiff's marriage could not be considered in determining whether the article was libelous per se. This court, however, rejected that argument. * * *

Defendant would have it that the *Sydney* decision (supra) turned on the taking of judicial notice that Arbuckle, a famous actor, was a person of bad repute. Not so. The dissenting opinion in *Sydney* not only analyzes the majority holding as permitting the allegation and proof of the fact of plaintiff's married status but says that the dissenter would have voted with the majority had the latter put its ruling on judicial notice of Fatty Arbuckle's reputation. The dissent correctly characterizes *Sydney* as a flat holding that such extrinsic facts as that the libeled person is already married can be alleged and proved to make a publication libelous per se. * * *.

We come now to the O'Connell v. Press Pub. Co. case * * * and the disputed and controversial "O'Connell rule" ("whatever it might mean", Henn, Libel by Extrinsic Fact, 47 Cornell L.Q. 14, 34). If the *O'Connell* case means that a libel per se action cannot stand if extrinsic facts must be read with it or into it, then *O'Connell* is directly opposed to the numerous decisions of our court above cited * * *.

Actually, the *O'Connell* decision (supra) is not in point here and not inconsistent with *Sydney* (supra). The reason for refusing to give it effect in *Sydney* was, it would seem, that *O'Connell* involved not "libel by extrinsic fact" but an effort to give defamatory meaning to the published words by ascribing to them an unnatural and unreasonable innuendo or ascribed meaning. The news article complained of in O'Connell's case discussed a Federal court criminal prosecution not against O'Connell but against certain sugar importers in which it was charged that the latter had arranged for fraudulent underweighing of sugar to avoid import duties. The newspaper story reported that O'Connell as a witness before the Grand Jury had testified that he had invented a steel spring device and that an officer of the corporation which was later indicted had referred plaintiff to an employee, also later indicted. The complaint in O'Connell's libel action alleged that these references to him meant that he had engaged in criminal conduct through the use of his invention on the weighing scales. The defendant moved to dismiss the complaint, alleging that the article was not a libel on its face but required the showing of extrinsic fact. This court held the complaint insufficient but not, it would seem, on that particular ground. * * * The *O'Connell* decision, therefore, must be understood as one dealing with the attempted use of an innuendo not justified by the words themselves. It is not, therefore, applicable here nor does it control or overrule the *Sydney* and other cases which allow not the utilization of innuendos but the pleading of extrinsic facts.

We conclude, therefore, that the complaint sufficiently alleges a publication libelous per se. It will be for a jury to say what damages (be they substantial or nominal) the several plaintiffs are entitled to.

The order appealed from should be reversed and the motions to dismiss the complaints denied, with costs in all courts.

NOTES

1. In 1937, *Restatement of Torts* § 569 adopted what we have seen was the position developed at English common law, namely that all libel was actionable without allegation and proof of special damages. The late Dean Prosser, the Reporter for the *Restatement (Second)*, was of the opinion that the majority of American jurisdictions did not follow the English rule but instead distinguished between libel per se, actionable without allegation and proof of special damages, and libel per quod which was only actionable upon such allegation and proof. As to what fell within the libel per se category, there was some uncertainty. Some jurisdictions required the libel to be clear on its face, others required the libel to fall within the slander per se categories, and perhaps others required the libel to be both clear on its face and within the slander per se categories. *Restatement (Second) of Torts* § 569, and accompanying note (Tent.Draft No. 11, 1965). Dean Prosser proposed changing § 569 to restrict liability for libel "without proof of special harm" to those situations where either the defamatory meaning is apparent from the publication itself, "without reference to extrinsic facts by way of inducement," or the statement falls within the slander per se categories. Prosser's proposal was attacked as being against the weight of authority by Lawrence H. Eldredge, one of the advisers to the project, who was then still active at the Philadelphia Bar. *See* 42 ALI Proceedings 411–16 (1965); 43 ALI Proceedings 434–37, 444–45 (1966). Eldredge and Prosser then took their dispute to the law reviews. *See* L. Eldredge, *Spurious Rule of Libel Per Quod,* 79 Harv. L.Rev. 733 (1966); L. Eldredge, *Variation on Libel Per Quod,* 25 Vand.L.Rev. 79 (1972); W. Prosser, *More Libel Per Quod*, 79 Harv.L.Rev. 1629 (1966). Professor Henn interjected, in the article cited by Desmond, C.J., that the situation, particularly in New York, was more confused than Prosser was prepared to admit. H. Henn, *Libel by Extrinsic Fact,* 47 Cornell L.Q. 14 (1961). Even in a state which follows the common law rule that all libel is actionable without allegation and proof of special damage, cases have arisen

where defendant was granted summary judgment because the plaintiff had such a poor reputation that he could not have suffered any damage from the publication of a false and defamatory statement. *See* Jackson v. Longcope, 394 Mass. 577, 476 N.E.2d 617 (1985). Although the court recognized that normally a defendant who has been defamed can at least recover nominal damages, it felt that, in the instant case involving an often convicted felon, it would be unfair to subject the defendant to the burden of trial when recovery of more than nominal damages was impossible. *Cf.* Kevorkian v. American Medical Ass'n., 237 Mich.App. 1, 602 N.W.2d 233 (1999). Kevorkian, a well-known advocate of assisted suicide, alleged he had been defamed by assertions of officers of the defendant and by the individual defendants that he was a murderer and a killer. In addition to noting that many of the statements could be considered as hyperbole or would otherwise receive "special solicitude" under the First Amendment, the court declared that the defendant was "virtually libel proof" on the issue of assisted suicide. *See also* Brooks v. American Broadcasting Co., 932 F.2d 495 (6th Cir. 1991).

As a consequence of the *Hinsdale* decision, Prosser abandoned the struggle. Except for minor changes in wording *Restatement (Second) of Torts* § 569, published in 1977, is identical to the original provision in the *Restatement.* All libel is actionable without allegation and proof of special damages. The Reporter's notes, reprinted in *Restatement (Second) of Torts* Appendix § 569 (1981), at p. 382, indicated that most state court decisions in the immediate aftermath of *Hinsdale* followed that case. This is not to say that, in many of those states which had previously adopted the distinction, it does not continue to be applied. For example, West's Ann.Cal.Civ.Code § 45a, which was added in 1945, provides that a plaintiff must allege and prove that he has suffered special damages, unless the defamatory language is libelous on its face. A statement is a "libel on its face" if it is "defamatory of the plaintiff without the necessity of explanatory matter, such as an inducement, innuendo, or other extrinsic fact."

2. It is not necessary that an allegedly defamatory statement be one that would lower the plaintiff's reputation in the entire community. It is enough if the statement would lower the plaintiff's esteem within what might be called a "significant" segment of "respectable society." Thus it has been held to be libelous to include the name of a Kosher butcher shop in an advertisement for bacon. Braun v. Armour & Co., 254 N.Y. 514, 173 N.E. 845 (1930). In a similar vein, the publication of the picture of a teetotaling nurse in a whiskey advertisement was held to be libelous in Peck v. Tribune Co., 214 U.S. 185, 29 S.Ct. 554, 53 L.Ed. 960 (1909), although it would seem that a modern court would want some extrinsic facts about the plaintiff's religious background and social circle before so concluding today. It has for example been more recently held that it is not defamatory to falsely write that a husband and wife were separated and getting a divorce. *See* Andreason v. Guard Publishing Co., 260 Or. 308, 489 P.2d 944 (1971). In Meyerson v. Hurlbut, 98 F.2d 232 (D.C.Cir. 1938), *cert. denied* 305 U.S. 610, 59 S.Ct. 69, 83 L.Ed. 388, it was held defamatory to call a businessman a "price cutter," but such a holding seems unlikely today. It has been argued that society is becoming more fragmented and that judges should be more open about the extent to which they are

engaging in a process of social idealization. *See* L. Lidsky, *Defamation, Reputation, and the Myth of Community,* 71 Wash.L.Rev. 1 (1996).

3. The cases are uniform in holding that it is not defamatory to call someone an informer. The decisions are based more on the public policy of encouraging cooperation with the police than on the assumption that no decent person would think ill of such a person. An amusing example is Byrne v. Deane, [1937] 1 K.B. 818 (C.A.). In that case, what appeared to be slot machines—they are identified as "diddler" machines—were on the premises of a golf club owned and operated by the defendants. Someone told the police about the machines and the machines were removed. The plaintiff was a member of the club. Someone posted the following doggerel verse at the spot where the machines had been:

For many years upon this spot

You heard the sound of a merry bell

Those who were rash and those who were not

Lost and made a spot of cash

But he who gave the game away

May he byrnn in hell and rue the day

Diddleramus

Although the defendants had not posted the verse, the court was prepared to hold them responsible for publishing it, since they were aware that the verse had been posted and allowed it to remain. Nevertheless, the Court of Appeal reversed a judgment for the plaintiff. The court was prepared to accept that the public might in fact think poorly of someone who informed about some crimes but noted, in addition to the public policy issue mentioned above, that it had no confidence in the ability of courts to determine which were the crimes as to which the public would look with scorn on an informant. On the question of liability for falsely accusing someone of being an informer, *see also* Connelly v. McKay, 176 Misc. 685, 28 N.Y.S.2d 327 (1941). For a more recent case reaffirming the traditional doctrine, *see* Clawson v. St. Louis Post Dispatch, L.L.C., 906 A.2d 308 (D.C. 2006).

4. Suppose that a headline and photograph accompanying a story are capable of a defamatory meaning but that when the entire article is read it is clear that there has been no defamation. What is the appropriate context: the headline and the photograph or the headline, the photograph, and the entire story? Compare *Restatement (Second) of Torts* § 563, Comment, *d*, with Charleston v. News Group Newspapers, [1995] 2 A.C. 65, 2 W.L.R. 450, 2 All E.R. 313. A more recent American case is Stanton v. Metro Corp., 438 F.3d 119 (1st Cir. 2006) in which a story about drinking and promiscuous behavior among students at a high school included a photograph of a group of five teenagers, one of whom was an out of state teenager who did not attend the school in question. The story made no specific reference to her and the story had an explicit disclaimer that the teenagers in the photograph were not related to the story. The court held that people could reasonably believe that she was one of the promiscuous teens about whom the story was written and

reversed the district court's dismissal of the case for failure to state a cause of action.

5. Unless the statement is obviously a spoof, as was the situation in the *Falwell* case presented in the previous chapter at p. 465, so long as the statement is false and defamatory, it is no defense that the persons to whom the defamatory communication was communicated did not believe the statement. That people do not believe the statement may have some effect on the damages awarded, but it does not affect liability. It is the tendency of the type of statement in question to injure a person in the plaintiff's position that is relevant. Moreover, a statement which is not initially believed may, over time, come to affect the plaintiff's reputation quite substantially, especially if it is repeated. It is a fairly common belief that "where there is smoke, there is fire." It should finally be noted that the republication of defamatory material, except in some limited circumstances to be discussed below in connection with a consideration of the defenses available in defamation actions, is itself defamatory, even if the statement is attributed to the original source.

YOUSSOUPOFF v. METRO–GOLDWYN–MAYER PICTURES, LTD.

Court of Appeal, 1934.
50 T.L.R. 581.

LORD JUSTICE SCRUTTON.—An English company called Metro–Goldwyn–Mayer Pictures, Limited, which produces films circulated to the cinemas in this country, and which, according to its solicitor and chairman, is controlled by a firm of similar name in America, produced in this country a film which dealt with the alleged circumstances in which the influence of a man called Rasputin, an alleged monk, on the Czar and Czarina brought about the destruction of Russia. The film also dealt with the undoubted fact that Rasputin was ultimately murdered by persons who conceived him to be the evil genius of Russia.

In the course of that film a lady who had relations of affection with the person represented as the murderer was represented as having also had relations, which might be either relations of seduction or relations of rape, with the man Rasputin, a man of the worst possible character. When the film was produced in this country the plaintiff alleged that reasonable people would understand that she was the woman who was represented as having had these illicit relations. The plaintiff is a member of the Russian Royal House, Princess Irina Alexandrovna of Russia, and she was married after the incidents in question to a man who undoubtedly was one of the persons concerned in the killing of Rasputin. She issued a writ for libel against the English company. The English company declined to stop presenting the film. The action for libel proceeded. It was tried before one of the most experienced Judges on the Bench and a special jury, the constitutional tribunal for trying actions of libel, and, after several days' hearing, and after the jury had twice gone to see the film itself, they returned a verdict for the plaintiff with £25,000 damages.

The defendants now appeal from that verdict, and, as I understand the argument put before us by Sir William Jowitt and Mr. Wallington, for the defendants, it falls under three heads. First of all, they say that there was no evidence on which a jury, properly directed, could find that reasonable people would understand the Princess Natasha of the film to be Princess Irina, the plaintiff. That was the first point—the question of identification. Secondly, they say that if we are to take the Princess Natasha of the film to be identified with the Princess Irina, the plaintiff, there was no evidence on which a jury, reasonably directed, could find the film to be defamatory of the plaintiff. Thirdly, they say: "Assuming both of those points are decided against us, the damages were excessive. They were such as no jury, properly directed, could give in the circumstances of the case."

I deal with each of those three points in turn. First of all, there is the question of identification. Now, if this case had been heard before 1910 there would undoubtedly have been scope for very elaborate arguments, and this Court would probably have had to reserve judgment to consider the numerous authorities which would have been cited. But since the decision in 1910 in a case which is always identified with the name of Mr. Artemus Jones, and since a subsequent decision of this Court in which somewhat similar principles were applied in a case which is identified with the name of General Corrigan, of the Mexican Army, there is, fortunately, no difficulty about the law. In Hulton and Co., Limited v. Jones (26 *The Times* L.R. 128; [1910] A.C. 20) a Manchester paper published by Messrs. Hulton published what was supposed to be an amusing article about a gentleman named Artemus Jones, who, on one side of his life, was a blameless churchwarden at Peckham and, on the other side of his life, indulged in wild careers unfitted for such a churchwarden at Le Touquet. A Mr. Artemus Jones—there may be several—conceived that that article was a libel upon him, and he brought an action for libel. The editor and proprietors of the paper said, rightly or wrongly, that they had never heard of Mr. Artemus Jones as an existing being, and that they had not the slightest intention of libelling him. There was some unfortunate doubt whether the gentleman who wrote the article had not a personal grudge against the real Mr. Artemus Jones,[a] but, at any rate, the proprietors and publishers of the paper said: "We are innocent of any intention to injure Mr. Artemus Jones, of whom we never heard."

The case resulted in this way. In spite of a very careful judgment by Lord Justice Moulton in the Court of Appeal, counterbalanced by an equally learned and convincing judgment of Lord Justice Farwell in the Court of Appeal, the House of Lords unanimously came to the conclusion which is expressed in the first lines of the headnote in this way: "In an action for libel it is no defence to show that the defendant did not intend to defame the plaintiff, if reasonable people would think the language to

a. [Ed. note.] There was some evidence that the plaintiff had at one time been employed by the defendant newspaper, but it was accepted by counsel that the publishers were unaware of who Artemus Jones was and that they thought it was a fictitious name.

be defamatory of the plaintiff"; and the Lord Chancellor quoted in his judgment this passage from the summing-up: "The real point upon which your verdict must turn is, ought or ought not sensible and reasonable people reading this article to think that it was a mere imaginary person such as I have said—Tom Jones, Mr. Pecksniff as a humbug, Mr. Stiggins, or any of that sort of names that one reads of in literature used as types? If you think any reasonable person would think that"—that is to say that it was mere type and did not mean anybody—"it is not actionable at all. If, on the other hand, you do not think that, but think that people would suppose it to mean some real person—those who did not know the plaintiff of course would not know who the real person was, but those who did know of the existence of the plaintiff would think that it was the plaintiff—then the action is maintainable."

A somewhat similar point was raised in the case where General Corrigan got damages—Cassidy v. Daily Mirror Newspapers, Limited (45 *The Times* L.R. 485; [1929] 2 K.B. 331). General Corrigan, who sometimes called himself Cassidy, being at a race meeting, conceived the idea of being photographed with a young lady to whom he said he was engaged. This photograph was sent up as an object of interest to a daily paper, which at once inserted it. Now, it so happened that the General was in fact married to a lady who lived in a London suburb, and was visited by the suburban ladies in the vicinity, who had hitherto considered that she was an honest married woman. When they took in the daily paper and saw that the gentleman describing himself as the husband of the lady was representing himself as being engaged to somebody else they very naturally, as respectable women, conceived evil ideas of the lady whom they had hitherto thought to be an honest woman and whom they now suspected of being a kept woman. Thereupon the lady brought an action against the paper, and the paper said what before 1910 would have been the sort of thing you would expect them to say: "Why, good gracious, madam, we never heard of you. We had no intention of libelling you. We did not know you existed, and all we have done is to publish an interesting photograph, stating that the gentleman in the photograph says he is engaged to the lady in the photograph." Just as *Hulton and Co., Limited v. Jones (supra)* had caused a difference of opinion with a very excellent judgment by Lord Justice Moulton, so again the case of the General did cause a difference of opinion with again, if I may say so, a very excellent judgment of my brother Greer, but, unfortunately, the majority of the Court, myself and Lord Russell, took another view, and this Court is now bound by the view laid down by the Lord Chancellor in the *Hulton* case (*supra*) and by the case of General Corrigan, and we follow the law that though the person who writes and publishes the libel may not intend to libel a particular person and, indeed, has never heard of that particular person, the plaintiff, yet, if evidence is produced that reasonable people knowing some of the circumstances, not necessarily all, would take the libel complained of to relate to the plaintiff, an action for libel will lie.

That, therefore, was the class of evidence put before the jury in this case. On the one side, various people, some of them representatives of England in Russia at the time of these occurrences, some of them people who had been merely reading books about Russia and thought they knew something about it, were called to say that they saw the film, and they understood it to relate to the present plaintiff, the Princess Irina. On the other side, other people who knew something about Russia, or who did not know anything about Russia, were called to say that they saw the film, that they did not think it related to the plaintiff, and they gave their views as to whom they did think the characters in the film related.

There was evidence [on] each side. I think counsel for the defendants agree that it would have been impossible for the [judge] to have stopped the case because the film was not capable of a defamatory meaning, and the jury, who are a tribunal particularly suited to try an action for libel, for the reason that I am going to allude to under the second head, came to the view that reasonable people would take the film to relate to the plaintiff in the action. It is not my business to express an opinion on the matter. It was the jury's business, and the only question for me is whether there was evidence on which the jury might come to the conclusion to which they have come. That being my position, I can quite see that there is a great deal of evidence on which the jury might take the view that the plaintiff was identified reasonably with the Princess Natasha.

* * *

Therefore, on the first point, I come to the conclusion that we cannot possibly interfere with the verdict of the jury, who are the constitutional tribunal, when they think, as they obviously have thought, that reasonable people, not all reasonable people but many reasonable people, would take the film representing Princess Natasha as also representing and referring to the plaintiff in the action, the Princess Irina. * * *

Now the second point is this, and it takes some courage to argue it, I think: suppose that the jury are right in treating Princess Irina, the plaintiff, as the Princess Natasha in real life, the film does not contain anything defamatory of her. There have been several formulae for describing what is defamation. The learned Judge at the trial uses the stock formula "calculated to bring into hatred, ridicule, or contempt," and because it has been clearly established some time ago that that is not exhaustive because there may be things which are defamatory which have nothing to do with hatred, ridicule, or contempt he adds the words "or causes them to be shunned or avoided." I, myself, have always preferred the language which Mr. Justice Cave used in Scott v. Sampson (8 Q.B.D. 491), a false statement about a man to his discredit. I think that satisfactorily expresses what has to be found. It has long been established that, with one modification, libel or no libel is for the jury, and the Court very rarely interferes with a finding by the jury that a particular statement is a libel or is no libel. The only exception is that it has been established with somewhat unfortunate results that a Judge may say: "No reasonable jury could possibly think this a libel, and consequently I will not ask the jury the question whether it is a libel or not.'' In a case in which that was conclusively established the law and the facts got so far from each other that the majority of the Judges—there was a great difference of opinion—held that a certain circular issued by a firm of brewers to their customers saying that they would not take the cheques of a particular bank was not capable of a defamatory meaning, though, in fact, it resulted in a run of a quarter of a million on the bank immediately it was issued.

Fortunately, however, in this case we have not to deal with that exception because it is not suggested that the Judge in this case could have withdrawn the question of this libel from the jury on the point that it was not capable of a defamatory meaning. When you get the matter going to the jury it is extremely rare that the Court interferes with the finding of the jury whether a thing is libel or no libel. That has resulted from the action of Parliament in Mr. Fox's Libel Act in settling a dispute between Lord Mansfield and another eminent Judge as to the powers of the Judge in dealing with questions of libel. Lord Mansfield was of opinion that if a libel came before the Courts the Judge was to say whether it was a libel, and it was only for the jury to assess damages or to find guilty or not guilty on the direction. That was considered so contrary to the constitution with regard to juries that Parliament intervened and passed an Act, known as Mr. Fox's Libel Act, by which the matter was left to the jury. * * *

If libel alone is for the jury on those lines, why is it said that the jury in this case have come to a wrong decision? I desire to approach this argument seriously if I can, because I have great difficulty in approaching it seriously. I understand the principal thing argued by the defendants is this: "This procedure, as it contains some spoken words, is slander and not libel. Slanders are not as a rule actionable unless you prove special damage. No special damage was proved in this case. Consequently, the plaintiff must get within the exceptions in which slander is actionable without proof of special damage.'' One of those exceptions is the exception which is amplified in the Slander of Women Act, 1891—namely, if the slander imports unchastity or adultery to a woman—and this is the argument as I understand it: "To say of a woman that she is raped does not impute unchastity.'' From that we get to this, which was solemnly put forward, that to say of a woman of good character that she has been ravished by a man of the worst possible character is not defamatory. That argument was solemnly presented to the jury, and I only wish the jury could have expressed, and that we could know, what they thought of it, because it seems to me to be one of the most legal arguments that were ever addressed to, I will not say a business body, but a sensible body.

That, really, as I understand it, is the argument upon which is based the contention that no reasonable jury could come to the conclusion that to say of a woman that she had been ravished by a man of very bad character when as a matter of fact she never saw the man at all and was never near him is not defamatory of the woman.

I really have no language to express my opinion of that argument. I therefore come, on the second point, to the view that there is no ground for interfering with the verdict of the jury (assuming the identification to stand, as I have assumed), that the words and the pictures in the film are defamatory of the lady whom they have found to be Princess Irina.

Then one comes to the third point, and that is the amount of damages. It is the law that in libel, though not in slander, you need not prove any particular damage in order to recover a verdict. What, then, is the position, the jury being the tribunal in libel or no libel, and, following from that, the tribunal as to the damages caused by libel, whose verdict is very rarely interfered with by the Court of Appeal? What have the jury to do? They have to give a verdict of amount without having any proof of actual damage. They need not have any proof of actual damage. They have to consider the nature of the libel as they understand it, the circumstances in which it was published, and the circumstances relating to the person who publishes it, right down to the time when they give their verdict, whether the defence made it true, and, if so, whether that defence has ever been withdrawn—the whole circumstances of the case. It is not the Judge who has to decide the amount. The constitution has thought, and I think there is great advantage in it, that the damages to be paid by a person who says false things about his neighbour are best decided by a jury representing the public, who may state the view of the public as to the action of the man who makes false statements about his neighbour, the plaintiff.

It is for that reason that it is extremely rare for the Court of Appeal to interfere with the verdict of the jury as to the amount of damages when the libel is established. It is very often the case that the individual Judges of the Court of Appeal, if they had been asked their verdict on the amount of damages, would have given a smaller sum. Sometimes they would have given a larger sum, but the question is not what amount the Judges would have given. The question is what amount the jury, as representing the public, the community, have fixed, and it is extremely rare to have that amount interfered with by the Court. A test has been formulated, and it is this, as has been correctly stated several times: the Courts will interfere only if the amount of damages is such that in all the circumstances no twelve reasonable men could have given it. If the Court comes to that view, it will interfere with the verdict, but even then it cannot fix the amount itself, but must send the case back to another jury who may very easily repeat the first verdict, and the Court cannot go on sending the case back to a jury until at last they get a verdict with which the Judges agree. Those are the reasons which justify the relation of the Court of Appeal to the amount of damages found by juries.

Applying that test to this case, * * * I find it quite impossible to say that the amount of damages here is such that no reasonable jury could have given it. There is the position of the plaintiff, a high position, although the Royal Family of Russia have fallen from their high position. There is the amount of publicity given by circulating the film through a large circle of cinemas to be seen at cheap prices by an enormous number of people. Apparently in this case there were performances for a week in more than 16, possibly 20, cinemas. Looking at all those matters, I come to the conclusion that, if the jury were properly directed, this Court cannot possibly interfere with the amount of the damages, even if any individual member of it, or all three members, had thought that if they had been on the jury they might have given a smaller sum.

* * *

For these reasons, in my opinion, this appeal should be dismissed, with costs.

* * *

LORD JUSTICE SLESSER.—This action is one of libel and raises at the outset an interesting and difficult problem which, I believe, to be a novel problem, whether the product of the combined photographic and talking instrument which produces these modern films does, if it throws upon the screen and impresses upon the ear defamatory matter, produce that which can be complained of as libel or as slander.

In my view, this action, as I have said, was properly framed in libel. There can be no doubt that, so far as the photographic part of the exhibition is concerned, that is a permanent matter to be seen by the eye, and is the proper subject of an action for libel, if defamatory. I regard the speech which is synchronized with the photographic reproduction and forms part of one complex, common exhibition as an ancillary circumstance, part of the surroundings explaining that which is to be seen.

* * *

SIR PATRICK HASTINGS.—The appeal will be dismissed, with costs?

LORD JUSTICE SCRUTTON.—Yes.

NOTES

1. Hulton and Co. v. Jones, [1910] A.C. 20, discussed by Scrutton, L.J., was followed in Corrigan v. Bobbs–Merrill Co., 228 N.Y. 58, 126 N.E. 260 (1920). *See also* Hanson v. Globe Newspaper Co., 159 Mass. 293, 34 N.E. 462 (1893), particularly the dissenting opinion of Holmes, J. For a more recent case, *see* Michaels v. Gannett Co., 10 A.D.2d 417, 199 N.Y.S.2d 778 (1960). In an article about a restauranteur against whom a tax lien had been filed, the defendants mistakenly published the plaintiff's address, the plaintiff having the same name. In a recent British article, it is argued that the development of the doctrine of strict liability in *Hulton v. Jones* was based on a mistaken interpretation of older cases. P. Mitchell, *Malice in Defamation*, 114 L.Q.Rev. 639 (1998). Be that as it may, with the intrusion, in recent years, of constitutional considerations into the American law of defamation that we shall examine later in this chapter, there seems to be very little room for liability for truly innocent defamation. Even before these constitutional devel-

opments a number of statutes have been passed absolving broadcasters from liability for innocent misrepresentation. *See* L. Eldredge, The Law of Defamation 86–90 (1978); D. Remmers, *Recent Legislative Trends in Defamation by Radio,* 64 Harv.L.Rev. 727, 739–46 (1951). Even where the defendant is unable to show lack of fault in publishing defamatory material, some of these statutes limit the plaintiff to recovery of actual damages only. Furthermore, even in Great Britain, as we shall see *infra* at p. 571, there has been some statutory attempt to limit the harsh consequences of the common-law rule, by limiting damages where a suitable offer of retraction is made.

It is common knowledge of course that many fictional characters in what clearly purport to be works of fiction—unlike the film involved in the *Youssoupoff* case, which purported to be a dramatization of an actual historical event—are modeled upon real persons. People who claim that they are in point of fact the model upon whom some fictional character is based have brought many defamation actions against authors. A well-publicized case is Bindrim v. Mitchell, 92 Cal.App.3d 61, 155 Cal.Rptr. 29 (1979), *cert. denied,* 444 U.S. 984, 100 S.Ct. 490, 62 L.Ed.2d 412 (1979). The particular problem such plaintiffs face is, of course, proving that they can be identified by the reader as the model for the character in question. Smith v. Stewart, 291 Ga.App. 86, 660 S.E.2d 822 (2008), is a more recent instance in which a character in a work of fiction was alleged to be recognizably based on a real person, and that some of the facts about that character were true but most of the unsavory facts about the character were false. The court held that she had adequately stated a cause of action. Subsidiary questions raised by the constitutionalization of the law of defamation, to which we shall turn shortly, include whether the author intentionally or recklessly or negligently misstated the allegedly defamatory facts. Some recent cases have attempted to accommodate these concerns by giving more breathing room to the defendant. *See* Tamkin v. CBS Broadcasting, Inc., 193 Cal.App.4th 133, 122 Cal.Rptr.3d 264 (2011) (television series); Muzikowski v. Paramount Pictures Corp., 477 F.3d 477 F.3d 899 (7th Cir. 2007) (movie based on non-fiction book about the plaintiff). In *Muzikowski.* the court relied in part on Illinois' having an innocent construction doctrine (i.e. a reasonable non-defamatory meaning) with respect to works of fiction.

2. While lack of intent to defame was no defense at common law, liability would not arise unless the publication to third parties were intended or at least the result of negligence. There was no liability for "accidental" publication. For a fairly recent case, *see* Smith v. Jones, 335 So.2d 896 (Miss.1976), in which the plaintiff's sons eavesdropped on the defendant's phone conversation with their mother. There was no liability because the defendants spoke "with the reasonable expectation that they would be heard by the plaintiff only." A letter to a child accusing him of theft, however, can be reasonably expected to be brought by the child to his parents. *See, e.g.,* Hedgpeth v. Coleman, 183 N.C. 309, 111 S.E. 517 (1922). There are also some situations in which an adult may be able to bring an action for defamation although he himself may be the person who publishes the defamatory matter to third persons. For a discussion of such cases of "compelled self-publication," *see* Note, 68 Tenn.L.Rev. 395 (2001).

3. The absolute liability of one who intentionally or negligently publishes defamatory material would impose a heavy burden on libraries, newspaper and magazine distributors, and newsstand and bookshop operators. To hold such persons liable they must, at the very least, be shown to have some knowledge of the defamatory content of the publication in question. *See, e.g.,* Balabanoff v. Fossani, 192 Misc. 615, 81 N.Y.S.2d 732 (1948); Weldon v. Times Book Co., 28 T.L.R. 143 (C.A.1911).

What about the Internet? To resolve the confusion created by somewhat conflicting court decisions, Congress, in 1996, enacted what is now 47 U.S.C. § 230, as amended, which provides that "[n]o provider or user of an interactive computer service shall be treated as the publisher or speaker of any information provided by another information content provider." It has been held that this immunity even applies to an interactive computer service provider who had paid someone to write a gossip column and who had even reserved the right to request changes in the column. Blumenthal v. Drudge, 992 F.Supp. 44 (D.D.C. 1998). On the general subject, *see* A. Cioli, *Defamatory Internet Speech: A Defense of the Status Quo.* 25 Quinnipiac L.Rev. 853 (2007).

4. Dictating a letter about a third party to a secretary is also generally considered to be a publication. *See* Ostrowe v. Lee, 256 N.Y. 36, 175 N.E. 505 (1931), also holding that dictating a letter is libel because of the transcription. If the person dictating the letter and the person taking the dictation are both employed by a common employer, and the letter pertains to the business of that employer, the publication may however be qualifiedly privileged. *See* p. 542, *infra.*

5. As Slesser, L.J., noted, the *Youssoupoff* case was one of the first involving the question of whether a motion picture film was libel or merely slander. In holding it to be libel, courts have been impressed with the permanent nature of the film as well as the fact that the medium appeals to the visual sense. The more difficult cases involved radio and now television. Some early cases held radio to be slander. *See, e.g.,* Meldrum v. Australian Broadcasting Co., [1932] Vict.L.R. 425; Summit Hotel Co. v. National Broadcasting Co., 336 Pa. 182, 8 A.2d 302 (1939); Kelly v. Hoffman, 137 N.J.L. 695, 61 A.2d 143 (1948). *Contra* Sorensen v. Wood, 123 Neb. 348, 243 N.W. 82 (1932), *appeal dismissed* 290 U.S. 599, 54 S.Ct. 209, 78 L.Ed. 527 (1933); Coffey v. Midland Broadcasting Co., 8 F.Supp. 889 (W.D.Mo.1934). A few states also passed statutes making radio broadcasting slander. *See* L. Eldredge, The Law of Defamation 87–88 (1978). In Hartmann v. Winchell, 296 N.Y. 296, 73 N.E.2d 30 (1947), the New York Court of Appeals held that a radio broadcast read from a written script was libel. Subsequently in Shor v. Billingsley, 4 Misc.2d 857, 158 N.Y.S.2d 476 (1956), *affirmed* 4 A.D.2d 1017, 169 N.Y.S.2d 416 (1957), ad lib remarks on television were held to be libel. The *Restatement of Torts* took no position on the subject but *Restatement (Second) of Torts* § 568A now declares that radio or television broadcasts are libel regardless of whether a script is used. Radio and television are also classified as libel in Great Britain under the Defamation Act of 1952. The act was amended in 1968 to extend the same treatment to words published in the course of the performance of a play.

6. Someone in possession of real or personal property, who fails to remove a defamatory statement affixed to his property by third persons within a reasonable time after notice, is himself liable for publishing the defamatory material. *See* Hellar v. Bianco, 111 Cal.App.2d 424, 244 P.2d 757 (1952) (defamatory statement about female plaintiff permitted to remain on wall in men's room toilet); Restatement (Second) of Torts § 577(2). *See also* Byrne v. Deane, [1937] 1 K.B. 818 (C.A.), discussed at p. 501, *supra.*

7. *Multiple Publication.* At common law each sale or delivery of a copy of a newspaper, magazine, or book was considered a separate publication, creating a new and distinct cause of action. *See* Duke of Brunswick v. Harmer, 14 Q.B. 185, 117 Eng.Rep. 75 (1849). This was the position taken by *Restatement of Torts* § 578, *Comment (b).* Most states have, however, now moved to some form of single publication rule as exemplified by *Restatement (Second) of Torts* § 577A(3) which provides that "[a]ny one edition of a book or newspaper or any one radio or television broadcast exhibition of a motion picture or similar aggregate communication is a single publication." The Uniform Single Publication Act, which was first propagated in 1952 and has been adopted in seven states, has similar provisions. *See* Unif. Single Publication Act, 14 U.L.A 377 (1990). Under the single publication rule, only one action for all damages suffered in all jurisdictions can be maintained and a judgment on the merits operates as a bar to any other action between the same parties in all jurisdictions. With regard to a motion picture, such as was involved in the *Youssoupoff* case, a single publication rule does not seem to deal with the problem presented by the *Youssoupoff* case in which the movie was shown repeatedly in a number of theaters. Accepting the *Restatement's* declaration that any "exhibition of a motion picture" is a single publication, then each showing of the film, and certainly each showing in a separate theater, would be a new publication. In point of fact, the issue, for most purposes, is largely a theoretical one. Modern rules of pleading and common sense would dictate that a plaintiff bring only one action and modern rules of collateral estoppel and res judicata would probably make the judgment in that action dispositive in any future action. Some states have insisted on maintaining the common law multiple publication rule for venue purposes in order to preserve the possibility that citizens of that state can bring an action in the courts of that state rather than being forced to bring the action in the defendant's principal place of business or in the jurisdiction in which a publication was printed. *See* Lewis v. Reader's Digest Association, 162 Mont. 401, 512 P.2d 702 (1973). The choice between a multiple and a single publication rule might also have a decisive impact on when the statute of limitations begins to run. *See* Finnegan v. Squire Publishers, Inc., 765 S.W.2d 703 (Mo.Ct.App.1989) in which the court held that the plaintiff's cause of action against a newspaper accrued in Kansas, where the article was published and later distributed in Missouri as well as Kansas. The court therefore ruled that Kansas' one-year statute of limitations would apply, rather than Missouri's two-year statute. *See also* Givens v. Quinn, 877 F.Supp. 485 (W.D.Mo.1994), in which the court held that only one cause of action would lie against the author of the syndicated column but opined that separate causes of action could be brought against each newspaper that reprinted her column.

8. In Keeton v. Hustler Magazine, Inc., 465 U.S. 770, 104 S.Ct. 1473, 79 L.Ed.2d 790 (1984), the statute of limitations on the plaintiff's claim for defamation had run in every jurisdiction except New Hampshire. The case was brought in the United States District Court for the District of New Hampshire on a diversity-of-citizenship basis. The only contact that the parties or the claim had with New Hampshire was the fact that some 10,000 to 15,000 copies of *Hustler* magazine were sold in New Hampshire each month. The plaintiff claimed to have been libeled in five separate issues of the magazine published between September 1975 and May 1976. The case had been dismissed by the lower courts on the ground that New Hampshire's interest in the litigation was too attenuated to permit an assertion of personal jurisdiction over *Hustler* magazine. The lower courts were influenced by the fact that New Hampshire followed the single-publication rule so that if the plaintiff succeeded in her claim she would be entitled to recover damages for the nationwide publication of the magazine, which, as noted, was time-barred in every jurisdiction but New Hampshire, which had an unusually long, six-year limitations period for libel actions. A unanimous Supreme Court reversed and held that there was sufficient contact with the forum state to permit the exercise of personal jurisdiction.

On the same day that *Keeton v. Hustler Magazine, Inc.* was decided, the court also handed down its decision in Calder v. Jones, 465 U.S. 783, 104 S.Ct. 1482, 79 L.Ed.2d 804 (1984), which involved some related jurisdictional issues. The plaintiff, a California resident, claimed that she had been libeled in an article written and edited by the two individual defendants in Florida. The article had been published in a national magazine with a large circulation in California, the *National Enquirer,* which was also a defendant in the case. The individual defendants were a reporter employed by the *Enquirer,* who resided in Florida and traveled frequently to California on business, and the president and editor of the *Enquirer,* who was also a Florida resident and who had only been to California twice, once on a pleasure trip prior to the publication of the article and once after the article's publication to testify in an unrelated trial. The question presented was whether the individual defendants could be served under California's "long-arm" statute. The Superior Court of California granted the individual defendants' motion to quash the service of process, but the California Court of Appeal reversed, noting that the defendants, under the allegations of the complaint, had intended to, and did, cause tortious injury to the plaintiff in California. The fact that these effects were caused by activities conducted outside of California did not prevent California from asserting jurisdiction over the case. A unanimous Supreme Court of the United States affirmed this decision.

BURTON v. CROWELL PUBLISHING CO.

United States Court of Appeals, Second Circuit, 1936.
82 F.2d 154.

L. HAND, CIRCUIT JUDGE.

This appeal arises upon a judgment dismissing a complaint for libel upon the pleadings. The complaint alleged that the defendant had published an advertisement—annexed and incorporated by reference—made up of text and photographs; that one of the photographs was "susceptible of being regarded as representing plaintiff as guilty of indecent exposure and as being a person physically deformed and mentally perverted"; that some of the text, read with the offending photograph, was "susceptible of being regarded as falsely representing plaintiff as an utterer of salacious and obscene language"; and finally that "by reason of the premises plaintiff has been subjected to frequent and conspicuous ridicule, scandal, reproach, scorn, and indignity." The advertisement was of "Camel" cigarettes; the plaintiff was a widely known gentleman steeple-chaser, and the text quoted him as declaring that "Camel" cigarettes "restored" him after "a crowded business day." Two photographs were inserted; the larger, a picture of the plaintiff in riding shirt and breeches, seated apparently outside a paddock with a cigarette in one hand and a cap and whip in the other. This contained the legend, "Get a lift with a Camel"; neither it, nor the photograph, is charged as part of the libel, except as the legend may be read upon the other and offending photograph. That represented him coming from a race to be weighed in; he is carrying his saddle in front of him with his right hand under the pommel and his left under the cantle; the line of the seat is about twelve inches below his waist. Over the pommel hangs, a stirrup; over the seat at his middle a white girth falls loosely in such a way that it seems to be attached to the plaintiff and not to the saddle. So regarded, the photograph becomes grotesque, monstrous, and obscene; and the legends, which without undue violence can be made to match, reinforce the ribald interpretation. That is the libel. The answer alleged that the plaintiff had posed for the photographs and been paid for their use as an advertisement; a reply, that they had never been shown to the plaintiff after they were taken. On this showing the judge held that the advertisement did not hold the plaintiff up to the hatred, ridicule, or contempt of fair-minded people, and that in any event he consented to its use and might not complain.

We dismiss at once so much of the complaint as alleged that the advertisement might be read to say that the plaintiff was deformed, or that he had indecently exposed himself, or was making obscene jokes by means of the legends. Nobody could be fatuous enough to believe any of these things; everybody would at once see that it was the camera, and the camera alone, that had made the unfortunate mistake. If the advertisement is a libel, it is such in spite of the fact that it asserts nothing whatever about the plaintiff, even by the remotest implications. It does not profess to depict him as he is; it does not exaggerate any part of his person so as to suggest that he is deformed; it is patently an optical illusion, and carries its correction on its face as much as though it were a verbal utterance which expressly declared that it was false. It would be hard for words so guarded to carry any sting, but the same is not true of caricatures, and this is an example; for, notwithstanding all we have just said, it exposed the plaintiff to overwhelming ridicule. The contrast between the drawn and serious face and the accompanying fantastic and lewd deformity was so extravagant that, though utterly unfair, it in fact made of the plaintiff a preposterously ridiculous spectacle; and the obvious mistake only added to the amusement. Had such a picture been deliberately produced, surely every right-minded person would agree that he would have had a genuine grievance; and the effect is the same whether it is deliberate or not. Such a caricature affects a man's reputation, if by that is meant his position in the minds of others; the association so established may be beyond repair; he may become known indefinitely as the absurd victim of this unhappy mischance. Literally, therefore, the injury falls within the accepted rubric; it exposes the sufferer to "ridicule" and "contempt." Nevertheless, we have not been able to find very much in the books that is in point, for although it has long been recognized that pictures may be libels, and in some cases they have been caricatures, in nearly all they have impugned the plaintiff at least by implication, directly or indirectly uttering some falsehood about him. * * *

The defendant answers that every libel must affect the plaintiff's character; but if by "character" is meant those moral qualities which the word ordinarily includes, the statement is certainly untrue, for there are many libels which do not affect the reputation of the victim in any such way. * * *

A more plausible challenge is that a libel must be something that can be true or false, since truth is always a defense. It would follow that if, as we agree, the picture was a mistake on its face and declared nothing about the plaintiff, it was not a libel. We have been able to find very little on the point. In Dunlop v. Dunlop Rubber Co. (1920) 1 Irish Ch. & Ld.Com. 280, 290–292, the picture represented the plaintiff in foppish clothes, and the opinion seems to rely merely upon the contempt which that alone might have aroused, but those who saw it might have taken it to imply that the plaintiff was in fact a fop. In Zbyszko v. New York American, 228 App.Div. 277, 239 N.Y.S. 411, however, though the decision certainly went far, nobody could possibly have read the picture as asserting anything which was in fact untrue; it was the mere association of the plaintiff with a gorilla that was thought to lower him in others' esteem. Nevertheless, although the question is almost tabula rasa, it seems to us that in principle there should be no doubt. The gravamen of the wrong in defamation is not so much the injury to reputation, measured by the opinions of others, as the feelings, that is, the repulsion or the light esteem, which those opinions engender. We are sensitive to the charge of murder only because our fellows deprecate it in most forms; but a head-hunter, or an aboriginal American Indian, or a gangster, would regard such an accusation as a distinction, and during the Great War an "ace," a man who had killed five others, was held in high regard. Usually it is difficult to arouse feelings without expressing an opinion, or asserting a fact; and the common law has so much regard for truth that it excuses the utterance of anything that is true. But it is a non sequitur to argue that whenever truth is not a defense, there can be no libel; that would invert the proper approach to the whole subject. In all wrongs we must first ascertain whether the interest invaded is one which the law will protect at all; that is indeed especially important in defamation, for the common law did not recognize all injuries to reputation, especially when the utterance was oral. But the interest here is by hypothesis one which the law does protect; the plaintiff has been substantially enough ridiculed to be in a position to complain. The defendant must therefore find some excuse, and truth would be an excuse if it could be pleaded. The only reason why the law makes truth a defense is not because a libel must be false, but because the utterance of truth is in all circumstances an interest paramount to reputation; it is like a privileged communication, which is privileged only because the law prefers it conditionally to reputation. When there is no such countervailing interest, there is no excuse; and that is the situation here. In conclusion therefore we hold that because the picture taken with the legends was calculated to expose the plaintiff to more than trivial ridicule, it was prima facie actionable; that the fact that it did not assume to state a fact or an opinion is irrelevant; and that in consequence the publication is actionable.

Finally, the plaintiff's consent to the use of the photographs for which he posed as an advertisement was not a consent to the use of the offending photograph; he had no reason to anticipate that the lens would so distort his appearance. If the defendant wished to fix him with responsibility for whatever the camera might turn out, the result should have been shown him before publication. Possibly any one who chooses to stir such a controversy in a court cannot have been very sensitive originally, but that is a consideration for the jury, which, if ever justified, is justified in actions for defamation.

Judgment reversed; cause remanded for trial.

NOTES

1. The picture involved in the *Burton* case was part of the record on appeal, and two of the editors of this casebook have a copy in their files. The picture makes it look very much as if the plaintiff were exposing himself in a bizarre and grotesque manner. The trial judge was not sympathetic, finding that no right-minded person would hold the plaintiff up to ridicule, hatred, or contempt and that, in any event, the plaintiff had consented to its use. On appeal, the plaintiff's attorneys argued that grotesque phalli had been used on the stage in ancient Greece and that, given the suggestion of the photograph, people might be prepared to think that the plaintiff was engaging in similar conduct. Appellant's Brief at pp. 11–12. If the court had been prepared to accept this contention, the case would easily have fit into the traditional format. For reasons of prudishness or whatever, the circuit court of appeals was unwilling to view the photograph in this light.

2. The leading case on ridicule as defamation is Triggs v. Sun Printing and Publishing Association, 179 N.Y. 144, 71 N.E. 739 (1904). In that case the defendant newspaper published a series of sarcastic articles about Professor Oscar L. Triggs, a well-known professor of English at the University of Chicago who, among other things, favored a simpler style of English than was

then currently fashionable. Triggs had turned down a substantial offer to give public lectures to the audiences who went to view the plays of a touring Shakespearean company. In bringing the action, Triggs' counsel argued that the articles implied that Triggs was an illiterate buffoon who was not professionally qualified to fill his high academic post and that such false factual implications made the articles libelous. The following extract is from one of the articles:

> The Shakespeare legend should be allowed to delude no more. Prof. Triggs * * * can be depended upon to reduce this man Shakespeare to his natural proportions, club the sawdust out of that wax figger of literature and preach to eager multitudes the superiority of the modern playrights, with all the modern improvements * * *. The so-called poetry and imagination visible in this Stratford Charlatan's plays must be torn out, deracinated, the fellow * * * would call it, in his fustian style * * *. If these plays are to be put upon the stage, they must be rewritten; and Prof. Triggs * * * is the destined rewriter, amender and reviser. The sapless, old-fashioned rhetoric must be cut down. The fresh and natural contemporary tongue, pure Triggsian, must be substituted. For example, who can read with patience these tinsel lines? 'Madam, an hour before the worshipped sun peered forth the golden window of the east, a troubled mind drave me to walk abroad.' This must be translated into Triggsian * * * somewhat like this: 'Say, lady, an hour before sun-up I was feeling wormy and took a walk around the block' * * *. Here is more Shakespearian rubbish:
>
> 'O, she doth teach the torches to burn bright!
>
> Her beauty hangs upon the cheek of night,
>
> As a rich jewel in an Ethiop's ear.'
>
> How much more forcible in clear, concise Triggsian: 'Say, she's a peach! A bird!' * * * Hear 'Pop' Capulet drivel: 'Go to, go to, You are a saucy boy!' In the Oscar * * * dialect, this is this: 'Come off, kid. You're too fresh.' * * * Compare the dropsical hifalutin:
>
> 'Night's candles are burnt out, and jocund day
>
> Stands tiptoe on the misty mountain's tops,'
>
> with the time-saving Triggsian version: 'I hear the milkman.' * * *
>
> The downfall of Shakespeare is only a matter of time and Triggs.

179 N.Y. at 148–50, 71 N.E. at 740–41. The New York Court of Appeals held that Triggs stated a good cause of action for libel but focused only on the ridicule. The court seemingly held that the ridicule alone made out the libel in the circumstances of the case before it.

3. Relying on cases like *Burton* and *Triggs,* the late Dean Prosser proposed adding to the *Restatement (Second)* a new section providing that "[a] defamatory communication may consist of words or other matter which ridicule another." *Restatement (Second) of Torts* § 567A (Tent.Draft No. 11, 1965). This provision was also included in Tentative Draft No. 20, 1974. In adding the section on ridicule Prosser was building on *Restatement of Torts* § 566, which provided that "[a] defamatory communication may consist of a

statement of opinion based upon facts known or assumed by both parties to the communication," and which it was proposed to retain in the *Restatement (Second)*. In illustrating § 566, the *Restatement* gave as an example a political speech in which "A * * * accurately relates certain conduct of his opponent blocking reform measures advocated by A. In the course of his argument, A declares that any person who would so conduct himself is no better than a murderer." The *Restatement* concluded that A has defamed his opponent. In preparing for the *Restatement (Second)* the illustration was changed to be a discussion involving the accurate description of a neighbor's abuse of his wife and followed by the "no better than a murderer" characterization. In reaching these conclusions on defamatory opinions on known facts, the American Law Institute glossed over two problems. The first is that there was only sparse case support for the position and no consideration was given to free speech considerations. English law seems to have been more solicitous of the defendant's freedom of speech. *See* Slim v. Daily Telegraph, [1968] 2 Q.B. 157, 2 W.L.R. 599, 1 All E.R. 497 (C.A.). *See also* A. Goodhart, *Restatement of the Law of Torts, Volume III: A Comparison Between American and English Law,* 89 U.Pa.L.Rev. 265, 273–84 (1944). The second, and conceptually more difficult one, is that, *contra* Hand J., in the *Burton* case, *Restatement of Torts* § 558 states that "[t]o create liability for defamation there must be an unprivileged publication of *false* and defamatory matter." (Emphasis supplied). An attempt, in May 1974, to delete the proposed §§ 566 and 567A from the *Restatement (Second)* failed. In June 1974, however, Gertz v. Robert Welch, Inc., 418 U.S. 323, 94 S.Ct. 2997, 41 L.Ed.2d 789 (1974), reprinted *infra,* p. 592, made it clear that the mere expression of opinion could not be the subject of an action for defamation and the provisions in question were dropped from the *Restatement (Second)*. The controversy and the issues are discussed in G. Christie, *Defamatory Opinions and the Restatement (Second) of Torts,* 75 Mich.L.Rev. 1621 (1977). *See also* Note, *Fact and Opinion After* Gertz v. Robert Welch, Inc.: *The Evolution of a Privilege,* 34 Rutgers L.Rev. 81 (1981). Actually distinguishing between what is fact and what is opinion can often be very difficult. We will address that question in note 7, p. 609, *infra*, following the presentation of the *Gertz* case.

4. The controversy noted above may have in part been influenced by what was once the fairly common practice of defendants, in defamation actions brought by well-known people against newspaper and other media defendants, of making the so-called "rolled-up plea" of "truth and fair comment." In most jurisdictions, the fair comment defense was only available if there were no misstatements of fact in the defendants' statements about the plaintiff. The leading case was Post Publishing Co. v. Hallam, 59 Fed. 530 (6th Cir.1893) (per Taft, J.), although there was a minority, as we shall see, prepared to excuse good-faith misstatements of fact at least in the context of political campaigns. *See* Coleman v. MacLennan, 78 Kan. 711, 98 P. 281 (1908). The recognition of the relevancy of a fair comment defense in a context in which there are no misstatements of fact suggests that, without the defense, some expressions of opinion or instances of ridicule might be actionable merely qua opinion or ridicule but that the courts will protect such material if the opinion or ridicule does not go too far. It was sometimes said that, to be fair, the comment had to have some basis in fact and be the

"honest" opinion of the critic and not published solely to harm the plaintiff. Although the issue of fair comment could be raised in an action brought by a public figure or official whose public life was being criticized, it most often figured in actions brought by artists, authors, and musical performers who were angry at the criticisms of their work published by the media. In point of fact, there are very few cases in which a defendant was held liable for expressing a derogatory opinion in the absence of there being a false implication of fact in the opinion,[2] and fewer still in which the comment was held to be "unfair." When literary, musical, or artistic endeavors were concerned some very biting criticism was routinely held non-actionable. In Cherry v. Des Moines Leader, 114 Iowa 298, 86 N.W. 323 (1901), the following review by a music critic of a group called the Cherry Sisters was held not to be actionable.

> Effie is an old jade of 50 summers, Jessie a friskie filly of 40, and Addie, the flower of the family, a capering monstrosity of 35. Their long skinny arms, equipped with talons at the extremities, swung mechanically, and anon waved frantically at the suffering audience. The mouths of their rancid features opened like caverns, and sounds like the wailings of damned souls issued therefrom. They pranced around the stage with a motion that suggested a cross between the danse du ventre and a fox trot,—strange creatures with painted faces and hideous mien. Effie is spavined, Addie is string halt, and Jessie, the only one who showed her stockings, has legs with calves as classic in their outlines as the curves of a broom handle.

5. We have already seen, in the previous chapter, that public officials and public figures cannot recover for ridicule or the expression of offensive and derogatory opinions by alleging that the defendant has, by his outrageous verbal conduct, intentionally inflicted severe emotional distress. *See* Hustler Magazine v. Falwell, 485 U.S. 46, 108 S.Ct. 876, 99 L.Ed.2d 41 (1988), reprinted at p. 465, *supra*.

FAWCETT PUBLICATIONS, INC. v. MORRIS

Supreme Court of Oklahoma, 1962.
377 P.2d 42, *cert. denied,* 376 U.S. 513, 84 S.Ct. 964, 11 L.Ed.2d 968.

JACKSON, JUSTICE.

In the trial court, plaintiff Dennit Morris sued Fawcett Publications, Inc., the publisher of "True" Magazine, and Mid–Continent News Company, its distributor, for damages for libel. The suit grew out of an article in a 1958 issue of "True" Magazine entitled "The Pill That Can Kill Sports", concerning the use of amphetamine and other similar drugs by athletes throughout the country.

Plaintiff alleged in his petition that he was a member of the 1956 Oklahoma University football team; that the article imputed to him a crime against the laws of the state of Oklahoma and was libelous per se;

2. For example, unless one is commenting on facts known to all parties to the conversation if one says "in my opinion, *X* is a thief" one is implying that he knows of facts which would justify the opinion.

and asked for general damages in the amount of $100,000, and punitive damages in the amount of $50,000.

At the conclusion of the evidence, the trial court instructed the jury to return a verdict against Fawcett, leaving only the amount of the damages for jury determination. Mid–Continent's motion for directed verdict in its favor was sustained.

The jury returned a verdict for plaintiff and against Fawcett in the amount of $75,000 for actual damages.

Fawcett is a foreign corporation without a service agent in this state, and service was had upon Fawcett herein by serving the Secretary of State pursuant to statute. On appeal, Fawcett, for its first proposition, argues that the court had no jurisdiction for the reason that Fawcett was not "doing business" in the state within the meaning of 18 O.S.1961, Sections 1.17 and 472, which authorize service upon the Secretary of State.

From uncontradicted evidence in the record, it appears that Fawcett had contracted with Mid–Continent to distribute its magazines in a portion of the State of Oklahoma. The "territory" is not described in the contract, and is left for all practical purposes to the discretion of Fawcett. Magazines were to be forwarded to Mid–Continent without specific orders, in amounts entirely within the discretion of Fawcett. Mid–Continent agreed to distribute not only the magazines and books named in the contract, but all "other matter" which Fawcett might choose to forward. All prices, sales dates and release dates were to be fixed by Fawcett and were subject to change at any time by Fawcett. Mid–Continent agreed to keep dealer records acceptable to Fawcett, showing "initial distribution, re-orders, pickups, returns and net sales". Provision was made for "returns", and credit thereon, and Mid–Continent agreed to dispose of unsold copies in any manner Fawcett should direct. Mid–Continent agreed to distribute to its retail dealers all "advertising, dealers' helps, posters, circulars, and other material" which Fawcett chose to supply. It agreed to furnish Fawcett a complete list of its dealers, showing address and line of business, and showing each dealer's "draw" of each of Fawcett's magazines, publications and other matter. The contract was for 10 years, but could be terminated by either party "at any time with or without cause by giving ten (10) days written notice" to the other party.

Fawcett also employed a "traveling representative" whose duty it was to call on both wholesalers and retailers, to "check up" on the manner of distribution, display and sale of Fawcett's publications and other matter. * * *

* * *

Considering the terms of the contract, and the activities of Fawcett's "traveling representative", we are forced to the conclusion that for all practical purposes Mid–Continent was little more than a mere conduit through which Fawcett exercised its own free and unhampered discretion as to all pertinent details of the business. Such being the case, * * *

Fawcett was doing business in Oklahoma within the meaning of 18 O.S.1961 §§ 1.17 and 472. It follows that service upon the Secretary of State was authorized in this case, and that the court had jurisdiction of the defendant so served. Defendant's first proposition is therefore without merit.

The remaining propositions urged on appeal go to the merits of the case, and we therefore summarize the alleged libelous publication. The article is approximately seven full pages in length; was studiously prepared after what purports to be painstaking research; and starts at pages 44 and 45 of the magazine. Across the center of pages 44 and 45, we find in large letters and bold type the following:

"The Pill That Can Kill Sports".

In the upper left hand corner of page 44 are these words: "Simply by using a phony letterhead, the author purchased by mail enough drugs to hop up over 100 football teams." Immediately under this statement is the following: "A SHOCKING REPORT:", which is emphasized by a red line underneath. In the middle of pages 44 and 45 is a picture of five bottles of pills; the sixth bottle is of the shape and type commonly used for hypodermic needle injections; and there are two hypodermic needles. In the upper right hand corner of page 45 is found the following:

> "You can go to jail for selling amphetamine to a truck driver or injecting it into a racehorse, yet this same drug is being handed out to high school and college athletes all over the country."

In the lower half of page 45, and flowing over onto page 44, is pictured a heavily loaded dual-wheeled truck bearing the sign or label on its side, "DOPE". In the body of the truck are two individuals labeled "Avarice" and "Ignorance" shovelling out dope to athletes, including football players, who are running behind the truck and catching the pills. Another person is handing out pills to a football player from the cab of the truck. Above the engine of the truck are these words: "Victory at any Cost".

Across the center of pages 46 and 47 is a picture of a stable with the heads of horses appearing from the windows. In front of the horses are what appear to be uniformed officials and trainers. Underneath this picture is printed the following: "Racehorses are scrupulously guarded against doping violations, yet the same drugs are given freely to young athletes."

While the article is too lengthy to be quoted, a few excerpts which appear to be fairly representative of the entire article are quoted as follows:

> "Definite proof that doping was a common practice came on September 13, 1956, when I received this report from the USOA's attorney, John T. McGovern. 'I have communicated with record executives of Olympic, university, A.A.U. organizations, athletic directors and others * * * At every point of contact I was informed * * * that

substantially the entire population in schools and colleges have been using this type drug * * * '.

* * *

"The *amphetamines are administered to athletes by* hypodermic injection, *nasal spray,* or in tablets or capsules, but pills are the most common form, at least according to those athletic figures who are willing to talk.

* * *

"There is, however, one statistic which is available, and which strongly indicates that consumption is rapidly increasing. Recently *I was able to buy 30 cc.'s of dextroamphetamine sulphate for 95 cents.* This amount—*enough to hop up an entire football team*—cost three times this much a few years ago. Also, I was able to buy a thousand amphetamine pills for $1.40 less than a third of the 1954 price. When sales go up, prices go down.

"Speaking of football teams, during the 1956 season, *while Oklahoma was increasing its sensational victory streak,* several *physicians observed Oklahoma players being sprayed in the nostrils with an atomizer. And during a televised game, a close-up showed Oklahoma spray jobs to the nation.* 'Ten years ago,' Dr. Howe observed acidly, 'when that was done to a horse, the case went to court. Medically, there is no reason for such treatment. If *players* need therapy, they shouldn't be on the field.'

* * *

"*The 'lifter'* (amphetamine user) can and *does become heroic, boisterous, pugnacious, or vicious.*

* * *

"*These results are what make amphetamines useful in the field of athletics.* They promote aggression, increase the competitive spirit, and work the same as the epinephrine (adrenalin) produced in your body. The adrenal cortex, however, is wiser than victory-hungry coaches and athletes, * * *." (Emphasis supplied.)

The article refers to several nationally known brutal crimes as being committed by users of amphetamine.

Plaintiff's evidence at the trial shows that the substance administered to Oklahoma players and members of the 1956 football team was "spirits of peppermint", a harmless substance used for the relief of "cotton mouth", or dryness of mouth, resulting from prolonged or extreme physical exertion; that plaintiff did not use amphetamine or any other narcotic drug, and there was no evidence that any other member of the team used amphetamine or narcotic drugs.

Plaintiff's evidence further shows that plaintiff was fullback on the alternate squad of the 1956 football team; that he played in all games during the 1956 season, except two, when he was "side-lined" because of injuries; that the team won all ten regular games during the season and won the Bowl game at the end of the season in Miami, Florida; that plaintiff played in the Bowl game; that plaintiff was a sophomore in 1956 and continued to play on the team in 1957 and 1958; and that he was a member of the University baseball team while at the university. That there were sixty or seventy members of the team in 1956.

Plaintiff's evidence further shows that many people asked plaintiff about the article in True, beginning shortly after its publication, and continuing until shortly before trial.

* * *

Having concluded that the article is defamatory and libelous on its face we think it follows that the article is *libelous per se.* * * *

* * *

The additional and final legal argument presented under Fawcett's second proposition is that a defamatory publication concerning a large group is not libelous per se as to an unnamed member of that group. In this connection it appears that the courts have generally held that defamatory words used broadly in respect to a large class or group will not support a libel action by an individual member of the group. 70 A.L.R.2d 1382. This doctrine appears to stem from the early decision of Sumner v. Buel, 12 Johns 475 (New York 1815), wherein the court concluded that a *civil* action would not lie for a libelous publication against all of the nine officers of three named rifle companies, because of the uncertainty as to who was libeled. In that case the court said:

> "* * * A writing which inveighs against mankind in general, or against a particular order of men, is no libel, nor is it even indictable. It must descend to particulars and individuals, to make it a libel. (3 Salk. 224, 1 Ld.Raym. 486)."

We have examined the cited [English] case, * * * In our examination of the case * * * it is apparent that it was a criminal case, [and] * * * it appears * * * that the reason why the indictment was set aside was because the jurors were unable from the proof to determine who had been libeled. * * *

Thus it is quite apparent that the case is not authority for the proposition that plaintiff in a suit based upon a libelous publication against nine identifiable officers of three named rifle companies could not recover in a libel action. In 34 Columbia Law Review, beginning at page 1332, is a very thorough and studiously prepared article entitled "Liability for Defamation of a Group." In the article it is said of Sumner v. Buel, supra, that "the misinterpretation of a dictum in an early English criminal libel case (King v. Alme, supra) gave rise to the doctrine that because of the absence of specific mention of any person, no action would lie for a statement of this nature."

* * *

From our examination of the authorities we have reached the conclusion that the English courts have never barred recovery in Group libel cases unless the group is extremely large. In Ortenberg v. Plamondon et al., Quebec Court of Appeals, 35 Can. Law Times 262, American Annotated Cases, Ann.Cas.1915C, Page 347, it was held that a member of the Jewish race in Quebec, consisting of 75 families out of a total city population of 80,000 people, could maintain an action of defamation of the entire group even though he was not assailed individually, but only as a member of the group.

* * *

While there is substantial precedent from other jurisdictions to the effect that a member of a "large group" may not recover in an individual action for a libelous publication unless he is referred to personally, we have found no substantial reason why *size* alone should be conclusive. We are not inclined to follow such a rule where, as here, the complaining member of the group is as well known and identified in connection with the group as was the plaintiff in this case. * * *

We hold, in answer to Fawcett's second proposition, that since the article is libelous on its face without the aid of extrinsic facts to make it so, it is libelous per se; that the article libels every member of the team, including the plaintiff, although he was not specifically named therein; that the average lay reader who was familiar with the team, and its members, would necessarily believe that the regular players, including the plaintiff, were using an amphetamine spray as set forth in the article; that the article strongly suggests that the use of amphetamine was criminal; and that plaintiff has sufficiently established his identity as one of those libeled by the publication.

In reaching the conclusion that plaintiff has established his identity in the mind of the average lay reader as one of those libeled, we are mindful that a full-back on the alternate squad of a university team who has played in nine out of eleven all victorious games in one season will not be overlooked by those who were familiar with the team, and the contribution made by its regular players. It should be remembered that plaintiff was a constant player, and not a part of the "changing" element of that group.

* * *

The judgment in favor of plaintiff and against Fawcett Publications, Inc., is affirmed; and the action of the trial court in sustaining the motion for directed verdict and entering judgment for the defendant, Mid–Continent News Company, is also affirmed.

NOTES

1. The case was decided by a divided court. Halley, J., dissented on the ground that the article was not libelous per se of Morris. Oklahoma is one of the states, now most probably a minority, that despite the *Hinsdale* case, p. 496, *supra,* and *Restatement (Second) of Torts* § 569 still retain a libel per se/libel per quod distinction. *See* Akins v. Altus Newspapers, Inc., 609 P.2d 1263 (Okl.1977), *as modified on denial of rehearing* (1980). Three other judges concurred in part and dissented in part in the *Morris* case, but published no opinion so that, given the many issues in the case, it is not clear what they dissented to.

2. How many members of the 1956 Oklahoma University football team could have brought an action? Morris seems to be the only one who actually did, but if the entire team brought an action and were sustained in the contention that the article libelled them, the damages would be very great indeed. Is this an argument for restricting the ability of members of a group to bring an action for statements that defame the group to which they belong? For a discussion of this general subject, *see* Note, *Group Defamation: Five Guiding Factors*, 64 Tex.L.Rev. 591 (1985).

3. In Owens v. Clark, 154 Okl. 108, 6 P.2d 755 (1931), discussed in an omitted portion of the *Morris* case, "certain members" of the Oklahoma Supreme Court were accused of making the Oklahoma courts an instrument for "looting" citizens of their property. It was held, by a special court, that the statement did not defame each of the nine members of the court. In the early case of Foxcroft v. Lacy, Hob. 89, 80 Eng.Rep. 239 (Ex.Ch.1613), the defendant had said, of seventeen men involved as defendants in a conspiracy suit in Star Chamber, that "[t]hese defendants are those that helped to murder Henry Farrar." It was held that each of the seventeen had been defamed.

4. It has been said that English law has never adequately found a means of handling group defamation. *See* Salmond & Heuston, Torts 145, n. 71 (21st ed. by R. Heuston and R. Buckley, 1996). The editor cites "a curious unreported case in which a newspaper thought it prudent to settle an action brought by 134 valuers of the London County Council." The leading modern English case is Knuppfer v. London Express Newspaper, Ltd., [1944] A.C. 116. In that case, the defendant newspaper had published an article accusing "an emigre group called * * * [the] Young Russia" party of being "quislings on whom Hitler flatters himself he can build a pro-German movement within the Soviet Union." The group, founded in France, and at the time headquartered in the United States, had some two thousand members. There were 24 members in Great Britain. The plaintiff was the British representative of the party. The House of Lords held, as a matter of law, that the article could not be interpreted as referring to the plaintiff. Lord Porter asked:

> Can an individual sue in respect of words which are defamatory of a body or class of persons generally? The answer as a rule must be 'No,' but the inquiry is really a wider one and is governed by no rule of thumb. The

> true question always is: 'Was the individual, or were the individuals, bringing the action personally pointed to by the words complained of?'

Id. at 124. Several of their lordships agreed that a charge that "all lawyers were thieves" was not actionable by any lawyers but mere "vulgar generalizations." But Lord Porter allowed that "I can imagine it being said that each member of a body, however large, was defamed where the libel consisted in the assertion that no one of the members of the community was elected as a member unless he had committed a murder."

5. Civil remedies in cases like Ortenberg v. Plamondon, 35 Can. Law Times 262, 37 Am. & Eng.Ann. Cases (1915c) 347 (1914) present difficulties. In theory in England and some American jurisdictions, group defamation could be handled by public prosecution for criminal libel. As a practical matter this is hardly an effective remedy. A British Government Report states:

> It is also a criminal libel to libel any sect, company, or class if it is proved that the object is to excite the hatred of the public against the class libelled. As far as we know there has been no prosecution for this offense this century and probably today any proceedings resulting from incitement to racial hatred would be taken under the Race Relations legislation.

Report of the Committee on Defamation, Cmd. 5909, at & 434(b) (1975).

In Beauharnais v. Illinois, 343 U.S. 250, 72 S.Ct. 725, 96 L.Ed. 919 (1952), an Illinois statute prohibiting the publishing of any publication portraying "depravity, criminality, unchastity, or lack of virtue of a class of citizens of any race, color, creed or religion" and which exposes such citizens "to contempt, derision or obloquy or which is productive of breach of the peace or riots" was applied to a scurrilous leaflet attacking the "encroachment, harassment and invasion of white people * * * by the Negro," etc. In upholding the conviction, the Court, per Frankfurter, J., relied on Chaplinsky v. New Hampshire, 315 U.S. 568, 62 S.Ct. 766, 86 L.Ed. 1031 (1942), discussed in the previous chapter at p. 479, which permitted a person to be prosecuted for uttering "fighting words," *i.e.* words calculated to incite an immediate breach of the peace. Justices Black, Douglas, Jackson, and Reed dissented in *Beauharnais.* Collin v. Smith, 578 F.2d 1197 (7th Cir.1978), *cert. denied* 439 U.S. 916, 99 S.Ct. 291, 58 L.Ed.2d 264, in which the Seventh Circuit affirmed a district court decision, *inter alia,* ruling unconstitutional an ordinance of Skokie, Illinois prohibiting the "dissemination of any materials * * * which promotes or incites hatred against persons by reason of their race, national origin, or religion, and is intended to do so * * *," seems, however, clearly inconsistent with *Beauharnais* and with any attempt, in a jurisdiction recognizing common law crimes, to prosecute on a criminal libel basis. The result in *Colin v. Smith* would also seem to be compelled by Brandenburg v. Ohio, 395 U.S. 444, 89 S.Ct. 1827, 23 L.Ed.2d 430 (1969) which held that, to be subject to criminal prosecution, the challenged speech must advocate "imminent lawless action." The result in the Skokie litigation is not of course universally applauded. K. Lasson has criticized the decision as well as the conclusions which the current editors draw from that litigation in *Racial Defamation as Free Speech: Abusing the First Amendment*, 17 Colum.Hum.Rts.L.Rev. 11 (1985); *Group Libel versus Free Speech: When Big*

Brother Should *Butt In*, 23 Duquesne L.Rev. 77 (1984). The limitations that the first amendment imposes upon attempts to punish inflammatory and scurrilous attacks on distinct classes of citizens are of course much too large and important subjects to be capable of adequate treatment in a course on torts. One may still wonder, however, whether the attempt to deal with scurrilous and offensive verbal attacks on discrete classes of citizens through the mechanism of criminal libel laws may not be an instance of the cure being worse than the disease.

6. The most frequently cited case on group defamation is Neiman–Marcus v. Lait, 13 F.R.D. 311 (S.D.N.Y.1952). In a book called "U.S.A. Confidential," the authors talked of "whores" or "call girls" or "party girls." They went on to say that "*some* Neiman models are call girls" commanding a price of "a hundred bucks a night." (Emphasis supplied). They then proceeded: "The salesgirls are good, too—pretty and often much cheaper—twenty bucks on average." They continued by discussing the men's store at Neiman's. "You wonder how all the faggots got to the wild and wooly. You thought those with talent ended up in New York or Hollywood and the plodders got government jobs in Washington. Then you learn the nucleus of the Dallas fairy colony is composed of many Neiman dress and millinery designers imported from New York and Paris, who sent for their boy friends when the men's store expanded. Now *most* of the sales staff are fairies, too." (Emphasis supplied). On this aspect of the case the plaintiffs fell into three classes (a) all nine of the models at the store as of the time of publication of the book; (b) fifteen of the twenty-five salesmen on behalf of themselves and of the class; and (c) thirty saleswomen out of 382, again suing on behalf of themselves and of the class. The court held that the models and salesmen had a cause of action, even though the authors did not say that all of them engaged in the activities charged, but that none of the saleswomen did. Even though all were seemingly charged, the group was too big. The court felt that "no reasonable man would take the writers seriously and conclude from the publication a reference to any individual saleswoman."

7. More recent cases dealing with group defamation include: Viola v. A & E Television Networks, 433 F.Supp.2d 613 (W.D.Pa. 2006), which involved an unsuccessful attempt by a priest, on behalf of the entire Roman Catholic Church, to bring an action against the producers of a TV program about the search for the real-life evidence on which the novel, *The Da Vinci Code,* had purportedly been based; and Berry v. Safer, 32 Media L.Rep. 2057 (S.D. Miss. 2004), an unsuccessful action based on the alleged defamation of juries in Jefferson County, Mississippi by the suggestion in the CBS program, *60 Minutes,* that these juries were biased in actions against big, out-of-state corporations brought by local people. In an attempt to create some certainty, some commentators have suggested that the so-called "25–member rule" derived from the *Nieman–Marcus* case should be the starting point of the analysis. *See* N. Stern, *The Certainty Principle as Justification for the Group Defamation Rule*, 40 Ariz. St. L.J. 951 (2008); J. King, *Reference to the Plaintiff Requirement in Defamatory Statements Directed at Groups*, 35 Wake Forest L.Rev. 343 (2000).

B. COMMON-LAW DEFENSES

CRANE v. NEW YORK WORLD TELEGRAM CORP.

Court of Appeals of New York, 1955.
308 N.Y. 470, 126 N.E.2d 753.

FULD, JUDGE.

On December 6, 1951, there appeared in a column of The *NEW YORK WORLD–TELEGRAM AND THE SUN,* a newspaper of wide daily circulation, this item:

> " 'John Crane, former president of the UFA now under indictment, isn't waiting for his own legal developments. Meanwhile his lawyers are launching a $,$$$,$$$ defamation suit.' "

The present action for libel followed; the individual defendant is the columnist who wrote the piece, the corporate defendant, the owner and publisher of the paper. The answer which defendants interposed includes two separate defenses, one complete, the other partial, both based on the premise and hypothesis that the charge is true in that plaintiff, though never "indicted" by a grand jury, had been accused of a number of indictable crimes by various people. By the motion under consideration, an order is sought striking both defenses as insufficient in law.

Plaintiff alleges that the publication was false and defamatory, that defendants knew or could have ascertained its falsity by the exercise of reasonable care and that they were guilty of "actual malice and wrongfully and wilfully intended to injure the plaintiff." Claiming, among other things, great injury to credit and reputation and an inability to secure or retain employment, he asks damages of $100,000.

Defendants deny all these allegations, except that of publication, and allege two separate defenses. The first of these purports to establish the truth of the publication. While nowhere stating that plaintiff was indicted by a grand jury—and, concededly, he never was—it asserts, nevertheless, that he was "under indictment" in an alleged nonlegal sense of that term; more specifically, it recites that he had been accused of various crimes by private individuals and was, in fact, guilty of those crimes. In support of the publication's truth under such a construction, it sets forth in considerable detail the substance of the New York City Fire Department scandals and investigations of 1950–1951, in which plaintiff, then president of an association of firemen, and others are depicted as playing a prominent part.

Little purpose would be served by repeating these allegations at any length. It is enough to observe that—while many of them touch on the derelictions of other firemen and relate to matters in which it is not clear that plaintiff was involved—it is recited that plaintiff misappropriated proceeds from the sale of tickets to the annual Firemen's Balls; that he had been accused of criminal activity by fellow firemen and others; and that, in testifying before a New York County grand jury and a committee of the United States Senate, he had admitted, without waiving immunity, facts which established his guilt of larceny and bribery.

* * *

The court at Special Term granted plaintiff's motion, directing that both defenses be stricken as insufficient in law, * * * on the ground that they had no relation to the truth of the publication. In the absence of qualifying language, the court said, the term "indictment" could be understood by reasonable people "in only one sense, namely, as a charge by a grand jury of the commission of a crime." The Appellate Division took a different view; it reversed, holding that "indictment" is reasonably susceptible to both the meaning "of an accusation by a grand jury, and of an accusation generally", and that it was for a jury to say in what sense it would be understood by the reader. The appeal is here by permission of the Appellate Division on certified questions.

In our judgment, the publication complained of, when considered in context as it must be, could reasonably be read and interpreted in only one way, that is, as charging that plaintiff had been indicted by the grand jury for some crime. * * * There can be no question that the "ordinary meaning" of the term "indictment" is that of the legal process, usually before a grand jury, whereby a person is formally charged with crime and a criminal prosecution begun. * * *

If, as defendants claim, the word permits of a looser, a highly rhetorical, use to signify an accusation by private persons, that sense of the term is so rare, as contrasted with the legal process of indictment, that no reader would so understand or accept it without some qualifying language to indicate that the ordinary meaning was not intended. An example would be a statement that John Doe stands "indicted in the court of public opinion." * * *

* * *

* * * A plea of truth as justification must be as broad as the alleged libel and must establish the truth of the precise charge therein made. * * *

Defendants contend, however, that, even though the complete defense be held insufficient, its allegations may properly be repeated in their entirety in the second numbered defense, as a partial defense in mitigation of damages, when coupled with the further allegations that "the facts" were widely known, that plaintiff's general reputation was bad, and that all such matters were known to defendants, relied upon by them and made them believe in the truth of the item in question. Before proceeding to a consideration of that defense, we examine some of the relevant principles governing damages in libel actions, as well as their mitigation or reduction by the proof of acts which fall short of those charged in the libel.

* * * Well settled is the basic rule that the amount of plaintiff's recovery may be reduced by proof of facts "tending but failing to prove the truth" of the libel's charge. * * * That proof is relevant in mitigation of punitive damages, for it may negative actual malice by showing that defendant, though mistaken, had reasonable grounds for belief in the truth of the charge contained in the publication. * * * And, turning to compensatory damages, such evidence may serve to reduce them as well, * * * on the theory that, if the actual facts "gave some color of verity to the statements contained in the published article, plaintiff would not be entitled to receive the same damages as if his reputation was beyond unfavorable criticism or comment." * * * But, of necessity, the facts that go to make up a partial defense in mitigation and reduction must *tend to prove the truth of the precise charge* made by the publication. * * *

In the case before us, however, the facts alleged are entirely unrelated to the truth of the charge that plaintiff had been indicted; they tend at most to prove that plaintiff had engaged in criminal activity and had been accused of wrong-doing by his fellow firemen. * * *

The situation might be different had defendants acknowledged that they had charged plaintiff with having been indicted and then proceeded to claim that they believed that to be true because plaintiff had been before the grand jury and had testified to his commission of crime. In such a case, those facts would tend, perhaps, toward proof of a belief in the charge actually made, but that is not this case. Here, by their very pleading, defendants seek to give a different and broader meaning to the published charge than reason permits. They do not even claim that they believed that plaintiff had been indicted * * *.

Defendants advance the additional contention that the pleading should be upheld and sustained, even if it does not tend to prove truth, because *some* of the facts alleged—as to particular acts of misconduct and bad reputation—may, nevertheless, be relevant to negative actual malice or reduce the value of plaintiff's injured reputation. Those allegations, the argument runs, may be used for that purpose irrespective of the form in which they are pleaded * * *.

Considerable doubt exists whether any of the matter pleaded is proper, for the rule is clear that, while defendant may offer proof of plaintiff's bad general reputation prior to the publication, to reduce the value of the injured interest, he may not plead or prove for that purpose "specific acts, or instances, of plaintiff's misconduct" having no connection with the charge of the libel. * * * Such specific misconduct, we have seen, may be admitted only if it also tends but fails to prove the truth of the libel's charge. * * *

However, regardless of what facts defendants might properly plead and prove, we may not approve the kind of pleading embodied in the second separate defense.

The entire thrust and purport of that defense is to establish defendants' belief in the truth of a different charge than the one made by the writing. Of the specific instances of misconduct alleged, which amount almost to a complete history of the Fire Department scandals, a considerable proportion would be inadmissible in evidence, as conclusory, irrelevant or prejudicial. The same is true of the list of newspaper headlines appended to the answer. Some of the items refer to the derelictions of fellow firemen with no suggestion that plaintiff was involved, while others purport to establish his guilt of divers acts on the basis of mere conjecture and rumor. * * * These allegations are certainly improper, and it is unthinkable that a defense, otherwise insufficient, should be saved and upheld by the device of simply adding a recital that plaintiff "enjoyed" a bad general reputation.[1]

* * *

We are not here deciding what facts defendants may adduce and prove in reduction of compensatory damages under the general denial, and nothing that we now say is to be taken as precluding defendants from seeking to amend their answer so as to plead properly matters in reduction of compensatory damages or in mitigation of those that are punitive in character. Nor are we suggesting that a partial defense must be pleaded in any particular form or that its purpose must be labeled. * * * All that we are holding is that the defense, aimed at establishing the truth of a charge different from that made in the publication, cannot stand. And it may not be saved by virtue of the fact that some of the items alleged might be pleaded properly in a different defense or that some of them might be proved at the trial.

* * *

Order reversed, etc.

NOTES

1. *Jennings v. Telegram–Tribune Co.* 164 Cal.App.3d 119, 210 Cal.Rptr. 485 (1985) involved an action brought by a locally prominent architect against the San Louis Obispo Telegram–Tribune. Plaintiff had pleaded no contest to " 'willfully and knowingly' failing to file federal income tax returns" for two calendar years. The defendant newspaper published a number of brief articles on plaintiff's difficulties. Plaintiff claimed that these articles contained a number of false and defamatory statements including statements that he had been "convicted of tax fraud" and that he had "pleaded no contest to income tax evasion charges." It was held that the statements in question were substantially fair and true reports of the criminal proceedings in which the plaintiff had been involved. Is *Jennings* inconsistent with *Crane*?

2. At common law truth was an affirmative defense which had to be raised and proved by the defendant. If the defamation consisted of charging the plaintiff with criminal conduct, the defense of truth had to be established only by the ordinary civil preponderance of the evidence standard. *See*

1. Proof of bad reputation is, of course, admissible under the general denial. * * *

Restatement (Second) of Torts § 581A, Comment *f*. Before the United States Supreme Court imposed constitutional limitations on the states' ability to formulate their own law of defamation in some states truth was only a complete defense if it was uttered without "malicious motives." *See* Johnson v. Johnson, 654 A.2d 1212 (R.I. 1995) (Ex-husband called his ex-wife, who was admittedly an extremely promiscuous person, a "whore" in a crowded restaurant and the court refused to consider any constitutional issues because they had not been raised at the trial stage.)

3. While one cannot justify a statement charging the plaintiff with having committed armed robbery by showing that the plaintiff has been convicted of embezzlement, slight discrepancies are permitted. For example, if, in *Crane,* the defendant had been able to show that criminal charges had been filed against the plaintiff by way of presentment, it probably would have succeeded in establishing the substantial truth of its charge that the plaintiff had been indicted.

4. In the light of the Supreme Court's injection of constitutional considerations into the law of defamation, a matter which we shall consider in the last section of this chapter, it is now undoubtedly part of the plaintiff's affirmative case in most, and perhaps even in all, defamation actions to establish the falsity of the defendant's allegedly defamatory statements. We shall discuss this specific question again at p. 634 *infra*.

LEE v. PAULSEN

Supreme Court of Oregon, 1975.
273 Or. 103, 539 P.2d 1079.

DENECKE, JUSTICE.

The plaintiff teacher brought this defamation action against the defendants who are school officials and school board members. The trial court granted defendants' motion for an involuntary nonsuit upon the ground that the publication was absolutely privileged.

The plaintiff was a nontenured teacher. He was notified his contract was not going to be renewed. Plaintiff's attorney wrote the school district's attorney asking to be provided with the specific reasons for the nonrenewal of the contract and for a public hearing. The district's attorney replied by letter furnishing the specific reasons. He further stated that no evidence would be provided by the district at the hearing and no school officials or board members could be questioned. Plaintiff read this letter.

At the public hearing or meeting the plaintiff's attorney requested that the reasons, as contained in the letter sent to him, be stated by the board. The statements were made and this publication is charged as defamation. We will assume for the purposes of this decision that the publication is defamatory.

The cases and scholars agree that there is an absolute privilege for publications that are consented to. * * *

It should be remembered that usually the question of whether or not a defamatory statement is privileged, either absolutely or conditionally, depends upon the balance that the court strikes between competing interests. In Ramstead v. Morgan, 219 Or. 383, 387, 347 P.2d 594 (1959), we held the communication involved was absolutely privileged because the relationship occasioning the communication was so important that the law freed the publishing party from liability regardless of the fact that the publishing party might use the occasion to publish defamatory and malicious statements. The important interest in *Ramstead* was having citizens communicate with the organized Bar concerning possible misconduct of attorneys. We were of the opinion that this interest was so important that the communication should be absolutely privileged.

* * *

In the consent cases Harper and James point out that no public interest is being served by encouraging publication which is free from the threat of being the subject of a defamation suit.

The reason for the imposition of the privilege when the plaintiff consents or requests the publication "is based upon the unwillingness of the courts to let the plaintiff 'lay the foundation of a lawsuit for his own pecuniary gain.'" Harper and James, supra at 400, quoting from Richardson v. Gunby, 88 Kan. 47, 54, 127 P. 533 (1912).

* * *

Shinglemeyer v. Wright, 124 Mich. 230, 82 N.W. 887, 890 (1900), illustrates this rationale. In a private conversation between the parties the defendant charged the plaintiff with stealing his wheel. Plaintiff called a policeman. When he came she told him that the defendant had accused her of stealing his wheel and, in effect, asked him to hear the defendant's version. Defendant told the officer that the plaintiff had stolen his wheel. Plaintiff brought a slander action based upon the defendant's statement to the officer.

The court held for defendant, stating:

> "In regard to the statement by defendant in the presence of the officer Henry, it was not a publication for which the law gives a remedy. She herself solicited the statement, and sent for the officer for the express purpose of having the defendant repeat the statement in his presence. It would not have been stated to him except by her invitation." * * *

We emphasize that in both the present case and *Shinglemeyer v. Wright,* supra, when the plaintiff requested the publication he or she knew the exact language that would be used in the publication. This knowledge is essential in order for the publication to be absolutely privileged, except in the circumstances present in Christensen v. Marvin, Or., 539 P.2d 1082 decided this date.

* * *

Nelson v. Whitten, 272 F. 135 (E.D.N.Y., 1921) illustrates the opposite circumstances. The plaintiff had been employed by the defendant as master of a vessel. Plaintiff asked defendant for a letter respecting his services. The defendant wrote in part:

> "As to your qualifications as a captain I can say you were an excellent housekeeper. Your knowledge of navigation is exceedingly meager.
>
> "I am so much in doubt as to your loyalty and integrity that I could not conscientiously give a recommendation to any one desiring to employ you." 272 F. at 136.

The letter was published to a third party and plaintiff brought a libel action. The defendant defended upon the ground that the plaintiff had consented. The court held for plaintiff stating, "Because of a request for such statement, plaintiff did not invite defendant to make public anything false and defamatory." 272 F. at 136.

In the present case the plaintiff did invite the defendant to make public a statement which plaintiff believed was false and defamatory. Defendants are absolutely privileged unless the publication falls within an exception to the rule that consent to publication creates an absolute privilege.

Plaintiff claims his case does fall within the exception stated in § 584, Restatement of Torts.

> "The republication of false and defamatory matter of another by one who has previously published it is not privileged although the person defamed in an honest effort to ascertain the source of the original defamatory publication procures the republication." § 584.

The drafters of the Restatement (Second) have recommended that the section be broadened to read:

> "An honest inquiry or investigation by the person defamed to ascertain the existence, source, content or meaning of a defamatory publication is not a defense to an action for its republication by the defamer." Restatement (Second), Torts, Tentative Draft No. 20 (1974) § 584, p. 158.

Assuming that the recommendation made in the Tentative Draft No. 20 correctly states the law, the plaintiff's case does not fall within the exception.

Cases cited by the reporter in Tentative Draft No. 20 in support of § 584 illustrate the intent of the section.

In Thorn v. Moser, 1 Denio (N.Y.) 488 (1845), plaintiff's agent had "heard that the defendant had charged this crime upon the plaintiff." 1 Denio (N.Y.) supra, at 488. He went to the defendant to inquire and defendant repeated the charge. In affirming a judgment for the plaintiff, the court commented: "An attempt by a person who deems himself injured to ascertain truly what slanderous imputations had already been cast upon him, could hardly be allowed to justify their renewal." * * * The agent's inquiry was to verify the existence and learn the content of a defamatory publication.

In Smith v. Dunlop Tire & Rubber Co., 186 S.C. 456, 458, 196 S.E. 174 (1938), one of the defendants stated to the plaintiff and his manager, "By God, I thought you birds were down here getting fat off of Dunlop. Now I know it." The plaintiff said he did not understand. The defendant replied, "you have been stealing." The court held the statement was not privileged. Plaintiff's inquiry was to determine the meaning of a possible defamatory publication.

In the present case, the request to the defendants to read the reasons for failure to renew, as stated in the defendants' letter previously sent plaintiff's attorney, was not "to ascertain the existence, source, content or meaning of a defamatory publication." * * *

Plaintiff contends one purpose in having the reasons read was to get a clarification of the reason, "Unprofessional conduct toward children." That contention cannot be substantiated. The school district's attorney informed the plaintiff and his attorney well before the meeting that the defendants and other school officials would not be open to questioning or offer any further explanation.

It must be remembered that the plaintiff is contending that this reading of the reasons for the defendants' refusal to renew plaintiff, which plaintiff requested, damaged his reputation.

The trial court commented, in regard to plaintiff's attorney requesting the reading of the statement, "you had no thought of setting up for entrapment in a libel suit." As we stated, the reason behind the rule that consent creates an absolute privilege is to prevent a plaintiff from "setting up" a lawsuit. However, it is not essential that the plaintiff in a particular case have that subjective intent. * * *. Affirmed.

NOTES

1. In *Lee v. Paulsen,* the court declared that, for consent to publication to be a defense, the person defamed must be aware of the "exact language that would be used in the publication * * * except in the circumstances present in" Christensen v. Marvin, 273 Or. 97, 539 P.2d 1082 (1975). In that case, decided on the same day as *Lee v. Paulsen,* a school teacher whose contract was not going to be renewed asked the school board for a statement of reasons. Unlike the situation in *Lee,* the plaintiff in *Christensen* did not know the exact language of what the school board would say but she had more than enough reason to know that the reasons would be unflattering. Citing what is now *Restatement (Second) of Torts* § 583, Comment *d* and Illustration *2,* the court held that the plaintiff's consent barred her action.

On the general subject of the pitfalls that the law of defamation may present to those providing employment references *see* Note, *Contracting Around the Law of Defamation and Employment References,* 79 Va.L.Rev. 517 (1993). In an important recent English case, a plaintiff who was unable to bring an action for defamation against a person giving an unfavorable employment reference because of the successful invocation of "qualified privilege", was held to be entitled to bring an action based on a negligence theory against the person providing the reference. Spring v. Guardian Assurance PLC, [1995] 2 A.C. 296, 3 W.L.R. 354, 3 All E.R. 129. Do you think it was wise to treat a negligently given employment reference as just another type of negligent misrepresentation?

The subject of employment references raises many interesting and difficult policy issues. On the one hand, a former employee understandably does not want to be blackballed by a vindictive former employer who can take advantage of the qualified privilege granted to such references. On the other hand, an employer does not want to risk the hassle of having to defend a defamation action by a disgruntled former employee for giving an honest letter of reference. The understandable tendency to give only the most bland or anodyne letters of recommendation not only burdens potential future employers but is also a disservice to the public, particularly when the position for which the applicant is applying is one which deals with the public and even more so when that position requires the exercise of special skills. Interesting articles on the subject include H. Verkerke, *Legal Regulation of Employment Reference Practices,* 65 U. Chi. L.Rev. 115 (1998) and D. Ballam, *Employment References—Speak No Evil, Hear No Evil: A Proposal for Meaningful Reform,* 39 Am. Bus. L.J. 445 (2002).

2. Defenses to defamation actions are classified as either absolute or qualified. Most of the absolute defenses are classified as privileges as are all of the qualified defenses. Most of the absolute defenses or privileges relate to statements made in the course of the participation in or the reporting of official or other public proceedings and will be discussed after the next principal case. We may mention at this stage, however, the absolute privilege, in most jurisdictions, to report suspected criminal conduct to the prosecuting authorities. *See Restatement (Second) of Torts* § 587. The court, in *Lee v. Paulsen,* referred to a case where it had extended the privilege to cover complaints to the "Organized Bar." *See also* Wiener v. Weintraub, 22 N.Y.2d 330, 292 N.Y.S.2d 667, 239 N.E.2d 540 (1968) (bar grievance committee). If the plaintiff has any redress in such situations his remedy would be an action for malicious prosecution, a subject to be discussed in Chapter Ten, *infra.* New York is one of the few states that continues to grant only a qualified privilege to reports furnished to prosecutorial authorities, on the ground that such reports are not part of judicial proceedings. *See* Pecue v. West, 233 N.Y. 316, 135 N.E. 515 (1922); Toker v. Pollak, 44 N.Y.2d 211, 405 N.Y.S.2d 1, 376 N.E.2d 163 (1978). A letter to the President, with copies to other officials, that criticized a prospective appointee to federal office was held not to be absolutely privileged under the right "to petition" clause. McDonald v. Smith, 472 U.S. 479, 105 S.Ct. 2787, 86 L.Ed.2d 384 (1985).

Of the absolute defenses available in defamation actions concerning private matters, as we have seen, two, truth and consent, are usually not classified as privileges. For practical purposes, it makes little difference whether an absolute defense is classified as a privilege or not; the practical consequences are the same. One absolute defense that is classified as a privilege and is also available in litigation not involving public matters concerns inter-spousal communications. Arguably, before the married women's property acts of the nineteenth century, it was also possible to argue that inter-spousal communication was not a publication, but that analytical approach is clearly not available today.

3. At common law a qualified privilege could be defeated by a showing of malice. One way of showing malice is by demonstrating that the speaker's *dominant* motive in uttering the defamatory statement was not to protect the interest which underlies the granting of the privilege but rather to hurt the plaintiff. Another way is by establishing excessive publication. For example, if one person asks another for information about the character of her fiance, the respondent's statements to her may be privileged but publication of the statement to the mutual friends of the parties would clearly be excessive, that is beyond the purposes for which the privilege was created. *See Restatement (Second) of Torts* § 604. The plaintiff bears the burden of showing that the defendant acted with malice. *See* Lundquist v. Reusser, 7 Cal.4th 1193, 875 P.2d 1279, 31 Cal.Rptr.2d 776 (1994).

Restatement of Torts § 601 took the position that a defendant's lack of reasonable grounds for belief in the truth of the statements he has made defeated a claim of qualified privilege even if the circumstances were such as to give rise to the privilege. English law was more favorable to the defendant. The House of Lords made it clear than an honest belief in the truth of the statement made, even if that belief is unreasonable, will permit the defendant to invoke a qualified privilege. See Horrocks v. Lowe, [1975] A.C. 135 (1974), [1974] 2 W.L.R. 282, 1 All E.R. 662. *See also* Clark v. Molyneaux, 3 Q.B.D. 237 (1877) (C.A.). In the light of the constitutional developments, to which we shall turn shortly, most American jurisdictions have now undoubtedly adopted the English position, and that is the position taken by *Restatement (Second) of Torts* § 600.

4. The qualified privilege of self defense, i.e., to defend oneself against the defamatory remarks of others, has some analogues to the defense of consent and to the qualified privilege that arises for statements made in defense of one's personal interests. A good case is Shenkman v. O'Malley, 2 A.D.2d 567, 157 N.Y.S.2d 290 (1956), in which the president of the Brooklyn Dodgers responded in kind to some defamatory charges, about the Dodgers' unwillingness to pay for medical services, made by a physician who had treated one of the team's star ballplayers. An example of a qualified privilege arising in the course of an attempt to protect one's interests is presented by Faber v. Byrle, 171 Kan. 38, 229 P.2d 718 (1951). One of the statements involved in that case was the defendant's statement to the plaintiff's brother that the plaintiff was stealing his gasoline and that the defendant feared for his life if he said anything to the plaintiff. The statement was held to be qualifiedly privileged.

WATT v. LONGSDON

Court of Appeal, 1929.
[1930] 1 K.B. 130.

SCRUTTON L.J. This case raises, amongst other matters, the extremely difficult question equally important in its legal and social aspect, as to the circumstances, if any, in which a person will be justified in giving to one partner to a marriage information which that person honestly believes to be correct, but which is in fact untrue, about the matrimonial delinquencies of the other party to the marriage. The question becomes more difficult if the answer in law turns on the existence or non-existence of a social or moral duty, a question which the judge is to determine, without any evidence, by the light of his own knowledge of the world, and his own views on social morality, a subject matter on which views vary in different ages, in different countries, and even as between man and man.

The Scottish Petroleum Company, which carried on business, amongst other places, in Morocco, had in Casa Blanca, a port in Morocco, a manager named Browne, and a managing director named Watt. The company had in England a chairman named Singer, who held a very large proportion of shares in the company, and also another director, Longsdon, a young man under thirty years of age. The latter had been in Morocco in business and friendly relations with Watt and Browne, and was a friend of Mrs. Watt, who had nursed him in an illness. * * * Under these circumstances Longsdon in England received at the beginning of May from Browne in Casa Blanca a letter stating that Watt had left for Lisbon to look for a job, that he had left a bill for 88*l*. for whisky unpaid, and that he had been for two months in immoral relations with his housemaid, who was now publicly raising claims against him for money matters. The woman was described as an old woman, stone deaf, almost blind, and with dyed hair. A number of details were given which Browne said Watt's cook had corroborated. The information was mixed up with an allegation that Watt had been scheming to compromise or seduce Mrs. Browne. The letter concluded: "From a letter shown to me by Mr. Watt I know how bitterly disappointed Mrs. Watt is, and how very much troubled she is. It would therefore perhaps be better not to show her this letter as it could only increase most terribly her own feelings in regard to her husband. These awful facts might be the cause of a breakdown to her, and I think she has enough to cope with at present. Mr. Singer, however, should perhaps know." On May 5, Longsdon, without making inquiries, sent Browne's letter on to Singer, the chairman of the board of directors. At the trial Watt's counsel put in Longsdon's answer to interrogatory 5 that he believed the statements in the letter to be true. On May 5 Longsdon wrote a long letter to Browne, in which he said that he had long suspected Watt's immorality, but had no proof; that he thought it wicked and cruel that Mrs. Watt, a very old friend of the writer's, should be in the dark when Watt might return to her—did not Browne agree?—that he (Longsdon) would not speak until he had a sworn statement in his possession, "and only with such proof would I speak, for an interferer between husband and wife nearly always comes off the worst." Could Browne get a sworn statement? "It may even be necessary for you to bribe the women to do such, and if only a matter of a few hundred francs I will pay it and of course the legal expenses." Longsdon's letter describes one of the women who was to make this sworn statement as "a prostitute all her life," a description not contained in Browne's letter. Watt returned to England in May. Without waiting for the sworn statement, on May 12, Longsdon sent the letter to Mrs. Watt. Mr. and Mrs. Watt separated, and Mrs. Watt instituted proceedings for divorce, which apparently are still pending.

Mr. Watt then instituted proceedings against Longsdon for libel—namely (1.) the publication of Browne's letter to Singer; (2.) the publication of the same letter to Mrs. Watt; (3.) Longsdon's letter of May 5 to Browne. * * * The plaintiff also put in at the trial the defendant's answers to interrogatories that his only information on the subject was derived from Browne's letter, that he made no further inquiries, and that he believed that all the statements in Browne's letter, and in the defendant's letter of May 12 were true. The defendant did not justify, but pleaded privilege. The case was tried before Horridge J. and a jury. The learned judge held that all three publications were privileged, and that there was no evidence of malice fit to be left to the jury. He therefore entered judgment for the defendant. The plaintiff appeals.

The learned judge appears to have taken the view that the authorities justify him in holding that if "there is an obvious interest in the person to whom a communication is made which causes him to be a proper recipient of a statement," even if the party making the communication had no moral or social duty to the party to whom the communication is made, the occasion is privileged. * * *

By the law of England there are occasions on which a person may make defamatory statements about another which are untrue without incurring any legal liability for his statements. These occasions are called privileged occasions. A reason frequently given for this privilege is that the allegation that the speaker has "unlawfully and maliciously published," is displaced by proof that the speaker had either a duty or an interest to publish, and that this duty or interest confers the privilege. But communications made on these occasions may lose their privilege: (1.) they may exceed the privilege of the occasion by going beyond the limits of the duty or interest, or (2.) they may be published with express malice, so that the occasion is not being legitimately used, but abused. * * * The classical definition of "privileged occasions" is that of Parke B. in *Toogood v. Spyring*[8] a case where the tenant of a farm complained to the agent of the landlord, who had sent a workman to do repairs, that the workman had broken into the tenant's cellar, got drunk on the tenant's cider, and spoilt the work he was sent to do. The workman sued the tenant. Parke B. gave the explanation of privileged occasions in these words: "In general, an action lies for the malicious publication of statements which are false in fact, and injurious to the character of another (within the well-known limits as to verbal slander), and the law considers such publication as malicious, unless it is fairly made by a person in the discharge of some public or private duty, whether legal or moral, or in the conduct of his own affairs, in matters where his interest is concerned. In such cases, the

8. 1 C.M. & R. 181.

occasion prevents the inference of malice, which the law draws from unauthorized communications, and affords a qualified defence depending upon the absence of actual malice. If fairly warranted by any reasonable occasion or exigency, and honestly made, such communications are protected for the common convenience and welfare of society; and the law has not restricted the right to make them within any narrow limits." It will be seen that the learned judge requires: (1.) a public or private duty to communicate, whether legal or moral; (2.) that the communication should be "fairly warranted by any reasonable occasion or exigency"; (3.) or a statement in the conduct of his own affairs where his interest is concerned. * * * This adds to the protection of his own interest * * * the protection of the interests of another where the situation of the writer requires him to protect those interests. This, I think, involves that his "situation" imposes on him a legal or moral duty. The question whether the occasion was privileged is for the judge, and so far as "duty" is concerned, the question is: Was there a duty, legal, moral, or social, to communicate? As to legal duty, the judge should have no difficulty; the judge should know the law; but as to moral or social duties of imperfect obligation, the task is far more troublesome. The judge has no evidence as to the view the community takes of moral or social duties. All the help the Court of Appeal can give him is contained in the judgment of Lindley L.J. in *Stuart v. Bell*[1]: "The question of moral or social duty being for the judge, each judge must decide it as best he can for himself. I take moral or social duty to mean a duty recognized by English people of ordinary intelligence and moral principle, but at the same time not a duty enforceable by legal proceedings, whether civil or criminal. My own conviction is that all or, at all events, the great mass of right-minded men in the position of the defendant would have considered it their duty, under the circumstances, to inform Stanley of the suspicion which had fallen on the plaintiff." Is the judge merely to give his own view of moral and social duty, though he thinks a considerable portion of the community hold a different opinion? Or is he to endeavour to ascertain what view "the great mass of right-minded men" would take? It is not surprising that with such a standard both judges and text-writers treat the matter as one of great difficulty in which no definite line can be drawn. * * * A conspicuous instance of the difficulties which arise when judges have to determine the existence of duties, not legal, but moral or social, by the inner light of their own conscience and judgment and knowledge of the world, is to be found in the case of *Coxhead v. Richards.*[2] A correct appreciation of what was the difference of opinion in that case is, in my opinion, of great importance in the decision of the present case. The short facts were that Cass, the mate of a ship, wrote to Richards, an intimate friend of his, a letter stating that on a voyage from the Channel to Wales, which was going to continue to Eastern ports, the captain, Coxhead, had by his drunkenness endangered the safety of the ship, and the lives of the crew;

1. [1891] 2 Q.B. 341, 350.
2. 2 C.B. 569.

and Cass asked Richards' advice what he should do in view of the risk of repetition of this danger on the voyage to the East. Richards, after consulting "an Elder Brother of the Trinity House, and an eminent shipowner," sent this letter to Ward, the owner of the ship. Richards did not know Ward, and had no interest in the ship. The owner dismissed the captain, who thereupon brought an action against Richards. The judge at the trial directed the jury, if they should think that the communication was strictly honest, and made solely in the execution of what he believed to be a duty, to find for the defendant. They did so, while finding that the plea of justification failed. The plaintiff then moved for a new trial, on which motion the Court after two hearings was equally divided. It is not very clear whether the judges differed on a general principle, or on its application to the facts of the case. I understand Tindal C.J. to have taken the view that if a man has information materially affecting the interests of another, and honestly communicates it to that other, he is protected, though he has no personal interest in the subject matter, and that his protection arises from "the various social duties by which men are bound to each other," and that it was the duty of the defendant to communicate this information to the owner. Erle J. appears to put the matter on "information given to protect damage from misconduct," "the importance of the information to the interest of the receiver," and says that a person having such information is justified in communicating it to the person interested, though the speaker did not stand in any relation to the recipient, and was a volunteer. He does not expressly refer to any social duty. On the other hand, Coltman and Cresswell JJ. both appear to me to hold that in such circumstances there was no moral duty, for that any tendency that way was counterbalanced by the moral duty not to slander your neighbour. In the subsequent case of *Bennett v. Deacon*[1] the same four judges repeated the same division of opinion, where Deacon, a man to whom the plaintiff owed 25*l*., volunteered to a tradesman, who was about to deal with the plaintiff, the statement that unless the tradesman was paid ready money he would lose the goods, and his money, or price, for he (Deacon) was about to seize the goods of the plaintiff for debt. I think it is clear that Tindal C.J. and Erle J. thought that a volunteer, with no personal interest, would be protected in giving information apparently material to the interest of the recipient, and that Coltman and Cresswell JJ. thought he would not. How far either set of judges meant to lay down a general principle applicable to all such cases is not very clear. They certainly differed in its application to the particular facts of those cases. I myself should have thought, and I think most of the judges who have considered the case * * * did think, that in the particular facts of *Coxhead v. Richards* Richards, if he believed the statements in the letter to be true, had a moral duty to forward them to the shipowner, who had obviously a vital interest in them, if they were true. * * *

Lastly, in *Stuart v. Bell* there was again a difference of opinion, though not an equal division of the judges, as in *Coxhead v. Richards*.

1. (1846) 2 C.B. 628.

Stanley, the explorer, and his valet, Stuart, were staying with the mayor of Newcastle, Bell. The Edinburgh police made a very carefully worded communication to the Newcastle police that there had been a robbery in Edinburgh at an hotel where Stuart was staying, and it might be well to make very careful and cautious inquiry into the matter. The Newcastle police showed the letter to the mayor, who after consideration showed it to Stanley, who dismissed Stuart. Stuart sued the mayor. Lindley and Kay L.JJ. held that the mayor had a moral duty to communicate, and Stanley a material interest to receive the communication; Lopes L.J. held that in the circumstances there was no moral duty to communicate, though in some circumstances there might be such a duty in a host towards a guest. I myself should have agreed with the majority, but the difference of opinion between such experienced judges shows the difficulty of the question.

In my opinion Horridge J. went too far in holding that there could be a privileged occasion on the ground of interest in the recipient without any duty to communicate on the part of the person making the communication. But that does not settle the question, for it is necessary to consider, in the present case, whether there was, as to each communication, a duty to communicate, and an interest in the recipient.

First as to the communication between Longsdon and Singer, I think the case must proceed on the admission that at all material times Watt, Longsdon and Browne were in the employment of the same company, and the evidence afforded by the answer to the interrogatory put in by the plaintiff that Longsdon believed the statements in Browne's letter. In my view on these facts there was a duty, both from a moral and a material point of view, on Longsdon to communicate the letter to Singer, the chairman of his company, who, apart from questions of present employment, might be asked by Watt for a testimonial to a future employer. Equally, I think Longsdon receiving the letter from Browne, might discuss the matter with him, and ask for further information, on the ground of a common interest in the affairs of the company, and to obtain further information for the chairman. I should therefore agree with the view of Horridge J. that these two occasions were privileged, though for different reasons. Horridge J. further held that there was no evidence of malice fit to be left to the jury, and, while I think some of Longsdon's action and language in this respect was unfortunate, as the plaintiff has put in the answer that Longsdon believed the truth of the statements in Browne's and his own letter, * * * I should not try excess with too nice scales, and I do not dissent from his view as to malice. As to the communications to Singer and Browne, in my opinion the appeal should fail, but as both my brethren take the view that there was evidence of malice which should be left to the jury, there must, of course, be a new trial as to the claim based on these two publications.

The communication to Mrs. Watt stands on a different footing. I have no intention of writing an exhaustive treatise on the circumstances when a stranger or a friend should communicate to husband or wife information he receives as to the conduct of the other party to the marriage. I am clear that it is impossible to say he is always under a moral or social duty to do so; it is equally impossible to say he is never under such a duty. It must depend on the circumstances of each case, the nature of the information, and the relation of speaker and recipient. It cannot, on the one hand, be the duty even of a friend to communicate all the gossip the friend hears at men's clubs or women's bridge parties to one of the spouses affected. On the other hand, most men would hold that it was the moral duty of a doctor who attended his sister in law, and believed her to be suffering from a miscarriage, for which an absent husband could not be responsible, to communicate that fact to his wife and the husband. * * * Using the best judgment I can in this difficult matter, I have come to the conclusion that there was not a moral or social duty in Longsdon to make this communication to Mrs. Watt such as to make the occasion privileged, and that there must be a new trial so far as it relates to the claim for publication of a libel to Mrs. Watt.

[The judgments of GREER and RUSSELL, L.JJ. have been omitted.]

NOTES

1. When a person against whom a defamation action has been brought claims a privilege on the ground that his statement was made to protect the interests of third parties there are three important factors to consider. The first is the importance of the interest in question. When life or serious bodily harm is thought to be at risk, as in Coxhead v. Richards, 2 C.B. 569, 135 Eng.Rep. 1069 (1846), discussed in *Watt,* even a third party with no interest of his own in the matter will have a qualified privilege to come forward with information. A similar privilege has been recognized when a person's significant property interests have been involved. *See* Doyle v. Clauss, 190 App.Div. 838, 180 N.Y.S. 671 (1920) (letter advising employer that an employee was embezzling the employer's money). The second factor is the relationship of the person claiming the privilege to the person whose interests are purportedly being protected. An "immediate" family member of the person whose interests are involved, *see Restatement (Second) of Torts* § 597, will have a privilege in circumstances where a friend or other busybody will not. This was one of the points involved in *Watt. See also* Burton v. Mattson, 50 Utah 133, 166 P. 979 (1917) (unsolicited letter advising wife that her husband, the plaintiff, had engaged in an adulterous relationship).[3] The third important factor is whether the defamatory communication has been solicited by the person whose interests are at stake or an immediate family member of that person, such as the parent of a person about to be married. *See Restatement (Second) of Torts* § 595(2)(a). *See also* Rude v. Nass, 79 Wis. 321, 48 N.W. 555 (1891) (defendant's letter had been solicited on behalf of father of girl whom plaintiff had been charged with seducing).

2. In addition to the common interests of employees of a common employer recognized in *Watt—see also* Ponticelli v. Mine Safety Appliance Co.,

---

3. In Nelson v. Whitten, 272 Fed. 135 (E.D.N.Y.1921), discussed in *Lee v. Paulsen, supra,* at p. 653, the court stressed that the former employer who made the defamatory statement had not been obliged to give the statement. Neither the plaintiff nor anyone else had invited the defendant to write anything that might be false or defamatory.

104 R.I. 549, 247 A.2d 303 (1968) (employer's statement to former co-workers of the reasons [alleged padding of production figures] for discharging that employee privileged on ground of discouraging similar conduct in other employees)—a common interest has been recognized among the members of a labor union. *See* Gabauer v. Woodcock, 520 F.2d 1084 (8th Cir.1975), *cert. denied* 423 U.S. 1061, 96 S.Ct. 800, 46 L.Ed.2d 653 (1976). *See also* Bereman v. Power Publishing Co., 93 Colo. 581, 27 P.2d 749 (1933) (statement about strike breakers in union newspaper; privilege not defeated because paper distributed to a few persons who are not union members). Among the other types of common interest that have been recognized is that of the members of a church. *See* Slocinski v. Radwan, 83 N.H. 501, 144 A. 787 (1929).

3. As courts have increasingly come to expect that relatively large groups of people, such as members of a church or stockholders of corporations, might be said to share a common interest, the question arose of why could not the members of a political society in a democratic country also share a common interest that could be called "the public interest." That is exactly what happened in the United Kingdom with the House of Lords decision in Reynolds v. Times Newspapers Ltd, [2001] 2 A.C. 127, [1999] 3 W.L.R. 1010, [1999] 4 All E.R. 609 (1999). The plaintiff in the case was a former Taoiseach (prime minister) of Ireland. Although the defendant newspaper lost the case, the House of Lords declared that the qualified privilege to comment on matters of common interest should be expanded to include shared public interest. In doing so it refused to hold that political speech was, as a general matter, of any greater public interest than other forms of speech. In Jameel v. Wall Street Journal Europe SPRL, [2007] 1 A.C. 359, [2006] 3 W.L.R. 642, [2006] 4 All E.R. 1279 (2006), the case that will now be presented, the House of Lords in ruling for the defendant newspaper gave guidance about how this privilege should be applied.

JAMEEL v. WALL STREET JOURNAL EUROPE SPRL

House of Lords, 2006
[2007] 1 A.C. 359, [2006] 3 W.L.R. 642, [2006] 4 All E.R. 1279

LORD BINGHAM OF CORNHILL

1. My Lords, this appeal raises two questions on the law of libel. The first concerns the entitlement of a trading corporation such as the second respondent to sue and recover damages without pleading or proving special damage. The second concerns the scope and application of what has come to be called Reynolds privilege, an important form of qualified privilege.

2. The appellant is the publisher of the "Wall Street Journal Europe", a respected, influential and unsensational newspaper ("the newspaper") carrying serious news about international business, finance and politics. It is edited, published and printed in Brussels for distribution throughout Europe and the Middle East. It shares some editorial and journalistic personnel and facilities with its elder sister in New York, the "Wall Street Journal", which has a large circulation in the United States.

3. The respondents, claimants in the proceedings, are Saudi Arabian. The first respondent is a prominent businessman and president of the Abdul Latif Jameel Group, an international trading conglomerate based in the Kingdom of Saudi Arabia comprising numerous companies and with interests in cars, shipping, property and distribution of electronic goods. The second respondent is a company incorporated in Saudi Arabia and is part of the Group. The first respondent is the general manager and president of the company, which does not itself own property or conduct any trade or business here, but which has a commercial reputation in England and Wales.

4. On 6 February 2002 the newspaper published the article which gave rise to these proceedings. It was headed "Saudi Officials Monitor Certain Bank Accounts" with a smaller sub-heading "Focus Is on Those With Potential Terrorist Ties". It bore the by-line of James M Dorsey, an Arabic-speaking reporter with specialist knowledge of Saudi Arabia, and acknowledged the contribution of Glenn Simpson, a staff writer in Washington. The gist of the article, succinctly stated in the first paragraph, was that the Saudi Arabian Monetary Authority, the kingdom's central bank, was, at the request of United States law enforcement agencies, monitoring bank accounts associated with some of the country's most prominent businessmen in a bid to prevent them from being used, wittingly or unwittingly, for the funnelling of funds to terrorist organisations. This information was attributed to "US officials and Saudis familiar with the issue". In the second paragraph a number of companies and individuals were named, among them "the Abdullatif Jamil Group of companies" who, it was stated later in the article, "couldn't be reached for comment".

5. The jury in due course found that the article referred to was defamatory of both respondents. They may have understood the article to mean that there were reasonable grounds to suspect the involvement of the respondents, or alternatively that there were reasonable grounds to investigate the involvement of the respondents, in the witting or unwitting funnelling of funds to terrorist organisations. For present purposes it is immaterial which defamatory meaning the jury gave the passage complained of, neither of which the newspaper sought to justify.

6. The article was published some five months after the catastrophic events which took place in New York and Washington on 11 September 2001. During the intervening months the United States authorities had taken determined steps, with strong international support, to cut off the flow of funds to terrorist organisations, including Al–Qaida. These steps were of particular importance in relation to Saudi Arabia, since a large majority of the suspected hijackers were of Saudi origin, and it was believed that much of their financial support came from Saudi sources. Yet the position of the Saudi authorities was one of some sensitivity. The kingdom was an ally of the United States and condemned terrorism. But among its devoutly Muslim population there were those who resented the kingdom's association with the United States and espoused the cause of Islamic jihad. Thus there were questions about whether, and to what

extent, the kingdom was co-operating with the United States authorities in cutting off funds to terrorist organisations. This was, without doubt, a matter of high international importance, a very appropriate matter for report by a serious newspaper. But it was a difficult matter to investigate and report since information was not freely available in the kingdom and the Saudi authorities, even if co-operating closely with those of the United States, might be embarrassed if that fact were to become generally known.

7. The trial of the action before Eady J and a jury lasted some three working weeks and culminated in verdicts for the respondents and awards of £30,000 and £10,000 respectively. Much evidence was called on both sides, of which the House has been referred to short excerpts only. The judge * * * rejected the newspaper's argument on the damage issue and the Court of Appeal agreed with him * * *. The judge also rejected the newspaper's claim to Reynolds privilege * * *. On this question also the Court of Appeal upheld his decision, but on a more limited ground. This calls for more detailed consideration.

8. The judge put a series of questions to the jury which, so far as relevant to Reynolds privilege, were directed to two matters: the sources on which Mr Dorsey, as reporter, relied; and his attempt to obtain the respondents' response to his inclusion of their names in his proposed article. Mr Dorsey testified that he had relied on information given by a prominent Saudi businessman (source A), confirmed by a banker (source B), a United States diplomat (source C), a United States embassy official (source D) and a senior Saudi official (source E). In answer to the judge's questions the jury found that the newspaper had proved that Mr Dorsey had received the information he claimed to have received from source A, but had not proved that Mr Dorsey had received the confirmation he claimed from sources B–E inclusive. The judge attached significance to these negative findings, since Mr Dorsey said in evidence that he would not have written the article in reliance on source A alone. In the Court of Appeal, the judge's reliance on these negative findings was criticised by the newspaper. At the outset of his direction to the jury the judge had pointed out that there was no plea of justification and that therefore, if the jury found the article defamatory of the respondents, they should assume it to be untrue. This direction, it was said, may well have infected the jury's approach to the questions concerning sources B–E. The Court of Appeal * * * refused the newspaper leave to raise a new ground of misdirection, and thought * * *, that the jury had "almost certainly" based their answers on the impression made by witnesses in court. But the Court of Appeal preferred to base its decision on the other ground relied on by the judge to deny privilege.

9. Mr Dorsey described attempts to obtain a response from the Group about his proposed article. He said he had telephoned the Group office at about 9 a m and left a recorded message. The jury found that the newspaper had not proved on the balance of probabilities that that was so. There was, it was agreed, a telephone conversation between Mr Dorsey and Mr Munajjed, an employee of the Group, on the evening of 5

February, the day before publication. During that conversation, according to Mr Munajjed, he had asked Mr Dorsey to wait until the following day for a comment by the Group. He had, he said, no authority to make a statement and the first respondent was in Japan, where the time was 3 a m. Mr Dorsey denied that Mr Munajjed had asked him to wait. But the jury found that Mr Munajjed had made that request. It was on this ground, as I understand, that the Court of Appeal upheld the judge's denial of Reynolds privilege:

* * *

10. I turn to the two issues raised in the appeal.

I Damage

11. The issue under this head is whether a trading company which itself conducts no business but which has a trading reputation within England and Wales should be entitled to recover general damages for libel without pleading and proving that the publication complained of has caused it special damage. To resolve this question it is helpful to distinguish three sub-issues: (1) whether such an entitlement exists under the current law of England and Wales; (2) whether, if so, article 10 of the European Convention on Human Rights requires revision of the current domestic law; and (3) whether, if not, the current domestic law should in any event be revised.

* * *

27. I do not on balance consider that the existing rule should be changed, provided always that where a trading corporation has suffered no actual financial loss any damages awarded should be kept strictly within modest bounds.

[LORD HOFFMAN and LADY HALE, two of the five law lords sitting on the jury dissented from this holding of the three-person majority.]

II Reynolds privilege

28. The decision of the House in Reynolds v Times Newspapers Ltd [2001] 2 AC 127 built on the traditional foundations of qualified privilege but carried the law forward in a way which gave much greater weight than the earlier law had done to the value of informed public debate of significant public issues. Both these aspects are, I think, important in understanding the decision.

29. Underlying the development of qualified privilege was the requirement of a reciprocal duty and interest between the publisher and the recipient of the statement in question. * * * Some of these cases concerned very limited publication, but * * * [some] did not, * * * Thus where a publication related to a matter of public interest, it was accepted that the reciprocal duty and interest could be found even where publication was by a newspaper to a section of the public or the public at large. In Reynolds [2001] 2 AC 127, 167, 177 the Court of Appeal restated these

tests, although it suggested a third supplemental test which the House held to be mistaken.

30. I do not understand the House to have rejected the duty/interest approach: * * * But Lord Nicholls * * * considered that matters relating to the nature and source of the information were matters to be taken into account in determining whether the duty-interest test was satisfied or, as he preferred to say "in a simpler and more direct way, whether the public was entitled to know the particular information".

31. The necessary precondition of reliance on qualified privilege in this context is that the matter published should be one of public interest. In the present case the subject matter of the article complained of was of undoubted public interest. But that is not always, perhaps not usually, so. It has been repeatedly and rightly said that what engages the interest of the public may not be material which engages the public interest.

32. Qualified privilege as a live issue only arises where a statement is defamatory and untrue. It was in this context, and assuming the matter to be one of public interest, that Lord Nicholls proposed * * * a test of responsible journalism * * * The rationale of this test is, as I understand, that there is no duty to publish and the public have no interest to read material which the publisher has not taken reasonable steps to verify. As Lord Hobhouse observed with characteristic pungency * * * "No public interest is served by publishing or communicating misinformation." But the publisher is protected if he has taken such steps as a responsible journalist would take to try and ensure that what is published is accurate and fit for publication.

33. Lord Nicholls * * * listed certain matters which might be taken into account in deciding whether the test of responsible journalism was satisfied. He intended these as pointers which might be more or less indicative, depending on the circumstances of a particular case, and not, I feel sure, as a series of hurdles to be negotiated by a publisher before he could successfully rely on qualified privilege. Lord Nicholls recognized * * * inevitably as I think, that it had to be a body other than the publisher, namely the court, which decided whether a publication was protected by qualified privilege. But this does not mean that the editorial decisions and judgments made at the time, without the knowledge of falsity which is a benefit of hindsight, are irrelevant. Weight should ordinarily be given to the professional judgment of an editor or journalist in the absence of some indication that it was made in a casual, cavalier, slipshod or careless manner.

34. Some misunderstanding may perhaps have been engendered by Lord Nicholls's references * * * to "the particular information". It is of course true that the defence of qualified privilege must be considered with reference to the particular publication complained of as defamatory, and where a whole article or story is complained of no difficulty arises. But difficulty can arise where the complaint relates to one particular ingredient of a composite story, since it is then open to a plaintiff to contend, as

in the present case, that the article could have been published without inclusion of the particular ingredient complained of. This may, in some instances, be a valid point. But consideration should be given to the thrust of the article which the publisher has published. If the thrust of the article is true, and the public interest condition is satisfied, the inclusion of an inaccurate fact may not have the same appearance of irresponsibility as it might if the whole thrust of the article is untrue.

35. These principles must be applied to the present case. * * * [T]he Court of Appeal upheld the judge's denial of Reynolds privilege on a single ground, discounting the jury's negative findings concerning Mr Dorsey's sources: that the newspaper had failed to delay publication of the respondents' names without waiting long enough for the respondents to comment. This seems to me, with respect, to be a very narrow ground on which to deny the privilege, and the ruling subverts the liberalising intention of the Reynolds decision. The subject matter was of great public interest, in the strictest sense. The article was written by an experienced specialist reporter and approved by senior staff on the newspaper and "Wall Street Journal" who themselves sought to verify its contents. The article was unsensational in tone and (apparently) factual in content. The respondents' response was sought, although at a late stage, and the newspaper's inability to obtain a comment recorded. It is very unlikely that a comment, if obtained, would have been revealing, since even if the respondents' accounts were being monitored it was unlikely that they would know. It might be thought that this was the sort of neutral, investigative journalism which Reynolds privilege exists to protect. I would accordingly allow the appeal and set aside the Court of Appeal judgment.

36. I am in much more doubt than my noble and learned friends what the consequence of that decision should be. The House has not, like the judge and the jury, heard the witnesses and seen the case develop day after day. It has read no more than a small sample of the evidence. It seems to me a large step for the House, thus disadvantaged, to hold that the publication was privileged, and I am not sure that counsel for the newspaper sought such a ruling. But I find myself in a minority, and it serves no useful purpose to do more than express my doubt.

LORD HOFFMANN

The issue

37. My Lords, on 6 February 2002 the "Wall Street Journal" published an article claiming that Saudi Arabian Monetary Authority ("SAMA"), at the request of the United States Treasury, was monitoring the accounts of certain named Saudi companies to trace whether any payments were finding their way to terrorist organisations. The jury found the article to be defamatory of the claimants, who are respectively the principal director and holding company of a group named in the article. The principal question is whether the newspaper was entitled to the defence of publication in the public interest established by the decision of this House in

Reynolds v Times Newspapers Ltd [2001] 2 AC 127. The judge (Eady J) [2004] 2 All ER 92 and the Court of Appeal (Lord Phillips of Worth Matravers MR, Sedley and Jonathan Parker LJJ) [2005] QB 904u rejected it. But in my opinion they gave it too narrow a scope. It should have been upheld and the action dismissed.

38. Until very recently, the law of defamation was weighted in favour of claimants and the law of privacy weighted against them. True but trivial intrusions into private life were safe. Reports of investigations by the newspaper into matters of public concern which could be construed as reflecting badly on public figures domestic or foreign were risky. The House attempted to redress the balance in favour of privacy in Campbell v MGN Ltd [2004] 2 AC 457 and in favour of greater freedom for the press to publish stories of genuine public interest in Reynolds v Times Newspapers Ltd [2001] 2 AC 127. But this case suggests that Reynolds has had little impact upon the way the law is applied at first instance. It is therefore necessary to restate the principles.

The article

39. The background to the article was the defining event of this century, the destruction of the World Trade Center and the other atrocities of 11 September 2001. It was quickly established that 15 out of the 19 hijackers had come from Saudi Arabia and it was strongly suspected that sources in the same country had financed them. Efforts to trace terrorist funds were high on the US and international agenda. On 28 September 2001 the Security Council passed resolution 1373 requiring all states to prevent and suppress the financing of terrorist acts. The United States made strong diplomatic efforts to secure the co-operation of SAMA. In the months that followed, there was much speculation and controversy about the extent to which the Saudi Government was really helping. Some United States newspapers and prominent politicians such as Senators McCain and Lieberman accused the Saudis of doing very little, appeasing domestic supporters of the terrorists in the controlled domestic media while publicly denouncing them in statements for overseas consumption. "Time to give Saudis an ultimatum" said the Boston "Globe" headline on 13 January 2002. But the official United States Government line was that they were co-operating fully with the United States Treasury. The subject was one of very considerable public interest, not least to the financial community served by the Wall Street Journal.

40. The article was written by Mr James Dorsey, the paper's special correspondent in Riyadh and checked by Mr Glenn R Simpson, a journalist based in Washington who was concentrating almost exclusively on terrorist funding and had daily contact with sources at the United States Treasury. It was published in the New York edition but the claimants have brought their proceedings in this country against the publishers of the European edition, the Wall Street Journal Europe, in which it also appeared. The defendants are based in Brussels but some 18,000 copies of

the paper are sold daily in the United Kingdom. The article was not the lead story but appeared on the front page:

"Saudi officials monitor certain bank accounts

"Focus is on those with potential terrorist ties

"RIYADH, Saudi Arabia–The Saudi Arabian Monetary Authority, the kingdom's central bank, is monitoring at the request of US law-enforcement agencies the bank accounts associated with some of the country's most prominent businessmen in a bid to prevent them from being used wittingly or unwittingly for the funnelling of funds to terrorist organizations, according to US officials and Saudis familiar with the issue. The accounts-belonging to Al Rajhi Banking & Investment Corp, headed by Saleh Abdulaziz al Rajhi; Al Rajhi Commercial Foreign Exchange, which isn't connected to Al Rajhi Banking; Islamic banking conglomerate Dallah Al Baraka Group, with $7 billion (& euro; 8.05 billion) in assets and whose chairman is Sheik Saleh Kamel; the Bin Mahfouz family, separate members of which own National Commercial Bank, Saudi Arabia's largest bank, and the Saudi Economic Development Co; and the Abdullatif Jamil Group of companies—are among 150 accounts being monitored by SAMA, said the Saudis and the US officials based in Riyadh. The US officials said the US presented the names of the accounts to Saudi Arabia since the Sept 11 terrorist attacks in America. They said four Saudi charities and eight businesses were also among 140 world-wide names given to Saudi Arabia last month. The US officials said the US had agreed not to publish the names of Saudi institutions and individuals provided that Saudi authorities took appropriate action. Many of the Saudi accounts on the US list belong to legitimate entities and businessmen who may in the past have had an association with institutions suspected of links to terrorism, the officials said. The officials said similar agreements had been reached with authorities in Kuwait and the United Arab Emirates. 'This arrangement sends out a warning to people,' a US official said. SAMA couldn't be reached for comment. In a recent report to the United Nations about combating terrorism, however, the Saudi government said: 'The kingdom took many urgent executive steps, amongst which SAMA sent a circular to all Saudi banks to uncover whether those listed in suspect lists have any real connection with terrorism.' "

41. The article went on to say that some of the named companies had denied that they were being monitored but that "the Abdullatif Jamil Group of companies couldn't be reached for comment". Abdul Latif Jameel Co Ltd, the second claimant, is a very substantial Saudi Arabian trading company with interests in a number of businesses, including the distribution of Toyota vehicles. It is part of an international group owned by the Jameel family which includes Hartwell plc, a company which distributes vehicles in the United Kingdom. Mr Mohammed Abdul Latif Jameel, the first claimant, is general manager and president of the second claimant and the principal figure in the group.

42. The jury found that the article was defamatory of both claimants. The newspaper did not attempt to justify any defamatory meaning and there is no appeal against the finding that it was defamatory. The absence of a plea of justification is not surprising. In the nature of things, the existence of covert surveillance by the highly secretive Saudi authorities would be impossible to prove by evidence in open court. That does not necessarily mean that it did not happen. Nor, on the other hand, does it follow that even if it did happen, the Jameel group had any connection with terrorism. The US intelligence agencies sometimes get things badly wrong.

The Reynolds defence

43. The newspaper's principal defence was based on Reynolds v Times Newspapers Ltd [2001] 2 AC 127. It is called in the trade "Reynolds privilege" but the use of the term privilege, although historically accurate, may be misleading. A defence of privilege in the usual sense is available when the defamatory statement was published on a privileged occasion and can be defeated only by showing that the privilege was abused. As Lord Diplock said in a well-known passage in Horrocks v Lowe [1975] AC 135, 149:

"The public interest that the law should provide an effective means whereby a man can vindicate his reputation against calumny has nevertheless to be accommodated to the competing public interest in permitting men to communicate frankly and freely with one another about matters in respect of which the law recognises that they have a duty to perform or an interest to protect in doing so. What is published in good faith on matters of these kinds is published on a privileged occasion. It is not actionable even though it be defamatory and turns out to be untrue. With some exceptions which are irrelevant to the instant appeal, the privilege is not absolute but qualified. It is lost if the occasion which gives rise to it is misused."

44. Misuse of the privileged occasion is technically known as "malice" and the burden is upon the claimant to prove it. In Reynolds, counsel for the newspaper invited the House to declare a similar privilege for the publication of political information. But the House refused to do so. Lord Nicholls of Birkenhead said that to allow publication of any defamatory statements of a political character, subject only to proof of malice, would provide inadequate protection for the reputation of defamed individuals.

45. Instead, Lord Nicholls said * * *:

"the common law solution is for the court to have regard to all the circumstances when deciding whether the publication of particular material was privileged because of its value to the public. Its value to the public depends upon its quality as well as its subject matter. This solution has the merit of elasticity. As observed by the Court of Appeal, this principle can be applied appropriately to the particular circumstances of individual cases in their infinite variety. It can be applied appropriately to all information published by a newspaper, whatever its source or origin."

46. Although Lord Nicholls uses the word "privilege", it is clearly not being used in the old sense. It is the material which is privileged, not the occasion on which it is published. There is no question of the privilege being defeated by proof of malice because the propriety of the conduct of the defendant is built into the conditions under which the material is privileged. The burden is upon the defendant to prove that those conditions are satisfied. I therefore agree with the opinion of the Court of Appeal in Loutchansky v Times Newspapers Ltd (Nos 2–5) [2002] QB 783, that "Reynolds privilege" is "a different jurisprudential creature from the traditional form of privilege from which it sprang". It might more appropriately be called the Reynolds public interest defence rather than privilege.

47. In Reynolds itself, the publication failed by a very considerable margin to satisfy the conditions for the new defence. The House was therefore able to deal with those conditions only in very general terms. Lord Nicholls offered guidance in the form of a non-exhaustive, illustrative list of matters which, depending on the circumstances, might be relevant. "Over time", he said* * * "a valuable corpus of case law will be built up". This case, in my opinion, illustrates the circumstances in which the defence should be available.

Applying Reynolds

The public interest of the material

48. The first question is whether the subject matter of the article was a matter of public interest. In answering this question, I think that one should consider the article as a whole and not isolate the defamatory statement. It is true that Lord Nicholls said, in the passage which I have quoted above, that the question is whether the publication of "particular material" was privileged because of its value to the public. But the term "particular material" was in my opinion being used by contrast with the generic privilege advocated by the newspaper. It was saying that one must consider the contents of each publication and not decide the matter simply by reference to whether it fell within a general category like political information. But that did not mean that it was necessary to find a separate public interest justification for each item of information within the publication. Whether it was justifiable to include the defamatory statement is a separate question, to which I shall return in a moment.

49. The question of whether the material concerned a matter of public interest is decided by the judge. As has often been said, the public tends to be interested in many things which are not of the slightest public interest and the newspapers are not often the best judges of where the line should be drawn. It is for the judge to apply the test of public interest. But this publication easily passes that test. The thrust of the article as a whole was to inform the public that the Saudis were co-operating with the United

States Treasury in monitoring accounts. It was a serious contribution in measured tone to a subject of very considerable importance

* * *

Inclusion of the defamatory statement

51. If the article as a whole concerned a matter of public interest, the next question is whether the inclusion of the defamatory statement was justifiable. The fact that the material was of public interest does not allow the newspaper to drag in damaging allegations which serve no public purpose. They must be part of the story. And the more serious the allegation, the more important it is that it should make a real contribution to the public interest element in the article. But whereas the question of whether the story as a whole was a matter of public interest must be decided by the judge without regard to what the editor's view may have been, the question of whether the defamatory statement should have been included is often a matter of how the story should have been presented. And on that question, allowance must be made for editorial judgment. If the article as a whole is in the public interest, opinions may reasonably differ over which details are needed to convey the general message. The fact that the judge, with the advantage of leisure and hindsight, might have made a different editorial decision should not destroy the defence. That would make the publication of articles which are, ex hypothesi, in the public interest, too risky and would discourage investigative reporting.

52. In the present case, the inclusion of the names of large and respectable Saudi businesses was an important part of the story. It showed that co-operation with the United States Treasury's requests was not confined to a few companies on the fringe of Saudi society but extended to companies which were by any test within the heartland of the Saudi business world. To convey this message, inclusion of the names was necessary. Generalisations such as "prominent Saudi companies", which can mean anything or nothing, would not have served the same purpose.

Responsible journalism

53. If the publication, including the defamatory statement, passes the public interest test, the inquiry then shifts to whether the steps taken to gather and publish the information were responsible and fair.

* * *

55. In this case, Eady J said that the concept of "responsible journalism" was too vague. It was, he said, "subjective". I am not certain what this means, except that it is obviously a term of disapproval. (In the jargon of the old Soviet Union, "objective" meant correct and in accordance with the Party line, while "subjective" meant deviationist and wrong.) But the standard of responsible journalism is as objective and no more vague than standards such as "reasonable care" which are regularly used in other branches of law. Greater certainty in its application is attained in two ways. First, as Lord Nicholls said, a body of illustrative case law builds up.

Secondly, just as the standard of reasonable care in particular areas, such as driving a vehicle, is made more concrete by extra-statutory codes of behaviour like the Highway Code, so the standard of responsible journalism is made more specific by the Code of Practice which has been adopted by the newspapers and ratified by the Press Complaints Commission. This too, while not binding upon the courts, can provide valuable guidance.

56. In Reynolds, Lord Nicholls gave his well-known non-exhaustive list of ten matters which should in suitable cases be taken into account. They are not tests which the publication has to pass. In the hands of a judge hostile to the spirit of Reynolds, they can become ten hurdles at any of which the defence may fail. That is how Eady J treated them. The defence, he said, can be sustained only after "the closest and most rigorous scrutiny" by the application of what he called "Lord Nicholls's ten tests". But that, in my opinion, is not what Lord Nicholls meant. As he said in Bonnick, * * * the standard of conduct required of the newspaper must be applied in a practical and flexible manner. It must have regard to practical realities.

* * *

58. I therefore pass to the question of whether the newspaper satisfied the conditions of responsible journalism. This may be divided into three topics: the steps taken to verify the story, the opportunity given to the Jameel group to comment and the propriety of publication in the light of United States diplomatic policy at the time.

Verification of the story

In Saudi Arabia

59. Mr James Dorsey, the correspondent in Riyadh, said that his story was derived from five sources whom, in accordance with journalistic practice, he did not identify by name. The first was "a prominent Saudi businessman", referred to as A, whose information was second-hand, and the others were "a banker", "a US diplomat", "a US embassy official" and "a senior Saudi official", all of whom were in a position to know and were referred to as B to E respectively. In Reynolds * * * Lord Nicholls said that any disputes of primary fact about matters relevant to the defence should be left to the jury. The judge therefore asked the jury whether the defendant had proved, on a balance of probabilities, that Mr Dorsey had been informed by source A that the Abdul Latif Jameel group was on an unpublished list of names whose accounts were being monitored by SAMA at the request of the United States and whether this had been confirmed by sources B to E.

60. That was a perfectly proper question to leave to the jury, but what in my opinion vitiated the answers was the assumption which the judge instructed the jury to make in considering it. He said:

"If . . . you come to the view, after due consideration, that the article does in some way link one or other or both of them to the funding of terrorism, then we accept, as an absolute fundamental assumption in this case, that such allegation is untrue . . . You and I therefore proceed on the basis that neither claimant was being monitored nor suspected nor on any list of suspects provided to the Saudis by the United States Government or anyone else . . . To put it simply, what Mr Price argues is that if in fact it was not true that they were on the list and it is not true they were being monitored, how can his sources have given him that information? What matters at this stage is that I am stating, as the law requires me to state, that they are fully entitled to the presumption that they are not guilty of funding terror or on any list or suspected of doing so.''

61. In other words, the jury were told that in deciding whether sources B to E had given the information, they were to assume that they would have known that it was false. In the circumstances, it is not surprising that they were unconvinced that sources B to E had confirmed the story. It is true that they accepted that source A had provided Mr Dorsey with his lead, but that may have been because source A did not have first-hand knowledge and could not therefore be treated as having known that the information was false.

62. Telling the jury to make that assumption was * * * a misdirection. The fact that the defamatory statement is not established at the trial to have been true is not relevant to the Reynolds defence. It is a neutral circumstance. The elements of that defence are the public interest of the material and the conduct of the journalists at the time. In most cases the Reynolds defence will not get off the ground unless the journalist honestly and reasonably believed that the statement was true but there are cases (''reportage'') in which the public interest lies simply in the fact that the statement was made, when it may be clear that the publisher does not subscribe to any belief in its truth. In either case, the defence is not affected by the newspaper's inability to prove the truth of the statement at the trial.

63. Although the Court of Appeal accepted that this was a misdirection, they refused leave to appeal on the point, partly because counsel for the newspaper had not raised the matter at the trial and partly because they thought it would have made no difference to the outcome. But they agreed * * * that they should not rule out the Reynolds defence on the basis of the jury's answers to the questions about Mr Dorsey's sources and that ''if this appeal is to be dismissed, it should be on the basis of the findings in favour of the Jameels in respect of the other issues before us''. I agree * * *.

In Washington

64. In New York, the news editor Ms Blackshire had Mr Simpson in Washington check it with the United States Treasury, which was alleged to have provided SAMA with the list of accounts including those of the companies named in the story. The Washington staff reporter Mr Simpson gave evidence that he had given his contact at the Treasury the names

provided by Mr Dorsey and that the Treasury had confirmed to him that they were on the list.

* * *

Opportunity to comment

79. One of the matters which Lord Nicholls in Reynolds said should be taken into account was the opportunity, if any, which the claimant had been given to comment on the allegations before they were published. Items on the list [2001] 2 AC 197, 205, were:

> "7. Whether comment was sought from the plaintiff. He may have information others do not possess or have not disclosed. An approach to the plaintiff will not always be necessary. 8. Whether the article contained the gist of the plaintiff's side of the story."

80. But Lord Nicholls * * * rejected the suggestion that failure to obtain and report a comment should always be fatal to the defence: "Failure to report the plaintiff's explanation is a factor to be taken into account. Depending upon the circumstances, it may be a weighty factor. But it should not be elevated into a rigid rule of law."

81. In this case, Mr Dorsey telephoned to ask for a comment at 5 p m (Saudi time) on 5 February, the day before publication. (He said in evidence that he had left a recorded message that morning, but the jury did not accept this.) He spoke to Mr Jameel's secretary, who referred the call to a Mr Munajjed in Jeddah, who described himself as Mr Jameel's adviser. Mr Munajjed called back four hours later. Mr Munajjed said that he did not think it possible that the group's accounts would be monitored. They were a big and respectable organisation. Mr Dorsey asked whether he could quote this and Mr Munajjed said no, the only person who could speak on the record for the group was Mr Jameel. He was asleep in Tokyo and Mr Munajjed was not inclined to wake him. He asked whether publication could be postponed for 24 hours. Mr Dorsey said no, the article would be published with a statement that the Jameel group was not available for comment.

82. The judge and the Court of Appeal regarded this refusal to delay publication as fatal to the defence. The judge in particular drew attention to the fact that Mr Jameel subsequently obtained a denial from SAMA that they were monitoring his account and, if he had been given 24 hours, would very likely have been able to produce the denial to the Wall Street Journal before publication. In that case, said Eady J: "The importance of this front-page story would have been considerably blunted-even to the extent, perhaps, that no such story could be published."

83. I am bound to say that I regard this as unrealistic. There was no way in which SAMA would admit to monitoring the accounts of well known Saudi businesses at the request of the United States Treasury. A denial was exactly what one would inspect. (Mr Dorsey had approached SAMA directly for a comment but was unable to obtain one.) But I do not

imagine that SAMA's denial would have inhibited the Wall Street Journal from publishing a story which had been confirmed by the Treasury in Washington. While it is true—and Mr Dorsey admitted—that the story would have been no better or worse 24 hours later, this is only significant if the delay would have made a difference. In my opinion it would not.

84. Lord Nicholls said that the importance of approaching the claimant was that "he may have information others do not possess or have not disclosed". But that was not the case here. In the nature of things, Mr Jameel would have no knowledge of whether there was covert surveillance of his bank account. He could only say, as Mr Munajjed and the other named businesses approached by Mr Dorsey had said, that he knew of no reason why anyone should want to monitor his accounts. This Mr Dorsey would have reported if he had been allowed to do so.

85. It might have been better if the newspaper had delayed publication to give Mr Jameel an opportunity to comment in person. But I do not think that their failure to do so is enough to deprive them of the defence that they were reporting on a matter of public interest.

Diplomatic relations

86. The article, it will be recalled, said that "the United States had agreed not to publish the names of Saudi institutions and individuals provided that Saudi authorities took appropriate action". The judge rejected the newspaper's defence on the additional ground that it could not be in the public interest for the Wall Street Journal to publish information which the United States government had agreed not to publish. In principle, I would be very reluctant to accept the proposition that it cannot be in the public interest for a newspaper to publish information which one's government had agreed not to publish. But in any case, the position of the Wall Street Journal was that they had no wish to publish anything which might be damaging to the diplomatic interests of the United States or its attempts to secure Saudi co-operation in tracing terrorist funds. If the Treasury had indicated that the information should not be published, they probably would not have done so. But the Treasury cleared the article and that was good enough for them.

* * *

Disposal

88. In my opinion there was no basis for rejecting the newspaper's Reynolds defence. For the reasons I have given, no weight can be attached to the jury's rejection of the confirmation by sources in Saudi Arabia and they were asked no question about the confirmation in Washington. The failure to delay publication and the effect on diplomatic relations are insufficient reasons. The question is then whether the case should be remitted for a new trial or whether the appeal should be allowed and the action dismissed.

89. A new trial would in effect be to allow the jury to answer the question to which Mr Price objected, namely, whether Mr Simpson was telling the truth when he said that he had received confirmation in Washington. If this question had been answered in the newspaper's favour, it would have been bound to succeed. Indeed, such an answer, and a correction of the misdirection on the presumption of innocence, would be likely also to have affected the jury's answers to the questions on confirmation in Saudi Arabia. But Mr Simpson's evidence was, as I have said, essentially uncontradicted. I think that it is now too late for the claimants to change their minds and have the question of his veracity put to the jury. I would therefore allow the appeal and dismiss the action.

* * *

Appeal allowed in part.

NOTES

1. It is interesting that two of the law lords thought that a corporate body should not be able to recover without proof of actual financial damage. In the United States, the issue of whether corporations enjoy the same first-amendment rights as natural persons has become a contentious issue in recent years. It is a matter that is more appropriately dealt with in a constitutional law course. Lord Bingham seems correct in contending that corporations can have general reputational interests that cannot easily be translated into concrete pecuniary figures in particular cases. As will be seen when we examine the evolving constitutional dimensions of the law of defamation in the United States, the Supreme Court has not shown the slightest inclination to hold that corporate owners of newspapers and broadcast media are not entitled to the same protections against actions for defamation as would natural persons.

2. The courts in Canada (*see,* Grant v. Torstar Corp., [2009] 3 S.C.R. 640; Quan v. Cusson, [2009] 3 S.C.R. 712), Australia (*see* Lange v. Australian Broadcasting Corp., 189 C.L.R. 520 (1997)), and New Zealand (*see* Lange v. Atkinson, [2000] 3 N.Z.L.R. 385 (C.A.)) have similarly expanded the common-law privilege accorded the common interests of members of groups to include a broader common-law defense of public interest. Unlike the United Kingdom and Canada, the courts in Australia and New Zealand have been prepared to give a higher priority to political speech than to other forms of speech claiming the public interest defense. Indeed in New Zealand it appears that an honest belief in the truth of one's statement is a defense to an action for defamation for political speech which, except for putting the burden of persuasion on the defendant, approximates the way the law has evolved in the United States. In a more recent decision, Flood v. Times Newspapers Ltd, [2012] 2 W.L.R. 760 (S.C.), the Supreme Court of the United Kingdom held that the publication of the detailed allegations that prompted an official investigation of police corruption could constitute responsible journalism even if the allegations prompting the official investigation might not have been as extensively explored by the reporters as one might wish.

3. As we have seen in Chief Justice Roberts' opinion in *Snyder v. Phelps*, reprinted *supra* p. 471, and shall see again in the next section immediately following *Barr v. Matteo*, a number of Justices of the United States Supreme Court have suggested something like a public interest or public concern test to narrow the range of speech that is entitled to constitutional protection. For the moment it is enough to note that, outside the United States, it seems to be accepted, as declared by Lord Bingham, repeating Lord Nicholls' statement in *Reynolds*, that the issue is "whether the public is entitled to know the particular information." As we have also seen in *Jameel,* Lord Bingham followed that declaration by stating "[i]t has been repeatedly and rightly said that what engages the interest of the public may not be material which engages the public interest." If that is true, how do courts decide what expression is *really* in the public interest?

BARR v. MATTEO

Supreme Court of the United States, 1959.
360 U.S. 564, 79 S.Ct. 1335, 3 L.Ed.2d 1434.

MR. JUSTICE HARLAN announced the judgment of the Court, and delivered an opinion, in which MR. JUSTICE FRANKFURTER, MR. JUSTICE CLARK, and MR. JUSTICE WHITTAKER join.

* * *

This is a libel suit, brought in the District Court of the District of Columbia by respondents, former employees of the Office of Rent Stabilization. The alleged libel was contained in a press release issued by the office on February 5, 1953, at the direction of petitioner, then its Acting Director. The circumstances which gave rise to the issuance of the release follow.

In 1950 the statutory existence of the Office of Housing Expediter, the predecessor agency of the Office of Rent Stabilization, was about to expire. Respondent Madigan, then Deputy Director in charge of personnel and fiscal matters, and respondent Matteo, chief of the personnel branch, suggested to the Housing Expediter a plan designed to utilize some $2,600,000 of agency funds earmarked in the agency's appropriation for the fiscal year 1950 exclusively for terminal-leave payments. The effect of the plan would have been to obviate the possibility that the agency might have to make large terminal-leave payments during the next fiscal year out of general agency funds, should the life of the agency be extended by Congress. In essence, the mechanics of the plan were that agency employees would be discharged, paid accrued annual leave out of the $2,600,000 earmarked for terminal-leave payments, rehired immediately as temporary employees, and restored to permanent status should the agency's life in fact be extended.

Petitioner, at the time General Manager of the agency, opposed respondents' plan on the ground that it violated the spirit of the Thomas

Amendment, 64 Stat. 768,[2] and expressed his opposition to the Housing Expediter. The Expediter decided against general adoption of the plan, but at respondent Matteo's request gave permission for its use in connection with approximately fifty employees, including both respondents, on a voluntary basis.[3] Thereafter the life of the agency was in fact extended.

Some two and a half years later, on January 28, 1953, the Office of Rent Stabilization received a letter from Senator John J. Williams of Delaware, inquiring about the terminal-leave payments made under the plan in 1950. Respondent Madigan drafted a reply to the letter, which he did not attempt to bring to the attention of petitioner, and then prepared a reply which he sent to petitioner's office for his signature as Acting Director of the agency. Petitioner was out of the office, and a secretary signed the submitted letter, which was then delivered by Madigan to Senator Williams on the morning of February 3, 1953.

On February 4, 1953, Senator Williams delivered a speech on the floor of the Senate strongly criticizing the plan, stating that "to say the least it is an unjustifiable raid on the Federal Treasury, and heads of every agency in the Government who have condoned this practice should be called to task." The letter above referred to was ordered printed in the Congressional Record. Other Senators joined in the attack on the plan. Their comments were widely reported in the press on February 5, 1953, and petitioner, in his capacity as Acting Director of the agency, received a large number of inquiries from newspapers and other news media as to the agency's position on the matter.

On that day petitioner served upon respondents letters expressing his intention to suspend them from duty, and at the same time ordered issuance by the office of the press release which is the subject of this litigation, and the text of which appears in the margin.[5]

---

2. This statute, part of the General Appropriation Act of 1951, provided that:

"No part of the funds of, or available for expenditure by any corporation or agency included in this Act, including the government of the District of Columbia, shall be available to pay for annual leave accumulated by any civilian officer or employee during the calendar year 1950 and unused at the close of business on June 30, 1951 * * *."

3. The General Accounting Office subsequently ruled that the payments were illegal, and respondents were required to return them. Respondent Madigan challenged this determination in the Court of Claims, which held that the plan was not in violation of law. Madigan v. United States, 142 Ct.Cl. 641 [1958].

5. "William G. Barr, Acting Director of Rent Stabilization today served notice of suspension on the two officials of the agency who in June 1950 were responsible for the plan which allowed 53 of the agency's 2,681 employees to take their accumulated annual leave in cash.

"Mr. Barr's appointment as Acting Director becomes effective Monday, February 9, 1953, and the suspension of these employees will be his first act of duty. The employees are John J. Madigan, Deputy Director for Administration, and Linda Matteo, Director of Personnel.

" 'In June 1950,' Mr. Barr stated, 'my position in the agency was not one of authority which would have permitted me to stop the action. Furthermore, I did not know about it until it was almost completed.

" 'When I did learn that certain employees were receiving cash annual leave settlements and being returned to agency employment on a temporary basis, I specifically notified the employees under my supervision that if they applied for such cash settlements I would demand their resignations and the record will show that my immediate employees complied with my request.

" 'While I was advised that the action was legal, I took the position that it violated the spirit of the Thomas Amendment and I violently opposed it. Monday, February 9th, when my appointment

Respondents sued, charging that the press release, in itself and as coupled with the contemporaneous news reports of senatorial reaction to the plan, defamed them to their injury, and alleging that its publication and terms had been actuated by malice on the part of petitioner. Petitioner defended, *inter alia,* on the ground that the issuance of the press release was protected by either a qualified or an absolute privilege. The trial court overruled these contentions, and instructed the jury to return a verdict for respondents if it found the release defamatory. The jury found for respondents.

Petitioner appealed, raising only the issue of absolute privilege. The judgment of the trial court was affirmed by the Court of Appeals, which held that "in explaining his decision [to suspend respondents] to the general public [petitioner] * * * went entirely outside his line of duty" and that thus the absolute privilege, assumed otherwise to be available, did not attach. * * * We granted certiorari, vacated the Court of Appeals' judgment, and remanded the case "with directions to pass upon petitioner's claim of a qualified privilege." * * * On remand the Court of Appeals held that the press release was protected by a qualified privilege, but that there was evidence from which a jury could reasonably conclude that petitioner had acted maliciously, or had spoken with lack of reasonable grounds for believing that his statement was true, and that either conclusion would defeat the qualified privilege. Accordingly it remanded the case to the District Court for retrial. * * * At this point petitioner again sought, and we again granted certiorari, * * * to determine whether in the circumstances of this case petitioner's claim of absolute privilege should have stood as a bar to maintenance of the suit despite the allegations of malice made in the complaint.

The law of privilege as a defense by officers of government to civil damage suits for defamation and kindred torts has in large part been of judicial making, although the Constitution itself gives an absolute privilege to members of both Houses of Congress in respect to any speech, debate, vote, report, or action done in session. This Court early held that judges of courts of superior or general authority are absolutely privileged as respects civil suits to recover for actions taken by them in the exercise of their judicial functions, irrespective of the motives with which those acts are alleged to have been performed, * * * and that a like immunity extends to other officers of government whose duties are related to the judicial process. * * * Nor has the privilege been confined to officers of the legislative and judicial branches of the Government and executive officers of the kind involved in Yaselli. In Spalding v. Vilas, 161 U.S. 483, 16 S.Ct. 631, 40 L.Ed. 780, petitioner brought suit against the Postmaster

---

as Acting Director becomes effective, will be the first time my position in the agency has permitted me to take any action on this matter, and the suspension of these employees will be the first official act I shall take.'

"Mr. Barr also revealed that he has written to Senator Joseph McCarthy, Chairman of the Committee on Government Operations, and to Representative John Phillips, Chairman of the House Subcommittee on Independent Offices Appropriations, requesting an opportunity to be heard on the entire matter."

General, alleging that the latter had maliciously circulated widely among postmasters, past and present, information which he knew to be false and which was intended to deceive the postmasters to the detriment of the plaintiff. This Court sustained a plea by the Postmaster General of absolute privilege, * * *.

* * * The matter has been admirably expressed by Judge Learned Hand:

> "It does indeed go without saying that an official, who is in fact guilty of using his powers to vent his spleen upon others, or for any other personal motive not connected with the public good, should not escape liability for the injuries he may so cause; and, if it were possible in practice to confine such complaints to the guilty, it would be monstrous to deny recovery. The justification for doing so is that it is impossible to know whether the claim is well founded until the case has been tried, and that to submit all officials, the innocent as well as the guilty, to the burden of a trial and to the inevitable danger of its outcome would dampen the ardor of all but the most resolute, or the most irresponsible, in the unflinching discharge of their duties. Again and again the public interest calls for action which may turn out to be founded on a mistake, in the face of which an official may later find himself hard put to it to satisfy a jury of his good faith. There must indeed be means of punishing public officers who have been truant to their duties; but that is quite another matter from exposing such as have been honestly mistaken to suit by anyone who has suffered from their errors. As is so often the case, the answer must be found in a balance between the evils inevitable in either alternative. In this instance it has been thought in the end better to leave unredressed the wrongs done by dishonest officers than to subject those who try to do their duty to the constant dread of retaliation. * * *
>
> "The decisions have, indeed, always imposed as a limitation upon the immunity that the official's act must have been within the scope of his powers; and it can be argued that official powers, since they exist only for the public good, never cover occasions where the public good is not their aim, and hence that to exercise a power dishonestly is necessarily to overstep its bounds. A moment's reflection shows, however, that that cannot be the meaning of the limitation without defeating the whole doctrine. What is meant by saying that the officer must be acting within his power cannot be more than that the occasion must be such as would have justified the act, if he had been using his power for any of the purposes on whose account it was vested in him. * * *" Gregoire v. Biddle, 2 Cir., 177 F.2d 579, 581.

We do not think that the principle announced in Vilas can properly be restricted to executive officers of cabinet rank, and in fact it never has been so restricted by the lower federal courts. The privilege is not a badge or emolument of exalted office, but an expression of a policy designed to aid in the effective functioning of government. The complexities and magnitude of governmental activity have become so great that there must of necessity be a delegation and redelegation of authority as to many functions, and we cannot say that these functions become less important simply because they are exercised by officers of lower rank in the executive hierarchy.

To be sure, the occasions upon which the acts of the head of an executive department will be protected by the privilege are doubtless far broader than in the case of an officer with less sweeping functions. But that is because the higher the post, the broader the range of responsibilities and duties, and the wider the scope of discretion, it entails. It is not the title of his office but the duties with which the particular officer sought to be made to respond in damages is entrusted * * * which must provide the guide in delineating the scope of the rule which clothes the official acts of the executive officer with immunity from civil defamation suits.

Judged by these standards, we hold that petitioner's plea of absolute privilege in defense of the alleged libel published at his direction must be sustained. The question is a close one, but we cannot say that it was not an appropriate exercise of the discretion with which an executive officer of petitioner's rank is necessarily clothed to publish the press release here at issue in the circumstances disclosed by this record. * * * The integrity of the internal operations of the agency which he headed, and thus his own integrity in his public capacity, had been directly and severely challenged in charges made on the floor of the Senate and given wide publicity; and without his knowledge correspondence which could reasonably be read as impliedly defending a position very different from that which he had from the beginning taken in the matter had been sent to a Senator over his signature and incorporated in the Congressional Record. * * * It would be an unduly restrictive view of the scope of the duties of a policy-making executive official to hold that a public statement of agency policy in respect to matters of wide public interest and concern is not action in the line of duty. That petitioner was not *required* by law or by direction of his superiors to speak out cannot be controlling in the case of an official of policy-making rank, for the same considerations which underlie the recognition of the privilege as to acts done in connection with a mandatory duty apply with equal force to discretionary acts at those levels of government where the concept of duty encompasses the sound exercise of discretionary authority.

The fact that the action here taken was within the outer perimeter of petitioner's line of duty is enough to render the privilege applicable, despite the allegations of malice in the complaint * * *

We are told that we should forbear from sanctioning any such rule of absolute privilege lest it open the door to wholesale oppression and abuses on the part of unscrupulous government officials. It is perhaps enough to say that fears of this sort have not been realized within the wide area of government where a judicially formulated absolute privilege of broad scope has long existed. It seems to us wholly chimerical to suggest that what hangs in the balance here is the maintenance of high standards of conduct among those in the public service. To be sure, as with any rule of law which attempts to reconcile fundamentally antagonistic social policies, there may be occasional instances of actual injustice which will go unredressed, but we think that price a necessary one to pay for the greater good. And there are of course other sanctions than civil tort suits available to deter the executive official who may be prone to exercise his functions in an unworthy and irresponsible manner. We think that we should not be deterred from establishing the rule which we announce today by any such remote forebodings.

Reversed.

MR. JUSTICE BLACK, concurring.

I concur in the reversal of this judgment but briefly summarize my reasons because they are not altogether the same as those stated in the opinion of Mr. Justice Harlan.

* * *

The effective functioning of a free government like ours depends largely on the force of an informed public opinion. This calls for the widest possible understanding of the quality of government service rendered by all elective or appointed public officials or employees. Such an informed understanding depends, of course, on the freedom people have to applaud or to criticize the way public employees do their jobs, from the least to the most important.

* * * So far as I am concerned, if federal employees are to be subjected to such restraints in reporting their views about how to run the government better, the restraint will have to be imposed expressly by Congress and not by the general libel laws of the States or of the District of Columbia. How far the Congress itself could go in barring federal officials and employees from discussing public matters consistently with the First Amendment is a question we need not reach in this case. * * *

MR. CHIEF JUSTICE WARREN, with whom MR. JUSTICE DOUGLAS joins, dissenting.

The principal opinion in this case purports to launch the Court on a balancing process in order to reconcile the interest of the public in obtaining fearless executive performance and the interest of the individual in having redress for defamation. Even accepting for the moment that these are the proper interests to be balanced, the ultimate disposition is not the result of a balance. On the one hand, the principal opinion sets up a vague standard under which no government employee can tell with any certainty whether he will receive absolute immunity for his acts. On the other hand, it has not given even the slightest consideration to the interest of the individual who is defamed. It is a complete annihilation of his interest.

* * *

I.

The history of the privileges conferred upon the three branches of Government is a story of uneven development. Absolute legislative privilege dates back to at least 1399. This privilege is given to Congress in the United States Constitution and to State Legislatures in the Constitutions of almost all of the States of the Union. The absolute immunity arising out of judicial proceedings existed at least as early as 1608 in England.

But what of the executive privilege? Apparently, the earliest English case presenting the problem of immunity outside the legislative and judicial branches of government is Sutton v. Johnstone, 1 T.R. 493, decided in 1786. There, the plaintiff, captain of a warship, sued the commander-in-chief of his squadron for charging plaintiff, maliciously and without probable cause, with disobedience of orders and putting him under arrest and forcing him to face a court-martial. The Court of Exchequer took jurisdiction of the case but was reversed, 1 T.R. 510, on the ground that purely military matters were not within the cognizance of the civil courts. During the next century several other military cases were decided.

In Chatterton v. Secretary of State for India, [1895] 2 Q.B. 189, the defendant had been apprised that his action with respect to the plaintiff would be made the subject of a parliamentary inquiry. In the communication alleged to be libelous, the defendant told his Under Secretary what answer should be made if the question were asked him in Parliament. The court affirmed dismissal of the complaint relying on Fraser on The Law of Libel and Slander (1st ed.), p. 95, where the author, with no citations, observed, after relating the history of the military cases:

> "For reasons of public policy the same protection would, no doubt, be given to anything in the nature of an act of state, e.g., to every communication relating to state matters made by one minister to another, or to the Crown."

This was the actual birth of executive privilege in England.

Such was the state of English law when, the next year, this Court decided Spalding v. Vilas, supra. In granting the Postmaster General absolute immunity for "matters committed by law to his control or supervision," this Court relied exclusively on the judicial privilege cases and the English military cases. Thus, leaving aside the military cases, which are unique, the executive privilege in defamation actions would appear to be a judicial creature of less than 65 years' existence. Yet, without statute, this relatively new privilege is being extended to open the possibility of absolute privilege for innumerable government officials.

* * *

I would not extend Spalding v. Vilas to cover public statements of lesser officials. Releases to the public from the executive branch of government imply far greater dangers to the individual claiming to have been defamed than do internal libels. * * *

Giving officials below cabinet or equivalent rank qualified privilege for statements to the public would in no way hamper the internal operation of the executive department of government, nor would it unduly subordinate the interest of the individual in obtaining redress for the public defamation uttered against him. * * *

II.

* * *

It is clear that public discussion of the action of the Government and its officials is accorded no more than qualified privilege. In most States, even that privilege is further restricted to situations in which the speaker is accurate as to his facts and where the claimed defamation results from conclusions or opinions based on those facts. Only in a minority of States is a public critic of Government even qualifiedly privileged where his facts are wrong. Thus, at best, a public critic of the Government has a qualified privilege. Yet here the Court has given some amorphous group of officials—who have the most direct and personal contact with the public—an absolute privilege when their agency or their action is criticized. In this situation, it will take a brave person to criticize government officials knowing that in reply they may libel him with immunity in the name of defending the agency and their own position. * * *

* * *

I would affirm.

MR. JUSTICE STEWART, dissenting.

My brother Harlan's opinion contains, it seems to me, a lucid and persuasive analysis of the principles that should guide decision in this troublesome area of law. Where I part company is in the application of these principles to the facts of the present case.

I cannot agree that the issuance by the petitioner of this press release was "action in the line of duty." * * *

* * *

MR. JUSTICE BRENNAN, dissenting.

I think it is demonstrable that the solution of Mr. Justice Harlan's opinion to the question whether an absolute privilege should be allowed in these cases is not justified by the considerations offered to support it, and unnecessarily deprives the individual citizen of all redress against malicious defamation. Surely the opinion must recognize the existence of the deep-rooted policy of the common law generally to provide redress against defamation. But the opinion in sweeping terms extinguishes that remedy, if the defamation is committed by a federal official, by erecting the barrier of an absolute privilege. In my view, only a qualified privilege is necessary here, and that is all I would afford the officials. A qualified privilege would be the most the law would allow private citizens under comparable circumstances. * * *

* * *

There is an even more basic objection to the opinion. * * * It denies the defamed citizen a recovery by characterizing the policy favoring absolute immunity as "an expression of a policy designed to aid in the effective functioning of government." * * * To come to this conclusion, and to shift the line from the already extensive protection given the public officer by the qualified privilege doctrine, demands the resolution of large imponderables which one might have thought would be better the business of the Legislative Branch. * * *

* * *

NOTES

1. In Westfall v. Erwin, 484 U.S. 292, 108 S.Ct. 580, 98 L.Ed.2d 619 (1988), the Court held that the absolute state tort law immunity for actions taken by federal officials within the outer perimeter of their official duties only extended to the exercise of discretionary functions. Congress responded by enacting the Federal Employees Liability Reform and Tort Compensation Act of 1988 (popularly known as the "Westfall Act"), 102 Stat. 4563 (1988), which amended the Federal Tort Claims Act (F.T.C.A.) to provide for the substitution of the United States as the party defendant in all tort actions against federal employees that fall within the coverage of the F.T.C.A. 28 U.S.C. § 2679. Actions for defamation do not, however, fall within the coverage of the F.T.C.A.

2. With regard to the legislative privilege several questions deserve brief consideration. The first is when is a legislator acting in a legislative capacity? The Supreme Court has held that, while the privilege extends to committee meetings and the insertion of material in the Congressional Record, the privilege does not extend to press releases or newsletters sent to a legislator's constituents. *See* Hutchinson v. Proxmire, 443 U.S. 111, 99 S.Ct. 2675, 61 L.Ed.2d 411 (1979). The privilege also protects legislative staff members insofar as the staff members are assisting a legislator in the performance of what might be called a "legislative act." *Cf.* Gravel v. United States, 408 U.S. 606, 92 S.Ct. 2614, 33 L.Ed.2d 583 (1972). Witnesses before legislative bodies are granted an absolute privilege at least if their remarks are germane to the issue under legislative consideration. *See Restatement (Second) of Torts* § 590A. In a case where the alleged defamatory remarks were made at a city council hearing by a witness who had neither been subpoenaed to appear nor sworn and who was not responding to a question put to her by the council, a divided court held that she was only entitled to qualified, and not absolute, immunity. Vultaggio v. Yasko, 215 Wis.2d 326, 572 N.W.2d 450 (1998). Relying on McDonald v. Smith, 472 U.S. 479, 105 S.Ct. 2787, 86 L.Ed.2d 384 (1985), in which the Court held that an unsolicited letter to the President, copies of which were also sent to members of Congress and government officials, enjoyed no special constitutional status, the Michigan Supreme Court

held that defamatory material concerning a private entity in an unsolicited statement made to a city council was entitled to no privilege at all. J & J Construction Co. v. Bricklayers and Allied Craftsmen, Local 1, 468 Mich. 722, 664 N.W.2d 728 (2003).

The other question worth mentioning is that some states distinguish between state legislators, who are granted an absolute privilege, and the members of subordinate legislatures such as city councils and school boards, who are only granted a qualified privilege. With a few exceptions—*see, e.g.*, McClendon v. Coverdale, 57 Del. 568, 203 A.2d 815 (1964); Mills v. Denny, 245 Iowa 584, 63 N.W.2d 222 (1954)—the cases granting members of subordinate legislative bodies only a qualified privilege are from the nineteenth or early twentieth centuries. The predominant view is that members are entitled to an absolute privilege. *See* Board of Education v. Buffalo Council of Supervisors, 52 A.D.2d 220, 383 N.Y.S.2d 732 (1976); Larson v. Doner, 32 Ill.App.2d 471, 178 N.E.2d 399 (1961). *See also Restatement (Second) of Torts* § 590.

3. With regard to the absolute privilege of the judiciary, the issue sometimes arises whether a judge, who has made a defamatory statement, was acting in a judicial capacity. In Murray v. Brancato, 290 N.Y. 52, 48 N.E.2d 257 (1943), a lower court judge sent his opinions, in which he defamed a defense attorney, to the New York Law Journal and to the West Publishing Company for inclusion in the New York Supplement. In a 4–3 decision, it was held that while publication in the official reports (New York Miscellaneous Reports) was privileged, the judge exceeded his privilege by sending the opinions to the New York Law Journal and to West. *Cf.* Douglas v. Collins, 243 App.Div. 546, 276 N.Y.S. 87 (1934), *affirmed without opinion* 267 N.Y. 557, 196 N.E. 577 (1935) (judge's remarks after court had adjourned and he had stepped down from the bench not privileged). *Murray v. Brancato* now seems to be a questionable decision. Indeed, in Beary v. West Publishing Co., 763 F.2d 66 (2d Cir.1985), the federal court of appeal ruled that the full and accurate report of a case in an unofficial report (New York Supplement 2d Advance Sheets) was absolutely privileged. The federal court relied on § 74 of the New York Civil Rights Law which, *inter alia*, provides that no action can be maintained for "a fair and true report of any judicial proceeding." The New York Court of Appeals in *Murray v. Brancato*, had noted the possible application of § 74 but did not rule on the issue because it had not been raised in the pleadings and because the prevailing majority had doubts whether it applied to publication by the judge himself.

The absolute privilege extends to statements made by parties, witnesses, jurors, and attorneys in the course of judicial proceedings, although the privilege they may claim is restricted by a requirement that the statements have some relevance to the judicial proceedings in question. *See Restatement (Second) of Torts* §§ 586–89. Under English law it has been stressed that what would be considered relevant would be given a very wide interpretation and that any relevance at all would probably suffice. *See* Duncan and Neill on Defamation § 15.26 (2009).

4. Prior to *Barr v. Matteo,* most states distinguished between major executive officers such as governors and the state equivalents of federal

cabinet officers, on the one hand, and lesser executive officials on the other. Only the former were granted an absolute privilege; lesser officials were granted only a qualified privilege. Since *Barr v. Matteo,* the situation on the state level is less clear. This uncertainty is reflected in a series of New York decisions. In Lombardo v. Stoke, 18 N.Y.2d 394, 276 N.Y.S.2d 97, 222 N.E.2d 721 (1966), an absolute privilege was granted to the New York City Board of Higher Education. The court relied on an earlier case recognizing an absolute privilege on the part of the Borough President of Queens. Sheridan v. Crisona, 14 N.Y.2d 108, 249 N.Y.S.2d 161, 198 N.E.2d 359 (1964). The court in *Lombardo* left open the question of whether the president of a municipal college was also able to claim an absolute privilege. In Stukuls v. State of New York, 42 N.Y.2d 272, 397 N.Y.S.2d 740, 366 N.E.2d 829 (1977), the court held that the acting president of the State University College at Cortland could only claim a qualified privilege. But then, in Ward Telecommunications and Computer Services, Inc. v. State of New York, 42 N.Y.2d 289, 397 N.Y.S.2d 751, 366 N.E.2d 840 (1977), the court held that members of the staff of the Comptroller of New York State were absolutely privileged. A good recent discussion of the present state of the law regarding the types of immunity enjoyed by government officials is contained in the majority opinions and the dissent in Zutz v. Nelson, 788 N.W.2d 58 (Minn. 2010).

5. *The Reporting Privilege.* Reports of official proceedings, if accurate, are absolutely privileged. The privilege has been extended to cover "public meetings." A report of a stockholders' meeting, that was not open to the public, has been held not to be privileged. *See* Kimball v. Post Publishing Co., 199 Mass. 248, 85 N.E. 103 (1908) (distinguishing an earlier case, Barrows v. Bell, 73 Mass. (7 Gray) 301 (1856) holding a report of a meeting of the Massachusetts Medical Society to be privileged). In the light of the constitutional developments, to which we are about to turn, however, it is questionable whether a case like *Kimball* would be followed today. Indeed, in Edwards v. National Audubon Society, Inc., 556 F.2d 113 (2d Cir.1977), *cert. denied* 434 U.S. 1002, 98 S.Ct. 647, 54 L.Ed.2d 498, the New York Times reported the charges and countercharges between the plaintiff scientists and the Audubon Society on the issue of whether the use of DDT was affecting bird life. The court of appeals held that the Times articles were privileged as "neutral reportage" of a public dispute. *See also* Krauss v. Champaign News Gazette, Inc., 59 Ill.App.3d 745, 17 Ill.Dec. 78, 375 N.E.2d 1362 (1978). The *Edwards* case was rejected by another circuit in Dickey v. CBS Inc., 583 F.2d 1221 (3d Cir.1978). *Edwards* was not applied by a later case, Cianci v. New Times Publishing Co., 639 F.2d 54 (2d Cir.1980), in which the court held that "a jury could well find that the New Times did not simply report the charges [of rape] but espoused or concurred in them. * * * " The *Edwards* case was likewise rejected by the New York state courts in Hogan v. Herald Co., 84 A.D.2d 470, 446 N.Y.S.2d 836 (4th Dept.1982), *affirmed on opinion below* 58 N.Y.2d 630, 458 N.Y.S.2d 538, 444 N.E.2d 1002. A California case has, however, applied an analogous privilege based on state-law grounds. Stockton Newspapers, Inc. v. Superior Court, 206 Cal.App.3d 966, 254 Cal.Rptr. 389 (1988) (report of a claim of official misconduct against the plaintiff, who was a public official, made by a third party). The scope of any such privilege in California is undoubtedly rather limited. It certainly does not include situations in which

the newspaper itself participated in creating the event which it is purporting to report or situations involving private parties. *See* Brown v. Kelly Broadcasting Co., 48 Cal.3d 711, 771 P.2d 406, 257 Cal.Rptr. 708 (1989). For a general discussion of the broader aspects of the subject, *see* J. Wade, *The Tort Liability of Investigative Reporters*, 37 Vand.L.J. 301 (1984). It should finally be noted that in Farmers Educational & Cooperative Union v. WDAY, Inc., 360 U.S. 525, 79 S.Ct. 1302, 3 L.Ed.2d 1407 (1959), the Court construed the Federal Communications Act (47 U.S.C. § 315(a)) to absolutely immunize broadcasters for defamatory remarks made by candidates for public office if the broadcaster permits such candidates to use its facilities. For a critical discussion of the press reports of a recent *cause célèbre, see* Note, *A Libel Law Analysis of Media Abuses in Reporting on the Duke Lacrosse Fabricated Rape Charges*, 11 Vand. J. Ent. & Tech.L. 99 (2008).

There has been some controversy over whether the mere filing of a complaint is such a public act as to permit a newspaper that accurately reports the substance of the complaint to claim the reporting privilege. Relying on cases like Sanford v. Boston Herald–Traveler Corp., 318 Mass. 156, 61 N.E.2d 5 (1945), *Restatement (Second)* § 611, Comment *e,* continues to take the position that the mere filing of a complaint does not give rise to a reporting privilege. Some official action on the complaint is necessary. *See also* Stern v. Piper, [1996] 3 All E.R. 385 (C.A.). New York has for many years taken the opposite position—*see* Campbell v. New York Evening Post, Inc., 245 N.Y. 320, 157 N.E. 153 (1927) (relying on a statutory provision)—and the modern trend is clearly in this direction. *See* Johnson v. Johnson Publishing Co., 271 A.2d 696 (D.C.App.1970); *cf.* O'Brien v. Franich, 19 Wash.App. 189, 575 P.2d 258 (1978); Hurley v. Northwest Publications, Inc., 273 F.Supp. 967 (D.Minn.1967), *affirmed* 398 F.2d 346 (8th Cir.1968). A reportorial privilege to reprint complaints and other material on file in public record offices may now indeed be constitutionally required.

That is not to say that there may not be some circumstances where the reporting privilege may not be applicable. For example, in Williams v. Williams, 23 N.Y.2d 592, 298 N.Y.S.2d 473, 246 N.E.2d 333 (1969), at the instigation of the defendants, an action was instituted against the plaintiff by his former employer charging him with misappropriating money and other derelictions while he was an employee. After the filing of the complaint, the defendants circulated copies of the complaint among the trade. The New York Court of Appeals, with two judges dissenting, held that this public circulation of the complaint could not claim the protection of the reporting privilege. The court held, however, that the trial of the libel action should await the results of the employer's action against the plaintiff. The *Williams* case was distinguished in Stover v. Journal Pub. Co., 105 N.M. 291, 731 P.2d 1335 (App. 1985), *cert. denied* 484 U.S. 897, 108 S.Ct. 230, 98 L.Ed.2d 189 (1987). In the *Stover* case the defendant newspaper had been a defendant in another action. In the course of that other action, the newspaper, pursuant to the trial court's order, filed an affidavit from a witness whose testimony the defendant intended to use in that other action. The affidavit indicated that Stover, who was a candidate for sheriff, and a former governor of New Mexico, who was a candidate for the United States Senate, had connections with Mafia figures. The attorneys for the former governor advised the trial court that they intended to call a press conference and to release an affidavit which they had filed with the court in order to rebut the contents of the affidavit filed by the newspaper, as it applied to the former governor. The newspaper then filed an unopposed motion to unseal this affidavit. The affidavit was unsealed and the newspaper, on the following day, published an article concerning the affidavit and the denials of Stover and others. Stover then brought his action for defamation against the newspaper. It was held that the newspaper's article was a fair and accurate report of the affidavit which had been filed with the trial court in the other action and that consequently the newspaper article was absolutely privileged. The *Williams* case was distinguished. Unlike the situation in *Williams*, the newspaper had not instigated the other judicial proceedings in which the affidavit had been filed; rather it was an unwilling defendant. The newspaper pointed out that the affidavit had been unsealed and was readily available for public examination. Indeed, the contents of the affidavit had already been the subject of reports presented by several local television stations.

6. *Retraction.* A timely retraction is of course normally relevant on the issue of damages. A few states, *e.g.,* West's Ann.Cal.Civ.Code § 48a; Or.Rev. Stat. § 30.160, provide that unless a retraction is demanded and refused, the plaintiff may not recover any general damages from a media defendant. The California statute, which applies only to newspapers and broadcasters, expressly limits the plaintiff in such a situation to his "special damages." The Oregon statute extends also to magazine publishers. Although the California and Oregon statutes have withstood constitutional attack in the courts of those states, a somewhat similar Montana statute was held unconstitutional in Madison v. Yunker, 180 Mont. 54, 589 P.2d 126 (1978). The Montana statute went further than the other statutes in conditioning even the right to bring an action for actual damages on a prior request for a retraction. It should finally be noted that, in Miami Herald Publishing Co. v. Tornillo, 418 U.S. 241, 94 S.Ct. 2831, 41 L.Ed.2d 730 (1974), a unanimous Court struck down a Florida statute requiring newspapers to publish a reply by any candidate for public office whom the newspaper had attacked.

In Great Britain, under § 4 of the Defamation Act of 1952, a person who published material "defamatory of another" and who claimed that "the words were published by him innocently of another" could make an "offer of amends." An offer of amends was defined to include an offer to publish "a suitable correction" and "a sufficient apology" and to take steps to notify persons to whom the person making the offer of amends knew the allegedly defamatory material had been distributed. If the party alleged to be defamed accepted the offer, a jury trial was avoided and, if the parties were unable to agree, the courts were given jurisdiction to award legal costs and other reasonable expenses incurred by the party allegedly defamed. If the party defamed rejected a timely offer of amends, the making of the offer served as a defense to an action of defamation if the defendant could show that he acted with reasonable care and that "the words complained of were published by him innocently in relation to the plaintiff." Sections 2, 3, and 4 of the Defamation Act of 1996 continue and expand the "offer to make amends" procedure. If the offer is accepted, a jury trial is avoided and the courts are empowered, in the absence of agreement by the parties, to determine the appropriate damages to be paid to the plaintiff. If an offer to make amends is not accepted and the defendant is prepared to waive all other defenses, the defendant can plead the offer to make amends as a complete defense if the defendant neither knew nor had reason to believe (a) that the material referred to the plaintiff or was likely to be understood as referring to the plaintiff *and* (b) that the material was both false and defamatory. The burden of showing defendant's knowledge of falsity or reason to believe that the material was false is apparently on the plaintiff.

7. *Alternative remedies.* It has often been urged that there should be alternate remedies for defamation. The principal such remedy that has been suggested over the years involves the use of declaratory judgment proceedings to establish the falsity of derogatory statements that have been made about the plaintiff. Given the constitutionalization of much of the law of defamation, we will postpone our discussion of these possible alternative remedies until p. 635, *infra,* because all these proposed remedies raise some first amendment issues.

C. CONSTITUTIONAL DEVELOPMENTS

NEW YORK TIMES CO. v. SULLIVAN

Supreme Court of the United States, 1964.
376 U.S. 254, 84 S.Ct. 710, 11 L.Ed.2d 686.

MR. JUSTICE BRENNAN delivered the opinion of the Court.

We are required in this case to determine for the first time the extent to which the constitutional protections for speech and press limit a State's power to award damages in a libel action brought by a public official against critics of his official conduct.

Respondent L. B. Sullivan is one of the three elected Commissioners of the City of Montgomery, Alabama. He testified that he was "Commissioner of Public Affairs and the duties are supervision of the Police Department, Fire Department, Department of Cemetery and Department of Scales." He brought this civil libel action against the four individual petitioners, who are Negroes and Alabama clergymen, and against petitioner the New York Times Company, a New York corporation which publishes the New York Times, a daily newspaper. A jury in the Circuit Court of Montgomery County awarded him damages of $500,000, the full amount claimed, against all the petitioners, and the Supreme Court of Alabama affirmed. 273 Ala. 656, 144 So.2d 25.

* * *

Of the 10 paragraphs of text in the advertisement, the third and a portion of the sixth were the basis of respondent's claim of libel. They read as follows:

Third paragraph:

> "In Montgomery, Alabama, after students sang 'My Country, 'Tis of Thee' on the State Capitol steps, their leaders were expelled from

> school, and truckloads of police armed with shotguns and tear-gas ringed the Alabama State College Campus. When the entire student body protested to state authorities by refusing to re-register, their dining hall was padlocked in an attempt to starve them into submission."

Sixth paragraph:

> "Again and again the Southern violators have answered Dr. King's peaceful protests with intimidation and violence. They have bombed his home almost killing his wife and child. They have assaulted his person. They have arrested him seven times—for 'speeding,' 'loitering' and similar 'offenses.' And now they have charged him with 'perjury'—a *felony* under which they could imprison him for *ten years*. * * * "

Although neither of these statements mentions respondent by name, he contended that the word "police" in the third paragraph referred to him as the Montgomery Commissioner who supervised the Police Department, so that he was being accused of "ringing" the campus with police. He further claimed that the paragraph would be read as imputing to the police, and hence to him, the padlocking of the dining hall in order to starve the students into submission. As to the sixth paragraph, he contended that since arrests are ordinarily made by the police, the statement "They have arrested [Dr. King] seven times" would be read as referring to him; he further contended that the "They" who did the arresting would be equated with the "They" who committed the other described acts and with the "Southern violators." Thus, he argued, the paragraph would be read as accusing the Montgomery police, and hence him, of answering Dr. King's protests with "intimidation and violence," bombing his home, assaulting his person, and charging him with perjury. Respondent and six other Montgomery residents testified that they read some or all of the statements as referring to him in his capacity as Commissioner.

It is uncontroverted that some of the statements contained in the two paragraphs were not accurate descriptions of events which occurred in Montgomery. Although Negro students staged a demonstration on the State Capitol steps, they sang the National Anthem and not "My Country, 'Tis of Thee." Although nine students were expelled by the State Board of Education, this was not for leading the demonstration at the Capitol, but for demanding service at a lunch counter in the Montgomery County Courthouse on another day. Not the entire student body, but most of it, had protested the expulsion, not by refusing to register, but by boycotting classes on a single day; virtually all the students did register for the ensuing semester. The campus dining hall was not padlocked on any occasion, and the only students who may have been barred from eating there were the few who had neither signed a preregistration application nor requested temporary meal tickets. Although the police were deployed near the campus in large numbers on three occasions, they did not at any time "ring" the campus, and they were not called to the campus in connection with the demonstration on the State Capitol steps, as the third paragraph implied. Dr. King had not been arrested seven times, but only four; and although he claimed to have been assaulted some years earlier in connection with his arrest for loitering outside a courtroom, one of the officers who made the arrest denied that there was such an assault.

On the premise that the charges in the sixth paragraph could be read as referring to him, respondent was allowed to prove that he had not participated in the events described. Although Dr. King's home had in fact been bombed twice when his wife and child were there, both of these occasions antedated respondent's tenure as Commissioner, and the police were not only not implicated in the bombings, but had made every effort to apprehend those who were. Three of Dr. King's four arrests took place before respondent became Commissioner. Although Dr. King had in fact been indicted (he was subsequently acquitted) on two counts of perjury, each of which carried a possible five-year sentence, respondent had nothing to do with procuring the indictment.

Respondent made no effort to prove that he suffered actual pecuniary loss as a result of the alleged libel.[3] One of his witnesses, a former employer, testified that if he had believed the statements, he doubted whether he "would want to be associated with anybody who would be a party to such things that are stated in that ad," and that he would not re-employ respondent if he believed "that he allowed the Police Department to do the things that the paper say he did." But neither this witness nor any of the others testified that he had actually believed the statements in their supposed reference to respondent.

The cost of the advertisement was approximately $4800, and it was published by the Times upon an order from a New York advertising agency acting for the signatory Committee. The agency submitted the advertisement with a letter from A. Philip Randolph, Chairman of the Committee, certifying that the persons whose names appeared on the advertisement had given their permission. Mr. Randolph was known to the Times' Advertising Acceptability Department as a responsible person, and in accepting the letter as sufficient proof of authorization it followed its established practice. * * * Each of the individual petitioners testified that he had not authorized the use of his name, and that he had been unaware of its use until receipt of respondent's demand for a retraction. The manager of the Advertising Acceptability Department testified that he had approved the advertisement for publication because he knew nothing to cause him to believe that anything in it was false, and because it bore the endorsement of "a number of people who are well known and whose reputation" he "had no reason to question." Neither he nor anyone else at the Times made an effort to confirm the accuracy of the advertisement,

3. Approximately 394 copies of the edition of the Times containing the advertisement were circulated in Alabama. Of these, about 35 copies were distributed in Montgomery County. The total circulation of the Times for that day was approximately 650,000 copies. [Ed. note] The *Times* argued that the Alabama courts had no basis for asserting jurisdiction over it, but the Court, in note 4 to its opinion that has been omitted, upheld the Alabama courts' ruling that the *Times* waived this objection by making a general appearance.

either by checking it against recent Times news stories relating to some of the described events or by any other means.

Alabama law denies a public officer recovery of punitive damages in a libel action brought on account of a publication concerning his official conduct unless he first makes a written demand for a public retraction and the defendant fails or refuses to comply. * * * Respondent served such a demand upon each of the petitioners. None of the individual petitioners responded to the demand, primarily because each took the position that he had not authorized the use of his name on the advertisement and therefore had not published the statements that respondent alleged had libeled him. The Times did not publish a retraction in response to the demand, but wrote respondent a letter stating, among other things, that "we * * * are somewhat puzzled as to how you think the statements in any way reflect on you," and "you might, if you desire, let us know in what respect you claim that the statements in the advertisement reflect on you." Respondent filed this suit a few days later without answering the letter. The Times did, however, subsequently publish a retraction of the advertisement upon the demand of Governor John Patterson of Alabama, who asserted that the publication charged him with "grave misconduct and * * * improper actions and omissions as Governor of Alabama and Ex–Officio Chairman of the State Board of Education of Alabama." When asked to explain why there had been a retraction for the Governor but not for respondent, the Secretary of the Times testified: "We did that because we didn't want anything that was published by The Times to be a reflection on the State of Alabama and the Governor was, as far as we could see, the embodiment of the State of Alabama and the proper representative of the State and, furthermore, we had by that time learned more of the actual facts which the ad purported to recite and, finally, the ad did refer to the action of the State authorities and the Board of Education presumably of which the Governor is the ex-officio chairman * * *." On the other hand, he testified that he did not think that "any of the language in there referred to Mr. Sullivan."

* * * The jury was instructed that, because the statements were libelous *per se,* "the law * * * implies legal injury from the bare fact of publication itself," "falsity and malice are presumed," "general damages need not be alleged or proved but are presumed," and "punitive damages may be awarded by the jury even though the amount of actual damages is neither found nor shown." An award of punitive damages—as distinguished from "general" damages, which are compensatory in nature—apparently requires proof of actual malice under Alabama law, and the judge charged that "mere negligence or carelessness is not evidence of actual malice or malice in fact, and does not justify an award of exemplary or punitive damages." He refused to charge, however, that the jury must be "convinced" of malice, in the sense of "actual intent" to harm or "gross negligence and recklessness," to make such an award, and he also refused to require that a verdict for respondent differentiate between compensatory and punitive damages. The judge rejected petitioners' con-

tention that his rulings abridged the freedoms of speech and of the press that are guaranteed by the First and Fourteenth Amendments.

In affirming the judgment, the Supreme Court of Alabama sustained the trial judge's rulings and instructions in all respects. * * * In sustaining the trial court's determination that the verdict was not excessive, the court said that malice could be inferred from the Times' "irresponsibility" in printing the advertisement while "the Times in its own files had articles already published which would have demonstrated the falsity of the allegations in the advertisement"; from the Times' failure to retract for respondent while retracting for the Governor, whereas the falsity of some of the allegations was then known to the Times and "the matter contained in the advertisement was equally false as to both parties"; and from the testimony of the Times' Secretary that, apart from the statement that the dining hall was padlocked, he thought the two paragraphs were "substantially correct." * * * The court reaffirmed a statement in an earlier opinion that "There is no legal measure of damages in cases of this character." * * * It rejected petitioners' constitutional contentions with the brief statements that "The First Amendment of the U.S. Constitution does not protect libelous publications" and "The Fourteenth Amendment is directed against State action and not private action." * * *

Because of the importance of the constitutional issues involved, we granted the separate petitions for certiorari of the individual petitioners and of the Times. * * * We reverse the judgment. We hold that the rule of law applied by the Alabama courts is constitutionally deficient for failure to provide the safeguards for freedom of speech and of the press that are required by the First and Fourteenth Amendments in a libel action brought by a public official against critics of his official conduct. We further hold that under the proper safeguards the evidence presented in this case is constitutionally insufficient to support the judgment for respondent.

I.

We may dispose at the outset of two grounds asserted to insulate the judgment of the Alabama courts from constitutional scrutiny. The first is the proposition relied on by the State Supreme Court—that "The Fourteenth Amendment is directed against State action and not private action." That proposition has no application to this case. Although this is a civil lawsuit between private parties, the Alabama courts have applied a state rule of law which petitioners claim to impose invalid restrictions on their constitutional freedoms of speech and press. It matters not that that law has been applied in a civil action and that it is common law only, though supplemented by statute. * * *

The second contention is that the constitutional guarantees of freedom of speech and of the press are inapplicable here, at least so far as the Times is concerned, because the allegedly libelous statements were published as part of a paid, "commercial" advertisement. The argument relies on Valentine v. Chrestensen, 316 U.S. 52, 62 S.Ct. 920, 86 L.Ed. 1262, * * *.

The publication here was not a "commercial" advertisement in the sense in which the word was used in Chrestensen. It communicated information, expressed opinion, recited grievances, protested claimed abuses, and sought financial support on behalf of a movement whose existence and objectives are matters of the highest public interest and concern. * * *

II.

Under Alabama law as applied in this case, a publication is "libelous per se" if the words "tend to injure a person * * * in his reputation" or to "bring [him] into public contempt"; the trial court stated that the standard was met if the words are such as to "injure him in his public office, or impute misconduct to him in his office, or want of official integrity, or want of fidelity to a public trust * * *." The jury must find that the words were published "of and concerning" the plaintiff, but where the plaintiff is a public official his place in the governmental hierarchy is sufficient evidence to support a finding that his reputation has been affected by statements that reflect upon the agency of which he is in charge. Once "libel per se" has been established, the defendant has no defense as to stated facts unless he can persuade the jury that they were true in all their particulars. * * * His privilege of "fair comment" for expressions of opinion depends on the truth of the facts upon which the comment is based. * * * Unless he can discharge the burden of proving truth, general damages are presumed, and may be awarded without proof of pecuniary injury. A showing of actual malice is apparently a prerequisite to recovery of punitive damages, and the defendant may in any event forestall a punitive award by a retraction meeting the statutory requirements. Good motives and belief in truth do not negate an inference of malice, but are relevant only in mitigation of punitive damages if the jury chooses to accord them weight. * * *

The question before us is whether this rule of liability, as applied to an action brought by a public official against critics of his official conduct, abridges the freedom of speech and of the press that is guaranteed by the First and Fourteenth Amendments.

Respondent relies heavily, as did the Alabama courts, on statements of this Court to the effect that the Constitution does not protect libelous publications. Those statements do not foreclose our inquiry here. None of the cases sustained the use of libel laws to impose sanctions upon expression critical of the official conduct of public officials. * * * In the only previous case that did present the question of constitutional limitations upon the power to award damages for libel of a public official, the Court was equally divided and the question was not decided. Schenectady Union Publishing Co. v. Sweeney, 316 U.S. 642, 62 S.Ct. 1031, 86 L.Ed. 1727 (1942).

The general proposition that freedom of expression upon public questions is secured by the First Amendment has long been settled by our decisions.

Thus we consider this case against the background of a profound national commitment to the principle that debate on public issues should be uninhibited, robust, and wide-open, and that it may well include vehement, caustic, and sometimes unpleasantly sharp attacks on government and public officials. * * * The present advertisement, as an expression of grievance and protest on one of the major public issues of our time, would seem clearly to qualify for the constitutional protection. The question is whether it forfeits that protection by the falsity of some of its factual statements and by its alleged defamation of respondent.

Authoritative interpretations of the First Amendment guarantees have consistently refused to recognize an exception for any test of truth—whether administered by judges, juries, or administrative officials—and especially one that puts the burden of proving truth on the speaker. * * * As Madison said, "Some degree of abuse is inseparable from the proper use of every thing; and in no instance is this more true than in that of the press." 4 Elliot's Debates on the Federal Constitution (1876), p. 571. * * *

Injury to official reputation affords no more warrant for repressing speech that would otherwise be free than does factual error. * * *

If neither factual error nor defamatory content suffices to remove the constitutional shield from criticism of official conduct, the combination of the two elements is no less inadequate. This is the lesson to be drawn from the great controversy over the Sedition Act of 1798, 1 Stat. 596, which first crystallized a national awareness of the central meaning of the First Amendment. * * * That statute made it a crime, punishable by a $5,000 fine and five years in prison, "if any person shall write, print, utter or publish * * * any false, scandalous and malicious writing or writings against the government of the United States, or either house of the Congress * * *, or the President * * *, with intent to defame * * * or to bring them, or either of them, into contempt or disrepute; or to excite against them, or either or any of them, the hatred of the good people of the United States." The Act allowed the defendant the defense of truth, and provided that the jury were to be judges both of the law and the facts. Despite these qualifications, the Act was vigorously condemned as unconstitutional in an attack joined in by Jefferson and Madison. * * *

Although the Sedition Act was never tested in this Court,[16] the attack upon its validity has carried the day in the court of history. Fines levied in its prosecution were repaid by Act of Congress on the ground that it was unconstitutional. See, e.g., Act of July 4, 1840, c. 45, 6 Stat. 802, accompanied by H.R.Rep. No. 86, 26th Cong., 1st Sess. (1840). Calhoun, reporting to the Senate on February 4, 1836, assumed that its invalidity was a matter "which no one now doubts." Report with Senate bill No. 122, 24th Cong., 1st Sess., p. 3. Jefferson, as President, pardoned those who had

16. The Act expired by its terms in 1801.

been convicted and sentenced under the Act and remitted their fines, stating: "I discharged every person under punishment or prosecution under the sedition law, because I considered, and now consider, that law to be a nullity, as absolute and as palpable as if Congress had ordered us to fall down and worship a golden image." Letter to Mrs. Adams, July 22, 1804, 4 Jefferson's Works (Washington ed.), pp. 555, 556. The invalidity of the Act has also been assumed by Justices of this Court. * * * These views reflect a broad consensus that the Act, because of the restraint it imposed upon criticism of government and public officials, was inconsistent with the First Amendment.

There is no force in respondent's argument that the constitutional limitations implicit in the history of the Sedition Act apply only to Congress and not to the States. It is true that the First Amendment was originally addressed only to action by the Federal Government, and that Jefferson, for one, while denying the power of Congress "to controul the freedom of the press," recognized such a power in the States. See the 1804 Letter to Abigail Adams quoted in Dennis v. United States, 341 U.S. 494 * * *.

What a State may not constitutionally bring about by means of a criminal statute is likewise beyond the reach of its civil law of libel. The fear of damage awards under a rule such as that invoked by the Alabama courts here may be markedly more inhibiting than the fear of prosecution under a criminal statute. * * * Alabama, for example, has a criminal libel law which subjects to prosecution "any person who speaks, writes, or prints of and concerning another any accusation falsely and maliciously importing the commission by such person of a felony, or any other indictable offense involving moral turpitude," and which allows as punishment upon conviction a fine not exceeding $500 and a prison sentence of six months. Alabama Code, Tit. 14, § 350. Presumably a person charged with violation of this statute enjoys ordinary criminal-law safeguards such as the requirements of an indictment and of proof beyond a reasonable doubt. These safeguards are not available to the defendant in a civil action. The judgment awarded in this case—without the need for any proof of actual pecuniary loss—was one thousand times greater than the maximum fine provided by the Alabama criminal statute, and one hundred times greater than that provided by the Sedition Act. And since there is no double-jeopardy limitation applicable to civil lawsuits, this is not the only judgment that may be awarded against petitioners for the same publication.[18] Whether or not a newspaper can survive a succession of such judgments, the pall of fear and timidity imposed upon those who would give voice to public criticism is an atmosphere in which the First Amendment freedoms cannot survive. * * *

18. The Times states that four other libel suits based on the advertisement have been filed against it by others who have served as Montgomery City Commissioners and by the Governor of Alabama; that another $500,000 verdict has been awarded in the only one of these cases that has yet gone to trial; and that the damages sought in the other three total $2,000,000.

The state rule of law is not saved by its allowance of the defense of truth. * * * A rule compelling the critic of official conduct to guarantee the truth of all his factual assertions—and to do so on pain of libel judgments virtually unlimited in amount—leads to a comparable "self-censorship." Allowance of the defense of truth, with the burden of proving it on the defendant, does not mean that only false speech will be deterred.[19] Even courts accepting this defense as an adequate safeguard have recognized the difficulties of adducing legal proofs that the alleged libel was true in all its factual particulars. * * * Under such a rule, would-be critics of official conduct may be deterred from voicing their criticism, even though it is believed to be true and even though it is in fact true, because of doubt whether it can be proved in court or fear of the expense of having to do so. * * * The rule thus dampens the vigor and limits the variety of public debate. It is inconsistent with the First and Fourteenth Amendments.

The constitutional guarantees require, we think, a federal rule that prohibits a public official from recovering damages for a defamatory falsehood relating to his official conduct unless he proves that the statement was made with "actual malice"—that is, with knowledge that it was false or with reckless disregard of whether it was false or not. An oft-cited statement of a like rule, which has been adopted by a number of state courts, is found in the Kansas case of Coleman v. MacLennan, 78 Kan. 711, 98 P. 281 (1908). * * *

Such a privilege for criticism of official conduct is appropriately analogous to the protection accorded a public official when *he* is sued for libel by a private citizen. In Barr v. Matteo, * * * this Court held the utterance of a federal official to be absolutely privileged if made "within the outer perimeter" of his duties. The States accord the same immunity to statements of their highest officers, although some differentiate their lesser officials and qualify the privilege they enjoy. But all hold that all officials are protected unless actual malice can be proved. The reason for the official privilege is said to be that the threat of damage suits would otherwise "inhibit the fearless, vigorous, and effective administration of policies of government" and "dampen the ardor of all but the most resolute, or the most irresponsible, in the unflinching discharge of their duties." Barr v. Matteo, supra, * * * Analogous considerations support the privilege for the citizen-critic of government. It is as much his duty to criticize as it is the official's duty to administer. * * * As Madison said, * * * "the censorial power is in the people over the Government, and not in the Government over the people." It would give public servants an unjustified preference over the public they serve, if critics of official conduct did not have a fair equivalent of the immunity granted to the officials themselves.

---

19. Even a false statement may be deemed to make a valuable contribution to public debate, since it brings about "the clearer perception and livelier impression of truth, produced by its collision with error." Mill, On Liberty (Oxford: Blackwell, 1947), at 15; see also Milton, Areopagitica, in Prose Works (Yale, 1959), Vol. II, at 561.

We conclude that such a privilege is required by the First and Fourteenth Amendments.

III.

We hold today that the Constitution delimits a State's power to award damages for libel in actions brought by public officials against critics of their official conduct. Since this is such an action,[23] the rule requiring proof of actual malice is applicable. While Alabama law apparently requires proof of actual malice for an award of punitive damages, where general damages are concerned malice is "presumed." Such a presumption is inconsistent with the federal rule. * * * Since the trial judge did not instruct the jury to differentiate between general and punitive damages, it may be that the verdict was wholly an award of one or the other. But it is impossible to know, in view of the general verdict returned. Because of this uncertainty, the judgment must be reversed and the case remanded. * * *

Since respondent may seek a new trial, we deem that considerations of effective judicial administration require us to review the evidence in the present record to determine whether it could constitutionally support a judgment for respondent. This Court's duty is not limited to the elaboration of constitutional principles; we must also in proper cases review the evidence to make certain that those principles have been constitutionally applied. This is such a case * * *.

Applying these standards, we consider that the proof presented to show actual malice lacks the convincing clarity which the constitutional standard demands, and hence that it would not constitutionally sustain the judgment for respondent under the proper rule of law. The case of the individual petitioners requires little discussion. Even assuming that they could constitutionally be found to have authorized the use of their names on the advertisement, there was no evidence whatever that they were aware of any erroneous statements or were in any way reckless in that regard. The judgment against them is thus without constitutional support.

As to the Times, we similarly conclude that the facts do not support a finding of actual malice. The statement by the Times' Secretary that, apart from the padlocking allegation, he thought the advertisement was "substantially correct," affords no constitutional warrant for the Alabama Supreme Court's conclusion that it was a "cavalier ignoring of the falsity of the advertisement [from which], the jury could not have but been impressed with the bad faith of The Times, and its maliciousness inferable therefrom." The statement does not indicate malice at the time of the publication; even if the advertisement was not "substantially correct"—although respondent's own proofs tend to show that it was—that opinion was at least a reasonable one, and there was no evidence to impeach the

23. We have no occasion here to determine how far down into the lower ranks of government employees the "public official" designation would extend for purposes of this rule, or otherwise to specify categories of persons who would or would not be included. * * * Nor need we here determine the boundaries of the "official conduct" concept. * * *

witness' good faith in holding it. The Times' failure to retract upon respondent's demand, although it later retracted upon the demand of Governor Patterson, is likewise not adequate evidence of malice for constitutional purposes. Whether or not a failure to retract may ever constitute such evidence, there are two reasons why it does not here. *First,* the letter written by the Times reflected a reasonable doubt on its part as to whether the advertisement could reasonably be taken to refer to respondent at all. *Second,* it was not a final refusal, since it asked for an explanation on this point—a request that respondent chose to ignore. Nor does the retraction upon the demand of the Governor supply the necessary proof. It may be doubted that a failure to retract which is not itself evidence of malice can retroactively become such by virtue of a retraction subsequently made to another party. But in any event that did not happen here, since the explanation given by the Times' Secretary for the distinction drawn between respondent and the Governor was a reasonable one, the good faith of which was not impeached.

Finally, there is evidence that the Times published the advertisement without checking its accuracy against the news stories in the Times' own files. The mere presence of the stories in the files does not, of course, establish that the Times "knew" the advertisement was false, since the state of mind required for actual malice would have to be brought home to the persons in the Times' organization having responsibility for the publication of the advertisement. * * * We think the evidence against the Times supports at most a finding of negligence in failing to discover the misstatements, and is constitutionally insufficient to show the recklessness that is required for a finding of actual malice. * * * We think the evidence was constitutionally defective in another respect: it was incapable of supporting the jury's finding that the allegedly libelous statements were made "of and concerning" respondent. Respondent relies on the words of the advertisement and the testimony of six witnesses to establish a connection between it and himself. Thus, in his brief to this Court, he states:

> "The reference to respondent as police commissioner is clear from the ad. In addition, the jury heard the testimony of a newspaper editor * * *; a real estate and insurance man * * *; the sales manager of a men's clothing store * * *; a food equipment man * * *; a service station operator * * *; and the operator of a truck line for whom respondent had formerly worked * * *. Each of these witnesses stated that he associated the statements with respondent * * *." (Citations to record omitted.)

There was no reference to respondent in the advertisement, either by name or official position. A number of the allegedly libelous statements—the charges that the dining hall was padlocked and that Dr. King's home was bombed, his person assaulted, and a perjury prosecution instituted against him—did not even concern the police; despite the ingenuity of the arguments which would attach this significance to the word "They," it is plain that these statements could not reasonably be read as accusing respondent of personal involvement in the acts in question. The statements upon which respondent principally relies as referring to him are the two allegations that did concern the police or police functions: that "truckloads of police * * * ringed the Alabama State College Campus" after the demonstration on the State Capitol steps, and that Dr. King had been "arrested * * * seven times." These statements were false only in that the police had been "deployed near" the campus but had not actually "ringed" it and had not gone there in connection with the State Capitol demonstration, and in that Dr. King had been arrested only four times. The ruling that these discrepancies between what was true and what was asserted were sufficient to injure respondent's reputation may itself raise constitutional problems, but we need not consider them here. Although the statements may be taken as referring to the police, they did not on their face make even an oblique reference to respondent as an individual. Support for the asserted reference must, therefore, be sought in the testimony of respondent's witnesses. But none of them suggested any basis for the belief that respondent himself was attacked in the advertisement beyond the bare fact that he was in overall charge of the Police Department and thus bore official responsibility for police conduct; to the extent that some of the witnesses thought respondent to have been charged with ordering or approving the conduct or otherwise being personally involved in it, they based this notion not on any statements in the advertisement, and not on any evidence that he had in fact been so involved, but solely on the unsupported assumption that, because of his official position, he must have been. This reliance on the bare fact of respondent's official position was made explicit by the Supreme Court of Alabama. * * *

This proposition has disquieting implications for criticism of governmental conduct. * * *

The judgment of the Supreme Court of Alabama is reversed and the case is remanded to that court for further proceedings not inconsistent with this opinion.

Reversed and remanded.

MR. JUSTICE BLACK, with whom MR. JUSTICE DOUGLAS joins (concurring).

I concur in reversing this half-million-dollar judgment against the New York Times Company and the four individual defendants. In reversing the Court holds that "the Constitution delimits a State's power to award damages for libel in actions brought by public officials against critics of their official conduct." * * * I base my vote to reverse on the belief that the First and Fourteenth Amendments not merely "delimit" a State's power to award damages to "public officials against critics of their official conduct" but completely prohibit a State from exercising such a power. * * *

* * *

MR. JUSTICE GOLDBERG, with whom MR. JUSTICE DOUGLAS joins (concurring in the result).

* * *

In my view, the First and Fourteenth Amendments to the Constitution afford to the citizen and to the press an absolute, unconditional privilege to criticize official conduct despite the harm which may flow from excesses and abuses. * * * The right should not depend upon a probing by the jury of the motivation[2] of the citizen or press. * * *

* * *

We must recognize that we are writing upon a clean slate. * * * It may be urged that deliberately and maliciously false statements have no conceivable value as free speech. That argument, however, is not responsive to the real issue presented by this case, which is whether that freedom of speech which all agree is constitutionally protected can be effectively safeguarded by a rule allowing the imposition of liability upon a jury's evaluation of the speaker's state of mind. If individual citizens may be held liable in damages for strong words, which a jury finds false and maliciously motivated, there can be little doubt that public debate and advocacy will be constrained. And if newspapers, publishing advertisements dealing with public issues, thereby risk liability, there can also be little doubt that the ability of minority groups to secure publication of their views on public affairs and to seek support for their causes will be greatly diminished. * * *

* * *

This is not to say that the Constitution protects defamatory statements directed against the private conduct of a public official or private citizen. Freedom of press and of speech insures that government will respond to the will of the people and that changes may be obtained by peaceful means. Purely private defamation has little to do with the political ends of a self-governing society. The imposition of liability for private defamation does not abridge the freedom of public speech or any other freedom protected by the First Amendment.[4] * * *

* * *

For these reasons, I strongly believe that the Constitution accords citizens and press an unconditional freedom to criticize official conduct. It necessarily follows that in a case such as this, where all agree that the

---

2. The requirement of proving actual malice or reckless disregard may, in the mind of the jury, add little to the requirement of proving falsity, a requirement which the Court recognizes not to be an adequate safeguard. * * *

4. In most cases, as in the case at bar, there will be little difficulty in distinguishing defamatory speech relating to private conduct from that relating to official conduct. I recognize, of course, that there will be a gray area. The difficulties of applying a public-private standard are, however, certainly, of a different genre from those attending the differentiation between a malicious and nonmalicious state of mind. * * *

allegedly defamatory statements related to official conduct, the judgments for libel cannot constitutionally be sustained.

NOTES

1. *Sullivan's* requirement that the plaintiff prove either knowledge of falsity or reckless disregard of falsity was extended to cover actions brought by relatively low-ranking public officials or former public officials, at least when the action was based upon statements about the plaintiff's official conduct. *See* Rosenblatt v. Baer, 383 U.S. 75, 86 S.Ct. 669, 15 L.Ed.2d 597 (1966) (former supervisor of county recreation facility). The Court has, however, remarked that, while it "has not provided precise boundaries for the category of 'public official,' it cannot be thought to include all public employees. * * * " Hutchinson v. Proxmire, 443 U.S. 111, 119 n. 8, 99 S.Ct. 2675, 2680 n. 8, 61 L.Ed.2d 411, 421 n. 8 (1979). Anaya v. CBS Broadcasting, Inc., 626 F.Supp.2d 1158 (D.N.M. 2009) contains a good discussion of factors to be considered in determining whether someone who might be considered a public employee should be classed as a "public official." These factors include whether the person had any supervisory authority of other employees, the amount of discretion the person had in exercising her responsibilities, and how the person would be perceived by the public.

2. The Court also made clear that recklessness could only be proven by some showing of conscious indifference to truth; a *mere* failure to investigate is not enough. *See* St. Amant v. Thompson, 390 U.S. 727, 88 S.Ct. 1323, 20 L.Ed.2d 262 (1968); Beckley Newspapers Corp. v. Hanks, 389 U.S. 81, 88 S.Ct. 197, 19 L.Ed.2d 248 (1967) (per curiam).

3. The Court, following the lead of some lower courts, also soon extended the scope of application of the *Sullivan* standard to statements concerning at least the non-private aspects of the lives of public figures, even those who were not involved in politics. *See* Curtis Publishing Co. v. Butts, 388 U.S. 130, 87 S.Ct. 1975, 18 L.Ed.2d 1094 (1967); Associated Press v. Walker, reported *sub. nom.* Curtis Publishing Co. v. Butts. Justice Harlan suggested in *Butts* and *Walker* that public figures who were not public officials might be able to recover on a showing of only gross negligence but he later abandoned that position in the *Rosenbloom* case, *infra*. Concurrently in a privacy case, the Court also indicated that a relatively unknown person could, by accidental involvement in an event of major newsworthiness, become a public figure, at least with regard to matters involving the newsworthy event. *See* Time, Inc. v. Hill, 385 U.S. 374, 87 S.Ct. 534, 17 L.Ed.2d 456 (1967). We shall return to the subject of involuntary public figures as the discussion proceeds, particularly in the notes after *Time, Inc. v. Firestone,* reprinted at p. 610, *infra*.

4. The last case in the expansive period of the application of *Sullivan* was Rosenbloom v. Metromedia, Inc., 403 U.S. 29, 91 S.Ct. 1811, 29 L.Ed.2d 296 (1971). In that case the plaintiff was a magazine distributor. The police had arrested him and seized some of his magazines on the ground that they were obscene. In reporting these events, the defendant Philadelphia radio station stated that the police had "confiscated 3000 obscene books." The plaintiff claimed that at most the station could have said that the materials

seized were "allegedly" obscene. The plaintiff brought suit in the federal courts for the return of the materials. In reporting these developments, the defendant described the proceeding as one in which the defendant sought an injunction "ordering * * * [the authorities and the media] to lay off the smut literature racket." In the same vein the report declared: "The girlie-book peddlers say the police crack down and continued reference to their borderline literature as smut or filth is hurting their business." The report continued that "if the injunction is not granted * * * it could signal an even more intense effort to rid the city of pornography." Shortly thereafter the plaintiff complained to the radio station that "his magazines were 'found to be completely legal and legitimate by the United States Supreme Court.' " The newscaster for the station replied that the district attorney had said the magazines were obscene. The plaintiff replied that he had a statement from the district attorney that the magazines were "legal." At that point the conversation was terminated. There was no request for a retraction or correction and none was made. Subsequently, in a criminal prosecution against the plaintiff, a state court jury acquitted the plaintiff under instructions from the trial judge who ruled that, as a matter of law, the nudist magazines distributed by the plaintiff were not obscene. At this point the plaintiff brought his defamation action in the federal courts on the basis of diversity of citizenship. The district court refused to apply the *Sullivan* standards and the jury found for the plaintiff. The jury awarded the plaintiff $25,000 in compensatory damages and $725,000 in punitive damages. On remittitur, the trial judge reduced the punitive damages to $250,000. The United States Court of Appeals for the Third Circuit reversed and the Supreme Court affirmed.

Although five of the eight justices who heard the case voted to affirm (Justice Douglas did not participate in the decision of the case), there was no opinion for the Court. Writing for himself and two other Justices (Chief Justice Burger and Justice Blackmun), Justice Brennan began by noting that the Pennsylvania law of defamation tracked the *Restatement of Torts*. Justice Brennan then continued:

> We turn then to the question to be decided. Petitioner's argument that the Constitution should be held to require that the private individual prove only that the publisher failed to exercise "reasonable care" in publishing defamatory falsehoods proceeds along two lines. First, he argues that the private individual, unlike the public figure, does not have access to the media to counter the defamatory material and that the private individual, unlike the public figure, has not assumed the risk of defamation by thrusting himself into the public arena. Second, petitioner focuses on the important values served by the law of defamation in preventing and redressing attacks upon reputation.
>
> We have recognized the force of petitioner's arguments, Time, Inc. v. Hill, *supra,* 385 U.S., at 391, 87 S.Ct., at 543–544, and we adhere to the caution expressed in that case against "blind application," of the *New York Times* standard. * * * Analysis of the particular factors involved, however, convinces us that petitioner's arguments cannot be reconciled with the purposes of the First Amendment, with our cases, and with the traditional doctrines of libel law itself. Drawing a distinction between

"public" and "private" figures makes no sense in terms of the First Amendment guarantees. The *New York Times* standard was applied to libel of a public official or public figure to give effect to the Amendment's function to encourage ventilation of public issues, not because the public official has any less interest in protecting his reputation than an individual in private life. While the argument that public figures need less protection because they can command media attention to counter criticism may be true for some very prominent people, even then it is the rare case where the denial overtakes the original charge. Denials, retractions, and corrections are not "hot" news, and rarely receive the prominence of the original story. When the public official or public figure is a minor functionary, or has left the position that put him in the public eye, *see* Rosenblatt v. Baer, *supra,* the argument loses all of its force. In the vast majority of libels involving public officials or public figures, the ability to respond through the media will depend on the same complex factor on which the ability of a private individual depends: the unpredictable event of the media's continuing interest in the story. Thus the unproved, and highly improbable, generalization that an as yet undefined class of "public figures" involved in matters of public concern will be better able to respond through the media than private individuals also involved in such matters seems too insubstantial a reed on which to rest a constitutional distinction. Furthermore, in First Amendment terms, the cure seems far worse than the disease. If the States fear that private citizens will not be able to respond adequately to publicity involving them, the solution lies in the direction of ensuring their ability to respond, rather than in stifling public discussion of matters of public concern.[15]

Further reflection over the years since *New York Times* was decided persuades us that the view of the "public official" or "public figure" as assuming the risk of defamation by voluntarily thrusting himself into the public eye bears little relationship either to the values protected by the First Amendment or to the nature of our society. We have recognized that "[e]xposure of the self to others in varying degrees is a concomitant of life in a civilized community." Time, Inc. v. Hill, *supra,* * * * Voluntarily or not, we are all "public" men to some degree. Conversely, some aspects of the lives of even the most public men fall outside the area of matters of public or general concern. * * * Thus, the idea that certain "public" figures have voluntarily exposed their entire lives to public inspection, while private individuals have kept theirs carefully shrouded from public view is, at best, a legal fiction. In any event, such a distinction could easily produce the paradoxical result of dampening discussion of issues of public or general concern because they happen to involve private citizens while extending constitutional encouragement to discussion of aspects of the lives of "public figures" that are not in the area of public or general concern.

* * *

15. Some States have adopted retraction statutes or right-of-reply statutes. * * * [Ed. note] The Court has since declared right of reply statutes unconstitutional in the *Tornillo* case, discussed in note 6, p. 571, *supra.*

Moreover, we ordinarily decide civil litigation by the preponderance of the evidence. Indeed, the judge instructed the jury to decide the present case by that standard. In the normal civil suit where this standard is employed, "we view it as no more serious in general for there to be an erroneous verdict in the defendant's favor than for there to be an erroneous verdict in the plaintiff's favor." In re Winship, 397 U.S. 358, 371, 90 S.Ct. 1068, 1076, 25 L.Ed.2d 368 (1970) (Harlan, J., concurring). In libel cases, however, we view an erroneous verdict for the plaintiff as most serious. Not only does it mulct the defendant for an innocent misstatement—the three-quarter-million-dollar jury verdict in this case could rest on such an error—but the possibility of such error, even beyond the vagueness of the negligence standard itself, would create a strong impetus toward self-censorship, which the First Amendment cannot tolerate. These dangers for freedom of speech and press led us to reject the reasonable-man standard of liability as "simply inconsistent" with our national commitment under the First Amendment when sought to be applied to the conduct of a political campaign. Monitor Patriot Co. v. Roy, 401 U.S. 265, 276, 91 S.Ct. 621, 627, 28 L.Ed.2d 35 (1971). The same considerations lead us to reject that standard here.

* * *

* * * We thus hold that a libel action, as here, by a private individual against a licensed radio station for a defamatory falsehood in a newscast relating to his involvement in an event of public or general concern may be sustained only upon clear and convincing proof that the defamatory falsehood was published with knowledge that it was false or with reckless disregard of whether it was false or not. * * *

Justice Black concurred on familiar grounds. Justice White also concurred on the ground that the case involved a "report and comment upon the official actions of public servants," *i.e.* the police. Justice Harlan in dissent argued that the concerns of the majority could be met by prohibiting the award of presumed damages in any defamation action. Justice Marshall, writing for himself and Justice Stewart, joined in this proposal but also contended that punitive damages should not be allowed in defamation actions. Anticipating the *Gertz* case to which we shall shortly turn, all three dissenters concluded that public officials and public figures should continue to have to meet the standards enunciated in *Sullivan* but that plaintiffs like George Rosenbloom who did not fit into either category should be able to recover for genuinely injurious defamation upon a showing of negligence.

5. In imposing the requirement that the plaintiff must, at least in some defamation actions, show that the defendant was aware of the falsity of his statements or at the very least consciously indifferent to the truth or falsity of his statements the Court has obviously made the defendant's state of mind, or the state of mind of those for whom the defendant is legally accountable, a relevant consideration. In Herbert v. Lando, 441 U.S. 153, 99 S.Ct. 1635, 60 L.Ed.2d 115 (1979), the plaintiff was, *inter alia*, reported, in a television program produced by CBS, to have accused his superiors of war crimes to explain his relief from military command in Vietnam. Lando, the individual defendant who prepared the report for CBS, also subsequently repeated the

charges in an article published in the Atlantic Monthly. Herbert brought his defamation action against Lando, CBS, and the Atlantic Monthly. During the taking of depositions, Lando refused to answer questions concerning a variety of issues. In deciding whether Lando could refuse to answer the questions asked him, the Court relied upon and quoted the following summary of the matters in controversy prepared by the United States Court of Appeals for the Second Circuit:

> 1. Lando's conclusions during his research and investigations regarding people or leads to be pursued, or not to be pursued, in connection with the '60 Minutes' segment and the Atlantic Monthly article;
>
> 2. Lando's conclusions about facts imparted by interviewees and his state of mind with respect to the veracity of persons interviewed;
>
> 3. The basis for conclusions where Lando testified that he did reach a conclusion concerning the veracity of persons, information or events;
>
> 4. Conversations between Lando and Wallace about matter to be included or excluded from the broadcast publication; and
>
> 5. Lando's intentions as manifested by his decision to include or exclude certain material.

Lando claimed he had a constitutional privilege to refuse to answer on the ground that the first amendment prohibited "inquiry into the state of mind of those who edit, produce or publish, and into the editorial process." The district court rejected the claim of privilege and ordered Lando to answer the questions. A divided court of appeals reversed. The Supreme Court granted certiorari and in turn reversed the court of appeals. The opinion of the Court was written by Justice White and joined by five other Justices including Justice Powell, who also wrote a concurring opinion. Both Justice White and Justice Powell reminded district courts of their power to insist on relevancy as a means of preventing the abuse of discovery procedures. Justice Brennan dissented in part. He concluded that questions pertaining to Lando's state of mind were permissible but not questions concerning Lando's conversations with Wallace during the editorial process. Justice Stewart in dissent thought the questions asked Lando were too broadranging to be relevant. Moreover, inquiry into the publisher's motives was clearly irrelevant. Justice Marshall also dissented. He contended that discovery requests in such litigation should be governed by strict standards of relevance. He furthermore argued that, while a journalist's state of mind could be probed, he "would foreclose discovery in defamation cases as to the substance of editorial conversation." For scholarly comment on various aspects of the case, *see* M. Franklin, *Reflections on* Herbert v. Lando, 31 Stan.L.Rev. 1035 (1979); J. Friedenthal, Herbert v. Lando: *A Note on Discovery,* 31 Stan.L.Rev. 1059 (1979).

6. *Fictionalized Quotations*. In Masson v. New Yorker Magazine, Inc., 501 U.S. 496, 111 S.Ct. 2419, 115 L.Ed.2d 447 (1991), the Court was confronted with a case in which Janet Malcolm, a co-defendant and free lance journalist, wrote a story about the plaintiff, Jeffrey Masson, and his disputes with Anna Freud, the daughter of Sigmund Freud, and Dr. Kurt Eissler, the director of the Sigmund Freud Archives. The story was first published in two parts in the *New Yorker* and then in expanded form as a book. Masson had for

a time been projects director of the Freud Archives but soon became disillusioned with Freudian Psychology. After Masson expressed his disillusionment in a public lecture delivered at the meeting of a professional association, he was terminated. In her story Malcolm used what purported to be a number of direct quotes which, however, could not be found in the tapes of her extensive interviews with Masson. For example, Masson was quoted as saying that, after his book was published, the psychoanalytic establishment "will say that Masson is a great scholar, a major analyst—after Freud he's the greatest analyst who ever lived." These statements did not appear in the tapes. The most germane portion of the tapes contain statements that "no analyst in the country . . . will say a single word in favor of Masson's work," that for a time Masson thought that it was "me and Freud against the world, or me and Freud and Anna Freud and Kur[t] Eissler * * * [and a few others] against the rest of the world. Not so, it's me. It's me alone." The tapes also contained an exchange between Masson and Malcolm in which Masson said "analysis stands or falls with me now," to which Malcolm replied "[w]ell that's a very grandiose thing to say," and Masson rejoined: "Yeah, but it's got nothing to do with me. It's got to do with the thing I discovered." The Court also discussed 5 additional instances of variances between the quotations attributed to Masson and the transcript of the tapes. The district court granted the defendants summary judgment and the court of appeals affirmed, 895 F.2d 1535 (9th Cir.1989). According to the Ninth Circuit, so long as the quotations in Malcolm's story were a reasonable interpretation of the interview, the discrepancy between the material on the tapes and the published story did not establish either knowledge of falsity or reckless disregard of truth or falsity. The Court reversed as to all but one of the misquotations (having to do with why Masson at one time changed his middle name) and remanded. The Ninth Circuit's doctrine was too favorable to the defendant. Accepting that minor alterations of interviews to correct for mistakes of grammar or syntax were permissible, the Court concluded that "a deliberate alteration of the words uttered by a plaintiff does not equate with knowledge of falsity for purposes of New York Times Co. v. Sullivan * * * unless the alteration results in a material change in meaning." Justices White and Scalia dissented on that point. According to them, if a publication contains deliberate misquotations and the misquotations are defamatory, the plaintiff is entitled to go to the jury on the issue of whether the defendant made the statements with knowledge of falsity or with reckless disregard of truth or falsity.

7. Even leaving aside the problem of deliberate misquotation, establishing that the defendant was consciously or recklessly indifferent to the truth or falsity of statements is not always an easy matter. An instructive illustration is the involved litigation that gave rise to Tavoulareas v. Piro, 817 F.2d 762 (D.C.Cir.1987) (en banc), *cert. denied* 484 U.S. 870, 108 S.Ct. 200, 98 L.Ed.2d 151. The case involved a story that appeared in *The Washington Post* in which it was asserted that the plaintiff, William Tavoulareas, had used his influence as the president of Mobil Corporation to "set up" his son Peter, who was also a plaintiff in the litigation, as a partner in a shipping firm with a multimillion dollar management services contract with Mobil. The jury returned a verdict for the plaintiffs but this was vacated by the trial judge who awarded judgment notwithstanding the verdict to the *Post* and to its reporters and

editors who had been joined as defendants. A divided panel of the court of appeals reinstated the jury's verdict but the full court vacated that portion of the panel opinion and set the case for rehearing en banc. The full court of appeals, sitting en banc, affirmed in its entirety the district court's decision. The opinion for the court was filed by Judge Kenneth Starr and senior Judge J. Skelly Wright. The court of appeals first found that some of the most damning allegations in the *Post* story were substantially true. The court noted that ill-will towards the plaintiff or other bad motives are not elements of actual malice as that has been defined by the Supreme Court. Nevertheless, while admitting such evidence will undoubtedly have some chilling effect on honestly believed speech, the court was not prepared to rule out the possibility that, under some circumstances, the probative value of the evidence of ill-will, in establishing an intent to inflict harm through falsehood, would be sufficiently high that the value of admitting such evidence would outweigh that risk. The court found that the evidence of ill-will or bad motive in the case before it, however, lacked such high probative value. An extremely interesting part of the court's opinion was its dealing with the plaintiff's contention that an inference of reckless disregard for truth or falsity could be drawn from the fact that reporters were under managerial pressure to produce high impact stories. In the *Tavoulareas* case, a *Post* editor had testified at trial that he was looking for stories that would cause a person reading the *Post* to exclaim "holy shit".[a] The court held that, "managerial pressure to produce such stories cannot, as a matter of law, constitute evidence of actual malice." 817 F.2d at 796. In Harte–Hanks Communications, Inc. v. Connaughton, 491 U.S. 657, 109 S.Ct. 2678, 105 L.Ed.2d 562 (1989) the Court, citing *Lando* and *Tavoulareas,* declared that "it cannot be said that evidence concerning motive or care never bears any relation to the actual malice inquiry." Although "courts must be careful not to place too much reliance on such factors, a plaintiff is entitled to prove the defendant's state of mind through circumstantial evidence."

8. *Role of trial judge and jury.* As *Gertz* and the other Supreme Court cases described in this section indicate, the question of who is a public figure is a question of law to be decided by the court. *See also Restatement (Second) of Torts* § 580A, Comment *c.* When the issue at least is knowledge of falsity or reckless indifference to truth or falsity, the plaintiff must prove his case by "clear and convincing evidence" and not merely by the preponderance of the evidence. This is how the Court's declaration in *New York Times v. Sullivan* that constitutional malice must be shown with "convincing clarity" was interpreted by the lower federal courts and the state courts in cases such as Yiamouyiannis v. Consumers Union, 619 F.2d 932, 940 (2d Cir.1980), *cert. denied* 449 U.S. 839, 101 S.Ct. 117, 66 L.Ed.2d 46 and Burns v. Times Argus Association, Inc., 139 Vt. 381, 430 A.2d 773 (1981). This interpretation of *New York Times v. Sullivan* has been expressly accepted in a number of subsequent decisions of the Court. *See e.g.,* Bose Corp. v. Consumers Union of United States, Inc., 466 U.S. 485, 104 S.Ct. 1949, 80 L.Ed.2d 502 (1984). The Court in the *Bose* case also made clear that *New York Times v. Sullivan* made the issue of actual or constitutional malice one of "constitutional fact", that is

a. The evidence on this point is examined more fully in the earlier panel opinion of the District of Columbia Circuit, Tavoulareas v. Piro, 759 F.2d 90, 120–21 (D.C.Cir.1985).

a fact as to which a trial court deciding whether to accept a jury verdict or an appellate court reviewing a trial court decision must exercise an "independent judgment." It is not enough for there to be a reasonable basis for the decision being reviewed if the reviewing court is not convinced that the decision on this issue was the correct one. In ruling on a motion for summary judgment, however, the Court has more recently declared, in a case which arose in the federal courts, that, while a plaintiff may not avoid the granting of the motion if the evidence supporting his claim is "merely colorable", the motion should not be granted if there is "sufficient evidence favoring the non-moving party for a jury to return a verdict for that party." At this stage of litigation the trial judge is not to "weigh the evidence and determine the truth of the matter." But, at least in the federal courts, whether there is enough evidence to support a jury verdict in favor of the plaintiff must be determined in the light of the plaintiff's burden of proving constitutional malice by clear and convincing evidence. Anderson v. Liberty Lobby, Inc., 477 U.S. 242, 106 S.Ct. 2505, 91 L.Ed.2d 202 (1986). Several states, however, have expressly held that, in ruling on a motion for summary judgment, the trial court is merely to consider whether there is a "genuine issue of fact" and not to take into account the plaintiff's heightened burden of persuasion, because to do so would involve weighing the evidence which is the jury's prerogative. *See e.g.*, Dairy Stores, Inc. v. Sentinel Pub. Co., 104 N.J. 125, 516 A.2d 220 (1986); Moffatt v. Brown, 751 P.2d 939 (Alaska 1988). This of course makes it easier for the plaintiff to resist the granting of the motion.

GERTZ v. ROBERT WELCH, INC.

Supreme Court of the United States, 1974.
418 U.S. 323, 94 S.Ct. 2997, 41 L.Ed.2d 789.

MR. JUSTICE POWELL delivered the opinion of the Court.

This Court has struggled for nearly a decade to define the proper accommodation between the law of defamation and the freedoms of speech and press protected by the First Amendment. With this decision we return to that effort. We granted certiorari to reconsider the extent of a publisher's constitutional privilege against liability for defamation of a private citizen. * * *

I

In 1968 a Chicago policeman named Nuccio shot and killed a youth named Nelson. The state authorities prosecuted Nuccio for the homicide and ultimately obtained a conviction for murder in the second degree. The Nelson family retained petitioner Elmer Gertz, a reputable attorney, to represent them in civil litigation against Nuccio.

Respondent publishes American Opinion, a monthly outlet for the views of the John Birch Society. Early in the 1960's the magazine began to warn of a nationwide conspiracy to discredit local law enforcement agencies and create in their stead a national police force capable of supporting a communist dictatorship. As part of the continuing effort to alert the public to this assumed danger, the managing editor of American Opinion commissioned an article on the murder trial of officer Nuccio. For this purpose he engaged a regular contributor to the magazine. In March of 1969 respondent published the resulting article under the title "FRAME–UP: Richard Nuccio And The War On Police." The article purports to demonstrate that the testimony against Nuccio at his criminal trial was false and that his prosecution was part of the communist campaign against the police.

In his capacity as counsel for the Nelson family in the civil litigation, petitioner attended the coroner's inquest into the boy's death and initiated actions for damages, but he neither discussed officer Nuccio with the press nor played any part in the criminal proceeding. Notwithstanding petitioner's remote connection with the prosecution of Nuccio, respondent's magazine portrayed him as an architect of the "frame-up." According to the article, the police file on petitioner took "a big, Irish cop to lift." The article stated that petitioner had been an official of the "Marxist League for Industrial Democracy, originally known as the Intercollegiate Socialist Society, which has advocated the violent seizure of our government." It labelled Gertz a "Leninist" and a "Communist-fronter." It also stated that Gertz had been an officer of the National Lawyers Guild, described as a communist organization that "probably did more than any other outfit to plan the Communist attack on the Chicago police during the 1968 Democratic convention."

These statements contained serious inaccuracies. The implication that petitioner had a criminal record was false. Petitioner had been a member and officer of the National Lawyers Guild some 15 years earlier, but there was no evidence that he or that organization had taken any part in planning the 1968 demonstrations in Chicago. There was also no basis for the charge that petitioner was a "Leninist" or a "Communist-fronter." And he had never been a member of the "Marxist League for Industrial Democracy" or the "Intercollegiate Socialist Society."

The managing editor of American Opinion made no effort to verify or substantiate the charges against petitioner. Instead, he appended an editorial introduction stating that the author had "concluded extensive research into the Richard Nuccio case." And he included in the article a photograph of petitioner and wrote the caption that appeared under it: "Elmer Gertz of the Red Guild harrasses Nuccio." Respondent placed the issue of American Opinion containing the article on sale at newsstands throughout the country and distributed reprints of the article on the streets of Chicago.

Petitioner filed a diversity action for libel in the United States District Court for the Northern District of Illinois. He claimed that the falsehoods published by respondent injured his reputation as a lawyer and a citizen. Before filing an answer, respondent moved to dismiss the complaint for failure to state a claim upon which relief could be granted, apparently on the ground that petitioner failed to allege special damages. But the court ruled that statements contained in the article constituted libel *per se* under Illinois law and that consequently petitioner need not plead special damages. * * *

After answering the complaint, respondent filed a pretrial motion for summary judgment, claiming a constitutional privilege against liability for defamation. It asserted that petitioner was a public official or a public figure and that the article concerned an issue of public interest and concern. For these reasons, respondent argued, it was entitled to invoke the privilege enunciated in New York Times Co. v. Sullivan. * * * Under this rule respondent would escape liability unless petitioner could prove publication of defamatory falsehood "with 'actual malice'—that is, in the knowledge that it was false or with reckless disregard for whether it was true or not." * * * Respondent claimed that petitioner could not make such a showing and submitted a supporting affidavit by the magazine's managing editor. The editor denied any knowledge of the falsity of the statements concerning petitioner and stated that he had relied on the author's reputation and on his prior experience with the accuracy and authenticity of his contributions to American Opinion.

The District Court denied respondent's motion for summary judgment in a memorandum opinion of Sept. 16, 1970. The court did not dispute respondent's claim to the protection of the *New York Times* standard. Rather, it concluded that petitioner might overcome the constitutional privilege by making a factual showing sufficient to prove publication of defamatory falsehood in reckless disregard of the truth. During the course of the trial, however, it became clear that the trial court had not accepted all of respondent's asserted grounds for applying the *New York Times* rule to this case. It thought that respondent's claim to the protection of the constitutional privilege depended on the contention that petitioner was either a public official under the *New York Times* decision or a public figure under Curtis Publishing Co. v. Butts, * * * apparently discounting the argument that a privilege would arise from the presence of a public issue. After all the evidence had been presented but before submission of the case to the jury, the court ruled in effect that petitioner was neither a public official nor a public figure. It added that, if he were, the resulting application of the *New York Times* standard would require a directed verdict for respondent. Because some statements in the article constituted libel *per se* under Illinois law, the court submitted the case to the jury under instructions that withdrew from its consideration all issues save the measure of damages. The jury awarded $50,000 to petitioner.

Following the jury verdict and on further reflection, the District Court concluded that the *New York Times* standard should govern this case even though petitioner was not a public official or public figure. It accepted respondent's contention that that privilege protected discussion of any public issue without regard to the status of a person defamed therein. Accordingly, the court entered judgment for respondent notwithstanding the jury's verdict. This conclusion anticipated the reasoning of a plurality of this Court in Rosenbloom v. Metromedia, Inc. * * *

Petitioner appealed to contest the applicability of the *New York Times* standard to this case. Although the Court of Appeals for the Seventh Circuit doubted the correctness of the District Court's determination that petitioner was not a public figure, it did not overturn that finding. It agreed with the District Court that respondent could assert the constitutional privilege because the article concerned a matter of public interest, citing this Court's intervening decision in Rosenbloom v. Metromedia, Inc., *supra*. The Court of Appeals read *Rosenbloom* to require application of the *New York Times* standard to any publication or broadcast about an issue of significant public interest, without regard to the position, fame, or anonymity of the person defamed, and it concluded that respondent's statements concerned such an issue. After reviewing the record, the Court of Appeals endorsed the District Court's conclusion that petitioner had failed to show by clear and convincing evidence that respondent had acted with "actual malice" as defined by *New York Times*. There was no evidence that the managing editor of American Opinion knew of the falsity of the accusations made in the article. In fact, he knew nothing about petitioner except what he learned from the article. The court correctly noted that mere proof of failure to investigate, without more, cannot establish reckless disregard for the truth. Rather, the publisher must act with a "high degree of awareness of * * * probable falsity." St. Amant v. Thompson, 390 U.S. 727, 731, 88 S.Ct. 1323, 1325, 20 L.Ed.2d 262 (1968). * * * The evidence in this case did not reveal that respondent had cause for such an awareness. The Court of Appeals therefore affirmed * * *. For the reasons stated below, we reverse.

II

The principal issue in this case is whether a newspaper or broadcaster that publishes defamatory falsehoods about an individual who is neither a public official nor a public figure may claim a constitutional privilege against liability for the injury inflicted by those statements. The Court considered this question on the rather different set of facts presented in Rosenbloom v. Metromedia, Inc. * * * Rosenbloom, a distributor of nudist magazines, was arrested for selling allegedly obscene material while making a delivery to a retail dealer. The police obtained a warrant and seized his entire inventory of 3,000 books and magazines. He sought and obtained an injunction prohibiting further police interference with his business. He then sued a local radio station for failing to note in two of its newscasts that the 3,000 items seized were only "reportedly" or "allegedly" obscene and for broadcasting references to "the smut literature racket" and to "girlie-book peddlers" in its coverage of the court proceeding for injunctive relief. He obtained a judgment against the radio station, but the Court of Appeals for the Third Circuit held the *New York Times* privilege applicable to the broadcast and reversed. * * *

This Court affirmed the decision below, but no majority could agree on a controlling rationale. The eight Justices who participated in *Rosenbloom* announced their views in five separate opinions, none of which commanded more than three votes. The several statements not only reveal disagreement about the appropriate result in that case; they also reflect divergent traditions of thought about the general problem of reconciling the law of defamation with the First Amendment. One approach has been to extend the *New York Times* test to an expanding variety of situations. Another has been to vary the level of constitutional privilege for defamatory falsehood with the status of the person defamed. And a third view would grant to the press and broadcast media absolute immunity from liability for defamation. * * *

* * *

III

We begin with the common ground. Under the First Amendment there is no such thing as a false idea. However pernicious an opinion may seem, we depend for its correction not on the conscience of judges and juries but on the competition of other ideas. But there is no constitutional value in false statements of fact. Neither the intentional lie nor the careless error materially advances society's interest in "uninhibited, robust, and wide-open" debate on public issues. * * *

Although the erroneous statement of fact is not worthy of constitutional protection, it is nevertheless inevitable in free debate. * * * The First Amendment requires that we protect some falsehood in order to protect speech that matters.

The need to avoid self-censorship by the news media is, however, not the only societal value at issue. If it were, this Court would have embraced long ago the view that publishers and broadcasters enjoy an unconditional and indefeasible immunity from liability for defamation. * * * Such a rule would indeed obviate the fear that the prospect of civil liability for injurious falsehood might dissuade a timorous press from the effective exercise of First Amendment freedoms. Yet absolute protection for the communications media requires a total sacrifice of the competing value served by the law of defamation.

The legitimate state interest underlying the law of libel is the compensation of individuals for the harm inflicted on them by defamatory falsehoods. We would not lightly require the State to abandon this purpose. * * *

Some tension necessarily exists between the need for a vigorous and uninhibited press and the legitimate interest in redressing wrongful injury. * * * To that end this Court has extended a measure of strategic protection to defamatory falsehood.

The *New York Times* standard defines the level of constitutional protection appropriate to the context of defamation of a public person. Those who, by reason of the notoriety of their achievements or the vigor and success with which they seek the public's attention, are properly classed as public figures and those who hold governmental office may recover for injury to reputation only on clear and convincing proof that the defamatory falsehood was made with knowledge of its falsity or with reckless disregard for the truth. This standard administers an extremely powerful antidote to the inducement to media self-censorship of the common law rule of strict liability for libel and slander. And it exacts a correspondingly high price from the victims of defamatory falsehood. Plainly many deserving plaintiffs, including some intentionally subjected to injury, will be unable to surmount the barrier of the *New York Times* test. Despite this substantial abridgement of the state law right to compensation for wrongful hurt to one's reputation, the Court has concluded that the protection of the *New York Times* privilege should be available to publishers and broadcasters of defamatory falsehoods concerning public officials and public figures. * * * We think that these decisions are correct, but we do not find their holdings justified solely by reference to the interest of the press and broadcast media in immunity from liability. Rather, we believe that the *New York Times* rule states an accommodation between this concern and the limited state interest present in the context of libel actions brought by public persons. For the reasons stated below, we conclude that the state interest in compensating injury to the reputation of private individuals requires that a different rule should obtain with respect to them.

Theoretically, of course, the balance between the needs of the press and the individual's claim to compensation for wrongful injury might be struck on a case-by-case basis. * * * But this approach would lead to unpredictable results and uncertain expectations, and it could render our duty to supervise the lower courts unmanageable. Because an *ad hoc* resolution of the competing interests at stake in each particular case is not feasible, we must lay down broad rules of general application. Such rules necessarily treat alike various cases involving differences as well as similarities. Thus it is often true that not all of the considerations which justify adoption of a given rule will obtain in each particular case decided under its authority.

With that caveat we have no difficulty in distinguishing among defamation plaintiffs. The first remedy of any victim of defamation is self-help—using available opportunities to contradict the lie or correct the error and thereby to minimize its adverse impact on reputation. Public officials and public figures usually enjoy significantly greater access to the channels of effective communication and hence have a more realistic opportunity to counteract false statements than private individuals normally enjoy.[9] Private individuals are therefore more vulnerable to injury, and the state interest in protecting them is correspondingly greater.

More important than the likelihood that private individuals will lack effective opportunities for rebuttal, there is a compelling normative con-

9. Of course, an opportunity for rebuttal seldom suffices to undo harm of defamatory falsehood. Indeed, the law of defamation is rooted in our experience that the truth rarely catches up with a lie. But the fact that the self-help remedy of rebuttal, standing alone, is inadequate to its task does not mean that it is irrelevant to our inquiry.

sideration underlying the distinction between public and private defamation plaintiffs. An individual who decides to seek governmental office must accept certain necessary consequences of that involvement in public affairs. He runs the risk of closer public scrutiny than might otherwise be the case. And society's interest in the officers of government is not strictly limited to the formal discharge of official duties. * * *

Those classed as public figures stand in a similar position. Hypothetically, it may be possible for someone to become a public figure through no purposeful action of his own, but the instances of truly involuntary public figures must be exceedingly rare. For the most part those who attain this status have assumed roles of especial prominence in the affairs of society. Some occupy positions of such persuasive power and influence that they are deemed public figures for all purposes. More commonly, those classed as public figures have thrust themselves to the forefront of particular public controversies in order to influence the resolution of the issues involved. In either event, they invite attention and comment.

Even if the foregoing generalities do not obtain in every instance, the communications media are entitled to act on the assumption that public officials and public figures have voluntarily exposed themselves to increased risk of injury from defamatory falsehoods concerning them. No such assumption is justified with respect to a private individual. * * * He has relinquished no part of his interest in the protection of his own good name, and consequently he has a more compelling call on the courts for redress of injury inflicted by defamatory falsehood. Thus, private individuals are not only more vulnerable to injury than public officials and public figures; they are also more deserving of recovery.

For these reasons we conclude that the States should retain substantial latitude in their efforts to enforce a legal remedy for defamatory falsehood injurious to the reputation of a private individual. The extension of the *New York Times* test proposed by the *Rosenbloom* plurality would abridge this legitimate state interest to a degree that we find unacceptable. And it would occasion the additional difficulty of forcing state and federal judges to decide on an *ad hoc* basis which publications address issues of "general or public interest" and which do not—to determine, in the words of Mr. Justice Marshall, "what information is relevant to self-government." Rosenbloom v. Metromedia, Inc. * * * We doubt the wisdom of committing this task to the conscience of judges. Nor does the Constitution require us to draw so thin a line between the drastic alternatives of the *New York Times* privilege and the common law of strict liability for defamatory error. The "public or general interest" test for determining the applicability of the *New York Times* standard to private defamation actions inadequately serves both of the competing values at stake. On the one hand, a private individual whose reputation is injured by defamatory falsehood that does concern an issue of public or general interest has no recourse unless he can meet the rigorous requirements of *New York Times*. This is true despite the factors that distinguish the state interest in compensating private individuals from the analogous interest involved in the context of public persons. On the other hand, a publisher or broadcaster of a defamatory error which a court deems unrelated to an issue of public or general interest may be held liable in damages even if it took every reasonable precaution to ensure the accuracy of its assertions. And liability may far exceed compensation for any actual injury to the plaintiff, for the jury may be permitted to presume damages without proof of loss and even to award punitive damages.

We hold that, so long as they do not impose liability without fault, the States may define for themselves the appropriate standard of liability for a publisher or broadcaster of defamatory falsehood injurious to a private individual. This approach provides a more equitable boundary between the competing concerns involved here. It recognizes the strength of the legitimate state interest in compensating private individuals for wrongful injury to reputation, yet shields the press and broadcast media from the rigors of strict liability for defamation. At least this conclusion obtains where, as here, the substance of the defamatory statement "makes substantial danger to reputation apparent." This phrase places in perspective the conclusion we announce today. Our inquiry would involve considerations somewhat different from those discussed above if a State purported to condition civil liability on a factual misstatement whose content did not warn a reasonably prudent editor or broadcaster of its defamatory potential. Cf. Time, Inc. v. Hill. * * * Such a case is not now before us, and we intimate no view as to its proper resolution.

IV

Our accommodation of the competing values at stake in defamation suits by private individuals allows the States to impose liability on the publisher or broadcaster of defamatory falsehoods on a less demanding showing than that required by *New York Times*. This conclusion is not based on a belief that the considerations which prompted the adoption of the *New York Times* privilege for defamation of public officials and its extension to public figures are wholly inapplicable to the context of private individuals. Rather, we endorse this approach in recognition of the strong and legitimate state interest in compensating private individuals for injury to reputation. But this countervailing state interest extends no further than compensation for actual injury. For the reasons stated below, we hold that the States may not permit recovery of presumed or punitive damages, at least when liability is not based on a showing of knowledge of falsity or reckless disregard for the truth.

The common law of defamation is an oddity of tort law, for it allows recovery of purportedly compensatory damages without evidence of actual loss. Under the traditional rules pertaining to actions for libel, the existence of injury is presumed from the fact of publication. Juries may award substantial sums as compensation for supposed damage to reputation without any proof that such harm actually occurred. The largely uncontrolled discretion of juries to award damages where there is no loss unnecessarily compounds the potential of any system of liability for defamatory falsehood to inhibit the vigorous exercise of First Amendment freedoms. Additionally, the doctrine of presumed damages invites juries to punish unpopular opinion rather than to compensate individuals for injury sustained by the publication of a false fact. More to the point, the States have no substantial interest in securing for plaintiffs such as this petitioner gratuitous awards of money damages far in excess of any actual injury.

We would not, of course, invalidate state law simply because we doubt its wisdom, but here we are attempting to reconcile state law with a competing interest grounded in the constitutional command of the First Amendment. * * * We need not define "actual injury," as trial courts have wide experience in framing appropriate jury instructions in tort action. Suffice it to say that actual injury is not limited to out-of-pocket loss. Indeed, the more customary types of actual harm inflicted by defamatory falsehood include impairment of reputation and standing in the community, personal humiliation, and mental anguish and suffering. Of course, juries must be limited by appropriate instructions, and all awards must be supported by competent evidence concerning the injury, although there need be no evidence which assigns an actual dollar value to the injury.

We also find no justification for allowing awards of punitive damages against publishers and broadcasters held liable under state-defined standards of liability for defamation. In most jurisdictions jury discretion over the amounts awarded is limited only by the gentle rule that they not be excessive. Consequently, juries assess punitive damages in wholly unpredictable amounts bearing no necessary relation to the actual harm caused. And they remain free to use their discretion selectively to punish expressions of unpopular views. Like the doctrine of presumed damages, jury discretion to award punitive damages unnecessarily exacerbates the danger of media self-censorship, but, unlike the former rule, punitive damages are wholly irrelevant to the state interest that justifies a negligence standard for private defamation actions. * * * In short, the private defamation plaintiff who establishes liability under a less demanding standard than that stated by *New York Times* may recover only such damages as are sufficient to compensate him for actual injury.

V

Notwithstanding our refusal to extend the *New York Times* privilege to defamation of private individuals, respondent contends that we should affirm the judgment below on the ground that petitioner is either a public official or a public figure. There is little basis for the former assertion. Several years prior to the present incident, petitioner had served briefly on housing committees appointed by the mayor of Chicago, but at the time of publication he had never held any remunerative governmental position. Respondent admits this but argues that petitioner's appearance at the coroner's inquest rendered him a "de facto public official." Our cases recognized no such concept. Respondent's suggestion would sweep all lawyers under the *New York Times* rule as officers of the court and distort the plain meaning of the "public official" category beyond all recognition. We decline to follow it.

Respondent's characterization of petitioner as a public figure raises a different question. That designation may rest on either of two alternative bases. In some instances an individual may achieve such pervasive fame or notoriety that he becomes a public figure for all purposes and in all contexts. More commonly, an individual voluntarily injects himself or is drawn into a particular public controversy and thereby becomes a public figure for a limited range of issues. In either case such persons assume special prominence in the resolution of public questions.

Petitioner has long been active in community and professional affairs. He has served as an officer of local civil groups and of various professional organizations, and he has published several books and articles on legal subjects. Although petitioner was consequently well-known in some circles, he had achieved no general fame or notoriety in the community. None of the prospective jurors called at the trial had ever heard of petitioner prior to this litigation, and respondent offered no proof that this response was atypical of the local population. We would not lightly assume that a citizen's participation in community and professional affairs rendered him a public figure for all purposes. Absent clear evidence of general fame or notoriety in the community, and pervasive involvement in the affairs of society, an individual should not be deemed a public personality for all aspects of his life. It is preferable to reduce the public figure question to a more meaningful context by looking to the nature and extent of an individual's participation in the particular controversy giving rise to the defamation.

In this context it is plain that petitioner was not a public figure. * * *

We therefore conclude that the *New York Times* standard is inapplicable to this case and that the trial court erred in entering judgment for respondent. Because the jury was allowed to impose liability without fault and was permitted to presume damages without proof of injury, a new trial is necessary. We reverse and remand for further proceedings in accord with this opinion.

It is so ordered.

Reversed and remanded.

MR. JUSTICE BLACKMUN, concurring.

I joined Mr. Justice Brennan's opinion for the plurality in Rosenbloom v. Metromedia, Inc. * * *. I did so because I concluded that, given New York Times Co. v. Sullivan * * * and its progeny * * * the step taken in *Rosenbloom,* extending the *New York Times* doctrine to an event of public or general interest, was logical and inevitable. A majority of the Court evidently thought otherwise * * *.

The Court today refuses to apply *New York Times* to the private individual, as contrasted with the public official and the public figure. It thus withdraws to the factual limits of the pre-*Rosenbloom* cases. It thereby fixes the outer boundary of the *New York Times* doctrine and says that beyond that boundary, a State is free to define for itself the appropriate standard of a media's liability so long as it does not impose liability without fault. As my joinder in *Rosenbloom's* plurality opinion would intimate, I sense some illogic in this.

The Court, however, seeks today to strike a balance between competing values where necessarily uncertain assumptions about human behavior color the result. Although the Court's opinion in the present case departs from the rationale of the *Rosenbloom* plurality, in that the Court now conditions a libel action by a private person upon a showing of negligence, as contrasted with a showing of willful or reckless disregard, I am willing to join, and do join, the Court's opinion and its judgment for two reasons:

1. By removing the spectres of presumed and punitive damages in the absence of *New York Times* malice, the Court eliminates significant and powerful motives for self-censorship that otherwise are present in the traditional libel action. * * *

2. The Court was sadly fractionated in *Rosenbloom.* A result of that kind inevitably leads to uncertainty. I feel that it is of profound importance for the Court to come to rest in the defamation area and to have a clearly defined majority position that eliminates the unsureness engendered by *Rosenbloom's* diversity. If my vote were not needed to create a majority, I would adhere to my prior view. A definitive ruling, however, is paramount. * * *

For these reasons, I join the opinion and the judgment of the Court.

MR. CHIEF JUSTICE BURGER, dissenting.

The doctrines of the law of defamation have had a gradual evolution primarily in the state courts. In New York Times Co. v. Sullivan and its progeny this Court entered this field.

Agreement or disagreement with the law as it has evolved to this time does not alter the fact that it has been orderly development with a consistent basic rationale. In today's opinion the Court abandons the traditional thread so far as the ordinary private citizen is concerned and introduces the concept that the media will be liable for negligence in publishing defamatory statements with respect to such persons. Although I agree with much of what Mr. Justice White states, I do not read the Court's new doctrinal approach in quite the way he does. I am frank to say I do not know the parameters of a "negligence" doctrine as applied to the news media. Conceivably this new doctrine could inhibit some editors, as the dissents of Mr. Justice Douglas and Mr. Justice Brennan suggest. But I would prefer to allow this area of law to continue to evolve as it has up to now with respect to private citizens rather than embark on a new doctrinal theory which has no jurisprudential ancestry.

* * *

MR. JUSTICE DOUGLAS, dissenting.

The Court describes this case as a return to the struggle of "defin[ing] the proper accommodation between the law of defamation and the freedoms of speech and press protected by the First Amendment." * * * I would suggest that the struggle is a quite hopeless one, for, in light of the command of the First Amendment, no "accommodation" of its freedoms can be "proper" except those made by the Framers themselves.

Unlike the right of privacy which, by the terms of the Fourth Amendment, must be accommodated with reasonable searches and seizures and warrants issued by magistrates, the rights of free speech and of a free press were protected by the Framers in verbiage whose prescription seems clear. * * *

* * *

Since in my view the First and Fourteenth Amendments prohibit the imposition of damages upon respondent for this discussion of public affairs, I would affirm the judgment below.

MR. JUSTICE BRENNAN, dissenting.

I agree with the conclusion, expressed in Part V of the Court's opinion, that, at the time of publication of respondent's article, petitioner could not properly have been viewed as either a "public official" or "public figure"; instead, respondent's article, dealing with an alleged conspiracy to discredit local police forces, concerned petitioner's purported involvement in "an event of 'public or general interest.'" Rosenbloom v. Metromedia, Inc. * * * I cannot agree, however, that free and robust debate—so essential to the proper functioning of our system of government—is permitted adequate "breathing space," * * * when, as the Court holds, the States may impose all but strict liability for defamation if the defamed party is a private person and "the substance of the defamatory statement 'makes substantial danger to reputation apparent.'" * * * I adhere to my view expressed in Rosenbloom v. Metromedia, Inc., *supra,* that we strike the proper accommodation between avoidance of media self-censorship and protection of individual reputations only when we require States to apply the New York Times Co. v. Sullivan * * * knowing-or-reckless-falsity standard in civil libel actions concerning media reports of the involvement of private individuals in events of public or general interest.

* * *

Since petitioner failed, after having been given a full and fair opportunity, to prove that respondent published the disputed article with knowledge of its falsity or with reckless disregard of the truth * * *, I would affirm the judgment of the Court of Appeals.

MR. JUSTICE WHITE, dissenting.

For some 200 years—from the very founding of the Nation—the law of defamation and right of the ordinary citizen to recover for false publication injurious to his reputation have been almost exclusively the business of state courts and legislatures. Under typical state defamation law, the defamed private citizen had to prove only a false publication that would subject him to hatred, contempt or ridicule. Given such publication, general damages to reputation were presumed, while punitive damages required proof of additional facts. The law governing the defamation of private citizens remained untouched by the First Amendment because until relatively recently, the consistent view of the Court was that libelous words constitute a class of speech wholly unprotected by the First Amendment, subject only to limited exceptions carved out since 1964.

But now, using that amendment as the chosen instrument, the Court, in a few printed pages, has federalized major aspects of libel law by declaring unconstitutional in important respects the prevailing defamation law in all or most of the 50 States. That result is accomplished by requiring the plaintiff in each and every defamation action to prove not only the defendant's culpability beyond his act of publishing defamatory material but also actual damage to reputation resulting from the publication. Moreover, punitive damages may not be recovered by showing malice in the traditional sense of ill will; knowing falsehood or reckless disregard of the truth will now be required.

I assume these sweeping changes will be popular with the press, but this is not the road to salvation for a court of law. As I see it, there are wholly insufficient grounds for scuttling the libel laws of the States in such wholesale fashion, to say nothing of deprecating the reputation interest of ordinary citizens and rendering them powerless to protect themselves. I do not suggest that the decision is illegitimate or beyond the bounds of judicial review, but it is an ill-considered exercise of the power entrusted to this Court, particularly when the Court has not had the benefit of briefs and argument addressed to most of the major issues which the Court now decides. I respectfully dissent.

* * *

II

* * *

The central meaning of *New York Times,* and for me the First Amendment as it relates to libel laws, is that seditious libel—criticism of government and public officials—falls beyond the police power of the State. * * * In a democratic society such as ours, the citizen has the privilege of criticizing his government and its officials. But neither *New York Times* nor its progeny suggest that the First Amendment intended in all circumstances to deprive the private citizen of his historic recourse to redress published falsehoods damaging to reputation or that, contrary to history and precedent, the Amendment should now be so interpreted. * * *

* * *

V

In disagreeing with the Court on the First Amendment's reach in the area of state libel laws protecting nonpublic persons, I do not repudiate the principle that the First Amendment "rests on the assumption that the widest possible dissemination of information from diverse and antagonistic sources is essential to the welfare of the public, that a free press is a condition of a free society." Associated Press v. United States, 326 U.S. 1, 20, 65 S.Ct. 1416, 1425, 89 L.Ed. 2013 (1945). * * * I continue to subscribe to *New York Times* and those decisions extending its protection to defamatory falsehoods about public persons. My quarrel with the Court stems from its willingness "to sacrifice good sense to a syllogism"[39]—to find in the *New York Times* doctrine an infinite elasticity. Unfortunately, this expansion is the latest manifestation of the destructive potential of any good idea carried out to its logical extreme.

* * *

I fail to see how the quality or quantity of public debate will be promoted by further emasculation of state libel laws for the benefit of the news media. If anything, this trend may provoke a new and radical imbalance in the communications process. * * * It is not at all inconceivable that virtually unrestrained defamatory remarks about private citizens will discourage them from speaking out and concerning themselves with social problems. This would turn the First Amendment on its head. * * *

* * *

In our federal system, there must be room for allowing the States to take diverse approaches to these vexing questions. * * * Whether or not the course followed by the majority is wise, and I have indicated my doubts that it is, our constitutional scheme compels a proper respect for the role of the States in acquitting their duty to obey the Constitution. Finding no evidence that they have shirked this responsibility, particularly when the law of defamation is even now in transition, I would await some demonstration of the diminution of freedom of expression before acting.

* * *

NOTES

1. Most of Justice White's long dissent has been omitted. In describing the modern law of defamation, Justice White relied upon *Restatement (Second) of Torts* Tentative Draft No. 12, 1966. In particular he relied upon § 569 of the Tentative Draft No. 12, which distinguished between libel that was clear on its face and libel that was not. In our discussion, *supra*, p. 499, we saw that at one time the drafters of the *Restatement (Second)* had proposed making libelous statements that were not defamatory on their face actionable without proof of special damages only if they fell within the slander per se

39. O. Holmes, The Common Law 36 (1881).

categories. (Note Justice White's statement that the law of defamation of the several states was "in transition.") By the time of the *Gertz* decision, however, the drafters of the *Restatement (Second)* had abandoned that position and reverted to the English common-law position. *See Restatement (Second) of Torts* § 569 (Tent. Draft No. 20, 1974), and as we have already seen this is the position taken by the final version of the *Restatement (Second).*

2. One of the most striking aspects of Justice Powell's opinion for the Court was his rejection, see p. 598, *supra*, of the test enumerated by the plurality in *Rosenbloom* which he declared would require "state and federal judges to decide on an *ad hoc* basis which publications address issues of 'general or public' interest." Justice Powell doubted "the wisdom of committing this task to the conscience of judges." Instead, as we have seen, he adopted a test based on whether the plaintiff was either a public official or a public figure rather than a private person. In a fairly recent case, *Neill Grading and Const. Co. v. Lingafelt*, 168 N.C.App. 36, 606 S.E.2d 734 (2005), the court applied the negligence standard in a case involving a person classified as a private figure even though it believed the subject matter of the statement in question involved a matter of public concern.

As we saw in *Snyder v. Phelps* reprinted at p. 471, *supra*, and shall see again in *Dun & Bradstreet, Inc. v. Greenmoss Builders, Inc.*, reprinted at p. 620, *infra,* and shall also see in our discussion of privacy in Chapter Nine, there is continued pressure to include some notion of public interest or concern in any test for identifying the speech that qualifies for greater constitutional protection. As we recognized in the notes following *Snyder v. Phelps,* the crucial issue involved in this approach boils down to who is to decide what is an issue of public concern. Is it the courts based on their notion of what the public has a legitimate interest in knowing or is it possible to enunciate some more empirically based criteria for making that decision-making process less subjective?

3. It should be noted that Justice Powell, in writing the opinion of the Court in *Gertz,* spoke in terms of actions against a "publisher or broadcaster." It is thus possible to argue that *Gertz* only applies in actions by private figures against the news media; actions by private figures against non-media defendants would thus be governed by the traditional common law. In the portion of his dissent reprinted above, Chief Justice Burger indicates his view that Justice Powell was only speaking about actions against "news media." Justice Powell's opinion was also interpreted in this manner in M. Nimmer, *Introduction—Is Freedom of the Press a Redundancy: What Does It Add to Freedom of Speech?,* 26 Hastings L.J. 639 (1975). *See also* M. Nimmer, *Speech and Press: A Brief Reply,* 23 U.C.L.A.L.Rev. 120 (1975). Moreover, former Justice Stewart publicly expressed the view that the media are in fact granted special protection by the First Amendment. *See* P. Stewart, *"Or of the Press,"* 26 Hastings L.J. 631 (1975). And Justice Stewart joined in Justice Powell's opinion for the Court in *Gertz.* Nevertheless, by the time *Gertz* was decided, the Court had already rejected the notion that the press has any special privileges not enjoyed by the rest of society. *See* Branzburg v. Hayes, 408 U.S. 665, 92 S.Ct. 2646, 33 L.Ed.2d 626 (1972). *See also Herbert v. Lando,* discussed at p. 588, *supra.* Moreover, as is conceded by Professor Nimmer, it is generally agreed that the founding fathers used the terms "freedom of

speech" and "freedom of the press" interchangeably and that when they spoke about the "press" they were probably adverting to Blackstone's idea of "no prior restraint," *i.e.* to the freedom to publish. *See* L. Levy, Legacy of Suppression (1960); D. Lange, *The Speech and Press Clauses,* 23 U.C.L.A.L.Rev. 77 (1975).[a] *See also* D. Anderson, *Freedom of the Press,* 80 Tex.L.Rev. 429 (2002). Moreover, if the press does have special privileges, who constitutes the press? What about a professor researching a book? *Cf.* United States v. Doe, 460 F.2d 328 (1st Cir.1972), *cert. denied* 411 U.S. 909, 93 S.Ct. 1527, 36 L.Ed.2d 199 (1973) (professor at Harvard denied any privileges not enjoyed by citizens at large to refuse to answer questions before a grand jury concerning the leakage of the "Pentagon Papers.") Nevertheless, a few state courts have restricted *Gertz* to actions by private figures against the media. *See* Harley–Davidson Motorsports, Inc. v. Markley, 279 Or. 361, 568 P.2d 1359 (1977). *See also* Denny v. Mertz, 106 Wis.2d 636, 318 N.W.2d 141 (1982); Rowe v. Metz, 195 Colo. 424, 579 P.2d 83 (1978); Calero v. Del Chemical Corp., 68 Wis.2d 487, 228 N.W.2d 737 (1975). Most state courts that have considered the question, however, have concluded that no such distinction is possible. *See, e.g.,* Jacron Sales Co. v. Sindorf, 276 Md. 580, 350 A.2d 688 (1976); Ryder Truck Rentals v. Latham, 593 S.W.2d 334 (Tex.Civ.App.1979). *See also* Gray v. Allison Division, General Motors Corp., 52 Ohio App.2d 348, 370 N.E.2d 747 (1977). This is the position taken by the *Restatement (Second) of Torts* §§ 558, 580B, Comment *e.* We will return to this question again when we examine Dun & Bradstreet, Inc. v. Greenmoss Builders, Inc., 472 U.S. 749, 105 S.Ct. 2939, 86 L.Ed.2d 593 (1985) at p. 620, *infra.*

4. On the same day that the Court decided *Gertz,* it also decided Old Dominion Branch No. 496, National Association of Letter Carriers v. Austin, 418 U.S. 264, 94 S.Ct. 2770, 41 L.Ed.2d 745 (1974). In that case the three plaintiff letter carriers who were among a group of fifteen out of 435 who were not members of the defendant union, were described as "scabs" in the union newsletter and then likened to Esau, Judas, and Benedict Arnold. The newsletter continued by quoting Jack London's definition of a "scab" as "a traitor to his God, his country, his family and his class." The plaintiffs had recovered substantial damages for defamation in the trial courts and the Supreme Court of Virginia had affirmed. The Supreme Court of the United States, however, reversed. Writing through Justice Marshall, the Court, with three dissents, held that the *Sullivan* standards were applicable because the statements in question had been made in the course of what was arguably a "labor dispute." Although most of the opinion of the Court discusses the applicability of the *Sullivan* standards, the Court went on to hold in the alternative that the statements in the newsletter were in any event not

a. It is hard to tell exactly what regulation of speech is permitted by the first amendment because, as has often been very persuasively argued, there is a very strong and persuasive case that the first amendment was intended principally as a proposition about federalism, namely that regulation of speech was a matter for the states and not for Congress. *See* W. Van Alstyne, *Congressional Power and Free Speech: Levy's* Legacy *Revisited* (Book Review), 99 Harv.L.Rev. 1089 (1986). This is a review of L. Levy, Emergence of a Free Press (1985), which is in effect a second edition of Levy's *Legacy of Suppression* cited in the text. *See also* P. Kurland, *Public Policy, the Constitution and the Supreme Court,* 12 N.Ky.L.Rev. 181 (1985). This reading, which may very well be totally correct, may help explain why it is difficult to apply against the states, whom the founding fathers did believe had some authority to regulate speech, a provision which the founding fathers may well have thought absolutely prohibited any regulation by the Congress.

actionable because they involved mere expressions of opinion and the use of epithets. Can the *Old Dominion* case be confined to labor disputes or is it an indication that the newsworthiness issue cannot be avoided? Can debate about labor matters be freer than debate about politics, foreign relations, or social issues like abortion? The *Old Dominion* case, together with the immediate *post-Gertz* developments, is discussed in G. Christie, *Injury to Reputation and the Constitution: Confusion Amid Conflicting Approaches,* 75 Mich.L.Rev. 43 (1976). Decisions of the Court since *Old Dominion* rejecting content based regulation of speech activities makes it even harder to restrict *Old Dominion's* extension of the *Sullivan* standard in actions involving private figures as plaintiffs to the labor relations area. *See* G. Christie, *Underlying Contradictions in the Supreme Court's Classification of Defamation,* 1981 Duke L.J. 811.

5. While most state courts have accepted the distinction drawn in *Gertz* between public officials and public figures on the one hand and private persons on the other, some courts have refused to join the Court in its retreat from *Rosenbloom v. Metromedia, Inc.* and have continued to require a showing of intended falsehood or reckless disregard for truth, at least when the defamatory statement concerns an issue of public interest. *See, e.g.,* Walker v. Colorado Springs Sun, Inc., 188 Colo. 86, 538 P.2d 450 (1975), *cert. denied* 423 U.S. 1025, 96 S.Ct. 469, 46 L.Ed.2d 399, as extended by Diversified Management, Inc. v. Denver Post, Inc., 653 P.2d 1103 (Colo.1982); AAFCO Heating & Air Conditioning Co. v. Northwest Publications, Inc., 162 Ind.App. 671, 321 N.E.2d 580 (1974), *cert. denied* 424 U.S. 913, 96 S.Ct. 1112, 47 L.Ed.2d 318 (1976); Schaefer v. State Bar, 77 Wis.2d 120, 252 N.W.2d 343 (1977); Dairy Stores, Inc. v. Sentinel Pub. Co., 104 N.J. 125, 516 A.2d 220 (1986). See *also* Gay v. Williams, 486 F.Supp. 12 (D.Alaska 1979). New York has adopted an intermediate position. In a case reminiscent of *Rosenbloom v. Metromedia, Inc.,* the New York Court of Appeals held that when a private individual is defamed in an article whose

> content * * * is arguably within the sphere of legitimate public concern, which is reasonably related to matters warranting public exposition * * * [the plaintiff] must establish, by a preponderance of the evidence, that the publisher acted in a grossly irresponsible manner without due consideration for the standards of information gathering and dissemination ordinarily followed by responsible parties.

Chapadeau v. Utica Observer–Dispatch, Inc., 38 N.Y.2d 196, 199, 379 N.Y.S.2d 61, 64, 341 N.E.2d 569, 571 (1975). Somewhat dated compilations of how the various states have handled this question are contained in Lansdowne v. Beacon Journal Pub. Co., 32 Ohio St.3d 176, 186–87, 512 N.E.2d 979, 989–90 (1987) (concurring opinion); Rouch v. Enquirer & News of Battle Creek, 427 Mich. 157, 187–89, 398 N.W.2d 245, 259–60 (1986). In the *Rouch* case the court held that a police report was not an official proceeding. Someone who was defamed by a newspaper article based on such a report could recover on proof of falsity and negligence. M.C.L. § 600.291(3) was subsequently amended to make it clear that such reports fell within the absolute privilege for fair and true reports "of matters of public record, a public and official proceeding, or of a government notice, announcement written or recorded report or report generally available to the public, or act or action of a public body." *See* Northland Wheels Roller Skating Center, Inc. v. Detroit Free Press, Inc., 213 Mich.App. 317, 539 N.W.2d 774 (1995).

6. On retrial, the jury awarded Gertz $100,000 in compensatory damages and $300,000 in punitive damages. The Seventh Circuit affirmed, finding more than enough evidence that the article was published with "utter disregard for truth or falsity." Gertz v. Robert Welch, Inc., 680 F.2d 527 (7th Cir.1982), *cert. denied*, 459 U.S. 1226, 103 S.Ct. 1233, 75 L.Ed.2d 467 (1983).

7. *Fact vs. Opinion.* Actually deciding what is opinion and what is fact can sometimes be a very difficult task whose difficulty has been highlighted now that the Court has held that the distinction between fact and opinion is one of constitutional significance. It has long been recognized that the expression of some opinions clearly gives rise in the minds of a reasonable reader or listener to the conclusion that the speaker or writer has a factual basis for the statement that has been made. The Court, in Milkovich v. Lorain Journal Co., 497 U.S. 1, 110 S.Ct. 2695, 111 L.Ed.2d 1 (1990) has rebuked those who sought to read *Gertz* as providing a blanket immunity, on first amendment grounds, to all expressions of opinion. If an allegedly defamatory opinion reasonably implies a statement that is "sufficiently factual to be susceptible of being proved true or false," the so-called opinion is actionable provided the other hurdles to bringing an action for defamation are met.

But the awareness that some so-called expressions of opinion are capable of being interpreted as implicit statements of fact only begins to illustrate the difficulty that can sometimes be experienced in deciding what is opinion rather than fact. An important case is Ollman v. Evans, 750 F.2d 970 (D.C.Cir.1984) (en banc), in which the eleven judges who heard the case issued seven different opinions. The case involved nationally syndicated columnists Evans and Novak who had commented on a proposal to name the plaintiff, who had been a professor at New York University, as Chairman of the Department of Government and Politics at the University of Maryland. The columnists tried to draw a distinction between the plaintiff's qualifications as a scholar which they were prepared to recognize was not the crucial issue, and his allegedly active support for what they termed "political marxism". Nevertheless the columnists did include a statement from someone identified as a "political scientist in a major eastern university whose scholarship and reputation as a liberal are well known" that the plaintiff had "no status within the profession but is a pure and simple activist." On what they considered to be the main issue, the columnists had declared, partially using quotations that purported to be from the plaintiff's own work, that the plaintiff believed that the classroom should be a place to convert students to socialism and to dismantle the students' "bourgeois ideology" and that " 'our prior task' before the revolution he writes 'is to make more revolutionaries' ". The majority of the court of appeals held that all these statements represented mere statements of opinions. Writing for the majority of the court, Judge Kenneth Starr surveyed the several methods that had been put forward for distinguishing between fact and opinion. Some courts had treated the matter as a judgment call to be made by the judiciary and others have focused upon the lack of verifiability of the allegedly defamatory statements. Other courts have adopted a multifactor test under which they attempted to analyze the statements in question in the context of the totality of the circumstances in which they appeared. Judge Starr himself started by analyzing common usage, namely whether the language had a precise core of meaning or whether the statement in question was indefinite and ambiguous. He then considered the verifiability of the statement in question. Next he turned to the full textual context in which the statement appeared, that is the entire article. Finally, he considered the broader social context or setting in which the statement appeared. Judge Robert Bork, in the concurring opinion in which three other judges joined, felt that all of the allegedly libelous statements at issue were expressions of opinion but that the majority had not adequately explained why. Judge Bork rejected the suggestion that the Supreme Court had imposed any sharp dividing line between opinions which are not actionable as libel and facts which are. Judge Antonin Scalia, who after his elevation to the Supreme Court, was one of the Justices joining the Court's opinion in *Milkovich*, dissented from the conclusion that the statements about the plaintiff having no status in the profession was merely an opinion as to which no action would lie. Judges Patricia Wald and Harry Edwards both concurred with Judge Scalia.

The *Ollman* case gave rise to voluminous literature on this difficult subject. *See e.g.,* Note, *The Fact–Opinion Determination in Defamation,* 88 Colum.L.Rev. 809 (1988); Comment, *The Fact/Opinion Distinction: an Analysis of the Subjectivity of Language in Law,* 70 Marq.L.Rev. 673 (1987); Note, *The Fact–Opinion Dilemma and First Amendment Defamation Law,* 13 Wm. Mitchell L.Rev. 545 (1987); Comment, *Structuring Defamation Law to Eliminate the Fact–Opinion Determination: A Critique of* Ollman v. Evans, 71 Iowa L.Rev. 913 (1986). Since the Court's decision in *Milkovich,* whether the statement in question is capable of verification or falsification has undoubtedly taken on greater importance. In Wampler v. Higgins, 93 Ohio St.3d 111, 752 N.E.2d 962 (2001) the court relied on the state constitution to hold that statements that the plaintiff was charging "exorbitant rent" and that he was a "ruthless speculator" were non-actionable expressions of opinion. In Esposito–Hilder v. SFX Broadcasting Inc., 236 A.D.2d 186, 665 N.Y.S.2d 697 (1997), the court held that a plaintiff, who was unable to bring a defamation action because the derogatory statements were merely opinions, might nevertheless, if she were a private person and the matter which led to the statement was one of "virtually no 'public' interest," have a possible cause of action for intentional infliction of mental suffering. That possibility seems to have been left open by *Snyder v. Phelps*, reprinted in Chapter Seven at p. 471, *supra. See also Hustler Magazine v. Falwell*, reprinted in Chapter Seven, at p. 465, *supra.*

TIME, INC. v. FIRESTONE

Supreme Court of the United States, 1976.
424 U.S. 448, 96 S.Ct. 958, 47 L.Ed.2d 154.

MR. JUSTICE REHNQUIST delivered the opinion of the Court.

Petitioner is the publisher of Time, a weekly news magazine. The Supreme Court of Florida affirmed a $100,000 libel judgment against petitioner which was based on an item appearing in Time that purported to describe the result of domestic relations litigation between respondent and her husband. We granted certiorari * * * to review petitioner's claim that the judgment violates its rights under the First and Fourteenth Amendments to the United States Constitution.

I

Respondent, Mary Alice Firestone, married Russell Firestone, the scion of one of America's wealthier industrial families, in 1961. In 1964, they separated, and respondent filed a complaint for separate maintenance in the Circuit Court of Palm Beach County, Fla. Her husband counterclaimed for divorce on grounds of extreme cruelty and adultery. After a lengthy trial the Circuit Court issued a judgment granting the divorce requested by respondent's husband. In relevant part the court's final judgment read:

> "This cause came on for final hearing before the court upon the plaintiff wife's second amended complaint for separate maintenance (alimony unconnected with the causes of divorce), the defendant husband's answer and counterclaim for divorce on grounds of extreme cruelty and adultery, and the wife's answer thereto setting up certain affirmative defenses. * * *
>
> * * *
>
> "According to certain testimony in behalf of the defendant, extramarital escapades of the plaintiff were bizarre and of an amatory nature which would have made Dr. Freud's hair curl. Other testimony, in plaintiff's behalf, would indicate that defendant was guilty of bounding from one bedpartner to another with the erotic zest of a satyr. The court is inclined to discount much of this testimony as unreliable. Nevertheless, it is the conclusion and finding of the court that neither party is domesticated, within the meaning of that term as used by the Supreme Court of Florida. * * *
>
> * * *
>
> "In the present case, it is abundantly clear from the evidence of marital discord that neither of the parties has shown the least susceptibility to domestication, and that the marriage should be dissolved.
>
> * * *
>
> "The premises considered, it is thereupon
>
> "ORDERED AND ADJUDGED as follows:
>
> "1. That the equities in this cause are with the defendant; that defendant's counterclaim for divorce be and the same is hereby granted, and the bonds of matrimony which have heretofore existed between the parties are hereby forever dissolved.
>
> * * *
>
> "4. That the defendant shall pay unto the plaintiff the sum of $3,000 per month as alimony beginning January 1, 1968, and a like sum on

the first day of each and every month thereafter until the death or remarriage of the plaintiff." App. 523–525, 528.

Time's editorial staff, headquartered in New York, was alerted by a wire service report and an account in a New York newspaper to the fact that a judgment had been rendered in the Firestone divorce proceeding. The staff subsequently received further information regarding the Florida decision from Time's Miami bureau chief and from a "stringer" working on a special assignment basis in the Palm Beach area. On the basis of these four sources, Time's staff composed the following item which appeared in the magazine's "Milestones" section the following week:

> "DIVORCED. By Russell A. Firestone, Jr., 41, heir to the tire fortune: Mary Alice Sullivan Firestone, 32, his third wife; a onetime Palm Beach schoolteacher; on grounds of extreme cruelty and adultery; after six years of marriage, one son; in West Palm Beach, Fla. The 17–month intermittent trial produced enough testimony of extramarital adventures on both sides, said the judge, 'to make Dr. Freud's hair curl.' "

Within a few weeks of the publication of this article respondent demanded in writing a retraction from petitioner, alleging that a portion of the article was "false, malicious and defamatory." Petitioner declined to issue the requested retraction.[1]

Respondent then filed this libel action against petitioner in the Florida Circuit Court. Based on a jury verdict for respondent, that court entered judgment against petitioner for $100,000, and after review in both the Florida District Court of Appeal, 279 So.2d 389 and the Supreme Court of Florida, the judgment was ultimately affirmed. 305 So.2d 172 (1974). Petitioner advances several contentions as to why the judgment is contrary to decisions of this Court holding that the First and Fourteenth Amendments of the United States Constitution limit the authority of state courts to impose liability for damages based on defamation.

II

Petitioner initially contends that it cannot be liable for publishing any falsehood defaming respondent unless it is established that the publication was made "with actual malice," as that term is defined in New York Times Co. v. Sullivan * * *. Petitioner advances two arguments in support of this contention: that respondent is a "public figure" within this Court's decisions extending *New York Times* to defamation suits brought by such individuals * * *; and that the Time item constituted a report of a judicial proceeding, a class of subject matter which petitioner claims deserves the protection of the "actual malice" standard even if the story is proved to be defamatorily false or inaccurate. We reject both arguments.

1. Under Florida law the demand for retraction was a prerequisite for filing a libel action, and permits defendants to limit their potential liability to actual damages by complying with the demand. Fla.Stat.Ann. §§ 770.01–770.02 (1963).

In *Gertz v. Robert Welch, Inc.* * * * we have recently further defined the meaning of "public figure" * * *. Respondent did not assume any role of especial prominence in the affairs of society, other than perhaps Palm Beach society, and she did not thrust herself to the forefront of any particular public controversy in order to influence the resolution of the issues involved in it.

Petitioner contends that because the Firestone divorce was characterized by the Florida Supreme Court as a "cause célèbre," it must have been a public controversy and respondent must be considered a public figure. But in so doing petitioner seeks to equate "public controversy" with all controversies of interest to the public. Were we to accept this reasoning, we would reinstate the doctrine advanced in the plurality opinion in Rosenbloom v. Metromedia, Inc. * * *. In *Gertz,* however, the Court repudiated this position, stating that "extension of the *New York Times* test proposed by the *Rosenbloom* plurality would abridge [a] legitimate state interest to a degree that we find unacceptable." * * *

Dissolution of a marriage through judicial proceedings is not the sort of "public controversy" referred to in *Gertz,* even though the marital difficulties of extremely wealthy individuals may be of interest to some portion of the reading public. Nor did respondent freely choose to publicize issues as to the propriety of her married life. She was compelled to go to court by the State in order to obtain legal release from the bonds of matrimony. We have said that in such an instance "[r]esort to the judicial process * * * is no more voluntary in a realistic sense than that of the defendant called upon to defend his interests in court." Boddie v. Connecticut, 401 U.S. 371 (1971). Her actions, both in instituting the litigation and in its conduct, were quite different from those of General Walker in *Curtis Publishing Co., supra.*[3] She assumed no "special prominence in the resolution of public questions." * * * We hold respondent was not a "public figure" for the purpose of determining the constitutional protection afforded petitioner's report of the factual and legal basis for her divorce.

For similar reasons we likewise reject petitioner's claim for automatic extension of the *New York Times* privilege to all reports of judicial proceedings. It is argued that information concerning proceedings in our Nation's courts may have such importance to all citizens as to justify extending special First Amendment protection to the press when reporting on such events. We have recently accepted a significantly more confined version of this argument by holding that the Constitution precludes States from imposing civil liability based upon the publication of truthful infor-

3. Nor do we think the fact that respondent may have held a few press conferences during the divorce proceedings in an attempt to satisfy inquiring reporters converts her into a "public figure." Such interviews should have had no effect upon the merits of the legal dispute between respondent and her husband or the outcome of that trial, and we do not think it can be assumed that any such purpose was intended. Moreover, there is no indication that she sought to use the press conferences as a vehicle by which to thrust herself to the forefront of some unrelated controversy in order to influence its resolution. See *Gertz v. Robert Welch, Inc.* * * *

mation contained in official court records open to public inspection. Cox Broadcasting Corp. v. Cohn, 420 U.S. 469 (1975).[a]

Petitioner would have us extend the reasoning of *Cox Broadcasting* to safeguard even inaccurate and false statements, at least where "actual malice" has not been established. But its argument proves too much. It may be that all reports of judicial proceedings contain some informational value implicating the First Amendment, but recognizing this is little different from labeling all judicial proceedings matters of "public or general interest," as that phrase was used by the plurality in *Rosenbloom.* Whatever their general validity, use of such subject-matter classifications to determine the extent of constitutional protection afforded defamatory falsehoods may too often result in an improper balance between the competing interests in this area. It was our recognition and rejection of this weakness in the *Rosenbloom* test which led us in *Gertz* to eschew a subject-matter test for one focusing upon the character of the defamation plaintiff. * * *

Presumptively erecting the *New York Times* barrier against all plaintiffs seeking to recover for injuries from defamatory falsehoods published in what are alleged to be reports of judicial proceedings would effect substantial depreciation of the individual's interest in protection from such harm, without any convincing assurance that such a sacrifice is required under the First Amendment. And in some instances such an undiscriminating approach might achieve results directly at odds with the constitutional balance intended. Indeed, the article upon which the *Gertz* libel action was based purported to be a report on the murder trial of a Chicago police officer. * * * Our decision in that case should make it clear that no such blanket privilege for reports of judicial proceedings is to be found in the Constitution.

It may be argued that there is still room for application of the *New York Times* protections to more narrowly focused reports of what actually transpires in the courtroom. But even so narrowed, the suggested privilege is simply too broad. Imposing upon the law of private defamation the rather drastic limitations worked by *New York Times* cannot be justified by generalized references to the public interest in reports of judicial proceedings. The details of many, if not most, courtroom battles would add almost nothing toward advancing the uninhibited debate on public issues thought to provide principal support for the decision in *New York Times.* * * * And while participants in some litigation may be legitimate "public figures," either generally or for the limited purpose of that litigation, the majority will more likely resemble respondent, drawn into a public forum largely against their will in order to attempt to obtain the only redress available to them or to defend themselves against actions brought by the State or by others. There appears little reason why these individuals should substantially forfeit that degree of protection which the law of defamation would otherwise afford them simply by virtue of their being

a. [Ed. note] This case will be discussed at p. 695, *infra.*

drawn into a courtroom. The public interest in accurate reports of judicial proceedings is substantially protected by *Cox Broadcasting Co., supra.* As to inaccurate and defamatory reports of facts, matters deserving no First Amendment protection * * *; we think *Gertz* provides an adequate safeguard for the constitutionally protected interests of the press and affords it a tolerable margin for error by requiring some type of fault.

III

Petitioner has urged throughout this litigation that it could not be held liable for publication of the "Milestones" item because its report of respondent's divorce was factually correct. In its view the Time article faithfully reproduced the precise meaning of the divorce judgment. But this issue was submitted to the jury under an instruction intended to implement Florida's limited privilege for accurate reports of judicial proceedings. * * * By returning a verdict for respondent the jury necessarily found that the identity of meaning which petitioner claims does not exist even for laymen. The Supreme Court of Florida upheld this finding on appeal, rejecting petitioner's contention that its report was accurate as a matter of law. Because demonstration that an article was true would seem to preclude finding the publisher at fault, * * * we have examined the predicate for petitioner's contention. We believe the Florida courts properly could have found the "Milestones" item to be false.

For petitioner's report to have been accurate, the divorce granted Russell Firestone must have been based on a finding by the divorce court that his wife had committed extreme cruelty toward him *and* that she had been guilty of adultery. This is indisputably what petitioner reported in its "Milestones" item, but it is equally indisputable that these were not the facts. Russell Firestone alleged in his counterclaim that respondent had been guilty of adultery, but the divorce court never made any such finding. Its judgment provided that Russell Firestone's "counterclaim for divorce be and the same is hereby granted," but did not specify that the basis for the judgment was either of the two grounds alleged in the counterclaim. The Supreme Court of Florida on appeal concluded that the ground actually relied upon by the divorce court was "lack of domestication of the parties," a ground not theretofore recognized by Florida law. The Supreme Court nonetheless affirmed the judgment dissolving the bonds of matrimony because the record contained sufficient evidence to establish the ground of extreme cruelty. * * *

Petitioner may well argue that the meaning of the trial court's decree was unclear, but this does not license it to choose from among several conceivable interpretations the one most damaging to respondent. Having chosen to follow this tack, petitioner must be able to establish not merely that the item reported was a conceivable or plausible interpretation of the decree, but that the item was factually correct. We believe there is ample support for the jury's conclusion, affirmed by the Supreme Court of Florida, that this was not the case. * * *

* * * Petitioner has argued that because respondent withdrew her claim for damages to reputation on the eve of trial, there could be no recovery consistent with *Gertz*. Petitioner's theory seems to be that the only compensable injury in a defamation action is that which may be done to one's reputation, and that claims not predicated upon such injury are by definition not actions for defamation. But Florida has obviously decided to permit recovery for other injuries without regard to measuring the effect the falsehood may have had upon a plaintiff's reputation. This does not transform the action into something other than an action for defamation as that term is meant in *Gertz*. In that opinion we made it clear that States could base awards on elements other than injury to reputation, specifically listing "personal humiliation, and mental anguish and suffering" as examples of injuries which might be compensated consistently with the Constitution upon a showing of fault. Because respondent has decided to forgo recovery for injury to her reputation, she is not prevented from obtaining compensation for such other damages that a defamatory falsehood may have caused her.

* * * There was competent evidence introduced to permit the jury to assess the amount of injury. Several witnesses[6] testified to the extent of respondent's anxiety and concern over Time's inaccurately reporting that she had been found guilty of adultery, and she herself took the stand to elaborate on her fears that her young son would be adversely affected by this falsehood when he grew older. The jury decided these injuries should be compensated by an award of $100,000. We have no warrant for re-examining this determination. * * *

IV

Gertz established, however, that not only must there be evidence to support an award of compensatory damages, there must also be evidence of some fault on the part of a defendant charged with publishing defamatory material. No question of fault was submitted to the jury in this case, because under Florida law the only findings required for determination of liability were whether the article was defamatory, whether it was true, and whether the defamation, if any, caused respondent harm.

The failure to submit the question of fault to the jury does not of itself establish noncompliance with the constitutional requirements established in *Gertz,* however. Nothing in the Constitution requires that assessment of fault in a civil case tried in a state court be made by a jury, nor is there any prohibition against such a finding being made in the first instance by an appellate, rather than a trial, court. The First and Fourteenth Amendments do not impose upon the States any limitations as to how, within their own judicial systems, factfinding tasks shall be allocated. If we were satisfied that one of the Florida courts which

6. These included respondent's minister, her attorney in the divorce proceedings, plus several friends and neighbors, one of whom was a physician who testified to having to administer a sedative to respondent in an attempt to reduce discomfort wrought by her worrying about the article.

considered this case had supportably ascertained petitioner was at fault, we would be required to affirm the judgment below.

But the only alternative source of such a finding, given that the issue was not submitted to the jury, is the opinion of the Supreme Court of Florida. That opinion appears to proceed generally on the assumption that a showing of fault was not required, but then in the penultimate paragraph it recites:

> "Furthermore, this erroneous reporting is clear and convincing evidence of the negligence in certain segments of the news media in gathering the news. * * * Pursuant to Florida law in effect at the time of the divorce judgment (Section 61.08, Florida Statutes), a wife found guilty of adultery could not be awarded alimony. Since petitioner had been awarded alimony, she had not been found guilty of adultery nor had the divorce been granted on the ground of adultery. A careful examination of the final decree prior to publication would have clearly demonstrated that the divorce had been granted on the grounds of extreme cruelty, and thus the wife would have been saved the humiliation of being accused of adultery in a nationwide magazine. This is a flagrant example of 'journalistic negligence.' " * * *

It may be argued that this is sufficient indication the court found petitioner at fault within the meaning of *Gertz*. Nothing in that decision or in the First or Fourteenth Amendment requires that in a libel action an appellate court treat in detail by written opinion all contentions of the parties, and if the jury or trial judge had found fault in fact, we would be quite willing to read the quoted passage as affirming that conclusion. But without some finding of fault by the judge or jury in the Circuit Court, we would have to attribute to the Supreme Court of Florida from the quoted language not merely an intention to affirm the finding of the lower court, but an intention to find such a fact in the first instance.

* * *

It may well be that petitioner's account in its "Milestones" section was the product of some fault on its part, and that the libel judgment against it was, therefore, entirely consistent with *Gertz.* But in the absence of a finding in some element of the state court system that there was fault, we are not inclined to canvass the record to make such a determination in the first instance. * * * Accordingly, the judgment of the Supreme Court of Florida is vacated and the case remanded for further proceedings not inconsistent with this opinion.

So ordered.

NOTES

1. Justice Stevens did not participate in the "consideration or decision" of the case. Justice Powell, writing for himself and Justice Stewart, joined the opinion of the Court but wrote in a separate opinion that, given the "opaqueness" of the trial court's decree in the divorce proceedings, "there *was*

substantial evidence supportive of Time's defense that it was not guilty of actionable negligence." Justice Brennan dissented on the ground that the First Amendment protected the erroneous reporting of the results of a judicial proceeding and that there could be liability only under the circumstances outlined in *Rosenbloom v. Metromedia, Inc.* Justice White dissented for the reasons outlined in his dissent in *Gertz* and for the further reason that, "in any event, the requisite fault was properly found below." Justice Marshall dissented on the ground that "Mary Alice Firestone * * * [was] a 'public figure' within the meaning of our prior decisions."

2. Mrs. Firestone apparently decided not to proceed with the case on retrial on the ground that she felt vindicated by the original verdict. *See* Editor & Publisher, Sept. 16, 1978, p. 11.

3. Since *Firestone,* the Court, on June 26, 1979, handed down two further decisions on the question of who is a public figure. Hutchinson v. Proxmire, 443 U.S. 111, 99 S.Ct. 2675, 61 L.Ed.2d 411 (1979) and Wolston v. Reader's Digest Association, 443 U.S. 157, 99 S.Ct. 2701, 61 L.Ed.2d 450 (1979). *Hutchinson* involved a professor whose work on the emotional behavior of animals had been funded by the federal government. Some of this research involved the study of behavior patterns such as the clenching of jaws when the animals were exposed to certain stressful stimuli. The Court ruled that Hutchinson was a private figure; the public interest in the expenditure of government funds did not cause Hutchinson to be a public figure. Other related aspects of the *Hutchinson* case were discussed, *supra,* at p. 567 and p. 585.

The *Wolston* case involved the nephew of Myra and Jack Noble, who were arrested in 1957 on charges of spying for the Soviet Union and who later pleaded guilty to charges of espionage. After the Nobles' arrest Wolston was summoned before several grand juries. Having failed to appear before the grand jury in July of 1958, Wolston was held in contempt; given a suspended sentence; and placed on three year's probation conditioned on his cooperation with grand jury investigations of Soviet espionage. A number of newspapers reported these events. Nevertheless, although Wolston was identified as a Soviet agent in an FBI report in 1960, he was never prosecuted. Aside from the investigation in the late 1950's, Wolston had led a life of obscurity. In 1974 the defendants published a book entitled *KGB* that named Wolston, among others, as a Soviet agent in the United States. Wolston thereupon brought a defamation action. The district court classified Wolston as a public figure and granted summary judgment for Reader's Digest; the court of appeals affirmed. The Supreme Court, however, reversed, and held that Wolston was a private figure. The Court declared:

> Petitioner's failure to appear before the grand jury and citation for contempt no doubt were 'newsworthy,' but the simple fact that these events attracted media attention also is not conclusive of the public-figure issue. A private individual is not automatically transformed into a public figure just by becoming involved or associated with a matter that attracts public attention. To accept such reasoning would in effect re-establish the doctrine advanced by the plurality opinion in *Rosenbloom v. Metromedia, Inc.,* * * *.

4. Despite *Hutchinson* and *Wolston,* the chief prosecution witness in the famous "Scottsboro Boys" trial of 1931 and 1933 was held to have remained a public figure for the purposes of a television dramatization in 1976 of the 1933 trial. Street v. National Broadcasting Co., 645 F.2d 1227 (6th Cir.1981), *cert. granted* 454 U.S. 815, 102 S.Ct. 91, 70 L.Ed.2d 83 (1981), *cert. dismissed* by stipulation of the parties, 454 U.S. 1095, 102 S.Ct. 667, 70 L.Ed.2d 636 (1981). Earlier in Meeropol v. Nizer, 560 F.2d 1061 (2d Cir.1977), *cert. denied* 434 U.S. 1013, 98 S.Ct. 727, 54 L.Ed.2d 756 (1978), the children of Julius and Ethel Rosenberg, who were executed in 1953 for transmitting defense secrets to the Soviet Union, were deemed public figures with regard to a book published in 1973 about their parents' trial. On the other hand, a dissident shareholder and former corporate counsel of a publicly held company was not a public figure in the context of newspaper reports of management turnover at the company. Denny v. Mertz, 106 Wis.2d 636, 318 N.W.2d 141 (1982). In Dameron v. Washington Magazine, Inc., 779 F.2d 736 (D.C.Cir.1985), *cert. denied* 476 U.S. 1141, 106 S.Ct. 2247, 90 L.Ed.2d 693 (1986), an air traffic controller who was on duty at Dulles airport at the time an airliner crashed with 92 fatalities was held to be an involuntary public figure with respect to an article concerning the cause of the crash. On the other hand, a woman, who had dinner with Dr. Martin Luther King the night before his assassination and who the defendant in his book had alleged had had an affair with Dr. King, was held not to be a public figure for purposes of her defamation action against the defendant. Although the plaintiff had been a civil rights activist and had run for elected office, the court stressed that the subject matter of her defamation action was not related to any such public conduct. Naantaanbuu v. Abernathy, 816 F.Supp. 218 (S.D.N.Y.1993). The court nevertheless granted summary judgment in favor of the defendant because the defamation action involved a matter of public interest and, under New York law (see p. 608, *supra*), could only proceed if the defendant acted in a "grossly irresponsible manner." The earlier history of the *Milkovich* case, (*supra* p. 609) is also instructive on the difficulty the courts have had in deciding who is a public figure. In Milkovich v. News–Herald, 15 Ohio St.3d 292, 473 N.E.2d 1191 (1984), *cert. denied* 474 U.S. 953, 106 S.Ct. 322, 88 L.Ed.2d 305 (1985), the plaintiff, a head wrestling coach at a public high school who had been censured by the state athletic association after a fight had broken out at a meet when the referee had disqualified a wrestler on the coach's team, was held to be neither a public official nor a public figure.[a] This latter ruling was made despite the fact that the plaintiff was a nationally prominent high school wrestling coach who was well-known in the area. Dissenting from the denial of certiorari, Justice Brennan, joined by Justice Marshall, characterized the Ohio court's holding that the plaintiff was not a public figure "for purposes of discussion about the controversy" as "simply nonsense". 474 U.S. at 964, 106 S.Ct. at 330, 88 L.Ed.2d at 314. When the Ohio Supreme Court considered a companion case arising out of the same article, brought by the superintendent of the local public school system, it held that the school superintendent was a public official and that, furthermore, the alleged defamation was the expression of opinion. Scott v. News–Herald, 25 Ohio St.3d

a. The Ohio Supreme Court divided 4–3 in the case. The three dissenters felt that the statements in question were merely opinions. Two of the dissenters thought that Milkovich was a public figure.

243, 496 N.E.2d 699 (1986). In the process of ruling that the school superintendent was a "public official," the court took note of Justice Brennan's dissent and declared that it disavowed the "restrictive view of public officials" that it had taken in *Milkovich*.

5. "Defining public figures is much like trying to nail a jellyfish to the wall." Rosanova v. Playboy Enterprises, Inc., 411 F.Supp. 440, 443 (S.D.Ga. 1976), affirmed 580 F.2d 859 (5th Cir.1978) (plaintiff held to be a public figure because of newspaper and other media reports that he was associated with organized crime). For a criticism of using notoriety as the criterion for determining whether a person was a public figure, because it permits a person who is heavily involved on an issue of public concern, but who operates behind the scenes and is not generally known, to avoid the constitutional malice burden, *see* W. Krough, *The Anonymous Public Figure: Influence Without Notoriety and the Defamation Plaintiff,* 15 Geo. Mason L.Rev. 839 (2008). The cases require courts to make some very delicate value judgments in a vast variety of situations. In O'Connor v. Burningham, 165 P.3d 1214 (Utah 2007), the plaintiff, the coach of the women's high school basketball team at a small town in northern Utah and a public employee, was held not to be a public figure (nor a public official) in his action against the parents of some of his players for making defamatory statements about him. Similarly the secretary to a senior official of the Democratic National Committee, who was falsely accused of having some connection to the scandals surrounding the Watergate break-ins because she had used one of the phones that had been illegally tapped by the burglars, was held not to be an involuntary public figure. Wells v. Liddy, 186 F.3d 505 (4th Cir. 1999).

DUN & BRADSTREET, INC. v. GREENMOSS BUILDERS, INC.

Supreme Court of the United States, 1985.
472 U.S. 749, 105 S.Ct. 2939, 86 L.Ed.2d 593.

JUSTICE POWELL announced the judgment of the Court and delivered an opinion, in which JUSTICE REHNQUIST and JUSTICE O'CONNOR joined.

In *Gertz v. Robert Welch, Inc.*, * * * we held that the First Amendment restricted the damages that a private individual could obtain from a publisher for a libel that involved a matter of public concern. More specifically, we held that in these circumstances the First Amendment prohibited awards of presumed and punitive damages for false and defamatory statements unless the plaintiff shows "actual malice," that is, knowledge of falsity or reckless disregard for the truth. The question presented in this case is whether this rule of *Gertz* applies when the false and defamatory statements do not involve matters of public concern.

I

Petitioner Dun & Bradstreet, a credit reporting agency, provides subscribers with financial and related information about businesses. All the information is confidential; under the terms of the subscription agreement the subscribers may not reveal it to anyone else. On July 26,

1976, petitioner sent a report to five subscribers indicating that respondent, a construction contractor, had filed a voluntary petition for bankruptcy. This report was false and grossly misrepresented respondent's assets and liabilities. That same day, while discussing the possibility of future financing with its bank, respondent's president was told that the bank had received the defamatory report. He immediately called petitioner's regional office, explained the error, and asked for a correction. In addition, he requested the names of the firms that had received the false report in order to assure them that the company was solvent. Petitioner promised to look into the matter but refused to divulge the names of those who had received the report.

After determining that its report was indeed false, petitioner issued a corrective notice on or about August 3, 1976, to the five subscribers who had received the initial report. The notice stated that one of respondent's former employees, not respondent itself, had filed for bankruptcy and that respondent "continued in business as usual." Respondent told petitioner that it was dissatisfied with the notice, and it again asked for a list of subscribers who had seen the initial report. Again petitioner refused to divulge their names.

Respondent then brought this defamation action in Vermont state court. It alleged that the false report had injured its reputation and sought both compensatory and punitive damages. The trial established that the error in petitioner's report had been caused when one of its employees, a 17–year–old high school student paid to review Vermont bankruptcy pleadings, had inadvertently attributed to respondent a bankruptcy petition filed by one of respondent's former employees. Although petitioner's representative testified that it was routine practice to check the accuracy of such reports with the businesses themselves, it did not try to verify the information about respondent before reporting it.

After trial, the jury returned a verdict in favor of respondent and awarded $50,000 in compensatory or presumed damages and $300,000 in punitive damages. Petitioner moved for a new trial. It argued that in *Gertz v. Robert Welch, Inc.*, * * * this Court had ruled broadly that "the States may not permit recovery of presumed or punitive damages, at least when liability is not based on a showing of knowledge of falsity or reckless disregard for the truth," and it argued that the judge's instructions in this case permitted the jury to award such damages on a lesser showing. The trial court indicated some doubt as to whether *Gertz* applied to "nonmedia cases," but granted a new trial "[b]ecause of * * * dissatisfaction with its charge and * * * conviction that the interests of justice require[d]" it. App. 26.

The Vermont Supreme Court reversed. 143 Vt. 66, 461 A.2d 414 (1983). Although recognizing that "in certain instances the distinction between media and nonmedia defendants may be difficult to draw," the court stated that "no such difficulty is presented with credit reporting agencies, which are in the business of selling financial information to a limited number of subscribers who have paid substantial fees for their services." * * * Relying on this distinguishing characteristic of credit reporting firms, the court concluded that such firms are not "the type of media worthy of First Amendment protection as contemplated by *New York Times* * * * and its progeny." * * * It held that the balance between a private plaintiff's right to recover presumed and punitive damages without a showing of special fault and the First Amendment rights of "nonmedia" speakers "must be struck in favor of the private plaintiff defamed by a nonmedia defendant." * * * Accordingly, the court held "that as a matter of federal constitutional law, the media protections outlined in *Gertz* are inapplicable to nonmedia defamation actions." *Ibid.*

Recognizing disagreement among the lower courts about when the protections of *Gertz* apply, we granted certiorari. * * * We now affirm, although for reasons different from those relied upon by the Vermont Supreme Court.

II

As an initial matter, respondent contends that we need not determine whether *Gertz* applies in this case because the instructions, taken as a whole, required the jury to find "actual malice" before awarding presumed or punitive damages. The trial court instructed the jury that because the report was libelous *per se,* respondent was not required "to prove actual damages * * * since damage and loss [are] conclusively presumed." * * * It also instructed the jury that it could award punitive damages only if it found "actual malice." *Id.,* at 20. Its only other relevant instruction was that liability could not be established unless respondent showed "malice or lack of good faith on the part of the Defendant." *Id.,* at 18. Respondent contends that these references to "malice," "lack of good faith," and "actual malice" required the jury to find knowledge of falsity or reckless disregard for the truth—the "actual malice" of *New York Times Co. v. Sullivan,* * * *—before it awarded presumed or punitive damages.

We reject this claim because the trial court failed to define any of these terms adequately. It did not, for example, provide the jury with any definition of the term "actual malice." In fact, the only relevant term it defined was simple "malice." And its definitions of this term included not only the *New York Times* formulation but also other concepts such as "bad faith" and "reckless disregard of the [statement's] possible consequences." App. 19. The instructions thus permitted the jury to award presumed and punitive damages on a lesser showing than "actual malice." Consequently, the trial court's conclusion that the instructions did not satisfy *Gertz* was correct, and the Vermont Supreme Court's determination that *Gertz* was inapplicable was necessary to its decision that the trial court erred in granting the motion for a new trial. We therefore must consider whether *Gertz* applies to the case before us.

III

* * *

In *Gertz,* we held that the fact that expression concerned a public issue did not by itself entitle the libel defendant to the constitutional protections of *New York Times.* These protections, we found, were not "justified solely by reference to the interest of the press and broadcast media in immunity from liability." 418 U.S., at 343, 94 S.Ct., at 3008. Rather, they represented "an accommodation between [First Amendment] concern[s] and the limited state interest present in the context of libel actions brought by public persons." * * * Nothing in our opinion, however, indicated that this same balance would be struck regardless of the type of speech involved.

IV

We have never considered whether the *Gertz* balance obtains when the defamatory statements involve no issue of public concern. To make this determination, we must employ the approach approved in *Gertz* and balance the State's interest in compensating private individuals for injury to their reputation against the First Amendment interest in protecting this type of expression. This state interest is identical to the one weighed in *Gertz.* There we found that it was "strong and legitimate." * * *

The First Amendment interest, on the other hand, is less important than the one weighed in *Gertz.* We have long recognized that not all speech is of equal First Amendment importance. It is speech on " 'matters of public concern' " that is "at the heart of the First Amendment's protection." *First National Bank of Boston v. Bellotti,* 435 U.S. 765, 776, 98 S.Ct. 1407, 1415, 55 L.Ed.2d 707 (1978), citing *Thornhill v. Alabama,* 310 U.S. 88, 101, 60 S.Ct. 736, 743, 84 L.Ed. 1093 (1940). * * * In contrast, speech on matters of purely private concern is of less First Amendment concern. * * * As a number of state courts, including the court below, have recognized, the role of the Constitution in regulating state libel law is far more limited when the concerns that activated *New York Times* and *Gertz* are absent.[6]

While such speech is not totally unprotected by the First Amendment, see *Connick v. Myers, supra,* 461 U.S., at 147, 103 S.Ct., at 1690, its protections are less stringent. In *Gertz,* we found that the state interest in awarding presumed and punitive damages was not "substantial" in view of their effect on speech at the core of First Amendment concern. * * * This interest, however, *is* "substantial" relative to the incidental effect these remedies may have on speech of significantly less constitutional interest. The rationale of the common-law rules has been the experience and judgment of history that "proof of actual damage will be impossible in

6. As one commentator has remarked with respect to "the case of a commercial supplier of credit information that defames a person applying for credit"—the case before us today—"If the first amendment requirements outlined in *Gertz* apply, there is something clearly wrong with the first amendment or with *Gertz.*" Shiffrin, The First Amendment and Economic Regulation: Away From a General Theory of the First Amendment, 78 Nw.U.L.Rev. 1212, 1268 (1983).

a great many cases where, from the character of the defamatory words and the circumstances of publication, it is all but certain that serious harm has resulted in fact." W. Prosser, Law of Torts § 112, p. 765 (4th ed. 1971). * * * As a result, courts for centuries have allowed juries to presume that some damage occurred from many defamatory utterances and publications. * * * This rule furthers the state interest in providing remedies for defamation by ensuring that those remedies are effective. In light of the reduced constitutional value of speech involving no matters of public concern, we hold that the state interest adequately supports awards of presumed and punitive damages—even absent a showing of "actual malice."

V

ISSUE – PUBLIC CONCERN?

The only remaining issue is whether petitioner's credit report involved a matter of public concern. In a related context, we have held that "[w]hether * * * speech addresses a matter of public concern must be determined by [the expression's] content, form, and context * * * as revealed by the whole record." *Connick v. Myers, supra,* 461 U.S., at 147–148, 103 S.Ct., at 1690. These factors indicate that petitioner's credit report concerns no public issue.[8] It was speech solely in the individual interest of the speaker and its specific business audience. * * * This particular interest warrants no special protection when—as in this case—the speech is wholly false and clearly damaging to the victim's business reputation. * * * Moreover, since the credit report was made available to only five subscribers, who, under the terms of the subscription agreement, could not disseminate it further, it cannot be said that the report involves any "strong interest in the free flow of commercial information." * * * There is simply no credible argument that this type of credit reporting requires special protection to ensure that "debate on public issues [will] be uninhibited, robust, and wide-open." * * *

In addition, the speech here, like advertising, is hardy and unlikely to be deterred by incidental state regulation. * * * It is solely motivated by the desire for profit, which, we have noted, is a force less likely to be deterred than others. * * * Arguably, the reporting here was also more objectively verifiable than speech deserving of greater protection. * * * In any case, the market provides a powerful incentive to a credit reporting agency to be accurate, since false credit reporting is of no use to creditors. Thus, any incremental "chilling" effect of libel suits would be of decreased significance.[9]

---

8. The dissent suggests that our holding today leaves all credit reporting subject to reduced First Amendment protection. This is incorrect. The protection to be accorded a particular credit report depends on whether the report's "content, form, and context" indicate that it concerns a public matter. We also do not hold, as the dissent suggests we do, * * * that the report is subject to reduced constitutional protection because it constitutes economic or commercial speech. We discuss such speech, along with advertising, only to show how many of the same concerns that argue in favor of reduced constitutional protection in those areas apply here as well.

9. The Court of Appeals for the Fifth Circuit has noted that, while most States provide a qualified privilege against libel suits for commercial credit reporting agencies, in those States that do not there is a thriving credit reporting business and commercial credit transactions are not

VI

We conclude that permitting recovery of presumed and punitive damages in defamation cases absent a showing of "actual malice" does not violate the First Amendment when the defamatory statements do not involve matters of public concern. Accordingly, we affirm the judgment of the Vermont Supreme Court.

It is so ordered.

CHIEF JUSTICE BURGER, concurring in the judgment.

* * *

I dissented in *Gertz* because I believed that, insofar as the "ordinary private citizen" was concerned, * * * the Court's opinion "abandon[ed] the traditional thread," *id.,* at 354–355, 94 S.Ct., at 3014, that had been the theme of the law in this country up to that time. I preferred "to allow this area of law to continue to evolve as it [had] up to [then] with respect to private citizens rather than embark on a new doctrinal theory which [had] no jurisprudential ancestry." *Ibid. Gertz,* however, is now the law of the land, and until it is overruled, it must, under the principle of *stare decisis,* be applied by this Court.

The single question before the Court today is whether *Gertz* applies to this case. The plurality opinion holds that *Gertz* does not apply because, unlike the challenged expression in *Gertz,* the alleged defamatory expression in this case does not relate to a matter of public concern. I agree that *Gertz* is limited to circumstances in which the alleged defamatory expression concerns a matter of general public importance, and that the expression in question here relates to a matter of essentially private concern. I therefore agree with the plurality opinion to the extent that it holds that *Gertz* is inapplicable in this case for the two reasons indicated. No more is needed to dispose of the present case.

I continue to believe, however, that *Gertz* was ill-conceived, and therefore agree with Justice White that *Gertz* should be overruled. * * * The great rights guaranteed by the First Amendment carry with them certain responsibilities as well.

Consideration of these issues inevitably recalls an aphorism of journalism that "too much checking on the facts has ruined many a good news story."

JUSTICE WHITE, concurring in the judgment.

Until *New York Times Co. v. Sullivan,* * * * the law of defamation was almost exclusively the business of state courts and legislatures. Under the then prevailing state libel law, the defamed individual had only to prove a false written publication that subjected him to hatred, contempt,

inhibited. *Hood v. Dun & Bradstreet, Inc.,* 486 F.2d 25, 32 (1973), cert. denied, 415 U.S. 985, 94 S.Ct. 1580, 39 L.Ed.2d 882 (1974). The court cited an empirical study comparing credit transactions in Boise, Idaho, where there is no privilege, with those in Spokane, Washington, where there is one. 486 F.2d, at 32, and n. 18.

or ridicule. Truth was a defense; but given a defamatory false circulation, general injury to reputation was presumed; special damages, such as pecuniary loss and emotional distress, could be recovered; and punitive damages were available if common-law malice were shown. General damages for injury to reputation were presumed and awarded because the judgment of history was that "in many cases the effect of defamatory statements is so subtle and indirect that it is impossible directly to trace the effects thereof in loss to the person defamed." Restatement of Torts § 621, Comment *a,* p. 314 (1938). The defendant was permitted to show that there was no reputational injury; but at the very least, the prevailing rule was that at least nominal damages were to be awarded for any defamatory publication actionable *per se.* * * *

* * *

I joined the judgment and opinion in *New York Times.* I also joined later decisions extending the *New York Times* standard to other situations. But I came to have increasing doubts about the soundness of the Court's approach and about some of the assumptions underlying it. I could not join the plurality opinion in *Rosenbloom,* and I dissented in *Gertz,* asserting that the common-law remedies should be retained for private plaintiffs. I remain convinced that *Gertz* was erroneously decided. I have also become convinced that the Court struck an improvident balance in the *New York Times* case between the public's interest in being fully informed about public officials and public affairs and the competing interest of those who have been defamed in vindicating their reputation.

In a country like ours, where the people purport to be able to govern themselves through their elected representatives, adequate information about their government is of transcendent importance. That flow of intelligence deserves full First Amendment protection. Criticism and assessment of the performance of public officials and of government in general are not subject to penalties imposed by law. But these First Amendment values are not at all served by circulating false statements of fact about public officials. On the contrary, erroneous information frustrates these values. They are even more disserved when the statements falsely impugn the honesty of those men and women and hence lessen the confidence in government. As the Court said in *Gertz:* "[T]here is no constitutional value in false statements of fact. Neither the intentional lie nor the careless error materially advances society's interest in 'uninhibited, robust, and wide-open' debate on public issues." * * * Yet in *New York Times* cases, the public official's complaint will be dismissed unless he alleges and makes out a jury case of a knowing or reckless falsehood. Absent such proof, there will be no jury verdict or judgment of any kind in his favor, even if the challenged publication is admittedly false. The lie will stand, and the public continue to be misinformed about public matters. This will recurringly happen because the putative plaintiff's burden is so exceedingly difficult to satisfy and can be discharged only by expensive litigation. Even if the plaintiff sues, he frequently loses on summary judgment or never gets to the jury because of insufficient proof of malice. If he wins before the jury, verdicts are often overturned by appellate courts for failure to prove malice. Furthermore, when the plaintiff loses, the jury will likely return a general verdict and there will be no judgment that the publication was false, even though it was without foundation in reality.[2] The public is left to conclude that the challenged statement was true after all. Their only chance of being accurately informed is measured by the public official's ability himself to counter the lie, unaided by the courts. That is a decidedly weak reed to depend on for the vindication of First Amendment interests * * *.

* * *

The *New York Times* rule thus countenances two evils: first, the stream of information about public officials and public affairs is polluted and often remains polluted by false information; and second, the reputation and professional life of the defeated plaintiff may be destroyed by falsehoods that might have been avoided with a reasonable effort to investigate the facts. In terms of the First Amendment and reputational interests at stake, these seem grossly perverse results.

* * *

In *New York Times,* instead of escalating the plaintiff's burden of proof to an almost impossible level, we could have achieved our stated goal by limiting the recoverable damages to a level that would not unduly threaten the press. Punitive damages might have been scrutinized as Justice Harlan suggested in *Rosenbloom, supra,* 403 U.S., at 77, 91 S.Ct., at 1836, or perhaps even entirely forbidden. Presumed damages to reputation might have been prohibited, or limited, as in *Gertz.* Had that course been taken and the common-law standard of liability been retained, the defamed public official, upon proving falsity, could at least have had a judgment to that effect. His reputation would then be vindicated; and to the extent possible, the misinformation circulated would have been countered. He might have also recovered a modest amount, enough perhaps to pay his litigation expenses. At the very least, the public official should not have been required to satisfy the actual malice standard where he sought

2. If the plaintiff succeeds in proving a jury case of malice, it may be that the jury will be asked to bring in separate verdicts on falsity and malice. In that event, there could be a verdict in favor of the plaintiff on falsity, but against him on malice. There would be no judgment in his favor, but the verdict on falsity would be a public one and would tend to set the record right and clear the plaintiff's name.

It might be suggested that courts, as organs of the government, cannot be trusted to discern what the truth is. But the logical consequence of that view is that the First Amendment forbids all libel and slander suits, for in each such suit, there will be no recovery unless the court finds the publication at issue to be factually false. Of course, no forum is perfect, but that is not a justification for leaving whole classes of defamed individuals without redress or a realistic opportunity to clear their names. We entrust to juries and the courts the responsibility of decisions affecting the life and liberty of persons. It is perverse indeed to say that these bodies are incompetent to inquire into the truth of a statement of fact in a defamation case. I can therefore discern nothing in the Constitution which forbids a plaintiff to obtain a judicial decree that a statement is false—a decree he can then use in the community to clear his name and to prevent further damage from a defamation already published.

no damages but only to clear his name. In this way, both First Amendment and reputational interests would have been far better served.

We are not talking in these cases about mere criticism or opinion, but about misstatements of fact that seriously harm the reputation of another, by lowering him in the estimation of the community or to deter third persons from associating or dealing with him. * * *

I still believe the common-law rules should have been retained where the plaintiff is not a public official or public figure. As I see it, the Court undervalued the reputational interest at stake in such cases. I have also come to doubt the easy assumption that the common-law rules would muzzle the press. But even accepting the *Gertz* premise that the press also needed protection in suits by private parties, there was no need to modify the common-law requirements for establishing liability and to increase the burden of proof that must be satisfied to secure a judgment authorizing at least nominal damages and the recovery of additional sums within the limitations that the Court might have set.[3]

It is interesting that Justice Powell declines to follow the *Gertz* approach in this case. I had thought that the decision in *Gertz* was intended to reach cases that involve any false statements of fact injurious to reputation, whether the statement is made privately or publicly and whether or not it implicates a matter of public importance. Justice Powell, however, distinguishes *Gertz* as a case that involved a matter of public concern, an element absent here. Wisely, in my view, Justice Powell does not rest his application of a different rule here on a distinction drawn between media and nonmedia defendants. On that issue, I agree with Justice Brennan that the First Amendment gives no more protection to the press in defamation suits than it does to others exercising their freedom of speech. None of our cases affords such a distinction; to the contrary, the Court has rejected it at every turn. It should be rejected again, particularly in this context, since it makes no sense to give the most protection to those publishers who reach the most readers and therefore pollute the channels of communication with the most misinformation and do the most damage to private reputation. If *Gertz* is to be distinguished from this case, on the ground that it applies only where the allegedly false publication deals with a matter of general or public importance, then where the false publication does not deal with such a matter, the common-law rules would apply whether the defendant is a member of the media or other public disseminator or a nonmedia individual publishing privately. Although Justice Powell speaks only of the inapplicability of the *Gertz* rule with respect to presumed and punitive damages, it must be that the *Gertz* requirement of some kind of fault on the part of the defendant is also inapplicable in cases such as this.

3. The Court was unresponsive to my suggestion in dissent, 418 U.S., at 391–392, 94 S.Ct., at 3032, that the plaintiff should be able to prove and obtain a judgment of falsehood without having to establish any kind of fault.

As I have said, I dissented in *Gertz,* and I doubt that the decision in that case has made any measurable contribution to First Amendment or reputational values since its announcement. Nor am I sure that it has saved the press a great deal of money. Like the *New York Times* decision, the burden that plaintiffs must meet invites long and complicated discovery involving detailed investigation of the workings of the press, how a news story is developed, and the state of mind of the reporter and publisher. See *Herbert v. Lando,* 441 U.S. 153, 99 S.Ct. 1635, 60 L.Ed.2d 115 (1979).[a] That kind of litigation is very expensive. I suspect that the press would be no worse off financially if the common-law rules were to apply and if the judiciary was careful to insist that damages awards be kept within bounds. A legislative solution to the damages problem would also be appropriate. Moreover, since libel plaintiffs are very likely more interested in clearing their names than in damages, I doubt that limiting recoveries would deter or be unfair to them. In any event, I cannot assume that the press, as successful and powerful as it is, will be intimidated into withholding news that by decent journalistic standards it believes to be true.

The question before us is whether *Gertz* is to be applied in this case. For either of two reasons, I believe that it should not. First, I am unreconciled to the *Gertz* holding and believe that it should be overruled. Second, as Justice Powell indicates, the defamatory publication in this case does not deal with a matter of public importance. Consequently, I concur in the Court's judgment.

JUSTICE BRENNAN, with whom JUSTICE MARSHALL, JUSTICE BLACKMUN, and JUSTICE STEVENS join, dissenting.

This case involves a difficult question of the proper application of *Gertz v. Robert Welch, Inc.,* * * * to credit reporting—a type of speech at some remove from that which first gave rise to explicit First Amendment restrictions on state defamation law—and has produced a diversity of considered opinions, none of which speaks for the Court. * * *

* * *

II

The question presented here is narrow. Neither the parties nor the courts below have suggested that respondent Greenmoss Builders should be required to show actual malice to obtain a judgment and actual compensatory damages. Nor do the parties question the requirement of *Gertz* that respondent must show fault to obtain a judgment and actual damages. The only question presented is whether a jury award of presumed and punitive damages based on less than a showing of actual malice is constitutionally permissible. *Gertz* provides a forthright negative answer. To preserve the jury verdict in this case, therefore, the opinions of

a. [Ed. note] discussed at p. 588, *supra.*

Justice Powell and Justice White have cut away the protective mantle of *Gertz.*

* * *

A

* * *

The free speech guarantee gives each citizen an equal right to self-expression and to participation in self-government. * * * This guarantee also protects the rights of listeners to "the widest possible dissemination of information from diverse and antagonistic sources." *Associated Press v. United States,* 326 U.S. 1, 20, 65 S.Ct. 1416, 1424, 89 L.Ed. 2013 (1945).[9] Accordingly, at least six Members of this Court (the four who join this opinion and Justice White and The Chief Justice) agree today that, in the context of defamation law, the rights of the institutional media are no greater and no less than those enjoyed by other individuals or organizations engaged in the same activities. See *ante,* * * * (opinion concurring in judgment).[10]

B

Eschewing the media/nonmedia distinction, the opinions of both Justice White and Justice Powell focus primarily on the content of the credit report as a reason for restricting the applicability of *Gertz.* Arguing that at most *Gertz* should protect speech that "deals with a matter of public or general importance," * * * Justice White, without analysis or explanation, decides that the credit report at issue here falls outside this protected category. The plurality opinion of Justice Powell offers virtually the same conclusion with at least a garnish of substantive analysis.

* * *

In professing allegiance to *Gertz,* the plurality opinion protests too much. As Justice White correctly observes, Justice Powell departs completely from the analytic framework and result of that case: "*Gertz* was intended to reach cases that involve any false statements * * * whether or not [they] implicat[e] a matter of public importance." *Ante,* * * * (concurring in judgment).[11] Even accepting the notion that a distinction can and

9. In light of the "increasingly prominent role of mass media in our society, and the awesome power it has placed in the hands of a select few," *Gertz,* 418 U.S., at 402, 94 S.Ct., at 3037 (White, J., dissenting), protection for the speech of nonmedia defendants is essential to ensure a diversity of perspectives. See J. Barron, Freedom of the Press for Whom? (1973). * * *

10. Justice Powell's opinion does not expressly reject the media/nonmedia distinction, but does expressly decline to apply that distinction to resolve this case.

11. One searches *Gertz* in vain for a single word to support the proposition that limits on presumed and punitive damages obtained only when speech involved matters of public concern. *Gertz* could not have been grounded in such a premise. Distrust of placing in the courts the power to decide what speech was of public concern was precisely the rationale *Gertz* offered for rejecting the *Rosenbloom* plurality approach. * * * It would have been incongruous for the Court to go on to circumscribe the protection against presumed and punitive damages by reference to a judicial judgment as to whether the speech at issue involved matters of public concern. At several points should be drawn between matters of public concern and matters of purely private concern, however, the analyses presented by both Justice Powell and Justice White fail on their own terms. Both, by virtue of what they hold in this case, propose an impoverished definition of "matters of public concern" that is irreconcilable with First Amendment principles. The credit reporting at issue here surely involves a subject matter of sufficient public concern to require the comprehensive protections of *Gertz.* Were this speech appropriately characterized as a matter of only private concern, moreover, the elimination of the *Gertz* restrictions on presumed and punitive damages would still violate basic First Amendment requirements.

(1)

The five Members of the Court voting to affirm the damages award in this case have provided almost no guidance as to what constitutes a protected "matter of public concern." * * *

In evaluating the subject matter of expression, this Court has consistently rejected the argument that speech is entitled to diminished First Amendment protection simply because it concerns economic matters or is in the economic interest of the speaker or the audience. * * *

The credit reporting of Dun & Bradstreet falls within any reasonable definition of "public concern" consistent with our precedents. Justice Powell's reliance on the fact that Dun & Bradstreet publishes credit reports "for profit," * * * is wholly unwarranted. Time and again we have made clear that speech loses none of its constitutional protection "even though it is carried in a form that is 'sold' for profit." *Virginia Pharmacy Bd.,* 425 U.S., at 761, 96 S.Ct., at 1825. * * * More importantly, an announcement of the bankruptcy of a local company is information of potentially great concern to residents of the community where the company is located; * * * such a bankruptcy "in a single factory may have economic repercussions upon a whole region." And knowledge about solvency and the effect and prevalence of bankruptcy certainly would inform citizen opinions about questions of economic regulation. It is difficult to suggest that a bankruptcy is not a subject matter of public concern when federal law requires invocation of judicial mechanisms to effectuate it and makes the fact of the bankruptcy a matter of public record. * * *

Speech about commercial or economic matters, even if not directly implicating "the central meaning of the First Amendment," * * * is an important part of our public discourse. * * *

---

the Court in *Gertz* makes perfectly clear the restrictions of presumed and punitive damages were to apply in all cases. * * *

Indeed, Justice Powell's opinion today is fairly read as embracing the approach of the *Rosenbloom* plurality to deciding when the Constitution should limit state defamation law. The limits imposed, however, are less stringent than those suggested by the *Rosenbloom* plurality. Under the approach of today's plurality, speech about matters of public or general interest receives only the *Gertz* protections against unrestrained presumed and punitive damages, not the full *New York Times Co. v. Sullivan* protections against any recovery absent a showing of actual malice.

Given that the subject matter of credit reporting directly implicates matters of public concern, the balancing analysis the Court today employs should properly lead to the conclusion that the type of expression here at issue should receive First Amendment protection from the chilling potential of unrestrained presumed and punitive damages in defamation actions.

(2)

Even if the subject matter of credit reporting were properly considered—in the terms of Justice White and Justice Powell—as purely a matter of private discourse, this speech would fall well within the range of valuable expression for which the First Amendment demands protection. Much expression that does not directly involve public issues receives significant protection. Our cases do permit some diminution in the degree of protection afforded one category of speech about economic or commercial matters. "Commercial speech"—defined as advertisements that "[do] no more than propose a commercial transaction," *Pittsburgh Press Co. v. Pittsburgh Comm'n on Human Relations,* 413 U.S. 376, 385, 93 S.Ct. 2553, 2558, 37 L.Ed.2d 669 (1973)—may be more closely regulated than other types of speech. Even commercial speech, however, receives substantial First Amendment protection. * * *

* * *

The credit reports of Dun & Bradstreet bear few of the earmarks of commercial speech that might be entitled to somewhat less rigorous protection. In *every* case in which we have permitted more extensive state regulation on the basis of a commercial speech rationale the speech being regulated was pure advertising—an offer to buy or sell goods and services or encouraging such buying and selling. Credit reports are not commercial advertisements for a good or service or a proposal to buy or sell such a product. We have been extremely chary about extending the "commercial speech" doctrine beyond this narrowly circumscribed category of advertising because often vitally important speech will be uttered to advance economic interests and because the profit motive making such speech hardy dissipates rapidly when the speech is not advertising. * * *

It is worth noting in this regard that the common law of most States, although apparently not of Vermont, 143 Vt. 66, 76, 461 A.2d 414, 419 (1983), recognizes a qualified privilege for reports like that at issue here. See Maurer, Common Law Defamation and the Fair Credit Reporting Act, 72 Geo.L.J. 95, 99–105 (1983). The privilege typically precludes recovery for false and defamatory credit information without a showing of bad faith or malice, a standard of proof which is often defined according to the *New York Times* formulation. See, *e.g., Datacon, Inc. v. Dun & Bradstreet, Inc.,* 465 F.Supp. 706, 708 (N.D.Tex.1979). The common law thus recognizes that credit reporting is quite susceptible to libel's chill; this accumulated learning is worthy of respect.

Even if Justice Powell's characterization of the credit reporting at issue here were accepted in its entirety, his opinion would have done no more than demonstrate that this speech is the equivalent of commercial speech. The opinion, after all, relies on analogy to advertising. Credit reporting is said to be hardy, motivated by desire for profit, and relatively verifiable. * * * But this does not justify the elimination of restrictions on presumed and punitive damages. State efforts to regulate commercial speech in the form of advertising must abide by the requirement that the regulatory means chosen be narrowly tailored so as to avoid any unnecessary chilling of protected expression. * * *[16]

* * *

(3)

Even if not at "the essence of self-government," *Garrison v. Louisiana,* 379 U.S. 64, 74–75, 85 S.Ct. 209, 216, 13 L.Ed.2d 125 (1964), the expression at issue in this case is important to both our public discourse and our private welfare. That its motivation might be the economic interest of the speaker or listeners does not diminish its First Amendment value. * * * Whether or not such speech is sufficiently central to First Amendment values to require actual malice as a standard of liability, this speech certainly falls within the range of speech that *Gertz* sought to protect from the chill of unrestrained presumed and punitive damage awards.

Of course, the commercial context of Dun & Bradstreet's reports is relevant to the constitutional analysis insofar as it implicates the strong state interest "in protecting consumers and regulating commercial transactions," *Ohralik v. Ohio State Bar Assn.,* 436 U.S. 447, 460, 98 S.Ct. 1912, 1920, 56 L.Ed.2d 444 (1978). * * * The special harms caused by inaccurate credit reports, the lack of public sophistication about or access to such reports, and the fact that such reports by and large contain statements that are fairly readily susceptible of verification, all may justify appropriate regulation designed to prevent the social losses caused by false credit reports. And in the libel context, the States' regulatory interest in protecting reputation is served by rules permitting recovery for actual compensatory damages upon a showing of fault. Any further interest in deterring potential defamation through case-by-case judicial imposition of presumed and punitive damages awards on less than a showing of actual malice simply exacts too high a toll on First Amendment values. Accordingly, Greenmoss Builders should be permitted to recover for any actual damage it can show resulted from Dun & Bradstreet's negligently false credit report, but should be required to show actual malice to receive

16. Indeed Justice Powell has chosen a particularly inept set of facts as a basis for urging a return to the common law. Though the individual's interest in reputation is certainly at the core of notions of human dignity, * * * the reputational interest at stake here is that of a corporation. Similarly, that this speech is solely commercial in nature undercuts the argument that presumed damages should be unrestrained in actions like this one because actual harm will be difficult to prove. If the credit report is viewed as commercial expression, proving that actual damages occurred is relatively easy. * * *

presumed or punitive damages. Because the jury was not instructed in accordance with these principles, we would reverse and remand for further proceedings not inconsistent with this opinion.

NOTES

1. Is *Dun & Bradstreet v. Greenmoss Builders* consistent with the *Gertz* case? Recall that in *Gertz* the Court, in its opinion written by Justice Powell, rejected the *Rosenbloom* "public or general interest" distinction because "[w]e doubt the wisdom of committing this task to the conscience of judges." (See p. 598, *supra*). Justice White and Justice Brennan thought it was not. It should be noted that Justice Powell's plurality opinion in *Dun & Bradstreet* was only joined in by two other justices whereas Justice Brennan's dissent represented the votes of four justices including himself. Justice Brennan's opinion was by far the longest opinion filed in the case. It is hoped that the extracts printed above give the reader a fairly accurate feel for the arguments that he presented.

2. It is obvious that, with the change in personnel on the Court, there is a fair amount of uncertainty as to what direction the Court will take in the future. For example, in Philadelphia Newspapers, Inc. v. Hepps, 475 U.S. 767, 106 S.Ct. 1558, 89 L.Ed.2d 783 (1986) the Court by only a five-four vote held that *Gertz* required that the burden of persuasion on the issue of truth, in a defamation action brought by a private figure against a newspaper about articles of public concern, be placed on the plaintiff. The *Restatement (Second) of Torts* § 580B, Comment *j* (1977) thought that, after *New York Times* and its progeny, this was a foregone conclusion. If the plaintiff must show that the defendant intentionally published a false statement, or was recklessly indifferent or negligent with regard to that statement, it does not seem to make much sense to place the burden of persuasion on the question of truth or falsity on the defendant. Writing per Justice O'Connor, the Court, moreover, made the following curious reservation in a footnote:

> We also have no occasion to consider the quantity of proof of falsity that a private-figure plaintiff must present to recover damages. Nor need we consider what standards would apply if the plaintiff sues a non-media defendant, *see* Hutchinson v. Proxmire, 443 U.S. 111, 133, n. 16, 99 S.Ct. 2675, 61 L.Ed.2d 411 (1979), or if the state were to provide a plaintiff with the opportunity to obtain a judgment that declared the speech at issue to be false but not give rise to liability for damages.

Id. at 779, n. 4, 106 S.Ct. at 1565, 89 L.Ed.2d at 794. Justice Brennan, joined by Justice Blackmun, both of whom otherwise concurred in the majority opinion, wrote that, while the Court reserved the question whether the doctrine it announced applied to non-media defendants, he continued to adhere to the view he expressed in *Dun & Bradstreet v. Greenmoss Builders* that such a distinction is irreconcilable with the fundamental principles of the first amendment. One wonders why Justice O'Connor wanted to reserve the question of whether the press had some special privilege when a year earlier in Dun & Bradstreet v. Greenmoss Builders, six Justices, as noted by Justice Brennan in his dissent in that case, thought there was no constitutional justification for that distinction. As hard as it might have been in 1986 to decide who qualifies as a member of the media or the press, now with a new form of internet sources the problem of drawing sensible lines of demarcation would be infinitely harder.

3. Justice Powell's plurality opinion in *Dun & Bradstreet v. Greenmoss Builders* said nothing about whether, in litigation between private persons not involving matters of public concern, the states are free to return to the common law doctrine that someone who publishes a statement that turns out to be defamatory of another is strictly liable if the statement turns out to be false. Nevertheless, as we have just seen, Justice White, in his concurring opinion in that case (*supra*, p. 628), opined that the logic of the plurality opinion rendered the *Gertz* requirement of fault inapplicable. And, indeed a few state courts have shown themselves prepared so to read *Dun & Bradstreet v. Greenmoss Builders*. For example, although the case before it involved a matter of public interest, the Arizona Supreme Court, in Dombey v. Phoenix Newspapers, Inc., 150 Ariz. 476, 481, 724 P.2d 562, 567 (1986), declared that the decisions of the United States Supreme Court "establish that when a plaintiff is a private figure and the speech is of private concern, the states are free to retain common law principles." A more recent such decision is Klentzman v. Brady, 312 S.W.3d 886, 898 (Tex. App. 2009), relying on Philadelphia Newspapers, Inc. v. Hepps, discussed in note 2, *supra*. *See also* Nelson v. Lapeyrouse Grain Corp., 534 So.2d 1085, 1092 n. 2 (Ala.1988) (dictum); Cox v. Hatch, 761 P.2d 556, 559–60 (Utah 1988) (dictum). In Ross v. Bricker, 770 F.Supp. 1038, 1043–44 (D.Vi.1991), the court also so interpreted *Dun & Bradstreet v. Greenmoss Builders*, but ruled that the Virgin islands would continue to follow the *Gertz* standards. On the other hand a federal district court in a diversity case ruled, in what might be considered an alternate holding rather than dictum, that North Carolina law could be interpreted as having recognized, in a limited class of libel cases between private parties, liability without proof of negligence. Sleem v. Yale University, 843 F.Supp. 57, 63–64 (M.D.N.C.1993). There is, however, a recent case insisting that neither the Supreme Court nor the Eleventh Circuit had addressed the issue of whether *Dun & Bradstreet* limited the reach of *Gertz*. *See* Log Creek, L.L.C. v. Kessler, 717 F.Supp.2d 1239 (N.D. Fla. 2010). As noted in note 1, *supra*, a majority of the Justices who decided *Dun & Bradstreet* declared that the case did not change the *Gertz* requirement of fault.

4. *Alternative remedies*. Justice White is not the first person to claim that many people, and particularly political figures, are more interested in establishing that derogatory statements made about them are false than in recovering any damages. Among such proposals are: M. Franklin, *A Declaratory Judgment Alternative to Current Libel Law,* 74 Calif.L.Rev. 809 (1986) and D. Barrett, *Declaratory Judgments for Libel: A Better Alternative,* 74 Calif.L.Rev. 847 (1986). On the general subject, *see also* R. Smolla and M. Gaertner, *The Annenberg Libel Reform Proposal: The Case for Enactment,* 31 Wm. & Mary L.Rev. 25 (1989). Barrett's proposal tracked H.R. 2846, 99th Cong., 1st Sess. (1985), that was introduced by then Representative Charles Schumer. That bill only covered actions by public officials or public figures who are the "subject of a publication or broadcast which is published or

broadcast in the print or electronic media." It permitted either the plaintiff or the defendant in such an action to designate the action as one for declaratory judgment in which no proof of the state of mind of the defendant is required and in which no damages are to be awarded. At the same time the Schumer bill prohibited punitive damages "in any action [for defamation] arising out of a publication or broadcast which is alleged to be false and defamatory" and provided for a one year statute of limitations on any such actions. Awards of attorneys' fees to prevailing parties were permitted. The Franklin proposal was not restricted to media defendants or to actions brought by public officials or public figures. Franklin's proposal ruled out the award of punitive damages in any "action for libel, or slander or false-light invasion of privacy." In an action for declaratory judgment no proof of the state of mind of the defendant would be required but no damages would be awarded. With some exceptions, Franklin also allowed the award of attorneys' fees to the prevailing party.

One *assumption* in all these proposals is that by removing the state of mind of the defendant as an issue and eliminating damages the cost of bringing or defending defamation actions would not be so great as either to discourage people from seeking redress or discourage potential defendants' willingness from speaking out. These proposals also assume that awarding attorneys' fees to the prevailing party will not reintroduce those same inhibiting concerns. In the very famous litigation between Arial Sharon and *Time Magazine* in 1984–1985, Judge Abraham Sofaer sent the case to the jury with a tripartite instruction. The jury was to first decide if Sharon had been defamed. If the jury concluded that he had been, the jury was then to decide if Sharon had proved that the defamatory statements made about him were false. If the jury decided this question in the affirmative as well, it was then to decide on the question of constitutional or actual malice. The jury decided these questions seriatim and reported its conclusions as it reached them. It eventually decided the first two questions in the affirmative. *See* New York Times Sat. Jan., 1985, p. 1, col. 5. The jury subsequently ruled that Sharon had not proved that *Time Magazine* published the article knowing it was false or with serious doubts about its truth. In effect Judge Sofaer allowed Sharon to have a declaratory judgment that false derogatory statements had been made about him. In the absence of statute one may have some doubts about the propriety of this procedure. It certainly introduces a greater judicial involvement in the jury's deliberations than is customary in defamation actions and goes against the spirit of Fox's libel act (32 Geo. 3, c. 60 (1792)) empowering juries to bring in general verdicts in criminal libel prosecutions. Although that statute only applied to criminal prosecutions, it has been taken in England to make the question of "libel or no libel" a jury question in civil actions and the usual practice there, as in the United States, has been to use general verdicts in defamation actions. It is also not at all clear that the greater volume of actions that a newspaper or other frequent defendants in defamation actions may expect to be brought against them will not cumulatively lead to the incurring of costs equal to those now being incurred when the potential recovery is much greater but the procedural hurdles which the plaintiff must overcome are much greater. M. Massing, *The Libel Chill: How Cold is It out There?* Colum.J.Rev., May/June 1985 at 31 is a frequently cited source for the proposition that the costs of defending libel actions can seriously threaten the media, particularly smaller newspapers. One incident that he described involved the Alton, Illinois *Telegraph* which was threatened with bankruptcy by a $9.2 million verdict in a defamation action. The defendant in that case decided to settle the action with the help of its libel insurer rather than take the chance that the entire award might be upheld on appeal.

5. *Libel tourism.* As American law has become more protective of speech than the law in civil law countries and other common-law countries, there have been a number of instances in which people, who had published material that had for the most part circulated in the United States, have been successfully sued in jurisdictions whose law was less protective of speech. In some of these instances there was minimal distribution of the material in question in the jurisdiction in which the action was brought. One response on the part of American courts has been to deny enforcement of any such judgments in the United States. *See* Ehrenfeld v. Mahfouz, 518 F.3d 102 (2d Cir. 2008). In 2010 Congress passed a statute stating that no foreign judgment for defamation shall be recognized in a domestic court of the United States if the law as stated or applied in a foreign jurisdiction does not provide as much protection for freedom of speech or the press as is provided by the first amendment to the United States Constitution and the constitution and laws of the state in which the domestic court is located, nor to any foreign judgment in an action for defamation in which the exercise of jurisdiction by the foreign court fails to comport with the due process requirements that are imposed on domestic courts by the Constitution of the United States. 28 U.S.C. § 4102. The burden of establishing compliance with these requirements is placed on the party seeking enforcement of the foreign judgment. This legislation also permits the defendant to remove an action for the enforcement of any such foreign judgment to the federal courts. *Id.* at § 4103. Prior to the federal enactment, a number of states, including New York, had enacted similar legislation. *See, e.g.,* N.Y.C.L.R. §§ 302 and 5304.

6. *Anti–SLAPP laws.* A number of states have passed such laws, including most prominently California. Cal. Code of Civ. Proc. § 425.16. These laws have been used as a basis for dismissing actions for defamation that are brought to harass people who have been critical of the plaintiff. SLAPP is an acronym for "strategic lawsuits against public participation." For an overview of these statutes *see* J. Ho, *I'll Huff and I'll Puff—But Then You'll Blow My Case Away: Dealing with Dismissed and Bad–Faith Defendants under California's Anti–SLAPP Statute*, 30 Whittier L. Rev. 533 (2009). For a recent judicial discussion of the California statute *see* Tamkin v. CBS Broadcasting, Inc., 193 Cal.App.4th 133, 122 Cal.Rptr.3d 264 (2011).

Chapter 9

Privacy

■ ■ ■

ROBERSON v. ROCHESTER FOLDING BOX CO.

Court of Appeals of New York, 1902.
171 N.Y. 538, 64 N.E. 442.

* * * From a judgment of the appellate division (71 N.Y.Supp. 876) affirming a judgment in favor of plaintiff overruling a demurrer to the complaint, defendants appeal. Reversed.

* * *

PARKER, C. J. The appellate division has certified that the following questions of law have arisen in this case, and ought to be reviewed by this court: (1) Does the complaint herein state a cause of action at law against the defendants, or either of them? (2) Does the complaint herein state a cause of action in equity against the defendants, or either of them? These questions are presented by a demurrer to the complaint, which is put upon the ground that the complaint does not state facts sufficient to constitute a cause of action.

* * * The complaint alleges that the Franklin Mills Company, one of the defendants, was engaged in a general milling business and in the manufacture and sale of flour; that before the commencement of the action, without the knowledge or consent of plaintiff, defendants, knowing that they had no right or authority so to do, had obtained, made, printed, sold, and circulated about 25,000 lithographic prints, photographs, and likenesses of plaintiff, made in a manner particularly set up in the complaint; that upon the paper upon which the likenesses were printed and above the portrait there were printed, in large, plain letters, the words, "Flour of the Family," and below the portrait, in large capital letters, "Franklin Mills Flour," and in the lower right-hand corner, in smaller capital letters, "Rochester Folding Box Co., Rochester, N.Y."; that upon the same sheet were other advertisements of the flour of the Franklin Mills Company; that those 25,000 likenesses of the plaintiff thus ornamented have been conspicuously posted and displayed in stores, warehouses, saloons, and other public places; that they have been recognized by friends of the plaintiff and other people, with the result that

plaintiff has been greatly humiliated by the scoffs and jeers of persons who have recognized her face and picture on this advertisement, and her good name has been attacked, causing her great distress and suffering, both in body and mind; that she was made sick, and suffered a severe nervous shock, was confined to her bed, and compelled to employ a physician, because of these facts; that defendants had continued to print, make, use, sell, and circulate the said lithographs, and that by reason of the foregoing facts plaintiff had suffered damages in the sum of $15,000. The complaint prays that defendants be enjoined from making, printing, publishing, circulating, or using in any manner any likenesses of plaintiff in any form whatever; for further relief (which it is not necessary to consider here); and for damages.

It will be observed that there is no complaint made that plaintiff was libeled by this publication of her portrait. The likeness is said to be a very good one, and one that her friends and acquaintances were able to recognize. Indeed, her grievance is that a good portrait of her, and therefore one easily recognized, has been used to attract attention toward the paper upon which defendant mill company's advertisements appear. Such publicity, which some find agreeable, is to plaintiff very distasteful, and thus, because of defendants' impertinence in using her picture, without her consent, for their own business purposes, she has been caused to suffer mental distress where others would have appreciated the compliment to their beauty implied in the selection of the picture for such purposes; but, as it is distasteful to her, she seeks the aid of the courts to enjoin a further circulation of the lithographic prints containing her portrait made as alleged in the complaint, and, as an incident thereto, to reimburse her for the damages to her feelings, which the complaint fixes at the sum of $15,000. There is no precedent for such an action to be found in the decisions of this court. Indeed, the learned judge who wrote the very able and interesting opinion in the appellate division said, while upon the threshold of the discussion of the question: "It may be said, in the first place, that the theory upon which this action is predicated is new, at least in instance, if not in principle, and that few precedents can be found to sustain the claim made by the plaintiff, if, indeed, it can be said that there are any authoritative cases establishing her right to recover in this action." Nevertheless that court reached the conclusion that plaintiff had a good cause of action against defendants, in that defendants had invaded what is called a "right of privacy"; in other words, the right to be let alone. Mention of such a right is not to be found in Blackstone, Kent, or any other of the great commentators upon the law; nor, so far as the learning of counsel or the courts in this case have been able to discover, does its existence seem to have been asserted prior to about the year 1890, when it was presented with attractiveness, and no inconsiderable ability, in the Harvard Law Review (volume 4, p. 193) in an article entitled "Rights of a Citizen to His Reputation." The so-called "right of privacy" is, as the phrase suggests, founded upon the claim that a man has the right to pass through this world, if he wills, without having his picture published, his business enterprises discussed, his successful experiments written up for the benefit of others, or his eccentricities commented upon either in handbills, circulars, catalogues, periodicals, or newspapers; and, necessarily, that the things which may not be written and published of him must not be spoken of him by his neighbors, whether the comment be favorable or otherwise. While most persons would much prefer to have a good likeness of themselves appear in a responsible periodical or leading newspaper rather than upon an advertising card or sheet, the doctrine which the courts are asked to create for this case would apply as well to the one publication as to the other, for the principle which a court of equity is asked to assert in support of a recovery in this action is that the right of privacy exists and is enforceable in equity, and that the publication of that which purports to be a portrait of another person, even if obtained upon the street by an impertinent individual with a camera, will be restrained in equity on the ground that an individual has the right to prevent his features from becoming known to those outside of his circle of friends and acquaintances. If such a principle be incorporated into the body of the law through the instrumentality of a court of equity, the attempts to logically apply the principle will necessarily result not only in a vast amount of litigation, but in litigation bordering upon the absurd, for the right of privacy, once established as a legal doctrine, cannot be confined to the restraint of the publication of a likeness, but must necessarily embrace as well the publication of a word picture, a comment upon one's looks, conduct, domestic relations or habits. And, were the right of privacy once legally asserted, it would necessarily be held to include the same things if spoken instead of printed, for one, as well as the other, invades the right to be absolutely let alone. An insult would certainly be in violation of such a right, and with many persons would more seriously wound the feelings than would the publication of their picture. And so we might add to the list of things that are spoken and done day by day which seriously offend the sensibilities of good people to which the principle which the plaintiff seeks to have imbedded in the doctrine of the law would seem to apply. I have gone only far enough to barely suggest the vast field of litigation which would necessarily be opened up should this court hold that privacy exists as a legal right enforceable in equity by injunction, and by damages where they seem necessary to give complete relief.

The legislative body could very well interfere and arbitrarily provide that no one should be permitted for his own selfish purpose to use the picture or the name of another for advertising purposes without his consent. In such event no embarrassment would result to the general body of the law, for the rule would be applicable only to cases provided for by the statute. The courts, however, being without authority to legislate, are required to decide cases upon principle, and so are necessarily embarrassed by precedents created by an extreme, and therefore unjustifiable, application of an old principle. The court below properly said that: "While it may be true that the fact that no precedent can be found to sustain an action in any given case is cogent evidence that a principle does not exist upon which the right may be based, it is not the rule that the want of a precedent is a sufficient reason for turning the plaintiff out of court," provided (I think should be added) there can be found a clear and unequivocal principle of the common law, which either directly or mediately governs it, or which, by analogy or parity of reasoning, ought to govern it. It is undoubtedly true that in the early days of chancery jurisdiction in England the chancellors were accustomed to deliver their judgments without regard to principles or precedents, and in that way the process of building up the system of equity went on, the chancellor disregarding absolutely many established principles of the common law. * * * In their work the chancellors were guided not only by what they regarded as the eternal principles of absolute right, but also by their individual consciences; but after a time, when "the period of infancy was passed, and an orderly system of equitable principles, doctrines, and rules began to be developed out of the increasing mass of precedents, this theory of a personal conscience was abandoned; and 'the conscience,' which is an element of the equitable jurisdiction, came to be regarded, and has so continued to the present day, as a metaphorical term, designating the common standard of civil right and expediency combined, based upon general principles, and limited by established doctrines to which the court appeals, and by which it tests the conduct and rights of suitors,—a juridical, and not a personal, conscience." Pom.Eq.Jur.§ 57.

The importance of observing the spirit of this rule cannot be overestimated; for, while justice in a given case may be worked out by a decision of the court according to the notions of right which govern the individual judge or body of judges comprising the court, the mischief which will finally result may be almost incalculable under our system, which makes a decision in one case a precedent for decisions in all future cases which are akin to it in the essential facts. So, in a case like the one before us, which is concededly new to this court, it is important that the court should have in mind the effect upon future litigation and upon the development of the law which would necessarily result from a step so far outside of the beaten paths of both common law and equity, assuming—what I shall attempt to show in a moment—that the right of privacy, as a legal doctrine enforceable in equity, has not, down to this time, been established by decisions. The history of the phrase "right of privacy" in this country seems to have begun in 1890, in a clever article in the Harvard Law Review,—already referred to,—in which a number of English cases were analyzed, and, reasoning by analogy, the conclusion was reached that, notwithstanding the unanimity of the courts in resting their decisions upon property rights in cases where publication is prevented by injunction, in reality such prevention was due to the necessity of affording protection to thoughts and sentiments expressed through the medium of writing, printing, and the arts, which is like the right not to be assaulted or beaten; in other words, that the principle actually involved, though not always appreciated, was that of an inviolate personality, not that of private property. This article brought forth a reply from the Northwestern Review (volume 3, p. 1) urging that equity has no concern with the feelings of an individual, or with considerations of moral fitness, except as the inconvenience or discomfort which the person may suffer is connected with the possession or enjoyment of property, and that the English authorities cited are consistent with such view. Those authorities are now to be examined, in order that we may see whether they were intended to and did mark a departure from the established rule which had been enforced for generations; or, on the other hand, are entirely consistent with it.

The first case is Prince Albert v. Strange, 1 Macn. & G. 25; Id., 2 De Gex & S. 652. The queen and the prince, having made etchings and drawings for their own amusement, decided to have copies struck off from the etched plates for presentation to friends and for their own use. The workman employed, however, printed some copies on his own account, which afterwards came into the hands of Strange, who purposed exhibiting them, and published a descriptive catalogue. Prince Albert applied for an injunction as to both exhibition and catalogue, and the vice chancellor granted it, restraining defendant from publishing, "at least by printing or writing, though not by copy or resemblance," a description of the etchings. An examination of the opinion of the vice chancellor discloses that he found two reasons for granting the injunction, namely, that the property rights of Prince Albert had been infringed, and that there was a breach of trust by the workman in retaining some impressions for himself. The opinion contained no hint whatever of a right of privacy separate and distinct from the right of property.

Pollard v. Photographic Co., 40 Ch.Div. 345, is certainly not an authority for granting an injunction on the ground of threatened injury to the feelings, although it is true, as stated in the opinion of the appellate division, that the court did say in the course of the discussion that the right to grant an injunction does not depend upon the existence of property; but the decision was, in fact, placed upon the ground that there was a breach of an implied contract. The facts, briefly stated, were that a photographer had been applied to by a woman to take her photograph, she ordering a certain number of copies, as is usual in such cases. The photographer made copies for himself, and undertook to exhibit them, and also sold copies to a stationer, who used them as Christmas cards. Their action was restrained by the court on the ground that there was an implied contract not to use the negative for any other purpose than to supply the sitter with copies of it for a price. During the argument of plaintiff's counsel the court asked this question: "Do you dispute that, if the negative likeness were taken on the sly, the person who took it might exhibit copies?" Counsel replied, "In that case there would be no consideration to support a contract."

* * *

In Duke of Queensbury v. Shebbeare, 2 Eden, 329, the Earl of Clarendon delivered to one Gwynne an original manuscript of his father's

"Lord Clarendon's History." Gwynne's administrator afterwards sold it to Shebbeare, and the court, upon the application of the personal representatives of Lord Clarendon, restrained its publication on the ground that they had a property right in the manuscript which it was not intended that Gwynne should have the benefit of by multiplying the number of copies in print for profit.

In not one of these cases, therefore, was it the basis of the decision that the defendant could be restrained from performing the act he was doing or threatening to do on the ground that the feelings of the plaintiff would be thereby injured; but, on the contrary, each decision was rested either upon the ground of breach of trust, or that plaintiff had a property right in the subject of litigation which the court could protect.

* * *

The case that seems to have been more relied upon than any other by the learned appellate division in reaching the conclusion that the complaint in this case states a cause of action is Schuyler v. Curtis, 147 N.Y. 434, 42 N.E. 22. * * * In that case certain persons attempted to erect a statue or bust of a woman no longer living, and one of her relatives commenced an action in equity to restrain such erection, alleging that his feelings and the feelings of other relatives of deceased would be injured thereby. At special term an injunction was granted on that ground. 19 N.Y.Supp. 264. The general term affirmed the decision. 64 Hun, 594. This court reversed the judgment, Judge Peckham writing, and, so far as the decision is concerned, therefore, it is not authority for the existence of a right of privacy which entitles a party to restrain another from doing an act which, though not actionable at common law, occasions plaintiff mental distress. In the course of the argument, however, expressions were used which it is now claimed indicate that the court recognized the existence of such a right. A sufficient answer to that contention is to be found in the opinion written on the motion for reargument in Colonial City Traction Co. v. Kingston City R. Co., 154 N.Y. 493, 48 N.E. 900, in which it was said: "It was not our intention to decide any case but the one before us. * * * If, as sometimes happens, broader statements were made by way of argument or otherwise than were essential to the decision of the questions presented, they are the dicta of the writer of the opinion, and not the decision of the court. A judicial opinion, like evidence, is only binding so far as it is relevant; and when it wanders from the point at issue it no longer has force as an official utterance." The question up for decision in the Schuyler Case was whether the relatives could restrain the threatened action of defendants, and not whether Mrs. Schuyler could have restrained it had she been living. The latter question not being before the court, it was not called upon to decide it, and, as we read the opinion, there is no expression in it which indicates an intention either to decide it or to seriously consider it; but, rather, it proceeds upon the assumption that, if such a right did exist in Mrs. Schuyler, her relatives did not succeed to it upon her death. * * *

* * *

An examination of the authorities leads us to the conclusion that the so-called "right of privacy" has not as yet found an abiding place in our jurisprudence, and, as we view it, the doctrine cannot now be incorporated without doing violence to settled principles of law by which the profession and the public have long been guided.

* * *

The judgment of the appellate division and of the special term should be reversed and [the] questions certified answered in the negative. * * *

GRAY, J. (dissenting).

* * *

* * * As I have suggested, that the exercise of this peculiar preventive power of a court of equity is not found in some precisely analogous case, furnishes no valid objection at all to the assumption of jurisdiction if the particular circumstances of the case show the performance, or the threatened performance, of an act by a defendant, which is wrongful, because constituting an invasion, in some novel form, of a right to something which is, or should be conceded to be, the plaintiff's, and as to which the law provides no adequate remedy. It would be a justifiable exercise of power whether the principle of interference be rested upon analogy to some established common-law principle, or whether it is one of natural justice. In an article in the Harvard Law Review of December 15, 1890, which contains an impressive argument upon the subject of the "right of privacy," it was well said by the authors: "That the individual shall have full protection in person and in property is a principle as old as the common law; but it has been found necessary from time to time to define anew the exact nature and extent of such protection. * * * The right to life has come to mean the right to enjoy life,—the right to be let alone; the right to liberty secures the exercise of extensive civil privileges; and the term 'property' has grown to comprise every form of possession, intangible as well as tangible." * * * The proposition is, to me, an inconceivable one that these defendants may, unauthorizedly, use the likeness of this young woman upon their advertisement as a method of attracting widespread public attention to their wares, and that she must submit to the mortifying notoriety, without right to invoke the exercise of the preventive power of a court of equity.

Such a view, as it seems to me, must have been unduly influenced by a failure to find precedents in analogous cases, or some declaration by the great commentators upon the law of a common-law principle which would precisely apply to and govern the action, without taking into consideration that in the existing state of society new conditions affecting the relations of persons demand the broader extension of those legal principles which underlie the immunity of one's person from attack. I think that such a view is unduly restricted, too, by a search for some property which has been invaded by the defendants' acts. Property is not, necessarily, the thing itself which is owned; it is the right of the owner in relation to it. The right to be protected in one's possession of a thing or in one's privileges, belonging to him as an individual, or secured to him as a member of the commonwealth, is property, and as such entitled to the protection of the law. The protective power of equity is not exercised upon the tangible thing, but upon the right to enjoy it; and so it is called forth for the protection of the right to that which is one's exclusive possession as a property right. It seems to me that the principle which is applicable is analogous to that upon which courts of equity have interfered to protect the right of privacy in cases of private writings, or of other unpublished products of the mind. The writer or the lecturer has been protected in his right to a literary property in a letter or a lecture, against its unauthorized publication, because it is property to which the right of privacy attaches. * * * I think that this plaintiff has the same property in the right to be protected against the use of her face for defendant's commercial purposes as she would have if they were publishing her literary compositions. The right would be conceded if she had sat for her photograph; but if her face or her portraiture has a value, the value is hers exclusively, until the use be granted away to the public. Any other principle of decision, in my opinion, is as repugnant to equity as it is shocking to reason.

* * *

The right to grant the injunction does not depend upon the existence of property which one has in some contractual form. It depends upon the existence of property in any right which belongs to a person * * *. It would be, in my opinion, an extraordinary view, which, while conceding the right of a person to be protected against the unauthorized circulation of an unpublished lecture, letter, drawing, or other ideal property, yet would deny the same protection to a person whose portrait was unauthorizedly obtained and made use of for commercial purposes. The injury to the plaintiff is irreparable, because she cannot be wholly compensated in damages for the various consequences entailed by defendants' acts. The only complete relief is an injunction restraining their continuance. Whether, as incidental to that equitable relief, she should be able to recover only nominal damages, is not material, for the issuance of the injunction does not, in such a case, depend upon the amount of the damages in dollars and cents.

* * *

O'BRIEN, CULLEN, and WERNER, JJ., concur with PARKER, C. J. BARTLETT and HAIGHT, JJ., concur with GRAY, J.

Judgment reversed, etc.

NOTES

1. S. Warren and L. Brandeis, *The Right to Privacy,* 4 Harv.L.Rev. 193 (1890), has been one of the most frequently cited law review articles ever written. The conventional wisdom has been that the article was prompted by Warren's annoyance over the manner in which the wedding of his daughter was covered by the press. *See* W. Prosser, *Privacy,* 48 Cal.L.Rev. 383 (1960); H. Kalven, Jr., *Privacy in Tort Law—Were Warren and Brandeis Wrong?,* 31 Law & Contemp. Probs. 326, 329 n. 22 (1966). More recent and more exhaustive scholarship contends that if there was any impetus for Warren and Brandeis' article, it was press criticism of Warren's father-in-law, Thomas Bayard, Sr., who had been a United States Senator from Delaware and who had been Secretary of State in the first Cleveland administration. *See* J. Barron, *Warren and Brandeis, The Right to Privacy,* 4 Harv.L.Rev. 193 (1890): *Demystifying a Landmark Citation*, 13 Suffolk U.L.Rev. 875 (1979). Barron points out that Warren's daughter was only seven years old in 1890. A cousin of Warren's had been married in 1890, but the press coverage had been fairly sedate.

Kalven's critical comments regarding the judicial creation of the tort of privacy have been followed by those of others, including D. Zimmerman, *Requiem for a Heavyweight: A Farewell to Warren and Brandeis's Privacy Tort,* 68 Cornell L.Rev. 291 (1983); R. Bezanson, *The Right to Privacy Revisited: Privacy, News, and Social Change, 1890–1990*, 80 Cal.L.Rev. 1133 (1992); Comment, *Privacy in Photographs: Misconception Since Inception,* 18 John Marshall L.Rev. 969 (1985). The Zimmerman article begins with a fairly comprehensive review of the law of privacy as of 1983. She concludes that the interests sought to be protected by the "so-called right to privacy" might better be served by narrowly drawn statutory provisions that focus on the point of origin of the information in question rather than the ultimate dissemination of that information to the public at large. She also advocates adequate sanctions for the breach of "special confidential relationships". Bezanson also maintains that the principal focus of the common-law tort of privacy should be the protection of confidentiality with perhaps a more expanded notion of the range of confidentiality.

2. The New York legislature in 1903 responded to the decision in *Roberson* by enacting what, after reenactment in 1909, became §§ 50–51 of the New York Civil Rights Law. The complete current wording of these provisions, as most recently amended in 1995, is as follows:

§ 50. Right of privacy

A person, firm or corporation that uses for advertising purposes, or for the purposes of trade, the name, portrait or picture of any living person without having first obtained the written consent of such person, or if a minor of his or her parent or guardian, is guilty of a misdemeanor.

§ 51. Action for injunction and for damages

Any person whose name, portrait, picture or voice is used within this state for advertising purposes or for the purposes of trade without the written consent first obtained as above provided may maintain an equitable action in the supreme court of this state against the person, firm or corporation so using his name, portrait, picture or voice, to prevent and restrain the use thereof; and may also sue and recover damages for any injuries sustained by reason of such use and if the defendant shall have knowingly used such person's name, portrait, picture or voice in such manner as is forbidden or declared to be unlawful by section fifty of this article, the jury, in its discretion, may award exemplary damages. But nothing contained in this article shall be so construed as to prevent any person, firm or corporation from selling or otherwise transferring any material containing such name, portrait, picture or voice in whatever medium to any user of such name, portrait, picture or voice, or to any third party for sale or transfer directly or indirectly to such a user, for use in a manner lawful under this article; nothing contained in this article shall be so construed as to prevent any person, firm or corporation, practicing the profession of photography, from exhibiting in or about his or its establishment specimens of the work of such establishment, unless the same is continued by such person, firm or corporation after written notice objecting thereto has been given by the person portrayed; and nothing contained in this article shall be so construed as to prevent any person, firm or corporation from using the name, portrait, picture or voice of any manufacturer or dealer in connection with the goods, wares and merchandise manufactured, produced or dealt in by him which he has sold or disposed of with such name, portrait, picture or voice used in connection therewith; or from using the name, portrait, picture or voice of any author, composer or artist in connection with his literary, musical or artistic productions which he has sold or disposed of with such name, portrait, picture or voice used in connection therewith. Nothing contained in this section shall be construed to prohibit the copyright owner of a sound recording from disposing of, dealing in, licensing or selling that sound recording to any party, if the right to dispose of, deal in, license or sell such sound recording has been conferred by contract or other written document by such living person or the holder of such right. Nothing contained in the foregoing sentence shall be deemed to abrogate or otherwise limit any rights or remedies otherwise conferred by federal law or state law.

In 1979, an additional provision was added. As amended most recently in 2006, it provides:

§ 50–b. Right of privacy; victims of sex offenses or offenses involving the transmission of the human immunodeficiency virus

1. The identity of any victim of a sex offense, as defined in article one hundred thirty or sections 255.25, 255.26 or 255.27 of the penal law, or of an offense involving the alleged transmission of the human immunodeficiency virus, shall be confidential. No report, paper, picture, photograph, court file or other documents, in the custody or possession of any public officer or employee, which identifies such a victim shall be made available for public inspection. No such public officer or employee shall disclose any portion of any police report, court file, or other document, which tends to

identify such a victim except as provided in subdivision two of this section.

2. The provisions of subdivision one of this section shall not be construed to prohibit disclosure of information to:

a. Any person charged with the commission of an offense, as defined in subdivision one of this section, against the same victim; the counsel or guardian of such person; the public officers and employees charged with the duty of investigating, prosecuting, keeping records relating to the offense, or any other act when done pursuant to the lawful discharge of their duties; and any necessary witnesses for either party; or

b. Any person who, upon application to a court having jurisdiction over the alleged offense, demonstrates to the satisfaction of the court that good cause exists for disclosure to that person. Such application shall be made upon notice to the victim or other person legally responsible for the care of the victim, and the public officer or employee charged with the duty of prosecuting the offense; or

c. Any person or agency, upon written consent of the victim or other person legally responsible for the care of the victim, except as may be otherwise required or provided by the order of a court.

3. The court having jurisdiction over the alleged offense may order any restrictions upon disclosure authorized in subdivision two of this section, as it deems necessary and proper to preserve the confidentiality of the identity of the victim.

4. Nothing contained in this section shall be construed to require the court to exclude the public from any stage of the criminal proceeding.

5. No disclosure of confidential HIV related information, as defined in section twenty-seven hundred eighty of the public health law, including the identity of the victim of an offense involving transmission of the human immunodeficiency virus, shall be permitted under this section contrary to article twenty-seven-F of the public health law.

As we shall see, p. 681 *infra*, attempts to prohibit the publication of the names of the victims of sexual offenses have had difficulty passing constitutional muster. We shall thus have occasion to consider whether a narrowly drawn statute like § 50–b is able to avoid the pitfalls of more broadly worded provisions. For a detailed discussion of the New York statute, *see* L. Savell, *Right of Privacy—Appropriation of a Person's Name, Portrait, or Picture for Advertising or Trade Purposes without Prior Written Consent: History and Scope in New York*, 48 Albany L.Rev. 1 (1983). *Roberson* was rejected in Pavesich v. New England Life Insurance Co., 122 Ga. 190, 50 S.E. 68 (1905).

3. In an article written in 1960 the late Dean Prosser categorized and summarized the development of the law up until that time as follows:

> What has emerged from the decisions is no simple matter. It is not one tort, but a complex of four. The law of privacy comprises four distinct kinds of invasion of four different interests of the plaintiff, which are tied together by the common name, but otherwise have almost nothing in

common except that each represents an interference with the right of the plaintiff, in the phrase coined by Judge Cooley, "to be let alone." Without any attempt to exact definition, these four torts may be described as follows:

1. Intrusion upon the plaintiff's seclusion or solitude, or into his private affairs.

2. Public disclosure of embarrassing private facts about the plaintiff.

3. Publicity which places the plaintiff in a false light in the public eye.

4. Appropriation, for the defendant's advantage, of the plaintiff's name or likeness.

It should be obvious at once that these four types of invasion may be subject, in some respects at least, to different rules; and that when what is said about any one of them is carried over to another, it may not be at all applicable, and confusion may follow.

W. Prosser, *supra* note 1, at 389. Prosser's characterization of the tort has become extremely influential and it may be helpful to keep it in mind in analyzing the remaining cases presented in this chapter. Nevertheless, while Prosser's analytical framework is widely used in legal analysis, it has almost from the beginning met with the assertion that there really is a core notion of privacy. *See, e.g.*, E. Bloustein, *Privacy as an Aspect of Human Dignity: an Answer to Dean Prosser,* 39 N.Y.U.L.Rev. 962 (1964). Bloustein also has attacked what might be characterized as the suggestion in Kalven, *supra* note 1, that privacy is a "trivial tort." *See* E. Bloustein, *Privacy, Tort Law, and the Constitution: Is Warren and Brandeis' Tort Petty and Unconstitutional as Well?,* 46 Tex.L.Rev. 611 (1968). More recent discussion of Prosser's approach to privacy include N. Richards and D. Solove, *Prosser's Privacy Law: A Mixed Legacy,* 98 Calif. L.Rev. 1887 (2010). *See also* P.M. Schwartz and K–N. Peifer, *Prosser's* Privacy *and the German Right of Personality: Are Four Privacy Torts Better than One Unitary Concept?,* 98 Calif. L.Rev. 1925 (2010). For a lively discussion of the dangers to individual privacy posed by modern technological innovations, *see* A. Miller, The Assault on Privacy: Computers, Data Banks, and Dossiers (1971). For a different view as to where the legal lines should be drawn, *see* G. Christie, *The Right to Privacy and the Freedom to Know: A Comment on Professor Miller's the Assault on Privacy,* 119 U.Pa. L.Rev. 970 (1971).

4. For a stimulating discussion of the philosophical foundation of the notion of privacy, *see* C. Fried, *Privacy,* 77 Yale L.J. 475 (1968). *See also* R. Gavison, *Privacy and the Limits of Law,* 89 Yale L.J. 421 (1980); J. Reiman, *Privacy, Intimacy and Personhood,* 6 Phil. & Pub. Aff. 26 (1976). A good analysis of the various interests that have been subsumed under the rubric "privacy" is contained in H. Gross, *The Concept of Privacy,* 42 N.Y.U. L.Rev. 34 (1967). For a more recent discussion of the theoretical justifications for protecting "privacy", *see* Symposium: *The Right to Privacy*, 17 Soc. Phil. & Pol. 1 *et seq.* (Summer 2000). A key issue is whether the right of privacy is a reflection of some basic inherent values or merely solely the reflection of a

society's current conventional values. *See also* D. Solove, *Conceptualizing Privacy*, 90 Calif. L.Rev. 1087 (2002).

On the comparative aspects of privacy, *see* H. Krause, *The Right to Privacy in Germany—Pointers for American Legislation?*, 1965 Duke L.J. 481; J. Weeks, *The Comparative Law of Privacy,* 12 Clev.–Mar.L.Rev. 484 (1963). An important article discussing the different philosophical underpinnings of the notion of privacy in the United States and Europe is J. Whitman, *The Two Western Cultures of Privacy: Dignity Versus Liberty*, 113 Yale L.J. 1151 (2004). *See also* P.M. Schwartz and K–N. Peifer,, *supra* note 3, and S. Simitis, *Privacy—An Endless Debate?,* 98 Calif. L.Rev. 1989 (2010). Later in this chapter, pp. 699–730, *infra*, we shall examine some material on the European approach to privacy. For a long time the tort of privacy was not recognized under English law. That is now changing as the result in part of the United Kingdom's membership in the Council of Europe and the European Union. As far as English law is concerned, as we shall see later in this chapter, the two most important developments are, as already noted, the incorporation of the European Convention on Human Rights into the law of the United Kingdom and a broad judicial expansion of the traditional common law of confidentiality.

CANTRELL v. FOREST CITY PUBLISHING CO.

Supreme Court of the United States, 1974.
419 U.S. 245, 95 S.Ct. 465, 42 L.Ed.2d 419.

MR. JUSTICE STEWART delivered the opinion of the Court.

Margaret Cantrell and four of her minor children brought this diversity action in a Federal District Court for invasion of privacy against the Forest City Publishing Co., publisher of a Cleveland newspaper, the Plain Dealer, and against Joseph Eszterhas, a reporter formerly employed by the Plain Dealer, and Richard Conway, a Plain Dealer photographer. The Cantrells alleged that an article published in the Plain Dealer Sunday Magazine unreasonably placed their family in a false light before the public through its many inaccuracies and untruths. The District Judge struck the claims relating to punitive damages as to all the plaintiffs and dismissed the actions of three of the Cantrell children in their entirety, but allowed the case to go to the jury as to Mrs. Cantrell and her oldest son, William. The jury returned a verdict against all three of the respondents for compensatory money damages in favor of these two plaintiffs.

The Court of Appeals for the Sixth Circuit reversed, holding that, in the light of the First and Fourteenth Amendments, the District Judge should have granted the respondents' motion for a directed verdict as to all the Cantrells' claims. * * *

I

In December 1967, Margaret Cantrell's husband Melvin was killed along with 43 other people when the Silver Bridge across the Ohio River at Point Pleasant, W.Va., collapsed. The respondent Eszterhas was assigned by the Plain Dealer to cover the story of the disaster. He wrote a "news feature" story focusing on the funeral of Melvin Cantrell and the impact of his death on the Cantrell family.

Five months later, after conferring with the Sunday Magazine editor of the Plain Dealer, Eszterhas and photographer Conway returned to the Point Pleasant area to write a follow-up feature. The two men went to the Cantrell residence, where Eszterhas talked with the children and Conway took 50 pictures. Mrs. Cantrell was not at home at any time during the 60 to 90 minutes that the men were at the Cantrell residence.

Eszterhas' story appeared as the lead feature in the August 4, 1968, edition of the Plain Dealer Sunday Magazine. The article stressed the family's abject poverty; the children's old, ill-fitting clothes and the deteriorating condition of their home were detailed in both the text and accompanying photographs. As he had done in his original, prize-winning article on the Silver Bridge disaster, Eszterhas used the Cantrell family to illustrate the impact of the bridge collapse on the lives of the people in the Point Pleasant area.

It is conceded that the story contained a number of inaccuracies and false statements. Most conspicuously, although Mrs. Cantrell was not present at any time during the reporter's visit to her home, Eszterhas wrote, "Margaret Cantrell will talk neither about what happened nor about how they are doing. She wears the same mask of non-expression she wore at the funeral. She is a proud woman. Her world has changed. She says that after it happened, the people in town offered to help them out with money and they refused to take it." Other significant misrepresentations were contained in details of Eszterhas' descriptions of the poverty in which the Cantrells were living and the dirty and dilapidated conditions of the Cantrell home.

The case went to the jury on a so-called "false light" theory of invasion of privacy. In essence, the theory of the case was that by publishing the false feature story about the Cantrells and thereby making them the objects of pity and ridicule, the respondents damaged Mrs. Cantrell and her son William by causing them to suffer outrage, mental distress, shame, and humiliation.

II

In Time, Inc. v. Hill, 385 U.S. 374, the Court considered a similar false-light, invasion-of-privacy action. The New York Court of Appeals had interpreted New York Civil Rights Law, McKinney's Consol.Laws, c. 6, §§ 50–51 to give a "newsworthy person" a right of action when his or her name, picture or portrait was the subject of a "fictitious" report or article. Material and substantial falsification was the test for recovery. * * * Under this doctrine the New York courts awarded the plaintiff James Hill compensatory damages based on his complaint that Life Magazine had falsely reported that a new Broadway play portrayed the Hill family's experience in being held hostage by three escaped convicts. This Court, guided by its decision in New York Times Co. v. Sullivan, * * * which recognized constitutional limits on a State's power to award damages for libel in actions brought by public officials, held that the constitutional protections for speech and press precluded the application of the New York statute to allow recovery for "false reports of matters of public interest in the absence of proof that the defendant published the report with knowledge of its falsity or in reckless disregard of the truth." * * * Although the jury could have reasonably concluded from the evidence in the *Hill* case that Life had engaged in knowing falsehood or had recklessly disregarded the truth in stating in the article that "the story re-enacted" the Hill family's experience, the Court concluded that the trial judge's instructions had not confined the jury to such a finding as a predicate for liability as required by the Constitution. * * *

The District Judge in the case before us, in contrast to the trial judge in Time, Inc. v. Hill, did instruct the jury that liability could be imposed only if it concluded that the false statements in the Sunday Magazine feature article on the Cantrells had been made with knowledge of their falsity or in reckless disregard of the truth. No objection was made by any of the parties to this knowing-or-reckless-falsehood instruction. Consequently, this case presents no occasion to consider whether a State may constitutionally apply a more relaxed standard of liability for a publisher or broadcaster of false statements injurious to a private individual under a false-light theory of invasion of privacy, or whether the constitutional standard announced in Time, Inc. v. Hill applies to all false-light cases. Cf. Gertz v. Robert Welch, Inc. * * *. Rather, the sole question that we need decide is whether the Court of Appeals erred in setting aside the jury's verdict.

III

At the close of the petitioners' case-in-chief, the District Judge struck the demand for punitive damages. He found that Mrs. Cantrell had failed to present any evidence to support the charges that the invasion of privacy "was done maliciously within the legal definition of that term." The Court of Appeals interpreted this finding to be a determination by the District Judge that there was no evidence of knowing falsity or reckless disregard of the truth introduced at the trial. Having made such a determination, the Court of Appeals held that the District Judge should have granted the motion for a directed verdict for respondents as to all the Cantrells' claims. * * *

The Court of Appeals appears to have assumed that the District Judge's finding of no malice "within the legal definition of that term" was a finding based on the definition of "actual malice" established by this Court in New York Times Co. v. Sullivan * * *. As so defined, of course, "actual malice" is a term of art, created to provide a convenient shorthand expression for the standard of liability that must be established before a State may constitutionally permit public officials to recover for libel in actions brought against publishers. As such, it is quite different from the common-law standard of "malice" generally required under state tort law to support an award of punitive damages. In a false-light case, common-law malice—frequently expressed in terms of either personal ill will toward the plaintiff or reckless or wanton disregard of the plaintiff's rights—would focus on the defendant's attitude toward the plaintiff's privacy, not toward the truth or falsity of the material published. * * *

Although the verbal record of the District Court proceedings is not entirely unambiguous, the conclusion is inescapable that the District Judge was referring to the common-law standard of malice rather than to the *New York Times* "actual malice" standard when he dismissed the punitive damages claims. For at the same time that he dismissed the demands for punitive damages, the District Judge refused to grant the respondents' motion for directed verdicts as to Mrs. Cantrell's and William's claims for compensatory damages. And, as his instructions to the jury made clear, the District Judge was fully aware that the Time, Inc. v. Hill meaning of the *New York Times* "actual malice" standard had to be satisfied for the Cantrells to recover actual damages. Thus, the only way to harmonize these two virtually simultaneous rulings by the District Judge is to conclude, contrary to the decision of the Court of Appeals, that in dismissing the punitive damages claims he was not determining that Mrs. Cantrell had failed to introduce any evidence of knowing falsity or reckless disregard of the truth. * * *

Moreover, the District Judge was clearly correct in believing that the evidence introduced at trial was sufficient to support a jury finding that the respondents Joseph Eszterhas and Forest City Publishing Co. had published knowing or reckless falsehoods about the Cantrells. There was no dispute during the trial that Eszterhas, who did not testify, must have known that a number of the statements in the feature story were untrue. In particular, his article plainly implied that Mrs. Cantrell had been present during his visit to her home and that Eszterhas had observed her "wear[ing] the same mask of nonexpression she wore [at her husband's] funeral." These were "calculated falsehoods," and the jury was plainly justified in finding that Eszterhas had portrayed the Cantrells in a false light through knowing or reckless untruth.

* * *

For the foregoing reasons, the judgment of the Court of Appeals is reversed and the case is remanded to that court with directions to enter a judgment affirming the judgment of the District Court as to the respondents Forest City Publishing Co. and Joseph Eszterhas.

It is so ordered.

Reversed and remanded.

MR. JUSTICE DOUGLAS, dissenting.

I adhere to the views which I expressed in Time, Inc. v. Hill, 385 U.S. 374 (1967). * * * Freedom of the press is "abridged" in violation of the First and Fourteenth Amendments by what we do today. This line of cases, which of course includes New York Times Co. v. Sullivan, * * * seems to me to place First Amendment rights of the press at a midway point similar to what our ill-fated Betts v. Brady, 316 U.S. 455 (1942) did to the right to counsel. The press will be "free" in the First Amendment sense when the judge-made qualifications of that freedom are withdrawn and the substance of the First Amendment restored to what I believe was the purpose of its enactment.

A bridge accident catapulted the Cantrells into the public eye and their disaster became newsworthy. To make the First Amendment freedom to report the news turn on subtle differences between common-law malice and actual malice is to stand the Amendment on its head. Those who write the current news seldom have the objective, dispassionate point of view—or the time—of scientific analysts. They deal in fast-moving events and the need for "spot" reporting. The jury under today's formula sits as a censor with broad powers—not to impose a prior restraint, but to lay heavy damages on the press. The press is "free" only if the jury is sufficiently disenchanted with the Cantrells to let the press be free of this damages claim. * * * Whatever might be the ultimate reach of the doctrine Mr. Justice Black and I have embraced, it seems clear that in matters of public import such as the present news reporting, there must be freedom from damages lest the press be frightened into playing a more ignoble role than the Framers visualized.

I would affirm the judgment of the Court of Appeals.

NOTES

1. In Time, Inc. v. Hill, 385 U.S. 374, 87 S.Ct. 534, 17 L.Ed.2d 456 (1967), the Court noted that on their face §§ 50–51 of the New York Civil Rights Law

> proscribe only conduct of the kind involved in *Roberson,* that is, appropriation and use in advertising or to promote the sale of goods, of another's name, portrait or picture without his consent. An application of that limited scope would present different questions of violation of the constitutional protections for speech and press.
>
> The New York courts have, however, construed the statute to operate much more broadly. * * *

385 U.S. at 381, 87 S.Ct. at 538–39, 17 L.Ed.2d at 463. Nevertheless, the Court noted that the New York Court of Appeals had held, in Spahn v. Julian Messner, Inc., 18 N.Y.2d 324, 274 N.Y.S.2d 877, 221 N.E.2d 543 (1966), that "truth is a complete defense in actions under the statute based upon reports of newsworthy people or events".* The Court in *Hill* went on to hold that,

* *Spahn* involved the partially fictionalized (though not unflattering) biography of a well-known baseball player. Furthermore, the New York court had also held that "minor errors" were not actionable. The New York Court of Appeals subsequently reheard the case after its original judgment had been vacated by the United States Supreme Court for reconsideration in the light of *Time, Inc. v. Hill,* 385 U.S. 374, 87 S.Ct. 534, 17 L.Ed.2d 456 (1967), and ultimately reinstated the judgment in favor of Spahn, 21 N.Y.2d 124, 286 N.Y.S.2d 832, 233 N.E.2d 840 (1967). Two judges dissented on the ground that a public figure should not be able to recover the fictionalization of his life unless he could show that it "hurt him and [... was] designed to hurt him."

accepting this construction of the New York statutes, no action could constitutionally lie unless there were proof of knowledge of falsity or reckless disregard for truth. An interesting part of the Court's opinion, written by Justice Brennan, is footnote 7, the pertinent parts of which read as follows:

> This limitation to newsworthy person and events does not of course foreclose an interpretation of the statute to allow damages where "Revelations may be so intimate and so unwarranted in view of the victim's position to outrage the community's sense of decency." *Sidis v. F–R Pub. Corp* [reprinted *infra*, p. 675] * * *. This case presents no question whether truthful publication of such matter could be constitutionally proscribed.
>
> It has been said that a 'right of privacy' has been recognized at common law in 30 States plus the District of Columbia and by statute in four States. See Prosser, Law of Torts 831–832 (3d ed. 1964). Professor Kalven notes, however, that since Warren and Brandeis championed an action against the press for public disclosure of truthful but private details about the individual which caused emotional upset to him, "it has been agreed that there is a generous privilege to serve the public interest in news. * * * What is at issue, it seems to me, is whether the claim of privilege is not so overpowering as virtually to swallow the tort. What can be left of the vaunted new right after the claims of privilege have been confronted?" Kalven, "Privacy in Tort Law—Were Warren and Brandeis Wrong?" 31 Law & Contemp.Prob. 326, 335–336 (1966).

2. Justice Stewart, in *Cantrell,* left open the question whether the *Gertz* standard may not be applicable in false-light privacy cases brought by private figures. Declaring that the *Gertz* negligence standard does replace the *Hill* standard in such cases is Rinsley v. Brandt, 446 F.Supp. 850 (D.Kan.1977), which was followed in Tomson v. Stephan, 696 F.Supp. 1407, 1413 (D.Kan. 1988). *See also* Wood v. Hustler Magazine, Inc., 736 F.2d 1084 (5th Cir.1984), *cert. denied* 469 U.S. 1107, 105 S.Ct. 783, 83 L.Ed.2d 777 (1985). This is also the position taken more recently in West v. Media Gen'l Convergence, Inc., 53 S.W.3d 640 (Tenn. 2001). *C.f.* A. Hill, *Defamation and Privacy Under the First Amendment,* 76 Colum.L.Rev. 1205, 1274 (1976); J. Phillips, *Defamation, Invasion of Privacy and the Constitutional Standard of Care,* 16 Santa Clara L.Rev. 77, 99 (1975). On the other hand, in Dodrill v. Arkansas Democrat Co., 265 Ark. 628, 590 S.W.2d 840 (1979) *cert. denied* 444 U.S. 1076, 100 S.Ct. 1024, 62 L.Ed.2d 759 (1980), the court held that until the Supreme Court held otherwise it was obliged to follow *Hill* and apply the *Sullivan* standard in false-light privacy cases. This appears to be the position taken by the majority of courts that have considered the question. *See e.g.* Colbert v. World Pub. Co., 747 P.2d 286 (Okl.1987); Machleder v. Diaz, 618 F.Supp. 1367, 1373 n. 4 (S.D.N.Y.1985), *reversed on other grounds* 801 F.2d 46 (2d Cir.1986). *Restatement (Second) of Torts* § 652E also applies the *Sullivan* standard to all false-light privacy cases. In this regard, it should be noted that in *Gertz,* Justice Powell, who wrote for the Court, specifically said, in conjunction with explaining why private figures could recover in defamation actions merely on a showing of "fault," "[o]ur inquiry would involve considerations somewhat different from those discussed above if a State purported to condition civil liability on a factual misstatement whose content did not warn a reasonably

prudent editor or broadcaster of its defamatory potential. *Cf.* Time, Inc. v. Hill, * * * Such a case is not now before us, and we intimate no view as to its proper resolution." *See* p. 599, *supra*.

3. Because of the similarities with defamation, most of the restrictions applied against plaintiffs in defamation actions have been applied to plaintiffs in false-light invasion of privacy actions. *See* Fellows v. National Enquirer, Inc., 42 Cal.3d 234, 228 Cal.Rptr. 215, 721 P.2d 97 (1986) which, in a false-light invasion of privacy action, applied the California doctrine that, if a false statement is not defamatory on its face, recovery is only permitted upon allegation and proof of special damages.

4. In Renwick v. News and Observer Pub. Co., 310 N.C. 312, 312 S.E.2d 405 (1984), *cert. denied* 469 U.S. 858, 105 S.Ct. 187, 83 L.Ed.2d 121 the court declared that North Carolina would not recognize actions for false-light invasion of privacy. Recovery for the dissemination of false information about a person may only be had in actions for libel or slander. Do you approve of this approach? *See* D. Zimmerman, *False Light Invasion of Privacy: The Light That Failed*, 64 N.Y.U.L.Rev. 364 (1989) which strongly approves of the approach taken in cases like *Renwick*. In Godbehere v. Phoenix Newspapers, Inc., 162 Ariz. 335, 783 P.2d 781 (1989) the court would not permit a false-light invasion of privacy action to be brought for publications relating to the public life or duties of public officials. More recently, the tort of false-light invasion of privacy was rejected in Denver Pub. Co. v. Bueno, 54 P.3d 893 (Colo. 2002), although the court noted that about thirty jurisdictions had recognized it. A more recent rejection of the tort is Jews for Jesus, Inc. v. Rapp, 997 So.2d 1098 (Fla. 2008), while a more recent recognition of the tort is Welling v. Weinfeld, 113 Ohio St.3d 464, 866 N.E.2d 1051 (2007).

NADER v. GENERAL MOTORS CORP.

New York Court of Appeals, 1970.
25 N.Y.2d 560, 307 N.Y.S.2d 647, 255 N.E.2d 765.

FULD, CHIEF JUDGE.

On this appeal, taken by permission of the Appellate Division on a certified question, we are called upon to determine the reach of the tort of invasion of privacy as it exists under the law of the District of Columbia.

The complaint, in this action by Ralph Nader, pleads four causes of action against the appellant, General Motors Corporation, and three other defendants allegedly acting as its agents. The first two causes of action charge an invasion of privacy, the third is predicated on the intentional infliction of severe emotional distress and the fourth on interference with the plaintiff's economic advantage. This appeal concerns only the legal sufficiency of the first two causes of action, which were upheld in the courts below as against the appellant's motion to dismiss * * *.

The plaintiff, an author and lecturer on automotive safety, has, for some years, been an articulate and severe critic of General Motors' products from the standpoint of safety and design. According to the complaint—which, for present purposes, we must assume to be true—the appellant, having learned of the imminent publication of the plaintiff's book "Unsafe at any Speed," decided to conduct a campaign of intimidation against him in order to "suppress plaintiff's criticism of and prevent his disclosure of information" about its products. To that end, the appellant authorized and directed the other defendants to engage in a series of activities which, the plaintiff claims in his first two causes of action, violated his right to privacy.

Specifically, the plaintiff alleges that the appellant's agents (1) conducted a series of interviews with acquaintances of the plaintiff, "questioning them about, and casting aspersions upon [his] political, social * * * racial and religious views * * *; his integrity; his sexual proclivities and inclinations; and his personal habits" (Complaint, par. 9[b]); (2) kept him under surveillance in public places for an unreasonable length of time (par. 9[c]); (3) caused him to be accosted by girls for the purpose of entrapping him into illicit relationships (par. 9[d]); (4) made threatening, harassing and obnoxious telephone calls to him (par. 9[e]); (5) tapped his telephone and eavesdropped, by means of mechanical and electronic equipment, on his private conversations with others (par. 9[f]); and (6) conducted a "continuing" and harassing investigation of him (par. 9[g]). These charges are amplified in the plaintiff's bill of particulars, and those particulars are, of course, to be taken into account in considering the sufficiency of the challenged causes of action. * * *

The threshold choice of law question requires no extended discussion. In point of fact, the parties have agreed—at least for purposes of this motion—that the sufficiency of these allegations is to be determined under the law of the District of Columbia. The District is the jurisdiction in which most of the acts are alleged to have occurred, and it was there, too, that the plaintiff lived and suffered the impact of those acts. It is, in short, the place which has the most significant relationship with the subject matter of the tort charged. * * *

Turning, then, to the law of the District of Columbia, it appears that its courts have not only recognized a common-law action for invasion of privacy but have broadened the scope of that tort beyond its traditional limits. * * * Thus, in the most recent of its cases on the subject, Pearson v. Dodd (133 U.S.App.D.C. 279, 410 F.2d 701, *supra*), the Federal Court of Appeals for the District of Columbia declared (p. 704):

> "We approve the extension of the tort of invasion of privacy to instances of *intrusion,* whether by physical trespass or not, into spheres from which an ordinary man in a plaintiff's position could reasonably expect that the particular defendant should be excluded." (Italics supplied.)

It is this form of invasion of privacy—initially termed "intrusion" by Dean Prosser in 1960 (Privacy, 48 Cal.L.Rev. 383, 389 et seq.; Torts, § 112)—on which the two challenged causes of action are predicated.

Quite obviously, some intrusions into one's private sphere are inevitable concomitants of life in an industrial and densely populated society, which the law does not seek to proscribe even if it were possible to do so. "The law does not provide a remedy for every annoyance that occurs in everyday life." (Kelley v. Post Publishing Co., 327 Mass. 275, 278, 98 N.E.2d 286, 287 (1951)). However, the District of Columbia courts have held that the law should and does protect against certain types of intrusive conduct, and we must, therefore, determine whether the plaintiff's allegations are actionable as violations of the right to privacy under the law of that jurisdiction. To do so, we must, in effect, predict what the judges of that jurisdiction's highest court would hold if this case were presented to them. * * * In other words, what would the Court of Appeals for the District of Columbia say is the character of the "privacy" sought to be protected? More specifically, would that court accord an individual a right, as the plaintiff before us insists, to be protected against any interference whatsoever with his personal seclusion and solitude? Or would it adopt a more restrictive view of the right, as the appellant urges, merely protecting the individual from intrusion into "something secret," from snooping and prying into his private affairs?

The classic article by Warren and Brandeis (The Right to Privacy, 4 Harv.L.Rev. 193)—to which the court in the *Pearson* case referred as the source of the District's common-law action for invasion of privacy (410 F.2d, at p. 703)—was premised, to a large extent, on principles originally developed in the field of copyright law. The authors thus based their thesis on a right granted by the common law to "each individual * * * of determining, ordinarily, to what extent his thoughts, sentiments and emotions shall be communicated to others" (4 Harv.L.Rev., at p. 198). Their principal concern appeared to be not with a broad "right to be let alone" (Cooley, Torts [2d ed.], p. 29) but, rather, with the right to protect oneself from having one's private affairs known to others and to keep secret or intimate facts about oneself from the prying eyes or ears of others.

In recognizing the existence of a common-law cause of action for invasion of privacy in the District of Columbia, the Court of Appeals has expressly adopted this latter formulation of the nature of the right. * * * And, in *Pearson,* where the court extended the tort of invasion of privacy to instances of "intrusion," it again indicated, contrary to the plaintiff's submission, that the interest protected was one's right to keep knowledge about oneself from exposure to others, the right to prevent *"the obtaining of the information* by improperly intrusive means" * * *. In other jurisdictions, too, the cases which have recognized a remedy for invasion of privacy founded upon intrusive conduct have generally involved the gathering of private facts or information through improper means. * * *

It should be emphasized that the mere gathering of information about a particular individual does not give rise to a cause of action under this theory. Privacy is invaded only if the information sought is of a confidential nature and the defendant's conduct was unreasonably intrusive. Just as a common-law copyright is lost when material is published, so, too, there can be no invasion of privacy where the information sought is open to public view or has been voluntarily revealed to others. * * * In order to sustain a cause of action for invasion of privacy, therefore, the plaintiff must show that the appellant's conduct was truly "intrusive" and that it was designed to elicit information which would not be available through normal inquiry or observation.

The majority of the Appellate Division in the present case stated that *all of "[t]he activities complained of"* in the first two counts constituted actionable invasions of privacy under the law of the District of Columbia * * *. We do not agree with that sweeping determination. At most, only two of the activities charged to the appellant are, in our view, actionable as invasions of privacy under the law of the District of Columbia * * *. However, since the first two counts include allegations which are sufficient to state a cause of action, we could—as the concurring opinion notes—merely affirm the order before us without further elaboration. To do so, though, would be a disservice both to the judge who will be called upon to try this case and to the litigants themselves. In other words, we deem it desirable, nay essential, that we go further and, for the guidance of the trial court and counsel, indicate the extent to which the plaintiff is entitled to rely on the various allegations in support of his privacy claim.

In following such a course, we are prompted not only by a desire to avoid any misconceptions that might stem from the opinion below but also by recognition of the fact that we are dealing with a new and developing area of the law. Indeed, we would fail to meet our responsibility if we were to withhold determination—particularly since the parties have fully briefed and argued the points involved—and thereby thrust upon the trial judge the initial burden of appraising the impact of a doctrine still in the process of growth and of predicting its reach in another jurisdiction.

Turning, then, to the particular acts charged in the complaint, we cannot find any basis for a claim of invasion of privacy, under District of Columbia law, in the allegations that the appellant, through its agents or employees, interviewed many persons who knew the plaintiff, asking questions about him and casting aspersions on his character. Although those inquiries may have uncovered information of a personal nature, it is difficult to see how they may be said to have invaded the plaintiff's privacy. Information about the plaintiff which was already known to others could hardly be regarded as private to the plaintiff. Presumably, the plaintiff had previously revealed the information to such other persons, and he would necessarily assume the risk that a friend or acquaintance in whom he had confided might breach the confidence. If, as alleged, the questions tended to disparage the plaintiff's character, his remedy would seem to be by way of an action for defamation, not for breach of his right to privacy. * * *

Nor can we find any actionable invasion of privacy in the allegations that the appellant caused the plaintiff to be accosted by girls with illicit proposals, or that it was responsible for the making of a large number of threatening and harassing telephone calls to the plaintiff's home at odd hours. Neither of these activities, howsoever offensive and disturbing, involved intrusion for the purpose of gathering information of a private and confidential nature.

As already indicated, it is manifestly neither practical nor desirable for the law to provide a remedy against any and all activity which an individual might find annoying. On the other hand, where severe mental pain or anguish is inflicted through a deliberate and malicious campaign of harassment or intimidation, a remedy is available in the form of an action for the intentional infliction of emotional distress—the theory underlying the plaintiff's third cause of action. But the elements of such an action are decidedly different from those governing the tort of invasion of privacy, and just as we have carefully guarded against the use of the prima facie tort doctrine to circumvent the limitations relating to other established tort remedies * * *, we should be wary of any attempt to rely on the tort of invasion of privacy as a means of avoiding the more stringent pleading and proof requirements for an action for infliction of emotional distress. * * *

Apart, however, from the foregoing allegations which we find inadequate to spell out a cause of action for invasion of privacy under District of Columbia law, the complaint contains allegations concerning other activities by the appellant or its agents which do satisfy the requirements for such a cause of action. The one which most clearly meets those requirements is the charge that the appellant and its codefendants engaged in unauthorized wiretapping and eavesdropping by mechanical and electronic means. The Court of Appeals in the *Pearson* case expressly recognized that such conduct constitutes a tortious intrusion and other jurisdictions have reached a similar conclusion. * * * In point of fact, the appellant does not dispute this, acknowledging that, to the extent the two challenged counts charge it with wiretapping and eavesdropping, an actionable invasion of privacy has been stated.

There are additional allegations that the appellant hired people to shadow the plaintiff and keep him under surveillance. In particular, he claims that, on one occasion, one of its agents followed him into a bank, getting sufficiently close to him to see the denomination of the bills he was withdrawing from his account. From what we have already said, it is manifest that the mere observation of the plaintiff in a public place does not amount to an invasion of his privacy. But, under certain circumstances, surveillance may be so "overzealous" as to render it actionable. * * * Whether or not the surveillance in the present case falls into this latter category will depend on the nature of the proof. A person does not automatically make public everything he does merely by being in a public place, and the mere fact that Nader was in a bank did not give anyone the right to try to discover the amount of money he was withdrawing. On the other hand, if the plaintiff acted in such a way as to reveal that fact to any casual observer, then, it may not be said that the appellant intruded into his private sphere. In any event, though, it is enough for present purposes to say that the surveillance allegation is not insufficient as a matter of law.

Since, then, the first two causes of action do contain allegations which are adequate to state a cause of action for invasion of privacy under District of Columbia law, the courts below properly denied the appellant's motion to dismiss those causes of action. It is settled that, so long as a pleading sets forth allegations which suffice to spell out a claim for relief, it is not subject to dismissal by reason of the inclusion therein of additional nonactionable allegations. * * *

We would but add that the allegations concerning the interviewing of third persons, the accosting by girls and the annoying and threatening telephone calls, though insufficient to support a cause of action for invasion of privacy, are pertinent to the plaintiff's third cause of action—in which those allegations are reiterated—charging the intentional infliction of emotional distress. However, as already noted, it will be necessary for the plaintiff to meet the additional requirements prescribed by the law of the District of Columbia for the maintenance of a cause of action under that theory.

The order appealed from should be affirmed, with costs, and the question certified answered in the affirmative.

BREITEL, JUDGE (concurring in result).

There is no doubt that the first and second causes of action are sufficient in alleging an invasion of privacy under what appears to be the applicable law in the District of Columbia * * *. This should be the end of this court's proper concern with the pleadings, the only matter before the court being a motion to dismiss specified causes of action for insufficiency.

Thus it is not proper, it is submitted, for the court directly or indirectly to analyze particular allegations in the pleadings, once the causes of action are found sufficient, in order to determine whether they would alternatively sustain one cause of action or another, or whether evidence offered in support of the allegations is relevant only as to one rather than to another cause of action. Particularly, it is inappropriate to decide that several of the allegations as they now appear are referable only to the more restricted tort of intentional infliction of mental distress rather than to the common-law right of privacy upon which the first and second causes of action depend. The third cause of action is quite restricted. Thus many of the quite offensive acts charged will not be actionable unless plaintiff succeeds in the very difficult, if not impossible, task of showing that defendants' activities were designed, actually or virtually, to make plaintiff unhappy and not to uncover disgraceful information about him. The real issue in the volatile and developing law of privacy is whether a private person is entitled to be free of certain grave offensive intrusions unsupported by palpable social or economic excuse or justification.

True, scholars, in trying to define the elusive concept of the right of privacy, have, as of the present, subdivided the common law right into separate classifications, most significantly distinguishing between unreasonable intrusion and unreasonable publicity. * * * This does not mean, however, that the classifications are either frozen or exhausted, or that several of the classifications may not overlap.

Concretely applied to this case, it is suggested, for example, that it is premature to hold that the attempted entrapment of plaintiff in a public place by seemingly promiscuous ladies is no invasion of any of the categories of the right to privacy and is restricted to a much more limited cause of action for intentional infliction of mental distress. Moreover, it does not strain credulity or imagination to conceive of the systematic "public" surveillance of another as being the implementation of a plan to intrude on the privacy of another. Although acts performed in "public", especially if taken singly or in small numbers, may not be confidential, at least arguably a right to privacy may nevertheless be invaded through extensive or exhaustive monitoring and cataloguing of acts normally disconnected and anonymous.

* * *

It is not unimportant that plaintiff contends that a giant corporation had allegedly sought by surreptitious and unusual methods to silence an unusually effective critic. If there was such a plan, and only a trial would show that, it is unduly restrictive of the future trial to allocate the evidence beforehand based only on a pleader's specification of overt acts on the bold assumption that they are not connected causally or do not bear on intent and motive.

* * *

There is still further difficulty. In this State thus far there has been no recognition of a common law right of privacy, but only that which derives from a statute of rather limited scope * * *. Consequently, this court must undertake the hazardous task of applying what is at present the quite different law of the District of Columbia. True, this may be the court's burden eventually, if the case were to return to it for review after trial, especially if the plaintiff were to prevail upon such a trial. However, there is no occasion to advance, now, into a complicated, subtle and still-changing field of law of another jurisdiction, solely to determine before trial the relevancy and allocability among pleaded causes of action or projected but not yet offered items of evidence. * * *

* * *

NOTES

1. In Pearson v. Dodd, 410 F.2d 701 (D.C.Cir.1969), *cert. denied* 395 U.S. 947, 89 S.Ct. 2021, 23 L.Ed.2d 465, the defendants, Drew Pearson and Jack Anderson, had published a number of nationally syndicated newspaper

columns concerning then Senator Thomas Dodd's relations with lobbyists representing "foreign interests." The defendants obtained their information from xerox copies of materials in Dodd's files. The xerox copies had been made by former employees of Dodd with the assistance of some of Dodd's current employees. In his complaint, Dodd charged the defendants with invasion of privacy and conversion. Although Dodd charged Pearson and Anderson with aiding and abetting in the unauthorized removal of documents from Dodd's files, it was undisputed that it could only be shown that Pearson and Anderson received the documents knowing that the documents were removed and copied without Dodd's permission. The district court denied Dodd's request for summary judgment on the privacy count but granted Dodd's request for summary judgment on the conversion count. The court of appeals reversed on the conversion count because "appellants committed no conversion of the physical documents." Recognizing that the ambit of legal protection had expanded, principally through the avenue of "common-law copyright," the court of appeals nevertheless held that no relief was possible here because "[i]nsofar as we can tell, none of it [i.e. the information] amounts to literary property, to scientific invention, or to secret plans formulated * * * for the conduct of commerce. Nor does it appear to be information held in any way for sale * * * analogous to the fresh news copy produced by a wire service." On the privacy count, after the discussion that was relied on in *Nader,* the court of appeals affirmed the district court's refusal to grant partial summary judgment in favor of Dodd. Obtaining information from an intruder was not itself intrusion.

2. One of the leading cases on intrusion is Hamberger v. Eastman, 106 N.H. 107, 206 A.2d 239, 11 A.L.R.3d 1288 (1964), a case mentioned several times in omitted portions of the majority's and Breitel, J.'s opinions in *Nader.* There was no trespass in *Hamberger* because the defendant landlord had placed the listening device in the wall of the bedroom before the plaintiffs took possession of the premises. Other cases holding that there may be liability for intrusion include Roach v. Harper, 143 W.Va. 869, 105 S.E.2d 564 (1958) (factually very similar to *Hamberger*) and Fowler v. Southern Bell Telephone & Telegraph Co., 343 F.2d 150 (5th Cir.1965) (tapping of a telephone; issue to be determined on remand was whether defendants acted at behest of federal agents acting within outer limits of their authority). Should the obtaining by an unauthorized person of someone's social security number from a credit reporting agency be actionable? *See* Remsburg v. Docusearch, Inc., 149 N.H. 148, 816 A.2d 1001 (2003). What about the renting, by a credit card company, of the names and purchasing patterns of its cardholders? *See* Dwyer v. American Express Co., 273 Ill.App.3d 742, 210 Ill.Dec. 375, 652 N.E.2d 1351 (1995).

A frequently cited case is Dietemann v. Time, Inc., 449 F.2d 245 (9th Cir.1971). In that case, two reporters for *Life* magazine, pursuant to an arrangement with the Los Angeles District Attorney's office, visited the plaintiff for the purpose of obtaining, in the words of the trial judge, "facts and pictures" concerning the plaintiff's "practice of healing with clay, minerals, and herbs" and with "some equipment which could at best be described as gadgets, not equipment which had anything to do with the practice of medicine." Using the name of a friend of the plaintiff's as a ruse to obtain entrance to his home, the male reporter surreptitiously photographed the plaintiff while he was examining the female reporter. One of these photographs was subsequently published in *Life* as part of a story entitled "Crackdown on Quackery." The plaintiff's conversation with the female reporter was transmitted by a radio transmitter hidden in her purse to an automobile occupied by another employee of *Life* magazine and employees of the District Attorney's office and the State Department of Public Health. A few days later the plaintiff was arrested on a charge of practicing medicine without a license. A *Life* photographer was present and took many photographs. The district court ruled that the surreptitious photographing of the plaintiff in his home on the first occasion was an actionable invasion of the plaintiff's privacy and the court of appeals affirmed. As to the second set of photographs the defendant claimed they were obtained by consent. The plaintiff, however, claimed he had permitted the photographing because he thought the *Life* photographer was a police officer. There was no ruling on this issue. How would you decide it? The whole subject is discussed in Note, *Press Passes and Trespasses: Newsgathering on Private Property*, 84 Colum.L.Rev. 1298 (1984). An interesting more recent case is Shulman v. Group W Productions, Inc., 18 Cal.4th 200, 955 P.2d 469, 74 Cal.Rptr.2d 843 (1998). The Supreme Court has now made it clear that law enforcement authorities who, without the property-holder's consent, permit members of the press to accompany them when they intrude on his property to make an arrest or execute some legal process are liable for violating the property-holder's constitutional rights. *See* Wilson v. Layne, 526 U.S. 603, 119 S.Ct. 1692, 143 L.Ed.2d 818 (1999). Because the Court held that the law had not been clearly established prior to its decision, the officers who were the defendants in the *Wilson* case were entitled to raise the qualified immunity defense that will be discussed in Chapter Eleven, at p. 790, *infra*.

It should be noted that, when the basis of the action is intrusion, the tort is complete when the intrusion is committed. It is not necessary for the plaintiff to show that any information gathered as a result of the intrusion has been published to third parties, although such factors will obviously be relevant on the issue of damages.

A case worth noting is Howell v. New York Post, Inc., 81 N.Y.2d 115, 612 N.E.2d 699, 596 N.Y.S.2d 350 (1993). The plaintiff was a patient in a private psychiatric hospital who alleged that it was essential for her recovery to keep her hospitalization secret from all but her immediate family. One of the other patients was a woman who was the subject of intense public interest because she had been the live-in lover of a man accused of killing his six-year old daughter. A photographer employed by the defendant trespassed on the grounds of the hospital and, using a telephoto lens, took a photograph of this other woman who happened to be walking on the hospital grounds in the company of the plaintiff. The hospital's medical director phoned the defendant to ask it not to publish any photographs of the patients but the defendant published the photograph as part of a news story about the "live-in lover." The plaintiff brought an action based on invasion of privacy, intentional and negligent infliction of emotional distress, trespass, and harassment. The Supreme Court (in New York the trial court) dismissed all causes of action other than those based on intentional infliction of emotional distress. On the cross appeals, the appellate division also dismissed the causes of action for intentional infliction of emotional distress. The case was then appealed to the New York Court of Appeals solely on the issue of the propriety of the dismissal of the privacy and intentional infliction of emotional distress counts. That court affirmed. It noted that the limited right of privacy recognized by statute in New York only covered the use of a photograph for advertising or trade purposes and held that the use of the photograph as part of a newsworthy article was not covered by the statute, nor did such "privileged conduct" constitute, in the case before the court, the tortious intentional infliction of emotional distress. The court noted that it had taken an extremely restrictive approach to intentional infliction of emotional distress claims and that all such claims that had thus far reached the court had been found not to be based on conduct that was sufficiently outrageous.

3. Since 1968, under Title III of the Omnibus Crime Control and Safe Streets Act (18 U.S.C. §§ 2510–20), it is now a federal crime for anyone not a party to the communication to intercept any wire or oral communication or to disclose or use its contents. A civil action for damages is granted to those whose conversations have been intercepted, disclosed, or used. (18 U.S.C. § 2520). The statutory protection extends to all "oral communication uttered by a person exhibiting an expectation that such communication is not subject to interception under circumstances justifying such expectation." 18 U.S.C. § 2510(2). To avoid the constitutional problems presented when a conversation is carried on loudly where it may be overheard without the use of any electronic or mechanical listening or amplifying devices, it has been held that there cannot be a justifiable expectation that a conversation will not be recorded by third parties unless the conversation was conducted under circumstances justifying an actual expectation of privacy. *See* United States v. Carroll, 337 F.Supp. 1260 (D.D.C.1971).

What about civil liability independent of any applicable criminal statute? In Sanders v. American Broadcasting Cos., 20 Cal.4th 907, 85 Cal.Rptr.2d 909, 978 P.2d 67 (1999) one of the defendant's investigative reporters had, without disclosing her affiliation, secured employment at the firm which employed the plaintiff. The reporter covertly videotaped conversations of her new co-workers. One of them brought an action and succeeded. The Court was prepared to recognize that an employee did not have a complete expectation of privacy in the circumstances, because his conversations could be overheard by his co-workers, but the employee could reasonably expect that his conversations would not be overheard by strangers.

4. About one third of the states have so-called "Peeping Tom" criminal statutes. At least one-half of these statutes require a trespass upon the victim's property before a criminal charge may be brought. As such they present relatively little constitutional difficulty. The remaining statutes permit a construction that does not require a physical intrusion unto the land of another. *See, e.g.,* LSA–Rev.Stat. § 14:284; Mich.Comp.Laws Ann. § 750.167 ("window peeper"); N.C.Gen.Stat. § 14–202 (secretly peeping "into any room occupied by a female person"). There is very little case authority on these statutes and that which does exist largely involves trespassing "peepers." *See, e.g.,* State v. Bivins, 262 N.C. 93, 136 S.E.2d 250 (1964); Butts v. State, 97 Ga.App. 465, 103 S.E.2d 450 (1958).

Despite the oft-cited Katz v. United States, 389 U.S. 347, 88 S.Ct. 507, 19 L.Ed.2d 576 (1967), which allowed the defendant to object to the use of conversations recorded by a listening device placed in a phone booth, on the ground that the defendant had a reasonable expectation of privacy, it has been held that a criminal defendant cannot object to non-trespassory visual surveillance conducted with the aid of strong binoculars. *See* Commonwealth v. Hernley, 216 Pa.Super. 177, 263 A.2d 904 (1970), *cert. denied,* 401 U.S. 914, 91 S.Ct. 886, 27 L.Ed.2d 813 (1971); State v. Manly, 85 Wash.2d 120, 530 P.2d 306 (1975). *But see* United States v. Kim, 415 F.Supp. 1252 (D.Hawai'i 1976). It seems doubtful that a civil action for intrusion could constitutionally lie for any non-trespassory visual observations, particularly if the observations are made from a public place or the defendant's own premises, even if binoculars are used, and almost inconceivable that an action could lie if the observations are made with the naked eye. *Cf.* Texas v. Brown, 460 U.S. 730, 103 S.Ct. 1535, 75 L.Ed.2d 502 (1983) (discussing ambit of "plain view" doctrine); United States v. Lee, 274 U.S. 559, 47 S.Ct. 746, 71 L.Ed. 1202 (1927) (examination of a boat by searchlight is not an unconstitutional search and declared to be similar to use of a "field glass"). With regard to observation by overflying aircraft, *see* Florida v. Riley, 488 U.S. 445, 109 S.Ct. 693, 102 L.Ed.2d 835 (1989). Cal. Civ. Code § 1708.8 (b) provides that a person "is liable for constructive invasion of privacy" if he "attempts to capture, in a manner that is offensive to a reasonable person, any type of visual image, sound recording, or other physical impression of the plaintiff engaging in a personal or familial activity under circumstances in which the plaintiff had a reasonable expectation of privacy . . . regardless of whether there is a physical trespass, if the image, sound recording, or other physical impression could not have been achieved without a trespass unless the visual or auditory enhancing device was used." More recent important criminal cases that would be germane in deciding what is a "reasonable expectation of privacy" include Kyllo v. United States, 533 U.S. 27, 121 S.Ct. 2038, 150 L.Ed.2d 94 (2001) (use of thermal imaging device to discern what was going on in a house by tracking heat patterns) and United States v. Jones, 565 U.S. ___, 132 S.Ct. 945, 181 L.Ed.2d 911 (2012) (police attached a G.P.S. device to the defendant's vehicle to track his movements over the course of a month). In both cases the Court ruled that the use of such devices without a warrant was unconstitutional.

5. On the subject of surveillance by governmental authorities during the Vietnamese war, see G. Christie, *Government Surveillance and Individual Freedom: A Proposed Statutory Response to* Laird v. Tatum *and the Broader Problem of Government Surveillance of the Individual,* 47 N.Y.U.L.Rev. 871 (1972). The issue of course continues to surface. *See* J. Rubenfeld, *The End of Privacy,* 61 Stan. L.Rev. 101 (2008).

6. As has already been noted, this chapter has been organized around the late Dean Prosser's division of the law of privacy into four separate categories, which do not pretend to exhaust the total range of activities which might be said to affect human privacy. The purpose of Prosser's analytical suggestion was to make what would otherwise be a subject of infinite scope sufficiently manageable. There will always, however, be some centrifugal tendencies. Whether these tendencies are desirable is another question. For

example, in Phillips v. Smalley Maintenance Services, Inc., 435 So.2d 705 (Ala.1983), a woman employee had been discharged for refusing to have oral and other forms of sex with her supervisor. She was awarded damages in federal court for wrongful discharge under Title VII, 42 U.S.C. § 2000e *et seq.*, of the Civil Rights Act of 1964. The plaintiff had joined to her federal claim a claim for damages for invasion of privacy. The United States Court of Appeals for the Eleventh Circuit certified to the Alabama Supreme Court the question whether Alabama law recognized a cause of action for invasion of privacy on the assumed facts of the case. The Alabama court held that it did despite the fact that there was nothing resembling a trespassory invasion of physical space or a public disclosure of embarrassing information about the plaintiff. Rather, the court held that an action would lie for invasion of the plaintiff's "emotional sanctum". Subsequently, the "intrusion" into one's emotional space was found not to be sufficiently "offensive" to be actionable in Logan v. Sears, Roebuck & Co., 466 So.2d 121 (Ala.1985), where a customer overheard a Sears employee, who had phoned him to inquire whether he had paid his bill, tell someone "[t]his guy is as queer as a three-dollar bill." The customer was in fact a homosexual. A lack of sufficient offensiveness was also found in McIsaac v. WZEW–FM Corp., 495 So.2d 649 (Ala.1986), which involved a less extreme form of sexual harassment than *Phillips*. On the other hand, in K–Mart Corp. v. Weston, 530 So.2d 736 (Ala.1988), a jury verdict for the plaintiff was upheld where a customer was told, in front of other customers, that he could not use a check-cashing card because his wife had given K–Mart a bad check. The check had been returned due to a bank error. The action had also been brought, in the alternative, on a defamation theory. Finally, in Hogin v. Cottingham, 533 So.2d 525 (Ala.1988), an attorney who, on behalf of a client, tried unsuccessfully to identify a young girl, whose picture was published in a Birmingham newspaper, by making inquiries at the girl's school was sued by the girl's irate parents "for invasion of privacy, outrageous conduct and intentional or reckless infliction of emotional distress". The trial court awarded the defendant summary judgment. The Supreme Court of Alabama reversed (5–3) on the privacy claim, affirmed the awarding of summary judgement on the other claims, and remanded the case for trial. What constitutes the invasion of privacy? Wanting to know the girl's name and address or trying, unsuccessfully, to secure that information from her school? Does the case raise constitutional questions?

We have already seen, Chapter Seven, *supra*, other instances in which actions for what normally would be considered the intentional infliction of severe emotional distress by outrageous conduct are sometimes framed, in the alternative, as actions for invasion of privacy. *See e.g.*, Guinn v. Church of Christ of Collinsville, 775 P.2d 766 (Okl.1989), discussed at p. 463, *supra*. That case is perhaps a less extreme expansion of the scope of an invasion of privacy action because it arguably involved the publication of embarrassing information that had been secured under a promise of confidentiality. Should labelling the complaint as one for the invasion of privacy make it easier for the plaintiff to recover than if the action were labelled as one for the intentional infliction of severe emotional distress? Should it be possible by doing so to avoid the strictures of Hustler Magazine, Inc. v. Falwell, 485 U.S. 46, 108 S.Ct. 876, 99 L.Ed.2d 41 (1988), presented at p. 465, *supra?* Do all these centrifugal tendencies confirm once again that the concept of privacy is capable of encompassing a good part of both morality and law?

GALELLA v. ONASSIS

United States Court of Appeals, Second Circuit, 1973.
487 F.2d 986.

Before SMITH, HAYS and TIMBERS, CIRCUIT JUDGES.

J. JOSEPH SMITH, CIRCUIT JUDGE:

Donald Galella, a free-lance photographer, appeals from a summary judgment dismissing his complaint against three Secret Service agents for false arrest, malicious prosecution, and interference with trade (S.D.N.Y., Edward C. McLean, Judge), the dismissal after trial of his identical complaint against Jacqueline Onassis and the grant of injunctive relief to defendant Onassis on her counterclaim and to the intervenor, the United States, on its intervening complaint and a third judgment retaxing transcript costs to plaintiff (S.D.N.Y., Irving Ben Cooper, Judge), 353 F.Supp. 196 (1972). In addition to numerous alleged procedural errors, Galella raises the First Amendment as an absolute shield against liability to any sanctions. The judgments dismissing the complaints are affirmed; the grant of injunctive relief is affirmed as herein modified. Taxation of costs against the plaintiff is affirmed in part, reversed in part.

Galella is a free-lance photographer specializing in the making and sale of photographs of well-known persons. Defendant Onassis is the widow of the late President, John F. Kennedy, mother of the two Kennedy children, John and Caroline, and is the wife of Aristotle Onassis, widely known shipping figure and reputed multimillionaire. John Walsh, James Kalafatis and John Connelly are U.S. Secret Service agents assigned to the duty of protecting the Kennedy children under 18 U.S.C. § 3056, which provides for protection of the children of deceased presidents up to the age of 16.

Galella fancies himself as a "paparazzo" (literally a kind of annoying insect, perhaps roughly equivalent to the English "gadfly.") Paparazzi make themselves as visible to the public and obnoxious to their photographic subjects as possible to aid in the advertisement and wide sale of their works.[2]

Some examples of Galella's conduct brought out at trial are illustrative. Galella took pictures of John Kennedy riding his bicycle in Central Park across the way from his home. He jumped out into the boy's path, causing the agents concern for John's safety. The agents' reaction and interrogation of Galella led to Galella's arrest and his action against the agents; Galella on other occasions interrupted Caroline at tennis, and invaded the children's private schools. At one time he came uncomfortably close in a power boat to Mrs. Onassis swimming. He often jumped and

---

2. The newspapers report a recent incident in which one Marlon Brando, annoyed by Galella, punched Galella, breaking Galella's jaw and infecting Brando's hand.

postured around while taking pictures of her party notably at a theater opening but also on numerous other occasions. He followed a practice of bribing apartment house, restaurant and nightclub doormen as well as romancing a family servant to keep him advised of the movements of the family.

After detention and arrest following complaint by the Secret Service agents protecting Mrs. Onassis' son and his acquittal in the state court, Galella filed suit in state court against the agents and Mrs. Onassis. Galella claimed that under orders from Mrs. Onassis, the three agents had falsely arrested and maliciously prosecuted him, and that this incident in addition to several others described in the complaint constituted an unlawful interference with his trade.

Mrs. Onassis answered denying any role in the arrest or any part in the claimed interference with his attempts to photograph her, and counterclaimed for damages and injunctive relief, charging that Galella had invaded her privacy, assaulted and battered her, intentionally inflicted emotional distress and engaged in a campaign of harassment.

The action was removed under 28 U.S.C. § 1442(a) to the United States District Court. On a motion for summary judgment, Galella's claim against the Secret Service agents was dismissed, the court finding that the agents were acting within the scope of their authority and thus were immune from prosecution. At the same time, the government intervened requesting injunctive relief from the activities of Galella which obstructed the Secret Service's ability to protect Mrs. Onassis' children. Galella's motion to remand the case to state court, just prior to trial, was denied.

Certain incidents of photographic coverage by Galella, subsequent to an agreement among the parties for Galella not to so engage, resulted in the issuance of a temporary restraining order to prevent further harassment of Mrs. Onassis and the children. Galella was enjoined from "harassing, alarming, startling, tormenting, touching the person of the defendant * * * or her children * * * and from blocking their movements in the public places and thoroughfares, invading their immediate zone of privacy by means of physical movements, gestures or with photographic equipment and from performing any act reasonably calculated to place the lives and safety of the defendant * * * and her children in jeopardy." Within two months, Galella was charged with violation of the temporary restraining order; a new order was signed which required that the photographer keep 100 yards from the Onassis apartment and 50 yards from the person of the defendant and her children. Surveillance was also prohibited.

Upon notice of consolidation of the preliminary injunction hearing and trial for permanent injunction, plaintiff moved for a jury trial—nine months after answer was served, and to remand to state court. The first motion was denied as untimely, the second on grounds of judicial economy. Just prior to trial Galella deposed Mrs. Onassis. Under protective order of this court, the defendant was allowed to testify at the office of the U.S. Attorney and outside the presence of Galella.

After a six-week trial the court dismissed Galella's claim and granted relief to both the defendant and the intervenor. Galella was enjoined from (1) keeping the defendant and her children under surveillance or following any of them; (2) approaching within 100 yards of the home of defendant or her children, or within 100 yards of either child's school or within 75 yards of either child or 50 yards of defendant; (3) using the name, portrait or picture of defendant or her children for advertising; (4) attempting to communicate with defendant or her children except through her attorney.

We conclude that grant of summary judgment and dismissal of Galella's claim against the Secret Service agents was proper. Federal agents when charged with duties which require the exercise of discretion are immune from liability for actions within the scope of their authority. Ordinarily enforcement agents charged with the duty of arrest are not so immune. * * * The protective duties assigned the agents under this statute, however, require the instant exercise of judgment which should be protected. The agents saw Galella jump into the path of John Kennedy who was forced to swerve his bike dangerously as he left Central Park and was about to enter Fifth Avenue, whereupon the agents gave chase to the photographer. Galella indicated that he was a press photographer listed with the New York City Police; he and the agents went to the police station to check on the story, where one of the agents made the complaint on which the state court charges were based. Certainly it was reasonable that the agents "check out" an individual who has endangered their charge, and seek prosecution for apparent violation of state law which interferes with them in the discharge of their duties.

* * *

Discrediting all of Galella's testimony the court found the photographer guilty of harassment, intentional infliction of emotional distress, assault and battery, commercial exploitation of defendant's personality, and invasion of privacy. Fully crediting defendant's testimony, the court found no liability on Galella's claim. Evidence offered by the defense showed that Galella had on occasion intentionally physically touched Mrs. Onassis and her daughter, caused fear of physical contact in his frenzied attempts to get their pictures, followed defendant and her children too closely in an automobile, endangered the safety of the children while they were swimming, water skiing and horseback riding. Galella cannot successfully challenge the court's finding of tortious conduct.[11]

Finding that Galella had "insinuated himself into the very fabric of Mrs. Onassis' life * * * " the court framed its relief in part on the need to prevent further invasion of the defendant's privacy. Whether or not this accords with present New York law, there is no doubt that it is sustainable under New York's proscription of harassment.

---

11. Harassment is a criminal violation under New York Penal Law § 240.25 (McKinney's Consol.Laws, c. 40, 1967) when with intent to harass a person follows another in a public place, inflicts physical contact or engages in any annoying conduct without legitimate cause. Galella was found to have engaged in this proscribed conduct. Conduct sufficient to invoke criminal liability for harassment may be the basis for private action. * * *

Of course legitimate countervailing social needs may warrant some intrusion despite an individual's reasonable expectation of privacy and freedom from harassment. However the interference allowed may be no greater than that necessary to protect the overriding public interest. Mrs. Onassis was properly found to be a public figure and thus subject to news coverage. * * * Nonetheless, Galella's action went far beyond the reasonable bounds of news gathering. When weighed against the *de minimis* public importance of the daily activities of the defendant, Galella's constant surveillance, his obtrusive and intruding presence, was unwarranted and unreasonable. If there were any doubt in our minds, Galella's inexcusable conduct toward defendant's minor children would resolve it.

Galella does not seriously dispute the court's finding of tortious conduct. Rather, he sets up the First Amendment as a wall of immunity protecting newsmen from any liability for their conduct while gathering news. There is no such scope to the First Amendment right. Crimes and torts committed in news gathering are not protected. * * *

* * *

Injunctive relief is appropriate. Galella has stated his intention to continue his coverage of defendant so long as she is newsworthy, and his continued harassment even while the temporary restraining orders were in effect indicate that no voluntary change in his technique can be expected. New York courts have found similar conduct sufficient to support a claim for injunctive relief. Flamm v. Van Nierop, 56 Misc.2d 1059, 291 N.Y.S.2d 189 (1968).[20]

The injunction, however, is broader than is required to protect the defendant. Relief must be tailored to protect Mrs. Onassis from the "paparazzo" attack which distinguishes Galella's behavior from that of other photographers; it should not unnecessarily infringe on reasonable efforts to "cover" defendant. Therefore, we modify the court's order to prohibit only (1) any approach within twenty-five (25) feet of defendant or any touching of the person of the defendant Jacqueline Onassis; (2) any blocking of her movement in public places and thoroughfares; (3) any act foreseeably or reasonably calculated to place the life and safety of defendant in jeopardy; and (4) any conduct which would reasonably be foreseen to harass, alarm or frighten the defendant.

Any further restriction on Galella's taking and selling pictures of defendant for news coverage is, however, improper and unwarranted by the evidence. * * *

Likewise, we affirm the grant of injunctive relief to the government modified to prohibit any action interfering with Secret Service agents'

20. The defendant in *Flamm* was sued for intentional infliction of emotional distress. He was charged with having dashed at the plaintiff in a threatening manner in various public places with threatening gestures, grimaces, leers, distorted faces and malign looks, accompanied by ridiculous utterances and laughs, driven his automobile behind that of the plaintiff at a dangerously close distance; walked behind or beside or in front of the plaintiff on the public streets; and consistently telephoned the plaintiff at home and place of business and hung up or remained on the line in silence.

protective duties. Galella thus may be enjoined from (a) entering the children's schools or play areas; (b) engaging in action calculated or reasonably foreseen to place the children's safety or well being in jeopardy, or which would threaten or create physical injury; (c) taking any action which could reasonably be foreseen to harass, alarm, or frighten the children; and (d) from approaching within thirty (30) feet of the children.

* * *

As modified, the relief granted fully allows Galella the opportunity to photograph and report on Mrs. Onassis' public activities. Any prior restraint on news gathering is miniscule and fully supported by the findings.

* * *

TIMBERS, CIRCUIT JUDGE (concurring in part and dissenting in part):

With one exception, I concur in the judgment of the Court and in the able majority opinion of Judge Smith.

With the utmost deference to and respect for my colleagues, however, I am constrained to dissent from the judgment of the Court and the majority opinion to the extent that they modify the injunctive relief found necessary by the district court to protect Jacqueline Onassis and her children, Caroline B. and John F. Kennedy, Jr., from the continued predatory conduct of the self-proclaimed paparazzo Galella.

* * *

In the instant case, after a six week trial at which 25 witnesses testified, hundreds of exhibits were received and a 4,714 page record was compiled, Judge Cooper filed a careful, comprehensive 40 page opinion, 353 F.Supp. 194, which meticulously sets forth detailed findings of fact and conclusions of law. * * *

* * *

* * * I feel very strongly that such findings should not be set aside or drastically modified by our Court unless they are clearly erroneous; and I do not understand the majority to suggest that they are.

But here is what the majority's modification of the critical distance provisions of the injunction has done:

DISTANCES GALELLA IS REQUIRED TO MAINTAIN	AS PROVIDED IN DISTRICT COURT INJUNCTION	AS MODIFIED BY COURT OF APPEALS MAJORITY
From home of Mrs. Onassis and her children	100 yards	No restriction
From children's schools	100 yards	Restricted only from entering schools or play areas*
From Mrs. Onassis personally	50 *yards*	25 *feet* and not to touch her
From children personally	75 *yards*	30 *feet*

* As pointed out below, the majority appears further to have modified the injunction by limiting the protection of the children to the "grant of injunctive relief to the *government* modified to

In addition to modifying the distance restrictions of the injunction, the majority also has directed that Galella be prohibited from blocking Mrs. Onassis' movement in public places and thoroughfares; from any act "foreseeably or reasonably calculated" to place Mrs. Onassis' life and safety in jeopardy (and similarly with respect to her children); and from any conduct which would "reasonably be foreseen" to harass, alarm or frighten Mrs. Onassis (and similarly with respect to her children).

With deference, I believe the majority's modification of the injunction in the respects indicated above to be unwarranted and unworkable. * * *

* * *

NOTES

1. Galella was subsequently held in contempt for violating the modified injunction in 1981. Galella v. Onassis, 533 F.Supp. 1076 (S.D.N.Y.1982). In settlement of the contempt proceedings, Galella agreed to pay Mrs. Onassis $10,000 and to give up forever his legal right to take pictures of Mrs. Onassis or her two children. *See* N.Y. Times, Mar. 25, 1982, at A25, col. 1.

2. In Gill v. Hearst Publishing Co., 40 Cal.2d 224, 253 P.2d 441 (1953), a couple, who embraced at the Farmer's Market in Los Angeles, were photographed by a wandering photographer. The photograph appeared in a widely circulated magazine. The couple was denied recovery on the ground that, by acting voluntarily in public, they relinquished any right to prevent a photograph of their actions from being published in a magazine. Would a contrary decision be constitutionally sound? *See also* Gautier v. Pro–Football, Inc., 304 N.Y. 354, 107 N.E.2d 485 (1952). The unsuccessful plaintiff was performing as an animal trainer during halftime at a Redskins–Giants football game and was televised, as part of the halftime festivities, by the company telecasting the game. The *Gautier* case presents some different considerations because the plaintiff's complaint as a professional performer is not so much that he was televised but that he was not paid for being televised. *Cf.* the *Zacchini* case, *infra* p. 741. On the general subject, *see* Comment, *Privacy in Photographs: Misconception Since Inception*, 18 John Marshall L.Rev. 968 (1985).

3. In Blumenthal v. Picture Classics, 235 App.Div. 570, 257 N.Y.S. 800 (1932), *affirmed on procedural grounds* 261 N.Y. 504, 185 N.E. 713, inclusion of a six second sequence of the plaintiff selling bread and photographed through the glass window of a bakery in a documentary about New York City was held actionable. The case does not appear to have been followed.[1] Moreover, the possible suggestion in that case that motion pictures are different than print media is no longer constitutionally sustainable. *See*

---

prohibit any action interfering with Secret Service agents' protective duties." (emphasis added). The district court injunction was not so limited. It granted injunctive relief for the protection of the children as specifically prayed for *by Mrs. Onassis*. The distinction introduced by the majority * * * substantially reduces the protection provided for the children.

1. The majority's opinion in *Blumenthal* is extremely cursory. A subsequent New York lower court case has tried to explain *Blumenthal* as involving some element of fictionalization. *See* Sarat Lahiri v. Daily Mirror, 162 Misc. 776, 295 N.Y.S. 382 (1937).

Joseph Burstyn, Inc. v. Wilson, 343 U.S. 495, 72 S.Ct. 777, 96 L.Ed. 1098 (1952).

4. The New York Penal Law Provisions cited (*supra*, p. 670) in note 11 of the court's opinion in *Galella* is part of a set of statutes that has been amplified over the years and now consists of four provisions, N.Y. Penal Law §§ 240.25, 240.26, 240.30 and 240.31 (Mckinney) that cover first and second degree harassment and first and second degree aggravated harassment. Aggravated harassment in the first degree is a class E felony; aggravated harassment in the second degree is a class A misdemeanor; and harassment in the first degree is a class B misdemeanor. Second degree harassment is only a "violation." All these provisions cover a variety of conduct, some of which include physical threats. Several provisions, however, present serious constitutional problems. Harassment in the first degree (§ 240.25) includes repeatedly following a person in public places and second degree aggravated harassment (§ 240.30) includes making telephone calls with intent to harass and "no purpose of legitimate communication" and the making, with intent to harass, of any communications in a manner likely to cause annoyance or alarm. Second degree harassment (§ 240.26) includes "a course of conduct or repeatedly committed acts which alarm or seriously annoy * * * [an]other person and which serve no legitimate purpose." There is an exception for activities covered by federal labor relations laws. A provision of an earlier version of this statutory scheme that made it a violation, punishable by 15 days imprisonment, to threaten someone with physical contact or to use "abusive or obscene language" in a public place was struck down as unconstitutional in a prosecution of a woman who called a mentally retarded woman a "bitch," referred to the woman's mentally retarded son as a "dog", and who said that she "would beat the crap out of [the complainant] some day or night on the street." People v. Dietze, 75 N.Y.2d 47, 549 N.E.2d 1166, 550 N.Y.S.2d 595 (1989). Most cases involve either second degree harassment or second degree aggravated harassment. There have been few convictions under any of these statutes as the courts have insisted on extremely outrageous behavior usually with strong implications of physical threat. *But see* People v. Miguez, 147 Misc.2d 482, 556 N.Y.S.2d 231 (1990), where the court submitted to the jury the question of whether daily telephone calls over a five-month period from a woman to the man she loved constituted aggravated harassment. On the other hand, soliciting, at 3:00 a.m., three young women whom the defendant mistakenly took for prostitutes did not constitute harassment. People v. Malausky, 127 Misc.2d 84, 485 N.Y.S.2d 925 (1985). A message sent to an internet newsgroup asking the recipients to "please kill" a named police officer was held to fall within the ambit of second degree aggravated harassment. People v. Munn, 179 Misc.2d 903, 688 N.Y.S.2d 384 (1999) *See also* People v. Singh, 187 Misc.2d 465, 722 N.Y.S.2d 368 (2001). The more recent cases strongly indicate that, absent a serious threat of physical violence, verbal harassment is not punishable under these statutes. See People v. Mangano, 100 N.Y.2d 569, 796 N.E.2d 470, 764 N.Y.S.2d 379 (2003); Vives v. City of New York, 405 F.3d 115 (2d Cir. 2005). *See also* People v. Louis, 34 Misc.3d 703, 927 N.Y.S.2d 592 (2011)

An illustration of what might be the basis of a tort action for stalking or harassment is Summers v. Bailey, 55 F.3d 1564 (11th Cir.1995). In that case the plaintiff had purchased a store from the defendant. A few years later, in the midst of bankruptcy proceedings, the plaintiff, who had been operating the store with her husband, negotiated the sale of the store to a third party. The defendant did not approve of this resale. It was alleged that he appeared at the store with a large hand gun, that he would park outside the store for hours and tell the plaintiff and her customers that he wanted her out of the store, that he would follow her in his truck when she ran errands, that he sometimes parked on her property, and that he followed her as she departed from her house. The plaintiff brought her action on grounds of malicious abuse and use of process, intentional infliction of emotional distress, and invasion of privacy. The district court granted the defendant summary judgment as to all plaintiff's causes of action, but the court of appeals held that the plaintiff was entitled to go to trial on her invasion of privacy claim. Certainly there seems here to be not only some element of trespass or intrusion but also a reasonable apprehension of physical violence. A common type of case involves insurance investigators who follow the plaintiff on the public streets and observe the plaintiff while he engages in public activities. These actions are normally unsuccessful. *See* Forster v. Manchester, 410 Pa. 192, 189 A.2d 147 (1963). Figured v. Paralegal Technical Services, 231 N.J.Super. 251, 555 A.2d 663 (1989). The *Figured* case contains a good discussion of the law. In McLain v. Boise Cascade Corp., 271 Or. 549, 533 P.2d 343 (1975), the court reached the same result even though the investigators may have trespassed on the far corner of the plaintiff's land. The plaintiff was seeking worker's compensation for a back injury. Surveillance conducted in a manner that might frighten a reasonable person might, however, be actionable. *See* Pinkerton Nat'l Detective Agency, Inc. v. Stevens, 108 Ga.App. 159, 132 S.E.2d 119 (1963) and, more recently, Anderson v. Mergenhagen, 283 Ga.App. 546, 642 S.E.2d 105 (2007) In both cases the court noted that the stalking could be said to be aimed at frightening the plaintiff.

In September 1996, Congress made interstate stalking a federal crime. The statute, 18 U.S.C. § 2261A, however, required that the person stalked should be put in reasonable fear of death or serious bodily injury to himself or to a member of his immediate family. In 2006, as noted on p. 480 *supra*, the statute was amended to cover causing "substantial emotional distress" as well as using the "mail" or "any interactive internet service" to cause "substantial emotional distress." The statute, as applied to messages posted on "Twitter" and "Internet Websites," was declared unconstitutional in United States v. Cassidy, 814 F.Supp.2d 574 (D.Md.2011).

SIDIS v. F–R PUBLISHING CORP.

Circuit Court of Appeals, Second Circuit, 1940.
113 F.2d 806.

Before SWAN, CLARK, and PATTERSON, CIRCUIT JUDGES.

CLARK, CIRCUIT JUDGE.

William James Sidis was the unwilling subject of a brief biographical sketch and cartoon printed in The New Yorker weekly magazine for August 14, 1937. Further references were made to him in the issue of

December 25, 1937, and in a newspaper advertisement announcing the August 14 issue. He brought an action in the district court against the publisher, FBR Publishing Corporation. His complaint stated three "causes of action" * * * Defendant's motion to dismiss the first two "causes of action" was granted, and plaintiff has filed an appeal from the order of dismissal. * * *

William James Sidis was a famous child prodigy in 1910. His name and prowess were well known to newspaper readers of the period. At the age of eleven, he lectured to distinguished mathematicians on the subject of Four–Dimensional Bodies. When he was sixteen, he was graduated from Harvard College, amid considerable public attention. Since then, his name has appeared in the press only sporadically, and he has sought to live as unobtrusively as possible. Until the articles objected to appeared in The New Yorker, he had apparently succeeded in his endeavor to avoid the public gaze.

Among The New Yorker's features are brief biographical sketches of current and past personalities. In the latter department, which appears haphazardly under the title of "Where Are They Now?" the article on Sidis was printed with a subtitle "April Fool." The author describes his subject's early accomplishments in mathematics and the wide-spread attention he received, then recounts his general breakdown and the revulsion which Sidis thereafter felt for his former life of fame and study. The unfortunate prodigy is traced over the years that followed, through his attempts to conceal his identity, through his chosen career as an insignificant clerk who would not need to employ unusual mathematical talents, and through the bizarre ways in which his genius flowered, as in his enthusiasm for collecting streetcar transfers and in his proficiency with an adding machine. The article closes with an account of an interview with Sidis at his present lodgings, "a hall bedroom of Boston's shabby south end." The untidiness of his room, his curious laugh, his manner of speech, and other personal habits are commented upon at length, as is his present interest in the lore of the Okamakammessett Indians. The subtitle is explained by the closing sentence, quoting Sidis as saying "with a grin" that it was strange, "but, you know, I was born on April Fool's Day." Accompanying the biography is a small cartoon showing the genius of eleven years lecturing to a group of astounded professors.

It is not contended that any of the matter printed is untrue. Nor is the manner of the author unfriendly; Sidis today is described as having "a certain childlike charm." But the article is merciless in its dissection of intimate details of its subject's personal life, and this in company with elaborate accounts of Sidis' passion for privacy and the pitiable lengths to which he has gone in order to avoid public scrutiny. The work possesses great reader interest, for it is both amusing and instructive; but it may be fairly described as a ruthless exposure of a once public character, who has since sought and has now been deprived of the seclusion of private life.

The article of December 25, 1937, was a biographical sketch of another former child prodigy, in the course of which William James Sidis and the recent account of him were mentioned. The advertisement published in the New York World–Telegram of August 13, 1937, read: "Out Today. Harvard Prodigy. Biography of the man who astonished Harvard at age 11. Where are they now? by J.L. Manley. Page 22. The New Yorker."

The complaint contains a general allegation, repeated for all the claims, of publication by the defendant of The New Yorker, "a weekly magazine of wide circulation throughout the United States." Then each separate "cause" contains an allegation that the defendant publicly circulated the articles or caused them to be circulated in the particular states upon whose law that cause is assumed to be founded. Circulation of the New York World–Telegram advertisement is, however, alleged only with respect to the second "cause," for asserted violation of New York law.

1. Under the first "cause of action" we are asked to declare that this exposure transgresses upon plaintiff's right of privacy, as recognized in California, Georgia, Kansas, Kentucky, and Missouri. Each of these states except California grants to the individual a common law right, and California a constitutional right, to be let alone to a certain extent. The decisions have been carefully analyzed by the court below[3] and we need not examine them further. None of the cited rulings goes so far as to prevent a newspaper or magazine from publishing the truth about a person, however intimate, revealing, or harmful the truth may be. Nor are there any decided cases that confer such a privilege upon the press. Under the mandate of Erie R. Co. v. Tompkins, 304 U.S. 64, 58 S.Ct. 817, 82 L.Ed. 1188, 114 A.L.R. 1487, we face the unenviable duty of determining the law of five states on a broad and vital public issue which the courts of those states have not even discussed.

All comment upon the right of privacy must stem from the famous article by Warren and Brandeis on The Right of Privacy in 4 Harv.L.Rev. 193. The learned authors of that paper were convinced that some limits ought to be imposed upon the privilege of newspapers to publish truthful items of a personal nature. * * *

* * *

It must be conceded that under the strict standards suggested by these authors plaintiff's right of privacy has been invaded. Sidis today is neither politician, public administrator, nor statesman. Even if he were, some of the personal details revealed were of the sort that Warren and Brandeis believed "all men alike are entitled to keep from popular curiosity."

3. Judge Goddard's decision is reported in 34 F.Supp. 19. * * * [Ed. note] Among the cases mentioned as having been considered by Judge Goddard is Melvin v. Reid, 112 Cal.App. 285, 297 P. 91 (1931), discussed in Note 2, *infra*.

But despite eminent opinion to the contrary, we are not yet disposed to afford to all of the intimate details of private life an absolute immunity from the prying of the press. Everyone will agree that at some point the public interest in obtaining information becomes dominant over the individual's desire for privacy. Warren and Brandeis were willing to lift the veil somewhat in the case of public officers. We would go further, though we are not yet prepared to say how far. At least we would permit limited scrutiny of the "private" life of any person who has achieved, or has had thrust upon him, the questionable and indefinable status of a "public figure." * * *

William James Sidis was once a public figure. As a child prodigy, he excited both admiration and curiosity. Of him great deeds were expected. In 1910, he was a person about whom the newspapers might display a legitimate intellectual interest, in the sense meant by Warren and Brandeis, as distinguished from a trivial and unseemly curiosity. But the precise motives of the press we regard as unimportant. And even if Sidis had loathed public attention at that time, we think his uncommon achievements and personality would have made the attention permissible. Since then Sidis has cloaked himself in obscurity, but his subsequent history, containing as it did the answer to the question of whether or not he had fulfilled his early promise, was still a matter of public concern. The article in The New Yorker sketched the life of an unusual personality, and it possessed considerable popular news interest.

We express no comment on whether or not the news worthiness of the matter printed will always constitute a complete defense. Revelations may be so intimate and so unwarranted in view of the victim's position as to outrage the community's notions of decency. But when focused upon public characters, truthful comments upon dress, speech, habits, and the ordinary aspects of personality will usually not transgress this line. Regrettably or not, the misfortunes and frailties of neighbors and "public figures" are subjects of considerable interest and discussion to the rest of the population. And when such are the mores of the community, it would be unwise for a court to bar their expression in the newspapers, books, and magazines of the day.

Plaintiff in his first "cause of action" charged actual malice in the publication, and now claims that an order of dismissal was improper in the face of such an allegation. We cannot agree. If plaintiff's right of privacy was not invaded by the article, the existence of actual malice in its publication would not change that result. Unless made so by statute, a truthful and therefore non-libelous statement will not become libelous when uttered maliciously. * * * A similar rule should prevail on invasions of the right of privacy. * * *

* * *

2. The second "cause of action" charged invasion of the rights conferred on plaintiff by §§ 50 and 51 of the N.Y. Civil Rights Law. * * * The statute forbids the use of a name or picture only when employed "for

advertising purposes, or for the purposes of trade." In this context, it is clear that "for the purposes of trade" does not contemplate the publication of a newspaper, magazine, or book which imparts truthful news or other factual information to the public. Though a publisher sells a commodity, and expects to profit from the sale of his product, he is immune from the interdict of §§ 50 and 51 so long as he confines himself to the unembroidered dissemination of facts. Publishers and motion picture producers have occasionally been held to transgress the statute in New York, but in each case the factual presentation was embellished by some degree of fictionalization. * * * The New Yorker articles limit themselves to the unvarnished, unfictionalized truth.

The case as to the newspaper advertisement announcing the August 14 article is somewhat different, for it was undoubtedly inserted in the World–Telegram "for advertising purposes." But since it was to advertise the article on Sidis, and the article itself was unobjectionable, the advertisement shares the privilege enjoyed by the article. * * *

* * *

Affirmed.

NOTES

1. The Harvard Law Record, April 14, 1978, p. 1, col. 3 (Vol. 66, no. 8), reports the continued notoriety of the descendants and other surviving relatives of Helen Palsgraf.

2. Nine years before the *Sidis* case was decided, a California district court of appeal decided Melvin v. Reid, 112 Cal.App. 285, 297 P. 91 (1931) which quickly became a much cited classic case. As noted in *Sidis* (in footnote 3), it was cited but not followed by the trial court in that case. *Melvin v. Reid* involved a movie that was based on the plaintiff's early life during which she had been a prostitute and had been charged and acquitted of murder after a lengthy trial which had attracted much public attention. The movie appeared seven years after this by which time she had married and lived among people who were unaware of her past life. The gravamen of her action was that the producers of the film had used her real maiden name. The court noted the absence of any statutory or case law to support the plaintiff's claim but it found sufficient support in section 1 of article 1 of the California constitution which declared that "[a]ll men . . . have certain inalienable rights, among which are . . . pursuing and obtaining safety and happiness."

Melvin v. Reid was relied on in *Briscoe v. Reader's Digest Ass'n, Inc.,* 4 Cal.3d 529, 93 Cal.Rptr. 866, 483 P.2d 34 (1971) to sustain a complaint against a motion to dismiss concerning an article about truck hijacking which mentioned the plaintiff by name as having participated in a truck hijacking in Kentucky some eleven years previously which involved a gun battle with police and in which it turned out the truck only contained four bowling pin spotter machines. After serving his sentence the plaintiff had started a new life. He alleged that after publication of the article his daughter and new friends learned about his past life and scorned and abandoned him . . . One might note two things about the case. The article in question was a condensed reprint of an article that had already appeared in the *Chicago American Magazine*. In *Briscoe* the court, relying on Time, Inc. v. Hill, 385 U.S. 374, 87 S.Ct. 534, 17 L.Ed.2d 456 (1967) discussed in the *Cantrell* case, *supra* p. 650, held that if the trier of fact found that the "plaintiff had become a rehabilitated member of society," and that identifying the plaintiff as a former criminal would be "highly offensive and injurious to the reasonable man" the publication of that information without any independent justification, would be actionable. It is rarely noted that, upon remand for trial, the case was removed to federal court which granted the defendant's motion to dismiss on the ground that the article disclosed "no private facts" about the plaintiff. Briscoe v. Reader's Digest Ass'n, Inc., 1972 WL 7259 (C.D.Cal. 1972).

A few years later the Supreme Court of the United States began to decide a series of cases that significantly undermined the presuppositions of the California Supreme Court in *Briscoe*. These decisions are described in *The Florida Star v. B.J.F.*, the most recent of them, to which we shall shortly turn. Before doing so, another California case that was similarly removed to the federal courts is worth examining. That case, Virgil v. Time, Inc., 527 F.2d 1122 (9th Cir.1975), *cert. denied* (with Justices Brennan and Stewart dissenting), 425 U.S. 998, 96 S.Ct. 2215, 48 L.Ed.2d 823 (1976), involved a story in *Sports Illustrated* about the sport of "body surfing." The plaintiff, Virgil, was described as the most daredevil of all the body surfers. Among the details of Virgil's life revealed in the article were that he dove headfirst down a flight of stairs to impress some "chicks;" and that he would take construction jobs and "dive off billboards or drop loads on myself so that I could collect unemployment compensation so that I could surf at the Wedge." The article reported that, according to Virgil's wife, Virgil ate "spiders and other insects and things." The article noted that "[p]erhaps because most of his time was spent engaged in such activity, Virgil never learned how to read." The author of the article obtained his information from long talks with Virgil and from conversations with his wife and friends. The plaintiff admitted he talked freely with the reporter but claimed he "revoked all consent" upon learning that the article was not confined to describing his physical prowess. The plaintiff learned about the contents of the article and first made known his desire not to have references to his private life in the article during a conversation with a Time, Inc. "checker" who was trying to verify the factual correctness of the article. The district court had refused Time, Inc.'s motion for summary judgment and Time, Inc. brought an interlocutory appeal. In disposing of the case, the court of appeals concluded:

> Talking freely to a member of the press, knowing the listener to be a member of the press, is not then in itself making public. Such communication can be said to anticipate that what is said will be made public since making public is the function of the press, and accordingly such communication can be construed as consent to publicize. Thus if publicity results it can be said to have been consented to. However, if consent is withdrawn prior to the act of publicizing, the consequent publicity is without consent.

The court of appeals noted that the Supreme Court had yet to reach the broad question of whether "truthful publication may ever be subject to civil or criminal liability." Accordingly, unless the information were "newsworthy * * * the publicizing of private facts is not protected by the First Amendment." The case was therefore remanded for reconsideration in light of the views expressed by the court of appeals. On remand, the district court granted Time, Inc.'s motion for summary judgment on the grounds first that the information about Virgil was not so offensive and second that, even if it were so offensive, the facts revealed were newsworthy. Virgil v. Sports Illustrated, 424 F.Supp. 1286 (S.D.Cal.1976). What is very much worth noting is that, while the court of appeals had questioned whether the "identity of Virgil as the one to whom such facts apply is a matter of public interest," the district court held that "compelling need" was not the test for newsworthiness. Moreover, unlike *Briscoe,* there was no "serious danger that revelation of the person's identity will lead to stigmatization and possible ostracism."

If the information had been gained in the course of a confidential relationship would it matter that the information was newsworthy? In this regard it should be noted that the Supreme Court has held that the First Amendment is no bar to an action for damages for breach of a promise of confidentiality, even if the information revealed is newsworthy. Cohen v. Cowles Media Co., 501 U.S. 663, 111 S.Ct. 2513, 115 L.Ed.2d 586 (1991). The question of when confidential information contained in medical records may be revealed because of pressing countervailing considerations is a complex one. *See e.g.* Doe v. City of New York, 15 F.3d 264 (2d Cir.1994) (revelation of plaintiff's infection with HIV); W. v. Egdell, [1990] Ch. 359, 2 W.L.R. 471, 1 A11 E.R. 835 (C.A.) (Mass killer applying for release from mental institution objecting to revelation of report of examining psychiatrist). New York now has a statutory prohibition against disclosure of possible HIV infection by public employees. *See* N.Y. Civil Right L. § 50–b, reprinted at the beginning of this chapter at p. 647, *supra*. In a suit in the federal courts by a prisoner as in *Doe*, even if the disclosure was improper, there can now be no recovery for "mental or emotional injury" without a showing of physical injury, as a result of 42 U.S.C. § 1997e(e), discussed in Chapter Eleven, at p. 781, *infra*.

THE FLORIDA STAR v. B.J.F.

Supreme Court of the United States, 1989.
491 U.S. 524, 109 S.Ct. 2603, 105 L.Ed.2d 443.

MARSHALL, J., delivered the opinion of the Court, in which BRENNAN, BLACKMUN, STEVENS, and KENNEDY, JJ,. joined. SCALIA, J., filed an opinion concurring in part and concurring in the judgment. WHITE, J., filed a dissenting opinion, in which REHNQUIST, C.J., and O'CONNOR, J. joined

Florida Stat. § 794.03 (1987) makes it unlawful to "print, publish, or broadcast . . . in any instrument of mass communication" the name of the victim of a sexual offense. Pursuant to this statute, appellant The Florida Star was found civilly liable for publishing the name of a rape victim which it had obtained from a publicly released police report. The issue presented here is whether this result comports with the First Amendment. We hold that it does not.

I

The Florida Star is a weekly newspaper which serves the community of Jacksonville, Florida, and which has an average circulation of approximately 18,000 copies. A regular feature of the newspaper is its "Police Reports" section. That section, typically two to three pages in length, contains brief articles describing local criminal incidents under police investigation.

On October 20, 1983, appellee B.J.F.[1] reported to the Duval County, Florida, Sheriff's Department (Department) that she had been robbed and sexually assaulted by an unknown assailant. The Department prepared a report on the incident which identified B.J.F. by her full name. The Department then placed the report in its pressroom. The Department does not restrict access either to the pressroom or to the reports made available therein.

A Florida Star reporter-trainee sent to the pressroom copied the police report verbatim, including B.J.F.'s full name, on a blank duplicate of the Department's forms. A Florida Star reporter then prepared a one-paragraph article about the crime, derived entirely from the trainee's copy of the police report. The article included B.J.F.'s full name. It appeared in the "Robberies" subsection of the "Police Reports" section on October 29, 1983, one of 54 police blotter stories in that day's edition. The article read:

> "[B.J.F.] reported on Thursday, October 20, she was crossing Brentwood Park, which is in the 500 block of Golfair Boulevard, enroute to her bus stop, when an unknown black man ran up behind the lady and placed a knife to her neck and told her not to yell. The suspect then undressed the lady and had sexual intercourse with her before fleeing the scene with her 60 cents, Timex watch and gold necklace. Patrol efforts have been suspended concerning this incident because of a lack of evidence."

In printing B.J.F.'s full name, The Florida Star violated its internal policy of not publishing the names of sexual offense victims.

On September 26, 1984, B.J.F. filed suit in the Circuit Court of Duval County against the Department and The Florida Star, alleging that these parties negligently violated § 794.03. * * * Before trial, the Department settled with B.J.F. for $2,500. The Florida Star moved to dismiss, claiming, *inter alia,* that imposing civil sanctions on the newspaper pursuant to § 794.03 violated the First Amendment. The trial judge rejected the motion. * * *

At the ensuing daylong trial, B.J.F. testified that she had suffered emotional distress from the publication of her name. She stated that she had heard about the article from fellow workers and acquaintances; that

---

1. In filing this lawsuit, appellee used her full name in the caption of the case. On appeal, the Florida District Court of Appeal *sua sponte* revised the caption, stating that it would refer to the appellee by her initials, "in order to preserve [her] privacy interests." * * * Respecting those interests, we, too, refer to appellee by her initials, both in the caption and in our discussion (Ed. Note. The footnotes that have been retained have been renumbered.).

her mother had received several threatening phone calls from a man who stated that he would rape B.J.F. again; and that these events had forced B.J.F. to change her phone number and residence, to seek police protection, and to obtain mental health counseling. In defense, The Florida Star put forth evidence indicating that the newspaper had learned B.J.F.'s name from the incident report released by the Department, and that the newspaper's violation of its internal rule against publishing the names of sexual offense victims was inadvertent.

At the close of B.J.F.'s case, and again at the close of its defense, The Florida Star moved for a directed verdict. On both occasions, the trial judge denied these motions. He ruled from the bench that § 794.03 was constitutional because it reflected a proper balance between the First Amendment and privacy rights, as it applied only to a narrow set of "rather sensitive . . . criminal offenses." * * * At the close of the newspaper's defense, the judge granted B.J.F.'s motion for a directed verdict on the issue of negligence, finding the newspaper *per se* negligent based upon its violation of § 794.03. * * * This ruling left the jury to consider only the questions of causation and damages. The judge instructed the jury that it could award B.J.F. punitive damages if it found that the newspaper had "acted with reckless indifference to the rights of others." * * * The jury awarded B.J.F. $75,000 in compensatory damages and $25,000 in punitive damages. Against the actual damages award, the judge set off B.J.F.'s settlement with the Department.

The First District Court of Appeal affirmed in a three-paragraph *per curiam* opinion. 499 So.2d 883 (1986). In the paragraph devoted to The Florida Star's First Amendment claim, the court stated that the directed verdict for B.J.F. had been properly entered because, under § 794.03, a rape victim's name is "of a private nature and not to be published as a matter of law." * * *. The Supreme Court of Florida denied discretionary review.

The Florida Star appealed to this Court. We noted probable jurisdiction. * * *

II

The tension between the right which the First Amendment accords to a free press, on the one hand, and the protections which various statutes and common-law doctrines accord to personal privacy against the publication of truthful information, on the other, is a subject we have addressed several times in recent years. Our decisions in cases involving government attempts to sanction the accurate dissemination of information as invasive of privacy, have not, however, exhaustively considered this conflict. On the contrary, although our decisions have without exception upheld the press' right to publish, we have emphasized each time that we were resolving this conflict only as it arose in a discrete factual context.[2]

2. The somewhat uncharted state of the law in this area thus contrasts markedly with the well-mapped area of defamatory falsehoods, where a long line of decisions has produced relatively

The parties to this case frame their contentions in light of a trilogy of cases which have presented, in different contexts, the conflict between truthful reporting and state-protected privacy interests. In *Cox Broadcasting Corp. v. Cohn,* 420 U.S. 469, 95 S.Ct. 1029, 43 L.Ed.2d 328 (1975), we found unconstitutional a civil damages award entered against a television station for broadcasting the name of a rape-murder victim which the station had obtained from courthouse records. In *Oklahoma Publishing Co. v. Oklahoma County District Court,* 430 U.S. 308, 97 S.Ct. 1045, 51 L.Ed.2d 355 (1977), we found unconstitutional a state court's pretrial order enjoining the media from publishing the name or photograph of an 11–year–old boy in connection with a juvenile proceeding involving that child which reporters had attended. Finally, in *Smith v. Daily Mail Publishing Co.,* 443 U.S. 97, 99 S.Ct. 2667, 61 L.Ed.2d 399 (1979), we found unconstitutional the indictment of two newspapers for violating a state statute forbidding newspapers to publish, without written approval of the juvenile court, the name of any youth charged as a juvenile offender. The papers had learned about a shooting by monitoring a police band radio frequency and had obtained the name of the alleged juvenile assailant from witnesses, the police, and a local prosecutor.

Appellant takes the position that this case is indistinguishable from *Cox Broadcasting.* * * * Alternatively, it urges that our decisions in the above trilogy, and in other cases in which we have held that the right of the press to publish truth overcame asserted interests other than personal privacy, can be distilled to yield a broader First Amendment principle that the press may never be punished, civilly or criminally, for publishing the truth. * * * Appellee counters that the privacy trilogy is inapposite, because in each case the private information already appeared on a "public record," * * * and because the privacy interests at stake were far less profound than in the present case. * * * In the alternative, appellee urges that *Cox Broadcasting* be overruled and replaced with a categorical rule that publication of the name of a rape victim never enjoys constitutional protection. * * *

We conclude that imposing damages on appellant for publishing B.J.F.'s name violates the First Amendment, although not for either of the reasons appellant urges. Despite the strong resemblance this case bears to *Cox Broadcasting,* that case cannot fairly be read as controlling here. The name of the rape victim in that case was obtained from courthouse records that were open to public inspection, a fact which Justice WHITE's opinion for the Court repeatedly noted. * * * Significantly, one of the reasons we gave in *Cox Broadcasting* for invalidating the challenged damages award was the important role the press plays in subjecting trials to public scrutiny and thereby helping guarantee their fairness.[3] * * * That role is

detailed legal standards governing the multifarious situations in which individuals aggrieved by the dissemination of damaging untruths seek redress. * * *

3. We also recognized that privacy interests fade once information already appears on the public record, 420 U.S., at 494–495, 95 S.Ct., at 1045–1046, and that making public records generally available to the media while allowing their publication to be punished if offensive would

not directly compromised where, as here, the information in question comes from a police report prepared and disseminated at a time at which not only had no adversarial criminal proceedings begun, but no suspect had been identified.

Nor need we accept appellant's invitation to hold broadly that truthful publication may never be punished consistent with the First Amendment. Our cases have carefully eschewed reaching this ultimate question, mindful that the future may bring scenarios which prudence counsels our not resolving anticipatorily. See, *e.g., Near v. Minnesota ex rel. Olson,* 283 U.S. 697, 716, 51 S.Ct. 625, 75 L.Ed. 1357 (1931) (hypothesizing "publication of the sailing dates of transports or the number and location of troops"); see also *Garrison v. Louisiana,* 379 U.S. 64, 72, n. 8, 74, 85 S.Ct. 209, 215, n. 8, 216, 13 L.Ed.2d 125 (1964) (endorsing absolute defense of truth "where discussion of public affairs is concerned," but leaving unsettled the constitutional implications of truthfulness "in the discrete area of purely private libels"); * * * Indeed, in *Cox Broadcasting,* we pointedly refused to answer even the less sweeping question "whether truthful publications may ever be subjected to civil or criminal liability" for invading "an area of privacy" defined by the State. * * * Respecting the fact that press freedom and privacy rights are both "plainly rooted in the traditions and significant concerns of our society," we instead focused on the less sweeping issue "whether the State may impose sanctions on the accurate publication of the name of a rape victim obtained from public records-more specifically, from judicial records which are maintained in connection with a public prosecution and which themselves are open to public inspection." * * * We continue to believe that the sensitivity and significance of the interests presented in clashes between First Amendment and privacy rights counsel relying on limited principles that sweep no more broadly than the appropriate context of the instant case.

In our view, this case is appropriately analyzed with reference to such a limited First Amendment principle. It is the one, in fact, which we articulated in *Daily Mail* in our synthesis of prior cases involving attempts to punish truthful publication: "[I]f a newspaper lawfully obtains truthful information about a matter of public significance then state officials may not constitutionally punish publication of the information, absent a need to further a state interest of the highest order." * * * According the press the ample protection provided by that principle is supported by at least three separate considerations, in addition to, of course, the overarching " 'public interest, secured by the Constitution, in the dissemination of truth.' " * * * The cases on which the *Daily Mail* synthesis relied demonstrate these considerations.

First, because the *Daily Mail* formulation only protects the publication of information which a newspaper has "lawfully obtain[ed]," * * * the government retains ample means of safeguarding significant interests

invite "self-censorship and very likely lead to the suppression of many items that ... should be made available to the public." *Id.,* at 496, 95 S.Ct., at 1046–47 upon which publication may impinge, including protecting a rape victim's anonymity. To the extent sensitive information rests in private hands, the government may under some circumstances forbid its nonconsensual acquisition, thereby bringing outside of the *Daily Mail* principle the publication of any information so acquired. To the extent sensitive information is in the government's custody, it has even greater power to forestall or mitigate the injury caused by its release. The government may classify certain information, establish and enforce procedures ensuring its redacted release, and extend a damages remedy against the government or its officials where the government's mishandling of sensitive information leads to its dissemination. Where information is entrusted to the government, a less drastic means than punishing truthful publication almost always exists for guarding against the dissemination of private facts. See, *e.g., Landmark Communications, supra,* * * * ("[M]uch of the risk [from disclosure of sensitive information regarding judicial disciplinary proceedings] can be eliminated through careful internal procedures to protect the confidentiality of Commission proceedings"); * * * (noting trial judge's failure to avail himself of the opportunity, provided by a state statute, to close juvenile hearing to the public, including members of the press, who later broadcast juvenile defendant's name); * * * ("If there are privacy interests to be protected in judicial proceedings, the States must respond by means which avoid public documentation or other exposure of private information").[4]

A second consideration undergirding the *Daily Mail* principle is the fact that punishing the press for its dissemination of information which is already publicly available is relatively unlikely to advance the interests in the service of which the State seeks to act. It is not, of course, always the case that information lawfully acquired by the press is known, or accessible, to others. But where the government has made certain information publicly available, it is highly anomalous to sanction persons other than the source of its release. We noted this anomaly in *Cox Broadcasting:* "By placing the information in the public domain on official court records, the State must be presumed to have concluded that the public interest was thereby being served." * * * The *Daily Mail* formulation reflects the fact that it is a limited set of cases indeed where, despite the accessibility of the public to certain information, a meaningful public interest is served by restricting its further release by other entities, like the press. As *Daily Mail* observed in its summary of *Oklahoma Publishing,* "once the truthful information was 'publicly revealed' or 'in the public domain' the court could not constitutionally restrain its dissemination." 443 U.S., at 103, 99 S.Ct., at 2671.

---

4. The *Daily Mail* principle does not settle the issue whether, in cases where information has been acquired *unlawfully* by a newspaper or by a source, government may ever punish not only the unlawful acquisition, but the ensuing publication as well. This issue was raised but not definitively resolved in *New York Times Co. v. United States,* 403 U.S. 713, 91 S.Ct. 2140, 29 L.Ed.2d 822 (1971), and reserved in *Landmark Communications,* 435 U.S., at 837, 98 S.Ct., at 1540–41. We have no occasion to address it here.

A third and final consideration is the "timidity and self-censorship" which may result from allowing the media to be punished for publishing certain truthful information. * * * *Cox Broadcasting* noted this concern with overdeterrence in the context of information made public through official court records, but the fear of excessive media self-suppression is applicable as well to other information released, without qualification, by the government. A contrary rule, depriving protection to those who rely on the government's implied representations of the lawfulness of dissemination, would force upon the media the onerous obligation of sifting through government press releases, reports, and pronouncements to prune out material arguably unlawful for publication. This situation could inhere even where the newspaper's sole object was to reproduce, with no substantial change, the government's rendition of the event in question.

Applied to the instant case, the *Daily Mail* principle clearly commands reversal. The first inquiry is whether the newspaper "lawfully obtain[ed] truthful information about a matter of public significance." * * * It is undisputed that the news article describing the assault on B.J.F. was accurate. In addition, appellant lawfully obtained B.J.F.'s name. Appellee's argument to the contrary is based on the fact that under Florida law, police reports which reveal the identity of the victim of a sexual offense are not among the matters of "public record" which the public, by law, is entitled to inspect. * * * But the fact that state officials are not required to disclose such reports does not make it unlawful for a newspaper to receive them when furnished by the government. Nor does the fact that the Department apparently failed to fulfill its obligation under § 794.03 not to "cause or allow to be ... published" the name of a sexual offense victim make the newspaper's ensuing receipt of this information unlawful. Even assuming the Constitution permitted a State to proscribe *receipt* of information, Florida has not taken this step. It is, clear, furthermore, that the news article concerned "a matter of public significance," * * * in the sense in which the *Daily Mail* synthesis of prior cases used that term. That is, the article generally, as opposed to the specific identity contained within it, involved a matter of paramount public import: the commission, and investigation, of a violent crime which had been reported to authorities. * * *

The second inquiry is whether imposing liability on appellant pursuant to § 794.03 serves "a need to further a state interest of the highest order." * * * Appellee argues that a rule punishing publication furthers three closely related interests: the privacy of victims of sexual offenses; the physical safety of such victims, who may be targeted for retaliation if their names become known to their assailants; and the goal of encouraging victims of such crimes to report these offenses without fear of exposure. * * *

At a time in which we are daily reminded of the tragic reality of rape, it is undeniable that these are highly significant interests, a fact underscored by the Florida Legislature's explicit attempt to protect these interests by enacting a criminal statute prohibiting much dissemination of victim identities. We accordingly do not rule out the possibility that, in a proper case, imposing civil sanctions for publication of the name of a rape victim might be so overwhelmingly necessary to advance these interests as to satisfy the *Daily Mail* standard. For three independent reasons, however, imposing liability for publication under the circumstances of this case is too precipitous a means of advancing these interests to convince us that there is a "need" within the meaning of the *Daily Mail* formulation for Florida to take this extreme step. Cf. *Landmark Communications, supra* (invalidating penalty on publication despite State's expressed interest in nondissemination, reflected in statute prohibiting unauthorized divulging of names of judges under investigation).

First is the manner in which appellant obtained the identifying information in question. As we have noted, where the government itself provides information to the media, it is most appropriate to assume that the government had, but failed to utilize, far more limited means of guarding against dissemination than the extreme step of punishing truthful speech. That assumption is richly borne out in this case. B.J.F.'s identity would never have come to light were it not for the erroneous, if inadvertent, inclusion by the Department of her full name in an incident report made available in a pressroom open to the public. Florida's policy against disclosure of rape victims' identities, reflected in § 794.03, was undercut by the Department's failure to abide by this policy. Where, as here, the government has failed to police itself in disseminating information, it is clear under *Cox Broadcasting, Oklahoma Publishing,* and *Landmark Communications* that the imposition of damages against the press for its subsequent publication can hardly be said to be a narrowly tailored means of safeguarding anonymity. * * * Once the government has placed such information in the public domain, "reliance must rest upon the judgment of those who decide what to publish or broadcast," *Cox Broadcasting,* 420 U.S., at 496, 95 S.Ct., at 1047, and hopes for restitution must rest upon the willingness of the government to compensate victims for their loss of privacy and to protect them from the other consequences of its mishandling of the information which these victims provided in confidence.

That appellant gained access to the information in question through a government news release makes it especially likely that, if liability were to be imposed, self-censorship would result. Reliance on a news release is a paradigmatically "routine newspaper reporting techniqu[e]." * * * The government's issuance of such a release, without qualification, can only convey to recipients that the government considered dissemination lawful, and indeed expected the recipients to disseminate the information further. Had appellant merely reproduced the news release prepared and released by the Department, imposing civil damages would surely violate the First Amendment. The fact that appellant converted the police report into a news story by adding the linguistic connecting tissue necessary to transform the report's facts into full sentences cannot change this result.

A second problem with Florida's imposition of liability for publication is the broad sweep of the negligence *per se* standard applied under the civil cause of action implied from § 794.03. Unlike claims based on the common law tort of invasion of privacy, see Restatement (Second) of Torts § 652D (1977), civil actions based on § 794.03 require no case-by-case findings that the disclosure of a fact about a person's private life was one that a reasonable person would find highly offensive. On the contrary, under the *per se* theory of negligence adopted by the courts below, liability follows automatically from publication. This is so regardless of whether the identity of the victim is already known throughout the community; whether the victim has voluntarily called public attention to the offense; or whether the identity of the victim has otherwise become a reasonable subject of public concern-because, perhaps, questions have arisen whether the victim fabricated an assault by a particular person. Nor is there a scienter requirement of any kind under § 794.03, engendering the perverse result that truthful publications challenged pursuant to this cause of action are less protected by the First Amendment than even the least protected defamatory falsehoods: those involving purely private figures, where liability is evaluated under a standard, usually applied by a jury, of ordinary negligence. * * * We have previously noted the impermissibility of categorical prohibitions upon media access where important First Amendment interests are at stake. * * * More individualized adjudication is no less indispensable where the State, seeking to safeguard the anonymity of crime victims, sets its face against publication of their names.

Third and finally, the facial underinclusiveness of § 794.03 raises serious doubts about whether Florida is, in fact, serving, with this statute, the significant interests which appellee invokes in support of affirmance. Section 794.03 prohibits the publication of identifying information only if this information appears in an "instrument of mass communication," a term the statute does not define. Section 794.03 does not prohibit the spread by other means of the identities of victims of sexual offenses. An individual who maliciously spreads word of the identity of a rape victim is thus not covered, despite the fact that the communication of such information to persons who live near, or work with, the victim may have consequences as devastating as the exposure of her name to large numbers of strangers. See Tr. of Oral Arg. 49–50 (appellee acknowledges that § 794.03 would not apply to "the backyard gossip who tells 50 people that don't have to know").

When a State attempts the extraordinary measure of punishing truthful publication in the name of privacy, it must demonstrate its commitment to advancing this interest by applying its prohibition evenhandedly, to the smalltime disseminator as well as the media giant.

III

Our holding today is limited. We do not hold that truthful publication is automatically constitutionally protected, or that there is no zone of personal privacy within which the State may protect the individual from intrusion by the press, or even that a State may never punish publication of the name of a victim of a sexual offense. We hold only that where a newspaper publishes truthful information which it has lawfully obtained, punishment may lawfully be imposed, if at all, only when narrowly tailored to a state interest of the highest order, and that no such interest is satisfactorily served by imposing liability under § 794.03 to appellant under the facts of this case. The decision below is therefore

Reversed.

JUSTICE SCALIA, concurring in part and concurring in the judgment.

I think it sufficient to decide this case to rely upon the third ground set forth in the Court's opinion, *ante,* * * * that a law cannot be regarded as protecting an interest "of the highest order," * * * and thus as justifying a restriction upon truthful speech, when it leaves appreciable damage to that supposedly vital interest unprohibited. In the present case, I would anticipate that the rape victim's discomfort at the dissemination of news of her misfortune among friends and acquaintances would be at least as great as her discomfort at its publication by the media to people to whom she is only a name. Yet the law in question does not prohibit the former in either oral or written form. Nor is it at all clear, as I think it must be to validate this statute, that Florida's general privacy law would prohibit such gossip. Nor, finally, is it credible that the interest meant to be served by the statute is the protection of the victim against a rapist still at large—an interest that arguably would extend only to mass publication. There would be little reason to limit a statute with that objective to rape alone; or to extend it to all rapes, whether or not the felon has been apprehended and confined. In any case, the instructions here did not require the jury to find that the rapist was at large.

This law has every appearance of a prohibition that society is prepared to impose upon the press but not upon itself. Such a prohibition does not protect an interest "of the highest order." For that reason, I agree that the judgment of the court below must be reversed.

JUSTICE WHITE, with whom THE CHIEF JUSTICE and JUSTICE O'CONNOR join, dissenting.

"Short of homicide, [rape] is the 'ultimate violation of self.' " *Coker v. Georgia,* 433 U.S. 584, 597, 97 S.Ct. 2861, 2869, 53 L.Ed.2d 982 (1977) (opinion of WHITE, J.). For B.J.F., however, the violation she suffered at a rapist's knifepoint marked only the beginning of her ordeal. A week later, while her assailant was still at large, an account of this assault—identifying by name B.J.F. as the victim—was published by The Florida Star. As a result, B.J.F. received harassing phone calls, required mental health counseling, was forced to move from her home, and was even threatened with being raped again. Yet today, the Court holds that a jury award of $75,000 to compensate B.J.F. for the harm she suffered due to the Star's negligence is at odds with the First Amendment. I do not accept this result.

The Court reaches its conclusion based on an analysis of three of our precedents and a concern with three particular aspects of the judgment against appellant. I consider each of these points in turn, and then consider some of the larger issues implicated by today's decision.

But even taking the Court's concerns in the abstract, they miss the mark. Permitting liability under a negligence *per se* theory does not mean that defendants will be held liable without a showing of negligence, but rather, that the standard of care has been set by the legislature, instead of the courts. The Court says that negligence *per se* permits a plaintiff to hold a defendant liable without a showing that the disclosure was "of a fact about a person's private life . . . that a reasonable person would find highly offensive." *Ibid.* But the point here is that the legislature—reflecting popular sentiment—has determined that disclosure of the fact that a person was raped is categorically a revelation that reasonable people find offensive. And as for the Court's suggestion that the Florida courts' theory permits liability without regard for whether the victim's identity is already known, or whether she herself has made it known—these are facts that would surely enter into the calculation of damages in such a case. In any event, none of these mitigating factors was present here; whatever the force of these arguments generally, they do not justify the Court's ruling against B.J.F. in this case.

Third, the Court faults the Florida criminal statute for being underinclusive: § 794.03 covers disclosure of rape victims' names in " 'instrument[s] of mass communication,' " but not other means of distribution, the Court observes. *Ante,* at 2612–2613. But our cases which have struck down laws that limit or burden the press due to their underinclusiveness have involved situations where a legislature has singled out one segment of the news media or press for adverse treatment, see, *e.g., Daily Mail* (restricting newspapers and not radio or television), or singled out the press for adverse treatment when compared to other similarly situated enterprises, see, *e.g., Minneapolis Star & Tribune Co. v. Minnesota Comm'r of Revenue,* 460 U.S. 575, 578, 103 S.Ct. 1365, 1368, 75 L.Ed.2d 295 (1983). Here, the Florida law evenhandedly covers all "instrument[s] of mass communication" no matter their form, media, content, nature, or purpose. It excludes neighborhood gossips, cf. *ante,* at 2612–2613, because presumably the Florida Legislature has determined that neighborhood gossips do not pose the danger and intrusion to rape victims that "instrument[s] of mass communication" do. Simply put: Florida wanted to prevent the widespread distribution of rape victims' names, and therefore enacted a statute tailored almost as precisely as possible to achieving that end.

Moreover, the Court's "underinclusiveness" analysis itself is "underinclusive." After all, the lawsuit against the Star which is at issue here is not an action for violating the statute which the Court deems underinclusive, but is, more accurately, for the negligent publication of appellee's name. See App. to Juris. Statement A10. The scheme which the Court should review, then, is not only § 794.03 (which, as noted above, merely provided the standard of care in this litigation), but rather, the whole of Florida privacy tort law. As to the latter, Florida does recognize a tort of publication of private facts. Thus, it is quite possible that the neighborhood gossip whom the Court so fears being left scot free to spread news of a rape victim's identity would be subjected to the same (or similar) liability regime under which appellant was taxed. The Court's myopic focus on § 794.03 ignores the probability that Florida law is more comprehensive than the Court gives it credit for being.

Consequently, neither the State's "dissemination" of B.J.F.'s name, nor the standard of liability imposed here, nor the underinclusiveness of Florida tort law requires setting aside the verdict for B.J.F. And as noted above, such a result is not compelled by our cases. I turn, therefore, to the more general principles at issue here to see if they recommend the Court's result.

III

At issue in this case is whether there is any information about people, which—though true—may not be published in the press. By holding that only "a state interest of the highest order" permits the State to penalize the publication of truthful information, and by holding that protecting a rape victim's right to privacy is not among those state interests of the highest order, the Court accepts appellant's invitation, see Tr. of Oral Arg. 10–11, to obliterate one of the most noteworthy legal inventions of the 20th century: the tort of the publication of private facts. W. Prosser, J. Wade, & V. Schwartz, Torts 951–952 (8th ed. 1988). Even if the Court's opinion does not say as much today, such obliteration will follow inevitably from the Court's conclusion here. If the First Amendment prohibits wholly private persons (such as B.J.F.) from recovering for the publication of the fact that she was raped, I doubt that there remain any "private facts" which persons may assume will not be published in the newspapers or broadcast on television.[5]

* * *

I do not suggest that the Court's decision today is a radical departure from a previously charted course. The Court's ruling has been foreshadowed. In *Time, Inc. v. Hill,* * * * n. 7, 87 S.Ct. 534, 539–540, n. 7, 17 L.Ed.2d 456 (1967), we observed that—after a brief period early in this century where Brandeis' view was ascendant—the trend in "modern" jurisprudence has been to eclipse an individual's right to maintain private any truthful information that the press wished to publish. More recently, in *Cox Broadcasting,* we acknowledged the possibility that the First Amendment may prevent a State from ever subjecting the publication of truthful but private information to civil liability. Today, we hit the bottom of the slippery slope.

5. The consequences of the Court's ruling—that a State cannot prevent the publication of private facts about its citizens which the State inadvertently discloses—is particularly troubling when one considers the extensive powers of the State to collect information. * * *

I would find a place to draw the line higher on the hillside: a spot high enough to protect B.J.F.'s desire for privacy and peace-of-mind in the wake of a horrible personal tragedy. There is no public interest in publishing the names, addresses, and phone numbers of persons who are the victims of crime—and no public interest in immunizing the press from liability in the rare cases where a State's efforts to protect a victim's privacy have failed. Consequently, I respectfully dissent.[6]

NOTES

1. Justice Marshall ended his opinion for the Court with two statement He declared that the Court was not holding that "truthful publication is automatically protected, or that there is no zone of personal privacy within which the State may protect the individual from intrusion by the press, or even that a state may never publish the name of the victim of a sexual offense." He also said that "[w]e hold only that where a newspaper publishes truthful information which it has lawfully obtained, punishment may lawfully be imposed, *if at all*, only when tailored to a state interest of the highest order." (Emphasis supplied.) The only examples of "highest state interest" that he supplied involved national security affairs. Why is the Court unwilling to declare that, in litigation involving only private people, the publication of truthful information which has not been obtained unlawfully or under some recognized obligation of confidentiality is under all circumstances privileged, at least with regard to an action for invasion of privacy? The possible national security concerns, to which he alluded, that might warrant the punishment of those who publish truthful information, are not present in a private action for invasion of privacy. It is worth noting in this regard that, in Butterworth v. Smith, 494 U.S. 624, 110 S.Ct. 1376, 108 L.Ed.2d 572 (1990), a unanimous Court struck down as unconstitutional a Florida statute that prohibited a person who had testified before a grand jury from ever disclosing his testimony except in response to the order of a court. The Court held that, after the term of the grand jury had expired, the witness was free to make whatever truthful statement he wished of information he had acquired on his own.

2. Suppose a person comes into possession of material that he knows has been illegally obtained. If that person neither instigated nor took any part in the illegal obtaining of the material, say a taped telephone conversation, may he publish it to the world? In Bartnicki v. Vopper, 532 U.S. 514, 121 S.Ct. 1753, 149 L.Ed.2d 787 (2001), the Court, in a six-to-three decision, said that he could because the communications, involving compromising conversations between union officials engaged in contentious negotiations with a local school board concerned a newsworthy event. The Court was prepared to accept that the defendants knew or should have known that that the intentional publishing of illegally intercepted communications was itself illegal. The provision making it illegal for a person to disclose the contents of communications that he knows were illegally obtained by others is 18 U.S.C. § 2511(1)(d). Whether

6. The Court does not address the distinct constitutional questions raised by the award of punitive damages in this case.* * *. Consequently, I do not do so either. That award is more troublesome than the compensatory award discussed above. Cf. Note, Punitive Damages and Libel Law, 98 Harv.L.Rev. 847 (1985).

that provision is constitutional is another matter. The *Pentagon Papers* case—New York Times v. United States, 403 U.S. 713, 91 S.Ct. 2140, 29 L.Ed.2d 822 (1971)—only concerned whether the press could be prevented from publishing classified material that it knew had been improperly obtained by others. As noted in a footnote to Justice Marshall's opinion for the Court in *The Florida Star*, *see* p. 686, *supra*, the Court did not answer that question in *Pentagon Papers* nor did it do so in *The Florida Star*.

3. Given how infrequently the Supreme Court decides privacy cases of the type that we have been examining and what many people consider the increasing ideological division among the members of the Court, it is hard to say with certainty how the law in this emotionally charged area will evolve. As we shall see in the next case, the California Supreme Court has been reluctant to make more than the constitutionally required minimum in its traditional more generous protection of privacy interests.

GATES v. DISCOVERY COMMUNICATIONS, INC.

Supreme Court of California, 2004.
34 Cal.4th 679, 21 Cal.Rptr.3d 663, 101 P.3d 552.

WERDEGAR, J.

We must decide whether the producers and presenters of a television documentary program may be held liable in tort for publishing therein information they gathered from public official court records concerning a person who many years previously served a prison term for a felony conviction but who has since lived an obscure, lawful life and become a respected member of the community. The Court of Appeal concluded defendants may not be held liable under such circumstances. We affirm the judgment of the Court of Appeal.

Background

Plaintiff served a prison sentence of three years (with time off for good behavior) that was imposed after he was convicted upon pleading guilty in 1992 to being an accessory after the fact to a murder for hire that occurred in 1988. The victim was an automobile salesman who was shot and killed by hired "hitmen" at the door of his Southern California home. A prominent automobile dealer was convicted of masterminding the murder in order to deter a class action lawsuit the victim had filed against an automobile dealership owned by the dealer's parents. Plaintiff, who was employed as the automobile dealers assistant manager at the time of the murder, originally was charged as a coconspirator, but the charges were later reduced. Defendants are television production and transmission companies that aired an account of the crime in 2001—more than a dozen years after the crime occurred.

After defendants' documentary was broadcast, plaintiff filed this action, pleading causes of action for defamation and invasion of privacy. With respect to his defamation claim, plaintiff alleged that since he was released from prison he has a led an obscure, productive, lawful life. He further alleged that defendants' program falsely portrayed him as being involved in a conspiracy to murder, falsely depicted him as participating in a telephone wiretap to develop evidence, and falsely suggested he was a self-confessed murderer. With respect to his invasion of privacy cause of action, plaintiff alleged he was damaged by "the revelation that Plaintiff pleaded guilty to being an accessory after the fact to a murder for hire plot and the airing by Defendants of Plaintiff's photograph."

Defendants demurred to both causes of action, contending plaintiff was a limited-purpose public figure and could not demonstrate that defendants had made any defamatory statements with malice. Defendants also filed a special motion to strike the invasion of privacy claim under Code of Civil Procedure section 425.16 (section 425.16), the anti-SLAPP statute.

Stating that "the gist or sting of [defendants'] report was accurate," the trial court sustained without leave to amend defendants' demurrer to the defamation cause of action. On the ground that "there is no authority which precludes civil liability for truthful publication of private facts regardless of whether the information is newsworthy," however, the court overruled the demurrer to the invasion of privacy cause of action. The court also denied defendants' anti-SLAPP motion as to the invasion of privacy cause of action, concluding that plaintiff had demonstrated a likelihood of prevailing thereon. * * *

Defendants appealed from the order denying the anti-SLAPP motion. (§ 425.16, subd. (j).) The Court of Appeal reversed, relying primarily on Cox Broadcasting Corporation v. Cohn (1975) 420 U.S. 469, 95 S.Ct. 1029, 43 L.Ed.2d 328, wherein the United States Supreme Court held that the State of Georgia could not constitutionally sanction a television station for publishing the identity of a deceased 17–year–old rape victim whose name the station's reporter had obtained by examining public court records. (Id. at pp. 494–495, 95 S.Ct. 1029.) The Court of Appeal held that, as a matter of law, plaintiff could not prevail on his invasion of privacy cause of action because defendants' disclosures were of truthful information contained in the public official records of a judicial proceeding and were, accordingly, protected under the First Amendment to the United States Constitution, as construed by the high court in Cox. We granted review.

Discussion

The question presented is whether the trial court erred in concluding that plaintiff is likely to prevail on his cause of action for invasion of privacy. Plaintiff bases the cause of action on Briscoe v. Reader's Digest Association, Inc. (1971) 4 Cal.3d 529, 93 Cal.Rptr. 866, 483 P.2d 34 (Briscoe), wherein we held that actionable invasion of privacy may occur through the reckless, offensive, injurious publication of true, but not newsworthy, information concerning the criminal past of a rehabilitated convict. * * * Defendants argue that Briscoe has been overruled by subsequent high court decisions, at least with respect to information a publisher obtains from public (i.e., not sealed) official records of judicial proceedings. For the following reasons, we agree with defendants.

Briscoe involved an action for invasion of privacy brought against a magazine publisher. The dispute arose when the defendant published an article disclosing that the plaintiff had committed a truck hijacking 11 years previously. The plaintiff alleged that his friends and his 11–year–old daughter, after learning for the first time from the defendant's article these true but embarrassing facts about his past life, had scorned and abandoned him. Conceding the truth of the disclosures, the plaintiff nevertheless contended that because the offense had occurred many years earlier and he had subsequently led a lawful, obscure life and achieved a place in respectable society, the use of his name in the defendant's article was not "newsworthy" and constituted therefore a tortious invasion of his privacy. * * *

In a unanimous opinion authored by Justice Peters, we held the plaintiff had stated a cause of action. * * * In reaching that conclusion, we traced the concept of the legal right to privacy from the seminal law review article by Warren and Brandeis, The Right to Privacy (1890) 4 Harv. L.Rev. 193. We noted that acceptance of the privacy right "has grown with the increasing capacity of the mass media and electronic devices with their capacity to destroy an individual's anonymity, intrude upon his most intimate activities, and expose his most personal characteristics to public gaze." * * * Accordingly, we reasoned, a truthful publication is protected only if it is newsworthy and does not reveal facts so offensive as to shock the community's notion of decency. (Id. at p. 541, 93 Cal.Rptr. 866, 483 P.2d 34.) We also discussed factors for determining whether an incident is newsworthy: " '[1] the social value of the facts published, [2] the depth of the article's intrusion into ostensibly private affairs, and [3] the extent to which the party voluntarily acceded to a position of public notoriety.' " (Ibid.)

Applying the foregoing, we concluded in Briscoe that "a jury could reasonably find that plaintiff's identity as a former hijacker was not newsworthy" * * *, that "revealing one's criminal past for all to see is grossly offensive to most people in America" * * *, and that the plaintiff had not voluntarily consented to the publicity accorded him. Therefore, we held, the plaintiff had stated a valid cause of action. * * *

* * * Pursuant to Briscoe, * * *, plaintiff contends a jury could reasonably find that the fact he long ago pled guilty to being an accessory after the fact to murder is not newsworthy because he is rehabilitated and has lived for over 10 years as an obscure and law-abiding citizen, that revealing the criminal past of someone in his circumstances is offensive to most Americans, and that he did not voluntarily consent to the injurious publicity accorded him. In denying defendants' anti-SLAPP motion, the trial court expressly agreed with plaintiff.

* * * As noted, we granted review in order to determine to what extent, if at all, theories of tort liability paralleling the one we validated in

Briscoe remain viable. Since Briscoe was decided, the United States Supreme Court has issued a number of relevant decisions. The Court of Appeal below accurately described this intervening jurisprudence:

"After Briscoe the United States Supreme Court decided a series of cases dealing with the same broad issue of the tension between the right to privacy and the rights of free speech and free press.

* * *

"The court first acknowledged a growing body of law recognizing a right to privacy. Cox argued the press could not be held criminally or civilly liable for publishing information that was neither false nor misleading. The court noted that in defamation actions truth was generally viewed as a defense. The court stated, however, it had 'carefully' left open the question of whether the Constitution required that truth be recognized as a defense in a defamation action brought by a private person rather than a public figure. The court stated the same degree of caution should exist in dealing with the issue of the effect of truth on the tort of invasion of privacy. (Cox, supra, 420 U.S. at pp. 489–491 * * *)".

* * *

We conclude that the high court's decision in Cox and its subsequent pronouncements in Oklahoma Publishing, Daily Mail, The Florida Star, and Bartnicki have fatally undermined Briscoe's holding that a media defendant may be held liable in tort for recklessly publishing true but not newsworthy facts concerning a rehabilitated former criminal (see Briscoe, supra * * *), insofar as that holding applies to facts obtained from public official court records. As explained, the high court in Cox flatly stated that "the States may not impose sanctions on the publication of truthful information contained in official court records open to public inspection" (Cox, supra, 420 U.S. at p. 495, 95 S.Ct. 1029) and specifically reaffirmed that rule in Oklahoma Publishing, supra, 430 U.S. at page 311, 97 S.Ct. 1045 ("the press may not be prohibited from 'truthfully publishing information released to the public in official court records' "). On matters of federal constitutional law, of course, we are bound by the decisions of the United States Supreme Court. * * *

It is true that in subsequently articulating the more general principle of which Cox's rule is an instance—viz., that "state officials may not constitutionally punish publication of [truthful] information" that "a newspaper lawfully obtains ... about a matter of public significance" * * *—the high court excepted circumstances involving "a need to further a state interest of the highest order" * * * But in light of the needs and interests the high court, as previously noted, has determined not to be "of the highest order" for these purposes, we conclude, contrary to plaintiff's suggestion, that any state interest in protecting for rehabilitative purposes the long-term anonymity of former convicts falls similarly short.

Plaintiff requests that we distinguish Cox and its progeny on their facts, principally the fact that "all of these cases involve situations in which the events reported on occurred within a few days, weeks or months of the offending publication, not years after the fact as in Briscoe...." But as the Court of Appeal below recognized, the high court has never suggested, in Cox or in any subsequent case, that the fact the public record of a criminal proceeding may have come into existence years previously affects the absolute right of the press to report its contents. Cox's holding was unqualified: "Once true information is disclosed in public court documents open to public inspection, the press cannot be sanctioned for publishing it." * * * Cox's rationale, moreover, related to the "very nature" * * * of court records per se, not the age of the particular records at issue in that case. As the high court explained, "[p]ublic records by their very nature are of interest to those concerned with the administration of government, and a public benefit is performed by the reporting of the true contents of the records by the media." * * *

* * *

For the foregoing reasons, we decline to distinguish Cox in the manner plaintiff advocates. We, like the high court, are "reluctant to embark on a course that would make public records generally available to the media but forbid their publication if offensive to the sensibilities of the supposed reasonable man. Such a rule would make it very difficult for the media to inform citizens about the public business and yet stay within the law. The rule would invite timidity and self-censorship and very likely lead to the suppression of many items that would otherwise be published and that should be made available to the public." (Cox, supra, 420 U.S. at p. 496, 95 S.Ct. 1029.)

Accordingly, following Cox and its progeny, we conclude that an invasion of privacy claim based on allegations of harm caused by a media defendant's publication of facts obtained from public official records of a criminal proceeding is barred by the First Amendment to the United States Constitution. * * * The complaint states: "The basis for Plaintiff's invasion of privacy claim is the revelation that Plaintiff pleaded guilty to being an accessory after the fact to a murder for hire plot and the airing by Defendants of Plaintiff's photograph." Both that fact and the photograph appear in the public official records relating to plaintiff's 1992 arrest and conviction. Therefore, plaintiff's invasion of privacy claim based thereon is barred.

It follows that defendants' anti-SLAPP motion should have been granted, because, as a matter of law, plaintiff cannot prevail on his invasion of privacy claim. The trial court erred insofar as it concluded to the contrary.

Disposition

The judgment of the Court of Appeal is affirmed.[7]

7. Briscoe v. Reader's Digest Association, Inc. (1971) 4 Cal.3d 529, 93 Cal.Rptr. 866, 483 P.2d 34 is overruled to the extent it conflicts with the views set forth herein.

NOTE

The court's disposition of this case strongly suggests that, if the information does not come from public records or concern a public figure as in the *Falwell* case, *supra* p. 465, an action will still lie in California for the publication of true facts that, to use the language of the *Restatement (Second) of Torts* § 652D "are of a kind that (a) would be highly offensive to a reasonable person, and (b) is not of legitimate concern of the public." This liability would accrue even if the information in question had not been obtained illegally or in the course of a confidential relationship. This of course is to adopt something of the European approach to which we shall now turn. One must note that there was some indication that the Supreme Court of the United States might be open to this possibility in *Snyder v. Phelps*, reprinted *supra* at p. 471, where, in denying recovery for intentional infliction of emotional distress caused by the vulgar and clearly offensive demonstration at the funeral for a Marine killed in Iraq, the Court relied on the fact that the demonstration involved a matter of public concern.

CAMPBELL v. MGN LTD

House of Lords, 2004.
[2004] 2 AC 457, 2 W.L.R. 1232, 2 All ER 995.

LORD NICHOLLS OF BIRKENHEAD:

[1] My Lords, Naomi Campbell is a celebrated fashion model. Hers is a household name, nationally and internationally. Her face is instantly recognisable. Whatever she does and wherever she goes is news.

[2] On 1 February 2001 the Daily Mirror (the Mirror) newspaper carried as its first story on its front page a prominent article headed: 'Naomi: I am a drug addict.' The article was supported on one side by a picture of Miss Campbell as a glamorous model, on the other side by a slightly indistinct picture of a smiling, relaxed Miss Campbell, dressed in baseball cap and jeans, over the caption: 'THERAPY: Naomi outside meeting.' The article read:

'SUPERMODEL Naomi Campbell is attending Narcotics Anonymous meetings in a courageous bid to beat her addiction to drink and drugs. The 30–year–old has been a regular at counselling sessions for three months, often attending twice a day. Dressed in jeans and baseball cap, she arrived at one of NA's lunchtime meetings this week. Hours later at a different venue she made a low-key entrance to a women-only gathering of recovered addicts. Despite her £14million fortune Naomi is treated as just another addict trying to put her life back together. A source close to her said last night: "She wants to clean up her life for good. She went into modelling when she was very young and it is easy to be led astray. Drink and drugs are unfortunately widely available in the fashion world. But Naomi has realised she has a problem and has bravely vowed to do something about it. Everyone wishes her well." Her spokeswoman at Elite Models declined to comment.'

[3] The story continued inside, with a longer article spread across two pages. The inside article was headed: 'Naomi's finally trying to beat the demons that have been haunting her.' The opening paragraphs read:

'She's just another face in the crowd, but the gleaming smile is unmistakeably Naomi Campbell's.

In our picture, the catwalk queen emerges from a gruelling two-hour session at Narcotics Anonymous and gives a friend a loving hug.

This is one of the world's most beautiful women facing up to her drink and drugs addiction-and clearly winning.

The London-born supermodel has been going to NA meetings for the past three months as she tries to change her wild lifestyle.

Such is her commitment to conquering her problem that she regularly goes twice a day to group counselling . . .

To the rest of the group she is simply Naomi, the addict. Not the supermodel. Not the style icon.'

[4] The article made mention of Miss Campbell's efforts to rehabilitate herself, and that one of her friends said she was still fragile but 'getting healthy'. The article gave a general description of Narcotics Anonymous (NA) therapy, and referred to some of Miss Campbell's recent publicised activities. These included an occasion when Miss Campbell was rushed to hospital and had her stomach pumped. She claimed it was an allergic reaction to antibiotics and that she had never had a drug problem: but 'those closest to her knew the truth'.

[5] In the middle of the double-page spread, between several innocuous pictures of Miss Campbell, was a dominating picture over the caption: 'HUGS: Naomi, dressed in jeans and baseball hat, arrives for a lunchtime group meeting this week.' The picture showed her in the street on the doorstep of a building as the central figure in a small group. She was being embraced by two people whose faces had been pixelated. Standing on the pavement was a board advertising a named cafe. The article did not name the venue of the meeting, but anyone who knew the district well would be able to identify the place shown in the photograph.

[6] The general tone of the articles was sympathetic and supportive with, perhaps, the barest undertone of smugness that Miss Campbell had been caught out by the Mirror. The source of the newspaper's information was either an associate of Miss Campbell or a fellow addict attending meetings of NA. The photographs of her attending a meeting were taken by a freelance photographer specifically employed by the newspaper to do the job. He took the photographs covertly, while concealed some distance away inside a parked car.

[7] In certain respects the articles were inaccurate. Miss Campbell had been attending NA meetings, in this country and abroad, for two years, not three months. The frequency of her attendance at meetings was greatly exaggerated. She did not regularly attend meetings twice a day.

The street photographs showed her leaving a meeting, not arriving, contrary to the caption in the newspaper article.

THE PROCEEDINGS AND THE FURTHER ARTICLES

[8] On the same day as the articles were published Miss Campbell commenced proceedings against MGN Ltd, the publisher of the Mirror. The newspaper's response was to publish further articles, this time highly critical of Miss Campbell. On 5 February 2001 the newspaper published an article headed, in large letters, 'PATHETIC'. Below was a photograph of Miss Campbell over the caption: 'HELP: Naomi leaves Narcotics Anonymous meeting last week after receiving therapy in her battle against illegal drugs.' This photograph was similar to the street scene picture published on 1 February. The text of the article was headed: 'After years of self-publicity and illegal drug abuse, Naomi Campbell whinges about privacy.' The article mentioned that 'the Mirror revealed last week how she is attending daily meetings of Narcotics Anonymous'. Elsewhere in the same edition an editorial article, with the heading 'No hiding Naomi', concluded with the words:

> 'If Naomi Campbell wants to live like a nun, let her join a nunnery. If she wants the excitement of a showbusiness life, she must accept what comes with it.'

[9] Two days later, on 7 February, the Mirror returned to the attack with an offensive and disparaging article. Under the heading 'Fame on you, Ms Campbell', an article referred to her plans 'to launch a campaign for better rights for celebrities or "artists" as she calls them'. The article included the sentence: 'As a campaigner, Naomi's about as effective as a chocolate soldier.'

[10] In the proceedings Miss Campbell claimed damages for breach of confidence and compensation under the Data Protection Act 1998. The article of 7 February formed the main basis of a claim for aggravated damages. Morland J upheld Miss Campbell's claim * * *. He made her a modest award of £2,500 plus £1,000 aggravated damages in respect of both claims. The newspaper appealed. The Court of Appeal, comprising Lord Phillips of Worth Matravers MR, Chadwick and Keene LJJ, allowed the appeal and discharged the judge's order * * *. Miss Campbell has now appealed to your Lordships' House.

BREACH OF CONFIDENCE: MISUSE OF PRIVATE INFORMATION

[11] In this country, unlike the United States of America, there is no overarching, all-embracing cause of action for 'invasion of privacy': * * *. But protection of various aspects of privacy is a fast developing area of the law, here and in some other common law jurisdictions. The recent decision of the Court of Appeal of New Zealand in Hosking v Runting (25 March 2004, unreported) is an example of this. In this country development of the law has been spurred by enactment of the Human Rights Act 1998.

[12] The present case concerns one aspect of invasion of privacy: wrongful disclosure of private information. The case involves the familiar competition between freedom of expression and respect for an individual's privacy. Both are vitally important rights. Neither has precedence over the other. The importance of freedom of expression has been stressed often and eloquently, the importance of privacy less so. But it, too, lies at the heart of liberty in a modern state. A proper degree of privacy is essential for the well-being and development of an individual. And restraints imposed on government to pry into the lives of the citizen go to the essence of a democratic state * * *.

[13] The common law or, more precisely, courts of equity have long afforded protection to the wrongful use of private information by means of the cause of action which became known as breach of confidence. A breach of confidence was restrained as a form of unconscionable conduct, akin to a breach of trust. Today this nomenclature is misleading. The breach of confidence label harks back to the time when the cause of action was based on improper use of information disclosed by one person to another in confidence. To attract protection the information had to be of a confidential nature. But the gist of the cause of action was that information of this character had been disclosed by one person to another in circumstances 'importing an obligation of confidence' even though no contract of non-disclosure existed * * *. The confidence referred to in the phrase 'breach of confidence' was the confidence arising out of a confidential relationship.

[14] This cause of action has now firmly shaken off the limiting constraint of the need for an initial confidential relationship. In doing so it has changed its nature. In this country this development was recognised clearly in the judgment of Lord Goff of Chieveley in A–G v Guardian Newspapers Ltd (No 2) [1988] 3 All ER 545 at 658–659, [1990] 1 AC 109 at 281. Now the law imposes a 'duty of confidence' whenever a person receives information he knows or ought to know is fairly and reasonably to be regarded as confidential. Even this formulation is awkward. The continuing use of the phrase 'duty of confidence' and the description of the information as 'confidential' is not altogether comfortable. Information about an individual's private life would not, in ordinary usage, be called 'confidential'. The more natural description today is that such information is private. The essence of the tort is better encapsulated now as misuse of private information.

[15] In the case of individuals this tort, however labelled, affords respect for one aspect of an individual's privacy. That is the value underlying this cause of action. An individual's privacy can be invaded in ways not involving publication of information. Strip searches are an example. The extent to which the common law as developed thus far in this country protects other forms of invasion of privacy is not a matter arising in the present case. It does not arise because, although pleaded more widely, Miss Campbell's common law claim was throughout present-

ed in court exclusively on the basis of breach of confidence, that is, the wrongful publication by the Mirror of private information.

[16] The European Convention for the Protection of Human Rights and Fundamental Freedoms * * * and the Strasbourg jurisprudence, have undoubtedly had a significant influence in this area of the common law for some years. The provisions of art 8, concerning respect for private and family life, and art 10, concerning freedom of expression, and the interaction of these two articles, have prompted the courts of this country to identify more clearly the different factors involved in cases where one or other of these two interests is present. Where both are present the courts are increasingly explicit in evaluating the competing considerations involved. When identifying and evaluating these factors the courts, including your Lordships' House, have tested the common law against the values encapsulated in these two articles. * * *

[17] The time has come to recognise that the values enshrined in arts 8 and 10 are now part of the cause of action for breach of confidence.* * * Further, it should now be recognised that for this purpose these values are of general application. The values embodied in arts 8 and 10 are as much applicable in disputes between individuals or between an individual and a non-governmental body such as a newspaper as they are in disputes between individuals and a public authority.

[18] In reaching this conclusion it is not necessary to pursue the controversial question whether the convention itself has this wider effect. Nor is it necessary to decide whether the duty imposed on courts by s 6 of the 1998 Act extends to questions of substantive law as distinct from questions of practice and procedure. It is sufficient to recognise that the values underlying arts 8 and 10 are not confined to disputes between individuals and public authorities. This approach has been adopted by the courts in several recent decisions, reported and unreported, where individuals have complained of press intrusion. * * *

[19] In applying this approach, and giving effect to the values protected by art 8, courts will often be aided by adopting the structure of art 8 in the same way as they now habitually apply the Strasbourg court's approach to art 10 when resolving questions concerning freedom of expression. * * *

[20] I should take this a little further on one point. Article 8(1) recognises the need to respect private and family life. Article 8(2) recognises there are occasions when intrusion into private and family life may be justified. One of these is where the intrusion is necessary for the protection of the rights and freedoms of others. Article 10(1) recognises the importance of freedom of expression. But art 10(2), like art 8(2), recognises there are occasions when protection of the rights of others may make it necessary for freedom of expression to give way. When both these articles are engaged a difficult question of proportionality may arise. This question is distinct from the initial question of whether the published information

engaged art 8 at all by being within the sphere of the complainant's private or family life.

[21] Accordingly, in deciding what was the ambit of an individual's 'private life' in particular circumstances courts need to be on guard against using as a touchstone a test which brings into account considerations which should more properly be considered at the later stage of proportionality. Essentially the touchstone of private life is whether in respect of the disclosed facts the person in question had a reasonable expectation of privacy.

[22] Different forms of words, usually to much the same effect, have been suggested from time to time. The second Restatement of Torts in the United States (1977) p 394, art 652D, uses the formulation of disclosure of matter which 'would be highly offensive to a reasonable person'. In Australian Broadcasting Corp v Lenah Game Meats Pty Ltd (2001) 185 ALR 1 at 13 (para 42), Gleeson CJ used words, widely quoted, having a similar meaning. This particular formulation should be used with care, for two reasons. First, the 'highly offensive' phrase is suggestive of a stricter test of private information than a reasonable expectation of privacy. Second, the 'highly offensive' formulation can all too easily bring into account, when deciding whether the disclosed information was private, considerations which go more properly to issues of proportionality, for instance, the degree of intrusion into private life, and the extent to which publication was a matter of proper public concern. This could be a recipe for confusion.

THE PRESENT CASE

[23] I turn to the present case and consider first whether the information whose disclosure is in dispute was private. Mr Caldecott QC placed the information published by the newspaper into five categories: (1) the fact of Miss Campbell's drug addiction; (2) the fact that she was receiving treatment; (3) the fact that she was receiving treatment at NA; (4) the details of the treatment—how long she had been attending meetings, how often she went, how she was treated within the sessions themselves, the extent of her commitment, and the nature of her entrance on the specific occasion; and (5) the visual portrayal of her leaving a specific meeting with other addicts.

[24] It was common ground between the parties that in the ordinary course the information in all five categories would attract the protection of art 8. But Mr Caldecott recognised that, as he put it, Miss Campbell's 'public lies' precluded her from claiming protection for categories (1) and (2). When talking to the media Miss Campbell went out of her way to say that, unlike many fashion models, she did not take drugs. By repeatedly making these assertions in public Miss Campbell could no longer have a reasonable expectation that this aspect of her life should be private. Public disclosure that, contrary to her assertions, she did in fact take drugs and had a serious drug problem for which she was being treated was not disclosure of private information. As the Court of Appeal noted, where a

public figure chooses to present a false image and make untrue pronouncements about his or her life, the press will normally be entitled to put the record straight. Thus the area of dispute at the trial concerned the other three categories of information.

[25] Of these three categories I shall consider first the information in categories (3) and (4), concerning Miss Campbell's attendance at NA meetings. In this regard it is important to note this is a highly unusual case. On any view of the matter, this information related closely to the fact, which admittedly could be published, that Miss Campbell was receiving treatment for drug addiction. Thus when considering whether Miss Campbell had a reasonable expectation of privacy in respect of information relating to her attendance at NA meetings the relevant question can be framed along the following lines: Miss Campbell having put her addiction and treatment into the public domain, did the further information relating to her attendance at NA meetings retain its character of private information sufficiently to engage the protection afforded by art 8?

[26] I doubt whether it did. Treatment by attendance at NA meetings is a form of therapy for drug addiction which is well known, widely used and much respected. Disclosure that Miss Campbell had opted for this form of treatment was not a disclosure of any more significance than saying that a person who has fractured a limb has his limb in plaster or that a person suffering from cancer is undergoing a course of chemotherapy. Given the extent of the information, otherwise of a highly private character, which admittedly could properly be disclosed, the additional information was of such an unremarkable and consequential nature that to divide the one from the other would be to apply altogether too fine a toothcomb. Human rights are concerned with substance, not with such fine distinctions.

[27] For the same reason I doubt whether the brief details of how long Miss Campbell had been undergoing treatment, and how often she attended meetings, stand differently. The brief reference to the way she was treated at the meetings did no more than spell out and apply to Miss Campbell common knowledge of how NA meetings are conducted.

[28] But I would not wish to found my conclusion solely on this point. I prefer to proceed to the next stage and consider how the tension between privacy and freedom of expression should be resolved in this case, on the assumption that the information regarding Miss Campbell's attendance at NA meetings retained its private character. At this stage I consider Miss Campbell's claim must fail. I can state my reason very shortly. On the one hand, publication of this information in the unusual circumstances of this case represents, at most, an intrusion into Miss Campbell's private life to a comparatively minor degree. On the other hand, non-publication of this information would have robbed a legitimate and sympathetic newspaper story of attendant detail which added colour and conviction. This information was published in order to demonstrate Miss Campbell's commitment to tackling her drug problem. The balance

ought not to be held at a point which would preclude, in this case, a degree of journalistic latitude in respect of information published for this purpose.

[29] It is at this point I respectfully consider Morland J fell into error. Having held that the details of Miss Campbell's attendance at NA had the necessary quality of confidentiality, the judge seems to have put nothing into the scales under art 10 when striking the balance between arts 8 and 10. This was a misdirection. The need to be free to disseminate information regarding Miss Campbell's drug addiction is of a lower order than the need for freedom to disseminate information on some other subjects such as political information. The degree of latitude reasonably to be accorded to journalists is correspondingly reduced, but it is not excluded altogether.

[30] There remains category (5): the photographs taken covertly of Miss Campbell in the road outside the building she was attending for a meeting of NA. I say at once that I wholly understand why Miss Campbell felt she was being hounded by the Mirror. I understand also that this could be deeply distressing, even damaging, to a person whose health was still fragile. But this is not the subject of complaint. Miss Campbell, expressly, makes no complaint about the taking of the photographs. She does not assert that the taking of the photographs was itself an invasion of privacy which attracts a legal remedy. The complaint regarding the photographs is of precisely the same character as the nature of the complaints regarding the text of the articles: the information conveyed by the photographs was private information. Thus the fact that the photographs were taken surreptitiously adds nothing to the only complaint being made.

[31] In general photographs of people contain more information than textual description. That is why they are more vivid. That is why they are worth a thousand words. But the pictorial information in the photographs illustrating the offending article of 1 February 2001 added nothing of an essentially private nature. They showed nothing untoward. They conveyed no private information beyond that discussed in the article. The group photograph showed Miss Campbell in the street exchanging warm greetings with others on the doorstep of a building. There was nothing undignified or distrait about her appearance. The same is true of the smaller picture on the front page. Until spotted by counsel in the course of preparing the case for oral argument in your Lordships' House no one seems to have noticed that a sharp eye could just about make out the name of the cafe on the advertising board on the pavement.

[32] For these reasons and those given by my noble and learned friend Lord Hoffmann, I agree with the Court of Appeal that Miss Campbell's claim fails. It is not necessary for me to pursue the claim based on the Data Protection Act 1998. The parties were agreed that this claim stands or falls with the outcome of the main claim.

[33] In reaching this overall conclusion I have well in mind the distress that publication of the article on 1 February 2001 must have caused Miss Campbell. Public exposure of this sort, especially for someone striving to cope with a serious medical condition, would almost inevitably be extremely painful. But it is right to recognise the source of this pain and distress. First, Miss Campbell realised she had been betrayed by an associate or fellow sufferer. Someone whom she trusted had told the newspaper she was attending NA meetings. This sense of betrayal, and consequential anxiety about continuing to attend NA meetings, flowed from her becoming aware she had been betrayed. The newspaper articles were only the means by which she became aware of her betrayal. Secondly, Miss Campbell realised her addiction was now public knowledge, as was the fact she was undergoing treatment. She realised also that it was now public knowledge that she had repeatedly lied. Thirdly, as already mentioned, Miss Campbell would readily feel she was being harassed by the Mirror employing a photographer to 'spy' on her.

[34] That Miss Campbell should suffer real distress under all these heads is wholly understandable. But in respect of none of these causes of distress does she have reason for complaint against the newspaper for misuse of private information. Against this background I find it difficult to envisage Miss Campbell suffered any significant additional distress based on public disclosure that her chosen form of treatment was attendance at NA meetings.

[35] Nor have I overlooked the further distress caused by the subsequent mean-spirited attack, with its shabby reference to a chocolate soldier, made by the Mirror on a person known to be peculiarly vulnerable. If Miss Campbell had a well-founded cause of action against the newspaper the trial judge rightly recognised that an award of aggravated damages was called for. But for reasons already given I would dismiss this appeal.

LORD HOFFMANN:

[36] My Lords, the House is divided as to the outcome of this appeal, but the difference of opinion relates to a very narrow point which arises on the unusual facts of this case. The facts are unusual because the plaintiff is a public figure who had made very public false statements about a matter in respect of which even a public figure would ordinarily be entitled to privacy, namely her use of drugs. It was these falsehoods which, as was conceded, made it justifiable, for a newspaper to report the fact that she was addicted. The division of opinion is whether in doing so the newspaper went too far in publishing associated facts about her private life. But the importance of this case lies in the statements of general principle on the way in which the law should strike a balance between the right to privacy and the right to freedom of expression, on which the House is unanimous. The principles are expressed in varying language but speaking for myself I can see no significant differences.

* * *

[59] The question is then whether the Mirror should have confined itself to these bare facts or whether it was entitled to reveal more of the circumstantial detail and print the photographs. If one applies the test of necessity or proportionality which I have suggested, this is a matter on which different people may have different views. That appears clearly enough from the judgments which have been delivered in this case. But judges are not newspaper editors. It may have been possible for the Mirror to satisfy the public interest in publication with a story which contained less detail and omitted the photographs. But the Mirror said that they wanted to show themselves sympathetic to Ms Campbell's efforts to overcome her dependency. For this purpose, some details about her frequency of attendance at NA meetings were needed. I agree with the observation of the Court of Appeal * * * that it is harsh to criticise the editor for 'painting a somewhat fuller picture in order to show her in a sympathetic light'.

* * *

[66] It is only in connection with the degree of latitude which must be allowed to the press in the way it chooses to present its story that I think it is relevant to consider Ms Campbell's relationship with the media. She and they have for many years both fed upon each other. She has given them stories to sell their papers and they have given her publicity to promote her career. This does not deprive Ms Campbell of the right to privacy in respect of areas of her life which she has not chosen to make public. But I think it means that when a newspaper publishes what is in substance a legitimate story, she cannot insist upon too great a nicety of judgment in the circumstantial detail with which the story is presented.

* * *

[72] That leaves the question of the photographs. In my opinion a photograph is in principle information no different from any other information. It may be a more vivid form of information than the written word ('a picture is worth a thousand words'). That has to be taken into account in deciding whether its publication infringes the right to privacy of personal information. The publication of a photograph cannot necessarily be justified by saying that one would be entitled to publish a verbal description of the scene: see Douglas v Hello! Ltd [2001] 2 All ER 289, [2001] QB 967. But the principles by which one decides whether or not the publication of a photograph is an unjustified invasion of the privacy of personal information are in my opinion the same as those which I have already discussed.

[73] In the present case, the pictures were taken without Ms Campbell's consent. That in my opinion is not enough to amount to a wrongful invasion of privacy. The famous and even the not so famous who go out in public must accept that they may be photographed without their consent, just as they may be observed by others without their consent. * * *

[74] But the fact that we cannot avoid being photographed does not mean that anyone who takes or obtains such photographs can publish them to the world at large. In the recent case of Peck v UK (2003) 13 BHRC 669 Mr Peck was filmed on a public street in an embarrassing moment by a closed circuit television camera. Subsequently, the film was broadcast several times on the television. The Strasbourg court said (at 684) that this was an invasion of his privacy contrary to art 8:

'. . . the relevant moment was viewed to an extent which far exceeded any exposure to a passer-by or to security observation . . . and to a degree surpassing that which the applicant could possibly have foreseen when he walked in Brentwood on 20 August 1995.'

[75] In my opinion, therefore, the widespread publication of a photograph of someone which reveals him to be in a situation of humiliation or severe embarrassment, even if taken in a public place, may be an infringement of the privacy of his personal information. Likewise, the publication of a photograph taken by intrusion into a private place (for example, by a long distance lens) may in itself be such an infringement, even if there is nothing embarrassing about the picture itself * * *:

'An infringement of privacy is an affront to the personality, which is damaged both by the violation and by the demonstration that the personal space is not inviolate.'

[76] In the present case, however, there was nothing embarrassing about the picture, which showed Ms Campbell neatly dressed and smiling among a number of other people. Nor did the taking of the picture involve an intrusion into private space. Hundreds of such 'candid' pictures of Ms Campbell, taken perhaps on more glamorous occasions, must have been published in the past without objection. The only ground for claiming that the picture was a wrongful disclosure of personal information was by virtue of the caption, which said that she was going to or coming from a meeting of NA. But this in my opinion added nothing to what was said in the text.

[77] No doubt it would have been possible for the Mirror to have published the article without pictures. But that would in my opinion again be to ignore the realities of this kind of journalism as much as to expect precision of judgment about the amount of circumstantial detail to be included in the text. We value the freedom of the press but the press is a commercial enterprise and can flourish only by selling newspapers. From a journalistic point of view, photographs are an essential part of the story. The picture carried the message, more strongly than anything in the text alone, that the Mirror's story was true. So the decision to publish the pictures was in my opinion within the margin of editorial judgment and something for which appropriate latitude should be allowed.

[78] I would therefore dismiss the appeal.

LORD HOPE OF CRAIGHEAD:

[79] My Lords, the facts of this case have been described by my noble and learned friend Lord Nicholls of Birkenhead, and I gratefully

adopt his account of them. But I should like to say a few more words about the general background before I explain why I have reached the conclusion that this appeal must be allowed.

THE BACKGROUND

[80] The business of fashion modelling, in which the appellant Naomi Campbell has built up such a powerful reputation internationally, is conducted under the constant gaze of the media. It is also highly competitive. It is a context where public reputation as a forceful and colourful personality adds value to the physical appearance of the individual. Much good can come of this, if the process is carefully and correctly handled. But there are aspects of Miss Campbell's exploitation of her status as a celebrity that have attracted criticism. She has been manipulative and selective in what she has revealed about herself. She has engaged in a deliberately false presentation of herself as someone who, in contrast to many models, has managed to keep clear of illegal drugs. The true position, it is now agreed, is that she has made a practice of abusing drugs. This has caused her medical problems, and it has affected her behaviour to such an extent that she has required and has received therapy for her addiction.

[81] Paradoxically, for someone in Miss Campbell's position, there are few areas of the life of an individual that are more in need of protection on the grounds of privacy than the combating of addiction to drugs or to alcohol. It is hard to break the habit which has led to the addiction. It is all too easy to give up the struggle if efforts to do so are exposed to public scrutiny. The struggle, after all, is an intensely personal one. It involves a high degree of commitment and of self-criticism. The sense of shame that comes with it is one of the most powerful of all the tools that are used to break the habit. But shame increases the individual's vulnerability as the barriers that the habit has engendered are broken down. The smallest hint that the process is being watched by the public may be enough to persuade the individual to delay or curtail the treatment. At the least it is likely to cause distress, even to those who in other circumstances like to court publicity and regard publicity as a benefit.

[82] The question in this case is whether the publicity which the respondents gave to Miss Campbell's drug addiction and to the therapy which she was receiving for it in an article which was published in the Daily Mirror (the Mirror) newspaper on 1 February 2001 is actionable on the ground of breach of confidence. Miss Campbell cannot complain about the fact that publicity was given in this article to the fact that she was a drug addict. This was a matter of legitimate public comment, as she had not only lied about her addiction but had sought to benefit from this by comparing herself with others in the fashion business who were addicted. As the Court of Appeal observed * * *, where a public figure chooses to make untrue pronouncements about his or her private life, the press will normally be entitled to put the record straight.

[83] Miss Campbell's case is that information about the details of the treatment which she was receiving for the addiction falls to be treated differently. This is because it was not the subject of any falsehood that was in need of correction and because it was information which any reasonable person who came into possession of it would realise was obtained in confidence. The argument was put succinctly in the particulars of her claim, where it was stated:

'Information about whether a person is receiving medical or similar treatment for addiction, and in particular details relating to such treatment or the person's reaction to it, is obviously confidential. The confidentiality is the stronger where, as here, disclosure would tend to disrupt the treatment and/or its benefits for the person concerned and others sharing in, or giving, or wishing to take or participate in, the treatment. The very name "Narcotics Anonymous" underlines the importance of privacy in the context of treatment as do the defendants' own words—"To the rest of the group she is simply Naomi, the addict." '

[84] The respondents' answer is based on the proposition that the information that was published about her treatment was peripheral and not sufficiently significant to amount to a breach of the duty of confidence that was owed to her. They also maintain that the right balance was struck between Miss Campbell's right to respect for her private life under art 8(1) of the European Convention for the Protection of Human Rights and Fundamental Freedoms 1950 (as set out in Sch 1 to the Human Rights Act 1998) and the right to freedom of expression that is enshrined in art 10(1) of the convention.

[85] The questions that I have just described seem to me to be essentially questions of fact and degree and not to raise any new issues of principle. As Lord Woolf CJ said in A v B (a company) [2002] EWCA Civ 337 at [11](ix), (x), [2002] 2 All ER 545 at [11](ix), (x), [2003] QB 195, the need for the existence of a confidential relationship should not give rise to problems as to the law because a duty of confidence will arise whenever the party subject to the duty is in a situation where he knows or ought to know that the other person can reasonably expect his privacy to be protected. The difficulty will be as to the relevant facts, bearing in mind that, if there is an intrusion in a situation where a person can reasonably expect his privacy to be respected, that intrusion will be capable of giving rise to liability unless the intrusion can be justified: see also the exposition in A–G v Guardian Newspapers Ltd (No 2) [1988] 3 All ER 545 at 659, [1990] 1 AC 109 at 282 by Lord Goff of Chieveley, where he set out the three limiting principles to the broad general principle that a duty of confidence arises when confidential information comes to the knowledge of a person where he has notice that the information is confidential. The third limiting principle is particularly relevant in this case. This is the principle which may require a court to carry out a balancing operation, weighing the public interest in maintaining confidence against a countervailing public interest favouring disclosure.

[86] The language has changed following the coming into operation of the 1998 Act and the incorporation into domestic law of arts 8 and 10 of the convention. We now talk about the right to respect for private life and the countervailing right to freedom of expression. The jurisprudence of the European Court of Human Rights offers important guidance as to how these competing rights ought to be approached and analysed. I doubt whether the result is that the centre of gravity, as my noble and learned friend Lord Hoffmann says, has shifted. It seems to me that the balancing exercise to which that guidance is directed is essentially the same exercise, although it is plainly now more carefully focussed and more penetrating. As Lord Woolf CJ said in A v B new breadth and strength is given to the action for breach of confidence by these articles.

[87] Where a case has gone to trial it would normally be right to attach a great deal of weight to the views which the judge has formed about the facts and where he thought the balance should be struck after reading and hearing the evidence. The fact that the Court of Appeal felt able to differ from the conclusions which Morland J reached on these issues * * * brings me to the first point on which I wish to comment.

WAS THE INFORMATION CONFIDENTIAL?

[88] The information contained in the article consisted of the following five elements: (1) the fact that Miss Campbell was a drug addict; (2) the fact that she was receiving treatment for her addiction; (3) the fact that the treatment which she was receiving was provided by Narcotics Anonymous (NA); (4) details of the treatment—for how long, how frequently and at what times of day she had been receiving it, the nature of it and extent of her commitment to the process; and (5) a visual portrayal by means of photographs of her when she was leaving the place where treatment had been taking place.

[89] The trial judge drew the line between the first two and the last three elements. Mr Caldecott QC for Miss Campbell said that he was content with this distinction. So the fact that she was a drug addict was open to public comment in view of her denials, although he maintained that this would normally be treated as a medical condition that was entitled to protection. He accepted that the fact that she was receiving treatment for the condition was not in itself intrusive in this context. Moreover disclosure of this fact in itself could not harm her therapy. But he said that the line was crossed as soon as details of the nature and frequency of the treatment were given, especially when these details were accompanied by a covertly taken photograph which showed her leaving one of the places where she had been undertaking it. This was an area of privacy where she was entitled to be protected by an obligation of confidence.

[90] The Court of Appeal recognised at the start of their discussion of this point that some categories of information are well recognised as confidential * * *. They noted that these include details of a medical condition or its treatment. But they were not prepared to accept that

information that Miss Campbell was receiving therapy from NA was to be equated with disclosure of clinical details of the treatment of a medical condition (see [48]). This was contrary to the view which Morland J appears to have taken when he said * * * that it mattered not whether therapy was obtained by means of professional medical input or by alternative means such as group counselling or by organised meetings between sufferers. The Court of Appeal were also of the view that the publication of this information was not, in its context, sufficiently significant to shock the conscience and thus to amount to a breach of the duty of confidence which was owed to her. They accepted the respondents' argument that disclosure of these details was peripheral. They had regard too to the fact that some of the additional information that was given in the article was inaccurate.

[91] I do not think that the Court of Appeal were right to reject the analogy which the judge drew between information that Miss Campbell was receiving therapy from NA and information about details of a medical condition or its treatment. Mr Brown QC for the respondents said that it was not his case that there was an essential difference or, as he put it, a bright line distinction between therapy and medical treatment. He maintained that the Court of Appeal were simply drawing attention to a difference of degree. But it seems to me that there is more in this passage in the Court of Appeal's judgment and its criticism of the judge's analogy than a difference of degree. The implication of the Court of Appeal's criticism of the judge's reasoning is that the details of non-medical therapy are less deserving of protection than the details of a medical condition or its treatment. That seems to be why, as they put it* * *, the two are not 'to be equated'.

[92] The underlying question in all cases where it is alleged that there has been a breach of the duty of confidence is whether the information that was disclosed was private and not public. There must be some interest of a private nature that the claimant wishes to protect: * * *. In some cases, as the Court of Appeal said in that case, the answer to the question whether the information is public or private will be obvious. Where it is not, the broad test is whether disclosure of the information about the individual (A) would give substantial offence to A, assuming that A was placed in similar circumstances and was a person of ordinary sensibilities.

* * *

[94] * * *. The test is not needed where the information can easily be identified as private. It is also important to bear in mind its source, and the guidance which the source offers as to whether the information is public or private. It is taken from the definition of the privacy tort in the United States, where the right of privacy is invaded if the matter which is publicised is of a kind that (a) would be highly offensive to a reasonable person, and (b) is not of legitimate concern to the public: Restatement of the Law of Torts (Second) (1977) p 383, art 652D. The reference to a

person of ordinary sensibilities is * * * a quotation from William L Prosser Privacy (1960) 48 Calif LR 383. As Dean Prosser put it (pp 396–397), the matter made public must be one which would be offensive and objectionable to a reasonable man of ordinary sensibilities, who must expect some reporting of his daily activities. The law of privacy is not intended for the protection of the unduly sensitive.

[95] I think that the judge was right to regard the details of Miss Campbell's attendance at NA as private information which imported a duty of confidence. He said that information relating to Miss Campbell's therapy for drug addiction giving details that it was by regular attendance at NA meetings was easily identifiable as private. * * *Views may differ as to what is the best treatment for an addiction. But it is well known that persons who are addicted to the taking of illegal drugs or to alcohol can benefit from meetings at which they discuss and face up to their addiction. The private nature of these meetings encourages addicts to attend them in the belief that they can do so anonymously. The assurance of privacy is an essential part of the exercise. The therapy is at risk of being damaged if the duty of confidence which the participants owe to each other is breached by making details of the therapy, such as where, when and how often it is being undertaken, public. I would hold that these details are obviously private.

[96] If the information is obviously private, the situation will be one where the person to whom it relates can reasonably expect his privacy to be respected. So there is normally no need to go on and ask whether it would be highly offensive for it to be published. * * *

* * *

[98] Where the person is suffering from a condition that is in need of treatment one has to try, in order to assess whether the disclosure would be objectionable, to put oneself into the shoes of a reasonable person who is in need of that treatment. Otherwise the exercise is divorced from its context. The fact that no objection could be taken to disclosure of the first two elements in the article does not mean that they must be left out of account in a consideration as to whether disclosure of the other elements was objectionable. The article must be read as whole along with the photographs to give a proper perspective to each element. The context was that of a drug addict who was receiving treatment. It is her sensibilities that needed to be taken into account. Critical to this exercise was an assessment of whether disclosure of the details would be liable to disrupt her treatment. It does not require much imagination to appreciate the sense of unease that disclosure of these details would be liable to engender, especially when they were accompanied by a covertly taken photograph. The message that it conveyed was that somebody, somewhere, was following her, was well aware of what was going on and was prepared to disclose the facts to the media. I would expect a drug addict who was trying to benefit from meetings to discuss her problem anonymously with other addicts to find this distressing and highly offensive.

[99] The approach which the Court of Appeal took to this issue seems to me, with great respect, to be quite unreal. I do not think that they had a sound basis for differing from the conclusion reached by the trial judge as to whether the information was private. They were also in error, in my opinion, when they were asking themselves whether the disclosure would have offended the reasonable man of ordinary susceptibilities. The mind that they examined was the mind of the reader * * *. This is wrong. It greatly reduces the level of protection that is afforded to the right of privacy. The mind that has to be examined is that, not of the reader in general, but of the person who is affected by the publicity. The question is what a reasonable person of ordinary sensibilities would feel if she was placed in the same position as the claimant and faced with the same publicity.

* * *

STRIKING THE BALANCE

[112] There is no doubt that the presentation of the material that it was legitimate to convey to the public in this case without breaching the duty of confidence was a matter for the journalists. The choice of language used to convey information and ideas, and decisions as to whether or not to accompany the printed word by the use of photographs, are pre-eminently editorial matters with which the court will not interfere. The respondents are also entitled to claim that they should be accorded a reasonable margin of appreciation in taking decisions as to what details needed to be included in the article to give it credibility. This is an essential part of the journalistic exercise.

[113] But decisions about the publication of material that is private to the individual raise issues that are not simply about presentation and editing. Any interference with the public interest in disclosure has to be balanced against the interference with the right of the individual to respect for their private life. The decisions that are then taken are open to review by the court. The tests which the court must apply are the familiar ones. They are whether publication of the material pursues a legitimate aim and whether the benefits that will be achieved by its publication are proportionate to the harm that may be done by the interference with the right to privacy. The jurisprudence of the European Court of Human Rights explains how these principles are to be understood and applied in the context of the facts of each case. Any restriction of the right to freedom of expression must be subjected to very close scrutiny. But so too must any restriction of the right to respect for private life. Neither art 8 nor art 10 has any pre-eminence over the other in the conduct of this exercise. As Resolution 1165 of the Parliamentary Assembly of the Council of Europe (1998), para 11, pointed out, they are neither absolute nor in any hierarchical order, since they are of equal value in a democratic society.

THE ARTICLE 10 RIGHT

[114] In the present case it is convenient to begin by looking at the matter from the standpoint of the respondents' assertion of the art 10 right and the court's duty as a public authority under s 6(1) of the 1998 Act, which s 12(4) reinforces, not to act in a way which is incompatible with that convention right.

[115] The first question is whether the objective of the restriction on the art 10 right—the protection of Miss Campbell's right under art 8 to respect for her private life—is sufficiently important to justify limiting the fundamental right to freedom of expression which the press assert on behalf of the public. It follows from my conclusion that the details of Miss Campbell's treatment were private that I would answer this question in the affirmative. The second question is whether the means chosen to limit the art 10 right are rational, fair and not arbitrary and impair the right as minimally as is reasonably possible. It is not enough to assert that it would be reasonable to exclude these details from the article. A close examination of the factual justification for the restriction on the freedom of expression is needed if the fundamental right enshrined in art 10 is to remain practical and effective. The restrictions which the court imposes on the art 10 right must be rational, fair and not arbitrary, and they must impair the right no more than is necessary.

[116] In my opinion the factors that need to be weighed are, on the one hand, the duty that was recognised in Jersild v Denmark (1995) 19 EHRR 1 at 25–26 (para 31) to impart information and ideas of public interest which the public has a right to receive, and the need that was recognised in Fressoz and Roire v France (1999) 5 BHRC 654 at 669 (para 54) for the court to leave it to journalists to decide what material needs to be reproduced to ensure credibility; and, on the other hand, the degree of privacy to which Miss Campbell was entitled under the law of confidence as to the details of her therapy. Account should therefore be taken of the respondents' wish to put forward a story that was credible and to present Miss Campbell in a way that commended her for her efforts to overcome her addiction.

[117] But it should also be recognised that the right of the public to receive information about the details of her treatment was of a much lower order than the undoubted right to know that she was misleading the public when she said that she did not take drugs. * * * Clayton and Tomlinson The Law of Human Rights (2000) vol 1, p 1067 (para 15.162) point out that the court has distinguished three kinds of expression: political expression, artistic expression and commercial expression, and that it consistently attaches great importance to political expression and applies rather less rigorous principles to expression which is artistic and commercial. According to the court's well-established case law, freedom of expression constitutes one of the essential foundations of a democratic society and one of the basic conditions for its progress and the self-fulfillment of each individual: * * * But there were no political or demo-

cratic values at stake here, nor has any pressing social need been identified: * * *.

[118] As for the other side of the balance, Keene LJ said in Douglas v Hello! Ltd * * * that any consideration of art 8 rights must reflect the fact that there are different degrees of privacy. In the present context the potential for disclosure of the information to cause harm is an important factor to be taken into account in the assessment of the extent of the restriction that was needed to protect Miss Campbell's right to privacy.

THE ARTICLE 8 RIGHT

[119] Looking at the matter from Miss Campbell's point of view and the protection of her art 8 convention right, publication of details of the treatment which she was undertaking to cure her addiction—that she was attending NA, for how long, how frequently and at what times of day she had been attending this therapy, the nature of it and extent of her commitment to the process and the publication of the covertly taken photographs (the third, fourth and fifth of the five elements contained in the article)—had the potential to cause harm to her, for the reasons which I have already given. So I would attach a good deal of weight to this factor.

[120] As for the other side of the balance, a person's right to privacy may be limited by the public's interest in knowing about certain traits of her personality and certain aspects of her private life * * *. But it is not enough to deprive Miss Campbell of her right to privacy that she is a celebrity and that her private life is newsworthy. A margin of appreciation must, of course, be given to the journalist. Weight must be given to this. But to treat these details merely as background was to undervalue the importance that was to be attached to the need, if Miss Campbell was to be protected, to keep these details private. And it is hard to see that there was any compelling need for the public to know the name of the organisation that she was attending for the therapy, or for the other details of it to be set out. The presentation of the article indicates that this was not fully appreciated when the decision was taken to publish these details. The decision to publish the photographs suggests that greater weight was being given to the wish to publish a story that would attract interest rather than to the wish to maintain its credibility.

[121] Had it not been for the publication of the photographs, and looking to the text only, I would have been inclined to regard the balance between these rights as about even. Such is the effect of the margin of appreciation that must, in a doubtful case, be given to the journalist. In that situation the proper conclusion to draw would have been that it had not been shown that the restriction on the art 10 right for which Miss Campbell argues was justified on grounds of proportionality. But the text cannot be separated from the photographs. The words 'Therapy: Naomi outside meeting' underneath the photograph on the front page and the words 'Hugs: Naomi, dressed in jeans and baseball hat, arrives for a lunchtime group meeting this week' underneath the photograph on p 13 were designed to link that what might otherwise have been anonymous

and uninformative pictures with the main text. The reader would undoubtedly make that link, and so too would the reasonable person of ordinary sensibilities. The reasonable person of ordinary sensibilities would also regard publication of the covertly taken photographs, and the fact that they were linked with the text in this way, as adding greatly overall to the intrusion which the article as a whole made into her private life.

[122] The photographs were taken of Miss Campbell while she was in a public place, as she was in the street outside the premises where she had been receiving therapy. The taking of photographs in a public street must * * * be taken to be one of the ordinary incidents of living in a free community. The real issue is whether publicising the content of the photographs would be offensive: * * *. A person who just happens to be in the street when the photograph was taken and appears in it only incidentally cannot as a general rule object to the publication of the photograph * * *. But the situation is different if the public nature of the place where a photograph is taken was simply used as background for one or more persons who constitute the true subject of the photograph. The question then arises, balancing the rights at issue, where the public's right to information can justify dissemination of a photograph taken without authorisation: * * * The European Court of Human Rights has recognised that a person who walks down a public street will inevitably be visible to any member of the public who is also present and, in the same way, to a security guard viewing the scene through closed circuit television * * *. But, as the court pointed out in the same paragraph, private life considerations may arise once any systematic or permanent record comes into existence of such material from the public domain. In Peck v UK (2003) 13 BHRC 669 at 683–684 (para 62) the court held that the release and publication of closed circuit television footage which showed the applicant in the process of attempting to commit suicide resulted in the moment being viewed to an extent that far exceeded any exposure to a passer-by or to security observation that he could have foreseen when he was in that street.

[123] The same process of reasoning that led to the findings in Peck's case that the art 8 right had been violated and by the majority in Aubry's case that there had been an infringement of the claimant's right to respect for her private life can be applied here. Miss Campbell could not have complained if the photographs had been taken to show the scene in the street by a passer-by and later published simply as street scenes. But these were not just pictures of a street scene where she happened to be when the photographs were taken. They were taken deliberately, in secret and with a view to their publication in conjunction with the article. The zoom lens was directed at the doorway of the place where the meeting had been taking place. The faces of others in the doorway were pixilated so as not to reveal their identity. Hers was not, the photographs were published and her privacy was invaded. The argument that the publication of the photograph added credibility to the story has little weight. The photo-

graph was not self-explanatory. Neither the place nor the person were instantly recognisable. The reader only had the editor's word as to the truth of these details.

[124] Any person in Miss Campbell's position, assuming her to be of ordinary sensibilities but assuming also that she had been photographed surreptitiously outside the place where she had been receiving therapy for drug addiction, would have known what they were and would have been distressed on seeing the photographs. She would have seen their publication, in conjunction with the article which revealed what she had been doing when she was photographed and other details about her engagement in the therapy, as a gross interference with her right to respect for her private life. In my opinion this additional element in the publication is more than enough to outweigh the right to freedom of expression which the defendants are asserting in this case.

CONCLUSION

[125] Despite the weight that must be given to the right to freedom of expression that the press needs if it is to play its role effectively, I would hold that there was here an infringement of Miss Campbell's right to privacy that cannot be justified. In my opinion publication of the third, fourth and fifth elements in the article (see [88], above) was an invasion of that right for which she is entitled to damages. I would allow the appeal and restore the orders that were made by the trial judge.

BARONESS HALE OF RICHMOND:

[126] My Lords, this case raises some big questions. How is the balance to be struck between everyone's right to respect for their private and family life under art 8 of the European Convention for the Protection of Human Rights and Fundamental Freedoms 1950 (as set out in Sch 1 to the Human Rights Act 1998) and everyone's right to freedom of expression, including the freedom to receive and impart information and ideas under art 10? How do those rights come into play in a dispute between two private persons? But the parties are largely agreed about the answers to these. They disagree about where that balance is to be struck in the individual case. In particular, how far is a newspaper able to go in publishing what would otherwise be confidential information about a celebrity in order to set the record straight? And does it matter that the article was illustrated by a covertly taken photograph?

* * *

[128] The original source of the story was either a fellow sufferer attending NA meetings or a member of Miss Campbell's staff or entourage. The Mirror had sent along a photographer in the hope of catching her outside the meeting. This done, the editor rang her agent the evening before publication. He pretended that the photographer had happened to be in the street when he saw Miss Campbell coming out of a shop and followed her to the meeting. The agent told the editor that she had 'no

comment' but that NA was a 'medical thing' and that it would be 'morally wrong' to publish it.

[129] At trial and ever since, however, it has been accepted that the Mirror was entitled to publish the fact that Miss Campbell was a drug addict and was having therapy. She had publicly denied any involvement with illegal drugs, in particular in a television interview after an admission to a clinic in America in 1997, and the paper was entitled to put the record straight. It was also entitled, even obliged, to balance that disclosure with the fact that she was addressing the problem by having therapy. But, it was argued, the paper was not entitled to disclose that she was attending meetings of NA, or that she had been doing so for some time and with some frequency. Nor was it entitled to illustrate the story with covert photography of Miss Campbell in the company of other participants in the meeting.

* * *

THE BASIC PRINCIPLES

[132] Neither party to this appeal has challenged the basic principles which have emerged from the Court of Appeal in the wake of the 1998 Act. The 1998 Act does not create any new cause of action between private persons. But if there is a relevant cause of action applicable, the court as a public authority must act compatibly with both parties' convention rights. In a case such as this, the relevant vehicle will usually be the action for breach of confidence * * *.

* * *

[137] It should be emphasised that the 'reasonable expectation of privacy' is a threshold test which brings the balancing exercise into play. It is not the end of the story. Once the information is identified as 'private' in this way, the court must balance the claimant's interest in keeping the information private against the countervailing interest of the recipient in publishing it. Very often, it can be expected that the countervailing rights of the recipient will prevail.

[138] The parties agree that neither right takes precedence over the other. This is consistent with Resolution 1165 of 1998 of the Parliamentary Assembly of the Council of Europe (para 10):

'The Assembly reaffirms the importance of everyone's right to privacy, and of the right to freedom of expression, as fundamental to a democratic society. These rights are neither absolute nor in any hierarchical order, since they are of equal value.'

[139] Each right has the same structure. Article 8(1) states: 'Everyone has the right to respect for his private and family life, his home and his correspondence.' Article 10(1) states:

'Everyone has the right to freedom of expression. This right shall include freedom to hold opinions and to receive and impart information and ideas without interference by public authority and regardless of frontiers . . .'

Unlike the art 8 right, however, it is accepted in art 10(2) that the exercise of this right 'carries with it duties and responsibilities'. Both rights are qualified. They may respectively be interfered with or restricted provided that three conditions are fulfilled. (a) The interference or restriction must be 'in accordance with the law'; it must have a basis in national law which conforms to the convention standards of legality. (b) It must pursue one of the legitimate aims set out in each article. Article 8(2) provides for 'the protection of the rights and freedoms of others'. Article 10(2) provides for 'the protection of the reputation or rights of others' and for 'preventing the disclosure of information received in confidence'. The rights referred to may either be rights protected under the national law or, as in this case, other convention rights. (c) Above all, the interference or restriction must be 'necessary in a democratic society'; it must meet a 'pressing social need' and be no greater than is proportionate to the legitimate aim pursued; the reasons given for it must be both 'relevant' and 'sufficient' for this purpose.

[140] The application of the proportionality test is more straightforward when only one convention right is in play: the question then is whether the private right claimed offers sufficient justification for the degree of interference with the fundamental right. It is much less straightforward when two convention rights are in play, and the proportionality of interfering with one has to be balanced against the proportionality of restricting the other. As each is a fundamental right, there is evidently a 'pressing social need' to protect it. The convention jurisprudence offers us little help with this. * * * In the national court, the problem of balancing two rights of equal importance arises most acutely in the context of disputes between private persons.

[141] Both parties accepted the basic approach of the Court of Appeal in Re S [2003] 2 FCR 577 at [54]–[60]. This involves looking first at the comparative importance of the actual rights being claimed in the individual case; then at the justifications for interfering with or restricting each of those rights; and applying the proportionality test to each. The parties in this case differed about whether the trial judge or the Court of Appeal had done this, the appellant arguing that the Court of Appeal had assumed primacy for the art 10 right while the respondent argued that the trial judge had assumed primacy for the art 8 right.

STRIKING THE BALANCE

* * *

[143] No one can pretend that the interests at stake on either side of this case are anywhere near as serious as the interests involved in Re S. Some might even regard them as trivial. Put crudely, it is a prima donna celebrity against a celebrity-exploiting tabloid newspaper. Each in their time has profited from the other. Both are assumed to be grown-ups who

know the score. On the one hand is the interest of a woman who wants to give up her dependence on illegal and harmful drugs and wants the peace and space in which to pursue the help which she finds useful. On the other hand is a newspaper which wants to keep its readers informed of the activities of celebrity figures, and to expose their weaknesses, lies, evasions and hypocrisies. This sort of story, especially if it has photographs attached, is just the sort of thing that fills, sells and enhances the reputation of the newspaper which gets it first. One reason why press freedom is so important is that we need newspapers to sell in order to ensure that we still have newspapers at all. It may be said that newspapers should be allowed considerable latitude in their intrusions into private grief so that they can maintain circulation and the rest of us can then continue to enjoy the variety of newspapers and other mass media which are available in this country. It may also be said that newspaper editors often have to make their decisions at great speed and in difficult circumstances, so that to expect too minute an analysis of the position is in itself a restriction on their freedom of expression.

[144] Examined more closely, however, this case is far from trivial. What is the nature of the private life, respect for which is in issue here? The information revealed by the article was information relating to Miss Campbell's health, both physical and mental. Drug abuse can be seriously damaging to physical health; indeed it is sometimes life-threatening. It can also lead to a wide variety of recognised mental disorders (see the ICD–10 Classification of Mental and Behavioural Disorders (WHO 1992) F10–F19). Drug addiction needs treatment if it is to be overcome. Treatment is at several levels. There is the quick 'detox' to rid the body of the harmful substances. This will remove the immediate physical danger but does nothing to tackle the underlying dependence. Then there is therapy aimed at tackling that underlying dependence, which may be combined with a transfer of the dependence from illegal drugs to legally prescribed substitutes. Then there is therapy aimed at maintaining and reinforcing the resolve to keep up the abstinence achieved and prevent relapse. This is vital. Anyone who has had anything to do with drug addiction knows how easy it is to relapse once returned to the temptations of the life in which it began and how necessary it is to try, try and try again to achieve success.

[145] It has always been accepted that information about a person's health and treatment for ill-health is both private and confidential. This stems not only from the confidentiality of the doctor-patient relationship but from the nature of the information itself. * * *

* * *

[146] The Court of Appeal in this case held that the information revealed here was not in the same category as clinical medical records. That may be so, in the sense that it was not the notes made by a doctor when consulted by a patient. But the information was of exactly the same kind as that which would be recorded by a doctor on those notes: the presenting problem was addiction to illegal drugs, the diagnosis was no

doubt the same, and the prescription was therapy, including the self-help group therapy offered by regular attendance at NA.

[147] I start, therefore, from the fact—indeed, it is common ground—that all of the information about Miss Campbell's addiction and attendance at NA which was revealed in the Mirror article was both private and confidential, because it related to an important aspect of Miss Campbell's physical and mental health and the treatment she was receiving for it. It had also been received from an insider in breach of confidence. That simple fact has been obscured by the concession properly made on her behalf that the newspaper's countervailing freedom of expression did serve to justify the publication of some of this information. But the starting point must be that it was all private and its publication required specific justification.

[148] What was the nature of the freedom of expression which was being asserted on the other side? There are undoubtedly different types of speech, just as there are different types of private information, some of which are more deserving of protection in a democratic society than others. Top of the list is political speech. The free exchange of information and ideas on matters relevant to the organisation of the economic, social and political life of the country is crucial to any democracy. Without this, it can scarcely be called a democracy at all. This includes revealing information about public figures, especially those in elective office, which would otherwise be private but is relevant to their participation in public life. Intellectual and educational speech and expression are also important in a democracy, not least because they enable the development of individuals' potential to play a full part in society and in our democratic life. Artistic speech and expression is important for similar reasons, in fostering both individual originality and creativity and the free-thinking and dynamic society we so much value. No doubt there are other kinds of speech and expression for which similar claims can be made.

[149] But it is difficult to make such claims on behalf of the publication with which we are concerned here. The political and social life of the community, and the intellectual, artistic or personal development of individuals, are not obviously assisted by pouring over the intimate details of a fashion model's private life. However, there is one way in which the article could be said to be educational. The editor had considered running a highly critical piece, adding the new information to the not inconsiderable list of Miss Campbell's faults and follies detailed in the article, emphasising the lies and hypocrisy it revealed. Instead he chose to run a sympathetic piece, still listing her faults and follies, but setting them in the context of her now-revealed addiction and her even more important efforts to overcome it. Newspapers and magazines often carry such pieces and they may well have a beneficial educational effect.

[150] The crucial difference here is that such pieces are normally run with the co-operation of those involved. Private people are not identified without their consent. It is taken for granted that this is

otherwise confidential information. The editor did offer Miss Campbell the opportunity of being involved with the story but this was refused. Her evidence suggests that she was concerned for the other people in the group. What entitled him to reveal this private information about her without her consent?

[151] The answer which she herself accepts is that she had presented herself to the public as someone who was not involved in drugs. It would have been a very good thing if she were not. If other young women do see her as someone to be admired and emulated, then it is all to the good if she is not addicted to narcotic substances. It might be questioned why, if a role model has adopted a stance which all would agree is beneficial rather than detrimental to society, it is so important to reveal that she has feet of clay. But the possession and use of illegal drugs is a criminal offence and a matter of serious public concern. The press must be free to expose the truth and put the record straight.

[152] That consideration justified the publication of the fact that, contrary to her previous statements, Miss Campbell had been involved with illegal drugs. It also justified publication of the fact that she was trying to do something about it by seeking treatment. It was not necessary for those purposes to publish any further information, especially if this might jeopardise the continued success of that treatment.

[153] The further information includes the fact that she was attending NA meetings, the fact that she had been doing so for some time, and with some regularity, and the photographs of her either arriving at or leaving the premises where meetings took place. All of these things are interrelated with one another and with the effect which revealing them might have upon her. Revealing that she was attending NA enabled the paper to print the headline 'Naomi: I am a drug addict', not because she had said so to the paper but because it could assume that she had said this or something like it in a meeting. It also enabled the paper to talk about the meetings and how she was treated there, in a way which made it look as if the information came from someone who had been there with her, even if it simply came from general knowledge of how these meetings work. This all contributed to the sense of betrayal by someone close to her of which she spoke and which destroyed the value of NA as a safe haven for her.

[154] Publishing the photographs contributed both to the revelation and to the harm that it might do. By themselves, they are not objectionable. Unlike France and Quebec, in this country we do not recognise a right to one's own image: cf Aubry v Editions Vice–Versa Inc [1998] 1 SCR 591. We have not so far held that the mere fact of covert photography is sufficient to make the information contained in the photograph confidential. The activity photographed must be private. If this had been, and had been presented as, a picture of Naomi Campbell going about her business in a public street, there could have been no complaint. She makes a substantial part of her living out of being photographed looking stunning

in designer clothing. Readers will obviously be interested to see how she looks if and when she pops out to the shops for a bottle of milk. There is nothing essentially private about that information nor can it be expected to damage her private life. It may not be a high order of freedom of speech but there is nothing to justify interfering with it. * * *

[155] But here the accompanying text made it plain that these photographs were different. They showed her coming either to or from the NA meeting. They showed her in the company of others, some of whom were undoubtedly part of the group. They showed the place where the meeting was taking place, which will have been entirely recognisable to anyone who knew the locality. A picture is 'worth a thousand words' because it adds to the impact of what the words convey; but it also adds to the information given in those words. If nothing else, it tells the reader what everyone looked like; in this case it also told the reader what the place looked like. In context, it also added to the potential harm, by making her think that she was being followed or betrayed, and deterring her from going back to the same place again.

[156] There was no need to do this. The editor accepted that even without the photographs, it would have been a front page story. He had his basic information and he had his quotes. There is no shortage of photographs with which to illustrate and brighten up a story about Naomi Campbell. No doubt some of those available are less flattering than others, so that if he had wanted to run a hostile piece he could have done so. The fact that it was a sympathetic story is neither here nor there. The way in which he chose to present the information he was entitled to reveal was entirely a matter for him. The photographs would have been useful in proving the truth of the story had this been challenged, but there was no need to publish them for this purpose. The credibility of the story with the public would stand or fall with the credibility of Mirror stories generally.

[157] The weight to be attached to these various considerations is a matter of fact and degree. Not every statement about a person's health will carry the badge of confidentiality or risk doing harm to that person's physical or moral integrity. The privacy interest in the fact that a public figure has a cold or a broken leg is unlikely to be strong enough to justify restricting the press's freedom to report it. What harm could it possibly do? Sometimes there will be other justifications for publishing, especially where the information is relevant to the capacity of a public figure to do the job. But that is not this case and in this case there was, as the judge found, a risk that publication would do harm. The risk of harm is what matters at this stage, rather than the proof that actual harm has occurred. People trying to recover from drug addiction need considerable dedication and commitment, along with constant reinforcement from those around them. That is why organisations like NA were set up and why they can do so much good. Blundering in when matters are acknowledged to be at a 'fragile' stage may do great harm.

[158] The trial judge was well placed to assess these matters. He could tell whether the impact of the story on her was serious or trivial. The fact that the story had been published at all was bound to cause distress and possibly interfere with her progress. But he was best placed to judge whether the additional information and the photographs had added significantly both to the distress and the potential harm. He accepted her evidence that it had done so. He could also tell how serious an interference with press freedom it would have been to publish the essential parts of the story without the additional material and how difficult a decision this would have been for an editor who had been told that it was a medical matter and that it would be morally wrong to publish it.

* * *

LORD CARSWELL:

[161] My Lords, I have had the advantage of reading in draft the opinions of my noble and learned friends, Lord Hope of Craighead and Baroness Hale of Richmond, and I agree with them that the appeal should be allowed.

* * *

[167] One must then move to the balancing exercise, which involves consideration of arts 8 and 10 of the European Convention for the Protection of Human Rights and Fundamental Freedoms 1950 * * *. The carrying out of the balancing is at the centre of this case and forms the point at which the two currents of opinion divide. I agree with the analysis contained in paras [105]–[113] of Lord Hope's opinion in the present appeal and am gratefully content to adopt it. I also agree with him that in order to justify limiting the art 10 right to freedom of expression the restrictions imposed must be rational, fair and not arbitrary, and they must impair the right no more than necessary.

[168] Resolution of this question depends on the weight which one attributes to several factors, the extent of the distress to the appellant and the potential adverse effects on her drug therapy, the extent to which one judges the material in categories (3), (4) and (5) to have gone beyond that contained in categories (1) and (2), and the degree of latitude which should be allowed to the press in the way in which it chooses to present a story. Weighing and balancing these factors is a process which may well lead different people to different conclusions, as one may readily see from consideration of the judgments of the courts below and the opinions given by the several members of the Appellate Committee of your Lordships' House.

* * *

[170] In my opinion the balance comes down in favour of the appellant on the issues in this appeal. I would not myself attempt to isolate which of the contents of categories (3), (4) and (5) is more harmful

or tips the balance. I find it sufficient to hold that the information contained in categories (3) and (4), allied to the photographs in category (5), went significantly beyond the revelation that the appellant was a drug addict and was engaged in drug therapy. I consider that it constituted such an intrusion into the appellant's private affairs that the factors relied upon by respondents do not suffice to justify publication. I am unable to accept that such publication was necessary to maintain the newspaper's credibility.

[171] I would accordingly hold that the publication of the third, fourth and fifth elements in the article constituted an infringement of the appellant's right to privacy that cannot be justified and that she is entitled to a remedy. I would allow the appeal and restore the judge's order.

NOTES

1. The text of Articles 8 and 10 of the European Convention for the Protection of Fundamental Rights and Freedoms is as follows:

ARTICLE 8

1. Everyone has the right to respect for his private and family life, his home and his correspondence.
2. There shall be no interference by a public authority with the exercise of this right except such as is in accordance with the law and is necessary in a democratic society in the interests of national security, public safety or the economic well-being of the country, for the prevention of disorder or crime, for the protection of health or morals, or for the protection of the rights and freedoms of others.

ARTICLE 10

1. Everyone has the right to freedom of expression. This right shall include freedom to hold opinions and to receive and impart information and ideas without interference by public authority and regardless of frontiers. This article shall not prevent States from requiring the licensing of broadcasting, television or cinema enterprises.
2. The exercise of these freedoms, since it carries with it duties and responsibilities, may be subject to such formalities, conditions, restrictions or penalties as are prescribed by law and are necessary in a democratic society, in the interests of national security, territorial integrity or public safety, for the prevention of disorder or crime, for the protection of health or morals, for the protection of the reputation or the rights of others, for preventing the disclosure of information received in confidence, or for maintaining the authority and impartiality of the judiciary

2. The European Court of Human Rights upheld the judgment in *Campbell* on the merits with one dissent among the seven judges who heard the case, but struck down the assessment of costs made by the British courts. MGN Ltd, v. United Kingdom, Application No. 39401/04. Judgment of Janu-

ary 18, 2011. It will be recalled that Ms. Campbell was awarded £3,500 in compensatory and aggravated damages. She was subsequently awarded £1,086,195.47 for costs including attorney's fees. In upholding the judgment on the merits in the *MGN* case, the European Court relied on its decision in the *von Hannover* case which is described in the following note. In dissenting on the merits Judge Thór Bjögvinsson declared that "[f]rom the point of view of journalistic discretion in the presentation of a legitimate story, it is the restriction on freedom of expression that must be justified by reference to 'necessity' and not the publication." (*Id.* at ¶ 4.)

A more recent British case is Murray v. Express Newspapers LLC, [2008] 3 W.L.R. 1360 (C.A.). The case involved photographs of the 19–month–old son of J.K. Rowling being pushed by his father in a "buggy" as he accompanied his parents to and from a café. It was conceded that the child himself was unaware of what was happening but recovery was allowed on the basis that it interfered with the family life of his family. In a New Zealand case involving practically identical facts, the Court of Appeal ruled that no action would lie even though, in a three-to-two decision, the majority declared that New Zealand recognized the action for breach of confidence along the lines articulated by the courts of the United Kingdom. Hosking v. Runting, [2005] 1 N.Z.L.R. 1 (C.A.).

3. Shortly after the *Campbell* case a section of the European Court of Human Rights decided von Hannover v. Germany, Application No. 59320/00, Judgment of June 24, 2004, 40 Eur.H.R. Rep. 1 (2005). In that case, Princess Caroline of Monaco sought legal relief under Article 8 of the European Convention for the publication of photographs of herself, sometimes with her children and sometimes with a male companion. All the photographs were taken while she was in a public space or in a space visible from a public space. She received some relief in the German courts for the pictures taken of her with her children and for a photograph taken of her and a male companion taken from public space while seated in a secluded outdoor part of a restaurant on the ground that she had legitimate expectation of privacy in that instance. As to the other photographs, including a picture of her on a private beach visible from public space, she was denied recovery on the ground that she was "a figure of contemporary society 'par excellence' ". The Court held that not only public figures but even political figures and officials enjoyed some respect for their privacy, even in public space. In an approach similar to that taken by the House of Lords in the *Campbell* case, the European Court declared that for expression to escape liability when challenged for invading someone's expectation of privacy, as in the case before it, the expression must be shown to "contribute to a debate of general interest." (*Id.* at ¶ 65.) In a related case involving Princess Caroline a Grand Chamber (of seventeen judges) reaffirmed that statement of principles. *See* von Hannover v. Germany (No. 2), Application No. 60641/08, Judgment of 7 February 2012.

As was recognized in *Campbell* and also by the concurring judges in the section judgment of the *von Hannover* case described above, these cases turn on largely factual issues on which different judges might come to different conclusions while at the same time involving matters on which coming to the right decision is important because of the great importance of the values involved. Inevitably to reach some sort of consistency one or more of the competing values, expression or privacy, will be given prima facie preference, despite the rhetorical acceptance that expression and privacy are of equal value. The British and European decisions seem to be making privacy the preferred value in close cases. That was the point of Judge Bjögvinsson's dissent in *MGN* to which we referred above. In the United States there is no question that the preferred value will be expression in such situations. This matter is discussed in some depth in G. Christie, Philosopher Kings? The Adjudication of Conflicting Human Rights and Social Values (2011).

4. The judges that decided the *Campbell* and the *von Hannover* cases made it clear that there was a public interest in discouraging paparazzi. That aversion is shared by many in the United States. California has what is often called an anti-paparazzi statute that includes a provision imposing civil liability for trespassing on someone's property "to capture any type of visual image, sound recording, or other physical impression of the plaintiff engaging in a personal or familial activity and the physical invasion occurs in a manner that is offensive to a reasonable person." Cal. Civ. Code § 1708.8(a). Another provision, *id.* § 1708.8(b) is more questionable. It provides for liability for "constructive trespass" even in the absence of a physical trespass for attempting to capture these visual images, sound recordings or other physical impressions "of the plaintiff engaging in a personal or familiar activity under circumstances in which the plaintiff had a reasonable expectation of privacy through the use of a visual or an auditory enhancement device" in circumstances in which those images, recordings, or physical impressions could not have been obtained without resort to those devices. One should note that the statute says nothing about using enhancement devices just to look at people. See note 4 (after the *Nader* case) on pp. 665–66, *supra*.

5. An approach to the problem of information gathering that presents fewer constitutional problems is not to restrict the ability to gather information but to restrict the uses that may be made of the information obtained. For example, it might be made illegal to deny consumer credit on the basis of arrests, convictions or bankruptcies that have occurred sufficiently far in the past. The Fair Credit Reporting Act of 1970, however, takes the tack of prohibiting consumer reporting agencies from furnishing reports containing arrests, convictions, or judgments more than seven years old and bankruptcies more than ten years old (15 U.S.C. § 1681c, as amended). On some of the problems presented by the Act, *see* G. Christie, *The Right to Privacy and the Freedom to Know: A Comment on Professor Miller's* The Assault on Privacy, 119 U.Pa.L.Rev. 970, 975–80 (1971). Another approach is not to try to restrict access to information or even dissemination of information but rather to make sure that the information is accurate. Thus, the Fair Credit Reporting Act has provisions requiring the notification of the consumer that information may be obtained about him (15 U.S.C. § 1681d(a)). The Act also provides procedures by which a consumer can find out what information has been obtained about him (15 U.S.C. §§ 1681g(a), 1681m(b)) and procedures whereby consumer credit records can be corrected (15 U.S.C. § 1681i). The subsequent Federal Privacy Act of 1974, 5 U.S.C. § 552a, also contains procedures whereby an individual may find out if the Government is keeping records about him—he may also be able to obtain this information under the Freedom of Information Act, 5 U.S.C. § 552, as amended. Moreover, procedures also exist, under the

Privacy Act, whereby an individual can seek correction of government records concerning him.

6. The problem of providing a legal remedy for publication of private facts in breach of a traditionally recognized confidential relationship presents somewhat different considerations. Consider Commonwealth v. Wiseman, 356 Mass. 251, 249 N.E.2d 610 (1969), *cert. denied* 398 U.S. 960, 90 S.Ct. 2165, 26 L.Ed.2d 546 (1970), *decree modified in minor respects* 360 Mass. 857, 275 N.E.2d 148 (1971). For a more detailed discussion of the case and its background, see Comment, *The "Titicut Follies" Case: Limiting the Public Interest Privilege,* 70 Colum.L.Rev. 359 (1970). Wiseman had obtained official permission to make an educational documentary film of the Massachusetts Correctional Institute at Bridgewater. The permission was subject to certain conditions designed to protect the privacy of the inmates and patients. Wiseman in due course produced a film about the criminally insane entitled *Titicut Follies.* The film is not without sympathy for the staff, who were struggling with excruciatingly difficult problems in an obsolete institution with inadequate resources, or for the depressing plight of the inmates, but it shows inmates in pathetic and embarrassingly indecent situations. The film contains scenes of forced nose feeding, skin searches of naked patients, and pathetic attempts of prisoners to hide their genitals. Unknown to the Massachusetts authorities, the film was shown at two film festivals, in one of which it won first prize as the best documentary film of the year. Wiseman contracted for the commercial distribution of the film, and it was first shown in New York where it was advertised as making " 'Marat Sade' look like 'Holiday on Ice.' " The Attorney General of Massachusetts, concluding that the film went beyond the scope of the consent granted by Massachusetts authorities and that the film was an unauthorized invasion of the inmates' privacy, brought suit to enjoin future exhibitions. Wiseman argued that the distribution of the film was in the public interest as a means of bringing the plight of the inmates to the public's attention. The Supreme Judicial Court of Massachusetts agreed with the trial court that Wiseman had not adequately complied with the conditions of the permission to make the film, one of which was to photograph only inmates legally competent to sign releases. Treating Wiseman as primarily a collector of information who had breached the conditions under which he was allowed to make the film, one can see little difficulty with the legal system's providing remedies to protect the interests of the inmates. Furthermore, regardless of the conditions that were or were not imposed, perhaps a court should have held that no one may grant permission to photograph mentally incompetent inmates within a state institution unless the photographs are necessary for treatment of the patients or would aid in the efficient administration of the institution such as for identification purposes. What is curious, however, is that the appellate court modified the trial court's decree that the film be destroyed, in order to permit exhibition to specialized audiences, such as "legislators, judges, lawyers, sociologists, social workers, doctors, psychiatrists, students in these or related fields, and organizations dealing with the social problems of custodial care and mental infirmity," provided that "a brief explanation that changes and improvements have taken place in the institution" be included in the film. Relying on this modification of the original decree the film was shown from time to time at a

number of law schools and other educational institutions. Does the court's order imply that some people's right to know is better than others? Should public interest or concern be irrelevant in these sorts of situations? An earlier federal district court decision, Cullen v. Grove Press, Inc., 276 F.Supp. 727 (S.D.N.Y.1967), denied relief to guards at Bridgewater who sought to enjoin the film's showing in New York. The restrictions on the distribution of *Titicut Follies* have now been lifted by the Massachusetts' courts. See N.Y. Times, Saturday, August 3, 1991, § 1, p. 6, col. 6. The passage of time was a decisive factor. What if all the inmates portrayed in the film had not died. Should that have been the decisive factor? For the actual order, *see* Commonwealth v. Wiseman, Civ. Action No. 87538 (Mass. Superior Ct., Suffolk Cty., July 29, 1991). (Wiseman, however, was not permitted to reveal the names of inmates who appeared in the film.)

TAGGART v. WADLEIGH–MAURICE LTD.

United States Court of Appeals, Third Circuit, 1973.
489 F.2d 434, *cert. denied* 417 U.S. 937, 94 S.Ct. 2653, 41 L.Ed.2d 241 (1974).

Opinion of the Court

GIBBONS, CIRCUIT JUDGE.

This is an appeal from the grant of defendants' motion for summary judgment. The pleadings, affidavits, and depositions on file establish that the appellant Taggart is an employee of Port–O–San, a corporation engaged in the business of furnishing and servicing portable latrines. Taggart was sent by his employer to Bethel, New York in August, 1969 to service such portable latrines furnished by Port–O–San to the promoters of the Woodstock music festival. While he was servicing the Port–O–San latrines he was, according to his complaint and deposition, diverted from that work and engaged in conversation by agents of defendant Wadleigh–Maurice, Ltd., who were filming the festival, and photographed by sound motion picture. Wadleigh–Maurice, Ltd. during the course of the festival took over 315,000 feet of film (about 120 hours of viewing). From this 315,000 feet of film a feature length "documentary" was assembled, which defendant Warner Bros. Inc. undertook to distribute for commercial viewing. There is no dispute that the festival, the preparation of the film, and its distribution to theatres were all undertaken for commercial profit-making purposes. In those parts of the 315,000 feet of film chosen for inclusion in the "documentary" and thereby given widespread public dissemination is a sequence of approximately two minutes depicting Taggart emptying latrines. Taggart's deposition discloses the circumstances in which he was photographed:

"Q. Basically, at the time you were at Woodstock and you were approached by these two men, had you ever seen them before?

A. No, I never did.

Q. Did you know who they were?

A. No, I have no idea.

Q. How did they engage you in conversation?

A. Well, as I said before, as I was working these two men just came up and started talking to me. What are you doing there, I think was the key sentence. What are you doing there, they said.

Q. You responded to the conversation that ensued?

A. Yes. From there on, I went on about my business, about doing my work. As I was, they spoke to me and asked me what was this, and so forth.

Q. Did you respond to anything they asked you?

A. I responded to the questions they asked me.

Q. You mentioned before that they had cameras. How big were the cameras they had? Can you show us?

A. They looked like the little square box or something like that.

MR. FARLEY: Indicating about six inches long.

A. Maybe rectangular.

Q. Do you have a home movie camera yourself at home?

A. I have one, yes. It would be not in that category. It would be more like my son's. Thomas has one with a zoom thing on it and stuff like that.

Q. The camera that the man was holding, was that similar to the camera your son has?

A. It would be something like that.

Q. So the cameras were like home movie type cameras?

A. Yes.

Q. Did you see any of those large cameras that they used to depict when they show the news?

A. No.

Q. You didn't see anything like that?

A. No. Whatever it was they had was strapped. They had them in a strap on their neck.

Q. A strap to hold the camera?

A. Yes, a little bit of a strap.

Q. In the general vicinity through these days you were at the festival, were there many people with cameras of various types?

A. As I recall, I saw different types of cameras. I wouldn't say there was a wholesale thing with cameras there, you know.

Q. At any time did anyone ask your permission to take the picture?

A. Well, not that they asked me. Nobody came up to me and said, can I take your picture, nothing like that. They just came up and started talking. As they were talking—

Q. Was one talking to you and the other took the picture?

A. It was a combination. I don't know if I'm making myself clear here * * *.

* * *

Q. In relation to the two men taking your picture did you know that they were taking it for any public released [sic]?

A. No. I had no idea of that."

Taggart contends that the sequence in which he was interrogated while performing his necessary though not necessarily pleasant employment was edited into the "documentary" in such a way as to achieve, at his expense, a comic effect. That this may well have been the intended and actual effect is supported by evidence in the record of the reaction of critics. For example, Kathleen Carroll, the critic, stated "[T]he funniest scene shows the latrine attendant proudly demonstrating his job." Craig McGregor, writing in the New York Times, April 19, 1970, stated " * * * and the man who is the real schizophrenic hero of Woodstock, the Port–O–San man, who empties the latrines of the beautiful people and has one son there at Woodstock and another flying a DMZ helicopter in Vietnam." Taggart contends that while he was engaged in his ordinary work he was without warning, and without consent, drawn into a conversation and photographed so that the sequence could be used as a key part of the theme of the "documentary" which was being prepared as a commercial enterprise.

When Taggart learned that he had been included in the commercial film he protested to the defendants, but they refused to delete the scene and proceeded to distribute the film nationwide. As a result, he alleges, he has suffered mental anguish, embarrassment, public ridicule, and invasion of his right to privacy which has detrimentally affected his social and family life and his employment. His deposition supports his contention that such ongoing damaging effects have occurred and are continuing. In this diversity civil action he seeks damages and an injunction against continued distribution of the offending scene. * * *

Moving for summary judgment, the defendants placed principal reliance on Man v. Warner Bros. Inc., 317 F.Supp. 50 (S.D.N.Y.1970). In that case Man, a professional musician, was at Woodstock, where at 4 A.M. he mounted the stage and played "Mess Call" on his Flugelhorn. His performance was photographed by the Wadleigh–Maurice camera crews, and was edited into the documentary without his consent. He brought a diversity action for injunctive relief pursuant to New York's right of privacy statute * * * and moved for a preliminary injunction. The defendant made a cross motion for summary judgment, which was granted. * * * In justification for the grant of summary judgment the court pointed out (1) that a professional musician who mounts a stage to give a performance before an audience of 400,000 is a public figure, (2) that in any event the depiction of his performance was merely a factual depiction of his participation in a newsworthy event, and (3) that plaintiff's forty-five second performance was *de minimis*.

The transcript of the argument on the motion for summary judgment in this case discloses that the district court appreciated several distinctions between this case and *Man*. First, Taggart was not a professional musician performing before an audience of 400,000. He was an ordinary working man going about his lowly task. Second, the reaction of the critics suffices to prevent the entry of summary judgment on a *de minimis* basis. The latrine sequence apparently makes a significant and memorable contribution to the film's overall impact. Thus, if summary judgment is to be sustained, it must be sustained solely because Taggart was a participant in a newsworthy event, and as such, outside the protection of § 51 or some other statutory or common law right of privacy. The district judge recognized, however, that it would be one thing to photograph Taggart as he went about his duties at a newsworthy event and to include such a photograph in a factual description of the event, but quite another thing to deliberately draw him out in conversation for the purpose of making him an inadvertent performer in a sequence intended to be exploited for its artistic effect. Recognizing this distinction, the district judge viewed the offending film sequence, and ruled:

> "I react, as Mr. Dershowitz's remarks indicate, as the reasonable man might react after seeing the film. I come to a different conclusion after having seen the film than I did from reading just the dialogue. It was not so much a drawing out as to expose him to a substantial participation in the film. The event fits in a perspective of moving from one aspect of this festival to the next. He was not diverted from the work he was doing and brought, so to speak, upon the stage and made somebody separate and apart from the fellow who was working at the time they focused the camera on him. It is a very difficult line to draw.
>
> I believe as you do, as I indicated before the luncheon recess, that there still is an area left where somebody does set out deliberately to make somebody participate in gaining a profit without compensation to him. But there is still an area where that is not protected by the First Amendment cases. I do not think that falls on this side of the line. I feel that summary judgment is indicated and I will grant the motion." (Tr. at 32).

The difficulty with this ruling is that it chooses between Taggart's version, that he was drawn out and made an involuntary performer, and the defendants' version, that he was a mere participant in a newsworthy event. The sequence which * * * [the judge] viewed undoubtedly was significant evidence in support of the defendants' position. But it was only evidence to be weighed against Taggart's testimony and the reaction of the critics. * * *

Clearly, then, the record presents disputed fact issues. We can affirm the grant of summary judgment on such a record only if we are prepared to hold that as a matter of law the defendants are entitled to judgment even if Taggart was deliberately drawn out as a performer in a commercial film. Such a ruling would leave very little to § 51 or to any similar statutory or common law right of privacy. It would be predicated upon a more absolutist interpretation of the first amendment than has yet been espoused by a majority of the Supreme Court. * * * We realize that requiring the defendants to defend in a trial rather than to obtain summary judgment puts them to additional expense, and arguably subjects their first amendment rights, should those rights ultimately be held to prevail over Taggart's right to privacy, to that much extra "chill." In the context of the problem—their commercial exploitation of Taggart's allegedly induced performance—this degree of "chill" seems to us *de minimis* when compared with the unsatisfactory alternative of ruling on a potentially serious conflict between legally protected rights without a complete record.

Judge Van Dusen, dissenting, urges that where "constitutional fact" is involved a district court may on a motion for summary judgment, or an appellate court may on appeal, resolve disputed fact issues. * * * Just as disputed facts in a nonjury case are determined by trial and not on summary judgment motion, a trial judge's decision to instruct the jury with the *New York Times* standard or an appellate court's de novo review of "constitutional fact" are both made after a full trial on the contested factual issues. Properly viewed these represent nothing more than the application of a governing legal standard to undisputed facts or to facts that are viewed in a light more favorable to one party. They do not involve the resolution of such credibility issues as whether or not Taggart was drawn out or was a willing participant. The label "constitutional fact" does not permit even an appellate court reviewing a full record to resolve credibility issues.

The judgment of the district court will be reversed and the case remanded for further proceedings consistent with this opinion.

VAN DUSEN, CIRCUIT JUDGE (dissenting):

I respectfully dissent and would affirm the granting of summary judgment by the district court.

The court has today characterized the issue before the district court as whether Mr. Taggart was "drawn out" and made an involuntary performer or whether he was a mere participant in a newsworthy event and concluded that such factual determinations are for the jury. If this case involved only the application of the New York statute to the factual situation presented here, I would agree that summary judgment was improperly granted.

However, the central issue before the district court was whether the rule of Time, Inc. v. Hill * * * applied to the facts of this case. The question of whether or not Mr. Taggart was a participant in a newsworthy event, even if properly characterized as one of fact, involves a constitutional decision as to the proper application of a First Amendment standard. It must, therefore, be considered one of "constitutional fact" which the Supreme Court has said to be subject to de novo review. Rosenbloom v. Metromedia, * * *. It follows that at trial such issues are properly decided by the judge on a motion for summary judgment, where there are no other genuine issues of material fact.

* * *

There is no question that the Woodstock festival itself was an event of public interest nor that Mr. Taggart, by his presence there, was a participant in it. Furthermore, counsel for appellant has conceded in oral argument that if Mr. Taggart had only been filmed and not interviewed, this action would be barred. I fail to see why the mere fact of the brief questions asked should alter that result.

There may arise cases where a reporter or film maker conducts an interview in such a way as to lose the constitutional privilege of Time, Inc. v. Hill, *supra*. For example, where an incident is staged, as in the television series "Candid Camera," it would not seem to be an event of public interest. But here Mr. Taggart was simply filmed going about his ordinary occupation and asked a few questions that directly related to his participation in, and opinions on, a clearly newsworthy event. This is a common and important technique of investigative reporting and should enjoy the same constitutional protection as would a written or filmed account of that event. I would affirm the district court's granting of summary judgment.

NOTES

1. We have already discussed the question of the degree of scrutiny which courts should exercise over factual issues arising in the course of litigation over the scope of the first amendment in connection with our discussion of defamation where these questions are presented more frequently. It, therefore, may be helpful to review the discussion at p. 591, *supra*. There is no question that the Court has made many factual issues which arise in the course of such litigation questions of "constitutional fact" as to which a trial court deciding whether to accept a jury verdict or an appellate court reviewing a lower court decision must exercise an "independent judgment". On the other hand, the Court has also made clear that, in deciding whether to grant summary judgment, the trial court is only to ask whether a reasonable jury could decide in the plaintiff's favor. The more searching independent judgment doctrine only comes into play once the jury has rendered its verdict. *See* Anderson v. Liberty Lobby, Inc., 477 U.S. 242, 106 S.Ct. 2505, 91 L.Ed.2d 202 (1986). The Court has of course recognized that the question of credibility is a particularly difficult one for an appellate court to handle. *See* Bose Corp. v. Consumers Union of United States, Inc., 466 U.S. 485, 104 S.Ct. 1949, 80 L.Ed.2d 502 (1984).

2. We have also already briefly considered p. 673, *supra*, the question whether the incidental inclusion of someone in a documentary motion picture is an invasion of someone's privacy. *See* Blumenthal v. Picture Classics, 235

App.Div. 570, 257 N.Y.S. 800 (1932), *aff'd on procedural grounds*, 261 N.Y. 504, 185 N.E. 713. The clear implication of *Taggart v. Wadleigh–Maurice Ltd.* is that it is not. The question left for decision on remand was whether Taggert's inclusion was more than incidental. In a case somewhat analogous to *Taggert,* Lane v. MRA Holdings, LLC., 242 F.Supp.2d 1205 (M.D. Fla. 2002), in which the plaintiff's inclusion in the finished film was arguably more than incidental, the plaintiff was denied recovery.

In Town and Country Property, Inc. v. Riggins, 249 Va. 387, 457 S.E.2d 356 (1995), the plaintiff, a former professional football player, recovered, under a Virginia statute modeled after the New York statute that has been discussed in many of the cases of this chapter, $50,000 in compensatory and punitive damages in the following circumstances. As a result of a divorce settlement, the plaintiff had conveyed to his ex-wife his interest in the former matrimonial home that was located in the Virginia suburbs of Washington D.C. His ex-wife became a sales representative of the defendant realty company. When she decided to sell the house she prepared a flyer that exhorted real estate brokers to "come see John Riggins' former home." Three type sizes were used with "John Riggins'" in the largest type size and "former home" in the smallest. The court held that the use of the plaintiff's name "was not relevant to dissemination of information to consumers about the physical condition, architectural features, or quality of the home." Are these the only relevant considerations? The question of commercial appropriation of a person's name, likeness, etc. will be further pursued in the next two cases. Although the present purpose is only to give the student an overview of an important topic, several points are worth noting. As we saw in the *Sidis* case, supra p. 675, as well as in other instances, and is expressly declared in Cal. Civ. § 3344 (d), use of a name, photograph likeness, etc. "in connection with any news, public affairs, or sport broadcast or account, or any political campaign" would not be considered commercial expropriation. Furthermore courts have been solicitous to protect artistic expression. *See, e.g.,* Winter v. DC Comics, 30 Cal.4th 881, 69 P.3d 473, 134 Cal.Rptr.2d 634 (2003); Altbach v. Kulon, 302 A.D.2d 655, 754 N.Y.S.2d 709 (2003); Simeonov v. Tiegs, 159 Misc.2d 54, 602 N.Y.S.2d 1014 (Civ. Ct. 1993).

GRANT v. ESQUIRE, INC.

United States District Court, Southern District of New York, 1973.
367 F.Supp. 876.

WHITMAN KNAPP, DISTRICT JUDGE.

The essential facts relevant to the cross motions for summary judgment in this diversity action are not in dispute, and are relatively simple. Back in 1946, Esquire published an article about the clothing tastes and habits of six Hollywood stars, including plaintiff Cary Grant. This article was illustrated with posed pictures of these stars, obtained with their consent. The caption under Mr. Grant's picture was as follows:

> "Hollywood Luminary Cary Grant—Cary Grant, ever coming up with the unexpected in pictures (as witness his roles in films from Gunga Din to Notorious with Ingrid Bergman), leans to conservative dress in

> his private life. Accordingly you see him in his favorite town suit of blue-striped unfinished worsted. The jacket, designed with slightly extended shoulders, has long rolled lapels which emphasize a trim waistline. The shirt, of off-white silk shantung, has a full collar. The black and white small-figured tie is typical of his taste in neckwear. He designs his own easygoing dress shirts, by the way. Made with a fly front, they fasten informally with buttons. As a concession to usage, they have studs but these purely decorative devices go only through the flap of the shirt."

It is to be observed that the foregoing caption provides the reader—in succinct form—with a fair amount of information about Mr. Grant's habits and life style. A considerable segment of the population might well consider this both interesting and informative.

In 1971, Esquire republished the same picture with one modification: everything below the collar line had been replaced with the figure of a model clothed in a cardigan sweater-jacket. Under the picture was the following caption:

> "To give a proper good riddance to the excesses of the Peacock Revolution we have tried a little trickery. And what better way to show the longevity of tradition than by taking the pictures of six modish men that appeared in Esquire in 1946 and garbing the ageless enchantment of these performers in the styles of the Seventies. Above, Cary Grant in a descendant of the classic cardigan, an Orlon doubleknit navy, rust, and buff sweater-coat (Forum, $22.50)."

It is to be observed that neither the picture nor the caption tells the reader anything about Mr. Grant. One is not told whether Mr. Grant ever wore a cardigan sweater jacket, or anything else about him except his one-time appearance in the pages of Esquire. Mr. Grant's face serves no function but to attract attention to the article. Presumably the model who posed for the torso got a professional fee for his part in the enterprise. The question presented is whether Esquire had the right to compel Mr. Grant to contribute his face for free.

It is plaintiff's claim that the 1971 Esquire article gives rise to three causes of action: for libel; for invasion of plaintiff's statutory right of privacy; and, while not made explicit in the complaint, for violation of plaintiff's "right of publicity."

Defendants contend that the complaint fails to state any claim as a matter of state law; and that, in any event, all of its claims are barred by the First Amendment and must therefore be dismissed.

It is readily apparent that these claims and contentions pose two basic questions: 1) Has plaintiff stated one or more valid claims under state law? 2) If so, is there a constitutional bar to plaintiff's enforcement of such otherwise valid state claim?

I.

Turning to state law, there is no difficulty in disposing of the claim for libel. * * *

* * * The publication * * * is not, as a matter of law, libelous. The first cause of action is accordingly dismissed.

Plaintiff's remaining state claims rest on § 51 of the New York Civil Rights Law * * * and upon the somewhat related common law "right of publicity". * * *

The two key expressions in this section are "for advertising purposes" and "for the purposes of trade". We shall first consider the expression "for advertising purposes". As to that, the Court rules as a matter of law that the article on its face does not constitute an advertisement. * * *

Plaintiff contends, however, that he should be allowed to prove that defendants had some covert arrangement with each other which converted the Esquire article into a paid advertisement for the co-defendant Forum. As to that, it seems highly unlikely—in light of the detailed affidavits submitted by defendants on this motion—that plaintiff will be able to establish such a contention. However, the facts—if any—being wholly within defendants' control, plaintiff should have the opportunity to establish its case by pre-trial discovery if he can. * * *

The statutory phrase "for the purposes of trade" is not so easily disposed of. The statutory right to recover damages for the use of one's name for the purpose described in that phrase has had a development influenced by and intertwined with a somewhat disparate common law right known as the right of publicity. * * * The "right of publicity" is somewhat akin to the exclusive right of a commercial enterprise to the benefits to be derived from the goodwill and secondary meaning that it has managed to build up in its name. * * *

* * *

As above indicated, two distinct interests appear to be protected under the general rubric of a "right to privacy". The first protects that right in its more conventional sense, and permits a private individual to recover damages for injured feelings and general embarrassment if for purposes of trade he is unjustifiably subjected to the harsh and—to him—unwelcome glare of publicity. * * * The second—almost the obverse of the first—protects public figures from having the publicity value of their names and reputations unlawfully appropriated by others. * * * It is the second of these aspects that plaintiff Grant seems particularly to be invoking in this litigation.

There is obvious difficulty in defining a "right of privacy" for public personages. Moreover, plaintiff Grant has complicated the difficulty by asserting that he does not want anyone—himself included—to profit by the publicity value of his name and reputation.

To obviate at least the latter difficulty, let us shift our focus from the reticent Mr. Grant and consider the problem from the point of view of one who makes no bones about the commercial exploitation of publicity, the famous English fashion model, Leslie Hornby, commonly known as "Twiggy". Two things are clear in her case: (a) she has amassed a small fortune by exploiting the publicity value of her looks, name and reputation; and (b) in the process, she has become a public personage. In the latter capacity she has become fair game for the media. If she should appear, for example, at the opera in a Givenchy creation she could not complain if her photograph appeared in a newspaper, a magazine, or on television in connection with a story about the opera, about fashions, or about the life and times of Twiggy herself. However, it by no means follows that publishers could present an apparently posed picture of Twiggy and—without her consent—use it in competition with other pictures for which she had professionally posed or in competition with (or in substitution for) the professionally posed pictures of other models. *A fortiori,* no magazine could without her consent crop her head off a posed photograph and superimpose it on the torso of another model.

The question then arises whether the rights of plaintiff Grant—because of his renunciation of any desire to exploit the commercial value of his own name and fame—should be any different than those of Twiggy. We think not. If the owner of Blackacre decides for reasons of his own not to use his land but to keep it in reserve he is not precluded from prosecuting trespassers.

It follows that—absent any constitutional prohibition—the motion for summary judgment will be denied as to the "for purposes of trade" phase of the complaint, and the jury will be asked to decide whether defendant Esquire has appropriated plaintiff Grant's picture for purposes of trade—e.g. merely to attract attention—or whether the picture was used in the course of some legitimate comment on a public figure or subject of public interest with which plaintiff has voluntarily associated himself. * * *

A word about damages. If the jury decides in plaintiff Grant's favor he will of course be entitled to recover for any lacerations to his feelings that he may be able to establish. More importantly, however, he will be able to recover the fair market value of the use for the purposes of trade of his face, name and reputation. The Court has no present suggestion as to how this should be proved. However, the Court can take judicial notice that there is a fairly active market for exploitation of the faces, names and reputations of celebrities, and such market—like any other—must have its recognized rules and experts. One element of damage will probably be the fact—if it be a fact—that Mr. Grant has never sanctioned his commercial use as a photographic model. There may well be a recognized first-time value (which diminishes with use) which the jury might find defendants to have appropriated.

With respect to the "advertising" phase of plaintiff's claim, he would, of course, be entitled to punitive damages should he be able to establish that defendants had secretly and deliberately used his likeness in a commercial advertisement. Punitive damages would not be available under the other phases of his claim as nothing in the affidavits submitted would appear to support a finding of bad faith.

* * *

NOTE

The use of the photograph of someone engaged in an activity as an illustration of the matter discussed in an article or book has been considered in a number of cases. Whether there will or will not be liability for invasion of privacy depends to a considerable extent on how newsworthy the matter discussed is and how closely involved with that activity is the plaintiff. *Compare* Oma v. Hillman Periodicals, Inc., 281 A.D. 240, 118 N.Y.S.2d 720 (1953) and Samuel v. Curtis Pub. Co., 122 F.Supp. 327 (N.D. Cal. 1954) *with* Ainsworth v. Century Supply Co., 295 Ill.App.3d 644, 230 Ill.Dec. 381, 693 N.E.2d 510 (1998). For a case involving the unsuccessful attempt of people who were portrayed in a dramatic presentation of a true incident to recover damages, *see* Tyne v. Time Warner Entertainment Co., 204 F.Supp.2d 1338 (M.D. Fla. 2002) (Case involved the motion picture *The Perfect Storm*).

ZACCHINI v. SCRIPPS–HOWARD BROADCASTING CO.

Supreme Court of the United States, 1977.
433 U.S. 562, 97 S.Ct. 2849, 53 L.Ed.2d 965.

MR. JUSTICE WHITE delivered the opinion of the Court.

Petitioner, Hugo Zacchini, is an entertainer. He performs a "human cannonball" act in which he is shot from a cannon into a net some 200 feet away. Each performance occupies some 15 seconds. In August and September 1972, petitioner was engaged to perform his act on a regular basis at the Geauga County Fair in Burton, Ohio. He performed in a fenced area, surrounded by grandstands, at the fair grounds. Members of the public attending the fair were not charged a separate admission fee to observe his act.

On August 30, a freelance reporter for Scripps–Howard Broadcasting Co., the operator of a television broadcasting station and respondent in this case, attended the fair. He carried a small movie camera. Petitioner noticed the reporter and asked him not to film the performance. The reporter did not do so on that day; but on the instructions of the producer of respondent's daily newscast, he returned the following day and videotaped the entire act. This film clip approximately 15 seconds in length, was shown on the 11 o'clock news program that night, together with favorable commentary.[1]

---

1. The script of the commentary accompanying the film clip read as follows:

"This * * * now * * * is the story of a *true spectator* sport * * * the sport of human cannonballing * * * in fact, the great *Zacchini* is about the only human cannonball around, these days * * * just happens that, *where* he is, is the Great Geauga County Fair, in Burton

Petitioner then brought this action for damages, alleging that he is "engaged in the entertainment business," that the act he performs is one "invented by his father and * * * performed only by his family for the last fifty years," that respondent "showed and commercialized the film of his act without his consent," and that such conduct was an "unlawful appropriation of plaintiff's professional property." * * * Respondent answered and moved for summary judgment, which was granted by the trial court.

The Court of Appeals of Ohio reversed. The majority held that petitioner's complaint stated a cause of action for conversion and for infringement of a common-law copyright, and one judge concurred in the judgment on the ground that the complaint stated a cause of action for appropriation of petitioner's "right of publicity" in the film of his act. All three judges agreed that the First Amendment did not privilege the press to show the entire performance on a news program without compensating petitioner for any financial injury he could prove at trial.

Like the concurring judge in the Court of Appeals, the Supreme Court of Ohio rested petitioner's cause of action under state law on his "right to the publicity value of his performance." * * * The opinion syllabus, to which we are to look for the rule of law used to decide the case, declared first that one may not use for his own benefit the name or likeness of another, whether or not the use or benefit is a commercial one, and second that respondent would be liable for the appropriation over petitioner's objection and in the absence of license or privilege, of petitioner's right to the publicity value of his performance. * * * The court nevertheless gave judgment for respondent because, in the words of the syllabus:

> "A TV station has a privilege to report in its newscasts matters of legitimate public interest which would otherwise be protected by an individual's right of publicity, unless the actual intent of the TV station was to appropriate the benefit of the publicity for some non-privileged private use, or unless the actual intent was to injure the individual."

We granted certiorari * * * to consider an issue unresolved by this Court: whether the First and Fourteenth Amendments immunized respondent from damages for its alleged infringement of petitioner's state-law "right of publicity." * * * Insofar as the Ohio Supreme Court held that the First and Fourteenth Amendments of the United States Constitution required judgment for respondent, we reverse the judgment of that court.

I

* * *

Even if the judgment in favor of respondent must nevertheless be understood as ultimately resting on Ohio law, it appears that at the very

* * * and believe me, although it's not a *long* act, it's a thriller * * * and you really need to see it *in person* * * * to appreciate it. * * * " (Emphasis in original.) App. 12.

least the Ohio court felt compelled by what it understood to be federal constitutional considerations to construe and apply its own law in the manner it did. In this event, we have jurisdiction and should decide the federal issue; for if the state court erred in its understanding of our cases and of the First and Fourteenth Amendments, we should so declare, leaving the state court free to decide the privilege issue solely as a matter of Ohio law. * * *

II

The Ohio Supreme Court held that respondent is constitutionally privileged to include in its newscasts matters of public interest that would otherwise be protected by the right of publicity, absent an intent to injure or to appropriate for some nonprivileged purpose. If under this standard respondent had merely reported that petitioner was performing at the fair and described or commented on his act, with or without showing his picture on television, we would have a very different case. But petitioner is not contending that his appearance at the fair and his performance could not be reported by the press as newsworthy items. His complaint is that respondent filmed his entire act and displayed that film on television for the public to see and enjoy. This, he claimed, was an appropriation of his professional property. The Ohio Supreme Court agreed that petitioner had "a right of publicity" that gave him "personal control over commercial display and exploitation of his personality and the exercise of his talents." This right of "exclusive control over the publicity given to his performances" was said to be such a "valuable part of the benefit which may be attained by his talents and efforts" that it was entitled to legal protection. It was also observed, or at least expressly assumed, that petitioner had not abandoned his rights by performing under the circumstances present at the Geauga County Fair Grounds.

The Ohio Supreme Court nevertheless held that the challenged invasion was privileged, saying that the press "must be accorded broad latitude in its choice of how much it presents of each story or incident, and of the emphasis to be given to such presentation. No fixed standard which would bar the press from reporting or depicting either an entire occurrence or an entire discrete part of a public performance can be formulated which would not unduly restrict the 'breathing room' in reporting which freedom of the press requires." Under this view, respondent was thus constitutionally free to film and display petitioner's entire act.

The Ohio Supreme Court relied heavily on *Time, Inc. v. Hill,* * * * but that case does not mandate a media privilege to televise a performer's entire act without his consent. * * *

Time, Inc. v. Hill, which was hotly contested and decided by a divided Court, involved an entirely different tort from the "right of publicity" recognized by the Ohio Supreme Court. As the opinion reveals in *Time, Inc. v. Hill,* the Court was steeped in the literature of privacy law and was aware of the developing distinctions and nuances in this branch of the law. * * * The Court was aware that it was adjudicating a "false light" privacy case involving a matter of public interest, not a case involving "intrusion," * * * "appropriation" of a name or likeness for the purposes of trade, * * * or "private details" about a non-newsworthy person or event * * *. It is also abundantly clear that *Time, Inc. v. Hill* did not involve a performer, a person with a name having commercial value, or any claim to a "right of publicity." This discrete kind of "appropriation" case was plainly identified in the literature cited by the Court and had been adjudicated in the reported cases.

The differences between these two torts are important. First, the State's interests in providing a cause of action in each instance are different. "The interest protected" in permitting recovery for placing the plaintiff in a false light "is clearly that of reputation, with the same overtones of mental distress as in defamation." Prosser, *supra*, 48 Calif.L.Rev., at 400. By contrast, the State's interest in permitting a "right of publicity" is in protecting the proprietary interest of the individual in his act in part to encourage such entertainment. As we later note, the State's interest is closely analogous to the goals of patent and copyright law, focusing on the right of the individual to reap the reward of his endeavors and having little to do with protecting feelings or reputation. Second, the two torts differ in the degree to which they intrude on dissemination of information to the public. In "false light" cases the only way to protect the interests involved is to attempt to minimize publication of the damaging matter, while in "right of publicity" cases the only question is who gets to do the publishing. An entertainer such as petitioner usually has no objection to the widespread publication of his act as long as he gets the commercial benefit of such publication. Indeed, in the present case petitioner did not seek to enjoin the broadcast of his act; he simply sought compensation for the broadcast in the form of damages.

Nor does it appear that our later cases * * * require or furnish substantial support for the Ohio court's privilege ruling. These cases, like *New York Times* emphasize the protection extended to the press by the First Amendment in defamation cases, particularly when suit is brought by a public official or a public figure. None of them involve an alleged appropriation by the press of a right of publicity existing under state law.

Moreover, *Time, Inc. v. Hill, New York Times, Metromedia, Gertz,* and *Firestone* all involved the reporting of events; in none of them was there an attempt to broadcast or publish an entire act for which the performer ordinarily gets paid. It is evident, and there is no claim here to the contrary, that petitioner's state-law right of publicity would not serve to prevent respondent from reporting the newsworthy facts about petitioner's act. Wherever the line in particular situations is to be drawn between media reports that are protected and those that are not, we are quite sure that the First and Fourteenth Amendments do not immunize the media when they broadcast a performer's entire act without his consent. The Constitution no more prevents a State from requiring respondent to compensate petitioner for broadcasting his act on television than it would privilege respondent to film and broadcast a copyrighted dramatic work without liability to the copyright owner, * * * or to film and broadcast a prize fight, * * * or a baseball game, * * * where the promoters or the participants had other plans for publicizing the event. There are ample reasons for reaching this conclusion.

The broadcast of a film of petitioner's entire act poses a substantial threat to the economic value of that performance. As the Ohio court recognized, this act is the product of petitioner's own talents and energy, the end result of much time, effort, and expense. Much of its economic value lies in the "right of exclusive control over the publicity given to his performance"; if the public can see the act free on television, it will be less willing to pay to see it at the fair. The effect of a public broadcast of the performance is similar to preventing petitioner from charging an admission fee. * * * Moreover, the broadcast of petitioner's entire performance, unlike the unauthorized use of another's name for purposes of trade or the incidental use of a name or picture by the press, goes to the heart of petitioner's ability to earn a living as an entertainer. Thus, in this case, Ohio has recognized what may be the strongest case for a "right of publicity"—involving, not the appropriation of an entertainer's reputation to enhance the attractiveness of a commercial product, but the appropriation of the very activity by which the entertainer acquired his reputation in the first place.

Of course, Ohio's decision to protect petitioner's right of publicity here rests on more than a desire to compensate the performer for the time and effort invested in his act; the protection provides an economic incentive for him to make the investment required to produce a performance of interest to the public. This same consideration underlies the patent and copyright laws long enforced by this Court. * * *

These laws perhaps regard the "reward to the owner [as] a secondary consideration," * * * but they were "intended definitely to grant valuable, enforceable rights" in order to afford greater encouragement to the production of works of benefit to the public. * * * The Constitution does not prevent Ohio from making a similar choice here in deciding to protect the entertainer's incentive in order to encourage the production of this type of work. * * *

There is no doubt that entertainment, as well as news, enjoys First Amendment protection. It is also true that entertainment itself can be important news. *Time, Inc. v. Hill.* But it is important to note that neither the public nor respondent will be deprived of the benefit of petitioner's performance as long as his commercial stake in his act is appropriately recognized. Petitioner does not seek to enjoin the broadcast of his performance; he simply wants to be paid for it. Nor do we think that a state-law damages remedy against respondent would represent a species of liability without fault contrary to the letter or spirit of *Gertz v. Robert Welch, Inc.* * * * Respondent knew that petitioner objected to televising his act, but nevertheless displayed the entire film.

We conclude that although the State of Ohio may as a matter of its own law privilege the press in the circumstances of this case, the First and Fourteenth Amendments do not require it to do so.

Reversed.

MR. JUSTICE POWELL, with whom MR. JUSTICE BRENNAN and MR. JUSTICE MARSHALL join, dissenting.

Disclaiming any attempt to do more than decide the narrow case before us, the Court reverses the decision of the Supreme Court of Ohio based on repeated incantation of a single formula: "a performer's entire act." * * * I doubt that his formula provides a standard clear enough even for resolution of this case. In any event, I am not persuaded that the Court's opinion is appropriately sensitive to the First Amendment values at stake, and I therefore dissent.

Although the Court would draw no distinction, * * * I do not view respondent's action as comparable to unauthorized commercial broadcasts of sporting events, theatrical performances, and the like where the broadcaster keeps the profits. There is no suggestion here that respondent made any such use of the film. Instead, it simply reported on what petitioner concedes to be a newsworthy event, in a way hardly surprising for a television station—by means of film coverage. The report was part of an ordinary daily news program, consuming a total of 15 seconds. It is a routine example of the press' fulfilling the informing function so vital to our system.

The Court's holding that the station's ordinary news report may give rise to substantial liability has disturbing implications, for the decision could lead to a degree of media self-censorship. * * * Hereafter, whenever a television news editor is unsure whether certain film footage received from a camera crew might be held to portray an "entire act," he may decline coverage—even of clearly newsworthy events—or confine the broadcast to watered-down verbal reporting, perhaps with an occasional still picture. The public is then the loser. This is hardly the kind of news reportage that the First Amendment is meant to foster. * * *

In my view the First Amendment commands a different analytical starting point from the one selected by the Court. Rather than begin with a quantitative analysis of the performer's behavior—is this or is this not his entire act?—we should direct initial attention to the actions of the news media: what use did the station make of the film footage? When a film is used, as here, for a routine portion of a regular news program, I would hold that the First Amendment protects the station from a "right of publicity" or "appropriation" suit, absent a strong showing by the plaintiff that the news broadcast was a subterfuge or cover for private or commercial exploitation.

I emphasize that this is a "reappropriation" suit, rather than one of the other varieties of "right of privacy" tort suits identified by Dean Prosser * * *. In those other causes of action the competing interests are considerably different. The plaintiff generally seeks to avoid any sort of public exposure, and the existence of constitutional privilege is therefore less likely to turn on whether the publication occurred in a news broadcast or in some other fashion. In a suit like the one before us, however, the plaintiff does not complain about the fact of exposure to the public, but rather about its timing or manner. He welcomes some publicity, but seeks to retain control over means and manner as a way to maximize for himself the monetary benefits that flow from such publication. But having made the matter public—having chosen, in essence, to make it newsworthy—he cannot, consistent with the First Amendment, complain of routine news reportage. * * *

Since the film clip here was undeniably treated as news and since there is no claim that the use was subterfuge, respondent's actions were constitutionally privileged. I would affirm.

MR. JUSTICE STEVENS, dissenting.

* * *

As I read the state court's explanation of the limits on the concept of privilege, they define the substantive reach of a common-law tort rather than anything I recognize as a limit on a federal constitutional right. The decision was unquestionably influenced by the Ohio court's proper sensitivity to First Amendment principles, and to this Court's cases construing the First Amendment; indeed, I must confess that the opinion can be read as resting entirely on federal constitutional grounds. Nevertheless, the basis of the state court's action is sufficiently doubtful that I would remand the case to that court for clarification of its holding before deciding the federal constitutional issue.

NOTES

1. Is it crucial for this decision that Zacchini performed at a county fair to which no one was admitted unless he paid an admission fee? Suppose Zacchini had not been paid for the particular performance that was filmed but did make his living from performing that act? Do you think Man v. Warner Brothers, Inc., 317 F.Supp. 50 (S.D.N.Y.1970), discussed in the *Taggart* case at p. 733, *supra,* was correctly decided?

2. Generally, just as one cannot defame the dead, so one cannot invade the privacy of the dead. *See Restatement (Second) of Torts* § 652I. The question has arisen, however, whether the right of commercial appropriation of a famous person's name, likeness, etc., is descendible to his heirs or otherwise survives the person's death. In Factors Etc., Inc. v. Pro Arts, Inc., 579 F.2d 215 (2d Cir.1978), *cert. denied* 440 U.S. 908, 99 S.Ct. 1215, 59 L.Ed.2d 455 (1979), the court, applying what it believed to be New York law, enjoined the sale of posters bearing Elvis Presley's photograph. The court noted that Presley had commercially exploited his name and likeness in his lifetime. A few months later a different federal court refused to rule that either the making of a large bronze statue of Elvis Presley *or* the distribution

of an eight-inch replica to anyone who contributed twenty-five dollars or more to the project infringed Factors Etc., Inc.'s license, given in Presley's lifetime, to exploit his name or likeness. Memphis Development Foundation v. Factors Etc., Inc., 616 F.2d 956 (6th Cir.1980), *cert. denied* 449 U.S. 953, 101 S.Ct. 358, 66 L.Ed.2d 217. Because the court felt that the matter was governed by Tennessee law, the Second Circuit reluctantly followed the Sixth Circuit's decision in Factors Etc., Inc. v. Pro Arts, Inc., 652 F.2d 278 (2d Cir.1981), *cert. denied* 456 U.S. 927, 102 S.Ct. 1973, 72 L.Ed.2d 442 (1982). On the other hand in the Estate of Elvis Presley v. Russen, 513 F.Supp. 1339 (D.N.J.1981), it was held that Elvis Presley's right of publicity would be descendible under New Jersey law. And, in State ex rel. Elvis Presley v. Crowell, 733 S.W.2d 89 (Tenn.App.1987), it was held that, under Tennessee law, Elvis Presley's right to control his name and image had in fact descended to his estate at his death. This latter decision by a Tennessee state court of course meant that the Sixth Circuit's decision in the *Memphis Development* case had been incorrect. However, in a somewhat ironic twist, the Second Circuit has now decided that its 1978 interpretation of New York law, in the first *Pro Arts* case, was also incorrect. It concluded that there is no descendible right of publicity under new York law. Pirone v. MacMillan, Inc., 894 F.2d 579 (2d Cir.1990) (the plaintiffs included the two daughters of Babe Ruth).

In Lugosi v. Universal Pictures, 25 Cal.3d 813, 160 Cal.Rptr. 323, 603 P.2d 425 (1979), the court held that the late Bela Lugosi had not commercially exploited his name and likeness in association with the character of Dracula and therefore his heirs had no such right of exclusive commercial exploitation. Accord, Guglielmi v. Spelling–Goldberg Productions, 25 Cal.3d 860, 160 Cal. Rptr. 352, 603 P.2d 454 (1979) (plaintiff was the nephew and "legal heir" of Rudolph Valentino). The California legislature responded to these decisions by enacting Cal.Civ.Code § 990 in 1984 giving persons to whom the deceased may have passed his right by contract or by establishing a trust or by testamentary disposition or, in the absence of such arrangements, by the deceased's next of kin the right to control the use of "a deceased personality's name, voice, signature, photograph or likeness * * * on or in products, merchandise, or goods or for purposes of advertising or selling, or soliciting purchases of, products, merchandise, goods, or services * * *" with minimum damages of $750 for any unauthorized use. Uses in connection with news, public affairs, sports broadcasts or political campaigns are expressly defined as uses for which consent is not required. The use of a personality's name, etc. in a play, book, magazine, musical composition, film, radio or television program, other than an advertisement or commercial announcement, is also not prohibited as is any material that is "of political or newsworthy value" or "[s]ingle and original works of fine art." There is no requirement that the personality have commercially exploited any aspects of his public persona. In Martin Luther King, Jr., Center for Social Change, Inc. v. American Heritage Products, Inc., 250 Ga. 135, 296 S.E.2d 697 (1982) responding to a question certified by the Eleventh Circuit as to Georgia law, the Supreme Court of Georgia held that a descendible right of publicity exists under Georgia law and, furthermore, that it was not necessary that "the owner have commercially exploited the right before it can survive his death". The case involved a suit to prohibit the defendant from manufacturing and selling plastic busts of the late Dr. Martin Luther King, Jr. In Southeast Bank, N.A. v. Lawrence, 66 N.Y.2d 910, 498 N.Y.S.2d 775, 489 N.E.2d 744 (1985), the personal representative of the late Tennessee Williams brought a suit to enjoin the defendants from renaming their theatre on West 48th Street in Manhattan the "Tennessee Williams". The lower courts granted the plaintiff's motion for preliminary injunction but the New York Court of Appeals reversed. It held that the matter was governed by Florida law, because at the time of his death Williams was domiciled in Florida and it interpreted West's Fla.Stats.Ann. § 540.08 as giving a descendible right of publicity only to a person to whom a license had been issued during the decedent's lifetime or to the decedent's surviving spouse and children. It cited Loft v. Fuller, 408 So.2d 619 (Fla.App.1981) for the proposition that the statute was not to be extended beyond its "contours". The New York Court of Appeals expressly refused to rule on the question decided in the New York lower courts, namely "whether a common-law descendible right of publicity exists in this State." For the moment that still seems to be the situation although there have been attempts, thus far unsuccessful, to enact a statute specifically recognizing that right. For a recent commentary, *see* L. Henderson. *Protecting a Celebrity's Legacy: Living in California or New York Becomes the Deciding Factor,* 3 J. Bus. Entrepreneurship & L., 165 (2009). One issue raised by statutory recognition of descendible rights of publicity is their applicability to people who died many years before the enactment of these statutes. *Compare* Milton H. Greene Archives, Inc. v. CMG Worldwide, Inc., 568 F.Supp.2d 1152 (C.D. Cal. 2008) *with* Dillinger, L.L.C. v. Electronic Arts, Inc., 795 F.Supp.2d 829 (S.D. Ind. 2011).

CHAPTER 10

FALSE IMPRISONMENT AND MISUSE OF LEGAL PROCESS

■ ■ ■

A. FALSE IMPRISONMENT

SERPICO v. MENARD, INC.

United States District Court, Northern District of Illinois, 1996.
927 F.Supp. 276.

GETTLEMAN, DISTRICT JUDGE.

The moral of this case is never to put someone else's nuts in your pocket. Plaintiff's amended complaint concerns an incident in which defendant accused plaintiff of shoplifting a machine nut from one of defendant's Menards [sic] stores. In his amended complaint plaintiff alleges that defendant: falsely arrested/imprisoned him (Count I); intentionally inflicted emotional distress upon him (Count II); and violated the Illinois Consumer Fraud and Deceptive Business Practices Act, 815 ILCS 505/1 et seq. (Count III). After filing an answer and affirmative defenses to the amended complaint, defendant filed a motion for judgment on the pleadings pursuant to Fed.R.Civ.P. 12(c).

Facts

On December 12, 1994, plaintiff, who is seventy years old, went to one of defendant's stores located at Hall Plaza in Chicago to pick up supplies that he needed to fix a broken sprinkler system for his employer. The first item plaintiff looked for and located was a nut. After picking out a nut, which had a value of less than 70 cents, plaintiff asked several of defendant's employees where he could locate pipe wrap.

During his search for the pipe wrap plaintiff put the "solitary, little nut" in his pocket so that he would not drop the nut or misplace it while he searched for the pipe wrap. Plaintiff found and picked up some pipe wrap, went to a cash register and paid for the pipe wrap, but forgot to remove or pay for the nut he had put in his pocket. Plaintiff then proceeded to exit the store without paying for the nut. After plaintiff exited, one of defendant's representatives stopped plaintiff and forced him to accompany the representative to a closed room within the store. In the room, defendant's representative demanded that plaintiff empty his pockets. Plaintiff proceeded to remove the nut, money, and a cash register receipt for the pipe wrap.

Defendant refused to listen to plaintiff's explanation that he had merely forgotten to pay for the nut. Defendant's representative then took plaintiff's picture and displayed it on a bulletin board along with numerous other pictures labeled as criminals who had stolen merchandise, and called the Chicago Police Department to have an officer come to defendant's store to file a criminal complaint against plaintiff for shoplifting. The police officer tried to dissuade defendant's store manager from filing a complaint against plaintiff, telling the manager that plaintiff did not intend to steal the nut and that plaintiff had made an honest mistake. Nonetheless, the manager insisted on filing a criminal complaint, and the police took plaintiff to the station where he was fingerprinted.

As a result of defendant's insistence that plaintiff be prosecuted for theft of the 70 cent nut, plaintiff was forced to retain a lawyer. The lawyer called defendant's store manager who told the attorney that defendant intended to prosecute plaintiff for shoplifting. When plaintiff's employer learned what had happened, one of its representatives called defendant's store manager, vouched for plaintiff's integrity, stated that plaintiff had not intended to steal the item, and explained that the employer always reimbursed plaintiff for all purchases plaintiff made for repairs for the employer (thus negating any motive or intent by plaintiff to steal the nut).

After further calls and investigation, the vice president of plaintiff's employer told a manager at defendant's corporate headquarters that the store manager had decided that plaintiff had not intended to steal the nut. Defendant's corporate headquarters, however, told plaintiff's attorney that regardless of whether plaintiff intended to steal the nut, defendant still intended to prosecute plaintiff because it was defendant's company policy to prosecute every case. Despite defendant's repeated insistence on having plaintiff prosecuted for shoplifting, on the date set for plaintiff's criminal trial no one from defendant's company appeared, and the judge dismissed the charges.

After the trial date William Payne, defendant's "legal enforcement manager," sent plaintiff a letter dated April 10, 1995, making a "civil restitution settlement demand." In the April 10 letter Payne wrote that plaintiff had been apprehended for concealing and taking unpaid merchandise from the store on December 12, 1994. The letter further stated that under "Illinois Statutes" Chapter 38 Sections 16A–3 & 16A–7, any person who commits retail theft (shoplifts) can be sued civilly by the owner of the property. The letter offered that to avoid additional time and expense to plaintiff of defending a law suit, defendant was "willing to settle the matter for [defendant's] actual costs in processing [plaintiff's] case." Defendant offered to settle all civil claims against plaintiff for $100. The letter noted that settlement of defendant's civil claim did not prevent local authorities from proceeding with a criminal prosecution.

Defendant, through Payne, then sent plaintiff a follow up letter dated May 16, 1995, giving plaintiff "final notice" to "amicably settle" the matter, stating that if defendant did not receive a $100 payment by May 30, 1995, defendant would file a lawsuit. Plaintiff filed the instant case against defendant on June 14, 1995. Defendant has not filed a counterclaim or otherwise made good on its "legal enforcement manager's" threat to sue plaintiff for the 70 cent nut.

* * *

False Arrest/Imprisonment

Defendant raises two arguments in support of its motion for judgment on the pleadings as to plaintiff's claim for false arrest/imprisonment. First, defendant asserts that it had probable cause to arrest and detain plaintiff. Under Illinois law, a claim for false arrest must allege the restraint of an individual's liberty without probable cause. * * * Probable cause is an absolute defense to an action for false arrest and false imprisonment. * * *

The existence of probable cause is a question of law for the court to determine. * * * Under Illinois law, probable cause is defined as "a state of facts that would lead a [person] of ordinary caution and prudence to believe, or to entertain an honest and strong suspicion, that the person arrested committed the offense charged." * * * "It is the state of mind of the one commencing the [arrest or imprisonment], and not the actual facts of the case or the guilt or innocence of the accused which is at issue." * * * In the instant case plaintiff was detained and turned over to the police for alleged retail theft actionable under § 16A–3 of the Illinois Criminal Code of 1961 * * *, which provides in part: A person commits the offense of retail theft when he or she knowingly: (a) Takes possession of, * * * any merchandise * * * offered for sale in a retail mercantile establishment with the intention of retaining such merchandise or with the intention of depriving the merchant permanently of the possession, * * * of such merchandise without paying the full retail value. * * *

Therefore, the issue presented by defendant's motion is whether plaintiff's allegations can support a finding that a person of ordinary caution and prudence would not believe or even entertain an honest and strong suspicion that plaintiff took the nut without intending to pay for it. They can. It is hard to imagine that under the facts alleged any person of ordinary caution could strongly suspect that plaintiff intended to pay for the more expensive pipe wrap but also intended to steal the 70 cent nut. Of particular import is the allegation that the police officer believed, and told defendant that he believed, that it was an honest mistake. Accordingly, the court concludes that if plaintiff proves the allegations of the complaint, he will establish that defendant did not have probable cause to arrest and detain him.

Next, defendant argues that it is entitled to judgment on its affirmative defense based on section 16A–6 because even if it did not have probable cause, its actions were reasonable under sections 16A–4 and 5 of the Criminal Code. Section 16A–4 provides:

> If any person: (a) conceals upon his or her person or among his or her belongings, unpurchased merchandise displayed, held, stored or offered for sale in a retail mercantile establishment; and (b) removes that merchandise beyond the last known station for receiving payments for that merchandise in that retail mercantile establishment such person shall be presumed to have possessed, carried away or transferred such merchandise with the intention of retaining it or with the intention of depriving the merchant permanently of the possession, use or benefit of such merchandise without paying the full retail value of such merchandise.

Section 16A–5 provides:

> Any merchant who has reasonable grounds to believe that a person has committed retail theft may detain such person, on or off the premises of a retail mercantile establishment, in a reasonable manner and for a reasonable length of time for all or any of the following purposes: (a) To request identification; (b) To verify such identification; (c) To make reasonable inquiry as to whether such person has in his possession unpurchased merchandise and, to make reasonable investigation of the ownership of such merchandise; (d) To inform a peace officer of the detention of the person and surrender that person to the custody of a peace officer;

* * *

Section 16A–6 provides that: A detention as permitted in this Article does not constitute an arrest or an unlawful restraint, as defined in Section 10–3 of the Code, nor shall it render the merchant liable to the person so detained.

Whether defendant's detention of plaintiff was permitted under the Article depends on whether it was "reasonable." 720 ILCS 5/16A–5. It was most likely reasonable for defendant to stop plaintiff initially, because under section 16A–4 it could presume that plaintiff intended to "steal" the nut. Under section 16A–5, however, defendant had to have reasonable grounds to believe that plaintiff committed retail theft and could only detain plaintiff a reasonable amount of time to make that determination. Defendant has the burden of proving that the actions of its security force were "reasonable." * * * Whether defendant's agents acted "reasonably" in continuing to detain plaintiff after refusing to hear plaintiff's explanation and after the police officer told defendant that plaintiff did not intend to steal the nut is a question for the jury to determine. * * *

Accordingly, the court concludes that under the facts alleged, defendant is not entitled to a finding as a matter of law that the entire length of detention at defendant's store and then at the police station was reasonable and permitted under the statute. Therefore, defendant's motion for judgment on the pleadings on Count I is denied.

[The court's discussion of the claim under intentional infliction of emotional distress and the claim for violation of the Illinois Consumer Fraud and Deceptive Trade Practices Act is omitted. The court found that no reasonable jury could find the acts of the defendant "so severe that no reasonable man could be expected to endure it" and dismissed the claim. The consumer fraud claim was dismissed because plaintiff was not a purchaser of the nut.]

NOTES

1. Frequently, when a customer is detained by store security personnel, the customer is questioned about the alleged theft and is given the opportunity to sign statements admitting liability for the theft of store merchandise. In a subsequent criminal trial this evidence may be offered against the customer to establish guilt when charged with shoplifting or theft. Customers have challenged the admissibility of these statements claiming that the security personnel were acting to enforce the state criminal law and were, therefore, subject to constitutionally imposed restrictions on the use of their state-granted authority. The United States Supreme Court in Colorado v. Connelly, 479 U.S. 157, 107 S.Ct. 515, 93 L.Ed.2d 473 (1986), required police involvement before these protections would be violated. Based on this decision, some states which had previously excluded these statements because the store security personnel were acting pursuant to a state statutory authority have reversed their position. *See, e.g.*, State v. Muegge, 178 W.Va. 439, 360 S.E.2d 216 (1987), rev'd on this issue by State v. Honaker, 193 W.Va. 51, 59, 454 S.E.2d 96, 104 (1994).

In Bowman v. State, 468 N.E.2d 1064 (Ind.App.1984), it was held that, when an off-duty police officer working as a security guard detains someone for investigation under a shoplifting statute, the person detained is "not in 'custody'," so as to bring into play the warnings required by Miranda v. Arizona, 384 U.S. 436, 86 S.Ct. 1602, 16 L.Ed.2d 694 (1966). The court declared that "the short duration allowed for such 'custody' and the authority given civilians under the statute indicates official custody was neither contemplated nor authorized by the legislature."[1]

One possibility is to bring an action under 42 U.S.C. § 1983 which grants a federal remedy against those who, under color of state law, deprive people of their rights under the Constitution and laws of the United States. We shall briefly discuss such actions in the next chapter devoted to "Constitutional Torts." The other possibility is a common law tort action for false imprisonment (or false arrest). In Alvarado v. City of Dodge City, 238 Kan. 48, 708 P.2d 174 (1985) the court held that an off-duty police officer working as a private security guard who detained someone under a shoplifting statute was in point of fact acting under color of state law but the court also held,

---

1. *But see* Owen v. State, 490 N.E.2d 1130 (Ind.App.1986) which distinguished between off-duty police officers who were subject to the *Miranda* requirements and private persons who were not.

probably mistakenly, that there was no cause of action under 42 U.S.C. § 1983 because "the Kansas tort actions for false imprisonment, battery and defamation provide an adequate post-deprivation remedy sufficient to satisfy the requirements of due process under the Fourteenth Amendment." It has been suggested in cases like *People v. Raitano*, 81 Ill.App.3d 373, 36 Ill.Dec. 597, 401 N.E.2d 278 (1980), that constitutional prohibitions may not apply to persons acting pursuant to shoplifting statutes on the ground that these statutes are "merely a codification of the common law shopkeepers' privilege." Such a statement shows first the plasticity of the term "common law"—the shopkeepers' privilege is, as we shall see in the succeeding notes, a quite recent development—and is also almost certainly incorrect. We have already seen in *New York Times v. Sullivan, supra*, p. 572, that the enforcement of a state's common law clearly is state action and clearly can be subject to constitutional restraints. *See also Tennessee v. Garner,* discussed in note 2, *infra*.

2. False arrest may usefully be considered a subcategory of false imprisonment. What makes the detention of a person an arrest, rather than merely an imprisonment, is the assertion of state authority to detain someone because that person is suspected of having committed a crime. Generally, both police officers and private persons may arrest someone pursuant to a warrant that is valid on its face. Arrests pursuant to a warrant will be discussed briefly in *Boose v. City of Rochester,* the next principal case. The major tort problems arise when the arrest is made without a warrant. The common law on the subject is summarized in *Restatement (Second) of Torts,* §§ 119, 120, and 121. At common law a private person could arrest another without a warrant for the commission of a felony if the person arrested had in fact committed the felony for which he had been arrested or if a felony had in fact been committed and the person making the arrest reasonably believed that the other had committed that felony. A private person could also arrest a person without a warrant for the commission of a misdemeanor *if* the person arrested had, in the presence of the person making the arrest, committed a breach of the peace. A police officer could arrest a person without a warrant in all the circumstances in which a private person could make an arrest. In addition, a police officer could arrest someone without a warrant for a crime constituting a felony, even if no such felony had been committed, if the officer reasonably believed that such a felony had been committed and that the person arrested had committed the felony. Most states now have statutes governing the matter. Subject to the requirement of probable cause (or reasonable belief) many of these statutes enlarge the circumstances in which an arrest can be made. In Minnesota, for example, an officer may arrest someone for the commission of any misdemeanor committed in the officer's presence and, in certain circumstances, for some other gross misdemeanors even if not committed in the officer's presence. Minn.Stat.Ann. § 629.34 (West 2003). In New York a police officer has the authority to arrest anyone whom the officer has "reasonable cause" to believe has committed any crime whether the crime was committed in the officer's presence or not and a private person has the power to arrest anyone who has committed any offense in his/her presence. N.Y. Crim.Proc. §§ 140.10, 140.30 (McKinney).

Shoplifting came to be considered a problem because, if the amount thought to be stolen was relatively small, the crime involved would be petty larceny which is only a misdemeanor. Since the commission of such a crime usually does not involve a breach of the peace, under common law neither a police officer nor a private citizen would have any authority to arrest without a warrant. If the amount thought to have been taken was sufficient to make the suspected crime a felony, the situation was somewhat eased. But, if in fact the person arrested had not taken the goods nor had the goods been taken by any other person, a private person would have had no authority to make an arrest regardless of how reasonable the belief that a felony had been committed or that the person arrested had been the one who committed the felony.

At common law, one could use reasonable force in making the arrest. If the offense for which the person being arrested was a felony, even deadly force could be used if resort to such force was reasonably believed to be necessary in order to make the arrest. *See Restatement (Second) of Torts* § 131. In Tennessee v. Garner, 471 U.S. 1, 105 S.Ct. 1694, 85 L.Ed.2d 1 (1985), however, the Court held that deadly force could only be used in the course of arresting a fleeing felon when there are reasonable grounds to believe that the fleeing felon poses a serious risk of death or serious harm to others. The use of deadly force could not be justified merely because it was necessary to resort to such force in order to apprehend the fleeing felon. In the *Garner* case, the Court upheld the reinstatement of a claim under 42 U.S.C. § 1983, a subject to be discussed in the next chapter, against a police officer who shot a fleeing felon who had broken into a dwelling house at night. The Court held that the fact that the person shot had broken into a dwelling house at night did not by itself prove that he was dangerous. Justice O'Connor dissented. She noted that a large percentage of rapes and robberies are committed by burglars (i.e., those who break and enter into dwellings).

3. Reacting to the perceived problem of how to deal with shoplifters, some courts began to permit the detention of suspected shoplifters under circumstances in which, under the common law, the shopkeeper would have had no right to arrest the suspect. For example, in Collyer v. S.H. Kress Co., 5 Cal.2d 175, 54 P.2d 20 (1936), the court held that a seventy-year-old man who was detained, questioned, and searched did not have a cause of action for false imprisonment against the store and its personnel. The defendants' conduct was held to be reasonable under the circumstances. Plaintiff had been seen by several persons putting a string of Christmas tree lights in his pocket. Plaintiff claimed that he had bought the items but had asked that they not be wrapped. Whether this was true or not, a jury had acquitted him in a criminal prosecution. Building on cases like *Collyer,* the *Restatement (Second) of Torts* added the following new provision which had not appeared in the original *Restatement.*

§ 120A. Temporary Detention for Investigation

One who reasonably believes that another has tortiously taken a chattel upon his premises, or has failed to make due cash payment for a chattel purchased or services rendered there, is privileged, without arresting the other, to detain him on the premises for the time necessary for a reasonable investigation of the facts.

Many states either judicially adopted the *Restatement (Second)* provision or adopted statutes like the Illinois statute noted in the *Serpico* case, above. Consider the following two representative statutes.

Minn.Stat.Ann.[2] § 629.366 Theft in business establishments; detaining suspects

Subdivision 1. Circumstances justifying detention. (a) A merchant or merchant's employee may detain a person if the merchant or employee has reasonable cause to believe:

(1) that the person has taken, or is taking, an article of value without paying for it, from the possession of the merchant in the merchant's place of business or from a vehicle or premises under the merchant's control;

(2) that the taking is done with the intent to wrongfully deprive the merchant of the property or the use or benefit of it; or

(3) that the taking is done with the intent to appropriate the use of the property to the taker or any other person.

(b) Subject to the limitations in paragraph (a), a merchant or merchant's employee may detain a person for any of the following purposes:

(1) to require the person to provide identification or verify identification;

(2) to inquire as to whether the person possesses unpurchased merchandise taken from the merchant and, if so, to receive the merchandise;

(3) to inform a peace officer; or

(4) to institute criminal proceedings against the person.

(c) The person detained shall be informed promptly of the purpose of the detention and may not be subjected to unnecessary or unreasonable force, nor to interrogation against the person's will. A merchant or merchant's employee may not detain a person for more than one hour unless:

(1) the merchant or employee is waiting to surrender the person to a peace officer, in which case the person may be detained until a peace officer has accepted custody of or released the person; or

(2) the person is a minor, or claims to be, and the merchant or employee is waiting to surrender the minor to a peace officer or the minor's parent, guardian, or custodian, in which case the minor may be detained until the peace officer, parent, guardian, or custodian has accepted custody of the minor.

(d) If at any time the person detained requests that a peace officer be summoned, the merchant or merchant's employee must notify a peace officer immediately.

Subd. 2. Arrest. Upon a charge being made by a merchant or merchant's employee, a peace officer may arrest a person without a warrant,

2. (West 2009).

if the officer has reasonable cause for believing that the person has committed or attempted to commit the offense described in subdivision 1.

Subd. 3. Immunity. No merchant, merchant's employee, or peace officer is criminally or civilly liable for any action authorized under subdivision 1 or 2 if the arresting person's action is based upon reasonable cause.

N.C.Gen.Stat.[3] § 14–72.1 Concealment of merchandise in mercantile establishments.

(a) Whoever, without authority, willfully conceals the goods or merchandise of any store, not theretofore purchased by such person, while still upon the premises of such store, shall be guilty of a misdemeanor and, upon conviction, shall be punished as provided in subsection (e). Such goods or merchandise found concealed upon or about the person and which have not theretofore been purchased by such person shall be prima facie evidence of a willful concealment.

* * *

(c) A merchant, or his agent or employee, or a peace officer who detains or causes the arrest of any person shall not be held civilly liable for detention, malicious prosecution, false imprisonment, or false arrest of the person detained or arrested, where such detention is in a reasonable manner for a reasonable length of time, and if in detaining or in causing the arrest of such person, the merchant, or his agent or employee, or the peace officer had at the time of the detention or arrest probable cause to believe that the person committed the offense created by this section. If the person being detained by the merchant, or his agent or employee, is a minor 18 years of age or younger, the merchant or his agent or employee, shall call or notify, or make a reasonable effort to call or notify the parent or guardian of the minor, during the period of detention. * * *

(d) Whoever, without authority, willfully transfers any price tag from goods or merchandise to other goods or merchandise having a higher selling price or marks said goods at a lower price or substitutes or superimposes thereon a false price tag and then presents said goods or merchandise for purchase shall be guilty of a misdemeanor and, upon conviction, shall be punished as provided in subsection (e).

Nothing herein shall be construed to provide that the mere possession of goods or the production by shoppers of improperly priced merchandise for checkout shall constitute prima facie evidence of guilt.

* * *

4. In addition to false imprisonment actions brought by customers against stores, frequently actions are being brought by employees against their employers for conduct during the course of a loss prevention investigation. In these cases a key issue becomes whether the claim is barred by the exclusivity provisions of the state's worker's compensation statute. *See* Fermino v. Fedco, Inc., 7 Cal.4th 701, 872 P.2d 559, 30 Cal.Rptr.2d 18 (1994) (holding a false imprisonment not to be part of the normal employer-employee

3. (Supp. 2010).

relationship and, therefore, a tort cause of action is not barred by the California worker's compensation statute); *see also* McGowan v. Warwick Corp., 691 So.2d 265 (La. App. 1997). *But see,* Dunn v. United States, 516 F.Supp. 1373 (E.D.Pa.1981).

5. The essence of the common law tort of false imprisonment is the intentional confinement of another person, without that person's consent within boundaries set by the actor.[4] Confinement may be accomplished by physical barriers, by physical force, or by the threat of physical force. A display of actual authority by a police officer or of purported authority by someone such as a railroad conductor ordering a passenger to remain on a train will also be enough to sustain the action. These situations in which confinement is achieved through a purported exercise of authority might perhaps be considered as situations involving the implicit threat of physical force. A person who is under a legal duty to release another from a place of confinement will also be liable for false imprisonment if he intentionally refuses to try to release him. *See* Bennett v. Ohio Dep't of Rehabilitation and Correction, 60 Ohio St.3d 107, 573 N.E.2d 633 (1991) (false imprisonment claim properly pled when State parole board wrongly held prisoner for six months after the end of sentence term). Also a shopkeeper who, upon discovering that a customer is locked in the store's washroom, refuses to take steps to release the customer will be liable for false imprisonment. *Cf.* Talcott v. National Exhib. Co., 144 App.Div. 337, 128 N.Y.S. 1059 (1911) (ballpark failed to advise patron of alternate exit after main gate locked because of the crush of the crowd). Confinement may also be accomplished by means of duress in the form of a physical threat to one's own property or to a third person. Consider, for example, the case in which one person takes another's purse to prevent her from leaving a place and she remains because there is a large amount of money in her purse. She has been falsely imprisoned. *See* Ashland Dry Goods Co. v. Wages, 302 Ky. 577, 195 S.W.2d 312 (1946). For the tort to lie, the confinement must be complete, that is to say there must be no reasonable escape route *known* to the person confined. *See Talcott v. National Exhib. Co., supra.* A reasonable escape route is one whose use does not involve any serious risk of physical injury or extreme degree of social embarrassment. One who is intentionally confined in a building is not obliged to incur the risk of injury by jumping out of an open second-story window nor would a person whose clothes have been taken as a prank while he was taking a shower be required to leave the building naked. An interesting, though not very often litigated question, is how large must the area of confinement be and still constitute a "prison". In Allen v. Fromme, 141 App.Div. 362, 126 N.Y.S. 520 (1910), a law student who was confined to the city of New York during vacation time under invalid civil process was held to have a cause of action for false imprisonment. A more recent example is presented by Helstrom v. North Slope Borough, 797 P.2d 1192 (Alaska 1990), in which it was held that

---

4. "Imprisonment is the restraint of a man's liberty whether it be in the open field, or in the stocks or cage in the street, or in a man's own house, as well as in the common goal. And in all these places the party so restrained is said to be a prisoner, so long as he has not his liberty freely to go at all times to all places whither he will, without bail or mainprize." Termes de la Ley (c.1520), quoted in Winfield and Jolowicz on Tort 81 (16 ed. by W. Rogers 2002). The *Restatement (Second) of Torts* treats the subject of false imprisonment in §§ 35 *through* 45A.

confinement within the Borough was sufficient to constitute false imprisonment.

The traditional common law definition of false imprisonment has been thought to require that the person confined be conscious of the confinement. *See* Herring v. Boyle, 1 Cr.M. & R. 377, 149 Eng.Rep. 1126 (Exch. 1834). *But see* Meering v. Graham White Aviation Co., 122 L.T. 44 (C.A.1920), discussed in Winfield and Jolowicz on Tort 81–83 (16th ed. by W. Rogers 2002). In *Herring,* a headmaster refused to allow a mother to take home her son because the mother had not paid the school fees. The mother eventually secured the release of her son through a writ of habeas corpus. An action for false imprisonment was dismissed because the boy was unaware that he was being detained against his mother's wishes. *The Restatement (Second of Torts)* §§ 35, 42, broadens the common law, permitting an action for false imprisonment for physical confinement of a person to either (1) one who knows or is conscious of the confinement or (2) one who is harmed by the confinement. One of the examples given under § 42 is that of a child six days old who was locked in the vault of a bank for two days and suffers from hunger and thirst and whose health is affected by the confinement. Would not such a person have a cause of action against the persons confining him under a negligence theory? Does the *Restatement Second*'s attempt to broaden the scope of the action serve any practical needs?

6. Note that in *Serpico* the plaintiff tried to use two other claims, in addition to the false imprisonment claim. In these cases several other torts are frequently pled. In addition to a claim for intentional infliction of emotional distress, which is quite common in these cases, other possibilities, as already noted, include a Section 1983 claim. If the confinement is followed by court action, a malicious prosecution claim is frequently added, as noted in the next section of this chapter. If there is any touching or threatened touching, an assault or battery claim may be included. For an example of a case asserting multiple, alternative claims and also dealing with the issue of governmental immunity, *see* Sena v. Commonwealth, 417 Mass. 250, 629 N.E.2d 986 (1994).

B. MALICIOUS PROSECUTION AND RELATED TORTS

BOOSE v. CITY OF ROCHESTER

Supreme Court of New York, Appellate Division, 1979.
71 A.D.2d 59, 421 N.Y.S.2d 740.

SIMONS, JUSTICE PRESIDING:

Plaintiff commenced this action for malicious prosecution alleging that defendant, acting through its police officers, wrongfully procured her indictment for assault second degree. At the conclusion of plaintiff's case, the Trial Court dismissed the cause of action for malicious prosecution, but permitted the trial to proceed. At the close of the evidence, the court solicited a motion to conform the pleadings to the proof and it then submitted the cause to the jury for recovery based upon negligence and false imprisonment. The jury returned a verdict of $6,000 in plaintiff's favor and defendant appeals.

Plaintiff was arrested for two crimes apparently committed by others. In the first instance, the perpetrator of the crime identified herself to police by use of plaintiff's name, and a warrant was issued charging "Gloria Jean Booth" with obstruction of governmental administration, a misdemeanor. In the second instance, the police had no identification but assuming that the crime was committed by the same defendant, they procured a warrant for "Jane Doe Booze" and arrested plaintiff for assault second degree. The charge was subsequently submitted to the Grand Jury and an indictment was handed up, later to be superseded by a no bill and dismissal.

At the root of the case is plaintiff's right to damages, by whatever legal theory, for injury occasioned to her because of the alleged inadequate investigation by the police into the identity of a criminal defendant before obtaining a warrant and making an arrest. The jury in this trial was asked to decide in essence, whether the police had been negligent in their preparation of plaintiff's assault case. Plaintiff may not recover under broad general principles of negligence, however, but must proceed by way of the traditional remedies of false arrest and imprisonment and malicious prosecution. Her right to be free of restraint or unjustified and unreasonable litigation is limited by the obvious policy of the law to encourage proceedings against those who are apparently guilty of criminal conduct and to let finished litigation remain undisturbed and unchallenged. To that end, plaintiff's recovery must be determined by established rules defining the torts of false arrest and imprisonment and malicious prosecution, rules which permit damages only under circumstances in which the law regards the imprisonment or prosecution as improper and unjustified * * *.

At the time of these events plaintiff was 23 years old, employed by Eastman Kodak Company and a part-time college student. She resided at 167 Pennsylvania Avenue in Rochester with her mother and seven sisters and she had an older, married sister who lived one or two houses away.

On June 22, 1975 one Miguel Pabon was driving down Pennsylvania Avenue near the Boose home when someone in a group of children threw a rock at his car. Mr. Pabon stopped and got out. Intending to find the child's parent, he followed the child as it ran to a nearby house. A "fair number" of people came out of the house, including one woman with a hammer and another with a club, and they started to chase him. Mr. Pabon tried to run to his car but before he could safely reach it he was assaulted and robbed. The next day, after reporting the incident to the police, he went to the house on Pennsylvania Avenue to investigate with Sergeant Scacchetti and Officer Zigarowicz of the Rochester police. A young lady came to the door and Mr. Pabon identified her as the one who had hit him. When she was asked, she answered that her name was "Gloria Jean Boosey" but Officer Scacchetti testified that a confrontation soon began to develop and the men decided to leave rather than risk "having a riot on [their] hands". Officer Scacchetti returned to the house on several subsequent occasions to investigate but no one answered the door. He described the person who gave her name as Gloria Jean Boose as 18 or 19 years of age.

Several months later, on October 16, 1975, a warrant was issued on the basis of these facts charging "Gloria Jean Booth" with obstruction. At trial Officer Scacchetti admitted that plaintiff was not the person whom he had met on Pennsylvania Avenue in June and who identified herself as "Gloria Jean Boosey".

A second incident occurred on August 20, 1975. On that day Anthony Kasper was driving his car down Pennsylvania Avenue when a young child threw a rock at him. Mr. Kasper also got out of his car to locate the child's parents and when he did so he was assaulted by two females, one heavy set and around 40 years of age, and the other between 14 and 17 years old. Before the Grand Jury and during the trial, Mr. Kasper identified one Ossie Boose as the older woman and as the individual who had hit him with a board causing his injuries. She was the mother of the child and, as it turns out she is plaintiff's mother.

On October 23, 1975 a warrant was procured based upon this August incident charging "Jane Doe Booze" with assault, second degree. Officer Scacchetti explained that a Jane Doe warrant was used because Kasper had not identified the defendant to him and he (Scacchetti) "assumed that it was one of the two (females, the younger one) from the previous (incident) * * *." It is this charge on which plaintiff was indicted and which is the basis of this action. At the trial Officer Scacchetti admitted that he was unsure at the time that he procured the warrants in October whether Gloria Jean Boose was the person he actually wanted or whether it was some other person in the Pennsylvania Avenue house.

Plaintiff appeared at the police station in response to these warrants at about 10:30 a.m. on October 30, 1975. She was booked, photographed and fingerprinted and then held in a cell until release on her own recognizance at about 5:00 p.m. Officer Scacchetti was in the building at the time and he was notified of her arrest, but he did not investigate further to determine whether the right person had been taken into custody. Plaintiff was first served with the obstruction warrant and later that afternoon, she was served with the Jane Doe warrant for assault.

Plaintiff was arraigned the next morning and a preliminary examination was requested but never took place, apparently because of plaintiff's failure to appear. The Monroe County Grand Jury indicted her for assault second degree January 30, 1976 and she was arraigned in County Court on the indictment February 5, 1976. It subsequently appeared that there was no identification testimony before the Grand Jury, and the indictment was superseded by a no bill dated February 17. County Court dismissed the indictment on February 18, 1976 and this action followed.

It will be helpful at the outset to recite the difference between the torts of false arrest and imprisonment and malicious prosecution as they have been defined by the Court of Appeals in Broughton v. State of New York, 37 N.Y.2d 451, 373 N.Y.S.2d 87, 335 N.E.2d 310: " * * * The tort of malicious prosecution protects the personal interest of freedom from unjustifiable litigation * * *. The essence of malicious prosecution is the perversion of proper legal procedures. Thus, it has been held that some sort of prior judicial proceeding is the *sine qua non* of a cause of action in malicious prosecution * * *. Such a judicial proceeding may be either an evaluation by a Magistrate of an affidavit supporting an arrest warrant application, or an arraignment or an indictment by a Grand Jury. The elements of the tort of malicious prosecution are: (1) the commencement or continuation of a criminal proceeding by the defendant against the plaintiff, (2) the termination of the proceeding in favor of the accused, (3) the absence of probable cause for the criminal proceeding and (4) actual malice * * *."

Further than that, however, an action for false arrest and imprisonment was not made out on the facts. An arrest made pursuant to a warrant valid on its face and issued by a court having jurisdiction of the crime and person is privileged * * * and this is so even though the process may have been erroneously or improvidently issued * * *. The arresting officer having reasonably carried out the instruction on the warrant, the appropriate remedy to challenge an unlawful arrest is malicious prosecution * * *.

There are exceptions to this privilege. As we have noted, an arrest is not privileged if the issuing court lacks jurisdiction * * *.

Further, if there is more than one individual with the same name, the arresting officer must exercise reasonable care and due diligence in executing the warrant * * *. This is not a misnomer case, however, because plaintiff was the person intended to be apprehended under the warrant. The police error was in determining the true identity of the party to be named in the warrant, not in determining that plaintiff was the person named.

Finally, it has been held that an arresting officer may not insulate himself from liability for false arrest or imprisonment by procuring the issuance of a warrant based upon his own false or unsubstantiated evidence * * *. In executing his affidavit, Officer Scacchetti did not knowingly supply any false evidence to support issuance of the warrant. He erroneously assumed on the basis of his limited knowledge that the same defendant who was involved in the Kasper assault was involved in the Pabon matter. The gravity of that mistake could be tested by an action for malicious prosecution, but it did not give plaintiff a cause of action for false imprisonment. * * *

Turning now to malicious prosecution, we hold that the Trial Court erroneously dismissed that cause of action. Plaintiff's uncontroverted evidence established the initiation of a criminal proceeding against her by defendant which terminated in her favor. The evidence also established *prima facie* that the proceeding was commenced without probable cause and with actual malice.

Probable cause consists of such facts and circumstances as would lead a reasonably prudent man in like circumstances to believe plaintiff guilty * * *. A mistake of fact as to the identity of a criminal may be consistent with probable cause if the defendant acted reasonably under the circumstances and in good faith * * *, but failure to make inquiry of plaintiff or further inquiry about her when a reasonable man would have done so may be evidence of a lack of probable cause * * *. In short, a defendant may be said to act with probable cause to arrest only if a reasonable man in the same position would believe, and defendant did in fact believe, that he had sufficient information to justify initiating a criminal proceeding against plaintiff without further investigation or inquiry * * *.

Plaintiff's arrest for assault was based upon affidavits made without any verification of her identity. Kasper could not name his assailant and Officer Zigarowicz, who interviewed him before preparing a police report, listed two female defendants, one in her forties and another named Roxanne, 14 to 16 years old, residing at an address listed as 173 Pennsylvania Avenue. This information differed significantly from the information Scacchetti acquired after the Pabon incident. He testified that the girl involved in that assault and identified as Gloria Jean Boose appeared to him to be 18 or 19 years of age and she resided at 167 Pennsylvania Avenue (where seven other Boose children resided). Furthermore, Scacchetti testified that he harbored some doubt that the name of Gloria Jean Boose given to him on June 22 during the Pabon incident was correct and he had returned to Pennsylvania Avenue several times to inquire further. Because of this doubt Scacchetti applied for the "Jane Doe Booze" warrant, rather than naming Gloria Jean Boose, but he did so without checking further or resolving the discrepancies in Officer Zigarowicz's report because he assumed that the August assault must have involved the same person as the Pabon incident in June. Plaintiff's name "stuck" in his mind.

It was defendant's contention that further investigation might prove futile or dangerous. The jury was entitled to weigh this claim, but it could also consider that the investigation had been dormant for several months and that nothing in the evidence indicated a need for plaintiff's prompt arrest. * * * Whatever the jury's resolution of those competing contentions, the evidence established, prima facie, that the police procured a warrant for plaintiff's arrest without probable cause to believe her to be the guilty party and the issue should have been submitted to the jury to decide.

There is a further contention to be addressed. The general rule is that a Grand Jury indictment is *prima facie* evidence of probable cause. The plaintiff in a malicious prosecution action must meet this evidence with proof that defendant has not made a full and complete statement of the facts either to the Grand Jury or the District Attorney, has misrepresented or falsified the evidence or else kept back evidence which would affect the result * * *. The rule is based upon the reasoning that the Grand Jury acts judicially and it may be presumed that it has acted regularly on the matter. The burden is placed upon plaintiff, therefore, to rebut this presumption. One may well question whether there is any basis for application of the rule in this case when the Grand Jury superseded its original indictment three weeks later with a no-bill * * *, but be that as it may, there was evidence at the trial that the prosecution was transferred by the police to the District Attorney for Grand Jury action naming plaintiff as the defendant although the police knew that there was no evidence identifying her and in fact no witness testified before the Grand Jury to supply that evidence. This was sufficient to overcome any presumption in defendant's favor because of the Grand Jury indictment.

The remaining element necessary to prove the cause of action is malice. Malice means "malice in fact" or "actual malice", not malice implied by law * * *. The only justification for a criminal proceeding is to bring an offender to justice and malice exists if the jury can find from the evidence that defendant commenced the proceeding because of a wrong or improper motive, something other than a desire to see the ends of justice served * * *. Thus, plaintiff is not required to prove that defendant was motivated by spite or ill will, although such proof will satisfy the legal requirements * * *. The existence of malice may be presumed by proof that probable cause was lacking or by proof of defendant's reckless or grossly negligent conduct * * *. Indeed, it has been said that it is difficult to conceive how a prosecution initiated without probable cause could be initiated with any other than bad motives * * *. The issue is a matter for the jury, however, * * * and it may infer malice from the lack of probable cause insofar as it tends to show that defendant did not believe in the guilt of the accused and that he did not initiate the proceedings for a proper purpose * * *. It has been held that malice exists where a prosecution is commenced to discover who might have committed a crime * * *. Viewing the evidence in a way most favorable to plaintiff, as we must on this appeal, the jury in this case might well have inferred from it that defendant's officers had arrested this plaintiff without probable cause and with actual malice for just that purpose.

The judgment should be reversed and a new trial granted.

NOTES

1. *See* Sheldon Appel Co. v. Albert & Oliker, 47 Cal.3d 863, 871, 765 P.2d 498, 501–02, 254 Cal.Rptr. 336, 340 (1989):

> The common law tort of malicious prosecution originated as a remedy for an individual who had been subjected to a maliciously instituted criminal charge, but in California, as in most common law jurisdictions, the tort was long ago extended to afford a remedy for malicious prosecution of a civil action.

* * *

Although the malicious prosecution tort has ancient roots, courts have long recognized that the tort has the potential to impose an undue "chilling effect" on the ordinary citizen's willingness to report criminal conduct or to bring a civil dispute to court, and, as a consequence, the tort has traditionally been regarded as a disfavored cause of action. * * * In a number of other states, the disfavored status of the tort is reflected in a requirement that a plaintiff demonstrate some "special injury" beyond that ordinarily incurred in defending a lawsuit in order to prevail in a malicious prosecution action. (*See* O'Toole v. Franklin (1977) 279 Or. 513, 569 P.2d 561, 564, fn. 3 [listing 17 states adhering to special-injury rule][5]; Friedman v. Dozorc (1981) 412 Mich. 1, 312 N.W.2d 585, 596 [applying special-injury rule].) Even in jurisdictions, like California, which do not impose a special-injury requirement, the elements of the tort have historically been carefully circumscribed so that litigants with potentially valid claims will not be deterred from bringing their claims to court by the prospect of a subsequent malicious prosecution claim.

2. Since a malicious prosecution action may not be brought without a showing that the original proceeding was instituted without probable cause and since want of probable cause will justify a finding of malice, how important an element is the requirement of actual malice? The *Restatement (Second) of Torts* uses the term "improper purpose" in place of the traditional term "malice". In § 669 the *Restatement (Second)* specifically declares that "lack of probable cause for the initiation of criminal proceedings, insofar as it tends to show that the accuser did not believe in the guilt of the accused, is evidence that he did not initiate the proceedings for a proper purpose". If there is probable cause will a showing of malice permit the bringing of a malicious prosecution action? Consider that *Restatement (Second) of Torts* § 669A specifically provides that an "improper purpose" is *not* evidence of lack of probable cause.

3. In *Boose* the action had to be brought against the city for the actions of its police officers because a prosecuting attorney cannot be the subject of a malicious prosecution action for any criminal proceedings instituted in the prosecuting officer's official capacity. *See Restatement (Second) of Torts* § 656. A similar absolute privilege attaches to judges who might hear, or rule on, any issues involved in the proceedings. An instructive case is Belcher v. Paine, 136 N.H. 137, 612 A.2d 1318 (1992). Plaintiffs were indicted for aggravated felonious sexual assault. After the indictments were nol prossed by the defendant, the County Attorney, the plaintiffs filed an action for malicious prosecution. The New Hampshire Supreme Court affirmed summary judgment for the defendant based upon his claim of absolute privilege from civil liability whenever the claimed activity is "functionally related to the initiation of criminal process or to the prosecution of criminal charges."

4. The defendant in a malicious prosecution action can relitigate the question of the plaintiff's guilt. Moreover, in the civil action the question of guilt will be resolved by the preponderance-of-the-evidence standard, not the beyond-a-reasonable-doubt standard. *See Restatement (Second) of Torts* § 657

5. [Ed. note: Lee v. Mitchell, 152 Or.App. 159, 953 P.2d 414 (1998) states that the *O'Toole* case and the English Rule requiring special injury have been overruled by Or. Rev. Stat. 30.895(1).]

and Comments; Wal–Mart Stores, Inc. v. Blackford, 264 Ga. 612, 449 S.E.2d 293 (1994).

5. A defendant who can establish that he relied in good faith upon the advice of an apparently disinterested attorney given upon a "full disclosure of the facts," will conclusively establish probable cause. *See Restatement (Second) of Torts* § 666. An instructive case is Peoples Bank & Trust Co. v. Stock, 181 Ind.App. 483, 392 N.E.2d 505 (1979). That was a case for malicious "civil" prosecution, a cause of action that has arisen by analogy to the malicious prosecution of criminal proceedings. In *Stock* the bank had agreed to serve as executor of an estate at the request of an attorney representing the deceased's former wife. In that capacity it prevented, for a substantial period of time, the payment of the proceeds of the deceased's insurance policy to the named beneficiary, the woman with whom the deceased had been living at the time of his death. The court held that the attorney was not a disinterested party upon whom the bank could rely.

6. The question of probable cause and the question of whether the prior proceedings terminated in favor of the plaintiff are among the issues to be decided by the court. *See Restatement (Second) of Torts* § 673; Solitro v. Moffatt, 523 A.2d 858 (R.I.1987).

BANK OF LYONS v. SCHULTZ

Supreme Court of Illinois, 1980.
78 Ill.2d 235, 35 Ill.Dec. 758, 399 N.E.2d 1286.

WARD, JUSTICE:

The plaintiff, Mary Schultz, brought an action in October 1975 in the circuit court of Cook County against the Bank of Lyons for malicious prosecution for damages allegedly sustained as a result of two suits filed against her by the bank, both of which were decided in her favor. The trial court dismissed her complaint and the appellate court reversed. * * * We granted the bank's petition for leave to appeal.

The plaintiff's claim of malicious prosecution by the bank is founded upon the following events. In April of 1962 the bank filed a creditor's suit against the plaintiff and her late husband, Alvin Schultz, who died during the pendency of that suit. As the beneficiary of his life insurance policies the plaintiff was to receive $61,533.27. The bank filed a suit in equity in June 1963 petitioning for an accounting and for an injunction to restrain distribution of the insurance proceeds to the plaintiff. The trial court issued a preliminary injunction enjoining the insurance companies from making payments to the plaintiff and ordering that the funds be deposited with the clerk of the circuit court. The trial court, however, following the recommendation of a master in chancery to whom the matter was referred, dissolved the injunction on July 2, 1963, and dismissed the complaint in equity. The plaintiff was also granted leave to file a suggestion of her damages on account of the injunction's issuance as provided for in section 12 of the Injunction Act (Ill.Rev.Stat.1963, ch. 69, par. 12). She was subsequently awarded $2,369.67 on her suggestion of damages to cover interest she would have earned on the insurance proceeds held by the clerk of the court, attorneys' fees and costs.

Seventeen days after the injunction was dissolved, the bank was given leave to amend the complaint in its pending creditor's suit by adding a second count, and in it the bank again prayed for an accounting and for a preliminary injunction prohibiting distribution of the insurance proceeds. A preliminary injunction was entered on July 19, but almost two years later, on September 24, 1965, the court dismissed the second count, stating that the injunction had been wrongfully issued. The court also dissolved this injunction and ordered the clerk of the court to release to the plaintiff those insurance proceeds in excess of $30,000. The plaintiff was also given leave to file a suggestion of damages under section 12.

In November of 1965 the bank, with leave of court, filed another count to its creditor's suit. This third count alleged conversion and unlawful withholding of funds based on claims that the bank had been induced to issue cashier's checks to Alvin Schultz without consideration and that the bank had erroneously credited the plaintiff's account in the amount of $10,200. A master in chancery found, however, that the bank failed to prove a *prima facie* cause of action, and the circuit court, following the recommendation of the master, dismissed this third count. This was in September 1969.

The court also ordered the release of the balance of the insurance proceeds to the plaintiff. The bank appealed, and the appellate court remanded to the trial court to determine whether the plaintiff was a holder in due course. * * * On remand the trial court found the plaintiff was a holder in due course and again dismissed the third count.

On June 21, 1972, the trial court dismissed count I of the bank's creditor's suit because of a failure to allege fraud. No appeal was taken by the bank. On August 1, 1972, the plaintiff filed her second suggestion of damages pursuant to the September 1965 order and, on March 6, 1973, was awarded a total of $24,103.52, representing unearned interest on the proceeds of insurance, attorneys' fees and costs. Upon the bank's appeal, the appellate court affirmed. * * *

Plaintiff filed this suit for malicious prosecution in October 1975, claiming $49,848.13 in compensatory damages for the forfeiture of her interest in a house which she had owned jointly with her late husband, Alvin Schultz, which interest was foreclosed, she alleged, as a result of the injunction which prevented her from using the insurance proceeds to make mortgage payments. She also claimed $300,000 in punitive damages.

It appears that the plaintiff's complaint for malicious prosecution was dismissed by the trial court on the ground that the damages claimed should have been requested when she filed her second statutory suggestion of damages, and that recovery was barred under the doctrine of *res judicata,* and, further, because she failed to allege an arrest of her person, seizure of property, or some other special injury. The appellate court, in reversing, held that the wrongful issuance of the preliminary injunction constituted a seizure of property for purposes of establishing a cause of action for malicious prosecution and that the plaintiff's claim for compensatory and punitive damages was not barred by the doctrine of *res judicata*.

In this jurisdiction a plaintiff, in a suit for malicious prosecution founded on the defendant's wrongful bringing of a civil suit, must show that the suit he claims was wrongfully filed was terminated in his favor. He must also prove that it was brought maliciously and without probable cause and, further, he must establish evidence of his arrest, the seizure of his property, or some other special injury which exceeds the usual expense and annoyance and inconvenience of defending a lawsuit. * * *

Clearly as a result of the preliminary injunctions the plaintiff was prevented from using the insurance proceeds for a period of more than nine years. There have been holdings in jurisdictions, which have the same requirements for malicious prosecution as we do, to the effect that an injunction may constitute a sufficient interference with property for purposes of bringing a malicious prosecution suit. * * *

We are not persuaded by the bank's contention that there must be an actual seizure of property, as opposed to an interference with it, before a cause of action for malicious prosecution can arise. There obviously can be harm from interference with one's property. In principle the harm may be the same in both cases. Even in jurisdictions which appear to focus on whether there has been a seizure of property rather than an interference, there have been holdings that events resembling those here amounted to seizures. For example, in Multiple Realty, Inc. v. Walker (1969), 119 Ga.App. 393, 167 S.E.2d 380, the court determined there had been a seizure where the plaintiff's funds were held in the registry of the court and not released until a writ of attachment was dissolved. In Balsiger v. American Steel & Supply Co. (1969), 254 Or. 204, 458 P.2d 932, it was held that though there had been no actual seizure, causing a petition for bankruptcy to be filed constituted interference with the debtor's property so as to satisfy the requirement of a seizure. * * *

Here injunctions were issued during the pendency of the suit filed by the bank in 1962 restraining the distribution of over $60,000 to the plaintiff, $30,000 of which was not released until 1973, more than nine years after her husband's death. This constituted an interference with the plaintiff's property interests sufficient to satisfy the requirement of a seizure or special injury in bringing an action for malicious prosecution.

We do not consider there is merit to the bank's contention that the plaintiff could have claimed damages for the loss of her house under section 12 of the Injunction Act, and that, as she did not do so, her claim for malicious prosecution is barred under the doctrine of *res judicata*. It is clear that the damages recoverable under section 12 are limited to damages actually suffered during the life or pendency of the injunction. * * * The plaintiff in her complaint for malicious prosecution sets out that her statutory right to redeem following the foreclosure did not expire until the second injunction obtained by the bank had been dissolved and, assuming for this discussion that damages of this character could be recovered under section 12, she could not claim under that section, as she did not sustain this loss during the pendency of the injunction. Too, as we have observed, to have a cause of action for malicious prosecution, the suit which was wrongfully brought must have been determined in favor of the plaintiff. At the time the second injunction obtained by the bank had been dissolved, and when the plaintiff filed her second suggestion of damages, no cause of action for malicious prosecution could have arisen because the litigation brought against her by the bank had not yet been concluded in her favor.

For the reasons given, the judgment of the appellate court is affirmed and the cause is remanded to the circuit court for further proceedings not inconsistent with this opinion.

NOTES

1. Some courts have held that no cause of action will lie for malicious institution of civil proceedings unless there is some interference with the plaintiff's person or property or some other form of special damage. This approach is sometimes called the "English" rule. The English Rule is a minority position, followed by about one-third of the states. 1 Harper, James & Gray, The Law of Torts, § 4.8, at 4.69 (3d Ed. 1995). *See also,* L. Anderson, *"Special Injury" in the Torts of Malicious Prosecution and Injurious Falsehood: Will They Get You Into or Keep You Out of Court?*, 26 For the Defense 22 (May 1984) in which it is stated that sixteen jurisdictions still require some form of special injury, thirty jurisdictions follow the "American" rule, and five jurisdictions have yet to rule on the issue. Even some of the minority states will permit an action to be brought for wrongful instigation of civil proceedings when the defendant is accused of having brought repetitious civil actions against the plaintiff for the purposes of harassment, as for example a landlord bringing multiple unsuccessful eviction actions to rid himself of a tenant whom he does not like. *See, e.g.,* Weisman v. Middleton, 390 A.2d 996 (D.C.App.1978) (tenant had tried to organize other tenants to complain about landlord's maintenance of the building), relying on Soffos v. Eaton, 152 F.2d 682 (D.C.Cir.1945); *cf.* Timeplan Loan & Investment Corp. v. Colbert, 108 Ga.App. 753, 134 S.E.2d 476 (1963). Ohio and Illinois have recently reaffirmed their use of the special damages rule, emphasizing the need to strike an appropriate balance between the interest in discouraging frivolous and vexatious law suits, on the one hand, but not chilling resort to the courts to settle disputes peacefully, on the other. *See* Robb v. Chagrin Lagoons Yacht Club, Inc., 75 Ohio St.3d 264, 662 N.E.2d 9 (1996) (involving repeated litigation growing out of disciplinary action and finally expulsion of some members of a private yacht club); Levin v. King, 271 Ill.App.3d 728, 208 Ill.Dec. 186, 648 N.E.2d 1108 (1995), *appeal dismissed*, 163 Ill.2d 560, 212 Ill.Dec. 422, 657 N.E.2d 623 (1995) (involving litigation growing out of a dispute over building a housing project). One court has observed:

> The [special damage] rule has been criticized by Dean Prosser and rejected by the Restatement of Torts. The argument is that the mere award of costs to the successful defendant, without the attorney fees included in England, is not full compensation for an unfounded lawsuit, which is true; and that while honest litigants should be encouraged to seek justice, "surely there is no policy in favor of vexatious suits known to be groundless, which are a real and often a serious injury". Prosser, The Law of Torts 851, § 120 (4th ed., 1971). Adequate protection for bona fide litigants, according to this view, exists in "the heavy burden of proof upon the plaintiff, to establish both lack of probable cause and an improper purpose," *ibid.*

O'Toole v. Franklin, 279 Or. 513, 569 P.2d 561 (1977). This case had held that the English Rule was still the governing law in Oregon and included an excellent discussion of the Rule and its rationale. However, shortly thereafter the Oregon legislature passed a statute effectively overruling the case. Or. Rev. Stat 30.895 (1). *See* Lee v. Mitchell, 152 Or.App. 159, 953 P.2d 414 (1998). It has been held by some courts that the anti-SLAPP statutes, discussed in Chapter Eight, p. 637, *supra,* also apply to malicious prosecution cases, since bringing a law suit is a constitutionally protected right. See Jarrow Formulas, Inc. v. LaMarche, 31 Cal.4th 728, 74 P.3d 737, 3 Cal. Rptr.3d 636 (2003). This would probably increase the plaintiff's burden because to defeat a motion to dismiss he must demonstrate "a probability of prevailing" on his malicious prosecution claim.

2. Some states now deal with these abuse of process causes of action in statutes. An example is the statute passed by Georgia in 1989 (Ga. Code Ann.):

> § 51–7–80 Definitions.
>
> As used in this article, the term:
>
> (1) "Civil proceeding" includes any action, suit, proceeding, counter-claim, cross-claim, third-party claim, or other claim at law or in equity.
>
> (2) "Claim" includes any allegation or contention of fact or law asserted in support of or in opposition to any civil proceeding, defense, motion, or appeal.
>
> (3) "Defense" includes any denial of allegations made by another party in any pleading, motion, or other paper submitted to the court for the purpose of seeking affirmative or negative relief, and any affirmative defense or matter asserted in confession or avoidance.
>
> (4) "Good faith," when used with reference to any civil proceeding, claim, defense, motion, appeal, or other position, means that to the best of a person's or his or her attorney's knowledge, information, and belief, formed honestly after reasonable inquiry, that such civil proceeding, claim, defense, motion, appeal, or other position is well grounded in fact and is either warranted by existing law or by reasonable grounds to believe that an argument for the extension, modification, or reversal of existing law may be successful.
>
> (5) "Malice" means acting with ill will or for a wrongful purpose and may be inferred in an action if the party initiated, continued, or procured

civil proceedings or process in a harassing manner or used process for a purpose other than that of securing the proper adjudication of the claim upon which the proceedings are based.

(6) "Person" means an individual, corporation, company, association, firm, partnership, society, joint-stock company, or any other entity, including any governmental entity or unincorporated association of persons with capacity to sue or be sued.

(7) "Without substantial justification," when used with reference to any civil proceeding, claim, defense, motion, appeal, or other position, means that such civil proceeding, claim, defense, motion, appeal, or other position is:

(A) Frivolous;

(B) Groundless in fact or in law; or

(C) Vexatious.

(8) "Wrongful purpose" when used with reference to any civil proceeding, claim, defense, motion, appeal, or other position results in or has the effect of:

(A) Attempting to unjustifiably harass or intimidate another party or witness to the proceeding; or

(B) Attempting to unjustifiably accomplish some ulterior or collateral purpose other than resolving the subject controversy on its merits.

§ 51–7–81 Liability for abusive litigation.

Any person who takes an active part in the initiation, continuation, or procurement of civil proceedings against another shall be liable for abusive litigation if such person acts:

(1) With malice; and

(2) Without substantial justification.

§ 51–7–82 Defenses.

(a) It shall be a complete defense to any claim for abusive litigation that the person against whom a claim of abusive litigation is asserted has voluntarily withdrawn, abandoned, discontinued, or dismissed the civil proceeding, claim, defense, motion, appeal, civil process, or other position which the injured person claims constitutes abusive litigation within 30 days after the mailing of the notice required by subsection (a) of Code Section 51–7–84 or prior to a ruling by the court relative to the civil proceeding, claim, defense, motion, appeal, civil process, or other position, whichever shall first occur; provided, however, that this defense shall not apply where the alleged act of abusive litigation involves the seizure or interference with the use of the injured person's property by process of attachment, execution, garnishment, writ of possession, lis pendens, injunction, restraining order, or similar process which results in special damage to the injured person.

(b) It shall be a complete defense to any claim for abusive litigation that the person against whom a claim of abusive litigation is asserted acted in good faith; provided, however, that good faith shall be an affirmative defense and the burden of proof shall be on the person asserting the actions were taken in good faith.

(c) It shall be a complete defense to any claim for abusive litigation that the person against whom a claim of abusive litigation is asserted was substantially successful on the issue forming the basis for the claim of abusive litigation in the underlying civil proceeding.

Sections 51–7–84 and 51–7–85 deal with procedural aspects, damages recoverable, and makes the remedy exclusive.

3. A lawyer can be subject to an action for the wrongful institution of civil proceedings. However, it has been recognized that the line between zealous advocacy and wrongful institution of civil proceedings or misuse of legal process is a difficult one. *Restatement (Second) of Torts* § 674, Comment *d* tries to resolve the problem in the following statement which is not without its own difficulties:

d. Attorneys. An attorney who initiates a civil proceeding on behalf of his client or one who takes any steps in the proceeding is not liable if he has probable cause for his action (*see* § 675); and even if he has no probable cause and is convinced that his client's claim is unfounded, he is still not liable if he acts primarily for the purpose of aiding his client in obtaining a proper adjudication of his claim. (See § 676).[6] An attorney is not required or expected to prejudge his client's claim, and although he is fully aware that its chances of success are comparatively slight, it is his responsibility to present it to the court for adjudication if his client so insists after he has explained to the client the nature of the chances. If, however, the attorney acts without probable cause for belief in the possibility that the claim will succeed, and for an improper purpose, as, for example, to put pressure upon the person proceeded against in order to compel payment of another claim of his own or solely to harass the person proceeded against by bringing a claim known to be invalid, he is subject to the same liability as any other person. There is one situation that sometimes arises in civil proceedings but does not occur in criminal proceedings. An attorney who initiates civil proceedings on a contingent-fee basis with his client is not for that reason to be charged with an improper motive or purpose, since the contingent fee is a legitimate arrangement and the interest of the attorney in receiving it is merely the ordinary interest of a professional man in being paid for his services. But by obtaining the authority of the client to bring the action he procures its initiation; and if he does so without probable cause and for an improper purpose other than the fee, he is subject to liability under the rule stated in this Section. An attorney may also be subject to liability if he takes an active part in continuing a civil proceeding properly begun, for an improper purpose and without probable cause.

In Junot v. Lee, 372 So.2d 707 (La.App.1979), the court affirmed dismissal of an action against an attorney for instituting multiple proceedings in a custody

6. [Ed. note] *Restatement (Second) of Torts* § 676 provides as follows:

To subject a person to liability for wrongful civil proceedings, the proceeding must have been initiated or continued primarily for a purpose other than that of securing the proper adjudication of the claim on which they are based.

dispute on the ground that given the increased overruling of older cases in recent years it was reluctant, except in "a clear case," to permit an action to be brought against an attorney who "urges a position which has little or no chance of success under current jurisprudence."

One of the few cases in which a physician has been able to win an action for wrongful institution of civil proceedings or, as it was called in that case, "malicious prosecution," against an attorney is Raine v. Drasin, 621 S.W.2d 895 (Ky.1981). *See also*, Nelson v. Miller, 227 Kan. 271, 607 P.2d 438 (1980); Peerman v. Sidicane, 605 S.W.2d 242 (Tenn.App.1980). In these cases the attorneys either knew that there was no basis for their bringing an action or brought the action without any investigation or continued the process after they knew that there was no basis for the action. The cases and the issues are discussed in H. Hirsch, *Physician Countersuit—To Sue or Better Not to Sue*, 34 Medical Trial Techniques Quarterly 59 (Winter 1987). Earlier discussions include H. Greenbaum, *Physician Countersuits: A Cause Without Action*, 12 Pac.L.J. 745 (1981); S. Reuter, *Physician Countersuits: A Catch–22*, 14 U.S.F.L.Rev. 203 (1980).

In Bird v. Rothman, 128 Ariz. 599, 627 P.2d 1097, *cert. denied*, 454 U.S. 865, 102 S.Ct. 327, 70 L.Ed.2d 166 (1981), the action was brought by an architect against two attorneys who had instigated a malpractice action against him. After upholding dismissal of a malicious prosecution count because of the presence of probable cause, the court turned to the negligence count and declared:

> * * * Our courts must be held open to litigating parties without fear or subsequent prosecution for calling upon the court to decide a contested issue. The lawyer's role in this process is unlike that of other professionals. His relationship with the opposing party is by its very nature adverse, not mutually beneficial. The party who is forced to defend a groundless lawsuit may institute disciplinary proceedings against the offending lawyer, as well as bringing a malicious prosecution action.
>
> Since we hold that there can be no liability in negligence for an attorney who allegedly brings a groundless suit against another party, the summary judgment on this count was properly granted.
>
> In summary, despite appellant's arguments that negligence suits, such as the underlying suit in this action, against architects and engineers have a significant impact on malpractice liability insurance rates and serve to impugn the reputation of conscientious professionals, we are persuaded that in the absence of proof of malicious prosecution on the part of the injured party or his attorney, the interest of freedom of access to our courts compels the conclusions we have reached. * * *

In an action brought by a physician, Nelson v. Miller, 227 Kan. 271, 607 P.2d 438 (1980), referred to earlier in this note, the court, relying upon *Restatement (Second) of Torts* § 674, Comment *d,* quoted above in note 3, reversed the dismissal by the trial court of "the claim * * * based upon a theory of malicious prosecution of a civil action." The court, however, upheld dismissal of a claim based upon "professional negligence." The essence of the court's opinion is contained in the following extract:

* * * The traditional rule has been that an attorney will be held liable for negligence only to his client. The rationale of that rule is that there can be no action against an attorney for professional negligence in the absence of some privity of contract between the plaintiff and the attorney. More recently, the strict requirement of privity of contract has been eased in situations where an attorney has rendered services which he should recognize as involving a foreseeable injury to some third-party beneficiary of the contract. These cases usually involve the negligence of attorneys in will drafting and in the examination of real estate titles. We have been cited no cases, and we have found none, where an attorney has been held liable to his client's adversary in prior civil litigation on the basis of professional negligence alone.

In representing their clients, lawyers are expected to use the legitimate sidearms of a warrior. It is only when a lawyer uses the dagger of an assassin that he should be subjected to discipline or to personal liability. We believe that the public is adequately protected from harassment and abuse by an unprofessional member of the bar through the means of the traditional cause of action for malicious prosecution. We, therefore, hold in accordance with established law, that an attorney cannot be held liable for the consequence of his professional negligence to his client's adversary. We further hold that a violation of the Code of Professional Responsibility does not alone create a cause of action against an attorney in favor of a third party. The remedy provided a third-party adversary is solely through an action for malicious prosecution of a civil action. It follows that the district court was correct in dismissing the plaintiff's second cause of action based upon a theory of professional negligence.

In Comment, *Attorney Professional Responsibility: Competence Through Malpractice Liability,* 77 N.W.U.L.Rev. 633 (1982), the argument is made that an attorney should be held liable for failure to meet the level of conduct (including fairness to adversaries, etc.) contained in the American Bar Association's Model Code of Professional Responsibility. On some of the more technical problems involved in bringing an action for the malicious instigation of civil proceedings, *see* C. Aragon, *Favorable Termination in Malicious Prosecution of Civil Proceedings,* 15 S.W.U.L.Rev. 65 (1984) which discusses the not uncommon situation where the prior case was discontinued without a ruling on the "merits."

4. An interesting new development is the common law creation of the tort of "malicious defense". The New Hampshire Supreme Court recognized this new cause of action building upon the suggestions made in Van Patten & Willard, *The Limits of Advocacy: A Proposal for the Tort of Malicious Defense in Civil Litigation,* 35 Hastings L.J. 891 (1994). This variation on the malicious prosecution action is composed of essentially the same elements. The plaintiff must prove the following: (1) acting without probable cause, the defendant forwarded a defense "without any credible basis in fact and such action is not warranted by existing law or established equitable principles or a good faith argument for the extension, modification or reversal of existing law", (2) the defendant had knowledge of the lack of merit for the defense, (3) the defendant acted primarily for a purpose other than the adjudication of the defense (*i.e.,* to vexate, injure, harass, or delay the opponent), (4) the proceed-

ings are terminated in favor of the party claiming malicious defense, and (5) injury or damage to the claimant. Aranson v. Schroeder, 140 N.H. 359, 671 A.2d 1023 (1995).

5. A recent *cause célèbre* is Franklin Mint Co. v. Manatt, Phelps & Phillips, LLP, 184 Cal.App.4th 313, 109 Cal.Rptr.3d 143 (2010). The case was eventually settled for $25,000,000. *See*. Ashby Jones, *Manatt Phelps Pays $25 Million to End Malicious Prosecution Case*, WSJ LAW BLOG (Jan. 21, 2011, 4:16 PM), http://blogs.wsj.com/law/2011/01/21/manatt-phelps-pays–25–million-to-end-malicious-prosecution-case/.

CHAPTER 11

CONSTITUTIONAL TORTS

■ ■ ■

It was one of the glories of the common law that everyone, except the king himself, was answerable in the courts of law to those whom he had legally wronged.[1] The king's ministers could be, and often were, hauled before the courts by those whom they had allegedly wronged. As we shall see, over the course of years, certain privileges arose which immunized some public servants from some types of litigation arising out of their attempts to perform their official duties. For example, since the English Bill of Rights, (1 W. & M. Sess. 2, c. 2 (1689)), "the freedom of speech and debates or proceedings in Parliament ought not to be impeached or questioned in any court or place out of Parliament." Compare Article 1, § 6, cl. 1 of the United States Constitution which provides that members of Congress "shall in all cases, except Treason, Felony, or Breach of the Peace, be privileged from Arrest during their Attendance at the Session of their respective Houses, and in going to or returning from the same; and for any Speech or Debate in either House, they shall not be questioned in any other Place." Judges also came to be immune from suit for anything they may have done in the course of performing their judicial function.

The common-law notion that even government ministers are answerable in the courts of law for their torts, like the freedom of debate in Parliament, was carried over to this country. Over the course of time, however, there came to be a common perception that the threat of a tort action was less likely to deter an official who abused his authority in the United States than was the case in Great Britain. Policemen and federal law enforcement officials are the public servants most likely to be involved in this type of litigation and it came to be considered that the poor and underprivileged, who were most likely to suffer from police abuse, would be unable to find sympathy among state court jurors. There thus came to

1. Although it was often said that the king can do no wrong, the reason the king was not personally answerable in the courts of law was a conceptual one, namely how could a person be a judge in a legal action involving himself? This formalistic problem arose because the judges were the servants of the king and pronounced judgment in his name. Since at least Magna Carta (1215), a subject who was aggrieved by the Crown could file a "petition of right" seeking redress for injuries. The granting of the petition was totally a matter of discretion. The most famous of these petitions was the "Petition of Right" of 1628 in which Parliament presented Charles I with a list of grievances.

be increasing pressure to find some method for bringing these actions into federal courts. In Bell v. Hood, 327 U.S. 678, 66 S.Ct. 773, 90 L.Ed. 939 (1946) the question was presented whether conduct on the part of FBI agents which might provide the basis for a "common law action in trespass under state law" might also be actionable in the federal courts as an action arising "under the Constitution or laws of the United States" under Congress' grant of federal question jurisdiction to the United States District Courts. The Court, in *Bell* held that this question was itself a federal question and remanded the case to the lower federal courts. It did not, however, itself express any opinion on this matter.

Beginning in 1961, however, first in cases involving state officers or those who acted under color of state law and then later, from 1971, in cases involving federal officials, a new category of tort litigation, "constitutional torts", was born and has since rapidly expanded. By 1976 it was estimated that "one out of three 'private' federal question suits filed in the federal courts was a civil rights action against the state or a local official." C. Whitman, *Constitutional Torts,* 79 Mich.L.Rev. 5, 6 (1980). Not all of these suits were tort actions, of course. Perhaps one half involved petitions by state prisoners seeking some change in the conditions of their incarceration. Unfortunately, the statistics kept by the Administrative Office of the United States Courts do not break down the data on the caseload of the federal courts in such a way as to permit the reader to arrive at an accurate determination of how many cases were constitutional tort actions brought against state officials or those who acted under color of state law or constitutional tort actions brought against federal officials. In the fiscal year ending September 30, 2010, 282,895 civil cases were commenced in the United States District Courts. Of these, 138,655, or 49%, involved federal questions and of the federal question cases, 15,651 involved "other civil rights" and 16,951 involved prisoner petitions concerned with "civil rights". Presumably litigation in which damages or other remedies are sought for conduct that amounts to a constitutional tort would be subsumed within these categories. Judicial Business of the United States Courts (2010), at 144–46 (Table C2).

It is impossible in a general course on torts to exhaustively treat the important subject of constitutional torts. Many law schools cover the subject in narrowly-focused upper-class courses or seminars. The most that we can do is sketch out the history and development of the notion of constitutional torts in the United States and to highlight some of the important questions that have arisen, particularly those which have close analogues in the common-law torts which form the background out of which the constitutional torts have evolved.

A. ACTIONS AGAINST STATE OFFICIALS AND OTHERS ACTING UNDER "COLOR OF STATE LAW"

1. HISTORICAL DEVELOPMENT

Rev.Stat. § 1979, more commonly referred to as 42 U.S.C. § 1983, first enacted in 1871 as part of the "Ku Klux" Act, provides that:

> every person who, under color of statute, ordinance, regulation, custom, or usage, of any State or Territory * * * or the District of Columbia subjects, or causes to be subjected, any citizen of the United States or other person within the jurisdiction thereof to the deprivation of any rights, privileges, or immunities secured by the Constitution and laws, shall be liable to the party injured in an action at law, suit in equity, or other proper proceeding for redress.

In *Monroe v. Pape,* 365 U.S. 167, 81 S.Ct. 473, 5 L.Ed.2d 492 (1961), the Court held that the actions of officials—in that case thirteen Chicago police officers who allegedly broke into petitioners' home in the early morning, routed them from bed, made them stand naked in the living room, and ransacked every room emptying drawers and ripping mattress covers—were activities conducted "under color of" state law, despite the fact that what these officers did was clearly in violation of the constitution and laws of Illinois and that legal redress was theoretically available in the Illinois courts for this outrageous conduct.[2] At the same time, the Court held that 42 U.S.C. § 1983 did not impose liability on a municipal corporation (in the case before them, the city of Chicago). Justice Frankfurter dissented from the holding that conduct which is forbidden by state law might nonetheless be "under color of" state law. For the position that Justice Frankfurter's view of the meaning of "under color" of the state law is without historical support *see* S. Winter, *The Meaning of "Under Color" of Law,* 91 Mich.L.Rev. 323 (1992). Even an official acting without any pretense of performing a legitimate public office can be found to be acting "under color" of state law as, for example, a police officer who at the time claimed his official status permitted him to assault with impunity his wife's former lover. *See* United States v. Tarpley, 945 F.2d 806 (5th Cir. 1991). Whether a private party has been sufficiently clothed with state authority to permit a § 1983 action to be brought against him is a difficult question. The Court has wrestled with the question in a number of different factual circumstances. *See* Jackson v. Metropolitan Edison Co., 419 U.S. 345, 95 S.Ct. 449, 42 L.Ed.2d 477 (1974); Rendell–Baker v. Kohn, 457 U.S. 830, 102 S.Ct. 2764, 73 L.Ed.2d 418 (1982); Blum v. Yaretsky, 457 U.S. 991, 102 S.Ct. 2777, 73 L.Ed.2d 534 (1982). *See also* Lebron v. National R.R. Passenger Corp., 513 U.S. 374, 115 S.Ct. 961, 130 L.Ed.2d

2. *See also* Patsy v. Board of Regents of Fla., 457 U.S. 496, 102 S.Ct. 2557, 73 L.Ed.2d 172 (1982) (no requirement to exhaust state administrative procedures). The special case of actions by prison inmates is discussed later in the text.

902 (1995), where the Court held that Amtrak was an entity of the United States even though the statute creating it specifically declared it was not "an agency or establishment of the United States Government." How about a statewide non-profit membership corporation regulating interscholastic athletic competition among public and private high schools, most of whose members were public high schools? *See* Brentwood Academy v. Tennessee Secondary Sch'l Athletic Ass'n., 531 U.S. 288, 121 S.Ct. 924, 148 L.Ed.2d 807 (2001), distinguishing National Collegiate Athletic Ass'n. v. Tarkanian, 488 U.S. 179, 109 S.Ct. 454, 102 L.Ed.2d 469 (1988). Finally the Court has intimated, but not definitively decided, that a guard employed at a "private" prison can be subject to a § 1983 action. *See* Richardson v. McKnight, 521 U.S. 399, 117 S.Ct. 2100, 138 L.Ed.2d 540 (1997). *See also,* Thompson v. Davidson Transit Organization, 563 F.Supp.2d 820 (M.D. Tenn. 2008). In Minneci v. Pollard, 565 U.S. ___, 132 S.Ct. 617, 181 L.Ed.2d 606 (2012) the Court held that a prisoner could not bring a federal action for violation of his eighth amendment right to adequate medical care against employees of a privately operated federal prison because the matter was adequately covered by state law.

Once the Court had held that state officials who acted unlawfully were nonetheless acting "under color" of state law, the modern constitutional tort was born. In Monell v. New York City Dept. of Social Services, 436 U.S. 658, 98 S.Ct. 2018, 56 L.Ed.2d 611 (1978), the Court overruled that portion of *Monroe v. Pape* which held that municipalities were not subject to liability under § 1983. Municipalities could be liable under § 1983 when the acts complained of were acts done in execution of official policy or were the acts of senior officials who might be said to make the policy of the municipality. In Pembaur v. City of Cincinnati, 475 U.S. 469, 106 S.Ct. 1292, 89 L.Ed.2d 452 (1986) the Court held that a single decision of a high-ranking official with final authority over the issue involved—in that case the County Prosecutor—could be considered the making of a "policy" for which a governmental entity may be liable in an action under § 1983. The mere fact that a government employee has been delegated final decision-making authority over an issue does not by itself, however, establish that such a person can make governmental policy. *See* City of St. Louis v. Praprotnik, 485 U.S. 112, 108 S.Ct. 915, 99 L.Ed.2d 107 (1988) where the Court held that the director of the city's "Community Development Agency" was not a municipal policymaker despite his authority to initiate transfers and layoffs and despite the fact that the director was given substantial discretion in making these decisions. It would have been a different case if, through a series of decisions, "a 'custom or usage' had been established" of which the persons delegating the authority "must have been aware". Moreover, a single decision by some officials with policy-making authority, such as a sheriff's decision to hire a deputy is not attributable to the municipality. *See* Board of City Comm'rs v. Brown, 520 U.S. 397, 117 S.Ct. 1382, 137 L.Ed.2d 626 (1997). The Court has continued to hold, however, that Congress, in § 1983, did not provide the specific authorization required by the Court's reading of the eleventh amendment in order to permit a suit in the federal courts against the state. *See* Quern v. Jordan, 440 U.S. 332, 99 S.Ct. 1139, 59 L.Ed.2d 358 (1979).[3] It should finally be noted that, in fleshing out the scope of the tort created by § 1983, the Court has held in Maine v. Thiboutot, 448 U.S. 1, 100 S.Ct. 2502, 65 L.Ed.2d 555 (1980), that the language in § 1983 covering "deprivation of any rights, privileges and immunities secured by the Constitution and laws" covered all federal law and not just those federal statutes concerned with "equal rights." The Court has since ruled that actions for violations of the Commerce Clause may also be brought under § 1983. Dennis v. Higgins, 498 U.S. 439, 111 S.Ct. 865, 112 L.Ed.2d 969 (1991). The two dissenters argued that the Commerce Clause is only concerned with delimiting the regulatory power of the state and federal governments and not the creation of "rights."

2. ATTORNEYS FEES AND NON-COMPENSATORY DAMAGES

Under an amendment to 42 U.S.C. § 1988, enacted in 1976, *attorneys' fees* can now be granted to prevailing parties in actions under § 1983 and related statutes. While prevailing plaintiffs are almost routinely granted counsel fees, the Court has construed the statutory authorization to permit prevailing defendants to recover counsel fees only when the plaintiff's action was "frivolous, unreasonable or without foundation." Christiansburg Garment Co. v. EEOC, 434 U.S. 412, 98 S.Ct. 694, 54 L.Ed.2d 648 (1978). In City of Riverside v. Rivera, 477 U.S. 561, 106 S.Ct. 2686, 91 L.Ed.2d 466 (1986) the Court held that the fee awarded to a prevailing plaintiff is not required to be proportional to the actual monetary award that was recovered. To be a prevailing party, however, some relief on the merits must be granted, either in the form of damages or an injunction or in a declaratory judgment. While the award of nominal damages may make the recipient a prevailing party, the receipt of such damages does not automatically entitle such a party to the award of attorney's fees. *See* Farrar v. Hobby, 506 U.S. 103, 113 S.Ct. 566, 121 L.Ed.2d 494 (1992). Congress, in 1996, amended 42 U.S.C. § 1997e, to prohibit, in any civil action brought in a federal court, by a prisoner, the award of damages for "mental or emotional injury in the absence of" a prior showing of physical injury. *Id.* at § 1997e (e). In addition no action may be brought under any federal law relating to prison conditions unless the plaintiff has first exhausted all available administrative remedies. *Id.* at § 1997e (a).

The Court has held that *punitive damages* are available in § 1983 actions against individuals upon a showing that "the defendant's conduct * * * [was] motivated by evil motives or intent, or when it involves reckless or callous indifference to the federally protected rights of others." Smith v. Wade, 461 U.S. 30, 103 S.Ct. 1625, 75 L.Ed.2d 632 (1983).

3. The Court has subsequently held that, even if the action is brought in a state court, a state is not a person within the meaning of § 1983. Will v. Michigan Dept. of State Police, 491 U.S. 58, 109 S.Ct. 2304, 105 L.Ed.2d 45 (1989), and thus cannot be sued in a state court even if the state has waived its sovereign immunity.

Punitive damages are not available, however, in § 1983 actions against municipalities. City of Newport v. Fact Concerts, Inc., 453 U.S. 247, 101 S.Ct. 2748, 69 L.Ed.2d 616 (1981). In Carey v. Piphus, 435 U.S. 247, 98 S.Ct. 1042, 55 L.Ed.2d 252 (1978), the Court held, in an action brought by school children who claimed they had been suspended without being given the proper procedural safeguards, that there could be no *presumed damages* in § 1983 actions, at least where the claim was based upon a denial of procedural due process. Subsequently, in Memphis Community School District v. Stachura, 477 U.S. 299, 106 S.Ct. 2537, 91 L.Ed.2d 249 (1986), the Court amplified this holding by ruling that there could be no recovery of damages for the abstract deprivation of rights although it left open the possibility that presumed damages might possibly be appropriate in circumstances where compensatory damages are difficult to measure.

3. THE ROLE OF STATE COURTS AND STATE LAW

It was soon held by a number of state courts, *see e.g.,* Clark v. Bond Stores, Inc., 41 A.D.2d 620, 340 N.Y.S.2d 847 (1973); Ingram v. Moody, 382 So.2d 522 (Ala.1980), that § 1983 actions were also cognizable in the state courts. This state court practice was recognized and accepted by the Court in a number of cases. *See e.g.,* Martinez v. California, 444 U.S. 277, 100 S.Ct. 553, 62 L.Ed.2d 481 (1980) (n. 7 of Court's opinion); Maine v. Thiboutot, 448 U.S. 1, 100 S.Ct. 2502, 65 L.Ed.2d 555 (1980) (n. 1 of Court's opinion). The Court has ruled, however, that, if a § 1983 action is brought in the state courts, the states may not apply provisions of state law which would impose restrictions upon the plaintiff that would not be applicable if the action had been brought in the federal courts. *See* Felder v. Casey, 487 U.S. 131, 108 S.Ct. 2302, 101 L.Ed.2d 123 (1988). In the *Felder* case the restriction was a state statute which provided that no action could be brought against any state governmental subdivision, agency, or officer unless the claimant had provided a written notice of claim within 120 days of the alleged injury or could demonstrate that the defendant had actual notice of the claim and had not been prejudiced by lack of written notice. Subsequently, in Howlett v. Rose, 496 U.S. 356, 110 S.Ct. 2430, 110 L.Ed.2d 332 (1990), the Court held that a school district for which sovereign immunity had been waived for state law claims is subject to suit in state court under § 1983. State courts may not entertain state law actions but refuse to entertain similar federal claims. As already noted previously, however, the Court in *Will v. Michigan Dept. of State Police, supra,* has held, that even if a state has waived its sovereign immunity, an action against a state cannot be maintained in a state court because a state, unlike a municipality or a school district, is not a "person" within the meaning of § 1983.

The relationship between state law and federal law in § 1983 actions is complicated by the fact that in 42 U.S.C. § 1988, Congress has specifically declared, that, where federal law is not "suitable" to achieve the purposes of the various civil rights statutes or "are deficient in the provisions necessary to furnish suitable remedies * * *, the common law, as modified and changed by the constitution and statutes of the State wherein the court having jurisdiction of such * * * causes is held, so far as the same is not inconsistent with the Constitution and laws of the United States, shall be extended to and govern the said courts in the trial and disposition of the cause * * *." This portion of § 1988 dates from 1866. Relying on § 1988, in Wilson v. Garcia, 471 U.S. 261, 105 S.Ct. 1938, 85 L.Ed.2d 254 (1985), the Court held that the characterization of § 1983 actions for purposes of applying a statute of limitations would be governed by federal law, but state law would then provide the appropriate limitation period. The Court went on to hold that § 1988 required the selection in each state of a single statute of limitations for all § 1983 claims rather than the use of different statutes of limitations depending upon the nature of the particular § 1983 claim involved. It then finally held, in *Garcia,* that all § 1983 claims should be characterized as "personal injury actions" for purposes of applying statutes of limitations. Subsequently, in Owens v. Okure, 488 U.S. 235, 109 S.Ct. 573, 102 L.Ed.2d 594 (1989), the Court held that, in a state with more than one statute of limitations for personal injury actions, § 1983 actions are to be governed by the residual or general personal injury statute of limitations rather than the statute of limitations for enumerated, intentional torts. Finally, in Hardin v. Straub, 490 U.S. 536, 109 S.Ct. 1998, 104 L.Ed.2d 582 (1989), the Court held that a Michigan provision tolling the three-year limitation period for personal injury actions during the period a person is under a legal disability—in the instant case, the petitioner was incarcerated in prison—was not inconsistent with the purposes of § 1983 and should be applied in the case at bar. The lower court had recognized that it was normally obligated to apply state tolling provisions but felt that, in cases like the instant case in which the application of the state tolling provision could lead to a very lengthy tolling period, such a potentially long delay would be contrary to the federal policy of attempting to deal with § 1983 claims as promptly as was practicable. The Court disagreed. The issue arose again in Wallace v. Kato, 549 U.S. 384, 127 S.Ct. 1091, 166 L.Ed.2d 973 (2007). The plaintiff had been arrested without probable cause or a warrant. Between his arrest and his remand for trial by a magistrate, he confessed to a murder for which he was tried and convicted; but the conviction was reversed because it was the result of a false arrest. The issue was whether the Illinois statute of limitations began to run from the moment of his arraignment by the magistrate, at which point his detention was no longer unlawful, or from the date of the reversal of his conviction. As a matter of federal law, the Court held that it ran from the time his unlawful detention ended, which meant that his § 1983 action was barred.

Despite the statement in *Monroe v. Pape* that resort to § 1983 does not require exhaustion of available state remedies, the Court has shown a reluctance to allow the § 1983 action to become, in essence, a substitute for state tort law when the defendant is a state official whose official actions are alleged to have injured the plaintiff. For example, in Paul v. Davis, 424 U.S. 693, 96 S.Ct. 1155, 47 L.Ed.2d 405 (1976), the Court held that, what was in substance a claim that the defendant police chiefs had libeled the plaintiff in a flyer about shoplifters, could not be brought under § 1983. *See also* Siegert v. Gilley, 500 U.S. 226, 111 S.Ct. 1789, 114 L.Ed.2d 277 (1991), where the Court held that a defamatory letter in response to a request for information about his job performance could not be the basis of an action against a federal official under the federal equivalent of a § 1983 action that will be discussed shortly. Furthermore in Ingraham v. Wright, 430 U.S. 651, 97 S.Ct. 1401, 51 L.Ed.2d 711 (1977), the Court held that students who had been "paddled" did not have an eighth amendment ("cruel and unusual punishment") claim, because they were not being punished for commission of a crime and that whatever due process claims the students might have because of the manner in which the paddlings were administered could be redressed under Florida statutory and common law. *See also* Minneci v. Pollard, 565 U.S. ___, 132 S.Ct. 617, 181 L.Ed.2d 606 (2012).

4. ACTIONS BASED ON A NEGLIGENCE THEORY

A question with which the Court has wrestled for a considerable length of time is whether a § 1983 action can be based on a negligence theory. The Court deliberately left the question open in Parratt v. Taylor, 451 U.S. 527, 101 S.Ct. 1908, 68 L.Ed.2d 420 (1981), which involved a claim by a state prisoner whose mail-ordered hobby materials were negligently lost when the normal procedures for the receipt of mailed packages had not been followed by prison officials. The Court held that the prisoner did not have a § 1983 claim based on a deprivation of "due process of law" because he had an adequate state remedy against the offending officials. The case thus seemed to suggest, at least when merely negligence was involved, that, contrary to *Monroe v. Pape,* whether a person had a valid § 1983 claim depended upon the adequacy of state remedies although the actual holding in *Parratt* appears to have been that the § 1983 wrong, if any, would not have been the negligent loss of the hobby materials but a failure to provide some kind of adequate state remedy for this loss. *Cf.* Hudson v. Palmer, 468 U.S. 517, 104 S.Ct. 3194, 82 L.Ed.2d 393 (1984) where the Court reiterated that, where the plaintiff complains of a deprivation of property, there is no violation of due process if meaningful post-deprivation remedies are available under state law.

The Court, however, expressly overruled *Parratt* in Daniels v. Williams, 474 U.S. 327, 106 S.Ct. 662, 88 L.Ed.2d 662 (1986), and held that, regardless of whether an adequate state remedy existed, injuries suffered by an inmate in a state prison as a result of the negligence of the state prison authorities were not redressable in a § 1983 action based on a "deprivation of due process of law." The Court expressly noted that it had "no occasion to consider whether something less than intentional conduct such as recklessness or 'gross negligence,' is enough to trigger the protections of the Due Process Clause." *Id.* at n. 3. In a case decided on the same day, Davidson v. Cannon, 474 U.S. 344, 106 S.Ct. 668, 88 L.Ed.2d 677 (1986), the Court held that negligence could not be the basis of a § 1983 claim for depriving a person of rights under the due process clause, regardless of whether the rights involved were procedural or substantive. In *Daniels* the plaintiff was injured in the Richmond, Va. city jail when he slipped on a pillow negligently left on the stairs by one of the jailers. The plaintiff argued that the respondent's conduct had deprived him of due process because the respondent claimed that he was "entitled to the defense of sovereign immunity in a state tort suit." In *Davidson* the plaintiff claimed that the New Jersey prison authorities had negligently failed to respond to his written note advising them that he had been threatened by a fellow inmate who subsequently attacked him. Justice Brennan, in a concurring opinion, agreed "that merely negligent conduct by a state official does not constitute a deprivation of liberty under the Due Process Clause" but he believed that the case should be remanded so that the court of appeals could review the district court's holding that the respondent's conduct was not reckless. Justice Blackmun, joined by Justice Marshall, agreed that the case should be remanded for consideration of the recklessness issue, but he also believed that, under the circumstances involved in *Davidson,* namely the failure to protect someone in the custody of the state, a § 1983 action would also lie for mere negligence.

Six weeks after *Daniels* and *Davidson* were decided the Court was again confronted with the issue in Whitley v. Albers, 475 U.S. 312, 106 S.Ct. 1078, 89 L.Ed.2d 251 (1986). In *Whitley* the plaintiff was an inmate in the Oregon State Penitentiary who was shot by prison guards while he was trying to protect elderly prisoners during the course of a prison riot during which a guard had been taken hostage. The plaintiff based his claim on both the eighth amendment right not to be subjected to "cruel or unusual punishment" and more generally on the deprivation of "a protected liberty interest without due process of law." The Court reinstated the district court's grant of summary judgment to the defendants. No action would lie for mere negligence and, in the circumstances, there was insufficient evidence from which to infer "a wanton willingness to inflict unjustified suffering" on the plaintiff. Justice Marshall, joined by Justices Brennan, Blackmun, and Stevens, dissented. In their view, there was enough evidence of wantonness to take the case to the jury. In a subsequent case a transsexual brought an analogous action against federal prison officials for placing him in the general prison population where he alleged he was injured by other inmates. Farmer v. Brennan, 511 U.S. 825, 114 S.Ct. 1970, 128 L.Ed.2d 811 (1994). The Court held that the prison officials would only be liable if it could be shown that they knew that a prisoner faced a substantial risk of serious harm and then exhibited deliberate indifference to that risk. The Court adopted the "subjective" recklessness test of the criminal law. *See also* Fagan v. City of Vineland, 22 F.3d 1296 (3d Cir. 1994) (high speed police chase). More recently the

Court considered whether deliberate indifference to the need to train his subordinates to follow constitutional requirements could be shown by a single act of indifference by the defendant district attorney or whether it required a pattern of such indifference. Connick v. Thompson, 563 U.S ___, 131 S.Ct. 1350, 179 L.Ed.2d 417 (2011). In a five five-to-four decision written by Justice Thomas the Court held that a pattern of such indifference was required. *See also* Ashcroft v. Iqbal, 556 U.S. 662, 129 S.Ct. 1937, 173 L.Ed.2d 868 (2009).

The extensive litigation under § 1983 has generated a very extensive literature. This literature includes P. Schuck, Suing Government: Citizen Remedies for Official Wrongs (1983); H. Monaghan, State Law Wrongs, State Law Remedies, and the Fourteenth Amendment, 86 Colum.L.Rev. 979 (1986); S. Schwab & T. Eisenberg, *Explaining Constitutional Tort Litigation: The Influence of the Attorney Fees Statute and the Government as Defendant,* 73 Cornell L.Rev. 719 (1988); (Hon.) H. Blackmun, *Section 1983 and the Federal Protection of Human Rights—Will the Statute Remain Alive or Fade Away,* 60 N.Y.U.L.Rev. 1 (1985) (Justice Blackmun disputed the contention that the federal courts are being overwhelmed by these actions); T. Eisenberg, *Section 1983: The Final Foundations and an Empirical Study,* 67 Cornell L.Rev. 482 (1982); R. Cass, *Damage Suits Against Public Officers,* 129 U.Pa.L.Rev. 1110 (1981); C. Whitman, *Constitutional Torts,* 79 Mich.L.Rev. 5 (1980). For a discussion of the interplay between the liability of municipalities and the liability or immunity of the officials who act for the municipality, *see* M. Brown, *Correlating Municipal Liability and Official Immunity under Section 1983,* 1989 Ill.L. Forum 625. For a critical reaction to the Court's refusal to permit a constitutional tort action to be brought in negligence, *see* W. Burnham, *Separating Constitutional and Common–Law Torts: A Critique and a Proposed Constitutional Theory of Duty,* 73 Minn.L.Rev. 515 (1989). It has been suggested that a more nuanced approach to constitutional torts is required than has thus far been taken by the Court. *See* J. Jeffries, Jr., *Disaggregating Constitutional Torts*, 110 Yale L.J. 259 (2000). More recent scholarship includes G. Rutherglen, *Custom and Usage as Action Under Color of State Law: An Essay on the Forgotten Terms of Section 1983*, 89 Va. L.Rev. 525 (2003); J. Preis, *Alternative Remedies in Constitutional Torts,* 40 Conn. L.Rev. 723 (2008); D. Zaring, *Three Models of Constitutional Torts*, 2 J. Tort L. 3 (2008)

Finally, it should be noted, that some states now allow actions based on violations of the state constitution. *See, e.g.*, Brown v. State of New York, 89 N.Y.2d 172, 674 N.E.2d 1129, 652 N.Y.S.2d 223 (1996); Prince George's County, Md. v. Longtin, 190 Md.App. 97, 988 A.2d 20 (Ct. Spec. 2010). *But see* Jones v. City of Philadelphia, 890 A.2d 1188 (Pa. Commw. Ct. 2006).

B. ACTIONS AGAINST FEDERAL OFFICIALS

In 1971 the Court finally decided the question left open in *Bell v. Hood, supra* p. 778. The case in which this important issue was resolved was Bivens v. Six Unknown Named Agents of Federal Bureau of Narcotics, 403 U.S. 388, 91 S.Ct. 1999, 29 L.Ed.2d 619 (1971). Like *Bell v. Hood* and *Monroe v. Pape,* the case involved an improper arrest and consequent search. It was alleged that agents of the Federal Bureau of Narcotics, acting under a claim of federal authority, entered Bivens' apartment and arrested him for alleged narcotics violations. They manacled him in front of his wife and children and threatened to arrest the entire family. The agents then searched the apartment "from stem to stern." He was eventually taken to the Federal Court House in Brooklyn, N.Y., where he was interrogated, booked and subjected to a "visual strip search." The complaint was dismissed by the district court on the ground, *inter alia,* that it failed to state a cause of action. The Second Circuit affirmed. The respondents argued that Bivens had a remedy under state law to which he should have resorted by bringing an action in the state courts. They were forced to admit, however, that, if the action had been brought in the state courts, the Department of Justice would, as a matter of policy, have removed the case to federal court under 28 U.S.C. § 1442(a)(1) which permits removal to the federal courts of any civil action or criminal prosecution commenced in a state court against an officer of the United States for any acts "under color of such office" or "on account of any right, title or authority claimed under any Act of Congress for the apprehension or punishment of criminals or the collection of the revenue." Respondent's point, however, was that all such actions would be governed by state law.

Writing for the majority, Justice Brennan declared that "[t]he interests protected by state laws regulating trespass and the invasion of privacy, and those protected by the Fourth Amendment's guarantee against unreasonable searches and seizures, may be inconsistent or even hostile. Thus, we may bar the door against an unwelcome private intruder or call the police if he persists in seeking entrance. The availability of such alternate means for the protection of privacy may lead the State to restrict imposition of liability for any consequent trespass * * *." In a footnote (n. 8) Justice Brennan noted that, while no state had as yet limited the common-law doctrine that one may use reasonable force to resist arrest by a private person, some states had made it unlawful to resist an unlawful arrest when the arrest is made by a person known to be an officer of the law. He then concluded that "petitioner's complaint states a cause of action under the Fourth Amendment * * * [for which the] petitioner is entitled to receive money damages for any injuries he has suffered as a result * * *." Justice Brennan also noted that a private citizen confronting a federal agent cannot normally either resist or seek the help of local police. The claim of authority alone may lead him to acquiesce in the violation of his constitutional rights.

The district court in *Bivens* had also ruled that the respondents were immune from liability by virtue of their official position. The Court did not rule on that question but, rather, reversed the judgment below and remanded the case for further proceedings. Justice Harlan concurred in a separate opinion. There were three dissenters. Chief Justice Burger believed that "an entirely different remedy is necessary but it was one that in my view is as much beyond judicial power as the step the Court takes today * * *." The Chief Justice felt that "Congress should develop an administrative or 'quasi-judicial' remedy against the government itself to afford compensation and restitution for persons whose Fourth Amendment rights had been violated * * *." Justice Black, whose opinion for the Court in *Bell v. Hood* had left the question now being decided open, thought that it was up to Congress to create a remedy. Even if the Court "had the legislative power to create a remedy" there were important reasons why the Court should decline to do so. He particularly stressed the plethora of "lawsuits" with which "[t]he courts of the United States as well as those of the States are choked * * *." Justice Blackmun also dissented. He relied principally on the reasons expressed by Chief Judge Lumbard who wrote the opinion for the court of appeals (409 F.2d 718 (2d Cir.1969)). Judge Lumbard stressed that the framers of the fourth amendment did not seem to contemplate a new federal cause of action and that, while the federal courts now had the power under their general grant of jurisdiction to provide a federal remedy, they should only do so if the provision of such a remedy "is essential to insure the vitality of a constitutional right."

On remand of the *Bivens* case to the Second Circuit, that court held that no absolute immunity, such as that recognized in *Barr v. Matteo, supra* p. 559, for defamatory remarks made by federal officials acting within the outer perimeter of their official duties, would apply. Federal law enforcement officers, however, were entitled to defend damage actions based upon unconstitutional searches and seizures by showing good faith and reasonable grounds for believing that they were acting properly. 456 F.2d 1339 (2d Cir.1972). The case was then returned to the district court. The question of immunities is common to both actions pursuant to § 1983 brought against those acting "under color of state law" and to *Bivens*-type actions brought against federal officials. The resolution of the question has been much influenced by common-law developments which cover a wide variety of torts. The question will be discussed at length in *Butz v. Economou, infra* and in the notes following that case.

In November 1981, Deputy Attorney General Edward C. Schmults testified before the Subcommittee on Agency Administration of the Senate Judiciary Committee that there were over 2,000 *Bivens*-type actions against federal officials pending in the federal courts at the time. Deputy Attorney General Schmults further testified that as of that time only nine money judgments against federal officials had ever been entered in any of these actions. Of these nine judgments some had been reversed on appeal; in a few others appeals were pending. Interestingly, the *Bivens* case itself is not mentioned in the list of successful actions. The largest judgment that had been entered was in Dellums v. Powell, 566 F.2d 167 (D.C.Cir. 1977), which was a class action on behalf of some 2,000 people whose demonstration on the steps of the United States Capitol against the Vietnamese war was broken up by the police. The defendants included the Chiefs of the District of Columbia and United States Capitol police. According to Mr. Schmults a judgment of $2,500,000 was eventually entered in favor of 1,200 plaintiffs. The judgment, together with accrued interest, was eventually paid through congressional appropriations. The pattern in almost all the cases in which the plaintiffs had been successful had been for the damages to run between 1,000 to 7,500 dollars. *See Federal Tort Claims Act: Hearings Before Subcomm. on Agency Administration of the Senate Comm. on the Judiciary*, 97th Cong., 1st Sess. 2–18 (1981) (statement of Dep. Att'y Gen. Schmults). Unfortunately there are no subsequent figures as to how many of the "other civil rights" actions filed annually in the federal courts, *see* statistics discussed at p. 778, *supra*, are *Bivens*-type actions against federal officials.

In 1974, the Federal Tort Claims Act was amended to provide that "with regard to acts or omissions of investigative or law enforcement officers of the United States" claims could be brought against the United States "arising * * * out of assault, battery, false imprisonment, false arrest, abuse of process, or malicious prosecution." 28 U.S.C. § 2680(h), as amended. While the 1974 amendment was enacted with *Bivens* in the background, the immediate precipitating factor was a series of actions brought against federal agents who, by mistake, broke into the wrong houses at night during raids for drugs in Collinsville, Illinois in 1973. The agents were operating without warrants. At that time, since-repealed legislation specifically authorized agents, under certain circumstances, to "break open an outer or inner door or window of a building" in search of "controlled substances." 84 Stat. 1274 (1970). This was the so-called "no-knock" authority. On the 1974 amendment and its background, see J. Boger, M. Gitenstein, and P. Verkuil, *The Federal Tort Claims Act Intentional Tort Amendment: An Interpretative Analysis*, 54 N.C.L.Rev. 497 (1976).

In 1988, in the "Westfall Act," (Federal Employees Liability Reform and Tort Compensation Act of 1988, 102 Stat. 4563 (1988)) Congress provided for the substitution of the United States as the party defendant in all actions, against federal employees, whose subject matter falls within the coverage of the Federal Tort Claims Act (28 U.S.C. § 2679). The Westfall Act, however, specifically declares that the provisions making the remedy against the United States the exclusive remedy do *not* apply to actions against federal employees "for a violation of the Constitution of the United States" (28 U.S.C. § 2679(b)(2)A). The statute codified the result the Court had earlier reached in Carlson v. Green, 446 U.S. 14, 100 S.Ct. 1468, 64 L.Ed.2d 15 (1980), where the Court specifically noted the possibility of recovery of punitive damages and the availability of a jury in *Bivens*-type actions and also established a uniform federal rule of survival for all such actions. While the availability of a Federal Tort Act claim against the United States does not pre-empt a *Bivens*-type action, it has been asserted that the federal courts are becoming increasingly reluctant to infer a *Bivens*-type action when the plaintiff's case is based upon a general claim of maladministration of a federal program, particularly if Congress has provided any kind of a remedial scheme, even if it is inadequate in particular cases. *See* B. Grey, *Preemption of* Bivens *Claims: How Clearly Must Congress Speak,* 70 Wash.U.L.Q. 1087 (1992), commenting on, *inter alia,* Schweiker v. Chilicky, 487 U.S. 412, 108 S.Ct. 2460, 101 L.Ed.2d 370 (1988). *See also* La Compania Ocho, Inc. v. United States Forest Service, 874 F.Supp. 1242 (D.N.M.1995). If there had ever been any doubt about the matter, the Court has now unanimously held that an independent federal agency, even if it has otherwise waived sovereign immunity, cannot be the subject of a *Bivens*-type action. Federal Deposit Insurance Corp. v. Meyer, 510 U.S. 471, 114 S.Ct. 996, 127 L.Ed.2d 308 (1994). Such actions can only be brought against federal officials. While it may well be the case that a *Bivens*-type action could be brought against a private individual exercising what might be called a federal function, a sharply divided Court has held that, unlike a § 1983 action, a *Bivens*-type action may not be maintained against a private juridical entity. Correctional Services Corp. v. Malesko, 534 U.S. 61, 122 S.Ct. 515, 151 L.Ed.2d 456 (2001) (private operator of halfway house for federal prisoners).

Academic discussions of *Bivens*-type actions against federal officials have usually been conducted in a larger context that includes § 1983 actions against state officials. *See* p. 786, *supra*. *See also* Note, *The Limits of Implied Constitutional Damages Actions: New Boundaries for* Bivens, 55 N.Y.U.L.Rev. 1238 (1980). A comprehensive recent review of the history and development of *Bivens*-type actions is W. Kratzke, *Some Recommendations Concerning Tort Liability of Government and its Employees for Torts and Constitutional Torts,* 9 Admin.L.J.Am.U. 1105 (1996).

C. IMMUNITIES

BUTZ v. ECONOMOU

Supreme Court of the United States, 1978.
438 U.S. 478, 98 S.Ct. 2894, 57 L.Ed.2d 895.

MR. JUSTICE WHITE delivered the opinion of the Court.

This case concerns the personal immunity of federal officials in the Executive Branch from claims for damages arising from their violations of citizens' constitutional rights. Respondent filed suit against a number of officials in the Department of Agriculture claiming that they had instituted an investigation and an administrative proceeding against him in retaliation for his criticism of that agency. The District Court dismissed the action on the ground that the individual defendants, as federal officials, were entitled to absolute immunity for all discretionary acts within the scope of their authority. The Court of Appeals reversed, holding that the defendants were entitled only to the qualified immunity available to their counterparts in state government. * * * Because of the importance of immunity doctrine to both the vindication of constitutional guarantees and the effective functioning of government, we granted certiorari. * * *

I

Respondent controls Arthur N. Economou and Co., Inc., which was at one time registered with the Department of Agriculture as a commodity futures commission merchant. Most of respondent's factual allegations in this lawsuit focus on an earlier administrative proceeding in which the Department of Agriculture sought to revoke or suspend the company's registration. On February 19, 1970, following an audit, the Department of Agriculture issued an administrative complaint alleging that respondent, while a registered merchant, had willfully failed to maintain the minimum financial requirements prescribed by the Department. After another audit, an amended complaint was issued on June 22, 1970. A hearing was held before the Chief Hearing Examiner of the Department, who filed a recommendation sustaining the administrative complaint. The Judicial Officer of the Department, to whom the Secretary had delegated his decisional authority in enforcement proceedings, affirmed the Chief Hearing Examiner's decision. On respondent's petition for review, the Court of Appeals for the Second Circuit vacated the order of the Judicial Officer. It reasoned that "the essential finding of willfulness * * * was made in a proceeding instituted without the customary warning letter, which the Judicial Officer conceded might well have resulted in prompt correction of the claimed insufficiencies." * * *

While the administrative complaint was pending before the Judicial Officer, respondent filed this lawsuit in Federal District Court. Respondent sought initially to enjoin the progress of the administrative proceeding, but he was unsuccessful in that regard. On March 31, 1975, respondent filed a second amended complaint seeking damages. Named as defendants were the individuals who had served as Secretary and Assistant Secretary of Agriculture during the relevant events; the Judicial Officer and Chief Hearing Examiner; several officials in the Commodity Exchange Authority; the Agriculture Department attorney who had prosecuted the enforcement proceeding; and several of the auditors who had investigated respondent or were witnesses against respondent.

The complaint stated that prior to the issuance of the administrative complaints respondent had been "sharply critical of the staff and operations of Defendants and carried on a vociferous campaign for the reform of Defendant Commodity Exchange Authority to obtain more effective regulation of commodity trading." * * * The complaint also stated that some time prior to the issuance of the February 19 complaint, respondent and his company had ceased to engage in activities regulated by the defendants. The complaint charged that each of the administrative complaints had been issued without the notice or warning required by law; that the defendants had furnished the complaints "to interested persons and others without furnishing respondent's answers as well"; and that following the issuance of the amended complaint, the defendants had issued a "deceptive" press release that "falsely indicated to the public that [respondent's] financial resources had deteriorated, when Defendants knew that their statement was untrue and so acknowledge[d] previously that said assertion was untrue." * * *

The complaint then presented 10 "causes of action," some of which purported to state claims for damages under the United States Constitution. For example, the first "cause of action" alleged that respondent had been denied due process of law because the defendants had instituted unauthorized proceedings against him without proper notice and with the knowledge that respondent was no longer subject to their regulatory jurisdiction. The third "cause of action" stated that by means of such actions "the Defendants discouraged and chilled the campaign of criticism [plaintiff] directed against them, and thereby deprived the [plaintiff] of [his] rights to free expression guaranteed by the First Amendment of the United States Constitution."

The defendants moved to dismiss the complaint on the ground that "as to the individual defendants it is barred by the doctrine of official immunity * * *." * * * The defendants relied on an affidavit submitted earlier in the litigation by the attorney who had prosecuted the original administrative complaint against respondent. He stated that the Secretary of Agriculture had had no involvement with the case and that each of the other named defendants had acted "within the course of his official duties." * * *

The District Court, apparently relying on the plurality opinion in Barr v. Matteo, * * * held that the individual defendants would be entitled to immunity if they could show that "their alleged unconstitutional acts were within the outer perimeter of their authority and discretionary." * * * After examining the nature of the acts alleged in the complaint, the District Court concluded: "Since the individual defendants have shown that their alleged unconstitutional acts were both within the scope of their authority and discretionary, we dismiss the second amended complaint as to them." * * *

The Court of Appeals for the Second Circuit reversed the District Court's judgment of dismissal with respect to the individual defendants. * * * The Court of Appeals reasoned that Barr v. Matteo, supra, did not "represen[t] the last word in this evolving area," * * * because principles governing the immunity of officials of the Executive Branch had been elucidated in later decisions dealing with constitutional claims against state officials. * * * These opinions were understood to establish that officials of the Executive Branch exercising discretionary functions did not need the protection of an absolute immunity from suit, but only a qualified immunity based on good faith and reasonable grounds. The Court of Appeals rejected a proposed distinction between suits against state officials sued pursuant to 42 U.S.C. § 1983 and suits against federal officials under the Constitution, noting that "[o]ther circuits have also concluded that the Supreme Court's development of official immunity doctrine in § 1983 suits against state officials applies with equal force to federal officers sued on a cause of action derived directly from the Constitution, since both types of suits serve the same function of protecting citizens against violations of their constitutional rights by government officials." * * * The Court of Appeals recognized that under Imbler v. Pachtman, 424 U.S. 409, 96 S.Ct. 984, 47 L.Ed.2d 128 (1976), state prosecutors were entitled to absolute immunity from § 1983 damages liability but reasoned that Agriculture Department officials performing analogous functions did not require such an immunity because their cases turned more on documentary proof than on the veracity of witnesses and because their work did not generally involve the same constraints of time and information present in criminal cases. * * * The court concluded that all of the defendants were "adequately protected by permitting them to avail themselves of the defense of qualified 'good faith, reasonable grounds' immunity of the type approved by the Supreme Court in Scheuer and Wood." * * * After noting that summary judgment would be available to the defendants if there were no genuine factual issues for trial, the Court of Appeals remanded the case for further proceedings.

II

The single submission by the United States on behalf of petitioners is that all of the federal officials sued in this case are absolutely immune from any liability for damages even if in the course of enforcing the relevant statutes they infringed respondent's constitutional rights and even if the violation was knowing and deliberate. Although the position is earnestly and ably presented by the United States, we are quite sure that it is unsound and consequently reject it.

* * *

The Government places principal reliance on Barr v. Matteo * * *.

* * *

Barr does not control this case. It did not address the liability of the acting director had his conduct not been within the outer limits of his duties, but from the care with which the Court inquired into the scope of his authority, it may be inferred that had the release been unauthorized, and surely if the issuance of press releases had been expressly forbidden by statute, the claim of absolute immunity would not have been upheld. The inference is supported by the fact that Mr. Justice Stewart, although agreeing with the principles announced by Mr. Justice Harlan, dissented and would have rejected the immunity claim because the press release, in his view, was not action in the line of duty. * * * It is apparent also that a quite different question would have been presented had the officer ignored an express statutory or constitutional limitation on his authority.

Barr did not, therefore, purport to depart from the general rule, which long prevailed, that a federal official may not with impunity ignore the limitations which the controlling law has placed on his powers. The immunity of federal executive officials began as a means of protecting them in the execution of their federal statutory duties from criminal or civil actions based on state law. * * * A federal official who acted outside of his federal statutory authority would be held strictly liable for his trespassory acts. For example, Little v. Barreme, 2 Cranch 170, 2 L.Ed. 243 (1804), held the commander of an American warship liable in damages for the seizure of a Danish cargo ship on the high seas. Congress had directed the President to intercept any vessels reasonably suspected of being en route *to* a French port, but the President had authorized the seizure of suspected vessels whether going *to* or *from* French ports, and the Danish vessel seized was en route *from* a forbidden destination. The Court, speaking through Mr. Chief Justice Marshall, held that the President's instructions could not "change the nature of the transaction, or legalize an act which, without those instructions, would have been a plain trespass." * * * Although there was probable cause to believe that the ship was engaged in traffic with the French, the seizure at issue was not among that class of seizures that the Executive had been authorized by statute to effect. * * *

* * *

As these cases demonstrate, a federal official was protected for action tortious under state law only if his acts were authorized by controlling federal law. * * * Since an unconstitutional act, even if authorized by statute, was viewed as not authorized in contemplation of law, there could be no immunity defense. * * *

* * * Kendall v. Stokes, 44 U.S. (3 How.) 87, 11 L.Ed. 506 (1845), addressed a different situation. The case involved a suit against the Postmaster General for erroneously suspending payments to a creditor of the Post Office. Examining and, if necessary, suspending payments to creditors were among the Postmaster's normal duties, and it appeared that he had simply made a mistake in the exercise of the discretion conferred upon him. He was held not liable in damages since "a public officer, acting to the best of his judgment and from a sense of duty, in a matter of account with an individual [is not] liable in an action for an error of judgment." * * * Having "the right to examine into this account" and the right to suspend it in the proper circumstances, * * * the officer was not liable in damages if he fell into error, provided, however, that he acted "from a sense of public duty and without malice." * * *

Four years later, in a case involving military discipline, the Court issued a similar ruling, exculpating the defendant officer because of the failure to prove that he had exceeded his jurisdiction or had exercised it in a malicious or willfully erroneous manner * * *. Wilkes v. Dinsman, 48 U.S. (7 How.) 89, 131, 12 L.Ed. 618 (1849).

In Spalding v. Vilas, 161 U.S. 483, 16 S.Ct. 631, 40 L.Ed. 780 (1896), on which the Government relies, the principal issue was whether the malicious motive of an officer would render him liable in damages for injury inflicted by his official act that otherwise was within the scope of his authority. * * *

Spalding made clear that a malicious intent will not subject a public officer to liability for performing his authorized duties as to which he would otherwise not be subject to damages liability. But Spalding did not involve conduct manifestly or otherwise beyond the authority of the official, nor did it involve a mistake of either law or fact in construing or applying the statute. It did not purport to immunize officials who ignore limitations on their authority imposed by law. * * * It is also evident that Spalding presented no claim that the officer was liable in damages because he had acted in violation of a limitation placed upon his conduct by the United States Constitution. If any inference is to be drawn from Spalding in any of these respects, it is that the official would not be excused from liability if he failed to observe obvious statutory or constitutional limitations on his powers or if his conduct was a manifestly erroneous application of the statute.

Insofar as cases in this Court dealing with the immunity or privilege of federal officers are concerned, this is where the matter stood until Barr v. Matteo. There, as we have set out above, immunity was granted even though the publication contained a factual error, which was not the case in Spalding. The plurality opinion and judgment in Barr also appear—although without any discussion of the matter—to have extended absolute immunity to an officer who was authorized to issue press releases, who was assumed to know that the press release he issued was false and who therefore was deliberately misusing his authority. Accepting this extension of immunity with respect to state tort claims, however, we are confident that Barr did not purport to protect an official who has not only committed a wrong under local law, but also violated those fundamental principles of fairness embodied in the Constitution. Whatever level of protection from state interference is appropriate for federal officials executing their duties under federal law, it cannot be doubted that these officials, even when acting pursuant to congressional authorization, are subject to the restraints imposed by the Federal Constitution.

The liability of officials who have exceeded constitutional limits was not confronted in either Barr or Spalding. Neither of those cases supports the Government's position. Beyond that, however, neither case purported to abolish the liability of federal officers for actions manifestly beyond their line of duty; and if they are accountable when they stray beyond the plain limits of their statutory authority, it would be incongruous to hold that they may nevertheless willfully or knowingly violate constitutional rights without fear of liability.

Although it is true that the Court has not dealt with this issue with respect to federal officers, we have several times addressed the immunity of state officers when sued under 42 U.S.C. § 1983 for alleged violations of constitutional rights. These decisions are instructive for present purposes.

III

Pierson v. Ray, 386 U.S. 547, 87 S.Ct. 1213, 18 L.Ed.2d 288 (1967), decided that § 1983 was not intended to abrogate the immunity of state judges which existed under the common law and which the Court had held applicable to federal judges in Bradley v. Fisher, 13 Wall. 335 (1872). Pierson also presented the issue "whether immunity was available to that segment of the executive branch of a state government that is * * * most frequently exposed to situations which can give rise to claims under § 1983—the local police officer." Scheuer v. Rhodes, 416 U.S. at 244–245, 94 S.Ct., at 1690 [1974]. Relying on the common law, we held that police officers were entitled to a defense of "good faith and probable cause," even though an arrest might subsequently be proved to be unconstitutional. We observed, however, that "[t]he common law has never granted police officers an absolute and unqualified immunity, and the officers in this case do not claim that they are entitled to one." 386 U.S. at 555.

In Scheuer v. Rhodes, supra, the issue was whether "higher officers of the executive branch" of state governments were immune from liability under § 1983 for violations of constitutionally protected rights. * * * There, the Governor of a State, the senior and subordinate officers of the state National Guard, and a state university president had been sued on the allegation that they had suppressed a civil disturbance in an unconstitutional manner. We explained that the doctrine of official immunity from § 1983 liability, although not constitutionally grounded and essentially a matter of statutory construction, was based on two mutually dependent rationales:

> "(1) the injustice, particularly in the absence of bad faith, of subjecting to liability an officer who is required, by the legal obligations of his position, to exercise discretion; (2) the danger that the threat of such liability would deter his willingness to execute his office with the decisiveness and the judgment required by the public good." * * *

The opinion also recognized that executive branch officers must often act swiftly and on the basis of factual information supplied by others, constraints which become even more acute in the "atmosphere of confusion, ambiguity, and swiftly moving events" created by a civil disturbance. * * * Although quoting at length from Barr v. Matteo, we did not believe that there was a need for absolute immunity from § 1983 liability for these high-ranking state officials. Rather the considerations discussed above indicated:

"[I]n varying scope, a qualified immunity is available to officers of the executive branch of government, the variation being dependent upon the scope of discretion and responsibilities of the office and all the circumstances as they reasonably appeared at the time of the action on which liability is sought to be based. It is the existence of reasonable grounds for the belief formed at the time and in light of all the circumstances, coupled with good-faith belief, that affords a basis for qualified immunity of executive officers for acts performed in the course of official conduct." 416 U.S. at 247–248, 94 S.Ct., at 1692.

Subsequent decisions have applied the Scheuer standard in other contexts. In Wood v. Strickland, 420 U.S. 308, 95 S.Ct. 992, 43 L.Ed.2d 214 (1975), school administrators were held entitled to claim a similar qualified immunity. A school board member would lose his immunity from a § 1983 suit only if "he knew or reasonably should have known that the action he took within his sphere of official responsibility would violate the constitutional rights of the student affected, or if he took the action with the malicious intention to cause a deprivation of constitutional rights or other injury to the student." * * * In O'Connor v. Donaldson, 422 U.S. 563, 95 S.Ct. 2486, 45 L.Ed.2d 396 (1975), we applied the same standard to the superintendent of a state hospital. In Procunier v. Navarette, 434 U.S. 555, 98 S.Ct. 855, 55 L.Ed.2d 24 (1978), we held that prison administrators would be adequately protected by the qualified immunity outlined in Scheuer and Wood. We emphasized, however, that, at least in the absence of some showing of malice, an official would not be held liable in damages under § 1983 unless the constitutional right he was alleged to have violated was "clearly established" at the time of the violation.

None of these decisions with respect to state officials furnishes any support for the submission of the United States that federal officials are absolutely immune from liability for their constitutional transgressions. On the contrary, with impressive unanimity, the Federal Courts of Appeals have concluded that federal officials should receive no greater degree of protection from *constitutional* claims than their counterparts in state government. * * *

* * *

The Government argues that the cases involving state officials are distinguishable because they reflect the need to preserve the effectiveness of the right of action authorized by § 1983. * * *

* * *

The presence or absence of congressional authorization for suits against federal officials is, of course, relevant to the question whether to infer a right of action for damages for a particular violation of the Constitution. * * *

But once this analysis is completed, there is no reason to return again to the absence of congressional authorization in resolving the question of immunity. Having determined that the plaintiff is entitled to a remedy in damages for a constitutional violation, the court then must address how best to reconcile the plaintiff's right to compensation with the need to protect the decisionmaking processes of an executive department. Since our decision in Scheuer was intended to guide the federal courts in resolving this tension in the myriad factual situations in which it might arise, we see no reason why it should not supply the governing principles for resolving this dilemma in the case of federal officials. The Court's opinion in Scheuer relied on precedents dealing with federal as well as state officials, analyzed the issue of executive immunity in terms of general policy considerations, and stated its conclusion, quoted supra, in the same universal terms. The analysis presented in that case cannot be limited to actions against state officials.

* * * To create a system in which the Bill of Rights monitors more closely the conduct of state officials than it does that of federal officials is to stand the constitutional design on its head.

IV

* * *

Our opinion in Bivens put aside the immunity question; but we could not have contemplated that immunity would be absolute. If, as the Government argues, all officials exercising discretion were exempt from personal liability, a suit under the Constitution could provide no redress to the injured citizen, nor would it in any degree deter federal officials from committing constitutional wrongs. Moreover, no compensation would be available from the Government, for the Tort Claims Act prohibits recovery for injuries stemming from discretionary acts, even when that discretion has been abused.

The extension of absolute immunity from damages liability to all federal executive officials would seriously erode the protection provided by basic constitutional guarantees. The broad authority possessed by these officials enables them to direct their subordinates to undertake a wide range of projects—including some which may infringe such important personal interests as liberty, property, and free speech. It makes little sense to hold that a Government agent is liable for warrantless and forcible entry into a citizen's house in pursuit of evidence, but that an official of higher rank who actually orders such a burglary is immune simply because of his greater authority. Indeed, the greater power of such officials affords a greater potential for a regime of lawless conduct. Extensive Government operations offer opportunities for unconstitutional action on a massive scale. In situations of abuse, an action for damages against the responsible official can be an important means of vindicating constitutional guarantees.

Our system of jurisprudence rests on the assumption that all individuals, whatever their position in government, are subject to federal law:

* * *

This is not to say that considerations of public policy fail to support a limited immunity for federal executive officials. We consider here, as we did in Scheuer, the need to protect officials who are required to exercise their discretion and the related public interest in encouraging the vigorous exercise of official authority. Yet Scheuer and other cases have recognized that it is not unfair to hold liable the official who knows or should know he is acting outside the law, and that insisting on an awareness of clearly established constitutional limits will not unduly interfere with the exercise of official judgment. We therefore hold that, in a suit for damages arising from unconstitutional action, federal executive officials exercising discretion are entitled only to the qualified immunity specified in Scheuer, subject to those exceptional situations where it is demonstrated that absolute immunity is essential for the conduct of the public business.

* * * Insubstantial lawsuits can be quickly terminated by federal courts alert to the possibilities of artful pleading. Unless the complaint states a compensable claim for relief under the Federal Constitution, it should not survive a motion to dismiss. Moreover, the Court recognized in Scheuer that damages suits concerning constitutional violations need not proceed to trial, but can be terminated on a properly supported motion for summary judgment based on the defense of immunity. * * * In responding to such a motion, plaintiffs may not play dog in the manger; and firm application of the Federal Rules of Civil Procedure will ensure that federal officials are not harassed by frivolous lawsuits.

V

Although a qualified immunity from damages liability should be the general rule for executive officials charged with constitutional violations, our decisions recognize that there are some officials whose special functions require a full exemption from liability. * * * In each case, we have undertaken "a considered inquiry into the immunity historically accorded the relevant official at common law and the interests behind it." Id., at 421.

In Bradley v. Fisher, the Court analyzed the need for absolute immunity to protect judges from lawsuits claiming that their decisions had been tainted by improper motives. The Court began by noting that the principle of immunity for acts done by judges "in the exercise of their judicial functions" had been "the settled doctrine of the English courts for many centuries, and has never been denied, that we are aware of, in the courts of this country." 13 Wall, at 347. * * *

The principle of Bradley was extended to federal prosecutors through the summary affirmance in Yaselli v. Goff, 275 U.S. 503, 48 S.Ct. 155, 72 L.Ed. 395 (1927) * * *.

We recently reaffirmed the holding of Yaselli v. Goff in Imbler v. Pachtman, supra, a suit against a state prosecutor under § 1983. * * *

Despite these precedents, the Court of Appeals concluded that all of the defendants in this case—including the Chief Hearing Examiner, Judicial Officer, and prosecuting attorney—were entitled to only a qualified immunity. The Court of Appeals reasoned that officials within the Executive Branch generally have more circumscribed discretion and pointed out that, unlike a judge, officials of the Executive Branch would face no conflict of interest if their legal representation was provided by the Executive Branch. The Court of Appeals recognized that "some of the Agriculture Department officials may be analogized to criminal prosecutors, in that they initiated the proceedings against [respondent], and presented evidence therein," * * * but found that attorneys in administrative proceedings did not face the same "serious constraints of time and even information" which this Court has found to be present frequently in criminal cases. * * *

We think that the Court of Appeals placed undue emphasis on the fact that the officials sued here are—from an administrative perspective—employees of the Executive Branch. Judges have absolute immunity not because of their particular location within the Government but because of the special nature of their responsibilities. This point is underlined by the fact that prosecutors—themselves members of the Executive Branch—are also absolutely immune. * * *

The cluster of immunities protecting the various participants in judge-supervised trials stems from the characteristics of the judicial process rather than its location. * * *

At the same time, the safeguards built into the judicial process tend to reduce the need for private damages actions as a means of controlling unconstitutional conduct. The insulation of the judge from political influence, the importance of precedent in resolving controversies, the adversary nature of the process, and the correctability of error on appeal are just a few of the many checks on malicious action by judges. Advocates are restrained not only by their professional obligations, but by the knowledge that their assertions will be contested by their adversaries in open court. Jurors are carefully screened to remove all possibility of bias. Witnesses are, of course, subject to the rigors of cross-examination and the penalty of perjury. Because these features of the judicial process tend to enhance the reliability of information and the impartiality of the decisionmaking process, there is a less pressing need for individual suits to correct constitutional error.

We think that adjudication within a federal administrative agency shares enough of the characteristics of the judicial process that those who participate in such adjudication should also be immune from suits for damages. The conflicts which federal hearing examiners seek to resolve are every bit as fractious as those which come to court. * * * Moreover, federal administrative law requires that agency adjudication contain many of the same safeguards as are available in the judicial process. * * *

There can be little doubt that the role of the modern federal hearing examiner or administrative law judge within this framework is "functionally comparable" to that of a judge. His powers are often, if not generally, comparable to those of a trial judge: * * *

We also believe that agency officials performing certain functions analogous to those of a prosecutor should be able to claim absolute immunity with respect to such acts. The decision to initiate administrative proceedings against an individual or corporation is very much like the prosecutor's decision to initiate or move forward with a criminal prosecution. An agency official, like a prosecutor, may have broad discretion in deciding whether a proceeding should be brought and what sanctions should be sought. * * *

The discretion which executive officials exercise with respect to the initiation of administrative proceedings might be distorted if their immunity from damages arising from that decision was less than complete. * * * While there is not likely to be anyone willing and legally able to seek damages from the officials if they do not authorize the administrative proceeding, * * * there is a serious danger that the decision to authorize proceedings will provoke a retaliatory response. An individual targeted by an administrative proceeding will react angrily and may seek vengeance in the courts. A corporation will muster all of its financial and legal resources in an effort to prevent administrative sanctions. "When millions may turn on regulatory decisions, there is a strong incentive to counter-attack."[39]

The defendant in an enforcement proceeding has ample opportunity to challenge the legality of the proceeding. An administrator's decision to proceed with a case is subject to scrutiny in the proceeding itself. The respondent may present his evidence to an impartial trier of fact and obtain an independent judgment as to whether the prosecution is justified. His claims that the proceeding is unconstitutional may also be heard by the courts. Indeed, respondent in this case was able to quash the administrative order entered against him by means of judicial review. * * *

We believe that agency officials must make the decision to move forward with an administrative proceeding free from intimidation or harassment. Because the legal remedies already available to the defendant in such a proceeding provide sufficient checks on agency zeal, we hold that those officials who are responsible for the decision to initiate or continue a proceeding subject to agency adjudication are entitled to absolute immunity from damages liability for their parts in that decision.

We turn finally to the role of an agency attorney in conducting a trial and presenting evidence on the record to the trier of fact. We can see no substantial difference between the function of the agency attorney in presenting evidence in an agency hearing and the function of the prosecutor who brings evidence before a court. In either case, the evidence will be subject to attack through cross-examination, rebuttal, or reinterpretation by opposing counsel. Evidence which is false or unpersuasive should be rejected upon analysis by an impartial trier of fact. If agency attorneys were held personally liable in damages as guarantors of the quality of their evidence, they might hesitate to bring forward some witnesses or documents. * * * Apart from the possible unfairness to agency personnel, the agency would often be denied relevant evidence. * * * Administrative

39. Expeditions Unlimited Aquatic Enterprises, Inc. v. Smithsonian Institution, 184 U.S.App. D.C. 397, 401, 566 F.2d 289, 293 (1977), cert. pending, 76–418.

agencies can act in the public interest only if they can adjudicate on the basis of a complete record. We therefore hold that an agency attorney who arranges for the presentation of evidence on the record in the course of an adjudication is absolutely immune from suits based on the introduction of such evidence.

VI

There remains the task of applying the foregoing principles to the claims against the particular petitioner-defendants involved in this case. Rather than attempt this here in the first instance, we vacate the judgment of the Court of Appeals and remand the case to that court with instructions to remand the case to the District Court for further proceedings consistent with this opinion.

So ordered.

MR. JUSTICE REHNQUIST, with whom THE CHIEF JUSTICE, MR. JUSTICE STEWART, and MR. JUSTICE STEVENS join, concurring in part and dissenting in part.

I concur in that part of the Court's judgment which affords absolute immunity to those persons performing adjudicatory functions within a federal agency, * * * those who are responsible for the decision to initiate or continue a proceeding subject to agency adjudication, * * * and those agency personnel who present evidence on the record in the course of an adjudication * * *. I cannot agree, however, with the Court's conclusion that in a suit for damages arising from allegedly unconstitutional action federal executive officials, regardless of their rank or the scope of their responsibilities, are entitled to only qualified immunity even when acting within the outer limits of their authority. The Court's protestations to the contrary notwithstanding, this decision seriously misconstrues our prior decisions, finds little support as a matter of logic or precedent, and perhaps most importantly, will, I fear, seriously "dampen the ardor of all but the most resolute, or the most irresponsible, in the unflinching discharge of their duties," Gregoire v. Biddle, 177 F.2d 579, 581 (C.A.2 1949) (Learned Hand, J.).

Most noticeable is the Court's unnaturally constrained reading of the landmark case of Spalding v. Vilas, * * *. The Court in that case did indeed hold that the actions taken by the Postmaster General were within the authority conferred upon him by Congress, and went on to hold that even though he had acted maliciously in carrying out the duties conferred upon him by Congress he was protected by official immunity. But the Court left no doubt that it would have reached the same result had it been alleged the official acts were unconstitutional.

> "We are of the opinion that the same general considerations of public policy and convenience which demand for judges of courts of superior jurisdiction immunity from civil suits for damages arising from acts done by them in the course of the performance of their judicial functions, apply to a large extent to official communications made by

heads of Executive Departments when engaged in the discharge of duties imposed upon them by law. The interests of the people require that due protection be accorded to them in respect of their official acts." * * *

* * *

Indeed, the language from Spalding quoted above unquestionably applies with equal force in the case at bar. No one seriously contends that the Secretary of Agriculture or the Assistant Secretary, who are being sued for $32 million in damages, had wandered completely off the official reservation in authorizing prosecution of respondent for violation of regulations promulgated by the Secretary for the regulation of "futures commission merchants," 7 U.S.C. § 6 (1976 ed.). * * * This is precisely what the Secretary and his assistants were empowered and required to do. That they would on occasion be mistaken in their judgment that a particular merchant had in fact violated the regulations is a necessary concomitant of any known system of administrative adjudication; that they acted "maliciously" gives no support to respondent's claim against them unless we are to overrule Spalding.

The Court's attempt to distinguish Spalding may be predicated on a simpler but equally erroneous concept of immunity. At one point the Court observes that even under Spalding "an executive officer would be vulnerable if he took action 'manifestly or palpably' beyond his authority or ignored a clear limitation on his enforcement powers." * * * From that proposition, which is undeniably accurate, the Court appears to conclude that anytime a plaintiff can paint his grievance in constitutional colors, the official is subject to damages unless he can prove he acted in good faith. After all, Congress would never "authorize" an official to engage in unconstitutional conduct. That this notion in fact underlies the Court's decision is strongly suggested by its discussion of numerous cases which supposedly support its position, but all of which in fact deal not with the question of what level of immunity a federal official may claim when acting within the outer limits of his authority, but rather with the question of whether he was in fact so acting. * * *

Putting to one side the illogic and impracticability of distinguishing between constitutional and common-law claims for purposes of immunity, which will be discussed shortly, this sort of immunity analysis badly misses the mark. It amounts to saying that an official has immunity until someone alleges he has acted unconstitutionally. But that is no immunity at all: The "immunity" disappears at the very moment when it is needed. The critical inquiry in determining whether an official is entitled to claim immunity is not whether someone has in fact been injured by his action; that is part of the plaintiff's case in chief. The immunity defense turns on * * * whether the official was acting within the outer bounds of his authority. Only if the immunity inquiry is approached in this manner does it have any meaning. That such a rule may occasionally result in individual injustices has never been doubted, but at least until today, immunity has been accorded nevertheless. * * *

Barr v. Matteo * * * unfortunately fares little better at the Court's hand than Spalding. Here the Court at least recognizes and reaffirms the minimum proposition for which Barr stands—that executive officials are absolutely immune at least from actions predicated on common-law claims as long as they are acting within the outer limits of their authority. * * * Barr is distinguished, however, on the ground that it did not involve a violation of "those fundamental principles of fairness embodied in the Constitution." * * * But if we allow a mere allegation of unconstitutionality, obviously unproved at the time made, to require a Cabinet-level official, charged with the enforcement of the responsibilities to which the complaint pertains, to lay aside his duties and defend such an action on the merits, the defense of official immunity will have been abolished in fact if not in form. The ease with which a constitutional claim may be pleaded in a case such as this, where a violation of statutory or judicial limits on agency action may be readily converted by any legal neophyte into a claim of denial of procedural due process under the Fifth Amendment, will assure that. The fact that the claim fails when put to trial will not prevent the consumption of time, effort, and money on the part of the defendant official in defending his actions on the merits. * * *

It likewise cannot seriously be argued that an official will be less deterred by the threat of liability for unconstitutional conduct than for activities which might constitute a common-law tort. The fear that inhibits is that of a long, involved lawsuit and a significant money judgment, not the fear of liability for a certain type of claim. Thus, even viewing the question functionally—indeed, *especially* viewing the question functionally—the basis for a distinction between constitutional and common-law torts in this context is open to serious question. Even the logical justification for raising such a novel distinction is far from clear. That the Framers thought some rights sufficiently susceptible of legislative derogation that they should be enshrined in the Constitution does not necessarily indicate that the Framers likewise intended to establish an immutable hierarchy of right in terms of their importance to individuals. The most heinous common-law tort surely cannot be less important to, or have less of an impact on, the aggrieved individual than a mere technical violation of a constitutional proscription.

* * *

The Court also looks to the question of immunity of state officials for causes arising under § 1983 * * *. * * * [E]ven a moment's reflection on the nature of the Bivens-type action and the purposes of § 1983, as made abundantly clear in this Court's prior cases, supplies a compelling reason for distinguishing between the two different situations. In the first place, as made clear above, a grant of absolute immunity to high-ranking executive officials on the federal side would not eviscerate the cause of action recognized in Bivens. The officials who are the most likely defendants in a Bivens-type action have generally been accorded only a qualified immunity. But more importantly, Congress has expressly waived sovereign immunity for this type of suit. This permits a direct action against the Government * * *. And the Federal Government can internally supervise and check its own officers. The Federal Government is not so situated that it can control state officials or strike this same balance, however. Hence the necessity of § 1983 and the differing standards of immunity. * * *

* * *

My biggest concern, however, is not with the illogic or impracticality of today's decision, but rather with the potential for disruption of Government that it invites. The steady increase in litigation, much of it directed against governmental officials and virtually all of which could be framed in constitutional terms, cannot escape the notice of even the most casual observer. From 1961 to 1977, the number of cases brought in the federal courts under civil rights statutes increased from 296 to 13,113. See Director of the Administrative Office of the United States Courts Ann. Rep. 189, Table 11 (1977); Ann.Rep. 173, Table 17 (1976). It simply defies logic and common experience to suggest that officials will not have this in the back of their minds when considering what official course to pursue. It likewise strains credulity to suggest that this threat will only inhibit officials from taking action which they should not take in any event. It is the cases in which the grounds for action are doubtful, or in which the actor is timid, which will be affected by today's decision.

The Court, of course, recognizes this problem and suggests two solutions. First, judges, ever alert to the artful pleader, supposedly will weed out insubstantial claims. * * * That, I fear, shows more optimism than prescience. Indeed, this very case, unquestionably frivolous in the extreme, belies any hope in that direction. And summary judgment on affidavits and the like is even more inappropriate when the central, and perhaps only, inquiry is the official's state of mind. * * *

The second solution offered by the Court is even less satisfactory. The Court holds that in those special circumstances "where it is demonstrated that absolute immunity is essential for the conduct of the public business," absolute immunity will be extended. * * * But this is a form of "absolute immunity" which in truth exists in name only. If, for example, the Secretary of Agriculture may never know until inquiry by a trial court whether there is a possibility that vexatious constitutional litigation will interfere with his decisionmaking process, the Secretary will obviously think not only twice but thrice about whether to prosecute a litigious commodities merchant who has played fast and loose with the regulations for his own profit. Careful consideration of the rights of every individual subject to his jurisdiction is one thing; a timorous reluctance to prosecute any of such individuals who have a reputation for using litigation as a defense weapon is quite another. Since Cabinet officials are mortal, it is not likely that we shall get the precise judgmental balance desired in each of them, and it is because of these very human failings that the principals of Spalding, 161 U.S. at 498, 16 S.Ct., at 637, dictate that absolute immunity be accorded once it be concluded by a court that a high-level executive official was "engaged in the discharge of duties imposed upon [him] by law.*

* * *

NOTES

1. Does not the continued vitality of *Barr v. Matteo,* reprinted *supra* p. 559, now depend on the Court's continued adherence to the holding in Paul v. Davis, 424 U.S. 693, 96 S.Ct. 1155, 47 L.Ed.2d 405 (1976), discussed at p. 784, *supra,* that defamatory statements made by officials acting in their official capacity only give rise to common-law actions? This may be a hard position for the Court to maintain. *See* G. Christie, *Injury to Reputation and the Constitution: Confusion Amid Conflicting Approaches,* 75 Mich.L.Rev. 43 (1976).

2. Do you think that Justice Rehnquist's attempts to distinguish between state officials subject to § 1983 actions and federal officials subject to *Bivens*-type actions are persuasive?

3. On remand, the claims against all the defendants in the *Economou* case were dismissed by the district court in two separate decisions: Economou v. Butz, 466 F.Supp. 1351 (S.D.N.Y.1979) and Economou v. Butz, 84 F.R.D. 678 (S.D.N.Y.1979). Subsequently, in an action brought against a court reporter for failure to provide a transcript to a person seeking to appeal a criminal conviction, the Court held that court reporters are not entitled to the absolute immunity granted to judges. Antoine v. Byers & Anderson, Inc., 508 U.S. 429, 113 S.Ct. 2167, 124 L.Ed.2d 391 (1993). As indicated in the *Economou* case, prosecutors are entitled to absolute immunity, but only when engaged in prosecutorial functions. Thus in Burns v. Reed, 500 U.S. 478, 111 S.Ct. 1934, 114 L.Ed.2d 547 (1991), the Court held that a prosecutor enjoyed absolute immunity for matters arising in the course of a probable cause hearing but did not enjoy absolute immunity for legal advice he had given the police. Subsequently, in Buckley v. Fitzsimmons, 509 U.S. 259, 113 S.Ct. 2606, 125 L.Ed.2d 209 (1993), the Court held that a prosecutor engaged in trying to determine if a footprint left at the scene of a crime was that of the plaintiff was engaged in an investigatory function which, as a type of administrative

* The ultimate irony of today's decision is that in the area of common-law official immunity, a body of law fashioned and applied by judges, absolute immunity within the federal system is extended only to judges and prosecutors functioning in the judicial system. * * * Similarly, where this Court has interpreted 42 U.S.C. § 1983 in the light of common-law doctrines of official immunity, again only judges and prosecutors are accorded absolute immunity. * * * If one were to hazard an informed guess as to why such a distinction in treatment between judges and prosecutors, on the one hand, and other public officials on the other, obtains, mine would be that those who decide the common law know through personal experience the sort of pressures that might exist for such decisionmakers in the absence of absolute immunity, but may not know or may have forgotten that similar pressures exist in the case of nonjudicial public officials to whom difficult decisions are committed. But the cynical among us might not unreasonably feel that this is simply another unfortunate example of judges treating those who are not part of the judicial machinery as "lesser breeds without the law."

function, did not entitle him to absolute immunity. In that case, the plaintiff also claimed that the defendant prosecutor had, by defaming him in a press conference, denied him a fair trial by turning the jury against him and leading the jury to deadlock rather than acquit him. The Court held that this activity of the prosecutor also was not entitled to absolute immunity. A similar result was reached when a prosecutor swore to the truth of the evidence presented in a "certification for determining probable cause," on the ground that this was a function that could be exercised by a police officer or even a mere witness. Kalina v. Fletcher, 522 U.S. 118, 118 S.Ct. 502, 139 L.Ed.2d 471 (1997). Of course, when denied absolute immunity, a prosecutor can still claim the normal qualified immunity enjoyed by government officials. The absolute immunity of persons serving in a quasi-judicial role has been extended by the lower courts to court-appointed mediators. *See* Wagshal v. Foster, 28 F.3d 1249 (D.C.Cir.1994), *cert. denied*, 514 U.S. 1004, 115 S.Ct. 1314, 131 L.Ed.2d 196 (1995).

4. Even prior to *Monroe v. Pape*, discussed *supra* p. 779, decided in 1961, the Court had held that an action brought under § 1983 and a companion statute would not lie against a state legislator who, it was alleged, had called the plaintiff before a California state senate legislative committee not "for a legislative purpose" but "to intimidate and silence the plaintiff and deter and prevent him from effectively exercising his constitutional rights of free speech. * * * " Tenney v. Brandhove, 341 U.S. 367, 71 S.Ct. 783, 95 L.Ed. 1019 (1951). Subsequently, in Davis v. Passman, 442 U.S. 228, 99 S.Ct. 2264, 60 L.Ed.2d 846 (1979), the Court was confronted with a claim by a former deputy administrative assistant of the defendant-Congressman that she had been discharged because he preferred to have a man in that position. A majority of the Court held that the plaintiff had stated a valid *Bivens*-type claim for violation of her rights, under the due process clause of the Fifth Amendment, not to be subject to discrimination based on sex. The Court did not, however, rule on whether the defendant could successfully claim that his conduct was immunized by the "speech or debate" clause of the Constitution. Since the court of appeals had not ruled on that issue, the Court remanded the case for further proceedings. If there were any further proceedings, there is no report of them. Subsequently, in Forrester v. White, 484 U.S. 219, 108 S.Ct. 538, 98 L.Ed.2d 555 (1988), the Court held that a state court judge who allegedly demoted and later discharged a probation officer on account of her sex did not enjoy absolute immunity in a resulting § 1983 action. Finally, a unanimous Court has ruled that a municipal ordinance abolishing a city department, of which the plaintiff was the sole employee, and that was alleged to be based on racial animus and to be retaliation against the plaintiff for constitutionally protected speech, was nevertheless covered by absolute legislative immunity. Bogan v. Scott–Harris, 523 U.S. 44, 118 S.Ct. 966, 140 L.Ed.2d 79 (1998).

In Pulliam v. Allen, 466 U.S. 522, 104 S.Ct. 1970, 80 L.Ed.2d 565 (1984), the Court, in a 5–4 decision, held that, although one could not bring an action against a judge for damages arising out of the judge's exercise of a judicial role, the plaintiff could sue her for an injunction and, having obtained the injunction, could be awarded attorney's fees. Although at common law one could not obtain an injunction against a judge, the majority noted that errant judges could and were controlled by writs of prohibition and mandamus issued by King's Bench. The Court relied on the common-law practice to support its conclusion that there was no inconsistency in allowing a judge to be immune from damage actions while making her susceptible to suits seeking prospective "collateral relief." Following common law precedent the Court has held that witnesses before a grand jury as well as witnesses at trials enjoy an absolute immunity regarding their testimony. *See* Rehberg v. Paulk, 566 U.S. ___, 132 S.Ct. 1497, 182 L.Ed.2d 593 (2012) (grand jury); Briscoe v. LaHue, 460 U.S. 325,460 U.S. 325, 103 S.Ct. 1108, 75 L.Ed.2d 96 (1983) (trial).

5. In Halperin v. Kissinger, 606 F.2d 1192 (D.C.Cir.1979), *affirmed by an equally divided court*, 452 U.S. 713, 101 S.Ct. 3132, 69 L.Ed.2d 367 (1981) (Justice Rehnquist not sitting), it was held that former President Nixon could be liable in damages for his role in authorizing, while he was President, unlawful wiretapping of the plaintiff's telephone. The plaintiff at the time in question was a member of the staff of the National Security Council and was suspected of leaking classified material to the press. Relying on *Butz v. Economou* and Scheuer v. Rhodes, 416 U.S. 232, 94 S.Ct. 1683, 40 L.Ed.2d 90 (1974), the court of appeals refused to accord Mr. Nixon any absolute immunity while serving as President. Mr. Nixon would be liable if he acted with " 'actual malice' " (Wood v. Strickland, 420 U.S. 308, 95 S.Ct. 992, 43 L.Ed.2d 214 (1975)), or "failed to meet a statutory or constitutional obligation that was clear under the circumstances as understood at the time." The issue, however, reached the Court again. Nixon v. Fitzgerald, 457 U.S. 731, 102 S.Ct. 2690, 73 L.Ed.2d 349 (1982). With the entire Court sitting, the majority, in a 5–4 decision, held that a President is entitled to absolute immunity for acts within the "outer perimeter" of his official responsibilities. In a companion case, Harlow v. Fitzgerald, 457 U.S. 800, 102 S.Ct. 2727, 73 L.Ed.2d 396 (1982), the Court held that presidential assistants should enjoy only a qualified privilege. Chief Justice Burger, the sole dissenter, argued that presidential assistants should share the President's immunity. In a subsequent case, the Court held that President Nixon's Attorney General, John Mitchell, was entitled to a qualified but not an absolute immunity in an action brought by someone the warrantless tapping of whose phone had been authorized by Mitchell on national security grounds (a suspected plot to kidnap a presidential advisor and sabotage government buildings). Mitchell v. Forsyth, 472 U.S. 511, 105 S.Ct. 2806, 86 L.Ed.2d 411 (1985). The Court nevertheless reversed the decision below which had affirmed the district court's denial of summary judgment in favor of Mitchell. In his opinion concurring in the result, Justice Stevens declared that sometimes cabinet officials are exercising the "President's powers," and he thought that this is what Mitchell had done. Accordingly, he believed that Mitchell was entitled to absolute immunity. On the other hand, the Court has rejected the contention that "in all but the most exceptional cases the Constitution requires the federal courts to defer ... litigation [based on conduct occurring before the President took office] until his term ends." Clinton v. Jones, 520 U.S. 681, 117 S.Ct. 1636, 137 L.Ed.2d 945 (1997). Justice Stevens wrote the opinion of the Court in which seven other justices joined. Justice Breyer wrote a concurring opinion in which he expressed his fear that the majority opinion did not give enough emphasis to the principle that the President has the constitutional authority "to control his own time and energy."

6. In Owen v. City of Independence, Missouri, 445 U.S. 622, 100 S.Ct. 1398, 63 L.Ed.2d 673 (1980), a majority of the Court held that a municipality against which an action had been brought under § 1983 could not take advantage of any qualified immunity based upon the good-faith and absence of malice of the officials for whose conduct the municipality was responsible. The qualified immunity was only applicable in actions against the individual officials.

7. When the defendant in the typical § 1983 or *Bivens*-type action is an individual, does not the question of liability merge into the question of immunity more than it does in, say, defamation? Consider again the issue raised at p. 784 *supra,* whether civil-rights actions may be based upon negligence. Nevertheless, in Saucier v. Katz, 533 U.S. 194, 121 S.Ct. 2151, 150 L.Ed.2d 272 (2001), the Court ruled that the question of qualified immunity was to be decided by the trial judge independently of the question of liability. At issue was whether excessive force was used in arresting a person protesting the appearance of Vice President Gore at a public function held at a military base. The Court held that the question of whether excessive force was used was to be decided on the standard of objective reasonableness while the question of whether the officer was entitled to qualified immunity depended on whether the officer had a reasonable but mistaken view of the facts or a reasonable but mistaken view as to the legality of his actions. While the federal courts will allow interlocutory appeals from a denial of qualified immunity, *see Mitchell v. Forsyth, supra*, note 5, the Court has held the states are not obliged to permit interlocutory appeals in actions brought in state courts. Johnson v. Fankell, 520 U.S. 911, 117 S.Ct. 1800, 138 L.Ed.2d 108 (1997).

8. Over the years, the Court has decided a number of other cases involving the question of immunities. In Briscoe v. LaHue, 460 U.S. 325, 103 S.Ct. 1108, 75 L.Ed.2d 96 (1983), the Court held (6–3) that a policeman who, as a witness, had lied at the plaintiff's criminal trial was entitled to an absolute immunity in a § 1983 action *See also* Rehberg v. Paulk, 566 U.S. ___, 132 S.Ct. 1497, 182 L.Ed.2d 593 (2012) (witness before grand jury) In Cleavinger v. Saxner, 474 U.S. 193, 106 S.Ct. 496, 88 L.Ed.2d 507 (1985), however, the Court held 6–3 that the members of a prison "Discipline Committee" are only entitled to a qualified rather than an absolute immunity. Subsequently, in Malley v. Briggs, 475 U.S. 335, 106 S.Ct. 1092, 89 L.Ed.2d 271 (1986), the Court held that a police officer who applied for a warrant which was then issued by a judge only had a qualified immunity. The Court adopted the common-law rule applied in cases of malicious prosecution, namely that one who procures the issuance of a warrant will be liable if the complaint was maliciously made and without probable cause. Citing *Harlow v. Fitzgerald, supra*, the Court in *Malley* declared that an action could be brought against an officer who procures an arrest warrant "if, on an objective basis, it is obvious that no reasonably competent officer would have concluded that a warrant should issue * * *." Finally, the Court has held that a private prison guard at a private prison, whom the Court assumed for purposes of its decision could be subject to a § 1983 action, could not, because he was not a state official, claim any qualified immunity. Richardson v. McKnight, 521 U.S. 399, 117 S.Ct. 2100, 138 L.Ed.2d 540 (1997). A private person directly

employed by a municipality to investigate possibly fraudulent activity by a city employee claiming disability pay, was, however, held to be entitled to claim the same immunities as would be applicable to a regular city employee. Filarsky v. Delia, 566 U.S. ___, 132 S.Ct. 1657, 182 L.Ed.2d 662 (2012).

9. The question of immunities is discussed in some of the literature cited at p. 786, *supra,* in the course of our discussion of the history and general features of constitutional torts. More narrowly focused discussions centered on the question of immunities include K. Blum, *Qualified Immunity: A User's Manual,* 26 Ind.L.Rev. 187 (1993); D. Rudovsky, *The Qualified Immunity Doctrine in the Supreme Court: Judicial Activism and the Restriction of Constitutional Rights,* 138 U.Pa.L.Rev. 23 (1989); Note, *Qualified Immunity for Government Officials: The Problem of Unconstitutional Purpose in Civil Rights Litigation* 95 Yale L.J. 126 (1985); Comment, *Tort Immunity of Federal Executive Officials: The Mutable Scope of Absolute Immunity,* 37 Okla.L.Rev. 285 (1984); Comment, *Rejecting Absolute Immunity for Federal Officials,* 71 Cal.L.Rev. 1707 (1983); Note, *An Examination of Immunity for Federal Executive Officials,* 28 Villanova L.Rev. 956 (1983).

INDEX

References are to Pages

References are to Pages

References are to Pages

References are to Pages

References are to Pages

References are to Pages

References are to Pages

References are to Pages

References are to Pages

References are to Pages